MEDIEVAL SCIENCE, TECHNOLOGY, AND MEDICINE

AN ENCYCLOPEDIA

MEDIEVAL SCIENCE, TECHNOLOGY, AND MEDICINE

AN ENCYCLOPEDIA

Thomas Glick, Steven J. Livesey, Faith Wallis, Editors

Routledge
Taylor & Francis Group
New York   London

For the Brown Reference Group plc.
Picture Researchers: Susy Forbes, Laila Torsun
Senior Managing Editor: Tim Cooke
Editorial Director: Lindsey Lowe

Published in 2005 by
Routledge
Taylor & Francis Group
270 Madison Avenue
New York, NY 10016

Published in Great Britain by
Routledge
Taylor & Francis Group
2 Park Square
Milton Park, Abingdon
Oxon OX14 4RN

International Standard Book Number-10: 0-415-96930-1 (Hardcover)
International Standard Book Number-13: 978-0-415-96930-7 (Hardcover)

Library of Congress Cataloging-in-Publication Data

Catalog record is available from the Library of Congress

Taylor & Francis Group is the Academic Division of T&F Informa plc.

Visit the Taylor & Francis Web site at
http://www.taylorandfrancis.com

and the Routledge Web site at
http://www.routledge-ny.com

CONTENTS

INTRODUCTION

The focus of this volume—science, technology and medicine in the Middle Ages—reflects a discipline that is barely a century old. For in late autumn 1903, when the French physicist and philosopher of science Pierre Duhem began his investigations of the development of statics, he very much embraced the popular wisdom of the day, that there had been no science until the Renaissance. By the time he published the first volume of *Les origines de la statique* (Paris: A. Hermann 1905–1906), Duhem had encountered the work of Jordanus Nemorarius, whose writings he took to anticipate the work of Leonardo da Vinci (the subject of another of Duhem's historical investigations [1906-1913]). The subtitle of the Leonardo volume—*ceux qu'il a lus et ceux qui l'ont lu*—underscores the dramatic shift that Duhem continued to pursue until his death in 1916: that early modern science did not arise *ex nihilo*, but instead was the product of a long history that stretched back into the Middle Ages.

In the intervening century since the publication of *Les origines*, Duhem has been rightly criticized for many of his historical and methodological constructions, but one that underlies many of them was his belief in the strong similarity if not virtual identity of the scientific enterprise in the Middle Ages and the early modern world. When he read Buridan's accounts of impetus, he could see classical theories of inertial motion; when he found formulations of the mean-speed theorem, he observed its later role when $v = at$; and when he read fourteenth-century hypothetical discussions of diurnal terrestrial motions, he could see their consequences in the Copernican debate.

While Duhem's investigations were largely confined to the physical sciences—after being offered a Parisian chair in history of science late in life, he declined it because he considered himself primarily a physicist—the same early historiographical inclinations *mutatis mutandis* may be seen in the other two areas explored by this volume. In particular, scholars of Duhem's generation often used terms "science," "technology," and "medicine" in a sense that implied, if not explicitly stated, the congruence of those terms with their modern counterparts. Medicine poses its own particular problems in this respect. This is because medicine itself is both science and technology—a system of ideas, but also a system of practices spread across a wide range of social actors. But scholarship in medieval medicine also has a complex history, one profoundly shaped by the modern medical profession and its sense of corporate confidence, based on the identity of medicine and science. The pioneering scholarship on medieval medicine in the nineteenth and early twentieth centuries was largely carried out by physicians themselves, often working within institutes of medical history embedded in university medical faculties. In consequence, medical history was accused by professional historians, sometimes unfairly, of being antiquarianism, or worse, Whig history. In the case of medieval medicine, the general prejudices against the Middle Ages seemed to encourage the tendency of this style of history towards self-congratulatory presentism. Most importantly, the older medical history was exclusively the story of doctors, or of institutions now controlled by doctors, such as hospitals. Non-physicians who worked on medieval themes gravitated towards editions of medical texts (particularly vernacular texts, and often edited by scholars of medieval literature).

Since the 1960s, non-physician historians trained in the methods of social history have surged into the field of medical history, bringing in their train new themes: the social and political context of disease and health care, the patient's experience, the history of the body, and the role of non-professional providers, to cite only a few examples. Medieval medical history, at first rather slow to take up this trend, has over the last two decades begun to reap the social history dividend in the form of new approaches to public health in the medieval city, to illness and the care of the ill in the context of Christian religious values, to the historic impact of epidemic disease, and to the functioning of a pluralistic "medical marketplace." Particularly in Europe, the venerable enterprise of text edition has begun to broaden out into the largely uncharted Latin medical material. More attention is being paid to the early medieval period, to the relationship of Islamic and European medicine, and to the development of medicine as a learned discipline within the nascent university. In sum, historians of medieval medicine, physicians as well as non-physicians, now have a clearer goal in view: understanding medieval medical knowledge as a coherent system of ideas about the body, its disorders, and the potential for intervention; and understanding how this knowledge did or did not affect actual practices, both on the level of individual care, and on the level of social or political arrangements.

The intellectual continuity between Islamic science and that of Latin Europe is an additional recurrent theme in this volume. This complex phenomenon was in great part owing to a common Greek heritage, which encompassed virtually the entire corpus of classical Greek science and philosophy that was extant when the Abbasid caliphs undertook to guide its translation into Arabic in the eighth century. Medieval Islamic science also had a strong Indian component, moreover, both astronomical (a tradition of celestial tables) and mathematical (Indian numerals and the place-value system). Elements of Greek science had reached India prior to Islam and were subsequently fed back, transformed, to the West. The translation movements of medieval times—Greek into Arabic, then Arabic into Latin, Hebrew and the European vernacular languages—bound the Islamic and European intellectual worlds into a coherent whole, disparity of ideologies notwithstanding. Finally, the great East-to-West diffusion of technology (but not science) from China to Europe ran parallel to and, to an extent, interacted with, the flow of science. Thus did Indian calculation and Indian agriculture follow the same routes of diffusion from East to West, fellow travelers in a vast movement of cultural change.

Medieval technology is today still a field that Lynn White, Jr. defined. In *Medieval Technology and Social Change* (1962), he not only touched the principal bases—agriculture, water power, military technology—but did so in a systemic way. His was not a "nuts and bolts" approach, but rather one that embedded technology in specific cultural and social systems. His construal of the agricultural revolution of the early Middle Ages, based on the substitution of horse power for that of humans, still undergirds much of recent work on agricultural history, although subsequent scholarship shows that the various innovations (the padded horse-collar, horse shoes, the heavy plow, and three-course rotations including oats) were not as synchronic as he would have liked and displayed many local variations. Like Joseph Needham, he sketches out the great east-to-west movement of diffusion, although both the stirrup and the horse-collar reached Western Europe not through the Arab world from China (as in the cases of paper and gunpowder) but from Central Asia via the chain of nomadic peoples. He recognized the crucial role of water power in medieval industry and the necessary linkage of the water-powered grist mill with the expansion of wheat cultivation. Because standard medieval documentation tends to be sparse in technical detail, White pioneered methodical expansion into iconography, philology, and archeology in particular, providing visual or semantic representations of some artifacts, or physical traces of the artifacts themselves, respectively.

The entries in this volume range in length from 500 to 3,000 words. We have created a small group of entries that can serve as launching points for the more specific entries in this volume: "Medicine, practical," "Medicine, theoretical," "Religion and science," "*Scientia*," "Technological diffusion," and "Women in science" all discuss issues that have strong affinities to the modern world, but the central theme of these entries is cautionary, including indications of ways in which medicine, religion, science, technology, and gender issues had distinct understandings and implications in the medieval world.

Aside from these platform entries, we have selected topics that generally fall within one of six categories: Apparatus, Equipment, Implements, Techniques; Biography; Disciplines; Geographical Places; Institutions; and Scientific Genres, Theories, Texts, Traditions. To the extent that it is possible, authors have cast their nets widely to explore political, social, religious, or broader intellectual traditions and influences. In addition, many of the authors have discussed their topics with an eye to the historiographical tradition, and the references at the end of each entry have been chosen in many cases to provide additional sources of the primary, secondary and historiographical material relevant to the topic. Illustrations and maps have been chosen by authors to reflect significant examples of issues discussed in the entry text. A particularly useful feature of the entries is the cross-referencing system: within the entry text, the reader is alerted to corresponding entries by an asterisk placed before the associated entry name; at the end of each entry, a short list of related entries directs the reader to material that expands upon issues discussed in the entry; and the index at the end of the volume provides a third means of mining the text for relevant information.

Thomas F. Glick
Steven J. Livesey
Faith Wallis

ACKNOWLEDGEMENTS

We wish to acknowledge assistance provided by the many individuals and institutions who contributed to the completion of this volume. We are indeed grateful first to the 148 authors who so generously shared their knowledge and time in writing the entries that appear in the following pages. But there are also a great many colleagues who because of time or circumstance were unable to write for the volume but offered suggestions of alternate authors and sometimes even commissioned entries themselves. Our encyclopedia has also drawn heavily on the resources of the libraries of our respective institutions, and we would like to thank the dedicated staff who have provided both information and materials. In particular: at the University of Oklahoma: Marilyn Ogilvie, Kerry Magruder and the staff of the History of Science Collections, Kay Womack and the Reference librarians of Bizzell Library, and Molly Murphy and her dedicated and talented staff in the Interlibrary Loan Department; at McGill University, the Reference librarians and the Interlibrary Loans staff at McLennan Library and the staff of the Osler Library of the History of Medicine.

This work was very much a collaborative effort among the three editors and the publications staff at The Brown Reference Group and Routledge. In particular, we wish to thank Tim Cooke, Peter Connor, and most recently Henry Russell, who read each of the entries and offered suggestions when problems arose. At Routledge, we wish to thank Marie-Claire Antoine for her interventions particularly in the final publication details. On a more personal note, each of us has family whose love and support transcend daily trials; to them we owe more than we can adequately express.

Thomas F. Glick
Steven J. Livesey
Faith Wallis

PUBLISHER'S NOTE

The Routledge Encyclopedias of the Middle Ages

Formerly the Garland Encyclopedias of the Middle Ages, this comprehensive series began in 1993 with the publication of Medieval Scandinavia. A major enterprise in medieval scholarship, the series brings the expertise of scholars specializing in myriad aspects of the medieval world together in a reference source accessible to students and the general public as well as to historians and scholars in related fields. Each volume focuses on a geographical area or theme important to medieval studies and is edited by a specialist in that field, who has called upon a board of consulting editors to establish the article list and review the articles. Each article is contributed by a scholar and followed by a bibliography and cross-references to guide further research.

Routledge is proud to carry on the tradition established by the first volumes in this important series. As the series continues to grow, we hope that it will provide the most comprehensive and detailed view of the medieval world in all its aspects ever presented in encyclopedia form.

Vol. 1   *Medieval Scandinavia: An Encyclopedia*. Edited by Phillip Pulsiano.

Vol. 2   *Medieval France: An Encyclopedia*. Edited by William W. Kibler and Grover A. Zinn.

Vol. 3   *Medieval England: An Encyclopedia*. Edited by Paul E. Szarmach, M. Teresa Tavormin, and Joel T. Rosenthal.

Vol. 4   *Medieval Archaeology: An Encyclopedia*. Edited by Pamela Crabtree.

Vol. 5   *Trade, Travel, and Exploration in the Middle Ages*. Edited by John Block Friedman and Kristen Mossler Figg.

Vol. 6   *Medieval Germany: An Encyclopedia*. Edited by John M. Jeep.

Vol. 7   *Medieval Jewish Civilization: An Encyclopedia*. Edited by Norman Roth.

Vol. 8   *Medieval Iberia: An Encyclopedia*. Edited by E. Michael Gerli.

Vol. 9   *Medieval Italy: An Encyclopedia*. Edited by Christopher Kleinhenz.

Vol. 10 *Medieval Ireland: An Encyclopedia*. Edited by Seán Duffy.

The present volume, *Medieval Science, Technology, and Medicine: An Encyclopedia*, edited by Thomas F. Glick, Stephen J. Livesey, and Faith Wallis is Volume 11 in the series.

CONTRIBUTORS

Cristina Álvarez Millán
*Universidad Nacional de Educación Distancia (UNED),
Madrid, Spain*

Stefano Arieti
University of Bologna, Italy

Jon Arrizabalaga
CSIC-IMF, Barcelona, Spain

Michael D. Bailey
Iowa State University

Hélène Bellosta
University of Paris, France

Pieter Beullens
Katholieke Universiteit Leuven (KUL), Belgium

Harald Berger
University of Graz, Austria

Jean-Patrice Boudet
University of Paris, France

Tod Brabner
Boston University

Sonja Brentjes
Aga Khan Unversity (International), London, England

Charles Burnett
The Warburg Institute, London, England

Robert I. Burns, S.J.
University of California, Los Angeles

H.L.L. Busard
Venlo, Netherlands

Emilia Calvo
University of Barcelona, Spain

William E. Carroll
University of Oxford, England

Jose Chabas Bergon
Universitat Pompeu Fabra, Barcelona, Spain

Joël Chandelier
University of Paris, France

Lluis Cifuentes
Universitat de Barcelona, Spain

Jeremy Citrome
Dalhousie University, Halifax, Nova Scotia, Canada

Luciano Cova
University of Trieste, Italy

Richard Cross
University of Oxford, England

Miguel de Asúa
Universidad Nacional de San Martín, Argentina

Pieter De Leemans
Katholieke Universiteit Leuven (KUL), Belgium

Jorge Lirola Delgado
Universidad de Almería, Spain

Luke Demaitre
University of Virginia, Charlottesville

Gregg De Young
The American University in Cairo, Egypt

Alnoor Dhanani
Institute of Ismaili Studies, London, England

Edith Wilks Dolnikowski
Michigan State University

Andrew Donnelly
Loyola University Chicago

Thérèse-Anne Druart
The Catholic University of America

Geneviève Dumas
Université de Sherbrooke, Quebec, Canada

Paul Edward Dutton
Simon Fraser University, Vancouver, Canada

Catherine Eagleton
The British Museum, London, England

Nader El-Bizri
Institute of Ismaili Studies, London, England

Maria G. Firneis
University of Vienna, Austria

Beth Marie Forrest
Boston University

Brenda Gardenour
Boston University

James R. Ginther
Saint Louis University

Thomas F. Glick
Boston University

André Goddu
Stonehill College, Easton, Massachusetts

Edward Grant
Indiana University, Bloomington

Monica H. Green
Arizona State University

Gregory G. Guzman
Bradley University

Jeremiah Hackett
University of South Carolina, Columbia

Petr Hadrava
Astronomical Institute, Academy of Sciences, Prague, Czech Republic

Alena Hadravová
Research Center for the History of Sciences and Humanities, Academy of Sciences, Prague, Czech Republic

Ruth Harvey
University of Toronto, Canada

Frank Hentschel
University of Hamburg, Germany

Debra Higgs Strickland
University of Edinburgh, Scotland

Kevin D. Hill
Iowa State University

Maarten J.F.M. Hoenen
University of Freiburg im Breisgau, Germany

Richard C. Hoffmann
York University, Toronto, Canada

Sue Ellen Holbrook
Southern Connecticut State University

Richard Holt
University of Tromsø, Norway

George R. Keiser
Kansas State University

David A. King
Johann Wolfgang Goethe University, Frankfurt am Main, Germany

Jo Kirby
The National Gallery, London, England

Dr. Helena Kirchner Granell
Universitat Autonoma, Barcelona, Spain

Matthew Klemm
Johns Hopkins University

Adam Knobler
The College of New Jersey

Toke Knudsen
Brown University

Jill Kraye
The Warburg Institute, London, England

John Langdon
University of Alberta, Edmonton, Canada

David C. Lindberg
University of Wisconsin, Madison

Steven J. Livesey
University of Oklahoma

John Longeway
University of Wisconsin-Parkside

Richard Lorch
University of Munich, Germany

Charles Lohr, SJ
University of Freiburg

Graham J. McAleer
Loyola University, New Orleans

Roberta Magnuson
Oklahoma University

Steven P. Marrone
Tufts University

Craig Martin
University of Oklahoma

Luis Pablo Martinez
University of Valencia, Spain

José Francisco Meirinhos
University of Porto, Portugal

Elizabeth W. Mellyn
Harvard University

Constant J. Mews
Monash University, Australia

Burkhard Mojsisch
University of Bochum, Germany

Dermot Moran
University College Dublin, Ireland

Maria Muccillo
University of Rome, Italy

Paul Needham
Princeton University

Cornelius O'Boyle
University of Notre Dame (London Centre)

Jennifer Ottman
Stanford University

Alison Peden
Holy Trinity Church, Stirling

Anna Pikulska
University of Lodz, Poland

Dominique Poirel
Institut de Recherche et D'Histoire des Textes, Paris, France

B.B. Price
York University, Toronto, Canada

Jacob Primley
London, England

Cynthia M. Pyle
New York University

Felix Retamero Serralvo
Universita Autonoma de Barcelona, Spain

Bernard Ribémont
University of Orléans, France

Monica Rius
Universitat de Barcelona, Spain

Fernando Salmón
University of Cantabria, Spain

Julio Samso
University of Barcelona, Spain

Jürgen Sarnowsky
University of Hamburg, Germany

Walton O. Schalick, III
Washington University in St. Louis

Shlomo Sela
Bar-Ilan University, Israel

Michael Shank
University of Wisconsin

Colette Sirat
CNRS, Paris, France

Keith Snedegar
Utah Valley State College

Victoria Sweet
University of California, San Francisco

Frank J. Swetz
Pennsylvania State University at Harrisburg

Edith Dudley Sylla
North Carolina State University

Mariken Teeuwen
Constantijn Huygens Institute, The Hague, Netherlands

J.M.M.H. Thijssen
Radboud University Nijmegen, Netherlands

Ron B. Thomson
University of Toronto, Canada

Roy Thomson
The Leather Conservation Centre, Northampton, England

Marina Tolmacheva
Washington State University

Alain Touwaide
Smithsonian Institution

Katherine A. Tredwell
University of Oklahoma

Cecilia Trifogli
University of Oxford, England

Richard W. Unger
University of British Columbia, Canada

Sabetai Unguru
University of Tel Aviv, Israel

Glen Van Brummelen
Bennington College

Baudouin Van den Abeele
Université catholique de Louvain, Belgium

Raphaela Veit
Tübingen University, Germany

Iolanda Ventura
University of Münster, Germany

Jacques Verger
École Normale Superieure, Paris, France

Romana Martorelli Vico
University of Pisa, Italy

Faith Wallis
McGill University, Montreal, Canada

Michael C. Weber
Salem State College

Olga Weijers
Huygens Instituut (KNAW), The Hague, Netherlands

Melitta Weiss Adamson
University of Western Ontario, Canada

David Whitehouse
The Corning Museum of Glass, New York

Clemency Williams
Brown University

Rega Wood
Stanford University

Julia Xenakis
Bennington College

Joseph Ziegler
University of Haifa, Israel

Mauro Zonta
University of Rome, Italy

Marco Zuccato
University of Melbourne, Australia

Jack Zupko
Emory University

ALPHABETICAL LIST OF ENTRIES

ENTRIES BY THEME

Apparatus, Equipment, Implements, Techniques
Agriculture
Alum
Arms and armor
Artillery and fire arms
Brewing
Bridges
Canals
Catapults and trebuchets
Cathedral building
Clepsydra
Clocks and timekeeping
Coinage, Minting of
Communication
Eyeglasses
Fishing
Food storage and preservation
Gunpowder
Harnessing
House building, housing
Instruments, agricultural
Instruments, medical
Irrigation and drainage
Leather production
Military architecture
Navigation
Noria
Paints, pigments, dyes
Paper
Pottery
Printing
Roads
Shipbuilding
Stirrup
Stone masonry
Transportation
Water supply and sewerage
Watermills

Weights and measures
Windmills

Biography
Abelard, Peter
Abraham bar Hiyya
Abu Ma'shar al Balkh (Albumasar)
Adelard of Bath
Albert of Saxony
Albertus Magnus
Alderotti, Taddeo
Alfonso X the Wise
Alfred of Sareschel
Andalusi, Sa'id al-
Aquinas, Thomas
Archimedes
Arnau de Vilanova
Bacon, Roger
Bartholomaeus Anglicus
Bartholomaeus of Bruges
Bartholomaeus of Salerno
Bartolomeo da Varignana
Battani, al- (Albategnius)
Bede
Benzi, Ugo
Bernard de Gordon
Bernard of Verdun
Bernard Silvester
Biruni, al-
Boethius
Boethius of Dacia
Borgognoni, Teodorico
Bradwardine, Thomas
Bredon, Simon
Burgundio of Pisa
Buridan, John
Campanus de Novara
Cecco d'Ascoli

Vincent of Beauvais
William of Conches
William of Moerbeke
William of Ockham
Witelo
Zacuto, Abraham
Zahrawi, al

Disciplines
Agronomy
Alchemy
Algebra
Anatomy
Arithmetic
Astrology
Astronomy
Cartography
Computus
Cosmology
Geography, chorography
Geometry
Illumination
Logic
Medicine, theoretical
Metaphysics
Meteorology
Mineralogy
Music theory
Natural history
Optics and catoptrics
Pharmacology
Pharmacy
Physiognomy
Psychology
Quadrivium
Surgery
Trigonometry
Weights, science of
Zoology

Geographical Places
Monte Cassino
Ravenna
Salerno
Toledo

Institutions
Astrolabes and quadrants
Bayt al-Hikma
Cathedral schools
Hospitals
Patronage of science
Universities

Platform Articles
Medicine, practical
Religion and science
Scientia
South-central Asian science
Technological diffusion
Women in science

Scientific Genres, Theories, Texts, Traditions
Agrimensores
Almanacs
Arabic numerals
Aristotelianism
Articella
Bestiaries
Calendar
Commercial arithmetic
Condemnation of 1277
Consilia
Elements and qualities
Encyclopedias
Gender in medicine and natural history
Generation
God in Christianity
God in Islam
Gynecology and midwifery
Herbals
Hylomorphism
Illustration, scientific
Impetus
Lapidaries
"Latin Averroists"
Latitude of forms
Magic and the occult
Magnet and magnetism
Microcosm/macrocosm
Miracle
Monsters
Nature: the structure of the physical world
Nature: diverse medieval interpretations
Pharmaceutic handbooks
Plague tractates
Planetary tables
Reason
Regimen sanitatis
Scholasticism
Tacuinum sanitatis
Theorica planetarum
Translation movements
Vocabulary

A

ABELARD, PETER

Peter Abelard (1079–1142) (Pierre Abélard or Abailard; the Latin form, Petrus Abaelardus) first achieved fame as a dialectician who rejected the authority of William of Champeaux on the question of universals. In *Dialectica* (c. 1112–1117) and *Logica "Ingredientibus"* (c. 1118–1122), Abelard argued that a universal term was a word signifying some attribute of an individual, rather than a real thing in itself. He attached great importance to the singularity of individual objects, and questioned the notion that identical individuals shared a common essence. Abelard had no direct knowledge of the scientific works of Aristotle. He was also critical of those scholars who were so fascinated by *Plato's *Timaeus* that they identified the world soul with the Holy Spirit. Nonetheless, Abelard was intrigued by the rational order of the universe, and interpreted Plato's world soul as a poetic image of divine goodness sustaining creation.

Abelard attained notoriety through engaging in a celebrated love affair with Héloïse, then living in the house of her uncle, Fulbert, a canon of the cathedral of Notre Dame, Paris. In his *Historia calamitatum*, written c. 1132, Abelard recalls how their exchange of frequent messages led to physical intimacy, and eventually to her becoming pregnant. Héloïse gave their child the unusual name of Astralabius, perhaps as a reflection of her fascination with a scientific instrument still relatively new to the Latin West in the early twelfth century. It may also be significant that "*Astralabius Puer Dei*" ("child of God") is an anagram of "*Petrus Abaelardus II*." Héloïse may have seen the child as having fallen from the stars, or perhaps as a means through which she and her lover could look at each other. In their letters Abelard and Héloïse frequently call each other "my sun" and "my star." Although Abelard tried to placate her uncle by marrying Héloïse, Fulbert had him castrated in revenge. Abelard then became a monk at St. Denis, while Héloïse became a nun at the abbey of Argenteuil. Abelard returned to the teaching of logic, and began to develop his ideas on theology.

Abelard was always more skilled in the arts of language than in the natural sciences of the *quadrivium. According to a contemporary anecdote, he did once try to follow scientific lectures (*mathematicas lectiones*) given by *Thierry of Chartres, but found them more difficult than he imagined. (This story was subsequently embellished by someone who confused Abelard's reputation in the trivium with that of *Adelard of Bath in the quadrivium). Whereas Thierry was an expert in *physica*, Abelard preferred the domains of *logica* and *ethica*. In the *Theologia "Summi boni"* (c. 1120), revised as *Theologia Christiana* (c. 1122–1126), Abelard considered theology from the perspective of linguistic statements about God rather than through observation of the natural world. He laid great emphasis on pagan philosophers, whom he believed capable of grasping the supreme good as much as the prophets of the Old Testament, a theme he developed further in *Collationes* (c. 1129–1133), the dialogue of a philosopher with a Jew and a Christian.

The love affair of Abelard and Héloïse was often retold in fictionalized versions. This illustration is taken from an edition of the poems of Charles, Duc d'Orléans (1394–1465). (Topham/The British Library/HIP)

In 1129 Abelard invited Héloïse to take over the Paraclete, which he had founded near Nogent-sur-Seine in 1122 as an oratory and philosophical retreat. At her instigation, Abelard then began to support Héloïse in building it up as a monastic community. They exchanged an important series of letters after she read the *Historia calamitatum*, and Héloïse inspired Abelard to produce a number of significant writings for the Paraclete, notably his *Expositio in Hexaemeron* (c. 1135–1137), a commentary on the six days of creation. Unlike Thierry of Chartres, Abelard did not give much emphasis in this commentary to the physical structure of creation, such as the question of whether the waters above the heavens had crystallized into ice. He was more interested in the underlying rationality of creation as revealing the wisdom and goodness of God. Peter Abelard was broadly sympathetic to the project of finding harmony between *physica* and scripture. In his view natural processes have their foundation in natural forces implanted by God in creation. Abelard is particularly critical of those who invoke *astronomia* in order to justify the claim that the stars exercise influence over humanity. He argues that this would effectively deny the possibility of free will.

Abelard rejected the notion that humanity had somehow been in legitimate bondage to the devil as a result of Adam's sin. In his commentary on St. Paul's Epistle to the Romans, he emphasizes that Christ redeemed humanity through the example of love manifested in His life and death. While not directly concerned with natural science, Abelard adopted a fundamentally more optimistic anthropology than that offered by Augustine in his later writings.

See also **Astrolabes and quadrants; Logic**

Bibliography

Primary Sources
Abelard, Peter. *Opera omnia*, ed. Jacques-Paul Migne. Paris: Patrologia Latina 178, 1885.
———. *Opera Theologica I–III, Corpus Christianorum Continuatio Mediaeualis 11-13.* Turnhout: Brepols, 1969 and 1987.
———. *Historia calamitatum*, ed. Jacques Monfrin. Paris: Vrin, 1959.
———. *Dialectica*, ed. Lambert Marie de Rijk, 2nd ed. Assen: Van Gorcum, 1970.
———. *Logica 'Ingredientibus'*, ed. Bernhard Geyer, *Beiträge zur Geschichte der Philosophie des Mittelalters* 21. 1–3. Münster: Aschendorff, 1919–1927.
———. *Expositio in Hexaemeron.* Paris: Patrologia Latina 178: 731–784.

Secondary Sources
Brower, Jeffrey E. and Kevin Guilfoy, eds. *The Cambridge Companion to Abelard.* New York: Cambridge University Press, 2004.
Clanchy, Michael T. *Abelard. A Medieval Life.* Malden, Mass: Blackwell, 1998.
East, William G. Abelard's Anagram. *Notes and Queries* (1995) 240.
Marenbon, John. *The Philosophy of Peter Abelard.* New York: Cambridge University Press, 1997.

Mews, Constant J. "In Search of a Name and Its Significance: A Twelfth-Century Anecdote About Thierry and Peter Abaelard." *Traditio* (1988) 44: 175–200.
———. *The Lost Love Letters of Héloïse and Abelard: Perceptions of Dialogue in Twelfth-Century France.* New York: Palgrave, 1999.
———. *Abelard and Héloïse.* New York: Oxford University Press, 2005.

CONSTANT J. MEWS

ABRAHAM BAR HIYYA

Abraham Bar Hiyya (c. 1065–c. 1140) is the genuine pioneer in the rise of medieval Hebrew science, a process in which Jewish scholars gradually abandoned Arabic and adopted Hebrew as the language for expressing secular and scientific ideas. After the completion of the Islamic conquests in the eighth century, Jews had willingly adopted the Arabic language, spoke it fluently, and participated, together with Muslims, Christians, and members of other religions, in the reception and integration of the Greek worldview into Arabic culture and language. This honeymoon between Jewish intellectuals and the Arabic language did not, however, outlast the successive invasions of Muslim Spain by the fundamentalist Berber dynasties of the Almoravides (1090) and the Almohades (1145). As a result, a remarkable transition from Arabic to Hebrew ensued, of which Abraham Bar Hiyya was the first, and perhaps the greatest, exponent.

Little is known about Abraham Bar Hiyya's life. However, he left significant information about his scientific career in the final paragraph of an epistle that he addressed at an elderly age to Rabbi Judah ben Barzilai of Barcelona. In it he reports that he was held in high esteem by grandees and kings, and that he was engrossed from his youth by learning, dealing with, inquiring into, and teaching the so-called "science of the stars"—*hokhmat ha-kokhavim*, a calque translation of the Arabic *'ilm al-nujum*, a term employed by *al-Farabi (c. 870–c. 950) in his *Ihsa al-'ulum* (*Classification of the Sciences*). Like al-Farabi, Bar Hiyya defined the "science of the stars" in two of his works as a composite body of learning that included astronomy as well as *astrology.

Bar Hiyya's reference to his connections with grandees and kings is borne out by his appellation "Savasorda," a corruption of *sahib al-shurta* (chief of the guard). It has been surmised by some commentators that he lived in Huesca, in the Arabic kingdom of Zaragoza-Lerida, where he attained mastery of Arabic sciences and high dignity under the rule of the Banu Hud dynasty. Bar Hiyya was probably also a scion of an important Jewish family, a fact which is indicated by his title *ha-Nasi* (the Prince).

Abraham Bar Hiyya's scientific work is truly encyclopedic and covers five main areas of medieval science: astronomy, mathematics, the Jewish *calendar, astrology, and philosophy. Whereas the astronomical, mathematical, and philosophical components are clearly flagged in the list of Bar Hiyya's scientific works, none of his output has astrology in its title. Nonetheless, substantial astrological material may be found in three of his non-astrological works. All of Bar Hiyya's original scientific works were written in Hebrew, thus testifying that he developed his scientific career principally among Jews. His scientific works are now presented separately.

Yesodey ha-tevuna u-migdal ha-'emuna (*Foundations of Understanding and Tower of Faith*) is the first medieval Hebrew encyclopedia of science. The title suggests that it was planned as a work in two parts, the first covering all scientific learning and the second intended as a summary of religious knowledge. Only the introduction and the beginning of the first part are extant, and it is not clear if Bar Hiyya ever completed his encyclopedia. In the introduction, Bar Hiyya informs the reader that he wrote the encyclopedia at the request of the Jews of France, i.e., Provence; he elaborates on wisdom and the tripartite human soul, and gives a hierarchical classification of the sciences, presenting a table of contents of the whole planned encyclopedia. The first part of the extant segment follows Nicomachus of Gerasa and *Muhammad ibn Musa al-Khwarizmi and deals with the theory of numbers, arithmetical operations, and rules for mercantile calculations (*regula mercatorum*); the second part follows *Euclid, Menelaus of Alexandria, *Archimedes, Hero, and notably al-Farabi, and deals with geometry, optics, and music.

Hibbur ha-meshiha ve ha-tishboret (*Treatise on Mensuration and Calculation*) is a mathematical work conceived as a nontechnical textbook for the use of land-holders and judges. Bar Hiyya, however, went far beyond the practical needs of elementary land measurements and added in many cases relevant theorems and their mathematical demonstrations. The work was translated into Latin by Plato of Tivoli under the title *Liber embadorum*, Bar Hiyya perhaps collaborating in the enterprise. The treatise is divided into four parts: the initial section defines general concepts and terms such as point, straight line, area, and various types of angles. The second part, the largest section of the treatise, is devoted to problems of mensuration; the third follows a lost work by Euclid and deals with the division of parcels of land, while the fourth is devoted to the calculation of the volume of various bodies. A main characteristic of this treatise is that Bar Hiyya consistently avoided the measurement of angles, with the exception of right angles.

Astronomy in Bar Hiyya's oeuvre is represented by two treatises—*Surat ha-ares* (*The Shape of the Earth*) and *Heshbon mahalakhot ha-kokhavim* (*Computation of the Motions of Stars*)—and a set of astronomical tables. The treatises were written in Barcelona in 1136 and are presented in the introduction to *Surat ha-ares* not as isolated works but, together with an astrological work that is not extant, as an interwoven trilogy meant to deal with the various features of the science of the stars. *Surat ha-ares* follows al-Farghani's *Kitab fi harakat alsamawiyya wa yawami 'ilm al-nujum* (*Treatise on the Motion of the Heavens and the Complete Science of the Stars*), and its rationale was presented by Bar Hiyya as the need to deal with the "shape of the configuration in the heavens and in the earth, and the order of the motion visible in the skies and in the stars, and its path and measure in each of them, and the proofs demonstrating it." Bar Hiyya drew up a set of planetary tables called *Luhot ha-nasi* (*Tables of the Prince*) or *Jerusalem Tables* since their radix is Jerusalem. The canons of these tables are found in *Heshbon mahalakhot ha-kokhavim*, a work that follows closely *al-Battani's *Zij al-Sabi*, and which was aimed by Bar Hiyya at expounding the "way of computing the course of these moving celestial bodies, and how you can ascertain the position of the stars in the sky at any time you may wish."

On the subject of the Jewish calendar, Bar Hiyya wrote *Sefer ha-'Ibbur* (*Book of Intercalation*), which was in all likelihood the first Hebrew work of this type. This treatise includes, beside typical calendrical material and a strong dose of polemics, rich astronomical materials whose counterpart may be found in Bar Hiyya's astronomical work. The first part introduces basic astronomical and cosmographic concepts, such as lunar and solar motions, and the relation of the seven climates and latitudes to the duration of day and night. The second and third parts of the book deal respectively with the lunar month and the solar year, their astronomical characterization and calendrical implications.

Astrological Predictions

Bar Hiyya devoted the whole of *Megillat ha-megalleh* (*Scroll of the Revealer*) to foretelling the exact date of the coming of the Messiah, mainly by means of Scriptural data. Its fifth chapter, however, is an impressive astrological work in which Bar Hiyya included a voluminous Jewish and universal astrological history, and provided a parallel astrological prognostication of the days of coming of the Messiah. Four main parts may be discerned. Its introduction is devoted to a justification of the use of astrology to predict the time of coming of the Messiah, in particular, and to analyze the course of history in general. In the second part, Bar Hiyya correlates the biblical account of Jewish history, from the birth of Moses and the exodus from Egypt to the destruction of the second temple, with a series of consecutive conjunctions of Saturn and Jupiter, as well as other celestial phenomena. Next, Bar Hiyya shows the correspondence between the subsequent conjunctions of Saturn and Jupiter and a general universal history, from the birth of Jesus and the founding of the Christian religion to the conquest of Palestine by the Crusaders. In the fourth and final part, Bar Hiyya utilizes the ensuing Saturn–Jupiter conjunctions to provide a futuristic view of world history from the beginning of the first quarter of the twelfth century, that is, from his own times, to the coming of the Messiah, which, according to his calculations, should have supervened in 1448 or 1468. The most marked feature in the astrological history is the interpretation of horoscopes cast at the vernal equinoxes of the years in which there are conjunctions of Saturn and Jupiter. Besides the three traditional types of conjunctions (small: every 20 years; great: every 238 years, and strong:

every 953 years), Bar Hiyya introduced an unprecedented "huge" conjunction with a period of 2,869 years, which serves as the chronological framework into which he built his complete astrological history.

Bar Hiyya also wrote a long, apologetic epistle to Rabbi Judah ben Barzilai of Barcelona, justifying the study and use of a specific astrological approach. Bar Hiyya shows that his permissible version of astrology is in perfect harmony with main tenets of Judaism, as well as closely related to astronomy, but disconnected from astrological magic. From this epistle we may infer that Bar Hiyya endorsed the main tenets of astrology and that he integrated astrological considerations into his tasks as a rabbi. We know also from this letter that his astrologically oriented activities while serving as a rabbi aroused sharp criticism and that he adopted an apologetic stance vis-à-vis his attackers. We know for certain from the introduction to *Surat ha-ares* that Bar Hiyya planned a whole astrological textbook. This book, however, is not extant; the possibility should not be excluded that it was never written. The last three chapters of the *Heshbon mahalakhot ha-kokhavim* were devoted to the explanation of astronomical procedures which actually embody typically astrological tasks such as the calculation of the twelve astrological houses and of the astrological aspects. It has been suggested that Bar Hiyya assisted Plato of Tivoli in the translation of astrological works into Latin.

Besides the first part of *Megillat ha-megalleh*, Bar Hiyya expounded his Neoplatonic philosophical thinking in *Hegyon ha-nefesh ha-asuvah* (*Meditation of the Sad Soul*). In the first cosmological part of this work Bar Hiyya deals with the creation of the world as it is narrated in Genesis. The three other chapters are devoted to morality and penitence, repentance, good and evil, and the saintly life. The emphasis is ethical, the approach is generally homiletical and based on the exposition of biblical passages. It is less frequently quoted than Bar Hiyya's other works.

See also **Astrolabes and quadrants; Optics and catoptrics**

Bibliography

Baron, S. *A Social and Religious History of the Jews*. New York: Columbia University Press, 1958.

Langermann, Y.T. *The Jews and the Sciences in the Middle Ages*. Brookfield, Vt: Ashgate/Variorum, 1999. I: 10–16, 32.

Lévy, T. Les débuts de la littérature mathématique hébraïque: La géométrie d'Abraham Bar Hiyya (XIe–XIIe siècle). *Micrologus, Nature, Sciences and Medieval Societies* (2001) 9: 35–64.

Sela, S. Abraham. *Ibn Ezra and the Rise of Medieval Hebrew Science*. Leiden: E.J. Brill, 2003.

Sirat, C. *A History of Jewish Philosophy in the Middle Ages*. New York: Cambridge University Press, 1990.

Steinschneider, M. "Abraham Judaeus—Savasorda und Ibn Esra." In *Gesamelte Schriften*. Berlin, 1925: 327–387

Stitskin, Leon D. *Judaism as a Philosophy—The Philosophy of Abraham Bar Hiyya (1065–1143)*. New York: Bloch, 1960.
SHLOMO SELA

ABU MA'SHAR

Abu Ma'shar Ja'far ibn Muhammad ibn 'Umar al-Balkhi (Albumasar) is the best-known astrologer of the Middle Ages. He was born in Balkh in the Persian province of Khurasan in 787 C.E., and died in al-Wasit in central Iraq in 886. He apparently spent most of his life in Baghdad, where he lived by the Khurasan Gate. His extant works were written in Arabic, but he retained his allegiance to the Persian cause; he refers to Persian astronomical tables (the *zij al-Shahriyar*), and he gave currency to an account of the history of science which privileged the Persian contribution. According to a story in the **Fihrist*, Ibn al-Nadim's tenth-century bio-bibliography, Abu Ma'shar was a student of Islamic tradition, until, at the age of forty-seven, he was tricked into studying *arithmetic and geometry by the "Philosopher of the Arabs," *al-Kindi, and consequently turned to the study of the stars. Although there is one arithmetical work, on amicable numbers, attributed to Abu Ma'shar, and references to astronomical tables drawn up by him, all the other texts that survive in his name are on the subject of *astrology. The best-known of these is his *Great Introduction to Astrology*. This work, of which two versions appear to have been written, one in 848 and the other in 876, sets astrology firmly within the framework of Aristotelian natural philosophy, and provides, in the first of its eight books, a detailed defense of astrology. His *Book of Religions and Dynasties* (known in its Latin version as *On the Great Conjunctions*) is of similar dimensions, and deals with the effects on whole nations, on dynasties, and on rulership, of conjunctions of the superior planets, and of other celestial phenomena. Other works deal with the remaining principal branches of astrology: natal horoscopes, anniversary horoscopes, choices, questions, and weather forecasting. Abu Ma'shar is eclectic by nature, drawing on both ancient Greek astrology (especially *Ptolemy's *Tetrabiblos* and Dorotheus's *Carmen Astrologicum*), and Middle Persian sources (which in turn incorporate Indian elements), apparently using previous translations and interpretations of the Greek and Persian material (especially those of *Masha'allah) rather than the original texts directly. His work became well known in Western Europe, first through the translation of a shorter version of his *Great Introduction to Astrology* by *Adelard of Bath, then through two independent translations of the *Great Introduction* itself made by *John of Seville (1133) and *Hermann of Carinthia (1140), and finally by translations of his major works in the various branches of astrology made in the circle of John of Seville in *Toledo in the mid-twelfth century, with two texts translated from Greek by Stephen of Messina in the mid-thirteenth century: *De revolutionibus nativitatum* (on anniversary horoscopes), and *Albumasar in Sadan* (anecdotes concerning Abu Ma'shar recorded by his pupil Shadhan). Abu Ma'shar's discussions of natural science and astrology were an important source for Western writers on philosophy in the twelfth century (especially Hermann of Carinthia and Daniel of Morley); his "conjunctionalism" became very popular in the political and eschatological astrology of the later medieval and early modern period (e.g., *Pierre d'Ailly), while his defense of astrology was the starting point of many of the arguments for and against the science (e.g., those of Pietro Pomponazzi and Giovanni Pico della Mirandola).

See also **Aristotelianism**

Bibliography

Primary Sources
Abu Ma'shar. *The Abbreviation of the Introduction to Astrology, together with the Medieval Latin Translation of Adelard of Bath.* Edited and translated by C. Burnett, K. Yamamoto, and M. Yano. Leiden: E.J. Brill, 1994.
———. *On Historical Astrology.* Edited by Keiji Yamamoto and Charles Burnett, 2 vols. Leiden: E.J. Brill, 2000.
Abu Ma'sar al-Balhi. *Liber introductorii maioris ad scientiam judiciorum astrorum.* Edited by Richard Lemay. 9 vols. Naples: Istituto universtaria orientale, 1995–1996, vol. V.
Albumasaris De revolutionibus nativitatum [Greek translation]. Edited by David Pingree. Leipzig: Teubner, 1968.

Secondary Sources
The Fihrist of al-Nadim. Translated by Bayard Dodge, 2 vols. New York: Columbia University Press, 1977.
Lemay, Richard. *Abu Ma'shar and Latin Aristotelianism in the Twelfth Century: The Recovery of Aristotle's Natural Philosophy through Arabic Astrology.* Beirut: American University of Beirut, 1962.
Pingree, David. *The Thousands of Abu Ma'shar.* London: Warburg Institute, 1968.
———. "The Sayings of Abu Ma'shar in Arabic, Greek, and Latin." In *Ratio et Superstitio: Essays in Honor of Graziella Federici Vescovini*, ed. G. Marchetti, Orsola Rignani, and Valeria Sorge. Louvain-la-Neuve: Fédération Internationale des Instituts d'Études Médiévales, 2003, pp. 41–57.
Saliba, George. Islamic Astronomy in Context: Attacks on Astrology and the Rise of the *Hay'a* Tradition. *Bulletin of the Royal Institute of Inter-Faith Studies* (2002) 4: 24–46.
Smoller, L.A. *History, Prophecy and the Stars: the Christian Astrology of Pierre d'Ailly, 1350–1420.* Princeton: Princeton University Press, 1994.

CHARLES BURNETT

ADELARD OF BATH

Adelard of Bath was a pioneer in introducing Arabic science into the Latin curriculum of the liberal arts. Born c. 1080 in Bath in the west of England, he went abroad to study—first to France, and then, following in the wake of the First Crusade, to the Principality of Antioch, Magna Graecia (Southern Italy), and Sicily. After seven years' absence he returned to England, probably spending most of his time in Bath, but during the troubled years of the civil war (1135–1154) he seems to have joined the household of the Duke of Normandy, since he dedicated his *De opere astrolapsus* (*On the Use of the Astrolabe*), to Henry, the son of the Duke, and the future King Henry II, early in 1150. Since we have no later record concerning him, Adelard may have died soon after this dedication. His works were well known both in northern France (e.g., at Mont-Saint-Michel and Chartres), and in England, where several students and followers of his can be identified.

Adelard regarded "philosophy" (the seven liberal arts that were the backbone of education in the secular arts since late antiquity) as a single entity, whose parts could not be studied without each other. He aimed to show this in an exhortation to the study of philosophy, which he called *De eodem et diverso* (*On the Same and the Different*), in which each of the seven liberal arts is described in a dramatic setting. Some notes on music theory survive, and there is evidence that Adelard wrote a text on rhetoric. Nevertheless, it is to geometry and astronomy that he paid most attention. He made the first complete translation (from Arabic) of *Euclid's Elements, and his adaptation of this version for teaching (the so-called *Adelard II Version*) became the standard geometry textbook for several generations of students. He also translated a set of astronomical tables by *al-Khwarizmi (early ninth century), together with the rules for using them. The starting-point of the tables is 1126, and one of the half-dozen extant manuscripts preserves a copy made in the scriptorium of Worcester Cathedral before 1140. The tables follow the Indian models of computation that had been used by early generations of astronomers of the Abbasid period in Baghdad, but which had been superseded by Ptolemaic models in the Islamic Orient by Adelard's time. Adelard's treatise on the astrolabe (*De opere astrolapsus*) draws on his translation of the *Elements* and on the *Tables*, as well as on earlier texts on the instrument, and includes a summary of Ptolemaic cosmology. Adelard regarded the ultimate aim of astronomy as enabling one "not only to declare the present condition of earthly things, but also their past or future conditions," and to further this aim he translated two Arabic texts on *astrology: the *Abbreviation of the Introduction to Astrology* of *Abu Ma'shar, and the *Hundred Aphorisms* attributed falsely to *Ptolemy. To Adelard or his circle also belong some marginal notes comparing the doctrines of Arabic astrology to those of the Latin textbook of Firmicus Maternus. Another application of astronomy was magic, to which Adelard contributed by translating a text on the manufacture of talismans by *Thabit ibn Qurra.

Luminary Among Mathematicians

Through his translations of Euclid's *Elements* and the *Tables* of al-Khwarizmi, Adelard considerably expanded the range of the traditional seven liberal arts (both texts were included in the well-known two-volume "Library of the Liberal Arts"—the *Heptateuchon* of *Thierry of Chartres of the early 1140s). His version or versions of Euclid's *Elements* in particular gained him a reputation as one of the "luminaries among geometricians," according to a comment in a mid-twelfth century manuscript from Coventry. However, he also ventured outside this curriculum by introducing the science of nature, or physics, in the form of a series of questions concerning topics arranged in ascending order, from the seeds within the

Earth to the highest heaven (his *Quaestiones naturales*). The physical questions concerning the heavenly bodies include: "Why is the Moon deprived of light?"; "Why do the planets not move with a constant motion?"; "Why do the planets move in the opposite direction from the fixed stars?"; "Why do stars appear to fall from the sky?"; and "Whether the heavenly bodies are animate." Adelard alleges that the teaching in this book comes from the "Arabic studies" (*studia Arabica*) to which he devoted himself during his seven-year absence from England. While it is likely that he took part in scientific discussions in the Middle East (he refers to meeting a philosopher in Tarsus, and experiencing an earthquake in Mamistra), no specific Arabic source is cited or identifiable in his work. It is possible that he knew some Greek medical and philosophical works (by Hippocrates and Nemesius) that had been translated into Latin from Arabic in southern Italy. However, it is not his doctrine so much as his method that he attributes to the Arabs: that of finding the causes of things through the use of reason rather than by following authorities. The *Quaestiones naturales* exemplifies this method throughout, by using the dialogue situation to counter one argument with another, taking observations from nature, and using analogy.

Adelard's influence on the teaching of geometry in Western Europe was much greater than on that of astronomy, since the *Tables* of al-Khwarizmi were soon eclipsed by those of *Toledo, and other texts on the astrolabe and astrology issuing especially from Toledo proved more popular than his own. However, the popularity of the *Quaestiones naturales* ensured that his discussions of cosmology were well known, and at least one English scholar, Daniel of Morley (fl. 1175), knew the cosmological section of the *De opere astrolapsus*, which he quotes in his own cosmology, the *Philosophia*. The *Quaestiones naturales* were printed three times in the Renaissance (twice in 1475, and again between 1488 and 1491), and were still being quoted by scholars such as Pico della Mirandola and Elias Ashmole.

See also **Astrolabes and quadrants; Cosmology; Magic and the occult; Music theory; Quadrivium; Translation movements; Translation, norms and practices**

Bibliography

Primary Sources
Adelard of Bath: Conversations with His Nephew: On the Same and the Different, Question on Natural Science and On Birds. Translated and edited by Charles Burnett, *et al.* New York: Cambridge University Press, 1998.
Boncompagni, Baldassare. Regulae Abaci di Adelardo di Bath. *Bulletino di bibliografia e di storia delle scienze matematiche e fisiche* (1881) 14: 1–134.
Dickey, Bruce G. "Adelard of Bath: An Examination Based on Heretofore Unexamined Manuscripts." Unpublished Ph.D. dissertation, University of Toronto, 1982 (includes *De opere astrolapsus*).
Suter, H., A. A. Bjørnbo and R. O. Besthorn. *Die astronomischen Tafeln des Muhammed ibn Musa al-Khwarizmi in der Bearbeitung des Maslama ibn Ahmed al-Madjriti und der latein. Ubersetzung des Athelhard von Bath.* Det Kongelige Danske Videnskabernes Selskab, Skrifter, 7 Række, hist.-filos. Afd. 3, Copenhagen, 1963.

Secondary Sources
Burnett, C., ed. *Adelard of Bath: An English Scientist and Arabist of the Early Twelfth Century.* London: The Warburg Institute, 1987 (Warburg Surveys and Texts 14).
Cochrane, L. *Adelard of Bath: The First English Scientist.* London: The British Library, 1994.

CHARLES BURNETT

AGRICULTURE

Medieval agriculture was a knowledge-intensive activity. That is, its practice was predicated on local knowledge guiding the application of generalized tool-kits to specific micro-regional settings. Technological constraints made for a medieval agricultural which, although low in yields by modern standards, was surprisingly resilient and endowed with enough flexibility to permit a fine-tuned relationship with the environment. In general terms, traditional agro-systems were surprisingly well-adapted to their environments. Although Arab, Mediterranean, and northern European agricultural will be dealt with separately here, a number of introductory considerations provides context for all cases. First, because of relatively small yields, medieval agriculture was highly sensitive to adverse weather conditions, both summer droughts, winter freezes, and periods of overabundance of rain. This meant that a certain level of crop variety was necessary as insurance against the possible destruction of an important staple. Therefore, all viable local microclimates tended to be used. Moreover, since medieval farmers lacked the technical ability to be able to standardize seeds or even to sort them by variety, sown cereals always involved some kind of mixture (where for example, spelt and emmer, growing as weeds, would turn up in a wheat field). All crop varieties changed over time, in obedience both to natural selection, which fine-tuned the adaptation of varieties to local habitats, and also to unconscious selection of cultivars. Thus, while we know in a general way what was planted (e.g., bread wheat, oats, rye, and so forth) we cannot specify the exact make-up of local varieties (at least, not without paleobotanical evidence).

All three agricultural systems had a standard approach to the balance among agricultural sectors: cereal cultivation, livestocking, and arboriculture, including grapevines. By livestocking, we refer not to transhumant or nomadic herding, but to local herds, specifically the number of animals that could be wintered over, which in turn set the level of cereal production, especially in northern Europe. Because medieval cultivators knew of no way to refurbish soil fertility other than fallowing and letting the local herds graze the fallow fields, supplying them with their manure. Domestic animals, in any case, can easily be switched from one agricultural role (e.g., source of dietary protein) to another (e.g., food stored against possible need; or, a medium of exchange) and as such are key elements in the agricultural economy.

Northern European Regimes

The Germans of late antiquity were a semi-nomadic hunting and grazing people. When they farmed they would cultivate new land for a while, until it was exhausted, then move on. Low population density is a prerequisite for this kind of agriculture. Because the barbarians generally (not just the Germans, but Slavs, Mongols, Huns, etc.) could not produce enough cereals, they needed to maintain large herds. And because they devoted so much space to their herds, they could not produce enough cereals. This kind of agricultural economy had some advantages over that of the Romans: it produced a more varied diet, with more protein. Semi-nomadic peoples had greater familiarity with domestic animals than the Romans had, and more animals were available to the peasant, for leaving manure on fallow fields. Medieval agriculture as it developed was a mixture of Roman and German styles.

Open Fields

The style of cerealculture that developed in northern Europe is known as the open field system. Open field agriculture is based on the heavy or wheeled plow, which is capable of turning over a furrow. This required a heavy team to pull it along, typically with eight oxen. Since it was cumbersome to turn a big team very often, fields tended to be about ten times longer than they were wide. The heavy plow enabled farmers to cultivate the lowland clay-earth areas of the northern European river valleys which had been uncultivatable with the Roman plow.

Open fields refer to fields surrounding a village. Toward the end of the first millennium the most common format was a system of two fields, one sown in wheat or rye ("wintercorn"), the other lying fallow with animals grazing on it. This was called biennial rotation; villagers had strips in each field and all had to follow the same rotation of crops. In the later Middle Ages, three-field agriculture became the dominant form. The third field was devoted to "springcorn"—oats, peas, beans, and barley—sown in the spring, and harvested in the fall. Note that oats, peas, and beans are nitrogen-fixing. Medieval farmers did not know any method of restoring exhausted land except to leave it alone and put as much manure on it as possible. Nor did they know anything about planting hay: it was always gathered wild. Meadowland—land in hay—was always more valuable than arable because the extent of meadow determined the number of animals you could keep through the winter. Feudalism privileged wheat in that, when rents were paid in kind, wheat was normally the specific medium of payment.

According to White's famous hypothesis the European economy entered a long phase of growth around 1000 C.E. as a result of the conjunction of three different technical elements. The first was the shift from the Roman plow (generically called an ard) to the heavy plow. The share of an ard does not turn over the soil and makes cross-plowing necessary. A single plowing will leave a wedge of undisturbed soil between each furrow. Cross-plowing pulverizes the soil, which prevents excessive evaporation of moisture in dry climates and helps keep fertility high by bringing up subsoil minerals through capillary action. The heavy plow had three advantages over the ard: (1) It was so powerful it broke up the clods without the need for cross-plowing. This saves the peasant's time and increases the areas of land which he can cultivate in a day; (2) It changes the shape of fields from squarish to long and narrow. With the passage of the years the ridges and furrows became accentuated. The farmer could be sure of getting a crop on the ridge in a wet year and one in the furrow in a dry one. It promoted more efficient drainage; (3) The heavy lowland soils which it could plow gave higher yields than the light upland soils plowed with the scratch plow.

The second element was the development of a new system of animal traction that included the modern harness, harnessing in file, the whippletree, traces, and horseshoes. Oxen had been used as the plow beast of choice because they suffer less from hoof breakage than do either horses or mules. Horses' hooves are especially sensitive to moisture, meaning that they could not be used in northern Europe before the introduction of the nailed horseshoe. The first common references to shod hooves are found in the ninth century. But a shod horse is useless for plowing unless it is harnessed in a way that utilizes its power. The yoke harness was well suited to oxen, but was applied to horses in such a way that from each end of the yoke two flexible straps encircled the belly and neck of the horse. As soon as the horse began to pull, the neck strap pressed on its windpipe and jugular vein, choking it and cutting down the circulation of blood to its brain. The modern harness of a work horse has a padded collar which rests on the horse's shoulders, permitting free breathing and circulation, and attached with traces so that the horse can throw its whole weight into pulling. A horse can pull four or five times more with a collar harness than with a yoke harness. The Germans appear to have learned about the horse collar from the Slavs in the late eighth or early ninth century, earlier than harnessing in file (tenth or eleventh centuries) and the whippletree (twelfth century).

The third element is three-field rotation. Again, the earliest documented evidence appears in the late eighth century. If a village had 600 acres (242 hectares), in the two-field system half of that area would have crops and the other half would lie fallow. In a three-field system, there would be 400 acres (160 hectares) under crops. In both systems all 600 acres must be plowed (800 if the fallow were plowed twice), but 100 more acres are producing than was the case before. White viewed the spread of three-field agriculture as a major impetus in bringing new land into cultivation, reclaiming swamps, and cutting down forests.

Three-field agriculture also had the crucial effect of diversifying crops. The spring crops (oats, peas, beans, and barley) while not as remunerative as wheat, brought a number of benefits. It lessened the risk of hunger in a bad cereal year. Spring crops provided a large amount of vegetable proteins which diversified a diet that had been top-heavy with carbohydrates. With triennial rotation, northern European peasants were able to grow enough oats—and oats of a high enough quality—needed to support plow horses. Southern European peasants had no choice between the ox and horse: they could not grow enough oats in a biennial rotation to support horses. Where the horse was the plow animal, the harrow was also found (this instrument seems not to have been much drawn by oxen). The harrow was used to remove weeds, to break up heavy clods, and to spread manure. (For the harrow to be much used, therefore, all the rest of the elements of the complex—plow, horse harness, horse-shoes, oat supply—have to be in place first.)

White correctly identified the most important elements of a technological complex typical of the agriculture of medieval northern Europe whose key element was the moldboard plow. Rather than a revolution however, medieval agricultural change was gradual, incremental and, in many areas, incomplete. In specific places, such as southern Jutland, however, the technological changeover appears to have happened according to the chronology suggested by White, that is around 900–1000 C.E., while for Scandinavia as a whole, three-field agriculture appears gradually in the course of the eleventh through thirteenth centuries. According to data presented by Langdon for England, although plow horses (*equi arantes*) are documented in the tenth century, and the use of horses increases to the end of the twelfth, oxen predominated overall. By 1500, rather than a wholesale replacement of oxen by horses there was patchwork of horse-only and oxen-only areas. The choice between the horse and the ox was determined by a complex set of factors, including the availability of pasture and meadows, soil (and therefore plow) type, and climate. Areas where oxen predominated used swing or foot plows on heavy lowland terrain with wetter climates, and used two-course rotations. With horses, one finds wheeled plows upland, drier climate with lighter soils, and three-course rotation schemes. In economic terms, horses represented lower costs, not increased production. Lords continued to prefer eight-oxen teams, while peasant teams were typically of four oxen or four horses. The fewer the draft animals a farm had, the more likely it was that those animals would be horses; hence peasants were more apt to adopt the horse than were lords. Langdon's conclusions with respect to the Middle Ages generally, that smallholders were the technologically most progressive sector of society, agree with those of Bois for the early medieval expansion that made seizure of peasant property by the emerging feudal nobility such an attractive course.

An overly sharp distinction between two- and three-field systems may also be an oversimplification. According to Hilton, the rotation was among strips (furlongs, as the basic unit of cultivation) rather than fields. The reduction of fallowing was not necessarily the result of the introduction of spring crops, nor were they planted as massively as White pretends.

To a great degree, the classical "Mediterranean triad" of wheat, the olive tree, and grapevines continued to dominate the agricultural landscape of this region in the Middle Ages. Wheat was especially privileged in areas where feudal dues were taken in kind. Elsewhere cereal culture was better able to respond to local environments. The olive was widely grown wherever the environment could accommodate it; the northern climatic limit of olive cultivation in Spain was conterminous with the Christian/ Muslim frontier of the early Middle Ages.

Mediterranean agricultural regimes were risk-driven. Because of the structural probability of summer drought, or torrential rains particularly in the autumn and spring, it was necessary to diversify crops to the maximum in order to ensure that at least some would survive. The diversification strategy was implemented in the context of a topography fragmented into microregions with different ecological characteristics and a variety of niches. In particular, it was common to grow a variety of cereals, not only wheat, but also spelt, barley, and millet or sorghum. Traditional wheat varieties were normally adapted to different microregional habitats over the course of centuries. Rough pasture, forests, and wetlands were all managed entities, integrated into agricultural economies. In addition, the numerous plants gathered wild were an important complement to cultivated crops.

Mediterranean agriculture was normally under a regime of two-course, biennial rotation. If the climate were arid enough, sometimes fields were fallowed for more than one year. In the Castilian system called *año y vez*, a field was planted to wheat one year and left fallow the next. In many areas of Spain no rotation was practiced, but in others a two-course rotation appeared when organized fallowing became an economic necessity. The advantage of a two-course rotation was that local herds could be grazed on half of the fields annually, a stratagem that was unnecessary as long as there was abundant uncultivated land (*monte*). In areas where local herding was particularly strong, a further adaptation was made by increasing the fallowing from one year to two (or more), which providing more fallow grazing. Given the summer aridity and the continued use of the light Roman plow, it was never feasible to introduce the northern European three-course rotation, with a spring sowing; the only way to increase wheat cultivation was by extending the arable land at the expense of pasture and woodland and, later, even of vineyards and irrigated fields. The increasing trend away from local towards transhumant herding—also an effect of increased use of land for agriculture—heightened the dependence of cultivators on fallowing, to make up for the loss of local sources of fertilizer. Yields were accordingly very low, from 3.4 to 4.2 to 1, for wheat and barley compared to the normal northern European yield of 5:1 for wheat and 8:1 for barley. When Christians captured irrigated *huertas*, like that of Valencia, what they did was install three-course rotation, grew the usual spring crops—oats, peas, and beans—and continued to fallow. As a consequence of cross-plowing, fields were square in shape and frequently bounded by irrigation canals or drainage ditches.

The Arab conquests of the seventh and eighth centuries created, in the Islamic Empire, a vast zone propitious for the diffusion of ideas and techniques, particularly from east to west through the great Eurasian continental land mass. Chief among these techniques were a roster of Indian cultivars (rice, sugar cane, citrus fruits, and old world cotton being the most important) grown under monsoon conditions in their hearths of origin, but which, when imported into the Mediterranean basin had to be grown under irrigation. The Arabs called the resultant style of cultivation "Indian agriculture" (*filaha hindiyya*). As this lore passed through Iran, it gained Persian accretions, both in crops and techniques. Thus the eggplant and the artichoke (Arabic *baranjana* and *karshuf*, respectively, both terms from Persian) were added to the crop roster; while irrigation technology picked up the *qanat* or filtration gallery and the waterwheel (in particular the fluvial *noria, generically called the Persian Wheel). In addition, specific plowing techniques, such as the comb furrow, known today from Afghanistan to Spain, probably represents a medieval irradiation both eastward and westward from a Persian hearth.

Inasmuch as these crops required heat, they were grown in the summer. Thus a rotation of crops became the norm, and irrigated fields yielded as many as four harvests yearly. The far greater number of annual plowings required by the new crop succession and the resultant water loss tended to make Muslim irrigators meticulous in their regard for the water-bearing capacities of each kind of soil. More kinds of soil were used than had been the custom in antiquity, and the agronomical handbooks indicate that each soil type should be fully exploited. The Andalusi agronomist Ibn Bassal, whose treatise was based completely on practical experience, distinguished between ten classes of soil, assigning to each a different life-sustaining capability, according to the season of the year, and he was insistent that fallow be plowed four times.

The Arabs were once thought responsible for the spread of hard wheat (*Triticum durum*), which was used for semolina, and could also be milled twice to make bread flour. It is now established that both the ancient Greeks and Romans had hard wheat, but when they made pasta from it, they cooked it fresh. The Arabs introduced dried pasta, which could be stored for long periods.

The Indian crops which were introduced into Europe through Spain were documented quite late, not before the tenth century. Noria pot finds around the same time suggest that the entire complex of crops and techniques was introduced together, as part of a unified peasant tool kit. Although medieval Arab historians have preserved anecdotes describing the introduction of specific varieties (such as the *safari* pomegranate or the *doñegal* fig) by palatine officials, and an impressive set of agronomical books emerged from the opulent courts of the "Party" kings of the eleventh and twelfth centuries, it cannot be concluded that princely acclimatization gardens were the principal motor of agricultural change. Rather the interaction of tribal settlement and the broken topography that produced a plethora of local "microregions" had the effect of generating dozens of slightly differing agricultural systems that were an ideal locus for acclimatizing crops. Ultimately there can be no standard "agricultural revolution" in societies, like those of the Mediterranean basin, characterized by a crazy-quilt of environmentally different regions. According to Horden and Purcell, "New crops were inserted within a spectrum of preexisting strategies," that is, the standard crops improved by generations of selection in the normal course of agricultural practice were more important in the long run than new cultivars.

See also **Agronomy; Irrigation and drainage**

Bibliography

Astill, Grenville and John Langdon, eds. *Medieval Farming and Technology: The Impact of Agricultural Change in Northwest Europe*. Leiden: E.J. Brill, 1977.

Bois, Guy. *The Transformation of the Year One Thousand*. Manchester: Manchester University Press, 1992.

Hilton, R. H. Technical Determinism: The Stirrup and the Plough. *Past and Present* (April 1963) 24: 01–100.

Horden, Peregrine and Nicholas Purcell. *The Corrupting Sea*. Oxford: Blackwell, 2000.

Langdon, John. *Horses, Oxen and Technological Innovation*. New York: Cambridge University Press, 1986.

Watson, Andrew M. *Agricultural Innovation in the Early Islamic World: The Diffusion of Crops and Farming Techniques, 700–1100*. New York: Cambridge University Press, 1983.

White Jr., L. *Medieval Technology and Social Change*. Oxford: Clarendon Press, 1962.

THOMAS F. GLICK

AGRIMENSORES

Agrimensura—the Latin term for the practice of land surveying—was always held in high esteem by the ancients. The tradition of surveying dates back to Babylon and Egypt. The ancient Greeks based their town planning on rectangular forms, and their practices were later adopted in Rome, where the earliest reference to surveyors (*agrimensores*) is dated July 597, during the pontificate of Pope Gregory I. For hundreds of years surveying was numbered among the liberal arts (*artes liberales*).

Medieval surveyors performed a range of public functions. Their duties included marking out and signing borders, mediating border disputes, and conducting geodetic works for road marking and aqueduct construction. All the issues were described in writing at the time, but most of the texts were subsequently modified, and those that have survived have reached us only in severely modified and truncated form. Such documents are technical tracts dated between 75 and 110 C.E. The authors are Sextus Julius Frontinus, Hyginus Gromaticus and Balbus, Siculus Flaccus, and Agennius Urbicus. The works include many interesting remarks on the education of surveyors, the professional knowledge they had to apply, and their approach to the profession. Surveyors are known to have had excellent writing and drawing skills; knowledge of solid geometry, optics, arithmetic, cartography, and law; and they were generally educated in history, philosophy, literature, music, and medical science.

Land measurement was a basic activity of the *agrimensores*. The applied procedure (*limitatio*) was based on marking out parallel lines from east to west and from south to north—the divided land looked like a chessboard. Traces of these divisions are still visible today, especially in North Africa, where they show up in aerial photographs.

Of the very precise instruments used by surveyors for measurement the most important was the groma (surveyor's cross), the main symbol of the profession, which was used for marking out angles and straight lines. Among the other commonly used instruments were chorobates, water tables with sighting devices, used for leveling, and decempeda, a ten-feet- (2.9m-) long measuring pole.

After measuring and dividing an area, the *agrimensores* then marked out its borders. The stones (*termini*) around the perimeter of the land were made of imported material so that they could be clearly distinguished from a distance; they were engraved with information, such as the location of the nearest river or lake.

Another of the surveyor's important functions was to draw charts of the land. The maps thus produced were made in two copies on bronze plates, and were always saved as evidence. Local authorities kept one copy; the other was taken to the central archive.

Plotting the courses of roads was another job for the *agrimensores*. The network of roads crossing the whole territory of the Roman Empire is shown on one of the oldest maps, *Tabula Peutningeriana*, the surviving twelfth-century copy of which is based on a map made in the third or fourth century C.E. The road lines marked on it are supplemented by distances, estimated traveling times, and information about the accommodation available in various places. In the Middle Ages travelers and pilgrims used copies of the maps made by Roman surveyors. These maps were made in the form of portable paper rolls.

In the early Empire *agrimensores* became imperial officials and carried out great geodetic operations that were usually connected with registering population and real estate in the Empire and were performed for fiscal reasons. One such survey of Orange, in the South of France, conducted in 77 C.E., gives information on private areas and includes a map.

Medieval Surveying

The art of surveying declined considerably during the early Middle Ages but was revived in the ninth and tenth centuries after the discovery of Roman surveyors' tracts (*gromatici veteres*), which were then transcribed. Authorship of the tracts is attributed to either *Boethius or *Gerbert of Aurillac. These works were quite common in the tenth and eleventh centuries, but they were used more for teaching than for practical applications in the countryside.

From the ninth century extensive if simple measurements were made of wide areas of Europe from England to Catalonia in order to evaluate the revenue due from the land. The range of measurements made for fiscal reasons was limited—land title books were very often made on the basis of the owner's declaration. The first real land registers date from the twelfth century.

It is difficult to date the first appearance of surveyors as a professional group. The earliest authorized source mentioning area measurement was written in 1139. From the early fourteenth century, however, there were numerous references to officials involved in measurements for royal properties in France.

By the late Middle Ages the measurement of land and the estimation of income from real estate for fiscal reasons had become commonplace. Literate and numerate people began to specialize in surveying, and by the fourteenth and fifteenth centuries surveying had become a profession, and practitioners began to write descriptions of their practical activities. One of the earliest works of this type, by Bernard Boysset of Arles (fourteenth century) is a comprehensive tract, illustrated by the author, that includes extensive information on the surveyor's profession, the techniques applied, and local customs. It reveals that surveyors of that epoch were involved in marking out the borderlines of the property, placing border stones, calculating the area of properties (which were typically divided into triangles and rectangles), compiling reports on all the activities performed, and even verifying weights and measures. The instruments used by medieval surveyors were simple and easy to construct: a wooden pole and a string marked for distance measurements, a T-square, and a trammel. As in the Roman period, border stones were regarded as sacrosanct: any violation of them or attempt to alter their positions was severely punished.

See also **House building, housing; Roads**

Bibliography

Campbell, Brian. *The Writings of the Roman Land Surveyors: Introduction, Text, Translation and Commentary*. London: Society for the Promotion of Roman Studies, 2000.

Guerreau, Alain. Remarques sur l'arpentage selon Bertrand Boysset (Arles, vers 1400–1410). In *Campagnes médiévales: l'homme et son space: études offertes à Robert Fossier*, ed. Elisabeth Mornet. Paris: Publications de la Sorbonne, 1995.

Dilke, Oswald A.W. *The Roman Land Surveyors: An Introduction to the agrimensores*. Newton Abbot, England: David and Charles, 1971.

ANNA PIKULSKA

AGRONOMY

In traditional societies, agronomy was the learned reflection of agricultural practice. It had both theoretical and applied components, bundled together in an attempt to synthesize a vast body of data.

The Roman agronomy tradition—*De re rustica*, the title of successive works by Cato, Varro, and Columella—was the immediate source of medieval writing on the subject. Cato the Censor (mid-second century B.C.E.), the first Roman agronomical writer, was said by Columella to have taught agriculture to speak Latin. His work was a compendium of practical information on estate management. Varro's treatise (37 B.C.E.) emphasizes the predominance of grapevines and fruit trees in Italian agriculture. Lucius Junius Columella (fl. mid-first century C.E.) was from Gades (Cádiz) in Roman Hispania. His book of the same title aimed, through a detailed presentation of agriculture techniques and farm management, to restore agriculture to its former primacy as a form of land investment, in a period when the aristocracy was investing in pasture. Finally Palladius (fl. late fourth century C.E.) in his *Opus agriculturae*, although as much as one-third of the work was based on Columella, became the most influential of Roman agricultural writers in medieval times (at least until the rediscovery of Columella in 1418) because his presentation—in the form of a calendar of agrarian tasks—proved more in tune with medieval farming. Palladius was well known in England through a versified Middle English translation titled *On husbondrie*. The hallmark of Roman agronomy was the interdependence of the various elements of mixed intensive farming: cereal and legume field crops, vineyards, fruit and olive trees, and animal husbandry whose close association with cultivation was stressed in particular by Varro.

English Estate Books

A common genre of agronomical writing is estate books, which describe managerial strategies for large estates, somewhat in the tradition of Varro and other Roman writers. First come various recensions of *Robert Grosseteste's rules (*Statuta*) for estate managers which he composed between 1235 and 1242 in Latin for the use of the management of his own household, as bishop of Lincoln. A French recension was later made for the Countess of Lincoln, and this version circulated widely. Grosseteste advised that crop yields be estimated in advance of harvesting so that lords could plan their budgets effectively.

Next came an anonymous treatise in French for the instruction of stewards and bailiffs called the *Seneschaucy*, written in the 1260s or 1270s. Stewards, it instructs, must keep track of how much of each crop of wintercorn (wheat, rye and barley) and springcorn (peas and beans) are sowed per acre; and what the plowing requirements of each is. The bailiff is in charge of soil quality (marling and manuring) and the apportionment of work between customary tenants and hired labor. In all estate books, these issues constitute the primary focus. Walter of Henley, a knight who later became a Dominican friar, wrote the most famous of these treatises, known as the *Husbandry*, also in French and based somewhat on the *Seneschaucy*, around 1285. The book is mainly about plowing, sowing and harvesting, in particular how costs and profits are to be calculated. Interestingly, Like the *Seneschaucy* Walter's treatise was read by and designed for not the owners of manors but rather estate lawyers, men trained in the common law on the particulars of estate management, conveyancing, and accounting in view of the demand for such services, whether in management or litigation.

Walter's treatise can be viewed as an operationalization of open field agriculture, whether with two- or three-course rotation. Walter based his cost calculations on a standard unit of 240 acres (97.1 hectares), the equivalent both of 160 acres (64.7 hectares) in a two-field system, with the fallow plowed twice, and 180 acres (72.8 hectares) in a three-field system, with the fallow plowed once. He then estimated the distance a team would travel per day in each system and, on this basis, calculated the labor requirements. Walter's theory of agriculture was roughly based on notions of the balance of the four qualities (dung is too "hot" to be used without cooling by mixing it with earth, for example.) Drainage was also a theme that Walter stressed in conjunction with soil types and quality: pooling water was an obvious cause of soil imbalance. The second part of the book is devoted to animal husbandry. As a counterpart to Walter's primer for lawyers, an anonymous *Husbandry*, copied mainly in monasteries, appears to have circulated mainly among estate owners and was probably designed to aid account audits.

Taken as a group, these didactic estate treatises reveal a characteristic pattern of linguistic *communication. Stewards and lawyers alike had to know both French and Latin. Accounts were always written in Latin, but French was the language of the nobility who owned and managed the estates.

Pietro de Crescenzi (1233–1321), a judge from Bologna, wrote the first medieval Latin work in the tradition of classical agronomy. His *Opus ruralium commodorum* (*Book of Practical Agriculture*) was based both on Roman authors and his own observations, was quickly translated into Italian, then French (by order of Charles V in 1373), and became the first agricultural work to be printed (Augsburg, 1471). He also drew on theoreticians like *Albertus Magnus and *Ibn Sina for information on plant growth. The work is divided into twelve books, covering farm location; practical botany; cereal cultivation; arboriculture and horticulture (with an account of one hundred eighty-five edible or medical plants); meadows and woods; gardens; animal husbandry; hunting; a recapitulation and summary; and finally a calendar of the farmer's year.

Ambrosoli characterizes Crescenzi's *Opus* as a reordering of medieval thought equal to that of Dante or *Aquinas. It is based mainly on Palladius, whose texts were frequently read together and compared with it. He provides general rules for growing every common field and garden crop and tree, in such a way that farmers with different requirements could mold his prescriptions to their own needs. In this sense, the *Opus* was an open text: readers practicing agriculture from different perspectives and under different conditions could adapt it to their needs. The French translation was at the same time an adaptation of Crescenzi's original text to the agrarian geography of France. He was read by persons interested in estate management, and also by those seeking information on specific agricultural products. He goes into great detail on the differences between emmer and spelt, although it is not clear whether he had direct experience of emmer or only knew of it through classical authors.

The Islamic Tradition

The *Nabatean Agriculture*, a tenth-century treatise, was a mixture of practical techniques and theosophical ideas compiled by Ibn Wahshiyya, reflecting the agricultural practice of central Mesopotamia (around Kufa). By "Nabatean" is meant the Syriac-speaking rural population. Although the treatise enjoyed wide fame in the Arabic-speaking world, the text reflects traditional agriculture in lowland Mesopotamia; there is only perfunctory mention of the new Indian crops, like rice, sugar, and cotton. The number of cultivated plants and fruit trees is substantially greater than those described in the Byzantine *Geoponika* (one hundred six versus seventy), with new coverage of garden vegetables (which became a hallmark of Arab agriculture) and medicinal plants, with strong integration of horticulture and arboriculture. The eleventh-century Andalusi agronomist, Ibn al-'Awwam, self-consciously relied on the *Nabatean Agriculture*, which he cites five hundred forty times, because the Middle East was located in the same clime as al-Andalus, as he ascertained by comparing harvest dates.

Acclimatization gardens were favored by the kings of the independent states that sprang up in eleventh-century al-Andalus in the wake of the dissolution of the Caliphate. Thus Ibn Bassal was employed as royal gardener in Toledo, Ibn al-'Awwam in Seville. Oddly, Andalusi agronomists devote scant attention to irrigation, even though it was central to the agricultural wealth of the country. Discussion of irrigation is limited to specifications about norias, with no mention of surface irrigation from canals. Ibn al-'Awwam describes a method of linking wells drawing from the same water table, adjacent with the depth stepped so that subsidiary wells supply water to the main one. This is the application of the filtration gallery (qanat) principle to noria wells, an example of which was excavated at an archeological site (Les Jovades) in Gandia, Spain. Abu'l-Khayr gives specifications regarding the kinds of wood appropriate to various noria components and how the pots should be arrayed on the rope of the pot-garland wheel.

On the other hand, considerable attention is paid to the water requirements of plants and how to design fields to facilitate irrigation. Homely surveying methods provide furrows with enough gradient to ensure both the flow of water and the equality of water depth throughout the area irrigated. All writers stress the objective of attaining equilibrium between plant, soil, and water.

The Arabic word *filaha* meant both agriculture and agronomy, as its study. For Ibn Khaldun *filaha* was both a science, a branch of physics, and a craft. As a science, "It concerns the study of the cultivation and growth of plants through irrigation, proper treatment, improvement of the soil... and the care for them by applying these things in a way that will benefit them and help them grow." The ancients, he goes on to say, considered plants not only with respect to their planting and cultivation, but also their properties and the relationship of their spiritual properties (*ruhaniyyat*) to that of the celestial bodies. He believes that the *Nabataean Agriculture* was a translation of a Greek work combining both agricultural

and magical lore, and that Ibn al-'Awwam had abridged it, excluding the magical portion which was transmitted separately by *Maslama of Madrid (III, 151–152). Agriculture was also the oldest craft, prior to and older than sedentary life (II, 356–357).

The Andalusis extended Ibn Wahshiyya's emphasis on soil types. Ibn Bassal describes ten such types, organizing them according to the Hippocratic four qualities (hot, cold, moist, and dry). The system functions analogically like that of humoral pathology. Soils must be balanced; therefore, water (cold and moist) can temper the overly hot and dry soils of arid and semi-arid regions. Plowing restores heat to soil which is cold and dry by nature. Similarly, fertilizers can supply heat. Ibn al-'Awwam—less theoretical—stressed the organic content and permeability of soils.

The Andalusis relied on the *Nabatean Agriculture*, but divested it of its neo-Platonic underpinnings and created a unique body of agronomical lore by conjoining the new Indian Agriculture with the collected experience of Andalusi peasant agriculture, systematized according to the Roman agronomical tradition, especially Columella, whom the Arabs knew as Yunius. In terms of theory, this was an agronomy of the tradition of Aristotle and Theophrastus which recognized the complexity of agricultural practice. It was also related to the traditions of classical *botany and *pharmacology. Ibn Wafid, for example, wrote on both agronomy and *materia medica*.

Indian agriculture (*filaha hindiyya*) followed the same path of diffusion as that taken by Indian *arithmetic (*hisab al-hind*)—from India to Persia to the Arabic-speaking world, to Spain. "Indian agriculture" referred to the particular roster of plants originating under monsoon conditions in India—rice, sugarcane, oranges and lemons, watermelon, old world cotton—together with the techniques—mainly Persian—required to irrigate them under the conditions of aridity prevailing in the Islamic world. In Persia, several additional crops—the artichoke and the eggplant—were assimilated to the roster of Indian cultivars.

The Chinese agronomical tradition was isolated from that of Europe until the eighteenth century. The earliest complete agronomical text that survives is the *Chhi Min Yao Shu* ("Essential Techniques for the Peasantry," c. 535 C.E.), by Chia Ssu-Hsieh. He says he wrote the book for his own children; therefore the text is plain and lacking in the rhetorical flourishes of the literary culture of the day and his approach is pragmatic. He describes crop rotations (e.g.; beans rotated with millet) which permitted constant cropping without fallowing. He names nearly one hundred varieties of millet. A later treatise was the *Nung Shu* (1313) by an official named Wang Chen. He apparently wrote for the bureaucratic class, because he believed that only official direction and instruction could improve peasant agriculture. He stresses the comparative advantages of northern (dry farming) and southern (irrigation agriculture) methods, and includes useful information on novel agricultural tools or techniques.

If one compares citations of authors in medieval Arab and Latin treatises and those of the Renaissance, the flow of information over time is sharply revealed. Ibn al-'Awwam's *Kitab al-filaha* contains one thousand nine hundred direct and indirect citations. Six hundred fifteen of these, or 32.5 percent, are to Byzantine sources, especially the *Geoponika* of Cassianus. Five hundred eighty-five (31 percent) are to near eastern sources and 85 percent of these are to Ibn Wahshiyya. Six hundred ninety citations (36.5 percent) are of earlier Sevillian agronomical writers. Classical sources were especially significant in the areas of arboriculture, olive and grape cultivation, and cereals, Near Eastern on soils and fertilizers, and Andalusi on irrigation, grafting and pruning, garden vegetables, condiments, and flowers.

In his *Opus*, Crescenzi cites thirty-four authors in four hundred twenty-eight citations. Palladius leads with one hundred twelve (26 percent of all citations), then Ibn Sina and Varro, fifty-nine (13.75 percent) each; and Albert the Great tied with Pliny, twenty-four (5.6 percent) each. There are thirteen mentions of Columella, whose work was not known first-hand to Crescenzi.

Gabriel Alonso de Herrera's *Obra de agricultura* is a sixteenth-century Spanish work that recapitulates the medieval tradition. The author's appetite for referencing dwarves that of his predecessors: he offers a total of 3,684. His top five are Crescenzi, eight hundred eighty-eight (24 percent), Pliny, six hundred ninety-two (16 percent), Palladius, five hundred twenty-nine (14.4 percent), Columella, five hundred seventeen (14 percent), and Theophrastus, two hundred sixty-two (7 percent). Two Muslim authorities, Ibn Sina and Ibn Wafid are cited one hundred forty-seven (4 percent) and one hundred two (3 percent) times, respectively.

Butzer concludes that the Mediterranean agrosystem, whether exploited by Greeks, Romans, Muslims or medieval Europeans, is "essentially the same, in terms of crops, methods, and strategies." There are only regional or cultural differences in crop emphasis and small-scale irrigation, while "At the academic level [agronomy proper] there are additional differences in the perception of agricultural goals or the different priorities set by religion, economics, or values." The problem is then how to interpret vastly different economic outcomes in the face of long-term continuity of agronomic ideas. The solution would seem to lie first in the application of similar principles and practices ("tool kits") to the myriad microregions of the Mediterranean world and second in the changing modalities of social appropriation of peasant work.

See also **Agriculture; Elements and qualities; Noria**

Bibliography

Bolens, Lucie. *Les méthodes culturales au Moyen-Age d'après les traités d'agronomie andalous: Traditions et techniques.* Geneva: Ed. Médicine et Hygiène, 1974.

Butzer, Karl W. The Islamic Traditions of Agroecology: Crosscultural Experience, Ideas and Innovations. *Ecumene: A Journal of Environment, Culture, Meaning* (1994) 1: 7–50.

Comet, Georges. "Le statut intellectuel des savoirs agricoles au Moyen Age." In *Traditions agronomiques européennes. Élaboration et transmission depuis l'Antiquité.* Edited by Marie-Claire Amouretti and F. Sigaut. Paris: CTHS, 1998, pp. 27–41.

———. "Les céréales du bas-Empire au Moyen Age." In *The Making of Feudal Agricultures?* Edited by Miquel Barceló and François Sigaut. Leiden: E.J. Brill, 2004, pp. 131–176.

Glick, Thomas F. "Introduction." In *Gabriel Alonso de Herrera, Obra de agricultura [1513].* Valencia: Hispaniae Scientia, 1979, pp. 14–49.

Ibn Khaldun. *The Muqaddimah. An Introduction to History.* Translated by Franz Rosenthal. 3 vols. Princeton: Princeton University Press, 1958.

Oschinsky, Dorothea. *Walter of Henley and other Treatises on Estate Management and Accounting.* Oxford: Clarendon Press, 1971.

THOMAS F. GLICK

ALBERT OF SAXONY

Albert of Saxony—otherwise known as Albert of Helmstedt, Albert of Rickmersdorf, or Albertutius—was one of the most influential Parisian masters of the fourteenth century, his works remaining widely read until the late sixteenth century. He was a secular cleric who taught at the Parisian Arts Faculty from 1351 to 1361/1362; he then helped to found the University of Vienna for Duke Rudolph IV of Austria (1363/64–1366), and died as Bishop of Halberstadt July 8, 1390.

The first secure biographical date is that of his determination at the Parisian Arts Faculty under master Albert of Bohemia in March 1351. Since the statutes of Paris require an age of at least twenty years to become a bachelor, Albert will have been born before 1331, probably rather around 1320. Before coming to Paris, he may have studied in Halberstadt, Magdeburg or even Erfurt, but not in Prague, which he probably visited later. After his determination and inception Albert probably started lecturing on Aristotle's *Physics* and other textbooks of *natural philosophy. In June 1353, Albert was elected rector of the Faculty (for three months of office), and from 1352 to 1362 he represented the English Nation on several occasions. Thus, in 1358, he took part in negotiations with the Picardian Nation concerning the border line of both nations—together with *John Buridan—and in 1361 he became receptor of the English Nation. He had more than fifty students that took at least one of the three parts of the master's examination under his supervision. After 1353, he probably also started studying in theology at the Sorbonne although he never finished his studies.

By November 1362 Albert had left Paris, for in that month he was named as a prebend at the cathedral chapter of Mainz on the yearly roll sent by the University of Paris to the pope to secure provision for its masters. Albert then probably went to Avignon, where he may have come into contact with the Austrian duke in July 1363, and followed Rudolph IV on a visit to Prague in April and May 1364. In September 1364 he returned to Pope Urban V as Austrian ambassador (and parish priest of Laa), and he achieved papal support for Rudolph's plan to establish a university in Vienna. Following Rudolph's foundation charter in March 1365, Albert secured a papal bull which established the Faculties of

Arts, Law and Medicine—but not a Faculty of Theology, perhaps because the emperor, Charles IV, had intervened. When Duke Rudolph died in July 1365, Albert reached an agreement over the endowment of the university. He became the first rector and imported the Parisian model for the first statutes, but actually only the Arts Faculty had been founded when he left Vienna (the university was re-founded in 1383/1384 by Duke Albert III).

Peak of Career

In October 1366 Albert was appointed Bishop of Halberstadt, and took office in February 1367; in doing so he became involved in politics. In September 1367 he lost a battle against Bishop Gerard of Hildesheim, and afterwards engaged in regional peace alliances. In 1372 he was suspected of determinism when Pope Gregory XI wrote to German inquisitors, but it seems that he was never formally accused. He stayed in office and remained quite successful until his death.

Probably mainly during his time in Paris, Albert wrote and published about thirty texts on logic and natural and moral philosophy, mainly commentaries on Aristotle, but also independent treatises. Although at times he relied heavily on Buridan or the highly original *Nicole Oresme, and also used the works of *William of Ockham, Walter Burley, *Thomas Bradwardine, and *William of Heytesbury (the last named is the only contemporary author he mentions explicitly), Albert was a quite independent thinker who sometimes combined the theories of his predecessors (especially those of Buridan, Oresme, and the English and Parisian masters) or chose to present problems in a didactic manner. His main contributions to the history of science concern "modern" logic, the theory of motion, and geology.

In *logic, he probably commented on the Ars Vetus, the Prior and Posterior Analytics and perhaps also on the Topics, although only one question on the latter is known to have survived (and some relevant problems also appear in his Perutilis Logica). Aside from some smaller texts, his main logical works are two different versions of Questiones logicales, his Perutilis Logica (or Logica nova), and his Sophismata, all of which survive in several manuscripts. The Perutilis Logica (which may even have influenced Buridan rather than vice versa) follows Ockham, but expands the problems of "modern" logic considerably into a handbook which is divided in six parts: the first deals with the elements of propositions, the second with the properties of terms, the third with different types of proposition, the fourth with consequences and syllogisms, the fifth with fallacies, and the sixth with insolubles and obligations. The work was very influential, and Albert's theory of consequences was an important step forward in the medieval theory of deduction by systematizing the forms of inference. The Questiones logicales, which have been termed "metalogical," treat various problems of logic and semantics, as well as of reference and truth. The Sophismata follow William of Heytesbury and deal intensively with infinity and the divisibility of the continuum.

In natural philosophy, Albert of Saxony contributed to the propagation of Bradwardine's Law (by his own Tractatus proportionum and in his commentary on the Physics), and of Buridan's concept of *impetus. His writings comprise different commentaries on the Physics, questions and an expositio on De Caelo, commentaries on De generatione, De anima (now lost), the Metheora and the Parva Naturalia. He also commented on *John of Sacrobosco's De Sphaera and perhaps on the so-called Philosophia pauperum, and a Questio de quadratura circuli has been attributed to him. His earlier questions on the Physics are an important work which influenced Buridan's ultima lectura. Although Albert took over Buridan's concept of *impetus or rather virtus impressa (impetus is the term used only in the ultima lectura) as not self-exhausting, and therefore had no problems explaining the celestial motions by an impressed force, there are also some changes in relation to Buridan's tertia lectura: he transferred the discussion of projectile motion into Book Eight, discussed also a different theory of motion similar to that of Ockham or Olivi, and was even more pragmatic. He was also the first to introduce the distinction between kinematics and dynamics into the Physics (relating them to Book Six and Book Seven, respectively), and he included an expanded discussion on vacuum. In the context of discussions on place and space, he also developed a theory of small movements of the Earth as a whole caused by erosion of earth by winds and rivers and resulting in geological changes which elevate lower layers. His Tractatus proportionum, which was widely copied and read, offers a more popular explanation than earlier texts of Bradwardine's Law.

Albert also contributed extensively to the field of moral philosophy through one widely read commentary on the Nicomachean Ethics and another on the Oeconomica. He lectured on the Aristotelian Politics, although no manuscripts of the text are known.

Many of the works of Albert of Saxony were distributed in several manuscripts and printed during the Renaissance period. They found wide reception at the central European and Italian universities, where they were known to a wide range of people including Leonardo da Vinci and the teachers of Galileo. In the end, even the concept of impetus was mainly linked with Albert's name (as well as with that of *Thomas Aquinas), not with Buridan's.

See also **Aristotelianism; Logic; Nature: diverse medieval interpretations**

Bibliography
Primary Sources
Albert of Saxony's Twenty-five disputed questions on logic: a critical edition of his Quaestiones circa logicam, ed. Michael J. Fitzgerald. (Studien und Texte zur Geistesgeschichte des Mittelalters, 79.) Leiden: E.J. Brill, 2002.
Albert von Sachsen. Tractatus proportionum, ed. Hubertus L. L. Busard. In Denkschriften der Österreichischen Akademie der Wissenschaften, math.-naturwiss. Kl. 116, 2. Wien: Springer in Komm 1971, pp. 43–72.

———. *Questiones subtilissime in libros De celo et mundo*, ed. Hieronymus Surianus. Venice: Bonetus Locatellus for Octavianus Scotus, 1492.

———. *Perutilis Logica*, ed. Petrus Aurelius Sanutus. Venice: Heredes Octaviani Scoti 1522 ; repr. Hildesheim-New York: Olms, 1974.

———. *Sophimata*, ed. Anthonius Chapiell. Paris: Dionysius Roce, 1502, repr. Hildesheim-New York: Olms, 1975.

Beltrán de Heredia, Vicente. Commentarios de San Alberto Magno [recte: de Saxonia] a los Económicos de Aristóteles. *La ciencia tomista* (1932) 46: 406–432.

Expositio et Quæstiones in Aristotelis Physicam ad Albertum de Saxonia Attributæ, ed. Benoît Patar. 3 volumes. (Philosophes médiévaux, XXXIX-XLI) Louvain-Paris: Institut supérieur de philosophie, Peeters, 1999.

Le Questiones de sensu attribuite a Oresme e Alberto de Sassonia, ed. Jole Agrimi. (Pubblicazioni della facoltà di lettere e filosofia dell'università di Pavia, 29) Firenze: La Nuova Italia, 1983.

Secondary Sources

Berger, Harald. "Albert von Sachsen." In *Die deutsche Literatur des Mittelalters, Verfasserlexikon*. 2nd ed. Berlin-NewYork: De Gruyter, 2000. Vol. 11, fasc. 1, col. 39–56.

———. "Bischof Albrecht III. (1366-1390) als Gelehrter von europäischem Rang (Albert von Sachsen)." In *Halberstadt. Das erste Bistum Mitteldeutschlands*. Edited by G. Maseberg and A. Schulze. (Veröffentlichungen des Städtischen Museums Halberstadt 29) Halberstadt: Städtisches Museum Halberstadt, 2004, pp. 81–92.

———. Albert von Sachsen († 1390), 4. Fortsetzung und Ergänzungen zur Bibliographie der Sekundärliteratur. *Acta Mediaevalia* (2004) 17: 253–279.

———. Albertus de Saxonia († 1390), Conradus de Waldhausen († 1369) und Ganderus recte Sanderus de Meppen († 1401/06). Eine Begegnung in Prag im Jahr 1364. Mitteilungen des Instituts für österreichische Geschichtsforschung (1998) 106: 31–50.

Biard, Joel, ed. *Itinéraires d'Albert de Saxe, Paris-Vienne au XIV siècle: actes du colloque organisé le 19-22 juin 1990 dans le cadre des activités de l'URA 1085 du CNRS à l'occasion du 600e anniversaire de la mort d'Albert de Saxe*. (Études de philosophie médiévale, 69). Paris: J. Vrin, 1991.

———. "Albert of Saxony." In *The Stanford Encyclopedia of Philosophy*. Edited by Edward Zalta. (Spring 2004 Edition). (http://plato.stanford.edu/entries/albert-saxony).

Kann, Christoph. *Die Eigenschaften der Termini. Eine Untersuchung zur Perutilis logica Alberts von Sachsen*. (Studien und Texte zur Geistesgeschichte des Mittelalters, 37.) Leiden: E.J. Brill, 1994.

Sarnowsky, Jürgen. "Albert von Sachsen und die 'Physik' des *ens mobile ad formam*." In *The Commentary Tradition on Aristotle's De generatione and corruptione. Ancient and Medieval and Early Modern*. Edited by J.M. Thijssen, H. Braakhuis. (Studia artistarum, 7) Turnhout: Brepols, 1999, pp. 163–181.

———. "Nicole Oresme and Albert of Saxony's Commentary on the *Physics*: the Problems of Vacuum and Motion in the Void." In Quia inter doctores est magna dissensio. *Les débats de philosophie naturelle à Paris au XIV siècle*. Edited by Stefano Caroti, Jean Celerette. Firenze : Leo S. Olschki 2004, pp. 161–174.

———. *Die aristotelisch-scholastische Theorie der Bewegung. Studien zum Kommentar Alberts von Sachsen zur Physik des Aristoteles*. (Beiträge zur Geschichte Philosophie und Theologie des Mittelalters, N.F. 32), Münster: Aschendorff, 1989.

———. Place and Space in Albert of Saxony's Commentaries on the *Physics*. *Arabic Sciences and Philosophy* (1999) 9: 25–45.

Thijssen, J.M.M.H. The Buridan School Reassessed. John Buridan and Albert of Saxony. *Vivarium* (2004) 42, 1: 18–42.

JÜRGEN SARNOWSKY

ALBERTUS MAGNUS

Albertus Magnus (known in English as Albert the Great) was born shortly before 1200 in Lauingen (present-day Swabia) into a knightly family in the service of the counts of Bollstadt. He died in Cologne on November 15, 1280. As a youth he was sent to study the liberal arts in Padua, where he probably began to read Aristotle and showed signs of an early interest in the study of the natural world. In the summer of 1223 he entered the Dominican order as a result of the preaching of Jordan of Saxony (the second master general of the order). Albert studied theology at the priory of Cologne, becoming lector (lecturer) there in 1228. He afterwards taught theology in various German Dominican priories (Hildesheim, Freiburg, Regensburg, and Strassburg), and during his wanderings visited the mines of the Harz mountains. During this period he wrote his first work, *De natura boni*, a theological treatise in which he cited several of Aristotle's books on nature. In the early 1240s he was sent to Paris to lecture on the *Sentences* of *Peter Lombard, and in 1245 he became Master of Theology, lecturing for three consecutive years at the Dominican priory of St.-Jacques, while he was engaged in the writing of a large theological work, the *Summa de creaturis*. Although at that time the ban on Aristotle's *libri naturales* (books on natural philosophy) decreed in 1210 and 1215 was still in effect at the University of Paris, Albert was able to absorb much of the new Aristotelian knowledge. He left Paris in 1248 together with *Thomas Aquinas (who had arrived in the city three years earlier) to serve as Regent Master at the recently established Dominican *studium* (college) in Cologne, where he remained until 1254. It was in Cologne that Albert finished his commentaries on Lombard and on the pseudo-Dionysian corpus begun in Paris. The period during which Albert wrote his paraphrase of Aristotle's works has long been a controversial issue, but in the most informed opinion it spanned about two decades, from 1250–1252 to 1270. Albert was elected provincial of the German province of the Order of the Preachers in 1254 and remained in office until 1257. He first traveled to Italy in 1256–1257, when he visited the papal court at Anagni. From 1257 Albert was back as lector at the Dominican study of Cologne, and in January 1260 he was appointed bishop of Regensburg by Pope Alexander IV, holding this office for almost two years. In the summer of 1261 Albert returned to Italy, where he remained until early 1263, initially at Viterbo and later at Orvieto. Immediately afterward he was sent to preach throughout Germany the crusade to the Holy Land launched by Pope Urban IV. From the end of 1264 to

MAGNVS · ALBERTVS · BOLSTADIVS · COGNOMENTO

Mitra pedumq̃ oneri tibi quondam Alberte, fuerunt.
Dulcius est Sophiæ delituiſſe ſinu.

Albertus Magnus taught Aristotelianism at the University of Paris. Thomas Aquinas was among his pupils. Albertus was canonized in 1931. (National Library of Medicine)

1267 Albert lived in Würzburg and, after a short stay in Strassburg in 1268, he remained in the Dominican convent in Cologne as lector emeritus from 1269 until his death. Albert's reputed participation in the Council of Lyons (1274) and his trip to Paris on the occasion of the condemnations of 1277 have been questioned by scholars.

Historical Significance and Scope

Albert the Great made available to the West a first complete, comprehensive version of the Aristotelian *scientia*. What could be taken as characteristic of Albert's approach to Aristotle—in contradistinction to that of authors such as *Robert Grosseteste and *Roger Bacon—is his emphasis on the observational, "empirical" branches of the Aristotelian encyclopedia of natural knowledge. Albert filled in the gaps in the sequence of the Aristotelian *libri naturales* with works of his own. Foremost among these were his treatises *On Plants* and *On Minerals* and his massive work *On Animals*, which

remained influential well into modern times. Moreover, Albert's treatment of physics, *cosmology, and the elements of matter provided a consistent interpretation of Aristotelian natural philosophy which was energetically pursued by Dominican authors, foremost among them Albert's disciple Aquinas. In the wake of the translation movement and the reception in the West of Aristotle, by the mid-thirteenth century the Christian world was confronted with the challenge of a comprehensive and consistent system of knowledge, a substantial part of which was related to the explanation of the natural world. Albert, a theologian turned philosopher, refurbished the Aristotelian encyclopedia to make it compatible with the Christian worldview, eliminating the tenet of the eternity of the world and considering nature as the result of divine creation. But while it seems legitimate to distinguish between Albert's philosophy and his theology inasmuch as he himself argues for it, his inquiry into nature is an integral part of his philosophy. What is sometimes termed Albert's "science" is actually natural philosophy (*philosophia naturalis*), a part of

Aristotelian *scientia* and as such an intellectual program that anticipates the modern distinction between science and philosophy.

Albert intended to make Aristotle "intelligible to the Latins." While at Cologne in the early 1250s he was asked by fellow Dominicans to write a paraphrase of Aristotle's *Physics*. He did more than that: he provided them with an exposition of the whole of natural knowledge along Peripatetic lines. In his works Albert repeatedly claims that what he intends to do is to expound the philosophy of the Peripatetics as faithfully as possible, correcting and completing it as necessary. His technique of commentary was the paraphrase of the Aristotelian text, which gave him the freedom to expound his own opinions as "digressions," to include a vast array of materials from other authors—in particular Arabic interpreters such as *Ibn Sina (Avicenna) and *Ibn Rushd (Averroes)—and to assimilate different kinds of disciplinary traditions and literary genres. Crucial to his project was the manner in which he handled and articulated different bodies of knowledge identified with authoritative authors. Albert himself distinguished between different fields of inquiry in terms of the authorities on whom he relied: Augustine in theology, *Galen and *Hippocrates in medicine, Aristotle "or anyone experienced in natural things" in matters of nature.

The Structure of Albert's Natural Philosophy

Albert adopts the Aristotelian scheme of a threefold division of philosophy into *metaphysics (concerning the intelligible), mathematics (dealing with the intelligible and imaginable), and physics (treating the intelligible, the imaginable, and the sensible). The object of physics is the natural, real body, considered with motion and sensible matter. Mathematics abstracts from real existence and deals with one aspect of body: its quantity as reconstructed in the imagination. Albert rejected the "Platonic" view supported by authors such as Grosseteste and Bacon that natural philosophy is founded on the principles of mathematics, and that mathematics in turn is founded on the principles of metaphysics. He endorsed the Aristotelian view that each science is autonomous within the limits of its principles, and that mathematics is only an aid to natural philosophy. Also, the ascent to metaphysics—the subject of which is not God but being as being—is through the natural sciences. The only known mathematical work ascribed to Albert is a commentary on the first four books of *Euclid's *Elements* which drew on a commentary by al-Narizi (Anaritius).

In the first book of the *Meteorology* Albert expounded his plan of commenting on Aristotle's *libri naturales*. According to this account, natural science (*scientia naturalis*) would involve three stages, considering: (1) The simple mobile body (*Physics*, *On the Heavens*, *On Generation and Corruption*); (2) The simple changeable body on its way to mixture (*Meteorology*); and (3) The mixed changeable body (minerals, plants, and animals). The *Physics* treats the principles of the mobile body, *On Heavens* discusses the motion from place to place of simple bodies, and *On Generation and Corruption* deals with simple bodies undergoing other kinds of change. In this section should also be included Albert's *On the Nature of Places*—a "physical *geography" which discusses coordinates and geographical accidents in terms of the seven climatic zones of the Earth—and *On the Causes of the Properties of the Elements*, which deals with the four elements and the action of the planets on them. The first three books of the *Meteorology* are about all the meteorological and geological phenomena resulting from the transition to mixture; the fourth book examines the compounds (a sort of "chemistry"). The third part of Albert's *philosophia naturalis* deals with the changeable body contracted to mineral, vegetal, and animal species. Thus, it comprehends inanimate bodies, which are discussed in his *On Minerals*, as well as bodies with soul, i.e., plants and animals, including human beings. Albert's exposition of living creatures opens with *On the Soul*, which is followed by a group of short treatises on the vital functions of living beings grouped under the title *Parva naturalia*—four of them were original works. Then came the treatise on plants and the various works on animals. Albert also wrote a commentary on the pseudo-Aristotelian *On Causes*, a work much influenced by pseudo-Dionysian philosophy.

Physics, Astronomy, and Alchemy

In his *Physics*, Albert affirms that the subject of natural science is the body as it undergoes any kind of natural change: generation and corruption (substantial change), increase and diminution (quantitative change), alteration (qualitative change), and local movement (locomotion). The principles of form and matter, characteristic of the doctrine of *hylomorphism, are also the active and passive principles of change. Explanations of the phenomena of change should be framed in terms of the four Aristotelian causes: material, formal, efficient, and final cause.

Albert drew a distinction between mathematical astronomy, subordinated to mathematics and providing hypotheses designed to "save the phenomena," and physical astronomy, which was concerned with the physical description of the universe and causal explanations. Albert depended on the geocentric physical world-pictures of Aristotle and al-Bitruji (Alpetragius) but did not altogether exclude *Ptolemy's system of mathematical astronomy, although he did not spell out the articulation of both approaches. He seems to have preferred the simpler system of the twelfth-century Arab astronomer, although he was aware that it was unable to explain the retrograde motion of the planets. Beside the first mover in the outermost sphere, identified with God and the ultimate cause of all movement in the universe, Albert postulated individual spiritual substances as movers for each sphere. The attribution of the *Speculum astronomiae* to Albert is considered doubtful by many scholars. Albert dealt with *astrology in several of his works and mostly in *On the Causes of the Properties of the Elements*. His principal authorities were Ptolemy and

Albumasar (*Abu Ma'shar). Albert believed in the influence of heavenly bodies on natural and social events on Earth, but in his theological works he underscored that the stars could not interfere with the exercise of free will in humans.

Albert's fame as an alchemist was great (as was his reputation as a magus), but it is now agreed that he did not write any work on *alchemy. Basing his conclusions mostly on Arabic sources, in the *Meteorology* and *On Minerals* Albert admitted the theoretical possibility of transmutation of metals but considered that it was very difficult to achieve. He was familiar with laboratory practice but was not himself an adept of the art and distrusted its hermetical and allegorical interpretations. In his theological works Albert condemned magic as the work of devils, but in his Aristotelian commentaries and original works his attitude is more nuanced: it seems as if he would have accepted "natural magic" as the result of the occult virtues of nature.

In *On Minerals* Albert deals with "stones," "minerals," and "intermediates." Minerals and stones are considered with respect to their essences ("origin" in terms of the four Aristotelian causes), accidental properties and, finally, their individual properties. The work draws on Aristotelian, Avicennan, and alchemical theories, as well as on Albert's considerable familiarity with metallurgical processes and his experience in the mining districts of Germany. Book II is a lapidary, preceded by a tract on "the causes and powers of stones" and followed by a treatise on sigils (images in stones) with a considerable amount of magical lore.

Plants and Animals

Two of the five books of *On Plants* are a commentary on the pseudo-Aristotelian *De Plantis* by Nicholas of Damascus; the remainder of the work is Albert's own. From the examples used it is clear that Albert was well acquainted with the flora of western Europe. Particular attention is paid to the habitat of plants, and there are numerous morphological observations concerning individual plants. Albert divided the plant kingdom into trees, shrubs, *olera virentia* (large leafy stems), and herbs; besides, he added a doubtful category for fungi. Book VI is a herbal, and Book VII deals with *agriculture and contains information about domestic and economic uses of plants, transplanting, and grafting.

Albert's study of animals is embodied in several works; the widest ranging is *On Animals*, his commentary on Michael Scot's Latin version of Aristotle's *History of Animals*, *On the Parts of Animals*, and *On Generation of Animals*, together with two original books and a "dictionary of animals." The last named drew heavily on *Thomas de Cantimpré's encyclopedia *On the Nature of Things*, and treated humans, quadrupeds, birds, aquatic animals, serpents, and *vermes* (vermin). In Book XI Albert discussed his methodology, distinguishing a two-step approach between a "narrative method" concerned with description, and the ulterior search for causal explanation of the facts. Humans, considered as the summit in the hierarchy of sentient beings, are the point of reference for Albert's study of animals. In *On Animals* Albert tried to reconcile the at times contradictory natural philosophical and medical doctrines of Aristotle and Galen and quite a lot of medical material—much of it taken from Ibn Sina's *Canon*—entered the work, including an account of human anatomy and a long discussion of human generation.

In an effort to show that Albert was a "scientist" or at least a "precursor" of a given scientific discipline, some have extolled, at times exaggeratedly, his personal observations and "discoveries." Undeniably, Albert had the cast of mind of a naturalist, a taste for the wilderness and the things of nature, and he was interested in the systematic and exhaustive study of all created beings. In philosophy, he argued for the need to arrive at general statements and principles proceeding from the study of particular species, and his understanding of Aristotle emphasized the latter's concern for the empirical basis of all knowledge. But Albert was also a scholastic: just as significant as his study of *natural history is his deployment of rhetorical devices and textual strategies to unify into a coherent synthesis different traditions of knowledge about nature within a christianized *Aristotelianism.

See also **Botany; Cosmology; Elements and qualities; Herbals; Lapidaries; Mineralogy; Natural history;** *Scientia*; **Translation movements; Universities; Zoology**

Bibliography

Primary sources

Albertus Magnus. *Opera omnia (Editio Coloniensis)*. Edited by the Albertus-Magnus-Institut. Münster: Aschendorff, 1951.

——. *Omnia opera*. 38 vols. Edited by Auguste Borgnet. Paris: L. Vivès, 1890–1899.

——. *De vegetabilibus libri septem*. Edited by Ernst Meyer and Carl Jessen. Berlin: G. Reimer, 1867.

——. *Albertus Magnus on Animals. A Medieval Summa Zoologica*. Translated by Kenneth F. Kitchell, Jr., and Irven M. Resnick. 2 vols. Baltimore: Johns Hopkins University Press, 1999.

——. *The Commentary of Albertus Magnus on Book I of Euclid's Elements of Geometry*. Edited by Anthony Lo Bello and Derek Robinson. Leiden: E.J. Brill, 2003.

——. *Albertus Magnus. Book of Minerals*. Translated by Dorothy Wyckoff. Oxford: Clarendon Press, 1967.

Secondary Sources

Anzulewicz, Henryk, ed. *De forma resultante in speculo. Die theologische Relevanz des Bildbegriffs und des Spiegelbildmodells in den Frühwerken des Albertus Magnus. Eine textkritische und begriffsgeschichtliche Untersuchung*. 2 vols. Münster: Aschendorff, 1999.

Asúa, Miguel de. "Minerals, Plants and Animals from A to Z. The Inventory of the Natural World in Albert the Great's *philosophia naturalis*." In *Albertus Magnus. Zum Gedenken nach 800 Jahren: Neue Zugänge, Aspekte und Perspektiven*. Edited by Walter Senner. Berlin: Akademie Verlag, 2001.

——. "The Organization of Discourse on Animals in the Thirteenth Century. Peter of Spain, Albert the Great, and the Commentaries on *De animalibus*." Ph.D. Dissertation. University of Notre Dame, 1991.

Bonin, Therese M. *Creation As Emanation: The Origin of Diversity in Albert the Great's on the Causes and the Procession of the Universe*. Notre Dame: University of Notre Dame Press, 2001.

Friedman, John B. "Albert the Great's Topoi of Direct Observation and his Debt to Thomas of Cantimpré." In *Pre-Modern Encyclopaedic Texts*. Edited by Peter Binkley. Leiden: E.J. Brill, 1997.

Jordan, Mark D. "Albert the Great and the Hierarchy of Sciences." *Faith and Philosophy* (1992) 9: 483–499.

Köhler, Theodor W. *Grundlagen des philosophisch-anthropologischen Diskurses im dreizenhten Jahrhundert. Die Erkentniss-bemühung um den Menschen im zeitgenössischen Verständniss*. Leiden: E.J. Brill, 2000.

Price, Betsey Barker. "The Physical Astronomy and Astrology of Albertus Magnus." In *Albertus Magnus and the Sciences*. Edited by James A. Weishepl, OP. Toronto: Pontifical Institute of Mediaeval Studies, 1980.

Stannard, Jerry. "The Botany of St. Albert the Great." In *Albertus Magnus Doctor Universalis, 1280/1980*. Edited by Gerbert Meyer and Albert Zimmermann. Mainz: Matthias-Grünewald-Verlag, 1980.

Thorndike, Lynn. "Albertus Magnus." In Lynn Thorndike, *A History of Magic and Experimental Science*. 8 vols. New York: University of Columbia Press (1923–1958).

Tilmann, Sister Jean P. *An Appraisal of the Geographical Works of Albertus Magnus and His Contributions to Geographical Thought*. Ann Arbor: University of Michigan Press, 1971.

Wallace, William. "The scientific methodology of St. Albert the Great." In *Albertus Magnus Doctor Universalis, 1280/1980*. Edited by Gerbert Meyer and Albert Zimmermann. Mainz: Matthias-Grünewald-Verlag, 1980.

Weisheipl, James A, OP. "Albertus Magnus and the Oxford Platonists." Proceedings of the American Catholic Philosophical Association (1958) 32: 124–139.

———. "The Life and Works of St. Albert the Great." In *Albertus Magnus and the Sciences*. Edited by James A. Weishepl, OP. Toronto: Pontifical Institute of Mediaeval Studies, 1980.

MIGUEL DE ASÚA

ALCHEMY

In the narrow sense of the word, alchemy refers to the attempt to transmute base metals into gold. In the broader sense, alchemy includes the enquiry into the scientific, theoretical, philosophical, theological, and mystical frameworks that encompass the application of chemical operations. Historically, the art of alchemy attempted to achieve two goals: (a) To produce or counterfeit precious metals from baser metals; and (b) To attain longevity and immortality through the *elixir vitae* (elixir of life).

The etymology of the word "alchemy" is debatable. It has been attributed to the ancient Egyptian *km* (black) or *kmt* (the black land), suggesting one of the ancient names for Egypt in relation to its rich alluvial soil along the Nile River. However, it has been noted that the Coptic word *keme* is never attributed to the concept of alchemy.

In addition, the Greek words *kymeia* (fusion), *kyma* (casting), and *kymos* (juice) have been associated with the origins of the English word; and it appears they were translated into the Syriac as *kimiya*, then into Arabic as *al-kimiya*, and later adopted by the Latin West in numerous phonetic forms (e.g., *alchimia, alkimia, alquimia, chymiae*).

The problem of identifying the origin of alchemy is further compounded when considering that early alchemical interests and efforts have been linked to ancient Mesopotamia, a point that becomes particularly complicated on the examination of specific equipment, technology, and religious beliefs of metallurgists and artisans at the time: (a) Sophisticated laboratory apparatuses (e.g., furnaces, bellows, crucibles, beakers, and weights); (b) Extant cuneiform tablets on the art of metallurgy (e.g., artificial lapis lazuli, copper, and silver); (c) The application of assaying gold by cupellation; and (d) The intrinsic association of metals and gods with *astrology. In addition, there appear to have been only minor technological advances made between Mesopotamian and Greek alchemical laboratory apparatus and those later adopted and improved by Muslim alchemists. For example, much of the equipment and many of the tools listed by the tenth-century Muslim physician and alchemist *Abu Bakr Mohammed al-Razi in his work *Sirr al-asrar* (*Secrets of Secrets*), are quite similar to earlier Mesopotamian technology: *al-tannur* (furnace), *minfakh aw ziqq* (bellows), *bawtaqa* (crucible), *qawarir* (flasks), etc. Furthermore, beginning in the fourth century B.C.E., over one hundred Taoist canonical texts covering the art of alchemy were written; many of the texts suggested that immortality was considered attainable through the application of medicines and other methods. Thus, by the first century B.C.E. a "gold elixir" (*chin-tan*) or "liquefied gold" (*chin-i*) appears in the texts; and as was true of Chinese alchemy, it appears most Muslim alchemical texts focused on the *iksir* (elixir). However, although similar ingredients and fractional distillation were employed by both cultures, the Muslim alchemists appear to have been introduced to the idea of the elixir by way of the Syriac term *ksirin* via the Greek word *iksirat*, representing powder used in medicine.

Even in light of these findings, it is still debatable whether or not Mesopotamian sources and Chinese alchemical literature were responsible for influencing the early Greek and Muslim alchemists. Moreover, it is not apparent when and what the Greeks truly knew about alchemy, since the majority of Greek alchemical texts are accessible only through uncatalogued and unpublished Arabic translations. Thus there are no extant Greek documents on the transmutation of base metals into gold until after the first centuries of the Common Era.

Early Alchemical Literature

At the same time, possibly the oldest Chinese alchemical treatise *Chou i ts' an t'ung ch' i* (*The Concordance of the Three*), which dates to c. 142 C.E., was considered to be an important interpretation of the *I ching* (*Book of*

Changes), and used simple chemical operations to represent metaphorically the cosmic balance between yin and yang. Subsequently, in the work entitled *Pao p'u tzu nei p'ien* (*The inner chapters of the philosopher Pao p'u tzu*), written c. 320 C.E., the first notable Chinese alchemist Ko Hung (283–343 C.E.), whose pseudonym, Pao p'u tzu, is used in the title, advocated the pursuit of alchemy for the sake of pure knowledge. The chapters consist of a collection of instructions, transmitted to Ko Hung by his great-uncle Ko Hsuan (c. third century C.E.), on the production of arsenic, mercury, and counterfeit silver- and gold-based elixirs for, among other things, ailments, longevity, invulnerability, immortality, and resurrection. By the seventh century, perhaps the most famous Chinese alchemical text compiled was by the author Sun Su-mo (c. 581–673 C.E.), and it was entitled *Tan ching yao chueh* (*Essential Formulas from the Alchemical Classics*). In the treatise, Su-mo detailed the construction of furnaces and specified recipes and apparatus needed for producing medicinal remedies and elixirs of immortality; again, it appears that the technology was similar to, if not slightly more advanced than, that of earlier Mesopotamian models.

At about the same time (100–300 C.E.), a mass of Greek philosophical, astrological, magical, and alchemical texts, purportedly compiled by Egyptians in Alexandria, was being attributed to Hermes Trismegistus ("Hermes the thrice-greatest"). The texts are collectively referred to as Hermetic literature or Hermetica, and primarily reflect mystical teachings on philosophy, theology, occultism, and astrology via Platonic dialogues. In Egypt, the Greeks superlatively praised (i.e., "thrice greatest") the Egyptian lunar deity Thoth or Djeheuty, whom they associated with Hermes, the messenger of the gods, the progenitor of writing, and the patron deity of good fortune, fraud, magic, and poetry. In addition, Hermes is frequently recorded by late antique and Byzantine writers as the initial transmitter of alchemy; and early Muslim scholars considered Hirmis (Hermes) to have been an exile of Babylonia, a Pharaoh of Egypt, a prolific commentator on magic, and the primary progenitor of alchemy. However, even though a consistent link between Pharaonic and Graeco-Eygptian magic has been reasonably established, at present it is not as evident that such a similar correlation existed within the alchemical corpora. Nevertheless, the Roman Emperor Diocletian (245–313 C.E.) did order the collection and burning of all magical and alchemical books, thus suggesting that both arts had possibly been developed for a considerable period of time prior to the decree. In the end, the quintessential alchemical work of Hermes is the *Emerald Tablet*, a text that was later translated from Arabic into Latin under the same title, *Tabula smaragdina*. In brief, the Arabic translation states that: (a) All things were from one; (b) The structure of the microcosm is in accordance with the macrocosm; and (c) The Sun and Moon represent father and mother, respectively.

By the late eighth and early ninth century C.E., late copies of Greek alchemical texts, initially translated into Syriac, appear to have been some of the first works ever translated into Arabic during early Abbasid times. The authorship of early Arabic alchemical texts is obscure until the late ninth and early tenth centuries. Thus, traditionally, the Umayyad prince Khalid ibn Yazid (660–704 C.E.) is credited not only with learning alchemy from a recluse named "Morienus the Greek," but also with ordering Greek and Coptic writings on alchemy to be translated into Arabic for the first time. Several centuries later, the English monastic scholar Robert of Chester or Robertus Castrenis (fl. 1142–1150 C.E.) translated the Khalid-Morienus work from Arabic to Latin in a treatise entitled *Liber de compositione alchimiae* (*The Book of the Composition of Alchemy*). The work is possibly the first book on alchemy translated from Arabic into Latin, and it appears to have been one of the precursors to the great proliferation of alchemical texts translated from Arabic into Latin, which took place in the Ebro valley and, somewhat later, in Toledo in the twelfth and thirteenth centuries. However, like its predecessor, its authenticity has been called into question. Nevertheless, apparently, the work served as one of the first introductions to alchemy in the Latin West.

Influence of Philosophy and Science in Alchemy

Due to the unsystematic manner in which the Greek-Syriac texts were translated into Arabic, errors were prevalent among many of the initial interpretations, and, therefore, had a lasting affect on Western scholarship. In one instance, the Muslim scholar *Jabir ibn Hayyan (c. 721–815 C.E.), known as Geber to the Latin West, appears to have been one of the initiators of the notion of an "assembly of philosophers," maintaining that Hermes, Pythagoras, Socrates, Aristotle, and Democritus all met at one time to discuss alchemical propositions. It has been suggested that the rationale for Jabir assimilating all of these early Greek philosophers into a single assembly, irrespective of their actual lifetime, is congruent with the idea of unity found in Islam. However, it also appears that the chronological dates of early Greek philosophers were simply not known to early Muslim scholars, which also seems to explain how so many alchemical references were indiscriminately credited to *Plato. Interestingly, the notion of the "assembly of philosophers" later re-emerged in some of the most prominent alchemical works in the Latin West. Translated from Arabic into Latin, the work *Turba philosophorum* ("Assembly of the Sages") surprisingly included the pre-Socratic philosophers (i.e., Anaximander, Anaximenes, Anaxagoras, Empedocles, Archelaos, Leucippus, Ecphantus, Pythagoras, and Xenophanes). Therefore, the translator not only included more Greek sources in the text, but clearly elaborated on an error entirely conceived by early Muslim scholarship.

During the late ninth and early tenth century, a number of Greek-Syriac texts dealing with the Greek subject of natural philosophy began to be incorporated into Muslim alchemic commentaries; and, by the twelfth century, these translated annotations would substantially influence the Latin West. One such concept, prevalent among many early Muslim scholars studying *tabi'yat* (natural philosophy), was the notion that all metals were literally prone to spontaneous growth. Basically, all base metals (e.g., lead) had the ability to "grow" into precious metals (e.g., gold). Thus, in essence, it was only for the alchemists to discover a catalyst that would expedite the process. It is a theme that re-emerged in the *De Mineralibus* (*Book of Minerals*) of the thirteenth-century Dominican friar and Scholastic philosopher *Albertus Magnus. In the book, Albertus upheld the hypothesis that a "natural" transmutation occurs between silver and gold because both are "noble" metals. However, Albertus remained doubtful that the process could be duplicated in a laboratory, and concluded that such alchemical claims were made by "deceivers" who preyed on the ignorant. Interestingly, although many early Muslim scholars accepted the idea that metals were living animate objects, which grew like plants or crystallized like minerals, the same scholars were also known to have rejected the alchemic claim of transmutation as being nothing more than deceptive. Thus, eventually, alchemic literature evolved into the realm of philosophical speculation; and soon the art of alchemy, itself, became a metaphor for examining a wide range of considerations focusing on whether or not alchemy was a science and to what degree ethics applied.

Early references to alchemic ethics can be found in the work entitled *Kitab al-Hind* (*The Book of India*) by the Muslim scholar *Abu Rayhan al-Biruni (973–1048 C.E.). In one particular chapter, al-Biruni discussed the alchemical work of Nagarjuna (c. 150–250 C.E.), whom he believed to have lived during the eighth century, but who was possibly the Indian Buddhist monk-philosopher who founded the Madhyanika school of Buddhism and who wrote the *Rasaratnakara* (i.e., a verse treatise on alchemy and metallic medicine). Retelling several gruesome alchemistic stories, in colourful moralistic overtones, al-Biruni rejected alchemy as being a "make-believe science," and adamantly condemned it on the grounds of its pernicious effects on the ignorant. Another example of moral and ethical speculation can be found in the work of the early Muslim philosopher *Abu Nasr al-Farabi (c. 870–950 C.E.), known to the Latin West as Alfarabius, who was credited for having argued for the validity of maintaining secrecy in the art of alchemy. Al-Farabi maintained that to prevent the collapse of the economic world order, which God had in fact established, one could not divulge the secrets of transmuting base metals into silver and gold. More than four centuries later, the Muslim historian Ibn Khaldun (1332–1406 C.E.) related a somewhat reverse-argument in his seminal work the *Muqaddimah* (*Introduction*) by claiming that the alchemic transmutation of silver and gold was not even scientifically obtainable, therefore it was not a matter to be considered seriously, simply because it would defy the laws of God which ensured "the standard of value by which the profits and capital accumulation of human beings are measured." Interestingly, the Muslim philosopher and physician *Abu Ali ibn Sina (980–c. 1036 C.E.), known as Avicenna to the Latin West, was

somewhat ambivalent about the question. He rejected the theory of transmutation, but is known to have praised the alchemists for their technological ability to imitate the properties of silver and gold. Similarly, the Italian Dominican theologian and disciple of Albertus Magnus, *Thomas Aquinas (1225–1274) later concluded in his *Summa Theologiae* that it was not unlawful to sell alchemical gold as "real gold" so long as it really possessed the same properties as gold: "For nothing prevents art from employing certain natural causes for the production of natural and true effects as Augustine says of things produced by the art of the demons."

Since alchemical texts can be interpreted literally, theoretically, allegorically, mystically, etc., there is no overall consensus that the art of alchemy shared a common origin or was de facto "the precursor to modern chemistry." Instead, alchemical literature appears to have been in some sense an internal exchange and refinement of unique regional and cultural perspectives on nature, philosophy, religion, etc., which became fundamental for

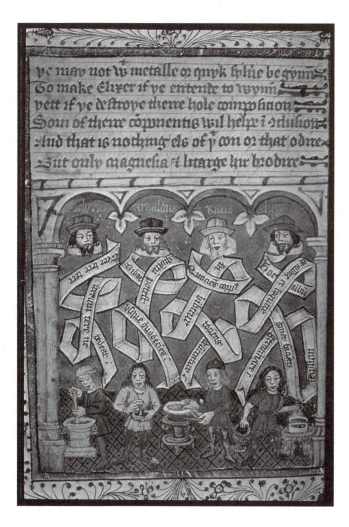

Alchemists at work in the fifteenth century. For the greater part of the medieval period the attempts of alchemists to convert base metal into gold were regarded as legitimate scientific studies. (Ancient Art and Architecture Collection)

the apprentice to comprehend. However, for an apprentice attempting to penetrate individual perspectives on the art of alchemy, prior to knowledge obtained from the teacher, proved to be increasingly cumbersome, if not impossible, over the centuries for a number of reasons. For example, the majority of writings were frequently disseminated, intentionally, in cipher under a nom de plume to ensure secrecy from the uninitiated and to protect the author from possible abduction or persecution. In addition, epigraphic pseudonyms were commonly assumed by other alchemists simply to add credibility to their own writings. Moreover, following earlier individual perceptions of alchemy, it became increasingly difficult to establish the true identity of any author; there was a whole list of prominent individuals who were frequently identified as alchemists, including the following: Thoth, Moses, Solomon, Mary, Jesus, Hermes, Democritus, Cleopatra, and Zarathustra.

Therefore, the practice of alchemy appears to have evolved into a collective art whose discursive developments far outweighed the minor advancements and contributions made to science and technology. Although the practice of alchemy borrowed from the laboratories of herbalists and physicians and employed materials and equipment used by other artisans, it should be clear that the objective of the alchemists was plain: either to produce or counterfeit precious metals from baser metals, or attain longevity and immortality through the *elixir vitae*.

See also **Magic and the occult; Mineralogy; Translation movements**

Bibliography

Biruni, Muhammad ibn Ahmad. *Alberuni's India*. Translated by Edward C. Sachau. New York: Norton 1971.

Copenhaver, B.P. Hermetica: *The Greek 'Corpus Hermeticum' and the Latin 'Asclepius.'* New York: Cambridge University Press, 1992.

Fowden, Garth. *The Egyptian Hermes: A Historical Approach to the Late Pagan Mind*. Princeton: Princeton University Press, 1993.

Holmyard, E.J. *Alchemy*. Baltimore: Penguin, 1968.

Ibn Khaldun. *The Muqaddimah*. Translated from Arabic by Franz Rosenthal. Princeton: Princeton University Press, 1967.

Levey, Martin. *Chemistry and Chemical Technology in Ancient Mesopotamia*. New York: Elsevier, 1959.

Magnus, Albertus. *De mineralibus*. Translated by Dorothy Wyckoff. Oxford: Clarendon Press, 1967.

Montgomery, Scott L. *Science in Translation: Movements of Knowledge Through Cultures of Time*. Chicago: University of Chicago Press, 2000.

Sivin, Nathan. *Chinese Alchemy: Preliminary Studies*. Cambridge: Harvard University Press, 1968.

Stavenhagen, Lee. *A Testament of Alchemy, Being the Revelations of Morienus, Ancient Adept and Hermit of Jerusalem to Khalid ibn Yazid ibn Mu'awiyya, King of the Arabs, of the Divine Secrets of the Magisterium and Accomplishment of the Alchemical Art*. Hanover, NH: University Press of New England for Brandeis University, 1974.

TOD BRABNER

ALDEROTTI, TADDEO

As a teacher, scholar, and practitioner of medicine in thirteenth-century Bologna, Taddeo Alderotti earned a reputation as the most celebrated physician of the late Middle Ages. He was instrumental in institutionalizing public medical teaching in Bologna, and he played a central role in the establishment of medicine as a learned discipline in the early *universities. He helped to introduce a curriculum of studies based on medical works that went beyond the basic texts of the *Articella. By initiating a series of public examinations, which qualified doctorate students to teach medicine and licensed them to practice it, Taddeo and his followers established a model for the professionalization of medicine in the late Middle Ages.

Taddeo was born in Florence, probably between 1206 and 1215, where he presumably received his basic education, possibly from the Franciscans or the Dominicans. By the mid-1260s he had moved to Bologna and had started teaching medicine in public. By this time Bologna had already gained a reputation as a center for the study and practice of medicine, so Taddeo probably acquired his expertise in his adopted city. Taddeo quickly established a reputation as an outstanding teacher, and over the next three decades attracted a group of talented students who were to form the next generation of Italy's leading teachers and practitioners of medicine. They included the logician Gentile da Cingoli, Taddeo's colleague (and later adversary) *Bartolomeo da Varignana, the papal physician Guglielmo da Brescia, the famous commentator on the *Canon* of *Ibn Sina (Avicenna) Dino del Garbo, the great commentator on *Galen *Torregiano de' Torregiani (Turisanus), and the renowned anatomist *Mondino de' Liuzzi.

Taddeo and his students produced detailed commentaries on many medical texts, especially the *Articella* and the *Canon* of Ibn Sina. Taddeo himself commented on the *Aphorisms*, *Prognostics*, and *De regimine acutorum morborum* of *Hippocrates, the *Tegni* and *De crisi* of Galen, the *Isagoge* of Johannitius (*Hunayn ibn Ishaq), sections of Ibn Sina's *Canon*, and possibly Galen's *De complexionibus* as well. In these expositions Taddeo emphasized the status of medicine as an autonomous, learned discipline by presenting it as an Aristotelian *scientia that needed to be taught according to the rules of logical demonstration. Moreover, he set Hippocratic-Galenic medicine within the framework of Aristotelian *natural philosophy, thus forging a link between medicine and philosophy. Using the format of the disputed question, Taddeo and his colleagues were also keen to resolve the apparent contradictions that arose between what Aristotle had said in his biological works and what Galen had said in his medical works. Taddeo and his group used these works, together with the texts of Hippocrates and the Arabic medical authors, to develop a unified theory of medicine grounded in the principles of Aristotelian natural philosophy, which pointed the way to good medical practice. Indeed, Taddeo himself composed two works on practical medicine, one dealing specifically with fevers.

Taddeo composed most of his medical writings between the late 1270s and the late 1280s. Even so, many of them were still incomplete when he died in 1295. By his own account he was often forced to put his writing aside because of the demands of his lucrative medical practice. In an attempt to keep him in the city, the Commune of Bologna had exempted Taddeo from many of the onerous tasks that city physicians were normally expected to perform. This gave Taddeo time to develop an extensive private practice within Bologna and beyond, in cities as far afield as Modena, Ferrara, Rome, Milan, and Venice. Several documents reflecting this extensive medical practice survive in the form of *consilia* and a *regimen sanitatis* written in the vernacular.

Taddeo appears to have fostered among his students an open-minded approach to intellectual enquiry, encouraging them to expand the medical curriculum with new texts and new translations, as they became available, and to develop their interests in anatomy and *surgery. Taddeo himself exhibited a strong interest in Aristotelian philosophy, at least at the beginning of his career, and he is said to have translated a compendium of Aristotle's *Nicomachean Ethics* into Italian.

Taddeo Alderotti. (National Library of Medicine)

On his death in 1295 Taddeo left a will indicating that his medical practice, his teaching, and his financial investments had made him a rich man. Largely as a result of his efforts, medicine had become more dialectical and philosophical. Under his influence Bolognese doctors had become highly organized and powerful, exerting a greater influence in urban affairs than ever before. Taddeo stood as an example of the new social and economic status to which university-trained physicians of the later Middle Ages could aspire.

See also **Anatomy, human; Aristotelianism; Medicine, practical; Medicine, theoretical;** *Regimen sanitatis*; **Scholasticism**

Bibliography

Bullough, Vern L. Medieval Bologna and the Development of Medical Education. *Bulletin of the History of Medicine* (1958) 32: 201-215 (reprinted in his *The Development of Medicine as a Profession: The Contribution of the Medieval University to Modern Medicine*. Basel and New York: Hafner, 1966).

Siraisi, Nancy G. *Taddeo Alderotti and his Pupils: Two Generations of Italian Medical Learning*. Princeton: Princeton University Press, 1981.

———. Pietro D'Abano and Taddeo Alderotti: Two Models of Medical Culture. *Medioevo: Rivista di storia della filosofia medievale* (1985) 11:139–162.

CORNELIUS O'BOYLE

ALFONSO, PEDRO

Pedro Alfonso (Petrus Alphonsi in Latin), also known as Moses Sephardi, was an outstanding pioneer as a translator, teacher, philosopher, and scientist of the twelfth-century renaissance. Alfonso was one of the most widely read medieval authors.

We know nothing of Alfonso's birth or early education. Unlike many other medieval scientists, he has left us some autobiographical description, although most of it is in the form of a semi-fictional dialogue between his "Jewish self" and his "Christian self." In one passage he tells us that he was baptized in 1106 in the northern Spanish kingdom of Aragon, taking his baptismal names from St. Peter and his patron Alfonso I, king of Aragon and of Navarre from 1104 to 1134. After this, Pedro may have lived for a while in Toledo, an important center of translation, served for a time as a teacher in northern France and England, and appears to have been a court physician to the English King Henry I (r. 1100–1135). Of the other details of his life, we know nothing except that he both presented himself and was regarded as a teacher of astronomy. Presumably he died near the middle of the twelfth century.

While Pedro Alfonso clearly regarded himself primarily as a teacher of astronomy, he also had a strong interest in the other physical sciences. He has four major works and a group of minor works, some of whose authorship is still disputed. His two most widely read books were the

Disciplina Clericalis (*The Secretary's Art*) and the *Dialogus Contra Judaeos* (*Dialog against the Jews*). Both exist in numerous manuscripts. Less well known, but of greater interest to historians of science, were the *Epistola ad peripateticos* (*Letter to the Peripatetics*) and a set of astronomical tables that he prepared while in England. Common to all these major works are discussions of astronomy, *cosmology, theoretical medicine, and element theory.

There is no question that Alfonso was an adult at the time of his conversion to Christianity and that he was by then already a fairly well-known man of letters having, as Tolan says, "knowledge of Hebrew, of the Bible, and of the Talmud. Alfonsi [*sic*] also had received an Arab education in letters, science, and philosophy." Alfonso was one of the earliest scholars who brought Arabic astronomy to Latin scholars. His writings reveal that he was thoroughly familiar with the corpus of Arabic scientific writing, which made up the contemporary scientific curriculum in Muslim Spain. In the preface to his Latin *Tables*, he wrote "I decided in my mind that I should publish a book on this [i.e., astronomy] and that, by knowledge of [the subject] its usefulness might become known.... This work, sweated over with much labor and brought over from the Arabs, Persians, and Egyptians with extreme industry, I intended to share in a friendly manner with the Latins."

Furthermore, Pedro Alfonso explicitly offered to teach what he knew to others: sometime in the first quarter of the twelfth century he addressed a "Letter to the Peripatetics of France," probably intending the students of the schools of Paris as the recipients. After praising the study of grammar, dialectic, arithmetic, and medicine, he encouraged his readers to get to know astronomy "since it is obvious that astronomy itself is more useful, more pleasant, and more worthy than the remaining arts." He then offered himself as their teacher and incorporated into his letter the preface to his translation and adaptation of the *Astronomical Tables*.

"Our Teacher"

Throughout the Middle Ages, scholars who wished to know astronomy needed to use astronomical tables adjusted to the latitude of their domicile. While in England, Alfonso reworked *al-Khwarizmi's ninth-century astronomical tables. While Alfonso's tables may have been of limited usefulness (they were somewhat muddled), he recalculated the parameters based on his observations of October 1, 1116. In addition, his *Dialogus Contra Judaeos* often lost sight of its polemical debate as his two personas (the Jewish "Moses" and the Christian "Peter") shared many discussions of science. This text included diagrams of the Sun's course around the Earth, and the division of the Earth into seven climatic zones along with (mostly accurate) descriptions of phenomena such as the water cycle. Even though Alfonso uses terminology such as "*experimentum*," it would be anachronistic to think of his science as being based in scientific method, for it was more akin to natural philosophy, a kind of scientific reasoning drawing necessary conclusions based on accepted principles rather than the results of experimentation. That Alfonso succeeded as a teacher is clear from *De dracone*, a minor astronomical text that he produced in 1121. It was clearly written while he was in England, and was translated by Walcher of Malvern, prior of one of the most important early centers of English scientific learning. Walcher called Alfonso "Our Teacher." On the basis of a study of textual similarities, Burnett (1997) has suggested the possibility that *Adelard of Bath was also taught by Alfonso. There is some question about Alfonso's knowledge of Latin; for, if fairly late in his career he needed Walcher to turn his teaching into Latin, his skill in that language may well have been limited. However, it was not uncommon in twelfth-century Spain for documents in foreign languages to be worked on by teams of translators. Pedro Alfonso is a crucial figure in the Middle Ages in the transmission to the Latin West of superior Arabic scientific knowledge, especially information pertaining to the study of the stars.

See also **Elements and qualities; Medicine, theoretical**

Bibliography

Burnett, Charles F. S. The Works of Petrus Alfonsi. *Medium aevum*. (1997) 66: 42–79.

Jones, Joseph R. and John E. Keller. *The Scholar's Guide.* Toronto: Pontifical Institute of Medieval Studies, 1969.

Lacarra, Maria Jesus, editor. *Estudios Sobre Pedro Alfonso de Huesca.* Huesca: Instituto de Estudios Altoaragonses, 1996.

Neugebauer, Otto. *The Astronomical Tables of al Khwarizmi.* Translated with Commentaries of the Latin Version. Copenhagen: Munksgaard, 1962.

Tolan, John. *Petrus Alfonsi and his Medieval Readers.* Gainesville: University Press of Florida, 1993.

MICHAEL C. WEBER

ALFONSO X THE WISE

Alfonso X, king of Castille, was born in Toledo on July 23, 1221, became king of Castille on June 1, 1252, and died in Seville on April 4, 1284. As a patron of literature and learning, he commissioned a series of translations into Castilian and, later, into Latin, of Arabic astronomical texts, probably as the result of the discovery of new manuscripts in Córdoba and Seville, two cities conquered by his father, Fernando III, in 1236 and 1248 respectively. Alfonso X also sponsored the compilation of original works; these mark the beginning of a new European astronomy which, for the first time, was written not in Latin but in a vernacular language.

Alfonso X or his collaborators set out to compile two great collections of scientific texts. The first was devoted to magic and included the translation of the *Picatrix* (already available in Latin), four *lapidaries (an index of contents of another ten is also extant) and the *Libro de la mágica de los signos*. The second collection was astronomical and astrological (*Libros del Saber de*

Astronomía or Astrología). Alfonso also supported the translation of several individual works such as *Ibn al-Haytham's *Cosmology*, *al-Battani's *Canons*, the treatise on the sine quadrant, two versions of the Alfonsine Tables, *Ptolemy's *Cuadripartito* (i.e., the *Tetrabiblos*) with the commentary of Ali ibn Ridwan, the *Libro conplido en los iudizios de las estrellas* of Ibn Aben Ragel and the *Libro de las Cruzes*. Some at least of these independent works could have been conceived as a part of the *Libros del Saber*, but they are not included in the royal codex of this anthology (MS Villamil 156, in the Library of Madrid University).

The analysis of the previous list shows the existence of a well-structured plan. The king's ambition was to compile a collection of treatises on astronomical instruments, mainly analogical computers (celestial sphere, spherical and plane astrolabes, universal astrolabes such as the *azafea* and the universal plate) designed to provide graphical solutions to the problems of spherical astronomy and *astrology (the division of the houses of a horoscope, for example). The purpose of other instruments was time-keeping (*cuadrante con cursor*, *clepsydra*), also necessary to cast a horoscope. A third group is formed by the two treatises on the equatorium, an instrument designed to give graphical solutions to the problem of computing planetary longitudes used in a horoscope. The king ordered that two treatises, one on construction and the other on use, be furnished for each instrument. If an Arabic text was available, a translation was made; otherwise, an original treatise was written. Because treatises on the use of instruments were more common than books dealing with their construction, most of the original books (written mainly by Rabiçag—see below) dealt with the techniques for the fabrication of instruments. This is the origin of the *Libros del Saber* in which only the first book (*Ochava Espera*, an updating of 'Abd al-Rahman al-Sufi's uranography) is unrelated to astronomical instruments; this work nonetheless has obvious astrological and magical applications.

The computation of planetary longitudes is the main purpose of the tabular works translated (*Almanac*, Battani's canons) or compiled (Alfonsine Tables) by the king's collaborators. Ptolemy's *Cuadripartito*, together with a commentary, as well as the *Libro conplido and Libro de las Cruzes*) provided the reader with the knowledge needed to interpret a horoscope and predict the future. Finally, a collection of magical texts taught how to fabricate talismans and not merely predict the future, but modify it. The basic scheme of the king's plan is, therefore, clear enough and it is obvious that it had a practical (astrological and magical) purpose: only one work (the translation of Ibn al-Haytham's *Cosmology*) falls outside this project and has a theoretical purpose (a description of a physical cosmos) unrelated to astrology.

The Scientific Collaborators of Alfonso X

Alfonso X's team of collaborators comprised one Muslim convert (Bernardo el Arábigo), four "Spanish" Christians (Fernando of Toledo, Garci Pérez, Guillén Arremón d'Aspa and Juan d'Aspa), four Italians (Giovanni of Cremona, Giovanni of Mesina, Pietro of Regio, and Egidio Tebaldi of Parma), and five Jews. The participation of Bernardo el Arábigo and of the four "Spaniards" had little importance and only one among the latter (Garci Pérez) seems to have been competent as an astronomer. As for the Italians, both Giovanni of Cremona and Giovanni of Mesina participated in the revision of the first translation of the treatise on the açafeha, whilst the other two worked in the retranslations into Latin of the *Libro conplido* and the *Cuadripartito*. The arrival at the Castilian chancellery of the group of Italians could be connected to the fact that between 1256 and 1275 King Alfonso was a candidate for the imperial title; this hypothesis might also explain his change of linguistic policy and his interest in preparing Latin translations of texts already translated into Spanish. The Jewish team (Yehudah ben Mosheh, Isaac ben Sid called Rabiçag, Abraham Alfaquín, Samuel ha-Levi and Don Mosheh) was far more important than the other groups and two of its members (Yehudah ben Mosheh and Rabiçag) were particularly relevant: far more productive than the others, they were also exclusively responsable for the Alfonsine Tables. Of these two, Yehudah was mainly a translator while Rabiçag, although he knew Arabic well, concentrated in writing original works, mainly related to the construction of astronomical instruments.

A Typology of Alfonsine Translations

Alfonsine translations vary from literal translations (*Ibn al-Zarqalluh's treatise on the açafeha, al-Battani's *Canons*) to very free adaptations of an Arabic original. Free translations are numerous and often contain interpolations. Such is the case of the Latin version of the *Picatrix* (derived from a lost previous Castilian translation) where the Alfonsine translator feels free to correct the Arabic original when he considers it obsolete. Alfonso X's interest in certain astrological matters also impelled his collaborators to add original chapters (e.g., on the division of the houses) to the translation of Qusta ibn Luqa's treatise on the celestial sphere. In other cases the translator rearranged the materials of his Arabic source: this happens in the Alfonsine Latin translation of Ibn al-Haytham's *Cosmology*, in which Abraham Hebraeus has subdivided the materials of the original Arabic text (one book, fifteen chapters) into two books and forty-eight shorter chapters. The order of exposition is also altered: Ibn al-Haytham describes the planetary spheres in ascending order, while the Latin translation uses a descending one. Finally, there are repetitions: Ibn al-Haytham dedicates one chapter to the three superior planets, and another to the two inferior ones; in Abraham's version there is one chapter on each planet, with a repetition of an identical text for Saturn, Jupiter, and Mars, on the one hand, and for Venus and Mercury on the other. Finally, some texts are adaptations and compilations: the original book written by Rabiçag on the construction of the *lámina universal* (universal plate) is a mere adaptation of Ibn al-Zarqalluh's treatise on the construction of a very similar instrument (*açafeha*). A similar case is that of the treatise on the use of the spherical astrolabe. The lack of an Arabic source on this instrument led the Alfonsine collaborators to adapt the treatise on the use of the planispheric astrolabe by *Ibn al-Samh (d. 1035): the Alfonsine book is divided into one hundred thirty-five chapters and only thirty are independent of the text of Ibn al-Samh. A most peculiar case is that of the *IIII Libros de la Ochaua Espera* in which books I–III contain the description of each one of the constellations, derived mainly from one Arabic source, al-Sufi. Al-Sufi's star catalogue represents each constellation in a wheel traced on the recto of each folio of the royal codex, while the corresponding textual description can be found in the verso of the preceding folio and, thus, faces the wheel. The texts of the descriptions are practically the same length, because the codex has been designed for aesthetic impact. Thus al-Sufi's texts were drastically abbreviated in cases where the constellation has a large number of stars, while they are supplemented with materials from other unidentified sources when the number of stars is small and the author has a blank space to fill in.

The Alfonsine Tables

The Alfonsine Tables are the most important contribution of Alfonsine astronomy. They were used in Europe from c. 1320 to 1551, the year of the publication of the Prutenic Tables computed by Erasmus Reinhold. They had an important influence on the astronomy of the Renaissance. Copernicus used parameters derived from them in his *Commentariolus*: as well, the tropical Alfonsine year (365 days, 5 hours, 49 minutes, and 16 seconds) is almost the same as the mean tropical year in the *De revolutionibus*, which became the basis of the Gregorian reform of the *calendar. The work poses important historical problems due to the existence of two different versions. The first is a set of canons or explanatory instructions in Castilian, but without tables, prepared by Rabiçag and Yehudah ben Mosheh between 1263 and 1272. These describe a collection of tables in the Zarqallian tradition: mean motions are sidereal, tropical longitudes can be calculated using trepidation tables, the obliquity of the ecliptic is obtained by means of a Zarqallian model, there are references to Ibn al-Zarqalluh's correction to the Ptolemaic lunar model, etc. A second set appears in Paris around 1320: these have numerical tables, with headings in Latin, but no canons which can be attributed to Alfonso X. These tables seem unrelated to the aforementioned Castilian canons and are clearly influenced by the *zij* of al-Battani: mean motions are tropical and most Zarqallian characteristics have disappeared. Many European authors, beginning with the Parisian group formed by *John of Saxony, *Jean de Meurs, and John of Lignières, wrote original canons which were added to the Alfonsine numerical tables. Some scholars conclude that the original Alfonsine Zarqallian tables were the object of a later adaptation probably in Paris, while others believe that the second version of the Tables was prepared by the Alfonsine collaborators themselves, after their translation of al-Battani's canons.

See also Clocks and timekeeping; Patronage of science; Translation movements; Translation norms and practice

Bibliography

Bossong, Georg. *Los Canones de Albateni. Herausgegeben sowie mit Einleitung, Anmerkungen und Glossar versehen.* Tübingen: Max Niemeyer Verlag, 1978.

Chabás, José and Bernard R. Goldstein. *The Alfonsine Tables of Toledo.* Dordrecht: Kluwer, 2003.

Comes, Mercè. *Ecuatorios andalusíes. Ibn al-Samh, al-Zarqulluh y Abu-l-S'alt.* Barcelona: Instituto de Cooperación con el Mundo Arabe y Universidad de Barcelona, 1991.

Comes, M., R. Puig and J. Samsó, eds. *De Astronomia Alphonsi Regis. Actas del Simposio sobre Astronomía Alfonsí celebrado en Berkeley (Agosto, 1985) y otros trabajos sobre el mismo tema.* Barcelona: Instituto "Millás Vallicrosa" de Historia de la Ciencia Arabe, 1987.

Comes, M., H. Mielgo and J. Samsó, eds. *"Ochava Espera" y "Astrofísica." Textos y Estudios sobre las Fuentes Arabes de la Astronomía de Alfonso X.* Barcelona: Instituto de Cooperación con el Mundo Arabe e Instituto "Millás Vallicrosa" de Historia de la Ciencia Arabe, 1990.

Hilty, Gerold. El libro conplido en los iudizios de las estrellas. *Al-Andalus* (1955) 20: 1–74.

Pingree, David. Picatrix. *The Latin Version of the Ghayat al-hakim.* London: The Warburg Institute, 1986.

Poulle, Emmanuel. *Les Tables Alphonsines avec les canons de Jean de Saxe.* Paris: C.N.R.S., 1984.

Procter, Evelyn S. *Alfonso X of Castile Patron of Literature and Learning.* Oxford: Clarendon Press, 1951.

Rico y Sinobas, Manuel. *Libros del Saber de Astronomía del Rey D. Alfonso X de Castilla, copilados, anotados y comentados.* 5 vols. Madrid: Real Academia de Ciencias, 1863–1867.

Samsó, Julio. *Islamic Astronomy and Medieval Spain.* Aldershot: Variorum Reprints, 1994.

Vernet, Juan, ed. *Textos y Estudios sobre Astronomía Española en el Siglo de Alfonso X.* Barcelona: Institución "Milà y Fontanals" del C.S.I.C. y Universidad Autónoma de Barcelona, 1981.

JULIO SAMSÓ

ALFRED OF SARESCHEL

Alfred of Shareshill or Sareschel, more commonly referred to as Alfredus Anglicus (Alfred the Englishman), probably owes his name to the village of Shareshill, ten miles (16 km) west of Lichfield, and is likely to be the "Magister Alueredus de Sarutehill canonicus Lich." mentioned in a charter of Ralph Neville, dean of Lichfield from 1214 to 1222 (BL, Harley MS 4799, fol. 62va). Lichfield was the diocese to which Oxford belonged, and the nature and diffusion of Alfred's writings imply that he was involved in teaching Aristotelian philosophy in the nascent university, along with *Alexander Nequam to whom he dedicates a work. His floruit must have been the late twelfth and early thirteenth century. Alfred continued the program of translating the corpus of texts on Aristotelian natural science set out in order in *al-Farabi's *On the Classification of the Sciences*, from the point where *Gerard of Cremona (d. 1187), the Toledan-based translator of texts from Arabic into Latin, left off. Gerard had translated Aristotle's *Physics*, *On Generation and Corruption*, *On the Heavens*, and completed the *Meteorology*, Alfred took the texts next in order: *On Minerals* and *On Plants*. This strongly suggests that Alfred himself spent some time in *Toledo, a hypothesis strengthened by the fact that several Spanish vernacular words are included in his translations. It was probably here that he studied with a Master Salomon Avenraza, "Israelita celeberrimus et modernorum philosophorum precipuus" ("the most famous Jew and leader of modern philosophers") (Alfred of Sareshel, *Commentary on the "Metheora,"* 51). Furthermore, Alfred wrote commentaries on many of these texts on natural science. His commentaries were quoted by Oxford masters lecturing on Aristotle's natural science in the mid-thirteenth century, such as Adam of Buckfield and "R. de Stanington."

The works on plants and mineralogy that Alfred of Shareshill translated as part of an Aristotelian corpus were two chapters, on stones and on metals, from Avicenna's (*Ibn Sina's) *summa* of Peripatetic philosophy, the *Shifa'* (these became three chapters in Latin), and the *On plants* of Nicholas of Damascus, which Alfred dedicated to Roger of Hereford. The three chapters on stones and plants were added to Gerard's translation of the first three books of Aristotle's *Meteorology* and Henricus Aristippus's translation of the fourth book, to form a single text. Alfred wrote commentaries on this composite text, as well as on the *On Plants*, and refers to his own commentary on *On Generation and Corruption*. According to a medieval catalog of the manuscripts of Beauvais Cathedral, he also wrote commentaries on Aristotle's *On the Soul*, *On Sleep*, *On Death and Life*, and *On the Heavens*.

Alfred's independent treatise—*On the Movement of the Heart* (*De motu cordis*)—was dedicated to Alexander Nequam, probably before c. 1197 when Alexander left Oxford to become a canon of Cirencester. It is concerned with the conditions necessary for life and ensoulment (a topic also covered in his commentary on *On Plants*), and adopts a strictly Aristotelian view in making the heart rather than the brain the seat of the soul. This work is remarkable for the large number of scientific texts it cites, which include, in addition to the above-mentioned works, Aristotle's *Physics*, *On Respiration*, *Metaphysics*, and *Ethics*, Qusta ibn Luqa's *On the Difference between the Spirit and the Soul*, Alexander of Aphrodisias's commentary on the *Meteorology*, and texts by *Hunayn ibn Ishaq and Ishaq Israeli (*Isaac Judaeus). Alfred's commentaries on the *Meteorology* and the *On Plants* had the same status as the commentaries by Averroes (*Ibn Rushd) on the other books of Aristotle's natural science among university teachers in Oxford and elsewhere from the mid-thirteenth century onward. He played an important role in the period during which Aristotle was being established as the key authority in natural science in the early universities.

See also **Aristotelianism**

Bibliography

Primary Sources
Alfred of Sareshel, *Commentary on the Metheora of Aristotle*, ed. J. K. Otte. Leiden: E. J. Brill, 1988.

Nicolas Damascenus, *De plantis*. Edited by H. J. Drossaart Lulofs and E. L. J. Poortman. North Holland Publishing Co.: Amsterdam, 1989, pp. 465–473.

R. J. Long, "Alfred of Sareshel's commentary on the pseudo-Aristotelian *De plantis*: a critical edition." *Mediaeval Studies* (1985) 47: 125–167.

Des Alfred von Sareshel (Alfredus Anglicus) Schrift De motu cordis. Edited by C. Baeumker. *Beiträge zur Geschichte der Philosophie des Mittelalters*, 23. Münster: Aschendorff, 1923.

Secondary Sources
Callus, D.A. Introduction of Aristotelian learning to Oxford. *Publications of the British Academy* (1943) 29: 229–281.

Southern, R.W. *Robert Grosseteste: the growth of an English mind in medieval Europe*, 2nd edn. Oxford: Clarendon Press, 1992, pp. 90–92.

CHARLES BURNETT

ALGEBRA

Defined as the science of determining unknown quantities in mathematical relations or equations, algebra has been studied by almost every culture, although in markedly different ways. Its appearance before the Renaissance would be foreign to modern readers; the symbolic language that we associate with algebra is a sixteenth-century invention. In ancient and medieval times algebraic expressions were written rhetorically, i.e., in words rather than symbols. Methods and goals differed as well: some relied on geometrical reasoning and others on arithmetic; some accepted approximation techniques while others looked for closed-form solutions. In China, for instance, polynomial equations were solved using a method—relying on the binomial theorem—that determines successive decimal places of the solution, whereas the Babylonians, Indians, and Muslims used procedures that led directly to the solution, as we learn today in high school. Greek mathematicians were especially interested in geometric proofs of what we now call algebraic identities, but in medieval India, as in ancient Babylon, the focus was on the steps that led to a numerical solution. Often these steps were given in verse, partly for ease of memorization. As early as Aryabhata's *Aryabhatiya* (499 C.E.), we find instructions for solving problems that can be reduced to quadratic equations ($ax^2 + bx + c = 0$). Similar instructions may be found in Brahmagupta's *Brahmasphutasiddhanta* (628 C.E.) and in later, more systematic works such as Bhaskara II's twelfth-century *Bijaganita*. Thus the form of Indian algebra differed dramatically from its Greek counterpart, and the stage was set for a synthesis in medieval Islam.

Early Islamic science was influenced heavily by Indian sources. A case can be made for at least some Hindu origin in the most important algebraic text of the medieval period, *Muhammad ibn Musa al-Khwarizmi's *al-Jabr wa'al-Muqabalah*. The two terms in the title refer to, respectively, moving a subtracted quantity on one side of an equation to the other side, and combining like terms on opposite sides of an equation. The phrase came to mean the entire science of algebra; in fact, *al-Jabr* is the origin of our word "algebra." The first part of al-Khwarizmi's book is a collection of algorithms to solve various types of quadratic equation (indeed, al-Khwarizmi's name is the origin of the word "algorithm"). Because the existence of negative numbers was not yet recognized, al-Khwarizmi needed to approach, say, $ax^2 + bx + c$ differently from $ax^2 + bx = c$; altogether he classified six types of equations, five of them quadratic. Although geometrical explanations of his methods are present, the work is mostly arithmetical in character. The second part of *al-Jabr wa'al-Muqabalah* deals with the science of measuring areas and volumes; the third and final part consists of solutions to problems of the disposition of inheritances under Islamic law.

The influence of *al-Jabr wa'al-Muqabalah* was dramatic. It immediately spawned a number of successors and commentaries, among them Abu Kamil's *Algebra* (900 C.E.). This work, not surprisingly very much in al-Khwarizmi's style, is innovative particularly for its general statements of algebraic rules (such as $\sqrt{a} + \sqrt{b} = \sqrt{a + 2\sqrt{ab} + b}$), as well as its treatment of irrational quantities as numbers rather than the Greek treatment as geometric magnitudes. (It also contains the rudiments of what was to become linear algebra.) Al-Khwarizmi's *Algebra*, meanwhile, became widely used as a textbook, and was to become a major impetus for the study of algebra in Europe after its translation into Latin in the twelfth century.

Al-Khwarizmi was a member of the House of Wisdom, a research institute founded by caliph al-Ma'mun in the early ninth century. One of the House of Wisdom's most important activities was the translation into Arabic of many of the most important texts of Greek mathematics, including those of *Euclid, *Archimedes, and Apollonius. These translations propagated Greek geometric and logical methods widely, and their impact was felt in algebra as well. For instance, *Thabit ibn Qurra (836–901 C.E.), one of the translators of Euclid's *Elements*, wrote *Discourse on the Establishment of the Correctness of Algebraic Problems*, in which he sets out to demonstrate the rules for solving quadratic equations. His main concern is for logical validity, and he achieves it by geometric deductions using propositions from Book II of the *Elements*.

However, this geometrization was not to last long; the quantities at the heart of algebra were increasingly being seen as numbers rather than geometric magnitudes. This trend came to fruition in the work of al-Karaji (1000 C.E.). His book *The Marvellous* contains the first set of rules to manipulate expressions involving terms x^n with arbitrary exponents; of course, only powers up to x^3 can be represented geometrically. He developed algebraic procedures not by proving them from the *Elements*, but rather by making an analogy with arithmetic: for instance, the expression $3x^2 + 5x + 8$ is analogous to the number 358, and arithmetic operations applied to

numbers can equally well apply to the corresponding polynomials. However, al-Karaji was unable to take certain vital steps, due to the lack of a concept of negative numbers. This prevented him from being able to perform the operations needed to divide polynomials. This shortcoming was addressed in the early twelfth century by the Iraqi Jewish scholar al-Samaw'al Ibn Yahya al-Maghribi, who at age nineteen wrote a systematization of algebra called *The Dazzling Book on Calculation*, in which we find a proper theory of negative quantities. Al-Samaw'al used it effectively, extending al-Karaji's approach to make possible not only polynomial division, but also the extraction of the square root of a polynomial. Curiously, however, when al-Samaw'al deals with quadratic equations later in the book, he returns to geometric demonstrations. Also found in *The Dazzling* are examples of recursive reasoning and a preservation of al-Karaji's computation of the binomial coefficients (now known as Pascal's triangle).

Geometry, however, plays a vital role in the next great Arab contribution to algebra. Having dealt so long with quadratic equations, it is natural to ask how one might solve a cubic (in modern form, $ax^3 + bx^2 + cx + d = 0$). Just as with quadratic equations, the lack of a concept of negative numbers broke the consideration of the cubic into a number of cases. Although attempts were made to solve cubics as early as the ninth century, only four of the fourteen types were solved before *'Umar al-Khayyam (1048–1131 C.E., known to the West as Omar Khayyam, author of the epic poem *The Rubaiyat*). Al-Khayyam's *Algebra* solves all fourteen types geometrically in a manner similar to his predecessors, by demonstrating that certain line segments in diagrams in which various conic sections such as circles, parabolas, and hyperbolas intersect satisfy the relation set out in the equation. He seems to have failed in an attempt to find a solution more recognizable to us, one which is calculated directly from the coefficients in the equation.

Less than a century later, Sharaf al-Din al-Tusi's *On the Equations* (1170 C.E.) took al-Khayyam's work on cubics in a new direction. It opens with a discussion of cubics using conic sections, similar to the method in al-Khayyam. However, the second half of the book contains a startlingly modern analysis of the existence of solutions to certain cubics. Representing the equation in the form $f(x) = k$, he considers the possibilities for the maximum value of $f(x)$, and determines the ranges of values of x for which $f(x)$ increases or decreases. While the mathematics of al-Tusi's method can be verified using differential calculus, the path that he might have taken to arrive at his conclusions remains controversial.

Europe

There is very little to say about algebra, or indeed mathematics of any sort, in early medieval Europe. Interest in the subject finally began to develop in 1145, when the first two parts of al-Khwarizmi's *Algebra* were translated into Latin—the first part by Robert of Chester (and again, later, by *Gerard of Cremona), and the second part (in an expanded edition by *Abraham bar Hiyya) by Plato of Tivoli. The first original contributions to algebra in Europe are found in the works of Leonardo of Pisa (1180?–1240? C.E.), also known as *Fibonacci. His best-known work, the *Liber abaci* (1202; revised 1228), contains an exposition of Hindu-Arabic arithmetic and uses algebra systematically to solve a variety of problems. Having traveled widely, Fibonacci was influenced greatly by both Greek and Arabic works; we find traces of the methods of al-Khwarizmi and al-Karaji within the pages, of his work, and many of the problems are Arabic in origin. Fibonacci handles problems related to quadratic equations, commercial interests, and number theory; he also delves into recreational mathematics, including a problem that leads to the famous Fibonacci sequence. Later, in his *Flos* (1225), he analyzes a cubic equation found in al-Khayyam's *Algebra* ($x^3 + 2x^2 + 10x = 20$), demonstrates that the solution is not one of the types of irrational magnitude found in Book X of Euclid's *Elements*, and gives an approximate solution accurate to the equivalent of about ten decimal places. Finally, in his *Liber quadratorum* (also 1225), Fibonacci solves expertly the system of indeterminate equations $x^2 + 5 = y^2$ and $x^2 - 5 = z^2$ in the manner of Diophantus. Even taking into account Fibonacci's reliance on his Greek and Arabic forebears, there is no doubt that he was the most creative algebraist in medieval Europe.

Fibonacci's contemporary *Jordanus de Nemore, most widely known for his work in mechanics, also wrote the algebraic treatise *De numeris datis*. This book, written in the style of Euclid's *Data*, was intended to be used in the practice of the first half of the paired ancient Greek techniques of analysis and synthesis; the propositions are in the form "if x, y… are given, then z is given." However, unlike the *Data*, its contents were intended to be used for algebraic rather than geometric purposes. It has been suggested that Jordanus here anticipated François Viète, sometimes called the father of symbolic algebra, in applying analysis to the solution of equations.

Although the books by Fibonacci and Jordanus contained much creative mathematics, they seem to have stirred only a little interest in the European scholarly community, and the algebraic tradition that followed them was not nearly as lively as it was in Islam. Through the fourteenth century solutions of cubic and even some quartic equations were sought, but substantial progress on these and other algebraic problems did not occur until the late fifteenth and sixteenth centuries, when the birth of symbolism changed the face of algebra forever.

See also **Arithmetic; Commercial arithmetic**

Bibliography

Berggren, J. L. *Episodes in the Mathematics of Medieval Islam.* New York: Springer-Verlag, 1986.

Franci, R. and L. Toti Rigatelli. "Fourteenth-century Italian algebra." In *Mathematics from Manuscript to Print 1300–1600.* Edited by Cynthia Hay. Oxford: Clarendon Press, 1988.

Hughes, Barnabas, ed. *Jordanus de Nemore, De numeris datis: A Critical Edition and Translation.* Berkeley: University of California Press, 1981.

Kasir, Daoud S., ed. *The Algebra of Omar Khayyam.* New York: Teacher's College, Columbia University, 1931.

Mahoney, Michael S. "Mathematics." In *Science in the Middle Ages.* Edited by David C. Lindberg. Chicago: University of Chicago Press, 1978.

Martzloff, Jean-Claude. *A History of Chinese Mathematics.* Berlin: Springer-Verlag, 1997.

Rashed, Roshdi. "Algebra." In *Encyclopedia of the History of Arabic Science.* 2 vols. Edited by Roshdi Rashed. London: Routledge, 1996.

Rosen, Frederic, ed. *The Algebra of Mohammed ben Musa.* London: Oriental Translation Fund, 1831. Reprinted by Elibron Classics, 2002.

Sigler, Laurence, ed. *Fibonacci's Liber abaci: A Translation into Modern English of Leonardo Pisano's Book of Calculation.* New York: Springer-Verlag, 2002.

Van Egmond, Warren. The algebra of Master Dardi of Pisa. *Historia Mathematica* (1983) 10: 399–421.

GLEN VAN BRUMMELEN

ALMANACS

Although its ultimate origin remains unknown, the word almanac appears as almanac in a text attributed to *Abraham Ibn Ezra (c. 1089–1167), only extant in Latin, and in the Arabic astronomical literature as *manakh*, in various texts associated with Ibn al-Banna' (d. 1321), an astronomer from Marrakesh who used this term to refer to "the ephemerides of the Sun and the Moon." Later, the term's semantic range increased and it was understood as a set of tables, whether accompanied or not by a text explaining their use, giving the daily (or at intervals of a few days) true positions in longitude of the Sun, the Moon, and the five planets for a period of time of different duration for each celestial body. These periods of recurrence, or cycles, were fixed at an integer number of years, after which the planet returns to its initial position, very nearly, thus giving the almanac a "perpetual" use. The planetary periods, usually called goal-year periods, were already known to Babylonian astronomers and were used for predicting lunar and planetary phenomena. In the *Almagest* IX. 3, *Ptolemy (second century C.E.) gives the values for such periods. See Table One (below), where N is the number of solar years spanning the same time as an integer number (very nearly) of revolutions in longitude (R), and corresponding to an integer number of returns in anomaly (A), i.e., returns of the planet with respect to the position of the Sun.

Planet	N	R	A
Saturn	59y + 1;45d	2 rev. + 1;43°	57
Jupiter	71y − 4;54d	6 rev. − 4;50°	65
Mars	79y + 3;13d	42 rev. + 3;10°	37
Venus	8y − 2;18d	8 rev. − 2;15°	5
Mercury	46y + 1; 2d	46 rev. + 1°	145

TABLE ONE

		Azarquiel (1088)	Jacob ben Makhir (1300)	Almanac of 1307	John of Lignères (1341)	Abraham Zacuto (1473)
Sun (longitude)	cycle	4y	4y	4y	–	4y
	frequency	1d	1d	1d		1d
	precision	0;1°	0;0,1°	0;0,1°		0;0,1°
Moon (longitude)	cycle	76y	76y	76y	–	31y
	frequency	1y, 1d	1y, 1d	1y, 1d		1d
	precision	0;1°	0;0,1°	0;0,1°		0;0,1°
Moon (anomaly)	cycle	180y	24y	86y	–	86y
	frequency	1y, 1d	1 d	1y, 1d		1y, 1d
	precision	1°	0,1°	0,1°		0,1°
Lunar Node	cycle	93y	93y	93y	–	93y
	frequency	1y, 5d	1y, 1d	1y, 3d		1y, 1d
	precision	0;1°	0;0,1°	0;1°		0;1°
Saturn (longitude)	cycle	59y	59y	59y	59y	59y
	frequency	10d (2)	10d (6)	10d (2)	10d (2)	10d (6)
	precision	1°	0;1°	1°	1°	0;1°
Jupiter (longitude)	cycle	83y	83y	83y	83y	83y
	frequency	10d (2)	10d (6)	10d (2)	10d (2)	8d (5)
	precision	1°	0;1°	1°	1°	0;1°
Mars (longitude)	cycle	79y	79y	79y	79y	79y
	frequency	5d (1)	10d (6)	5d (1)	10d (6)	5d (1)
	precision	1°	0;1°	1°	1°	0;1°
Venus (longitude)	cycle	8y	8y	8y	8y	8y
	frequency	5d (1)	5d (4)	5d (1)	5d (1)	1d
	precision	1°	0;1°	1°	1°	0;1°
Mercury (longitude)	cycle	46y	46y	46y	46y	125y
	frequency	5d (1)	5d (4)	5d (1)	5d (4)	4d (3)
	precision	1°	0;1°	1°	1°	0;1°

TABLE TWO

(1) Entries for days 1, 6, 11, 16, 21, and 26 of each month.
(2) Entries for days 1, 11, and 21 of each month.
(3) Entries for days 4, 8, 12, 16, 20, 26, and the last of each month.
(4) Entries for days 5, 10, 15, 20, 25, and the last of each month.
(5) Entries for days 8, 16, and 24.
(6) Entries for days 10, 20, and the last of each month.

The almanacs differ from other sets of tables in that the entries found in the almanacs give directly the positions of the celestial bodies and need no further computation, contrary to what is required with what are called "auxiliary astronomical tables" which are far more common and follow the pattern of the tables in Ptolemy's *Almagest*.

The oldest work of this kind compiled in the Iberian peninsula is known as the *Almanac of Azarquiel* (*Ibn al-Zarqalluh), but the extant copies of it do not include the word almanac. This set of tables was composed by Azarquiel, a leading astronomer in eleventh-century *Toledo, and consists of canons and tables. A Castilian version of the tables translated for *Alfonso X (1221–1284) also survives. The *Almanac of Azarquiel* uses Ptolemaic models and parameters, and seems to derive from a similar work by an Alexandrian astronomer, referred to as Awmatiyus, Armeniut, or

Humeniz, otherwise unknown. The *Almanac of Azarquiel* is based on almost the same periods as those mentioned by Ptolemy, and its entries were computed with the data in the *Toledan Tables*, a set of tables (*zij*) compiled in Toledo by a group of astronomers, including Azarquiel, led by *Sa'id al-Andalusi. The almanac provides the true daily positions of the Sun for four years from September 1, 1088 (beginning of year 1400, era of Alexander), and the five planets (in sidereal coordinates), as well as the mean positions of the Moon (longitude, anomaly, and node), and contains many more tables than those in other almanacs.

What has been traditionally called the *Almanac of Tortosa* is a perpetual almanac, consisting of a text and tables beginning in 1307. This designation was coined when the only known copy of it was a Latin version made in Tortosa, now in Catalonia, from an archetype in Arabic. This designation is no longer appropriate, for various copies in Latin, Catalan, Castilian, Portuguese, and Hebrew have recently been identified. The Arabic archetype, however, has not been found. Some of the characteristics of the Almanac of 1307 are listed below.

The Jewish-Provençal astronomer and translator Jacob ben Makhir Ibn Tibbon (c. 1236–1304), also called *Profatius Judaeus, is the author of an *Almanach* *perpetuum* compiled for the meridian of Montpellier in southern France. The tables for the daily positions of the Sun begin on March 1, 1301, and those for the planets on various days in March 1300 (see Table Two). Jacob ben Makhir's *Almanach* also contains tables for the computation of eclipses and several tables for purposes of interpolation. The longitudes tabulated in the *Almanach* are tropical and were calculated according to the Toledan Tables.

The astronomical genre of almanacs expanded greatly in the fourteenth century, and more so in the fifteenth century. We shall only mention a few of these works. John of Lignières, an astronomer active in Paris in the 1320s and 1340s, is the author of an almanac only very recently described by historians of astronomy and uniquely preserved in an incomplete copy. This almanac follows the pattern put in place by his predecessors. A contemporary of John of Lignères, *John of Saxony, also working in Paris, compiled an almanac of a different kind. It lists the true positions of the two luminaries and the planets, distributed in nine tables, covering the period 1336–1380. The almanac of John of Saxony is not organized according to the goal-year periods used by his predecessors, and no increments are given for each planet after these cycles, as is the case with all perpetual almanacs. There is evidence of various almanacs compiled in England, but no names are associated with them. In the Iberian peninsula, Pere Gilbert and Dalmau Ses Planes, two astronomers in the service of King Pere III of Catalonia (IV of Aragon), wrote a text called *Tables and Almanac*, partially preserved in Latin in a unique manuscript lacking the tables. The introduction explains that the tables were valid for a period spanning from 1360 to 1433, and that the tabulated longitudes were tropical. Ferrand Martines, from Seville, compiled an almanac preceded by a text in Castilian in fifteen chapters and consisting of tables adapted for 1391 from those in the Almanac of 1307.

Many almanacs were compiled during the fifteenth century, and among them stands out the *Almanach Perpetuum* associated with *Abraham Zacuto (1452–1515), the most celebrated astronomer in the Iberian Peninsula of his time. Zacuto produced the bulk of his astronomical work in Salamanca, although not at the university (as has often been said), until he left Spain for Portugal when the Jews were expelled from Spain in 1492. Zacuto's principal work is a set of astronomical tables called *Ha-hibbur ha-gadol* (*The Great Composition*), composed in 1478. The *Almanach Perpetuum*, on which Zacuto's fame rests, consists of a set of canons by Joseph Vizinus and a great number of astronomical tables, almost all drawn from the Hibbur. The *Almanach Perpetuum* was first printed in Leiria, Portugal, in 1496, probably without the intervention of Zacuto himself, and was reprinted several times, not always mentioning the author's name.

Table Two summarizes such features as the length of the cycle, the frequency of the entries ("1y, 1d" means that two tables are presented, one at intervals of one year, and one at intervals of one day), and the precision in several almanacs.

See also **Astronomy; Calendar**

Bibliography

Boffito, J. and C. Melzi d'Eril. *Almanach Dantis Aligherii sive Profhacii Judaei Montispessulani Almanach Perpetuum ad annum 1300 inchoatum*. Florence, 1908.

Chabás, J. 1996. "El almanaque perpetuo de Ferrand Martines (1391)." *Archives internationales d'histoire des sciences*, 46: 261–308.

Chabás, J. and B. R. Goldstein. *Astronomy in the Iberian Peninsula: Abraham Zacut and the Transition from Manuscript to Print*. Transactions of the American Philosophical Society, 90.2. Philadelphia, 2000.

Millás, J. M. *Estudios sobre Azarquiel*. Madrid-Granada, 1943–1950.

JOSÉ CHABÁS

ALUM

Alum is an important chemical substance that had multiple uses in the Middle Ages. Its high demand everywhere in western Europe and primary geographical location in the Black Sea area made it, along with timber and wheat, one of the commercial products that most configured the patterns of east-west shipping in the medieval Mediterranean.

Alum is a double sulfate of aluminum and potassium, or of aluminum and ammonium, or mixtures of the two. Raw alum was mined as a mineral (alunite), which had to be treated before it could be used industrially. The raw alum was baked in a kiln at high temperature, then slaked, then boiled, and then poured into oaken tanks where the refined alum formed as a precipitate. This process of crystallization produced a remarkably pure form of the substance. Because of its complex chemical nature, however, it was often confused with other substances. Yemen alum (*alum jamen*) was a relatively pure form of alum from southern Arabia, but was also confused with rock salt. "Feather alum" (*alumen plumeum*) was probably asbestos or talc. Scale alum (*lume scagiola*) was gypsum, calcium sulfate. Alum of lees (*alumen faecis*) was actually potassium carbonate made from burning the sediments of wine. *Isidore of Seville, in his *Etymologies*, explained that alum (*alumen*) is so called from light (*lumen*) because it gives lightness to the dyeing tints.

Industrial Uses: Dyeing

In the dyeing of woolen cloth, alum was commonly used as a mordant to fix non-fast dyes; other substances were added, particularly cream of tartar, perhaps to neutralize organic impurities in the alum. It was particularly recommended for use with weld (*Reseda luteola*) to make a yellow color. A late fourteenth-century English recipe for dyeing linen cloth is typical: "To every eight ells [ten yards] of cloth take one pound of alum…. For to alum thy cloth first take thy alum and pound it small. Put it in water and set in on the fire and stir. Then take thy cloth and wet it in another water and out it in the water that alum was melted in…. When thou alumest thy cloth, take a light linen clout [scrap] and alum it with thy cloth, for when thou makest thy colors thou mayest assay by thy clout if it be good or no." Such recipes were fairly standard and European ones do not differ substantially from the Persian recipes that a dyer from medieval Tabriz took along with him to India.

The cost of dyeing fluctuated with the price of alum. A mid-fifteenth century treatise entitled *Methods and Devices of Cloth-Making at Florence* specified that "No dyer must alum more than two pieces of cloth or ten dozen skeins of wool per cauldron. The prices are based on alum at sixty florins per thousand pounds. Dyeing fees may rise with price of alum."

Industrial Uses: Leather Preparation

In the leather trades, alum was used mainly in a preparatory process known as tawing. The cleaned hide was soaked in water, salt, egg yolk, and flour. It was then dried for a period of weeks: the longer the aluminum salts were left in, the more water-resistant the hide became. Tawing left the hide white and stiff and it had then to be softened by stretching it over a blunt wooden edge. The leather could then be colored or tanned, and some tanning recipes also included alum. There were alum mines in the south of Spain, including one close to Córdoba, the origin of Cordovan leather, tawed with local alum.

Alum had other diverse uses: *al-Razi suggested mixing alum and mastic to make cement for the filling of dental cavities. It was traditionally used as an additive in pickling brine, to firm up the pickles. Before the introduction of modern mechanical filtration methods, alum was used in traditional sugar refining. A mixture of alum and lime-water was added to the boiling cane syrup which coagulated and rose to the top, carrying impurities of the sugar with it.

The Alum Trade

Francesco di Balduccio Pegolotti, in his *Practice of Commerce*, gives an exhaustive account of the sources of alum in the fifteenth century. He says the best is from Karahissar, in Turkish Asia Minor, seven days inland from the port of Kerasont, near Trebizond. Fourteen thousand Genoese cantara—a measure equivalent to around 125 pounds 10 ounces (57 kg)—are produced there yearly in three different grades. Equal in output and almost as fine is alum of Phocaea on the coast of Asia Minor, near Smyrna. Pegolotti enumerates other Turkish sources of supply, as well as several sites on the Black Sea in the Byzantine Empire, of inferior quality. He specifies that alum will not spoil if kept dry, and that the higher grades are whiter and clearer than the poorer.

The Genoese controlled the Phocoea alum trade sporadically from the late thirteenth century until the Turks captured it in 1455. Subsequently a huge deposit was found at Tolfa, in southern Italy. This was first developed commercially under the direction of Pope Pius II, and represented abroad by the Medici Bank.

See also **Leather production**

Bibliography

Edelestein, S. and A. C. Borghetty. *The Plichto of Gioanventura Rosetti.* Cambridge, Mass.: MIT Press, 1969.
Pegolotti, F. di B. *La pratica della mercatura* [The Practice of Commerce]. Edited by Allan Evans. Cambridge: Mediaeval Academy of America, 1936.
Singer, C. *The Earliest Chemical Industry. An Essay in the Historical Relations of Economics & Technology illustrated from the Alum Trade.* London: The Folio Society, 1948.
Vest. M. "White Tawed Leather: Aspects of Conservation." Ninth International Congress of the IADA, Copenhagen, August 15–21, 1999. Reprint.
Wulff, H. E. *The Traditional Crafts of Persia.* Cambridge: MIT Press, 1966.

THOMAS F. GLICK

ANATOMY

In late medieval Latin the word *anatomia*, also spelled *anothomia*, had three principal meanings. It referred simultaneously to the structure of human or animal bodies, to the medical discipline devoted to the study of this structure, and to the practice of opening or eviscerating bodies. The last was used not only for the purposes of medical instruction and study (the practice we call dissection) but also in order to determine cause of death (the practice we call autopsy) and to preserve human corpses through techniques of embalming that involved evisceration. Of these three related practices, the earliest and most common was embalming; thus it is no coincidence that the only extensive study of human anatomy through dissection, before the late medieval era, took place in Hellenistic Egypt, where techniques of mummification were highly developed.

After the third century B.C.E., however, human dissection fell into disuse, as the culture of ancient Greeks and Romans, as well as of medieval Muslims, discouraged the mutilation of the human body after death. Thus the anatomical teaching of the most influential ancient Greek writers on anatomy and physiology, such as Aristotle, in the fourth century B.C.E., and *Galen in the second century C.E., relied instead on the dissection of animals. The treatment of human anatomy in the works of the most important medieval Arabic authors from the late ninth through twelfth centuries, including *Abu Bakr Muhammad ibn Zakariyya al-Razi (Rhazes), *Ibn Sina (Avicenna), and *Ibn Rushd (Averroes), was even less oriented toward observation of opened bodies; they drew for the most part on the descriptions of earlier Greek writers, supplemented by casual observations made in the course of medical and surgical practice. As a result, their discussions of human anatomy were relatively brief, intended for the most part to elucidate the nature and causes of disease.

The first signs of what was to become one of the distinguishing features of Western Christian medicine—its strong interest in the study of human anatomy, and its practice of dissection in this connection—are traceable to twelfth-century *Salerno, in southern Italy, the most important early center of medical study in Europe before 1200. Building on the work of their Greek and Arabic predecessors, several Salernitan masters wrote short, independent treatises on anatomy, one of which described the systematic dissection of a pig. This southern Italian orientation toward anatomy as basic to medical study and practice was ratified by *Emperor Frederick II in a decree of 1241, which required knowledge of anatomy on the part of all those seeking a license to practice medicine in the Kingdom of Naples. Frederick did not specify that this knowledge should be based on the dissection of human bodies, although it is worth noting that contemporaries attributed to him an experiment that involved killing two men and opening their bodies to study the process of digestion. Although the story of this experiment is probably apocryphal, it does suggest that the idea of opening and inspecting human corpses in the interests of advancing medical and physiological knowledge was in the air.

It was only in the late thirteenth century, however, in north-central Italy, that the study of anatomy based on human dissection was established as a permanent element in Western medical culture. This new practice had its roots in several contemporary developments. Thanks to the work of *Taddeo Alderotti, the years around 1300 saw the establishment in Bologna of a university medical curriculum that focused on the works of Galen and his followers and presupposed Aristotelian ideas about the functioning of animal (including human) bodies. Alderotti and his contemporaries looked in particular to two works attributed erroneously to Galen, although of Galenic inspiration: De interioribus (On Things Inside) and De juvamentis membrorum (On the Uses of the Members). Taddeo's interest in anatomy—he lamented that he had never seen the opening of a pregnant woman, suggesting that he had witnessed the dissection of other human bodies—was certainly reinforced by the elaboration of *surgery as a learned discipline at the hands of writers such as *Teodorico Borgognoni and Guglielmo of Saliceto. The study of anatomy based on dissection seems to have become a regular part of the medical curriculum in Bologna in the generation after Alderotti and was codified in an influential textbook, the Anothomia of Taddeo's student *Mondino de' Liuzzi, completed c. 1316. Over the course of the fourteenth century, this study spread to other Italian universities and medical corporations (primarily colleges of physicians and surgeons), including those in Perugia, Florence, Padua, and Venice, as well as to the university of Montpellier, in southern France.

Another development that facilitated the adoption of anatomical dissection in late medieval Italy was the practice of using autopsy to determine cause of death in criminal trials and to study epidemic diseases that posed a threat to public health. Autopsies of this sort seem also to have been pioneered initially in Bologna and other nearby cities. Equally important was the increasing use of evisceration to embalm the bodies of popes, holy men and women, and eventually civic leaders and rulers, whose corpses might be placed on public display. It was relatively straightforward to examine the viscera of people who had been embalmed to see if they had died of natural causes, or if their corpses showed signs of supernatural intervention or foul play.

As this last practice makes clear, there was nothing intrinsically degrading about having one's body opened or intrinsically un-Christian or impious about dissection. Indeed, medieval Christianity—a religion organized around the mutilated body of the crucified Christ and the corporeal relics of the Christian martyrs—contrasted markedly with Judaism, Greco-Roman paganism, and Islam in rejecting the idea of corpse pollution and the overriding importance of bodily integrity after death. Pope Boniface VIII's famous decree Detestande feritatis (1297), prohibited the dismembering and boiling of human corpses in order to reduce them to bones for easy transportation, but his rulings targeted funerary customs (including embalming by evisceration) rather than the nascent practices of autopsy and dissection. Nonetheless, the decree had a chilling effect on the spread of dissection in northern Europe, where the practice was widely understood as prohibited or as requiring a special ecclesiastical license. It is in part for this reason that the practice of autopsy and the study of anatomy based on dissection were slow to be adopted outside the Mediterranean basin, where they did not begin to make serious inroads until the late fifteenth century.

This fact may help to account for the flowering of anatomical illustration in fourteenth- and fifteenth-century France and Germany. *Henri de Mondeville, for example, who had studied surgery in Bologna, created a series of anatomical images for use in his teaching at the university of Montpellier, to substitute for the dissected cadaver. A generation later, Guido of Vigevano, also trained in Italy, commissioned elaborate illustrations for his own treatise on anatomy (1345)—based heavily on Mondino's Anothomia—which he addressed to the King of France.

Wherever the teaching of anatomy was based, at least in part, on the practice of dissection, universities, and medical corporations struggled with the limited supply of cadavers. While few Italians seem to have viewed the opening of the body as sacrilegious, it shamed and dishonored dead person and his or her family when performed in public, in front of an audience of unrelated men. It is for this reason that formal dissections, unlike autopsies, were typically carried out on the corpses of executed criminals. Because executions were relatively rare before the sixteenth century, this meant that cadavers—especially female cadavers—were in very short supply. As a result, although many university statutes called for at least one dissection a year by the end of the fifteenth century, the practice seems to have been infrequent, prompting petitions and protests from teachers and students in medical faculties. This situation was remedied in part by the increasing currency of autopsies, typically performed in domestic spaces at the request of the family, and what came to be called "private" dissections, attended by one or more medical masters and a small number of students, which were performed on private citizens and people who had died in *hospitals for the poor. It is worth noting that physicians and professors of medicine rarely carried out their own dissections, employing surgeons for this purpose.

The relative infrequency of dissections reflected in part the fact that they were ancillary to the study of anatomy, intended to supplement the university lectures and learned texts that were the principal sources of knowledge about the human body and its structure. Until the early sixteenth century, in fact, anatomy was primarily a text-based discipline, studied above all through Greek and Arabic treatises, principally the third book of Ibn Sina's *Canon*, which discussed human diseases and their treatments according to the organs affected, ordered spatially from head to foot. (This organization contrasted with that of Mondino's *Anothomia*, written specifically to accompany dissections, which was divided according to the order in which the parts of the body were opened, treating sequentially the organs of the quickly putrefying abdomen, followed by those of the chest and the head.) Dissections helped students understand and commit to memory their textbooks, but they were not for the most part intended to serve as independent sources of information or to create new knowledge. This situation began to change dramatically in the years around 1500, when learned medical men, inspired in part by the humanist recovery of Galen's lost text, *De anatomicis administrationibus* (*On Anatomical Procedures*), began to treat anatomy as an arena for research as well as teaching and practice. In the process, they began to compare their own observations with those recorded in ancient and medieval texts and to criticize these on the basis of their own experience; in this way, anatomy began to assume a quasi-autonomous status, as a source of natural philosophical knowledge concerning the human body, which it had not enjoyed before.

The new enthusiasm for dissection affected not only medical students and teaching masters but also artists such as Leonardo da Vinci and Michelangelo, who saw it as fundamental to the naturalistic portrayal of the human body. Although these new developments belong properly to the Renaissance and to the sixteenth century, however, they were by no means independent of the medieval tradition. Both the revival of Western interest in anatomy as a medical subfield and the institutionalization of anatomical practices of autopsy and human dissection were above all products of the medieval Western Christian world.

See also **Bartolomeo da Varignana; Henri de Mondeville; Liuzzi, Mondino de'; Medicine, practical; Medicine, theoretical**

Bibliography

Primary sources
Corner, George. *Anatomical texts of the Earlier Middle Ages: A Study in the Transmission of Culture, with a Revised Latin Text of Anatomia Cophonis and Translations of Four Texts.* Washington: Carnegie Institution of Washington, 1927.
Mondino de' Liuzzi. *Anothomia di Mondino de' Liuzzi da Bologna, XIV secolo.* Edited by Piero P. Giorgi and Gian Franco Pasini. Bologna: Istituto per la Storia dell'Università di Bologna, 1992.
Wickersheimer, Ernest. L' 'Anatomie' de Guido de Vigevano, médecin de la reine Jeanne de Bourgogne (1345). *Archiv für Geschichte der Medizin* (1913) 7: 2–25.
Wolf-Heidegger, Gerhard and Anna Maria Cetto. *Die anatomisches Sektion in bildlicher Darstellung.* Basel: S. Karger, 1967.

Secondary Sources
Alston, Mary Niven. The Attitude of the Church toward Dissection before 1500. *Bulletin of the History of Medicine* (1944) 16: 221–238.
French, Roger K. *Dissection and Vivisection in the European Renaissance.* Aldershot: Ashgate, 1999.
Herrlinger, Robert. *History of Medical Illustration, from Antiquity to A.D. 1600.* Translated by Graham Fulton-Smith. London, Pitman Medical, 1970.
Mondino de' Liuzzi, *Anothomia*, trans. Michael McVaugh. In *A Source Book of Medieval Science.* Edited by Edward Grant. Cambridge: Harvard University Press, 1974. (Partial translation.)
Park, Katharine. The Criminal and the Saintly Body: Autopsy and Dissection in Renaissance Italy. *Renaissance Quarterly* (1994) 47: 1–33.
Park, Katharine. The Life of the Corpse: Division and Dissection in Late Medieval Europe. *Journal of the History of Medicine and Allied Sciences* (1994) 50: 111–132.
Savage-Smith, Emilie. Attitudes toward Dissection in Medieval Islam. *Journal of the History of Medicine* (1994) 50: 67–110.
Siraisi, Nancy G. Medieval and Early Renaissance Medicine: An Introduction to Knowledge and Practice. Chicago: University of Chicago Press, 1990.

KATHARINE PARK

ANDALUSI, SA'ID AL-

Sa'id al-Andalusi was a religious scholar, judge, and patron of astronomy, born in Almería, Spain, in 1029. He moved to *Toledo in 1046, where he studied astronomy. He became friendly with the king, al-Ma'mun (reigned 1037–1064) who used Sa'id to attract astronomers to his court, possibly in conscious emulation of his namesake the Abbasid caliph al-Ma'mun, famous for his encouragement of translations of Greek scientific works. Sa'id wrote what amounts to a history of science viewed through the prism of the Arabic scientific movement, titled *Kitab Tabaqat al-'Umam* (*Book of the Categories of Nations*).

In his account of Indian science, he introduces the Sindhind astronomical system, later adopted by Muslim scientists including *al-Khwarizmi, the bias of which is the long-term cyclical nature of celestial movements. He also gives an account of Indian arithmetic, which he calls *hisab al-ghubar* (dust board calculations), and of the invention of chess. His account of the Greeks is surprisingly detailed, but he concentrates particularly on Aristotle ("the first to separate the art of proof... and to provide it with its syllogistic type of argument") and *Ptolemy, whose theoretical treatise the *Almagest* was so complete that no one since has even criticized it, although al-Nayrizi had clarified some of its points and *al-Battani had made it more accessible.

In a general chapter on Arab science, which he begins by noting the lack of interest that astronomy held for the ancient kings of Himyar, he praises the caliph al-Ma'mun for his efforts in promoting science, describes his contacts with the Byzantine emperors, his hiring of translators, and his encouraging his subjects to read the translated books: "As a result of his efforts, a scientific movement was firmly established during his reign." With the decline of the caliphate, which Sa'id ascribes to the influence of "women and Turks," came the neglect of science.

In a chapter on science in the Arab east, Sa'id elaborates on al-Ma'mun's particular love of astronomy, charging astronomers, once they were familiar with the *Almagest*, to construct the equipment of the kind that Ptolemy and the ancient Greeks had used, creating an observatory at Shamasiyah, near Damascus. The observations made there resulted in a collection of tables called *al-Rasd al-Ma'muni* (*Observations of al-Ma'mun*). The rest of the chapter describes the contributions to philosophy and logic by *al-Kindi and then *al-Farabi, who supplied the analytical method lacking in the works of the former. There is considerable detail on the compositions of astronomical tables, in particular by al-Battani, the leader in the Islamic world "in rectifying celestial observations and examining stellar movements."

In a long chapter on science in al-Andalus (Islamic Spain), he praises al-Kirmani, a Cordoban who had studied geometry and astronomy in the east and then settled in Saragossa where he introduced the astronomical works of the Banu Musa. Al-Kirmani was a practicing physician and surgeon and was known for medical experimentation, but not for observational astronomy. Sa'id says that he learned his information on al-Kirmani from Abu'l-Fadl ibn Hasdai, another member of the group of scientists and philosopher in the court of the Banu Hud—an important piece of information because the scientific library of Banu Hud ended up in Toledo when their kingdom was conquered in the early twelfth century. Sa'id's statement attests to the ongoing contact between scientists of the two courts.

Sa'id's most important colleague or disciple in Toledo was the astronomer *Ibn al-Zarqalluh, the principal author of the Toledan Tables, which in Latin translation became the most influential astronomical tables in Europe until supplanted by the Alfonsine Tables of *Alfonso X the Wise. The Toledan Tables in general reflect the Sindhind tradition that had been predominant in Andalusi astronomy from the time of Maslama al-Majriti (*Maslama of Madrid) (d. 1007) and his school. A study of the numerical parameters of the tables reveals a mélange of sources, including the Sindhind, Ptolemy, al-Khwarizmi, Maslama and his school, and al-Battani.

Oddly, Sa'id does not mention the work on the preparation of these tables, no doubt because the *Tabaqat* was written in 1068, and Sa'id died in 1070, just when the Tables were nearing completion. The original Arabic version of the Tables has been lost, but in the canons of the first Latin translation, attributed to *John of Seville, it is stated that "Abensahet (Ibn Sa'id) the judge of king Maymon of Toledo composed these tables, along with his disciple Arzachel (al-Zarqalluh) and others, but Arzachel handled the instruments and studied the positions." This account became the standard one: the fourteenth-century Toledan Jewish historian Isaac Israeli wrote in his *Yesod ha-'Olam* that Sa'id had directed the work of twelve astronomers, mainly Muslims but also including some Jews.

See also **Aristotelianism; Astronomy, Islamic; Astronomy, Latin; Planetary tables; South-central Asian science**

Bibliography

Sa'id al-Andalusi. *Kitab Tabaqat al-'Umam.* L. Cheikho, ed. Beirut: Imprimerie Catholique, 1912.
———. *Science in the Medieval World: Book of the Categories of Nations.* A. S. Salem and A. Kumar, eds. Austin: University of Texas Press, 1991.
Samsó, Julio. *Las ciencias de los antiguos en al-Andalus.* Madrid: Mapfre, 1992.

THOMAS F. GLICK

AQUINAS, THOMAS

Born near Naples in either 1224 or 1225 and expected by his family to spend his life as a Benedictine monk at Monte Cassino, Thomas Aquinas was instead attracted to the newly established Order of Preachers (Dominicans), founded early in the century by St. Dominic. As a young Dominican Aquinas was sent to Paris to study with *Albertus Magnus and went with him in 1248 as the latter founded a new Dominican house of studies in Cologne. He returned to Paris in 1252 to lecture on the *Sentences* of *Peter Lombard. In 1256 Aquinas became Master of Theology at the University of Paris. He returned to Italy in 1259 (teaching in Naples, Orvieto, and Rome), and then went back again to Paris, where he taught from 1268 to 1272. He returned to Naples in 1272, and died on March 7, 1274, at Fossanova, south of Rome, on his way to the Council of Lyon.

No doubt under the inspiration of Albertus Magnus, who sought to make Aristotle "intelligible to the Latins," Aquinas wrote extensive commentaries on Aristotle's books in the natural sciences. He also incorporated his knowledge of Aristotelian thought in his more famous works: *Summa theologiae* and *Summa contra gentiles.* The commentaries on Aristotle, especially on *Physics* and *De Anima*, and his own early work, *The Principles of Nature*, as well as important sections of *On the Power of God* and *On Truth*, manifest Aquinas's lively interest in fundamental questions of natural philosophy. Evidence of the importance Aquinas placed on a correct understanding of natural philosophy is the fact that his major commentaries on Aristotle were undertaken during his intellectually mature years.

Science and Faith

As a theologian and philosopher, Aquinas was especially concerned with questions involving the relationship between faith and reason. In the midst of debates about the role of Greek learning, especially the heritage of Aristotle in the context of religious belief, Aquinas sought to use the insights of that learning to help to understand what was believed. In this enterprise he was influenced by Muslim and Jewish predecessors, such as *Ibn Sina (Avicenna), *Ibn Rushd (Averroes), and *Maimonides, as well as by his teacher, Albertus.

In the tradition of Aristotle, Aquinas viewed science as sure and certain knowledge of a specific subject, achieved by the discovery of a necessary nexus between cause and effect. For the natural sciences, this meant an understanding of all four causes: formal, final, efficient, and material. Committed to the principles of Aristotelian metaphysics and natural science, Aquinas recognized that explanations of the natural world must employ the notions of form and matter, substance and accident, and act and potency. Following the analysis of science set forth in Aristotle's *Posterior Analytics*, Aquinas thought of scientific knowledge as including both theoretical and practical domains: from metaphysics and natural science to ethics and politics.

Since, for Aquinas, God is the author of all truth, the truths discovered by reason, including truths about nature, cannot in principle contradict the truths disclosed by God in Scripture. Conflicts, when they do arise, must be the result of an improper use of reason or a misunderstanding of faith, or both. Furthermore, he thought that specific truths about God, such as that He exists, is one, and that He is the creator, are discoverable by reason alone. One of his famous arguments for the existence of God proceeds from the reality of motion to the existence of an unmoved mover, Who is God. Since faith is an illumination of the intellect, there can be no radical disjunction between faith and reason. As he famously remarked: Grace does not abolish nature; it perfects nature. Faith presupposes and thus needs that knowledge of reality which reason provides.

In the very first question of the *Summa theologiae*, Aquinas argued that *sacra doctrina* (which includes both Scripture and theology) is truly a science, although, unlike all other sciences, it takes its first principles from God's own knowledge (as revealed in Scripture). Thus *sacra doctrina* has an inherently intelligible content even though the recognition of its truth depends on faith.

Throughout his career Aquinas sought to delineate the appropriate domains of theology, on the one hand, and the natural sciences and philosophy, on the other. He also sought to make clear the differences between metaphysics and natural philosophy, the latter being a more general science of nature than any one of the special empirical sciences. As such, natural philosophy, what Aristotle called physics, concerns itself with topics such as nature, change, and time. Although his ultimate concern was theological, Aquinas recognized the appropriate autonomy of the natural sciences—as well as of all the sciences based on reason alone.

Aquinas had no doubts that human beings are able to come to know the world, themselves, and (to some extent) God. Such knowledge is of two kinds: (1) Self-evident truths which are apprehended by a kind of intellectual intuition (including general notions such as the law of non-contradiction and the first principles proper to a given science, such as definitions of lines and points in geometry, or of motion in physics), and (2) Scientific knowledge, properly speaking, which is the result of demonstrations. Without the first, self-evident truths, there is no possibility to achieve the second. Scientific knowledge is of universals, not particulars: of what it means to be a bee, for example, not of an individual bee. Although scientific knowledge itself is the result of a deductive syllogism, it depends on sense experience. For Aquinas, all knowledge begins with sense experience. The human intellect has the ability to abstract from the particulars of sense experience to discover universals.

Motion and Change

Throughout his commentary on Aristotle's *Physics*, Aquinas defended and made his own Aristotle's understanding of nature and motion. The eight books of the *Physics* set forth general principles of the philosophy of nature which are necessary for detailed studies of celestial and terrestrial realities. Aquinas did not reduce all of motion or change to local motion. He defined motion (*mutatio*) in the broadest sense as the "act of the potential insofar as it is potential." Motion is a reality that can be identified neither with mere actuality (for the actual is no longer in motion) nor with mere potentiality (for the potential is not yet in motion). Motion or change is understood in four analogical senses. Substantial change is the most fundamental; it is the change from one kind of natural unit to another (e.g., the coming into existence of a new individual member of a particular species). There are three kinds of accidental changes: changes with respect to sensible qualities are called alterations; changes with respect to quantity are augmentation or diminution; changes with respect to place are locomotion. All substantial changes are instantaneous, although most are preceded by accidental changes, which involve time.

Any form of atomism, which reduces change to the mere rearrangement of fundamental elements (a kind of locomotion), must be rejected as rendering unintelligible both natural things and change.

Aquinas accepted Aristotle's distinction between natural and violent motion: for the former the source of the motion is intrinsic to the body, for the latter it is extrinsic.

At times, Aquinas rejected some of Averroes's interpretations of Aristotelian physics: for example, Averroes claimed that motion in a void is impossible, and that Aristotle's principle that everything that is moved is moved by another required that every motion have a conjoined mover. Aquinas also thought that almost all substantial changes can be accounted for by causes in nature, and that there was no need to appeal, as Avicenna did, to a supernatural "giver of forms" to account for the appearance of new substances.

Thomas Aquinas and Albertus Magnus advance to meet Dante and Beatrice in Heaven. Seated in a semicircle in the foreground are ten doctors of the church, including three mitred bishops, Gratianus, Peter Lombard, and Isidore of Seville. This illustration is taken from a copy of Dante's *The Divine Comedy* made for Alfonso V, King of Aragon (1416–1458) and Naples (as Alfonso I, 1442–1458). (Topham/The British Library/HIP)

Mathematics and Physics

Aquinas was especially insightful in distinguishing between mathematics and the natural sciences. Early in his career, in writing a commentary on *Boethius's *On the Trinity*, he argued that there is an important difference between what each discipline studies. The natural sciences have as their proper area of investigation that which exists in motion or is capable of motion: mobile being (*ens mobile*). As he remarked, such entities depend on matter for their existence and for their being understood: that is, the natural sciences, although leaving behind particular sensible bodies (this horse or that plant, for example), do not leave behind in their explanation all references to material things. As he put it: the natural scientist abstracts from individual sensible matter, but not from common sensible matter (from this flesh and these bones, when speaking of animals, but not from flesh and bones, taken in a universal sense). The mathematician, on the other hand, abstracts from any reference to material being and considers quantities as such: continuous (in geometry) and discontinuous (in arithmetic). Aquinas thought that quantity, as an accident, does not exist separately from the material substance in which it inheres; nevertheless, the human intellect can leave behind all other sensible features of physical things and consider quantity as such. Arithmetic and geometry are both sciences rooted in what exists, but they consider the real world in terms of categories abstracted from that world. Mathematics does not provide a deeper explanation of reality than the natural sciences do; nor does mathematics provide the true principles for all scientific inquiry.

Particularly important for the history of science is Aquinas's account of what he calls "intermediate sciences," which employ mathematical principles to study physical reality. Following Aristotle, Aquinas cited examples such as harmonics and optics in which principles drawn from arithmetic, in the first case, and geometry, in the second, result in sciences different from either the natural sciences or mathematics. Aquinas also thought that mathematical principles can be applied to motion: the resulting mathematical physics is an "intermediate science."

Aquinas was aware of the differences between Aristotelian cosmology and Ptolemaic astronomy, even though many in the Middle Ages conflated the two. The former seeks to discover the nature of the heavens in terms of causes; the latter, with its use of geometric entities such as epicycles, deferents, and equants, offers a mathematical description of observed phenomena in the heavens.

Creation and the Natural Sciences

Aquinas addressed the topic of creation in a magisterial way four times, and each time he noted that it is important to distinguish between creation and change; or as he would say: *creatio non est mutatio* (creation is not a change). The natural sciences study the world of changing things, and a self-evident principle of such a world is that something cannot come from nothing: all change requires an underlying material reality. Creation, however, is a concept in metaphysics and theology; it is a topic on which the natural sciences are not themselves competent to comment. Aquinas thought that "to create" means to be the complete cause of all that is. Creation refers to a metaphysical dependence in the order of being: were God not causing all that is, no things would exist. Thomas thought that the science of metaphysics is able to demonstrate that all things depend on God as the cause of their existence. As he wrote in his commentary on the *Sentences* of Peter Lombard: "Not only does faith hold that there is creation, but reason also demonstrates it."

Aquinas distinguished between the origin of the universe and the beginning of the universe. Although he thought that reason alone can demonstrate that the world is created, that is, has an origin, he did not think that reason can conclude whether or not the world is temporally finite. Here he set himself apart from some Muslim and Christian thinkers who thought that, on the basis of what reason tells us, one could indeed conclude that the world must have a temporal beginning. Following the tradition of the Church Fathers and the decree of the Fourth Lateran Council (1215), he accepted as a matter of faith that the world is temporally finite; nevertheless, he argued that a created, eternal world would involve no logical contradictions. He pointed to the limits of the natural sciences: in principle, they cannot conclude whether or not the world has a temporal beginning. He specifically rejected Aristotle's claim that it is demonstrably true that the world is eternal. He also warned believers to avoid using faulty scientific arguments which purport to show the temporal beginning of the world.

Although recognizing that God possesses an infinite power to produce beings ex nihilo, Aquinas did not think that such absolute power eliminates real secondary causes operating in nature: causes which it is the function of the natural sciences to discover. Aquinas did not think that one must choose between affirming God's complete causality of all that is and the existence of other causes— a dilemma which vexed both *mutakallimun* and Averroes. Only by understanding divine transcendence, and that God is a cause in a way quite different from the way creatures are causes, was Aquinas able to defend the view that both God and creatures are the complete causes of what occurs in the world. Aquinas, thus, was able to affirm both a robust notion of divine agency and a natural order susceptible to scientific understanding in terms of causes discoverable in that order.

Biology and Psychology

Questions of the origin, development, and nature of human beings were part of Aquinas's larger concern about understanding nature. He accepted Aristotle's comment that the developing human embryo first lives the life of a plant, then that of an animal, and finally becomes human. Unlike Albert the Great, Aquinas thought that embryogenesis involves a series of substantial changes, with each rational soul's being created immediately by God only when the embryo possesses the appropriate biological complexity to have such a soul as his or her substantial form. Each living being has a soul, which is the source of the being's characteristic activity.

Aquinas rejected the arguments of some of his contemporaries that a human being has three souls—vegetative, sensitive, and rational. He was always alert to defend the "unity of substantial form," that is, that each substance has only one informing principle which makes it the one thing which it is.

Aquinas is not a dualist. He did not think that a human being is the combination of two things: body and soul (or, more generally, matter and form). A human being is one thing, understood in terms of the unity of two principles, one material, the other spiritual. Aquinas's analysis of the human soul is part of his explanation of living things, which is itself part of his even broader understanding of the distinction between form and matter, the co-principles of all physical reality. That the rational soul is the informing principle of each human being follows from his view that each individual substance, inanimate and animate, must have an informing principle, and that the differences among informing principles are correlative to the differences among existing substances. Soul is not something added to, or which falls inside, or is united to a physical thing. Soul is what makes a living being the kind of living thing it is, and a human soul makes one a human being. The incorporeality of the human intellect means that human beings are of a very special sort, irreducible to physical things or sentient animals. In commenting on Aristotle's *De Anima*, Aquinas rejected Averroes's contention that there is a single "agent intellect" for all human beings; he locates an active power to come to know the world within each human being.

See also **Albertus Magnus; Aristotelianism; Condemnation of 1277; Ibn Rushd; Ibn Sina; Lombard, Peter; Maimonides; Nature: diverse medieval interpretations; Reason; Religion and science; Scholasticism; Universities**

Bibliography

Primary Texts

Aquinas, Thomas. *Commentary on the "Posterior Analytics" of Aristotle* (trans. by F.R. Larcher). Albany, NY: Magi Books, 1970.

——. *Commentary on Aristotle's "De Anima"* (trans. by Kenelm Foster and Silvester Humphries). Notre Dame: Dumb Ox Books, 1994.

——. *Commentary on Aristotle's "Physics"* (trans. by Richard J. Blackwell, Richard J. Spath, and W. Edmund Thirlkel). Notre Dame: Dumb Ox Books, 1999.

Baldner, Steven E. and William E. Carroll. *Aquinas on Creation: "Writings on the 'Sentences' of Peter Lombard" 2.1.1*. Translation, Introduction, and Notes. Toronto: Pontifical Institute of Mediaeval Studies Press, 1997.

Bobik, Joseph (trans. and ed.). *Aquinas on Matter and Form and the Elements. A Translation and Interpretation of the "De Principiis Naturae" and the "De Mixtione Elementorum" of Thomas Aquinas*. Notre Dame: University of Notre Dame Press, 1998.

Maurer, Armand (trans. and ed.). *Thomas Aquinas: The Division and Methods of the Sciences. Questions V and VI of His Commentary on the "De Trinitate" of Boethius*.

Toronto: Pontifical Institute of Mediaeval Studies Press, 1986.

Secondary Sourcss

Davies, Brian. *The Thought of Thomas Aquinas*. Oxford: Clarendon Press, 1992.

Elders, Leo. *The Philosophy of Nature of Saint Thomas Aquinas: Nature, The Universe, Man*. New York: Peter Lang, 1997.

Jenkins, John. *Knowledge and Faith in Thomas Aquinas*. New York: Cambridge University Press, 1997.

Kretzmann, Norman and Eleonore Stump (eds.). *The Cambridge Companion to Aquinas.* New York: Cambridge University Press, 1993.

Stump, Eleonore. *Aquinas*. London: Routledge, 2003.

Torrell, Jean-Pierre. *Saint Thomas Aquinas*, vol. 1, *The Person and His Work*; Vol. 2, *Spiritual Master* (trans. by Robert Royal). Washington, D.C.: The Catholic University of America Press, 1996.

Weisheipl, James A. *Friar Thomas D'Aquino: His Life, Thought, and Works*. New York: Doubleday, 1974.

———. *Nature and Motion in the Middle Ages* (edited by William E. Carroll). Washington, D.C.: The Catholic University of America Press, 1985.

Wippel, John. *The Metaphysical Thought of Thomas Aquinas*. Washington, D.C.: The Catholic University of America Press, 2000.

WILLIAM E. CARROLL

ARABIC NUMERALS

The Arabic numerals that are universally used nowadays were formerly called "Indian numerals," in recognition of their ultimate origin. The Indians developed a set of nine symbols to represent all numbers, to which, later, they added a symbol for zero. These numbers and their use in calculation were known to the Syrian scholar Severus Sebokht who wrote in 662 C.E. of the Indians' "subtle discoveries in the science of astronomy, which are more ingenious than those even of the Greeks and Babylonians, and their method of calculation which is beyond description—I mean that which is done with nine symbols." Indian mathematics and astronomy were introduced into the Arabic world, most conspicuously in a celebrated mission to the court of the caliph al-Mansur in Baghdad in 771 C.E., which included a set of astronomical tables. This, or another set of Indian astronomical tables—by Brahmagupta—was revised or translated by *Muhammad ibn Musa al-Khwarizmi. The same al-Khwarizmi wrote (c. 825 C.E.) a text on computation with Indian numerals (*kitab al-hisab al-hindi*) and another text on addition and subtraction (*kitab al-jam' wa'l-tafriq*), neither of which survives in Arabic. The earliest extant Arabic work on Indian arithmetic is the *Kitab al-fusul fi'l-hisab al-hindi* of *Abu'l-Hasan Ahmad ibn Ibrahim al-Uqlidisi, composed in Damascus in 952–953 C.E., and surviving in a unique manuscript written more than two centuries later, in 1186. The earliest Arabic examples of the use of Indian numerals are two legal documents written on papyrus in the Fayyum in Egypt which contain the Arabic numerals for the Hijra dates equivalent to 873–874 and 888–889 C.E.; the next oldest examples are not earlier than the eleventh century. By the twelfth century a difference in the writing of these Hindu-Arabic numerals in the Western and Eastern part of the Islamic world had developed. This difference is described by the Moroccan mathematician, Ibn al-Yasamin, who died c. 1204, but the earliest Arabic manuscript in which the Western forms have been identified is of 1284. It is rather in Latin manuscripts that we have the first certain examples of the use of Hindu-Arabic numerals outside India itself.

The first record of these coincides with the burgeoning of intellectual culture in al-Andalus under the first Western caliphs, 'Abd al-Rahman III and al-Hakam II: namely in a manuscript of *Isidore of Seville's *Etymologies* copied by the monk Vigila in the monastery of Albelda in the Rioja in 976. Vigila praises the Indians in similar terms to those of Severus Sebokht: "We must know that the Indians have a most subtle talent and all other races yield to them in arithmetic and geometry and the other liberal arts. And this is clear in the nine figures with which they are able to designate each and every degree of each order (of numbers). And these are the forms (the nine numerals follow)." Vigila may have acquired this familiarity with the numerals from Christians educated in al-Andalus ("Mozarabs") who emigrated to the north of Spain. Nine years earlier (967), *Gerbert of Aurillac was invited to go to Catalonia, where he studied mathematics for three years under the supervision of Hatto, Bishop of Vich. Gerbert appears to have been responsible for using the Western forms of the Arabic numerals to mark the counters of a particular kind of abacus, which was attributed to him in manuscripts before the end of the tenth century, and remained popular for teaching arithmetic and demonstrating the powers of numbers until at least the mid-twelfth century. Although not strictly necessary, a counter for zero, marked with a circle, was also used.

In the early twelfth century a new wave of Arabic science flowed into Europe via translations made in Spain, Italy, and the Crusader States. One of the Arabic texts was a version of al-Khwarizmi's writings on Indian calculation. We do not have a literal translation, but rather four Latin versions, three of which preserve some form of al-Khwarizmi's name in their titles or incipits: *Dixit Algorizmi* (*arismethica Alchoarismi*), *Liber alchoarismi de practica arismetice*, and *Liber ysagogarum alchorismi* (the fourth is the *Liber pulveris*). "Algorismus" as a term describing this Indian kind of calculation first appears in the mid-twelfth century, replacing a term "*helcep sarracenicum*" ("Saracen calculation"), which was briefly used. The abacus soon gave way to the algorism, in which calculations could be done easily with parchment and pen, and the zero became essential. Because of the dominance of Spain in this transmission, the Western forms of the numerals predominated, but in certain Latin texts that had affinities rather with Italy and the Crusader States, eastern forms are found, and it is these forms that were used in certain Greek mathematical manuscripts from the twelfth century onward.

By the end of the twelfth century the algorism was widespread. Based on these translations and on new Arabic material *Fibonacci (Leonard of Pisa) wrote his *Liber abaci* (1228), which raised the study of arithmetic to a new level. It is unclear whether he "reintroduced" Arabic numerals from Bugia (present-day Algeria), or used a form of the numerals that was already current in Tuscany. By the middle of the thirteenth century, the Arabic numerals were the subject of the popular textbooks of Alexander de Villa Dei (the *Carmen de algorismo*) and of *John of Sacrobosco (*Algorismus vulgaris*). These three works established the study of arithmetic with Arabic numerals as part of the Western curriculum of mathematical studies.

What distinguishes Arabic numerals from Roman numerals and the alphanumerical notation used by the Greeks, Arabs, and Jews, is that each each numeral has place value—i.e., the symbol "2" can be used for 2, 20, 200, 2,000, 20,000 etc., depending on which decimal place it occupies—while the zero marks the "empty" places. The arithmeticians went to considerable lengths to explain this versatility of symbols by using tables in which the same numerical symbol was repeated in each of the decimal places, and demonstrating the function of the zero. But Arabic numerals were not confined to arithmetical contexts. Among early examples is their use for writing the years (in chronicles), for recording large numbers, for numbering folios and roof beams, and for practicing onomancy.

See also Arithmetic

Bibliography

Primary Sources
al-Khwarizmi, Muhammad ibn Musa. *Le calcul indien (Algorismus): histoire des texts, edition critique, traduction et commentaire des plus anciennes versions latines remaniées du XIIe siècle*. Edited André Allard. Paris and Namur: A. Blanchard and Société des etudes classiques, 1992.
———. *Die älteste lateinische Schrift über das indische Rechnen nach al-Hwarizmi*. Ed., trans., and comm. by M. Folkerts, with the collaboration of P. Kunitzsch, Munich: Verlag der Bayerischen Akademie der Wissenschaften, 1997. English summary on pp. 163–183.
Halliwell, J.O. *Rara mathematica*. London: S. Maynard, 1841, pp. 1–26 (John of Sacrobosco) and 73–83 (Alexander de Villa Dei).
Leonard of Pisa. *Liber abbaci*. Edited by Baldassarre Boncampagni. Rome: Tipografia delle Scienze Matematiche e Fisiche, 1857.

Secondary Sources
Burnett, Charles. "Indian Numerals in the Mediterranean Basin in the Twelfth Century, with Special Reference to the 'Eastern Forms.'" In *From China to Paris: 2000 Years' Transmission of Mathematical Ideas*. Edited by Y. Dold-Samplonius, J. W. Dauben, M. Folkerts and B. van Dalen. Stuttgart: Steiner, 2002, pp. 237–288.
Grant, Edward, ed. *A Source Book in Medieval Science*. Cambridge: Harvard University Press, 1974, pp. 94–102.
Ifrah, Georges. *The Universal History of Numbers*. 2nd Edition. London: Harvill Press, 1998.
Kunitzsch, Paul. "The Transmission of Hindu-Arabic Numerals Reconsidered." In *The Enterprise of Science in Islam: New Perspectives*. Edited by Jan P. Hogendijk and Abdelhamid I. Sabra. Cambridge: MIT Press, 2003, pp. 3–21.
Lemay, Richard. *The Hispanic Origin of Our Present Numeral Forms. Viator* (1977) 8: 435–462.

CHARLES BURNETT

ARCHIMEDES

Through the works of Archimedes (d. 212 B.C.E.) and the commentaries on them by Eutocius the mathematicians of the Arabic-Islamic world, and later those of the Latin world, were introduced to such varied matters as an advanced form of the principle of exhaustion, methods of solving cubic equations, solutions of geometrical problems by *neusis* (verging), and hydrostatic theory. Short biographies of Archimedes circulated at least as early as that of *Vincent of Beauvais (d. c. 1256). They relied principally on the account by Valerius Maximus (first century C.E.) of Archimedes' death at the taking of Syracuse by the Roman general Marcellus: that he had hindered the Roman victory by constructing machines, and that he was killed after he had told a Roman soldier to go away from the mathematical diagram that he had drawn in the dust. The only mathematical work mentioned is the *Measurement of a Circle*.

At least two of Archimedes' major works were translated into Arabic: the *Sphere and Cylinder* and the *Measurement of a Circle*. The first of the two books of the *Sphere and Cylinder* is largely about determining the surface area or volume of a sphere (or a segment thereof) by applying exhaustion procedures to the figure formed by rotating a polygon inscribed in, or circumscribed round, a great circle on the sphere. Much of Book II is on cutting a sphere with a plane so that the areas (or volumes) of the segments are in a given ratio. In the *Measurement of a Circle* the area of a circle is approximated by considering inscribed and circumscribed polygons. *Nasir al-Din al-Tusi (d. 1274 C.E.), who made a *tahrir* (redaction) of the text, reports two translations of the *Sphere and Cylinder*, one by *Hunayn ibn Ishaq and one corrected by *Thabit ibn Qurra. An almost complete text (in MS Istanbul, Fatih 3414) corresponds well enough to al-Tusi's description of the text corrected by Thabit. In the Fatih manuscript, however, the translation is attributed to Qusta ibn Luqa, so perhaps we may speak of the Qusta-Thabit translation. We learn that the translation was made from Syriac, for the translator into Arabic complains that the Syriac translator has left out some definitions and other preliminary matter. To make this omission good, the scribe added a fragment from another translation.

Also translated into Arabic was Eutocius's sixth-century commentary on the *Sphere and Cylinder*; a translation apparently by Ishaq ibn Hunayn was known to al-Tusi. This work was particularly important in transmitting to the Arab world numerous Greek solutions to what a modern mathematician might call cubic equations.

The *Measurement of a Circle* was translated from Arabic into Latin twice in the twelfth century, once probably by Plato of Tivoli and once by *Gerard of Cremona. There were at least a dozen reworkings of the latter, most of them with Gerard's enunciations but supplied with new proofs. In some there are discussions of such matters as the meaning of the length of a curved line. Of the *Sphere and Cylinder* there is only a fragment in Latin, apparently translated by Gerard, consisting of six enunciations taken from the prefaces to the two books.

Material from both the *Sphere and Cylinder* and *Measurement of a Circle* was incorporated in the treatise usually known by its Latin title *Verba filiorum* or *Liber trium fratrum*, written by the three sons of Musa ibn Shakir. The book was translated into Latin by Gerard of Cremona and was later the subject of a *tahrir* by al-Tusi. In Latin Archimedes' ideas were also transmitted by the *De curvis superficiebus*, a text apparently translated from the Greek. This, too, was sometimes expanded or commented on. Archimedes' influence is clear to see on *Thomas Bradwardine (early fourteenth century) in his *Geometria speculativa* and on the anonymous fifteenth-century author of the *De inquisicione capacitatis figurarum*.

The *Sphere and Cylinder* was translated into Hebrew by Qalonymus ben Qalonymus (early fourteenth century, Provence) from an Arabic text apparently translated by Qusta—so perhaps our Qusta-Thabit translation. Most of Book I of Eutocius's commentary was also translated, probably by the same translator. Further research will be required before we know how influential these translations were among medieval Jewish mathematicians. We may note that the Latin and Hebrew translations imply the availability of Archimedes manuscripts in Arabic.

Archimedean results on areas and volumes were also transmitted in handbooks, of which one type went under the name *Practica geometrie*. Of these perhaps the best known is that of Leonardo of Pisa (*Fibonacci), which has the peculiarity of containing passages copied verbatim from the *Verba filiorum*.

Indirect Transmission

Archimedes was also influential through indirect transmission: through collections of results sometimes attributed to him, but not part of the Greek corpus. An example is the *Liber Archimedis de insidentibus in humidum* (the book of Archimedes on [things] floating in water). This is probably not a genuine work, but it contains the Principle of Archimedes and treats Archimedean problems such as determining the proportion of substances in an alloy. There are several collections of geometrical propositions usually attributed to Archimedes that appear to be of Greek origin but not directly by him. Thus one such collection, included by Heath in his translation of Archimedes' works under the title *Book of Lemmas*, mentions Archimedes by name. This text is known in the redaction of the eleventh-century mathematician Abu 'l-Hasan Ali ibn Ahmad al-Nasawi, which was later the subject of a *tahrir* by al-Tusi. Another collection is attributed in one manuscript

to Archimedes and in another to a certain Aqatun. A third collection, *On Tangent Circles* and a fourth, a treatment of the regular heptagon, are each attributed to Archimedes in the one known manuscript. Sometimes the same result appears in several collections, often in slightly different forms. An example is an elegant theorem attributed to Archimedes by *Abu al-Rayhan al-Biruni in his *Istikhraj al-autar* (*The Determination of Chords*) and used by *Ptolemy (second century C.E.) in the *Almagest* in the determination of chords: if AB and BC are chords in a circle and AB is the longer, and if the perpendicular ED from the mid-point E of arc ABC to AB is drawn, then $AD = DB + BC$. There are various presentations of this in the *Istikhraj*, in the *Book of Lemmas*, in *On Tangent Circles*, and in the treatise on the regular heptagon.

Archimedean ideas contained in these collections sometimes found their way into Latin. Thus a construction of the regular heptagon similar to that ascribed to Archimedes is in a fragment translated by Gerard of Cremona and later taken almost word-for-word into the *Liber de triangulis* once thought to be by *Jordanus de Nemore. Again, al-Biruni says in the *Istikhraj*—and presumably with good reason—that Archimedes enunciated the theorem that we now call "Hero's formula" for the area of a triangle. A proof of this result is to be found in the *Verba filiorum*; and another proof, in two Latin versions, was claimed to be from the Arabic.

In 1269 *William of Moerbeke translated almost all of Archimedes (and also Eutocius's commentary on the *Sphere and Cylinder*) direct from Greek. The translation is so literal that it was used to help establish the Greek text. William was a Flemish Dominican, at one time confessor of Pope Clement IV. He is most famous for his translations of Aristotle from Greek. *Witelo, the Polish writer on optics, was a close friend and dedicated his *Perspectiva* to him. Not surprisingly, Witelo was one of the first to use the material provided by the new translations—his treatment of ratios, inter alia the notion of the *denominatio* of a ratio, owed something to Eutocius's commentary on the *Sphere and Cylinder*.

The *Measurement of a Circle* (under the title *De quadratura circuli*) and the *Liber de curvis superficiebus* were explicitly cited by the thirteenth-century Gerard of Brussels—although without giving an author in either case—in his *Liber de motu* (*Book on Motion*), which in turn had some influence on the fourteenth-century masters of Oxford and Paris. The Moerbeke translations were used too: witness *Nicole Oresme's use of the *Spirals* in his *De configurationibus qualitatum et motuum* (*On the Configurations of Qualities and Motions*); Henry of Hesse's references to the *Floating Bodies* in his *Questiones super perspectivam* (*Questions on General Optics*); material taken from Eutocius on the duplication of the cube in the *De arte mensurandi* (*On the Art of Measurement*) by *Jean de Meurs; and many other examples.

In 1450 Jacobus Cremonensis made a new translation of Archimedes' works (almost complete) from the Greek at the behest of Pope Nicholas V, who sent a copy to Nicholas of Cusa (d. 1464). Whether the new translation was completely independent of Moerbeke's has yet to be investigated. Some printed editions of the sixteenth century were based on Moerbeke and other medieval material: these include the first two printed works of Archimedes, the *Quadrature of the Parabola* and the *Measurement of a Circle*, printed by Gaurico in 1503 from the Moerbeke translation. *Regiomontanus may be seen as a bridge between the medieval and the modern mathematical world. He copied one of the reworkings of Gerard's translation of the *Measurement of a Circle* and owned copies of the *Verba filiorum*, but he also copied Jacobus's new translations, making numerous emendations to them. He intended to reproduce them as part of his project to print the ancient classics of mathematics, but was prevented by his untimely death.

Many writings have been attributed to Archimedes. A book on water-clocks is ascribed to him, but without certainty. That he concerned himself with mechanical contrivances is clear (the machines he is supposed to have made to defend Syracuse are not meant), for Cicero describes his celestial globe and another, more complex, instrument. Whether they contained anything new we do not know. Again, according to ancient testimony Archimedes had written on catoptrics (on the reflection of light), and it has even been suggested that he is partly responsible for the pseudo-Euclidean *Catoptrics*, but we can only speculate about this. Much of Archimedes' enormous achievement must remain hidden.

See also **Clepsydra; Optics and catoptrics**

Bibliography

Clagett, M. *Archimedes in the Middle Ages*. Vol. I Madison: University of Wisconsin Press, 1964; vols. II–V. Philadelphia: The American Philosophical Society, 1976–1984.

Folkerts M., and R. Lorch. "Some Geometrical Theorems Attributed to Archimedes and their Appearance in the West." In *Archimede—Mito, Tradizione, Scienza…*, ed. Corrado Dollo, Nuncius, Studi e Testi IV, Florence 1992, pp. 61–79. Repr. in R. Lorch, *Arabic Mathematical Sciences: Instruments, Texts, Transmission*. Aldershot: Variorum, 1995.

Heath T.L. [translator]. *The Works of Archimedes*. New York: Dover Press, 1955.

Knorr, W.R. *Textual Studies in Ancient and Medieval Geometry*. Boston, Basel, Berlin: Birkhauser, 1989.

Lorch, R. The Arabic Transmission of Archimedes' Sphere and Cylinder and Eutocius' Commentary. *Zeitschrift für Geschichte der Arabisch-Islamischen Wissenschaften* (1989) 5: 94–114. Repr. in R. Lorch, *Arabic Mathematical Sciences: Instruments, Texts, Transmission* (op. cit.).

RICHARD LORCH

ARISTOTELIANISM

In *Nicomachean Ethics* VI 3–5 Aristotle distinguishes theoretical "science" from the practical "arts" and "prudence." In the Aristotelian tradition before the Latin Middle Ages the theoretical "sciences" rather than the practical disciplines in Aristotle's encyclopedia were stressed, and within the theoretical disciplines the systematic presentation of "true and certain" knowledge rather than the inductive search for its principles.

The edition of Aristotle's works made by Andronicus of Rhodes (fl. c. 70–c. 50 B.C.E.) established the knowledge of a comprehensive, structured body of demonstrated conclusions as Aristotle's ideal of science. The works of Alexander of Aphrodisias (fl. c. 193–217), the first great commentator on Aristotle, complemented this view of the Philosopher's scientific corpus. The Neoplatonic movement attempted to harmonize the thought of Plato and Aristotle as the two great representatives of the Greek tradition. The tradition of commentary on Aristotle as an introduction to the higher wisdom of Plato was represented at Athens by the *Elementatio theologica* and the *Elementatio physica* of Proclus (c. 410–485), which exhibit all forms of substance as deriving from a single first principle, the Platonic One.

Alexandrian exegesis of Aristotle's text, following Ammonius Hermeae, a pagan (fl. c. 500), was more independent. John Philoponus (fl. c. 529), a Christian follower of Ammonius, even contested various Aristotelian notions. His introduction of the Judaeo-Christian idea of creation into philosophy rendered Proclus' entire system questionable. These Alexandrian developments determined, in large measure, the approach to Aristotle's philosophy in the Byzantine world. Plato and Aristotle were regarded as representatives of "Hellenic philosophy," as part of a pagan tradition, generally opposed to "our [Christian] philosophy." The interest of Christian theologians in Aristotle was mostly limited to the parts of his logic necessary in theology. After the fall of Constantinople to the Crusaders in 1204 the necessity of answering the challenge of an increasingly sophisticated Latin theology led to the composition of comprehensive compendia of Aristotelian doctrine.

Arabic Aristotelianism

By the ninth century practically the entire corpus of Aristotle's works, together with the Greek commentators on them, had been made available in Arabic. Aristotle's classification of the natural sciences supplied the structure for an encyclopedia in which classical authors such as Hippocrates and *Galen, *Euclid, and *Ptolemy also found a place. But Muslim thinkers generally opposed studies concerned with their own way of life, called the "Arabic or traditional sciences" (the Qur'an, traditions, *kalam* or dialectical theology, and the like) to the "Greek or rational sciences" associated for the most part with Aristotle's name. *Kalam*'s task was to supply the faithful with logical proofs for their belief.

*Al-Farabi (d. 950) attempted to fit the "traditional sciences of the Arabs" into the Aristotelian division of the sciences. The doctrine of God was taken up under the theoretical science of metaphysics, whereas *kalam* was regarded as a part of politics, with the function of defending the articles of faith. About a century later, Avicenna (*Ibn Sina) undertook to reform *kalam* in accordance with the Aristotelian theory of demonstrative science and understood *kalam*, not as a part of politics, but rather as metaphysics. Averroes (*Ibn Rushd), writing in Muslim Spain, also confronted the theologians with Aristotle's idea of demonstrative science, stressing the truth and certainty of Aristotle's presentation of theoretical science.

Jewish and Medieval Latin Aristotelianism

Medieval Judaism also had need of Aristotelian science and the logic which went with it. Where conflicts between philosophy and the Jewish faith appeared, some thinkers—of whom *Moses Maimonides (1135–1204) is the best example—held that only when the philosophical and theological doctrines have been clearly defined can one ask how the two realms are related. But an increasingly critical evaluation of Aristotle's doctrines in the light of the Jewish faith appeared in the fourteenth century.

The works of Aristotle were made available in the Latin West in four clearly distinguishable stages. The first stage opened in the sixth century with translations by *Boethius of Aristotle's treatises on logic, along with some notions transmitted by Cicero (106–43 B.C.E.). But the monastic teacher of the times knew little of Greek philosophy and science, and less of Aristotle.

With the rise of the towns new schools appeared and with them a new type of teacher. This new teacher—*Peter Abelard (1079–1142) is the best known—slowly pieced together the original fabric of the Aristotelian logic with the exception of the theory of demonstration as it is found in the *Analytica posteriora*. But because Boethius in his *De hebdomadibus* had described the organization of scientific knowledge much as Aristotle had done, twelfth-century authors often sought to develop a general theory of scientific method from it. Gilbert of Poitiers (c. 1075–1154), for example, maintained that first principles can be established for all the liberal arts and in the same way for theology itself. Nicholas of Amiens (fl. c. 1190) in his *Ars fidei catholicae* attempted to present theological doctrine in accordance with Euclid's geometrical model.

The function of the masters was no longer simply that of transmitting traditional biblical wisdom. The "School of Chartres" confronted the Bible and the Church Fathers with the *Timaeus* of Plato, and Alain de Lille sought to work Platonic notions into Christian theology, employing the methodology of the newly translated *Liber de causis*. The translators of the period made immense additions to these sources, challenging the masters further: for geometry and optics Euclid, for astronomy Ptolemy, for medicine Hippocrates and Galen, and above all the works of Aristotle, together with his Muslim and Jewish commentators.

The consequent condemnation in 1210 and 1215 of Aristotle's *libri naturales* at Paris was followed by an intense effort to axiomatize the quadrivial sciences. The attempt was most successful in the science of optics, a science subalternate to geometry. But attention was also turned to Aristotle's theory of science directly. *Robert Grosseteste (c. 1168–1253) commented on Aristotle's *Analytica posteriora* and explained that "science" means true and certain knowledge derived by syllogistic demonstration from first principles. Accordingly, the theologians undertook to transform their discipline into an Aristotelian science. In his *Summa aurea*, William of Auxerre (1140/50–1231) proposed taking the articles of faith as the principles of theological demonstration, on the basis of which Catholic theology could be presented as a structured body of strictly demonstrated conclusions. This lead was followed in particular by the Dominican theologians of the early part of the thirteenth century.

The Aristotelian encyclopedia provided the framework not only for theology, but also for the new philosophical, medical, astrological, and natural sciences, both those of ancient Greece and those of past and contemporary Islam and Judaism. There is a manuscript at Barcelona, in the Archives of the Crown of Aragon, which contains a manual or guidebook for students in the arts faculty in Paris. This text, which was apparently based on early thirteenth-century practice, was composed about 1230–1240 by an unknown master of the faculty for the benefit of students having to prepare for examinations. It reveals very clearly the role which the Aristotelian encyclopedia played in mastering the ancient legacy.

For the author of the guide-book the arts are no longer simply the seven liberal arts of the trivium and *quadrivium; they comprise rather all the philosophical and scientific disciplines newly recovered at his time. The author divides his subject into three branches: rational, natural, and practical or moral philosophy. Under rational philosophy he takes up the subjects of the trivium, assigning to grammar the works of Priscian and Donatus, to rhetoric Cicero's *De inventione*, and to dialectic Aristotle's Organon together with the *Isagoge* of Porphyry and the logical treatises of Boethius. Natural philosophy is divided into metaphysics, mathematics, and physics. For metaphysics the standard texts are the hardly known *Metaphysica* of Aristotle and the pseudo-Aristotelian *Liber de causis*. Under mathematics the author takes up the subjects of the quadrivium, but assigns to some of its branches works which were unknown in the earlier Middle Ages. To astronomy he assigns *Ptolemy's *Almagest*, to geometry *Euclid's *Elements*, to arithmetic Boethius' *Institutio arithmetica*, and to music Boethius' *Institutio musica*. Then are included the works at that time ascribed to Aristotle on natural philosophy: *Physica*, dealing with the general principles of physical change; *De caelo*, dealing with the eternal motion of the celestial bodies; *De generatione et corruptione*, dealing with the four sublunary elements which explain generation and corruption; *Meteora*, dealing with a great variety of natural phenomena; *De plantis*, *De animalibus*, *De anima*, *Parva naturalia*, and *De motu cordis*, which deal with the whole range of animate nature. But for moral philosophy the author's assignment of texts to the different branches is less clear. He assigns the *Ethica* of Aristotle to the treatment of the life of the soul in itself. But the author does not yet know of Aristotle's *Oeconomica* and *Politica* and fills the gap with Cicero's *De officiis* and Roman and canon law. This students' guide marks a definite stage in the evolution of the medieval arts faculty, the final stage in the formation of a new, urban type of school. Although the author attempts to assign theology a place among the practical disciplines, his concern is rather with the Aristotelian system of the natural sciences. The Aristotelian classification supplied the framework for the vast amount of new scientific material which the translators of the late twelfth and early thirteenth centuries had made available.

By about 1240/1250 the Latins had at their disposal the complete body of Aristotelian doctrine together with Averroes' commentaries. Institutionally, the Aristotelian paradigm for science was established on March 19, 1255, when Aristotle's works were prescribed for the lectures in the Paris arts faculty. Working within this paradigm, the Latins made, in the course of the next two centuries, enormous progress not only in mathematics and the physical sciences, but also in the Aristotelian practical philosophy, following new translations of the *Ethics* and *Politics*. *Albertus Magnus (c. 1200–1280) was among the first to turn his attention to the complete Aristotelian encyclopedia. His paraphrases of all of the fundamental works in Aristotle's encyclopedia prepared the way for the vast commentatory literature through which the Middle Ages assimilated Aristotelian science.

More importantly, the Aristotelian system of the sciences was decisive for the formation of the medieval university. The arts faculty became what we might call a philosophical faculty, with a tendency to develop a teaching independent of the theological faculty. This development was bound to arouse a growing rivalry between the two faculties. The conflict had broken out at least as early as the students' guide. It concerned at first moral philosophy, but far more profound than such particular differences was the implicit distinction between theological and philosophical discourse to which our master of arts here appealed. Medieval exegesis had been concerned with the Bible. The task of the exegete was not the discovery of new truths, but rather the unveiling of the truth concealed in the words of the sacred text. In the twelfth century, as discrepancies among his authorities became increasingly obtrusive, Scholastic teachers, working in the tradition of the *concordia discordantium*, made the epoch-making decision not to try to separate—as the Byzantines and Muslims before them had done—their own religious disciplines from the profane sciences inherited from the ancients. They attempted rather to situate theological teaching within the Aristotelian classification of the sciences.

The prescription of the Aristotelian philosophy as the basis of instruction in the arts faculty brought with it for the masters the obligation of interpreting the texts they had sought after. Their commentaries on the works of Aristotle open a new epoch in the history of medieval exegesis. In Paris *Siger of Brabant (c. 1240–c. 1284) explained their purpose: "We seek what the philosophers meant in this matter, their intention rather than the truth, because we proceed philosophically." Siger and his fellow masters were the first to want to interpret philosophical texts "philosophically," that is, by abstracting from the question of the truth of the teaching. Their task was not—like that of the theologians—the unveiling of a truth already possessed, but hidden; it was rather the discussion of the opinion of a most distinguished colleague. Siger gave the following rule for the interpretation of Aristotle: "It should be noted by those who undertake to comment upon the books of the Philosopher that his opinion is not to be concealed, even though it be contrary to the truth." The interpreter of Aristotle's text, having abandoned the notion of truth possessed for the notion of truth to be sought, could approach the text of the Philosopher in a critical, questioning way. Behind this revolution lay no doubt the de facto conflicts between Aristotle's teachings and the doctrines of faith. The masters of arts were confronted with an important literature opposing various interpretations of Aristotle. In the face of such opposition it was difficult to maintain that Aristotle had spoken the whole truth.

The theologians had traditionally attempted to solve problems arising out of divergent authorities by seeking a standpoint from which all the relevant texts could be brought into harmony. But in the thirteenth century the newly translated philosophical and scientific sources rendered questionable the simple concordances which the twelfth century had made between authorities limited to the Latin ecclesiastical tradition. In this new situation some rejected the new literature and attempted by ecclesiastical condemnations to prevent its being read; still other theologians, like Albertus Magnus, showed themselves receptive to the new sources and tried in a new and very subtle way to continue the clerical enterprise of a *concordia discordantium*.

Influence on Aquinas

The Aristotelian paradigm was taken up by many theologians, most prominently by *Thomas Aquinas (1225–1274). At this period the theologians were faced with the same problem as that which confronted the masters of arts, the systematic presentation of a body of traditional knowledge. Thomas sought to establish a concord between revealed doctrine and Aristotle's conclusions. While revealed Christian doctrines could not be proved, their acceptance was thought to be able to be shown at least reasonable, because congruent with the basic philosophical conclusions which Aristotle was thought to have demonstrated. Thomas maintained that God had revealed not only strictly supernatural truths, but also some truths which are philosophically demonstrable. For example, God revealed his existence, for otherwise but few men would have attained certain knowledge of this truth. Nevertheless, Thomas argued, God's existence can be also rationally demonstrated on the basis of the principles of the philosophers and is that very being which the Christian by revelation knows as God.

The concord between philosophy and revelation which Thomas intended involved not only the demonstration of rationally accessible truths, but also the discovery of natural analogies to transcendent truths. It was in dealing with the Aristotelian astronomy that Thomas encountered a type of discourse different from that between dissenting theological authorities. The translators from

Arabic and Greek had made available two far more advanced, but mutually opposed, discussions of the problem of celestial motion: the *Almagest* of Ptolemy and Aristotle's *De caelo*. While the professional astronomers of the period adopted Ptolemy's theory of eccentrics and epicycles and paid little attention to Aristotle's theory of homocentric spheres, the theologians were very disturbed by the contradiction between Ptolemy's mathematical astronomy which claimed to save the phenomena and Aristotle's physical theory which was presented as a deduction from first principles. To the argument that Ptolemy's hypotheses are supported by experience, Thomas rejoined that the experimental verification of an hypothesis does not necessarily demonstrate the hypothesis.

Although Thomas thus formulated explicitly one of the most important principles in the theory of science, he employed it to render harmless the objections to his theological interpretation of Aristotle's astronomy—in the hope that some day a way might be found to make Aristotle's theory agree with experience. His appeal to the principle that verification does not demonstrate a hypothesis meant only that his conception of the concordance between philosophy and revelation need not be disturbed by the contrary data of experience. Armed with Thomas's principle, this clerical world-view was able to maintain itself and disappeared only with the new astronomical discoveries of the sixteenth and seventeenth centuries.

Other anomalies in the Aristotelian paradigm appeared even in the thirteenth century. About the year 1250, as Averroes' real position on the immortality of the human soul became known, the Latins came increasingly to distinguish between the teaching of Aristotle and that of Averroes. And in the year 1277 the Bishop of Paris condemned two hundred nineteen propositions, of which the majority represented Aristotelian positions, condemned because they entailed consequences contrary to revealed doctrine. The masters of arts regarded their work as philosophy, but it was meant to include the vast legacy they had inherited from antiquity—a legacy which embraced logic and mathematics, mechanics and astronomy, ethics and political theory. The "philosophical procedure" made it possible for the masters of arts to criticize Aristotle's idea of science and to ask the new logical and mathematical questions with which *William of Ockham (c. 1285–c. 1347), Walter Burley (c. 1275–c. 1346), and the Merton school led philosophy in the early fourteenth century into new paths.

No longer simply the gateway to theology, the arts faculty became an institution on an equal footing with the faculties of law, medicine, and theology. Aided by the Aristotelian idea that the individual sciences are autonomous in their own realm, philosophers such as *John Buridan (c. 1295–c. 1358) were able to develop theories in physics which were independent of Aristotle's treatment, while mathematicians such as *Nicole Oresme (c. 1320–1382) turned to areas which Aristotle had neglected. Oresme was able to fuse Mertonian mathematics with the Parisian physics of Buridan in the late fourteenth century, while Paul of Venice (c. 1370–1429) and others in Padua in the fifteenth century were able to bring these developments together with the Averroist attitude to form the secular Aristotelianism of the sixteenth-century Italian universities.

A fourth stage of the Aristotelian tradition appeared in the fifteenth century. This period can be said to have begun in the year 1438 with the arrival Georgius Gemistus Pletho (c. 1360–1452) at the Council of Florence. Pletho charged the Latins with misunderstanding Aristotle's teaching because they had been misled by Averroes to believe that Aristotle's works contained a demonstrative summary of scientific truth. The character of the new era became more philological than philosophical. New editions and vernacular translations of the Greek and Latin classics and new philosophical options—Platonism, Epicureanism, and Stoicism—began to appear. A last wave of editions, translations, and commentaries on the works of Aristotle began in the fifteenth century and lasted until about the middle of the seventeenth. But new sources, new scientific interests, new classes of students, new geographical divisions led such groups of scholars to attend to the various parts of philosophy without reference to Aristotle's organization of science.

See also **Condemnation of 1277**; *Scientia*; **Translation movements**; **Universities**

Bibliography

Callus, Daniel. Introduction of Aristotelian Learning to Oxford. *Proceedings of the British Academy* (1943) 29: 229–281.

Dreyer, M. *More mathematicorum: Rezeption und Transformation der antiken Gestalten wissenschaftlichen Wissens !m 12. Jahrhundert.* [Beiträge zur Geschichte der Philosophie und Theologie des Mittelalters NF 47] Münster: Aschendorff, 1996.

Gottschalk, H.B. "Aristotelian Philosophy in the Roman World from the time of Cicero to the end of the second century AD." In *Aufstieg und Niedergang der römischen Welt (ANRW): Geschichte und Kultur Rms im Spiegel der neueren Forschung.* 2 volumes. Berlin: W. de Gruyter, 1987. II. 36.2, 1079–1174.

Grabmann, M. "Eine für Examinazwecke abgefasste Quästionensammlung der Pariser Artistenfakultät aus der ersten Hälfte des XIII. Jahrhunderts." In *Mittelalterliches geistesleben.* 3 volumes. München: Hueber 1926–1956. vol. 2, pp. 183–199.

Hisette, R. *Enquête sur les 219 articles condamnés à Paris le 7 mars 1277.* Louvain: Nauwelaerts, 1977.

Kennedy, E.S. Late Medieval Planetary Theory. *Isis* (1966) 57: 365–378.

Krafft, F. Physikalische Realität oder mathematische Hypothese? *Philosophia naturalis* (1973) 14: 243–275 .

Lang, A. *Die Entfaltung des apologetischen Problems in der Scholastik des Mittelalters.* Freiburg: i.Br: Herder, 1962.

———. *Die theologische Prinzipienlehre der mittelalterlichen Scholastik.* Freiburg: i.Br.: Herder, 1964.

Lohr, C. H. "The Medieval Interpretation of Aristotle." In *The Cambridge History of Late Medieval Philosophy.* New York: Cambridge University Press, 1982.

———. Medieval Latin Aristotle Commentaries. *Traditio* (1967) 23: 314–413; (1968) 24: 149–245; (1970) 26: 135–215; (1971) 27: 251–351; (1972) 28: 281–396; (1973)

29: 93–197; (1974) 30: 119–144; and *Bulletin de philosophie médiévale* (1972) 14: 116–126.

————. *Latin Aristotle Commentaries: II. Renaissance Authors.* Florence: L.S. Olschki, 1988; III. *Index initiorum et finium.* Florence: L.S. Olschki, 1995; IV. *Bibliography of Secondary Literature.* Florence: L.S. Olschki, 2005.

Moraux, P. *Der Aristotelismus bei den Griechen von Andronikos bis Alexander von Aphrodisias.* 2 volumes. Berlin: De Gruyter, 1973–1984.

Peters, F. E. *Aristoteles arabus. The oriental translations and commentaries of the Aristotelian Corpus.* Leiden: E.J. Brill, 1968.

Podskalsky, G. *Theologie und Philosophie in Byzanz.* Munich: Beck, 1977.

Sorabji, R., ed. *Aristotle Transformed: The Ancient Commentators and Their Influence.* London: Duckworth, 1990.

Van Steenberghen, F. *Aristotle in the West; the origins of Latin Aristotelianism.* Translated by Leonard Johnston. Louvain: Nauwelaerts, 1970.

————. *Maître Siger de Brabant.* Louvain: Publications universitaires, 1977.

CHARLES H. LOHR

ARITHMETIC

The story of the growth of arithmetic from the ancient inheritance to the wealth passed on to the Renaissance is dramatic and passes through several cultures. The most groundbreaking achievement was the evolution of a positional number system, in which the position of a digit within a number determines its value according to powers (usually) of ten (e.g., in 3,285, the "2" refers to hundreds). Its extension to include decimal fractions and the procedures that were made possible by its adoption transformed the abilities of all who calculated, with an effect comparable to the modern invention of the electronic computer. Roughly speaking, this began in India, was transmitted to Islam, and then to the Latin West. (Although Chinese mathematics included many of the concepts discussed here from an early stage, it does not play a large role in the transmission of ideas.) By the Renaissance arithmetic was a powerful tool, prepared to meet the computational challenges of both science and commerce.

India

Unlike the geometrically- and logically-minded Greeks, Indian mathematicians emphasized computation; they readily accepted irrational quantities and zero as numbers and incorporated them easily into their arithmetic. Mathematics in India divides into two disciplines, *patiganita* (the "mathematics of algorithms," or arithmetic) and *bijaganita* (the "mathematics of seeds," or *algebra). Although this distinction is not yet found in Aryabhata's mathematical and astronomical work *Aryabhatiya* (499 C.E.), it is present in Brahmagupta's *Brahmasphutasiddhanta* (*The Opening of the Universe,* 628 C.E.) and afterward. We also find a progression in the notion of positional arithmetic from a mere hint in Aryabhata to a fully formed theory in Brahmagupta. Although Brahmagupta did not extend his system to include decimal fractions, he conceived such innovations as the beginnings of the system for notating fractions that we use today (numerator over denominator), and rules for handling zero and negative numbers. One of India's greatest works was the Bhaskara II's *Lilavati* (twelfth century), which became the most popular textbook on arithmetic and spawned numerous commentaries. Among the topics found in Indian treatises on arithmetic are the rule of three (essentially the solution to $a/b = c/x$), useful to merchants dealing with weights and measures; the solution of linear equations by the method of false position; the solution of linear indeterminate equations (*kuttaka*, or pulverizer), useful for calendrical work; and combinatorial problems.

Islam

Before the Indian presence began to be felt in the late eighth century, Islamic calculators relied primarily on finger reckoning. This primitive but surprisingly useful tool did not disappear immediately with the rise of Hindu methods; in fact, the two most important works on finger reckoning are by Abu'l-Wafa' (late tenth century) and al-Karaji (early eleventh century, who also introduced Pascal's triangle of binomial coefficients to Islam). However, it faded away gradually as the new methods proved their worth. Perhaps the earliest exposition of the new arithmetic was *Muhammed al-Khwarizmi's early ninth-century *Kitab hisab al-'adad al-hindi* (*Book on Calculation with Hindu Numerals*); it is now lost in Arabic, but it was to play a vital role in Europe through Latin translation. Although al-Khwarizmi used the Hindu system he did not extend it to fractions, instead still relying on the ancient representations using sums of unit fractions. As with many of his successors, al-Khwarizmi's procedures for the basic arithmetic operations (addition, subtraction, multiplication, division) were designed to be used on a dust board, which was compact and on which figures could be easily erased and replaced. Dust board arithmetic had staying power; it is found, for instance, in works by Kushyar ibn Labban in the late tenth century and by the famous astronomer *Nasir al-Din al-Tusi almost three centuries later. However, it was gradually replaced by algorithms performed with pen and paper. The earliest text to describe these new methods was *al-Uqlidisi's *Arithmetic*, written in Baghdad in 945 C.E.; in it the author argues for pen-and-paper techniques so that arithmeticists could be distinguished from the dust board-wielding astrologers. Also within its pages is an early appearance of decimal fractions, although a systematic treatment would not come until the twelfth century with al-Samaw'al. A complete mastery of pen-and-paper arithmetic with a positional number system, including decimal fractions, may be seen in the early fifteenth-century Iranian astronomer Jamshid al-Kashi's *Miftah al-hisab* (*The Calculator's Key*). Used as a textbook for centuries, this book contained all the arithmetic needed for astronomy, surveying, commerce, and architecture.

Concurrent with these developments, astronomers were using a full-fledged positional numeration system, with base 60, that dates back to the Babylonians. Authors of arithmetic texts such as Kushyar and al-Kashi described computational procedures for the so-called "astronomers' arithmetic" that were analogous to their decimal counterparts. Since the "digits" in this system range from zero to 59, the process of multiplication required the use of tables listing the products of all whole numbers up to 59 x 59. However, the great eleventh-century scholar *al-Biruni once remarked that many of his predecessors cheated by converting base 60 numbers into whole decimal numbers, then multiplying, then converting back.

Much Muslim work in arithmetic was inspired by Greek ideas; this included results on amicable numbers and sums of sequences, including squares and cubes. We also find explorations of binomial coefficients, and related algorithms for computing the nth root of a given number, at least as early as *'Umar al-Khayyam (around 1100 C.E.; known to the West as Omar Khayyam), and later in al-Samaw'al and al-Kashi. In the latter's Calculator's Key there is a truly impressive calculation of $\sqrt[5]{44,240,899,506,197}$, using an algorithm designed with the aid of the binomial theorem.

Europe

The main source for arithmetic in early medieval Europe was Nicomachus's *Introduction to Arithmetic*, through a paraphrased translation by *Boethius in the early sixth century. As one of the subjects in the *quadrivium, arithmetic was part of what it meant to be educated; Charlemagne even ordained its instruction, although over time it was subject to neglect. Although the available techniques were crude, they sufficed for the requirements of the day—especially the determination of the date of Easter, and probably numerology and divination. The science of the *computus* relied mostly on Roman numerals, finger reckoning, and the abacus, although textual evidence for the latter begins only in the late tenth century. At this time *Gerbert of Aurillac reintroduced mathematics in school and popularized a variant of the Roman abacus which used Hindu-Arabic numeration, although he did not include a symbol for zero and his calculation methods were not very effective. It is possible that he learned decimal numeration from contacts with Muslim science during his studies in Barcelona.

It was not until the twelfth century that needs arose requiring substantial improvement. The introduction of mathematical astronomy through translations into Latin of works by al-Khwarizmi, *al-Battani, and *Ptolemy placed higher demands on arithmetic than it could handle. Fortunately, the translation of al-Khwarizmi's *Arithmetic* by *Adelard of Bath contained sections on the base 60 astronomers' system as well as on Hindu-Arabic decimal numeration. Al-Khwarizmi's dust board computations transformed the practice of arithmetic; the abacus was soon supplanted by so-called "algorismus" texts propagating the new methods. Indeed, it is probable that the word "algorithm" arose from the Latinization of his

name within these texts. The two most influential algorismus works in the thirteenth century were Alexander de Villadieu's *Carmen de algorismo*, used extensively for calendar calculations; and *John of Sacrobosco's *Algorismus vulgaris*, which became a leading university text on the subject.

The switch from dust board to pen-and-paper calculations is due mainly to Leonardo of Pisa, known as *Fibonacci. His *Liber abaci* (1202; in Italy at this time the word "*abaco*" had come to mean computation in general) promoted the use of Hindu-Arabic numerals, including zero, but did not yet use decimal fractions. Although Fibonacci learned to compute on Gerbert's abacus using Hindu-Arabic numerals, the *Liber abaci* owes a large debt to Arabic sources. The advanced number theory in his other works was not really appreciated in his own time, but the *Liber abaci* did originate the Italian tradition of "abbacus" arithmetic of the fourteenth and fifteenth centuries. The abacus methods were essentially the same as those taught in schools today, and were inspired by commercial interests.

Hindu-Arabic arithmetic did not have a smooth reception in Italy; it was actually banned in Florence in 1299 and in several places early in the fourteenth century, presumably due to the possibility of fraud. However, its benefits in trade made it inevitable. Although ordinary Europeans would not become familiar with it until the seventeenth century, positional decimal arithmetic flourished in science and especially in business by the fifteenth century.

See also **Algebra; Arabic numerals; Commercial arithmetic; Translation norms and practice**

Bibliography

Al-Khwarizmi, Muhammed. *Mohammed ibn Musa Alchwarizmi's Algorismus. Das früheste Lehrbuch zum Rechnen mit indischen Ziffern. Nach der einzigen (lateinischen) Handschrift (Cambridge Un. Lib. Ms. Ii. 6. 5) in Faksimile mit Transkription und Kommentar herausgegeben.* Aalen: Zeller, 1963.

Al-Uqlidisi, Abu l-Hasan. *The Arithmetic of al-Uqlidisi.* Translated by Ahmad S. Saidan. Boston: Reidel, 1978.

Berggren, J. L. *Episodes in the Mathematics of Medieval Islam.* New York: Springer-Verlag, 1986.

———. "Medieval Arithmetic: Arabic Texts and European Motivations." In *Word, Image, Number. Communication in the Middle Ages.* Edited by John J. Contreni and Santa Casciani. Florence: SISMEL—Edizioni del Galluzzo, 2002, pp. 351–365.

Contreni, John J. and Santa Casciani, eds. *Word, Image, Number. Communication in the Middle Ages.* Florence: SISMEL—Edizioni del Galluzzo, 2002.

Evans, Gillian. From Abacus to Algorism: Theory and Practice in Medieval Arithmetic. *British Journal for the History of Science* (1977) 10: 114–131.

Kushyar ibn Labban. *Principles of Hindu Reckoning.* Translated by Martin Levey and Marvin Petruck. Madison/Milwaukee: University of Wisconsin Press, 1965.

Mahoney, Michael S. "Mathematics." In *Science in the Middle Ages.* Edited by David C. Lindberg. Chicago: University of Chicago Press, 1978.

Sigler, Laurence, ed. *Fibonacci's* Liber abaci: *A Translation into Modern English of Leonardo Pisano's Book of Calculation.* New York: Springer-Verlag, 2002.

Van Egmond, Warren. "Abbacus arithmetic." In *Companion Encyclopedia of the History and Philosophy of the Mathematical Sciences.* Edited by Ivor Grattan-Guinness. London/New York: Routledge, 1994. Vol. 1.

GLEN VAN BRUMMELEN

ARMS AND ARMOR

Iron ores are very widespread and may be reduced by heating with carbon (as charcoal) in small furnaces. The non-metallic elements in the ore form slag, which liquefies at around 1200°C, and runs away from the solid iron, leaving it as a lump or bloom, porous in form and containing much entrapped slag. Repeated heating and forging are necessary to expel most of the slag and consolidate the bloom.

If the bloom was left in the hearth for some time, then parts of it might absorb some carbon, and form steel. Steel is harder and stronger than iron. So the product of the bloomery might well be a heterogeneous lump, parts of which would be of higher carbon content than others. Early smiths would have found that some samples of "iron" were twice as hard as others, but whether they could be deliberately produced was another matter. A more efficient way of proceeding could be to make an artefact of iron, and then convert part of it to steel. This might be done by forge-welding a steel edge to an iron back, or by case-carburizing the edge (heating the iron in contact with carbon).

Many medieval smiths, and indeed Celtic and Roman smiths before them, attempted to overcome the difficulty of carburizing iron uniformly by treating only very small pieces, of which several could then be piled together, and forged into a blade.

The technique known as pattern-welding (sometimes called "false Damascus" or "twisted Damascus") grew out of piling as a means of making long blades from many small pieces of metal with varied compositions. Pieces of iron and steel were twisted as they were welded together, and then the surface ground and etched with fruit acids to reveal a pattern. The pattern visible on the surface may have contributed to their popularity, being reminiscent in appearance to blades made of true "Damascus steel." From about the third to the tenth century pattern-welded swords were common in Western Europe, but after about 1000 C.E. their occurrence diminishes, presumably because larger pieces of steel became available.

The relatively high cost of steel meant that smiths would often make swords and other weapons by forge-welding a steel edge, or edges, onto an iron body, thus making a scarce material go further. After fabrication, the red-hot blade could be quenched (plunged red-hot into cold water) to harden it. The process is a difficult one to manipulate, however, as the hardness is accompanied by embrittlement.

The Roman army was based on legionaries who were armed with javelins and swords and were armored by metal helmets and shirts of mail (interlinked rings), scale armor (small plates of metal fastened to a cloth backing) or lamellar armor. Lamellar armor can be traced back to the Assyrians and consists of small plates laced to each other (but not to the underlying garment) for maximum flexibility. It was to remain in use outside Europe throughout Central Asia, China, and Japan.

Effective at close quarters, the legionary armies proved unable to defend the frontiers of the Roman Empire successfully. A faster-moving army was required, and the elite of the army became the armored cavalry. A Near-Eastern influence, from Iran, on the use of cavalry has been suggested. Rock-carvings at Naqsh-i-Rustem, from the third to the fifth century C.E., show the Sassanid kings on horseback charging their enemies with lances, but without shields or stirrups. A graffito from Dura Europos shows a mailed cavalryman on a mailed horse also charging with a lance, and without stirrups or shield. Some writers have suggested that the adoption of the stirrup was of profound importance in enabling cavalry to fight as shocktroops, rather than mounted archers or scouts, by seating the warrior firmly. Certainly it improved the efficiency of cavalry considerably, but so did the invention of horseshoes (also perhaps from this period) which enormously extended the useful life of the horse.

It is also possible that armored lancers might have been practical even without stirrups if saddles could be gripped for leverage. Roman saddles show four "horns" which may have been grasped to steady the rider, as an alternative to stirrups, but of course, the left arm could not then manipulate a shield as well as reins.

The last Western Emperor was deposed in 476 and the old empire was succeeded by various Germanic kingdoms. Most of their armies still apparently consisted of foot-soldiers, but mailed cavalry continued to become steadily more important. The Franks in Gaul under Charles Martel seem to have been the first to use large numbers of mailed cavalry as their principal weapon. They certainly used stirrups by this time, but it may have been their organization which made the crucial difference. In 755 Pepin III changed the date of the muster from March to May, so that there would be enough grass for the horses to eat. The bulk of the Frankish army was mounted, costly though this was. The price of the equipment of a mailed horseman totaled as much as twenty-three oxen, according to Verbruggen. This enormous sum was justified by their complete supremacy on the battlefield.

In Western Europe any man who fought on horseback was known from the tenth century onward as a knight, whatever his precise social status. He had to be a fulltime soldier because the cost of his equipment, and the training required to use it effectively, left little time for any economic activity. If he could not be paid in cash, he would have to be paid in land. Many knights were not landowners of course, but they formed a social class which lived on the work of others who cultivated the land on their behalf.

Mail Armor

Throughout the early Middle Ages, the mail shirt was the principal body defense for those warriors fortunate enough to be able to afford it. Its adaptability, however, meant that it was frequently repaired and reused, so that very little has survived intact from this period. The links, made of lengths of strip or drawn wire, were formed into rings and then linked together. Each link is attached to four others, except of course, at the edges, where the garment ends. The links are then closed by riveting. An economy of effort may be made by closing half the links by hammer-welding, so that only alternate rows need to be riveted. Most medieval European mail shirts consist of all-riveted links; this arrangement is less common but still found in Oriental mail.

A series of boat-burials at Vendel in Sweden, Valsgarde, and elsewhere from the seventh to the ninth century have yielded samples of mail with rectangular reinforcing pieces of plate. This innovation might be ascribed to an Eastern influence. Certainly, Vikings employed the rivers of Russia to trade to the Black and Caspian seas as well as setting up the Kingdom of Kiev (864 C.E.), from which the nucleus of medieval Russia grew. Russian armor of the Middle Ages was a mixture of mail, scale, and lamellar not dissimilar to that depicted in Byzantine images of soldiers. Although sometimes reinforced with pieces of plate, mail remained the principal form of body armor in the Islamic world, as late as the Ottoman Empire, and in India, as well as Russia, until armor itself went out of use.

Carolingian manuscripts of the ninth and tenth centuries show mounted warriors wearing mail shirts extending from the elbow to the knee, and conical helmets. The armor for knights and also protection for their horses was extended steadily. By the eleventh century mail shirts are shown reaching down to the wrist, and separate leggings of mail to complete the protection of the limbs appear by the twelfth century, as do hoods of mail like balaclavas over the head and neck. Horses acquired some mail also, although cloth wrappers hide its extent in illustrations. Knights on the winning side could feel very safe, unless they were unhorsed. At the battle of Lincoln (1217) just three were killed, at Falkirk (1297) only one, although many lost their horses.

While the body defense made entirely of mail had reached a peak of completeness by the thirteenth century, some of its limitations were becoming apparent. Crossbows were growing in power, and while mail was generally a good defense against slashing weapons, always in conjunction with a quilted undergarment (gambeson), it was less effective against the points of arrows which were retained rather than deflected by its links.

Missile Weapons and Infantry

Despite the great effectiveness of knights, infantry that could withstand a charge of knights was not unknown. However, by the early fourteenth century, given favorable local circumstances, knights were being defeated by foot-soldiers in Flanders, Switzerland, and Scotland. The citizens of Ghent, Bruges, and Ypres are shown in contemporary illustrations as being armored from head to knee and carrying spiked maces ("goedendags") as well as pikes and crossbows. The pikes were set against the ground and used to stop a charge of knights. Then for hand-to-hand combat, heavy two-handed weapons which would reach up to a man in the saddle were needed. The goedendags of the Flemings, the halberds of the Swiss and the battleaxes of the Scots all belonged in this category.

In 1291 the farmers and herdsmen of Switzerland asserted their independence from Rudolph of Hapsburg. The terrain did not favor knights at the best of times, and the Swiss infantry won the battle of Morgarten (1315) against Austrian forces. They organized themselves into squares of pikemen which were eventually able to take the offensive against armies in the field and won famous victories over Charles the Bold at Grandson and Morat in 1476, and at Nancy in 1477.

In England, Edward I recruited large numbers of Welsh archers, and used them on the battlefield in thousands rather than in hundreds notably after Gerald of Wales had earlier described how during the siege of Abergavenny in 1182, Welsh arrows pierced an oak door four inches (10 cm) thick. Edward II failed to coordinate the use of his knights and archers, and lost the battle of Bannockburn (1314) to Scots pikemen. Edward III maintained his grandfather's faith in archers, recruiting even more of them, and making his knights dismount and fight on foot beside them. Such was the army that he took to France and used to win the Battle of Crecy (1346).

Miniature illustration of the Battle of Crecy from the *Chronique* of Jean Froissart (c. 1347–c. 1405). English longbows on the right face French crossbows. (Corbis/Bettmann)

Crossbows

The earliest crossbows were simply heavy bows fixed to a stock, with a trigger release which enabled it to be spanned with both hands, both feet being placed on the bow. Simply making a bow thicker does not make it more powerful. It may be more difficult to bend into a curve, but it still has to bend and straighten again quickly and without cracking. So overall the stiffness must be increased, rather than the thickness. One way of achieving this is by making a "compound" bow. Horn or whalebone (which resist compression) are placed on the inside, and animal sinew (which resists extension) on the outside, of a wooden bow, and the whole assembly glued together with fish glue and rendered waterproof with a skin covering.

As early as 1139 the crossbow had become such a dangerous weapon to knights that its use was banned by the Second Lateran Council in 1139. To span these stronger bows, a stirrup was added to the stock in the twelfth century, and a belt with a hook could be worn by the operator to enable his upper body as well as his arms to take part in drawing the bow. By the fourteenth century a belt such as this, improved by incorporating a pulley ("Samson's belt") or a "goat's foot" lever might be used. By the fifteenth century a windlass with a system of pulleys, or a cranequin (a rack and pinion gear) were needed to span the powerful steel crossbows then in use.

Plate Armor

The threat from crossbows meant that mail was regularly reinforced by some sort of rigid body defense from at least the thirteenth century. Several large plates of metal, or sometimes hardened leather ("cuir bouilli") would be formed as a defense to be worn on top of the hauberk, or a coat-of-plates. This would indeed protect the knight from missile weapons, but at the cost of extra weight.

So the combination of mail and plate steadily developed into a "harness" or suit of armor made up of articulated plates designed to cover the entire body except for the armpits and bottom, which had to remain protected by gussets of mail. This started to emerge in its final form in fourteenth-century Lombardy, and was fully developed by about 1400, when it remained in use for more than two hundred years. It required the production of large pieces of plate, made of steel of acceptable quality. A plate of armor which weighs between 5½ and 10 pounds (2.5–4.5 kg) will require billets of metal of 22 pounds (10 kg) or more and their production from a bloomery is difficult. However, during the fourteenth century in Italy, bloomeries had become large enough to make the production of such large plates possible, while their operators developed sufficient skill to prevent the furnace overheating and producing liquid "cast iron."

As a result, European armor starts to differ fundamentally in design from those forms of armor used in other parts of the world, namely Islam, India, China, and Japan. All of those cultures continued to use armor made up of a large number of small plates or rings joined together to form a flexible garment, rather than a rigid exoskeleton.

Asiatic Swords

"Damascus steel" swords were the famous blades with a "watered-silk" or "damask" pattern on their surfaces, made from a very high-carbon steel (wootz) formed by melting iron with carbonaceous material in a sealed crucible over several days until it wholly or partially melted into a cake of steel, and was then allowed to cool extremely slowly. These cakes were exported to centers of arms manufacture (such as Damascus) where they were carefully forged, with some difficulty, into sword blades. Since the melting-point of steel falls with increasing carbon content, a lower temperature than usual has to be employed to forge a harder blade of higher carbon content than usual (around 1.2–1.6 percent). This forging broke up network of iron carbide crystals left over from the casting, reducing brittleness, and producing the characteristic pattern ("watered silk") on the surface of the blade. The blade so formed needed no further heat treatment to harden it, nor did any amount of sharpening ever remove the edge.

However it has become clear, that wootz was only a small part, albeit a special part, of a crucible steel industry, active throughout the Middle East. Crucible steel that was not as slowly and carefully cooled would have a similar chemical composition to wootz, but without its surface pattern. Crucible steel weapons were expensive, and probably reserved for a tiny minority. But the vast topic of Indian arms and armor is still largely unexamined in any detail. Until the eighteenth century, Indian warriors wore body defenses of mail, sometimes reinforced with small plates, and fought with sword bow and spear like medieval Europeans, but without employing the shock tactics of knights.

See also **Artillery and firearms**

Bibliography

Blair, Claude. *European Armour*. London: Batsford 1958, reprinted 1972.

Boccia, Lionello. *Armi e Armature Lombarde*. Milan: Electa, 1980.

Elgood, Robert. *Islamic Arms and Armour*. London: Scolar Press, 1979.

ffoulkes, Charles. *The Armourer and his Craft*. New York: Dover, 1988.

Oakeshott, R.E. *The Sword in the Age of Chivalry*. Guildford: Lutterworth, 1964.

Robinson, H. Russell. *Oriental Armour*. London: Jenkins, 1967.

Sewter, E.R.A. *The Alexiad of Anna Comnena*. Harmondsworth: Penguin, 1969.

Smith, Cyril Stanley. *A History of Metallography*. Cambridge: MIT Press, 1988.

Strickland, Matthew and Robert Hardy. *The Great War Bow*. Stroud: Sutton, 2005.

Thomas, Bruno and Ortwin Gamber. *Katalog der Leibrüstkammer. I*. Vienna: Schroll, 1976.

Thordeman, Bengt. *Armour from the Battle of Wisby, 1361*. 2 vols. Stockholm: 1939–1940. Reprinted in one volume: Chivalry Bookshelf, 2001.

Trapp, Oswald Graf, and J.G. Mann. *The Armoury of the Castle of Churburg*. Udine: Magnus, 1995.

Verbruggen, J.F. *The Art of Warfare in Western Europe during the Middle Ages*. Woodbridge: Boydell. 1997.
Williams, Alan. *The Knight and the Blast Furnace*. Leiden: E.J. Brill, 2003.

ALAN WILLIAMS

ARNAU DE VILANOVA

Arnau de Vilanova's early life and education are not known with certainty. The agreed date of his birth is c. 1240 but the place, somewhere in the Crown of Aragon, is still a subject of debate. In the 1260s he was studying medicine at Montpellier, where he earned his degree. He married Agnès Blasi and established himself in Valencia. In 1281 Arnau moved to Barcelona to serve King Pere III as his personal physician. Despite this move and his many later travels, Arnau and his family kept strong personal and economic links with Valencia throughout their lives. After the death of Pere in 1285, Arnau became royal physician to the king's sons; first to Alfons II, and after his death in 1290 to his brother and successor Jaume II and to his youngest brother Frederic III, who become king of Sicily in 1296. As was the case with many of his colleagues at the royal courts, Arnau's activities went far beyond the strictly medical. A personal friend of the monarchs, he served them informally as a political and spiritual adviser and at a more formal level as representative of the Crown in some diplomatic negotiations. His role at the royal court was not an impediment to his development as a teacher and author of medical works at the medical school of Montpellier, to which he was attached from 1289 to 1301. The value of his presence at the Studium was recognized in 1309 by the papal bull that regulated its medical syllabus. In Montpellier, the flourishing of Arnau's medical production paralleled his growing interest in spiritual matters in line with the reformist views of certain Franciscans groups. Some historians have made an effort to show the crossing of boundaries in Arnau's interests between divine illumination and reason, between the religious and the medical; others have been readier to defend the independent development of both enterprises. By 1300 Arnau had already finished a number of religious works of a didactic nature (addressed to the Aragonese royal family), biblical exegeses, anti-Jewish apologetics, and prophetic and reform writings. Thereafter he did not occupy his chair at the medical school, instead devoting the bulk of his energies to diffusing his eschatological views and to defending himself in various conflicts with elements within the Church. However, he did not abandon his medical activities, and continued his service as physician to the Aragonese royal family and at the papal court, first to Pope Boniface VIII and later to his successor Benedict XI. After Benedict's death in 1304, Clement V took Peter's chair. The new pope was an old friend of Arnau and more sympathetic to his ideas than his predecessors. Consequently 1305 marked the beginning of a period of relative calm in Arnau's life. Enjoying the patronage of the pope as well as that of the kings of Aragon and Sicily,

Arnau envisaged the possibility of realizing his proposals for the social and religious reform of Christendom. The ideals of poverty, charity, and the need to preach evangelical truth to the poor led Arnau during these years to write a number of religious works in the vernacular that reflected and reinforced the ideals and practices of various groups of lay spirituals. However, the patronage of the king of Aragon that had been so important to Arnau, providing him with protection and a means for achieving his goals, was soon to be withdrawn. In 1309, the disclosure and prophetic interpretation of the dreams of the two monarchs, Jaume II and Frederic, to the papal curia in Avignon, caused the former to break with Arnau. Despite his indiscretion, Arnau kept the support of the younger brother, Frederic, who was the recipient in 1310 of the *Informació espiritual per al rey Frederic*, in which Arnau set out the guidelines to the perfect Christian king. Traveling by sea in the service of this monarch, Arnau died off the coast of Genoa in 1311.

Medical Writings

Despite his religious interests and their public impact, Arnau was regarded by his contemporaries principally as a physician. And it was as a physician that he was able to build his influential connections at the royal and papal courts. About his actual healing activities there is not much information, although his success and his patrons' appreciation of his application of the art are well documented. Further information about Arnau's medical thought can be obtained from the wide number of medical writings that he produced and that are extant in manuscript form or in sixteenth-century printed editions (Lyons, 1504, 1509, 1520, 1532; Venice, 1505, 1527; Basel, 1585).

Unfortunately there is no list of Arnau's medical works equivalent to that of his spiritual works, which he prepared himself in 1305. Neither do his medical writings contain references to dates and places of composition that might help to establish a genuine Arnaudian corpus and an accurate chronology. Manuscript tradition, cross-references, theoretical consistency, data from archival material, and the inventory of his possessions made after his death are the main tools that allow us to draw Arnau's professional profile. From the early 1280s to his death, Arnau touched on almost all medical genres and subjects: commentaries on medical authorities, monographs on particular diseases in the form of *consilia or epistles, aphorisms, medical compendia, and pharmacological treatises. He made translations too. Arnau confessed that he knew no Greek, but he mastered Arabic. In 1282, while staying in Barcelona, he translated several medical treatises from Arabic into Latin: the *De viribus cordis* of *Ibn Sina (Avicenna), *De rigore* by *Galen, and *De medicinis simplicibus*, a pharmacological work by Abu-Salt.

Arnau's main written production must surely be dated to 1290–1300, when he held his position as master at the Montpellier medical school. Before this period Arnau seems to have composed only a short treatise (*Tractatus de amore heroico*, composed before 1285) devoted to a single disease, love-sickness, a kind of mental alteration, and an epistle (*De reprobacione nigromantice ficcionis*, c. 1276–1281 or c. 1286–1288) condemning necromantic practices and arguing that those who believed that they had mastered the devil were in fact insane.

The first work produced by Arnau at Montpellier, *De intentione medicorum*, laid the ground for his medical epistemology. What is medicine, *scientia or ars? What are the nature and the aim of medical knowledge? What role must be performed by the university physician? And accordingly, what training will best suit him for this role? All these questions were contained in this programmatic text where Arnau explored the limits between medical and philosophical knowledge and proposed a duality of objectives and two levels of epistemological evaluation. The physician, according to Arnau, is an *artifex sensualis et operativus* and thus, at least rhetorically, his theoretical interests must be limited by their practical usefulness. This stance, which Michael McVaugh has called "medical instrumentalism," allowed Arnau to establish an intermediary space between an idea of medicine as science that would fulfil itself in theoretical speculation and an anti-intellectual empiricism. Arnau identified the first position with medical Averroism, against which he confessed that he wrote several works: *De intentione medicorum*; the *Epistola de dosi tyriacalium* (c. 1290–1299) on the effect of antidotes designed to refute the *De tyriaca* of *Ibn Rushd (Averroes); *De considerationibus operis medicine sive de flebotomia* (c. 1298–1300) on phlebotomy; and the *Aphorismi de gradibus*, a pharmacological work composed between 1295 and 1300. Historiography has highlighted Arnau's supposed anti-intellectualism and connected it with his religious views. However, this link has been based mostly on the erroneous ascription to Arnau of the work *Breviarium practice*. In fact, Arnau's position on medieval empirics, as stated in his *De consideracionibus* and elsewhere, is by no means a positive one.

The polemical tone employed by Arnau in some of his medical writings reflected a tense intellectual and professional environment at Montpellier where Arnau was strongly involved. Like other masters at Paris, Bologna, and Montpellier, Arnau was responsible for developing at the medical school a wider intellectual framework that overshadowed the one focused in the canonical texts of the so-called *Articella collection. The change, termed by García Ballester as the introduction of "the new Galen" to medical teaching and research, involved revaluations of more than thirty works of Galen and also revisiting Arabic works, which previous generations had not done. This no doubt helped to pose new questions and to offer new answers, both at a theoretical and a practical level. The rhetorical aspect of this movement is clear—it gave to university medicine a more convincing presentation within the academia and outside—but there is evidence of actual changes in diagnosis, prognosis, and therapy as a result of this new reading of Galenic works. Arnau's pedagogical impetus extended not only to his classroom expositions but also to other works devoted to a wider audience and composed with an aphoristic structure to make them easy to memorize: *Medicationis parabole*, dedicated in 1300 to King Philip IV of France; *Aphorismi particulares; Aphorismi extravagantes*. The pedagogical intention is also clear in Arnau's last complete work, the *Speculum medicine*, a compendium composed as an introduction to the principles of medicine following the scheme of the *Isagoge* of Johannitius (*Hunayn ibn Ishaq). There is debate about its date of composition. For some, it must be the product of Arnau's final activities at Montpellier in 1300–1301; for others, archival evidence suggests 1305–1308 as a more probable date range. Since the *Speculum*, according to Arnau, was composed as the theoretical part of medicine, it has been assumed that the unfinished *De parte operativa* was the practical sequel of Arnau's projected *summa*.

Pedagogical concerns of another sort inspired some of Arnau's practical writings: regimens of health (*Regimen sanitatis ad regem aragonum*, c. 1305–1308 and *Regimen Almarie*, c. 1309–1310), and *consilia* aimed not only at giving therapeutic advice but also at teaching certain regulations in the lifestyles of those to whom he addressed the works.

Historiography has traditionally adorned Arnau de Vilanova with features common to other heterodox figures in the history of science and medicine. As a supposed rebel against medical *Scholasticism, Arnau's clinical common sense and lust for empirical findings have been contrasted with the inane subtleties of his academic contemporaries. Yet the magical and the alchemical, too, have often been associated with Arnau. In both cases, however, the picture is highly distorted. In his theoretical and practical medical writings, Arnau was much like other university physicians in using the tools provided by scholasticism: the authority of the ancients, a logical apparatus based on Aristotelian principles, and recourse to experience in a variable degree. It is true that he wrote about the value of divine illumination in obtaining medical knowledge, and that he used some magical and alchemical concepts in his medical thinking. It is also true that he distrusted medical speculation and natural-philosophical intrusions into health matters. Nevertheless, Arnau was not the master of the arcane secrets of nature in the service of an alchemical dream any more than he was the avant-garde scientist molded by the patterns of experimental medicine.

A painstaking critical edition of the Arnaudian medical corpus accompanied by historical studies has been under way since 1975 and is establishing the foundation for a more balanced understanding of his thought.

See also **Alchemy; John of Saint-Amand; "Latin Averroists"; Medicine, practical; Medicine, theoretical; Patronage of science; Pharmaceutic handbooks;** *Regimen sanitatis***; Religion and science; Translation movements; Translation norms and practice; Universities**

Bibliography

Primary Sources
García Ballester, Luis and Michael McVaugh and Juan A. Paniagua, general editors. *Arnaldi de Vilanova Opera*

Medica Omnia. Granada/Barcelona: Universitat de Barcelona, 1975–.

Secondary Sources

Batllori, Miquel. *Arnau de Vilanova i l'arnaldisme*. Valencia: Tres I Quatre, 1994.

García Ballester, Luis. Arnau de Vilanova (c. 1240–1311) y la Reforma de los Estudios Médicos en Montpellier (1309): El Hipócrates latino y la introducción del nuevo Galeno. *Dynamis* (1982) 2: 119–146.

———. *Galen and Galenism. Theory and medical practice from Antiquity to the European Renaissance*. Aldershot: Ashgate, 2003.

Giralt, Sebastià. "Decus Arnaldi. Estudis entorn dels escrits de medicina pràctica, l'ocultisme i la pervivència del corpus atribuït a Arnau de Vilanova." PhD. Dissertation, Universitat Autònoma de Barcelona, Barcelona, 2002.

McVaugh, Michael. *Medicine before the Plague. Practitioners and Their Patients in the Crown of Aragon, 1285-1345*. New York: Cambridge University Press, 1993.

Mensa i Valls, J. and S. Giralt. *Bibliografía Arnaldiana (1994–2003)*. Arxiu de Textos Catalans Antics (2003) 22: 665–734.

Paniagua, Juan A. *Studia Arnaldiana. Trabajos en torno a la obra médica de Arnau de Vilanova, c. 1240-1311*. Barcelona: Uriach, 1994.

Perarnau, Josep, ed. *Actes de la I Trobada Internacional d'Estudis sobre Arnau de Vilanova*. Barcelona, Institut d'Estudis Catalans, 1995 (2 vols.).

Ziegler, Joseph. *Medicine and Religion c. 1300. The case of Arnau de Vilanova*. Oxford: Clarendon Press, 1998.

FERNANDO SALMÓN

ARTICELLA

Articella—an Italian word meaning "little art"—is one of many titles given to a collection of texts of Greek and Arabic origin that served as the basis of nearly all medical teaching in Europe from the twelfth to the sixteenth centuries. The collection was put together in *Salerno in the early twelfth century, and was adopted as the fundamental textbook of university medical education in the thirteenth century. The collection continued to be widely read and commented on in universities and was printed in at least sixteen editions between 1476 and 1534. As the introductory text to medicine, the *Articella* supplied the conceptual framework within which medicine was studied in the late Middle Ages.

The *Articella* was put together for the purpose of teaching medicine in a classroom setting. Initially, it comprised five texts: the *Isagoge* of Johannitius, the *Aphorisms* and *Prognostics* of *Hippocrates, the *Urines* of the Byzantine physician Theophilus Protospatharius, and the *Pulses* of Philaretus. By the middle of the twelfth century *Galen's *Tegni* had been added to the collection, creating a core of six texts.

These texts provide a systematic outline of Galenic medical theory together with the basics of Hippocratic medical practice. For the most part, the texts are short, introductory works written in summary fashion, containing easily memorized statements of fundamental medical concepts. The *Isagoge* is a short compendium that proceeds by division and definition to give a schematic overview of Galenic medicine in the form of brief summaries. Although attributed to an author named Johannitius, the text is an abridgement of a work by *Hunayn ibn Ishaq as an introduction to Galenic medicine. The *Tegni* (or *Techne*) was Galen's own summary of the medical system he had developed in the course of his practice and had expounded in his other medical writings.

The *Aphorisms*—probably the most famous medical text of the Middle Ages—is a collection of terse statements that encapsulate the wisdom of the medical art. The aphorisms are loosely grouped into topics dealing with purging and diet, sleep patterns, environmental factors of sickness, age-related illness, diagnosis from urine samples, spasms and epilepsy, women's ailments, prognosis and therapy, and identification of the stages of illness. The *Prognostics*—the companion text to the *Aphorisms*—tells the physician how to recognize acute illnesses, especially their past, present, and future states, and how to treat such ailments.

Pulses is a work of Byzantine origin which defines the function of the pulse and then describes it under ten categories, including dimension, type, consistency, and beat. Its companion text, *Urines*, categorizes urine in terms of its color, consistency, sediment, and odor, and then relates these characteristics to changes taking place in various parts of the body.

These two texts introduced students to the chief diagnostic tools of medieval medicine, and were being read by scholars in Salerno soon after 1100. By the middle of the century *Bartholomaeus of Salerno had commented on the entire collection, and by the end of the century all six texts had been commented on once again by *Maurus of Salerno. The commentaries marked a shift in interest among Salernitan masters from their traditional concern with practical medicine toward a new fascination with medical theory. In their commentaries they sought to establish a philosophical framework for medicine in which detailed theoretical explanations were given for the workings of the human body. Drawing on Aristotle's natural philosophy, the Salernitan masters offered explanations of health and disease in terms of human beings' relationships to the natural world.

The method of teaching medicine by commenting on the *Articella* was adopted at other centers of learning as well. For example, by the end of the twelfth century, the collection had been commented on in the schools of Chartres. In this process of dissemination, the collection was developed to suit different intellectual and pedagogical needs. The earliest changes involved supplementing the collection with works on practical medicine, such as the *De regimine acutorum morborum* of Hippocrates and *Gilles de Corbeil's verses on *Pulses* and *Urines*. A more substantial alteration was made when five Arabic texts on medical theory were added, namely, the *Viaticum* of Isaac (Ibn al-Jazzar) and four works by *Isaac Judaeus: the *Universal Diets*, the *Particular Diets*, a treatise on fevers, and a treatise on urines. This expanded *Articella* was recommended to medical students in Paris in the

1180s, and by the 1240s it had been commented on by *Petrus Hispanus in Siena and by Cardinalis in Montpellier. It was subsequently adopted as the basis of the medical curriculum in the universities of Paris (1270–1274), Naples (1278), and Salerno (1280).

University masters of medicine continued to develop the *Articella* in new ways. In particular, they drew on Galen's commentaries on the *Aphorisms*, the *Prognostics*, *De regimine acutorum morborum*, and Haly Ridwan's commentary on Galen's *Tegni* to develop more definitive interpretations of the *Articella*. These authoritative commentaries provided masters with models of exposition in which logical analysis and sophisticated tools of exegesis were used to create a philosophically more rigorous framework for medicine.

A fundamental change occurred in the middle of the thirteenth century when masters made these commentaries the primary object of their teaching. This shift in focus from text to commentary dramatically expanded the scope of university medical education. Accordingly, from the 1260s onwards, the *Articella* became a much bigger textbook, including not only the texts of the *Aphorisms*, *Prognostics*, *De regimine acutorum morborum*, and the *Tegni*, but also their respective commentaries.

This new version of the collection was being taught in Bologna by the end of the thirteenth century by *Taddeo Alderotti and *Mondino de' Liuzzi, and it was soon incorporated into the statutes of the medical faculties at Montpellier (1309) and Paris (1331). It also provided the basis of the medical curriculum at the new universities of central Europe, including Vienna (1389), Erfurt (1412), and Tübingen (1497).

The *Articella* presented a new view of medicine in which medical theory was grounded in authoritative texts and taught by means of textual exegesis. Originally a fairly flexible group of texts, in the context of the new universities the *Articella* took on a more elaborate and stable form as the centerpiece of a medical curriculum in which Galen was the ultimate authority.

See also **Aristotelianism; Cathedral schools; Constantine the African; Gerard of Cremona; Medicine, practical; Medicine, theoretical; Monte Cassino; Nequam, Alexander; Nicholas of Salerno; Scholasticism; Universities**

Bibliography

Arrizabalaga, Jon. *The Articella in the Early Press, c. 1476–1534*. Cambridge: Cambridge Wellcome Unit for the History of Medicine, 1998.

Beccaria, Augusto. "Sulle trace di un antico canone latino di Ippocrate e di Galeno." *Italia medioevale e umanistica* (1959) 2: 1–56; (1961) 4: 1–73; (1971) 14: 1-23.

Kristeller, Paul O. "Bartholomaeus, Musandinus and Maurus of Salerno and other Early Commentators on the Articella, with a Tentative List of Texts and Manuscripts." *Italia medioevale e umanistica* (1976) 19:57-87. Revised Italian edition in his *Studi sulla Scuola medica salernitana*. Naples: Istituto italiano per gli studi filosofici, 1986.

O'Boyle, Cornelius. *The Art of Medicine: Medical Teaching at the University of Paris, 1250-1400*. Leiden: Brill, 1998.

Pesenti, Tiziana. "Arti et medicina: la formazione del curriculum medico." In *Luoghi e metodi di insegnamento nell'Italia medioevale (secoli XII-XIV)*. Edited by L. Gargan and O. Limone. Galatina: Congedo, 1989.

———. "Articella dagli incunabula ai manoscritti: origini e vicende di un titolo." In *Mercurius in trivio: studi di bibliografia e di Biblioteconomia per Alfredo Serrai nel 60o compleanno (20 novembre 1992)*. Edited by M. Cochetti. Rome: Bulzoni, 1993.

Saffron, Morris H. *Maurus of Salerno, Twelfth-Century 'Optimus Physicus,' with his Commentary on the Prognostics of Hippocrates*. Philadelphia: American Philosophical Society, 1972.

CORNELIUS O'BOYLE

ARTILLERY AND FIREARMS

Gunpowder was first used as projectile propellant in thirteenth-century China. Between the tenth and twelfth centuries a wide variety of powder-based incendiary and explosive devices were developed by the Chinese, including bombs, grenades, rockets, land and sea mines, and flame-throwers, on the basis of the experience acquired with fireworks in civilian contexts.

True guns appeared later, as a development of the fire-lance. This flame-throwing device, closely related to the rocket, consisted of a tube socketed to a wooden shaft into which low-nitrate, slow-burning black powder was tightly packed, with solid debris and other chemicals intermixed, in order to cast a jet of sparkling fire, scattershot and toxic fumes on the enemy for several minutes. The substitution of the original bamboo cane by a metal barrel, and the use of high nitrate, explosive black powder, plus one single, bore-filling projectile, gave birth to the first gun. A bronze handgun dating to 1288 was found in the Manchurian province of Heilungchiang. The oldest representation of a firearm, the sculpture of a demon carrying a shooting gun, dated between 1250 and 1280, decorates one of the Buddist cave-temples at Ta-tsu in Szechuan province. Early Chinese guns, cast in bronze or iron, were muzzle-loaders of medium and small size, with a typical bulbous thickening of the explosive chamber, and a blunderbuss-like muzzle.

The first unquestionable European references to guns are noticed a few decades later. The illuminators of Walter de Milimete's treatise *De notabilibus, sapientiis et prudentiis regum* (*Concerning the Majesty, Wisdom and Prudence of Kings*), dated 1326, depicted the oldest representation of a gun. Milimete's gun, a vase-shaped artifact shooting a big crossbow bolt, looks close to early Chinese guns. A gun similar to Milimete's, although bigger, illustrates another contemporary English manuscript containing the work *Secretis secretorum Aristotelis* (*The Secrets of Secrets of Aristotle*). Also in 1326, the acquisition of iron pellets and metal cannons was ordered for the defense of Florence.

Wandering artisans looking for the jobs offered by the uncertain market of war quickly spread gun technology thoughout Western Europe. But how guns made their way from China to Europe is unclear. Competing theories identify either the Mongols or the Arabs as responsible for the *technological diffusion. The conquest of China, completed in 1276, put all the available knowledge on black powder weaponry in Mongol hands, who made use of it in their campaigns in Eastern Europe, the Middle East, and India. Some Europeans, including fellow friars of the Franciscan *Roger Bacon, who first described the explosive mixture in Latin Christendom, could have acquired first-hand knowledge of guns on their trips to the Mongol khans.

The Arabs were also aware of the new technology. Hasan al-Rammah's treatise *Kitab al-furusiya wa'l-munasab al-harbiya* (*Treatise on Horsemanship and Stratagems of War*), written by 1280, describes gunpowder recipes of clear Chinese filiation, and the fire-lance. Historical sources point to the Muslims as responsible for the introduction of guns in the Iberian Peninsula. In 1331, the Nasrid army besieging Elche made use of "iron pellets that were shot with fire." Guns are recorded in Mamluk Egypt in the 1360s.

Early guns were muzzle-loaders of medium and small size, cast in iron or bronze, that shot quarrels and lead and iron balls, making use of small amounts of gunpowder relative to the projectile's weight. These were low-power weapons, fairly inaccurate and slow to reload, that could only be used as anti-personnel weapons from secure positions in close-range fighting. But they were cheap, in comparison to the available projectile-throwing engines.

The static nature of siege and naval warfare provided the niche for the establishment and further development of early guns. Among the oldest references to their use, are the sieges of Cividale (1331), Cambrai (1339), Quesnoy (1340), and Stirling (1341). In 1337, an English cog had aboard "a certain iron instrument for firing quarrels and lead pellets, with powder, for the defense of the ship." Efficient gun use in ship-to-ship combat is reported in an Aragonese-Castilian engagement fought in 1359 in Barcelonan waters.

Early firearms were given long-lasting names like guns, cannons, and bombards. But they also received specific names that carry significant information on their relative size (the Italian distinction between *schioppi* and the larger *vasi*), their appearance (French *pots de fer*, iron pots), the sound they produced (English "crakys of war," Castillian *truenos*, thunderclaps), and even their resemblance to regard to traditional weaponry (Catalan *ballestes del tro*, thunder crossbows). But guns were still far from being a serious rival to the powerful and accurate crossbows of the day. The biggest siege engine, the counterweight trebuchet, was simply beyond their reach.

The Age of the Bombard

The first firearm capable of tearing down castles and city walls, the bombard, appeared in the early 1370s. Bombard development relied on the blacksmiths' wrought-iron techniques, and the adoption of round stone shot, used for centuries as projectiles by *catapults and trebuchets. Forged iron allowed the construction of bigger guns, overcoming the checks posed by deficient cast-iron techniques and the high costs of casting bronze.

And stone shot, of much lower density than lead and iron shot, did not cause primitive guns to break.

To produce the barrel of the gun, previously forged and heated iron bars were welded together around a wooden cylinder by means of hammering. White-hot forged iron hoops were placed along the barrel afterwards, which, in cooling, contracted, lending additional strength to the gun. The bombard was completed by the attachment of the chamber, of less diameter and thicker walls, to the barrel's end opposite to the muzzle. In some bombards, the hoop and stave wrought-iron dual structure was forged around a cast iron core. Bombards grew astoundingly in size in a few decades. The ones at the siege of Saint-Sauveur-le-Vicomte (1375) fired stone balls of about 100 pounds (45 kg), whereas the Austrian von Steyr bombard, forged by 1420, fired stones of over 1,500 pounds (700 kg). The success of the iron bombards stimulated the casting of expensive but more reliable giant bronze bombards, a challenge to the bellfounders' skills, that had the chamber and the barrel, of equal external diameter, bolted together.

To absorb the enormous recoil produced by each shot, bombards were placed on cumbersome wooden frames reinforced with ropes and backed by thick wooden wedges dug into the earth. Sometimes the barrels were simply spiked to the earth. Bombards, as early guns, still used only small amounts of gunpowder per shot. To inflict damage they had to be placed close to the bombarded ramparts, considering the great resistance offered by the inertial mass of the projectile. Bombards fell thus into the range of the defenders' crossbows, longbows, small firearms, and sorties, and their positions had to be protected by wooden screens, lifted in the moment of fire, palisades, gabions, earthworks and trenches. Giant bombards played a major role in the conduct of key sieges, such as those of Balaguer (1413), Harfleur (1415), Orléans (1429), Naples (1442), and Constantinople (1453). The monster guns were given individualized names such as *La plus du monde*, Luxembourg, or The King's Daughter.

The success of the bombards made the number of guns involved in siege trains increase, as bombardments grew in intensity, producing a sharp increase in gunpowder consumption. Only ten guns took part in the siege of Calais by the English in 1346–1347, whereas by 1410 Christine de Pizan stated in her *Livre des faicts d'armes et de chevalerie* (*Book on the Feasts of Arms and Chivalry*, an adapted translation of Flavius Vegetius Renatus's *Epitoma rei militaris*) that the siege of a stronghold defended by six hundred well-armed combatants should imply the use of two hundred forty-eight guns—forty-two shooting stones of 200 pounds (90 kg) or more—with an overall gunpowder consumption estimated at 30,000 pounds (13,600 kg). The development of saltpeter farming techniques, first reported in Frankfurt in 1388, made the success of the new artillery possible. The dependence on imported Eastern saltpeter was reduced, gunpowder production increased, and prices decreased sharply.

By the mid-fifteenth century, bombards were achieving perfection in design, but constituted a technological dead end in the evolution of artillery, which had already shifted to the development of smaller but powerful and versatile guns, and improved handguns. Small and medium-sized guns started their development in parallel to big bombards, as reflected in the proliferation of gunports for the defense of castles and city walls in the 1380s, and the irruption of firearms in European battlefields, as in Bevershoutsveld (1382), Aljubarrota (1385), and Castagnaro (1387).

The new trend was connected with the increasing use of corned powder, of greater ballistic performance than the flour-like powder used in primitive guns and big bombards. Granulated powder is mentioned in the oldest section of the *Feuerwerkbuch* (*Firework Book*), written in Germany by 1380, but its general diffusion was delayed until the 1420s because of the challenge posed to available guns by their highly explosive nature. Looking for the highest muzzle velocities then possible and increasing rates of fire, guns tended to grow in length, and breech-loaders with multiple chambers per barrel flourished. A wide variety of guns, designed to match specific commitments in combat, were developed. They were named after birds of prey (falcons), venemous reptiles (rattlesnakes), and mystical beasts (basilisks), as a recognition of their death-dealing swiftness.

Permanent artillery services developed by the powers involved in the final phases of the Hundred Years War became centers of innovation. The forgers, founders, carpenters, cartwrights, horse- and ox-herders, and sappers under the command of artillery masters did not disband after the end of each military campaign. Continuous exercise of gunnery fostered the introduction of improvements in gun design. These included mobile gun carriages (four-wheeled and two-wheeled), aiming mechanisms (perforated curved bars for fixing barrel elevations by means of safety bolts; trunnions), and hoisting devices (rings, "dolphins"). By the late 1440s the adoption of cast iron shot promoted standardization of guns around determined projectile weights. The new guns used specific gunpowders with different granule size and/or different proportions of saltpeter (the bigger the piece, the bigger the granule size and the smaller the saltpeter content). Bigger powder charges were used in relation to projectiles, obtaining higher muzzle velocities for smaller but denser projectiles. The big bombard was substituted by the battery of smaller but more efficient guns.

The expulsion of the English from Normandy and Gascony betwen 1449 and 1453 by the artillery train commanded by the brothers Gaspar and Jean Bureau forced the adoption of the new French guns and organizational techniques by their foes. The compact and mobile muzzle-loader, smooth-bore, cast-bronze gun, shooting cast-iron balls, provided with trunnions and mounted in two-wheeled, tailed wooden gun carriages, was the finest outcome of the French artillery service. Its design, with walls narrowing from the chamber to the muzzle, as gas pressures propelling the projectile decreased inside the barrel, reflected almost full mastery of the art of smooth-bore gunnery by the 1490s. Gun design remained stable for centuries. The artillery train used by King Charles VIII of France in his 1494 speedy campaign for the crown of Naples was equipped with cannons similar to those used in European warfare up to the nineteenth century.

Cannons forced radical changes in military architecture. Medieval walled towns and castles, that withstood the bombard's slow rate of fire by means of temporary reinforcements, were easily destroyed by the new artillery batteries. New fortifications able to resist cannonade and to use the new artillery in active defense were desperately sought. Multiple solutions were devised, from the erection of fortified earthen defenses (boulevards) to permanent low-level artillery platforms surrounding medieval fortifications, massive artillery towers, or low-profile artillery fortresses, which featured common traits such as round forms, scarped, thick walls, and wide, defensive dry ditches. But the future lay in the angle bastion, first reported in Italy in the mid-fifteenth century, whose design maximized the capability of flanking fire for inflicting damage on assailants.

Handguns underwent a parallel development, from short iron or bronze muzzle-loader guns, socketed to a wooden tiller or fastened to it by means of metal straps, to the arquebus, which began to diffuse in the 1470s. The arquebus incorporated improvements developed from the 1410s, like longer wrought iron barrels, wooden buttstocks, flash pan for priming powder, and the matchlock, a further refinement of the crude serpentine fire mechanism depicted in an Austrian manuscript dated 1411. Arquebusiers were capable of aiming without the help of an assistant in charge of putting fire to the touchhole, as in the case of early handguns. Nevertheless, because of smoothbore ballistics, arquebuses were still inaccurate weapons. More accurately rifled firearms, with spiral grooves cut along the bore to put spin on the bullet, first reported in Nuremberg in the 1490s, remained out of military use because ramming the tight-fitting bullet down the barrel imposed an unbearable delay in the already slow loading process.

Effective development of artillery and firearms on the battlefield derived from their tactical use. Close-range volley fire, able to stop a charge of cavalry or pikemen, made up for the lack of individual marksmanship. But gunners and handgunners were easily cut to pieces by enemy assault while reloading, so they had to fight under cover of either fortified positions or formations of pikemen. The wagon laager (*wagenburg*), a mobile fortress used by the Bohemian Hussites in their 1419–1434 wars, provided a successful and long-lasting solution and was introduced into the Ottoman army by the Hungarians. Earthworks and trenches made firepower victorious against frontal assault in Castillon (1453) and Cerignola (1503). Nevertheless, fixed positions were an easy target for enemy field artillery and subsequent cavalry charges, as happened in Ravenna (1512). Battlefield tactics of the sixteenth century, characterized by the coordinated action of field artillery, pikemen, arquebusiers, and cavalry, emerged as a response to the benefits and drawbacks of the available artillery and firearms technology.

Gun use in naval warfare increased in the 1370s. Contemporary chronicles refer to their use in the battles of La Rochelle (1372), Saint-Malo (1379), and Dunkirk (1387). Improvements in gun design fostered the adoption of firearms by military and merchant ships by the mid-fifteenth century. Breech-loader swivel guns shooting small stone balls or lead pellets, and bigger stone-shooting bombards, each one provided with multiple removable chambers, were placed by the dozens on round ships and galleys. Standardization was purposely sought. In 1447 Burgundian galleys defeated an Egyptian fleet off the Anatolian coast by rapid fire of their stern guns, fed with the interchangeable chambers of the rest of the guns, unable to fire. The bigger guns concentrated atop the round ship's lower flushdeck, and on the prow of the galleys. Numbers increased as the century progressed. The *Holy Ghost of the Tower* had two guns aboard in 1416. Six years later, it had six guns, plus twelve chambers. In 1497, the *Sovereign* had one hundred forty-one guns with four hundred nineteen chambers.

Cast-bronze cannon were incorporated into ships' arsenals by 1500, but stone shot remained in use and crossbows were not completely superseded by arquebuses until the mid-sixteenth century. Wrought-iron guns remained in service well into the century, as evidence found in the 1545 *Mary Rose* shipwreck proves. Stone-shot bronze guns known as perriers are also documented in sixteenth-century naval and land warfare. Mediterranean galleys easily placed big guns aboard, close to the waterline—typically one main centerline bow gun flanked by smaller pieces. Artillery duels resulted in sinkings, and naval warfare gradually changed its nature. But galleys could not deploy big guns along their sides, which were occupied by oarsmen. The adoption of gunports allowed round ships of new design, the carracks, to place plenty of guns on the lower decks of their broadsides. Galleys were soon widely surpassed in heavy ordnance by sailing ships, although further refinements in their design was required to guarantee stability, as the surprising sinking of the *Mary Rose* demonstrated. The refined offspring of the heavily armed round ships of the early 1500s, first galleons, then ships of the line, ruled naval warfare up to the nineteenth century. The maintenance of Portuguese supremacy in the Indian Ocean, in spite of the incursions of Ottoman galley fleets, inaugurated the new era.

See also **Albertus Magnus; Alchemy; Arms and armor; Metallurgy; Navigation; Shipbuilding; Transportation; Travel and exploration**

Bibliography

Buchanan, Brenda J., ed. *Gunpowder: The History of an International Technology.* Bath: Bath University Press, 1996.

Chase, Kenneth. *Firearms. A Global History to 1700.* New York: Cambridge University Press, 2003.

DeVries, Kelly. *Medieval Military Technology.* Peterborough, Ontario: Broadview Press Ltd., 1992.

———. *Guns and Men in Medieval Europe, 1200-1500. Studies in Military History and Technology.* Padstow, Cornwall: Variorum Collected Studies Series, 2002.

Guilmartin, John Francis. *Gunpowder & Galleys. Changing Technology & Mediterranean Warfare at Sea in the 16th Century.* New York: Cambridge University Press, 1974 [revised edition, Annapolis: Naval Institute Press, 2003].

Hall, Bert S. *Weapons and Warfare in Renaissance Europe. Gunpowder, Technology, and Tactics.* Baltimore: Johns Hopkins University Press, 1997.

Needham, Josep et al. *Science and Civilisation in China. Volume V. Chemistry and Chemical Technology. Part 7: The Gunpowder Epic.* New York: Cambidge University Press, 1986.

Partington, James Riddick. *A History of Greek Fire and Gunpowder.* Cambridge: W. Heffer & Sons, 1960 [new edition, with a new introduction by Bert S. Hall, Baltimore: Johns Hopkins University Press, 1999].

Rogers, Clifford J., ed. *The Military Revolution Debate. Readings on the Military Transformation of Early Modern Europe.* Boulder: Westview Press, 1995.

Smith, Robert D. and Ruth Rhynas Brown. *Bombards. Mons Meg and her Sisters.* Dorset: Royal Armouries Monograph 1, 1989.

LUIS PABLO MARTINEZ

ASTROLABES AND QUADRANTS

The astrolabe is a two-dimensional representation of the three-dimensional celestial sphere, a model of the universe that one can hold in one's hand. The representation is achieved by a mathematical procedure known as stereographic projection. There is a "celestial" part, consisting of a cutout frame known as a rete, with star-pointers for various bright stars and a ring for the ecliptic, or path of the Sun against the background of the stars. Then there is a terrestrial part, comprising a set of plates for different latitudes, with markings for the local horizon and altitude circles up to the zenith and azimuth circles around the horizon. The rete is placed on top of the appropriate plate, and the ensemble fits in a hollowed-out frame known as the mater. On the back of the mater is the alidade, a viewer for measuring the altitude of any celestial body, as well as scales for finding the position of the Sun from the date, for measuring shadows, and often more besides.

The configuration of the heavens relative to the horizon of a given locality is determined by the instantaneous altitude of the Sun or any star above that horizon. Having measured the altitude of the Sun or any star with the alidade and altitude scale on the back of the astrolabe, one sets the marker for the celestial body on the rete on top of the appropriate altitude circle on the plate: the instrument then shows the instantaneous configuration of the heavens relative to the local horizon. If one rotates the rete over one of the plates one can simulate the apparent daily rotation of the Sun or of the starry heavens above the horizon of the observer; the passage of time between two positions of the rete is measured by the rotation of the rete (360° correspond to twenty-four hours). In addition, one can investigate the position of the ecliptic relative to the local horizon and meridian, configurations of prime importance in *astrology. The astrolabe is thus a multifunctional analogue computer.

The astrolabe is a Greek invention that was inherited by the Muslims in the eighth century and much developed by them over the centuries. (Here we consider only standard astrolabes.) The astrolabe became known to Europeans in Islamic Spain in the tenth century only in its simplest form. Thus the Europeans essentially had to develop technical improvements to astrolabe design for themselves, as well as artistic details on the retes and thrones; this accounts for the very different appearance of medieval Islamic and European instruments. Occasional transfers of knowledge and skills and artistic design between the two cultural regions are attested.

Close to one hundred fifty brass European astrolabes survive from the period before c. 1500, and it was clearly the most popular instrument of the Middle Ages. For some we still do not know even a rough provenance and cannot suggest a reliable dating. Furthermore, some of the most historically important pieces have been dubbed fake by would-be specialists who did not understand them, or by medievalists confronted with their first instrument. There is no incontrovertible evidence that any of the purportedly fake medieval astrolabes ever actually existed.

Early Surviving Examples

The earliest known astrolabe with Latin inscriptions dates from the tenth century, and is now preserved in Paris. The rete is simple and barely decorated: it bears no resemblance to tenth-century Eastern or Western Islamic retes. The piece is rather crudely made (judging it by the standards of, say, tenth-century Islamic astrolabes), and the numbers are in a Latin alphanumerical notation inspired by the Western Arabic notation. The star-positions are not particularly accurate and the maker left out the star-names. The most important plate is for 41°30' and is labeled "Roma et Francia," the former perhaps an indication of a Greco-Roman tradition of astrolabe making, about which we otherwise know nothing, and the latter referring to Catalonia as the land of the Franks. The Latin names of the zodiacal signs in the later (thirteenth- or fourteenth-century) inscriptions on the ecliptic ring show Catalan influence. (This remarkable piece was first published by Marcel Destombes, the leading French instrument specialist, in 1962 as the oldest surviving European astrolabe, and was immediately labeled a fake by experts in Latin manuscripts who had never looked at any astrolabes.)

The distinctive form of rete design (a Y- or V-shaped frame inside the ecliptic ring) that is found in manuscripts of *Chaucer's Treatise on the Astrolabe* is attested on several surviving pieces. However, other English pieces display a different design with a single quatrefoil and some zoomorphic star-pointers. All of these are preceded temporally by the monumental Sloane astrolabe in the British Museum, London, England, with an imposing diameter of 18.3 inches (46.5 cm) and a complex arrangement of three quatrefoils, two trefoils, and a half-quatrefoil at each end of both perpendicular axes. Since this piece is datable c. 1300, it symbolizes how little we know about the introduction of the astrolabe to England. Clearly it came from continental Europe, and it is surely significant that we find the V-shaped rete on a Catalan astrolabe from c. 1300.

An astrolabe from fourteenth-century Picardy has all numbers marked in an ingenious cipher notation that was developed by Cistercian monks in the thirteenth century, proving that these ciphers were used on material objects as well as in manuscripts for listing, foliation, dates, and concordances. A later inscription on the instrument dated 1522 shows that it was given by Pascasius Berselius, a Humanist monk of Liège, to Hardianus Amerotius, his teacher of Greek in Louvain. The latter wrote one of the first histories of number notations, but did not realize that the monastic ciphers on his own astrolabe were based on an ancient Greek prototype.

The magnificent painting of *St. Jerome in his Study* associated with Jan van Eyck (d. 1441) shows the back of an astrolabe among a group of objects with symbolic significance. The piece is unusual in that there is no solar/calendrical scale, and the numbers in the scale are in a distinctive hand, also the throne is of a very early design. An Italian astrolabe from c. 1300 with a diameter of 2.4 inches (6 cm) with the same features on the back survives in Oxford. The scales on the astrolabe in the painting suggest that the original from which it was copied was even smaller; in any case, the artist drew it with a diameter of 0.8 inches (2 cm), larger than the saint's face.

Astrolabe design varied considerably in the major centers of instrumentation in Europe, and although no workshops or schools can be identified before c. 1425, by that time we know of instrument centers at least in Vienna and Paris. Since most medieval European astrolabes are unsigned, and very few are dated, it is pure speculation to suggest that there must have been workshops in cultural centers such as Montpellier, London or Milan, already before the appearance of the above schools.

However, we can identify designs and trends that can be associated with various regions. Also, regional influence on Latin names for the months and zodiacal signs, or names in vernaculars, offer clues to provenance, sometimes more than the latitudes and localities chosen for the plates. There was a tradition inherited from antiquity of representing the latitudes of the seven climates, roughly, 16°, 24°, 30°, 36°, 41°, 45°, and 48°, which tells us little about the provenance. But the presence of a plate with additional markings for, say, 52°, suggests an interest in London. And the presence of a plate for 32°, Jerusalem, reflects a wish to go on a pilgrimage or crusade, although we have no instruments that were clearly taken that far. A plate for, say, 30° marked "Babylonie" (Cairo) or 36° marked "Affrica" (Tunisia) is a reminder of the tradition of the climates.

We have no dated pieces from before the fourteenth century. It is instructive to look at some of the earliest pieces that are both signed or dedicated and dated or datable:

A German quatrefoil astrolabe now in Kraków was made for Ludolf de Scicte, treasurer of the Cathedral at Einbeck. Archival evidence yields the period of his tenure of this position as 1322–1342. The quatrefoil design on this, the earliest known German astrolabe, is second in complexity only to the London Sloane astrolabe mentioned above.

Thirteenth-century miniature depicting three scientists, one of whom is using an astrolabe to observe the sky. (Bettmann/Corbis)

An astrolabe now in Boston is dated Barcelona, 1375, and signed by Petrus Raimundus from Aragon. Further research is necessary to clarify the relationship of the maker to Pedro IV (1336–1387), ruler of the Crown of Aragon, well known for his astronomical, astrological, and cartographic interests.

An English astrolabe of the Chaucer type now in London is signed "Blakenei me fecit Anno Do' 1342." The name recalls towns in Gloucestershire and Lincolnshire. One set of markings is finished for latitude 52° and the other unfinished for 51°, which tells us little, not least because at the time the latitude of London had already been carefully measured as 51°34' (accurately 51°30'). Some other fourteenth-century English astrolabes have a plate for London at 51°34'.

An astrolabe in a German private collection with an unusual appearance bears a signature by Antonio de Pacent and the date 1420. The plates are labeled for different latitudes but their markings are all for latitude 45°, so that one might think that the piece could work only in the Po Valley. However, the star positions have been totally confused (ecliptic coordinates used equatorially), which explains the strange appearance of the rete. The ensemble is useless for any practical purposes.

It is fortunate that so many surviving astrolabes can be "read" in this way, once we can decode their "language." Perhaps the most colorful example is a quatrefoil astrolabe with inscriptions in Hebrew, Latin, and Arabic. It was constructed c. 1300, probably in *Toledo. The bare instrument was made by a Jewish craftsman who left scratches in Hebrew alphanumerical script for the latitudes of each of the plates. The quatrefoil design of the rete is European, with strong *mudéjar* influence. The inscriptions on the rete and the plates are in a scholastic Latin, with very distorted Arabic names for the stars, and some regional peculiarities that could eventually localize the engraver (a Tironian 9-like the abbreviation for *cum-*, *con-*, and *-us*, here used for a hard c, k, and q, as in ON9E for *onq/ke*, from Arabic *'unuq*). But the back was never completed by the Christian, and the piece fell into the hands of a Muslim Arab, who put his name, Mas'ud, on the shackle of the throne. He also had plans to emigrate to more hospitable climes: he replaced one of the plates with one of his own, serving Algiers and Mecca. He seems to have been at least partly successful for we have an Ibn Mas'ud born in Tlemcen at the right time, but his astrolabe ended up in northern France by the sixteenth century, as attested by a final set of numbers around the rim. It surfaced in Lorraine in the 1990s, and is now in a private collection.

Numerous manuscripts exist of treatises in Latin or the vernaculars on the construction and/or use of the astrolabe. They are of interest for transmission of textual knowledge and linguistic aspects but tell us little about the instruments themselves. For example, the star-names that we find on medieval astrolabes are often quite different from those we find in star-lists in medieval manuscripts. The manuscripts seldom give lists of latitudes for engraving on plates. Rarely do we find illustrations of retes, which would help in investigations of instruments and regional schools. No corpus of such illustrations has been gathered. One example must suffice:

The Brussels miniature of the monk Heinrich Suso and Sapientia shows an astrolabe of typical French design, which is "safely" datable to c. 1400. However, the same design is illustrated in a medieval French astrolabe treatise, now in Berlin, which is dated 1276.

Of particular interest are texts by people who actually made astrolabes. The best example is Jean Fusoris of Paris c. 1425. Some two dozen astrolabes that can be associated with his atelier survive. Although they are neither signed nor dated, all incorporate an error that is also found in his star-catalog.

Renaissance astrolabes appear almost, as it were, out of the blue, and all those known from Elizabethan England and sixteenth-century Flanders are now carefully described. However, they often cannot be properly understood without the medieval connection, Islamic or European. The astrolabe depicted in the intarsia of the *studiolo* in the palace of the Archduke Frederico at Urbino built in 1476 was copied from a Renaissance Italian astrolabe with a distinctive rete design. One such astrolabe, dated Urbino 1462, was stolen from a museum in Moulins in 1977. Its design was copied in turn from a medieval Italian astrolabe, and one with this same design datable c. 1400 survives in Florence. The design can be traced to Marrakesh c. 1200.

An astrolabe dedicated in 1462 by *Johannes Regiomontanus to his patron, Cardinal Bessarion, shows the transition from Gothic script to Antiqua as well as from Latinized Arabic star-names to Latin ones. The back is embellished by an Italian angel (Gabriel) bearing good news on a scroll: the dedication to Bessarion is a masterpiece of Renaissance Latin, with clever plays of words and numbers. Hidden in the text, for Bessarion to enjoy, is a reference to the four-hundredth anniversary of a splendid Byzantine astrolabe dated 1062, now preserved in Brescia, which Bessarion surely brought to Italy from Constantinople along with all his manuscripts. A text by Georg Hartmann of Nuremberg dated 1527 mentions a feature of all the astrolabes that Regiomontanus made which he had seen, and which we find on this astrolabe. This and another ten mid- and late-fifteenth-century German astrolabes from the same or related workshops all identified in the late 1980s bear witness to Italian influence and their design provides the model for Hartmann's prolific workshop half a century later.

The magnificent astrolabes of the Arsenius brothers in sixteenth-century Louvain have a cluster of pointers for the stars of the Plough. This proves that they owe something to a medieval French tradition, for the seven stars are included in Jean Fusoris' astrolabe treatise and feature on the instruments that can be associated with his atelier.

The serious study of medieval European astrolabes is still in its infancy. There is material for the epigrapher (forms of letters), the philologist (regional forms), the historian of number notations and numeral forms (unusual Roman numerals, developing Gothic forms of the Hindu-Arabic numerals), the specialist on calendars (lists of saints' days), the art historian (astrolabes are scientific works of art, often very beautiful), the general medievalist (there is not a single book on the Middle Ages that displays an astrolabe with a sensible caption), the historian of technology (how were they made?), the metallurgist (what were they made of?), the historian of astronomy (these were the principal tools of medieval astronomers and astrologers), and, last but not least, the cynic (did people actually use them?) and the devil's advocate (do we have a documented provenance over the centuries so that we can be sure that a given astrolabe is not a fake?).

Quadrants

The second most popular astronomical instrument of the European Middle Ages was the quadrant. It is essentially a device for timekeeping by the Sun. It bears a set of markings that are graphical representations of the altitude of the Sun at the hours throughout the year. One holds the quadrant vertically with one axis towards the sun, and a movable bead on a thread with plummet, set to the appropriate solar longitude, falls on the appropriate markings to indicate the hour of day. The horary markings are either for a specific latitude or for all latitudes, markings of the latter variety being necessarily approximate. Both kinds of quadrants were invented in Baghdad in the ninth century.

Quadrants for a fixed latitude are known for London (1398 and 1399, brass) and Vienna (1438, ivory). Medieval tables displaying the altitude of the Sun as a function of the time of day for, say, each sign of the ecliptic, which one needs to construct the markings on such a quadrant are known for many more cities from Rome to Oxford.

Quadrants for all latitudes are much more common, not least because they were usually included on the backs of astrolabes. The universal horary quadrant provides a quick means of finding the time in seasonal hours for any latitude, whereas with the front of the astrolabe one can, albeit with more effort, determine the time in equatorial hours or seasonal hours for any latitude represented by the plates.

The universal horary quadrant with six circular arcs for the seasonal hours is sufficient unto itself, but already in ninth-century Baghdad an optional movable calendrical-cum-solar scale was proposed. In this form the *quadrans vetus* was introduced into Europe (probably first to Montpellier, France, in the late twelfth century), and several examples from the medieval period survive. European astronomers do not seem to have understood that whereas the formula (actually of Indian origin) underlying the markings yielded good results throughout the year in Mediterranean latitudes, it produced increasingly inaccurate results in more northerly latitudes. In Montepellier in the late thirteenth century the Jewish scholar Ibn Ben Tibbon or *Profatius Judaeus proposed a *quadrans novus*, which combined the approximate horary markings of the *quadrans vetus* with accurate astrolabic projections of the ecliptic and the horizons of various latitudes. This unhappy combination could not be sensibly used for timekeeping, but the instrument became popular anyway, and several medieval European examples survive.

See also **Astronomy, Islamic; Astronomy, Latin; Calendar**

Bibliography

Gunther, Robert T. *The Astrolabes of the World.* 2 vols., Oxford: Oxford University Press, 1932. Reprinted in one vol. London: The Holland Press, 1976.

King, David A. "Astronomical Instruments between East and West." In *Kommunikation zwischen Orient und Okzident—Alltag und Sachkultur.* Edited by Harry Kühnel, Vienna: Österreichische Akademie der Wissenschaften, 1994, pp. 143–198.

———. *The Ciphers of the Monks–A Forgotten Number Notation of the Middle Ages.* Stuttgart: Franz Steiner, 2001.

———. *In Synchrony with the Heavens.* Vol. 2: *Instruments of Mass Calculation.* Leiden: E.J. Brill, 2005.

North, John D. *Chaucer's Universe.* Oxford: Clarendon Press, 1988.

Poulle, Emmanuel. *Un constructeur d'instruments astronomiques au 15e siècle–Jean Fusoris.* Paris: Honoré Champion, 1963.

Stevens, Wesley M. *et al.,* eds. *The Oldest Latin Astrolabe.* Florence: Leo S. Olschki, 1995. (a special issue of *Physis* 32: 2–3).

Zinner, Ernst. *Deutsche und niederländische astronomische Instrumente des 11.-18. Jahrhunderts.* 2nd ed. Munich: C.H. Beck, 1967, repr. 1972.

DAVID A. KING

ASTROLOGY

The modern distinction between astronomy and astrology is not pertinent for the medieval period. For Christian and Muslim scholars of the Middle Ages, in a world created by God and for man, where Earth occupies a central place in the cosmological representations of the universe, where the human being is a little world (*microcosmus*) corresponding with the entire creation (*macrocosmus*), the basic idea on which astrology is founded (i.e., belief that events on Earth are influenced by power emanating from the stars and planets) is a matter of consensus.

This consensus is broken when medieval scholars have to define the precise nature and extent of astral influence. Do the Sun, the Moon, the planets, and the stars have an effect on natural phenomena—tides, floods, meteorological catastrophes, earthquakes, epidemics? Do they also cause or determine, directly or through passions and humors, collective and individual human actions? Is there a good astrology, confined to the study and prevision of these natural phenomena, and a bad astrology, going through this frontier? The debate had a considerable echo in the Middle Ages, in the Arabic world, the Byzantine Empire, and Christian Europe. Supporters of a very deterministic astrology, such as the ninth-century philosophers *al-Kindi and *Abu Ma'shar (Albumasar) and their thirteenth-century Italian followers Guido Bonatti and *Pietro d'Abano, can thus be opposed to some of the main adversaries of astral divination, such as the famous doctor *Ibn Sina (Avicenna), the fourteenth-century historian Ibn Khaldun, the French theologians *Nicole Oresme (1322–1382) and Jean Gerson (1363–1429), and the Italian humanist Picco della Mirandola (1463–1494).

This controversy, however, must not obscure the main point: during the Middle Ages, astronomy and astrology were generally considered by scholars as two complementary faces of the same discipline. Astrological prevision was the primary purpose of astronomical calculations and a possible help for the practice of medicine. The fact that many doctors took astral influences into account and that *astronomia* was part of the late antique *quadrivium allowed astrology to claim a scientific status.

Origins and Diffusion

The scientific status of astrology went back to the first appearance of horoscopes in the fifth century B.C.E., in Babylonia, yet medieval Christian astrology is derived mainly from Greco-Arabic science. *Ptolemy's *Tetrabiblos*, written in the second century C.E., is the most famous astrological book ever written. This work and that of several Greek authors, including Dorotheus of Sidon and Vettius Valens, spread to Byzantium, and then to the Islamic world, where they were enriched by Indian and Persian elements. During the Abbassid period (eighth–thirteenth centuries), the judgment of the stars (*ahkam al-nujum*) featured prominently in the work of several famous authors including *Masha'allah (Messahalla), Abu Ali al-Khaiyat, Umar al-Tabari, and

Abu Ma'shar. One of the widespread works of Arabic astrology was the *Karpos* or *Centiloquium*, a collection of one hundred aphorisms falsely ascribed in the tenth century to Ptolemy; a manual frequently used was *The Introduction to Astrology* of al-Qabisi, astrologer of the Emir of Aleppo Sayf ad-Dawla (945–967); and the most complete compendium in this field was the *Kitab al-Bari*, written by Ali ibn Abi l-Rijal (Hali Abenragel), counsellor of the Zirid prince al-Mu'izz, in Kairouan (eleventh century). Byzantine astrology, very dynamic in the sphere of political horoscopes from the fifth century, benefited from Islamic contributions from the eighth century, and prospered until the fall of Constantinople, especially in the fourteenth century, with the astrological school of Johannes Abramius.

In the Latin West, the situation was radically different until the beginning of the twelfth century, since the work of Greek and Arab mathematical astronomers and astrologers was almost unknown there. During the High Middle Ages, astrology was not considered very differently from the augural divination condemned by the Fathers of the Church. Simple forms of astrological prevision translated from Greek flourished from the eighth century: spheres of life and death ascribed to Pythagoras, Petosiris, and Apuleus; predictions founded on the thirty days of an imaginary lunar cycle (*lunaria*) or the zodiacal positions of the Sun or the Moon (*zodiologia*). In the absence of accurate astronomical tables and instruments, horoscopes were totally ignored until the appearance in the second half of the tenth century of the "Alchandreana corpus," partly translated from Arabic, which allowed some horoscopes to be compiled on numerological principles.

The appearance in Christian Europe of a learned astrology, taking into account a great number of celestial parameters and forming a clearly organized and hierarchical system of knowledge, took place in the twelfth century, at a time when translations from Arabic to Latin were providing astronomical tables and instruments to place in horoscopes the position of the planets, ascendants and astrological houses, and were giving the basic rules of the "judgments of the stars." More than seventy astrological treatises were translated into Latin in the twelfth and thirteenth centuries. Among the clerks and courts, the diffusion of these translations and some original texts contributed to the promotion of a sophisticated astrological knowledge, potentially useful for medicine and political action. Inserting itself into a philosophy of nature taught in schools and universities, astrology claimed more than ever to be a real science. It is in this context that, before 1277, Guido Bonatti compiled the main summa of medieval Latin astrology, the *Liber introductorius ad judicia stellarum*, and managed to become, in Duke Guido da Montefeltro's service, the most notorious court astrologer of his time. The considerable attraction of Arabo-Latin astrology in the university world of the thirteenth century set off reactions in the Church. The most important response was that of the Bishop of Paris, Etienne Tempier, who, in 1277, condemned two hundred nineteen propositions,

some thirty of which led directly to astral determinism. But astrologers managed to avoid that difficulty by two means: first, they appropriated to themselves the famous sentence ascribed to Ptolemy and previously quoted by *Albertus Magnus and *Thomas Aquinas, *Vir sapiens dominabitur astris* ("the wise man will dominate the stars"); second, they declared that astrological predictions were compatible with God's absolute power and human free will.

Therefore, astrology was largely tolerated by the Church in the late Middle Ages and used by emperors and kings (*Frederick II, *Alfonso X and Peter I of Castille, Charles V of France, Matthias Corvinus of Hungary, etc.), popes (Clement VI, Sixtus IV, Alexander VI) and many princes and prelates. But the personal status of court astrologers was less in England and France than in Italy, Germany, and Poland, where they could be considered as spokesmen of their employers. And even in Italy, the seriousness with which astrology was taken was criticized by the likes of Pico della Mirandola and Girolamo Savonarola.

From 1470 the spread of printing gave a new stimulus to astrological output. It was vulgarized through almanacs and annual predictions, published notably in Italy and Germany and addressed to the whole of the learned public. At the start of the Renaissance, the practice of astrology nevertheless remained the prerogative of a small elite of clerics who were for the most part mainly doctors, the professional astrologer being an exception.

The Four Parts of Astrology

Medieval Arabic and Arabo-Latin astrology is commonly divided into four main branches: nativities, revolutions, elections, and interrogations.

The study of nativities (genethlialogy) is founded on the horoscope of birth of an individual and of the new or full moon preceding the birth. The astrologer calculates the position of the planets, the ascendant, the astrological houses, and the *partes* (lots) on the zodiacal circle. Then he selects the most significant parameters in the horoscope, notably the planet *hyleg* or *significator vite*, and he is supposed to be able to predict the main steps of the subject's life. But this implies that he knows the precise place, date, and hour of the birth, which was very rare outside the courtly milieu before the end of the Middle Ages. He is thus frequently obliged to verify the time of birth by a method called *annimodar*.

Revolutions are related to the return of the Sun to the precise zodiacal point occupied at an initial moment. The study of revolutions of nativities is based on the examination of the sky at the time of the subject's birthday, while that of the revolutions of years rested on the horoscope of the vernal equinox of a particular year, and of the new or full moon preceding it. Examining these horoscopes, the astrologer is supposed to predict the weather of the next year, natural catastrophes, epidemics, the immediate future of peoples, and other political events. He is helped in this by a system of relations between zodiacal signs, planets, countries, and social categories. These annual predictions appeared to have been regularly preserved in Europe from the end of the fourteenth century.

Connected to annual revolutions, analysis of the conjunctions of the three superior planets, Saturn, Jupiter, and Mars, as well as that of comets, belongs to historical astrology. Conjunctions of Saturn and Jupiter occur every twenty years, and conjunctions of Saturn and Mars in Cancer, supposed to be malefic, occur every thirty years. According to the doctrine of great conjunctions standardized by Albumasar, they influence the major natural, political, and religious events: the birth of Muhammad and of Islam after the conjunction of Saturn and Jupiter of 571; the demise of the Caliphate of Córdoba, related to the conjunction Saturn and Jupiter in 1007; the hypothetical tempests of 1186, linked to the presence of all the planets in the sign of Libra; the Black Death of 1348 and the Great Schism of 1378, interpreted *post eventum* as the consequences of the Saturn–Jupiter conjunctions of 1345 and 1365; the possible defeat of the king of France by the English after the conjunction of Saturn and Mars in 1357; the appearance of a false prophet after the conjunctions of 1484 and 1504; the false flood of 1524, and so on. As for comets, they were usually taken to foretell catastrophes, notably the imminent death of some king or prince, as in the case of Giovanni Galeazzo Visconti, Duke of Milan, in 1402.

Elections (or catarchic astrology) deal with the forecasting of undertakings and the choice of proper times for initiate actions: the mythical or real foundation or refoundation of cities such as Constantinople, Gaza, Baghdad (founded by al-Mansur in 762), Cairo, Vittoria (near Parma, founded by Frederick II in 1247), Florence, Venice, Bologna, and Milan; the foundation of a university such as that in Bratislava by Matthias Corvinus in 1467; declarations of war; consecrations of marriage; the begetting of a child; the beginning of a difficult medical operation, such as that performed on the cataract of the King John II of Aragon in 1468, etc. Elections may be established occasionally or by the use of an annual almanac, supposed to program all the owner's activities or, more modestly, indicate the good days for bleeding and purgatives, which were among the basic practices of medieval medicine.

Interrogations deal with responses to queries, which may be of special or general interest. Will my pregnant wife have a boy or a girl? Where is my stolen golden cup? Will a new pope be elected during the Council of Constance before Christmas? The astrologer draws up a horoscope of the precise moment of the question and tries to answer it.

With and after the condemnations of 1277, the attitude of Church to these different activities was clarified, but some ambiguities and contradictions remained. The ecclesiastical hierarchy tolerated nativities and revolutions up to a certain point, but condemned energetically elections and interrogations, which were considered to be forms of augural divination. Some astrologers who specialized in interrogations, such as Simon de Phares in France at the end of the fifteenth century, may thus have been easily suspected by the *vox populi* to be diviners, and might be quickly attacked and condemned as diviners, even if no astrologer was ever executed for such reason.

Astrology and Astrologers in Society

At first glance, a comparison would be useful between the two major historiographical sources, the *Faraj al-mahmum*, a history of astrologers completed in 1252 in Iraq by the Shi'ite scholar Ibn Tawus, and the *Recueil des plus célèbres astrologues* of Simon de Phares, written between 1494 and 1498 for Charles VIII of France. The former is very well documented but the latter is a largely mythical prosopography: even if astrologers played a more and more important role in the public life of European countries in the late Middle Ages, astrology was in fact a secondary way of counsel, information, propaganda, and power. It seems to have been quite different in Islamic lands, according to the work of Ibn Tawus and some other sources such as *Albumasar in Sadan*, a famous collection of scientific talks emanating from the caliphal court of Baghdad in the ninth century. These texts show the persistent favor of astrology in the courtly milieu during the Abbassid period and the deep integration of astrologers in social life: between the chief astrologer of the caliphal court and the modest street diviner, incomes were very different but the prestige of divinatory knowledge was the same. Astrology, as a guide to individual and collective initiatives, played an important role in the urban daily life of medieval Islam, particularly among Shi'ite people. The "science of the stars" also played a real part in politics in Samarkand in the fifteenth century, as well as in Baghdad and Córdoba five centuries earlier.

We may therefore conclude that, globally, astrology was assimilated more successfully by medieval Islam than by Christian Europe: for example, no cathedral was ever built after an astral election, like the Bibi Hanum mosque in Samarkand in 1399. But astrology has played, mainly from the twelfth century, an increasingly important role in the cultural and artistic life of European elites. Far from being a sign of obscurantism, the medieval "science of the stars" has contributed significantly to progress in several fields, most notably astronomy, horology, civil status, and hygiene.

See also **Almanacs; Condemnation of 1277**

Bibliography

Abu Ma'Shar al-Balhi [Albumasar]. *Liber introductorii majoris ad scientiam judiciorum astrorum*, édition critique par Richard Lemay, 9 vol., Napoli: Istituto Universitario Orientale, 1995–1996.

———. *Le Recueil des plus célèbres astrologues de Simon de Phares*, présenté par Jean-Patrice Boudet, 2 vol., Paris: Honoré Champion, 1997–1999.

Abu Ma'Shar on Historical Astrology. The Book of Religions and Dynasties (On the Great Conjunctions). K. Yamamoto, C. Burnett ed., 2 vols., Leiden: E.J. Brill, 2000.

Al-Qabisi (Alcabitius). *The Introduction of Astrology. Editions of the Arabic and Latin Texts and an English Translation.* C. Burnett, K. Yamamoto, M. Yano ed., London/Torino: The Warburg Institute—Nino Aragno Editore, 2004.

Blume, Dieter. *Regenten des Himmels. Astrologische Bilder in Mittelalter und Renaissance.* Berlin: Akademie Verlag, 2000.

Carey, Hilary M. *Courting Disaster. Astrology at the English Court and University in the Later Middle Ages.* London: Macmillan, 1992.

Carmody, Francis J. *Arabic Astronomical and Astrological Sciences in Latin Translations. A critical Bibliography.* Berkeley/Los Angeles: University of California Press, 1956.

Caroti, Stefano. *L'astrologia in Italia. Profezie, oroscopi e segreti celesti, dagli zodiaci romani alla tradizione islamica, dalle corti rinascimenti alle scuole moderne: storia, documenti, personaggi.* Roma: Newton Compton Editori, 1983.

Juste, David. "Les doctrines astrologiques du Liber Alchandrei." In I. Draelants, A. Tihon, B. van den Abeele ed., *Occident et Proche-Orient: contacts scientifiques au temps des Croisades.* Actes du colloque de Louvain-la-Neuve (24–25 mars 1997). Turnhout: Brepols, 2000, pp. 277–311.

Page, Sophie. *Astrology in Medieval Manuscripts.* London: The British Library, 2002.

Préaud, Maxime. *Les astrologues à la fin du Moyen Age.* Paris: Lattès, 1984.

Saliba, Georges. "The Role of the Astrologer in Medieval Islamic Society." *Bulletin d'études orientales* (1992) 44: 45–67, repr. in Savage-Smith, Emilie ed., *Magic and Divination in Early Islam.* Aldershot: Ashgate, 2004, pp. 341–370.

Sezgin, Fuat. *Geschichte des arabischen Schrifttums*, Band VII, *Astrologie—Meterologie und Verwandtes bis ca. 430 H.* Leiden: E.J. Brill, 1979.

Tester, Jim. *A History of Western Astrology.* Woodbridge: The Boydell Press, 1987.

Thorndike, Lynn. *A History of Magic and Experimental Science.* 8 volumes. New York: Columbia University Press, 1923–1958.

Weill-Parot, Nicolas. *Les «images astrologiques» au Moyen Age et à la Renaissance. Spéculations intellectuelles et pratiques magiques.* Paris: Honoré Champion, 2002.

Whitfield, Peter. *Astrology. A History.* New York, Harry N. Abrams, Inc., 2001.

Zambelli, Paola. *The Speculum astronomiae and its Enigma. Astrology, Theology and Science in Albertus Magnus and his Contemporaries.* Dordrecht/Boston/London: Kluwer Academic Publishers, 1992.

JEAN-PATRICE BOUDET

ASTRONOMY, ISLAMIC

Pre-Islamic Arabs living in the Arabian Peninsula had a very primitive knowledge of a certain kind of folk-astronomy mainly related to the stars, the Moon (their *calendar was luni-solar) and the Sun (a system of heliacal risings and achronical settings of certain stars formed the backbone of their luni-solar calendar). The arrival of Islam helped the development of a specialized kind of astronomy (*miqat*) applied to the needs of religious worship, notable establishing the *qibla*—the direction towards Mecca—prediction of the visibility of the new moon, and determination of the times of Muslim prayers. The solutions given for these kinds of problems were initially crude, but they developed in the course of time towards a fully scientific level.

Indo-Iranian Astronomy in Islam

The accession to the Caliphate of the Abbasid dynasty in 750 C.E. inaugurated a period of assimilation of the Indian, Iranian, and, especially, Greek heritage which lasted until the end of the tenth century. The Indo-Iranian astronomical tradition, which has a Greek, pre-Ptolemaic, origin, began to penetrate Islamic lands as early as the Umayyad period (from c. 679), and experienced an important development from the caliphate of al-Mansur (754–775). The first collections of astronomical tables, known as *zij* (*Arkand, Zij al-Shah, Sindhind*) began to arrive; these were translated into Arabic and used for the computation of horoscopes. The recension of the *Sindhind* prepared by *al-Khwarizmi (fl. 800–847) reached al-Andalus where it was adapted to the Islamic calendar and to the geographical coordinates of Córdoba by *Maslama of Madrid (d. 1007) and translated in the twelfth century, at least twice, into Latin. As a result of this, it knew a great success in Latin Europe.

Ptolemaic Astronomy and Islamic Observatories

The caliphate of al-Ma'mun (813–833) marked a turning point, for it was then that Ptolemaic astronomy was introduced. A Syriac translation of the *Almagest* was the first to appear, followed by three Arabic translations and several revisions, only two of which survive. Other Ptolemaic works such as the *Planetary Hypotheses* and the *Handy Tables* were also translated into Arabic. The three known traditions (Indian, Persian, and Greek) used different parameters and planetary models, and a program of astronomical observations was designed to solve the problem of their discrepancy. This was carried out in Baghdad (828–829) and near Damascus (831–832). Several Ptolemaic *zij* modelled on the *Handy Tables* were compiled using the results of these observations. These tables accepted Ptolemy's kinematic models but used new parameters; they rejected some dogmatic beliefs of the *Almagest*, such as the invariability of the obliquity of the ecliptic, the constant character of the precession of equinoxes, the immobility of the solar apogee, and the impossibility of annular solar eclipses. Some of the alterations are accurate improvements, while others are understandable mistakes due to the belief of Muslim astronomers in the accurateness of ancients, and of their own observations. This was the start of a process of critical analysis of Ptolemaic astronomy, as well as of a serious theoretical effort which continued through the ninth and tenth centuries. *Thabit ibn Qurra (d. 901) was one of its main representatives.

It also marked the appearance of one of the essential institutions of Islamic astronomy, the observatory; this began with al-Ma'mun and continued, almost without interruption, in small private observatories or in more or less organized institutions with official support. Fakhr al-Dawla (977–997) subsidized an observatory at Rayy (near Teheran) and the astronomer al-Khujandi (d. c. 1000) built a large sextant with a radius of c. 65 feet (20 m) for solar observations. Although it is possible that al-Ma'mun's observatories already used large instruments, al-Khujandi's sextant seems to be the earliest clear instance of this kind of Islamic device; these reappear in the observatory founded in Maragha (1259) by *Nasir al-Din al-Tusi (1201–1274), which survived until 1316. The Maragha model was imitated, notably in the observatory built in Samarkand in 1420 by prince Ulugh Beg, who was himself a highly competent astronomer. The buildings of the Samarkand observatory were still in place c. 1500 and they contained huge instruments, of which a good part of the meridian one (probably a sextant) still exists. Islamic observatories continued with the foundation of the Istanbul observatory in 1577, which was destroyed in 1580. This tradition survived until the 1700s for Jay Singh, Muslim maharajah of Amber (India) built between 1699 and 1734 five observatories, following the models of Maragha and Samarkand, in Jaypur, Delhi, Benares, Mathura, and Ujjayn. In the age of the telescope, these were already obsolete, but they testify to the persistence of the tradition.

Observations or simple computational work were the origin of new *zij*, of which we know of the existence of some two hundred twenty-five (eighth to nineteenth centuries). Planetary positions computed with a *zij* were in agreement with the observed ones for a short period of time (about forty years according to an Andalusi estimation). When the disagreement was clear, a new set of tables had to be computed. Corrections affected mainly mean motion parameters; equation tables, with the exception of those for the Sun and Venus, were usually taken from the *Handy Tables*. This effort to adjust computation to observation led to the conclusion, reached in Europe during the Scientific Revolution, that it was neessary to change the Ptolemaic paradigm. At the same time, these astronomical tables introduced a new spherical trigonometry which has remote Indian roots but is mainly an Islamic creation: all the trigonometry Copernicus knew was Islamic.

The Role of Al-Andalus

In the second half of the tenth century astronomy in al-Andalus benefited from an original development which preserved many elements of the Indo-Iranian tradition. This reached its summit in eleventh-century *Toledo where *Ibn al-Zarqalluh made important contributions to astronomical theory. These were continued both in the Iberian peninsula and in the Maghrib until the end of the fourteenth century and were well known by the astronomers of the European Renaissance. This was due to the translation of astronomical works from Arabic into Latin or Castilian which began around 1000 C.E. and reached its apogee during the twelfth and thirteenth centuries. This allowed Latin Europe to recover the

Greek astronomical tradition together with the modifications and criticisms made by eastern Islamic astronomers up to the end of the tenth century: translations could only be made of Eastern books which had reached al-Andalus before contact with the Islamic east was lost with the fall of the Cordovan Umayyad Caliphate c. 1031. Arabic astronomical works written in the eleventh century or later which were translated into Latin and known in Europe were usually Andalusi.

The *Hay'a* (Cosmology) Tradition

Ptolemy's *Almagest* is a mathematical tool, the purpose of which is to predict planetary longitudes. *Ptolemy also wrote the *Planetary Hypotheses*, a good part of which is only known through an Arabic translation, in which he defends his astronomical system in physical terms, projecting his geometrical models into three dimensions and using these to compute the sizes of planets and their distance from Earth. The interest in planetary sizes and distances appears in Islamic astronomy as early as the eighth century. Later, the great physicist *Ibn al-Haytham (945–c. 1040) made a serious attempt in his *Hay'at al-'alam* (*On the Configuration of the World*) to give a new interpretation of the geometrical models of the *Almagest* in physical terms. This led him to the criticism of Ptolemy which appears in his *al-Shukuk 'ala Batlamiyus* (*Doubts on Ptolemy*): Ibn al-Haytham discusses Ptolemy's failure in the *Hypotheses* to justify physically all the motions described in the *Almagest*, as well as certain aspects of the geometrical models of this latter work which he considers to be physically impossible. The most important of these criticisms is concerned with the equant point (the center of mean motion in longitude of Ptolemy's planetary models), a device which clearly violated the principle that any celestial motion must be a combination of uniform circular motions.

The problem of the equant point became crucial in all attempts to create a physically admissible astronomical system, and there were unsuccessful attempts to design planetary models without equant from the eleventh century onward. A great revival of this tradition took place shortly before the foundation of the Maragha observatory in 1259, but as many of the theoretical innovations were made by a group of astronomers who worked in this observatory, the denomination of "Maragha school" has often been applied to them. Mu'ayyad al-Din al-'Urdi (d. 1266) and Nasir al-Din al-Tusi described physically admissible non-Ptolemaic planetary models which are as successful as those of Ptolemy: many of them present remarkable similarities to those of Copernicus, although no mention is made of heliocentrism. This kind of enterprise was continued by al-Tusi's disciple Qutab ad-Din al-Shirazi (1236–1311) and, later, by the Syrian astronomer Ibn al-Shatir (c. 1305–c. 1375) who computed a new *zij* based in his own models (the lunar one is clearly better than Ptolemy's) and on the observations he made in Damascus. The geometrical models of the "Maragha school," like those of Copernicus, replace Ptolemy's equant by combinations of from two to four epicycles, the radii of which are linked like vectors of constant length rotating at uniform speed. Although it is not clear how the information about the Maragha models reached Copernicus (the best hypothesis points to a transmission through a Byzantine Greek translation) it is obvious that the great Renaissance astronomer knew about these theoretical efforts: besides many other similarities, his lunar model is identical to that of Ibn al-Shatir and he uses two lemmas discovered by al-'Urdi and al-Tusi which are the main mathematical tools of all the Maragha and Copernican models.

See also **Astronomy, Latin; Ptolemy; Translation movements; Translation norms and practice**

Bibliography

al-Hassan, A.Y., Maqbul Ahmed and A.Z. Iskandar, eds. The Different Aspects of Islamic Culture. Volume Four: Science and Technology in Islam. Part I: The Exact and Natural Sciences. Paris: UNESCO, 2001.

Kennedy, E.S. A Survey of Islamic Astronomical Tables. Transactions of the American Philosophical Society (1956) n.s. 46: 123-175.

———. Astronomy and Astrology in the Medieval Islamic World. Aldershot: Variorum, 1998.

Kennedy, E.S., Colleagues and Former Students. Studies in the Islamic Exact Sciences. Beirut: American University of Beirut, 1983.

Kennedy, E.S. and I. Ghanem, eds. The Life and Work of Ibn al-Shatir. An Arab Astronomer of the Fourteenth Century. Aleppo: Institute for the History of Arabic Science, 1976.

King, D.A. Islamic Mathematical Astronomy. London: Variorum, 1986.

———. Astronomy in the Service of Islam. Aldershot: Variorum, 1993.

———. World-maps for finding the direction and distance to Mecca. Innovation and tradition in Islamic science. Leiden: E.J. Brill, 1999.

———. In Synchrony with the Heavens. Studies in Astronomical Timekeeping and Instrumentation in Medieval Islamic Civilization (Studies I–IX). I: The Call of the Muezzin. Leiden: E.J. Brill, 2004.

King, D.A., J. Samsó and B.R. Goldstein. "Astronomical Handbooks and Tables from the Islamic World (750–1900): an Interim Report." Suhayl (2001) 2: 9–105.

Rashed, Roshdi, ed. Encyclopedia of the History of Arabic Science. Vol. I. London: Routledge, 1996.

Saliba, G. A History of Arabic Astronomy. Planetary Theories during the Golden Age of Islam. New York: New York University Press, 1994.

Samsó, J. Las ciencias de los antiguos en al-Andalus. Madrid: Mapfre, 1992.

———. Islamic Astronomy and Medieval Spain. Aldershot: Variorum, 1994.

Sayili, A. The Observatory in Islam and its Place in the General History of the Observatory. Ankara: Türk Tarih Kurumu Publications, 1969 (reprint Ankara, 1988).

Van Dalen, B. Al-Khwarizmi's astronomical tables revisited: analysis of the equation of time. In From Baghdad to Barcelona. Studies in the Islamic Exact Sciences in Honour of Prof. Juan Vernet. Edited by J. Casulleras and J. Samsó. Barcelona: Instituto Millás Vallicrosa de Historia de la Ciencia Arabe, 1996, 195–252.

JULIO SAMSÓ

ASTRONOMY, LATIN

Astronomy was well established as a scientific discipline in classical times. To the Greeks and their intellectual successors, not all study of the heavens qualified as astronomy. They regarded it as the mathematical study of the universe and of celestial bodies; in contrast, causal descriptions of the heavens were considered to be a part of physics or *cosmology. Ancient astronomy may be divided into three overlapping fields of study: (1) Measuring time and creating calendars based on the rising and setting of bright stars or constellations, often the signs of the zodiac; (2) Predicting the apparent positions of the seven planets, including the Sun and Moon, as measured against the background of the fixed stars; (3) Determining the diameters, volumes, and distances of the stars and planets. These activities had been developed to a sophisticated level by the Greeks, culminating with the Alexandrian mathematician *Ptolemy in the second century C.E.

Because Ptolemy and his predecessors wrote in Greek, their works became inaccessible to the medieval scholars of Western Europe, who read only Latin. Their knowledge was limited to the summaries of astronomy in *encyclopedias and handbooks by Roman and early Christian authors such as Pliny the Elder, *Macrobius, and *Isidore of Seville, along with a partial translation of *Plato's Timaeus. Christianity added a new science of time-reckoning named *computus, which centered on the problem of determining the date of Easter. Since it involved the reconciliation of solar and lunar cycles, computus required some astronomical knowledge. The *translation movements of the twelfth and thirteenth centuries introduced Greek and Arabic astronomy to Latin speakers, although the general level of understanding remained modest. Undoubtedly folk astronomy could also be found in many areas, but its practitioners were seldom literate and left few records of their art.

The Classical Legacy

In broad outline, the medieval idea of the cosmos was the same as that of Ptolemy, Plato, and Aristotle in the fourth century B.C.E. The center of the world was occupied by the four terrestrial elements. Earth, the heaviest element, collected in a sphere surrounded by layers of the other three elements, water, air, and fire. The celestial realm began with the sphere of the Moon, just beyond fire. The heavens consisted solely of spheres of the fifth element, aether, centered on the Earth. Most astronomers agreed that the Moon was closest to Earth, and that the planets were arranged in the order Moon–Mercury–Venus–Sun–Mars–Jupiter–Saturn, beyond which the fixed stars shared a single sphere. The order sometimes varied in ancient and medieval works, but there was general agreement that the Moon was nearest and the stars furthest away.

In contrast to the four elements, which moved in straight lines until reaching their natural place, aether moved perpetually in circles. All celestial objects complete a common revolution around the Earth in twenty-four hours, and we see them as rising and setting. But each object also has its own, more complicated motion. When compared to the fixed stars, the Sun appears to move through the zodiac on a path known as the ecliptic, which it completes in a year. The Moon takes about a month to complete its own revolution. Each of the five planets has its own cycle, in addition to drifting away from the ecliptic (motion in latitude) and periodically reversing its motion (retrogradation). Even the fixed stars share in a slow motion known as precession.

The variety of motions can be explained by attributing to each planet a set of orbs; combined, they cause the planet to appear to move irregularly. Aristotle adopted the system of Eudoxus (fourth century B.C.E.), in which each planet is assigned three or four orbs concentric with the Earth. But this scheme could neither predict planetary motion accurately, nor account for variations in brightness, which seemed to indicate changes in planetary distances.

In the *Almagest*, Ptolemy described an accurate system of prediction. The most basic element is the deferent ("carrying") circle, which moves the planet around the Earth. The Sun, which has the simplest motion, has an eccentric deferent, meaning that it is slightly off-center. Because the observer is not at the center of the eccentric, the Sun appears to move most slowly when furthest from Earth. In reality, however it maintains a constant speed around its circle. Each of the remaining planets also has an epicycle, a smaller circle carried by the deferent; the planet is placed on the epicycle. In the lunar model, the epicycle simply changes speed and distance. For the other planets, the epicycle explains retrogradation: the planet retrogrades when the epicycle carries the planet in a motion opposite to the deferent. Finally, the five planets have equants. The equant is a point separate from the center of the deferent; the center of the epicycle moves uniformly with respect to the equant. In *Planetary Hypotheses*, Ptolemy explained how to convert the circles of motion into three-dimensional orbs, and how to calculate the sizes of the planets and their orbs.

The Early Middle Ages

Only a fraction of classical astronomy was available in the early Middle Ages. Through the efforts of *Boethius to preserve knowledge of the seven liberal arts, astronomy retained its status as part of the mathematical *quadrivium, but the level of knowledge remained superficial. A reader of one of the common handbooks could have learned about the division of the cosmos into celestial and terrestrial realms; the shape of the Earth and perhaps its measurement by Eratosthenes; the Earth's five climatic zones (the torrid zone, two arctic zones, and two habitable temperate zones); the daily motion of the heavens; the names, natures, and arrangement of the seven planets; and the causes of eclipses. The most advanced treatments of astronomy included the approximate period of each planet, the Sun's motion through the ecliptic, eccentric circles as a cause of variable apparent speed, and a qualitative description of retrogradation. Individual texts added variations on the theme.

Macrobius, for example, gave a simple method of finding planetary distances in the *Commentary on the Dream of Scipio*. *Martianus Capella placed Mercury and Venus in motion around the Sun, not the Earth. Not one described details of astronomical models, such as the equant or the ratio of epicycle to deferent. With only these texts, it was impossible to predict planetary motion.

For prediction it was necessary to use the *computus*. Beginning as a method of predicting the date of Easter, *computus* developed into a mathematical art in its own right, demanding the ability to calculate celestial cycles. Some regarded it as a Christian response to the quadrivium, which was tainted by association with *astrology and pagan learning. *Bede wrote two books on *computus*. The longer of these, *De ratione temporum*, was among the most advanced Latin astronomical works of its time. Bede went beyond the creation of a *calendar to explain the underlying motions of the Sun and Moon, investigating such questions as the changing angle of the luminaries' rising and setting, and the connection between the Moon and tides.

The High Middle Ages

The rediscovery of Ptolemy and Aristotle was part of a broad revival of learning facilitated by contact with Islamic scholarship, heavily dependent in its first stages on translation of Arabic works and of Greek texts in Arabic. *Gerbert of Aurillac may have helped initiate the process by bringing mathematical texts from a visit to Spain. An important first step towards predictive astronomy was mastering the astrolabe, an astronomical instrument for observation and calculation. During the twelfth century, translators produced Latin versions of *zijat* (singular, *zij*), *planetary tables with canons (instructions for use), including the *Toledan Tables* of *Ibn al-Zarqalluh. Around 1270 a new set of tables was prepared in Spain. The *Alfonsine Tables*—named for their patron, *King Alfonso X—gradually replaced the translated *zijat* and remained the primary tables until after the publication of Copernicus's *De revolutionibus* (1543). Latin scholars also gave their attention to theoretical texts. The celebrated translator *Gerard of Cremona traveled to Spain and learned Arabic in order to study the *Almagest*, but few, if any, read and understood his translation of Ptolemy in toto.

Astronomy played a minor role in the curriculum of the new *universities. As part of the quadrivium, it was incorporated into the arts faculty, and as a prerequisite for astrology it supplemented the practice of medicine. New astronomical textbooks appeared in the thirteenth and fourteenth centuries to satisfy demand for instructional materials. Among the popular textbook authors were *Robert Grosseteste and *Campanus de Novara, but the most successful was *John of Sacrobosco. University statutes and manuscript anthologies confirm that three textbooks by Sacrobosco—the *Algorismus* on arithmetic, the *Computus ecclesiasticus*, and the *Sphaera* or "sphere" on elementary astronomy—formed the core of a course of astronomical studies, supplemented by books on instruments, an advanced genre of textbook called *theorica planetarum*, and the *Alfonsine Tables*. Modern accounts of "epicycles on epicycles" are simply untrue; the planetary models of medieval texts are essentially identical to those of Ptolemy. The major exception is the theory of trepidation ascribed to *Thabit ibn Qurra, according to which a rotation of the sphere of fixed stars causes the equinoxes to oscillate.

Scholastic philosophers debated whether the eccentric circles and epicycles of astronomers could exist as ethereal orbs in the heavens. Many assented to the possibility that such orbs existed, but Averroists (followers of *Ibn Rushd, the great Islamic commentator on Aristotle) insisted that all celestial motion must be strictly concentric with the Earth, in accordance with Aristotelian physical doctrine. Averroists adopted a modified form of the Eudoxan system of homocentric orbs and dismissed Ptolemaic models as fictions meant only for predicting appearances from Earth.

The Renaissance

In the mid-fifteenth century Viennese professor *Georg Peuerbach began a commentary on the *Almagest* but was prevented by death from completing it. His student *Johannes Regiomontanus took up the task; in his hands, the *Epitome of the Almagest* became an invaluable technical supplement and critique of Ptolemy, based on an understanding of astronomy unmatched in the West since antiquity. Regiomontanus moved to Nuremberg in 1471 where he became the first scientific publisher; his publications included Peuerbach's *Theoricae novae planetarum*, which he had transcribed while a student at Vienna. The *Epitome* was published posthumously in 1496. For over a century the methods, problems, and even many of the standard texts in astronomy continued to be what they had been in the Middle Ages. But printing and the new textbooks helped to create a critical mass of skilled astronomers who would ultimately discard the legacy of the classical world.

See also **Almanacs; Aristotelianism; Astrolabes and quadrants; Astrology; Astronomy, Islamic; Cosmology; Elements and qualities; Latin Averroists; Macrobius; Martianus Capella; Michael Scot; Planetary tables**

Bibliography

Bede. *Bede: The Reckoning of Time*. Translated with introduction, notes, and commentary by Faith Wallis. Liverpool: Liverpool University Press, 1999.

Grant, Edward, ed. *A Source Book in Medieval Science*. Cambridge: Harvard University Press, 1974.

Lindberg, David. *The Beginnings of Western Science: The European Scientific Tradition in Philosophical, Religious, and Institutional Context, 600 B.C. to A.D. 1450*. Chicago: University of Chicago Press, 1992.

McCluskey, Stephen. *Astronomies and Cultures in Early Medieval Europe*. New York: Cambridge University Press, 1997.

Pedersen, Olaf. "The *Corpus astronomicum* and the Traditions of Mediaeval Latin Astronomy: A Tentative Interpretation." In *Colloquia Copernicana III: Astronomy of Copernicus & Its Background*, 57-96. Studia Copernicana 13. Wroclaw: Ossolineum, 1975.

———. *Early Physics and Astronomy: A Historical Introduction*. Revised edition. New York: Cambridge University Press, 1993.

Stahl, William Harris. *Roman Science: Origins, Development and Influence to the Later Middle Ages*. Madison: University of Wisconsin Press, 1962.

Stahl, William Harris, Richard Johnson, and E.L. Burge. *Martianus Capella and the Seven Liberal Arts*. 2 vols. New York: Columbia University Press, 1971–1977.

Thorndike, Lynn. *The "Sphere" of Sacrobosco and Its Commentators*. Chicago: University of Chicago Press, 1949.

KATHERINE A. TREDWELL

B

BACON, ROGER

Roger Bacon (c. 1214/20–1292?) was trained in the liberal arts (arts and sciences) at Oxford. Although not a student of *Robert Grosseteste, he could have met the retired Professor, Chancellor and lector for the Franciscans at Oxford (1229–1235). Bacon was trained in the reading of the "new" Aristotle, yet his reading included significant non-Aristotelian authors such as *Boethius and writers from the School of Chartres. It is widely believed that Bacon lectured in Paris sometime after 1237. He was preceded in this task by his later opponent, *Richard Rufus of Cornwall. Bacon himself tells us that he lectured in the arts longer than was normal, and that he assisted in M.A. examinations in natural philosophy. It is probable that Bacon returned to Oxford sometime after 1247. It is most likely that at this time he was influenced in his understanding of the relation of biblical interpretation and natural science by Adam Marsh, the Franciscan regent of studies and a close friend of Grosseteste. It would appear that Bacon gained access to Grosseteste's scientific works at this time. One should not rule out the possibility that he may have visited the English city of Lincoln. Bacon was back in Paris in 1251. He may have entered the Franciscan Order by 1257.

The common view of Bacon, outlined by Stewart C. Easton (1953), as one who developed his notion of a Universal Science based almost single-handedly on his edition of the *Secretum secretorum* c. 1245, cannot now be sustained. The influence of this work only shows up in the late 1260s, and his edition was not completed until about 1280 at Oxford. This work clearly influenced Bacon's views on science, technology, and medicine. It is an important influence on Bacon's understanding of the applications of mathematical sciences, yet it is just one among many significant philosophical and scientific works from the Greek, Arabic, and Latin worlds that influenced Bacon's new "scientific" directions after 1247.

Bacon tells us that the period from about 1256 to 1266 was one of "exile" from scholarly teaching and research.

Further, he informs us that even with the patronage of Cardinal Guy le Gros de Foulques (Pope Clement IV: spring 1265–fall 1268) he had great difficulty in producing his *Opus maius*, *Opus minus*, *Opus tertium*, and related works. It is clear that by July 1266, when he received the papal mandate to write his work on philosophy and educational reform at the University of Paris, Bacon had produced no formal work in philosophy. Hence, his later works, including his more scientific texts such as the *Perspectiva*, *De speculis comburentibus*, *De scientia experimentali*, and the miscellaneous writings on medicine and other subjects, were largely incomplete short treatises. By means of a skilful use of a rhetorical *persuasio* in his *Opus maius*, Bacon managed to provide a philosophical context for these works. All this was aimed at an educational reform of the curriculum at Paris. Because of Bacon's demand for a connection between Grammar–Logic and Rhetoric and Poetics, together with primary emphasis on the applications of mathematics, he can be seen as a Proto-Humanist.

Bacon attacks the Aristotelian synthesis of the Faculty of Arts and Theology at Paris. His argument is as follows: the logicians, natural philosophers, and theologians, with their emphasis on "partial" versions of Aristotle, ignore the "greater philosophers." These greater philosophers are the Neoplatonists of Late Antiquity, the Arab world, and modern Christian Neoplatonists such as William of Auvergne and Robert Grosseteste. Yet, implicit in the term "Neoplatonist" is a distinct commitment to the traditional Stoic division of Philosophy: Logic/Epistemology–Physics–Ethics. Indeed, Bacon organizes all his later philosophy and science around this division.

It is clear that Bacon, as a retired professor and later as a Franciscan, took an interest in the development of the science, medicine, and technology of his times. It is most unlikely, however, that he had either the leisure or the opportunity to carry out serious experimental work. Instead, he reports on that of others such as Robert Grosseteste, the mathematicians John of London and *Campanus de Novara, and the French experimentalist Pierre de Maricourt (*Peter Peregrinus). Bacon developed a moral philosophy capable of dealing with the critical implications of scientific work for the *Respublica christiana*. It is not insignificant that, whereas Bacon wrote his *Opus maius* for Pope Clement IV, his edition of the *Secretum secretorum* was written for an English royal, possibly Henry III or his son Edward I. Rather than a practicing experimentalist, Bacon should be seen as a philosopher of science who addressed the moral and social implications of scientific research especially in relation to statecraft. Hence the importance of his *Secretum secretorum* as a unique but significant representative of the genre "Mirrors of Princes."

Bacon returned from Paris to Oxford in about 1280. He engaged in theological polemic at the Franciscan house in Oxford. It was here that he completed his *Compendium studii theologiae* (c. 1292), in which he laments the practices of Oxford theologians. Again, his argument is humanistic: the scholastic theologians, particularly Richard Rufus of Cornwall, allow the scholastic *quaestio* to displace both the text of Scripture and the histories.

Bacon's Division of the Sciences

The "Aristotelian Commentaries" of Roger Bacon in the 1240s are concerned with problems from the *Physics* and the *Metaphysics*. The remaining works from this period are concerned with Grammar and Logic.

It was during the 1260s in the *Opus maius* and the *Communia naturalium* that there emerged a new schema for a division of the sciences. In the latter work, Bacon gives an account of the organization of natural science, the number of the sciences, and the method or procedure in the sciences. Broadly, all science can be divided into the following: language study, including logic; mathematics (common and special); natural philosophy, both the common exposition of Aristotle and the seven sciences; metaphysics; and moral philosophy. For Bacon, moral philosophy is the telos of all the other sciences.

Perhaps the most significant new development here is Bacon's explicit criticisms of Aristotle's natural philosophy. He argues that even in special treatises such as *De caelo et mundo*, Aristotle fails to give precise and detailed account of the phenomena. In other words, Aristotle's teaching on the heavens, the stars, light, and the planets is too general and lacks experimental detail. Further, Aristotle's account of the physical and chemical elements is deficient. In Bacon's view, there are seven new sciences which are superior to the "philosophical" sciences taught in the universities. These are: perspective, astronomy (judicial and operative), the science of weights, *alchemy, *agriculture, medicine, and experimental science. All these sciences differ from the common teaching on Aristotle's natural philosophy in that they involve the strict application of mathematics and detailed study of experiences.

In *Opus maius* Part Six Bacon locates these sciences of nature in the context of his effort to distinguish a true "art and science of nature" from magic and moral philosophy. Moral philosophy also includes religion. It may seem strange that the seventh science is called "experimental science." The reason for this is that Bacon is concerned with the establishment of canons of legitimate verifiability. Many sciences in the Middle Ages were "speculative," and a consideration of "formal logic" would have been a sufficient condition for their validity. In Bacon's view, natural science required a set of "practical criteria," analogous to "formal logic," that would set out the boundaries between natural science and other concerns such as magic, ethics, sociology, and religion. Hence, in *Opus maius* Part Six he provides examples or case studies of this method: the study of the rainbow, chemical development, and medicine.

The outline of this division in the *Opus maius* is slightly different: physics, *astrology, computistics, geography, perspective, experimental sciences. Yet there is a consistency to his general criticism of the natural philosophy of the common scholars (*vulgus studentium*) at the University of Paris.

Bacon as an Aristotelian Commentator

Recent research has shown that Bacon's *Summa grammatica*, *Summa de sophismatibus et distinctionibus*, and especially the *Summulae dialectices* take up the concerns of "speculative grammar." In this, the author was influenced by *Robert Kilwardby and possibly also by Richard Fishacre. Bacon is opposed to any mechanical application of grammatical rules. He places great emphasis on discovering the intention of the speaker in the context of the speech. Bacon returned to the question of meaning and language in the 1260s, by which time his main concerns were with theology and the methods of an experimental science. There is, therefore, a continuity between early and late Bacon in his teaching on language. We might say in modern terms that Bacon is very much aware of the nature of the speech act in the communication of meaning. The intention of the speaker, the different linguistic expressions, and the sense gained by the listener/reader are analyzed in detail. One can call this Bacon's analysis of the *generatio sermonis*. The *Summulae dialectices* ought to be called Bacon's *Summulae super totam logicam*. It is comparable with similar works by Peter of Spain (*Petrus Hispanus) and Lambert of Auxerre. In fact, it is superior to other contemporary works in the manner in which it treats of Aristotle and a variety of new works in philosophy. This work introduces two new doctrines to semantics: the doctrine of univocal appellation, and the doctrine of predication in reference to "empty classes." Much of this doctrine formed the basis of Bacon's later theological disagreements with Richard Rufus. Above all, Bacon introduced a set of rules for the fixing of prepositional sense. He makes the doctrine of the imposition of meaning for present things fundamental to his account. All this logical analysis would become central to his doctrine of signs as applied to the study of nature and medicine in his later works.

Bacon's commentaries on the *Physics* and *Metaphysics* exhibit a concern with the genesis of the experimental universal as set out by Aristotle. Relevant here too are his numerous references to the *Posterior Analytics*. It would seem that in these commentaries from the 1240s he was already acquainted with the *Commentary* on the *Posterior Analytics* by Robert Grosseteste. Indeed, his development of an interest in experience (*experimentum*) in a more "experimental" manner in the 1260s is closely connected with these Aristotelian concerns. And yet there are new and non-Aristotelian elements which derive from the Stoic tradition and from the world of Arabic philosophy.

Bacon's Program for Educational Reform

What is the actual context for Bacon's publication of his views on science, philosophy, and religion from 1266 to 1292, and why did he react so strongly to the practices of the common philosophers at Paris and Oxford? Bacon saw the problem of Averroism and the sciences as central to the debates in thirteenth-century theology. His works from 1266 to 1292 are an explicit attack on the Averroism of the philosophers and theologians. They are also a sustained argument for the importance of language study, mathematics, and the sciences in the study of theology. Bacon represents an "Avicennian–Augustinian" synthesis which argues for the limitations of the introductory philosophy courses of the *universities.

It would be a mistake to think that Roger Bacon was an "experimental philosopher" in the sense of one who carried out significant contrived experiments. That he had an interest in the scientific methodology of experience and experiment is not doubted. The nineteenth-century view, much published by historians of science and religion, that Bacon was the inventor of modern science, cannot be sustained. Roger Bacon was very much a medieval thinker. Yet he was one who had some sense of how that thought might develop in the future. To summarize: Bacon acquired most of his knowledge of "experiments" from *books*. Books, for the medieval academic, were the Mirrors of Nature. When Bacon ceased being a professor of philosophy at Paris in about 1247, he devoted the next twenty years and many resources to "experimental books" and to training students in their use. Even in the more experimental parts of his philosophy, such as the *Perspectiva*, *De speculis comburentibus*, and *De scientia experimentali*, Bacon offers the general reader a synthesis of the new knowledge lately available from the Greek, Roman, and Islamic worlds. This is especially true of his own "Mirror of Princes," the *Secretum secretorum*. It is largely an account of the uses of science, medicine, and technology for statecraft in the Islamic world. Still, it would be pejorative to dismiss Bacon's experimental concerns as just warmed-over Aristotle or simple transcription of ancient texts. There is a development of new avenues of research in the work of Bacon and they foreshadow significant work in the Renaissance. In this sense, the classification of Bacon as an Aristotelian is inadequate. He does contribute new vistas to the development of science.

Drawing on the critical spirit of twelfth-century thinkers such as *Adelard of Bath, and the cosmological interests of the School of Chartres, Bacon in *Opus maius*

Eighteenth-century engraved plate portrait of Roger Bacon, originally from the collection of Friderici Roth. (SCETI)

Part One offered a criticism of the common scholastic thought. He argued that it was based on custom and unworthy authority. Even the uses of Aristotle and Scripture were scientifically deficient. Overall, the *Opus maius* is a scientific–philosophical–theological synthesis. Following on the development in *Opus maius* Part Two of the notion of a history of wisdom which incorporates literature, science, philosophy, and theology, and which is based on the principles of interpretation in Augustine's *De doctrina christiana*, Bacon sets out the major Stoic division of philosophy in the remainder of the work. In all the work, Bacon takes up and transcends Aristotelian themes in a Stoic/Neoplatonic synthesis. In this, he contrasts the positions of the "greater philosophers" with the common teaching of the schools, which was based on the literal reading of the available texts of Aristotle on logic.

In *Opus maius* Part Three Bacon outlines his basic philosophy of language. He presents a range of linguistic study from basic grammar to philosophical grammar. His section on semiotics, *De signis*, presents a fruitful synthesis of Aristotle and Augustine. It presents an account of natural inference and deals with the phenomena of ambiguity and equivocation. It has implications for natural sign phenomena and for intentional meaning.

In *Opus maius* Parts Four, Five, and Six, Bacon presents his account of physics in the sense of natural philosophy. Part Four deals with the applications of mathematics, Part Five with *perspectiva*, and Part Six with "experimental science."

Part Four presents a digest of Bacon's account of force and natural agency. The more complete account is found in "On the multiplication of species" (*De multiplicatione specierum*), the treatise that is fundamental for his natural philosophy. Agency in nature is closely related to the self-diffusion of light rays. Each kind of thing generates its "image" or product. A species is the natural outcome of a specific agent. Bacon's account of matter is significant. Matter has a positive element; it is an inchoate thing with a tendency. It needs form for completion. In his own words: "By 'species' we do not mean Porphyry's fifth universal; rather this name is meant to designate the first-effect of any naturally-acting thing." Further: "*Lux* [light] is the source, the quality of a luminous body, such as fire or a star; but *lumen* is that which is multiplied and generated from that *lux* and which is produced in air and other rare bodies, which are called *media*, because species are multiplied by their mediation." Hence Bacon's very significant doctrine of the multiplication of species. The doctrine would be fundamental for his concerns about the theory of vision, experience, and medicine. One central result is the bifurcation of things into the realms of strictly material agency in the world and strictly immaterial mental reality. Immaterial species operating on the body from natural objects are ruled out as fantasy. This distinction did not have to await the mind of Descartes: it became the Frenchman's philosophical inheritance.

Following on this, Bacon presents an account of a polemic at Paris concerning the status of astrology. Since astrology plays a major role in his account of science and medicine, it required a defense in view of the fact that Augustine had offered strong criticisms of its deterministic implications. Bacon bases his case on the *Introduction to Astrology* of *Abu Ma'shar (Albumassar). This work, even with its deterministic tendencies, is fundamental to Bacon's science. It forces him to hold to a strict dualism between determinism in nature and an independent freedom of the will and mind. He qualifies some of these deterministic tendencies by means of two other texts, the *Commentary on the Centiloquium* (Pseudo-Ptolemy), and the Pseudo-Ptolemaic *De dispositione sphaerae* (= Geminus, *Introduction to Astronomy*). All this material is represented in the important introduction and notes to the *Secretum secretorum*.

Also in Part Four of the *Opus maius*, Bacon presents an account of computistics and calendar reform, an account of world geography, and a digest of astrology. Bacon's account of geography and cartography has been acknowledged as innovative: in it he demanded a systematic mathematical mapping of the world using astronomical instruments and Ptolemy a century before it was accomplished.

The fifth and sixth parts of the *Opus maius* form the basis of Bacon's model of an experimental science. Part Five is named *Perspectiva*. This treatise is very broad in scope. First, it involves a Latin rendition of the intromission teaching on vision taken from *Ibn al-Haytham (Alhacen). Second, it consists of a working of this teaching into the common teaching on the body–mind relation taken from Aristotle, Augustine, and Avicenna (*Ibn Sina), and into the common medical tradition. In Part One of this work, Bacon presents a very fine synthesis of basic medieval theory of mind as a preface to theory of vision. Parts Two and Three contain a generic account of reflection and refraction.

In his 1983 study of Bacon, David C. Lindberg asked: "Were the optical achievements discussed above made possible by the application of a new (and perhaps modern) scientific methodology?" Nineteenth-century experts absolutely believed that Bacon did apply this "new" scientific methodology. In summary, Lindberg's analysis was that, following Euclid, Ptolemy, Alhacen and other predecessors, Bacon in the *Perspectiva* makes geometrical, mathematical analysis fundamental. The rectilinear propagation of light is geometrical. Reflection and refraction are subjected to careful geometrical analysis. Visual phenomena including the act of vision are given careful geometrical analysis. Double vision, and optical illusions including the Moon-phenomenon are subject to mathematical analysis. But in Lindberg's judgment this analysis did not extend "to the most fundamental principles of *perspectiva*." The problem is that when Bacon came to the explanation of the phenomena of reflection and refraction, he fell back on mechanical analogies and metaphysical principles. It would seem that Bacon's fundamental scientific principles in optics were not geometrical at all, but rather "physical, metaphysical and perceptual." Despite the fact that experience and experiment are scattered throughout his works, the terms cover a range of phenomena from ordinary observation to spiritual illumination. Lindberg concludes that "Bacon's perspectival theories were not primarily the product of his own empirical activity" (the sources of his experiments are the written word, books). Bacon has a knowledge of perspectival phenomena that goes well beyond ordinary, everyday observation, but he does not always carefully integrate it into his theory. Nevertheless, some of Bacon's observations can be classified as artificial experiments with the use of instruments, such as for example his correct measurement, most likely with an astrolabe, of the maximum elevation of the rainbow. Further, Bacon's analysis of the halo likewise exhibits an ease with mathematical analysis applied to observed natural phenomena. And in the *Perspectiva* there is an account of an experimental apparatus designed to study double-vision. Observation and experiments (real or imaginary) serve a theoretical function for Bacon. But the more usual experiments in Bacon are used to "confirm, refute, or challenge theoretical claims" of his contemporaries.

Bacon did not live up to his "methodology." But then, one must ask about his purpose and his resources in the *Opus maius*. He had almost no resources, and his superiors tried to dissuade him from these activities. As

Lindberg correctly states "Bacon's primary purpose was basically pedagogical...." And in this he was successful, reporting on the actual experimental work of his Parisian contemporary, *Peter Peregrinus, the author of the treatise on the magnet. He tells us so in the *Opus tertium*. Bacon skilfully, although not always successfully, informs the educated leadership in Europe about matters which had only lately been learned from the Arab world.

In *Opus maius* Part Six, Bacon sets out his "methodology" for an experimental science. His starting point is Aristotle's remarks in the *Posterior Analytics*, *Metaphysics*, and *Nicomachean Ethics*. His goal is to provide by way of case studies certain criteria for experimental science. First, it must be separated from magic, religion, and morals. Second, it must involve more than general theory of science or indeed of optics. It must incorporate detailed studies of individual phenomena such as the rainbow and halo. And these studies must consist of a combination of mathematics and experimental observations. Further, astronomical instruments must be developed, chemical compounds must be produced, and new forms developed; medicine must be encouraged, and techniques of warfare such as Greek fire and gunpowder must be developed. All of this is to be put at the disposal of the head of state by the scientist. Bacon's treatise must be seen as his attempt to take up and improve on Robert Grosseteste's theory of the rainbow. It is an important step on the way to the more complete theory formulated in 1307 by *Theodoric of Freiberg.

For many years it was thought that Bacon's contributions to alchemy and medicine were his most important work. Research in the late twentieth century, specifically that of William Newman (1997), has accentuated the "highly idiosyncratic nature" of Bacon's alchemical theory. Newman views Bacon's account "as in some respects highly original." It plays a central role in Bacon's reform of studies and in his proposal for a transformation of both nature and human life. Bacon's program for a microbiotic transformation of the human body differs in kind from the restriction of alchemy to nature's processes in both *Albertus Magnus and in Gerber (*Jabir ibn Hayyan). Ultimately, Bacon's interest in transformative alchemy is intimately tied to his ideas on the resurrection of the whole human being.

Bacon's reputation in medicine is due to his having been made an emblem of English medicine in the later Middle Ages and Renaissance. Bacon can be seen as one who inherited a tradition of learning about human medicine from the time of *Bede up to *Bartholomaeus Anglicus. Faye Getz holds that the example of medicine in this part of the *Opus maius* "is the most detailed and carefully crafted of Bacon's medical writings." He places great emphasis on a "regimen of health," and sees medicine just like alchemy as the means by which to retard the process of aging. In this, he depends on *Dioscorides, *'Ali ibn al 'Abbas al-Majusi (Haly Abbas), *al-Razi, and Ibn Sina (Avicenna). The whole aim was to return the body to its prelapsarian state, just like that of Adam. Bacon's *De erroribus medicorum* can be seen as a practically oriented humanistic criticism of

the common "theoretical" scholastic treatments of medicine. A. Paravicini-Bagliani has demonstrated that not all of the ascribed medical works in Volume Nine of the Steele edition are authentic.

Opus maius Part Seven presents Bacon's synthesis of Metaphysics, Social Philosophy, Theory of Virtue, Astrological Sociology of Religions, Rhetoric/Poetics and Forensic Logic.

Continuity and Influence of Bacon's Thought

General philosophical themes from Bacon are repeated throughout the English Franciscan tradition, for example in Peter John Olivi, *Duns Scotus, *William of Ockham, and others. The preservation of Bacon's manuscripts owes much to John Dee in the sixteenth century and Sir Kenelm Digby in the seventeenth century. His works on alchemy and astrology were published in the sixteenth century. The *Perspectiva* was published in Frankfurt in 1614, and the first edition of the *Opus maius* was edited by Samuel Jebb in 1733 in London. But because Bacon lacked the institutional backing of a Bonaventure or a Duns Scotus, he did not get the historical publicity that his works merit. There was a revival of interest in Roger Bacon in the nineteenth century, during which he again became an emblem of English medicine and science. In the early twentieth century there was a successful effort to provide a working edition of his texts. In the latter part of the twentieth century a more measured and careful picture of Bacon's work emerged. He is now seen as a medieval scholar who contributed significantly to science, philosophy, and theology. He was not, however, the founder of modern science. This has not prevented writers from repeating the hagiography of nineteenth-century historians of science. Bacon is perhaps best described as a late scholastic proto-humanist. He is a medieval thinker who anticipates some of the scientific concerns of the Renaissance.

See also "Latin Averroists"; Optics and catoptrics; Ptolemy; Scholasticism; Weights, Science of

Bibliography

Primary Sources

Brewer, J. S., ed. *Fr. Rogeri Bacon Opera Quaedam Hactenus Inedita: Opus tertium, Opus minus, Compendium studii philosophiae*. London: Longman, Green, Longman and Roberts, 1859; [N.p.]: Kraus Reprint, 1965.

Bridges, John Henry, ed. *The "Opus maius" of Roger Bacon*. 3 vols. Oxford: Clarendon Press, 1897–1900; Reprint, Frankfurt: Minerva, 1964.

De Libera, Alain, ed. Les *Summulae dialectices* de Roger Bacon [parts 1 and 2]. *Archives d'Histoire Doctrinale et Litteraire du Moyen Age* (1986) 53: 139–289.

Duhem, Pierre, ed. *Un Fragment Inedit de L'Opus Tertium de Roger Bacon*. Quarrachi: Collegio St. Bonaventure, 1909.

Fredborg, K.M., Lauge Nielsen and Jan Pinborg. An Unedited Part of Roger Bacon's *Opus Maius: De Signis*. *Traditio* (1978) 34: 75–136.

Gasquet, F.A. An Unpublished Fragment of a Work by Roger Bacon. *English Historical Review* (1897) 12: 494–517.

Hackett, J.M.G., ed. *Tractatus de experientia*. In idem, "The Meaning of Experimental Science (Scientia Experimentalis) in Roger Bacon." Ph.D. Dissertation, University of Toronto, 1983.

Lindberg, David C., ed. *Roger Bacon and the Origins of Perspectiva in the Middle Ages: A Critical Edition and English Translation of Bacon's Perspectiva with Notes and Introduction*. Oxford: Clarendon Press, 1996.

———. *Roger Bacon's Philosophy of Nature: A Critical Edition, with English Translation, Introduction, and Notes, of De multiplicatione specierum and De speculis comburentibus*. Oxford: Clarendon Press, 1983.

Little, A.G., ed. *Part of the Opus tertium of Roger Bacon including a Fragment Now Printed for the First Time*. Aberdeen: University Press, 1912; reprinted Farnborough: Gregg Press, 1966.

Maloney, Thomas S., ed. *Compendium Of The Study of Theology*. Leiden: E.J. Brill, 1988.

Massa, Eugenio, ed. *Rogeri Baconis Moralis Philosophia*. Zurich: Thesaurus Mundi, 1953.

Molland, George, ed. and trans. "Roger Bacon's *Geometria speculativa*." In Folkerts, M. and J. P. Hogendijk, eds. *Vestigia mathematica: studies in medieval and early modern mathematics in honour of H.L.L. Busard*. Amsterdam/Atlanta: Editions Rodopi, 1993, pp. 265–303.

Steele, Robert, ed. *Opera hactenus inedita Rogeri Baconi*. 16 volumes. Oxford: Clarendon Press, 1905–1940.

Secondary Sources

Alessio, Franco. Un secolo di studi su Ruggero Bacone (1848–1957). *Revista critica di storia della filosofia* (1959) 14: 81–102.

Crombie, A.C. *Styles of Scientific Thinking in the European Tradition: The History of Argument and Explanation especially in the Mathematical and Biomedical Sciences and Arts*. 3 volumes. London: Duckworth, 1994, Volume 1.

Hackett, Jeremiah M. G. "Aristotle, *Astrologia*, and Controversy at the University of Paris (1266–1274)." In John Van Engen, ed. *Learning Institutionalized: Teaching in the Medieval University*. Notre Dame: University of Notre Dame Press, 2000, 69–110.

———. "*Experientia, Experimentum* and the Perception of Objects in Space." In Jan A. Aertsen and Andreas Speer, eds. *Raum und Raumvorstellungen im Mittelalter*. [Miscellania Medievallia, 25] Berlin: De Gruyter, 1997, pp. 101–120.

———. "Robert Grosseteste and Roger Bacon on the *Posterior Analytics*." In Matthias Lutz-Bachmann, Alexander Fidora and Pia Antolic, eds. *Erkenntnis und Wissenschaft: Probleme der Epistemologie in der Philosophie des Mittelalters = Knowledge and science: problems of epistemology in medieval philosophy*. Berlin: Akademie Verlag, 2004, pp. 161–212.

———. "*Scientia experimentalis*: From Robert Grosseteste to Roger Bacon." In James McEvoy, ed. *Robert Grosseteste: New Perspectives on his Thought and Scholarship*. Turnhout: Brepols, 1995, pp. 89–119.

———, ed. *Roger Bacon and the Sciences: Commemorative Essays*. Leiden: E.J. Brill, 1997. [Papers by De Libera, Getz, Hackett, Howe, Lemay, Lindberg, Maloney, Molland, Newman, Rosier-Catach, Van Deusen, Williams, Woodward]

———, ed. *Roger Bacon and Aristotelianism*. [*Vivarium* (1997) 35.2] [Papers by Donati, Hackett, Long, Noone, Trifolgi, Wood]

———. The Published Works of Roger Bacon. *Vivarium* (1997) 35.2: 315–320.

Hackett, Jeremiah and Thomas S. Maloney. A Roger Bacon Bibliography (1957–1985). *The New Scholasticism* (1987) 61: 184–207.

Huber, Mara. Bibliographie zu Roger Bacon. *Franziskanicsne Studien* (1983) 65: 98–102.

Linden, Stanton J. *The Mirror of Alchemy*. New York: Garland Press, 1992.

Maloney, Thomas S. *Three Treatments of Universals by Roger Bacon*. Binghamton, New York: Medieval & Renaissance Texts and Studies, 1989.

———. "A Roger Bacon Bibliography (1985–95)." In Hackett, ed. cit., *Roger Bacon and the Sciences*, pp. 395–403.

Rosier-Catach, Irène. *La parole comme acte: sur la grammaire et la semantique au XIII siècle*. Paris: Vrin, 1994.

Paravicini-Bagliani, Agostino. Ruggero Bacone autore del *De retardatione accidentium senectutis? Studi Medievali* (1987) 28: 707–728.

———. "Storia della scienza e storia della mentalità. Ruggero Bacone, Bonifacio VIII e la teoria della 'prolongatio vitae'." In *Aspetti della letteratura latina nel secolo XIII*, ed. Leonardi, Claudio & Orlandi, Giovanni. [Atti del primo convegno internazionale di studi dell'AMUL, Perugia, 3–5 ottobre 1983.] Perugia-Firenze: Regione dell'Umbria; "La Nuova Italia," 1986, pp. 243–280.

———. *Medicina, e scienza della natura, alla corte dei papi nel Ducento*. Spoleto: Centro Italiano di Studi sull' Alto Medioevo, 1991.

Sharpe, Richard. *A Handlist of Latin Writers of Great Britain and Ireland before 1540*. Turnhout: Brepols 1997, pp. 580–583.

Tachau, Katherine H. *Vision and Certitude in the Age of Ockham: Optics, Epistemology and the Foundations of Semantics*. Leiden: E.J. Brill, 1988.

JEREMIAH HACKETT

BARTHOLOMAEUS ANGLICUS

Bartholomaeus Anglicus (Bartholomew the Englishman) composed *De proprietatibus rerum* (*On the Properties of Things*) during the 1220s while a teaching master at the Franciscan school in Paris; he revised or completed it in about 1235 while supervising the education of Franciscans in Magdeburg. *De proprietatibus rerum* belongs to the tradition of *encyclopedias, such as *Isidore of Seville's *Etymologies*. To fulfill his avowed purpose of compiling passages from diverse tracts, not writing his own commentary, Bartholomew assembled and identified more than one hundred sources, intending to aid those lacking access to such books. These items are concerned primarily with physics, specifically the properties of material things; hence, *De proprietatibus rerum* falls into the division of natural philosophy, not theology. In justifying this concern, Bartholomew explains that one must consider what is perceptible before ascending to contemplate what God has veiled.

Unlike the alphabetical arrangement expected in modern encyclopedias, no standard plan ruled early compilations; instead, authors devised their own systems. Bartholomew organizes his topics into nineteen books ordered in a descending hierarchy. Books One, Two, and Three survey the properties of forms separated from matter: God, angels, and the soul. Turning to the properties of

Illustration from an early fifteenth-century French translation of *De proprietatibus rerum* by Bartholomaeus Anglicus. (Topham/The British Library/HIP)

forms in matter, the next four books are concerned with the human body: the theory of the four elements is introduced (Book Four) and then applied to the body's outer and inner workings (Book Five), ages and sexes (Book Six), illnesses and their treatment (Book Seven tract on medicine). Next come the properties of things in the remaining perceptible world, beginning first with celestial phenomena and then time, which results from the effects of celestial movements on earth (Books Eight and Nine, astronomy tracts). The subsequent nine books move down through the properties of things in the nether world according to the four elements: fire (Book Ten); air and its ornaments, birds (Books Eleven and Twelve); water and its ornaments, fish (Book Thirteen); earth and its physical and social geography (Books Fourteen and Fifteen); earth's ornaments, namely metals and stones, which lie in the interior (Book Sixteen, the lapidary); plants, which grow out of it (Book Seventeen, the herbal); and beasts, which move on the surface (Book Eighteen, the bestiary). The final book (Book Nineteen) turns to "accidents" and other forms apart from matter, notably color, odor, savor, numbers, geometry, measures, weights, and music.

Its subject matter, methodically ordered exposition, and systematic organization into separable parts made *De proprietatibus rerum* useful well into the sixteenth century. It was documented as a textbook at the *universities of Paris, Oxford, and Cambridge and in numerous conventual libraries. *De proprietatibus rerum* was also used, in Latin or vernacular languages, outside formal academic communities. For instance, writing about *alchemy, Thomas Norton drew on the final book's color theory. Charles V commissioned a French translation (1372) from Jean Corbichon as part of his royal program for replacing Latin with French as the language of learning. Thomas Lord Berkeley of Somerset commissioned John Trevisa to make an English version (1398), printed by Wynkyn de Worde (1495). Although not planned by Bartholomew, illustrations in copies of *De proprietatibus rerum* provide evidence of instruments, autopsies, loci, and other matters valued by historians of science.

See also **Bestiaries; Elements and qualities; Geography, chorography; Herbals; Instruments, medical; Lapidaries; Medicine, practical; Medicine, theoretical; Meteorology; Weights and measures**

Bibliography

Primary Sources

Bartholomaeus Angelicus [*sic*]. *De rerum Proprietatibus.* Frankfurt: Wolfgang Richter, 1601; repr. Frankfurt: Minerva, 1964.

Le Livre des propriétés des choses: Une encyclopédie au XIVe siècle. Paris: Stock, 1992.

Trevisa, John. *On the Properties of Things.* 3 vols. Edited by M.C. Seymour et al. Oxford: Clarendon Press, 1975–1988.

Secondary Sources

Holbrook, Sue Ellen. "Picturing Time in Bartholomew's Encyclopaedia on the Properties of Things." *Time and*

Eternity: The Medieval Discourse. Ed. by Gerhard Jaritz and Gerson Moreno-Riaño. Turnhout: Brepols, 2003.

———. A Medieval Scientific Encyclopedia "Renewed by Goodly Printing": Wynkyn de Worde's English De Proprietatibus Rerum. *Early Science and Medicine* (1998) 3, 2: 119–156.

Seymour, M. C. and Colleagues. *Bartholomaeus Anglicus and His Encyclopedia*. Aldershot: Variorum, 1992.

SUE ELLEN HOLBROOK

BARTHOLOMAEUS OF BRUGES

Bartholomaeus of Bruges, a renowned teacher at the universities of Paris and Montpellier during the first half of the fourteenth century, was a prolific commentator on Aristotle and the basic works of the university medical curriculum. His philosophical expositions formed part of a broader attempt to reinstitute Aristotle's natural philosophy in the curriculum of the arts faculty in Paris following the *Condemnation of 1277. Bartholomaeus's medical commentaries are good examples of the attempt by masters to make medicine more philosophically respectable and thereby secure its reputation as a learned discipline in the early *universities.

Bartholomaeus was probably born into a family connected with trade in Bruges in about 1286; he matriculated in the arts faculty at the University of Paris in about 1300, and became a master of arts in about 1306. He then taught in the faculty as a regent master from about 1306 to 1310. During this time he wrote commentaries on a broad range of Aristotelian texts as well as numerous sophisms (records of disputations held by masters of arts on topics of a predominantly logical nature).

Bartholomaeus's commentaries on Aristotle's *De anima*, *Physics*, *Meteorics*, and *On Generation and Corruption*, as well as his (apparently lost) commentary on Aristotle's *Metaphysics* closely reflect the requirements of the arts curriculum in early-fourteenth-century Paris. But his commentary on Aristotle's *Poetics* and his expositions of two pseudo-Aristotelian works, the *Economics* and the *Inundation of the Nile*, reveal an interest in broadening the range of texts taught in the faculty at the time. Bartholomaeus's commentaries incorporate the methods of late *Scholasticism, combining line-by-line expositions of the text with disputed questions in which broader issues arising from the text are treated at length separately from the text. They also reveal a desire to make use of the most recent translations of Aristotle. For example, Bartholomaeus based his exposition of the *Economics* on Durand of Auvergne's new Latin rendering of the text taken directly from the Greek.

Bartholomaeus also wrote at least fifteen sophisms. These works place him at the heart of numerous disagreements on points of Aristotelian philosophy that emerged among contemporary Parisian masters of arts. They reveal that Bartholomaeus was engaged in an effort to defend orthodox interpretations of Aristotle against the heterodox interpretations of *"Latin Averroists" such as Ramon Llull and John of Jandun.

By 1315 Bartholomaeus had become a doctor of medicine and had been elected a fellow of the Sorbonne. Given that he had been active in Paris as a master of arts during the first decade of the fourteenth century, it seems likely that he undertook his medical training in Paris as well. But by 1329 Bartholomaeus was teaching medicine at Montpellier, a position he held until at least 1333. While there, Bartholomaeus commented on sections of the *Canon* of *Ibn Sina (Avicenna) and parts of the *Articella (*Galen's *Tegni*, the *Isagoge* of Johannitius (*Hunayn ibn Ishaq), and the *Aphorisms* of *Hippocrates). Once again, these commentaries exhibit Bartholomaeus's commitment to *Aristotelianism. They represent an attempt to locate medical knowledge within an Aristotelian framework by presenting it in the form of an Aristotelian *scientia and teaching it according to the rules of logical demonstration.

Bartholomaeus was also a practicing physician. In the early 1330s he was called to Paris to take care of certain members of the royal family, and from 1329 until at least 1343 he was retained by the counts of Blois to provide medical services for the family. Bartholomaeus's practice is reflected in two medical recipes and a plague tractate, written in 1348, in which he offered advice on how to avoid the Black Death.

Bartholomaeus acquired substantial wealth from his teaching and his practice as well as from his ecclesiastical benefices (he was a perpetual chaplain at Vieux-Ville in the diocese of Liège, a non-resident prebendary canon at St. Begge in Andenne-sur-Meuse, and a prebendary canon in Cambrai Cathedral). But in 1350 he began to dispose of much of his money in the form of benefactions to the University of Paris, establishing three scholarships at the Collège de Saint Nicholas-du-Louvre and four scholarships at the Collège de Bourgogne. Bartholomaeus died in March 1356, having made benefactions to the Collège de Bourgogne, the Sorbonne, and the Abbey of Sainte-Geneviève for the establishment of masses to be celebrated for the repose of his soul.

Bartholomaeus's life and work show how university medical faculties defended the status of medicine as an intellectually respectable discipline and opened to their members new paths of social and economic advancement.

See also **Medicine, practical; Medicine, theoretical; Plague tractates; Pseudo-Aristotle; Universities**

Bibliography

Ebbesen, S. and J. Pinborg. Bartholomew of Bruges and his Sophisma on the Nature of Logic. *Cahiers de l'Institut du Moyen Age grec et latin* (1981) 39: i-xxvi, 1–80.

Ermatinger, C.J. More Manuscript Evidence of Philosophical Controversies between John of Jandun and Bartholomew of Bruges. *Manuscripta* (1982) 26:6.

O'Boyle, C. An Updated Survey of the Life and Works of Bartholomew of Bruges. *Manuscripta* (1996) 40: 67–95.

Pattin, A. Trois questions de Barthélemy de Bruges dans le MS Vaticanus lat. 2173. *Bulletin de philosophie médiévale* (1973) 15: 141–144.

Roos, H. Bartholomaeus de Brugis: question circa significatum generis. *Cahiers de l'Institut du Moyen Age grec et latin* (1978) 24: 65–84.

Wickersheimer, E. "Barthélemy de Bruges." In *Dictionnaire biographique des médecins en France au Moyen Age*. 2 vols. Edited by Ernest Wickersheimer. Paris: E. Droz, 1936.
CORNELIUS O'BOYLE

BARTHOLOMAEUS OF SALERNO

The physician and teacher Bartholomaeus of Salerno (fl. c. 1150–1180) composed a manual of practical medicine which was both widely diffused in its original Latin form and also translated and adapted into vernacular versions, especially German. In addition, he was the author of an innovative suite of commentaries on the *Articella*; indeed, his are the first commentaries on the entire *Articella* anthology to be ascribed to a named author. Bartholomaeus was responsible for the insertion of *Galen's *Ars medica* (*Tegni*) into the *Articella* anthology and pioneered the use of Aristotelian works on *logic and natural philosophy for elucidating medical concepts. Moreover, in his commentary on the *Isagoge* of *Hunayn ibn Ishaq (Johannitius), Bartholomaeus states that he had composed a commentary on the *Liber graduum* of *Constantine the African: this suggests that further works by Bartholomaeus may someday be found among the numerous unascribed and unedited twelfth-century glosses and texts on medicine.

Despite his literary reputation, there are few details which enable us to fix Bartholomaeus's career in space and time. He may be identical with the physician named Bartholomaeus to whom Peter the Venerable, abbot of Cluny, wrote for advice, probably in 1151, about recurrent bouts of catarrh. This identification has been contested on the grounds that Peter's doctor Bartholomaeus offered to send assistance to Cluny at the hands of his *amicus et socius* Bernard, and stipulated that Bernard could make the journey to Cluny and back in a month. This Bernard could be Bernard of Provence, author of a commentary on the *Tabulae Salerni* and perhaps on the works of Bartholomaeus himself, but if Bartholomaeus were teaching at Salerno, and Bernard were with him, a journey to and from Cluny in one month would have been impossible. To be sure, these objections rest on the assumption that Bartholomaeus resided in Salerno. Another of his students, Petrus Musandinus, definitely taught at Salerno, and Bartholomaeus had documented Italian connections: for example, he commissioned *Burgundio of Pisa (c. 1110–1193) to translate a passage of the *Tegni* that was missing from the vulgate Latin recension. However, the discovery of a second letter by a magister Bartholomaeus, this time to King Louis VII of France (r. 1137–1180), whose contents closely resemble passages in the *Practica*, indicates that Bartholomaeus was a consultant well known in elite circles of French society. Some of the advice in this letter is duplicated in Bartholomaeus's commentary on the *Isagoge*, which leaves little doubt that the king's correspondent was Bartholomaeus of Salerno. These links with the French royal court, and the fact that (apart from Bartholomaeus himself) the Parisian master

Adam of the Petit-Pont was apparently the first to teach the expanded six-book *Articella* on which Bartholomaeus composed the first suite of commentaries, opens up the possibility that he taught in northern France. If his *socius* Bernard were with him in Paris, a journey to and from Cluny in a month would not have been impossible.

Bartholomaeus's *Articella* commentaries survive in at least twenty-three manuscripts from the twelfth to the fourteenth centuries. The glosses on all texts except *Hippocrates' *Prognostics* and Philaretus's *De pulsibus* circulated in two recensions. In the case of Johannitius's *Isagoge* and the *Tegni*, one of these recensions was assembled from *reportata* of Bartholomaeus's lectures by Petrus Musandinus, whom *Gilles de Corbeil names in his *De laudibus et virtutibus compositorum medicaminum* as one of his teachers at Salerno. Bartholomaeus, in sum, stood at the head of an influential medical teaching lineage.

Although Bartholomaeus's *Practica* is essentially an overview of therapeutic interventions, particularly drugs, followed by a synopsis of diseases and remedies, its text also reveals the author's strong attraction to Greek philology and etymology, as well as his familiarity with the medical literature associated with Constantine the African. In the *Articella* commentaries, these features are magnified; in particular, medicinal concepts are subjected to rigorous grammatical and logical analysis, based on Aristotle's *Categories* and *On Interpretation*. Bartholomaeus shows a formidable knowledge of ancient literature (especially Cicero, Boethius, and Plato's *Timaeus*), but the most significant feature of his *Articella* commentaries is his precocious use of Aristotle's natural philosophy. His commentary on the *Isagoge* quotes the Greco-Latin translations of the *Physics* and *On Generation and Corruption*, and there are unmistakable allusions to the *Metaphysics*. Finally, by highlighting Galen's *Tegni* as the key to the *Articella* anthology, and by cross-referencing within each commentary to other texts in the collection, Bartholomaeus transformed what had hitherto been a group of texts on diagnosis and prognosis into a coherent introduction to theoretical medicine. Bartholomaeus launched the *Articella*'s long career as the foundation text of an academic medical curriculum grounded on a philosophical definition of medical *scientia.

See also **Aristotelianism; Medicine, practical; Medicine, theoretical; Nature: diverse medieval interpretations; Nature: the structure of the physical world**

Bibliography

Primary sources
Practica magistri Bartholomaei Salernitani. In *Collectio Salernitana*. Edited by Salvatore De Renzi. Naples: Tipografia del Filiatre-Sebezio, 1852–1859, volume 4, pp. 321–406.
———.Translated [into modern Italian] by A. Capparoni. Rome: Istituto di storia della medicina dell'Università di Roma, 1960.
———. [Medieval German] *The Middle High German Bartholomaeus: Text, with Critical Commentary*. Edited by Walter L. Wardale. Dundee: James Fallon, 1993.

The Letters of Peter the Venerable. Edited by Giles Constable. Cambridge: Harvard University Press, 1967. 1. 379–383; 2. 58; 2. 82–83; 2. 205; 2. 247–252; 2. 302–303 and appendix M.

Quentin, H. "Une correspondence médicale de Pierre le Vénérable avec Magister Bartholomaeus." In *Miscellanea Francesco Ehrle: Scritti di storia e paleografia*. 6 volumes. Rome: Biblioteca Apostolica Vaticana, 1924, volume 1, pp. 8–86.

Talbot, C.H. A Letter from Bartholomew of Salerno to King Louis of France. *Bulletin of the History of Medicine* 30 (1956): 321–328.

Secondary Sources

Enrico Borlone, La practica dermatologica salernitana in Maestro Petroncello e in maestro Bartolomeo. *Medicina nei secoli 5* (1968): 108–121

Jacquart, Danielle. "Aristotelian Thought in Salerno." In *A History of Twelfth-Century Philosophy*. Edited by Peter Dronke. New York: Cambridge University Press, 1988, pp. 407–428.

———. Minima in Twelfth-Century Medical Texts from Salerno. In *Late Medieval and Early Modern Corpuscular Matter Theories*. Edited by Christoph Lüthy, John E. Murdoch and William R. Newman. Medieval and Early Modern Science, 1. Leiden: E.J. Brill, 200, pp. 39–56.

———. "'Theorica' et 'practica' dans l'enseignement de la médecine à Salerne au XIIe siècle." In *Vocabulaire des écoles et des méthodes d'enseignement au moyen âge*. Edited by Olga Weijers. Études sur le vocabulaire intellectuel du moyen âge, 5. Turnhout: Brepols, 1992, pp. 102–110.

Jordan, Mark D. Medicine as Science in the Early Commentaries on 'Johannitius.' *Traditio* 43 (1987): 121–145.

Keil, Gundolf. "Bartholomaeus Salernitanus." In *Die deutsche Literatur des Mittelalters Verfasserlexikon*. 2nd ed. New York: Walter de Gruyter, 1977–, volume 1, pp. 623–626.

Kristeller, Paul Oskar. Bartholomaeus, Musandinus and Maurus of Salerno and other Early Commentators of the Articella, with a Tentative List of Texts and Manuscripts. *Italia medioevale e umanistica* 29 (1976): 57–87.

Morpurgo, Piero. "I commenti salernitani all'Articella." In *Knowledge and the Sciences in Medieval Philosophy, Proceedings of the Eighth International Congress of Medieval Philosophy, Helsinki 24–29 August 1987*. Helsinki: Yliopistopaino 1990. volume 2, pp. 97–105.

Segrè, Marcello. Malattie polmonari nella 'Practica' di Bartholomeo, maestro Salernitano. *Medicina nei secoli 5* (1968): 9–14.

FAITH WALLIS

BARTOLOMEO DA VARIGNANA

Bartolomeo da Varignana, son of Giovanni, was born in Bologna in the mid-thirteenth century. He was probably a pupil of *Taddeo Alderotti. As a member of the Guelf (papal) party, Bartolomeo did not suffer when the Ghibelline (imperial) Lambertazzi were expelled from the city in 1274. He became a magister in 1278, and in 1292 qualified as a professor of medicine. In 1301 he was elected to the Consiglio degli Anziani e dei Consoli, one of the Courts of Bologna, and became its prior in 1303.

Bartolomeo da Varignana met Henry VII during the Holy Roman Emperor's first visit to Italy and later became his doctor. He was banished from Bologna on October 15, 1311, after falling out of favor with the Guelf government. He remained at the court of Henry VII until the emperor's death on August 24, 1313. After this date our knowledge of Bartolomeo becomes incomplete and contradictory. Some historians of Bologna, particularly Sarti and Fattorini, take the view that he moved to Genoa in 1318. They base that on the Book of the Ufficio dei Memoriali (Registrar's Office), in which it is reported that a certain Simone da Venola confessed to robbing Bartolomeo of two thousand lire while he was "*in civitate Januae cum Magistro Bartholomeo de Varignana.*" Notwithstanding, it is probable that the notary drawing up this document misunderstood the name of the town in which the theft occurred and changed Jadrae (Zara) to Januae (Genoa). This theory is supported by another error in *Secreta Medicinae* (1597) by Bartolomeo's son, Guglielmo, according to which the work was finished "*in veneranda curia Januae* [Genoa] *sub anno Domine MCC-CXIX die sabbati secundo exeunte decembris,*" and not, as reported correctly in the MS Latino 2163 of the Marciana Library in Venice, "*in veneranda curia Jadrae* [Zara]." The links between Bologna and Dalmatia were strong at the time, making it more likely that the place in question was Zara, not Genoa. The date of Bartolomeo's death is unknown, although it was probably after June 14, 1321, when the Major Council of Venice appointed him for two years.

Bartolomeo is best remembered for his work as a civic physician after 1265, the year in which judges in Bologna first turned to medical practitioners for help in prosecutions. This was the first proper medical-legal organization in Italy, and the Bolognese prototype was soon followed by the Republic of Venice. Bartolomeo is also important for the originality of his teaching at the University of Bologna. He introduced into the curricula of the School of Medicine the previously neglected work of *Galen, particularly *De accidenti et morbo*, *De complexionibus*, and *De interioribus*. Like *Pietro d'Abano in Padua, Bartolomeo also tried to reconcile the ideas of *Ibn Sina (Avicenna) with those of Galen: some of Bartolomeo's work in this area is preserved in his annotations on the fourth chapter of Avicenna's *Canon*. Bartolomeo's commentary on the pseudo-Aristotelian *Economica* is also interesting because it reflects the rapprochement between Bologna University's schools of law and medicine.

Bartolomeo also wrote *Pratica a capite usque ad pedes*, in which the treatments of various diseases were considered synthetically. The work followed a schema which was later taken up by Bartolomeo's son, Guglielmo, in his work *Secreta Medicinae*. The *Pratica* began with a treatise on diseases in single organs, and was followed by further treatises on the treatment of fevers, smallpox, wounds, and abscesses. The final part of the work considers antidotes to animal and vegetable poisons and medicaments for skin afflictions.

See also **Medicine, practical; Medicine, theoretical**

Bibliography

Arieti, Stefano. "Una famiglia di medici illustri: Bartolomeo e Guglielmo da Varignana." In Procedings of XXXI International Congress on the History of Medicine. Edited by R.A. Bernabeo. Bologna, 1988.

Ortalli, Gherardo. La perizia medica a Bologna nei secoli XII e XIV. Atti e Memorie della Deputazione di Storia Patria per le Provincie di Romagna (1969) XVII–XIX: 223–259.

Samoggia, Luigi. I Varignana. Bologna: Gamma Tipografia, 1963.

Siraisi, Nancy G. The libri Morales in the Faculty of Arts and Medicine at Bologna: Bartolomeo da Varignana and the psuedoaristotelian Economics. Manuscripta (1976) 20: 105–118.

———. Taddeo Alderotti and his Pupils. Princeton: Princeton University Press,1981.

STEFANO ARIETI

BATTANI, AL-

Abu 'Abd Allah Muhammad Ibn Jabir Ibn Sinan al-Raqqi al-Harrani al-Sabi' was an extremely important Islamic astronomer of the ninth–tenth centuries (b. before 858–d. 929). He was probably born in Harran and, although he himself was clearly a Muslim, his ancestors had probably professed the astral religion of the Harranian Sabians. His interest in Astronomy probably developed from the fact that his father was the famous instrument-maker Jabir ibn Sinan al-Harrani. Al-Battani lived most of his life in Raqqa (Syria, on the left bank of the Euphrates River) but there is also evidence that he visited Baghdad and Antioch. His death took place in Qasir near Samarra' on his return from Baghdad.

Apart from a few astrological tracts (including a commentary to *Ptolemy's Tetrabiblos and an astrological history of early Islam) which have not been studied so far, he compiled (after 901) his Zij (astronomical handbook with tables) also called al-Zij al-Sabi' (Sabian Zij). Only one complete manuscript of the second recension of this work is extant in the Library of El Escorial (Spain). This work marks the stage of full assimilation of Ptolemaic astronomy in Islam and the abandonment, in the Islamic East, of the Indian-Iranian tradition which had a long survival in al-Andalus and the Maghrib. This process had given its first results c. 830 with the zijes (al-Mumtahan, zijes compiled by Habash al-Hasib, etc.) which were the consequence of the program of observations undertaken in Baghdad and Damascus under the patronage of Caliph al-Ma'mun. Al-Battani's astronomical observations, often carefully described, were made in Raqqa: according to Ibn al-Nadim and Ibn Qifti the first ones correspond to 877 and his observational activity continued until 918. On January 23 and August 2, 901, he observed, in Antioch, a solar and a lunar eclipse respectively. The epoch of his catalogue of 533 stars is 911. He mentions two observational instruments (a mural quadrant and a triquetrum), as well as a sundial indicating unequal hours and a kind of mixed instrument which seems to combine elements of a solid celestial sphere with others derived from the tradition of the armillary sphere, which receives the name of al-bayda ("the egg"). It seems that this instrument was known in Latin Western Europe at a very early date: the collection of Latin astronomical texts with an Arabic origin which was assembled in Catalonia at the end of the tenth century contains a short tract entitled De horologio secundum alkoram id est speram rotundam, which contains a description of the applications to timekeeping of a solid sphere similar to al-Battani's bayda. As the Andalusi astronomer *Maslama of Madrid (d. 1007) was well acquainted with al-Battani's zij and the texts on the astrolabe written by him and by his disciples were very influential in the old corpus of Latin texts on astronomical instruments, it seems clear that Maslama's works were the channel for this early Latin diffusion of al-Battani.

Al-Battani's zij contains a set of instructions for the use of the numerical tables which have an essentially practical character. We do not find in them careful descriptions of the Ptolemaic models implied in the tables and the author employs surprising simplifications, such as giving a common description for all planetary models (both superior and inferior), without any reference to Ptolemy's complicated model for Mercury or even to the equant point around which the mean motion of the center of the epicycle takes place: according to Chapter Thirty-one of the Zij, the mean motion of the planets takes place around the center of the deferent (!). This is only one of the errors in the Escorial copy of the Zij, as well as in the extant Latin and Spanish translations (see below) which seem to correspond to the same manuscript tradition, and it is clear that it is the result of the mistakes made by a careless copyist, for the rest of the work attests that al-Battani was a highly competent astronomer.

New Parameters

Al-Battani's detailed observations enabled him to establish new and more precise planetary mean motion parameters, a new eccentricity for the Sun and Venus, the longitude of the apogee (82.17°) of these two celestial bodies, a very accurate determination of the obliquity of the ecliptic (23.35°), measurements of the apparent diameters of the Sun and the Moon and their variation in a solar year and anomalistic month respectively. He accepted *Thabit ibn Qurra's estimation of the precession of equinoxes (1° in sixty-six years). These new parameters show a clear improvement over those of Ptolemy and led al-Battani to follow the path initiated by the astronomers of Caliph al-Ma'mun and to establish clearly some important corrections on Ptolemaic theory such as the mobility of the solar apogee, the fact that the obliquity of the ecliptic is not a fixed value, and the possibility of solar annular eclipses. Although he favored precession and criticized the ancient theories of trepidation, he studied carefully the possibility—which was later used by Western Islamic astronomers—of combining constant precession with variable trepidation in order to justify the different historical estimations of the rate of precession.

Apart from the Almagest and the Planetary Hypotheses (which were used indirectly by Battani to determine the geocentric distances and sizes of the planets), Theon's *Handy Tables* constitute a major Ptolemaic influence in the *Zij*: the planetary equation tables (with the obvious exception of those for the equation of the center of Venus), for example, derive from Theon and al-Battani's work constitutes one of the important instruments for the diffusion of the *Handy Tables* during the Middle Ages.

The *Zij* was well known in al-Andalus toward the end of the tenth century: the aforementioned Maslama al-Majriti used al-Battani's values for precession and obliquity of the ecliptic and added astrological tables to the corpus. A copy, at least, of this work was circulated in the northeastern part of the Iberian Peninsula (it was probably a part of the library of king al-Mu'taman who reigned in Zaragoza between 1081 and 1085) for it was translated into Latin by Plato of Tivoli (fl. Barcelona 1132–1146) who also used it to cast the horoscope of the beginning of his translations of the *Iudicia Almansoris* (1136) and of the *Liber embadorum* (1145).

Another Latin translation, apparently lost, was also prepared by Robert of Ketton (fl. Tudela 1141–1157). The *Zij* was also the main source used by Plato's collaborator, the Jewish astronomer *Abraham bar Hiyya (d. c. 1136), in his *Sefer heshbon mahlekot ha-kokabim* (*On the computation of the motion of celestial bodies*). It was used in the second half of the twelfth century by *Maimonides (d. 1204) in his book "On the Sanctification of the New Moon," within his *Mishneh Torah*. In the thirteenth century it was translated into Spanish by the collaborators of *Alfonso X, king of Castile. It influenced strongly the Latin version of the *Alfonsine Tables* and was quoted by European astronomers until the seventeenth century.

See also **Astronomy, Islamic**

Bibliography

Bossong, Georg. *Los Canones de Albateni*. Herausgegeben sowie mit Einleitung, Anmerkungen und Glossar versehen. Tübingen: Max Niemeyer Verlag, 1978.

Kennedy, Edward S. A Survey of Islamic Astronomical Tables. *Transactions of the American Philosophical Society (Philadelphia)* (1956) 46 (2): 32–34.

Nallino, Carlo A. *Al-Battani sive Albatenii Opus Astronomicum*. 3 vols. Milan: Pubblicazioni del Reale Osservatorio di Brera in Milano, 1899–1907. Reprint Frankfurt: Minerva, 1969.

Ragep, F.J. "Al-Battani, Cosmology and the Early History of Trepidation in Islam." In *From Baghdad to Barcelona. Studies in the Islamic Exact Sciences in Honour of Prof. Juan Vernet*. Edited by J. Casulleras and J. Samsó. Barcelona: Instituto Millás-Vallicrosa de Historia de la Ciencia Arabe, 1996, pp. 267–298.

JULIO SAMSÓ

BAYT AL-HIKMA

Bayt al-Hikma (literally "house of wisdom") was a caliphal institution in Baghdad that is best characterized as a library with a number of limited scholarly functions (such as the translation and copying of books) but without most of the attributes of scholarly interchange that historians have sought to embody in it. It was also known as *dar al-hikma* and *hizanat al-hikma* ("store-house of wisdom," in the sense of "library"). It had been supposed that Abbasid caliphs, particularly Harun al-Rashid (786–809) and al-Ma'mun (813–833), established a kind of translation bureau with this name. But *bayt al-hikma* is most likely just an Arabic translation of the Sasanid Persian term for library, in particular a palace library established by the rulers to preserve books on Persian history. The Abbasid *bayt al-hikma* then appears to be a continuation of a Sasanid palace bureau, mainly a library but with scribal services and some translation activity, particularly from Persian into Arabic. No translation from Greek into Arabic has been explicitly located there, and the great translators are not mentioned in the context of the Bayt.

In the *Fihrist*, Ibn al-Nadim reports the meticulous way in which the Persian rulers preserved cultural documents: they chose the best writing materials (the bark of the white poplar tree) and sought safe storage places. One such vaulted building, Ibn al-Nadim adds, cracked open in 961/962 and the books that were found there were in a language people did not know how to read.

The successor of the Sasanid palace library would appear to have been the *bayt al-hikma*, the principal among a number of royal libraries. An official named al-Sanawbar is described as "director of the Bayt al-Hikma among the libraries of al-Ma'mun" (*sahib bayt al-hikma min buyut hikam al-Ma'mun*). Persons explicitly associated with the Bayt al-Hikma were administrators, copyists, and binders. Ibn al-Nadim reports that the astrologer al-Fadl ibn Nawbaht "was at the *hizanat al-hikma* for Harun al-Rashid; he translated from Persian into Arabic and relied in his scholarship on the books of Iran." Ibn al-Qifti adds that Ibn Nawbaht was the head of this library (*sahib bayt al-hikma*). Ibn al-Nadim also mentions a Persian scholar, 'Allan al-Shu'ubi, a copyist who "transcribed in the Bayt al-Hikmah for al-Rashid and al-Ma'mun," and ibn Abi'l-Harish, who was a bookbinder there. We know, too, that the mathematician and astronomer *al-Khwarizmi frequented the Bayt al-Hikma in the times of al-Ma'mun, one of the few solid indications that activities other than translation from Persian into Arabic took place there. The great translator *Hunayn ibn Ishaq was called "chief of translation" (*amin 'ala'l-targama*) under al-Mutawakkil (847–861), as Yuhanna ibn Masawayh had been under Harun al-Rashid, but these activities, apparently, were unconnected with the Bayt al-Hikma.

Ibn al-Nadim links another director of the Bayt, Salman, with a group of scholars sent out by al-Ma'mun to secure Greek manuscripts and translate them, before Hunayn ibn Ishaq and Qusta ibn Luqa were dispatched. But there is no direct evidence linking the library with the Greek translation movement.

In the western historiographical tradition, the translation movement from Greek into Arabic has been conflated with the palace library of Persian tradition. Thus Hitti wrote: "In pursuance of his policy [of assimilating the Greek corpus] al-Ma'mun in 830 established in Baghdad his famous Bayt al-Hikmah... a combination library, academy, and translation bureau which in many respects proved the most important educational institution since the foundation of the Alexandrian Museum in the first half of the third century B.C.E." But there is no direct evidence that translation from the Greek went on there, or that it was in any way an "academy." Al-Ma'mun appears to have held scholarly discussion there about religious issues, but it seems unlikely that any teaching, in the accepted sense, went on. Teaching scholarly subjects was conventionally practiced in the private homes of teachers. The most we can say about the Bayt al-Hikmah is that it was the main palace library, the one which continued the Sassanid tradition as a repository for great works on national culture, and copying from Persian into Arabic went on there (ostensibly because it held the inherited collection of Persian materials), and that the personnel associated with it were mainly technical: librarians, copyists, bookbinders, and the like.

See also **Translation movements**

Bibliography
Balty-Guesdon, M.-G. Le Bayt al-Hikma de Baghdad. *Arabica* (1992) 39: 131–150.
Gutas, Dmitri. *Greek Thought, Arabic Culture*. London: Routledge, 1998.
Hitti, Philip K. *History of the Arabs*. 7th ed. London: Macmillan, 1960.

THOMAS F. GLICK

BEDE

The Venerable Bede (c. 675–735) is most familiar to modern students as the author of the *Historia ecclesiastica gentis Anglorum* (*Ecclesiastical History of the English People*). To medieval readers, he was primarily an exegete, but he was also renowned as the author of an authoritative guide to *computus*, *De temporum ratione* (*The Reckoning of Time*), completed in 725. This work expanded Bede's earlier textbook *De temporibus* (*On Times*, c. 703), while at the same time incorporating a significant amount of the material previously included in his *De natura rerum* (*The Nature of Things*, c. 703). Although Bede's interest in cosmology, number and time, as well as in geography, medicine, and other topics, can be traced throughout his theological and historical writings, it is these three works which constitute his principal contribution to medieval science.

Most literature on *computus* prior to Bede took the form of polemics on behalf of one of the many solutions to the problem of determining valid dates for Easter, and establishing a reliable Easter cycle. In *De temporibus*, Bede struck out in a different direction by composing a didactic manual, but one based on the Alexandrian system of Paschal reckoning which Dionysius Exiguus had adapted for the Roman calendar. Taking his cue from

*Isidore of Seville (*De natura rerum* 1–7 and *Etymologiae* Book 5) and from Irish computists of the seventh century, Bede structured *De temporibus* according to the magnitude of the various units of time-reckoning, beginning with the smallest (the *punctus*) and ascending to the world-age. Into this framework he inserted explanations of the two essential documents of *computus*, namely the Roman solar calendar and the Paschal table; he also included a universal chronicle in the final section on the world ages. *De natura rerum*, on the other hand, surveyed the physical structure of the cosmos from the top downwards: the heavens, the atmosphere, oceans and rivers, land masses, and subterranean phenomena. Bede's structural model was Isidore's *De natura rerum*, but he drew on sources unavailable to Isidore, notably Pliny's *Historia naturalis*.

De temporibus proved to be both popular and notorious. Bede's *Letter to Plegwin* indicates that the revised chronology of world history presented in its universal chronicle prompted an apparently frivolous but deeply shocking accusation of heresy against the author. This lingering infamy, combined with his students' complaints that *De temporibus* was brief and obscure, motivated Bede to revise and enlarge *De temporibus* as *De temporum ratione*. In this work, the sequence of the units of time again serves as a framework for the calendar and Paschal table; but the material is both more extensive, and somewhat different in character.

Original Contributions

Bede's first innovation was to incorporate much of the cosmology of *De natura rerum* into his account of *computus*: for example, the section on the year provides an opportunity to dilate on the seasons and the variations in the length of the day at different latitudes. Most striking is the inclusion in Chapter Twenty-nine of a discussion, noteworthy for its originality and critical clarity, of the relationship of tides to the lunar month. Here Bede evaluates and corrects a number of earlier theories about tides, notably those recorded by Pliny, Philippus Presbyter (a disciple of St. Jerome), and the Irish cosmographers of the seventh century. Only a few ancient Mediterranean sources actually mentioned that there are two tides each day, or that the tides exhibit semi-monthly variations, or that there is a relationship between the tides and the phases of the Moon. Most theories about the cause of tides assumed that tides occur at the same time everywhere on Earth. Bede, on the other hand, knew about the monthly cycle of spring and neap tides from two anonymous Irish treatises, the *Liber de mirabilibus sacrae scripturae* and the *Liber de ordine creaturatum*; these works reflected the experience of dwellers on the Atlantic coast, where tides are higher and more noticeable than in the Mediterranean. Bede made a number of significant corrections to all these sources. Firstly, he explicitly connected the fact that the Moon rises about fifty minutes later each day with the pattern of the retardation of the tides. Pliny's calculation of tidal retardation at forty-seven and a half minutes (recorded

Detail of an illuminated manuscript of Bede's *Historia ecclesiastica gentis Anglorum*. (Corbis/David Reed)

by Bede in *De temporibus*) is corrected in *De temporum ratione* to forty-eight minutes. Though still short of the correct figure, this stands as evidence of Bede's active reflection and research on tides. Secondly, Bede proposed a new explanation for the cause of tides, namely that the passage of the Moon drags (*protrahitur*) the waters of the ocean along. He points out that the number of tides within a given space of time corresponds to the number of times the Moon has circled the Earth in the same period, and that the time of high tide follows a consistent pattern throughout the lunar month. Both these correlations prove that the motion of the Moon causes the tides. Thirdly, Bede corrects the statement found in his Irish sources that the four periods of the tidal month framing the spring and neap tides are equal in length, and corrects Pliny's claim that unusually high tides occur at the solstices as well as at the equinoxes. Finally, Bede enunciates for the first time the concept of "port," that is, that the time of high tide is affected locally by geographic situation, topographic features, or prevailing winds. Dwellers on the North Sea coast, he says, know that the tides arrive in some places earlier than in others. Indeed, there is evidence that Bede actively collected information about local tides from his network of monastic correspondents.

Bede's second innovation was to expand his discussion of the Paschal table considerably in order to refute in detail the perceived errors of both Victorius of Aquitaine (whose tables were used in Gaul and probably parts of southern Ireland) and the so-called "Celtic" system of Easter reckoning still employed by the British churches. This part of *De temporum ratione* marshaled considerable astronomical and mathematical evidence (notably concerning the date of the spring equinox, and the correlation of lunar and solar periods to produce a great Paschal cycle of five hundred thirty-two years) to resolve a quarrel that no lay or ecclesiastical authority in the West had the capacity or resources to adjudicate. It thus represents an important instance when rational argumentation based on mathematical and natural data resulted in practical changes affecting church and state. It was its widespread use as a textbook that effected this.

Bede often laments that it is easier to explain astronomy or drill students in mathematical operations through face to face instruction rather than in writing. Nonetheless, *De temporum ratione* allows us to glimpse something of the scientific pedagogy of an early monastic school. When introducing a formula, Bede customarily includes several worked examples, starting with a simple problem, and proceeding to more difficult ones. Finally, he demonstrates the validity of the formula by showing how it works with incontestably true data. Bede also "streams" his readership according to their level of background preparation, offering alternative methods, both mathematical and in the form of tables, for arriving at the same information. In Chapter Twenty-six, he even proposes an ingenious experiment with hanging lamps in a darkened church to prove that a heavenly body which appears to the earthbound observer to be higher in the sky than another heavenly body may in fact be closer to Earth. In sum, Bede's computistical writings furnished Carolingian and later schoolmasters with a paradigm of how to use problem-solving and visual models to teach scientific subject-matter. Not unsurprisingly, mathematical and astronomical pseudepigrapha came to be ascribed to him.

See also **Calendar; Computus; Navigation**

Bibliography

Primary sources

Bede. "*De temporum ratione.*" In *Bedae opera didascalica*, 241–544. Edited by C.W. Jones. CCSL 123A–C. Turnhout: Brepols, 1875–1980. English translation with introduction and commentary by Faith Wallis, *Bede: The Reckoning of Time*. Translated Texts for Historians 29. Liverpool: Liverpool University Press, 1999 (rev. ed. 2004).

———. *De natura rerum*. In *Bedae opera didascalica*, 174–234.

———. *De temporibus*. In *Bedae opera didascalica*, 580–611.

Secondary Sources

Di Pilla, Alessandra. Cosmologia e uso delle fonte nel *De natura rerum* di Beda. *Romanobarbarica* (1991) 11: 128–147.

Eckenrode, Thomas. The Growth of a Scientific Mind: Bede's Early and late Scientific Writings. *Downside Review* (1966) 84: 197–212.

Folkerts, Menso. Pseudo-Beda, *De arithmeticis propositionibus*: Eine mathematische Schrift aus der Karolingerzeit. *Sudhoffs Archiv* (1972) 56: 22–43.

Jones, C.W. *Bedae opera de temporibus*. Cambridge: Mediaeval Academy of America, 1943.

———. "Bede's Place in the Medieval Schools." In *Famulus Christi. Essays in Commemoration of the Thirteenth Centenary of the Birth of the Venerable Bede*. Edited Gerald Bonner. London: SPCK, 1976, pp. 261–285.

Kleist, Aaron. "The Influence of Bede's *De temporum ratione* on Aelfric's Understanding of Time." In *Time and Eternity: The Medieval Discourse*. Edited by Gerhard Jaritz and Gerson Moreno-Riaño. International Medieval Research 9. Turnhout: Brepols, 2003, pp. 81–97.

Moreton, Jennifer. Doubts about the Calendar. Bede and the Eclipse of 664. *Isis* (1998) 89: 50–65.

Ó Cróinín, Dáibhí. The Irish Provenance of Bede's Computus. *Peritia* (1983) 2: 238–242.

Smyth, Marina. *Understanding the Universe in Seventh-Century Ireland*. Studies in Celtic History 15. Woodbridge: Boydell, 1996.

Stevens, Wesley. *Bede's Scientific Achievement*. Jarrow Lecture 1985. Jarrow, Durham: St. Paul's Church 1985. Reprinted in *Bede and His World*. Edited by Michael Lapidge. 2 volumes. Aldershot: Ashgate, 1994, pp. 645–688.

FAITH WALLIS

BENZI, UGO

Philosopher and physician Ugo Benzi was born in Siena on February 24, 1376, the son of Minoccia and Andrea, a local magistrate allied to the faction of the Twelve. Ugo died on November 30, 1439, in Ferrara where he was buried in the church of San Domenico.

Thanks to the *Vita Ugonis* composed by his son Socino, the facts of Benzi's life are well attested. His education in the liberal arts (grammar, logic, dialectic, arithmetic, geometry, music, and astronomy) began in 1393 at Florence, and concluded at the University of Bologna in 1395 under Peter of Mantua. In 1396 he was invited to Pavia, and then to Bologna in 1403 where he taught philosophy and logic. While teaching at Bologna, he undertook the formal study of medicine under Marsilio de Sancta Sophia.

In 1405, Benzi returned to Siena specifically to teach medicine only to be driven out four years later, according to Socino by political enemies. The *Vita* makes no mention of his brief stay in Pisa during the Council of 1409. Before the Council had concluded, however, he was in the service of Cardinal Baldassare Cossa. By July of that year he was again teaching at the University of Bologna. On the occasion of Cossa's elevation to the papacy as John XXIII in May of 1410, Benzi is said to have defeated the philosophers and theologians among the French delegation during a public disputation held at Bologna. This victory of Italian over French *metaphysics may explain the later myth that he had taught at the University of Paris.

Benzi's growing reputation attracted the patronage of Niccolo d'Este, who invited him to teach at Parma at the newly established university in 1412. The failure of the university to attract students, however, provided Benzi with the leisure necessary to compile three of his principal medical commentaries as well as to issue his *Quaestiones rerum naturalium* in only four years.

Benzi was subsequently invited back to Siena to teach medicine and remained there until 1421 when, in Socino's account, political rivalries again induced him to flee. Correspondence between the cities of Siena and Florence indicate, however, that Florence managed to lure him to its university for the next two years until he was again engaged as a lecturer in medicine at the University of Bologna. Perhaps to honor his excellence as a physician, Cardinal Gabriele Condulmer, later Pope Eugene IV, conferred Bolognese citizenship on Ugo and his brother, Bonsignore, in 1424.

In 1425 Filippo Maria Visconti appointed Benzi ordinary lecturer at the University of Pavia, a post he held until 1429. The years 1429 to 1431 saw Benzi as chief lecturer on theoretical medicine at the University of Padua, a highly coveted post, until he was summoned to the court of Niccolo d'Este, in whose service he remained until his death. Engaged primarily as a court physician, Ugo did not resume university teaching, although he counted the notable humanist Angelo Decembrio among his private students.

During the ecumenical council of Ferrara in 1438, Benzi is said to have entertained Greek and Latin dignitaries at a symposium in which he spoke to great effect on various philosophical topics. Aeneas Sylvius Piccolomini, later Pope Pius II, also recorded this episode in his *Europa descripta*, where he described Ugo as the prince of physicians.

Works

Benzi is part of a tradition of western medicine in Europe from about 1300 to 1600 in which the study and exposition of certain authoritative texts came to be established in a university context. Medical education required a firm basis in the precepts of Aristotelian logic and consisted of lectures on the classical Greek, Roman, and Arabic medical authorities, most notably *Hippocrates, *Galen, *al-Razi, and Avicenna (*Ibn Sina). Because medical theory drew so heavily on Aristotelian philosophy, Benzi's initial training and teaching in the liberal arts, particularly logic and dialectic, laid the framework for advanced study in medicine.

Benzi's scholarly works are representative of the kind of scholastic literature generated in medieval Italian universities, and provide a rough outline of the content of medical education in this period. From 1396 to 1405, before formally professing medicine, Benzi compiled the philosophical treatises *De logicae artis ratione*, a basic introduction to logic which is no longer extant, and a commentary on Aristotle's *Parva naturalia*. Like many of his colleagues, he also produced commentaries on the medical texts contained in the *Articella*, including Hippocrates' *Aphorisms* with Galen's commentary, Galen's *Tegni* with the commentary by Haly Abbas (*'Ali ibn al'Abbas al Majusi), and select parts of Avicenna's *Canon*.

However theoretical it may seem, the medical curriculum in universities was designed above all to train practitioners. Efforts to apply theory to practice are evident in the development and increasing interest in practical medical literature in the form of *practicae*, medical manuals used in the course of practice, and *consilia*, narrative accounts of treatment recommended for individual cases. Although he did not compile a *practica*, Benzi is best known for his collection of over one hundred *consilia*. Issued in five separate printed editions in the sixteenth century, Benzi's *consilia* enjoyed a degree of popularity in learned medical circles probably as aids to practicing physicians and to enrich the teaching of standard medical texts.

While his university lectures and public disputations attracted many students, his reputation as prince of physicians won him hundreds of patients and noble patronage. Benzi also expressed interest in the intellectual world beyond the university. He read the new Latin translation of Aristotle's *Nichomachean Ethics* by Leonardo Bruni, and even corresponded with Bruni to discuss it.

A man of culture and learning, Benzi's life and career offer insight into the connections that link medicine to culture as a whole. His career also sheds light on the growth of medicine as a profession and its increasing prestige as a repository of authoritative knowledge and a skill worthy of patronage.

See also **Alderotti, Taddeo; Aristotelianism; Galen; Hippocrates; Ibn Sina; Medicine, practical; Medicine, theoretical; Metaphysics; Nature: diverse medieval interpretations; Nature: the structure of the physical world; Patronage of science; Scholasticism;** *Scientia*; **Universities**

Bibliography

Benzi, Ugo. *Scriptum de somno et vigilia*. Edited by Gianfranco Fioravanti and A. Idato. Siena: Università degli studi di Siena, 1991.

Conrad, Lawrence. *The Western Medical Tradition, 800 BC to AD 1800*. New York: Cambridge University Press, 1995.

Crisciani, Chiara. History, Novelty, and Progress in Scholastic Medicine. *Osiris* (1990) 6: 118–139.

Fioravanti, Gianfranco. Il commento di Ugo Benzi agli Economici (Pseudo) Aristotelici. *Rinascimento* (1995) 35: 125–152.

Lockwood, D.P. *Ugo Benzi: Medieval Philosopher and Physician, 1376–1439*. Chicago: University of Chicago Press, 1951.

Siraisi, Nancy. Anatomizing the Past: Physicians and History in Renaissance Culture. *Renaissance Quarterly* (Spring, 2000) 53, 1: 1–30.

_____. *Medieval and Early Renaissance Medicine: An Introduction to Knowledge and Practice*. Chicago: University of Chicago Press, 1990.

_____. Some Current Trends in the Study of Renaissance Medicine. *Renaissance Quarterly*. (Winter, 1984) 37, 4: 585–600.

ELIZABETH W. MELLYN

BERNARD DE GORDON

By the mid-nineteenth century Bernard de Gordon had become the prototypical medieval physician, "Gordonius the Divine" for the nineteenth-century poet Longfellow ("Christus: A Mystery"). Historians, however, have lost track of Bernard's origins, upbringing, and personal life. It is reasonable to surmise that he was a son of Fontanier II de Gourdon (d. c. 1260), a feudal lord in the Quercy region of southwest France. From his own account, we know that Bernard studied medicine at the University of Montpellier, began to teach there in 1283, and was still active in 1308. He is not remembered as a faculty official or court physician, but as an author and, indirectly but most importantly, as a teacher. All his books, thirteen or more in number, suggest that they were intended for the classroom rather than the private study. Their educational setting is reflected in their content and style.

Bernard de Gordon's work incorporated the curriculum that was becoming standardized as "the Art of Medicine," later known as the *Articella*. At its core were the precepts of *Hippocrates, with their focus on careful and comprehensive observation, which most visibly governed Bernard's *Management of Acute Diseases* and his *Book of Prognostication*. The Hippocratic emphasis on the everyday factors affecting health induced Bernard to have an Arabic text on dietetics translated into Latin. In his synopsis *On the Method of Treating Diseases*, the Montpellier master fused and simplified the principal textbooks of *Galen, the prolific interpreter of the Greek legacy and dominant force in the curriculum. Galen's authority not only framed a four-book collection *On the Preservation of Human Life* (1308) that culminated in a *Regimen of Health*, but also pervaded Bernard's thought and accounted for more than half of his citations. These included references to at least seven of the texts that reached Montpellier in translation during the first two decades of Bernard's teaching career in the consequential wave of what is now recognized as the "new Galen." It may seem surprising that no masters of *Salerno were mentioned and, even more, that the emerging dominance of the *Canon of Medicine* by *Ibn Sina (Avicenna) was not more visible, even when it affected the scope and arrangement of subject matter. Extracurricular sources, on the other hand, especially translations from Arabic, stimulated him to devote two treatises, *On Theriac* and *On Degrees*, to the compounding and measurement of drugs.

Authoritative writings, rational foundations, and sense-experience—personal or hearsay—constituted for Bernard the three pillars of correct teaching and sound practice. Reasoning took many forms, ranging from logical classification, formalized *quaestiones*, and dialectic arguments, to a conceptual pursuit of causes. The associated tendency to bookishness and sophistry neither precluded his consistently practical orientation nor turned him into a philosopher-physician. When venturing into speculation about life and death in his treatise *On Marasmus*, Bernard expressly preferred "the way of the physicians" to explanations based on the teachings of Aristotle; his ultimate interest in emaciation lay in the relation between diet and the radical moisture. The priority of concrete concerns over rationalization is particularly evident in Bernard's most famous work, the manual of practice known as the *Lilium medicine (Lily of Medicine)*.

Medical Authority

Comprehensiveness, organization, and clarity made the *Lilium* a prized encyclopedia that was aimed at giving broad access to medicine. Following a section on fevers, which consisted of afflictions ranging from malaria to pestilence and pustules, six parts covered diseases in head-to-toe order. Each chapter followed the structure of the *Art of Medicine*, beginning with a definition and its elaboration, proceeding to the causes, signs, and treatment, and concluding with "clarifications" of remaining questions. Humoral constructs and issues of natural philosophy were explained in dialectical but relatively simple terms, while practical recommendations were reinforced.

The *Lilium*'s section on therapeutics gained wide circulation, as the recommendations of "Gordon's pills" demonstrate. It also evinced Bernard's familiarity with surgical procedures, although he frequently relinquished difficult cases to "the hand of the restorer," and he persuaded *Henri de Mondeville to devote a special volume to *surgery. He seemed ambivalent about three of the auxiliary sciences. His patent knowledge of chemical processes and instruments contrasts with his warning that "uncounted numbers have perished" in the practice of *alchemy. He taught that the authentic Art condemned "every art" of *magic, yet his prescriptions included incantations and talismans. While claiming that the physician needed to know only the basics of astronomy, he commissioned *Profatius Judaeus to draw up an armillary sphere, and he may have translated two texts of *astrology, one on geomancy and the other on seals. In 1477 Bernard even drew the admiration of the celebrated astrologer Conrad Heingarter.

The *Lilium* and, to a lesser extent, the other works of Bernard de Gordon were further admired on account of his sensible instructions for bedside conduct, his precise definitions, and his diagnostic acuity. He figured as an authority on various baffling diseases, such as epilepsy,

lovesickness, and sterility. Successive generations at the University of Montpellier saw him as a representative of "our school." At the same time, this stature allowed for frank expressions of disagreement, for example by the Montpellier master Jean de Tornamira.

The *Lilium* was still recommended reading at the University of Vienna in 1520 and in circulation at the University of Padua past 1586. The translations of the *Lilium* and the *Liber Pronosticorum* into seven languages attest to the breadth of their appeal beyond the Latin academe. An overall indicator of Bernard's place in history is the number of copies in manuscript and print, citations by medical authors from the fourteenth to the seventeenth century, and references by modern historians. In 1458, the sworn town physician of Frankfurt rested his diagnosis of leprosy on the teachings of a trio of *Meister* (masters), namely "Avicenna, Liliator, Galienus." In 1621, when Robert Burton compiled his encyclopedic *The Anatomy of Melancholy* from scores of authors, he bestowed his highest praise on "Gordonius, who is worth them all."

See also Encyclopedias; Medicine, practical; Medicine, theoretical; *Regimen sanitatis*; Translation movements

Bibliography

Demaitre, Luke. *Doctor Bernard de Gordon, Professor and Practitioner*. Toronto: Pontifical Institute of Medieval Studies, 1980.

———. The medical notion of "withering" from Galen to the fourteenth century: the treatise on marasmus by Bernard of Gordon. *Traditio* (1992) 34: 259–307.

———. The *Articella* in teaching *De urinis* as exemplified by Bernard de Gordon. Articella Studies, Texts and Interpretations in Medieval and Renaissance Medical Teaching (Cambridge Wellcome Unit for the History of Medicine) (1998) 3: 29–37.

Lennox, William Gordon. Bernard de Gordon on epilepsy. *Annals of Medical History* (1941) 3: 372–383.

McVaugh, Michael R. Theriac at Montpellier, 1285–1325. *Sudhoffs Archiv* (1972) 56: 113–144.

LUKE DEMAITRE

BERNARD OF VERDUN

A French astronomer of the second half of the thirteenth century, Bernard of Verdun (Bernardus de Virduno) was probably born in Verdun, a town in the French region of Lorraine, in the department of Meuse. Other than the fact that he was a Franciscan monk, nothing is known about his life. His place in the history of astronomy is assured through his *Tractatus super totam astrologiam (Treatise on all of Astrology)*, which is thought to have been written at the end of the thirteenth century. The treatise did not attempt to explain *astrology (there was no well-defined boundary between astrology and astronomy in Bernard's epoch, and both notions were often interchanged) but is instead a clearly presented didactic explanation of *Ptolemy's geocentric teaching intended for Bernard's students. It begins with a description of the four basic elements in the sense used by Aristotle and

Ptolemy, and deals with the nature of the celestial sphere and its circular motion. Bernard then treats the tables of arcs and chords, and covers the basic astronomical notions. He studies in detail the motions of the Sun and Moon and their related effects (above all eclipses), as well as the motions of the other five planets then known. Some efforts to formulate an alternative view of the movements of celestial bodies to replace Ptolemy's teaching had already been made in Bernard's lifetime. One of the most serious such attempts was the *De motibus celorum* of *al-Bitruji (Alpetragius), the twelfth-century Spanish-Islamic astronomer who was active in Córdoba and Seville. His system, however, was not sufficiently developed to challenge Ptolemy's teachings, and Bernard himself rejected it utterly and conceived his own work as a defense of Ptolemy. Bernard also rejected the hypothesis of the ninth-century Baghdad astronomer *Thabit ibn Qurra that trepidation (*trepidatio* as "agitated" movement of the intersections of the equator and the ecliptic) caused the assumed unevenness of precession, even though that explanation was widely accepted until the late sixteenth century, when it was disproved by Tycho Brahe. On the other hand, Bernard's work has many similarities to the *Theorica planetarum* by *Campanus de Novara, as well as to the work of *al-Battani, Muslim astronomer of the ninth to tenth centuries. Of major importance is the final, tenth part of Bernard's book, in which he describes the principles of the torquetum and the noctilabium. The torquetum is one of the oldest astronomical instruments, measuring angles in horizontal, equatorial, and ecliptic coordinate systems. The inclination of the first oblique board to the instrument's horizontal base reproduces the equator's inclination to the horizon; the second oblique board is adjusted with regard to the first board to the ecliptic's inclination to the equator. The ecliptic latitudes are measured on the circle, which is perpendicular to the ecliptic, and then on the freely hanging semicircle by means of the plumb line of the height above the horizon. The noctilabium is an instrument that determines the time at night (assuming that the day's date is known) using the Pole Star and other bright stars in its vicinity.

See also **Aristotelianism; Elements and qualities**

Bibliography

Primary Source
Bernard of Verdun. *Tractatus super totam astrologiam*. Edited by Polykarp Hartmann. Vol. XV. Series Franziskanische Forschungen. Werl 1961.

Secondary Sources
Duhem, Pierre. *Le système du monde I-XII*. Paris, 1914–1959. (Bernard of Verdun: III. Paris 1958, pp. 442–460.)
Gunther, R. T. *Early Science in Oxford. II, Astronomy*. Oxford: Oxford University Press, 1923.
Poulle, Emmanuel. Bernard de Verdun et le turquet. In *Isis*, 55, 1964, pp. 200-208.
Thorndike, Lynn and Pearl Kibre. *A Catalogue of Incipits of Mediaeval Scientific Writings in Latin*. London: The Mediaeval Academy of America, 1963.

ALENA HADRAVOVÁ AND PETR HADRAVA

BERNARD SILVESTER

Bernard Silvester was confused for a long time with Bernard of Chartres and Bernard of Moelan and so was involved in the questionable "School of Chartres." Although he had contacts with *Thierry of Chartres and shares with him a similar humanist and neo-platonic interest in a cosmology expressed through integumenta, he is now clearly distinguished from other authors named Bernard. Native of the region of Tours, he taught in that city around the middle of the twelfth century. He was the master of Mathieu of Vendôme and died between 1159 and 1178.

Bernard Silvester's written production offers two sides, literary and scientific. On the one hand, he is the author of a still unauthenticated *Summa dictaminis* (there are many *Artes dictaminis* attributed to a "Magister Bernardus"), and he wrote unfinished commentaries on books I-VI of Virgil's *Aeneid* and the beginning of *Martianus Capella's *De nuptiis Philologiae et Mercurii* (I, 1–37). On the other hand, three treatises ascribed to him show a special concern for sciences. The *Experimentarius* is a book of spells, of Arabic origin, in which the precise role of Bernard (as adaptor or transmitter) remains unclear. Inspired by the fourth Pseudo-Quintilian *Declamation*, the *Mathematicus* or *Parricida* is a verse story telling of a son's suicide after he fulfilled an astrological prediction by killing his father. John of Salisbury quotes some verses of it.

Bernard's most famous work is *De mundi universitate* or *Cosmographia*. Dedicated to Thierry of Chartres, it was written under Pope Eugenius III (1145–1153) and seems to have been read in his presence during the Council of Rheims (1148). Its two parts successively deal with the organization of the universe (*Megacosmus*) and the production of man, its conclusion, masterpiece and condensed image (*Microcosmus*). Like Martianus and Boethius, Bernard alternates prose and poetry and uses a mythological language crowded with allegorical entities: *Noys* (divine wisdom), *Silva-Yle* (informed matter), *Endelechia* (wife and soul of the world), *Imarmene* (continuity of time), *Tugathon* (God), Urania and *Physis* (in charge of spiritual and biological life of man), etc. In both parts, *Noys* tries to bring creation to the perfection of a well-balanced order: it gives occasion to a descriptive itinerary, freely combining Christian, astrological and pagan theories, like eternity of the world or matter.

Neither a pagan, pantheist or monist author, nor a theologian, nor even a natural philosopher, Bernard is the creator of a fascinating integumentum, in which he shows a special talent to express in a poetic and mythic form the most recent scientific conceptions of his time. To the wide range of classical authors he imitated, he adds neo-platonic sources including the *Timaeus*, Calcidius, Macrobius, Martianus Capella, Boethius, Asclepius, and John Scot, and even some knowledge of new Aristotelian and Arabic scientific theories, which he consulted through *Hermann of Carinthia's translation of Albumasar (*Abu Ma'shar). In turn, Bernard's works, especially the *Cosmographia*, had a wide influence on, among others,

Alain de Lille, Peter Cantor, Eberhart de Béthune, *Vincent of Beauvais, Jean de Meung, Boccaccio, probably Dante, and even C.S. Lewis (*Out of the Silent Planet*).

See also **Cosmology; Microcosm/macrocosm**

Bibliography

Primary Sources

Barach, Carl Sigmund and Johann Wrobel. *Bernardi Silvestris De mundi universitate libri duo sive Megacosmus et Microcosmus, nach handschriftlicher Ueberlieferung zum ersten Male herausgegeben.* (Bibliotheca philosophorum mediae aetatis, 1) Innsbruck: Verlag der Wagner'schen Universitäts-Buchhandlung, 1876; repr. Frankfurt am Main: Minerva, 1964.

Brini Savorelli, Mirella. Un manuale di geomanzia presentato da Bernardo Silvestre de Tours (XII secolo): l'Experimentarius. *Rivista critica di storia della filosofia* (1959) 14: 283–342.

———. Il Dictamen di Bernardo Silvestre. *Rivista critica di storia della filosofia* (1965) 20: 182–230.

Dronke, Peter. *Bernardus Silvestris, Cosmographia, edited with an Introduction and Notes.* Leiden: E.J. Brill, 1978.

Hauréau, Barthélemy. *Le "Mathematicus" de Bernard Silvestris et la "Passio Sanctae Agnetis" de Pierre Riga.* Paris: C. Klincksieck, 1895.

Jones, Julian Ward and Elisabeth Frances Jones. *Commentum quod dicitur Bernardi Silvestris super sex libros Eneidos Virgilii (The Commentary of the First Six Books of the Aeneid of Vergil Commonly Attributed to Bernardus Silvestris).* Lincoln: University of Nebraska Press, 1977.

Westra, Haijo W. *The Commentary on Martianus Capella's De nuptiis Philologiae et Mercurii Attributed to Bernardus Silvestris.* (Pontifical Institute of Mediaeval Studies. Studies and texts, 80). Toronto: Pontifical Institute of Mediaeval Studies, 1986.

Secondary Sources

Burnett, Charles S. F. What is the Experimentarius of Bernardus Silvestris? A Preliminary Survey of the Material. *Archives d'histoire doctrinale et littéraire du Moyen Age* (1977) 44: 79–125.

Gilson, Etienne. La cosmogonie de Bernardus Silvestris. *Archives d'histoire doctrinale et littéraire du Moyen Age* (1928) 3: 5–24.

Jeauneau, Edouard. Berkeley, University of California, Bancroft Library MS. 2 (notes de lecture). *Mediaeval Studies* (1988) 50: 438–456.

Silverstein, Theodore. The Fabulous Cosmogony of Bernardus Silvestris. *Modern Philology* (1948) 46: 92–116.

Stock, Brian. *Myth and Science in the Twelfth Century. A Study of Bernard Silvester.* Princeton: Princeton University Press, 1972.

Tauste Alcocer, Francisco. *Opus naturae. La influencia de la tradición del Timeo en la Cosmographia de Bernardo Silvestre.* Barcelona: Promociones y publicaciones universitarias, 1995.

Thorndike, Lynn. *A History of Magic and Experimental Science.* New York: Columbia University Press, 1923, vol. 2, pp. 99–123 (ch. XXXIX: Bernard Silvester: astrology and geomancy).

Vernet, André. "Bernardus Silvestris et sa Cosmographie." Unpublished dissertation, Ecole nationale des chartes, Positions des thèses, 1937, pp. 167–174.

DOMINIQUE POIREL

BESTIARIES

Bestiaries are books that illustrate and describe selected mammals, birds, reptiles, plants, stones, and other related subjects. During the Middle Ages, they reached their height of popularity in thirteenth- and fourteenth-century England and France. The earliest twelfth-century examples were written in Latin prose, but by the thirteenth century bestiaries were produced all over Western Europe in vernacular languages in both prose and metrical forms. Valued especially for their illustrations, bestiaries contain some of the earliest medieval collections of natural history imagery, based partly on empirical observation but primarily on imaginative invention. They were a highly influential source of animal lore that informed Christian art and literature throughout the later Middle Ages and the Renaissance.

The variable bestiary texts combine excerpts from a wide range of sources. The most important for defining the genre are the Bible, *Isidore of Seville's seventh-century *Etymologies*, and the anonymous *Physiologus* (*The Naturalist*), probably composed during the second century. The *Physiologus* forms the moralizing core of the bestiary, in which evidence of God's plan for humans is found in the appearance and behavior of non-human creatures. For example, the sawfish that races against the boat but ultimately gives up signifies those who follow the path of God but retreat in the face of hardship; the hoopoe chicks that nurture their aging parents by pecking away their eye scales and preening their wings signify those who honor their mother and father. The phoenix rising intact from the flames signifies resurrection, and the dragon repelled by the panther's sweet breath symbolizes the Devil.

Manuscript inscriptions indicate that bestiaries were patronized by monasteries at an early date. It has been hypothesized that bestiaries were an Augustinian invention, although the evidence for this is inconclusive. They clearly had a didactic function, and may have been used in the moral education of the lay brotherhood. There is also some evidence that the *Physiologus* functioned independently as a schoolbook. A few scholars have argued for a natural history or scientific function for bestiaries by claiming that even the imaginary animals, such as the yale and the unicorn, represent real animals. However, such an agenda is not really consonant with the spirit of the bestiarists, and other later medieval thinkers, such as *Albertus Magnus, compiled more empirically-based information for those seeking to learn about actual animal behavior.

Over time, the changing contents of the bestiaries suggest a shift in emphasis from strictly religious to more social and political concerns relevant to lay patrons, including women. This is especially apparent in the later thirteenth-century bestiaries, which contain the most extensive range of texts and images. The most radical reworking of the bestiary was undertaken during the later thirteenth century by Richard of Fournival (c. 1190–1260), whose *Bestiary of Love* recasts the traditional bestiary animals as symbols of courtly love. During the Renaissance, bestiarists adopted a more scientific tone derived from Classical rather than Christian authorities, but still retained much of the imaginative animal lore that characterizes the medieval genre.

See also Encyclopedias; Lapidaries; Natural history; Nature: the structure of the physical world; Religion and science; Zoology

Bibliography

Beer, Jeanette. *Beasts of Love: Richard de Fournival's Bestiaire d'amour and a Woman's Response.* Toronto: University of Toronto Press, 2003.

George, Wilma and Brunsdon Yapp. *The Naming of the Beasts: Natural History in the Medieval Bestiary.* London: Duckworth, 1991.

Hassig, Debra, ed. *The Mark of the Beast: The Medieval Bestiary in Art, Life, and Literature.* New York: Garland, 1999.

Hassig, Debra. *Medieval Bestiaries: Text, Image, Ideology.* New York: Cambridge University Press, 1995.

White, T. H., ed. and trans. *The Book of Beasts: Being a Translation from a Latin Bestiary of the Twelfth Century.* New York: G. P. Putnam's Sons, 1954.

DEBRA HIGGS STRICKLAND

BIRUNI, AL-

The polymath Muhammad ibn Ahmad al-Biruni was born in Kath, Khwarizm (now Kara-Kalpakskaya, Uzbekistan) in 973 and died in Ghazna (now Ghazni, Afghanistan) in 1048. Much of his youth was spent in Jurjan (now Kunya Urgench, Turkmenistan). He studied astronomy and mathematics as a boy. He must have been precocious because when he was seventeen he determined the latitude of Kath by observing the meridian solar altitude with a ring graduated in half-degrees. He was apparently in the service of the shah of Khwarizm, and fled when the emir of Jurjania killed the shah and took his title. Al-Biruni was thus forced into exile, possibly in Rayy, Iran. There the Buwayhid ruler Fakhr al-Dawla had the astronomer al-Khujandi build a mural sextant on a nearby mountain, where al-Khujandi observed meridian transits in 994. Al-Biruni wrote an account of the observations (*Tahdid al-amakin*) and another treatise on the instrument itself, the *Hikayat al-alat al-musammat al-suds al-fakhri* (*Account of the Instrument known as the Fakhri Sextant*).

Around 1000 C.E., al-Biruni appears to have been in Jurjan in the service of the Ziyarid Qabus, to whom he dedicated his *Chronology*. Around this time he polemicized by letter with *Ibn Sina, still an adolescent. Biruni sent Ibn Sina a list of ten questions suggested by Aristotle's *De Caelo*, plus an additional eight, each of which was answered by Ibn Sina. Here Ibn Sina defends orthodox Aristotelian positions questioned by the independent-minded Biruni, who criticizes Aristotle for relying too heavily on authority with regard to the nature of the heavens, and not using his own observations. If heat rises, how does sunlight reach us?

He returned sometime in 1003 or 1004 and entered the service of Abu'l-Hasan Ali. When the Sultan of Ghazna (now in Afghanistan) conquered Khwarizm in 1017, he obliged al-Biruni and other scholars to accompany him to his court. While there he accompanied the sultan on expeditions to India where he learned Sanskrit and made the observations that he embodied in his great *Description of India* (*Kitab fi tahqiq ma li'l-Hind*), completed in 1030.

Al-Biruni in India

In the preface to his India Book, al-Biruni states that his intent is not to write a polemical book, but rather to "place before the reader the theories of the Hindus exactly as they are, and I shall mention in connection with them similar theories of the Greeks in order to show the relationship existing between them." He wishes neither to attack Hindu doctrines nor to defend Islamic ones. Although much of the work can properly be described as ethnographic, he also surveys Indian mathematics and astronomy, the computation of time, and the astronomical regulation of the religious calendar. His discussion of arithmetic shares a chapter with writing and writing materials (he repeats the well-known story of the introduction of *paper in the Islamic world by Chinese prisoners in Samarkand). He notes that while all people whom he has studied understand a place-unit decimal concept, none go beyond the unit one thousand, except the Indians who, for religious reasons, extend the units to the eighteenth order. In another account of the Indian system Biruni explains that "the conventional grouping of numbers, depending on their relative position, used in the operations of *arithmetic... Should any group lack a number, a sign is used to indicate the vacancy. We employ for this purpose a small circle, o, and call it a cipher, sifr, or zero, but the Hindus use a point." He then provides an explanatory chart followed by a brief account of *algebra (*al-jabr wa'l-muqabalah*).

Practical Mathematics

Al-Biruni liked to point out that there were various religious benefits to be gained from observations. For example, once you determine the longitude and latitude of one's town, you can then compute the hours of canonical prayer and the visibility of the new moon, even though the Prophet ordered their determination with the unaided eye.

Like many Muslim astronomers, al-Biruni devoted much effort to devising methods for establishing the beginnings of months, the canonical prayer times, and the qibla, or direction of prayer from any city. *The Exhaustive Treatise on Shadows* is mainly about gnomons and the use of human shadows for determining the times of canonical prayer, how much technical training a muezzin needed to ascertain the prayer times, how to determine prayer time with instruments, particularly the astrolabe, and relatively simple trigonometric surveying that can be accomplished with astrolabes or gnomons. His discussion, in several books, of calendrical problems, is always comparative and highly practical. The beginning of day and night is conventional, but the arrival of the sun at the horizon or a meridian is most convenient. Astronomers prefer the meridian to the horizon, because it is easier to carry out some of their operations. Only astrologers pay attention to the horizon, because the rising and setting of the Sun are so obvious. The People of the Book and Muslims who place night before day regard the setting of sun as the beginning of the civil day.

Al-Biruni was highly critical of astrologers who debase the Sindhind astronomical tables by using them to frighten the ingenuous, thereby exciting "suspicions against—and bring[ing] discredit upon—astronomers and mathematicians, by counting themselves among their ranks." (*Chronology*, 31) When he wrote about astrology at the behest of a royal patron he was careful to distinguish between what he reported of astrological lore and what he himself believed.

Chess

In The India Book, al-Biruni includes in his chapter on mathematics an account of chess as played by four persons using dice. The culture of chess included at least one much-discussed mathematical component, a geometrical progression puzzle known as the "doubling of squares": if you put a coin on one square and double it until all sixty-four squares are filled, how many coins are there? (The answer is $2^{64} - 1$.) This is originally an Indian calculation that Muslim scientists took up enthusiastically. Al-Biruni mentions it both in his *Chronology* and in *The Exhaustive Treatise on Shadows*, wherein he describes an experiment involving directing a beam of light through an aperture with angles casting a shadow of a polygon "having sides whose number is the double of the angles of the hole. Then the polygon also undergoes what happened to the hole. And in this manner the number of the angles continues to increase by doubling, like the doubling at chess, by the property of the double of the double" (*Shadows*, p. 51).

Observation and Instrumentation

A general technical problem with celestial determination of latitude (*Tahdid*, 51) is the discrepancy between the huge extension of celestial spheres and minute gradations of human instrumentation. For this reason, such observations can only yield approximations. Therefore he liked to use big instruments. He recounts (*Tahdid*, 50) observing the meridian altitude in Jurjaniya (407 H) with "a quadrant of a circle of diameter six cubits, whose circumference was graduated in minutes." He describes *al-Battani's observations at Raqqa with a mural quadrant equipped with an alidade and mentions observations made at Balkh, by al-Samarqandi, with a mural quadrant eight cubits in diameter, also with an alidade (*Tahdid*, 65). In his treatise on the astrolabe—*Kitab fi isti'ab al-wujuh al-mumkina fi sana't al-asturlab* (*Book on the Full Comprehensiveness of the Possible Methods for Constructing the Astrolabe*, unpublished)—he describes a mechanical calendar in the form of an assembly of eight geared wheels mounted on a disk or on the back of an astrolabe.

Al-Biruni had access to the geography of *Ptolemy and others and "corrected the distances given as well as the names of the places and countries from what I had heard from the mouth of these who had traveled these roads and gathered from those who had been there.... I made for this purpose half a globe, the diameter of which was ten yards, traced upon it the longitudes and latitudes from the route-indications when time was lacking to work out the mathematical account of them because of their multitude and length."

Materia Medica

Al-Biruni's native language was Balukhi, but he enthusiastically adopted Arabic as the international language of science and culture. There is a problem with the scientific use of Arabic, however, and that is that many words are similar, differentiated from each other only by diacritical marks and inflections. If scribes are negligent, texts depending on terminological accuracy, such as pharmacology, are seriously compromised. In *materia medica*, therefore, it is important to provide the names of plants in various languages and in different Arabic dialects, so that simples mentioned by *Galen and *Dioscorides can be identified locally. These medications he listed in rigorous alphabetical with attention to diacriticals and second letters, to facilitate the location of entries. After the principal name in Arabic, he supplies Arabic variants, then Persian, Greek, Syriac and other foreign equivalents.

When he was eighty, Al-Biruni's sight and hearing had weakened to the point where he hired a secretary (Abu Hamid Nahasha'i) to assist him. One of Abu Hamid's duties was to bring plants to him "so that I may closely examine them and describe their properties." Al-Biruni's emphasis on observation, that is, was not limited to the realm of astronomy.

Scientific Method and Theory of Errors

Many authors have observed al-Biruni's prescience. With regard to scientific method, al-Biruni was concerned with how to conceptualize and therefore prevent both systematic observations and random errors. Small errors that result from the application of trigonometric tables become particularly appreciable when "added to errors caused by the use of small instruments and errors made by human observers" (Sheynin, 301). We have seen with regard to instrumental accuracy his predilection for large observational instruments, and the larger the better. In his book on the distances between cities he discusses a variety of errors due to methods of observation and even errors due to the nature of the astronomical model employed. Such errors are systemic, but he also understood the inevitability of random errors, both in astronomical observation and in other areas such as the measurement of time (clepsydras for example and subject to random errors owing to the qualities of the water used to run them). If instruments, because of their imperfections or idiosyncratic qualities, produce random errors, then multiple observations had to be taken, analyzed qualitatively, and on this basis arrive at a "common-sense single value for the constant sought" (Sheynin, 304) whether an arithmetical mean or a "reliable estimate."

Biruni and the West

Establishing the qibla by using astronomical tables was one method explained by Biruni in the *Tahdid* and may have been the source of a passage in the trigonometry treatise of Mu'adh of Jaén (d. 1093). Al-Biruni had devised the "prime vertical" method for demarcating the houses of the horoscope, which divides the ecliptic into six great circles traversing the horizon from north to south, thirty degrees apart. The method reached al-Andalus in the lifetime of Biruni, because *Ibn al-Samh (d. 1035) used it (and through him it appears in the Alfonsine *Libro de la açafeha*). Biruni said the longitudes of the houses were difficult to ascertain by calculatation but easy to determine with an astrolabe, for which purpose he signed a special astrolabe plate. An alternative method, the equatorial projection of an astrolabe, was also discussed by al-Biruni, whose treatise on the astrolabe (*Kitab al-isti'ab*) appears to be the ultimate source of two treatises commissioned by *Alfonso X the Wise, the *Libro de las Armellas* and the *Libro del Ataçyr* (Arabic, *taysir*, the twelve-fold division of the heavens).

See also Astrolabes and quadrants; Astrology; Astronomy, Islamic; Astronomy, Latin; Battani, al-; Clepsydra; Ibn al-Samh; Pharmacology

Bibliography

Primary Sources
al-Athar al-Baqiyah. *The Chronology of Ancient Nations.* Translated and edited by C. Edward Sachau. London, 1879. Reprint ed. Frankfurt: Minerva GMBH, 1969.
Kitab fi ifrad al-maqal fi amr al-zilal. The Exhaustive Treatise on Shadows. Edited and Translated by E.S. Kennedy. 2 vols. Aleppo: Institute for the History of Arabic Science, 1976.
Kitab al-Tafhim li-'Awa'il Sina'at al-Tanjim. The Book of Instruction in the Elements of the Art of Astrology. Translated by R. Ramsay Wright. London: Luzac, 1934.
Kitab Tahdid al-Amakin. The Determination of Coordinates of Positions for the Correction of Distances Between Cities. Translated by Jamil Ali. Beirut: American University, 1967.
Kitab fi Tahqiq ma li'l-Hind. Alberuni's India. Edited by Edward C. Sachau. 2 vols. London: Kegan Paul, 1910.
al-Saydanah. *Al-Biruni's Book on Pharmacy and Materia Medica.* Edited with English Translation by Hakim Mohammed Said. Karachi. Hamdard National Foundation, 1973.
Al-Biruni and Ibn Sina. *Al-As'ilah wa'l-ajwibah (Questions and Answers).* Teheran, 1975. Edited by Seyyid Hossein Nasr and Mahdi Mohaghegh.
Richter-Bernburg, Lutz. *Al-Biruni's Maqala fi tastih al-suwar wa-tabtikh al-kuwar. A Translation of the Preface with Notes and Commentary. Journal of the History of Arabic Science* (1982) 6: 113–122.

Secondary Sources
Berggren, J. L. Al-Biruni on Plane Maps of the Sphere. *Journal of the History of Arabic Science* (1982) 6: 47–112.
Hill, Donald R. Al-Biruni's Mechanical Calendar. *Annals of Science* (1985) 42: 139–163.
Krenkow, F. "Beruni and the MS Sultan Fatich No. 3386." In *Al-Biruni Commemoration Volume, A.H. 362-A.H. 1362.* Calcutta: Iran Society,1951: 195–208.
Rosenfeld, B.A. and L.G. Utseha. Some Mathematical Discoveries on al-Biruni's *Shadows. Journal of the History of Arabic Science* (1980) 4: 332–336.
Saliba, George. *A History of Arabic Astronomy.* New York: New York University Press, 1994.
Samsó, Julio. "Al-Biruni in al-Andalus." In *From Baghdad de Barcelona: Studies in the Islamic Exact Sciences in Honour of Prof. Juan Vernet.* Vol. II. Barcelona: Instituto Millás Vallicrosa, 1996, pp. 583–612.
Sheynin, Oscar. Al-Biruni and the Mathematical Treatment of Observations. *Arabic Sciences and Philosophy* (1992): 299–306.

THOMAS F. GLICK

BOETHIUS

Anicius Manlius Severinus Boethius (c. 480–524 C.E.), the last of the ancient philosophers in the West, transmitted to the Middle Ages the elementary portion of the ancient philosophical curriculum as it existed in his time. In the course of the fifth century knowledge of Greek had virtually disappeared in the West, and the first task in Boethius's work of preservation was the translation of the Greek curriculum to Latin. He wrote Latin compilations from the Greek texts of Nicomachus of Gerasa and *Euclid, on *arithmetic, geometry, and music (treated as a mathematical discipline related to astronomy), and translated Aristotle's logical works, with Porphyry's *Isagoge* (*Introduction*), and planned, but never executed, translations of the rest of Aristotle and *Plato. He also wrote Latin commentaries, largely compilations in the Neoplatonic tradition, on the elementary logical treatises of Aristotle and Porphyry, and more advanced works on syllogism, both categorical and hypothetical, on division, on topical differences, and on Cicero's *Topics*. In addition, he wrote, in defense of orthodoxy, a number of theological tracts which received considerable attention with the revival of letters in the eleventh and twelfth centuries—*On the Trinity, Against Eutyches and Nestorius, On the Person and Two Natures of Christ, How Substances are Goods in Virtue of their Existence without being Substantial Goods* (*On the Hebdomads*), and *Whether Father, Son and Holy Spirit are Substantially Predicated of the Divinity.* Another treatise, *On the Catholic Faith,* was written as a handbook, perhaps as a catechetical exercise under his teacher, John the Deacon, and lacks the dialectical depth of the other works. Finally, while awaiting execution in prison, Boethius wrote the *Consolation of Philosophy,* one of the most popular works of the Middle Ages, translated into Anglo-Saxon by King Alfred the Great (c. 890), into German by Notker (c. 1000), into French by Jean de Meung (c. 1300), and

Illustration from fifteenth-century French manuscript of *Consolation of Philosophy* showing Boethius talking with the visionary figure of Philosophy. (Mary Evans Picture Library)

echoed in *Chaucer, Dante, Boccaccio, and the popular poetry of Normandy and Provence. Boethius's works formed the bulk of the classical curriculum revived in the course of the ninth through the twelfth centuries, and the initial focus on his work contributed to Western philosophy's interest in dialectic and language, commentary, and the philosophical explication and defense of Christian doctrine. Together with St. Augustine, he provided the initial Platonic formation of Western thought, and, in his *Consolation of Philosophy*, an acceptable example of serious philosophical reflection carried on independently, but in support of revelation.

Boethius belonged to one of the richest and most powerful senatorial families in Italy. He was born sometime shortly after 476, when the last Roman Emperor, a puppet ruler, had been forced into retirement by his Ostrogothic general, Ordovocar. Hence Italy was under the rule of Theodoric, a barbarian king, but a barbarian educated in Constantinople and bent on preserving the old Roman order for the good of his own people. Theodoric was treated by the Italians as de facto emperor. If he was not officially recognized as such by Byzantium,

he willingly played the role, and the emperor did recognize him as king and had granted him the exercise of some of the powers of the emperor, such as the nomination of consuls. Though an Arian like all his people, he tolerated the Roman Orthodoxy, and endeavored to rule the country together with the Roman upper classes. His was a precarious position that strained his abilities to the utmost, and doomed his successors. On the one hand, he feared, entirely reasonably, the intentions of the Eastern emperor, whose refusal to recognize him as his Western colleague suggested a hope eventually to bring about his downfall, replacing him with an Orthodox, Roman ruler. So he was nervous about the loyalty of his Roman subjects, particularly after 519, when the long schism within the Orthodox Church was put to an end, with Justinian taking considerable heat from his own Monophysites for his concessions to Rome. Theodoric correctly saw this as a calculated move with a view to intervention in the West with the support of the Roman Church, which had hitherto favored an heretical, but tolerant, barbarian ruler over union with an intolerant, heretical Eastern Church. On the other hand, Theodoric had to maintain his status with his own people. It would have been impossible to convert to Orthodoxy, and before the Goths he had to be the war leader on horseback, not the cultured administrator. He was in danger of overthrow by one of his own people, someone not educated among Romans, not in league with the hated Roman aristocracy. It is not surprising that he eventually gave way to paranoia, striking out at enemies that he knew were there, even if he was uncertain who they might be.

While Boethius was still young, his father died, and the orphan was adopted by an even more powerful family, moving in with Q. Memmius Symmachus, whom the boy came to admire and imitate, and whose daughter Rusticiana he married. Symmachus was a scholar, the author of a Roman history and several treatises on rhetoric. He perceived talent in the boy, and lavished attention on his education. We do not know if Boethius attended the Neoplatonic schools at Athens or Alexandria, but he did somehow gain a mastery of Greek, and was steeped in the latest Neoplatonic lore from the East. As a very young man, it seems, he produced his works on arithmetic and music, and a lost work on geometry, and gained a reputation as a philosopher. In 507 he was entrusted with several diplomatic missions abroad by Theodoric. In 522 Theodoric made Boethius his "Master of Offices," the highest post available in his administration. He also nominated Boethius's two young sons as consuls, no doubt because he knew the nomination would be received favorably as part of Justinian's conciliatory policies toward the Pope, given Boethius's theological opuscula in defense of Rome's position. For the moment, relations with Byzantium were good, and Boethius could expect to prosper as long as they stayed that way.

But they did not. Theodoric found evidence that the distinguished and devout senator Albinus was engaged in treasonable correspondence with people close to the emperor. Boethius, who had made influential enemies in his new office, even among Romans, by his attacks on official corruption, and was suspected by some of sorcery because of his learning, unwisely objected to Albinus's condemnation without a trial, and declared that if he was guilty, the whole Senate was. Theodoric, a suspicious old man encircled by enemies whose dynastic arrangements were falling apart, took this in the worst possible way, and, encouraged, Boethius says, by forged letters produced by his senatorial enemies, he imprisoned Boethius. The *Consolation of Philosophy* was written while awaiting execution. The work must have been smuggled out of prison, for it is anything but ingratiating toward Theodoric. By 526 he had been executed, along with his father-in-law Symmachus and Pope John II, probably John the Deacon, whom Boethius had recommended for the office.

Boethius left behind meticulous translations of Aristotle's *Categories*, *On Interpretation*, *Prior and Posterior Analytics*, *Topics* and *Sophistical Refutations*, as well as short commentaries on the first two works, and a full-length commentary on *On Interpretation*. He had begun by writing a commentary on Victorinus's translation of Porphyry's *Introduction* to the *Categories*, and, becoming frustrated with the translation, he wrote his own, with a second, longer commentary. Of these works, the translations and commentaries on the *Categories* (drawing on the lost commentary of Iamblichus), on Porphyry, and on *On Interpretation* form the foundation for the resurrection of logical studies in Europe in the eleventh and twelfth centuries, the *logica vetus*. The remainder of his translations of Aristotle's *Logic* began to circulate only around 1120, and contributed to the Western resurrection of Aristotle in the twelfth century and the *Logica*. Most notable here is Boethius's discussion of universals in his second commentary on Porphyry, in which he lays out the arguments for and against the existence of real universals, and provides an Aristotelian resolution of the problem, avoiding postulation of the Forms, drawn from Alexander of Aphrodisias. The discussion inaugurated the famous dispute in the Middle Ages, and the initial stages of that dispute consist of commentaries on it, most notably that by *Peter Abelard.

Boethius also produced a number of more advanced logical treatises. *On Division* concerns the Platonic method for arriving at real definitions. *On Categorical Syllogism* covers the Aristotelian syllogistic of the *Prior Analytics*. *On Hypothetical Syllogism* concerns the Stoic sentential logic and its reconciliation with Aristotle's syllogistic, and is the most informative work on this topic we have from the Ancient world. *On Cicero's Topics* concerns Cicero's work on the discovery of arguments, utilizing a classification of argument types based, like that in Aristotle's *Topics*, on the "predicables" discussed in Porphyry's *Introduction*, that is, genus, species, definition, difference, property, and accident. A topic is primarily a strategy of argumentation, but it is also viewed as a principle on which the arguments derived from it are based. *On Topical Differences* is a more advanced work on this subject, which attempts to reconcile the topical schemes of Cicero and Themistius. The chief interest in these works is dialectic, but rhetorical topics are also treated. Boethius did not live to treat of the *Posterior Analytics* and the logic of Aristotelian science.

The theological works apply the logical scheme of Porphyry's predicables to the problems of Christ's dual nature and his place as a single person in the Trinity. This had already been done by Cyril of Alexandria, but much work remained, and Greek writers seemed to have welcomed Boethius's contributions after Justinian's shift away from Monophysitism. Boethius insisted that Christ was always of two natures. The Monophysites held that Christ was of one nature after the union of man and God, even though two natures were involved in that union, the human nature being transformed into the divine. Boethius balances the Monophysite doctrine against the Nestorian in *Against Eutyches*, holding that Nestorius posited two natures, but failed to combine them in one individual person. In both cases the salvation of man is made impossible, for the one person, Christ, must be wholly man if he is rightly to pay man's debt, and wholly God if his suffering is to be effective payment. The theological works, in particular *Against Eutyches*, set the stage for the discussion of salvation and incarnation in medieval Europe, and were enormously influential, for instance, on the speculations on these topics in Anselm's works.

Another of Boethius's theological works, *How Substances Are Goods in Virtue of Their Existence*, argues for a Neoplatonic approach to the problem of evil, asserting that evil is always an absence of a good, and so nothing, every actual being being a good. The Neoplatonic strain in early Christian speculation, from *John Scottus Eriugena to Anselm and the twelfth-century Platonists, is rooted as much in Boethius as Augustine, and it is Boethius more than Augustine who set the high standards of argumentative cogency that we find Anselm and Abelard responding to, and which is one of the glories of Scholastic thought.

But Boethius was respected also for his poetry, and it was the *Consolation of Philosophy* that drew the early Middle Ages into his dialectical works. The work begins with the arrival of a metaphorical Philosophia in Boethius's prison cell, where she puts the Muses, who are trying to comfort him, to flight, and takes over the job herself. She points out first that Fortune cannot be expected to be constant, so that it is irrational to expect a permanent good from Fortune. She then points out that the goods of Fortune are of little value, in fact, and that we mistake them for the true goods found in true happiness, so that money is mistaken for security, high office for respect, and so on. Then Philosophy points out that all these true goods are but aspects of a single highest good which is rationally sought because it cannot be lost, as the goods of Fortune can. (Here Boethius is following the same thoughts as Augustine in the *Confessions* and *On Free Choice of the Will*). Finally, returning to Boethius's initial complaints, she points out that the simple fact of being evil is sufficient punishment for the evil, since it rules out happiness by dividing the soul against itself. Only that good which cannot be lost and brings unity to the soul is rationally sought—only God. Then Boethius launches an intricate discussion, in the last book, of the problem of how God's foreknowledge of human actions can be compatible with human free will. He argues that God's eternity, "unending life, entirely, perfectly and all at once" (a notion drawn from Plotinus), means that He knows the future in the way that we know the present. Of course, one can know that someone is now doing something without it being the case that they are in any way necessitated to do it by causes in place beforehand, even if a human being, being temporal instead of eternal, cannot know a future event that is not necessitated by its causes in the present.

Even in the twelfth century it was noted by some that Boethius does not seem to be a Christian in his *Consolation*, instead proposing a distinctly Platonic view of the world, even to the point of a doctrine of reincarnation in the very center of the book, the ninth poem in Book III, which presents a Platonic cosmogony after the *Timaeus*. Probably the fact that the form of the work is Menippean Satire, alternating poetry and prose, is significant here, for that form was generally reserved for satirical treatments of intellectually pretentious themes.

Boethius seems to hint that he is showing us the best that Philosophy can do to console us, which, though it is better than the Muse of Poetry can do, is nonetheless inadequate. Philosophy thinks rather more of herself than she should. As is hinted by Boethius's increasing hesitations by the end of Book IV, one must actually *find* Plato's God to attain the end, and Philosophy, though she can reassure us about God's existence and providence, cannot bring us to Him, and even makes mistakes about Him. God is reconciled with the sinner only within the Christian revelation. What Philosophy can do is revealed in Book V, when Boethius politely turns her aside from her own course to the task—she can resolve intellectual difficulties within the Christian faith. The *Consolation* seems to authorize a certain independence in philosophical investigation, and to suggest that Philosophy, done well, will not go far wrong. Boethius took Christians a long way toward the independent investigation of philosophy and science under the supervision of theology that became a hallmark of medieval European culture. His work was largely responsible for the development of the European educational system, with its independent study of the Liberal Arts, which formed the institutional basis for the scientific and scholarly revolutions of the sixteenth and seventeenth centuries.

See also **Aristotelianism; Astronomy, Islamic; Astronomy, Latin; God in Christianity; Quadrivium**

Bibliography

Primary Sources

Translations of Aristotle. Edited by L. Minio-Paluello and B. Dod, in *Aristoteles Latinus*, vols I–VI. Bruges: De Brouwer, 1966–1975.

In Isagogen Porphyrii commenta. Edited by S. Brandt. *Corpus Scriptorum Ecclesiasticorum Latinorum* 48. Vienna: Tempsky, 1906.

Commentaries on *Categories*. *De Divisione. De syllogismo categorico. De topicis differentiis*. In J.P. Migne, ed., *Patrologia Latina* 64, Paris, 1860.

Anicii Manlii Severini Boetii in librum Aristotelis Peri hermeneias. Edited by R. Meiser. 2 volumes. Leipzig: Teubner, 1877–1880.

In Ciceronis Topica. In J.C. Orelli and J.G Baiter (eds.), *Ciceronis Opera* Vol. V, Part I, Zurich: Fuesslini, 1833.

De hypotheticis syllogismis. Ed. L. Obertello. Brescia: Paideia, 1969.

De institutione arithmetica libri duo, De institutione musida libri quinque. Ed. G. Friedlein. Leipzig: Teubner, 1867.

Theological Tractates, Consolation of Philosophy. Translated, with Latin on facing pages, by H.F. Stewart, E.K. Rand and S.J. Tester. *Boethius: Theological Tractates, Consolation of Philosophy*. Cambridge: Harvard University Press, 1988.

On Topical Differences. Translated E. Stump, *Boethius's De topicis differentiis*, Ithaca, New York: Cornell University Press, 1978.

On Division. Translated E. Stump and N. Kretzmann, in *The Cambridge Translation of Medieval Philosophical Texts* I, Cambridge: Cambridge University Press, 1988.

On Cicero's Topics. Translated E. Stump, *Boethius's In Ciceronis Topica*, Ithaca, New York: Cornell University Press, 1988.

Secondary Sources

Chadwick, H. *Boethius, The Consolations of Music, Logic, Theology and Philosophy*. Oxford: Clarendon Press, 1981.

Gibson, M.T., ed. *Boethius, His Life, Thought and Influence*. Oxford: Blackwell, 1981.

Sorabji, R., ed. *Aristotle Transformed*. London: Duckworth, 1990.

Stump, E. and N. Kretzmann. "Eternity." *The Journal of Philosophy* (1981) 78: 429–458.

JOHN LONGEWAY

BOETHIUS OF DACIA

Little is known about the life and academic career of Boethius of Dacia. He originated from Denmark, and was active as a master of arts at the University of Paris during the 1270s. It is possible that he became a Dominican at a later stage in his life. He is best known for his involvement in the *Condemnation of 1277, issued by Etienne Tempier, Bishop of Paris. A number of the two hundred nineteen theses that were prohibited were taken from his works and those by *Siger of Brabant. In particular Tempier's proposition that philosophy is the most excellent kind of life may have been derived from Boethius' *De summo bono* (*On the Supreme Good*). In this small treatise, Boethius argues that happiness in this life is possible for human beings, and that it is available through the exercise of reason. In line with Aristotle, Boethius distinguishes practical reason, i.e., to know what to do in a certain situation, from the theoretical or speculative reason, i.e., to know what is true. The supreme good that is available to us consists, according to Boethius, in knowing what is true and doing what is good, and taking delight in both. The treatise is inspired by Aristotle's *Nicomachean Ethics*, especially Book X, which addresses the nature of human happiness and indicates that the pursuit of philosophy is the ideal method to achieve it. Although *On the Supreme Good* seems to deal with ethics, the work is relevant for the history of science as well, not because it is some kind of rationalist manifesto, as some interpreters have believed, but because it grapples with the question of how the domains of (natural) philosophy and faith can be kept apart. Boethius' treatise argues from the principles of philosophy, without relying on the truths of faith. The happiness that one expects in the life to come, and that, according to Christian faith, constitutes perfect happiness, falls beyond the domain of rational inquiry. This is not to say that Boethius denies the truths of faith, but that he does not take them into consideration when he is doing philosophy.

The same perspective is also present in another treatise by Boethius, *De aeternitate mundi* (*On the Eternity of the World*), which addresses a topic that is more directly relevant to the history of science, namely the eternity of the universe. On the basis of principles such as "nothing comes from nothing" (*ex nihilo nihil fit*) and "something is not caused by nothing," Aristotle, in Book Eight of his *Physics*, had argued that the universe did not have a beginning, but had always existed. This view had been identified in 1270s as one of the main Aristotelian errors, and had one of the things been prohibited by Tempier in his 1277 strictures.

In this treatise, Boethius of Dacia takes a stance similar to the one taken in *On the Supreme Good*. He does not deny the truth of faith, set down in Genesis, that the world was created, but he explores, as a natural philosopher, Aristotle's position and arguments. Arguing on this basis, Boethius concluded that Aristotle's proofs for the universe's beginninglessness were convincing. In Boethius' view, the account in Genesis about the creation of the universe out of nothing could be understood as an event that occurred outside the normal cause of nature, as a supernatural event. A natural philosopher reasoning as a natural philosopher has nothing to say about creation, because it supersedes the priniciples of his science. At the same time, Boethius confirmed that it is true according to Christian faith that the world was created. He made the important methodological point that the conclusions in a science are relative to the principles from which they are argued. On the basis of this same methodology, Boethius could claim at the end of his treatise that the natural philosopher and the Christian were not contradicting each other.

Boethius' methodology of thus distinguishing various disciplines from each other and from faith was attacked by Tempier, who believed that one should never contradict faith, even when doing natural philosophy. He accused unnamed philosopers of holding that certain things were true according to philosophy but not according to faith "as if there were two contrary truths." This reference to a so-called theory of double truth has been taken to imply Boethius. There is generally agreement, however, that his point was much more subtle.

Boethius also wrote on logic and grammar. His *Quaestiones super libros Physicorum* (*Questions on Aristotle's Physics*) and on Aristotle's *Quaestiones de generatione et corruptione* (*On Generation and Corruption*) are little studied yet.

See also **Aristotelianism; Nature: diverse medieval interpretations; Religion and science; Universities**

Bibliography

Primary Sources

Boethius of Dacia. *Opera*. Edited by Jan Pinborg, Heinrich Roos, Niels J. Green-Pedersen, Sten Ebbese, Irène Rosier. Corpus Philosophorum Danicorum Medii Aevi, vols. IV–XI. Copenhagen: DSL-Gad, 1969–.

Boethius of Dacia, *On the Supreme Good. On the Eternity of the World. On Dreams*. Translated by J.F. Wippel. Toronto: Pontifical Institute of Mediaeval Studies, 1987.

Secondary Source

Wippel, John F. *Mediaeval Reactions to the Encounter Between Faith and Reason*. Milwaukee: Marquette University Press, 1995.

JOHANNES M.M.H. THIJSSEN

BORGOGNONI, TEODORICO

Also known as Teodorico dei Borgognoni, Teodorico of Lucca, and Teodorico of Cervia, Teodorico Borgognoni was born in Lucca (Tuscany) in 1205. He was the last of the five children of the Luccan surgeon Ugo Borgognoni (d. c. 1259). Teodorico moved to Bologna in 1214 when his father was hired as town physician, possibly at the instigation of count Rodolfo Borgognoni, the city's mayor and a possible relative. He entered the Dominican Order at an early age (c. 1230–1231), probably in the monastery at Bologna. Under the pontificate of Innocent IV (1243–1254) he became a *penitentiarius minor* (confessor) in the Apostolic Penitentiary, a body devoted to the absolution of those sins and censures reserved to the pope. In 1262 Urban IV named him bishop of Bitonto (Puglia). He apparently never resided in his diocese, since documents indicate his presence during that period in Lucca, where he owned a house (1262), and where Clement IV sent him letters urging him to persuade the Luccans to participate in the war against Manfred of Sicily (1265). In 1266 Clement IV transferred him to the diocese of Cervia (Romagna), where he was confirmed *sede vacante* in 1270. However, he resided in the nearby university city of Bologna, where he owned considerable real estate. In 1290 Nicholas IV increased his episcopal income, granting him the rights to the saltworks of Cervia. Borgognoni dictated his last will and testament on October 17, 1298, and died in Bologna at the age of ninety-three on December 24 of that same year.

Teodorico is a good example, still frequent at the time (*Albertus Magnus, *Petrus Hispanus), of the interest in natural philosophy and medicine among the cultivated high clergy. Like some of his siblings, Teodorico learned the art of surgery from his father, an art he exercised with notable success both inside and outside the monastery. Shortly after 1243, while he was still a member of the Apostolic Penitentiary, he composed a short treatise in Latin on the treatment of wounds. In the Roman Curia, Teodorico became the chaplain of the Catalan Dominican, Andreu d'Albalat, who shared his interest in natural philosophy and medicine. After he was named bishop of Valencia (1248), Albalat asked Teodorico for the more extensive version of the treatise that Teodorico had promised to send him. However, dissatisfied with the results, it took Teodorico nearly twenty years to produce the greatly amplified version that incorporated the latest knowledge and his readings of both surgical writings and works in such other fields as alchemy. Although the treatise would later undergo slight modifications, the version (*Cyrurgia seu Filia principis*) that he sent to Valencia while he was bishop of Bitonto (1262–1266), with a dedication to Albalat, is considered canonical. This text comprises a prologue (including the aforementioned dedication and the definition of surgery) and four books that discuss: (1) General surgery and diet; (2) Wounds inflicted to different body parts, fractures, and dislocations; (3) Fistulas, abscesses, hernias, and other pathologies that require surgery; and (4) the preparation of medicines used in surgery, along with observations on

certain diseases. Many Latin manuscripts of the *Chirurgia* have been preserved, thus permitting us to reconstruct the various redactions the work underwent. The treatise continued to be consulted until the first years of the printing press (surgical collections were printed in Venice, 1497; Bergamo, 1498; Venice 1499, 1513, 1519, and 1546).

As proof of the interest in Teodorico's treatise outside academic circles, it was soon translated from Latin into the vernacular languages of Western Europe (two Catalan versions as well as Castilian, French, Italian, English, and German versions), and into Hebrew (probably based on the second Catalan translation). The first Catalan translation is of exceptional interest. It was made c. 1302–1304 by the Mallorcan surgeon Guillem Corretger, and was widely disseminated in the Crown of Aragon in the fourteenth and fifteenth centuries, especially among barbers and surgeons. Historians of the Dominican Order rediscovered this translation at the beginning of the eighteenth century, and, ignorant of the author's true identity, attributed it to one "Teodoricus Catalanus," an error that was then widely repeated.

Teodorico's is one of the most prominent treatises of the so-called "new surgery" that arose in northern Italian medical schools in the second half of the thirteenth century. This "new surgery" was characterized by the contextualization of surgical technique within scholastic medicine founded on Galenism, according to Islamic patterns. Teodorico's reading of the *Chirurgia magna* of Bruno da Longobucco (1252–1253), the first text belonging to the "new surgery," was crucial for his intellectual development and was incorporated almost word for word into the expanded versions of his own treatise. This procedure, so typical of medieval authors, clashed with the evolution of compositional techniques—hence *Guy de Chauliac's criticism of Teodorico's borrowings (1363)—and with the ignorance of the *ordinatio partium* shown by many historians. Teodorico's text had a considerable advantage over Bruno's, for it met the social demand, much stronger in his time, of those without academic training who sought in such manuals an instrument of social and professional advancement. Additionally, vernacular translations of Teodorico's treatise enhanced its usefulness.

Teodorico contrasts information received from Bruno and the ancient and Muslim authors (*Galen, *Ibn Sina, *al-Majusi, *al-Zahrawi, etc.) with Ugo's teachings and his own personal experience. Among his contributions we can underscore his defense of the use of wine as a disinfectant, the complete suturing and dry dressing of wounds, in which he follows Ugo, as opposed to the Galenic approach, championed by the Salernitan School and later by Chauliac, which sought to promote suppuration (*pus bonum et laudabile*). Teodorico is also notable for prescribing for convalescents an abundant diet, especially rich in foods productive of blood (meat and wine), once again in accordance with Ugo and in contrast to the traditional advocacy of frugality in the nourishment of the wounded. Teodorico also recommended the use of an ancient method of narcosis (*spongia* *somnifera*) to lessen the patient's pain and the suture of intestinal wounds. Teodorico taught surgery in Bologna. The Frenchman *Henri de Mondeville (d. c. 1320), the author of an important *Chirurgia*, was one of his pupils as well as the most famous of his followers.

Teodorico was also the author of a *Mulomedicina* (also known as *Practica equorum* or *De medela equorum*), a veterinary treatise in Latin dedicated to Pope Honorius IV (1285–1287). Divided into three books (generalities, pathology, antidotary), the treatise is based on the works of Vegetius, Giordano Ruffo, and Albertus Magnus. It is notable for its inscription of veterinary practice into the context of Galenism. It is preserved at least in nine manuscripts (but never printed), and was translated into Occitan, Catalan (lost), and Castilian. It served as the source of the Castilian *Libro de los caballos*, written at the court of Alfonso XI of Castile (1325-1350), one of the most important veterinary treatises in the medieval West. On the other hand, the traditional attribution to Teodorico of a treatise on falconry (*De cura accipitrum*) appears to be erroneous. Some manuscripts copy at least two alchemical treatises (*De sublimatione arsenici* and *De aluminibus et salibus*) attributed to Teodorico. These yet to be studied texts would help to explain Teodorico's intellectual evolution—manifest in his surgical treatise— towards an acceptance of medical-surgical possibilities in alchemy. Lastly, some of Teodorico's sermons have been preserved.

See also **Medicine, theoretical; Nature: diverse medieval interpretations**

Bibliography

Campbell, Eldridge C. and James B. Colton. *The Surgery of Theodoric, ca. A.D. 1267*. 2 vols. New York: Appleton-Century-Crofts, 1955 and 1960.

Cifuentes, Lluís. "Vernacularization as an Intellectual and Social Bridge: the Catalan translations of Teodorico's Chirurgia and of Arnau de Vilanova's Regimen sanitatis." *Early Science and Medicine* (1999) 4: 127–148.

Fernández de Viana y Vietes, José Ignacio, Luis García Ballester and Asencio Gallego Gómez. "Una traducción castellana del siglo XVI de la Cyrurgia del dominico Teodorico Borgognoni." *Arquivo Histórico Dominicano Português* (1986) 3: 111–118.

Keil, Gundolf. "Thiederik von Cervia (Tederico dei Borgognoni) OP." In *Die deutsche Literatur des Mittelalters. Verfasserlexikon*. 10 vols. New York: Walter de Gruyter, 1977–1999, 9: 792–793.

McVaugh, Michael. "Alchemy in the Chirurgia of Teodorico Borgognoni." In *Alchimia e medicina nel Medioevo*. Edited by Chiara Crisciani and Agostino Paravicini Bagliani. Florence: SISMEL-Ed. del Galluzzo (Micrologus Library, IX), 2003, 55–76.

Poulle-Drieux, Yvonne. *L'hippiatrie dans l'Occident latin du XIIIe au XVe siècle*. In Guy Beaujouan, Yvonne Poulle-Drieux and Jeanne-Marie Dureau-Lapeyssonnie. *Médecine humaine et vétérinaire à la fin du Moyen Age*. Geneva-Paris: Droz-Minard, 1966, 9–168, in 22–24.

Tabanelli, Mario. *La chirurgia italiana nell'Alto Medioevo*. 2 vols. Florence: Leo S. Olschki, 1965, 1 (Ruggero-Rolando-Teodorico): 198–495.

Thomas, Antoine. "Traduction provençale abrégée de la Mulomedicina de Teodorico Borgognoni, suivie de recettes pour le vin." *Romania* (1911) 40: 353–370.

LLUÍS CIFUENTES

BOTANY

Plant knowledge in the Middle Ages was deeply rooted in the legacy of classical antiquity and was mainly of a practical nature, particularly the uses of plants as medicines. Theoretical botany was not totally absent, however, even though works in the field had a complex destiny. *De plantis* by Aristotle (384–322 B.C.E.), which dealt with the genesis and growth of plants, their parts, properties and qualities, and their classification, has been soon lost and was known only in the commented version by Nicholas of Damascus (first century B.C.E./C.E.). This work, in turn, was translated several times during the Middle Ages from one language into another successively: from Greek into Syriac (sixth century [?]), Arabic (late ninth century), and Latin (c. 1200). In Byzantium, it was lost and was not recovered until the fourteenth century, when its Latin version was translated into Greek by the Calabrese bilingual monk Barlaam of Seminari (c. 1290–1348). The *Enquiry on plants* and *Causes of plants* by Theophrastus (372/370–288/286 B.C.E.), respectively dealing with the parts of plants and their classification on this basis, and plant physiology and reproduction, did not circulate widely, either in the East (Byzantium and the Arabic World) or in the West.

In Byzantium, botany was mainly represented by *Dioscorides' De materia medica (first century C.E.). The work deals with all the natural products used as medicines (plants, animals, and minerals), and contains one chapter for each such substance with a total of more than one thousand chapters. Plants constitute the large majority (seventy percent). With the exception of the most common ones, they are described so that herb gatherers, physicians, and practitioners could recognize and collect them in the field. Descriptions do not proceed in a systematic way, but by main characteristics according to Theophrastus's method, which had been further developed, possibly in Alexandria. Several manuscripts of *De materia medica* also contain color representations of the plants, whose authenticity and origin are still debated. The work includes an implicit classification of plants, of a cosmogonic nature: the sequence of chapters corresponds to the gradual appearance of the plants during the mythological creation of the universe, with several ages from gold to iron. The paradigm of decline underlying such classification is also present in the description of the single species where the wild varieties are usually credited with superior botanical features and medical properties to the cultivated ones. In such classificatory system, plant names played a certain role, be it to group or distinguish species with similar names according to the cases. The work, supposedly divided into five books (which might correspond in fact to five papyrus rolls at the origin), was widely distributed and used through the entire Mediterranean basin as the number and origin of extant manuscripts suggests. As a consequence it underwent several modifications, the first of which might have been an alphabetical ordering of its chapters (whatever the nature of the substances). As early as the sixth century C.E., about three hundred chapters dealing with common plants were selected out of this hypothetical alphabetical version so as to constitute a herbal where plants were listed alphabetically. In the tenth century at least, most of the chapters left out of such selection were recovered and grouped in such a way as to constitute five books according to the nature of the substances dealt with (plants, animals, oils, trees, wines, and minerals). Within such books, chapters were listed alphabetically. Oriental drugs, still missing in the tenth-century version, were reintroduced during the eleventh. During the fourteenth century all extant previous versions of De materia medica were brought together in Constantinople and collated so as to produce a new edition. At the same time, oriental plants seem to have been better known and used in therapeutics.

In the East, De materia medica was translated into Syriac by Sergius of Ra's al-'Ayn (d. 536), as was also the major pharmacological treatise of *Galen, De simplicium medicamentorum temperamentis et facultatibus (On the mixtures and properties of single medicines). The two works were further translated into Arabic in Baghdad by *Hunayn ibn Ishaq (808–873) and his collaborators, first from Sergius' Syriac version and then directly from Greek. A major problem was the identification of the plants and, on this basis, the proper translation of their names. According to traditional historiography, translators did not necessarily know the plants and their names, and just reproduced their Greek names, which they transliterated into the Arabic alphabet, however. Such strategy might result, instead, from a deliberate decision to keep Greek names so as to conserve the information they implicitly contained for the classification of plants. Two new translations of De materia medica were made during the twelfth century from the Syriac in Northern Mesopotamia, in order to fully assimilate the text into Arabic. Several extant manuscripts include plant representations made not by observing nature, but by reproducing Greek models. Over time, such illustrations evolved in two opposite directions: they were gradually more stylized, and they integrated plants in their natural environment (rocks, water, and animals). Together with Galen's Treatise on Simple Medicines, De materia medica was extremely influential in the Arabic world in such works as those by *al-Razi, *al-Biruni, and *Ibn Sina. Plant knowledge was also present in agriculture and horticultural treatises, whose material went back to ancient and Byzantine works (the Georgika of Demokritos/Bolos of Mendes (c. 200 B.C.E.), Anatolios of Berytos (=? Vindonius Anatolius, d. 360 C.E.), and Kassianos Bassos (sixth century C.E.) and the Nabatean agriculture encyclopedia translated from Syriac into Arabic in the late eighth century. The eleventh-century physician Ibn Butlan (d. 1063 [?]) introduced a new way to present data on plants used for medical purposes by tabulating them in his Taqwim as-sihha. During the

thirteenth century, ninth-century illustrated manuscripts were reproduced in the context of a revival of Abbassid ideology and culture. One of them contains an illustration supposedly produced by direct impression of a leaf. This suggests that plant knowledge was not limited to reading reference works, but also included collecting leaving plants.

Medieval Islamic Spain

In the Western Arabic world, al-Andalus was an important center of plant study. As early as the eighth century C.E., the Umayyad Emir of Córdoba, Abd al-Rahman I (756–788) ordered plants from Syria be transferred to, and acclimated in, Spain. According to contemporary historiography, this was the origin of the productive Andalusian school of botany and pharmacology. During the tenth century at the Court of Abd al-Rahman III (912–961), emir and, from 929, caliph of Córdoba, local scientists knew Hunayn's and Istafan's translation of Dioscorides' De materia medica. In 948 (?), the Caliph received an illustrated copy of Dioscorides' Greek text from a Byzantine Emperor named Romanos, who is not exactly identified because of a contradiction in the report of the story. Working with a Byzantine monk sent to Córdoba by the emperor at the caliph's request, Arabic scientists identified the plants described by Dioscorides to local species, and revised Hunayn's and Istifan's Arabic text on this basis, without translating afresh the Greek text into Arabic. The local school reached its zenith with the two pharmaco-botanists al-Ghafiqi (twelfth century) and ibn al-Baytar (c. 1190–1248).

In the Latin West, treatises of therapeutics proliferated in late antiquity with the works of Gargilius Martialis (third century), Serenus Sammonicus (between second and third centuries), the Medicina Plinii (early fourth century), the Pseudo-Apuleius (fourth century [?]), Sextus Placitus Papyriensis (early fifth century), Vindicianus (fourth/fifth century), Theodorus Priscianus (fourth/fifth century), Marcellus of Bordeaux (fourth/fifth century), Caelius Aurelianus (early fifth century), Cassius Felix (fifth century), and anonymous treatises such as the Ex herbis feminis attributed to Dioscorides, the Pseudo-Hippocratic Dynamidia, and De herba vettonica, whose exact origin and period are unknown. Such treatises associated classical material (not only from Dioscorides, but also from Pliny's Natural History) and local knowledge of healers. Dioscorides' De materia medica and the medical encyclopedia of Oribasius (fourth century), which includes a section on medicinal plants, were translated into Latin: the former maybe in the sixth century in North Africa or Southern Europe, and the latter in Ravenna in the sixth century. Cassiodorus (c. 490–583) recommended reading Dioscorides to the members of the Vivarium (it is not known if in the Greek original text or in the Latin version), and *Isidore of Seville (c. 602–636) used ancient botanical data in the Etymologies. The classical tradition, weakened but not interrupted until the Carolingians, was reinvigorated with them. In this transition period, plant knowledge was transferred from the lay to the religious world, particularly the newly founded monasteries, their hospitals, and gardens of plants. Plant knowledge was also transformed: divine creationism left little space for scientific and philosophical speculation on the genesis and growth of plants, their sensory characteristics, and medicinal properties. Greek botanico-therapeutic texts might have been available again before 800 C.E. as the recipe book of the Lorsch abbey (Germany) suggests. Charlemagne's *Capitulare de villis* (c. 795), Walahfrid Strabo (c. 808–849), and *Hildegard of Bingen (1098–1179) confirm the new development, location, and science of plants. Classical material was also transferred to England and translated into Old English.

In southern Europe, Eastern plants were acclimated in Arabic Sicily as had already happened in Spain. Contacts between Arabic- and Greek-speaking groups led to the translation of Arabic texts into Greek (for example the *Efodia*, translated from the *Zad al-musfir* of ibn al-Gazzir, which contains a section on medicinal plants). Latin scholars were also in contact with Constantinople as early as Alfanus of Salerno (1015/1020–1087). *Constantine the African (d. after 1087) followed and amplified earlier practice of translation and rendered into Latin a large corpus of medical texts, including works on therapeutics. The school of *Salerno further developed this first material with such treatises as the *Circa instans* (or *Tractatus de simplicibus medicinis*) of a Platearius not better identified (twelfth century), the *Secreta Salernitana*, and the *Liber de plantis et herbis*. In Sicily the *Taqwim as-sihha* of ibn Butlan was translated into Latin by Faraj ibn Salim (thirteenth century) (*Tacuinum sanitatis*), and in the fourteenth century the Salernitan physician Mattheus Sylvaticus (d. c. 1342) wrote the *Pandectae medicinae*. Medical botany also entered the university curriculum, for example with *Albertus Magnus (c. 1200–1280), author of a *De vegetabilibus* (*On plants*). The many translations and adaptations of earlier material reproduced a problem already met in Baghdad during the ninth century: the inaccurate or mistaken translation of plant names and the frequent use of transliteration. Simo Januensis (d. after 1304) systematized the profusion of such names in his *Synonima medicinae sive Clavis sanationis*.

After these translations and their problems, scholars had again direct access to Greek material as early as the Fourth Crusade and the Latin Kingdom (1204–1261). Later *Pietro d'Abano (1257–c. 1315), for example, traveled to Constantinople and saw the Latin herbal of Dioscorides. On his return he commented on *De materia medica* Latin translation in Padua, also introducing textual passages from Galen. Around the same time plant representations in manuscripts, which had followed so far the classical tradition and its codes, started to become more realistic. The manuscript Egerton 747 of the British Library (Southern Italy [?], c. 1300) is supposed to be the first witness of this renewal attributed to direct observation of plants in nature. A profusion of pre-Renaissance manuscripts with nature-like plant representations was produced in Italy, which culminated in the *Libro dei semplici* of Nicolò Roccabonella (d. 1549) (Venice, Biblioteca Marciana, lat.

VI.59 [coll. 2548]). At the Court of the Visconti in Milan, the *Tacuinum sanitatis* had an extraordinary success and was lavishly illustrated in a reduced group of manuscripts: illustrations covered the entire surface of the page and represented the plants in a natural or human context suggesting their properties, uses, and cultural meanings. Texts in the vernacular became more frequent, as the *Livre des simples mèdecines* widely distributed in the late Middle Ages.

The printing press in Germany diffused *herbals with crude wood blocks from 1475 on, with the *Buch der natur* of Konrad von Megenberg (1475), the *Herbarium Apulei* (1481), the Latin *Herbarius* (1484), the *Herbarius zu Teutsch* (also called *Gart der Geshundheit*) of Johann von Cube (1485) and the *Ortus sanitatis* (1491). Ancient texts were also printed and not only in Germany: the *Natural History* of Pliny from 1469 and many times during the late fifteenth century; the Latin translation of Dioscorides' *De materia medica* commented on by Pietro d'Abano in 1478, and the Latin translation of the *Enquiry of plants* and *Causes of plants* of Theophrastus by Theodorus of Gaza (1398–1478) in 1483. In 1492, the booklet by Nicolao Leoniceno (1428–1524) *De Plinii aliorumque in medicina erroribus* (*On the mistakes of Pliny and others in medicine*), published in Ferrara, put an end to this first efflorescence of botanical interest by attempting to identify the material dealt with, rather than doing strictly philological work. New works were not published until the *Herbarum vivae eicones* (*Pictures of leaving plants*) (1532) of Otto Brunfels (c. 1498–1534) and the *Historia plantarum* (*History of plants*) (1540) of Leonhart Fuchs (1501–1566), which opened a new era in plant science.

See also **Aristotelianism; Mineralogy; Translation movements; Zoology**

Bibliography

Collins, Minta. *Medieval Herbals: The Illustrative Traditions.* Toronto: University of Toronto Press, 2000
De Vriend, Hubert Jan, ed. *The Old English Herbarium and Medicina de quadrupedibus.* Oxford: Oxford University Press, 1984.
Fortenbaugh, William W. and Robert W. Sharples, eds. *Theophrastean Studies: On Natural Science, Physics and Metaphysics, Ethics, Religion, and Rhetoric.* New Brunswick: Transaction Books, 1988.
Reeds, Karen. *Botany in Medieval and Renaissance Universities.* New York: Garland, 1991.
Stannard, Jerry. *Herbs and Herbalism in the Middle Ages and Renaissance.* Edited by Katherine E. Stannard and Richard Kay. Aldershot: Ashgate Variorum, 1999.

ALAIN TOUWAIDE

BRADWARDINE, THOMAS

Thomas Bradwardine was born in England sometime in the last decade of the thirteenth century. His birthplace is unknown, although a reference to his father's living in

Chichester in one of his writings has led to the supposition that he may have born in that vicinity. Unfortunately, little else is known about his early life. According to Oxford University records he was a fellow of Balliol College from 1321 to 1323. From 1323 to 1325 he was a fellow of Merton College. In 1333 he held the post of canon of Lincoln Cathedral. Although it cannot be verified, the assumption is that he remained at Merton until 1335.

While at Merton Bradwardine was an active participant in a circle of mathematicians, logicians, physicians, and astronomers whose work established Oxford University as a leading center for the study of natural philosophy in the fourteenth century. In the 1320s Bradwardine established his mastery of natural philosophy by writing treatises encompassing a wide variety of topics including geometry, velocity, proportionality, continuity, contingency, and memory. Several of his treatises continued to be used as teaching texts long after his death in 1349.

In 1335 Richard of Bury, the Bishop of Durham and a patron of Merton College, invited Bradwardine to join a select group of natural philosophers he had assembled in his household. In 1337 Bradwardine was appointed chancellor of St. Paul's Cathedral in London. Two years later he became the chaplain and confessor to King Edward III, a responsibility that required him to travel extensively in England and France and to engage in a variety of diplomatic missions. His active participation in civil affairs is implied in the text of his *Sermo epinicius*, a sermon commemorating the 1346 victories of English forces at the battle of Crécy in France, which he witnessed personally, and at Neville's Cross in Scotland.

During this period Bradwardine developed a reputation for excellence in preaching and teaching. He continued to lecture in natural philosophy and theology, earning the honorific title "the profound doctor." Bradwardine completed his major theological work, *De causa Dei contra Pelagium*, in 1346. This treatise represents his contribution to a lively academic debate in the mid-fourteenth century about the nature and extent of God's foreknowledge. Bradwardine's thorough knowledge of Aristotelian natural philosophy and mathematics is manifest in his approach to the question of whether God's perfect knowledge of future contingent events can be reconciled with the doctrine of human free will.

Bradwardine's distinguished service to king and church culminated in his consecration as Archbishop of Canterbury in July 1349 in Avignon, France. Unfortunately, Bradwardine was exposed to the plague while on the continent and he died in England on August 26, 1349, before he was able to assume his new role.

Apart from the *De causa Dei contra Pelagium*, Bradwardine's principal works date from the 1320s and show a steady progression from simpler to more sophisticated philosophical inquiry. His *Geometria speculativa*, written in the early 1320s, is a concise summary of the principles of Euclidean geometry. Most of his subsequent works of natural philosophy demonstrate a keen interest in Aristotle's theories about the physics of motion and time. His *De incipit and desinit*, written in 1323, explores the logical problem of assigning beginning- and end-points for permanent and successive things, largely restating Aristotle's position. In 1328 Bradwardine completed his *Tractatus de proportionibus*, which offered a mathematical approach to the study of motion. At about the same time he presented a philosophical justification of Aristotle's theory of infinite divisibility in his *Tractatus de continuo*. Also attributed to Bradwardine is a short treatise on artificial memory entitled *De arte memorativa*.

In the mid-1320s Bradwardine wrote one treatise that attempted to bridge the gap between purely physical definitions of time and motion with more metaphysical or theological understandings of these phenomena. In his *Tractatus de futuris contingentibus*, he addressed the question of whether events in the future can really be contingent if the omniscient God already knows their outcome. Drawing on authorities such as Augustine and Boethius, Bradwardine concluded, rather conservatively, that the future cannot be contingent from God's perspective, although human beings can and do perceive the future as being open to many possible events.

Bradwardine's longest and most mature work is the *De causa Dei contra Pelagium*. As the title suggests, this was a somewhat polemical work directed against contemporary theologians, whom he labeled as Pelagians because of their emphasis on the paramount importance of human free will. Bradwardine argued that his contemporaries, not unlike the fourth-century theologian Pelagius, wrongly sacrificed God's complete and perfect omniscience for the sake of extending the limits of human freedom. Augustine had accused Pelagius of denying the transmission of original sin in his assertion that human beings, created in God's image, are capable of choosing to be good. Similarly, Bradwardine argued, some contemporary "pelagian" theologians undermined the doctrine of God's omniscience by insisting so strongly on the extent of human free will. Although the *De causa Dei contra Pelagium* is an explicitly theological work, Bradwardine drew extensively from mathematics and natural philosophy to support or illustrate many of his theological propositions. While he was not by any means the only theologian of his time to apply mathematical or philosophical principles to theological problems, his facility at moving across these disciplines was remarkable even to his contemporaries.

Significance

Because Bradwardine excelled in so many areas—as a natural philosopher, mathematician, theologian, priest, preacher and public servant—his influence has been considerable. His works were widely studied well beyond Oxford University, and some of his mathematical treatises were used as teaching texts throughout Europe. His particular interests in continuity, contingency, contiguity, and time drew him into lively debates with such contemporary scholars as Thomas Buckingham, Robert Holcot, Adam Wodeham, John of Mirecourt. and Gregory of Rimini. Bradwardine's views about predestination, free will, and grace influenced the English theologian, John Wyclif (c. 1330–1384). Through Wyclif, Bradwardine has sometimes been associated with Reformation theology. This connection can be misleading because Bradwardine's writings, while innovative in form and sometimes polemical in style, reflect traditional positions and fit well within the mainstream of fourteenth-century thought.

See also **Aristotelianism; Religion and science**

Bibliography

Primary Sources

Crosby, H. Lamar. *Thomas of Bradwardine, His Tractatus de proportionibus: Its Significance for the Development of Mathematical Physics.* Madison, Wisconsin: University of Wisconsin Press, 1955.

Genest, M. Jean-François, ed. Le De futuris contingentibus de Thomas Bradwardine. *Recherches augustiniennes* (1979) 14: 249–336.

Gillmeister, Hüner. An Intriguing Fourteenth-Century Document: Thomas Bradwardine's De arte memorativa. *Archiv für das Studium des neueren Sprachen und Literaturen* (1983) 220: 111–114.

Green-Pedersen, Niels Jorgen. Bradwardine (?) on Ockham's Doctrine of Consequences: An Edition. *Cahiers de l'Institute du moyen âge grec et latin* (1982) 42: 85–105.

Molland, A. G., ed. *Thomas Bradwardine, Geometria speculativa: Latin text and English translation with an introduction and a commentary.* Stuttgart: Springer Verlag, 1989.

Murdoch, John Emery. "Geometry and the Continuum in the Fourteenth Century: A Philosophical Analysis of Thomas Bradwardine's Tractatus de continuo." Ph. D. Dissertation, University of Wisconsin, 1957.

Nielsen, Lauge Olaf. Thomas Bradwardine's treatise on "incipit" and "desinit": Edition and Introduction. *Cahiers de l'Institute du moyen âge grec et latin* (1982) 42: 1–83.

Savile, Henry, ed. *De causa Dei contra Pelagium et de virtute causarum ad suos Mertonenses, libri tres.* London: Ex officina Nortoniana apud Johannem Billium, 1618.

Secondary Sources

Dolnikowski, Edith W. *Thomas Bradwardine: A View of Time and a Vision of Eternity in Fourteenth-century Thought.* Leiden: E. J. Brill, 1995.

Fleming, Brian. "Thomas Bradwardine: Oxford Scholar, Royal Servant and Archbishop of Canterbury." Thesis, Université catholique de Louvain, 1964.

Genest, M. Jean-François and Tachau, Katherine H. Le lecture de Thomas Bradwardine sur le Sentences. *Archives d'histoire doctrinaire et littéraire du moyen âge* (1990) 56: 301–306.

Kaluza, Zenon. La prétendu discussion parisienne de Thomas de Bradwardine avec Thomas de Buckingham: témoignage de Thomas de Cracovie. *Recherches de théologie ancienne et medieval* (1976) 43: 209–236.

Kaluza, Zenon. Le problème du "Deum non esse" chez Étienne du Chaumont, Nicolas Aston et Thomas Bradwardine. *Mediaevalia Philosophia Polonorum* (1979) 24: 3–19.

Leff, Gordon. *Bradwardine and the Pelagians.* New York: Cambridge University Press, 1957.

McCarthy, Donald J. "Free Choice and Liberty according to Thomas Bradwardine." Ph. D. Thesis, University of Toronto, 1965.

McGrath, Alister E. The Anti-Pelagian Structure of "Nominalist" Doctrines of Justification. *Ephemerides Theologicae Lovanienses* (1981) 57: 107–119.

Molland, A. G. Assessing Ancient Authority: Thomas Bradwardine and Prisca sapientia. *Annals of Science* (1996) 53: 213–233.

———. An Examination of Bradwardine's Geometry. *Archive for the History of Exact Sciences* (1978) 19: 113–175.

———. The Geometrical Background to the "Merton School": An Exploration into the Application of Mathematics to Natural Philosophy in the Fourteenth Century. *British Journal for the History of Science* (1968) 4: 108–125.

Oberman, Heiko. *Archbishop Thomas Bradwardine: A Fourteenth-Century Augustinian: A Study of his Theology in its Historical Context.* Utrecht: Kemink and Zoon, 1958.

———. Thomas Bradwardine: un precurseur du Luther? *Revue d'histoire et de philosophie religieuse* (1960) 40: 146–151.

Robson, John Adam. *Wyclif and the Oxford Schools.* New York: Cambridge University Press, 1961.

Rouré, Marie Louise. La problématique des propositions insolubles au XIII siècle—William Shyreswood, Walter Burleigh et Thomas Bradwardine. *Archives d'histoire doctrinale et littéraire du moyen âge* (1970) 37: 205–326.

Rowland, Beryl. Bishop Bradwardine on the Artificial Memory. Journal of the Warburg and Courtauld Institutes (1978) 41: 307–312.

Spade, Paul Vincent. Insolubilia and Bradwardine's Theory of Signification. *Medioevo* (1981) 7: 115–134.

Stump, Eleonore and Norman Kretzman. Eternity. *Journal of Philosophy* (1981) 78: 429–458.

Sylla, Edith Dudley. "Compounding Ratios: Bradwardine, Oresme, and the First Edition of Newton's Principia." In *Transformation and Tradition in the Sciences: Essays in Honor of I. Bernard Cohen.* Ed. Everett Mendelsohn. New York: Cambridge University Press, 1984, pp. 11–43.

Weisheipl, James A. *The Development of Physical Theory in the Middle Ages.* New York: Sheed and Ward, 1959.

———. The Curriculum of the Faculty of Arts at Oxford in the Early Fourteenth Century. *Mediaeval Studies* (1964) 26: 143–185.

Weisheipl, James A. "Ockham and the Mertonians." In *The History of the University of Oxford*, Volume I. Ed. Jeremy I. Catto. Oxford: Clarendon Press, 1984, pp. 607–658.

Weisheipl, James A. Ockham and Some Mertonians. *Mediaeval Studies* (1968) 30: 163–213.

Weisheipl, James A. Repertorium Mertonense. *Mediaeval Studies* (1969) 31: 174–224.

Weisheipl, James A. and Oberman, Heiko. The Sermo Epinicius Ascribed to Thomas Bradwardine (1346). *Archives d'histoire doctrinale et littéraire du moyen âge* (1958) 26: 295–329.

EDITH WILKS DOLNIKOWSKI

BREDON, SIMON

Simon Bredon (c.1310–1372), an astronomer, bibliophile, mathematician, and physician, exemplifies the scientific life and social ambition of a university scholar in fourteenth-century England. A relatively full outline of Bredon's life can be gleaned from his last will and testament, the several extant books from his personal library, and records of his activities at Merton College,

Oxford. Bredon had family ties to the English county of Lincolnshire. He came up to Oxford as a student in Balliol College in the late 1320s. By 1330 he had become a fellow of Merton, where he was a colleague of the mathematician *Thomas Bradwardine, the natural philosopher *William of Heytesbury, and the astrologer John Ashenden. He left Merton after 1341, but remained in Oxford to study medicine. Bredon's post-university career was as a physician to high nobility. Joanna, queen of Scotland, Richard Fitzalan, earl of Arundel, Simon Islip, Archbishop of Canterbury, and Elizabeth de Burgh, Lady Clare were among his patients. His scholarly reputation and ability to garner lucrative patronage made Bredon the very image of the "doctour of physic" in *Chaucer's The Canterbury Tales. However, his career declined sharply after he brought a lawsuit against the prior of Lewes, who had canceled an annuity paid to Bredon for medical services. The trial record indicates that Bredon had refused to attend, counsel, or provide medication for the prior when he fell ill in 1364. A panel of judges affirmed the legal necessity for a physician to attend to his patient. The cancellation of the annuity was upheld. Sometime after this judgment Bredon retired to Battle Abbey, where he died in spring 1372.

Work in Mathematics, Astronomy, Astrology

As an Oxford master in the 1330s Bredon lectured on the mathematical subjects of the *quadrivium (arithmetic, geometry, astronomy, and music) and wrote commentaries on traditional texts in the university curriculum. Most influential was his guide to the arithmetic of *Boethius, entitled Expositio arsmetrice Boicii, which explained basic arithmetical operations and number theory after the fashion of the classical text. The Expositio was a pedagogical success, continuing to be used by Oxford teachers for over a century, and even reaching continental universities. In 1495 Pedro Cirvelo published the work at Paris under the title Arithmetica speculativa. Only a few of Bredon's notes on geometry and music have survived, but it is intriguing that the fifteenth-century composer John Dunstaple was among the copyists of Bredon's mathematical writings.

While lecturing on astronomy, Bredon updated the traditional *Theorica planetarum textbook on the motion of planets in a geocentric system. Bredon's edition of the Theorica is noteworthy for its consistent use of sexagesimal numbers and its references to the Alfonsine Tables, which were only becoming widely known in England in the 1330s. Bredon's Theorica also borrowed the uniformiter/difformiter terminology describing states of motion from the kinematical theories of contemporary Mertonians, notably William of Heytesbury. Apart from the Theorica, Bredon focused his astrological and astronomical scholarship on the corpus of Ptolemaic writings. He assiduously collected works attributed to *Ptolemy, including apocryphal works such as the Introductorium ad artem spericam (which was actually a Latin translation of the Isagoge of Geminos). Dissatisfied with existing Latin translations of Ptolemy's astrological handbook, the

Quadripartitum, he drafted his own version with special attention to the clear definition of technical terms. Merton colleague John Ashenden utilized Bredon's Quadripartitum in his own astrological compilation, Summa judicialis de accidentibus mundi, concerning the prediction of famines, plagues, wars, and other global events. At a more advanced level, Bredon began a mathematical commentary on Ptolemy's Almagest, incorporating in his analysis references to the spherical geometry and trigonometry of Menelaos, Theodosius, *Thabit ibn Qurra, Jabir ibn Aflah, and Richard of Wallingford.

Bredon was one of the few medieval astronomers to go beyond textual study and attempt to measure astronomical parameters by observation. In his copy of Ptolemy's star catalog Bredon recorded two observations made in 1347—of a close approach of Venus to the star Regulus, and a lunar occultation of the star Aldebaran—with the purpose of determining the precession (movement of the Earth's axis) that had occurred since Ptolemy's time. Bredon did not record what, if any, instruments he used to make his observations, but he did own an astrolabe and is credited with a manual on the use of this instrument. (Although the Equatorie of the Planetis, a treatise on the equatorium instrument, was previously attributed to Bredon, it is now known that he could not have been its author.) Bredon evidently set aside his Ptolemaic studies, including the incomplete Almagest commentary, to pursue medicine.

Medical Scholarship and Practice

No specific records of Bredon's medical training exist. Even so, it is reasonable to think that his studies were academic rather than clinical in nature. Like many other university-trained physicians of the time, Bredon proved his scholarship by compiling a manual derived from the writings of acknowledged authorities. His Trifolium de re medica, as its name implies, is divided into three parts, (1) on the analysis of urine, (2) on the efficacy of drugs, and (3) on the interpretation of the pulse. It is chiefly a patchwork of references from *Galen, Avicenna (*Ibn Sina), *Constantine the African, Theophilus, and *John of St. Amand. The most original aspect of the Trifolium is Bredon's approach to pharmacology: He attempted to establish degrees of potency for a compound medicine based on the mathematical proportions of its active ingredients. *Bernard de Gordon and *Arnau de Vilanova had pioneered de gradibus pharmacology a generation earlier, but Bredon's inspiration was most likely the De proportionibus of Thomas Bradwardine. It was as if he wanted to treat medicine as applied mathematics.

An extensive herbal index written by Bredon suggests that his medical practice often involved drug treatments. In the single documented case of treatment, he prescribed medicines for a London apothecary to prepare for the queen of Scotland. It is not known how the queen or any of his other patients responded to his treatments.

At the time of his death Bredon had a personal library of some sixty volumes, mainly astronomical, mathematical, and medical titles. The library was the most valuable asset of his estate. Texts copied, purchased, shared, and traded over a lifetime formed the currency of his reputation. Despite his astronomical observations and clinical experiences, valuable though they may have been, textual study remained central to Bredon's scholarship, and the possession of books reinforced his standing as a professional. It is significant, too, that Bredon left most of his library to Merton College or to former Merton colleagues. Alumni loyalty was already an important element of university culture in the fourteenth century.

See also **Astrology; Astronomy, Latin; Medicine, practical; Pharmacology**

Bibliography

Snedegar K.V. "The Works and Days of Simon Bredon, a fourteenth-century astronomer and physician." In *Between Demonstration and Imagination. Essays in the History of Science and Philosophy Presented to John D. North*. Lodi Nauta and Arjo Vanderjagt, eds. Dordrecht: Kluwer Academic Publishers, 1999, pp. 285–309.

KEITH SNEDEGAR

BREWING

Brewing is the process of making an infusion of germinated grain, that is of malt, and letting it ferment after being cooled and then clarifying it before consumption was a traditional art until the seventeenth century. Techniques were not informed by any theoretical considerations or even descriptions until the Renaissance. Brewing began in Mesopotamia and Egypt and was firmly in place by the fourth millennium B.C.E. The production of beer continued in the eastern Mediterranean through the Roman era and was common among the indigenous Roman and Celtic populations and immigrants who spoke Germanic languages. The Celtic word for malt was *brace*, which is probably the origin of the French *brasser*, the German *brauen*, and the English *brew*. The drink made by early medieval brewers contained grain or other vegetable matter, water, and additives for flavor that also helped to preserve a drink which was subject to invasion by various bacteria that caused it to sour. One way around the problem of preservation was to consume the drink almost immediately. Another was to make it strong, the higher alcohol content fending off infection. Hops have certain oils that help preserve beer, and brewers by the Carolingian era if not earlier knew that. Adding hops was not common, however, possibly because of the difficulty of finding the right proportions. The large monasteries of the ninth century had their own breweries, sizable operations to supply the monks, who drank beer daily, and visitors. Farmers, typically the women of the household, made beer in the countryside for family use, selling to or trading with other villagers any surplus. With increasing urbanization in the eleventh and twelfth centuries professional brewers appeared in towns, making beer for sale to those who did not have the skill or the space to make it themselves. The new urban professionals had opportunities to improve production through investment in better equipment and experimentation with a range of different additives.

Brewers in northern Europe typically used a combination of various herbs known as gruit, probably containing mostly bog myrtle to flavor and preserve their product. Around 1,200 brewers in north German towns, especially Bremen and Hamburg, perfected the skill of producing beer of consistent quality with hops. Since the hopped beer could last for six months or more it was possible to ship the drink over some distance. Towns standardized the size of beer casks to make it easier to sell the beer and reduce the cost of making barrels. Common sizes meant the same barrels could be used anywhere. German beer found markets in the Low Countries and in England. Brewers first in Holland in the fourteenth century and later in Flanders and Brabant and then in the fifteenth century in England imitated German practices, producing hopped beer. The new high quality drink found wider markets, and beer invaded areas where wine had previously been the alcoholic beverage of choice. The new drink was typically named "beer," in England the word used to distinguish hopped beer from the older drink which retained a name of Celtic origin, "ale." In some parts of northern Europe, for example Sweden, *öl* was the name for hopped beer with no distinction made between it and the earlier type of drink. Hopped beer enjoyed unprecedented success in the last years of the Middle Ages. Consumption levels rose in the cities of the Low Countries and England to around 60–66 gallons (275–300 liters) per person per year on average. People in both town and country drank beer at all meals of the day, downing thin beers with low alcohol content for breakfast and stronger, heavier drinks with their other meals. Beer brought variety to a rather boring diet as well as nutrition and alcohol. The beer came from small operations, the typical brewery having no more than eight or ten employees. Most of the workers were typically members of the brewer's family. Large towns had dozens of breweries. Cities such as Hamburg and Wismar in Germany and Delft and Gouda in Holland exported hundreds of thousands of liters of beer annually. While the scale of production rose somewhat as beer became more popular, the equipment and methods changed little. The biochemical process was very much like that of the earliest known brewing but the product was certainly of higher and much more consistent quality. Brewing enjoyed even greater success in the Renaissance with production and consumption rising and the region where beer was the dominant drink expanding. That success, which continued into the seventeenth century, was based firmly on the development of methods of producing hopped beer in the closing centuries of the Middle Ages.

See also **Water supplies and sewerage**

Bibliography

Bennett, Judith M. *Ale, Beer, and Brewsters in England: Women's Work in a Changing World, 1300–1600*. New York: Oxford University Press, 1996.

Corran, H. S. *A History of Brewing*. Newton Abbot: David and Charles, 1975.

Nordlund, Odd. *Brewing and Beer Traditions in Norway: The Social Anthropological Background of the Brewing Industry*. Oslo: Universitetsforlaget, 1969.

Unger, Richard W. *Beer in the Middle Ages and the Renaissance*. Philadelphia: University of Pennsylvania Press, 2004.

———. *A History of Brewing in Holland 900–1900. Economy, Technology and the State*. Leiden: E. J. Brill, 2001.

RICHARD W. UNGER

BRIDGES

Bridges were engineered nodal points within an under-developed road system, over which they exercised considerable influence. If a bridge's site was changed, the connecting roads were moved accordingly. The Romans had built bridges of stone and also of timber, resting on stone piers. In some areas of the former Roman Empire, still standing stone bridges provided ready models for medieval bridge-builders. But in England, most Roman bridges had been made of timber and did not survive. In early eighth-century England, fords were the rule and are recalled in place names such as Bradford, Longford, Shalford, Sartford (indicating a broad ford, long, and shallow ford, respectively, and one built on the line of a Roman road).

The scale of bridge-building in medieval England was huge. Medieval bridges were built on piers, on piles set in such a way as to even out the foundations on which the arches sat. Groups of piles called staddles were driven in close together and then surrounded by starlings—pile-supported platforms filled with rubble on which the piers sat. The piles were set with special apparatus called (in England) the gin and the ram. The gin was a lifting device used to maneuver the pile into position. The pile (usually a trunk of elm or oak) fitted with an iron tip known as a "pile shoe" was driven with the ram, a pile driver that caused a heavy weight to fall on the head of the pile. Bridges were both built and repaired by carpenters and stone masons. On a bridge made completely of stone, a carpenter was needed to build scaffolding. On a wooden bridge, the stone mason built the piers, the carpenter the plank road and superstructure.

Roman stone bridges were built on semicircular arches, barrel vaults that required scaffolding during construction while the arch was not self-supporting. In the later Middle Ages, rib vaulting was sometimes preferred, because each rib is self supporting and less stone is required. To the semicircular arch, medieval masons added segmental and pointed (ogival) arches. As bridges were repaired, some came to have arches of different styles. The relatively flat segmental arches were stronger and had a gentler gradient than semicircular arches. Vaulting for bridges followed the styles used in the naves of churches. In the thirteenth century some older bridges were replaced with pointed arches and groined vaults. Many medieval bridges are humped, where the road rose over pointed Gothic arches.

Spans of arches varied from five feet (1.5 m) in small bridges to twenty feet (6 m) in some large ones. In swampy areas bridges were long, with stone causeways leading up to cross a floodplain. Such causeways had arches, although without channels of water flowing through them.

Roman bridges had cutwaters on the upstream side in order to soften the scouring effect of the river current. Medieval bridges frequently had cutwaters on both the upstream and downstream sides, the latter to reduce scouring by whirlpools. Bridges were easily damaged by flood waters which might wash an arch or two, or an entire bridge, away.

Causeways

Causeways were built up with stonework and timber, much in the same way as true bridges over water which they also encompassed. Ely in the English Fens was linked to surrounding areas by three causeways (Aldreth, Earith, and Soham). There is no technical account of their construction but they had to be repaired constantly, especially the little bridges (*ponticulos*) that dotted their courses. The official in charge of the repair was the sacristan of the church of Ely and his accounts in the fourteenth century record expenses for repair of the causeway, its small and large bridges, and boat rental fees. Sand was brought from "le gravelpitte." At times the causeways were completely broken down and traffic interrupted, sometimes for years. The St. Saviour section of a causeway to the south of Boston, Lincolnshire, had thirty bridges, each ten feet (3 m) wide and eight feet (2.4 m) high, wide enough for two carts to pass. In 1331 thirteen were out of repair at the same time.

In the Islamic world, pontoon bridges were common, such as one comprising thirty boats that connected Fustat to the island of Rawda, and another of sixty boats connecting the same island to the other bank of the Nile. There was another in Murcia, Spain, described by al-Himyari. Such boats were strung together on steel cables anchored to either bank of a river. Navigable rivers were spanned with masonry bridges, many with semicircular arches although segmental arches were used in the Islamic world long before their first use in Europe in the thirteenth century. An eighth-century segmental arch bridge over the Tab River in Iran had a span of 200 feet (60 m) and a rise of 30 feet (10 m). Segmental arches permit longer spans but add a horizontal load to the vertical load on the abutments, and so are used where solid root footings are available on the banks.

Specialization and Financing

There were specialists in bridge building, such as Henry Yvele, warden of London Bridge, who was involved in the reconstruction of Rochester Bridge in the 1390s. Two Spanish masons were canonized for building bridges on the pilgrimage road to Santiago de Compostela. Santo Domingo de la Calzada (Saint Dominic of the Highway), built (perhaps rebuilt) the bridge over the Oja River, with pillars of stone and a wooden superstructure. His disciple, San Juan de Ortega, also built numerous bridges including those of Logroño, Nájera, Santo Domingo de la Calzada, and Cubo. The qualification of these eleventh-century builders for sainthood was their ability to build such works with scarce resources. Bridges had a semi-religious aura (quite a few had chapels built on them or hospitals next to them) and so they attracted pious donations.

The individuals (lords) or corporate entities (towns, monasteries) that built the bridges often charged a toll (called pontage in English, *potentate* in French, *pontazgo* in Spanish) for their use. The law code of *Alfonso X of Castile, the *Siete Partidas*, charges localities with the upkeep of roads and bridges (Partida I, Law 54, Title 6). In Asturias there was a customary obligation (the *sestaferia*) on all men to work Fridays on bridge and road maintenance. In return for such service, the community had the right to collect *pontazgo* and other taxes. In Valencia bridges on royal roads were the responsibility of the city. Its officials had to see "that bridges be made in all places which pass over small irrigation canals so that fields can be reached." Bridges, like the roads themselves, were public property and, when crossing a canal, had to be supported on public space on either side.

See also **Transportation**

Bibliography

Al-Hasan, Ahmad Y. and Donald R. Hill. *Islamic Technology: An Illustrated History*. New York: Cambridge University Press, 1986: 79–80.

Boyer, Marjorie Nice. *Medieval French Bridges: A History*. Cambridge, Mass: Mediaeval Academy of America, 1976.

Cook, Martin. *Medieval Bridges*. Princes Risborough: Shire Publications, 1998.

Harrison, David F. *The Bridges of Medieval England: Transport and Society, 400–1800*. Oxford: Clarendon Press, 2004.

Menéndez Pidal, Gonzalo. *Los caminos en la historia de España*. Madrid: Cultura Hispánica, 1951.

Steane, John. *Medieval Bridges in Oxfordshire*. Wantage: Vale and Down Museum Trust, 1997.

Vázquez de Parga, Luis *et al*. *Las peregrinaciones a Santiago de Compostela*. 3 vols. Madrid: Consejo Superior de Investigaciones Científicas, 1948–1949: II, 162–173.

Yates, Nigel and James M. Gibson. *Traffic and Politics: The Construction and Management of Rochester Bridge, AD 43–1993*. Woodbridge: Boydell, 1994.

THOMAS F. GLICK

BURGUNDIO OF PISA

Burgundio (in Latin usually "Burgundius") was probably born around 1110. Although he was of Pisan origin, it is likely that he spent part of his youth in Greece, where he acquired his excellent knowledge of Greek. For this ability, he was chosen to assist the German bishop Anselm of Havelberg at a theological dispute with archbishop Nicetas about the nature of the Holy Spirit in Constantinople on April 10, 1136. In their company were also *James of Venice and Moses of Bergamo. While nothing is known about his formation as a legist, Burgundio's name is mentioned in several Pisan legal documents from 1140 onwards, first as *advocatus*, later as *iudex*. According to his own statement, he was in contact with the emperor Frederick I Barbarossa. From 1168 to 1171, he was on a diplomatic mission to the Byzantine emperor on behalf of his native city to restore the original location of the Pisan quarter in the city of Constantinople. In March 1179 he attended the Third Lateran Council, where he presented his translation of John Chrysostom's sermons on St. John's Gospel. He died on October 30, 1193. His body was buried in the Church of San Paolo a Ripa d'Arno in Pisa, where his sarcophagus and epitaph are still in place.

Burgundio translated numerous theological, philosophical, and medical works from Greek into Latin. He dedicated his versions of John Chrysostom's sermons on St. Matthew's Gospel (1151) and of John of Damascus's *De fide orthodoxa* (1153–1154) to Pope Eugene III, while the translation of Nemesius of Emesa's *De natura hominis* (1164–1165) was offered to Frederick Barbarossa. According to the preface, his work on Chrysostom's sermons on St. John's Gospel (1171) was meant for the salvation of his son, who died accompanying Burgundio on his second trip to Constantinople. It has been suggested that he also authored a translation of Basilius's commentary on the *Hexaemeron*. The translations of other patristic texts that were ascribed to him seem to be lost. Burgundio was identified as the translator of the oldest versions of Aristotle's *De generatione et corruptione* and *Ethica Nicomachea* (*Ethica Vetus* and *Nova*, as well as the fragments of the *Ethica Hoferiana* and *Borghesiana*). His name is found in the subscriptions of approximately ten medical treatises by *Galen, but with the exception of the texts that have been critically edited, the accuracy of these reports has not yet been examined. As for Galen's *De sectis medicorum* (1185), dedicated to "King Henry," Burgundio's translation must not be confused with an older Latin version that incorporated Galen's text within the commentary by a certain Johannes Alexandrinus. Finally, Burgundio translated the Greek passages in the *Digesta*, a part of the legal *Codex Iustiniani*, and sections about viniculture from the *Geoponica*, a Byzantine work about *agriculture.

Method

In the prefaces to several of his works, Burgundio defends his considered choice to render each Greek word with a Latin parallel. He thus followed the method advocated by St. Jerome for the translation of sacred texts. As it was impossible to always find a perfect match for a Greek term in Latin, he often added second or even third equivalents for the same word—a feature of his translation method which cannot always be fully appreciated from the modern critical editions, as not all editors were aware of his practice. Burgundio also glossed his text with syntactical explanations and sometimes translated notes he found in his Greek manuscripts. Several of the Greek models that he used for his translations have been identified: mss. Firenze, Laur. 74.5 and 74.30 (Galen), Laur. 87.7 and 81.18 (Aristotle), and possibly Vatican, Chig. R. IV. 13 (Nemesius). Most of these manuscripts were written and annotated in Constantinople or southern Italy in the first half of the thirteenth century by a certain Ioannikios and his "anonymous colleague" of Italian origin. They each contain Burgundio's preparatory notes in Latin, and most likely also in Greek, and thus allow a privileged view into the production process prior to the translation itself. His annotations in ms. Firenze, Laur. 87.7 confirm that he studied the content of Aristotle's treatises *De caelo* and *Meteora*, which according to his preface to *De natura hominis* he intended to translate. No extant manuscripts confirm that he ever brought that project to an end. Similarly, a number of Greek manuscripts of Galen's works contain his notes, although it is unknown whether Burgundio ever translated these treatises into Latin.

In his *Metalogicon* (1159), Burgundio's contemporary John of Salisbury cited him as an authority without peer in the field of Greek philosophy. The influence of his philosophical translations can be gathered from the number of manuscripts in which they survive. Aristotle's *De generatione et corruptione* is preserved in roughly one hundred codices, while more than one hundred twenty copies of *De fide orthodoxa* from the thirteenth through the fifteenth century are known. The latter work was used by *Peter Lombard in his influential *Sentences*, and by virtually all scholastic authors of the thirteenth century, including *Albertus Magnus and *Thomas Aquinas. Some of Burgundio's works were revised in the thirteenth century by the famous translators *William of Moerbeke (*De generatione et corruptione*) and *Robert Grosseteste (*De fide orthodoxa* and *Ethica*). In the case of Aristotle's *Ethica*, the transmission became extremely intricate. The original translation by Burgundio was fragmentarily preserved in different forms. After the revision by Grosseteste, who must still have had Burgundio's complete version at his disposal, William of Moerbeke reworked the text a second time. As for the medical works, many attributions remain uncertain. Claims that *Niccolò da Reggio revised some of Burgundio's works need renewed research in the light of increased understanding of his translation method. The reliability of the colophons stating that *Taddeo Alderotti made a compilation of Burgundio's *De interioribus* by comparing it with the Arabo-Latin translation, and that *Pietro d'Abano completed several fragmentary translations of Galen's works by Burgundio has not yet been fully assessed.

See also **Aristotelianism; Translation movements; Translation, norms and practice**

Bibliography

Primary sources

Aristoteles Latinus Database. Release 1. Under the direction of Jozef Brams and Paul Tombeur. Turnhout: Brepols, 2003.
Buytaert, Eligius M., ed. *Saint John Damascene. De fide orthodoxa. Versions of Burgundio and Cerbanus* (Franciscan Institute Publications, Text Series, 8). Saint Bonaventure, N.Y.: The Franciscan Institute, 1955.
Gauthier, Renatus Antonius, ed. *Ethica Nicomachea.* Aristoteles Latinus XXVI. 1–3. 5 vol. Leiden: E.J. Brill–Desclée De Brouwer, 1974.
Judycka, Joanna, ed. *De generatione et corruptione. Translatio vetus.* Aristoteles Latinus IX.1. Leiden: E.J. Brill, 1986.
Verbeke, G. and J.R. Moncho, eds. *Némésius d'Emèse. De natura hominis. Traduction de Burgundio de Pise.* Leiden: E.J. Brill, 1975.

Secondary Sources

Backus, Irene. John of Damascus *De fide orthodoxa.* Translations by Burgundio (1153/54), Grosstest (1235/40) and Lefèvre d'Etaples (1507). *Journal of the Warburg and Courtauld Institutes* (1986) 49: 211–217.
Bossier, Fernand. "L'élaboration du vocabulaire philosophique chez Burgundio de Pise." In *Aux origins du lexique philosophique européen. L'influence de la* latinitas. Actes du Colloque international organisé à Rome (Academia Belgica, 23–25 mai 1996). Edited by Jacqueline Hamesse. Fédération Internationale des Instituts d'Etudes Médiévales. Textes et Etudes du Moyen Age, 8. Louvain-la-Neuve, 1997, pp. 81–116.
Classen, Peter. *Burgundio von Pisa. Richter—Gesandter—Übersetzer.* Sitzungsberichte der Heidelberger Akademie der Wissenschaften, Philosophisch-historische Klasse, 1974, 4. Heidelberg: Carl Winter Verlag, 1974.
d'Alverny, M. Th. Review of: Pritchet, C.D., ed. *Iohannis Alexandrini Commentaria in Librum de sectis Galeni.* Leiden: E.J. Brill, 1982. *Scriptorium* (1984) 38: 361–366.
Durling, Richard J. The Anonymous Translation of Aristotle's *De generatione et corruptione (Translatio Vetus). Traditio* (1994) 49: 320–330.
Gaulin, Jean-Louis. Sur le vin au moyen âge. Pietro de' Crescenzi lecteur et utilisateur des Géoponiques traduites par Burgundio de Pise. *Mélanges de l'école française de Rome. Moyen âge–temps modernes* 1984 (96): 95: 127.
Gryson, Roger and Thomas P. Osborne. Un faux témoin de la "Vetus Latina": la version latine du Commentaire pseudo-basilien sur Isaie. Avec une note sur le ms. 179 de la "Vetus Latina." *Revue bénédictine* (1985) 95: 280–292.
Röhle, R. Bemerkungen zu einer Neuausgave der 'Versio Modestinianorum a Burgundione facta.' *Studia et documenta historiae et iuris* (1983) 49: 372–374.
Vuillemin-Diem, Gudrun and Marwan Rashed. Burgundio de Pise et ses manuscrits grecs d'Aristote: Laur. 87.7 et Laur. 81.18. *Recherches de Théologie et Philosophie médiévales* (1997) 64: 136–198.
Wilson, Nigel G. New Light on Burgundio of Pisa. *Studi italiani di filologia classica.* Terza serie (1986) 4: 113–118.
———. Ioannikios and Burgundio: a Survey of the Problem. In *Scritture, libri e testi nelle aree provinciali di Bisanzio.* Atti del seminario di Erice (18–25 settembre 1988). Edited by G. Cavallo. Spoleto, 1991: 447–455.

PIETER BEULLENS

BURIDAN, JOHN

John Buridan (c. 1300–1361) was a renowned philosopher and arts master who taught at the University of Paris in the mid-fourteenth century. His application of logical methods to traditional problems in metaphysics and natural philosophy, and his commitment to philosophy as an independent, secular enterprise—rather than as *ancilla theologiae* ("handmaiden to theology"), as *Thomas Aquinas put it—helped to pave the way for the modern conception of philosophy as an autonomous academic discipline. Buridan's commentaries on Aristotle were immensely popular, first at Paris and later at the newly-founded universities of Heidelberg, Vienna, Kraków, Pisa, and Florence, where they continued to influence the way philosophy was practiced for the next two centuries.

Life and Works

We know only a few details of Buridan's life. He hailed from Picardy, in northeastern France, and probably came as a young man to study at the University of Paris, where he received his Master of Arts degree and formal license to teach by the mid-1320s. He was awarded a stipend for needy students, suggesting that he was of limited means when he first arrived in the city, but the award of several benefices (lifetime income from church property) during his career eventually made him wealthy enough to purchase a house in the university precinct, which was later used as a student residence for his fellow Picards. He twice served as rector of the university, and was sometimes asked to adjudicate internal disputes. He is last mentioned in a document of 1358, and must have been dead by 1361 because in that year one of his benefices went to another person.

Unlike most philosophers in the faculty of arts, Buridan never moved on to study for a doctoral degree in theology. This was the career path followed by most of the figures we now think of as medieval philosophers, including Aquinas, *Duns Scotus, and *William of Ockham (although political circumstances prevented Ockham from finishing his degree). There had been a few career arts masters before Buridan, but the best known of these—*Pietro d'Abano, *Boethius of Dacia, *Siger of Brabant, and John of Jandun—were associated with the heterodox teachings of Latin Averroism, which held, among other things, that true *scientia* is the province of philosophy, not theology. Naturally, this upset the theologians, and the doctrine was eventually declared to be in error by the Bishop of Paris in the *Condemnation of 1277. Only two generations later, Buridan allowed his readers to reach essentially the same conclusion by shrewdly bracketing the question of whether theology counts as a science, leaving it for the theologians to decide (in doing so, he could say that he was adhering to university statutes that forbade arts masters to teach or write about theology). At the same time, he unambiguously asserts that philosophy counts as knowledge because it begins from what is evident to our senses and intellect—unlike theology, which begins from non-evident truths revealed in scripture and church doctrine. So, whatever else we say about it, philosophy was for Buridan an activity of the arts masters, or *artistae* (artists), as they were known.

Buridan was also different in that he remained his whole life a secular cleric: he never joined a religious order such as the Dominicans or Franciscans. This was an important consideration in an age when virtually all the leading thinkers had religious and intellectual affiliations outside their university: Aquinas was a Dominican, Ockham a Franciscan, Gregory of Rimini an Augustinian, and so on. Among other things, this freed Buridan from the obligation to enter into the ferocious disputes that sometimes arose between religious orders or between an order and the church hierarchy. Thus, whereas Ockham spent his entire later career away from philosophy, crusading against the papacy on apostolic poverty and eventually being excommunicated for his troubles, Buridan was bound only by the intellectual and pedagogical traditions of his university. His confessional independence also meant that he could help himself to insights from a variety of sources, something that emerges in the occasionally eclectic character of his thought.

Buridan was an astonishingly productive scholar, even by medieval standards. Most of his works are in the form of commentaries on Aristotle. He wrote both *expositiones* (expositions)—literal commentaries featuring line-by-line explanations of the meaning of Aristotle's remarks—and *quaestiones* (questions), longer, critical studies of the philosophical issues raised by those remarks. Both genres originated in the classroom, a fact that can still be seen in student queries that survive in the text. Like a modern professor teaching different versions of the same course, Buridan also lectured more than once on the same text during his career, with the result that there are sometimes multiple versions of his commentary on the same work. These show the development of his thought in the sense that they become longer and more sophisticated over time, but in general Buridan was a very consistent thinker. Only rarely do we find changes in doctrine.

The works of Buridan that had the most immediate impact on medieval science were his commentaries on Aristotle's *Physics*, *On the Heavens*, *On Generation and Corruption*, *De Anima*, *Parva Naturalia*, and *Metaphysics*, as well as his independent treatise on the nature of points. But Buridan was primarily a logician, and here his masterwork was the *Summulae de dialectica* (Compendium of Dialectic), a comprehensive textbook that showed how the analysis of terms in a proposition could be used to solve—or just as often to dissolve—philosophical problems.

Although his mother tongue was French, Buridan always lectured and wrote in Latin. Unfortunately, there have been few modern editions and translations of his works. The situation has improved with the appearance of a translation of the entire *Summulae*, along with studies containing excerpts of other texts, but on the whole it is fair to say that his impact on premodern science has not been fully appreciated.

Contributions

Buridan's main contribution to medieval science was to extend and hone the analytical methods of Aristotelian natural philosophy. Like most of his contemporaries, he assumed that science is primarily about how we represent the world to ourselves in thought and language. What he brought to the discussion was a more systematic way of analyzing terms, propositions, and arguments, set forth in the chapters of his *Summulae*, the popularity of which helped to raise the profile of natural philosophy within the university. Indeed, when the influence of the *via Buridani* or "Buridanian way" began to wane some two centuries later, it was not because it was replaced by something newer and more powerful, but because the whole concept of scientific knowledge had changed. Thus, when Francis Bacon (1561–1626), one of the heralds of modern empirical science, writes about the Aristotelian logic used by his predecessors, he can barely hide his contempt: "Aristotle," he says, "utterly enslaved his natural philosophy to his logic, and made it a matter of disputation and almost useless" (*Novum Organum*, I.64). These are the words of someone already in the grip of a new paradigm.

Buridan's dialectical approach was ideally suited to the medieval view of nature as a closed system whose rational order testifies to the goodness of its maker. On this view, careful analysis of the significance of the concepts and terms through which we try to understand the world, and of the way they function in propositions, can go a long way toward clarifying questions and identifying pseudo-problems. For example, in the debate over the composition of continuous magnitudes, Henry of Harclay (1270–1317) had argued that lines, surfaces, and solids must ultimately be composed of indivisibles, even if only God has the power to "see" them. To prove this, he used some compelling examples, including one that has become known as the "touch-at-a-point" argument: imagine a perfect sphere slowly descending onto a perfectly flat surface; it must first touch the surface at some indivisible part of itself, because contact with any divisible part of itself would be divisible into smaller parts, one of which must touch the surface before the others, and so on; therefore, the first point of contact must be indivisible. Buridan replies that one can reach this conclusion only by failing to understand what the word *punctum* (point) means. Divisible entities, such as spheres and surfaces, cannot have indivisible points as parts because indivisible points by definition have no parts. Accordingly, we can say that the sphere will touch the surface at a point only if we interpret "point" in its correct sense as "some last part" of the sphere, but any last part of the sphere will likewise be divisible ad infinitum. It matters greatly to Buridan to identify the literally true sense of a proposition because only true propositions are knowledge-producing on the Aristotelian view. Of course, Buridan readily acknowledged that there are other, more metaphorical, uses of the term "point," such as when we speak "in keeping with the concepts of the mathematicians [*secundum imaginationem mathematicorum*], as if there were indivisible points—not because they believe that there really are, but because they revert to that assumption in measuring" (*Questions on Aristotle's Physics*, VI.4). Mathematical points belong to a different order of discourse, one in which we "speak figuratively

[*transsumptive*]… according to a different signification" (*Summulae* 4.3.2). They have no more relevance for natural science than the arbitrary starting points a cloth merchant uses when measuring a bolt of cloth.

Buridan sometimes uses this figurative mode of expression to explore the limits of natural philosophy. For example, although philosophers can ask whether God could make a space outside the cosmos or annihilate everything inside the sphere of the Moon, speculation about such hypothetical cases is not part of natural philosophy because to discuss them "one must so to speak beg the intellect [*ideo quasi mendicare oportet intellectum humanum*]" (*Questions on Aristotle's Physics*, IV.15). The key difference is that the truth or falsity of such propositions is not evident to us—for all we know, God could have created a space outside the cosmos; our belief that He did not in fact do so is based on scripture and church teaching, but here we assent with our will, not our intellect. Purely theological assumptions are irrelevant to philosophy: "One might assume that there are many more separate substances than there are celestial spheres and celestial motions, viz., great legions of angels, but this cannot be proved by demonstrative arguments originating from sense perception" (*Questions on Aristotle's Metaphysics*, II.9).

Buridan also contributed to the demise of Aristotelian cosmology by popularizing the theory of *impetus, or impressed force, to explain projectile motion. Rejecting the Aristotelian theory of antiperistasis, according to which the continued motion of a javelin after it leaves a thrower's hand is due to the motion of the surrounding air (it is "pushed along" by the air rushing in to fill the empty space behind it), Buridan argues that only an internal motive force, transmitted from the mover to the projectile, can explain the phenomenon. Although impetus theory did not originate with him, his account differs from earlier treatments in Philoponus and *Ibn Sina (Avicenna) in that he entertains the possibility that impetus may not be self-dissipating: "After leaving the arm of the thrower, the projectile would be moved by an impetus given to it by the thrower, and would continue to be moved as long as the impetus remained stronger than the resistance, and would be of infinite duration were it not diminished and corrupted by a contrary force resisting it or by something inclining it to a contrary motion" (*Questions on Aristotle's Metaphysics* XII.9). He even suggests that the acceleration of a falling body can be understood in terms of its accumulation of units of impetus.

Despite its revolutionary implications, however, Buridan did not take the further step of using impetus to transform the science of mechanics, and so he did not anticipate Galileo, as some historians of science have suggested. He was in too many other respects an unapologetic Aristotelian, as for example in his insistence that motion and rest are contrary states of bodies and that the world is finite in extent. It would be more accurate to think of Buridan as a philosopher who tried to reshape Aristotelian natural philosophy as best he could in the face of challenges from an increasingly mechanistic worldview.

See also **Aristotelianism; Impetus;** *Scientia*

Bibliography

Primary Sources

Clagett, Marshall (ed. & tr.). *The Science of Mechanics in the Middle Ages*. Madison: University of Wisconsin Press, 1959.

Hyman, Arthur, and James J. Walsh, eds. *Philosophy in the Middle Ages: The Christian, Islamic, and Jewish Traditions*. Second Edition. Indianapolis: Hackett, 1987.

Klima, Gyula (tr.). *John Buridan: 'Summulae de Dialectica'*. New Haven: Yale University Press, 2001.

Patar, Benoît (ed.). *Ioannis Buridani, Expositio et Quaestiones in Aristotelis 'De Caelo'*. Louvain-Paris: Éditions de l'Institut Supérieur de Philosophie-Éditions du Préambule–Éditions Peeters, 1991.

——— (ed.). *Le Traité de l'âme de Jean Buridan [De prima lectura]*. Louvain-Longueuil (Québec): Éditions de l'Institut Supérieur de Philosophie-Éditions du Préambule, 1991.

Scott, Frederick, and Herman Shapiro (ed.). John Buridan's *De motibus animalium*. *Isis* (1967) 58: 533–552.

Sobol, Peter G. (tr.). "Jean Buridan on Sensation." In *Readings in Medieval Philosophy*, ed. Andrew B. Schoedinger. New York: Oxford University Press, 1996.

Thijssen, J. M. M. H. (ed.). *John Buridan's 'Tractatus de Infinito'*. Nijmegen: Ingenium, 1991.

Secondary Sources

Duhem, Pierre. *Études sur Léonard de Vinci*. 3 vols. Paris: Hermann, 1906–1913.

Michael, Bernd. "Johannes Buridan: Studien zu seinem Leben, seinen Werken und zu Rezeption seiner Theorien im Europa des späten Mittelalters." 2 vols. Ph.D. Dissertation: University of Berlin, 1985.

Maier, Anneliese. *Metaphysische Hintergründe der spätscholastischen Naturphilosophie*. Roma: Storia e Letteratura, 1955.

Sylla, Edith D. Aristotelian Commentaries and Scientific Change: The Parisian Nominalists on the Cause of the Natural Motion of Inanimate Bodies. *Vivarium* (1993) 32: 37-83.

Thijssen, J.M.M.H., and Jack Zupko (eds.). *The Metaphysics and Natural Philosophy of John Buridan*. Leiden: Brill, 2001.

Zupko, Jack. *John Buridan: Portrait of a Fourteenth-Century Arts Master*. Notre Dame, Ind: University of Notre Dame Press, 2003.

———. Nominalism Meets Indivisibilism. *Medieval Philosophy and Theology* (1993) 3: 158–185.

Zoubov, Vassili (ed.). Jean Buridan et les concepts du point au quatorzième siècle. *Medieval and Renaissance Studies* (1961) 5: 63–95.

JACK ZUPKO

C

CALENDAR

The medieval calendar was made up of a number of overlapping components: the solar day and year, lunar month, the natural seasons, and artificial divisions (such as the reign of a king). In 725 C.E. the Venerable *Bede wrote that "all the courses of mortal life are measured in moments, hours, days, months, years, ages." He went on to say that there are three kinds of time reckoning, operating according to nature, custom, or authority. Thus, the natural passage of the seasons is a different kind of time-reckoning than the thirty-day month or the divine requirement that the seventh day be a day of rest. The rest of Bede's work, titled *The Reckoning of Time*, discusses the calendars, starting with the day, ending with the Ages of the World, and clarifying how to reckon dates according to each.

The Passing of Years

For Christian writers, the whole of history stretched out in a continuous line which started with Adam at year one, and the line divided into ages and generations. According to Bede, the first age—from Adam to Noah—is ten generations; the second—from Noah to Abraham—is also ten generations. Each age could be compared to a stage of life, with the first likened to infancy, the second to childhood, the third to adolescence, and so on. By parallel with the resurrection of Christ, the world will be destroyed at the end of the Sixth Age, and reborn in the Eighth Age. *Isidore of Seville organized his chronology of the Six Ages (*Etymologiae* book 5) according to the reigns of patriarchs, judges, and kings, dating each reign by its final year; he also fixed the beginning of the Sixth Age at Christ's birth, as distinct from his earthly ministry or passion. Eusebius (263–339), who synchronized biblical and secular dates in a time-line chronicle beginning with Abraham. The fusions of world-chronicle and the Six Ages proposed by medieval authors was not unproblematic, however, since there are difficulties with the versions of the Bible—the Septuagint translation gives

different numbers of years and generations from the Hebrew version, and many texts equated one age with one thousand years. Nonetheless, medieval authors continued to work on chronologies of the world, and in the later Middle Ages chronologies such as the Nuremberg Chronicle were among the earliest printed books. Another two hundred years later, in the seventeenth century, Bishop James Ussher famously combined biblical, secular and astronomical dates to calculate that the Creation had taken place on Sunday October 23, 4004 B.C.E.

Conflicts between various sets of criteria (astronomical, theological, and calendrical), notably between Rome and Alexandria, culminated in Dionysius Exiguus' reworking in 526 C.E. of Alexandrian tables for a Roman calendar. An incidental but ultimately influential side-effect of his new Easter table was that it was projected according to an innovative dating system: the *annus domini*, calculated from the beginning of the reign of Diocletian, which had hitherto prevailed. The Dionysian Paschal table and its chronological scheme spread rapidly, although it was not until the Synod of Whitby in 664 C.E. that the English Church united and accepted the new way of determining the date of Easter.

To locate an event in time, it had to be given a year-number. One system, used in Europe from the eighth century onwards, particularly for official and administrative documents, was to number the years according to the reign of a particular monarch or pope. The regnal years began on the date of the king's coronation. This system ran alongside year-numbers fixed according to the Christian Era, and difficulties for historians are compounded by the fact that there is no standardization about when the year began. Bede, Dionysius, and other writers considered that the year began with the Nativity (December 25). During the twelfth and thirteenth centuries this was replaced in many (but not all) places by dating from the Annunciation (March 25). The French Chancery used a year which started on the moveable feast of Easter, meaning that each year had a different number of days from the previous one. In the Roman calendar

January was considered the first month, and January 1 was considered the first day of the solar year for the purposes of calculating feast days. The different systems were adopted by different cities and countries, as seen in the famous example given by R.L. Poole. If we suppose a traveler to set out from Venice on March 1, 1245, the first day of the Venetian year, he would find himself in 1244 when he reached Florence: and if after a short stay he went to Pisa, the year 1246 would already have begun there. Continuing his journey westward, he would find himself again in 1245 when he entered Provence, and on arriving in France before Easter (April 16) he would once more be in 1244.

Dividing the Year

The seasons of the year governed life for many people in medieval Europe—the planting, nurturing, and harvesting of crops was the cycle according to which life was lived. Celebrations of the end of winter and the start of spring were followed by periods of plowing the fields and planting crops. In the summer there was hay to be cut, wheat to be harvested and stored, and grapes to be harvested and made into wine. The fall was taken up with storing and preserving food, and preparing the fields for winter crops, and the winter was a cold and dormant time, occupied with keeping warm and well fed until the beginning of spring started the cycle again. The sequence of agricultural tasks is depicted in many medieval calendar manuscripts, as well as in books of hours made for the nobility. Each month would be illustrated with the task to be carried out at that time, an iconographic tradition seen in sculture, tapestry, and illuminated manuscripts including the sumptuous *Très Riches Heures* made for the Duc de Berry.

The year could also be divided into months according to the Julian calendar, with twelve months of around thirty days each, and an extra day every four years to keep the calendar in step with the solar year. According to the Roman system the days within each month were numbered according to the kalends, ides, and nones, and in the Middle Ages this system was used in parallel with the now more familiar one of the sequential numbering of days within a month. The first day of May could also be referred to as the kalends of May, and since the Julian calendar counted back from the kalends, the twentieth day of April was twelve days before the kalends of May.

Although the Christian calendar dominated medieval Europe, the Jewish and Islamic calendars were also used in some areas and by some groups of people. The Islamic calendar is a strictly lunar calendar of twelve months of twenty-nine or thirty days, instituted in 642 C.E. (ten years after the death of Muhammed). Years are numbered from the Hijira (the flight of Muhammed from Mecca to Medina): July 16, 622 in the Julian calendar. The Jewish calendar is also lunar, with twelve months of twenty-nine or thirty days, and the new year beginning on Rosh Hashanah, the first day of the seventh month (Tishri). Years are counted from the creation, which was in 3760 B.C.E. of the Julian calendar.

Days for Feasting and Fasting

As a quarter of the lunar month, the seven-day week has been used for thousands of years. It probably has Assyrian origins, and many cultures have taken one of the days of the week as a day of rest. Because there were also seven planets known, the days were linked to planets, according them cosmological significance and forming the basis for astrological calculations. Indeed, many of the weekday names used in Europe relate to the names of the planets.

As well as the numbering of days according to the Julian calendar's ides, nones, and kalends, or the sequential numbering of days in a month, medieval scholars used a wealth of different systems for identifying days in the year, and giving information about them. Each day was allocated a letter A–G, starting with A on January 1, and the letter of the first Sunday of the year is called the dominical letter of the year. Linked to the dominical letters are the concurrents, which also indicate what day of the week a particular date is: the number indicates the number of days between the last Sunday of the year and January 1. The year also had a golden number: to calculate this add one to the number of the year in the Christian Era, divide this by nineteen, and the remainder will be the golden number, which gives the year's position in the nineteen-year lunar cycle, useful for calculating the date of Easter. The indiction number for a year, a system originating with the Roman tax system, ranged from one to fifteen, and the epact indicted how old the moon was on March 22. Astronomical dates could be given in terms of the position of the Sun in the zodiac, in relation to the zodiac rather than the calendar months. Ecclesiastical dates might be given in relation to festivals and saints' days, for example, the octave was the eighth day after a feast day (counted inclusively). In 1232 Pope Gregory IX established a standard list of eighty-five feasts and fixed their dates, but there was still much freedom to introduce local variations both with respect to which saints were commemorated, and on which dates.

Calendars and Calculations

All this information was gathered together in calendar manuscripts, of which there survive hundreds of examples from medieval Europe. Ranging from beautiful illuminated codices to small notebooks, one particular medieval calendar manuscript might look very different from another. Despite their differing physical appearance, most calendars are organized with a month to a page and the data for that month arranged in columns. With one row per day, the information given usually includes the golden number and dominical letters, to allow calculation of the date of Easter, new moons, times of sunrise and sunset, eclipses of the Sun and Moon, and, depending on the function of the manuscript, saints' days and feast names might be listed, or astronomical data such as the rising and setting of stars. If saints' days are listed, this can help date and locate the calendar by the particular selection of saints included, by matching the celebration of a particular saint on a particular day to a known local practice. If times of the rising and setting of the Sun and stars are given, this can again help to locate the calendar since these values change with latitude.

The medieval calendar thus contained all the information that might be needed to calculate the dates of moveable Church feasts, or the positions of the Sun and Moon, and the methods for these calculations were described in *computus texts. These could be in verse or prose, and were circulated attached to or separate from the tables of calendrical data. By following the methods described, a medieval scholar could calculate divisions of time, days, weeks, months, and seasons, solstices and equinoxes, solar and lunar cycles, and (most importantly) the date of Easter.

Easter was defined as the first Sunday after the first (calculated) full moon following the vernal equinox, which was fixed on March 21. The calendar dates for the Paschal full moons run in a nineteen-year cycle—called the Metonic Cycle—at the end of which the cycle repeats, and Easter is on the Sunday following the paschal full moon, or Easter limit. The golden number of a year refers to its position in this cycle, and for any year the golden number can be used to determine the date of the paschal full moon by consulting a set of tables or a calendar. Then, the dominical letter indicates which days that year are Sundays, allowing the date of Easter to be fixed. In addition to the longhand methods, computus manuscripts often included mnemonics and lists for easy reference. One example of this is the medieval mnemonic "post epi pri pri pri di di di pascha fi," which reminds the reader that in a given year Easter is the third Sunday after the third new moon after Epiphany, a system that works in all but two very specific cases.

A common variation on the standard computus manuscript was the so-called *computus manualis* which explained how to use the hand as a way to calculate by counting along the fingers and around the palm, and allocating each joint of each finger to the months, dominical letters, and other important pieces of information. Material from the computus manuscripts was also extracted and included in texts including encyclopedias, astronomical and medical texts, and religious texts. For quick reference on the move, there survive a number of folded almanac manuscripts, which were worn hanging from the belt. Linked in particular to astrological medicine, and probably originating in late fourteenth-century England, these small books contain summaries of calendrical, astrological, and medical information. In addition, tables of calendrical information were made into instruments (such as the *annulus* of John of Northampton), or engraved onto quadrants, sundials, and astronomical compendia.

Moving away from the written books, which after all would have required a certain level of numeracy or literacy, there is evidence that mnemonic verses were circulating, which would have made basic calendrical information available to the non-literate. There were many versions of a poem often called *Cisio Janus* which provided a way of remembering the most important saints' days of the year. The origins of this poem date back to the twelfth century, and it often appears in Latin *computus* manuscripts and, later, in vernacular versions. Other rhymes reminded people how to calculate Easter, how to divide the day into hours, minutes, and seconds, or how many days were in each month, as in this short poem, found in a number of English and French manuscripts:

"Thirti dayes hath nouembir
April, iune and septembir;
Of xxviijti is but oon,
and all the remenaunt xxxti and j."

See also **Almanacs; Astrology; Astronomy; Clocks and timekeeping**

Bibliography

Carey, Hilary. Astrological medicine and the medieval English folded almanac. *Social History of Medicine* (2003) 16.3: 481–509.

Cheney, C. R., and Michael Jones. *A Handbook of Dates for Students of British History*. New York: Cambridge University Press, 2000.

Fussell, Stephen. *Chronicle of the World: the Complete and Annotated Nuremberg Chronicle of 1493*. Cologne: Tashen, 2001.

Heinsch, Bridget A. *The Medieval Calendar Year*. University Park, PA: Pennsylvania State University Press, 1999.

Higuera, Teresa P. *Medieval Calendars*. London: Weidenfield and Nicolson, 1998.

Means, Laurel. Ffor as moche as yche man may not haue the astrolabe: popular Middle English variations on the computus. *Speculum* (1992) 67: 595–623.

Mooney, Linne M. *The Kalendarium of John Somer*. Atlanta: University of Georgia Press, 1999.

Richards, E. G. *Mapping Time: the Calendar and its History*. Oxford: Oxford University Press, 2000.

Wallis, Faith. *Bede: The Reckoning of Time*. Liverpool: Liverpool University Press, 1999.

CATHERINE EAGLETON

CAMPANUS DE NOVARA

Campanus was born in the first quarter of the thirteenth century, possibly as early as the first decade. He was very probably from Novara in Italy, for he referred to himself as Campanus Novariensis, and used the meridian of Novara in his astronomical works. He accumulated a series of benefices and served as chaplain to three popes: Urban IV, Nicholas IV, and Boniface VIII. Campanus wrote several books on mathematics and astronomy, and many more works are ascribed to him. He was most famous for his redaction of the *Elements* of *Euclid. An edition of *Tractatus de sphaera* published in 1531 identifies the author as *magistro campano euclidis interpraete* (Master Campanus, interpreter of Euclid). The title Magister often given to him may indicate that he was part of a university faculty. Since Campanus's will was drawn up on September 9, 1296, and a letter of Boniface VIII dated September 17, 1296, informs us that

Campanus had just died at Viterbo, his death must fall between those two dates.

Astronomical Works

In addition to his fame as "interpreter of Euclid," Campanus enjoyed a reputation as a skilled astronomer and astrologer. Benjamin and Toomer, in their authoritative study of Campanus, identify him as the certain or probable author of five works on astronomy and a set of *planetary tables. Manuscripts and early printed books inconsistently ascribe other texts on astronomy and *astrology to him, although in most cases the attribution is dubious.

The most important astronomical work by Campanus is his *Theorica planetarum. Its dedication to his patron Urban IV places its composition between 1261 and 1264, the period of Urban's papacy. Campanus's *Theorica* explains the manufacture and use of the equatorium, a calculating instrument ostensibly for use by those who cannot calculate planetary motions from tables. An equatorium imitates the orbs of a planetary model in cross-section. An outer circle indicates the ecliptic. Disks within the ecliptic represent the deferent and epicycle; a third disk is used to create equant motion (although astronomers did not consider the equant to be a physical orb). By turning the disks, the user recreates the motion of the planet, then reads its position from the outer circle.

The *Theorica* is the first known Latin description of an equatorium. The version Campanus describes is completely impractical, requiring several large wooden plates. No example survives, and it is possible that no one, not even Campanus himself, constructed the instrument according to these directions. Later Latin equatoria were compact and usable. Yet despite the near uselessness of the *Theorica* as a book on the equatorium, it was widely copied and cited. In order to explain the instrument, Campanus first had to explain *Ptolemy's planetary models and the motion of each circle or orb. Readers therefore turned to the *Theorica* as a textbook of advanced astronomy that explained the motions of the planets.

In addition, Campanus gave the least and greatest distances for the planets. Ptolemy explained the calculation of celestial distances in the *Planetary Hypotheses*; Latin astronomers knew the work indirectly through translations of Arabic works. Ptolemy assumed that the planets were arranged in nested orbs with no intervening space. Given the relative least and greatest distances of the planets (fixed by the *Almagest* models), it becomes possible to find the sizes of their orbs, and hence their distances from Earth. Campanus used al-Farghani's models to find celestial distances in terms of the Earth's size, then, unusually, converted them into miles. Campanus's values were adopted by Robertus Anglicus in his commentary on *John of Sacrobosco.

Campanus also wrote a *computus on the medieval art of time-reckoning. Astronomers sometimes wrote on this subject since it was based on the solar and lunar cycles. Campanus's *Computus maior* followed the approach to time-reckoning standardized by *Bede in the eighth century, but with the introduction of more elaborate astronomy, including the theory of trepidation (oscillation of the equinoxes) associated with *Thabit ibn Qurra.

Campanus's third major astronomical work was the *Tractatus de sphaera*, one of a group of medieval textbooks on elementary astronomy. Like others of its kind, the *Sphaera* concentrated on introductory *cosmology and on the celestial phenomena associated with the twenty-four hour rotation of the heavens. Unlike Sacrobosco, author of a popular alternative *sphaera*, Campanus discusses some details of planetary motion. Since it cites the *Theorica* and the *Computus*, the *Sphaera* must have been written later than either.

A minor work of Campanus, *De quadrante*, describes the manufacture and use of the quadrant, a standard instrument for measuring the altitude of celestial objects. A second, rarely copied work gives problems to be solved with yet another instrument, the astrolabe.

Campanus prepared a set of astronomical tables, based on the popular Toledan Tables but recalculated for the meridian of Novara. Tables for the Moon were extracted and circulated separately.

As an astronomer, Campanus was not innovative in the modern sense. His importance lies rather in his ability to understand and utilize the recently rediscovered astronomy of the ancients. His direct impact on the Renaissance was small: some of his astronomical works went through a few printed editions, while his *Theorica* was sometimes read but not printed. However, his works helped to establish the foundation on which later generations of astronomers would build their critical re-examinations of Ptolemy. In the early fifteenth century, *John of Gmunden prepared an extract of Campanus's *Theorica*. John, a frequent lecturer in astronomy, helped to establish Vienna as a center of astronomical studies that soon produced *Georg Peuerbach and *Johannes Regiomontanus.

KATHERINE A. TREDWELL

Mathematical Works of Campanus

In the twelfth century, the *Elements* of *Euclid—including the non-Euclidean Books XIV and XV—were translated from Arabic into Latin by *Adelard of Bath, *Hermann of Carinthia, and *Gerard of Cremona. Besides these Arabic-Latin translations, a translation directly from the Greek was produced in Sicily in the twelfth century. The so-called *Adelard II*, very likely written by Robert of Chester, was by far the most popular and most influential Euclid text in the Latin West in the twelfth and thirteenth centuries. It is not a translation, but a compilation, and in almost all cases the Latin commentaries on the *Elements* composed in the thirteenth and fourteenth centuries used the definitions, postulates, axioms, and enunciations of Version II.

The best-known representative of the Robert tradition is the redaction of the *Elements* prepared by Campanus de Novara. A *terminus ante quem* of 1259 for Campanus's version can be derived from what seems to be the earliest dated extant codex of the work, Firenze, BNC Magliab. XI, 112. The Campanus version dominated Latin mathematics until printed editions were made from Greek manuscripts in the sixteenth century. This medieval version was printed in Venice by Erhard Ratdolt in 1482, thus becoming the first printed edition of Euclid's *Elements* in any language. Campanus borrowed most of his definitions, axioms, postulates, and enunciations from the Robert redaction, but he added to Book VII a number of definitions, as well as postulates and axioms derived from the *Arithmetica* of *Jordanus de Nemore (ed. Busard 1991), and there are indications that he also used Johannes de Tinemue's version as a source. In Book V., Def. 16, he cites Ahmad ibn Yusuf's *Epistola de proportione et proportionalitate*, translated by Gerard of Cremona from Arabic into Latin, while in his commentary on the same definition he refers to Jordanus's *Arithmetica*, and later, in XIII. 9, he mentions *Ptolemy's *Almagest*. It is very probable that Campanus was acquainted with the Greek-Latin translation of the *Elements* as well as Anaritius's commentary on the *Elements* translated by Gerard of Cremona.

Campanus's Euclid version was very influential. In 1267 *Roger Bacon, in a work addressed to Pope Clement IV, ranked Campanus among the excellent mathematicians (Benjamin/ Toomer 1971, 7). *Witelo was acquainted with Campanus's edition, for he gives Prop. V. 26–29 of Campanus in his *Perspectiva* Prop. I.6, I.10-12 (Unguru 1977, 218, 219–221). In the fourteenth century, *Bradwardine (d. 1349) says in his *Geometria speculativa*: "I have not seen a discussion of them, except only by Campanus, who only casually touches on the pentagon a little" (Molland 1989, 37), and "On account of this Campanus says in the first comment of the tenth book of Geometry that any rectilinear angle is infinitely greater than an angle of contingency" (Molland 1989, 71). The Campanus manuscript Nuremberg, Stadtbibliothek Cent. VI 13 belonged to *Regiomontanus (1436–1476); the first fourteen folios (up to *Elements* III. 8) are in the hand of Regiomontanus himself, while the remainder of the text in another hand contains long additions and marginal comments by Regiomontanus (Folkerts 1990, 367). Some indication of the popularity of Campanus's version and commentary is provided by Folkerts' (1989, 38–43) census of one hundred and thirty-one manuscripts containing the whole Campanus redaction or parts thereof.

Beyond this highly influential work, other mathematical texts have been attributed to Campanus with varying degrees of certainty. *De proportione et proportionabilitate* (*On Composed Ratios*, ed. Busard, 1971), written probably in the thirteenth century, depends ultimately on the transversal theorem of Menelaus through intermediate works by Ametus filius Josephi and *Thabit ibn Qurra that were translated in the twelfth century by Gerard of Cremona. It begins with four definitions, the first of which reads as follows: *Proportio est duarum quantitatum eiusdem generis ad invicem habitudo* (A ratio is the mutual relationship of two quantities of the same kind). Positive evidence that Campanus wrote the work is slight, consisting of attestations in two manuscripts. The fact that seven of the fourteen manuscripts are Italian might be thought to favor claims for Campanus's authorship.

A related text, *De figura sectore* (*On the Sector-Figure*, ed. Lorch, 2001, 436–442), is aimed at proving the theorem of Menelaus for a spherical surface. It directly follows the Campanus text *De proportione et proportionabilitate* in five manuscripts and one manuscript contains both texts, but not consecutively. Therefore, it is very likely that Campanus wrote both *De figura sectore* and *De proportione*, for the two treatises together form a unit, reproducing the content of Thabit's *De figura sectore*, with the exception of §7 and §8.

We have evidence that Campanus not only borrowed from Jordanus, but also added to the latter's *Arithmetica*. In the manuscript P4 (Paris, BnF lat. 16198, fol. 150r), at the conclusion of Book X of the *Arithmetica* we find the following as a prefatory note to three appended propositions: *Istas propositiones apposuit magister Campanus post 78^{am} 9^i libri vel secundum alium ordinem post 71^{am} ita quod inter 78 et 79 vel 71 et 72 9^i libri interseruit*. Thus, Campanus added these three propositions to the *Arithmetica* of Jordanus (Busard 1991, 240f). The available manuscripts of the *Arithmetica* are divided into three distinct families. The manuscripts P4 and V1 (Venice, Bibl. Naz. Marc., fondo antico 332 [= 1647]), representing the second family, contain 25 (P4) and 31 (V1) added propositions. An indication that Campanus adjoined some added propositions is found in the margin of V1.

In addition to the foregoing works, other mathematical works have been attributed more tenuously to Campanus. Lorch (1996, 169) ascribed one of two Latin versions of the *Sphaerica* of Theodosius (c. 200 B.C.E.) to Campanus. Bjornbo (1902, 152) speculated that notes to Menelaus of Alexandria's *Sphaerica* might have been written by Campanus, but this question needs further research. The *De quadratura circuli* (ed. Clagett 1964, 588–607 with an English translation) attributed to Campanus by *Albert of Saxony is sufficiently elementary and trivial to deny that Campanus had written it.

H.L.L. BUSARD

See also **Arithmetic; Astrolabes and quadrants; Astronomy; Euclid; Gerard of Cremona; Jordanus de Nemore; Ptolemy; Quadrivium; *Theorica planetarum*; Toledo; Translation movements**

Bibliography

Benjamin, Francis S. John of Gmunden and Campanus of Novara. *Osiris* (1954), 1st ser., 11: 221–246.

Benjamin, Jr., Francis S. and G. J. Toomer. *Campanus of Novara and Medieval Planetary Theory: "Theorica Planetarum."* Madison: University of Wisconsin Press, 1971.

Bjornbo, Axel A. Studien über Menelaos' Sphärik: Beiträge zur Geschichte des Sphärik und Trigonometrie der Griechen. *Abhandlungen zur Geschichte der rnathematischen Wissenschaften* (1902) 14: 1–154.

Busard, Hubert L.L. Die Traktate De proportionibus von Jordanus und Campanus. *Centaurus* (1971) 15: 193–227.

———. *Jordanus de Nemore, De elementis arithmetice artis. A medieval treatise on number theory.* Stuttgart: Franz Steiner Verlag, 1991.

Clagett, Marshall. *Archimedes in the Middle Ages, Volume I. Arabo-Latin Tradition.* Madison: University of Wisconsin Press, 1964.

Duhem, Pierre. *Le système du monde.* Paris: Hermann, 1958.

Grant, Edward. *A Source Book in Medieval Science.* Cambridge: Harvard University Press, 1974, pp. 136–150.

Folkerts, Menso. "Euclid in Medieval Europe." In: *The Benjamin Catalogue for History of Science, Questio II de rerum natura.* Winnipeg, 1989.

———. "New Results on the Mathematical Activity of Regiomontanus." In Ernst Zinner, *Regiomontanus: His life and Work*, translated by Ezra Brown. New York: North-Holland, 1990, pp. 363–372.

Lorch, Richard. "The Transmission of Theodosius' Sphaerica." In *Mathematische Probleme im Mittelalter Der lateinische und arabische Sprachbereich*, ed. M. Folkerts. Wiesbaden: Harrassowitz Verlag, 1996, pp. 159–183.

———. *Thabit ibn Qurra On the Sector-Figure and Related Texts.* Islamic Mathematics and Astronomy 108. Frankfurt am Main, Germany: Institute for the History of Arabic Science at the Johann Wolfgang Goethe University, 2001.

Molland, George. *Thomas Bradwardine, Geometria speculativa.* Stuttgart: Franz Steiner Verlag, 1989.

Price, Derek J. *The Equatorie of the Planetis.* New York: Cambridge University Press, 1955.

Unguru, Sabetai. *Witelonis perspectivae, liber primus. Book I of Witelo's Perspectiva.* Warsaw, Poland: The Polish Academy of Sciences Press, 1977.

Van Helden, Albert. *Measuring the Universe: Cosmic Dimensions from Aristarchus to Halley.* Chicago: University of Chicago Press, 1985.

CANALS

Digging canals implied a process of repeated surveying or leveling operations in order to ensure that the water ran downhill. An eleventh-century Iraqi document, probably dictated by a surveyor or contractor with practical experience, describes three different kinds of instruments used to survey irrigation canals. The one most used was a canal-level, a pipe filled with water that had been described by Hero of Alexandria in his *Dioptra*. This level is called *anbub*, "pipe," in Arabic. "If the water issues from the two ends at the same time, it is because the surface is horizontal. But if it flows only from one end, it is because the side on which it flows is lower than the other." The operation, which is to be repeated along the entire length of the proposed course, was the one used at the time in "most of the districts of Iraq and Khurasan" (Cahen). There was also a learned science associated with leveling called *'ilm al-mizan* ("science of the balance").

The same document gives specific details regarding the digging of canals. The author states that before any work is done, one must first estimate the depth desired and the debit of the canal. He then gives sample problems for computing work and salaries. "Take a canal 400 cubits long by one-half plus one-third [cubit] wide and two-thirds deep, with a spade and two porters. How much work will there be?" The earth removed was measured in units of 100 cubic cubits. A service road was constructed alongside the canal (or the proposed route), and the number of men required to do the job calculated mathematically. For each man digging with a spade, one or two porters were required to remove the earth or silt in baskets. This standard modus operandi appears to have been continuously practiced in Mesopotamia since the times of the ancient empires. In the irrigation systems ancient of the ancient Near East, where silting was such a massive problem, digging out canals was quite literally reduced to a science. The state had to pay workers to dig out silt and had therefore to calculate how much was being removed. Old-Babylonian problem-texts survive on cuneiform tablets from around 1700 B.C.E., and give examples of how to calculate expenses for digging a canal of specific width, depth and length, the number of workers required to complete the task in a single day, or the costs of digging our or expanding the volume of an old canal that has been silted up (Neugebauer and Sachs).

In late medieval Valencia, the most common method of leveling canals was with an A-level, a large instrument carried about on a pack animal. A plumb-line was hung from the apex of the A. The legs of the instrument could be placed at any point on the proposed route and the gradient read from a scale on the bar of the A. Levelers (*llivelladors*) were generally master masons, used to working with levels, who specialized in canal surveys. They not only laid out the courses of new canals, or surveyed proposed courses, but also executed more precise measurements, especially of divisors, structures located at the point where a main canal splits into two branch canals carrying a specific proportion of the debit, generally 1:1. Any interference with the flow of the water in the environs of the divisor, or the deposition of silt in the structure itself, could alter the proportions, and thus divisors were frequently "leveled" by experts.

Ditching and Land Reclamation

The introduction of the iron-shod spade in the tenth and eleventh centuries greatly eased the labor involved in digging ditches and canals. Only then was it cost-effective to systematically dig drainage ditches around dry-farmed fields (in irrigated areas fields were commonly bounded by canals, on more than one side). In the Rijnland of medieval Holland, where excess water was a permanent, structural feature of agriculture, parcels were enclosed by ditches in the early Middle Ages, whether for bounding fields or for drainage. Reclamation of peat bogs in the late Middle Ages was accomplished purely by building drainage ditches, water from the top layers of the bog seeping into the ditches which carried it away. Parallel ditches or drainage canals were dug in these bogs around 120 yards (110 meters) apart, the channels constituting standard parcel boundaries, with houses located at the front of each parcel. The common length of ditches and parcels in the western Netherlands eventually stabilized at around 1,367 yards (1,250) meters, creating standardized parcels of around 35 acres (14 hectares).

In northern France, Guillerme describes "mini-Venices," with seven cities ranking ahead of Venice in the ratio of intramural waterways to total surface area. The canals of Beauvais were supplied by the Therain River. The floors of the canals were partially paved because they had been Roman streets. Canals dug down to the Roman street level were typically just over one yard (one meter) deep and six feet six inches (two meters) wide. In Nimes, too, a Roman road was converted into a canal; inasmuch as a clay substrate underlay the road, there was minimal seepage. The enlargement of moats surrounding these cities caused upstream fields to become waterlogged. Such marshlands were drained in the twelfth and thirteenth centuries where flax and hemp were cultivated from networks of shallow canals. Retting pits where flax was steeped in vats or stagnant ponds and fermented before being reduced to pulp constituted the hydraulic infrastructure of the linen cloth industry (and, later on, of *paper, which used the same preparation technology).

Further south, the coastline of much of the Mediterranean was naturally marshy. It was extremely difficult to build stable canals (whether for irrigation or drainage) when the water table was very high. In the swamplands (*marjals*) near the city of Valencia digging canals so close to the water table had the paradoxical effect of expanding the marsh. In the 1390s the city sought to stabilize the area by building new main canals and giving settlers tax breaks to encourage them to move there. Stability depended on sufficient population density to provide constant upkeep for the canal system.

See also **Agriculture; Instruments, agricultural; Irrigation and drainage; Water supply and sewerage**

Bibliography

Cahen, Claude. Le service de l'irrigation en Iraq au début du XIe siècle. *Bulletin d'Etudes Orientales* (1949–1950) 13: 117–143.

Glick, Thomas F. Levels and Levelers: Surveying Irrigation Canals in Medieval Valencia. *Technology and Culture* (1968) 9: 165–180.

———. *Irrigation and Society in Medieval Valencia*. Cambridge: Harvard University Press, 1970.

Guillerme, André E. *The Age of Water: The Urban Environment in the North of France, A.D. 300–1800*. College Station: Texas A&M University Press, 1988.

Neugebauer, O. and A. Sachs, eds. *Mathematical Cuneiform Texts*. New Haven: American Oriental Society, 1945.

THOMAS F. GLICK

CARTOGRAPHY

Medieval maps in Europe were shaped by several major, not always compatible traditions, and the various genres of cartography show little or no apparent relation to each other until the High Middle Ages. The superimposition of Christian cosmology on the pre-Christian Greek, mostly astronomical and theoretical, and Roman, mostly applied, cartographic traditions introduced a tension between the classical ideas of sphericity of the Earth and universe and the biblical ideas of a flat and rectangular Earth. The teaching of the spherical Earth prevailed, but the problems of projecting location of objects on the Earth's surface received little attention from medieval geographers until the thirteenth century. Apart from a few celestial maps, all known medieval maps focus on the inhabited part of the Earth, the equivalent of the Greek *oikumene*, limited to the northern part of the eastern hemisphere. Extant maps are found in copies dating from the eighth century C.E. Among them, world maps are the most numerous (over one thousand one hundred are known), although most are small and diagrammatic. Usually circular, they could also be oval or mandorla, in the almond shape of the Christian aura. Most other maps (regional, topographical, cadastral) date from the fourteenth and fifteenth centuries and are rectangular in shape.

Historians of cartography generally hold a low opinion of the role of geographical theory in medieval mapping, and indeed it was not until the rediscovery of *Ptolemy's *Geography* with its instructions for map production in the fourteenth and fifteenth centuries that major progress may be observed in the development of European cartographical method. Maps created during the Middle Ages had primarily narrative, historical, didactic, and symbolic, rather than scientific functions. The main type of circular world map in medieval western Europe is that of *mappamundi* (Latin: "picture of the world," plural *mappaemundi*). Based on a Roman prototype and usually inscribed in Latin, *mappaemundi* primarily followed the O-T template, in which the circular outline of the inhabited Earth (the *orbis terrarum*) was divided into three continents, Europe, Libya (Africa), and Asia—by prominent hydrographic features coming together to form the T: the Don (Tanais) river separating Europe from Asia, the Nile (or the Red Sea) separating Asia from Africa, and the Mediterranean Sea separating Africa from Europe. The O-shaped rim represented the Ocean, which early on was thought of as a river, but gradually became firmly associated with the sea (*Mare Oceanum*). Africa was thought to lie wholly in the northern hemisphere, but sometimes a fourth continent is shown in the southern hemisphere, as in the maps of Beatus (late eighth century). The early medieval author credited with popularizing this type of map as well as with bringing it into compliance with Christian theology was the encyclopedist *Isidore of Seville (c. 560–636). He oriented the map to the east, the site of earthly paradise, and designated Jerusalem as the center of the world. This type of map is also called T-O or O-Y, when the bodies of water are represented in a different schema. It includes a variation in which the dividing lines form the tau cross, symbolizing the passion of Christ. Isidore's T-O map was influential and popular, and became the first map printed in Europe (1477).

A more complex Christian symbolism is best seen in the Ebstorf map (c. 1240) where the head, hands, and feet of Christ are represented at the four cardinal directions, with the map itself standing for the body of Christ. From Eden flow the Four Rivers of Paradise, identified with the Tigris, Euphrates, Indus, and Ganges. In Africa, in addition to the Nile, the Niger is shown (as a land-locked river). The map, destroyed in 1943, was the largest *mappamundi* (140 x 141 inches/3.56 x 3.58m) known to have been drawn (on kidskin) during the Middle Ages (in Lüneburg, Germany). The late-thirteenth-century Hereford *mappamundi* is another instance of combining Roman and early Christian sources. Its legends cite among the sources Pliny, Solinus, Orosius, and Isidore, and its axis links the circular Paradise at the top with Jerusalem and Rome, then leading to the Pillars of Hercules at the western limits. The Hereford map outline and content correlate closely with the twelfth-century *mappamundi* by Henry of Mainz which, however, follows an ancient Greek tradition in placing at its center sacred Delos, rather than Jerusalem. The clearest example of the Roman (Agrippa) prototype is seen in the Cotton "Anglo-Saxon" map of the tenth or eleventh century.

Until the fourteenth century, travel information only slowly made its way into maps. For example, the influence of *Marco Polo's narratives shows clearly only as late as 1459, in the map by Fra Mauro and the 1492 globe by Martin Behaim. Earlier, however, St. Brendan's legendary voyage in the North Atlantic resulted in the appearance in the extreme northwest of the world maps of a Brendan Island. The circular, hemispherical world map in *Liber Floridus* (early twelfth-century France) names Norway and Venice. The Vinland map of the world, an alleged forgery outside the tradition of Scandinavian *mappaemundi*, claims to show both

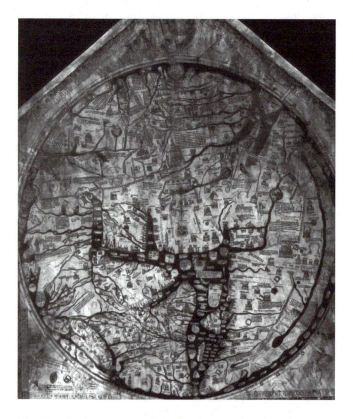

The Hereford *mappamundi* is of unknown date, but the scholarly consensus puts its completion at c. 1290. (Topham)

Greenland and Vinland (North America). The map seems to follow in outline Andrea Bianco's 1436 world map drawn in Venice. The Near Eastern Crusades had little immediate impact on general cartography, but dozens of diagrammatic and stylized maps of Jerusalem survive from 1140 on. The twelfth-century "Jerome" map of Palestine shows the rivers of Paradise as real watercourses. Burchard of Mount Sion, in his 1283 *Descriptio terrae sanctae* (*Description of the Holy Land*), proposed a division of Palestine into four quarters fanning out from a central point in Acre. Marino Sanudo's 1321 *Opus terrae sanctae* was accompanied by maps of the world, the Near East, and Jerusalem probably drawn by Pietro Vesconte. The map of the Holy Land contains a grid with each square representing two leagues, an important aid for travel or military purposes. As noted by Brincken, this pairing was the first European example of a map made essential to the interpretation of a corresponding text.

Medieval cartographers rarely articulated theoretical views or their methods. A book composed in the early 1120s by *Hugh of St. Victor, *Descriptio mappae mundi*, appears to be meant as a guide for mapmaking. Jerome's map of Asia uses an azimuthal logarithmic projection where the central part of the map—of most interest—is enlarged in scale, so that Asia Minor is almost as large as the rest of Asia. In 1178 Roger of Hereford calculated the longitudes of Hereford, Marseilles, and Toledo in relation to the meridian of Arin. *Roger Bacon discussed in his *Opus maius* (1268) a map, now lost, with a projection where he fixed the position of a point by its distance from the equator and a central meridian. Both these instances suggest an awareness of Arabic geographical concepts described below; in Ptolemaic geography, the prime meridian was drawn through the "Fortunate Islands" (now identified as the Canaries). An early Arabic connection also comes through in the use of "Mozarab" coloring by Beatus. Color coding in European maps is rare, but the Walsperger map of 1448 marks Christian cities in red and Muslim cities in black. The Red Sea was often colored in red, an exception.

Maps and Travel

The post-Crusade increase in travel and especially navigation was a major factor in cartographical progress prior to the Renaissance. Medieval books of sailing instructions were known as *portolani*, and the charts, sketched in Italy from at least the twelfth century, received the same name. Portolans were based on practical knowledge of the Mediterranean and were soon required to be carried on board. Drawn on parchment or vellum without a cartographic projection, the charts were based on coast outlines and were accurate only in small-scale versions. They were developed through careful measurement of directions and distances, and gradually corrected. For orientation, Mediterranean sailors originally used the directions of the eight winds named by the ancients. This skill was dramatically advanced by the appearance on the Mediterranean of the mariner's compass, first mentioned by *Nequam in 1187. The wind rose, with twenty-four and later thirty-two points, was added to the charts, and the bodies of water became crisscrossed with a network of color-coded rhumb lines, which helped the mariner hold the course. The first description of a nautical chart is by Ramon Llull (c. 1233–1315), a Majorcan Franciscan with direct experience at sea. The oldest extant is the Pisan Chart dating from between 1275 and 1291. From Italy chartmaking spread to the port cities of Spain and subsequently to Portugal, eventually reaching northwestern Europe. Some one hundred eighty portolan charts, all oriented to the north, survive from the fourteenth and fifteenth centuries.

The famed Catalan Atlas (1375) is a multi-sheet hybrid of a *mappamundi* and portolan chart. It was created in Barcelona for King Charles VI of France by the Catalan cartographers Abraham Cresques (1325–1387), his wife, and their son Jafuda Cresques, Jewish converts from Palma de Mallorca. The Atlas shows Asia and Africa considerably enriched by the recent information from the travels of Marco Polo, Mongol embassies, and the 1324 pilgrimage to Mecca of Mansa Musa, the Muslim ruler of Mali; it also has the first known example of an ornamental compass rose on a portolan chart. Portolans became conduits of information obtained in the Atlantic exploration by the Portuguese, although we have none from Portugal. The Canary Islands, discovered in 1336, appear on a chart dated 1339. The influence of portolan charts is seen in the Gough map of Britain (c. 1360). Pietro Vesconte, who worked in Venice c. 1310–1330, made portolan charts, and his world maps have distinctive depictions of the Black Sea and the eastern Mediterranean. On a map for navigation, scale was essential, and Vesconte's map of Palestine provides an early example of applying scale to a land-based map. Portolan charts also contributed to the new genre of *Isolarii*, or "books of islands," which proliferated between 1500 and 1700. Maps without coastal outlines were not commonly drawn to consistent scale until the sixteenth century.

Another link between maps and travel was maintained in itinerary maps. The Peutinger map is a twelfth- or early thirteenth-century copy of a fourth-century Roman itinerary map. Significant medieval itinerary maps come from England. In the mid-thirteenth century Matthew Paris produced pilgrim itinerary maps that are seen primarily as mnemonic devices and examples of sacred topography, but his maps of Britain and Palestine show attention to proportion and scale, are oriented to the north, and have four points of the compass marked on the edges. The more detailed and "modern" Gough map of England (mid- to late fourteenth century) is seen as a collection of itineraries with distances written in locally measured miles. Medieval regional and local maps made prior to 1350 are very few, but the numbers grow quickly from 1500. The Italian school again predominates: maps of Italian cities are included in some manuscripts of Ptolemy, and Genoa and Venice appear on some portolan maps; northern Italian district maps appear from the thirteenth century. As noted by Harvey, Venice appears to be the only state in fifteenth-century Europe to make regular use of maps in the work of government.

Byzantine Cartography

Byzantine cartography inherited both the Greek and Roman antecedents, but cartographical innovation lapsed, and few new maps were produced. Military maps are known to have existed. Emperor Theodosius II (r. 408–450) commissioned a map of the empire, which was described in the ninth century by the Irish monk Dicuil and probably owed much to the first-century map of Agrippa. From Byzantine Alexandria comes the *Christian Topography* of *Kosmas Indikopleustês (fl. 540), whose maps are the earliest to illustrate a biblical interpretation of the world. His visible world is shaped as the Ark. He makes the ocean into a rectangle surrounding a flat earth, with Jerusalem at the center. The sky consists of four walls meeting in the dome of heaven that is the ceiling of the tabernacle and also resembles the elongated vaults of the early churches. He shows the four seas (Mediterranean, Arabian, Persian Gulf, and the Caspian in the north) as gulfs of the ocean, but otherwise his map completely lacks practical information. Probably the best known Byzantine map is the Madaba mosaic in Jordan, datable to between 560 and 565 and originally measuring 72 feet 2 inches by 22 feet 11 inches (22 x 7m). Intended to instruct Christians and showing biblical lands, it gives a prominent place and exaggerated size to Jerusalem. The map is oriented to the east and configured on the basis of a Roman road map, with inscriptions in Greek. Byzantine world maps of the T-O type, though few, have been found as far east as Mosul (ninth century), and a Byzantine plan of Jerusalem was used in a tenth-century Latin treatise. An eighth-century instrument-maker Leontios of Constantinople recreated Aratus's globe and wrote instructions for constructing it (*De preparatione sphaerae Aratae*). Michael Psellus revived Byzantine cosmographical theory by writing c. 1050 *On the Geographical Maps*, based on the work of Strabo. Narrative land itineraries and *periploi*, books of sailing instructions, exist but lack accompanying maps. Greek charts of the fourteenth and fifteenth centuries show influence of the Italian portolan charts.

The few scientific achievements of the Byzantine millennium included archival preservation of Ptolemy's *Geography* and maintenance of map-making skills. In the late thirteenth century, the scholar Maximus Planudes (c. 1260–1310) undertook a search for Ptolemy's *Geography*, whose significance to geographical science he was one of the few to perceive. He found the text, but without maps, which he subsequently had drawn to Ptolemy's instructions. In 1350 one Nikephoros Gregoras, in producing a copy of the *Geography* in Constantinople, made four additional maps (of Asia, Europe, and Libya) with an original projection reminiscent of the much later Mercator's. Copies of the *Geography*, in two versions with twenty-seven or sixty-five maps, soon reached Italy, where the work was translated into Latin in 1406. These maps signaled the dawn of the "Ptolemaic revolution" in Western cartography. Together with the compass and the discoveries they made it no longer relevant to center maps on Jerusalem, facilitated reorientation of maps to the north, and made widespread the use of frame, scale and coordinates of latitude and longitude. About 1425 scholars associated with the University of Vienna and the Monastery of Klosterneuburg produced several world maps for which series of coordinates are preserved in table form from 1449. From 1477 on, Ptolemy's maps were frequently reproduced in print, sometimes with addition of more contemporary information.

Islamic Cartography

The first Islamic reference to map-making dates to 702 C.E., although most extant maps are copies dating from the thirteenth century onward. Pre-Islamic Arab concepts of cartography included an image of the Earth in the shape of a bird with spread wings whose head is in the east (China) and tail in the west. Islamic cartography proper, originating in ninth-century Baghdad, experienced strong Iranian influences, including map orientation to the east and the division of the Earth into seven regions (kishvar) with Iran at the center, for which Muslim scholars quickly substituted Iraq. In the corpus of round world maps forming the so-called Atlas of Islam the world became centered on Mecca, while the eleventh-century Turkish world map by Mahmud al-Kashghari is centered on Balasaghun, capital of the then Uighur state. From India was borrowed the idea of prime meridian passing through Mount Meru from the North Pole to Sri Lanka via the Cupola of the Earth, or Cupola of Arin (Arabic Arun, from Ujjain, site of an ancient Indian observatory). From the Greeks came the limitation of world maps to the inhabited quarter of the Earth, surrounded by the ocean, and the system of seven latitudinal climates (iqlim) marked on extant copies of authors from the ninth to the fourteenth century, including Ibn Khaldun. Ptolemy's Geography was translated several times in the ninth and tenth centuries, but apparently without his instructions for map-making and without maps. In the twelfth century *al-Idrisi, working at the Norman court of Sicily, produced a detailed world map that represents the highest achievement of Islamic cartography. Adopting Ptolemy's map of the world as a base (though oriented to the south), he subdivided each of the seven climates into ten longitudinal sections, starting from the west. The resulting seventy rectangular regional maps, filled with information compiled from contemporary and earlier sources, surpass all other Islamic maps in quantity and detail of cartographic data. Al-Idrisi reportedly created a silver planisphere, now lost, based on the so-called map of al-Ma'mun, in the projection of Marinus. Apart from al-Idrisi, few authors gave instructions for map production, and the projections used are not yet fully understood. City plans must have existed, but those extant date from the sixteenth century and later. There are no topographical maps, although some color-coding of features occurs. An important Islamic map genre is the special qibla (direction of the prayer) maps for orienting the Muslim viewer to the Ka'ba sanctuary in Mecca from any location. Nautical charts are mentioned in texts referring to the Indian

ocean, but none survives; the few extant North African charts, as also the more numerous post-1500 Turkish ones, strongly suggest European influence.

See also **Geography, chorography; Kosmas Indikopleustês; Ptolemy**

Bibliography

Arentzen, Jörg-Geerd. *Imago Mundi Cartographica: Studien zur Bildlichkeit mittelalterlicher Welt- und Ökumenekarten unter besonderer Berücksichtigung des Zusammenwirkens von Text und Bild.* Münstersche Mittelalter-Schriften 53. Munich: Wilhelm Fink, 1984.

Beazley, Charles Raymond. *The Dawn of Modern Geography: A History of Exploration and Geographical Science from the Conversion of the Roman Empire to A.D. 900.* 3 vols. London: J. Murray, 1897–1906. New York: Peter Smith, 1949.

Berthon, Simon and Andrew Robinson. *The Shape of the World: the Mapping and Discovery of the Earth.* Chicago: Rand McNally, 1991.

Brincken, Anna-Dorothee von den. *Fines terrae: Die Enden der Erde und der vierte Kontinent auf mittelalterlichen Weltkarten.* Monumenta Germaniae Historica, Schriften 36. Hanover: Hahn, 1992.

Brown, Lloyd A. *The Story of Maps.* Boston: Little Brown, 1949; London: Cresset Press, 1951; multiple reprints.

Edson, Evelyn. *Mapping Time and Space: How Medieval Mapmakers Viewed Their World.* London: British Library; Toronto: University of Toronto Press, 1997.

Harley, J.B. and David Woodward, eds. *The History of Cartography.* Vol. 1: *Cartography in Prehistoric, Ancient, and Medieval Europe and the Mediterranean,* esp. chapters 15–20. Vol. 2, Book 1, *Cartography in the Traditional Islamic and South Asian Societies,* esp. chapters 1–14. Chicago: Chicago University Press, 1987–1992.

The Image of the World: An Interactive Exploration of Ten Historic World Maps. CD-ROM. Produced by Karen Brookfield. London: British Library, 1995.

King, David A. *World-maps for Finding the Direction and Distance to Mecca: Innovation and Tradition in Islamic Science.* London: Al-Furqan Islamic Heritage Foundation, 1999.

Harvey, P.D.A. *Medieval Maps.* London: British Library, 1991.

Sezgin, Fuat. *The Contribution of Arabic-Islamic geographers to the Formation of the World Map.* Frankfurt: Institute for the History of Arabic-Islamic Sciences, 1987.

Skelton, R.A. *The Vinland Map and the Tartar Relation.* New Haven: Yale University Press, 1965.

Tolmacheva, Marina. "Ptolemaic Influence on Medieval Arab Geography: The Case Study of East Africa." In *Discovering New Worlds: Essays on Medieval Exploration and Imagination,* edited by Scott D. Westrem. New York: Garland, 1991, pp. 125–141.

———. Bertius and al-Idrisi: an Experiment in Orientalist Cartography. *Terrae Incognitae* (1996), 28: 36–45.

MARINA TOLMACHEVA

CATAPULTS AND TREBUCHETS

Scholars now generally agree that the successor states of the Roman empire in the early medieval West inherited two basic types of artillery from their imperial predecessors.

The first of these consisted of torsion-powered engines (Roman: *ballista, chieroballista, onager*; Medieval: *manga, mangonellus*) that propelled their projectiles through the transformation of potential energy stored in twisted fibrous material, ranging from gut to horsehair and hempen rope, into kinetic energy that drove a wooden beam. The wooden beam, which could be equipped with a basket attached directly to the beam, or with a sling attached to its end, then transferred this kinetic energy to a projectile, usually a stone, located in the basket or sling. These engines generally were light artillery with rounds weighing 22–33 pounds (10–15kg). The second type of artillery available in late antiquity and throughout the Middle Ages was tension-powered. Tension engines (known as *gastraphetes* in the ancient world but *balistae* in the medieval world) used the same principle as hand-held bows and crossbows, transferring the potential energy of the bow to the projectile, usually a long thin shaft equipped with an iron head, which looked like a large arrow or a crossbow bolt.

The range of engines (*petraria, trubecheta, blida*) that were probably the particular inventions of the Middle Ages employed the lever principle. Engines of this type were essentially long beams fixed to a fulcrum. The front, shorter end of the beam—i.e., the end closest to the target—is described by scholars as the target end, and the back, longer end is identified as the projectile end, because the projectile was attached there. Energy was generated by the rapid descent of the target end and the concomitant rapid rise of the projectile end.

Medieval engineers had two means of causing the rapid descent of the target end. The first method was to have a large number of well-trained men pull down, in unison, on ropes attached to the target end. Engines employing this method have been identified by scholars as a "traction type." The traction lever engine was the only type of lever engine available in the Latin West and in the Levant until the end of the twelfth century.

The second method used to cause the rapid descent of the target end was to attach a very heavy weight to it. These weights, called *trubae* in some medieval sources, could weigh up to 220 pounds (1,000kg) and varied considerably in material composition and construction. In many cases, artillery engineers used large lead castings. However, wooden containers filled with stone, or even clay, were also fixed to the target end. The projectile end, in this type of engine, although substantially longer, was therefore much lighter than the target end. In order to use this engine, the artillerymen had to drag down the projectile end and secure it. After it was loaded, the projectile end was set free and the much heavier weight on the target end fell rapidly, causing the projectile end to rise rapidly with the result that the projectile was sent on its way. Engines equipped with weights on their target ends have been designated by scholars as "counterweight" lever engines. Counterweight engines did not appear in the Latin West until the first quarter of the thirteenth century.

The technology available to artillery engineers remained relatively static from the late Roman period through the end of the twelfth century. Although some scholars have questioned whether torsion or, conversely, traction-lever artillery was produced in the Middle Ages, it is now generally agreed that both types of propulsion were used consistently. Nevertheless, there is even at present controversy on this point because of the nature of the sources of information that deal with artillery in the period before c. 1200. One of the major problems faced by scholars, who have tried to identify the types of artillery actually deployed in late antiquity and the Middle Ages, is the lack of precision in the use of terminology in contemporary narrative sources. Many of the authors of historical narratives, in which artillery is discussed, were personally unfamiliar with military technology and used generic terms, such as *instrumentum* (instrument), *machina* (machine), *ingenium* (engine), and *catapulta* (catapult) to describe the weapons that were deployed. Many authors of narrative sources also used terms such as *tormentum, scorpio, petraria*, and *onager*, which may have had a technical meaning as a particular type of artillery. The lack of description for these weapons, however, makes it virtually impossible to determine whether they were torsion- or lever-powered, much less their specific characteristics, e. g., one-armed or two, wheeled or stationary. Finally, the narrative sources frequently used closely related terms, e.g., *manga* and *mangonellus*, without making clear if these terms refer to the same type or to different types of artillery.

Perhaps the most famous example of terminological confusion concerns the type of artillery known to modern readers as the trebuchet. The Latin version of this word begins to appear in medieval narrative sources in the thirteenth century. The first mention of a *trubechetum* in England, for example, occurs in the context of Prince Louis of France's invasion of the island in 1216. Louis is reported to have brought a *trubechetum* with him to help conduct sieges. The thirteenth-century narrative sources, however, do not provide detailed information about the construction of the *trubechetum*. In light of this ambiguity, the English term trebuchet frequently has been used by scholars in a generic manner to refer to all lever-powered artillery from the ninth century onward. In fact, however, trebuchet was not used by contemporaries as simply another generic term for lever-powered artillery, but rather referred to a sophisticated technological improvement introduced by government officials to replace the older type of traction lever engine with a counterweight design. (The term for the counterweight engine as a whole may have been derived from the word *truba*, noted above, which some medieval authors used to designated counterweights.) Instead of deploying an engine that required dozens if not scores of well-trained men to operate, the trebuchet required only a small crew to lock the projectile end of the piece of artillery into position. It has been suggested by scholars that the counterweight engines could propel much heavier stones than their traction-lever cousins, with rounds weighing as much as 100–200 pounds (45–90kg), over distances of 328 yards (300m).

It is a happy coincidence that the first major development in the technology of artillery in many hundreds of years coincides with the survival of major new sources of information that shed significant light on how the trebuchet differed from earlier engines. The number of surviving administrative documents in England, where we have the best information about developments in the construction of artillery, increases dramatically for the period 1200 and after. These documents include large numbers of reports from engineers and military officials concerning the construction of artillery. This is significant because, unlike the contemporary authors of narrative sources, these engineers and officials were very familiar with military technology, and had a range of very precise terms to discuss the types of engines that they built. It is from these reports that it is possible to determine that the trebuchet was a relatively small type of counterweight lever artillery that began to be produced in England c. 1225. By the early 1240s, engineers in England began to build much larger counterweight lever artillery, which they at first designated as *blidae*, but then later simply referred to as engines (*ingenia*).

Cultural Significance

It is widely accepted by medieval military historians that sieges were the dominant form of warfare from the late Roman Empire until the massive introduction of gunpowder weapons at the end of the fifteenth century. The pursuit of politico-military objectives throughout this period required the capture, or the holding, of fortifications and major fortified cities. In the late antique West, the Roman government long maintained a monopoly on the ability to produce and deploy the sophisticated siege engines, particularly stone-throwers, that facilitated the reduction of these fortified places short of starving the population and garrison into submission or storming the walls with overwhelming numbers and concomitantly high rates of casualties. The late fourth-century Roman military officer and historian Ammianus Marcelinus emphasized in his works that barbarians were quite simply unable to capture Roman fortress towns, or even substantial forts, because they lacked "modern" technology. Attila the Hun likewise famously lacked sophisticated siege engines during his assault on the city of Orléans in the north of Gaul in 451 C.E., as his men were reduced to trying to pull down the walls stone by stone with hand tools. By contrast with the barbarians, the Christianized rulers of the Roman successor states devoted tremendous human, material, and financial resources both to producing artillery and to maintaining as well as improving the Roman military infrastructure of fortifications and fortified cities, that could withstand these engines. Indeed, medieval engineers engaged in an ongoing and increasingly expensive cycle of competitive development in the technology of siege engines and of fortifications. This pattern of military spending, what one might term part of the pre-modern "military industrial complex," continued throughout the Middle Ages.

Stone-throwing engines were constructed of specially designed wooden pieces, iron clamps and bolts, ropes, slings, baskets, and, in the case of trebuchets, counterweights. All of these elements of the engines' material construction had to be built or produced by highly trained specialists. Not every carpenter knew either the designs or the techniques necessary to build the wooden framework for a piece of artillery, much less all of the types of artillery deployed by his government. Similarly, not every blacksmith knew how to produce the fittings necessary to withstand the stresses of holding together an engine that could hurl hundreds of rounds of stone ammunition weighing 100–200 pounds (45–90 kg). In order to ensure that a sufficient number of the correct types of artillery were available at the right place at the right time in good working order, governments in late antiquity and throughout the Middle Ages required a thoroughly articulated logistical system supported by a well-financed and highly structured military administration.

The Norman and Angevin kings of England, like many other rulers in medieval Europe, employed a corps of specialists in the construction of artillery, including torsion, tension, and lever engines of both the traction and counterweight types. These specialists, identified in contemporary English administrative sources as engineers (*ingeniatores*), were among the most highly paid officers of the crown. Some of them even became substantial landowners as a result. Each of these engineers employed numerous carpenters, blacksmiths, ropemakers, leatherworkers, woodcutters, carters, sailors, and bargemen. To gain a mere glimpse of the effort required to sustain this work, one can note that the royal forests of England rang with the axes of woodsmen preparing thousands of logs to be shipped to London, Dover, Carlisle, and other towns that served as major production centers for hundreds of enormous wall-breaking engines, as well as the even more numerous smaller pieces of artillery used as antipersonnel weapons. The lead mines of Cornwall produced hundreds and hundreds of tons of lead that were carted or shipped out for use as counterweights. The hides of whole herds of cows were required to produce slings. Masons chipped and shaped tens of thousands of stones to be used as ammunition, some of which can still be found at the sites of medieval sieges. To these basic elements of construction, one might add the thousands of carts, wagons, barges, and ships that were required to transport these supplies, as well as the completed artillery and ammunition. It is also necessary to keep in mind the mountains of grain and other foodstuffs necessary to feed the animal and human personnel who undertook these transportation duties. In economic terms, the production of weapons, in general, and of artillery, in particular, was a big industry that employed many thousands of workers. In sum, if we are permitted, as modern politicians are, to see the commitment of resources as a gauge of the importance attached by the government to a particular program, it is clear that the kings of England, and they were certainly not alone, valued artillery, including the trebuchet, very highly indeed.

See also **Arms and armor**

Bibliography

Amt, Emilie. Besieging Bedford: Military Logistics in 1224. *Journal of Medieval Military History* (2002) 1: 101–124.

Bradbury, Jim. *The Medieval Siege*. Rochester: Boydell Press, 1992, pp. 250–270

Chevedden, Paul E., Zvi Shiller, Samuel R. Gilbert and Donald J. Kagay. The Traction Trebuchet: A Triumph of Four Civilizations. *Viator* (2000) 31: 433–486.

DeVries, Kelly. *Medieval Military Technology*. Peterborough, Ontario: Broadview Press, 1992, pp. 125–138

Dinzelbacher, Peter. Quellenprobleme bei der Erforschung hochmittelalterlicher Bewaffnung. *Mediaevistik* (1989) 2: 43–79.

Finó, J.-F. *Forteresses de la France médiévale: Construction–Attaque–Défense*. 3rd edition. Paris: A. et J. Picard, 1977, pp. 150–158.

———. Machines de jet médiévales. *Gladius* (1972) 10: 25–43.

Hill, Donald R. Trebuchets. *Viator* (1973) 4: 99–115.

Huuri, Kalervo. *Zur Geschichte des mittelalterlichen Geschützwesens aus orientalischen Quellen*. Helsinki: Societas Orientalis Fennica, 1941.

Köhler, Gustav. *Die Entwicklung des Kriegswesens und der Kriegführung in der Ritterzeit von Mitte des 11 Jahrhunderts bis zu den Hussitenkriegen*. 3 volumes in 4. Breslau: W. Koebner, 1886–1890. volume 3.

Nicolle, David C. *Arms and Armour of the Crusading Era 1050–1350*. White Plains: Kraus International Publications, 1988.

Rogers, Randall. *Latin Siege Warfare in the Twelfth Century*. Oxford: Clarendon Press, 1992, pp. 251–273.

Schneider, Rudolf. *Die Artillerie des Mittelalters. Nach den Angaben der Zeitgenossen dargestellt*. Berlin: Weidmannsche Buchhandlung, 1910.

DAVID S. BACHRACH

CATHEDRAL SCHOOLS

In late antiquity, Christians were generally satisfied with the existing urban schools and the classical training they offered, so that the Church did not consider it necessary to build up its own educative system. Nevertheless, it is likely that in the community of clerks organized by some bishops, such as Augustine in Hippo at the end of the fourth century or Caesarius in Arles a hundred years later, within the *domus ecclesiae*, some kind of education was already provided for the youngest people. But it is during the sixth century, when the ancient schools had disappeared, that formal cathedral schools were created. The first evidence is given by the Council of Toledo (527) which ordered the bishops to provide a teacher to educate the boys under eighteen of whom they were in charge. In the following centuries, other cathedral schools are mentioned in different episcopal sees in Gaul and Italy. These first cathedral schools were very modest, their main purpose being to give the young clerics a practical training in reading, song, and other liturgical duties; but the really educated members of the higher clergy were taught elsewhere, either within their families or in monastic schools which were, at this time, much more sophisticated.

School reform was an important part of the cultural policy of Charles the Great and his successors. The various directives issued for this purpose—*Admonitio generalis* in 789, *Epistola de litteris colendis* in 794, Council of Attigny in 822, Capitulary of Olonna for the kingdom of Italy in 825, etc.—are reminders that bishops were responsible for the education of their clergy and that they had to maintain one school in their cathedral—or even several, if the diocese was too large. In these schools, the pupils had to receive a good training in liberal arts, in particular in grammar, in order to be able to read and understand the Holy Scripture. This policy was not entirely effective: many cathedrals remained without a school and, with the exception of the brilliant cathedral school of Laon in the time of *John Scottus Eriugena, the monastic schools were always the great intellectual centers of the Carolingian Empire.

The eleventh and twelfth centuries were the golden age of cathedral schools in the West. This was due to the new context of that period. Many monastic schools were closed, and the new orders, such as Cîteaux, refused the admission of schoolboys; the towns were in rapid expansion, the reform of the Church required a competent and well-trained secular clergy. At this time, most episcopal sees had a more or less permanent school: this was the case in Italy, France, and Spain (at least in Catalonia) as well as in Germany and England. These schools were under the responsibility of the bishop and his chapter. Sometimes bishops, including Fulbert in Chartres, taught personally, but in most cases they entrusted the supervision of the schools to a canon who could be the archdeacon, the chancellor or a more specialized *scholasticus*. This man was the head of the school; he could appoint assistant teachers and, more generally, was entitled to grant after examination the *licentia docendi*, i.e., the right to teach, to anyone who wanted to open a new school in the diocese.

Cathedral schools were primarily intended for the training of young clerics, but they could also admit the male offspring of the local nobility, even if they were not destined for a career in the church. Learning in eleventh- and twelfth-century cathedral schools extended beyond the elementary level of reading and song, to the arts of trivium, biblical exegesis (*sacra pagina*), and even, in some cases, canon law. Normally, the role of a cathedral school did not exceed the boundaries of the diocese but after the end of the eleventh century some cathedral schools won a much larger reputation. Thanks to the professors whose fame and works were greatly widespread—Anselm at Laon, Bernard and Thierry at Chartres, Peter Comestor and Peter the Chanter at Paris—these schools attracted foreign students and became centers of intellectual innovation. The most famous cathedral schools were in northern France (Laon, Paris, Chartres, Reims) and in Germany (Liège, Cologne, Mainz, Bamberg, Magdeburg); naturally, these great cathedral schools had a tendency to become more and more autonomous, and increasingly acted independently of local authorities, bishops, and canons. There were cathedral schools in Mediterranean Europe too—Italy,

Provence, Languedoc—but they had to compete with private and lay schools of law and medicine.

The development of cathedral schools was strongly supported by the Papacy; Canon Eighteen of the Third Lateran Council (1179) ordered that in every cathedral a prebend should be reserved for the schoolmaster so that he could teach freely to poor students; this canon was repeated at the Fourth Lateran Council (1215) which added that this master would teach grammar and the various liberal arts, and that in metropolitan churches at least there should also be a master of divinity.

Yet these canons were, in some way, already outmoded because in the thirteenth century the emergence of universities led to the irreparable decline of cathedral schools. On the whole, the first *universities (Bologna, Oxford, Montpellier) did not arise out of cathedral schools; even in Paris, the origins of the university lie more with the private schools of the *rive gauche* than with the cathedral school of Notre-Dame, which was only partially integrated within the university. But other universities (Salamanca, Toulouse, Orléans) resulted from the transformation of cathedral schools into autonomous and privileged *studia generalia*, and, on the whole, the old institutions were depreciated by the new ones, both because the former were unable to deliver recognized degrees and because their teaching appeared more and more outdated and conservative, reluctant to admit the new Aristotelian philosophy.

Nonetheless cathedral schools did not disappear in the late Middle Ages and probably deserve greater attention than they have so far received. They obviously remained of particular importance in Germany, where universities emerged only at the end of the fourteenth century. But they usually confined themselves to a purely local role, delivering elementary training to the youngest members of the cathedral clergy; for some of them, it was a preparatory stage before going to the university.

See also **Aristotelianism; Quadrivium**

Bibliography

Benson, Robert L. and Giles Constable, eds. *Renaissance and Renewal in the Twelfth Century*. Cambridge: Harvard University Press, 1982.

Classen, Peter. Die hohen Schulen und die Gesellschaft im 12. Jahrhundert. *Archiv für Kulturgeschichte* (1966) 48: 155–180.

Delhaye, Philippe. L'organisation scolaire au XIIe siècle. *Traditio* (1947) 5: 211–268.

Ferruolo, Stephen C. *The Origins of the University. The Schools of Paris and their Critics, 1100-1215*. Stanford: Stanford University Press, 1985.

Paré, Gérard, A. Brunet, and Pierre Tremblay. *La Renaissance du XIIe siècle. Les écoles et l'enseignement*. Paris-Ottawa: Vrin-Institut d'Études médiévales, 1933.

Pixton, Paul B. The Misfiring of German Cultural Leadership in the Twelfth Century: The Evidence from the Cathedral Schools. *Paedagogica Historica* (1998) 34: 348–363.

Renardy, Christine. Les écoles liégeoises du IXe au XIIe siècle: grandes lignes de leur évolution. *Revue belge de philologie et d'histoire* (1979) 57: 309–328.

Riché, Pierre. *Écoles et enseignement dans le Haut Moyen Age*, 2nd ed. Paris: Picard, 1989.

Riché, Pierre. *Éducation et culture dans l'Occident barbare, VIe-VIIIe siècles*, 3rd ed. Paris: Éditions du Seuil, 1972.

La Scuola nell'Occidente latino dell'alto Medioevo, 2 vols., Spoleto: Centro italiano di Studi sull'Alto Medioevo, 1972.

Verger, Jacques. "Une étape dans le renouveau scolaire du XIIe siècle ?" In *Le XIIe siècle. Mutations et renouveau en France dans la première moitié du XIIe siècle*, éd. par Françoise Gasparri. Paris: Le Léopard d'or, 1994, pp. 123–145.

JACQUES VERGER

CECCO D'ASCOLI

Physician, astrologer, and poet, Cecco d'Ascoli (Francesco Stabili) was born in or near Ascoli Piceno around 1269. Nothing is known about his studies and life before 1320. Between 1322 and 1324 he was professor of *astrology at the University of Bologna. In 1324 he was dismissed and condemned for heresy by the inquisitor Lamberto da Cingoli. This first condemnation was probably caused by the discussion of magic and astrological theories during his lectures.

Following this sentence, he was prohibited from lecturing in every Italian university; his doctoral degree was withdrawn and his library confiscated. In 1326 he joined the court of Count Charles of Calabria (son of Robert of Anjou) as doctor and astrologer, and in 1327 followed him to Florence. There he came into disagreement with the physician Dino del Garbo; at the same time, he fell into disgrace with Charles, according to legend because he predicted that Giovanna, the count's daughter, would become a lustful woman. Investigated again by the Florentine inquisition, he was condemned by the inquisitor Accursio as a relapsed heretic and burned at the stake on September 16, 1327. According to the Florentine historian Giovanni Villani (*Cronica* 10, 39), Cecco's condemnation was determined by his own arrogance, which cost him the sympathies of protectors and colleagues, and by the unorthodox theories he developed in his works. The condemnation included a prohibition on reading his writings. Nevertheless, some of them survived in manuscript and were later printed.

Cecco's most representative writings are *L'Acerba*—a didactic poem in Italian whose alternative title, *Immature*, points to the unfinished character of the work and to its readers' difficulty in grasping it—and the Latin commentary on *John of Sacrobosco's *Sphaera*. He also composed a commentary on al-Qabisi's *De principiis astrologiae*, a treatise *De eccentricis et epicyclis*, and some sonnets of alchemical content.

L'Acerba was written between 1324 and 1327 and left unfinished. In it, he accused Dante of having written a poem based on fiction and reporting a vision, not describing reality. Cecco, on the other hand, intended to write a very didactic poem that provided scientific data useful to his readers, and for this reason, in his view, his own poem was to be preferred to *The Divine Comedy*. However, *L'Acerba* clearly shows the influence of Dante's poem, particularly in the use of terza rima. *L'Acerba* is divided into five books of composite character: the first deals with astronomy and *cosmology, the second combines a treatise on vices and virtues with elements of *physiognomy and astrology, and the third consists of a bestiary and a lapidary based on *encyclopedias such as the *De proprietatibus rerum* of *Bartholomaeus Anglicus and collections such as the *Physiologus*. The fourth book is structured in question-and-answer form, and concerns *alchemy, occultism, biology, astronomy, and *meteorology. Among its sources we find Aristotle's *Meteora* and the pseudo-Aristotelian *Problemata*. The fifth and final book, which was left incomplete, was planned to discuss moral philosophy and ethics. Cecco also started the composition of a commentary on *L'Acerba*, but finished only the first two books.

Despite the condemnation, *L'Acerba* was widely diffused—we know of approximately forty manuscripts—and first printed in 1476. Some selected passages of the second book were translated into Hebrew during the sixteenth century, probably by Abraham ben Hannaniah Yagel.

The commentary devoted to Sacrobosco's *Sphaera* was composed by Cecco before 1324, while he was professor of astrology at the University of Bologna, and left unfinished. Its content reproduces the lessons given by Cecco and the curriculum of lectures on astronomy established by the University of Bologna for the first year of studies, the bulk of which was represented by Sacrobosco's *Sphaera*. The commentary attracted the attention of the Inquisition and contributed to Cecco's condemnations in 1324 and 1327. Compared to other commentaries on Sacrobosco's work, which focuses exclusively on astronomy, Cecco's explanation is characterized by the interest in astrology, magic, and diabolic necromancy. Also particularly important in Cecco's view is the interpretation of history according to the principles of astrology.

In his commentary, Cecco showed a wide scientific culture. Some of his astrological, hermetic, and necromantic sources do not seem to have survived, and are also unknown to the author of one of the most complete lists of astrological and magical works, the *Speculum astronomiae*, formerly attributed to *Albertus Magnus.

Pico della Mirandola attributed to Cecco the redaction of a horoscope of Jesus Christ, which is not preserved. It has been assumed by some scholars that this horoscope was contained in a preliminary version of the commentary on Sacrobosco's *Sphaera*, and eliminated after Cecco's condemnation.

See also **Aristotelianism; Bestiaries; Lapidaries; Pseudo-Aristotle**

Bibliography

Primary Sources
Albertazzi, Marco, ed. *Cecco d'Ascoli, L'Acerba*. Trento: La Finestra, 2003.
Thorndike, Lynn, ed. *The Sphere of Sacrobosco and its Commentators*. Chicago: University of Chicago Press, 1949.

Illustration by an unknown artist from 1475 edition of Cecco d'Ascoli's *L'Acerba*. The painting shows (top to bottom) the virtue Nobility and the vices Anger and Envy. (Mary Evans Picture Library)

Secondary Sources
Albertazzi, Marco, ed. *Studi Stabiliani*. Trento: La Finestra, 2002.
Boudet, Jean-Patrice. Les who's who démonologiques de la Renaissance et leurs ancêtres médiévaux. In *Le diable en procès. Démonologie et sorcellerie à la fin du Moyen Age*. Edited by M. Ostotero and É. Anheim. Médiévales (2003) 44: 117–141.
Busetto, G. "Cecco d'Ascoli." In *Lexikon des Mittelalters*, vol. 3. München-Zürich: Artemis Verlag, 1983.
Camuffo, Maria Luisa. Presenze dantesche nell'Acerba di Cecco d'Ascoli. *Rivista di letteratura italiana* (1987) 5: 91–100.
Camuffo, Maria Luisa and Aldo M. Costantini. Il Fiore di Virtù: una nuova fonte per l'Acerba. *Rivista di Letteratura Italiana* (1988), 6: 247–258.
———. Il Lapidario dell'«Acerba». *Lettere Italiane* (1988) 40: 526–535.
Debenedetti Stow, Sandra. "A Judeo-Italian Version of Selected Passages from Cecco d'Ascoli's Acerba." In *Communication in the Jewish Diaspora. The Pre-Modern World*, edited by S. Menache, Leiden: E.J. Brill, 1996, pp. 283–311.

Faracovi, Ornella Pompeo. *Gli oroscopi di Cristo*. Venezia: Marsilio, 1999.

Frasca, Gabriele. «I' voglio qui che'l quare covi il quia». Cecco d'Ascoli "avversario" di Dante. In *Dante e la Scienza*, edited by P. Boyde and V. Russo. Ravenna: Longo, 1995, pp. 243–263.

Picchio Simonelli, Maria. L'Inquisizione e Dante: alcune osservazioni. *Dante Studies* (2000), 118: 303–321.

Tester, S. Jim. *A History of Western Astrology*. Woodbridge: Boydell Press, 1987, pp. 193–196.

Thorndike, Lynn. *A History of Magic and Experimental Science*. New York: Columbia University Press, 1923, vol. II, pp. 948–968.

———. More Light on Cecco d'Ascoli. *Romanic Review* (1946) 37: 293–306.

———. Relations of the Inquisitions to Peter of Abano and Cecco d'Ascoli. *Speculum* (1926) 1: 338–343.

Van der Lugt, Maike. *Le ver, le demon, la vièrge. Les théories médiévales de la génération extraordinaire*. Paris: Les Belles Lettres, 2003, pp. 309–315 and 453–454.

Weill-Parot, Nicolas. Dans le ciel ou sous le ciel? Les anges dans la magie astrale, XIIe-XIVe siècle. Mélanges de l'École française de Rome, Moyen Age (2002) 114: 753–771.

IOLANDA VENTURA

CHAUCER, GEOFFREY

Probably born in the early 1340s, the English poet Geoffrey Chaucer was the son of a wine merchant. By 1357 he was a page in the household of the Countess of Ulster and soon after this he was involved in the war in France, resulting in his capture and ransom for £16 in 1360. In 1366 he married Phillippa, and soon afterwards was employed in Edward III's household. More important positions followed: in 1374 Chaucer was appointed Controller of Customs, and in 1389 he became Clerk of the Works. In 1394 he was granted an annuity of £20 by Richard II, but all was not well financially and in 1398 there were actions against Chaucer for debt, from which he was protected by the king. In the following year, however, Richard was deposed, and Chaucer is last known to have been alive in 1400. No one is certain when, where or how he died, but a monument was raised to him in London's Westminster Abbey in the sixteenth century.

Despite being busy with all these responsibilities, Chaucer found time to write throughout his working life. His surviving writings include ten large works, among them *The Canterbury Tales* and *Troilus and Criseyde*, as well as more than twenty short poems, and he probably wrote other things that no longer survive. A quick glance at his works shows the variety of styles and subjects found in his writings: he was clearly an educated, witty, and intelligent man. We know that he traveled widely—to Spain, Italy and France—but we know surprisingly little about other aspects of his life, such as where or how he was educated, or what he was like as a man. Despite this, his learning shines through, and there are many references to scientific and medical subjects throughout Chaucer's literary works. The examples here are drawn from his most famous work, *The Canterbury Tales*, and give a picture of the breadth of his influences and interests.

Chaucer's works—especially *The Canterbury Tales* and *Troilus and Criseyde*—contain many references to astronomical events, and some scholars have used them to date his writings. Linne Mooney, however, argues that they give stronger evidence for Chaucer's interest in astronomy in general than for the dates of particular works. She links Chaucer's choice of such material to a fashion at court, influenced by Richard II's queen, Anne of Bohemia.

One astronomical reference is Chaucer's description in the General Prologue of *The Canterbury Tales* that the Sun has gone half way through Aries. This is one of the ways that he fixes the date of the pilgrimage in early April. Along with this astronomical date, there are descriptions of natural phenomena in springtime, and a direct statement that the date is early April. You can read this section without knowing any astronomy, but you will only get the full depth of meaning if you know a little about the motion of the Sun through the heavens.

There are also several references to the ways that the characters tell the time while on the pilgrimage. In "The Shipman's Tale" the lecherous monk uses a cylinder dial which he keeps in his pocket. In "The Parson's Tale" the manciple works out that it is four o'clock by looking at the length of shadows relative to the objects that cast them, presumably using a reference table rather than doing spherical trigonometry in his head.

Some of the astronomical references show that the depth of Chaucer's learning went beyond being able to use a sundial or *calendar. In "The Squire's Tale" the king has a wife named Elpheta, an Arabic star name, and his children also have names that can be linked to the heavens. In "The Miller's Tale" the shelves in the student's room include a copy of *Ptolemy's *Almagest*, as well as an astrolabe and a set of counting stones: tools of the student's astrological activities. The student lodges with a carpenter, who finds him locked in his room one day and blames too much astronomy for the student's condition, telling a story of an astronomer who was so busy looking at the stars that he fell into a clay pit because he wasn't looking where he was going. So even though we know that Chaucer was interested in astronomy, he has one of his characters tell us of the dangers of studying astronomy too much. This highlights a problem when we are assessing Chaucer's interests in scientific and medical subjects: to what extent, if any, can we work out his opinion on the more controversial subjects, such as *astrology or *alchemy, from the opinions expressed by his characters?

Throughout *The Canterbury Tales* Chaucer uses astrology to describe the characters, and as with the astronomical time and calendar references, you could understand the stories without knowing any astrology, but it adds more depth to the descriptions if you do. One area in which astrology was accepted, even encouraged, was in medicine. The description of the physician in the General Prologue shows us that he is learned and successful—he wears blue and red silk robes, and knows the causes of diseases. Another of the doctor's skills is astrology, which he uses to find the ascendant for his patient and so understand what is wrong with him.

Chaucer himself seems to have known much about the casting of horoscopes and the ways that the stars shaped peoples lives. There are horoscopes datable to 1392 in "The Nun's Priest's Tale"; the Wife of Bath explains in the Prologue to her tale that her character is shaped by the planets. She says that she has followed the inclination set out for her by the stars at the moment of her birth, implying that she might have chosen otherwise and therefore has some free will.

Alongside references in his fictional works, there is more direct evidence of Chaucer's astronomical skill and interests in his *Treatise on the Astrolabe*, compiled in the early 1390s. This remarkable work is among the first technical treatises in English, and was based on sources including the work on the astrolabe then attributed to *Masha'allah and the *De Sphaera* of *Sacrobosco. Chaucer reworked his sources, reordering the material he took from them, and adding and removing some sections. One of the additional sections discusses the ascendant, a measurement essential in casting a horoscope. But even here there is no definite statement for or against, say, predictions of the future based on the casting of horoscopes. Chaucer limits himself to saying that the measurements used by astrologers are often inaccurate.

Medieval alchemy took in a wide range of activities, including what might now be described as metallurgy and distillation alongside things that might more often be associated with the name, including the transmutation of base metals into gold. In "The Canon's Yeoman's Tale" Chaucer shows his knowledge of alchemical equipment and processes in a long description given by a servant about his master's alchemical activities. The alchemist is always unsuccessful though, despite spending large amounts of money and time on his search. Interestingly, despite Chaucer's apparent knowledge of alchemy and perhaps even experience of chemical processes, the tale ends with a warning that alchemy is an attempt to pry into matters that are God's, and that philosophers should leave it alone.

In *The Canterbury Tales* there are also references to magic, or to magical events and objects. In "The Squire's Tale" a knight visiting the court of Ghengis Khan brings with him four magical gifts—a flying brass horse, a mirror, a ring, and a sword. Onlookers marvel at the magical objects, trying to understand them using their book learning. It is not clear whether Chaucer was saying that knowledge of the natural world allows you to see through trickery and apparently magical things, or whether he is instead implying that you should not try to explain away every marvellous thing you see. To add to the confusion, the tale is unfinished.

In another example, in "The Franklin's Tale," the situation is a little clearer. At a critical point in the story, a group of rocks off the coast of Brittany are made to disappear by the Clerk of Orléans. Chaucer explains that this was done using the Toledan astronomical tables, and involved calculations of the position of the Moon. Rather than magically making the rocks disappear, the Clerk seems to have instead predicted when an extraordinarily high tide would cover the rocks naturally.

A fifteenth-century portrait of Geoffrey Chaucer. (Topham/The British Library)

Chaucer was happy to show off his astronomical learning throughout *The Canterbury Tales*, as well as in other of his works, and he clearly knew much about astrology, alchemy, and magic. However, he sometimes seems reluctant to commit himself to whether the more controversial aspects of this learning were acceptable. This was probably wise, given his positions in and around the court, and his reliance on the king for his income: he perhaps could not afford to find himself out of fashion and so avoided making strong statements about some of the more occult subjects when they were in vogue at court.

If Chaucer himself seems to have been reluctant to state clearly his opinion for or against astrology, alchemy or magic, later commentators seem not to have felt the same restraint: as early as 1477 Thomas Norton cited Chaucer as an authority on alchemy. Posthumously Chaucer's reputation grew and grew, and the audience for his writings widened from the courtiers and civil servants around him during his lifetime, in parallel with the increasing use of written English during the fifteenth century.

Sixteenth-century commentators sometimes emphasized Chaucer's learning, and some referred to him as an expert in alchemy, astrology, and the occult arts. There survive sixteenth-century prophecies for the end of the world and spurious astrological and alchemical works that are wrongly ascribed to Chaucer in the manuscripts. Other scholars concentrated on his learning, and specifically mentioned his astronomical and philosophical learning. In 1585 Gabriel Harvey wrote:

"Others commend Chaucer and Lydgate for their wit, pleasant vein, variety of poetical discourse, and all humanity: I specially note their astronomy, philosophy, and other parts of their profound or cunning art. Wherein few of their time were more exactly learned. It is not enough for poets to be superficial humanists: but they must be exquisite artists, and curious universal scholars."

See also **Astrolabes and quadrants; Magic and the occult; Medicine, practical; Medicine, theoretical**

Bibliography

Benson, Larry D. (ed.). *The Riverside Chaucer*. New York: Oxford University Press, 1987.

Crow, Martin M. and Olson, Clair C. (eds.). *Chaucer Life Records*. New York: Oxford University Press, 1966.

Curry, Walter C. *Chaucer and the Medieval Sciences*. London: George Allen and Unwin, rev. ed., 1960.

Mooney, Linne M. "Chaucer and Interest in Astronomy at the Court of Richard II." In *Chaucer in perspective: Middle English essays in honour of Norman Blake*. Edited by Geoffrey A. Lester. Sheffield: Sheffield Academic Press, 1999, pp. 139–160.

North, John D. *Chaucer's Universe*. Oxford: Clarendon Press, 1988.

Spurgeon, Caroline F. E. *Five Hundred Years of Chaucer Criticism and Allusion 1357–1900*. 7 vols. Chaucer Society Publications, Second Series, nos. 48–50, 52–56, London: K. Paul, Trench, Trubner & Co., and Oxford University Press, 1960.

Ussery, Huling. *Chaucer's Physician: Medicine and Literature in Fourteenth-century England*. New Orleans: Tulane University Press, 1971.

CATHERINE EAGLETON

CLEPSYDRA

Clepsydra ("water-thief") is the generic name for devices that use flowing water to measure time. They are of two types: one in which water fills a vessel (inflow clepsydra), the other where it flows out of one (outflow clepsydra). Very ancient outflow clepsydrae, where water drips out of a vessel whose dropping water level is calibrated to represent the passage of time, are documented in ancient China,

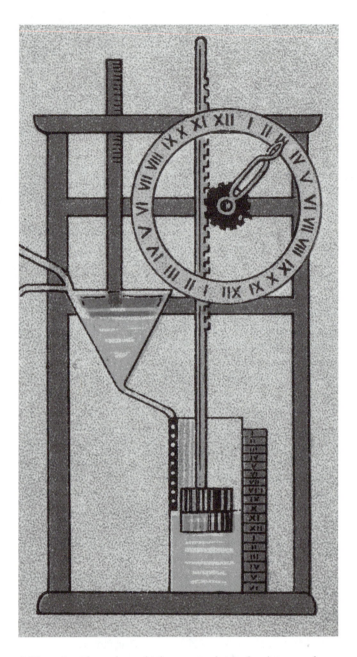

A Vitruvian clepsydra, which measured time by the rate of flow of water into the calibrated vase. (Mary Evans Picture Library)

India, Babylonia, and Egypt. Simple outflow clepsydrae were used in Athens to limit the time of speeches in law courts and assemblies. The use of clepsydrae to measure specific allotments of minutes is associated with irrigation: for example, in those areas of the Islamic world where water was sold or apportioned in time units, irrigation time was measured by sinking bowls (a simple inflow clepsydra that floats in a bucket of water till it sinks) or simple outflow clepsydrae, jars which empty through an orifice in their bottoms in a determinate time. In both instances, time is governed by the rate of flow through an orifice, which is the only regulating device.

Vitruvius describes an inflow clock, regulated by an outflow spout in such a way that the water level of a vessel fills uniformly. In this way a device attached to a float can be rigged to point to a scale, ring a bell, or—if converted to circular motion—cause a disk representing the heavens to revolve. Herophilus of Alexandria, physician of the third century B.C.E., used an outflow clepsydra to measure the pulse of patients, a practice still used by Nicholas of Cusa in the fifteenth century C.E.

In medieval monasteries, where the canonical hours of prayer were important, time was kept by sundials during the day, water-clocks by night. In the late tenth century, Abbo of Fleury had an outflow clock that signaled the time of the night offices in such a way that those on duty could awaken the monks with a hand-bell. This was most likely a dial with a pointer driven by a float and drum.

A series of complex and ingenious water-clocks is described by al-Jazari in his *Book of Knowledge of Ingenious Mechanical Devices* (*Kitab fi ma 'rifat al-hiyal al-handasiyya*). Al-Jazari entered the service of the Turcoman Artuqids in 1181 and completed his book in 1204 or 1206. Books on mechanical devices constituted a distinct genre of literature in medieval Arabic science, meant to illustrate points of mechanics (*'ilm al-hiyal*) rather than to serve any practical end. Al-Jazari's various water clocks all resemble astrolabes, having water-driven disks on which are presented the zodiac, the Sun, the Moon, and so forth. The problem in all such contrivances was how to regulate the flow of water in such a way as to keep it constant, or to shift from daytime to nighttime hours (which differed in length through the solar year). Circular motion was attained with different combinations of weights and pulleys. These were elaborate toys, for the most part. Muslims designed water clocks that could measure either equal or unequal (equinoctial) hours, while in Europe equal hours were not used before the invention of the mechanical clock. Hours of the night and day are equal in length only on the two equinoxes.

Such elaborate clocks no doubt had an ancient precedent that the Arabs continued. As early as 807, the Abbasid caliph, Harun al-Rashid, sent an embassy to Charlemagne bearing an elaborate water clock displaying twelve hours, marked by bronze bells dropping into a brass basin. The Arab tradition was continued by the astronomers in the court of *Alfonso X the Wise of Castile. One such clepsydra drove the dial of an astrolabe and was used for telling time when neither the Sun nor the stars were visible. Alfonso's famous mercury clock, which had an astrolabe set for the latitude of *Toledo, was a compartmented-clepsydra, the mercury passing from one compartment to another on the rim of a cylinder. The cylinder engaged the gears of a wheel on which twenty-four rods were mounted to strike each hour of the day on a bell.

Irrigation clocks, by contrast, were always very simple. Sinking bowls were commonly used in traditional irrigation systems in eastern Spain. Bowls of different sizes were used depending on the structure of water rights. In the Vall de Segó, a large bowl, the *olla*, sank in about an hour, while a smaller one sank in seven and a half

minutes—one-eighth of an hour. In North Africa, outflow clepsydrae were common. *Noria pots, which commonly had a hole in the bottom to allow air to escape as it scooped up water, were pressed into time-keeping duty. Such a pot, as described by al-Bakri for the oasis of Touzer, Tunisia, in the eleventh century, emptied in seven and a half minutes.

See also **Clocks** and timekeeping

Bibliography

Borst, Arno. *The Ordering of Time*. Chicago: University of Chicago Press, 1993.

Cipolla, Carlo. *Clocks and Culture, 1300–1700*. London: Collins, 1967.

Dohrn-van Rossum, Gerhard. *History of the Hour: Clocks and the Modern Temporal Order*. Chicago: University of Chicago Press, 1996.

Glick, Thomas F. Medieval Irrigation Clocks. *Technology and Culture* (1969) 10: 424–428.

al-Jazari, Ibn al-Razzaz. *The Book of Knowledge of Ingenious Mechanical Devices*. Donald R. Hill, trans. Dordrecht: D. Reidel, 1974.

Sánchez Pérez, José Augusto. *La personalidad científica y los relojes de Alfonso X el Sabio*. Murcia: Academia Alfonso X el Sabio, 1955.

THOMAS F. GLICK

CLOCKS AND TIMEKEEPING

In medieval Europe, the temporal location of an event could be measured in lives, years, seasons, months, days, hours, minutes; and instruments, tables, texts, and rules of thumb were used to find the time. One of the earliest Latin texts on measuring time was written by *Bede in 725 C.E., and one of the opening sections explains that "all the courses of mortal life are measured in moments, hours, days, months, years, ages." He goes on to say that there are three kinds of time reckoning, operating according to nature, custom, or authority. Thus, the natural passage of the seasons is a different kind of time-reckoning from the thirty-day month or the divine requirement that the seventh day be a day of rest.

One of the major motivations for dividing the day into hours was the fixing of times for prayers during the day: prime (sunrise), terce, sext (midday), none, vespers and compline (sunset). There were many ways in which churches and monasteries could determine the prayer times, including water clocks, candles, sundials, and the positions of the Sun and stars. In 1198 Jocelin Brakelond explains how, when putting out a fire, the monks of Bury St. Edmunds Abbey made a bucket chain to the clock to get water. Other monasteries had sundials, some with the prayer times marked on them as well as (or instead of) the twelve daytime hours. Other methods included the burning of graduated candles and the calculation of time from the position of certain stars, a method described in the sixth century by Gregory of Tours. Within the sequence of prayers, however, there was considerable flexibility about exactly when a particular office would take place, and the clock did not necessarily rule the religious life of an institution.

Monastic and church hours were unequal—daylight is divided into twelve hours, and nighttime into twelve. This means that the resulting hours will vary in length with the seasons, with daylight unequal hours being shorter in winter and longer in summer, and the day and night hours being the same length only at the equinoxes. Alongside this system, especially for astronomical and astrological purposes, time could be reckoned according to a system of equal hours, resulting from the division of day and night into twenty-four sections of equal length. And, in addition, different parts of Europe numbered the hours differently: "Italian hours" were counted from sunset, from one to twenty-four. In Italian hours, dawn could already be the twelfth hour. In England or Germany, by contrast, the hours were usually numbered one to twelve and one to twelve, starting at midday or midnight.

The choice of whether to use equal or unequal hours to tell the time was not the only one facing a medieval scholar. There are legal records showing that there was no universally accepted definition of the start of the day, no standardization of how to interpret temporal references in literary and administrative texts, and considerable philosophical debate about the structure of time. Alongside the variability in the ways that time could be conceived of and divided up, there were many possible ways of telling the time using instruments or rules of thumb. And a single instrument might tell the time in several different ways, using different methods. In contrast to philosophical discussions that divided minutes into smaller and smaller parts, measurements using instruments were not expected to be "accurate" in the modern sense: most medieval sundials are only marked with quarter-hours, even though astronomical tables and texts might give times accurate to minutes and seconds. Bede describes the difference between practical and theoretical divisions of hours, explaining that the *punctus* (a quarter of an hour) is named after the passage of the point on a sundial, and that there are smaller theoretical divisions of *minuta* (one tenth of an hour) and *partes* (one fifteenth of an hour). Later in the Middle Ages astronomical texts regularly discuss the division of an hour into sixty minutes and three hundred sixty seconds, although it is not until at least the sixteenth century that these were used in practical measurements of the time.

Timekeeping was closely linked to astronomy, since the year and the day were divided up according to the motion of the heavenly bodies. There survive many astronomical texts explaining how to make and use devices for telling the time, and how the various lines on them link to the structure of the heavens. Derek Price suggested that astronomical time-telling instruments were tangible models of the universe, useful for teaching astronomy, going as far as to say "I do not believe that then [in antiquity] or in the Middle Ages, instruments were used to tell the time, survey fields or navigate ships." For Price, instruments showed the truth of a system by physically modeling it. To tell the time using an astronomical instrument was to understand the structure of the universe: as *John of Saxony wrote in 1327 in his canons to the *Alfonsine Tables*: "Time is the measurement of the *primum mobile*."

Time-telling Instruments

In medieval Europe there were many varieties of sundial, quadrant, and astrolabe, all of which told the time. Hundreds of examples survive. Many astrolabes are preserved in museums all over the world, and these could tell the time in a multitude of ways from the Sun and stars, as well as convert between equal and unequal hours. Quadrants could tell the time from the Sun and, with the help of a method outlined in several manuscript texts on the instrument, by the stars as well. The cylinder dial was another popular instrument, to judge from the number of surviving manuscripts including instructions for its construction. Evidence from probate inventories and wills shows that wealthy people might own these kinds of objects, and medieval library booklists show them being kept alongside the astronomical books for the use of scholars.

However, it would probably be impossible, and definitely misleading, to try and give a typology of all the timekeeping instruments that were used in medieval Europe. The surviving evidence for the ownership of instruments is extremely patchy, and when combined with the material evidence preserved in museums shows only how much has been lost. Many of the instruments in use in the Middle Ages no longer survive, having been made from wood and paper. Others, if they were made of brass or copper, might have been melted down for their metal when they were no longer of interest as time-measuring instruments. For example, a number of fragments of small wood and brass compass dials dating from the fifteenth century have been found. However, references to them in texts and images are rare, one exception being an early sixteenth-century drawing by Urs Graaf showing a man holding a compass dial. This instrument, in common with several of the surviving instruments, has a nocturnal on the lid so that the owner could tell the time by day or by night. Another example is that of the sandglass, of which very few survive from the medieval period. If one were to consider only the fragmentary material evidence, it would be easy to dismiss this instrument as a rare and unimportant thing. But there are many artistic representations of people with sandglasses, and references to them in the accounts of navies and merchants, making it clear that the sandglass was in fact a relatively common object.

Nevertheless, it is likely that only a tiny fraction of the population of Europe could afford to own instruments designed for measuring the time. Most people instead probably told the time by listening for the bells ringing at the local church or monastery to signal the prayer times, or by rule-of-thumb methods. There survive notes explaining that an hour is the time it takes to say two nocturnes of the psalter, or that an hour is the time it takes to walk two miles in winter or three miles in summer. Medieval manuscript texts explain how to turn your hand into a basic sundial and tell the time, as well as how to calculate the date of Easter by counting along your fingers. In addition, people probably got to know the positions of the Sun relative to local landmarks, or to estimate time from the length of shadows. There are a number of surviving medieval copies of tables relating the length of a six-feet-tall man's shadow to the date and time, with equal-hour versions available from the late fourteenth century, and one of the pilgrims in *Chaucer's *The Canterbury Tales* uses this method to find the hour.

Clocks and Clockwork

In addition to these technologies and techniques, the Middle Ages saw a major development in timekeeping: the mechanical clock. There had been complex water clocks in antiquity and earlier in the Middle Ages, measuring the passage of time according to the flow of water into or out of a vessel graduated with scales. Cassiodorus explained the relationship between the sundial and the water clock in a letter sent to King Gundoband of Burgundy by Emperor Theoderic in 507: "We have provided you with a sundial for use during the day and a water clock for use at night and on the not infrequent days when there is no sunshine." Three hundred years later, in 807, Harun-al-Rashid, the Abbasid Caliph of Baghdad, gave an elaborate water clock to Charlemagne. It was described as: "A marvelous mechanical contraption, in which the course of the twelve hours moved according to a water clock, with as many brazen balls, which fell down on the hour and through their fall made a cymbal ring underneath. On this clock there were also twelve horsemen who at the end of each hour stepped out of twelve windows, closing the previously open windows by their movements."

Later, water clocks were fitted with elaborate mechanisms modeling the motion of the heavens, automata, and striking bells. Then in the thirteenth century there appear the first descriptions of weight-driven clocks. Robertus Anglicus described in 1271 the attempts of astronomers to construct a mechanical device that would accurately model the motion of the heavenly bodies, and so allow the equal hours to be determined, powered by weights. The first unambiguous evidence for the construction of weight-driven clocks dates from the fourteenth century, when clock-construction expenses appear in the accounts of several monasteries and towns, and literary descriptions attest to interest in the new device. These clocks relied on a new device: the escapement, a toothed wheel that converts the motion of the weights into the rotation of a wheel powering the gear train. This device, combined with the gears, automata, and striking mechanisms of the old water clocks, made mechanical weight-driven clocks possible. Some medieval clocks are still working, for example the clock at Salisbury Cathedral, England, built in 1386.

Just like the water clocks, the mechanical clock told the time during the day and night, and did not need a clear day to allow a reading to be taken. However, they still had to be regulated using sundials in order to keep them in time with the heavens. Anthony Turner has clarified the distinction between sundials and clocks, separating timekeeping instruments from time-finding instruments. Sundials are time-finding instruments since they measure time directly from the motion of the heavenly bodies; they track the motion of the heavens. Clocks are time-keeping instruments which keep track of the passage of time, but do not measure it directly from the heavens.

Jacques Le Goff, in his influential article on the impact of clocks, linked them to the need of merchants to control labor time in the expanding cities. This "merchant's time" and "clock time" is said to have replaced the "Church time" which had until that point dominated. Gerhard Dohrn-van Rossum, in his careful analysis of the transformations of time-consciousness linked to the mechanical clock, outlines the spread of the mechanical clock in the fourteenth century, starting in northern Italy. He shows that the introduction of a public clock in a particular town should be seen as part of a wider process of urban modernization, in conjunction with mills, foundries, and church organs, schools, and the improvement of financial and administrative governance: merchants and traders did not stand out from any other part of the political community.

The Passage of Time

In 1344 Jacopo Dondi installed a clock on the Palazzo del Capitano at Padua: it was no ordinary clock, but an astronomical clock that earned him the title "Dall'Orologio." His son Giovanni (1315–1389) completed an even more impressive clock, the *astrarium*, in 1364. This instrument had seven dials, one for each planet, and it showed the motions of the Ptolemaic system. Despite the fact that many early astronomical clocks were inaccurate, the metaphor of the universe as heavenly clockwork with God as a master-clockmaker proved popular. In an influential article, Derek Price linked the interest in clockwork, gears, and machines to the growth of mechanistic philosophy, suggesting that growing interest in the latter encouraged the making of automata and clocks. In around 1410, the author of an English manual titled *Dives et Pauper* used the metaphor of the clockwork universe to compare the influence of the planets and the clock on men's lives. He argues that just as the planets do not rule men, neither should the clock.

The mechanical clock also captured the imagination of medieval writers and artists. Some marvelled at the device, including Froissart, who wrote a poem titled *L'Orloge Amoureus*, in which he explained that the clock is beautiful and remarkable, pleasing and profitable, because it shows the hours night and day, even when there is no sunlight. Others were less positive; the Welsh poet Davydd ap Gwilym (1320–1370) described it as "churlish clock with foolish chatter." Later in the fourteenth century Chaucer includes several references to clock time in his writings, although many of his characters still tell the time using sundials and rules of thumb.

During the fourteenth and fifteenth centuries, there are increasingly frequent references to clock time, and a 1396 manual of useful phrases for Englishmen traveling to France includes how to ask "What has the clock struck?" and "What time is it?" Chronicles increasingly give the times of events in terms of clock hours rather than prayer times, and city decrees regulated working hours and breaks according to the clock.

At the same time, there was an increasing quantification of time and regulation of the day by equal hours. Schools began to set limits on the length of classes, often using sandglasses, and humanist authors worried about wasting time: Francesco Petrarch, in his *De vita solitaria* of 1366, described how study could enable a scholar to cheat time by producing knowledge that would live on after his death. In around 1404 Petrus Paulus Vergerius suggested that time-measuring devices should be installed in libraries so that scholars could literally see time slipping away. In paintings, clocks and other time-measuring instruments are often seen in the studies of scholars, and the clock quickly became a powerful symbol of the passage of time and an admonition not to waste it.

See also **Almanacs; Astrolabes and quadrants; Astrology; Astronomy; Calendar; Clepsydra; Cosmology; Navigation; Planetary tables**

Bibliography

Boullin, D. G. An Iconographic Study of Sandglasses. *Nuncius* (1989) 4: 67–85.
Calouste Gulbenkian Museum. *The Image of Time: European Manuscript Books*. Lisbon: Calouste Gulbenkian Foundation, 2000.
Dembowski, P.F. (ed.) *Le paradis d'amour. L'orloge amoureuse*. Geneva: Droz, 1986.
Dohrn-van Rossum, Gerhard. *History of the Hour: Clocks and Modern Temporal Orders*. Chicago: University of Chicago Press, 1996.
Hector, L.C. The Beginning of the 'Natural Day' in the Late Fourteenth Century. *Journal of the Society of Archivists* (1961) 2: 87–89.
Higgins, A. Medieval Notions of the Structure of Time. *Journal of Medieval and Renaissance Studies* (1989) 19: 227–258.
Landes, David S. *Revolution in Time: Clocks and the Making of the Modern World*. London: Viking, 2000.
Leclerq, J. The Experience of Time and its Interpretation in the Late Middle Ages. *Studies in Medieval Culture* (1976) 8–9: 137–150.
Le Goff, Jacques. *Time, work, and culture in the Middle Ages*. Chicago: University of Chicago Press, 1982.
Lippincott, Kirsten et al. *The Story of Time*. London: Merrell Holberton, 1999.
McCluskey, Stephen C. Gregory of Tours, Monastic Timekeeping, and Early Christian Attitudes to Astronomy. *Isis* (1990) 81: 8–22.
Mooney, Linne M. The Cock and the Clock: Telling the Time in Chaucer's Day. *Studies in the Age of Chaucer* (1993) 15: 91–109.
Price, Derek J. de Solla. Automata and the Origins of Mechanism and Mechanistic Philosophy. *Technology and Culture* (1964) 5: 9–23.
Rothwell, W. The Hours of the Day in Medieval French. *French Studies* (1959) 13: 240–251.
Travis, P. W. Chaucer's 'Chronographiae', the Confounded Reader, and Fourteenth-Century Measurements of Time. *Disputatio* (1997) 2: 1–34.
Turner, Anthony J. "Essential Complementarity: The Sundial and the Clock." In Hester K. Higton, ed. *Sundials at Greenwich*. Oxford: Oxford University Press, 2002, pp. 15–24.
Wallis, Faith. *Bede: the Reckoning of Time*. Liverpool: Liverpool University Press, 1999.
Ward, F. A.B. An Early Pocket Sundial Illustrated in Art. *Antiquarian Horology* (1979) 11: 484–487.
EPACT: Scientific Instruments of Medieval and Renaissance Europe www.mhs.ox.ac.uk/epact

CATHERINE EAGLETON

COINAGE, MINTING OF

The minting of coinage was a process whereby states and some seigniorial authorities created certain quantities of money as a monopoly. These coins were generally made from alloys containing variable proportions of gold, silver or bronze. Once the coins were put into circulation, they were used as media for the payment of commercial or other transactions and for fiscal payments. The conversion of pieces of metal into monetary signs required a stamp of authority on the flans (blank pieces of metal). To do this two dies had to be prepared, one for the obverse side and the other for the reverse. These dies were made of hardened steel, bronze or iron. The design of the die was made by melting it in a mold (bronze dies were most amenable to melting, normally in a matrix of lead), engraving the complete design directly on the surface, or else combining various punches with different forms (strokes, curves, and circles) or with part of an inscription. The lower pile or anvil-die was fixed, while the upper pile, known as the trussel, was movable, and operated with the left hand. A heated flan was placed between the dies before the trussel received a hammer-blow delivered with the right hand. This blow pressed the lower face of the flan into the hollows of the lower pile, creating an image in relief.

Normally, the flans were prepared by melting the metal in molds. The ingots thus obtained might take the form of a strip. Once heated, the ingots were treated on an anvil with a forging hammer to anneal the metal and obtain a uniform thickness. An image on a twelfth-century capital at the abbey of Souvigny (France) depicts a person working on a metal strip with a hammer in just this way. Then, blanks of the weight desired were cut from the metal strip with a chisel and rounded off with hammer and tongs. The ingots might also have a cylindrical or square form, such as those used by the mint of London in the thirteenth century, or as it is also explained in medieval Arabic treatises on the coining of money. These bars were cut into small pieces. After weighing and rounding off with a hammer, the blanks were heated, coined, and finally polished. The same Arabic treatises explained another procedure consisting of casting the blanks in molds. The pieces obtained were hammered to anneal the metal and to shape the blanks before making them into coins.

General Conditions of Coin Production

The production of coins required the prior establishment of legal standard for weight and value whose acceptance was obligatory. Only a continuous relationship between the pieces and the legally instituted units of weight and account could avoid the dissipation of coins into mere metallic objects. Similarly, all coinage contained an additional element of authority (seigneuriage) which increased the legal value of the piece beyond its metallic weight.

Once the legal system of weight and accounting was established, the authority could then proceed to mint coins. With them, the state or lord possessed a means with which to pay his own bills and to purchase services, especially those of a bureaucratic and military nature. At the same time, such payments constituted the initial channels for the distribution of coins. Nevertheless, markets were the principal agency for the diffusion of coinage. This necessary intervention of money in market exchanges can be clearly appreciated in, for example, the donations of *mercatum et moneta* made to the abbey of Corvey by the Carolingian kings in the mid-eighth century, or in the establishment of markets in burghs by English lords after the Norman conquest. The central role of the market in the circulation of coins was remarked by the eleventh-century Andalusi polymath Ibn Hazm when he described how coins—which he characterized as "snakes" and "scorpions"—came into the hands of peasants with the sale in markets of what they alone produced. In the final analysis, what underlay the need to acquire coinage in market exchanges was the obligation on subjects to satisfy some or most of the fiscal demands of rulers with money. In this way, the power that minted the pieces was assured not only that the metal would return to the mint but also of the liquidity of peasant production. In any case, the states or lords that produced coins habitually needed to obtain fresh metal to coin at least the same mass of metal as had been put into circulation. Evasion, fraud, and the imperfections of the system of tax and tribute collection resulted in the inevitable loss of metal. For this reason, the authorities strove to control the process of metal extraction. One of the habitual procedures, documented for example in tenth-century Italy and eleventh-century al-Andalus, was to acquire metal directly from miners—gold from placers in both cases—paying the price fixed by the state.

The manufacture of coins thus required mastery of various techniques, including melting and engraving of the dies used to stamp the coins, the refining of metals, the preparation of alloys, and polishing of the flans before being coined as well as of the coins already stamped. Eligius, a Frankish moneyer of the seventh century, patron saint of the goldsmiths, personified this technical relationship between the manufacture of coins and the production of other metallic objects. So important was the work of mint personnel that the authorities frequently confined moneyers to places in which they could have no contact with the outside world. In this way they tried to avoid the counterfeiting of coinage, a practice well documented throughout the Middle Ages.

Severe punishments were also prescribed. For example, in an edict of 643 the Lombard king Rothar ordered the amputation of the hand of anyone fabricating coins without royal authorization.

See also **Mineralogy**

Bibliography

Cooper, Denis R. *The Art and Craft of Coin Making. A History of Minting Technology.* London: Spink, 1988.

Grierson, Philip. "Note on Stamping of Coins and Other Objects." In *A History of Technology*, edited by Charles Joseph et al. Singer, ed. Oxford: Clarendon Press, 1954–1984. II, 485–492.

Sellwood, D. "Medieval Minting Techniques." *British Numismatic Journal* (1962) 31: 57–65.

Toll, Ch. "Minting Technique according to Arabic Literary Sources." *Orientalia Suecana* 19–20 (1970–1971), 125–139.

FÈLIX RETAMERO

COLUMBUS, CHRISTOPHER

The navigator Christopher Columbus (called Cristóbal Colón in Spain) was born Cristoforo Colombo in Genoa in 1451. Experience gained in sailing Atlantic waters as a merchant in the 1470s and 1480s (Iceland, Madeira, the Azores, and the Gulf of Guinea) convinced Columbus of the possibility of a westward voyage to India. Columbus established himself in Lisbon and between 1478 and 1484, when he left for Spain, he attempted to convince Portuguese officials to back his voyage westward. He presented his ideas to Ferdinand and Isabel in 1486 and 1487. Finally the king and queen convened a panel of experts (including "wise men, learned officials and mariners") at the University of Salamanca to evaluate his plan. The experts rejected Columbus's proposals, not because the Earth was flat (a false story that Spain's enemies concocted years later) but because, according to Columbus's biographer Bartolomé de Las Casas, it was not thought possible to sail to the Antipodes. It was widely believed that the "torrid zone" near the equator was both impassable and uninhabitable. To Columbus this was absurd: "The Torrid Zone is not uninhabitable, because the Portuguese sail through it nowadays, and it is densely populated.... Below the equator, where the days are always twelve hours long, is the king of Portugal's fortress. I was there and it was a temperate place." *Mandeville's *Book*, one of Columbus's sources, had debunked the Torrid Zone and Columbus had verified his conclusion by his own experience. The sovereigns finally relented in 1491, even though another royal commission had decided against Columbus, and he was granted the title of Admiral of the Ocean Sea and viceroy in whatever territories he might claim for Castile.

Columbus made four voyages across the ocean. He recruited his crew for the first expedition among experienced Atlantic seamen from the port of Palos de la Frontera, near Cádiz. Columbus's ship, the *Santa Maria*,

Unsigned fifteenth-century portrait of Christopher Columbus. (Getty Images/Hulton Archive)

belonged to a local ship owner named Juan de la Cosa, who sailed as Columbus's second in command and was to become the greatest cartographer of the early discovery period. The crossing actually began at Gomera in the Canary Islands on September 6, 1492, and made landfall in an island of the Bahamas on October 12. Columbus sailed the coasts of Cuba (which he first thought to be Japan, then mainland China) and Hispaniola, and began the voyage home on January 4, 1493. During the second voyage (1493–1496) he was involved with colonizing Hispaniola and sailing to the west of Cuba. On the third voyage (1496–1498), he explored the Paria Peninsula of Venezuela and the mouth of the Orinoco River, which he believed to be the entrance to the Terrestrial Paradise. On the fourth voyage (1500–1504) he sailed the coast of Central America and Panama (which he called Veragua). He was marooned on Jamaica (where he predicted a lunar eclipse) and returned to Spain on November 5, 1504. Juan de la Cosa was also on the second voyage, and after a third with Alonso de Ojeda in 1499–1500 he drew his famous world map depicting all Spanish and Portuguese exploration until that time.

In the process of conceptualizing his voyage, Columbus consulted all manner of sources in order to substantiate his conviction that the ocean was narrower than many thought. In order to convince both prospective patrons

and crew members he had to make a case for the trip's feasibility. Columbus had seen a letter written to the king of Portugal by Paolo Toscanelli, an Italian physician and amateur geographer, estimating the distance from the Canary Islands to China as five thousand nautical miles. He found corroboration of the assertion of the apocryphal book of Esdras that land covered six-sevenths of the Earth's surface in the *Imago Mundi*, a geographical encyclopedia compiled by *Pierre d'Ailly, who gave 225° for land and 135° for the sea (where *Ptolemy had had 180° for each). After further juggling of the figures, he finally arrived at a projected voyage from the Canary Islands to India of only 60°, a mere twenty percent of the real distance.

Columbus also used an overly small value for the mile. In a Latin marginal note to Pierre d'Ailly's *Imago Mundi* he wrote: "Note that from Lisbon south to Guinea I frequently observed the course carefully and afterwards I many times took the Sun's altitude with the quadrant and other instruments, and I found agreement with al-Farghani, that is, that 56 2/3 miles equaled one degree." He thus concluded that the circumference of the Earth at the equator was 20,400 miles (32,800 km).

Columbus reflected on this experience in a 1501 letter to Ferdinand and Isabel: "I have conversed and exchanged ideas with learned men, churchmen and laymen, Latins and Greeks, Jews and Moors and many others of other religions.... [God] endowed me abundantly in seamanship; of astrology He gave me sufficient, and of geometry and arithmetic too, with the wit and craftsmanship to make presentations of the globe and draw on them the cities, rivers and mountains, islands and harbors, all in their proper places."

Columbus's method of navigation and how good he was at it are matters of controversy. Judging from his methodical recording of distance in his logs (only those of the first voyage survive), he sailed by dead reckoning, using a compass, marking his course on a chart, and determining speed by watching flotsam floating by his ship. He habitually overestimated the speed of his ships. He made a series of latitude readings in the Caribbean and on the return voyage by determining the altitude of the Pole Star with a quadrant. His errors were so great that Morison thought he had mistaken other stars for Polaris. A more recent view holds that Columbus had read the tangent scale of his quadrant rather than the direct declination scale, in which case his readings were only a few degrees off instead of fifteen or more. His finding of 19° latitude for Jamaica on his fourth voyage, within one degree of accuracy, suggests that his skills at celestial navigation had improved. It is possible that many such observations were rough approximations made without the use of observational instruments.

Columbus was the first European to record the shifting of positive (northeast) to negative (northwest) magnetic declination as, on the night of September 12, 1492 (on his first voyage westward), he passed a point of zero declination: "The compass needles which until then had varied towards the northeast, suddenly changed one-quarter to the northwest." On subsequent voyages he used this

geomagnetic reference to establish his longitude roughly one hundred leagues west of the Azores.

It has been supposed, based on a fleeting reference to an "Almanach" in a passage of his *Book of Prophecies* describing his lunar eclipse prediction in Jamaica in 1505, that Columbus carried, at least on the fourth voyage, a copy of *Zacuto's *Almanach Perpetuum*. But the Almanach contains neither eclipse tables nor those for declination. Therefore he might have carried the tables of *Regiomontanus, either in book format or individual tables copied onto sheets. On a blank page of his copy of d'Ailly, he had copied a table of the longest day of the year for each degree of latitude and another of the number of degrees traversed by the Sun in each house of the zodiac. On occasion, he did attempt to ascertain latitude by the length of daylight, with mixed results.

Once his geographical views were formed, he held doggedly to them, an inflexibility made possible by the tremendous latitude allowed him by the great variety of medieval texts he consulted. Columbus insisted until he died (in 1506) that he been sailing off the Asian coast.

See also **Navigation**

Bibliography

Primary Sources
Columbus, Christopher. *The* Diario *of Christopher Columbus's First Voyage to America, 1492–1493*. Eited by Oliver Dunn and James E. Kelley, Jr. Norman: University of Oklahoma Press, 1988.
———. *The Book of Prophecies*. Edited by Roberto Rusconi. Berkeley: University of California Press, 1997.
D'Ailly, Pierre. *Ymago Mundi*. Edited by Edmond Buron. 3 vols. Paris: Maisonneuve, 1930.

Secondary Sources
Alvarez, Aldo. Geomagnetism and the Cartography of Juan de la Cosa: A New Perspective on the Great Antilles in the Age of Discovery. *Terra Incognitae* (2003): 35: 1–15.
Fernández-Armesto, Felipe. *Columbus*. New York: Oxford University Press, 1991.
Flint, Valerie. *The Imaginative Landscape of Christopher Columbus*. Princeton: Princeton University Press, 1992.
Morison, Samuel Eliot. *Admiral of the Ocean Sea*. 2 vols. Boston: Little, Brown, 1942.
Pickering, Keith A. Columbus and Celestial Navigation: www1.minn.net/~keithp/cn.htm
Russell, Jeffrey Burton. *Inventing the Flat Earth: Columbus and Modern Historians*. New York: Praeger, 1991.

Thomas F. Glick

COMMERCIAL ARITHMETIC

The increase in European trade from the tenth century onward led to the replacement of the individual, nomadic merchant by the established, sedentary, trading house. Initially, it was cities such as Pisa, Genoa, Venice, and Florence with their access to the Mediterranean and the markets of the Levant that became trade centers with *fondacos*, or large commercial houses. With their regional and international network of warehouses and agents, these houses became conduits for diverse goods, commodities, and information. During their travels, merchants were avid observers and recorders of customs and practices pertaining to mercantile success and efficiency. Their *ricordanze* (diaries) became a record of tariffs and custom duties, foreign weights and measures, methods of storing and transporting goods, and the mathematical methods used to protect investments, establish costs and ensure profits. One particular new form of knowledge, commercial arithmetic, as practiced by the Arabs, was brought by merchants into Europe where it was refined and expanded to meet the rising complexities of trade within the developing monied economies.

Since classical times, merchants have always been involved with arithmetic, establishing a value, reckoning prices and the terms of a sale necessary to realize a profit for their efforts. In Greek times and even into the late Roman period, this type of working with numbers was considered crass and vulgar because it was felt that numbers, their properties and associations should be the subject of philosophical speculation. It would be primarily in the merchant houses of medieval Europe that this concept of number and calculation would be radically changed. Traditionally in the medieval merchant house, calculation was performed on an abacus, a *mesa Pythagorica* or *tabula abaci*, a table with ruled columns or rows which designated assigned numerical magnitudes—tens, hundreds, etc—and along which "counters" would be moved to perform a reckoning process. These counters were round, flat metal disks used to mark numerical positions on the computing board or table. Known as *jittons* in French or, more tellingly, *Rechenpfennig* (reckoning-penny), in German, they eventually became standardized and resembled coins. The counters were manipulated according to specific rules in performing the four fundamental operations of arithmetic with division singled out as "*dura cosa e la partita*" (literally, "hard thing is division"). Merchants worked with whole numbers, fractions, and mixed numbers. Facility on the abacus or counting board was enhanced by the memorization of tables (*librettine*) of numerous multiplication facts which had to deal with a great variety of monetary systems and weights and measures. Such tables were far more extensive than those usually required today. A merchant calculator also had to be able "to hold numbers in his hand," that is, to use his hand and finger positions as a register to store numbers during abacus calculations. Finger mathematics was a practice employed since Roman times. Its various techniques and positions were transmitted through the writings of *Boethius. The results of calculations were usually checked by the "method of casting out nines" and recorded in account books using Roman numerals. Throughout the Middle Ages, the accounting table or board became the center of commercial transactions, giving rise to the modern expression "doing business over the counter."

But the real essence of commercial arithmetic was in its application to business situations: fair division of property and profit in partnership arrangements; computation of commissions and brokerage fees; monetary exchange; estimation of tare and tret (allowances and deductions); the determination of interest; alligation; the mechanics of barter and, even in some situations, calendrical reckoning and astrological readings. Within these applications, the calculator would usually apply specific arithmetical techniques such as "the rule of two" or "the rule of three" and "the chain rule." Although these were all regarded as powerful solution techniques, they were no more than simple applications of proportion. Italian merchants were the pioneers of commercial arithmetic on the European scene. As a result, many of the problem situations and solution techniques bore Italian names, even when they were used in Northern Europe. Merchants from all over Europe sent their sons to learn *l'arte della merchandanta* from the Italians.

The Rule of Three

An eastern import that found its way to Europe through Arabic sources, "the rule of three" was called *la regula de le tre cosa* in Italian and *regula trium rerum* in Latin but, reflecting on its use and value, in English it was more popularly known as the "Merchant's Rule" or the "Golden Rule." It involves the solving of a proportion where three values are known and from which a fourth, unknown, must be found, that is: *a* is to *b* as *c* is to *x*; from which *x* is found to be the product of *b* and *c* divided by *a*. The "rule of two" involved finding an unknown from a product of two knowns divided by their sum whereas the rule of five was a simple proportion between five known values and one related unknown. The chain rule, *regula del chataina*, particularly useful in determining monetary exchange, was a continuous proportion with different terms for different currencies.

Often the hazards and costs of a business venture were distributed by means of a partnership. If the venture failed, individual losses would be restricted, but if it was successful, profits had to be distributed fairly. Computations involving partnership almost always required an application of the rule of three. The problems encountered concerned two situations: (1) A number of partners contribute varying amounts of investment to a venture and at its successful completion must share the profits accordingly; and (2) The same scenario with time factors introduced, that is, when each partner has invested for a different period, and the duration of each's involvement has to be taken into account when distributing profit. Medieval writers of arithmetic such as Johannes Hispalensis (c. 1140) and Leonardo Pisano (1202) devoted sections to the mathematics of partnership, known in Latin as *Regula de societate*.

Before the standardization and ready availability of money, barter (*barattare*) was a common method of exchanging goods. For the medieval merchant, barter was a major form of commerce. Barter computations involved placing a value on the merchandise to be exchanged so that it offset the barter value and ensured the desired profit. Even when solvent monied economies existed, barter was still often employed. In such cases, two prices would be established for a good: a cash price and a barter price. The barter price was always higher.

Alligation (*legare e consolare le monete*) was a method of standardizing different currencies so that merchants could compare like with like. For tradespeople dealing with differing coinage that contained varied amounts of precious metals such as gold or silver, the actual value of money was often in question. The exchange of different coinage required appropriate calculations, and tables of information were available to assist merchants with this task. Often the value set for a product that, in itself, was comprised of a mixture of substances of different quality and price had to be determined. For example, different grades of grain, wool, oil or wine could be mixed to comprise saleable products.

Tare (*tara*) was the determination of the weight of a shipment of goods with appropriate deductions for the weight of the containers, such as crates or barrels. Tret (*tratto*) is the allowance made for possible damage to and/or deterioration of merchandise experienced during shipment. In the transport of any merchandise, calculations had to be made for tare and tret. Merchant handbooks (*pratica della mercantura*) contained advice and tables that assisted in this task.

Certain chronologically-based phenomena were important in the professional lives of merchants. Change of seasons, planting and harvesting times determined agricultural markets. The periodic flow of tides and the shifting of wind patterns controlled maritime trade. Rainy periods curtailed overland trade. In Christian Europe, church feast days and holidays disrupted money transactions and trade patterns. Merchants had to be able to coordinate their transactions according to these factors and thus, in this era before the appearance of reliable public calendars, had to be able to reckon dates in advance. The Christian *calendar is compiled around the occurrence of Easter, which was officially declared to be the first Sunday after the full moon following the vernal equinox on March 21. If the full moon happened to coincide with a Sunday, Easter would be the following Sunday. The astronomical computations involved in this issue were settled by the year 525 C.E., and the necessary tables of interpolation were compiled by Dionysius Exiguus and Bede to assist in determining the date of Easter. These tables were included in merchants' manuals. To use these tables one had to determine the "Golden Number," by adding 1 to the existing date and dividing by 19. The remainder was the "Golden Number," which allowed the tables to be referenced. Merchants, in their travels and business ventures, were constantly tempting the "fates." *Astrology was used to remedy this situation. Astrological advice was frequently directed towards the hazards of travel and the uncertainties of the marketplace. Many commercial reckoning books and manuals contained sections on astrological computations.

From the twelfth century onward, increased demand by merchants for a knowledge of and facility with commercial arithmetic stimulated the rise of two complementary industries: the writing and publishing of manuscripts and books devoted to the subject, and the development of a system of private schools and teachers to impart the new knowledge to students.

In their travels Arab merchants encountered new and effective mathematical techniques and applications which they refined and adopted for their own use. Italian traders in their contacts with the Arabs learned of these applications and began to use them themselves. Leonardo Pisano (c. 1175–1250), more commonly known as *Fibonacci (son of Bonacci), the child of a Pisan merchant, spent his youth in Bugia, a Pisan trading colony on the Barbary Coast. Leonardo was instructed in the methods of commercial arithmetic by local Arab teachers. During business travels through the Levant he further extended his knowledge of the subject. Impressed by the power of mathematics and its applications in the commercial world, he published his findings for a European audience. *Liber abaci* (Book of Calculations) appeared in 1202. Written in Latin, the book had a limited readership but a second edition appeared in 1228. While ostensibly written to convey information on the Hindu-Arabic numeral system to Europeans, over a third of the text is devoted to solving business-related problems: monetary conversion; barter computation; conversion methods for weights and measures; calculations involving partnership and the distribution of profits; simple and compound interest, and the alloying of money. As a *practica* or handbook of commercial arithmetic, the *Liber abaci* spawned numerous similar texts. Until this period of European history, arithmetic texts were rather scholarly, intended for those who wished to learn *arithmetica*, the philosophical and theoretical aspects of numbers, or to compute the Church calendar. The mathematics of the workplace had been left mainly to oral instruction between the master and his apprentices. Warren Van Egmond, in his research on this literature intended for merchants, termed such material "Abacus manuscripts." It should be noted that at this time the word "abacus" and its many variants referred not only to the computing table but also designated working with numbers, computing, and arithmetic itself. Many of the practica published did not bear the word "abacus" in their title but rather were algorisms, such as Jacopo da Firenze's *Tractatus algorismi* (1307). An algorism was any small treatise that explained the use of Hindu-Arabic numerals and their computing algorisms. Algorisms also served as handbooks of commercial arithmetic. In fact, partly through the influence of algorisms, Italian merchants became the first European professionals to adopt and extensively use the new numerals. As a result these numerical symbols were designated as *figura mercantesco* (the figures or numbers of the merchants), in contrast to the traditional *figura imperiale* (Roman numerals).

Further to accommodate the demand for knowledge of commercial arithmetic a new class of secular teachers arose in Europe: in Italy, they were known as *maestri d'abbaco*; in France, *maistres d'algorisme*, and in the Germanic regions, *Rechenmeister*. These men were practitioners of applied mathematics who sold their services and, in many cases, taught the subject. They opened schools of commercial arithmetic (*scuole d'abbaco*) for the instruction of merchants' sons. It is known that by 1338 there were six such schools in Florence.

In practicing commercial arithmetic, medieval merchants refined and extended its scope. The use of Hindu-Arabic numerals led the way for their adoption in the rest of Europe. In the use of arithmetic, merchants developed the techniques of double-entry bookkeeping and the concept of percentage (*per cento*). Many present-day applications of arithmetic owe their origins to the commercial arithmetic of the medieval merchant community.

See also **Arithmetic**

Bibliography

Lopez, Robert. "Stars and Spices: The Earliest Italian Manual of Commercial Practice." In *Economy, Society and Government in Medieval Italy*. Edited by David Herlihy, Robert Lopez and Vsevold Slessarev. Kent, Ohio: The Kent State Press, 1969, pp. 35–42.
Pullan, J. M. *The History of the Abacus*. New York: Frederick Praeger, 1969.
Sigler, Laurence. *Fibonacci's Liber Abaci: A Translation into Modern English of Leonardo Pisano's Book of Calculation*. New York: Springer-Verlag, 2003.
Smith, David. *History of Mathematics*. 2 volumes. New York: Dover Publications, 1958, pp. 552–582.
Swetz, Frank. "*Figura Mercantesco*: Merchants and the Evolution of a Number Concept in the Latter Middle Ages." In *Word, Image, Number: Communication in the Middle Ages*. Edited by John Contreni and Santa Casciani. Micrologus' Library 8. Florence: Edizioni del Galluzzo, 2002.
Van Egmond, Warren. "The Commercial Revolution and the Beginnings of Western Mathematics in Renaissance Florence, 1300–1500." Ph. D. Dissertation, Indiana University, 1976.

FRANK J. SWETZ

COMMUNICATION

The notion of scientific communication includes the ways in which scientific ideas are communicated to scientists and others, including personal interaction, the diffusion of texts, patterns of translation, literacy, and the rise of science in vernacular languages.

Scientific and medical communication can be understood in terms of textual communities. If the community changes, or is broadened, owing to translation or vernacularization, that may alter the way in which the text is perceived. Translation alone would not significantly alter the nature of the scholarly textual community, because in an Aristotelian world basic assumptions proved remarkably pliable in the face of the linguistic change. When an idea or set of ideas is the focus, rather than as discrete text, perhaps one might conceptualize multiple semantic communities clustered around the same text or set of texts. Such communities included both producers of texts (authors, translators, scribes) and consumers—all who had access to a text, listeners as well as readers.

The term "vernacular science" usually refers to the production of scientific texts in spoken languages, particularly in the cultural area where Latin was the language of learning. An analogue in the Muslim world was the relatively late, minoritarian production of scientific texts in Persian, rather than Arabic. However, the analogy is purely social, because Persian was every bit as much a classical language as were Arabic and Latin. So the discussion here will be limited to Europe. It must also be observed that Latin itself cannot be regarded as a single register of expression. When Arabic texts were said to have been translated *vulgariter*, what was often meant was that the target language was a Latin accessible to persons not trained in the Classics, not the vernacular.

Practical science was vernacularized earlier than that of a more theoretical nature: thus medicine, astrology, and alchemy all have rather strong vernacular traditions in late medieval Europe. In the thirteenth-century court of *Alfonso X the Wise of Castile, "The astronomical works translated from the Arabic were not of interest or important for what they revealed about the nature of the stars, but for how their movements influenced men's lives. For this reason they were translated into Castilian rather than Latin, which was the language of a minority" (Castro, 1971: 538).

Emerging vernacular science was, of course, sharply configured by the established conventions of Latin writing. But both in translations from Latin or Arabic into the vernacular and literary creation directly in vernacular languages, new means of expressing scientific ideas had to be invented. Of course, oral teaching practices had themselves figured in the development of forms of written scholarly discourse: *quaestiones*, commentary, and compilations all to some extent were formalized versions of vernacular discourse that could be repatriated to their original domain. Taavitsainen (51–59) identifies uroscopies, *Guy de Chauliac's surgeries, various Hippocratic and Galenic medical texts, and Beneventus Grassus's ophthalmological treatise as vernacular commentaries (signaled by the repeated allusions to scholarly opinion ("Galien saith…"). Grassus contributed an English vernacular commentary on *Hunayn ibn Ishaq's (Johannitius') treatise on the eye. Encyclopedias were the most obvious form of vernacular compilations, overlapping, at least stylistically, with the commentary.

Vernacular *quaestiones* were also popular, particularly in verse form, which facilitated the memorization of complex issues such as humoral pathology:

> "Telle me now, if that thou can
> The perilousest thinges than ben in man.
> Foure colours a man that him inne
> That of foure complexiouns bigynne…
>
> (Taavitsainen, 65)

Vernacular science was highly didactic, and much effort was devoted to the explanation of scientific and medical terms in plain language. That is why scientific vernacularization, as well as translation, were creators of new vernacular forms of expression.

Part of this process is revealed in the resolution of conceptual problems that translation presented. Castro argued that scientific translation in and of itself was a powerful force in the creation of literary Castilian generally, while Millás explained that the literalism of the Castilian translations from the Arabic of Alfonso X's translators can be explained by, e.g., the need to coin new and somewhat clumsy abstract nouns to represent a kind of abstract discourse that had not previously existed in the language. Word-for-word translations from Latin to vernaculars and from Arabic into Latin appear as relexified versions of Latin and Arabic linguistic structures, respectively. In extreme cases, translators even tried for morpheme-by-morpheme renderings.

In technology, it is less appropriate to speak of textual communities, as opposed to communities of users of the same or related tool kits. Related tool kits can admit indefinite variation, however, in consonance with varying cultural, economic or social conditions, without thereby altering their function. No two *watermills are exactly alike, to cite a notorious example, even though their builders and operators may partake of identical tool kits.

"Community of discourse" is an even more comprehensive concept than readership or textual community, because one need not have read anything to participate in one. Some scientific and medical concepts, moreover, were so broadly diffused that perhaps an even more inclusive concept, such as field of knowledge, may be appropriate. For example, the percentage of the population conversant with humoral pathology as diffused through folk medicine in Europe must have been very high. The same can be said for the notion of the four qualities as understood in medieval *agronomy. Many illiterate cultivators knew that cold, dry seeds required hot, wet soil for their nurture. They must have identified these qualities by touch, according to traditional norms passed down orally, because agronomical treatises do not say how the system worked on a practical basis. The same is true, in Chinese medicine, of basic concepts such as *yin-yang*, *qi*, the five-phase system (wood, fire, earth, metal, water), and so forth. Everyone who has heard of the concept is in the field, and that is a very large percentage of the population. The same is true of astrology, where one did not have to be literate or know anything about cosmological theory to understand the meaning of horoscopes.

Anglo-Saxon England was precocious—uniquely so in Western Europe—in vernacular scientific texts, particularly medical. The first extant French vernacular medical texts did not appear until the thirteenth century. By the fifteenth century, vernacular scientific texts appeared all over Europe. In the Spain of Alfonso X the Wise (r. 1252–1284), Romance vernacular was first used as a medium for science. This was ten years before France, and one hundred years before England. The language in which the Alfonsine corpus was written shows the influence of Arabic in its semantic, syntactic and stylistic makeup. Of the technical terms used in Arabized Castilian science, five percent are Arabisms, thirty percent Latinisms with Arabized meanings, and the remaining sixty-five percent linguistic calques. A calque is a literal translation, the original meaning of which is lost in the target language of translation. An example is Castilian *cuerda*, "sine," which retained the original Sanskrit meaning of "bowstring." The spoken language had been much simpler than that in which the translations were rendered. Syntax had to be expanded to represent the internal complexity of subordinate clauses, which were required in order to convey, for example, the hierarchical relations among the different terms of mathematical equations ("multiple subordination"), in an age before the development of modern mathematical notation.

*Chaucer's *Treatise on the Astrolabe* is a set-piece in the discussion of the creation of science in the vernacular. Chaucer begins the work by stating he is "but a lewd compilator of the labour of olde astrologiens." In fact, some parts of the work, composed for his son around 1391, are translations, direct or expanded, from *Masha'allah's *De operatione uel utilitate astrolabii* and from *John of Sacrobosco's *De sphaera*, while much is composed by Chaucer himself. The text has a higher percentage of Romance words than is usual for Chaucer, indicating that Latin prototypes determined his choice of word.

The combination of the specific problems posed by translation from the Arabic and vernacularization (of which Chaucer's *Treatise* is not only the first, but the best, exemplar from England) led to the creation of a new register of "nominalized" discourse which we recognize as scientific. Chaucer's *Treatise* is replete with both concrete/technical and abstract/scientific nouns, extended nominal groups typical of mathematical writing, and clause complexes that carry the argument forward. "Spoken gestures," another hallmark of vernacular scientific writing, are also found abundantly in Chaucer: "set the fix point of thy compass," "mak a marke," "loke in thyn almenak."

A comparative study of vernacular science writing would be even more revealing than those of single languages. For example, in both Spanish and English, translation from the Arabic forced the creation of new abstract nouns. Thus in Chaucer's *Treatise*, an abundance of nouns ending in *-ioun*, such as *declinacioun*, *solsticioun*, *operacioun*; in the Alfonsine translation of *Ibn al-Zarqalluh's *Treatise on the Saphea*, abstract nouns ending in *-iento* (*echamiento*, *ponimiento*, *minguamiento*, *catamiento*), in *-ura* (*longura*, *cortura*), and in *-ario* (*ascensionario*, *circulario*, *appositario*).

In English, vernacular science was expressed in a "plain style," shorn of rhetorical excess, that also characterized Chancery and legal English of the fourteenth century (law courts were obliged to use English in 1362), and unadorned vernacular translations of the Bible (Wycliffe, Tyndale). It is this tradition, after an interval of Elizabethan rhetoric, that reemerges among the members of the Royal Society, which enshrined plain writing as a norm of modern science.

Practical texts in particular were intended to memorized. For example, *materia medica* texts in the Dioscoridean tradition presupposed that the practitioner knew the systems of classification, whereby simples were indexed by their properties, according to humoral pathology, rather than by alphabetical order. (Medieval Latin authors shunned alphabetization as an organizing principle because it was not hierarchical.) Memorization of both diagnostic and remedial information turned the medical corpus into a hypertext: the physician could easily match diagnosis with cure because both were understood in terms of humoral pathology. In the vernacular realm, memorization was frequently aided by rhyming.

Code Switching

Code switching (or code mixing) refers to the use of more than one language in a single text. The process of scientific creation in medieval Europe reflects a kind of structural diglossia in that Latin texts were read by persons who presumably discussed and assimilated in the vernacular. But in many scientific and medical texts (nearly half of one hundred seventy-eight English manuscripts between 1375 and 1500 surveyed by Voigts, 1996) eighty-six contained more than one language. The mixing of languages can thus be viewed as a rhetorical or discursive strategy associated in particular with medical texts first and foremost, and then those on *astrology, astronomy, and *alchemy. In the case of a bilingual population, such as that of medieval England, the linguistic patterns are even more complex. In 1455, an English cleric named George Kirkeby compiled an alchemical miscellany drawn from the tradition of the Catalan Ramon Llull, with both Latin and Catalan versions. In a passage in Catalan on cosmology, Kirkeby intermingles Latin words and phrases with the Catalan, and in one place uses a Norman French adverbial expression. The Catalan version is given to enhance the authority and authenticity of the text, with Latin expressions perhaps used to sharpen technical points.

*Adelard of Bath in his translation of *Thabit ibn Qurras' book on talismanic magic, *Liber prestigiorum*, retains the original Arabic wording for spells, ostensibly so that their power would not be diminished through translation. In his translation of *al-Khwarizmi's astronomical tables, moreover, Adelard includes jingles with astrological content in transcribed Arabic, which reflects Andalusi pronunciation. In an explanation of the abacus, Adelard included a poem, as a mnemonic device, which explained the Arabic names of the counters, e.g., *Octo beatificos themenias exprimiti unus*: "One themenias [Arabic: thumun, 'eight') expresses the blessed eight" (Burnett, 22). All of this reflects (according to Burnett, 44) "an oral milieu of teaching, with a considerable amount of familiarity with the Arabic language." In a treatise of Indian mathematics, one Ocreatus slots in Arabic transliteration for a technical operation of finding a square: *cum vellem ducere finaph[s]ihi* (Arabic, *fi nafsihi*, by itself): "When I want to multiply (the number) by itself." Among a group of scholars who know only a little Arabic, conceptual clarity can still be maintained by switching into Arabic, particularly where there was no European tradition to fall back on. The resemblance of such astronomical/astrological jingles to incantations must have contributed to the perception of Arabic science as black magic.

Sometimes the languages used have different functions in the same text. For example a medical text in which the etiology of the illness appears in Latin, frequently followed by Middle English medicinal recipes. The provenance of some astrolabes has been identified by Romance vernacular influence detected in their Latin star names or zodiacal signs.

Some texts were interlinear with a vernacular translation given between the lines of Latin text; or technical terms in a Latin text could be glossed with vernacular equivalents in the margins. Vernacular writers might switch to Latin as an aide to organizing a text, by placing Latin rubrics in an otherwise vernacular text. One might switch from Latin to transliterated Arabic or from vernacular to Latin to introduce a voice of authority. Or Latin may hide something held secret or indecorous (women's ailments, for example). Latin blessings and charms appear in vernacular treatises, as when a specific prayer is included in a recipe for a specific condition. Polyglot *receptaria* (recipes for remedies or other technical operations) are particularly common. A vernacular recipe might end with Latin *sanabitur* ("it will cure"), for emphasis. "The code-switched special terms contribute to the precision and specificity required of scientific discourse" (Pahta, 83–92).

Scholars have noted with fascination the polylingual nature of translation, whereby translators might work in teams, mixing languages freely in the process of translation. But this easy mixing of languages was common and not confined to scientific pursuits. Medieval European society was everywhere multilingual and predominantly oral, according to Clanchy (206); a Latin charter might be read aloud in French or English, while a statement made at court in the vernacular might be recorded by a notary or scribe in Latin.

Scholarly Interaction

Collins observes that scientific creation obeys the "law of small numbers": original work occurs in very small groups displaying a high grade of connectivity. This is true of certain distinctive groups of medieval scientists. For example, the "trigonometrical revolution" occurred in the interacting circle of Central Asian Arab/Persian mathematicians active between 950 and 1000, including al-Khazin, al-Buzajani, al-Kuhi, al-Khujandi, al-Sijzi, and, somewhat younger, *al-Biruni. The Andalusi Aristotelians who developed a distinctive approach to cosmological theory (Ibn Bajja, al-Bitruji, etc.) certainly illustrate the point, although Collins (438) sees them as enmeshed in a geographically broader, interconnected group that includes *Ibn Rushd, *Maimonides, and *Abraham ibn Ezra.

In the Arab world, travel "in search of knowledge" (*fi talab al-ʿilm*) was a key modality of scientific communication. Merchant/scholars, both Jewish and Muslim, could support themselves by trade at the same time as they studied with eminent teachers. When they returned to their homelands, they disseminated both books and ideas among their more sedentary colleagues. The connectivity of a world already tightly linked by commercial networks explains the rapidity by which certain ideas and techniques spread. The "prime vertical" method of using fixed boundaries to divide the "houses" of the ecliptic, devised by *al-Biruni, was known to *Ibn al-Samh in Spain during Biruni's lifetime. Scholars also came from outside the Islamic sphere: *al-Razi told the story of an insistent Chinese who called at his house and demanded that his host read his medical works aloud so that he could record them in Chinese.

One way in which the new Arabized Greek science reached Europe was by travel. First, there was a stream of Latin scholars going to Spain, in particular *Toledo (*Gerard of Cremona, Adelard of Bath, *Michael Scot, Daniel of Morley, Robert of Ketton). The opposite current is represented by *Pedro Alfonso, who campaigned for the new science in his writings and also went to England, where he composed astronomical tables and instructed Englishmen in their use, and *Abraham ibn Ezra, who likewise made his living by traveling from town to town in Italy and France composing astronomical tables.

Circles of Affinity

Established scholars held open discussions (called *majlis*) with students and colleagues usually in their own studies. Ibn Bajja presided over a famous Aristotelian *majlis* in Zaragoza. Maimonides held his own *majlis* for his medical students in Cairo, and also attended a more philosophical *majlis*, that of the Arab courtier and judge, Ibn Sanaʾ al-Mulk. In Toledo, Gerard of Cremona's relationship with his *socii* (associates, but in the sense of Arabic *sahibuna*, our fellows [Weber]) is analogous. The circles of scholars that kings brought into their courts were centers of scholarly communication and production. Both Alfonso the Wise and *Frederick II of Sicily took active roles of scholarly discourse and presided over *majlis*-type meetings of their scientific courtiers, that included both Christians and Jews. Another affinity group, bridging Barcelona and Montpellier, was that whose central figure was Ibn Tibbon (*Profatius Judaeus).

On a more technical level, *scriptoria* were of course centers for the diffusion of science. Arabic numerals first appeared in Europe in the *scriptorium* of the Spanish monastery of Silos. Reading was a skill, but writing was a technique, not linked to reading. A specific technology had to be mastered because of the difficulty in writing on parchment with a quill pen. The arsenal of scribal tools included knife, pumice, and animal teeth to prepare the writing surface; stylus, pencil ruler, plumb line, and awl for ruling the lines; and finally quillpens, inkhorn, and various kinds of ink.

See also **Aristotelianism; Dioscorides; Herbals; Translation movements; Translation norms and practice**

Bibliography

Burnett, Charles. *The Introduction of Arabic Learning into England*. London: The British Library, 1997.

Castro, Américo. *The Structure of Spanish History*. Princeton: Princeton University Press, 1954.

———. *The Spaniards*. Berkeley: University of California Press, 1971.

Clanchy, Michael. *From Memory to Written Record: England 1066–1307*. 2nd ed. Oxford: Blackwell, 1993.

Collins, Randall. *The Sociology of Philosophies: A Global Theory of Intellectual Change*. Cambridge: Harvard University Press, 1998.

Comet, Georges. "Les céréales du Bas-Empire au Moyen Age." In Miquel Barceló and Grançois Sigaut, eds. *The Making Feudal Agricultures?* Leiden: E.J. Brill, 2004, pp. 131–176.

Halliday, M. A. K. "On the Language of Physical Science." In Mohsen Ghadessy, ed. *Registers of Written English: Situational Factors and Linguistic Features*. New York: Pinter, 1988, pp. 162–178.

Jones, Claire. "Discourse Communities and Medical Texts." In Taavitsainen and Pahta (2004), pp. 23–36.

Millás Vallicrosa, José M. "El literalismo de los traductores de la Corte de Alfonso el Sabio." In *Estudios sobre historia de la ciencia española*. Barcelona: CSIC, 1949, pp. 349–358.

Pahta, Päivi. "Code-Switching in Medieval Medical Writing." In Taavitsainen and Pahta (2004), pp. 73–99.

Pahta, Päivi and Irma Taavitsainen. "Vernacularisation of Scientific and Medical Writing in its Sociohistorical Context." In Taavitsainen and Pahta (2004), 1–18.

Pereira, Michela. Alchemy and the Use of Vernacular Languages in the Late Middle Ages. *Speculum* (1999) 74: 336–356.

Samsó, Julio. "Al-Biruni in al-Andalus." In *From Baghdad to Barcelona: Studies in the Islamic Exact Sciences in Honour of Prof. Juan Vernet*. 2 vols. Barcelona: Universitat de Barcelona, 1996, II: 583–612.

Taavitsainen, Irma. "Transferring Classical Discourse Conventions into the Vernacular." In Taavitsainen and Pahta (2004), 37–72.

Taavitsainen, Irma and Päivi Pahta, eds. *Medical and Scientific Writing in Late Medieval England*. New York: Cambridge University Press, 2004.

Tebeaux, Elizabeth. *The Emergence of a Tradition: Technical Writing in the English Renaissance, 1475–1640*. Amityville, NY: Baywood, 1997.

Wilson, R. M. "Linguistic Analysis." In Derek J. Price, ed. *The Equatories of the Planets*. New York: Cambridge University Press, 1955: 137–148.

Voigts, Linda E. What's the Word: Bilingualism in Late-Medieval England. *Speculum* (1996) 71: 813–826.

THOMAS F. GLICK

COMPUTUS

The term *computus* denotes any kind of reckoning or accounting, but is also used in a special sense to mean the calculation of *calendar adjustments, particularly in connection with determining the date of Easter. For historians of science, *computus* is significant for two reasons: first, it was one of the few problems of a scientific character to arouse sustained debate in the early medieval period; and secondly, it was the arena in which the capabilities of the mathematical astronomy introduced from Greek and Arabic sources in the central Middle Ages were first systematically tested. The issue at stake was the recalibration of the calendar to ensure its conformity with celestial phenomena; but that recalibration was necessitated by the religious and symbolic meaning of the date of Easter.

Computus and the Calendar

Because the Christian Church adopted the Julian solar calendar of Rome as its basic framework for time-reckoning, a medieval calendar found in any *computus* manuscript looks very much like a pre-Christian Roman calendar. It is a generic calendar of twelve months—the familiar Roman months used today—in which the dates are listed vertically, and numbered, according to the Roman convention, in relation to the marker-days of kalends, nones and ides. To the right of each date is the feast or saint commemorated on that day, along with astronomical notices (e.g., solstices and equinoxes, the entry of the Sun into zodiac signs). To the left of the dates are key letters used to customize the generic calendar for a particular year. The seven letters A–G, in sequence representing the seven days of the planetary week, permitted the adjustment of date to week-day in any given year (on years designated with A, all A-days were Sundays, etc.). These were known as the "dominical" or Sunday letters. A second set of key-letters translated calendar dates into days of the lunar month or the position of the Moon in the zodiac: two such lunar letter schemes, together with the counter-tables for converting the letters into lunar dates, are described by *Bede in *De temporum ratione* chapter nineteen and chapter twenty-three. The "Golden Numbers" placed to the left of certain dates indicate the year of the nineteen-year Paschal lunar cycle in which a new moon falls on that date; they serve as a handy reference point from which to calculate the lunar phase on any calendar date. Customizing the generic Julian calendar into the calendar for a particular year could, of course, also be carried out by mathematical formulae known as *argumenta*.

The Problem of Determining Easter

Determining the calendar date for Easter Sunday, however, was a challenge of a very different order. Easter commemorates Christ's death and resurrection at the Jewish feast of Passover, celebrated in the full moon of the first lunar month (Nisan 14 in the Jewish calendar). Since Passover is a spring festival, Christian writers assumed that it had to fall after the vernal equinox. In the original Julian calendar, the equinox was fixed at March 25, and so it remained in popular lore for many centuries. However, because the calculated solar year of 365.25 days is longer than its true tropical year (365.2422... days), the date of the astronomical equinox gradually moved backward with respect to the solar calendar. This problem was noticed in antiquity, and the Alexandrian Church, whose *computus* eventually formed the basis of both Eastern and Western Paschal reckoning, adopted the correct date of March 21 in the fourth century. But the root of the problem was neither recognized nor addressed, and the slippage of the equinox continued until Pope Gregory XIII mandated the reform of 1583.

The calculation of Easter involves solving several interlocking puzzles. First, one must know the age the moon will be on the next vernal equinox, since the full moon which follows this will be the *terminus a quo* of Easter. This lunar age will vary from year to year, because twelve lunar months of approximately 29.5 days each is about 11 days short of a solar year of 365.25 days. Hence the moon will be 11 days older on the spring equinox next year than it is this year. After about three years, this increment will amount to more than 30 days, so an entire lunar month (an "embolismic month") must be inserted to bring the lunar and solar years roughly into phase. To calculate the age of the moon on future equinoxes therefore requires a luni-solar cycle, that is, a whole number of solar years into which a whole number of lunar months can be inserted, so that the lunar phases fall on the same calendar dates after the end of the cyclic period. Several cycles already in use in antiquity were tried out, of which the most accurate was the nineteen-year cycle of Meton of Athens. The second problem arises from the custom of celebrating Easter only on a Sunday. The weekday of the Easter terminus must be known in order to locate Easter on the next following Sunday. The Julian calendar contains 52 weeks plus one day, which means that calendar dates advance one weekday each year, and two weekdays after February in leap years, over a cycle of 28 years (7 weekdays times 4 years in the leap-year cycle). The remaining issues are not so much scientific as theological. What is the permissible seven-day range of lunar dates (i.e., dates in Nisan) on which the Paschal terminus can fall? Termini of luna 14–20 implies that Easter is a Christian Passover, since Passover begins on Nisan 14. Opting for luna 16–22, on the other hand, puts the accent on the lunar anniversary of the Resurrection, which occurred on Nisan 16, while 15–21 aligns Easter with the Jewish Feast of Unleavened Bread. Finally, in the light of all the conditions enumerated above, within what range of dates in a Julian calendar could Easter fall?

Finding a formula for Easter therefore entailed grappling with some explosive theological problems (particularly the relationship of Easter to the Jewish Passover), reaching consensus on dating the vernal equinox, and proving that a luni-solar cycle could be translated into a pattern of lunar and calendar dates within agreed termini. The solution had to be a formula which would unfailingly produce correct Easter dates and which would present these in a table for ready consultation. The Alexandrian *computus* current in the Eastern Church held a position of preeminence, but it took Bede's *De temporum ratione* to provide a detailed and accessible exposition of this system in terms of the Julian calendar. The Alexandrian *computus* used the 19-year Metonic lunar cycle, the March 21 equinox, lunar limits of 15–21, and calendar limits of March 22–April 25. A table based on this system and adapted to the Julian calendar had been published by Dionysius Exiguus (c. 532), a Greek monk living in Rome, in response to the defective Easter table of Victorius of Aquitaine. *De temporum ratione* explained and defended Dionysius' table, exposing the failings not only of Victorius, but also of the version of the old Roman 84-year Paschal table current among the British and some sectors of the Irish church. It also demonstrated that Dionysius' system would produce a cycle of Easters over 532 years.

As knowledge of the Church's *computus* was considered an essential element of clerical training, Bede's text rapidly became a standard schoolbook. Carolingian schoolmasters such as Hrabanus Maurus simplified it, eleventh-century *scholastici* such as Abbo of Fleury devised new tables to supplement it, and in the twelfth century Alexander of Villedieu versified it for use in the new urban schools. Schemes for memorizing the Paschal data by mentally inscribing them on the joints of the hand, and then using the hand as a "calculator," were popularized through the sub-genre known as *computus manualis*. Vernacular *computi* first appear in Anglo-Saxon England (Byrhtferth, Aelfric), and are diffused in virtually every western European language by the later Middle Ages.

However, beginning in the late eleventh century, purely astronomical time-reckoning or *computus naturalis* emerged in the wake of newly available translations, planetary tables, and astronomical instruments such as the astrolabe. Late medieval calendar treatises such as those of John Somur and Nicholas of Lynn also contain tables of eclipses and even of planetary positions—evidence of the influence of *astrology. The advent of *computus naturalis* also highlighted the discrepancy between the crudely calculated positions of the Sun and Moon used for the *computus ecclesiasticus*, and the reality of the heavens. It thus fueled debates over calendar reform.

Computus and the Reform of the Calendar

Medieval projects to reform time-reckoning focused on two issues: chronology, and the relationship of the calculated calendar to astronomical reality. Debates over the inaccuracy of Dionysius' *annus domini* dominated the eleventh century, but did not result in any change to this system. From the perspective of the history of science, the controversies surrounding the defects in the calculation of the lunar and solar periods on which the Paschal *computus* rested are of greater interest. The drift of the equinox backward with respect to the calendar continued, and by the late twelfth century *computus naturalis* furnished computists such as Roger of Hereford, *Robert Grosseteste and *Roger Bacon with the means to calculate its rate. At the same time, computists tackled the problem of the embarrassing discrepancy between the calculated moon and the visible Moon, a consequence of the gap between the notional lunation of 29.5 days and the true mean synodic lunar month of 29.53059 days. From the early thirteenth century up to the Gregorian Reform of 1583, the calendar reform debate focused on how to bring the calendar back into line with the astronomical realities of the Sun and the Moon, and how to keep it there. The first goal could be accomplished simply by dropping a certain number of days from the Julian reckoning, and was a matter of communication and political will. The second problem was scientific: the tropical solar year was plainly shorter than 365.25 days, but by how much? In practical terms, how often would a leap year have to be omitted in order for the calendar to stay in step with the Sun? Estimates varied from once every 300 (Grosseteste) or 288 years (Sacrobosco), to 125 years (Bacon). A task force set up by Pope Clement VI proposed dropping one leap year in 134, and setting back the Golden Numbers by one day every 310 years, but no action was taken. The general councils of the early fifteenth century, and succeeding popes, also failed to enact a solution, although they commissioned studies of the true length of the tropical year by astronomers such as *John of Gmunden and *Johannes Regiomontanus. Copernicus' *De revolutionibus* was another contribution to the same debate. In sum, the purely religious-symbolic criteria for Easter—its relation to the astronomical spring and the cycle of lunations, and the necessity of plotting these against the grid of calendar-dates and weekdays—posed a very precise problem of exceptional scientific difficulty. What is intriguing about *computus* is that the Church's commitment to keeping its celebrations in line with the true aspect of the heavens opened up a channel of inquiry that flowed into the Scientific Revolution.

See also **Astronomy; Calendar; Clocks and timekeeping**

Bibliography

Blackburn, Bonnie and Leofranc Holford-Strevens. *The Oxford Companion to the Year.* Oxford: Oxford University Press, 1999.

Borst, Arno. *The Ordering of Time.* Chicago: University of Chicago Press, 1993.

Contreni, John. "Counting, Calendars and Cosmology: Numeracy in the Early Middle Ages." In *Word, Image, Number: Communication in the Middle Ages.* Edited by John J. Contreni and Santa Casciani. Micrologus' Library 8. Florence: SISMEL–Edizioni del Galluzzo, 2002, pp. 43–84.

Cordoliani, A. *Comput, calendriers, chronologie. L'Histoire et ses methodes.* Edited Charles Samaran. Paris: Gallimard, 1961, pp. 37–51.

Coyne, C.V., M.A. Hoskin, and O. Pedersen, eds. *Gregorian Reform of the Calendar.* Vatican City: Pontific Academia Scientiarum, Specola Vaticana, 1983.

Declercq, Georges. *Anno Domini: the Origins of the Christian Era.* Turnhout: Brepols, 2000.

Englisch, Brigitte. *Die Artes liberales im frühen Mittelalter (5.-9. Jh.): Das Quadrivium und der Komputus als Indikatoren für Kontinuität und Erneuerung der exacten Wissenschaften zwischen Antike und Mittelalter.* Sudhoffs Archiv, Beiheft 33. Stuttgart: Franz Steiner, 1994.

García Avilés, Alejandro. *El tiempo y los astros. Arte, Ciencia y religión en la alta edad media.* Murcia: Universidad de Murcia, 2001.

Ginzel, F.K. *Handbuch der mathematischen und technischen Chronologie.* 3 v. Leipzig: J.C. Hinrich, 1906–1914.

Gómez Pallarez, Joan. *Studia chronologica. Estudios sobre manuscritos latinos de cómputo.* Madrid: Ediciones Clásicas, 1999.

Jones, C.W. [introduction to] *Bedae opera de temporibus.* Cambridge: Mediaeval Academy of America, 1943.

Jones, C.W. *Bede, the Schools and the Computus.* Aldershot: Variorum, 1995.

McCarthy, Daniel and Aidan Breen. *The ante-Nicene Christian Pasch: the Paschal Tract of Anatolius, bishop of Laodicea.* Dublin: Four Courts, 2003.

McCluskey, Stephen C. *Astronomies and Cultures in Early Medieval Europe.* New York: Cambridge University Press, 1998.

Moreton, Jennifer. "Robert Grosseteste and the Calendar." In *Robert Grosseteste: New Perspectives on his Thought and Scholarship.* Edited by James McEvoy. Instrumenta patristica 27. Turnhout: Brepols, 1997, pp. 77–88.

——. Robert of Hereford and Calendar Reform in Eleventh and Twelfth-century England. *Isis* (1995) 86: 562–586.

——. John of Sacrobosco and the Calendar. *Viator* (1994) 25: 229–244.

Mundy, John. John of Gmünden. *Isis* (1943) 34:196–205.

The Kalendarium of Nicholas of Lynn. Edited Sigmund Eisner. Translated by Gary MacEoin and Sigmund Eisner. Athens: University of Georgia Press, 1980.

Ó Cróinín, D. *Early Irish History and Chronology.* Dublin: Four Courts Press, 2003.

Stevens, W. *Cycles of Time and Scientific Learning in Medieval Europe.* Aldershot: Variorum, 1995.

Strobel, August. *Ursprung und Geschichte des frühchristlichen Osterkalendars. Texte und Untersuchungen 121.* Berlin: Akademie-Verlag, 1977.

Van Wijk, Walter Emile. *Le numéro d'or: Étude de chronologie technique suivie du texts de la 'Massa compoti' d'Alexandre de Ville-Dieu.* The Hague: Nijhoff, 1936.

FAITH WALLIS

CONDEMNATION OF 1277

On March 7, 1277, Bishop Etienne Tempier issued a syllabus of two hundred nineteen erroneous propositions (*articuli*), and forbade their dissemination and defense at the arts faculty of the University of Paris. Tempier's prohibition has been widely considered to be the most dramatic and significant censure in the history of the University of Paris. Its impact on (natural) philosophy is clear from the many allusions in texts from the thirteenth and fourteenth centuries and from the debates it generated about whether or not *Thomas Aquinas was one of its targets. In addition, Tempier's action has played a crucial role in helping to shape the historiography of medieval science as a respectable discipline. This latter development is connected to the name of Pierre Duhem (1861–1916), and to the far-reaching interpretation he gave of the 1277 event in preparing the way for modern science. Before discussing the possible importance of Tempier's prohibition for the development of medieval science, it is useful to turn to the actual events.

The Events of 1277

The generally accepted picture of the events leading to the condemnation looks something like this. On January 18, 1277, Pope John XXI (1276–1277) informed Etienne Tempier that he had heard rumors of heresy, and charged the Bishop of Paris with the task of examining where and by whom these errors had been disseminated. Tempier's response did not take long to formulate. On March 7,

1277, the bishop issued a letter to which he attached a list of two hundred nineteen propositions and of some books that were thereby condemned. In the letter he rebukes "some scholars of arts at Paris" (*nonnulli Parisius studentes in artibus*) for discussing and holding disputations about "manifest and damned errors" (*manifesti et exsecrabiles errores*). The errors are the two hundred nineteen articles quoted in the attached rotulus. On pain of excommunication, members of the arts faculty are prohibited to disseminate in any way the errors collected by Tempier.

The prefatory letter also gives some indication as to the procedure which Tempier followed in establishing his list or errors. Tempier indicates that he had received information from "important people." In other words, the bishop reacted to complaints of false teaching, either from the pope or from local sources. As the leading ecclesiastical authority of the University of Paris, he had to investigate these allegations that "some scholars of arts at Paris" had been "transgressing the limits of their own faculty" (*proprie facultatis limites excedentes*). Tempier established an advisory board, which consisted of theologians and "other wise men." Although the letter remains silent on the procedure that was followed, we know from similar cases that the theologians were probably charged with examining works or a prepared list of theses, and assess whether they contained any errors or heresies. The outcome is clear.

The Targets of the 1277 Condemnation

What we still do not know is who Tempier's targets were. As mentioned above, the prefatory letter merely refers to some people engaged in the arts at Paris. Yet, *Siger of Brabant and *Boethius of Dacia are usually identified as the main advocates of the prohibited errors. This identification derives from the rubrics of only two of the many medieval manuscripts of Tempier's condemnation. These clues proved not to be totally unfounded. The admirable study by Roland Hissette has established that seventy-nine of the two hundred nineteen theses can be identified with varying degrees of probability in the works by Siger and Boethius, and by three anonymous writings that originated at the arts faculty and that have so far been edited. The somewhat disappointing results in identifying the errors in specific works that were produced at the arts faculty may have their origin in wrong assumptions about Tempier's targets. As the prefatory letter states, the two hundred nineteen errors were propagated by members at the arts faculty. It does not say that they were the authors. In other words, only a limited number of theses represent the proprietary views of masters of arts, whereas for others one has to cast the net further, and investigate Greek and Arabic sources that were translated into Latin. It is still controversial whether Thomas Aquinas was implied.

The long list of two hundred nineteen prohibited theses lacks any thematic organization. Possibly the theses appear in the order in which they were culled from the works that were examined, or from other lists, for the 1277 condemnation was by no means the only prohibition of (allegedly) false teaching. Shortly after 1277, the list was reorganized, as it was again at the beginning of the twentieth century by Pierre Mandonnet. He distinguished one hundred seventy-nine philosophical theses from forty theological ones in an edition that came to be widely used by historians.

A very helpful thematic survey of the condemned propositions has been provided by John F. Wippel. The first seven of the philosophical propositions bear on the nature and excellence of philosophy. Propositions eight through twelve (in the numbering of Mandonnet) have a bearing on the knowability and nature of God. Propositions 13–15 concern divine knowledge, and 16 through 26 divine omnipotence. Many of the articles, notably numbers 34 to 61, regard the separate intelligences (angels). Another interesting group of articles is 67–69. By condemning these articles, Tempier endorsed God's absolute power to do whatever He wills. Other interesting themes that are touched in the philosophical articles are the world's eternity (80 through 89), the unicity of the human intellect and its implications (117–133), and human freedom and free will (151 through 166). Among the theological articles, themes that appear are theology as a science (180–186), the doctrine of the Eucharist (196–199), Christian morality (202–205), and human immortality and reward and punishment in the life to come (213–219). It should be emphasized that Tempier's theses express positions that cannot be maintained in the light of revealed truth, and for this reason each is followed by the qualification "error."

Condemnation of 1277 and Medieval Science

Tempier's 1277 condemnation should be seen as a stage in the appropriation of Aristotelian (natural) philosophy in the West, and, more specifically, as a reaction against a certain variation of *Aristotelianism which in the older literature has been labelled "heterodox Aristotelianism" or "Latin Averroism." At an institutional level, the events of 1277 can be seen as an interdisciplinary struggle between the faculties of arts and theology. At a doctrinal level, Tempier's action reveals theological concerns over certain views in physics, metaphysics, and ethics that harked back to Aristotle's treatises and that were embraced by masters of arts and by some theologians as well. Already in the 1270s masters of arts were prohibited to discuss philosophical questions in a way that was contrary to the faith. In his preface, Tempier ridicules the hermeneutical method of distinguishing between a philosophical treatment of a topic and a discussion of that same topic according to the truths of faith "as if there were two contrary truths, and as if against the truth of Sacred Scripture, there is truth in the sayings of the condemned pagans." In reality, no thinker held a theory of double truth, but Tempier's attack shows a high level of suspicion toward those thinkers who claimed to uphold the truths of faith, while at the same time saving the "scientific" conclusions reached through natural reasoning. On the basis of such passages and specific articles in the syllabus, historians have viewed the condemnation as evidence for the presence of rationalist tendencies at the University of Paris, i.e., as signs of the existence of an autonomous (natural) philosophy, pursued for its own sake, which Tempier attempted to curb.

A different assessment of Tempier's role was given by Pierre Duhem. He believed that 1277 marked the birth of modern science, because it was then that Christian thought was liberated from the yoke of Aristotelian natural philosophy and thus came to produce modern science. Duhem focused in particular on articles 34 (Mandonnet, art. 27: "that the first cause [God] could not make several worlds") and 49 (Mandonnet, art. 66: "That God could not move the heavens with a rectilinear motion and the reason is that a vacuum would remain"). These articles were in line with Aristotle's views. He had demonstrated that it is impossible for there to be other worlds beyond our own, and that it is impossible for a vacuum to occur naturally. If this is the case, so these natural philosophers claimed, then even God cannot make a plurality of worlds or a vacuum. Tempier declared these articles as erroneous, because they subjected God's omnipotence to the principles and conclusions of Aristotle's physics. In his view, God was not constrained by what is possible or impossible in Aristotle's natural philosophy. For Duhem, this attitude provided the key to rejecting Aristotelian physics, and thus opened up the way to the Scientific Revolution. The condemned articles encouraged speculation about the possibility that God could create a plurality of worlds, or could move the world with a rectilinear motion. They carried with them the destruction of Aristotelian notions of space and time and cosmology. Duhem's thesis about the importance of Tempier's condemnation was severely criticized. Yet its impact was tremendous, because of the documentation of medieval science that it brought with it, both by Duhem and his critics. In this way, Duhem set the topics for the subsequent historiography of medieval science and thus helped to establish it as an autonomous discipline.

See also "Latin Averroists"; Religion and science; Universities

Bibliography

Primary Sources

Denifle, Heinrich and Emile Châtelain, eds. *Chartularium Universitatis Parisiensis*. 4 volumes. Paris: ex typis fratrum Delalain, 1889–1897, vol. 1, pp. 543–558.

Grant, Edward. *A Source Book in Medieval Science*. Cambridge: Harvard University Press, 1974.

Mandonnet, P. *Siger de Brabant et l'averroïsme latin au XIIIme siècle; étude critique et documents inédits*. Fribourg: Librairie de l'Université, 1899.

Piché, David, ed. *La condemnation parisienne de 1277. Texte latin, traduction, introduction et commentaire*. Paris: Vrin, 1999.

Secondary Sources

Aertsen, Jan A., Kent Emery, Jr. and Andreas Speer, eds. *Nach der Verurteilung von 1277. Philosophie und Theologie an der Universität von Paris im letzten Viertel des 13. Jahrhunderts*. New York: De Gruyter, 2001.

Bianchi, Luca. "1277: A Turning Point in Medieval Philosophy?" In *Was ist Philosophie im Mittelalter?* Edited by Jan A. Aertsen and Andreas Speer. New York: De Gruyter, 1998, pp. 90–110.

Grant, Edward. *The Foundations of Modern Science in the Middle Ages. Their Religious, Institutional, and Intellectual Contexts*. New York: Cambridge University Press, 1996.

Hissette, Roland. *Enquête sur les 219 articles condamnés à Paris le 7 mars 1277*. Louvain: Publications Universitaires, 1977.

Murdoch, John E. "Pierre Duhem and the History of Late Medieval Science and Philosophy in the Latin West." In *Gli studi di filosofia medievale fra otto e novecento*. Edited by Alfonso Maierù and Ruedi Imbach. Roma: Edizioni di Storia e Letteratura, 1991, pp. 253–302.

———. "1277 and Late Medieval Natural Philosophy." In *Was ist Philosophie im Mittelalter?* Edited by Jan A. Aertsen and Andreas Speer. New York: De Gruyter, 1998, pp. 111–121.

Thijssen, J.M.M.H. *Censure and Heresy at the University of Paris, 1200-1400*. Philadelphia: University of Pennsylvania Press, 1998.

Van Steenberghen, F. *Thomas Aquinas and Radical Aristotelianism*. Washington, D.C: The Catholic University of America Press, 1980.

Wippel, John F. The Condemnations of 1270 and 1277 at Paris. *Journal of Medieval and Renaissance Studies* (1977) 7: 169–201.

JOHANNES M.M.H. THIJSSEN

CONSILIA

The medical *consilium* was a text in which a learned physician wrote a response to a specific medical question put to him either directly by a patient or indirectly by another physician with respect to a particular case. A physician need not have been present himself to consult on the case, and many *consilia* were composed in absentia. They were written predominantly in Latin and issued together in collections. Vernacular versions of *consilia* do exist. Plague *consilia*, which became popular after 1348 as a consequence of the Black Death, often circulated on their own in the vernacular.

The ideal text commonly comprised three main sections. The first described the patient (name, place of residence, occupation, social status, sex, age), signs and symptoms of disease, diagnosis (in the medieval context, often merely a brief description of the patient's complaint), and sometimes an identification of causes. The second part, most of which was dedicated to dietary recommendations, provided directions for the daily routine and care of the patient according to the six Galenic nonnaturals (air and habitation, exercise and rest, food and drink, sleep and waking, evacuation and retention, and the emotions). The third part addressed therapeutic medicines, baths, and surgical procedures such as cauterization and phlebotomy. Although primarily produced in the course of practice, *consilia* also served as aids to teaching and study. When asked for advice on a particular case, Guglielmo da Brescia, for example, suggested that a fellow doctor read a *consilium* he had written on a like case.

The general form and structure of the medieval western *consilium* seem to have first appeared at the University of Bologna in the thirteenth century. Earlier examples exist, but the earliest collections of medical *consilia* appear to be those produced by *Taddeo Alderotti (1223–1295) and his associates. Although there are analogues in the works of *Arnau de Vilanova, the genre was developed and predominated above all in northern Italy.

Antecedents and Influences

Hippocratic antecedents include the *Epidemics* (I–III), which describe particular cases in detail, but offer little therapeutic advice, and *Affections and Diseases of Women*, which outlines therapies for specific diseases. *Galen's *De locis affectis*, *De methodo medendi ad Glauconem*, and *Methodus medendi* illustrate clinical cases with the purpose of demonstrating and confirming the validity of theoretical doctrines outlined in the treatises. This technique of relating the theoretical to the practical seems to have most influenced the development of medieval practical medical literature from 1250 to 1500. Galen's written response to a young man, which appeared as *Pro puero epileptico consilium*, may have been the ultimate model of the *consilium*, although it was not available to Latin readers until the Renaissance. Despite ancient antecedents, the development of legal *consilia* at Bologna in the twelfth century and their proliferation in the thirteenth may have provided the most direct model. Arabic authors also produced and translated accounts of clinical cases. These accounts, however, were not generally available to western physicians until the twentieth century, and consequently do not seem to have influenced the western medical *consilium* directly.

Relationship to Other Genres

Consilia should not necessarily be viewed as constituting an autonomous genre. It may be more constructive to consider them in the context of other forms of practical medical literature emerging between 1250 and 1500, which increasingly sought to apply medical theory to practice. Other practical genres developing concurrently were collections of remedies, *experimenta* (tried and tested medical regimens), regimens of health, and *practicae* (large medical manuals geared toward the treatment of specific diseases). Like the *consilia*, the regimen of health was often addressed to a particular individual. *Ugo Benzi, for example, wrote the *Libro da conservare la persona in sanitate* for Niccolo d'Este, who was said to suffer from obesity. Generally the purpose of a regimen of health was the maintenance of wellbeing rather than the treatment of a specific disease. Sometimes distinctions between these genres, however, were sufficiently unclear that a physician entitled his text *consilium sive regimen* or *regimen sive consilium*.

Some *consilia* by virtue of their length and formality resemble treatises even though they exist as parts of *consilia* collections as in Alderotti's *De ruptura sifac*, Ugo Benzi's *On the Kidney Stone*, or the enormous treatise-like *consilia* on defects of the bladder by Bartolomeo Montagnana (d. 1460). Other *consilia* written at the request of a particular patient were, in fact, circulated as individual treatises as in the *Tractatus de hernia* by *Gentile da Foligno (d. 1348), or the *Ad appariciones fantasticas oculorum* by Guglielmo Corvi (1250–1326).

Medieval Developments

The thirteenth century saw the birth and development of the medieval medical *consilium* in the work of Taddeo Alderotti, Baviero Baviera (d. 1480), Guglielmo Corvi, and Guillaume Boucher (fl. 1400). *Consilia* written in this period vary in form and structure, exhibit a variety of terminology and vocabulary, and are generally more pragmatic in tone than those composed later. Of Alderotti's one hundred eighty-five *consilia*, more than one hundred are merely medical recipes and very few describe the patient's symptoms.

Those of Gentile da Foligno bridge the first phase of the genre and its further evolution in the fifteenth century. His *consilia* are generally more abstract and theoretical, diagnosis is often treated in greater depth, and terminology is more precise. The inclusion of the opinions of medical authorities may indicate that these *consilia* were produced for didactic as well as professional purposes.

In the fifteenth-century *consilia* of Bartolomeo Montagnana, Antonio Cermisone (d. 1441), and Ugo Benzi, the theoretical element is developed to such an extent that the works sometimes resemble small scholastic treatises. In some cases, descriptions of the disease and its treatment appear in the form of doctrinal debates, and it is not uncommon to come across a scholastic exposition on possible interpretations according to the opinions of the ancient and Arabic authorities, namely, *Hippocrates, Galen, *al-Razi, and *Ibn Sina. There is also present a more pronounced interest in nomenclature. Some *consilia* contain etymological examinations of Greek, Latin, and Arabic terminology. In contrast to the scholastic *consilia* influenced by university medical learning, however, the *consilia* of Antonio Benivieni (c. 1443–1502) draw heavily on fifteenth-century philosophical movements such as neo-Platonism, which thrived outside the university.

This genre was well suited to serve as a form of self-advertisement or self-aggrandizement. Because of the highly personalized nature of the individual *consilium*, a learned physician could use *consilia* collections to showcase the fame and prestige of his clientele. Alderotti, for example, wrote *consilia* for a doge of Venice, two bishops, two counts, one of the Malatesta, and nine other people of high rank. Although men of high rank account for the greatest number of *consilia* produced in the Middle Ages, many also address the illnesses of men, women, and children from more modest backgrounds, and show the diversity of patients treated by learned physicians.

Medieval medical works in general reflect the intellectual and social world in which learned physicians lived and practiced. *Consilia* in particular are rich sources for studying the influence of classical and Arabic authors on medieval medicine and the developments and transformations of medical doctrines. Because they often include detailed medical recipes they are also useful in the history of medieval *pharmacology. They can further shed light on how learned physicians applied the theoretical training of the universities to therapeutic practice. Furthermore, they are important for establishing the social context in which a professional physician worked. It should be noted, however, that the social context they recreate is commonly an aristocratic one. They are, therefore, not useful in establishing general disease patterns, or for exploring the types of diseases brought about by famine or poverty.

See also **Medicine, practical**; **Medicine, theoretical**; *Regimen sanitatis*; Scholasticism; *Scientia*; Universities

Bibliography

Agrimi, Jole and Chiara Crisciani. *Les consilia médicaux.* Turnhout: Brepols, 1994.

Crisciani, Chiara. History, Novelty, and Progress in Scholastic Medicine. *Osiris* (1990) 6: 118–139.

Lockwood, D.P. *Ugo Benzi: Medieval Philosopher and Physician, 1376–1439.* Chicago: University of Chicago Press, 1951.

Park, Katharine. *Doctors and Medicine in Early Renaissance Florence.* Princeton: Princeton University Press, 1985.

Siraisi, Nancy. Anatomizing the Past: Physicians and History in Renaissance Culture. *Renaissance Quarterly* (Spring, 2000) 53, 1: 1–30.

_____. *Medieval and Early Renaissance Medicine: An Introduction to Knowledge and Practice.* Chicago: University of Chicago Press, 1990.

_____. *Taddeo Alderotti and his Pupils: Two Generations of Italian Medical Learning.* Princeton: Princeton University Press, 1981.

ELIZABETH W. MELLYN

CONSTANTINE THE AFRICAN

Constantine the African was the first major translator of Arabic medical writings into Latin and hence the most important figure in the revival of scientific medicine in the West from the late eleventh century on. The only biographical data that can be firmly documented are his arrival in Salerno in 1077 and his death at the Italian Benedictine monastery of *Monte Cassino by 1098–1099 at the latest. (The death date of 1087 that is often cited in secondary accounts has no documentary foundation.)

Peter the Deacon (d. after 1154), another monk at Monte Cassino, provides the earliest account of Constantine's life: he came originally, Peter claims, from Carthage, and traveled to "Babilonia" (Cairo), India, Ethiopia, and Egypt. Another telling of Constantine's activities by the mid-twelfth-century physician Matheus Ferrarius of Salerno claims that Constantine initially visited Italy and, finding the Latins impoverished in their medical literature, returned to Africa to gather books, though several were lost when he was shipwrecked on his return. A third, entirely different account (perhaps written by a partisan for the rival school of Montpellier) presents him as a fugitive from Spain who nearly killed his royal patient. Given his clear associations with the medical community of the Tunisian city of Qayrawan (see below), it may well be that his origins lie there.

Although clearly of African origin, Constantine's original religion remains unclear. Ferrarius explicitly refers to him as a "Saracen," but it has been noted that Arabic-speaking Christian communities are documented in Tunisia. Ferrarius comments on Constantine's initial need to rely on a Muslim slave as his translator, while another twelfth-century Salernitan writer, *Johannes de Sancto Paulo, ascribes Constantine's linguistic limitations in Latin to his African origin. Even Constantine's medical qualifications are not securely documented. Peter the Deacon never specifically calls him a physician (*medicus*) while Ferrarius claims he was a spice merchant.

Works and Sources

Peter the Deacon included in his biography of Constantine the earliest comprehensive list of his works. It includes such items as the *De genecia* (*On gynecology*) and *Cyrurgia* (*Surgery*) that were probably independently circulating excerpts of the translation of *al-Majusi's *Kamil as-sina'a at-tibbiya* ("The Whole Art of Medicine," in Latin the *Pantegni*). Omitted from the list (perhaps due to oversight) were the *Isagoge* ("Introduction [to the Medical Art]") by *Hunayn ibn Ishaq (Johannitius), the *De stomacho* ("On the Stomach") and *De melancholia* ("On Melancholy") by the Tunisian writer Ishaq ibn Imran (d. before 907), the *De oblivione* ("On Forgetfulness") by Ibn al-Jazzar (d. 979/980), and a work on charms and amulets by Qusta ibn Luqa (d. early tenth century). In all, Constantine translated some two dozen different texts from Arabic into Latin.

Although Constantine (or his early copyists at Monte Cassino) omitted the names of all his sources save for the Jew, Isaac Israeli (*Isaac Judaeus, d. 932), thanks to increasing knowledge of the corpus of medieval Arabic medical writing it is possible to identify the sources for at least half of Constantine's oeuvre. Besides Hunayn, al-Majusi, and Qusta ibn Luqa, Constantine's sources were writers active in Tunisia, specifically Qayrawan, in the tenth century. Ibn al-Jazzar was Constantine's most important source, including not only his general work on medical pathology, the *Viaticum*, but also works on leprosy, sexual intercourse, and degrees of medicines. The predominance of North African texts suggests that Constantine did not, in fact, travel very far to assemble his treasure trove of works; Ibn al-Jazzar's work was available on Sicily itself where it was translated into Greek in the twelfth century.

Very few of Constantine's works have yet been critically edited, so it is still difficult to pinpoint his unique stylistic characteristics as a translator. Indeed, it is still unclear how much of the Constantinian corpus is really by Constantine. Beside a peculiar text on impotence caused by magic (which is attested only in thirteenth-century manuscripts), there are several works associated with Constantine in medieval manuscripts or in Renaissance editions that are either spurious or of suspect authenticity. Particularly puzzling is the origin of the second major part of the *Pantegni*, the *Practica* ("Practical Medicine"), which has been shown to be a pastiche from a variety of different sources, not a direct translation of al-Majusi's Arabic text.

In terms of the larger significance of Constantine's translation project, two principal questions are pressing: how does it relate to work that went before him, and how was his work carried on after his death? There may have been other translators from Arabic in southern Italy either just before or contemporaneously with Constantine. There was also considerable translation activity going on from Greek into Latin, including the important work on urines and pulses by, respectively, Theophilus and Philaretus. The interactions between Muslims and Greek Christians on Sicily have not yet been sufficiently examined, nor the role of the latter in serving as linguistic and cultural intermediaries between the Muslim world and the Latin-speaking Christians of mainland southern Italy.

Constantine had two pupils, both of them also monks at Monte Cassino: Johannes Afflacius (sometimes called Johannes Saracenus) and a former chaplain to the empress Agnes named Azo (or Adzo). Johannes was the dedicatee of five of Constantine's translations, including the *Viaticum* itself. He also wrote his own original medical work, the *Liber aureus* ("Golden Book"), and may have retranslated Ibn al-Jazzar's treatise on lovesickness. This was apparently the same Johannes who, together with a certain "Pisan rustic," completed Constantine's *Surgery* in 1113–1114. Johannes is perhaps the most likely individual to have also completed the second half of Constantine's *Pantegni*, which makes use of the *Liber aureus*. As for Adzo, he was the dedicatee of Constantine's translation of *Galen's commentary on the Hippocratic *Aphorisms* and reportedly polished Constantine's rough Latin prose.

Influence

As the first major translator of Arabic medical texts into Latin, Constantine was by necessity an innovator in creating new medical and pharmaceutical terminology. He displays a fondness for the use of pseudo-classical terminology (like "Pantegni") though he also introduced many Arabic terms into Latin (like *nucha* for the spinal cord). Likewise, Constantine introduced from his Arabic sources new philosophical and nosological concepts, such as lovesickness (*amor hereos*), as formal disease categories.

No doubt due to Monte Cassino's central position within the Benedictine order, Constantine's works enjoyed rapid dissemination throughout western Europe. His works are documented beyond the Alps as early as the 1130s (in England even earlier). *William of Conches eagerly exploited the theoretical volume of the *Pantegni* and we can see Constantine's influence in other twelfth-century writers such as *Hildegard of Bingen.

Constantine's influence on the physicians of the "school" of *Salerno was perhaps not as immediate as would be expected given Constantine's direct ties with the city (he had arrived there when he first came to Italy). If Constantine is indeed to be credited with the translation of Hunayn ibn Ishaq's *Isagoge*, then his most immediate impact was in providing this foundational text of the Salernitan medical curriculum. The early Salernitan writer Copho makes little direct use of the Constantinian corpus; his employment of Arabic terminology and *materia medica* (like sugar or the compound remedy, *trifera saracenica*) may well be due to influences coming directly from Muslim practitioners in Sicily or their Greek-speaking intermediaries. By the time of Johannes Platearius in the mid-century, however, the influence of the *Viaticum* is apparent, and Constantine's works on diets and urines would become increasingly influential as the century progressed.

Constantine's works probably had their most powerful impact in the thirteenth century, when they were heavily exploited by the great mendicant encyclopedists, especially *Bartholomaeus Anglicus and *Thomas of Cantimpré. Also during this period, the *Viaticum* was subjected to several commentaries; aside from the *Isagoge*, it was probably the most widely circulated of all of Constantine's works. After the middle of the thirteenth century, however, the new Arabic medicine coming out of Spain (particularly Avicenna's massive *Canon*) began to eclipse the Constantinian corpus.

Only a few vernacular translations of Constantine's works are known: his treatise on intercourse was translated into English in the mid-fifteenth century, that on melancholy into French. Constantine is cited in such literary works as the *Romance of the Rose* and *Geoffrey Chaucer's *The Canterbury Tales*; in the latter, he appears both as a respected medical authority known well by the Doctor of Physick and, in the Merchant's Tale, as a "cursed monk" who wrote on coitus.

Constantine's works appeared in print principally in two different Renaissance editions: a collection of works attributed to Isaac Judaeus (only some of the works are in fact Isaac's), and an *Opera omnia* that appeared in two volumes at Basel in 1536–1539. There are few translations into modern languages besides Italian.

See also **Medicine, practical; Medicine, theoretical**

Bibliography

Ammar, Sleim. *Ibn Al Jazzar et l'Ecole médicale de Kairouan*. Ben Arous: Presses d'Imprimerie Principale, 1994.

Burnett, Charles, and Danielle Jacquart, eds. *Constantine the African and 'Ali ibn al-Abbas al-Magusi: The 'Pantegni' and Related Texts*. Studies in Ancient Medicine 10. Leiden: E.J. Brill, 1994.

Constantinus Africanus. *Omnia opera Ysaac*. Lyons: Bartholomeus Trot, 1515.

———. *Opera*. 2 vols. Basel: Henricus Petrus, 1536–1539.

Matheson, Lister M. Constantinus Africanus: *Liber de coitu (Liber creatoris)*. In *Sex, Aging, and Death in a Medieval Medical Compendium: TCC R.14.52, Its Language, Scribe and Text*, ed. M. Teresa Tavormina. Tempe: Arizona State University, 2005.

Martín Ferreira, Ana Isabel, ed. *Tratado médico de*

Constantino el Africano: Constantini Liber de elephancia. Valladolid: Universidad de Valladolid, 1996.

Sezgin, Fuat, ed. *Constantinus Africanus (11th cent.) and His Arabic sources: Texts and Studies.* Frankfurt am Main: Institute for the History of Arabic-Islamic Science at the Johann Wolfgang Goethe University, 1996.

Veit, Raphaela. Quellenkundliches zu Leben und Werk von Constantinus Africanus. *Deutsches Archiv für Erforschung des Mittelalters* 59 (2003), 121–152.

MONICA H. GREEN

COSMOLOGY

Although there was no Latin term for "cosmology" in the Middle Ages, scientific cosmology in that period was a fundamental part of natural philosophy, not of astronomy. The understanding of cosmic structure and operations was overwhelmingly derived from the natural philosophy of Aristotle, whose relevant treatises in natural philosophy were translated from Greek and Arabic during the twelfth and thirteenth centuries and became the basic subject of study in the arts curriculum of medieval universities, especially at Paris and Oxford.

Most of Aristotle's ideas about the cosmos were acceptable to Christians, but his firm conviction that the world is eternal—without beginning or end—was not. In effect, Aristotle rejected the idea that the world was created, and his views implied not only a denial of the divine creation of our world in six days, as described in Genesis, but also a denial of the basic Christian belief in the eventual destruction of the world (John 1.2–3 and 17.5). Although Christians were obligated by faith to accept these basic tenets, many of them also accepted *St. Thomas Aquinas's argument that it is logically possible that God could have created an eternally existent world—that is, a world without a temporal beginning. But few believed that He had done so.

The account of creation in Genesis posed serious problems for Aristotle's followers. They had somehow to reconcile statements in Genesis with Aristotle's secular cosmos. What, for example, was the firmament, which God called heaven, created on the second day? And what were the waters it divided above and below? How did the firmament, or heaven, created on the second day differ from the heaven created on the first day? How does the light created on the first day differ from the light created on the fourth day? Most of the answers to these questions did not do violence to Aristotle's cosmology and physics.

The cosmic sphere of the universe extends from the center of our spherical Earth, which coincides with the geometric center of the universe, to the sphere of the fixed stars and beyond. *Campanus de Novara estimated the distance from the Earth's center to the sphere of the fixed stars as approximately seventy-three million miles. Although minuscule by modern estimates, those who contemplated it during the Middle Ages regarded the universe as a gigantic sphere that is everywhere filled with matter, thereby leaving no void spaces. Beyond the convex surface of the outermost sphere of the universe nothing whatever exists: no body, no void, no place, no time. Aristotle convinced his medieval followers that the universe is divided into two radically different parts: one celestial, the other terrestrial. The world as a whole was linked by a hierarchical ladder of perfection ranging from the least perfect Earth at the center of the world to the most perfect and noble parts at the outermost reaches of the cosmos. Perfection was measured by the degree of change that substances undergo. The greatest amount of change occurs in the Earth at the center of the world, and gradually diminishes as the distance from Earth increases. The dividing line between the terrestrial and celestial regions was assumed to be the concave surface of the lunar sphere. At that surface, change and corruptibility end, and changelessness and incorruptibility begin for the celestial region. That part of the cosmos—from the Moon to the sphere of the fixed stars and beyond—was regarded as the noblest and most perfect part of the world, as evidenced by its incorruptibility. Change of place is the only change that can occur in the celestial region as the planets and stars are carried around the heavens.

The Terrestrial and Celestial Regions

Below the concave surface of the lunar sphere, and descending all the way to the center of the Earth, is the terrestrial part of the world. In stark contrast to the celestial region, all material bodies in this part of the world continually undergo four kinds of change—change of substance, change of quality, change of quantity, and change of place. These changes are the result of the interaction of four basic elements out of which all terrestrial bodies—animate and inanimate—are compounded, namely earth, water, air, and fire. The terrestrial region is divided into four concentric spheres, each of which is the natural place of one of the elements. The innermost sphere is the natural place of earth; the next is the natural place of water; the third is the natural place of air; and the outermost concentric sphere is the natural place of fire. If unimpeded, each element would move innately toward its natural place, and the terrestrial region would become a series of four static elemental spheres. But this will never occur because the elements are always embedded in compound bodies that are continually changing. They are corrupted as their elements depart and re-associate with other elements to generate new compounds, a never-ending process. The radical distinction between the celestial and terrestrial regions, based on whether change did or did not occur, is nowhere better illustrated than in the location of comets, shooting stars, and other occasional "celestial" phenomena, which were all located in the natural place of fire, that is, in the uppermost reaches of the terrestrial region, just below the Moon. As changeable phenomena, they had to be excluded from the heavens and placed in the upper reaches of the terrestrial region.

The incorruptible ether that filled the celestial region was subdivided into a series of concentric spheres. For astronomical purposes, astronomers, and even Aristotle, assigned numerous orbs to account for the motion of each planet and the fixed stars. Aristotle assigned anywhere from forty-nine to fifty-five orbs, and *Ptolemy assigned as many as forty-one. But natural philosophers, who were the cosmologists of their day, viewed the cosmos in simpler terms. They assigned to each planet a single orb. Since there were seven planets (in ascending order: the Moon, Mercury, Venus, the Sun, Mars, Jupiter, and Saturn), there were seven orbs arranged concentrically—that is, one orb within another, all with the center of the Earth as their common center. The fixed stars were usually assigned three distinct orbs, one for the daily motion, another for the precession of the equinoxes, and one for trepidation, a motion that was imagined to exist, but did not. The creation account in Genesis played a role. The fixed stars were assigned to the eighth orb, which not only carried the stars around in their daily motion, but was also frequently identified with the biblical firmament. Apart from its astronomical function, the starless ninth sphere was usually regarded as the biblical waters above the firmament. The ninth sphere was often called the crystalline orb, because its waters were regarded as solid, like ice. The tenth orb, also starless, simply performed its astronomical function. Finally, surrounding them all is the Empyrean heaven, which, unlike all other orbs, was assumed to be immobile. The Empyrean had no astronomical function, but was a purely theological construct that was regarded as "the dwelling place of God and the elect." All told, natural philosophers assumed the existence of eleven concentric celestial orbs.

Although planets, stars, and orbs were made of the same celestial ether, the planets lay immobile in their respective spheres, which carried them around the heavens. Prior to the fourteenth century, the celestial ether was regarded as fluid, as were the celestial orbs, which were somehow imagined to retain their spherical shapes. This interpretation changed in the fourteenth century, when numerous natural philosophers came to assume that the planetary orbs were hard, shell-like objects arranged concentrically from the lunar sphere to the outermost sphere of the world. This became the predominant opinion until Tycho Brahe's astronomical researches, near the end of the sixteenth century, made the fluid theory the more plausible option.

The cause of the uniform circular motions of the celestial orbs was attributed primarily to external intelligences, and occasionally to internal forces. Following Aristotle, each celestial orb was assumed to have an immaterial, spiritual intelligence associated with it, but yet distinct from it. An intelligence functioned as an "unmoved mover" because it had the power to move its orb without itself being in motion. It did so, as Aristotle explained, by being loved by its celestial orb, a relationship that was not further explained. Immaterial intelligences were often equated with angels. Some natural philosophers, however, chose a different path from Aristotle, and held that at the creation God impressed an immaterial internal force into every celestial orb, providing the power for its incessant motion through a celestial ether that offered no resistance.

Celestial orbs were nested one within another as they moved around the sky, but whether they moved in the same direction or opposition directions, their touching surfaces produced no friction. Throughout the Middle Ages it was assumed that the nobler and incorruptible celestial bodies exerted a dominant and controlling influence over the corruptible and ever-changing material bodies in the terrestrial, or sub-lunar, region. These effects were exerted in three basic ways: (1) by the celestial motions; (2) by light from the Sun; and (3) by invisible influences that could penetrate where light could not (for example, into the bowels of the Earth where celestial influences were thought to cause the generation of metals). The overwhelming dominance of the celestial region over the terrestrial was the ultimate basis for belief in astrology.

It was generally believed that God had not created a perfect world, but one that was as perfect as it needed to be. Because God was assumed to have absolute power to do anything He pleased short of a logical contradiction, it was always assumed that, if He wished, God could create better and better worlds, or as many other worlds as He pleased.

Does Anything Exist Beyond Our World?

Although Aristotle had argued that it was impossible for anything to exist beyond our finite world, his medieval followers insisted that God, by His absolute power, could create anything beyond our world that He wished, including other worlds. In 1277, the bishop of Paris condemned 219 propositions among which were assertions that God could not create other worlds and that He could not move our whole spherical universe with a rectilinear motion, because the departure of the world from its place would leave a vacuum. Although Aristotle regarded both the existence of other worlds beyond ours, and the existence of extracosmic void spaces, as impossibilities, his medieval Christian followers were convinced that God, by His omnipotence, could create both. Thus where Aristotle regarded such extracosmic phenomena as impossible and absurd, medieval natural philosophers regarded them as possible by supernatural action, although virtually no one believed that God had actually done so, or would do so. University scholars began to imagine numerous scenarios in which they showed that if other worlds existed, they would be compatible with each other. The most popular hypothetical situation was one in which a multiplicity of identical, self-contained worlds existed each with its own center and circumference. The multiplicity of centers and circumferences violated Aristotle's conviction that only one center and circumference could exist, because only one world is possible. Scholastics also imagined that God annihilated matter within our world, thus creating a vacuum. They then argued—contrary to Aristotle—that successive, finite motions of material bodies would be possible in such a vacuum.

The most dramatic departure from Aristotle, however, was the assumption by some theologian-natural philosophers that an infinite, dimensionless, void space lay beyond our world. This was partly based on a strong intuitive sense that something must exist beyond our world. But it was on theological grounds that *Thomas Bradwardine (c. 1290–1349) identified God's infinite, omnipresent immensity with a dimensionless, infinite void space. Because God is an unextended being, it was deemed essential that the infinite void He "occupied" also be regarded as extensionless. Except for extension, scholastic theologians conferred much the same properties on infinite space as did the major scientists of the Scientific Revolution, most notably Sir Isaac Newton. Nevertheless, the contributions of Copernicus, Tycho Brahe, Galileo, and Newton in the sixteenth and seventeenth centuries produced a radically different cosmos that wholly replaced its medieval predecessor.

See also **Astrology; Astronomy; Nature: diverse medieval interpretations; Nature: the structure of the physical world; Scholasticism**

Bibliography

Grant, Edward, ed. *A Source Book in Medieval Science.* Cambridge: Harvard University Press, 1974, pp. 494–568.

———. *Much Ado About Nothing: Theories of Space and Vacuum from the Middle Ages to the Seventeenth Century.* New York: Cambridge University Press, 1981.

———. *Planets, Stars, and Orbs: The Medieval Cosmos 1200–1687.* New York: Cambridge University Press, 1994.

McCluskey, Stephen C. *Astronomies and Cultures in Early Medieval Europe.* New York: Cambridge University Press, 1998.

North, John. "Medieval Concepts of Celestial Influence: A Survey." In Patrick Curry, ed. *Astrology, Science and Society, Historical Essays.* Woodbridge: Boydell, 1987, pp. 5–17.

Sacrobosco, John of. *The "Sphere" of Sacrobosco and Its Commentators.* Ed. and tr. Lynn Thorndike. Chicago: University of Chicago Press, 1949.

Steneck, Nicholas H. *Science and Creation in the Middle Ages: Henry of Langenstein (d. 1397) on Genesis.* Notre Dame: University of Notre Dame Press, 1976.

EDWARD GRANT

D

DESPARS, JACQUES

Jacques Despars was born in Tournai, France, c. 1380, and died in Paris on January 3, 1458.

A knight's son from the old Capetian bishopric of Tournai, Jacques studied grammar in his native village and then went on to study primarily at the University of Paris, taking degrees from 1403 to 1410, including those in the arts as well as his licentiate and master of medicine; he was elected rector in 1406. Jacques also studied briefly at the University of Montpellier. From 1411 to 1419 he was regent master in medicine in Paris, representing the masters at the Council of Constance in 1415. From 1420 to 1450 he practiced medicine in Tournai, Cambrai, Bruges, and Audenarde, serving the local nobles as well as the House of Burgundy. Duke Philip the Good awarded him four ecclesiastical benefices in the late 1440s. He returned to Paris in 1450, living there until his death. He had at least three noteworthy students: Jean Spierinck, Guillaume de Naste, and Eudes de Creil.

Despar's commentary on the *Canon* of Avicenna (*Ibn Sina), written from 1432 to 1453, remains one of the great bastions of fifteenth-century medicine. After his death Jacques left his own fifteen-volume copy to the Paris Medical Faculty, where it had a profound impact on his students and followers. The work of a great scholastic, the commentary synthesizes Greek and Arabic authorities with some two hundred forty-four discriminative *quaestiones*, often argued in a neo-Albertian fashion, along with more than a modicum of clinical expertise. The commentary evaluates volumes I, II, and IV (fen 1) of Avicenna's text, and applies material found in *Galen, *Hippocrates, Aristotle, Alexander of Tralles (on whose work he also commented), Avenzoar (*Ibn Zuhr), Averroes (*Ibn Rushd), Mesue, Rhazes (*al-Razi), and Serapion.

Having written the treatise over some twenty-one years of direct clinical practice, Jacques struggled at times with the relationship of theory and practice, as in his wrestling with the seeming incurability of plague in his own patients. While Avicenna might evoke the image of human-to-human transmission, Jacques' clinical experience demanded a more miasmatic interpretation. Among many other technical points, Jacques used Avicenna's text as a vehicle for supporting the superiority of physicians over other practitioners in the field, including surgeons. Finally, from the point of view of retrospective diagnosis, the work is notable for a case of leptospirosis at the siege of Arras in 1414, and, it has been less successfully argued, a case of the rash of typhoid fever. The commentary was copied in numerous manuscripts and printed in 1498 with several excerpts printed in the sixteenth century.

Jacques' work displays a variety of tensions in the rapidly evolving academic and clinical marketplace of the day, especially in the realms of therapeutics and heuristics. For example, not above anatomical observations, Jacques examined skeletons at the Saint-Innocents cemetery in Paris. However, this paragon of the so-called *via scolaris* railed against the growing popularity of *astrology, which he found baseless. Its weakness lay in diverting the physician's attention away from bodily causes. Jacques did, however, acknowledge that the practice was useful in soothing patients, a concession perhaps made with the appearance of a rival at the court of the Duke of Burgundy. On the other hand, Jacques appears to have appreciated *alchemy, offering descriptions of alchemical processes and using its metaphors to support his arguments. Regarding the therapy of phlebotomy, unlike contemporary authors, Jacques could be almost reckless in its use, depending on the condition.

Jacques also wrote *Summula per alphabetum super plurimis remediis ex Mesue libris excerptis*, being a pharmaceutical study of prescriptions from the work of Mesue, an Arabic author of the ninth century; this work was added to printed editions of the *Articella* in the sixteenth century, suggesting its late scholastic role in education. Regimens of health written for Michel and Guillaume Bernard survive as well as a *consilium* on epilepsy and a number of pharmaceutical recipes. Jacques' commentary on a Hippocratic aphorism actually comments on the humoral effect of a variety of simple and compound medicines.

See also **Medicine, practical; Medicine, theoretical; Surgery**

Bibliography

Primary Source

Canon Avicenne cum explanatione Jacobi de Partibus. Lyons, 1498.

Secondary Sources

Jacquart, Danielle. *Le regard d'un médecin sur son temps: Jacques Despars (1380?–1458).* Bibliothèque de l'École des Chartes (1980) 138: 35–86.

Jacquart, Danielle. Theory, Everyday Practice, and Three Fifteenth-century Physicians. *Osiris* (1990) 6: 140–160.

Jacquart, Danielle. *La médecine médiévale dans le cadre Parisien.* Paris: Fayard, 1998.

Wickersheimer, Ernst. *Dictionnaire biographique des médecins en France au moyen-âge, t. 2.* Genève: Droz, 1979.

WALTON O. SCHALICK, III

DIOSCORIDES

Dioscorides Pedanius is known as the author of *De materia medica* (*MM*), the most influential treatise of classical antiquity in Greek on the natural substances used for the preparation of medicines. Identified as Pedanios Dioskorides Anazarbeus in Byzantine manuscripts, Dioscorides probably lived during the first century C.E., and was born in Anazarba (Cilicia, Asia Minor). Thought by modern scholars to have received his medical education in Pergamon and Alexandria (or, according to some research, in Tarsus), Dioscorides is thought to have then become a physician to the Roman army under the emperors Claudius (41–54 C.E.) or Nero (54–68 C.E.). During his extensive travels throughout the Empire, especially in the Middle East, Dioscorides would have been able to gain firsthand experence of many of the products he analyzed in *MM*.

MM, often considered a herbal, deals with all three natural kingdoms: plant, mineral, and animal. It describes all the natural substances known to Dioscorides that were used as primary ingredients for medicines (i.e., drugs), and constitutes an encyclopedia on the topic. A chapter is devoted to each drug. *MM* contains just over one thousand chapters and features 794 plants, 104 animals, and 105 minerals. Most of the chapters contain the following information: (a) The most common name of the drug and its possible synonyms; (b) A description of the natural element producing the drug (for a vegetal drug, the whole plant); (c) The part used as a drug, possibly with its preparation; (d) The therapeutic properties of the drug; (e) The disease(s) for which the drug was used, including the preparation and administration of the medicine; (f) When appropriate, the falsifications and methods of authentication of the drug; and (g) Other uses of the drug, such as in cosmetics, veterinary medicine, or handicraft.

In several Byzantine manuscripts, the text of *MM* is accompanied by illustrations of plants, animals, and minerals whose authenticity and style are still debated: were they in Dioscorides' originals or are they subsequent additions? Whatever their origin, were they originally realistic and became schematic over time due to successive copies? No definitive argument has been provided so far for either theory.

In its canonic form, *MM* is composed of five books of almost equal length, each of which supposedly deals with a specific topic. This division is thought to have been imposed by the length of the rolls of papyrus which were the medium of book production in Dioscorides' time. Whatever the truth of that, drugs are grouped so as to constitute major classes (e.g., perfumed plants, oil and perfumed oils, trees, fruit trees, animals, and cereals) and, within each class, groups with a specific therapeutic action. Within these groups, drugs are listed in order of the extent to which they demonstrate the degree of activity that is common to the group. Drug classes, in turn, are ordered so that their supposed therapeutic properties shift from hot and drying at the beginning of *MM* to cold and humidifying at the end. Differences between classes are gradual and constitute a proper *scala naturae*, each major step of which corresponds to a period of the mythological history of the cosmos (the five ages of the world and humankind), characterized by a gradual reduction of positive qualities.

Some *MM* manuscripts contain a treatise *On simple drugs* (in Greek) that lists drugs by diseases and is of uncertain authenticity; other manuscripts have transmitted under Dioscorides' name two treatises, *On poisons* and *On venomous animals*, which were associated with *MM* before the ninth century. Although they contain material dating back most probably to Dioscorides' period, they do not seem to be authentic, but were added to *MM* over time (maybe in two steps), as they supplement it.

Byzantium and the East

MM had a truly exceptional history from antiquity to the Renaissance. It was spread very soon across the entire Mediterranean world, from Egypt to Constantinople, from Syria to Rome. Its original structure seems to have been modified as early as the fourth century C.E. if not before: the new recension organized the text in alphabetical order by drug name. In *On simple drugs, mixtures, and properties*, *Galen, who relied on *MM* for the description of drugs, already used this order, as did also the authors of early Byzantine medical encyclopedias, Oribasius (fourth century), Aetius (sixth century), and Paul of Ægina (seventh century). In these encyclopedias, *MM* text is associated in different ways with Galen's treatise on simple drugs.

A certain number of *MM* chapters dealing with plants were extracted from this alphabetical version to form an alphabetical herbal. This new recension—the oldest known manuscript of which is the richly illustrated *Vindobonensis medicus graecus* 1, dated about 513, now preserved in Vienna (Austria)—necessarily predates such a codex. Its origin, which has never been accounted for, might be the result of an attempt to reduce the number of drugs in *MM* from the original thousand to about three hundred. Eastern drugs were not included in this herbal. Before the ninth century, the chapters of *MM* not included in the herbal were taken again from *MM* full text, divided into four groups (oils, animals, trees, and minerals), and added to the herbal so as to form again a five-book version of *MM*. In each of these books of a new kind, chapters were sequenced according to the alphabetic order of drug names. Oriental drugs seem not to have been reintroduced into this new version until the mid-eleventh century codex *Megistis Lavras* S 75 (Mount Athos, Greece).

The *MM* Greek text was translated into Syriac during the sixth century, and into Arabic during the ninth. *Hunayn ibn Ishaq (808–873), working in Baghdad in collaboration with Istifan ibn Basil, translated it first from Syriac and then a second time from Greek. Characteristically, many Greek names of drugs were not translated, but merely transliterated. Even though the translators stated that they did not know the exact translation of such terms, they could also have proceeded in this way to keep apparent the structure of *MM*, which relies in many cases on the similarity of drug names. Hunayn's translations were further revised, if not replaced, by later versions made at the court of eastern Arabic princes. Several Arabic copies of *MM* (whatever the version) contain polychromatic representations of plants and other *materia medica*, some in a highly stylized fashion. *MM* provided a basis for many new Arabic herbals and *materia medica* treatises.

After the Latin occupation (1204–1261) of Constantinople, the most important extant manuscripts of *MM* of the earlier periods seem to have been gathered all together in the same place in the capital, possibly the Katholikon Mouseion, that is, the school adjacent to the hospital of the king of Serbia Milutin (the so-called Xenodocheion tou Krale), in the Petra area of Constantinople. Damaged codices were restored and their texts collated to produce a revised edition (the so-called Byzantine recension), that is, a medically updated version. The illustrations were also revised. This new text replaced earlier versions and was widely spread, both in Constantinople and in the West in the Renaissance.

The West

Known in Rome at least at Galen's period, the *MM* Greek text was not as extensively revised in Italy during subsequent periods as it was in Byzantium. At some time after the ninth century C.E., one or more illustrated codices of *MM* could have arrived in Italy from Syria-Palestine and were copied.

A Latin translation supposedly referred to by Cassiodorus (c. 490–c. 583) was made, maybe during the sixth century, in North Africa or southern Europe. Its earliest copy is the *Dioscorides longobardus*, (manuscript Clm 337 of the Bayerische Staatsbibliothek in Munich). This document, written in the typical script of Benevento (Italy), has been recently attributed to the area of Naples and the tenth century, and is illustrated in simple color.

Contacts between East and West started before the translation enterprise whose beginning is traditionally attributed to *Constantine the African (d. after 1085), in southern Italy and southern Spain. Córdoba was in contact with Constantinople during the tenth century: an illustrated copy of the *MM* in Greek was sent to the emir as a present by the emperor. No new translation was made (contrary to what is often asserted in literature), but Hunayn's translation, which had arrived earlier, was revised and corrected by means of this Greek manuscript.

While it is generally affirmed that Western residents of Constantinople did not interact with local scientists between the end of the Fourth Crusade (1204) and 1261, a manuscript herbal (Copenhagen, Kongelige Bibliotek, Thot 190) contains plant representations similar to those of Greek manuscripts that were at the Katholikon Mouseion during the fourteenth century. Later, *Pietro d'Abano (1257–c. 1315), who traveled to Constantinople shortly after the end of the Latin Kingdom, referred to an alphabetical recension of the *MM* in his pharmacological work. He might have seen the Vindobonensis manuscript and, in any case, he seems to have taken note of variant readings from the herbal and compared them to those of the five-book recension.

A copy of the Byzantine five-book recension made during the early fourteenth century in Constantinople seems to have been in the milieu of Manouel Chrysoloras (c. 1350–1415), a Byzantine scholar who emigrated to Florence. Further on, this copy (which is now manuscript Florentinus Laurentianus 74.23) arrived in the collection gathered by Lorenzo de Medici (1449–1492), and was borrowed by Angelo Poliziano (1454–1494). Later on, such collectors as Cardinal Bessarion and Isidorus, Cardinal of Kiev (1380/90–1463), had copies of *MM*, which they brought to Italy and donated to the Republic of Venice and the Vatican Library respectively.

After the Fall of Constantinople (1453), the *MM* Greek text reached Italy through two main channels. One route was via Crete, where Michael Apostoles (c. 1420–1474 or 1486), a protégé of the Greek cardinal Bessarion (1400–1472), had created a scriptorium. His collaborators seem to have reproduced only an alphabetic version (which is not necessarily the one supposedly made in antiquity). The other route was across the Adriatic and through Venice, thanks to the manuscript now preserved at the Bibliothèque Nationale de France (Paris) under the shelf-mark graecus 2183, which contained the Byzantine recension and was used as a model for several copies, thus widely spreading this version of *MM*. Collectors and scholars such as Pico della Mirandola (1463–1494), Giorgio Valla (c. 1487–1500), Ermolao Barbaro (1453–1493), and Nicolao Leoniceno (1428–1524) had one or more copies of the *MM*.

MM Latin text commented on by Pietro d'Abano was printed as early as 1478 at Colle (Tuscany, Italy). Shortly after, Ermolao Barbaro wrote a Latin translation with commentary, which was not published before 1516, however. The *MM* Greek text was printed in 1499 by Aldo Manuzio (1449–c. 1515), on the basis of a copy of manuscript Parisinus graecus 2183, that is, the Byzantine recension. The Aldine edition could have been prepared by Nicolao Leoniceno in order to demonstrate the validity of the thesis that he first put forth in his booklet *De Plinii aliorumque in medicina erroribus* (Ferrara, 1492), according to which Greek scientific texts of classical antiquity (particularly *MM*) were superior to Pliny's *Natural History* and the medieval Latin translations of Arabic authors. Whatever the case, both the *De Plinii* and the 1499 Greek edition of *MM* closed the medieval period of *MM* history.

See also Herbals; Pharmacology

Bibliography

Primary Sources

Dioscorides: Pedanii Dioscuridis Anazarbei. De materia medica libri quinque. Edidit M. Wellmann. 3 vols. Berlin: Weidmann, 1906–1914 (reprinted 1958 and 1999).
Gunther, Robert T. *The Greek herbal of Dioscorides. Illustrated by a Byzantine A.D. 512, Englished by John Goodyer A.D. 1655, edited and first printed A.D. 1933.* New York: Oxford University Press, 1934.

Secondary Sources

Aufmesser, Max. *Etymologische und wortgeschichtliche Erläuterungen zu De materia medica des Pedanius Dioscurides Anazarbeus.* Hildesheim: Olms-Weidmann, 2000.
Riddle, John M. "Dioscorides." In *Catalogus translationum et commentariorum: Mediaeval and Renaissance Latin translations and commentaries 4.* Edited by F.E. Cranz and P.O. Kristeller. Washington, D.C.: Catholic University of America Press, 1980: 1–143.
———. *Dioscorides on Pharmacy and Medicine.* Austin: University of Texas Press, 1985.
Sadek, Mahmoud M. *The Arabic Materia Medica of Dioscorides.* St-Jean-Chrysostome: Les Editions du Sphinx, 1983.
Scarborough, John and V. Nutton. The Preface of Dioscorides' Materia Medica: introduction, translation, and commentary. *Transactions and studies of the College of Physicians of Philadelphia* (1982) 5.4: 187–227.
Touwaide Alain. L'authenticité et l'origine des deux traités de toxicologie attribués à Dioscoride. *Janus* (1983) 70: 1–53.
———. "Les deux traités de toxicologie attribués à Dioscoride. Tradition manuscrite, établissement du texte et critique d'authenticité." In *Tradizione e ecdotica dei testi medici tardoantichi e bizantini.* Edited by A. Garyz. Naples: M. D'Auria, 1992: 291–339.
———. "Le Traité de matière médicale de Dioscoride en Italie depuis la fin de l'Empire romain jusqu'aux débuts de l'école de Salerne. Essai de synthèse." In *From Epidaurus to Salerno.* Edited by A. Krug. Rixensart: PACT Belgium, 1992: 275–305.
———. "La botanique entre science et culture au Ier siècle de notre ère." In *Geschichte der Mathematik und der Naturwissenschaften in der Antike I: Biologie.* Edited by G. Wöhrle. Stuttgart: Franz Steiner, 1999: 219–252.
———. "Loquantur ipsi ut velint ... modo quis serpens sit tirus ... non ignorent: Leoniceno's contribution to Renaissance epistemological approach to scientific lexicology." In *Medical latin from the Late Middle Ages to the Eighteenth century.* Edited by W. Bracker, and H. Deumes. Brussels: Academy of Medicine, 2000: 151–173.
Wellmann, Max. *Die Schrift des Dioskurides peri aplôn farmakôn. Ein Beitrag zur Geschichte der Medizin.* Berlin: Weidmann, 1914.

ALAIN TOUWAIDE

DUNS SCOTUS, JOHANNES

It is usually accepted that Johannes (John) Duns Scotus was born in late 1265 or early 1266 in the small Scottish village of Duns just north of the border with England. He joined the Franciscan order, in which his distinguished scientific predecessors included *Roger Bacon and *John Pecham. He was studying in Oxford in 1291, during which time he began the composition of important sets of questions on the logical and metaphysical works of Aristotle, as well as a draft—the *Lectura*—of his major theological work, his Oxford commentary on *Peter Lombard's *Sentences*. The revision of this work—the *Ordinatio*—was under way by 1300. In about 1301 Scotus was sent to Paris to continue his theological studies, where he lectured for a second time on the *Sentences*. The work survives as a set of examined student notes—the *Reportatio*—and Scotus became regent master (professor) in theology at Paris in 1305, where he presided over one set of quodlibetal disputations. In 1307 he was moved to the Franciscan house of studies in Cologne, where he died on November 8, 1308, with most of his works extant only in more or less complete drafts.

Scotus's main philosophical achievements lay in the areas of *metaphysics and action theory. He attempted to solve the problem of the individuation by positing haecceities—thisnesses: non-qualitative features of substances, proper to each substance. His theory of transcendental concepts, reducing all knowledge to a set of simple, non-overlapping, non-definable concepts, is ancestor of the rationalist philosophy of figures such as was later developed by Leibniz. Scotus was the first to formulate a notion of logical possibility, conceiving the possible as the non-contradictory, irrespective of its real existence at some time or another (and thus independent of physical possibility). In line with this, he was the first to attempt a philosophical defense of human free will as a real power to choose different courses of action in exactly the same circumstances, something required by the *Condemnation of 1277.

The Nature of Science

Like all practitioners of *Scholasticism in the thirteenth and fourteenth centuries, Scotus was heavily indebted to the recently recovered thought of Aristotle. According to Aristotle, a science or *scientia* is an explanatory deductive system deriving theorems from necessarily true axioms. Aristotle holds that we can posit such axioms if required to explain some empirical fact. Scotus adds a probabilistic element that brings him somewhat closer to modern views of induction. He believes that through experiment (that is, experience), we know that such-and-such an event follows such-and-such a substance for the

Duns Scotus. Unattributed engraving (1584) after André Thevet (c. 1516?–1592). (Mary Evans Picture Library)

most part; we can infer from this that the event is caused by the substance, since causes of the same type by definition produce effects of the same type.

Unsurprisingly, Scotus follows Aristotle's division of the theoretical sciences, in *Metaphysics* bk 6, ch. 1, into mathematics, natural philosophy or physics, and first philosophy or metaphysics. Scotus accepts a version of Aristotle's *hylomorphism, according to which bodies are composites of matter and form. He holds that physics studies bodies insofar as they have "form, which is the principle of determinate operation, motion, and rest... which can be known by the way of sense." Scotus is happy to use mathematical tools in his physics, and like many medieval authors is perhaps more aware than Aristotle of the fundamentally mathematical structure of empirical reality.

Natural Philosophy

Scotus is remembered not so much for his scientific achievements as for other achievements in philosophy and theology; perhaps the reason for this is merely the extent of his achievements in these last two areas, for he makes some important contributions in natural philosophy. There is, however, little in his writings that implies a particular scientific relation to earlier Franciscan tradition.

One of Scotus's most important innovations is the rejection of a fundamental principle of Aristotelian physics, that self-motion is impossible, a principle that undergirds the Aristotelian argument for a first mover.

Scotus reasons that motion requires the notions of act and potency: an active power to cause, and a passive potency to be caused (to be made to exist in a certain state). Scotus argues that there is no reason why one and the same substance could not possess both the active power and the passive capacity, and thus change itself.

The version of hylomorphism that Scotus accepts differs from Aristotle's in various ways. One, which he inherited from his Franciscan (and other) predecessors is that, in order to explain the identity of a living body with a dead one it is necessary to posit a bodily form, giving the body its basic structure, and another form, the soul, giving the body the microstructure that allows it to live. Scotus also concludes that matter must have some reality in itself, such that it could exist without any form whatsoever, in order for matter to be the substrate of Aristotelian substantial change, the thing that "exists now in a different way than before." If matter lacked any reality in itself, then it would be impossible for it to remain constant over a change.

The Condemnation of 1277 allowed for the possibility both of an intracosmic vacuum and of extracosmic space. Scotus follows these anti-Aristotelian lines of thought, arguing that a notion akin to that of absolute space is required to deal with the Aristotelian problem of an immobile body surrounded by moving bodies, and that such a notion can be used to give an account of a vacuum and extracosmic space too. (Extracosmic space does not exist; it would, however, if God were to create something at a distance from this universe.)

Scotus follows Aristotle in wanting to give a non-atomistic account of motion, and thus of space and time, but he adds some important arguments of his own. Like Aristotle, he holds that extension requires divisibility, and that however far the process of division is carried, there is always more that can be done. He notes that the divisibility of space (or time) at any point does not entail divisibility at every point (as argued by an unnamed opponent), and thus that infinite divisibility does not entail composition from infinitely many points. And he makes use of two geometrical arguments to show that an extended magnitude cannot be composed of a finite number of unextended points. The first argues that, on the assumption of composition from such points, it would be possible for a line drawn from the centre of two concentric circles not to bisect both circles, and the second, derived from Bacon and (remotely) from *al-Ghazali, reasons from the incommensurability of the side and diagonal of a square. Scotus makes use of a version of his first argument to show that an extended magnitude could not be composed of a finite number of extended minimum particles either.

Scotus uses his anti-atomistic insights to develop an important new theory of the *latitude of forms. According to Scotus, kinds or species of qualities admit of degrees. Increases and decreases are explained by the addition and subtraction of new "parts" of the quality, such that lower degrees persist and are contained in higher degrees. Degrees of a quality thus admit of quantitative analysis in terms of more or less (of the quality). Against the opposing view that change in quality requires the production and destruction of complete qualities, Scotus argues that such a theory could not explain the continuity of a gradual change, requiring (impossibly) the production and destruction of infinitely many qualities in finite time. Seeing qualities in this quantitative way opened the way for the quantification of velocity (seen as a quality of motion), and thus for the formulation of the mean-speed theorem proposed by *Richard Swineshead and *William of Heytesbury.

Religion and Science

Scotus's theology has a marked influence on his scientific theories, although he is careful always to find non-theological arguments in favor of his scientific theories too. The context of the discussion of the latitude of forms is an account of increases (and decreases) in grace, conceived on the analogy of an Aristotelian quality. And Scotus makes use of his theory to give an account of the infinite perfections of God: God's perfections are like infinite degrees of qualities. This means, in turn, that in at least one important context, Scotus rejects Aristotle's denial of an actual infinity. Scotus supposes that God's infinite perfection can be pictured on the analogy of an actually infinite magnitude (just as the degrees of a quality are understood on the analogy of an extended quantity). Scotus's account of the plurality of forms is formulated in part to deal with the problem of the identity of Christ's dead body in the tomb, something

arising from the 1277 condemnation. Moreover, according to Scotus, the doctrine of transubstantiation entails the reality of quantity distinct from substance, that place is distinct from extension, and that substances are fundamentally unknowable, since it is impossible to know that God has not transubstantiated the whole universe into Himself.

See also **Aristotelianism**

Bibliography

Primary Sources

Joannes Duns Scotus. *Opera Omnia*. 12 vols. Edited by L. Wadding. Lyon, 1639.
———. *Opera Omnia*. Edited by C. Balíc. Vatican City: Vatican Polyglot Press, 1950–.
———. *God and Creatures: The Quodlibetal Questions*. Edited by Allan B. Wolter and Felix Alluntis. Princeton: Princeton University Press, 1975.
———. *Philosophical Writings: A Selection*. Edited by Allan B. Wolter. Indianapolis: Hackett, 1987.
———. *Opera Philosophica*. Edited by G. Etzkorn. St Bonaventure, NY: The Franciscan Institute, 1997–.

Secondary Sources

Cross, Richard. *The Physics of Duns Scotus: The Scientific Context of a Theological Vision*. Oxford: Clarendon Press, 1998.
Duhem, Pierre. *Medieval Cosmology: Theories of Infinity, Place, Time, Void, and the Plurality of Worlds*. Chicago: University of Chicago Press, 1985.
Grant, Edward. *Much Ado about Nothing: Theories of Space and Vacuum from the Middle Ages to the Scientific Revolution*. New York: Cambridge University Press, 1981.
King, Peter. "Duns Scotus on the Reality of Self-Change." In *Self-Motion from Aristotle to Newton*. Edited by Mary Louise Gill and James G. Lennox. Princeton: Princeton University Press, 1994.
Lewis, Neil. "Space and Time." In *The Cambridge Companion to Duns Scotus*. Edited by Thomas Williams. New York: Cambridge University Press, 2003.

RICHARD CROSS

E

ELEMENTS AND QUALITIES

According to Aristotle's *cosmology, the universe is divided into two distinct realms. In his geocentric account, beyond the border of the sphere of the Moon, all bodies are composed of the element ether. These bodies are eternal, experience neither generation nor corruption, and move in circles around the Earth. Below the sphere of the Moon, in the terrestrial region, all bodies are composed of mixtures of the four elements: earth, water, air, and fire. These elements were considered to be simple substances, and the matter from which all terrestrial substances were composed. They never exist separately in a pure form, and are characterized by four primary qualities: the hot, the cold, the wet, and the dry. These elements and their defining qualities explain the passive properties and active powers of corporeal substances. By and large medieval philosophers accepted Aristotle's framework as laid out in *De generatione et corruptione*, *Meteorologica* IV, the *Physics*, and the *De caelo*, although they debated some of the finer points of his theories. The general correspondence between Aristotle's elements and those of *Plato as described in the *Timaeus* gave additional authority to this understanding of the elements. Furthermore, medieval physicians, who derived their theories from Greek medical works attributed to *Galen and *Hippocrates, also used the prime qualities to define the temperaments of the body and to explain the causes of health and disease.

Elements and the Prime Qualities

In typical medieval accounts each element is defined by two of the four primary qualities. The qualities are divided into two groups: active and passive. The two opposites, the hot and the cold, are active, while the wet and the dry are passive. Each element is defined by one active and one passive element. Thus earth is cold and dry; water is cold and wet; air is hot and wet; and fire is hot and dry. The elements transform into each other when one of their prime qualities turns into its opposite.

For example, earth changes into water when it becomes wet, and water becomes air when it becomes hot. Elements can only transform one quality at a time. Therefore, earth must transform first into either water or fire before turning into air, its polar opposite.

Even though all the elements are defined by two primary qualities, one particular quality predominates in each element. Thus earth is dry; water is cold; air is wet, and fire is hot. The qualities themselves can be thought of both as tangible properties, such as heat, coldness, etc., as well as powers or principles of organization. The four primary qualities and their effects were thought to be responsible, either directly or indirectly, for all qualitative change, generation, and corruption in the sublunary realm. The active qualities "act" by participating in the generation and corruption of substances. The hot assimilates like substances and separates unlike ones, while the cold brings together both like and unlike substances. The passive qualities are responsible for the shape of the

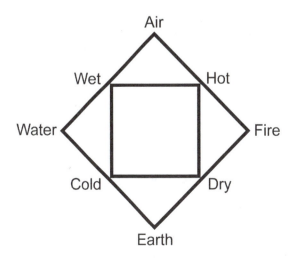

Schematic diagram showing the relation between each of the elements and the qualities that compose them.

157

substance in which they inhere. Thus wet substances are topologically fluid and conform to the shape of a container, while dry ones are solid and retain their shape. There was some debate over the rigid distinction between passive and active qualities, and some medieval scholars argued that the active qualities were only relatively more active than the passive ones, and that the passive qualities were in fact active. In particular it was argued that the wet was active since wet substances could turn dry substances into liquids through dissolution.

Medieval interpreters of Aristotle devoted much energy to discussions of how the four elements combine in mixtures. Since all sublunary bodies are composed of the four elements, it was a fundamental question of terrestrial physics. Approaches relied on the notions of substantial forms and matter, key concepts to Aristotelian theories of *hylomorphism. In particular, they questioned in what sense the elements acted as the matter of composites, and in what manner the qualities persisted in these mixtures. Since the elements did not remain perfectly complete in, for example, small particles side by side in composites, but rather fused to make new mixtures, scholars debated whether the substantial forms or the qualities of the elements were diminished or persisted intact.

Elements, Cosmology, and Secondary Qualities

While the elements are defined by the prime qualities, they are also distinguished by what is described in Aristotelian terms as their natural place. In this schema, each of the elements has a characteristic tendency to move to a particular region closer to or further away from the center of the Earth. The element earth was thought to be the heaviest, followed by water, which tends toward the surface of the Earth. Air naturally moves toward the region above the Earth; and fire, the lightest element, moves away from the Earth. Because of their natural motions, earth and fire were known as extreme elements (elementa extrema), while water and air were termed middle elements (elementa media). Since all sublunary bodies are compounds of the four elements, a given body's weight, or tendency to move toward the center of the Earth, was thought to be determined by the relative amounts of each element that it contains. Some scholars believed that the weights of compounds of the elements, that is, the weight of every terrestrial body, could be understood in terms of ratios of the elements that composed the given body. Additionally, the tendency of each of the elements to move toward its natural place partially explains why bodies in the sublunary region were constantly in a state of generation and corruption. No compound of the elements can be eternal because of the natural tendency of its components to break apart and move in different directions. Meanwhile, the temporally finite persistence of a body was dependent on the organizing powers of its substantial form that unified a compound of the elements.

Secondary qualities other than heaviness and lightness were said to derive from the hot, the cold, the wet, and the dry. Secondary tangible qualities, such as fineness and coarseness or hardness and softness, stemmed directly from the prime qualities. For example, the dry causes hardness. Other sensible but not tangible secondary qualities, such as color and odor, were widely regarded as the result of local motions (motus locales), which in turn were caused by the power of the active qualities to assimilate and separate substances, or the natural motions inherent to each of the elements.

Applications of the Elements and Qualities

The qualities were prominent not only in matter theory but also in medieval understanding of *meteorology and medical theory. The four seasons could be characterized by combinations of the primary qualities, just as the elements could be. Furthermore, according to Aristotelian meteorology, two exhalations characterized by the prime qualities, one wet, the other hot and dry, occurred in cycles between the surface of the Earth and the sphere of Moon. These cyclic exhalations caused atmospheric changes. Perhaps more significantly, the qualities were seen to be essential for medical diagnoses and cures. Standard medical textbooks of the Middle Ages, such as the Canon of Avicenna (*Ibn Sina), introduced students to medical theory with discussions of the elements and qualities. These were seen as pertinent topics for medical students because they could be used to explain pharmaceuticals and other cures, such as baths and diets.

Under the standard Galenic view, the human body was thought to contain four humors: black bile, blood, phlegm, and yellow bile. Each of these humors was characterized by one passive and one active primary quality, as well as associated with a corresponding season. This theory holds that black bile is cold and dry; phlegm is cold and wet; blood is hot and wet; and, yellow bile warm and dry. Health was widely considered to be the balance of these humors, while disease resulted from the predominance of one or more the humors. Thus explanation of cures depended on identifying the primary qualities of the components of the regimen. If a patient was diagnosed to be excessively hot, a drug or some other cure with a cooling property might be prescribed. As a result, discussions of the elements and the primary qualities abound in medical commentaries on the Canon and other texts used for teaching medicine in medieval universities.

The universal nature of the elements and the prime qualities, their broad correspondence to everyday experience, and the authority of ancient and medieval texts ensured their place in medieval accounts of the sublunary world. The explanatory power of these simple bodies was particularly broad, and thus the success of this theory was due in part to its applicability to a wide range of phenomena and branches of learning. As a result it was only with great reluctance and much polemic that the scientific world sought a more pluralistic understanding of the material elements of the world in the seventeenth and eighteenth centuries.

See also **Aristotelianism; Experiment, experimenta;**

Medicine, practical; Medicine, theoretical; Weights and measures

Bibliography

Aristotle. *De generatione et corruptione*. Translated by C. J. F. Williams. Oxford: Clarendon Press, 1982.

Galen. "On Mixtures." In *Selected Works*. Translated by P. N. Singer. Oxford: Oxford University Press, 1997.

Lang, Helen S. *Aristotle's Physics and its Medieval Varieties*. Albany: SUNY Press, 1992.

Lang, Helen S. *The Order of Nature in Aristotle's Physics: Place and the Elements*. New York: Cambridge University Press, 1998.

Maier, Analiese. *On the Threshold of Exact Science*. Edited and Translated by Steven D. Sargent. Philadelphia: University of Pennsylvania Press, 1982.

McKeon, Richard P. "Medicine and Philosophy in the Eleventh and Twelfth Centuries: The Problem of the Elements." *The Thomist* (1961) 24: 75–120.

CRAIG MARTIN

ENCYCLOPEDIAS

During the thirteenth century several voluminous texts were written in Latin and vernacular languages in which their authors attempted to gather the knowledge of their time for non-specialist audiences. Although it is strictly anachronistic to describe such works as "encyclopedias"—the first recorded use of the term in English is dated 1525—these medieval works satisfy the definition: their contents are arranged under several rubrics and focus on various fields such as theology, astronomy, mathematics, biology, and even daily life.

Among the most influential encyclopedias of the Middle Ages are *De naturis rerum* by *Alexander Nequam (end of the twelfth century), *De natura rerum* by *Thomas of Cantimpre (c. 1200–c. 1280), *De proprietatibus rerum* by *Bartholomaeus Anglicus (thirteenth century), *Le livre du trésor* (The Book of the Treasure) by Brunetto Latini (c. 1220–c. 1294), and *Speculum maius* by *Vincent of Beauvais (c. 1199–c. 1265). (The last named work is divided in three *Specula*: *naturale*, *historiale*, and *doctrinale*.) All five of these texts are composed of a collection of topics, which are classified by chapters and books. The works deal mainly with the "things of nature" (*naturae res*) or the "nature of things" (*natura rerum*), in other words, with all the elements surrounding humans on Earth and in heaven.

Although there was a profusion of encyclopedias in the thirteenth century, the form is much older than that: the originator is widely held to be *Isidore of Seville (d. 636), with his *Etymologiae*, a work that took as one of its major references the *Historia naturalis* of Pliny the Elder (23–79 C.E.). Isidore was soon imitated by *Bede, the English author of a *De natura rerum*, and by the German abbot of Fulda, Rabanus Maurus (c. 776–856) in his *De rerum naturis*. Also classifiable as an encyclopedia is the *imago mundi*, a form of geographical text that described the inhabited areas of the world and built a discourse on other disciplines such as astronomy. Leading examples of *imagines mundi* were by Honorius (twelfth century; Latin) and Gossuin de Metz (thirteenth century; French). Similar, too, were didactic texts that took the form of dialogues between master and pupil—works such as those of Placides and Timéo or the *Livre de Sydrach* (late thirteenth century), in which there are several reflections on natural phenomena.

The Founder

Isidore of Seville's *Etymologiae* played a major role in the transmission of ancient culture. Its title comes from the belief—common in the Middle Ages—that words are inextricably linked with the objects they describe. Thus, the practice of etymology is regarded as the best way both to discover the true "nature of things" and to organize the various rubrics of the encyclopedia. As a consequence, the encyclopedic text is not merely a simple compilation: it is organized according to a method that may be termed "the encyclopedic transposition process." Such a process is based on the transposition of the "scholarly knowledge"—mainly provided by ancient Latin texts, the Bible, and the writings of the Fathers of Church—into a more accessible fund of information. The idea of encyclopedic transposition is set out in a passage in the *Etymologiae* in which Isidore clarifies his method. According to him, the compiler is like an alchemist who combines various substances, bringing together the elements, the bonds, and the catalysts that produce, at the end of the process, a new form of matter.

Through the twenty books of the *Etymologiae*, Isidore influenced the whole medieval encyclopedic genre, especially through the coherence of his approach, which tends to limit references to the supernatural. The seven liberal arts occupied the main place in Isidore's text. They were put in an order that would be influential throughout the Middle Ages: grammar, rhetoric, dialectic, *arithmetic, geometry, music, and astronomy/*astrology. Moreover, the *Etymologiae* constitutes a turning point in the history of the encyclopedic style by gathering information on the things of nature without reference to scholarly disciplines. These objects of knowledge can be divided into three categories as they appear in Isidore's work: humans, lower nature (divided into three fundamental types: animals, plants, and minerals), and objects transformed by human activity (thus opening the path to mechanical arts). Later encyclopedists who worked on the things of nature were influenced by Isidore's ideas. They went further and apprehended nature in a more naturalistic way. This process was facilitated at the end of the twelfth century by the diffusion among encyclopedists of the works of Aristotle and various Arabic authors on the philosophy of nature.

The Golden Age of the Encyclopedic Genre

What is known as "medieval encyclopedism" is linked principally to the thirteenth century, during which most of the major works in the genre were written. With the growth of cities, the creation of *universities, the rise of urban intellectuals and an audience increasingly eager for knowledge but without a grounding in Aristotle and scholastic techniques, new cultural expectations appeared. In addition, following the Arabic and Latin translations of the twelfth century that brought new scientific learning to the Latin West, the general need for knowledge seemed to expand, and there was a consequent increase in the number of popular works. However, encyclopedists remained faithful to Isidore's tradition: etymology was still frequently used to introduce a topic, and references to the originator himself ("*ut dixit Isidorus*") remained numerous in later works. The modern study of encyclopedic texts written during this productive period involves not only reference to the works themselves but also consideration of what a medieval encyclopedia could really be.

It is also instructive to examine the words used by medieval authors to define what are now known as "encyclopedias." Two terms are recurrent: "*speculum*" and "*natura rerum*" or its equivalents. The first, systematically used by Vincent of Beauvais and often appearing in the prologues of encyclopedias, indicates that the encyclopedia is a book that reflects nature, in the manner of a mirror. In medieval representations, "mirror" also refers to the learning process: through it readers discover how to apprehend the things of nature and their wonders. They can then understand the will and power of God.

Miniature showing construction of a tower from the early encyclopedic work *The Sacred and Profane* in the Codex of Monte Cassino (1023). (Corbis/Bettmann)

Moreover, in the prologue, authors normally state their intention of dealing with the things of nature, i.e., the main elements of Creation. Lists compiled by encyclopedists show that their works aim at building an overview of these elements. In other words, they show a propensity to compose a *summa* (general survey).

In the *Livre du Trésor*, Brunetto Latini states that he has tried to "briefly write a *Summa*." The two terms—"briefly" and "*summa*"—may seem contradictory. However, they do not appear paradoxical to the author, who proceeds to explain his method of building a *summa* from collected data. The double reference to brevity and *summa* appears in the prologue of most medieval encyclopedias and seems to have been regarded as a necessary part of the exordium. Thus, the fact that such texts are often voluminous is not contradictory. For medieval encyclopedists, brevity was not necessarily the same as concision: their method was to compile the most relevant and important parts of the work of other philosophers; their effectiveness was measured by their choice of what to include, not by the number of words in the finished product.

Organization of Knowledge

In order to compile and arrange a large amount of data, encyclopedists had to structure their discourse. This was one of the fundamental premises of encyclopedic writing. Another was that the text was not written only to be consulted: according to Gossuin de Metz in his *Image du monde*, the work, in order to be effective, had to be read as a whole.

But a more modern idea of consultation progressively appears. It is linked with the emergence of rubrics classified by alphabetical order, then with the use of indexes (in, for example, the work of Bartholomaeus Anglicus and Vincent of Beauvais). However, this alphabetical order was never complete, and generally took the form of a "system of the world." For example, Vincent of Beauvais tried to build his text according to the structure of the Bible; Bartholomaeus Anglicus attempted to make his work conform to a neo-Platonic hierarchy of creatures, from God to matter; Brunetto Latini followed a Stoic division of sciences. Of course, considering the abundance of information, no encyclopedist managed to build a complete classification. One sees above all various kinds of juxtapositions, often marked by inconsistencies. These inconsistencies are all the more obvious as encyclopedists did not analyse their sources: they were then bound to repeat what earlier authors had said, sometimes in a contradictory way.

One can note in prologues the recurrence of the terms "brief *summa*," "to compile," "compilation," and "compendium." Most of the time, the encyclopedist specifies that he does not use his own knowledge, except to structure discourses extracted from the work of authorities. Consequently, a medieval equivalent for "encyclopaedia" could be "brief *summa*." A *summa* is a kind of aggregate of the things of nature, i.e., a mirror-book of nature. In that respect, nature is itself a mirror of

God. Each *summa* is brief because it is based on sources from which the encyclopedist extracts some data. Moreover, brevity implies a structure: the encyclopedist methodically organizes the philosophers' discourses.

The medieval encyclopedia is thus a literary genre between the *accessus* and the account of a synthetic vision of the Creation. Throughout prologues, the numerous quotations from the authorities, whose names and/or works are specified, reveal some of the conscious process by which scholarly knowledge was rendered into encyclopedic knowledge. The encyclopedist writes for an audience that has little time to spare, such as the mighty or people who lack the knowledge to read the scholarly works on which his work is based. He considers himself a teacher aiming at a large audience. Among his goals are to improve the reader's understanding of the Bible; to help preachers and train princes; to encourage people to study and then improve their moral standards; and to facilitate the reading of more technical texts.

Many medieval encyclopedias were highly successful. For example, the *De proprietatibus rerum* was translated into five languages beginning in the fourteenth century. The texts survive in many manuscripts of this period, and from the fifteenth century to the eighteenth century many encyclopedias also appeared in several editions. Numerous marginalia in the manuscripts and borrowings from medieval encyclopedias by many authors show that these texts were frequently consulted. Library catalogues also contain many references to these works. Thus it is clear that medieval encyclopedias played a major role in the culture of the Middle Ages and in the diffusion of scientific knowledge among a large audience.

See also **Aristotelianism; Astronomy, Latin; Bestiaries; Herbals; Lapidaries; Music theory; Natural history; Quadrivium; Vocabulary**

Bibliography

Binkley, P., ed. *Premodern Encyclopaedic Texts*. Leiden: E.J. Brill, 1997.

Lusignan, S., M. Paulmier-Foucart and A. Nadeau, eds. *Vincent de Beauvais. Intentions et réceptions d'une œuvre encyclopédique au Moyen Âge*. Paris: Vrin, 1990.

Lusignan, S and M. Paulmier-Foucart, eds. *Lector et compilator, Vincent de Beauvais, frère prêcheur. Un intellectuel et son milieu au XIIIe siècle*. Grâne, France: Créaphis, 1997.

Ribémont, B. *De natura rerum. Études des encyclopédies du Moyen Âge*. Orléans: Paradigme, 1995.

———. *Le Livre des propriétés des choses, une encyclopédie au XIVe siècle*. Paris: Stock, 1999.

———. *Les Origines des encyclopédies médiévales. D'Isidore de Séville aux Carolingiens*. Paris: Champion, Bibliothèque du Moyen Age, 2001.

———. *Littérature et encyclopédies du Moyen Âge*. Orléans: Paradigme, coll. Medievalia, 2002.

———. *La "renaissance" du XIIe siècle et l'encyclopédisme*. [Essais sur le Moyen Age 27] Paris, France: Champion, 2002.

Seymour, M.C. *Bartholomaeus Anglicus and his Encyclopedia*. London: Variorum, 1992.

B. RIBÉMONT

ERIUGENA, JOHN SCOTTUS

The Irish-born Johannes Eriugena—his seventeenth-century editor Thomas Gale named him "Johannes Scotus Erigena"—was "master" (*magister*) of the cathedral school at Laon and a scholar at the court of King Charles the Bald of France. In 850–851, Bishop Pardulus of Laon refers to "a certain Irishman, named Johannes, who is at the palace of the king." The appelation "*scottus*" or "*scotigena*" means "Irish"; the Vatican Librarian Anastasius, for instance, refers to him as "Joannes Scotigena." The name "Eriugena" ("Irish born")—corrupted to "Erigena" in twelfth-century catalogues—was a pen-name used to sign his translation of Pseudo-Dionysius.

Eriugena was probably born before 800 and died sometime around 877. Recognized for his erudition, he had a wide knowledge of Latin Christian sources: St. Augustine, *Martianus Capella, *Macrobius, Cassiodorus, *Bede, *Isidore of Seville, Ambrose, Hilary of Poitiers, and Jerome. He refers occasionally to *Boethius (*Opuscula sacra*) and possibly knew his *Consolation of Philosophy* (glosses, possibly in his hand, survive). Two partial commentaries, *Annotationes in Marcianum* (c. 840–c. 850), on Martianus' liberal arts handbook *De nuptiis Philologiae et Mercurii* (*The Marriage of Philolology and Mercury*) survive. Pierre Duhem thought that Eriugena, in Book Seven of this Commentary, offers a version of the non-Ptolemaic system subsequently associated with Tycho Brahe. In fact, Eriugena is accurately reporting Martianus' version of Heraclidus of Pontus' theory, but remarkably places Mars and Jupiter also in orbit around the Sun.

In the late 840s Eriugena was commissioned by two bishops to refute a treatise by a Saxon monk, Gottschalk (806–868), who interpreted St. Augustine as teaching a "twofold" or "twin predestination" (*gemina praedestinatio*) of the elect to heaven and of the damned to hell, based on the opinion of Isidore of Seville, *Sententiae* II, 6, I. Eriugena's *De divina praedestinatione* (*On Divine Predestination*, c. 851) rebuts Gottschalk, rejecting any predestination toward evil by appealing to God's unity, transcendence and goodness. This treatise proceeds through a rationalistic, dialectical analysis of key theological concepts, relying on argument rather than Scripture (something criticized by contemporaries, see PL CXV 1294a). Eriugena holds that "true philosophy is true religion and conversely" (following Augustine, *De uera religione* 5, 8).

In *De divina praedestinatione* Eriugena maintains that God wants all humans to be saved and does not predestine souls to damnation. Humans damn themselves through their own free choices: "Sin, death, unhappiness are not from God." God is outside time and cannot be said to foreknow or predestine. Eriugena locates Gottschalk's errors as midway between the Pelagian heresy that downplays divine grace, and the opposing heresy that denies human freedom. In turn Eriugena himself, due to his emphasis on free will, was accused of "Origenism" and "Pelagianism." Eriugena's treatise was condemned at the councils of Valence (855) and Langres (859): one reason for the verdict on the work was its reliance on "dialectic" (*dialectica*).

Around 860, Eriugena translated the works of (Pseudo-) Dionysius the Areopagite—his *Divine Names*, *Mystical Theology*, *Celestial Hierarchy*, and *Ecclesiastical Hierarchy*. He subsequently wrote a long commentary, *Expositiones in hierarchiam coelestem*, on the *Celestial Hierarchy*. In his *Divine Names*, Dionysius draws on Proclus' *Commentary on the Parmenides* to argue that affirmations are less worthy than negations in referring to entities that transcend being, since negations strip something away whereas affirmations involve "possession of form." Negations concerning God (such as, for example, "God is not good") are "more true" than affirmations (such as "God is good"). Divine names apply metaphorically and not literally to God, who is "beyond all that is." Pseudo-Dionysius maintains that God is not known directly except through *theophaniai*, divine appearances (*Divine Names*, ch. 7, PG III 869c-d). Eriugena also translated and commented on the work of Maximus Confessor, giving him access to a rich Greek Christian anthropology. These translations gave him both a familiarity with and a preference for the Eastern Fathers.

Eriugena's dialogue, *Periphyseon* or *De divisione naturae* (*On the Division of Nature*), enthusiastically adopts the Areopagite's main ideas, chiefly, his distinction between affirmative (*kataphatic*) and negative (*apophatic*) theology. He even extends the dialectic of affirmation and negation beyond theology to statements about human nature ("man is not an animal" is more true than "man is an animal"). Overall his outlook is rationalistic; true philosophy is true reason (*vera ratio*); authority is but right reason (*Periphyseon*, I.511b). One should introduce the "opinions of the holy Fathers" only where "the gravest necessity requires that human reason be supported for the sake of those who, being untrained in it, are more amenable to authority than reason" (*Periphyseon* IV.781c-d).

Eriugena's cosmology includes original views on creation, matter, space, and time, corporeal body, the nature of paradise and hell, and so on. For example, heaven and hell are not places. Paradise is perfect human nature (*Periphyseon* IV.840a), whereas souls trapped in their own fantasies are in "hell." He defines nature (*natura*) very broadly as the "totality of all things" including both beings and non-beings, both God and creation. All things emerge from and return to the one God, Who is beyond being and non-being. God "creates Himself by manifesting Himself in theophanies" (*Periphyseon* I.446d). This self-manifestation (I.455b) is identical with the speaking of the Word and the creation of all other things, since all things are contained in the Word. The Word contains the divine Ideas or "primary causes" (*causae primordiales*) of all creation, which proceed into their created effects. The timeless primordial causes are contrasted with the "mutable and imperfect and as yet formless procession of this sensible world" (*Periphyseon* II.549b).

Four Divisions of Divine Nature

Eriugena divides the divine nature into four "divisions" (*divisiones*), or "species" or "forms," namely:
nature which creates and is not created,
nature which creates and is created,
nature which is created and does not create, and
nature which is neither created nor creates.

God is present in all four divisions. The outgoing of all things in creation is balanced by their "return" (*epistrophe*, *reditus*, *reversio*) to God. There is a general return of all things to God. Corporeal things will return to their incorporeal causes, the temporal to the eternal, the finite will be absorbed in the infinite. The human mind will achieve reunification with the divine, and then the corporeal, temporal, material world will become essentially incorporeal, timeless and intellectual. The elect achieve "deification" (*deificatio*, *theosis*), merging with God as lights blend into the one light, as voices blend in the choir, as a droplet of water merges with the stream. God shall be all in all (*omnia in omnibus*, V 935c).

Eriugena controversially claims that God and the creature are ultimately "one and the same" (*Periphyseon*, III.678c), and that God is the "essence of all things" (*essentia omnium*) or "form of all things" (*forma omnium*), expressions that led to the accusation of pantheism. However, Eriugena also stresses the divine transcendence: God is the non-being above being as well as the principle or form of all things.

Eriugena's *Periphyseon* had influence in the schools of Laon, Auxerre, and Corbie, and was popular in the twelfth century, especially when circulated in the "edition" of William of Malmesbury and in the paraphrase, *Clavis physicae*, of Honorius Augustodunensis. His version of Dionysius was also influential in the twelfth and thirteenth centuries. Linked with two heretical Paris theologians, David of Dinant and Amaury of Bène, *Periphyseon* was condemned in 1210 and 1225. Meister Eckhart of Hochheim (c. 1260–c. 1328) and Nicholas of Cusa (1401–1464) were both familiar with the *Periphyseon*.

See also **God in Christianity; Nature: the structure of the physical world**

Bibliography

Primary Sources

Barbet, Jeanne. *Iohannis Scoti Eriugenae Expositiones in Ierarchiam coelestem*, Corpus Christianorum. Continuatio Mediaevalis XXI, Turnhout: Brepols, 1975.

Cappuyns, Maiul. Le *De imagine de Grégoire de Nysse traduit par Jean Scot Erigène*. *Recherches de théologie ancienne et médiévale* (1965) 32: 205–262.

Contreni, John J. and Pádraig P. Ó Néill. *Glossae Divinae Historiae. The Biblical Glosses of John Scottus Eriugena*. Firenze: Sismel–Edizioni del Galluzo, 1997.

Floss, H.-J., ed. *Johannis Scoti Opera quae supersunt Omnia*. Patrologia Latina CXXII. Paris, 1853.

Gale, Thomas. *Joannis Scoti Erigenae De Divisione Naturae Libri Quinque Diu Desiderati. Accedit Appendix ex Ambiguis S. Maximi Graece et Latine*. Oxford: Sheldonian Theatre, 1681.

Jeauneau, Édouard. *Jean Scot: Commentaire sur l'Evangile de Jean.* Sources Chrétiennes 180. Paris: Cerf, 1972.

———. *Jean Scot: L'Homélie sur le Prologue de Jean.* Sources Chrétiennes 151. Paris: Editions du Cerf, 1969.

———, ed. *Maximi Confessoris Ambigua ad Iohannem iuxta Iohannis Scotti Eriugenae latinam interpretationem.* Corpus Christianorum Series Graeca, 18. Turnout/Leuven: Brepols/Leuven University Press, 1988.

———, ed. *Iohannis Scotti seu Eriugenae Periphyseon, liber primus.* Corpus Christianorum Continuatio Medievalis 161. Turnhout: Brepols, 1996.

———, ed. *Iohannis Scotti seu Eriugenae Periphyseon, liber secundus.* Corpus Christianorum Continuatio Medievalis 162. Turnhout: Brepols, 1997.

———, ed. *Iohannis Scotti seu Eriugenae Periphyseon, liber tertius.* Corpus Christianorum Continuatio Medievalis 163. Turnhout: Brepols, 1999.

———, with the assistance of Mark A. Zier, eds. *Iohannis Scotti Eriugenae Periphyseon (De Divisione Naturae) Liber Quartus.* English Translation by John J. O'Meara and I.P. Sheldon-Williams, Scriptores Latini Hiberniae Volume XIII. Dublin: Dublin Institute for Advanced Studies, 1995.

Laga, Carl and Carlos Steel, eds. *Maximi Confessoris Quaestiones ad Thalassium II. Q. LVI-LXV una cum latina interpretatione Iohannies Scotti Eriugenae.* Corpus Christianorum Series Graeca, 22. Turnhout/Leuven: Brepols/Leuven University Press, 1990.

Lutz, Cora, ed. *Iohannis Scotti Annotationes in Marcianum.* Cambridge, MA: Medieval Academy of America, 1939.

Madec, Goulven, ed. *Iohannis Scotti de divina praedestinatione.* Turnhout: Brepols, 1978.

Sheldon-Williams, I.-P. *Iohannis Scotti Eriugenae Periphyseon.* Volumes I–III, Dublin: Institute for Advanced Studies, 1968, 1972, and 1981.

Secondary Sources

Allard, Guy, ed. *Jean Scot écrivain.* Montréal: Bellarmin, 1986.

Beierwaltes, Werner. *Eriugena. Grundzüge seines Denkens.* Frankfurt am Main: Vittorio Klostermann, 1994.

———, ed. *Eriugena Redivivus. Zur Wirkungsgeschichte seines Denkens im Mittelalter und im Übergang zur Neuzeit.* Heidelberg: Carl Winter Universitätsverlag, 1987.

———, ed. *Begriff und Metapher. Sprachform des Denkens bei Eriugena.* Heidelberg: Carl Winter Universitätsverlag, 1990.

———, ed. *Eriugena. Studien zu seinen Quellen. Vorträge der III. Internationalen Eriugena-Colloquiums, Freiburg im Breisgau, 27.-30. August 1979.* Heidelberg: Carl Winter Universitätsverlag, 1980.

Bett, Henry. *Johannes Scotus Erigena: A Study in Medieval Philosophy.* New York: Cambridge University Press, 1925.

Brennan, Mary. *A Guide to Eriugenian Studies. A Survey of Publications 1930–87.* Paris: Editions du Cerf, 1989.

———. A Bibliography of Publications in the Field of Eriugena Studies 1800–1975. *Studi Medievali* (1977) ser. 3a, 28: 401–447.

———. Materials for the Biography of Johannes Scottus Eriugena. *Studi Medievali* (1986), ser. 3a, 27: 413–460.

Brennan, Mary, tr. *John Scottus Eriugena. Treatise on Divine Predestination,* with an Introduction by Avital Wohlman, Notre Dame: University of Notre Dame Press, 1998.

Cappuyns, Maiul. *Jean Scot Erigène: sa vie, son oeuvre, sa pensée.* Louvain: Abbaye de Mont César, 1933.

Carabine, Deirdre. *John Scottus Eriugena.* Oxford: Oxford University Press, 2000.

Gardner, Alice. *Studies in John the Scot: A Philosopher of the Dark Ages.* London: Oxford University Press, 1900.

Gersh, Stephen. *From Iamblichus to Eriugena.* Leiden. E.J. Brill, 1978.

Huber, Johannes. *Johannes Scotus Erigena: Ein Beitrag zur Geschichte der Philosophie und Theologie im Mittelalter (1861).* Hildesheim: Olms, 1960.

Jeauneau, Édouard. *Études érigéniennes.* Paris: Études Augustiniennes, 1987.

Leonardi, Claudio and E. Mesesto, eds. *Giovanni Scoto nel suo tempo: L'organizzazione del sapere in età carolingia.* Spoleto: Centro Italiano di Studi sull'Alto Medioevo, 1989.

Madec, Goulven. *Jean Scot et ses auteurs. Annotations érigéniennes.* Paris: Études Augustiniennes, 1988.

Marenbon, John. *From the Circle of Alcuin to the School of Auxerre: Logic, Theology and Philosophy in the Early Middle Ages.* New York: Cambridge University Press, 1981.

McEvoy, James J. and Michael Dunne, eds. *History and Eschatology in John Scottus Eriugena and His Time. Proceedings of the Tenth International Conference of the Society for the Promotion of Eriugena Studies, Maynooth and Dublin, August 16-20, 2000.* Leuven: Leuven University Press, 2002.

McGinn, Bernard and Willemien Otten, eds. *Eriugena. East and West.* Notre Dame: Notre Dame University Press, 1994.

Moran, Dermot. *The Philosophy of John Scottus Eriugena. A Study of Idealism in the Middle Ages.* New York: Cambridge University Press, 1989.

———. Pantheism from John Scottus Eriugena to Nicholas of Cusa. *American Catholic Philosophical Quarterly* 1990, Vol. LXIV No. 1 (Winter): 131-152.

———. "Time, Space and Matter in the Periphyseon: an Examination of Eriugena's Understanding of the Physical World." In *At the Heart of the Real,* edited by F. O'Rourke. Dublin: Irish Academic Press, 1992.

———. "Origen and Eriugena: Aspects of Christian Gnosis." In *The Relationship Between Neoplatonism and Christianity,* edited by T. Finan and V. Twomey. Dublin: Four Courts Press, 1992.

———. "Eriugena's Theory of Language in the *Periphyseon*: Explorations in the Neoplatonic Tradition." In *Ireland and Europe in the Early Middle Ages IV. Language and Learning,* edited by Próinséas Ní Chatháin and Michael Richter. Frankfurt: Klett-Cotta, 1996, 240–260.

———. Idealism in Medieval Philosophy: The Case of Johannes Scottus Eriugena. *Medieval Philosophy and Theology* (1999) 8: 53–82.

O'Meara, John J. *Eriugena.* Cork: Mercier Press, 1988.

Otten, Willemien. *The Anthropology of Johannes Scottus Eriugena.* Leiden: E.J. Brill, 1991.

——— and Ludwig Bieler, eds. *The Mind of Eriugena.* Dublin: Irish University Press, 1973.

Riccati, C. *Processio et explicatio: La Doctrine de la création chez Jean Scot et Nicolas de Cues.* Naples: Bibliopolis, 1983.

Rudnick, Ulrich. *Das System des Johannes Scottus Eriugena. Eine theologisch-philosophische Studie zu seinem Werk.* Frankfurt am Main: Peter Lang, 1990.

Schrimpf, Gangolf. *Das Werk des Johannes Scottus Eriugena im Rahmen des Wissenschaftsverständnisses seiner Zeit. Eine Hinführung zu Periphyseon.* Münster: Beiträge zur Geschichte der Philosophie und Theologie des Mittelalters, 1982.

Sheldon-Williams, I.-P. "The Greek Platonist Tradition from the Cappadocians to Maximus and Eriugena." In *The Cambridge History of Later Greek and Early Medieval*

Thought, edited by A.H. Armstrong. New York: Cambridge University Press, 1970.

Sheldon-Williams, I.-P. and J.J. O'Meara, tr. *Eriugena. Periphyseon (The Division of Nature)*. Montreal/Paris: Bellarmin, 1987.

Uhlfelder, Myra and J. Potter, tr. *John the Scot. Periphyseon. On the Division of Nature*. Indianapolis: Bobbs-Merrill, 1976.

Van Riel, Gerd, Carlos Steel and James J. McEvoy, eds. *Iohannes Scottus Eriugena. The Bible and Hermeneutics. Proceedings of the Ninth International Conference of the Society for the Promotion of Eriugena Studies, held at Leuven and Louvain-La-Neuve, June 7–10, 1995*. Leuven: Leuven University Press, 1996.

DERMOT MORAN

EUCLID

Euclid lived around 300 B.C.E. in Alexandria. He authored the most influential textbook in the history of mathematics, the *Elements*. Additionally, he wrote at least five other geometrical works (*Data, Porisma, On Divisions, Conics, Plane loci, Pseudaria*), one text on astronomy (*Phainomena*), an influential text on optics (*Optics*) and a work on theoretical music (*Elements of Music*). Others texts on mechanics and on mirrors ascribed to him are not believed to be his works.

Certain axioms, postulates, definitions and theorems of the *Elements* have been contested since antiquity. During the greater part of the twentieth century, it was believed that Heiberg had successfully established the genuine Euclidean text in a critical edition. This belief was questioned at the end of the century by the works of Knorr, Vitrac, Djebbar, and Rommevaux. Similar shifts of understanding and approach occurred in the course of the century with regard to the medieval transmission of Euclid's *Elements*. This transmission embraces translations into Latin, Arabic, Syriac, and Hebrew either from Greek or from Arabic texts. A further strand of transmission, often ignored, comprises the translation from Arabic into Persian. The multiplicity of texts translated from one language into the other and transferred from one scholarly culture to the other makes the study of the history of Euclid's *Elements* one of the most difficult, but also most fascinating, subjects in textual history of medieval mathematics.

The first interest in the text is documented at the beginning of the Abbasid dynasty (750–1258), when caliph al-Mansur (r. 754–775) asked for a Greek manuscript. Yahya ibn Khalid (d. 805), vizier of al-Mansur's grandson Harun al-Rashid (r. 786–809), sponsored the first known Arabic translation by al-Hajjaj ibn Yusuf ibn Matar (d. after 825). No trace of this translation seems to be preserved. During the reign of Harun's second son, al-Ma'mun (r. 813–833), al-Hajjaj produced a second version, the character of which is highly disputed. While Arabic historical sources imply that this second version was a new translation, current research sees it more as a substantially revised edition. Fragments of this version or of editions based on it are extant in at least four different groups in Arabic and Latin, but the relationship between these four groups is far from being firmly established.

The second major textual transmission of the *Elements* had its start in the last third of the ninth century, when Ishaq ibn Hunayn (830–911) translated in Baghdad a different Greek version. This translation was edited and modified by his colleague *Thabit ibn Qurra (d. 901). Ishaq's translation is apparently lost except for a very small number of fragments. The extant manuscripts that are acknowledged as representing the two translation efforts contain highly mixed texts with substantial differences in some books. There is no agreement among historians as to what relationship exists between these manuscripts and the three scholars of the ninth century.

Parallel to the efforts of translating, scholars began in the early ninth century to edit the translated text according to either philosophical or mathematical priorities. Almost all evidence for this work seems to be lost except for small fragments of *al-Kindi (d. c. 870) and al-'Abbas b. Sa'id al-Jawhari (d. c. 860). The most important versions among those extant are the editions compiled by *Ibn Sina (d. 1037), Athir al-Din al-Abhari (d. 1263), Mu'ayyad al-Din al-'Urdi (d. c. 1266), Muhyi'l-Din al-Maghribi (d. c. 1290), *Nasir al-Din al-Tusi (1201–1274), and an anonymous version printed in Rome in 1594. The most influential of these revised editions was the one composed by al-Tusi. As pointed out recently by De Young, Tusi's text indicates that until the thirteenth century both major Arabic traditions (Hajjaj and Ishaq-Thabit) were used by scholars across the Muslim world. After the thirteenth century, they were replaced by al-Tusi's edition.

Other works on Euclid's *Elements* aimed to solve doubts, fill lacunae or add variants as well as new aspects. The most important authors of these kinds of commentaries were Abu'l-'Abbas al-Fadl al-Nayrizi (d. c. 922), Abu Sahl al-Kuhi (fourth/eleventh century), Ahmad ibn Muhammad al-Sijzi (d. c. 1025), *Ibn al-Haytham (d. c. 1041), *'Umar al-Khayyam (1048–1131), Muhyi'l-Din al-Maghribi (c. 1220–c. 1283), and Shams al-Din al-Khafri (d. 1550).

Translations of the *Elements*

Only a few Syriac texts are extant that testify to an interest in Euclid's work among Nestorian and Jacobite Christians. None is known for the period before 700. An undated fragment of Book I was edited in 1924. Historians continue to debate about the language from which it was translated (Greek or Arabic) and about its relationship to the Arabic and Arabic-Latin transmission. The second known Syriac extract of the *Elements* came from the pen of the Jacobite patriarch Abu'l-Faraj ibn al-'Ibri (1226–1286). It is related to the Arabic editions of the thirteenth century, but the precise character of this relationship has yet to be established.

The most influential translation from Greek into Latin before 1200 was made by *Boethius (c. 480–524/5) in c. 500. The four fragments that survive from this translation either come from northeast France (Corbie) or from

Lorraine. Each of them was transmitted within another text or set of texts: B(Ma) belongs to Cassidorus' *Institutiones*; B(Mb) belongs to *Corpus Agrimensorum*; B(Mc) belongs to *Geometria I*; B(Md) belongs to *Geometria II*. Folkerts reconstructed from the last named Boethius' original translation of books I–IV and of the definitions of Book V.

In the twelfth century, a new Latin translation of the *Elements* was made from a Greek text in Southern Italy or Sicily. Folkerts proposed *Leonardo Fibonacci (1170?–1250?) as the compiler of the present form of the text, which is not identical with the original translation. Furthermore, at least three other Latin translations from Arabic have been made by *Adelard of Bath (c. 1116–1142), *Hermann of Carinthia (c. 1110–1154 or 1160) and *Gerard of Cremona (c. 1114–1187). The relationship between these translations and Arabic versions of the *Elements* has been repeatedly debated, but no general consensus could be reached.

Robert of Chester (fl. 1136–1157) was the compiler of an edition of the *Elements* (previously called *Adelard II*) that combined extracts from Adelard of Bath's and Hermann of Carinthia's translations with independent work, partially based on additional Arabic manuscripts. This edition dominated the Latin transmission until the mid-thirteenth century. Four other compilations that mix various textual forms of the *Elements* such as Boethius, Robert of Chester and unidentified Arabic material originated in the course of the twelfth century—the *Liber Ysagogarum Alchorismi* (chapter on geometry in Book IV), the version of an anonymous compiler from northern Germany, the version of an anonymous compiler possibly linked to Chartres and the edition, previously known as *Adelard III*, but identified by Knorr as the work of an Englishman, John of Tynemouth (twelfth/thirteenth century?).

Latin scholars continued to edit, rework, and comment on the *Elements* in the following two and a half centuries before the *editio princeps* of the Greek text appeared in 1533. The version that dominated this period was produced by *Campanus de Novara (c. 1210–1296) in the 1350s. He adopted most of the enunciations from Robert, but provided his own proofs. Campanus had didactic interests and hence strove to make the text self-contained. The result became one of the most important books in the curriculum of the medieval university. Other important commentaries on or editions of (parts of) the *Elements* were composed by *Albertus Magnus (c. 1206–1280), *Roger Bacon (1214–1294) and *Nicole Oresme (c. 1323–1382).

Additionally to the *Elements*, Gerard of Cremona translated three Arabic commentaries on this work—the Arabic translation of Pappus of Alexandria's (fl. 300) commentary on Book X, al-Nayrizi's comments on and additions to Euclid's text (extant only Book I–Book VII, definitions) and an anonymous Arabic commentary on Book X.

The Hebrew transmission of the *Elements* consists of texts derived from the Ishaq–Thabit tradition and some fragments affiliated to the Hajjaj tradition. The main translators were Moses ibn Tibbon (*Profatius Judaeus) and Jacob ibn Makhir (1236?–1305?). Additionally, Hebrew scholars composed about fifteen commentaries and adaptations based on Arabic editions. An anonymous scholar translated the enunciations of Adelard of Bath's Arabic-Latin translation to which he added the diagrams. A Hebrew compilation, from which Book I and II are extant, quotes from Campanus' edition. According to Lévy, it may have been the work of Moses Provensali (fl. c. 1550).

The first Persian texts related to the *Elements* were written in the late tenth and early eleventh centuries. They are mainly chapters on geometry in encyclopedias based on earlier Arabic encyclopedias. The earliest Persian summary of an Arabic edition of the *Elements* was also produced in this period. The first known Persian translation of the entire work is found in Qutb al-Din al-Shirazi's encyclopedia *Durrat al-taj li-ghurrat al-Dibaj*, written in 1282. It is related to al-Tusi's Arabic edition, but the character of the relationship needs yet to be established. Until the nineteenth century, at least fourteen other Persian works on all or parts of the *Elements* appeared, among them at least three new translations.

Euclid's Other Works

The second most influential Euclidean work within Islamic societies was the *Data*. It was used by scholars as a guidebook for approaching and solving geometrical problems. Included in the so-called *Middle Books*, which had to be studied after the *Elements* and before Ptolemy's *Almagest*, it became available for mathematical training in the context of the *madrasa*, although it was not taken up in each and every one of them. Three Arabic translations of the *Data* are known and possibly extant. One was made in the circle of al-Kindi. The other two may have been the work of al-Hajjaj ibn Yusuf ibn Matar and Hunayn ibn Ishaq. One Arabic version of the *Data* was translated into Latin by Gerard of Cremona. *On Divisions* is extant in Arabic fragments in works by al-Sijzi and Abu'l-Wafa' al-Buzjani (940–998) and in an anonymous compilation. Latin quotations come from this background rather than from a direct knowledge of the Euclidean text. Traces of the *Porisms* are found in the anonymous Arabic translation *Book of Assumptions* of a lost Greek work by an unidentified author transliterated in Arabic as *Aqatun* and in works by al-Sijzi and Ibrahim ibn Sinan (908–946).

Euclid's *Optics*, which like the *Elements* has a complex textual history, was translated in one of its versions into Arabic by Hiliya ibn Sarjun (fl. early ninth century?). The author of the second Arabic version is unknown. The textual transmission included a substantial transformation of its theoretical content. It involved al-Kindi, who compiled an edition of the text as well as other treatises on Euclidean and Pseudo-Euclidean optical writings. As in the case of the *Elements* and the *Data*, al-Tusi reedited the *Optics*. Parallel to al-Tusi, Ibn Abi Jarada (c. 1277) composed a paraphrase. The Latin transmission of the *Optics* is also fairly diverse. Three Arabic-Latin versions and a Greek-Latin version are known to exist. They were studied by Catholic scholars such as *Roger Bacon, *John Pecham, and *Witelo. The Hebrew and the Persian transmission of the work did not yet attract much attention.

Ancient sources know nothing about two texts on mechanics ascribed in Arabic sources to Euclid—the *Maqala fi'l-mizan* (*Treatise on the Balance*) and *Kitab fi'l-thiql wa'l-khiffa* (*Book on Heaviness and Lightness*); the latter was edited by Thabit ibn Qurra; the translator or editor of the former is unknown. The axiomatic and deductive structure situates the two texts clearly in a Euclidean framework. Bulmer-Thomas proposed to regard them as parts of one single larger Greek text, now lost. Several scholars from Islamic societies between the ninth and thirteenth centuries contributed to a new science of mechanics by merging the content and methodology of the Pseudo-Euclidean texts into the dynamic tradition of the Pseudo-Aristotelian *Problemata Mechanica* to which they added concepts and methods taken from the works of *Archimedes (c. 287–212 B.C.E.). On this basis, according to Abattouy, Muzaffar ibn Isma'il al-Isfizari (fl. 1048–1116) achieved a unified theory of the balance. The second Pseudo-Euclidean text plus several Arabic texts on mechanics were translated by Gerard of Cremona and other scholars into Latin and provided the basis for the works of *Jordanus de Nemore (fl. c. 1220) and others in Europe.

See also **Abraham bar Hiyya; Algebra; Aristotelianism; Optics and catoptrics; Quadrivium; Uqlidisi, Al-; Weights, Science of**

Bibliography

Primary Sources
Arnzen, Rüdiger. *Abu l-'Abbas an-Nayrizis Exzerpte aus (Ps.-?) Simplicius' Kommentar zu den Definitionen, Postulaten und Axiomen in Euclids Elementa I. Eingeleitet, ediert und mit arabischen und lateinischen Glossaren versehen.* Köln, Essen: Arnzen, 2002.
Busard, H.L.L. *The Translation of the Elements of Euclid from the Arabic into Latin by Hermann of Carinthia (?): books I-VI, Janus,* (1967) 54: 1–140, and published separately (Leiden: E. J. Brill, 1968); books VII-IX, *Janus,* (1972) 59: 125–187; books VII–XII (Amsterdam: Mathematisch Centrum, 1977).
———. *The First Latin Translation of Euclid's Elements Commonly Ascribed to Adelard of Bath.* Toronto: Pontifical Institute of Mediaeval Studies, 1983.
———. *The Latin Translation of the Arabic Version of Euclid's Elements Commonly Ascribed to Gerard of Cremona.* Leiden: New Rhine Publishers, 1983.
———. *The Mediaeval Latin Translation of Euclid's Elements Made Directly from the Greek.* Stuttgart: Franz Steiner, 1987.
———. Ein mittelalterlicher Euklid-Kommentar, der Roger Bacon zugeschrieben werden kann. *Archives Internationales d'Histoire des Sciences* (1974) 24: 199–218.
———. A Latin Translation of an Arabic Commentary on Book X of Euclid's *Elements.* Mediaeval Studies (1997) 59: 19–110.
Busard, H.L.L. and M. Folkerts, eds. *Robert of Chester's (?) Redaction of Euclid's* Elements, *the so-called* Adelard II Version. 2 vols. Basel, Boston, Berlin: Birkhäuser, 1992.

Folkerts, Menso. *Boethius' Geometrie II, ein mathematisches Lehrbuch des Mittelalters.* Wiesbaden, 1970.
———. *Ein neuer Text des Euclides Latinus. Faksimiledruck der Handschrift Lüneburg D 4? 48, f.13-17v.* Hildesheim: Dr. H. A. Gerstenberg, 1970.
Hogendijk, Jan P. "The Arabic version of Euclid's On Divisions." In M. Folkerts and J. P. Hogendijk, eds. *Vestigia Mathematica. Studies in Medieval and Early Modern Mathematics in Honour of H. L. L. Busard.* Amsterdam: Rodopi, 1993: 143–162.
———. An Arabic Text on the Comparison of the Five Regular Polyhedra: "Book XV" of the *Revision of the Elements* by Muhyi al-Din al-Maghribi. *Zeitschrift für Geschichte der arabisch-islamischen Wissenschaften* (1994) 8: 133–233.
Ito, Shuntaro. *The Medieval Latin Translation of the Data of Euclid.* Basel: Birkhäuser, 1980.
Kheirandish, Elaheh. *The Arabic Version of Euclid's Optics (Kitab Uqlidis fi Ikhtilaf al-manazir).* Edited and Translated with Historical Introduction and Commentary. 2 vols. Heidelberg, New York: Springer, 1999. Sources in the History of Mathematics and Physical Sciences, vol. 16.
Theisen, W. R. "The Medieval Tradition of Euclid's Optics." Unpub. Doctoral Diss. University of Wisconsin, 1972.
Tummers, P. M.J.E. *Albertus (Magnus)' commentaar of Euclides' Elementen der geometrie,* deel II. Nijmegen, 1984.
———. *Anaritius' commentary on Euclid. The Latin translation, I–IV.* Nijmegen: Ingenium, 1994.

Secondary Sources
Abattouy, Mohammed. Greek Mechanics in Arabic Context: Thabit ibn Qurra, al-Isfizari and the Arabic Traditions of Aristotelian and Euclidean Mechanics. *Science in Context* (2001) 14: 179–247.
Baudoux, C. "La version syriaque des Eléments d'Euclide." In *Deuxième Congrès National des Sciences.* Brussels, 1935: 73–75.
Brentjes, Sonja. "Remarks about the proof sketches in Euclid's Elements, Book I as transmitted by Ms Paris, B.N., fonds latin 10257." In: *Mathematische Probleme im Mittelalter. Der lateinische und arabische Sprachbereich.* Wolfenbütteler Mittelalter-Studien, Menso Folkerts, ed. Wiesbaden: Harrassowitz, 1996: 115–137.
———. "On The Persian Transmission of Euclid's *Elements.*" In *La science dans le monde iranien à l'époque islamique.* Z. Vesel, H. Beikbaghban et B. Thierry de Crussol des Epesse, eds. Teheran: Institut Français de Recherche en Iran, 1998: 73–94.
———. Observations on Hermann of Carinthia's Version of the *Elements* and its Relation to the Arabic Transmission. *Science in Context* (2001) 14: 39–84.
De Young, Gregg. Al-Jawhari's Additions to Book V of Euclid's Elements. *Zeitschrift für Geschichte der arabisch-islamischen Wissenschaften* (1997) 11: 153–178.
———. The Arabic Version of Euclid's Elements by al-Hajjaj ibn Yusuf ibn Matar. New Light on A Submerged Tradition. *Zeitschrift für Geschichte der arabisch-islamischen Wissenschaften.* (2002/2003), 15: 125–164.
———. The Tahrir of Euclid's Elements by Nasir al-Din al-Tusi: Redressing the Balance. *Farhang* (2003) 15–16: 117–143.
Dold-Samplonius, Yvonne. *Book of Assumptions by Aqatun.* Amsterdam, 1977.
Furlani, G. Bruchstücke einer syrischen Paraphrase der Elemente des Euklid. *Zeitschrift für Semitistik und verwandte Gebiete* (1924) 3: 27–52, 212–235.

Hogendijk, Jan P. On Euclid's Lost *Porisms* and Its Arabic Traces. *Bolletino di Storia delle Scienze Matematiche* (1987) 7: 93–115.

Knorr, Wilbur R. John of Tynemouth alias John of London: Emerging Portrait of a Singular Medieval Mathematician. *British Journal for the History of Science* (1990) 23: 293–330.

———. The Wrong Text of Euclid: On Heiberg's Text and its Alternatives. *Centaurus* (1996), 38: 208–276.

———. *Ancient Sources of the Medieval Tradition of Mechanics: Greek, Arabic and Latin Studies of the Balance.* Firenze: Istituto e Museo di Sotira della Scienza, 1982.

Lévy, Tony. "Les *Éléments* d'Euclide en Hébreu (XIIIe-XVIe siècles)." In *Perspectives arabes et médiévales sur la tradition scientifique et philosophique grecque.* A. Hasnawi, A. Elamrani-Jamal, and M. Aouad, eds. Paris and Leuven: Institut du Monde Arabe, Peeters, 1997: 79–94.

———. "Une version hébraique inédite des Éléments d'Euclide." In *Les voies de la science grecque. Études sur la transmission des textes de l'Antiquité au dix-neuvième siècle.* D. Jacquart, ed. Paris: Droz, 1997: 181–239.

Murdoch, J. E. Euclides Graeco-Latinus. A Hitherto Unknown Medieval Latin Translation of the Elements Made Directly from the Greek. *Harvard Studies in Classical Philology,* (1966) 71: 249–302.

Rommevaux, Sabine. Rationalité, exprimabilité : une relecture médiévale du livre X des Éléments d'Euclide. *Revue d'Histoire des Mathématiques* (2001) 7: 91–119.

Rommevaux, Sabine, B. Vitrac and A. Djebbar. Remarques sur l'histoire du texte des Éléments d'Euclide. *Archive for History of Exact Sciences* (2001) 55: 221–295.

Theisen, W. R. Liber de Visu: the Greco-Latin Translation of Euclid's Optics. *Medieval Studies* (1979) 41: 44–105.

Vitrac, B. A Propos des Démonstrations Alternatives et Autres Substitutions de Preuves Dans les Éléments d'Euclide. *Archive for History of Exact Sciences* (2004) 59: 1–44.

Wright, W. *A Short History of Syriac Literature.* London: Adam and Charles Black, 1898.

SONJA BRENTJES

EYEGLASSES

The science of optics, which was highly developed in the Middle Ages, did not seem to have been directly related to the invention of eyeglasses, probably by a glassmaker of Pisa around 1286. The date however is suggestive, because it coincides with a spate of optical writing by *Roger Bacon, *Robert Grosseteste, *Witelo, and *John Pecham, all of whom were interested in problems of perspective and particularly of the geometry of light rays associated with burning mirrors, concave mirrors that could focus light rays in a beam that could ignite a fire, a set-piece in theoretical optics that goes back to *Archimedes. Although the properties of lenses were important in the discussion of burning mirrors, interest in them appears to have been almost wholly geometrical. We do not know of a technological interest in, for example, designing machinery to grind such mirrors, until Leonardo da Vinci's description of such machines in the early sixteenth century (even though Witelo had described a parabolic grinding template). Leonardo understood the differing effects of concave and convex mirrors. If you want to understand why the Moon appears larger than it is, he writes in Codex W (1508), take a lens which is convex on one side, concave on the other, and place the concave side near the eye, which will reproduce the optical effect of the atmosphere which accounts for the phenomenon (Ilardi, 1976, 351).

Magnifying glasses (*lapides ad legendum*), external optical instruments, had long been used and were quite well understood. But magnifying glasses were designed purely to enlarge objects, not to clarify vision generally. What eyeglasses do is to bend rays of light from nearby objects so that they focus on the retina properly. Eyeglasses become therefore an integral component of the optical system of the eye (Ilardi, 1993, 508). If one believes in an emissive theory of vision, however, there would be no reason to suspect that a lens placed close to the retina would enhance, rather than hinder, eyesight. The first eyeglasses with convex (converging) lenses for the correction of presbyopia (farsightedness) were apparently invented in Tuscany in the early 1280s. The date is an extrapolation from a sermon by Fra Giordano da Pisa in 1306: "It is not twenty years since there was discovered the art of making spectacles which help you to see well, and which is one of the best and most necessary in the world. I myself saw the man who discovered and practiced it, and I talked with him" (Cipolla, 145). The chronicle of the Dominican monastery of Saint Catherine in Pisa noted that in 1313, "when it happened that somebody else was the first to invent eyeglasses and was unwilling to communicate the invention to others, all by himself [Alessandro della Spina] made them and good-naturedly shared them with everybody" (Rosen, 1956, 14). Once invented, eyeglasses were not difficult to make.

The standard Italian term for eyeglasses was coined by Giordano da Rivalto, a brother at Spina's monastery, who used the word *occhiali* in another sermon of 1306 (Ilardi, 1993, 509), and certainly monks, as well as commercial glassmakers, became known for their skills in this craft. By the mid-fifteenth century spectacles were made everywhere in northern Italy by monks, glassmakers, goldsmiths, young women, and even children (*putti*—a sixteenth century song held that even "*qualche putto*" could be taught the art). There was an eyeglass shop in the monastery of Santa Brigida al Paradiso in Florence in the mid-fifteenth century.

Who purchased glasses? They were inexpensive and could easily be obtained by almost anyone. Aristocrats liked to buy them in large numbers to give them out to their courtiers. And they were certainly affordable by anyone involved in the exploding world of commerce whose generation of all kinds of paper documents was in itself a spur to greater literacy. The mention of eyeglasses in account books, wills, and literary works attest to their popularity in the fourteenth century. Petrarch wrote in his *Letter to Posterity* (1367) that at age sixty he felt the need for eyeglasses: "For long years [I was possessed of] a keen vision, which however deserted me, contrary to my hopes, after I reached my sixtieth birthday, and forced me, to my great annoyance, to resort to glasses" (Ilardi,

Detail of *St. Jerome in his Study* by Domenico Ghirlandaio (1449–1494). (Bridgeman Art Library)

1976, 356 n. 39). Convex-lens glasses were a godsend for scholars, whose active creative life they extended.

Mid-fifteenth century correspondence between Francesco Sforza, duke of Milan, and his ambassador in Florence makes clear that by then concave lenses for myopes were also available. Sforza, in 1462, asks his man in Florence to buy for him three dozen eyeglasses, one dozen "suitable for distance vision, that is for the young; another [dozen] that are suitable for near vision, that is for the elderly, and the third [dozen] for normal vision" (Ilardi, 1976, 345). Several years later, Sforza's successor in Milan wrote to Florence now ordering fifty pairs of glasses: fifteen for ages thirty, thirty-five, forty, forty-five, fifty; fifteen for ages forty, forty-five, fifty, fifty-five, sixty, sixty-five, and seventy; ten pairs for the medium vision of the young, and ten for distance vision of the young (Ilardi, 1976, 348-349). This means that spectacle-makers and customers alike were now aware that vision tends to diminish in five-year periods after the age of thirty, and that stages of myopia were expressed in two grades, medium and distant vision for the young. This was the beginning of the commercial custom of selling eyeglasses by age group.

That persons with normal vision should wear glasses is indicative of their stylishness. Wearing them had become a sign of prestige and refinement. In paintings of the four-teenth and fifteenth centuries, eyeglasses turn up anachronistically to denote learning: figures such as Pythagoras and Virgil are portrayed with spectacles on their noses or in their hands. Saint Jerome, in particular, was painted with eyeglasses, one of the best known depictions of him appearing in Domenico Ghirlandaio's 1480 painting, *St. Jerome in his Study*, with eyeglasses hanging on the saint's lectern (Ilardi, 1976, 358).

By the mid-fifteenth century Florence was established as the center of eyeglass production. The Medicis, who suffered from hereditary nearsightedness (myopia), were active and magnanimous patrons of the eyeglass trade, bestowing large numbers of the products on friends, family and courtiers.

The reason why eyeglasses first appeared in Italy in this period no doubt has to do with the intersection of a number of different phenomena, including the stimulus that the commercial revolution gave to literacy, learned interest in optics, and the interest among artists in devel-oping a geometrically consistent technique of perspective.

See also **Optics and catoptrics**

Bibliography

Cipolla, Carlo. *Before the Industrial Revolution: European Society and Economy, 1000–1700.* New York: W.W. Norton, 1994.

Ilardi, Vincent. Eyeglasses and Concave Lenses in Fifteenth Century Florence. *Renaissance Quarterly* (1976) 29: 341–366.

———. *Occhiali alla corte di Francesco e Galeazzo Maria Sforza.* Milan: Metal Lux, 1978.

———. Renaissance Florence: The Optical Capital of the World. *Journal of European Economic History* (1993) 22: 507–541.

Rosen, Edward. The Invention of Eyeglasses. *Journal of the History of Medicine* (1956) 11: 13–53, 183–218.

———. Did Roger Bacon Invent Eyeglasses? *Annales Internationales d'Histoire des Sciences* (1954) 7: 3–15.

THOMAS F. GLICK

F

FARABI, AL-

Al-Farabi (Abu Nasr Muhammad ibn Muhammad ibn Tarkhan ibn Awzalagh) (c. 870–950 C.E.) was well known among medieval Muslim intellectuals as "The Second Teacher," and as "Abunaser" or "Alfarabius" to medieval Christians. In view of his distinction, it is surprising how little we actually know of the life of this highly significant Neoplatonic philosopher. As his name implies, he was born in the Farabi district of Wasij, a town in Turkestan, a region that comprised the northeast border of the Islamic world until after his death. According to geographers, the town of his birth was a fortress, which accords well with the tradition that his father was an officer in the Turkish guard of the Caliph of Baghdad. In spite of that connection, al-Farabi does not appear to have been part of the court circles. It is believed that he learned Arabic in Baghdad and then philosophy from Yuhanna ibn Haylan, a Nestorian Christian who came to that city around 908 C.E. However, it is possible that he studied with Yuhanna before that scholar came to Baghdad from Merv. Whichever is the case, despite being a Muslim, al-Farabi was clearly part of the circle of Christian Aristotelian scholars that flourished in Baghdad in the first half of the tenth century, studying with Abu Bisr Matta ibn Yunus and teaching Yahya ibn Adi. Beyond these sketchy details, there are numerous legendary stories attached to al-Farabi by medieval biographers which attempt to give us a view of his personality; none is entirely trustworthy. In addition to his education, the one fact that is certain is that around 942 he moved from Baghdad to the court of the Shi'ite ruler of Aleppo, Sayf al-Dawla, who became his patron, and in whose company he remained until his death about eight years later.

We do not know where and in what circumstances al-Farabi wrote most of his works, but the principal reasons for his reputation as the second most important philosopher after Aristotle were the volume and the clarity of his writings on philosophy. While al-Farabi was not a scientist per se, he understood and advocated the notion that truth is discoverable by reason. In the late Abbasid period, because the earlier Mu'tazilite controversy had created friction between faith and reason, there was strong suspicion among the orthodox Sunnite theologians that Hellenistic rationalism created heretics. This controversy, which had played out in the generation before al-Farabi's birth, made it difficult for Muslim thinkers to pursue philosophy in its own right. Those who wanted to study philosophy had always to take account of religious thought and the theologians. Al-Farabi does not appear to have been intimidated by studying in such an atmosphere (although it may explain why he studied with Christian teachers), and in fact he may have paved a way for Muslim intellectuals to approach Aristotle. Before him, as a matter of practice, Christian and Islamic scholars had read the *Organon* only as far as *Prior Analytics* I.7; the material after this point had come to be called by a sort of technical term: "the part that is not read." In a curious episode, it appears that al-Farabi and his teacher Yuhanna ibn Haylan may have been the first to break that barrier in Baghdad; significantly, another of al-Farabi's teachers, Abu Bishr Matta ibn Yunus, was the translator of the *Posterior Analytics*. As Ibn Abi Usaybia relates this story, after al-Farabi the reading of "the part that is not read" became standard in logical study. In this way, al-Farabi is a pivotal figure in reinstating philosophical study (particularly of logical demonstration) to the status it had before religious strictures were placed on its instruction.

However, al-Farabi was not a thoroughgoing Aristotelian who had no room for revelation in his epistemology, for he clearly recognized that there were two ways of knowing, by philosophy or religious belief, and he did not see them as contradictory. In the chapter of the *Enumeration of the Sciences* (*Ihsa' al-culum*) devoted to "Divine Science," he shows how all being is derived from "the first being, to whom nothing is able to be prior and to whom nothing is able to take precedence." He goes on to conclude that this first being "is more worthy of the name and all that is signified by Unity and Being and Truth and the First," and "that this, such as is of its own nature, ought to be believed to be God"

(*Enumeration*, Ch. 4). It is from this being, through a series of Neoplatonic emanations, that humans ultimately gain life and knowledge. So while al-Farabi preserves a place for God and revelation in his metaphysics and epistemology, in his writings there was still a clear preference for rational comprehension: "In everything demonstrated by philosophy, religion employs persuasion" (*Attainment of Happiness*, 44). To any reader familiar with the Aristotelian system, demonstration attained on the basis of syllogistic logic was far superior to persuasion in pursuit of the truth. Al-Farabi says this explicitly in the excursus on the art of demonstration which forms the concluding section of the chapter on Logic in the *Enumeration of the Sciences*. He makes it clear that "certain knowledge of the truth is not to be had except through demonstration." He goes on to say that all the other parts of logic and all the kinds of argumentation—including persuasion—are, in one sense or another, subservient to demonstration, as taught in the *Posterior Analytics*. Because his conclusions were based on demonstration, the assertions of the philosopher demand assent and represent a kind of knowledge "fixed in the soul." Thus the philosopher came to certain knowledge, not mere belief. Al-Farabi's Neoplatonic system seemed to many of his contemporaries to bridge the gap between the "religious" and the "foreign" sciences. Of *The Philosophy of Plato and Aristotle*, the book in which al-Farabi explained this difference between the two ways of knowing, *Sa'id al-Andalusi wrote: "I do not know of a more helpful book for the study of philosophy, because it explains the common ground of all the sciences and provides the specifics for each one of these sciences."

Wideranging Influence

Al-Farabi was an unparalleled thinker, but he was first and foremost a teacher. We do not know the names of all the scholars he taught personally, but his writings served as both fundamental and advanced instruction for those who sought to truly know a subject. As logic was the foundation of all further study, including the sciences, reading al-Farabi's books was considered essential prerequisite preparation for anyone who wished to understand any field of knowledge. Sa'id al-Andalusi said that al-Farabi "surpassed all Muslim scholars in his knowledge of logic and in his research in the field. He explained its obscurities, uncovered its secrets, and facilitated its understanding." *Maimonides, too, added his recommendation in a letter to his pupil Samuel Ibn Tibbon in which he wrote: "Do not concern yourself with books on logic except for what the philosopher Abu Nasr al-Farabi composed." Al-Farabi's works were even helpful to some of the greatest thinkers of the Islamic world. The famous passage from *Ibn Sina's *Autobiography* is instructive: in it he states that he had read Aristotle's *Metaphysics* thirty times without understanding it and then, after reading al-Farabi's commentary on the work, he finally comprehended. Al-Farabi's works were useful not only to scholars of Ibn Sina's caliber: they were also greatly beneficial to students. *The Book of the Enumeration of the Sciences*, for example, was intended as a kind of description of all the "well-known sciences," and was of particular value to students of philosophy. More than that, the book also functioned as a kind of prescriptive syllabus. In the ninth and tenth centuries, many such texts were written as Muslim scholars attempted to come to grips with the ways in which Hellenistic science and philosophy could be useful. Because of the Mu'tazilites, teaching such subjects—especially in mosques where most teaching was done—was problematic. There was a need for an instructional resource from which students could discover which books they needed to read in order to truly learn a subject. In addition, scholars who wished to add a field of knowledge, or who wished to examine someone else's expertise, could use this book to "get up to speed" in each discipline. In the five books that comprised this work, al-Farabi outlined the major divisions of knowledge. While his categorization is based on earlier schemas, the divisions are uniquely his own: the first section was the Science of Language; the second the Science of Logic; the third, the Mathematical Sciences that include Arithmetic, Geometry, Optics, Astronomy, the science of weights, and the science of the Making of Mechanical Devices; the fourth section was about Physics and Metaphysics; the fifth dealt with Civil Science and its parts, including both the science of jurisprudence and the science of theology. Within these divisions are subdivisions in which al-Farabi discusses some thirty-six sciences in all.

In each of these divisions, al-Farabi outlined the content of the discipline (its "parts"), and at the end usually provided a list of the books to be read in order to comprehend this field of study. One can understand why Sa'id al-Andalusi said: "The student of any of the sciences cannot do without it or proceed without its guidance." In fact, that is probably exactly how it was used: students who wished to know some field of study not taught in the "circles" of professors in the mosque schools, could use this book to find out what they needed to read in order to be (or appear to be) learned in any science.

Al-Farabi also advocated the application of a rudimentary scientific method to various fields of inquiry. In discussing the ways in which the ruler should work to find the right stimuli for citizens in the state, he says that the power of a ruler consists of two strengths: one is awareness of the force of universal rules; the other is the faculty a man acquires by long, arduous study of operations of civil societies, of the deeds of one particular city, of individuals within a specific city, and of practical experience by experimentation and long observation, following the example of medical treatment. For a doctor only comes to a perfect treatment by two methods: first from the strength derived from knowing the universal conceptions and rules which he acquires from medical books; second, from the faculty which comes from long observation of the working of medicines on the disease and the practical experience which comes from long trials and observation of the bodies of individuals. By this power, the physician is able to decide the remedies and medical treatments required for each body and each condition. What goes for the practice of medicine also holds true for political leadership (*Enumeration*, Ch. 5).

Here we see the elements of a scientific method that is based on knowledge of universal principles and on testing hypothetical treatments and observing the results. The body of knowledge in a particular discipline grows from these experiments.

Outside the Islamic world, this text was rendered into Latin by two of the most prolific twelfth-century translators. One of them, *Domingo Gundisalvo, combined parts of his translation with other works on the knowledge of the sciences to produce a pastiche entitled *De Divisione Philosophiae*. Since the time of *Boethius, the study of anything beyond the trivium and theology had been minimal. Gundisalvo's translation and adaptation of al-Farabi's work introduced Christian scholars to an expanded *quadrivium that had long been in place in the Muslim world. It had an immediate effect. Recent scholarship has suggested that the text was instrumental in guiding the twelfth-century Christian translators in *Toledo and elsewhere in Spain to the very books they needed as they sought to gain the *doctrina Arabum*. Furthermore, within a century of the translations the nascent universities of Europe were requiring readings in these new sciences and the "new" Aristotle.

In addition to this broad introduction to the fields of knowledge, al-Farabi wrote several introductory books on logic, explaining for beginners the terminology and the logical expressions in easy-to-understand presentations. He also wrote at least two books extolling the virtues of philosophy as the "way to happiness" for a thinking person. He is perhaps best known for his book on political philosophy, *The Perfect State*. This work is often compared to Plato's *Republic* because of its orientation and structure; however, it is more than an adaptation of that great text and includes a place for the transcendent God of Neoplatonism while holding to the idea that only the city that adopts goodness and happiness as its goals will be virtuous or perfect. Finally, *The Great Book on Music* was the only work by al-Farabi on a specific "science." In the anecdotal materials, he is often presented as a very competent practicing musician as well as a theoretician.

Al-Farabi's influence was widespread in both the Christian and Islamic worlds of the Middle Ages. Netton (1992) has written of a "school of al-Farabi" that includes the philosophers al-Sijistani, al-'Amiri, and al-Tawhidi. Many other later Muslim thinkers, including *Ibn Rushd and Ibn Sina, were influenced by his thought; even as late as fifty years after it was translated and circulated in the Latin West, Muslim scholars such as Ibn Tumlus still depended heavily on al-Farabi's *Enumeration*. Maimonides knew al-Farabi's work and thought highly of it. Other Jewish scholars in the cultural orbit of al-Andalus were also interested in the issues raised by the classification of the sciences and were influenced by al-Farabi; both *Abraham ibn Ezra and Bayha ibn Paquda adapted the Farabian curricular scheme to their own purposes, as did Judah ha-Levi and Maimonides. In the Christian West, al-Farabi certainly was read by *Roger Bacon, who refers to him frequently. It has been argued that *Aquinas derived some of his ideas from al-Farabi through the medium of the *Avicenna Latinus* (Latin translations of Ibn Sina's works). In terms of scientific theory and methods, Ibn Sina certainly follows al-Farabi's conception that universals are known first and that experimentation comes in their wake. Ibn Sina's *Canon*, which was authoritative in medical circles until the eighteenth century, expounded this principle. Because nearly all of al-Farabi's *Enumeration of the Sciences* was included in both Gundisalvo's *De Divisione Philosophiae* and *Vincent of Beauvais' *Speculum doctrinale*, al-Farabi's concep- tualization of the number and hierarchy of the sciences became widespread in the Latin West.

See also **Aristotelianism; Music theory; Translation movements; Translation norms and practice**

Bibliography

Primary Sources

Al-Farabi. *Al-Farabi on the Perfect State*. Translated and edited by Richard Walzer Oxford: The Clarendon Press, 1985.

———. *Ihsa' al-culum*. [Enumeration of the Sciences]. *Catálogo de las Ciencias*. Edited by Angel González Palencia, 2nd ed. Madrid: CSIC, 1953.

———. The Attainment of Happiness. Edited and Translated by Muhsin Mahdi. In *The Philosophy of Plato and Aristotle*. New York: Free Press, 1962.

Dunlop, D. M. Chapters on What is Useful in the Art of Logic. *Islamic Quarterly* (1955) 2: 264–282.

———. Al-Farabi's Isagoge. *Islamic Quarterly*. (1956) 3: 117–138.

Najjar, Fauzi M. "Alfarabi: The Enumeration of the Sciences." In Lerner and Mahdi, eds, *Medieval Political Philosophy*. Ithaca: Cornell University Press, 1978, pp. 22–30.

Saliba, George. The Function of Mechanical Devices in Medieval Islamic Science. *Annals of the New York Academy of Sciences* (1985) 441: 141–151.

Sa'id al-Andalusi, Tabaqat al-Umam (Categories of the Nations). Translated and edited by Salem and Kumar. *Science in the Medieval World*. Austin: University of Texas Press, 1991.

Secondary Sources

Abed, Shukri B. *Aristotelian Logic and the Arabic Language in al-Farabi*. Albany: SUNY Press, 1991.

Burnett, Charles S. F. "The Institutional context of Arabic-Latin Translations of the Middle Ages: A Reassessment of the 'School of Toledo'." In *Vocabulary of Teaching and Research between Middle Ages and Renaissance*. Edited by Olga Weijers. Turnhout: Brepols, 1995, pp. 214–255.

Butterworth, C.E. and B.A. Kessel. *The Introduction of Arabic Philosophy into Europe*. Leiden: E. J. Brill, 1994.

Fakhry, Majid. *A History of Islamic Philosophy*, 2nd. ed. London: Longman, 1983.

Farmer, Henry George. The Influence of al-Farabi's Ihsa' al-culum. *Journal of the Royal Asiatic Society* (1932) 561–592.

Lindberg, David C., ed. *Studies in Medieval Science*. Chicago: University of Chicago Press, 1989.

Muhsin, Mahdi. "Science, Philosophy, and Religion in Al-Farabi's Enumeration of the Sciences." In *The Cultural Context of Medieval Learning*, edited by John Murdoch and Edith Sylla. Dordrecht and Boston: D. Reidel Publishing, 1975, pp. 113–150.

Netton, Ian R. *Al-Farabi and his School*. London: Routledge, 1992.

Rescher, Nicholas. *Al-Farabi: An Annotated Bibliography*. Pittsburgh: University of Pittsburgh Press, 1962.

———. "Al-Farabi on the Logical Tradition." *Journal of the History of Ideas* (1963) 24: 127–132.

Young, M.J.L., J.D. Latham, and R.B. Serjeant. *Religion, Learning and Sciences in the Abbasid Period*. New York: Cambridge University Press, 1990.

MICHAEL C. WEBER

FIBONACCI, LEONARDO

Leonardo Fibonacci (Leonardus Pisanus, Leonardo Pisano, Leonardo da Pisa) was born in Pisa in about 1170, and died there in or after 1240 or 1241.

According to Fibonacci himself in the prologue of the *Liber abaci* (Book of the Abacus), he began his study of mathematics in Bugia, a Pisan colony on the Barbary Coast of Africa (modern Bejaïa, Algeria), where he joined his father, Guglielmo Bonacci, who was working as *publicus scriba* (public notary). The young Fibonacci learned the "nine figures of the numbers used by the Hindus," i.e., Arabic ciphers. Later he became a merchant, visiting Egypt, Syria, Greece, Sicily, Provence, and Byzantium, and observing the manner in which mathematics was taught there. Fibonacci himself tells us that, on his travels, he engaged in public disputations and addressed specific mathematical questions posed to him by scholars of several countries, but especially at the court of the Holy Roman Emperor *Frederick II, including John of Palermo, "Master Theodoric," and, above all, *Michael Scot, the imperial astronomer, astrologer, and philosopher, who encouraged him to revise the *Liber abaci*. Originally completed in 1202, a new edition of the work was produced in 1228. In 1240 or 1241 the citizens of Pisa awarded Fibonacci twenty pounds (*denarii*) in recognition of his lifetime's service to the city state.

Fibonacci's works have been preserved in numerous manuscripts. The original *Liber abaci* is lost, but the later edition survives. Although it is based largely on the work of *Euclid and the Islamic mathematicians *al-Khwarizmi and Abu Kamil, it is not without original contributions by Fibonacci himself. It is composed of a prologue and fifteen chapters in which the arrangement of the material both conforms to and reflects principles of order and systematization. The result is a *summa*, a complete encyclopedia of the most advanced mathematical learning of the period, which influenced mathematicians for several centuries.

Chapters One to Seven deal with elementary notions of arithmetic: Hindu numbers, the advantages of their use, their representation using the fingers of the hand; the four operations with whole numbers; the criteria of divisibility by 2, 3, 5, and 9; the proofs for casting out 7, 9, and 11; and the method of finding the common denominator of fractions. The *Liber abaci* also treats more difficult concepts, such as those of arithmetical progressions, their addition and their squares, and of equations of the first degree, whose solution is found through the method of the false position. Chapter Twelve, the most extensive of the work, is dedicated to a great number of curious problems, the most famous of which concerns the multiplication of rabbits. Supposing that any newborn pair of rabbits requires one month to reach maturity, and that thereafter it reproduces itself every month, the question is: how many pairs will there be at the end of n months? The answer is u_n where every number in the series is the sum of the preceding two—1, 1, 2, 3, 5, 8, 13, 21, 34, 55, 89, 144, and so on. Fibonacci was able to demonstrate the truth of his theory, but he could not prove it. The principle of the Fibonacci Series is closely related to that of the Golden Ratio—a geometric proportion of ancient origin in which a line AB is divided at a point C such that AC:AB = CB:AC, which can be expressed numerically as:

$$\frac{1 + \sqrt{5}}{2} = 1.618033989$$

By dividing adjacent numbers in the Fibonacci Series it is possible to obtain an approximation of this ratio which becomes more and more precise as you go further up the series, tending to a limit that is the ratio at infinity. The Golden Ratio appears extensively in nature: the shells of snails, the heads of sunflowers, and phyllotaxy all conform to it. There are also instances of it in art and literature. A notable example of the use of the Golden Section in architecture is the Castel del Monte, a mysterious building in Apulia that was started during Fibonacci's lifetime, possibly under his influence. This high, isolated landmark is built around an octagonal courtyard in two stories of eight rooms. Strangely, in view of its location and period, it is not fortified. It is unknown whether those parts of the Castel's structure that reflect the Golden Ratio do so fortuitously or by design.

Chapter Thirteen of the *Liber abaci* concerns problems reducible to systems of five equations which Fibonacci solves using a method of double false position, the most advanced stage of pre-algebraic mathematics. Chapter Fourteen deals with the extraction of square and cubic roots, and with the problem of irrational squares. The last chapter (Chapter Fifteen) focuses on the theory of proportions, and "the method of algebra." Here Fibonacci explains how to solve equations of the first and second degree, sometimes using irrational coefficients and geometrical demonstrations, all explained through one hundred concrete problems. Not all the *Liber abaci* is theoretical, however: chapters Eight to Eleven treat *"commercial arithmetic," and suggest solutions to numerous commercial problems, especially those arising from the need to divide profits fairly in proportion to the amount of capital invested by each member of a company.

Fibonacci dedicated his *Practica geometriae*, written in 1220, to his friend the astrologer Domenico Ispano. Divided into eight parts, the work defines fundamental

It is uncertain whether the Castel del Monte in Apulia fortuitously conforms to the theories of Fibonacci or was designed deliberately to illustrate them. (AKG Images/ Schütze/Rodemann)

geometrical concepts (point, line, surface, angle, triangle, quadrangle); states the rules for extracting square and cube roots and shows some of their possible uses; and gives the formula for Heron's triangle. It gives solutions to various practical problems of geometry, such as rules for measuring the length and surface area of land, and formulae for calculating the surface areas and volumes of plain and solid figures. It also describes methods for comparing values in different monetary currencies. In addition, the *Practica geometriae* contains several other important techniques, including a simplification of the Archimedean method of calculating pi, the use of the quadrant to measure altitudes, and examples of indeterminate analysis. In the mid-fourteenth century, the first four parts of the work were translated into Italian, under the title *Savasorra id est libro di geometria*.

In 1225 or 1226 Fibonacci responded to various questions that had been put to him by Giovanni of Palermo and other scholars at the imperial court in two further works, the *Liber quadratorum*, which remained unfinished and was for a long time considered lost, and *Flos supersolutionibus quarundam questionum ad numerum et ad geometriam vel ad utrumque pertinentium*. The former is devoted to the solution of problems concerning quadratic numbers and their reciprocal relations. The latter features the first complete equation of the third degree. Fibonacci returned to equations in his

Quaestio mihi proposita a Magistro Theodoro domini imperatoris phylosopho. He was also the author of *Trattato di minor guisa* (a résumé of the *Liber abaci*), and a Commentary on the Tenth Book of Euclid, but both works have been lost.

See also **Algebra; Arithmetic; Khwarizmi, al-**

Bibliography

Primary sources
Fibonacci, Leonardo. *Liber abaci*. In Baldassarre Boncompagni: *Scritti di Leonardo Pisano, matematico del secolo decimoterzo, Vol. I. Il Liber Abbaci di Leonardo Pisano secondo la lezione del Codice Magliabechiano C.I, 2616, Badia Fiorentina, n.73*. Roma: Tipografia delle scienze matematiche e fisiche, 1857, pp. 1–459.

———. *Liber quadratorum; Flos super solutionibus quarundam questionum ad numerum et ad geometriam vel ad utrumque pertinentium; Questio mihi proposita a magistro Theodoro domini imperatoris phylosopho*. In Baldassarre Boncompagni: *Scritti di Leonardo Pisano, matematico del secolo decimoterzo. Vol. II. Opuscoli di Leonardo Pisano secondo un Codice della Biblioteca Ambrosiana di Milano contrassegnato E. 75. Parte superiore*. Roma: Tipografia delle scienze matematiche e fisiche, 1862, pp. 227–283.

———. *Practica geometriae*. In Baldassarre Boncompagni. *Scritti di Leonardo Pisano, matematico del secolo decimoterzo. Vol. II. La Practica geometriae di Leonardo*

Pisano secondo la lezione del Codice Urbinate n. 292 della Biblioteca Vaticana. Roma: Tipografia delle scienze matematiche e fisiche, 1862, pp. 1–224.

———. *La pratica di geometria: volgarizzata da Cristofano di Gherardo di Dino, cittadino pisano, dal codice 2186 della Biblioteca Riccardiana di Firenze.* Edited and with an Introduction by Gino Arrighi. Pisa: Domus Galilaeana, 1966.

———. *É chasi della terza parte del XV capitolo del Liber abaci nella trascelta a cura di maestro Benedetto, secondo la lezione del Codice L.IV.21 (sec. XV) della Biblioteca comunale di Siena.* Edited with an introduction by Lucia Salomone. Siena: Servizio editoriale dell'Università di Siena 1984.

———. *Fibonacci's Liber abaci: a translation into modern English of Leonardo Pisano's Book of calculation.* Translated by Laurence E. Sigler. New York: Springer, 2002.

———. *The Book of Squares.* Translated by Laurence E. Sigler. Boston: Academic Press, 1987.

———. *Le livre des nombres carrés.* Translated by Paul Ver Eecke. Bruges: Desclée de Brouwer, 1952.

Secondary Sources

Bartolozzi, Margherita and Raffaella Franci. La teoria delle proporzioni nella matematica dell'abaco da Leonardo Pisano a Luca Pacioli. *Bollettino di Storia delle Scienze Matematiche* (1990) 10: 3–28.

Folkerts, Menso. "Gli albori di una 'matematica pratica': Leonardo Fibonacci." In *Storia della Scienza. Medioevo. Rinascimento.* Vol. 4, Roma: Istituto dell'Enciclopedia Italiana, 2001, pp. 320–321.

Franci, Raffaella and Laura Toti Rigatelli. Towards a history of algebra from Leonardo of Pisa to Luca Pacioli. *Janus* (1985) 72: 17–82.

Gies, Joseph and Frances Gies. *Leonard of Pisa and the new mathematics of the Middle Ages.* New York: Crowell, 1969.

Giusti, Enrico. "Matematica e commercio nel Liber abaci." In *Un ponte sul Mediterraneo: Leonardo Pisano, la scienza araba e la rinascita della matematica in Occidente.* Edited by Enrico Giusti with di Raffaella Petti. Florence: Edizioni Polistampa, 2002, pp. 59–120.

Lüneburg, Heinz. *Leonardi Pisani Liber abbaci oder Lesevergnügen eines Mathematikers.* Mannheim: B.I. Wissenschaftsverlag, 1992.

Pepe, Luigi. "La riscoperta di Leonardo Pisano." In *Un ponte sul Mediterraneo: Leonardo Pisano, la scienza araba e la rinascita della matematica in Occidente.* Edited by Enrico Giusti with di Raffaella Petti. Florence: Edizioni Polistampa, 2002, pp. 161–175.

Picutti, Ettore. Il Libro dei quadrati di Leonardo Pisano e i problemi di analisi indeterminata nel Codice Palatino 577 della Biblioteca Nazionale di Firenze. Introduzione e commenti. *Physis* (1979) 21: 195–339.

———. Leonardo Pisano. *Le Scienze. Quaderni* (1984) 18: 30–39.

———. Sui numeri congruo-congruenti di Leonardo Pisano. *Physis* (1981) 23: 141–170.

Rashed, Roshdi. "Fibonacci e la matematica araba." In *Federico II e le scienze.* Edited by Pierre Toubert and Agostino Paravicini Bagliani. Palermo: Sellerio, 1994, pp. 324–337.

Tavolaro Aldo. *Federico II di Svevia Imperatore e Leonardo Fibonacci da Pisa Matematico.* Bari: Edizioni Fratelli Laterza, 1994, pp. 15–23 (concerning the Castel del Monte and Fibonacci numbers, pp. 25–35).

Ulivi, Elisabetta. "Scuole e maestri d'abaco in Italia tra Medioevo e Rinascimento." In *Un ponte sul Mediterraneo: Leonardo Pisano, la scienza araba e la rinascita della matematica in Occidente.* Edited by Enrico Giusti with di Raffaella Petti. Florence: Edizioni Polistampa, 2002, pp. 121–123, 155.

MARIA MUCCILLO

FIHRIST

The *Kitab al-Fihrist* ("Book of the Index") is a booksellers' catalogue of books written in Arabic (or translated into Arabic), ostensibly available for copying and sale. It was written in Baghdad in 987 C.E. by a bookseller named Abu'l-Faraj Muhammad ibn al-Nadim al-Warraq ("Warraq" meaning "paper maker," and by extension, copyist and bookseller). Ibn al-Nadim was a Shi'ite intellectual, whose father was also a bookseller; he lived in Baghdad and died there in 995.

The book is divided into ten sections (*maqalat*): (1) On language, calligraphy, and the various scriptural traditions; (2) On grammarians; (3) On historians and genealogists, government officials who wrote books, works by different courtiers, singers, jesters, and the like; (4) On poetry; (5) On speculative theology (*kalam*); (6) On the various schools and traditions of Islamic Law (*fiqh*); (7) On the ancient sciences (philosophy, mathematics, astronomy, and medicine); (8) On storytellers, magic, and fables; (9) On non-Abrahamic religions (Buddhism, Hinduism, etc.) together with information on India and China; and (10) Mainly on alchemical writers. The book circulated in versions of different lengths, some containing only the last four chapters.

The *Fihrist* was apparently intended to be a guide for booksellers presented with practical problems arising when a customer ordered a particular work to be copied. Ibn al-Nadim describes talking to book collectors and seeing what books they had on hand. He takes pains to declare that the information provided is either based on his personal experience or came to him on good authority. Thus he will interject phrases like "from what I have seen myself" or "I read what was written in the handwriting of...." There are details about who copied or corrected which book. So, for example, with regard to translations of *Plato (Dodge, 593): "Three dialogues which Ibn al-Batriq translated, and which *Hunayn ibn Ishaq either translated or else Hunayn corrected what Ibn al-Batriq had translated." If there were multiple versions of the same work, that is, the dealer had to know what to look for or suggest, and the customer, which version to order (and in the case of commentaries, which commentator). With the works of *Galen, for example, (evidently reflecting the multiplicity of copies and formats), he provides the name of the book, the name of the translator, how many sections; which sections were corrected by whom, and so forth. In some instances he gives a rough estimate of the number of leaves in a specific work, and such figures are given for all works of poetry so that the customer can judge whether he has been cheated with an abridged version.

The *Fihrist* provides a vivid picture of the great density of activities related to ancient sciences at this time. In the first chapter he recounts as fact the caliph al-Ma'mun's famous dream of Aristotle that ostensibly gave rise to his passion for Greek philosophy and science, and which led to his sending a delegation to Byzantium in search of manuscripts. There is dispersed, but detailed, information on how the translation movement was organized. For example, he says that the Banu Musa (three brothers, themselves mathematicians) financially supported a group of philosophers including Hunayn ibn Ishaq and *Thabit ibn Qurra: "Each month the translation and maintenance amounted to about five hundred dinars" (Dodge, 585). He describes the personnel and activities of various caliphal libraries, including the Bayt al-Hikma.

The *Fihrist* is well appreciated as an unusually complete documentation of the translation movement, and the introduction and growth of Aristotelian philosophy in the Arabic-speaking world. But it is also a key document of the cultural and intellectual impact of paper technology. Ibn al-Nadim provides copious details about the history of papermaking, although some details appear to be purely conventional. For example, he states that paper had been made of flax in Khurasan by Chinese craftsmen in imitation of Chinese paper, although modern studies of these same papers show them to be largely of rag (Bloom, 44–45). He identifies many different kinds of paper, ostensibly because they were identifiable to book dealers and were therefore another element in their ability to authenticate specific manuscripts. He calls papers made in Baghdad after the administrator who used it—an indication of the physical particularity of different paper stocks. He describes different kinds of script, in different alphabets, and the work originally included specimens of script forms as illustrations.

See also **Aristotelianism; Paper; Translation movements**

Bibliography

Bloom, Jonathan M. *Paper before Print: The History and Impact of Paper in the Islamic World*. New Haven: Yale University Press, 2001.

Dodge, Bayard, ed. and trans. *The Fihrist of al-Nadim: A Tenth-Century Survey of Muslim Culture*. 2 vols. (paginated consecutively). New York: Columbia University Press, 1970.

THOMAS F. GLICK

FISHING

Fishing was practiced on inland and coastal waters nearly everywhere in medieval Europe, although the target species, intensity, and economic orientation of this activity varied. As medieval fisheries evolved in response to economic and environmental change, so did the importance and scale of chosen techniques for capture, preservation, and marketing of the catch.

Religious taboos and the prestige derived from eating a costly food shaped medieval demand for fish. Latin Christian rules allowed fish on the one day in three when they forbade animal flesh. For medieval elites, lay and clerical, fish on the table showed off wealth and piety. Poorer folk had to be content with small portions of disfavored varieties about as often as they ate comparable meats. From a subsistence activity of peasants and those serving great households, medieval fishing developed further as a small, then large-scale, commercial enterprise supplying urban markets.

Up to the central medieval centuries (roughly 1000–1300 C.E.), Europeans ate almost exclusively those fishes naturally present in local and nearby waters. Available transport and preservatives could not get fish to distant consumers for later use. Growing human numbers increased fishing pressure against limited and even depleted natural stocks of inland, migratory, and coastal fishes. This encouraged privatization of lucrative fishing rights, governmental regulation, and development of new marine and artificial fisheries. From even before 1200 innovations in preservation and marketing were as key as capture techniques for expanding use of, for instance, herring and cod from the North Atlantic Ocean and tuna from the Mediterranean Sea. About that same time inland estate managers learned how to rear certain freshwater fishes in ponds for fresh local consumption.

Consistent success called for good local environmental knowledge of the quarry and conditions across the diverse inland and marine waters of Europe. Fishers chose among traditional techniques still predominant as late as 1900. Simple movable gear targeting certain species or locations was ubiquitous. Some fishers knew how to catch fish by hand, incapacitate them with botanical, chemical, or primitive explosive preparations, or use a spear. The hand line with a single baited hook was normal for northern cod, southern hake, and many inland fishes. Besides live and prepared baits, medieval fishers made artificial lures from feathers or metal. Fish seeking food or shelter entered funnel-shaped basket traps (called *retia, netz, weels, Reussen, vervaux*, etc.) designed to prevent escape. These devices of wicker or webbing could be set independently in likely spots or as the operative element in a weir, sluice, or barrier trap.

One or two fishers could deploy larger panels of netting passively or actively. Nets stretched between poles in estuaries held fish, particularly seasonal migrants such as salmon and sturgeon. Hanging appropriate mesh on frames or with weights below a float line let desired fish put the head through, then caught the gill cover. Gill nets took whitefishes from cold inland lakes and, perhaps since the 700s, herring from the North Sea and the Baltic Sea. The seine, an elongate strip of netting, was actively maneuvered from one or both ends to encircle a school, then pulled to shore or into a boat to collect the catch. Various seines gave good catches from large coastal and inland waters of northern and southern Europe. The trawl, a bag of netting dragged behind a boat to scoop up fish, needed more powerful equipment, which limited its use. In 1376 fishers in eastern England complained that a new bottom trawl called *wonderchoun* harmed marine habitat.

More permanent installations called "fishery" (*piscatura*, *piscaria*) blocked, concentrated, and held especially fishes on seasonal migration. Perhaps every water mill had traps for eel or salmon in its race and spillway. Specialized fish weirs, fences of posts supporting brushwood or woven panels, angled across a current to funnel migrants into a trap or chamber. English rivers still contain traces of Anglo-Saxon and Norman weirs. Analogous structures of stone occur along French rivers and tidal coasts. Rows of close-set stakes channeled herring schools at the mouth of the Schlei estuary since at least the sixth century. On the north coast of Sicily post and net tuna traps (*tonnara*) extending as much as a kilometre seawards evolved from Arab and Byzantine prototypes and, since the thirteenth century, supplied a major export industry. Like big seines and trawls, fixed fisheries employed larger work crews.

Seasonal abundance required storage for later use. Smoking and light salting offered short-term solutions. Drying worked for non-oily varieties where the climate provided dry heat (Mediterranean hake) or cold (Norwegian "stockfish," dried cod). Oil-rich herring, sardine, and mackerel had to be kept from the air or treated copiously with salt. Herring salted whole on North Sea beaches were sold in bundles of a thousand; they lasted the few cool months from late fall catch to Lenten consumption. A breakthrough came with probably thirteenth-century recognition that a partly gutted herring barrelled in salt brine kept much longer, allowing larger offshore catches to be shipped to consumers further inland. Similar packaging served Scottish salmon and Sicilian tuna. Much earlier many large consumers (castles, monasteries, towns) had facilities for live storage: net or wicker cages, wooden tanks, dug ponds (*servatoria*, *vivaria*, "stews"). This was not, however, aquaculture.

Fish farming meant control over selected animals for continual production. Probably in twelfth-century central France estate managers developed methods for controlling the water stored in dammed ponds, so that they could fill the pond to rear selected young fish and some years later drain it to harvest the adults. Specialized ponds for spawning selected brood stock and protecting the larvae followed. Techniques pioneered with a native western cyprinid, bream, were adapted around 1250 to the faster-growing carp, recently introduced from the Balkans, and spread across central Europe. Professional pond masters got big annual yields by staged rotation of several artificial water bodies, each covering hundreds of hectares.

See also **Food storage; Shipbuilding; Watermills; Zoology**

Bibliography

Aston, Michael, ed. *Medieval Fish, Fisheries and Fishponds in England*. 2 vols. BAR British series 182. Oxford: BAR, 1988.

Hoffmann, Richard C. Economic Development and Aquatic Ecosystems in Medieval Europe. *American Historical Review* (1996) 101: 631–669.

———. *Fishers' Craft and Lettered Art: Tracts on Fishing from the End of the Middle Ages*. Toronto: University of Toronto Press, 1997.

———. "Medieval Fishing" In *Working with Water in Medieval Europe: Technology and Resource Use*, edited by Paolo Squatriti. Leiden: E.J. Brill, 2000.

Kowaleski, Maryanne. The Expansion of the Southwestern Fisheries in Late Medieval England. *Economic History Review* (2000) 2d series 53: 429–454.

RICHARD C. HOFFMANN

FOOD STORAGE AND PRESERVATION

Societies in the medieval period had developed primarily into settled agricultural communities and cities, which were subject to food availability based on seasonal cycles of bounty and dearth, unpredictable weather, and transportation delays. The preservation and storage of foodstuffs to sustain the population throughout the year was imperative for its survival.

Various methods of food preservation had developed prior to the Middle Ages and remained largely unchanged until the development of canning in the nineteenth century, but even then the principle of the technology remained constant. Simply put, food preservation results from killing, or greatly hindering, the efficacy of microorganisms that cause decay and rot. Civilizations around the world used variants on universal methods that altered according to their climate and obtainable foodstuffs.

One way to preserve food was by physical means (drying or cooling), whereby the provisions were preserved for as long as the status remained unchanged. Air or sun provided the simplest means of preserving food by removing the moisture from it. Grains in Europe, rice in Asia, maize in the Americas—all staple products—were dried and stored in cellars or silos to use throughout the year. Fruits, including grapes (raisins), plums (prunes), and apricots, were sun-dried in the warmer climates of the Middle East, Mediterranean and Asia, while for more moderate temperatures, ovens dried out foodstuffs to be stored away in cellars, attics, or sometimes even in bedrooms. In the extreme north of Scandinavia, stockfish were left out in open to dehydrate in the cool, dry air, and South Americans in the altiplano freeze-dried potatoes. In the imperial palaces of China, ice was carried down from the mountains in the winter or spring and placed in deep pits to keep food frozen or cold during the summer months.

Le Menagier de Paris (1393) explains the common practice to preserve fish by drying:

"Cod. When it is taken in the far seas and it is desired to keep it for ten or twelve years, it is gutted and its head removed and it is dried in the air and sun...."

An alternative method of preservation was by chemical means (smoking, salting, brining, conserving, fermenting), which resulted in a shorter incubation period but offered alternatives that also enhanced or changed the flavors of the foods to be preserved. Smoking, by hanging the food in a chimney for several days, also dried food while imparting flavor to the food. To avoid feeding livestock through winters, extra animals were usually butchered in the fall, and chunks of meat, bacon, and sausages, as well as fresh- and salt-water fish were smoked and then hung from rafters away from rodents.

Salting food to extract moisture was common in various cultures, and in addition to meat and fish, vegetables were layered with salt and pressed into earthenware crocks and stored for the winter. Butter, too, was heavily salted. A variation of using salt as a preservative was pickling, or brining, whereby food was preserved in a salty liquid, sometimes with the addition of an acid (lemon, verjuice, or vinegar). The Arab cookery book *Kitab wasf al- at'ima al-Mu'tada* (c. 1373) lists turnips, cucumbers, eggs, plums, carrots, eggplants, hearts of garlic, and fish as ingredients to be pickled. The Chinese pickled crabs, while along the Mediterranean people stored pickled capers, eggplant, olives, limes, and fish in large jars until they were needed.

Preserves or comfits entailed the practice of covering foods with honey, or cooking them with sugar, which sealed the food from air and bacteria, while confits, or potting, preserved meats and poultry cooked in fat and stored in pots covered with fat. Again, this method was near universal, from cherries in China and oranges in France, to lamb in the Middle East.

So far from stopping or hindering living organisms from rotting foodstuffs, fermentation actually encouraged their introduction to convert desirable changes to provisions that made them more easily digestible and longer lasting. Throughout Europe, vintners turned grapes into wine, sometimes stored for years in wooden barrels and wine cellars. Alewives brewed grain into beer, a drink that provided a large part of the caloric makeup of peasants in Northern Europe. Andeans drank chichi, fermented grains and fruits, and in Mexico, the sap of the agave plant was fermented into pulque. In Asia, fermenting soy allowed easier digestion. The longevity of milk was also extended by fermenting it into cheese, which could be eaten immediately or salted and stored for years in a cellar. In al-Andalus, Spain, it was recommended that cheesemaking occur in March/April and that the product be left outside in the shade to cure until May. In India, earthen pots that held buttermilk (fermented milk) were stored underground and kept cold from Himalayan ice.

See also **Agriculture**

Bibliography

Carlin, Martha and Joel Rosenthal, eds. *Food and Eating in Medieval Europe*. London: The Hambleton Press, 1998.
Chang, K.E., ed. *Food in Chinese Culture: Anthropological and Historical Perspectives*. New Haven: Yale University Press, 1977.
Hörandner, Edith. "Storing and Preserving Meat in Europe: Historical Survey." *Food in Change: Eating Habits from the Middle Ages to the Present Day*. Edited by Alexander Fenton and Eszter Kisban. Atlantic Highlands: Humanities Press, 1986.
Mennell, Stephen. *All Manners of Food: Eating and Taste in England and France from the Middle Ages to the Present*. Chicago: University of Illinois Press, 1985.
Power, Eileen. *The Goodman of Paris*. New York: Harcourt, Brace, 1928.
Prakash, Om. *Food and Drinks in Ancient India*. Delhi: Munshi Ram Manohar Lal, 1961.
Rodinson, Maxime, A.J. Arberry and Charles Perry. *Medieval Arab Cookery*. Devon, England: Prospect Books, 2001.
Superk, John C. *Food, Conquest, and Colonization in Sixteenth-Century Spanish America*. Albuquerque: University of New Mexico Press, 1988.
Wheaton, Barbara Ketcham. *Savoring the Past: The French Kitchen and Table from 1300–1789*. New York: Simon and Schuster, 1983.

BETH MARIE FORREST

FREDERICK II

Frederick Hohenstaufen, son of emperor Henry VI and Constance, heiress to the Norman kingdom of Sicily, was born in 1194 in the march of Ancona. Educated in southern Italy, Frederick was crowned Holy Roman Emperor in 1220 after more than two decades of virtual interregnum. Immediately after his accession he tried to impose a strong rule in Sicily, eventually succeeding and thus gaining a strong basis of economic power in the south. His conflict with the northern Italian cities, virtually declared in the imperial diet of Cremona in 1226, turned by 1235 into an open war between the empire and the Lombard League—a protracted confrontation that lasted until Frederick's death in 1250 in Apulia. Reluctantly, Frederick led a crusade to the Holy Land between 1228 and 1230 with the diplomatic success of regaining Jerusalem for the West. His long struggle with Rome—which resulted in the emperor's deposition by Pope Innocent IV in Lyons—prompted accusations of heresy from the papal party answered by imperial propaganda.

In the eyes of his admirers Frederick was a patron of learning, the animator of a vital cosmopolitan court resulting from the Sicilian mixture of Latin, Greek, and Arab cultures. According to other interpreters, he was not the enlightened despot of legend but an overripe medieval knight. If Frederick's court culture were compared with that of thirteenth-century *Alfonso X, it would be to the disadvantage of the former. Frederick's most significant scholarly achievement is his treatise *On the Art of Falconry*, of which two versions have been preserved, the larger in six books. It includes an original discussion on the nature, anatomy, and habits of birds which draws on the author's experience and Aristotle's works on animals. Frederick's announcement that he will show "things as they are" and will oppose Aristotle on those matters in which he erred, has won for him a reputation as a "modern," empirical observer of nature. Considered in terms of medieval *scientia*, his treatise on hawking is hardly a "scientific" work and should be better seen as an accomplished example of technical literature. Besides, it has been claimed that Frederick's strictures on Aristotle reveal his dependence on the medical approach to the study of living beings developed in *Salerno. Anyway, this work is an outstanding contribution to the princely literature on animals, for which he had a passion. Frederick's itinerant court included a menagerie of exotic beasts with which he even crossed the Alps.

Frederick maintained a learned diplomatic correspondence, e.g., the "Sicilian letters," a group of questions on controversial natural philosophical topics circulated among Muslim rulers and philosophers. He also addressed a famous questionnaire on cosmology to *Michael Scot, his court astrologer from around 1227 until the former's death in 1236. Scot had translated Aristotle's On animals while in Toledo and dedicated to Frederick his translation of *Ibn Sina's Abbreviatio de animalibus. During his period in the emperor's service he wrote astrological treatises and a book on physiognomy and translated commentaries by *Ibn Rushd. *Leonardo Fibonacci, who introduced Arabic numerals into the West, met Frederick in Pisa in 1225 and dedicated to Scot the revised edition of his Liber abaci, besides including in his Liber quadratorum the answers to questions posed to him by scholars of Frederick's court such as Theodore of Antioch. Master Theodore succeeded Scot as Frederick's astrologer, wrote a treatise on hygiene for the emperor and translated from the Arabic Moamyn's On the Art of Hawking—it is said that Frederick himself supervised the translation. Jacob Anatoli, a Jewish scholar of the Ibn Tibbon family, enjoyed some kind of patronage from the emperor: he translated into Hebrew Ibn Rushd's commentary on Aristotle's logical works and Ptolemy's Almagest.

Frederick founded in 1224 in Naples the first state university, where *Thomas Aquinas was taught natural philosophy by John of Ireland. In 1231 the emperor regulated the curriculum and the practice of medicine at Salerno, demanding one year of practical training after five years of study and the obligatory teaching of *anatomy to surgeons. Some medical literature arose in connection with Frederick's patronage. *Petrus Hispanus (medicus) dedicated his treatise on diseases of the eye to a personage of the court and mentions Theodore as "my teacher." Adam, a chanter of Cremona in the north, dedicated to Frederick a treatise on hygiene for the crusading army, and Peter of Eboli wrote for the emperor a poem on the baths of Pozzuoli. Jordanus Rufus of Calabria wrote under Frederick his Latin treatise on veterinary medicine, but the work was not completed until after the emperor's death.

See also **Natural history; Patronage of science; Translation movements; Zoology**

Bibliography

Abulafia, David. Frederick II. A Medieval Emperor. Oxford: Oxford University Press, 1992.
Asúa, Miguel de. El De arte venandi cum avibus de Federico II. Veritas (1999) 44: 541–553.
Frederick II. The Art of Falconry being the De arte venandi cum avibus. Trans. by Casey A. Wood and F. Marjorie Fyfe. Stanford: Stanford University Press, 1943.
Haskins, Charles H. Studies in the History of Mediaeval Science. New York: Frederick Ungar, 1960.
Nitschke, August. "Federico II e gli scienziati del suo tempo." In Atti del Convegno di studi su Federico II, Jesi, 28–29 maggio 1966. Edited by Edoardo Pierpaolo. Jesi: Biblioteca Comunale, 1976.

MIGUEL DE ASÚA

FRUGARD, ROGER

Roger Frugard, an obscure teacher and surgeon who lived and worked in late twelfth-century Parma (c. 1170), was the first and perhaps the most important of the great medieval surgical authorities—a remarkable feat, given that he never actually wrote. It was Guido Arrezzo the Younger, himself the author of a handbook on medication, who, with the help of several of Roger's pupils, organized sets of lecture notes into a head-to-toe exposition on surgical treatment in four distinct sections. The resulting book, the Chirurgia, inaugurated the long and distinguished tradition of medieval surgery. The Chirurgia, like Roger's teachings on which it was based, was more empiric than academic, contained few references to established medical authorities, and reflected little of the Arabic scholarly activity that had perpetuated single-handedly the learned Greco-Roman traditions of medicine derailed in the fall of Alexandria. Nonetheless, the Chirurgia quickly captured the imagination of commentators at *Salerno, who produced "The First Salernitan Gloss" around the end of the century. In response, Roland, one of Roger's disciples at Parma, added his own set of commentaries in an extremely popular version that would become known as the "Rolandino." This version, in turn, was glossed yet further by the Salernitans, whose resulting text, known as "The Four Masters Gloss," replaced Guido's anatomical arrangement with one based instead on humors and pathology. The fame of Roger of Parma, as he eventually became known, was not confined to Salerno. Surgeons at Montpellier also found much to admire in the Chirurgia; not only the thirteenth-century surgeon and teacher Guillaume de Congenis but also one of his pupils wrote surgeries heavily indebted to Roger's teachings. Indeed, twenty manuscripts survive in Latin along with numerous translations, including Catalan, Old French, Anglo-Norman, and Middle English versions.

See also **Medicine, practical**

Bibliography

Hunt, Tony. Anglo-Norman Medicine. Cambridge: D.S. Brewer, 1994.
———. The Medieval Surgery. Woodbridge: Boydell, 1992.
Siraisi, Nancy. Medieval and Early Renaissance Medicine: An Introduction to Knowledge and Practice. Chicago: University of Chicago Press, 1990.

JEREMY CITROME

G

GALEN

A Greek physician, Galen (129–post 216 [?] C.E.) was the son of Nicon, a rich architect of Pergamum. After Galen first studied philosophy, he opted for medicine at the age of seventeen because Asclepius appeared to his father in a dream. He started learning it in his home town with Satyrus, Aiphicianus, and Stratonicus, and in 149 at Smyrna with Pelops. From there he left for Alexandria where he stayed from 151 to 157, studying with Heracleianus and Iulianus. He then returned to Pergamum and was appointed physician to the gladiators. In 162 he moved to Rome. By this time a renowned philosopher and a brilliant anatomist, he abruptly deserted the city in 166, supposedly because of an outbreak of plague. Back in Pergamum, he was ordered in 168 to Aquileia by Marcus Aurelius and Lucius Verus. He returned to Rome in 169 and stayed in the capital as the personal physician of the emperor until his death, possibly sometime after 216. Galen was a prolific writer, and gathered an immense book collection, which was partially destroyed by fire in 191.

The immense oeuvre of Galen covers all medical topics from physiology and anatomy to medical terminology and ethics. As a philosopher, Galen was well acquainted with the main schools of antiquity. An eclectic, he borrowed from the systems of both *Plato and Aristotle. He had a strong interest in geometry, *logic, and theories of knowledge, and firmly believed in logical and empirical demonstrations to establish facts. In the analysis of matter, he followed Aristotle. With Plato he admitted the interaction between soul and body, and wrote treatises on ethics at the end of his life.

In matter of medicine, Galen conceived the body according to the Hippocratic system best presented in *De natura hominis* (written c. 410–400 B.C.E., by Polybius, one of *Hippocrates' followers and his son-in-law). The body is made of four humors (blood, phlegm, black bile, and yellow bile), which are derived from the four elements (air, water, earth, and fire respectively) and associated with two of the four basic qualities (hot and moist, moist and cold, cold and dry, dry and hot respectively). The main bodily organs are the brain, the heart, and the liver. They originate the three major systems that control all bodily functions: the brain governs thoughts through the nervous system, the heart the movements through the arteries, and the liver the nourishment through the veins. Following Aristotelian teleology, Galen considered that each organ had a function for which it was made. These speculative conceptions were supported by an extraordinary knowledge of anatomy, which Galen derived not only from his medical training in Alexandria following the Hellenistic model of Herophilus (fl. c. 300 B.C.E.), but also from his activity as physician to the gladiators, and from the many dissections he performed. However, his use of animals for such demonstrations led to mistaken conclusions that were not corrected until the Renaissance and the dissections by Vesalius (1514–1564) in Padua.

Galen's system of pathology resulted directly from his conception of physiology. Apart from lesions of an accidental nature, illness results from imbalances in the quantity or the quality of the humors, which, in turn, disturb the function of the different organs. Diagnosis of illnesses relied on the perception of all possible signs (including urine and pulse) and logical reasoning. Therapy was surgical or pharmaceutical, accordingly. As a surgeon, Galen successfully performed a great number of operations with remarkable dexterity. In pharmacotherapy, he worked according to the principle of allopathy (*contraria contrariis*). He wrote major syntheses in the field—*De simplicium medicamentorum temperamentis et facultatibus* (*On the mixtures and properties of simple medicines*), *De compositione medicamentorum secundum locos* (*On the composition of medicines according to the places of the body*), *De compositione medicamentorum per genera* (*On the composition of medicines according to their types*)—and also compiled several preexistent works, which he transformed according to a materialistic system of nature (medicines interact with the body by exchanging particles of different shape, size, and weight).

Galen's all-embracing oeuvre is not necessarily the original synthesis it appears to be at first glance, since it relies at least in part on earlier compilations. Still, it had a deep impact on the knowledge and evaluation of earlier physicians by successive generations. Galen filtered, and indeed sometimes reinterpreted, earlier works according to his own agenda. So great was his reputation, and so widely were his works circulated, that his personal criteria often influenced whether other texts were preserved or discarded. As early as the fourth century the Byzantine encyclopedist Oribasius referred to Hippocrates only through Galen's quotations, and not directly from the original text.

In the school of Alexandria, a corpus of sixteen Galenic treatises is supposed to have constituted the core of the teaching from the fifth century. This body of work did not reproduce exactly the sequence in which Galen himself had suggested that his work should be studied, and was thus probably not originated by him. It was divided in four main units, with an introduction and three coherent groups. The introduction contained *On sects*, *Art of medicine*, *Short book on the pulse*, and *Method of healing, dedicated to Glaucon*. The three groups were as follows: (a) Anatomy and physiology: *Anatomy for beginners*, *On bones*, *On muscles*, *On nerves*, *On veins and arteries*, *On elements*, *On temperaments*, *On the natural faculties*; (b) Pathology: the *Book of Causes and Symptoms*, *On affected places*; (c) Diagnosis and therapeutic method: the sixteen books on the pulse, *On the differences between fevers*, *On crises*, *On critical days*, and *Method of Healing*. Such an approach to Galenic medicine was reproduced in the medical school at *Ravenna and transmitted to the Arabic world, where a further treatise was added to the third group: *On the preservation of health*.

Decline of Influence

In Byzantium and the West the Galenic oeuvre rapidly lost its influence. This might be attributed at least in part to the spread of Christianity. The materialistic conception of medicine promoted by Galen was not necessarily compatible with Christian creationism in which bodily features, illnesses, and cures, as well as the characteristics and properties of natural substances (including plants) used in therapeutic resulted from the action of God. In Byzantium, anthropology was dominated by such works as Nemesius' and Meletius' treatises on the nature of man; pathology was a matter of divine punishment or grace, and pharmaceutical therapy, often miraculously operated by several saints on the model of Cosmas and Damianos, followed rather the Hippocratic and Dioscoridean heritage. However, the Galenic textual tradition was not limited to late medieval copies, contrary to a widely diffused opinion. Some texts were used in Constantinople and passages were introduced in such other manuscripts as the early-sixth-century copy of *Dioscorides, and others made their way from Alexandria to Ravenna and Bobbio (northern Italy) during the eighth century. Nevertheless, only a very limited number of

works was translated into Latin in more or less reliable versions: *On sects*, *Medical art*, *On pulse beginners*, and *Method of healing*. In the East, a large number of texts and manuscripts was available to, or could be found by, sixth-century Syriac and ninth-century Arabic translators. Sergius of Ra's al-'Ayn (d. 536 C.E.) translated not only the sixteen works of the Alexandrian corpus, but also thirteen others dealing with such different topics as anatomy (*On the use of body parts*), pharmacology (*On the mixtures and properties of simple medicines* VI–XI), therapy (*On eye diseases and their cures*), dietetics (*On the properties of aliments*), and pharmacy (*On the preparation of medicines by types and according to the parts of the body*). Similarly *Hunayn ibn Ishaq (808–873 C.E.) translated first from Greek into Syriac, and then from Syriac or Greek into Arabic a great many of Galenic treatises. Working alone or in collaboration, he translated more than one hundred texts, sometimes having at his disposal several copies, which he collated before translating, sometimes repeating a translation because he found a better Greek manuscript. Through these translations, Galenic medicine deeply influenced Arabic medicine, particularly with such physicians as *al-Razi (865–925), *al-Biruni (943–1078), and *Ibn Sina (980–1037).

Tenth-Century Hellenic Revival

After its first decline in Byzantium, Galenic medicine was probably the object of some renewed interest from the tenth century among Greek-speaking groups. It is probably significant that Galen's treatises are often associated with other works. A precursor might be the manuscript of Apollonius of Citium (Florence, 74.7) of the late ninth or early tenth century, which also includes Galenic material. Four manuscripts date back to the tenth century. They contain the *Method of healing dedicated to Glaucon*; passages of the *Mixtures and properties of simple medicines* associated with extracts from Dioscorides' *De materia medica*; Galen's collection of rare words associated with the Hippocratic corpus; and a collection of several Greek medical texts, among which appear the *Method of healing dedicated to Glaucon* and *On the pulse to beginners*. While there was no particular interest in Galen in the eleventh century, during the twelfth many of his works were produced by the scribe Ioannikios, whose location, problematic for a long time (Italy—maybe Palermo—or Constantinople), has been recently linked with the translator *Burgundio of Pisa (c. 1110–1193). The origin of the manuscripts reproduced by Ioannikios is still unclear, however. While Burgundio visited Constantinople on at least two occasions, the texts themselves and the characteristics of many of the other manuscripts of that period indicate an Italian origin and perhaps also a certain antiquity. If so, Galen's text might have been better preserved from antiquity in Italy than in Constantinople. At any rate, it was not abundantly read and used as the concordance between these manuscripts as some late antique papyri suggest, but was reexhumed at that time.

Such a renewed interest might follow the eleventh-century translation activity best represented, but not necessarily initiated, by *Constantine the African (d. after 1087), who crossed the Mediterranean and settled in *Monte Cassino. There he translated or summarized Galenic commentaries on Hippocratic works (*Aphorisms*, *De victus ratione in morbis acutis*, and perhaps also *Prognostics*), as well as some of his original works, such as *On human nature* and *On mixtures and properties of simple medicines*. Before the mid-twelfth century, the commentaries on the Hippocratic *Aphorisms* and *Prognostics* were included in the so-called *Articella* collection, which also included the *Isagoge* by Constantine, two treatises *On urine* and *On pulse* respectively by Theophilus and Philaretus, and later the *Techne* by Galen (a translation from Greek of his *Small art*). These were circulated widely in the post-Salernitan world. The Italian enterprise of translation was soon followed by the Spanish one, with *Gerard of Cremona (c. 1114–1187) and *Mark of Toledo (fl. mid-twelfth century). Working from Arabic as did Constantine, they expanded the range of topics covered with the *Art of Medicine*, *On temperaments*, *Therapeutic method*, *On unclear movements*, and *On the use of pulse*. The translations spread from Spain to Italy.

During the second half of the twelfth century, Burgundio of Pisa translated several treatises of Galen from Greek into Latin. Acting on a request from Pisan physicians, he translated such works of propedeutic, physiological, pathological, diagnostic, and preventive medicine as *On sects*, *On temperaments*, *On the affected parts*, *On the differences between fevers*, *On the pulse for the beginners*, and *On the way to preserve health*. He might have commissioned the Greek models he worked on from the copyist Ioannikios. During the same period, *William of Moerbeke (c. 1220/1235–before October 26, 1286) translated On the faculties of aliments from Greek and, somewhat later, *Pietro d'Abano (c. 1257–c. 1315) completed and took over the work of Burgundio of Pisa. Not only did he achieve the incomplete translation of *On sects*, but he also translated a part of *Therapeutic method*, *On black bile*, *On palpitation*, and maybe also *On respiration*. During the fourteenth century, *Niccolò da Reggio (fl. c. 1308–1345)—a Greek-Latin bilingual physician from Calabria connected with the court of Anjou—went to search for manuscripts in Constantinople. There, according to Renaissance printed editions, he found and translated from Greek into Latin up to forty-eight Galenic treatises. He touched many of the topics covered by Galen's oeuvre: medical theory and history (*On the parts of the medical art*, *On the best sect*, *On sects*); medical reasoning (*On antecedent causes*); physiology and anatomy (*On the best constitution of the body*, *On the cause of respiration*, *On the dissection of the uterus*), including some special questions (*On the anatomy of the eye*, *On semen*); therapy (*On the method of healing, dedicated to Glaucon*); surgical treatment (*On the way of curing by cutting veins*); pharmaceutical treatment (*On the composition of medicines according to the places of the body*, *On the*

During the Middle Ages and Renaissance in Europe, Galen was widely regarded as the most important figure in medicine after Hippocrates. This illustration from the title page of a 1677 medical book by Justus Cortnumm shows the two men together beside a flowering bush. (Corbis)

medicines easy to procure, *On theriac*); dietetics (*On the good and bad juices from aliments*), and even ethics (*The soul's dependence on the body*).

Such massive importation of Galenic textual material in all fields of medical science had an impact on medical activity and, beyond, on medical teaching. New regulations were adopted by several universities across Europe: in Bologna in the 1280s thanks to *Taddeo Alderotti (c. 1206/15–1295), in Paris between 1285 and 1290 with Jean de Saint Amand (d. before 1307), and in Montpellier at the very end of the thirteenth century, principally thanks to the action of *Bernard of Gordon (c. 1258–c. 1320) and *Arnau de Vilanova (c. 1240–1311). This movement was further accentuated over time, such as in Montpellier where On temperaments, On crises, On the differences of fevers, and Therapeutic method among others were introduced into teaching in 1309.

Latin versions of Galen's works were not printed before 1490 (Venice). Giorgio Valla (d. 1499), probably taking his models from his personal collection of manuscripts, rendered in Latin treatises previously translated by Niccolò da Reggio, as well as a fragment of *On the constitution of medical art*, *On the signification of urine*, *Questions on Hippocratis on urine*, and *Presages*, previously untranslated into Latin. Nicolao Leoniceno (1428–1524), who also had a significant collection of manuscripts, initiated philological analysis of Galen's text and published Greek critical editions, Latin translations or commentaries of such fundamental treatises as *Therapeutic method*, *Medical art*, *On the differences of fevers*, *On the elements according to Hippocrates*, *On the natural faculties*, and *On Hippocrates' Aphorisms*, which had been previously translated. He also worked on less well-known Galenic treatises—*On diseases causes*, *On diseases differences*, Crises—and published the first Latin translation of *On muscle movement*, previously untranslated. Many of Leoniceno's works were republsihed several times during the sixteenth century and exerted a strong influence on medical and philological studies. In 1525, Gian Francesco d'Asola (c. 1498–1557/8) of Venice published the complete works in Greek in five volumes, before doing the same for the works of Hippocrates in the following year. Gunther von Andernach (1505–1574) translated and commented on Galenic treatises in his classes in Paris, definitively confirming the place and importance of Galen in medical teaching and practice.

See also **Aristotelianism; Medicine, practical; Medicine, theoretical; Translation movements; Translation norms and practice**

Bibliography

d'Alverny, M.-T. "Pietro d'Abano traducteur de Galien." *Medioevo* (1985) 11: 19–64.
Durling R.J. *A Dictionary of Medical Terms in Galen*. Leiden: E.J. Brill, 1993.
———. *Burgundio of Pisa's translation of Galen's Peri kraseôn "De complexionibus."* New York: De Gruyter, 1976.
———. *Burgundio of Pisa's translation of Galen's Peri tôn peponthotôn topôn "De interioribus."* 2 vols. New York: De Gruyter, 1992.
———. "Renaissance editions and translations of Galen". *Journal of the Warburg and Courtauld Institutes* (1961) 24 (3–4): 230–305.
García-Ballester, L. *Galen and Galenism*. Aldershot: Ashgate/Variorum, 2002.
Moraux P. *Galien de Pergame. Souvenirs d'un médecin*. Paris: Les Belles Lettres, 1985.
Nutton V., ed. *Galen: problems and prospects. A collection of papers submitted at the 1979 Cambridge conference*. London: The Wellcome Institute for the History of Medicine, 1981.
Pesenti T. "The Libri Galieni in Italian universities in the fourteenth century." *Italia medioevale e umanistica* (2001) 42: 119–147.
Sezgin, F. *Geschichte des arabischen Schrifttums, III. Medizin-Pharmazie-Zoologie- Tierheilkunde bis ca. 430 H*. Leiden: E.J. Brill, 1970, pp. 68–140.
Siegel, Rudolph E. *Galen's system of physiology and medicine. An analysis of his doctrines and observations on bloodflow, respiration, humors and internal diseases*. New York: S. Karger, 1968.
Temkin, O. *Galenism. Rise and Decline of a Medical Philosophy*. Ithaca: Cornell University Press, 1973.
Ullmann, M. *Die Medizin im Islam*. Leiden: E.J. Brill, 1970, pp. 35–68.
Wilson, N.G. Aspects of the Transmission of Galen. In *Le strade del testo*, edited by G. Cavallo. Bari: Adriatica Editrice, 1987, pp. 45–64.

ALAIN TOUWAIDE

GENDER IN MEDICINE AND NATURAL HISTORY

In antiquity, gender identity was bound closely to reproductive roles. Physicians and natural philosophers, including Hippocrates of Cos and those writing under his name, Aristotle, and Soranus of Ephesus wrote extensively on the subject of male and female bodies, and in so doing attempted to define the characteristics of each sex and its role in reproduction. While the works attributed to these three men were not the only ones in antiquity to approach the subject of the gendered body, they were the most influential; the ideas expressed in these works persisted into the Middle Ages and at an academic level influenced the construction of gender, as well as the characteristics and meaning of maleness and femaleness.

Of the sixty texts in the Hippocratic corpus, including the *Aphorisms*, *On the Nature of the Embryo*, *On the Nature of the Child*, and *On Generation*, ten discuss the qualities of male and female bodies as well as the processes of reproduction. Male bodies tended to be hot and dry in nature. Maleness was associated with the right side, the warmer, drier, and stronger side of the body; thus males were conceived on the right side of the womb, which also retained these characteristics. Because of their vital heat and vigorous activity level, men were able to burn off excess humors within their bodies and thus maintain proper humoral balance. Men contributed their vital heat, through sexual contact and resulting semen, to women, who were colder and drier than their counterparts. Femaleness was associated with the left side, the cooler, moister side of the body; thus female fetuses developed on the left side of the womb. Because women were cold and moist, they could not effectively burn off the excess humors produced by their bodies. To compensate for their lack of heat, women's bodies purged themselves of excess humors through menstruation, which Hippocratic authors argued was a natural and healthy process. Both male and female seed contributed to the conception of a fetus through a process known as pangenesis. Importantly, the Hippocratic view of male and female was not hierarchical; neither male nor female was "good" or "bad," but a balance between the two was best.

Aristotle (fourth century B.C.E.) utilized Hippocratic theories to develop a system of abstract male and female anatomy and physiology. Because he was a theoretician, Aristotle's writings, such as *De Generatione*, reveal his interest in creating categories of male and female, each of which contain a system of elements that either mirror or oppose those of the other. Furthermore, Aristotle assigned values to the hierarchical system which he created. Heat and dryness were the best qualities; males were warm and dry, thus maleness was associated with perfection. Conversely, cold and moisture were lesser qualities, and women were considered base and lesser than men. Men's bodies, being perfect, processed their humors effectively; women, imperfect, passed their bodily toxins out through menstruation. The man contributed semen containing vital heat and active principle to the woman's cold, passive womb. It was the male semen that purified toxic menstrual blood into a life-giving matrix for the fetus. Clearly, there was no impetus for balance within the Aristotelian system; for if men met women in the middle, they became less than what they already were: perfect.

Brief mention must be given to Soranus of Ephesus (second century C.E.), whose works came down to the Middle Ages via the school of Salerno. Soranus, a methodist, rejected theoretical approaches to medicine, opting instead for therapies that would relax or constrict tissues. Soranus was interested in the care of women as whole individuals, not only their reproductive organs. In his *Gynaecia*, Soranus argued that, while male and female bodies were equal, women had illnesses unique to their sex. He advocated for the use of midwives in the treatment of female patients, to prevent embarrassment. Through him the care of women in general, and midwifery in particular, were established in written tradition as gendered practices.

Flexibility of Medieval Gender

Medieval bodies were gendered bodies, and, as in antiquity, much of gender identity was bound to reproduction. Physicians and academicians accepted on the authority of antiquity that men were larger, hotter, and drier, and the combination of their vital heat and semen was largely responsible for the reproductive process. Women were smaller, cooler, and moister, and although natural philosophers argued that they must contribute seed of some sort, the role of this female seed was negligible. Both men and women experienced pleasure in intercourse, but women desired this pleasure more than men. Because of their different bodily constitutions, women were believed to be more passionate and emotional, and unable to control their desires. Thus women, cold and moist, continually desired sexual contact with hot, dry men, in an effort to balance their own constitutions.

Medievals, at all levels, had a strong sense of what constituted male and female; however, they did not limit gender identity to just these two groups. An individual might not just be one or the other, but both. Examples of this would include womanly men, manly women, and hermaphrodites. This range of gender variations was due in part to the concept, received from *Salerno, of the seven-celled uterus; the three cells on the right produced males, the left three cells produced females, and the middle cell produced a hermaphrodite. Paradoxically, the gendered womb was also seen as a gradient, with areas closer to the center producing more ambiguous sexes. A womanly man (characterized by hairlessness, slightness of frame, physical weakness, impetuousness, and tender-heartedness) was an individual who was conceived closer to the central uterine cell. A manly woman, similarly conceived, was characterized by her hairiness, her beard, her large frame, her strength, and her manly virtue. In rare cases, these ambiguously gendered individuals were lauded for their qualities; effeminate men were praised as more pious, while the virago was hailed as a hero among her degenerate sex. The predominant response to individuals in society at large who did not conform to gender expectations, however, was undoubtedly disapprobation.

Gender in Nature and Alchemy

Not only human bodies expressed varying degrees of male and female characteristics, but also the elements of nature itself were gendered. Physicians and pharmacists utilized the qualities of *materia medica*, which were often associated with gender, in the concoction of medicinal recipes; cold and wet, and thus female, elements were used to counteract diseases that were hot and dry, and vice versa. The gender of natural elements was especially evident in *magic, *astronomy, and *alchemy. Two types of magic were prevalent in the Middle Ages: demonic magic and natural magic. The efficacy of the former depended on the supposed participation of demons, and became a persistent *topoi* after the eleventh- and twelfth-century translation and dissemination of Greco-Arabic treatises on magic. The later, natural, magic was a much older art form in the West, and depended on the harnessing of occult natural forces to effect change. Whether we categorize their activities as magic or medicine, folk-healers used natural elements in a system of sympathies and antipathies. For example, in order to guarantee the conception of a boy, one recipe book recommended that the woman drink a beverage made from the dried testicles of a pig. For the learned, the elements of nature combined with the alignment of the planets and stars to create a grid of gendered alliances. Saturn was believed to be cold and moist, and so was "female," and thus facilitated or predicted the birth of a girl. When used for good, the purpose of the manipulation of these varied gendered natural elements was, as Hippocrates prescribed, to balance the male element with the female element, arriving at a point of harmony.

Where magicians and folk-healers were content with balance and harmony, alchemists sought perfect union, and through that union, an unearthly homeostasis of elements to be found only in the realm of perfection beyond the Moon or, on Earth, in the Philosopher's Stone. The processes of alchemy involved the harnessing of the hidden powers within nature. By manipulating these elements, the alchemist of pure heart and soul could combine and refine base metals into gold, and raw elements, such as antimony, into a product so pure that its transformative power affected everything with which it came into contact. Important to our discussion here is the role of gendered elements in the process of alchemical combination. Alchemists believed that, in combining the male elements represented by the Sun with the female elements associated with the Moon, they would create the hermaphrodite, or Hermetic Androgyn, the symbol of perfect balance and unity, and often representing the Philosopher's Stone. Perfection, in alchemy, was the balance between male and female, and expressed an ideal not of polarized gender, but of two genders in proportion with one another, meeting in the precise center of the alembic, womb, and all of creation.

See also **Aristotelianism; Gynecology and midwifery; Medicine, practical; Medicine, theoretical**

Bibliography

Bynum, Caroline Walker. *Jesus as Mother: Studies in the Spirituality of the High Middle Ages.* Berkeley: University of California Press, 1982.

Cadden, Joan. *Meanings of Sex Difference in the Middle Ages: Medicine, Science, and Culture.* New York: Cambridge University Press, 1993.

Dean-Jones, Lesley Ann. *Women's Bodies in Classical Greek Science.* Oxford: Oxford University Press, 1996.

Green, Monica. *The Trotula.* Philadelphia: University of Pennsylvania Press, 2000.

Jacquart, Danielle and Claude Thomasset. *Sexuality and Medicine in the Middle Ages.* Princeton: Princeton University Press, 1985.

Kieckhefer, Richard. *Magic in the Middle Ages.* New York: Cambridge University Press, 1989.

Laqueur, Thomas. *Making Sex: Body and Gender from the Greeks to Freud.* Cambridge: Harvard University Press, 1990.

Lindberg, David. *The Beginnings of Western Science: The European Scientific Tradition in Philosophical, Religious, and Institutional Context, 600 B.C. to A.D. 1450.* Chicago: Chicago University Press, 1992.

Newman, Barbara. "Visions and Validations." In *Church History*, 1985.

Soranus. *Gynecology,* translated by Owen Temkin. Baltimore: Johns Hopkins University Press, 1956.

BRENDA GARDENOUR

GENERATION

The English word "generation" is derived from the Latin *generatio* and the Greek *genesis.* Together with its opposite, "corruption" (*corruptio*; *phthora*), it constitutes the main theme of Aristotle's treatise *On Generation and Corruption* (*De generatione et corruptione*), also rendered as *On coming-to-be and passing-away.* Within the systematic ordering of Aristotle's works on *natural philosophy, it comes third, after the *Physics* and *De caelo*, and before the *Meterologica* (cf. Aristotle, *Met.* 338a20–338b20). The *Physics* discusses the first causes of nature, and all natural change. *De caelo* is devoted more specifically to motions in the incorruptible celestial region. In Aristotle's view, the celestial sphere, which stretches from the Moon to the fixed stars, is radically superior to the sublunar sphere. It reveals no changes,

with the exception of the change of position of the celestial bodies, which move in uniform circular motion. In contrast to the heavens, the sublunar, terrestrial region is the theater of incessant change. *De generatione et corruptione* studies the types of natural change to be found in all those things which come to be and perish, or, in brief, the processes of the natural world.

According to standard Aristotelian doctrine, there are four different types of change. The change most likely to be associated with generation and corruption, according to Aristotle, is alteration or qualitative change. Its main characteristic is that a perceptible substratum subsists through the change of qualities or properties that come and go, as when a white wall turns into a black one. Another type of change is quantitative change, or change of size, such as growth and diminution. A third type of change is motion or change of one place to another. But the most basic change involves generation and corruption.

Aristotle distinguishes two senses of generation or coming-to-be. The first involves coming to be something from being something, for instance, "coming to be well from being ill, or small from big" (Aristotle, *De gen. et corr.* 317a33). The other sense is generation properly speaking, or coming-to-be and perishing—period. In this sense, generation refers to the transition between something that was not, and then was, or, in other words, to coming to be from not being without qualification (Aristotle, *De gen. et corr.* 317b1–5). This latter definition has to be properly understood. It is not contradicting the ancient axiom of Parmenides and Zeno that "nothing can come to be out of nothing." On the contrary, Aristotle is searching for a way to save the phenomenon of change in nature, and to circumvent the conceptual dilemmas created by these two pre-Socratic philosophers. They had maintained that change is only apparent, since what comes to be, actually does so from what already is. The option that something comes to be from nothing at all was deemed absurd.

Aristotle too believes that nothing can come to be out of nothing, but at the same time, he believes that perceived change is real. How can this be so? According to Aristotle, the objects of the world are composites of the metaphysical principles form and matter. Matter is the raw material, the underlying substrate, which acquires the structure that constitutes an object into what it is through the imposition of form. From the perspective of matter, change involves continuation. The underlying substrate is already there, and does not change. From the perspective of form, however, change is real, because it consists of the successive replacement of one form by another. A good Aristotelian example of generation and corruption would be a log of wood that is turned into ash by fire. In this natural process, the form of wood perishes and is replaced by the form of ash, whereas the matter remains the same. The replacement of one form by another is not a transition from non-being to being, but rather a passage from potential being to actual being (the wood potentially is ash).

Generation is therefore not a coming to be out of what is not, and corruption is not the passing of things into nothing: the underlying matter is the cause of the perpetuity of generation and corruption. In this respect, generation is markedly different from another process, which came to play a crucial role with the advent of Christianity in the medieval West, namely creation. Creation, indeed, is coming into existence out of nothing, *ex nihilo*. This process is not natural, but supernatural, due to divine power. In nature, one only encounters generation and corruption.

Generation and the Elements

In Book Two of his treatise *De generatione et corruptione*, Aristotle studies the causes of generation and corruption. Here, his theory of the elements and the primary qualities play a key role. From a physical point of view, objects in the terrestial region are composites of the four elements: air, water, earth, and fire. Each of these elements corresponds to two fundamental pairs of contraries, wet–dry and hot–cold. The element fire, for instance, is dry and hot, whereas the element air is wet and hot. Since each element contains a contrary quality, it can change into any of the others. In this sense, generation and corruption of the elements occurs: one element is transformed into another one. However, the elements can also mix, depending on the balance between the primary qualities. When this occurs, the elements are somehow preserved in the mixture. All natural entities in the physical world that are not elements are mixtures.

The Intellectual Context

De generatione et corruptione came to be translated into Latin, together with Aristotle's other books on natural philosophy. The first translation was made from Arabic by *Gerard of Cremona (d. 1187). It was soon superseded by one made directly from Greek text by *Burgundio of Pisa (c. 1110–1193) and possibly revised by *William of Moerbeke. During the Renaissance, at least eight new translations appeared.

Aristotle's text had a regular place on the curriculum of the medieval universities. Many well-known thinkers wrote commentaries on this text: Giles of Orléans, *Albertus Magnus, *Thomas Aquinas, *Boethius of Dacia, *Giles of Rome, *John Buridan, *Albert of Saxony, *Nicholas Oresme, and *Marsilius of Inghen. The bulk of commentaries on this particular text was, however, written during the Renaissance, when ancient Greek commentaries became available in Latin translation.

The commentary literature of *De generatione et corruptione* provides a rich field of themes that are interesting for the study of medieval natural philosophy. Aristotle's account of mixture (*mixtio*) raised problems concerning the survival of the ingredients in a mixture. If these ingredients, i.e., the elements, remain somehow potentially in the mixture, what happens to their forms? And in what way is mixture still distinct from another natural process, that of aggregation? Related to this issue is the discussion about the existence of so-called *minima naturalia*, the smallest particles that are of the same

nature as the whole, and about infinite divisibility. The treatise also induced methodological discussions, such as whether change of form (*ens mobile ad formam*) is its proper object, and whether certain knowledge about things that have ceased to exist, or are temporarily non-existent, is possible.

Commentaries on the *Physics* can also contain material that is relevant for a better understanding of the concept of "generation," as those by John Buridan and Nicholas Oresme illustrate. One of the ontological problems discussed there is what generation precisely is. Does it or does it not substantially change the thing in which it inheres, i.e., the thing that is being generated? In other words, is generation an accidental property? Other proposed solutions were that generation is a way of being of the thing that is generated (*modus essendi*), or the way of how the thing that undergoes generation is being understood (*modus intelligendi*).

Generation also arises in Aristotle's biological works, in particular *Generation of Animals* (*De generatione animalium*) where he tries to explain the processes involved in the transmission and sustenance of life. There, too, he falls back on the familiar scheme of matter and form. The matter is contributed by the female menses, whereas the form is supplied by the male semen. Crucial in Aristotle's account of animal generation is his effort to explain why the offspring resemble the parents.

See also **Aristotelianism; Translation movements**

Bibliography

Aristotle's De generatione et corruptione. Translated with notes by C.J.F. Williams. Oxford: Clarendon Press, 1985.
Aristotle's de Partibus Animalium I and de Generatione Animalium. Translated with notes by D.M. Balme. Oxford: Clarendon Press, 1972.
Caroti, Stefano. *Generation/Generare*: Ontological Problems in John Buridan's Natural Philosophy. *Medioevo* (2002) 27: 373–413.
Thijssen, Johannes M.M.H. and Henk A.G. Braakhuis. *The Commentary Tradition on Aristotle's De generatione et corruptione*. Turnhout: Brepols, 1999.

JOHANNES M.M.H. THIJSSEN

GENTILE DA FOLIGNO

Gentile da Foligno was born in the last quarter of the thirteenth century, probably c. 1280–1290. His life remains largely unknown. He claimed his father was a physician himself, but we do not know which university he attended. The identity of his masters is still questionable, although it is likely that Dino del Garbo was one of them. From 1322 to 1324 he taught at the University of Siena. Then, in October 1324, he left Siena to teach at the University of Perugia, where he stayed at least until 1327. His trail evaporates from 1327 to 1338, at which point he reappears in our sources as a professor at the University of Perugia, where he remained until his death. He may very well have spent most of his career there.

Gentile da Foligno was also a renowned practitioner, as suggested by his *Consilia* and by the fact that he was called on to treat the sickly Ubertino da Carrara, ruler of Padua between 1338 and 1345.

Gentile da Foligno died on June 18, 1348, from the Black Death, while treating the sick and trying to find a cure for the epidemic. His heirs inherited a significant fortune, as several documents from Perugia and Foligno's archives show. He also left a few disciples, such as Francesco da Foligno, later a professor at the University of Perugia, who was present when his master died, and Tommaso del Garbo, the son of Dino del Garbo. At the time of his death, Gentile's reputation was great, as evidenced by his nicknames ("the Speculator" or the "Anima di Avicenna").

Gentile's masterpiece is his commentary on the *Canon* of *Ibn Sina (Avicenna). Others, including *Taddeo Alderotti, Dino del Garbo, and *Mondino da' Liuzzi had already commented on the *Canon*, which since the end of the thirteenth century had become the basis of medical instruction at Italian universities, but Gentile was the first to undertake the entire commentary, a daunting endeavor which spanned several decades. He paid particular attention to the first fen (part) of Book One, about the definition and principles of medicine, Book Three, about the illnesses of the body's different organs, and the first fen of Book Four, about fevers. This commentary was a compilation of all medieval scholastic science, and in it Gentile demonstrated extensive knowledge of the different Greek and Arabic authorities such as *Galen, *Hippocrates, Avicenna, *al-Razi, and Averroes (*Ibn Rushd). Not only did he refer to ancient scholars, but he also referred to the works of his medieval *moderni* as well as to the information he got from his own practical experience, in order to question the major scientific issues of his time.

Gentile wrote a number of other works, among which the most notable were commentaries on the first book of the *Tegni* by Galen, *Aphorisms* by Hippocrates, and *De urines* and *De pulsibus* by *Gilles de Corbeil. He wrote numerous treatises and short pieces on specific topics, compiled in 1520 into a volume entitled *Questiones et Tractatus extravagantes*. Gentile da Foligno also displayed a keen interest in the practice of medicine. In particular, he was drawn toward *anatomy, which he practiced himself, and which he considered one of the more appropriate means of attaining genuine knowledge in the medical sciences. His *Consilia* were prescriptions made for specific patients which were compiled posthumously. They were quite popular at the time, and they prefigured an important trend that flourished at the end of the fourteenth century and throughout the fifteenth century. Overall, his writings were largely circulated: more than one hundred fifty manuscripts have been preserved, and numerous editions were published between 1473 and 1606.

Opinions on Gentile da Foligno's legacy to medical sciences have varied greatly. During his time, his imposing work generated admiration from Michele Savonarola (in his *Libellus de magnificis ornamentis regie civitatis Padue*), but also disgust from Tommaso del Garbo, who fumed at his "tedious prolixity." Later, his commentary on Avicenna was widely read in the sixteenth century before falling into oblivion, its complexity making it an easy target for the adversaries of scholastic science. Although one cannot point to any major discovery he might have made in any specific field, Gentile can be credited with a painstaking reflection on the definition of medicine, as well as a furthering of the link between real medical practice and its theoretical teaching at universities, which kept close track of the latest scientific developments.

See also **Medicine, practical; Medicine, theoretical; Scholasticism**

Bibliography

Primary Sources

Questiones et Tractatus extravagantes clarissimi domini Gentilis de Fulgineo. Venice, 1520.
Avicenne medicorum principis Canonum Libri cum lucidissima Gentilis Fulgiensis expositione. Venice, 1520–1522.

Secondary Sources

Bonora, Fausto and George Kern. Does Anyone Really Know the Life of Gentile da Foligno? *Medicina nei secoli* (1972) 9: 29–53.
Chandelier, Joël. "Gentile da Foligno. Médecin et universitaire du XIVe siècle." In École nationale des chartes. Positions des thèses, 2002: 21–28.
French, Roger K. *Canonical Medicine. Gentile da Foligno and Scholasticism*. Leiden: E.J. Brill, 2001.

JOËL CHANDELIER

GEOGRAPHY, CHOROGRAPHY

Much of the Western medieval geography was inherited from Greek and Roman scholarship, although the word "geography" itself fell out of use until the Western rediscovery of *Ptolemy c. 1400. More frequently, the term "geometry" was used, and geographical material was included in the *quadrivium and considered as part of *physica*. The created world (*mundus*) consisted of Heaven and the Earth, so astronomical material often preceded geographical description in cosmographies. The Earth was both the globe (*orbis*) and one of the four elements; the Latin *terra* stood for the element and for the inhabited world, or the Greek *oikoumene*. The Latin writers accepted the Greek sub-genres of pictorial and narrative geographic description: *topographia*, *khorographia*, and *geographia*, each aiming to describe or depict respectively one location (*topos*), a region or country (*khoros*), and the whole earth (*ge*). The discipline of chorography was defined by Pomponius Mela (c. 44 C.E.) as a narrative genre that may follow an itinerary and includes the human and cultural geography of a region. In consequence, "chorography" may refer on occasion to literary descriptions or visual images created by travel writers. The lack of mathematical precision caused *Ptolemy to criticize chorography for its qualitative and impressionistic aspects to the detriment of universal completeness, mapping information, and scientific observation. Thus, *chorographia* is primarily descriptive regional geography, while *geographia* is a complete representation of the known world based on geometry and astronomy.

The early medieval geography in the West relied heavily on Mela, Pliny (c. 79 C.E.), and his follower Julius Solinus (c. 230–240), whose works were transmitted and interpreted for the early Christian scholars by Macrobius (c. 400), Paulus Orosius (c. 417), Martianus Capella (fl. c. 410–429), and *Isidore of Seville (c. 560–636). The new Christian context of science was recognized by Augustine (354–430), who taught that one should know about "the natures of things" to understand the Bible. Geographical knowledge was part of *scientia*, the knowledge of human things, meant to support *sapientia*, the knowledge of divine things. Lozovsky has pointed out that in the early Middle Ages geographical knowledge regarded the Earth as a physical testimony of God's work and thus provided an image to contemplate and interpret rather than a travel guide. Consequently, theoretical description often ignored contemporary information in favor of classical authorities and the Bible.

The Bible does not offer a definite geographical concept. The Old Testament sometimes refers to the Earth as a flat circle under a dome-shaped heaven. Some statements indicate that the Earth has ends, therefore is not a circle. The Heaven is supported by columns and pillars, it does not rest on the Earth directly. The shape of the heaven is like a tent or cloth spread above the Earth. The number and qualities of heavens vary. Waters, concentrated above the heavenly firmament, pour onto the Earth as rain through special windows. Earthly waters surround dry land; the extent of the Earth and the height of Heaven are impossible for the human to grasp or determine. From Isidore on, scriptural elements form a lasting pattern of the Christian worldview: Jerusalem in the center of the earth, the earthly Paradise in the Far East, the Four Rivers of Paradise including the Tigris and Euphrates, the heathen peoples of Gog and Magog beyond Asian mountains, the three continents divided among the three sons of Noah (Asia for the descendants of Shem, Europe of Japheth, and Africa of Ham). Von Brincken has carefully analyzed such scriptural references, finding some allegories and contradictions. For example, *Hugh of Saint-Victor (fl. c. 1120) imagined the world in the shape of Noah's ark, as described in Genesis 6:15. While the "four corners of the earth" of patristic authors such as *Kosmas Indikopleustês (see below) became part of medieval Christian cartography, the notion of a spherical Earth eventually prevailed and was firmly established with the acceptance of the Aristotelian view of a geocentric universe by the twelfth century. The shape of the universe was egg-like, with the spherical Earth like a yolk inside the white; some authors scaled it down to a drop of grease in the center of the yolk. The Earth was an unmoving sphere with a circumference of about 25,000 miles (40,000 km); its surface was divided, after the Greeks, into five climatic zones: two temperate, one torrid, and two frigid, sometimes illustrated with zonal maps. The *oikoumene* was in the northern temperate zone; it included Europe, Asia, Africa and some islands. The idea of an antipodean southern landmass, *terra australis*, remained a subject of intellectual speculation. By the thirteenth century Aristotle and Ptolemy were restored to scholarship, through Latin translations first from Arabic and then directly from Greek, but the concepts remained very naïve and the knowledge limited. Western translations from the Arabic helped spread not only Greek ideas of natural science: in the eleventh century Petrus Alphonsus has the mythical (Indian) city of Arin (see below) at the center of the inhabited world. *Adelard of Bath (c. 1070–c. 1142/1146), who translated *al-Khwarizmi's ninth-century astronomical work, held that the uneven level of the ocean, higher in the north than in the south, was due to the eccentricity of the two spheres of the Earth and water; the Earth floated on the ocean and, where it protruded above the waters, formed the dry land. Another view allowed for underground river courses that took their source from the ocean. They filtered through the Earth losing salt content, and rose to mountain tops whence they subsequently descended creating the great rivers. The rise was explained by hydrostatic pressure or the attractivve energy of the Sun and stars. Variations of the earthly relief also were explained by the lesser or greater distance of stars from the Earth.

Physical Geography

Physical geography was neglected; it was drawn primarily from antique authors and only secondarily and reluctantly from observation. Theory came mostly from the Greeks and descriptive information from the Romans, including the material excerpted from the Greek works by the Latin writers, especially Pliny and Solinus. Aristotle's *Meteorology* was highly influential in teaching that the four elements (fire, air, water, and earth) combined in various ways to produce tides, earthquakes, winds, thunder and lightning, and comets. *William of Conches of Chartres was unusual, presenting in his *De philosophia mundi* (before 1145) reasoned explanations of such atmospheric phenomena as clouds, rainfall, flood, and tides. Among the few authors who contradicted Aristotle's notion that the Earth was cold at the center was *Albertus Magnus (c. 1200–1280), who was instrumental in introducing Arabo-Islamic works into the philosophical mainstream. A teacher of *Thomas Aquinas, Albertus was a prodigious traveler and criticized Aristotle on the basis of his own personal observations. In *De natura locorum* he discussed earthquakes, comets, and fossils, and contributed an elaborate discussion of geographical theory in environmental terms. One fundamental error attributed to Ptolemy was an under-estimation of the size of the Earth: his Mediterranean Sea spanned an extra twenty degrees of longitude, and his Europe and Asia extended over half the globe, instead of the 130 degrees of their true extent, a miscalculation that later misled *Christopher

Columbus into underestimating the distances to Cathay and India.

Medieval understanding of the tides was based primarily on the *Introductorium in astronomiam* of Albumasar (*Abu Ma'shar), a ninth-century Arabic text translated into Latin in the twelfth century, although much earlier Bede (673–736) also had concluded that the Moon was involved. Abu Ma'shar taught that the Moon caused ebb and flood tides, discussed the tidal effect of the Moon's phases and its relation to the Sun, and commented on the effects of wind and topographical features on the tides. Other theories, such as *al-Bitruji's notion that the tides were caused by the general circulation of the heavens, also came to the Middle Ages through Latin translations of Muslim writers. Tides were not an important concern in the Mediterranean, but northern Europe developed "rutters"—vernacular booklets with information about the tides, harbors, hazards, landmarks, and coastal streams. Gerald of Wales in his thirteenth-century *Topographia Hiberniae* compiled information about high and low tides. The earliest known tidal table also dates from the thirteenth century and was compiled for London Bridge.

After Orosius, geography was closely tied to Christian history; his *History Against the Pagans* was frequently used and translated by Alfred the Great (r. 871–899) into Anglo-Saxon. It was in the service of history that new geographical knowledge was often developed through the use of independent sources, especially for northern Europe poorly known to the ancients. The regional histories of England by Bede; of northern Germany and Scandinavia, with possible references to America (Vinland) by Adam of Bremen (c. 1076); and of Ireland and Wales by Gerald of Wales contribute much to our knowledge of historical geography and ethnography. Northern regions are also prominent in the *Cosmographia* of Aethicus Ister (c. 700) and Dicuil's *Liber de mensura orbis terrae* (*Book on Measurements of the Terrestrial Globe*, c. 825). Scholastics may be credited with bringing back an interest in geography and exploration and fusing antique theory with medieval travel. Some travel narratives were fantastic or doubtful, like those of St. Brendan; others sometimes failed to circulate, and might even be forgotten. The Baltic Sea was recognized as closed in the north, and Scandinavia as a peninsula, only in the eleventh century. The voyages of the Danes and Norse, extending from the Baltic and White seas to America, remained unknown in southern Europe, even those of Columbus. In turn, northerners believed, especially after linking Iceland to Greenland and Newfoundland, that the Atlantic was a mediterranean sea, and that Vinland shared a coastline with Africa. The Caspian Sea was recognized as a lake in the thirteenth and not charted until the fourteenth century.

By about 1200, the increased commercial and pilgrim travel by land and sea contributed significantly to the development of geographical knowledge, scholarly narratives and map-making, and travel literature, which was increasingly in vernacular languages. The Crusades were a major landmark in promoting cultural interchange and expanding the practical knowledge of the Middle East and routes to Palestine from remote departure points in Europe. Adelard of Bath visited the Levant c. 1147, and John of Würzburg between 1160 and 1170, and the first Western records of a compass and compass instrument come down from *Peter Peregrinus, a thirteenth-century French crusader (c. 1269). Marino Sanudo proposed a sophisticated grid system for enhancing a topographical image of the Holy Land in his *Liber secretorum fidelium crucis* (*Book of Secrets for True Crusaders*, 1306–1321). In the age of Christian-Muslim hostilities, Jews were often intermediaries and long-distance merchants. Benjamin of Tudela (c. 1159–1173) traveled from Spain to Constantinople, Jerusalem, and Baghdad, expanding the western outlook toward Central Asia.

Another new era was created by the Mongol conquests of the mid-thirteenth century. Travel records of only two actual journeys to the Mongol court survive, by John of Plano Carpini (1245–1247) for the pope and by William of Rubruck (1252–1255) for King Louis IX. A fragment of Ascelin's embassy (1247) by Simon of St. Quentin is preserved by *Vincent of Beauvais. The appearance of the Mongols from the east produced expectations of Antichrist and confusion of the "Tartars" with the subjects of the Gog and Magog. On the other hand, the Mongols' association with Nestorian Christianity supported the proliferation of the legend of Prester John, a mythical potentate and potential ally for European Christians in Asia. The Mongols were also confused with the dog-headed people of the ancients, previously sometimes identified with Saracens.

Popular Guidebooks

A more broadly educated public became avid consumers of pilgrim and merchant guidebooks, cosmographies, and *encyclopedias now combining classical, Muslim, and newly discovered sources of information. Examples include *L'image du monde* (mid-thirteenth century), modeled after an earlier *Imago mundi* by Honorius of Autun (Augustodunensis, c. 1100), and *Speculum maius* of Vincent of Beauvais (c. 1244–1260). *Roger Bacon (1214–1292) recommended an accurate and complete survey of the known world and produced a world map, now lost. The Scandinavian *King's Mirror* (c. 1250) summarized the northerners' knowledge of the world. Itineraries and Christian histories of places became more personalized and impressionistic, such as the *Itinerary of King Richard I* (c. 1200). Francesco Petrarch (1304–1370) wrote his *Itinerarium syriacum* as a guide to the Holy Land filled with descriptions very different from the early lists of distances and locations. Discoveries in the Atlantic led to speculation on African circumnavigation by Ramon Llull (1232/1236–1315) and *Pietro d'Abano (d. 1316). *Marco Polo's book about his travels to China (1275–1295) may not have been believed, but was eagerly read and expanded his public's geographic horizons. Habitations of Gog and Magog, the Amazons, and imaginary monsters kept moving to the margins of the known world. Unlike popular versions of the

Romance of Alexander, probably the most famous traveler of medieval literature, *Mandeville's Travels* (1330s–1340s) combines legend with authentic and recent travel reports, the latter especially for the description of Asia beyond Palestine (Odoric of Pordenone, Peter Comestor, Jacques of Vitry, etc.). One of the most widely read vernacular texts of medieval Europe, it was translated into eight languages and served, along with Marco Polo's *Travels*, as an inspiration to Columbus. Significant advances in cartography achieved in the fourteenth and fifteenth centuries, primarily in the countries of southwestern Europe, were enabled by the acquisition of the compass, maritime exploration, and the rediscovery of Ptolemy. Pilgrimage guidebooks—to Jerusalem, Constantinople, Santiago de Compostela, and especially Rome—became increasingly popular in the fifteenth century and benefited from the introduction of printing. Supported by a growing interest in systematic and reliable mapping, European scholarship of the early Renaissance era rediscovered geography as a scientific discipline.

Byzantine geography experienced a decline both in theoretical and descriptive works. All Byzantine cosmography bore an imprint of Aristotelian thought. The difficulties experienced in trying to merge the biblical worldview with ancient scientific theory and observation resulted in the development of two early schools of *cosmology. The authors of the Antioch school, including Kosmas Indikopleustês and Anonymous Ravennatus, envisioned a flat, usually rectangular Earth surrounded by the ocean under a heaven shaped like a hat or tent. They placed Jerusalem at the center of the Earth, located the earthly Paradise in the east with the four rivers flowing out of it and argued against human ability to reach it. By contrast, scholars of the Alexandrian–Cappadocian school showed reliance on the antique tradition and greater independence of the Scriptures. They presented the Aristotelian view of a geocentric universe subject to the laws of physics, a spherical Earth divided into climatic zones, with the logical possibility of the antipodes opposite the known inhabited world. To this school belonged Philoponus of Alexandria (mid-sixth century), the Armenian scholar Anania Shirakatsi (610–685), and St. John of Damascus (c. 676–c.754), the last of the Greek Fathers of the Church, whose work *The Fountain of Wisdom* was translated into Slavonic in the tenth century and into Latin in the twelfth. A further development of the Hellenistic heritage in Byzantine cosmography came when Michael Psellos (1018–1078 or 1096) revived the geocentric Ptolemaic worldview, while drawing on Aristotle's *Meteorology* for discussion of natural phenomena.

Administrative geography was represented in the writings of some of the emperors and court officials. Several new genres developed, including textbooks, *encyclopedias, city guides, *metonomasias* (reference works correlating ancient Greek to contemporary Byzantine place names), and *notitias*. A *notitia* by Nilos Doxapatres, originally of Constantinople, was presented by him to the Norman King Roger II of Sicily in 1143, about the time when *al-Idrisi was working in Palermo on his world geography (see below). This example of "church geography" describing the Five Patriarchates (Rome, Alexandria, Antioch, Constantinople, and Jerusalem) was designed to persuade Roger to take his kingdom from under papal authority and transfer it to the patriarch of Constantinople.

Byzantine literature is not rich in travel writing. Kosmas's *Christian Topography* (c. 540), while respected as an early example of patristic geography, probably owed a degree of its popularity to his description of travels to Ethiopia, Ceylon, and possibly India; it was copied and translated in Slavic countries. The so-called Ravenna cosmography (early eighth century) is a list, in Latin, of some five thousand geographical names arranged in approximate topographical order, roughly from west to east. Most extant Greek-language itineraries record pilgrim routes to Palestine, including Johannes Phokas's 1185 record of pilgrim travel to Jerusalem and a fourteenth-century guide to Jerusalem in verse. Only one early secular itinerary survives, although city guides to Constantinople proliferated. Among the very few extant Byzantine *periploi* is one of all the coasts of the Black Sea (fifteenth century). Some foreign itineraries and embassy records of the fourteenth and fifteenth centuries added information on Russia, Crimea, Iran, Mongolia, Egypt, Scandinavia, and possibly Greenland. Among the Eastern Orthodox travelers associated with Russia were the pilgrim to the Holy Land Abbot Daniel (c. 1122), the future bishop of Kiev Isidore, who described his voyage from Constantinople to Syracuse (c. 1429), and Afanasii Nikitin, the first Russian to write a firsthand account of a journey to India (c. 1466–1472).

Byzantine writers' use of ancient authors revived in the period of the Macedonian Renaissance (867–1059). The works of Strabo and Ptolemy were taught in schools and became a major source of information for historians. The Ptolemaic revival initiated by Maximus Planudes c. 1300 was followed by intensive export of copies of Ptolemy's *Geography* and other ancient works to Italy, and helped to lay the scholarly foundations of Renaissance geography. Georgios Gemistos Plethon (1355–c. 1450), who knew the work of both Ptolemy and Strabo, proposed to correct Strabo on the basis of Ptolemy in a book to which he added more contemporary descriptions of Scandinavia, Russia, and the adjacent north. This encyclopedist, who met with Toscanelli, is an example of the Greek cultural and academic diaspora which grew as the empire shrank under the blows of the Turks and Crusaders.

Islamic Perspectives

Early Islamic geography absorbed the pre-Islamic cosmology reflected in the Qur'an and some hadiths, and pre-Islamic traditions recorded in the second and third centuries of Islam. One such view, recorded by al-Ya'qubi (late ninth century), represents the Earth as a bird with spread wings whose head is in the east (China), tail in the west (Maghrib), and the body encompasses the core of the early Islamic empire: Mecca, Hijaz, Syria, Iraq, and

Egypt. Scientific Islamic geography began in Baghdad in the early Abbasid period and was particularly encouraged by the Caliph al-Ma'mun (r. 813–833 C.E.). The first steps included the measurement of the degree of latitude, construction of observatories, production of maps and instruments, and translation and adaptation of Indian, Iranian, and Greek geographical and astronomical tracts. The great majority of geographical works combined aspects of science and literature and were composed in Arabic, although non-Arabs and even non-Muslims made important contributions.

In addition to mathematical geography, Greek influence was strong in cosmology (for example, in the teachings of the *Ikhwan al-Safa'* or Pure Brethren), cosmographic methods, and in physical geography. The Arabic authors understood that the changing positioning of the Sun resulted in differences between climatic zones: hot, temperate, and cold. They agreed that climate, topography, and soils conditioned the spatial distribution of life and water. They discussed the causes of wind, clouds, rain, tides, and earthquakes. The word *djughrafiya* was borrowed for the discipline and translated into Arabic as *sarat al-ard* ("picture" or "description of the earth"). The Earth in the universe was thought of as a sphere, resembling the yoke within the white of the egg. The Inhabited Quarter, *al-Ma'mura*, was surrounded by the Ocean, *al-Bahr al-Muhit*, and divided into three continents. The names of Europe, Libya, and Ethiopia for Africa, and Scythia for Asia were transcribed, but little used. The Fortunate Isles (*jaza'ir al-Khalidat*) and the Pillars of Hercules formed the western boundary of the inhabited Earth, while the Wall of Alexander separated the civilized world from Gog and Magog in the far northeast. The Greek notions of zonal geography promoted the adoption of the seven-climate system and influenced the authors who wrote that the parts of the earth south of the equator were uninhabitable due to excessive heat. Ptolemy's *Geography* was translated several times in the ninth and tenth centuries, though apparently without the maps. Extant works of mathematical geography, developed by *al-Khwarizmi, al-Farghani, and *al-Battani contain tables of astronomical coordinates of locations and geographical features, and descriptions of maps with coordinates (very few maps survive). Ptolemy's idea of the Indian Ocean as a landlocked sea was never fully accepted, although tropical Africa was depicted extending eastward. The bulk of extant works are represented by the various narrative genres; some scholars treated geography as part of history, and it was also customary to discuss other sciences in the introductions to geographical works.

The newly reordered, vast Islamic empire required geographical information for administrative purposes. The genre of "Routes and Kingdoms," *Masalik wa Mamalik*, comprised reference books describing the topography, district boundaries, and commercial and postal routes of the empire. Another early genre was that of *fada'il*, descriptions of "advantages" of places sacred to Muslims in some ways, which later acquired an increasingly secular nature. The geographers of the Balkhi school, also known as the school of the Atlas of Islam, focused on the world of Islam, which they divided into twenty climes or regions, and attached central importance to Mecca. The last and most original representative of this school was al-Muqaddasi (c. 1000).

Unique among the geographers of the late classical period of Islam is *al-Biruni (c. 1050). Apart from his important contribution to regional geography, he compared and critically evaluated the contributions to geography of the Arabs, Greeks, Indians, and Iranians. An advanced theoretician of geography and astronomy, he discussed the difference in seasons between the northern and southern hemispheres and argued that, contrary to the prevailing views, life was possible south of the equator; he alone among Muslim geographers conjectured that the Indian Ocean communicated with the Atlantic.

The rise of the Islamic empire provided new impetus and opportunities for travel, exploration, and long-distance trade. For some parts of the world, or certain periods of their history, medieval Islamic geographers provide major, if not the only, sources of information. Travel information fed the later genres of geographical dictionaries and encyclopedias, cosmographies and books of marvels (*'adja'ib*), pilgrim guides (*ziyarat*) and personal travel narratives (*rihla*), such as the famous "Journey" of Ibn Battuta (1368/69 or 1377), who traveled over distances three times as great as those covered by Marco Polo, but unlike him, remained largely unknown to his contemporaries.

Marine geography for the most part remained outside the mainstream of Islamic scholarship. Only works of *Ahmad Ibn Majid (second half of the fifteenth century) and Sulayman al-Mahri (first half of the sixteenth century) survive. Among them are sailing manuals and nautical instructions for the Mediterranean and Red seas and for the Indian Ocean. Yet despite the far reach of travelers and navigators, later formal geographical works say disappointingly little about distant areas, overlook new facts or try to fit them into the old theoretically devised patterns. Some fifteenth-century cosmographies still speak of the Mount Qaf surrounding the ocean and the Isles of Waq-Waq where fantastic trees bear fruit of human heads. This conservative attitude forced practical geography to yield to theory and gradually led to scientific stagnation.

See also **Cartography; Encyclopedias; Mandeville, John, Travel and exploration**

Bibliography

Ahmad, S. Maqbul. *A History of Arab-Islamic Geography (9th–16th century A.D.)*. Amman: Al al-Bayit University, 1995.

Alington, Gabriel and Dominic Harbour. *The Hereford Mappamundi: A Medieval View of the World*. Leominster: Fowler Wright Books, 1996.

Beazley, Charles Raymond. *The Dawn of Modern Geography: A History of Exploration and Geographical Science from the Conversion of the Roman Empire to A.D. 900*. 3 vols.

London: J. Murray, 1897–1906. New York: Peter Smith, 1949.

Brincken, Anna Dorethee von. Mappa mundi und Chorographie. *Deutsches Archiv für Erforschung des Mittelalters* (1968) 24: 118–186.

Campbell, Mary B. *The Witness and the Other World: Exotic European Travel Writing, 400–1600.* Ithaca: Cornell University Press, 1988.

Donini, Pier Giovanni. *Arab Travelers and Geographers.* London: IMMEL, 1991.

Harley, J.B. and David Woodward, eds. *The History of Cartography.* Vol. 1: *Cartography in Prehistoric, Ancient, and Medieval Europe and the Mediterranean,* esp. chs 15–20. Vol. 2, Book 1, *Cartography in the Traditional Islamic and South Asian Societies,* esp. chapters 1–14. Chicago: Chicago University Press, 1987–1992.

Ibn Battuta. *The Travels of Ibn Battuta, A.D. 1325–1354.* Translated with revisions and notes from the Arabic text edited by C. Defrémery and B.R. Sanguinetti by H.A.R. Gibb. 5 vols. Cambridge: Hakluyt Society, 1971–2000.

Kamal, Youssouf. *Monumenta cartographica Africae et Aegypti.* 5 vols. In 16 pts. Cairo, 1926–1951. Reprinted in 6 vols. Frankfurt: Institut für Geschichte der Arabisch-Islamischen Wissenschaften, 1987.

Lozovsky, Natalia. *The Earth is Our Book: Geographical Knowledge in the Latin West ca. 400–1000.* Ann Arbor: University of Michigan Press, 2000.

Marco Polo. *The Travels of Marco Polo.* Translated by Ronald Latham. London: Folio Society, 1968; reprinted Penguin Books, 1972.

Miquel, André. *La géographie humaine du monde musulman jusqu'au milieu du XIe siècle.* 4 vols. Paris: Mouton, 1967–1988.

Newton, A.P., ed. *Travel and Travellers in the Middle Ages.* New York: Routledge, 1996; London: Kegan Paul International, 2003.

Schmithüsen, Josef. *Geschichte der geographischen Wissenschaft von den ersten Anfängen bis zum Ende des 18. Jahrhunderts.* Mannheim: Bibliographisches Institut, 1970.

Tolmacheva, Marina. "Intercultural Transmission and Selection: Greek Toponyms in Arabic Geography." In *Tradition, Transmission, Transformation.* Edited by F. Jamil Ragep and Sally P. Ragep with Steven Livesey. Leiden: E.J. Brill, 1996, pp. 419–440.

Westrem, Scott, ed. *Discovering New Worlds: Essays on Medieval Exploration and Imagination.* New York: Garland, 1991.

Wright, John Kirtland. *The Geographical Lore of Time of the Crusades: A Study in the History of medieval Science and Tradition in Western Europe.* American Geographical Society Research Series no. 15. New York: American Geographical Society, 1925; republished with additions, New York: Dover, 1965.

Zumthor, Paul. *La mesure du monde: representation de l'éspace au moyen âge.* Paris: Editions du Seuil, 1993.

MARINA TOLMACHEVA

GERARD OF CREMONA

Gerard of Cremona was the foremost translator of scientific works from Arabic into Latin. According to the brief biography accompanying a list of his works drawn up by his pupils after his death Gerard was born in Cremona, and passed his life in *Toledo where he was the "glory of the clergy" and died at the age of seventy-three in 1187. He is probably to be identified with the "Gerardus dictus magister" who attestates two documents, in 1174 and 1176, as a canon of the cathedral (a third document, of 1157, mentions simply "Gerardus"). Daniel of Morley recounts his experiences listening to Gerard lecture on astrology and learning "the doctrine of the Arabs" from Gerard's assistant, Galippus. He would have been working alongside *Domingo Gundisalvo, who was translating works on psychology and metaphysics, and may have revised Gerard's translation of the *Classification of the Sciences* of *al-Farabi.

Work

Gerard seems in some way to have continued the work of *John of Seville in the science of the stars, and his own work on Aristotle's natural science was in turn continued by *Alfred of Sareschel and *Michael Scot. Gerard's pupils list seventy-one works, classifying them under the categories of dialectic, geometry, astronomy, medicine, alchemy, and geomancy, and adding at the end a translation of an Arabic Christian calendar (the *Liber anoe*). Almost all the texts listed have survived, and a few more translations have been added to the list on the grounds of their style or manuscript affiliation. The translations were evidently made in response to a need for basic texts in philosophy, mathematics and medicine in the nascent European universities and Gerard was evidently following a program. For Aristotle he seems to have followed the order of works established in al-Farabi's *Classification of the Sciences,* which he translated. The works of *Galen that he chose either were those on the ancient curriculum of the school of Alexandria or had a particular bearing on element-theory, the temperaments and therapeutic method. His choice also reflects the interests of Islamic scholars in the Almohad Court in Córdoba in a radical *Aristotelianism, and includes several texts written by Andalusi scholars (those of Jabir ibn Aflah, *Abu'l-Qasim al-Zahrawi, Ibn al-Wafid, and 'Arib ibn Sa'd). His translations were eagerly copied by visitors to *Toledo, and several of the earliest surviving manuscripts were produced in northern Italy. Those translations which became standard works for the study of their respective subjects include *Archimedes' *On the Measurement of the Circle,* al-Nayrizi's *Commentary on Euclid's Elements,* al-Farghani's *Rudiments of Astronomy,* *Ptolemy's *Almagest,* several texts by Jabir ibn Aflah and *Thabit ibn Qurra dependent on the *Almagest,* Aristotle's *Physics* and *De caelo,* and the first three books of his *Meteora,* *Pseudo-Aristotle's *De causis,* several works on medicine by Galen, *Isaac Judaeus and *al-Razi (Rhazes), the *Surgery* of Abu'l-Qasim al-Zahrawi and the *Canon on Medicine* by Avicenna (*Ibn Sina). Gerard's pupils state that Gerard came to Toledo in the first place because of his desire for the *Almagest,* and the translation of this substantial and advanced work on mathematical astronomy marks a highpoint in the history of the transmission of Arabic learning. His version of Avicenna's *Canon* became the principal text for the study of medicine from the thirteenth to the seventeenth century, and his versions of Aristotle's *Physics*, *De caelo*, and *Meteora* joined translations from Greek to form the *Corpus vetustius* of Aristotle's natural philosophy studied in the *universities. His translations are characterized by extreme literalness, and the frequent retention of Arabic terms in Latin transcription. Diagrams (in the mathematical works) and illustrations (e.g., in Abu'l-Qasim's *Surgery*) were also reproduced with extreme accuracy. Often, however, an obscure term or phrase would be explained with a clearer Latin expression in the margin. Gerard himself is credited with more extensive explanatory notes to his translation of al-Razi's *Book of Almansor*. Sometimes (as with the *Almagest*) a translation would be revised and improved in the light of a second Arabic manuscript. After the age of printing his translations would still be used as the basis for revised texts (such as Andreas Alpago's revision of Avicenna's *Canon*). Whether Gerard wrote any independent works is more debatable. One of the several versions of the Toledan tables that became the basis for European astronomical tables for the next one hundred fifty years, is likely to be by him. A very popular *Theorica planetarum* (an account of the movements of the planets) circulated under his name and led to Gerard being sharply criticized by *Regiomontanus. His reputation as a doctor, an astronomer, and a philosopher lived on, especially in his native Cremona, to which, according to stories first encountered in the early fourteenth century, his books and his body were returned after his death.

See also **Aristotelianism; Translation movements; Translation norms and practice**

Bibliography

Primary Sources
Gerard's version of Almagest bks VII–VIII is included in Paul Kunitzsch, *Der Sternkatalog des Almagest.* 3 vols. Wiesbaden: Harrassowitz, 1986–1991.
The Latin Translation of the Arabic Version of Euclid's Elements Commonly Ascribed to Gerard of Cremona. Edited by Hubertus L.L. Busard. Leiden: E.J. Brill, 1984.
Biography and list of works drawn up by his pupils, in Charles Burnett, The Coherence of the Arabic-Latin Translation Program in Toledo in the Twelfth Century. *Science in Context* (2001) 14: 249–288.
Daniel of Morley. *Philosophia.* Edited by Gregor Maurach. *Mittellateinisches Jahrbuch* (1979) 14: 204–255.
Aristotle, *Meteora I–III*, translated by Gerard of Cremona. Edited by Pieter Schoonheim. In *Aristotle's Meteorology in the Arbico-Latin Tradition.* Leiden: E.J. Brill, 2000.

Secondary Sources
Leino, Marika and Charles Burnett. Myth and Astronomy in the Frescoes at Sant' Abbondio in Cremona. *Journal of the Warburg and Courtauld Institutes* (2003) 66: 273–288.
Pizzamiglio, Pierluigi, ed. *Gerardo da Cremona.* Annali della Biblioteca statale e libreria civica di Cremona XLI. Cremona: Biblioteca statle e libreria civica, 1992.

CHARLES BURNETT

GERBERT OF AURILLAC

Gerbert of Aurillac, later Pope Sylvester II (999–1003), was born around 945–950 somewhere in Aquitania of humble parents, and died at Rome on May 12, 1003. He received his early education at the monastery of Saint-Géraud d'Aurillac where, according to his biographer Richer of St.-Rémy, his studies focused on *grammatica*. In 967 the abbot there entrusted the young monk to Borrel II, count of Barcelona, then visiting the French monastery on a pilgrimage. Borrel introduced Gerbert to the *quadrivium and then passed the student on to Atto, bishop of Vic. Three years later Gerbert, Borrel, and Atto visited the papal court in Rome, where Gerbert's knowledge of *mathesis* greatly impressed Pope John XIII, and the Holy Roman Emperor Otto I. In consequence, Gerbert was invited to remain in Rome as a teacher, an invitation that initiated a meteoric career in both scholarship and politics. In 972 Gerbert left Rome to study logic in Rheims under Bishop Adalbero, at the same time teaching mathematics at the cathedral school. In January 981 in Ravenna, in the presence of Emperor Otto II, Gerbert held a successful disputation with Otric, schoolmaster of the cathedral school at Magdeburg, on the classification of knowledge, in particular on the relationship between mathematics and physics. This episode resulted, a year later, in Otto appointing Gerbert abbot of the prestigious monastery of St. Columban of Bobbio in northern Italy. But after the death of his patron, Otto II, Gerbert had to flee Bobbio and returned to Rheims. A few years later, he was elected bishop of Rheims but unfavorable political circumstances forced him to leave France in 997. Under the protection of emperor Otto III, he was elected archbishop of Ravenna in 998 and then pope in 999, with the name of Sylvester II.

Gerbert's contemporary reputation for exceptional scholarship, especially in mathematics and astronomy, has echoed through the centuries, and not long after his death a "dark legend" circulated, implying that he acquired some of his knowledge from Saracens (who were reputed to have taught him necromancy). He was also supposed to have made a pact with the devil in order to learn the secrets of astrology. Modern scholarship, however, tends to deny any great originality to Gerbert, nor does it accept that he interacted with Arabic regions. Yet there is much indirect evidence in favour of the traditional view: Gerbert may well have been the scholar who first brought Arabic science to the West.

Although little is known from primary sources about the three years that Gerbert spent in Spain, it is possible that Gerbert did acquire there some knowledge of Arabic science. First, favorable cultural and political conditions for traveling from Catalonia to al-Andalus were already in place at least as early as 940. Second, it has been shown that Atto of Vic, Gerbert's Catalan mentor, served as archdeacon of Girona before becoming bishop of Vic, and that he had a strong cultural and political relationship with Gotmar, bishop of Girona. The latter did travel to Córdoba accompanied by Hasday ibn Shaprut, a leading figure in both the political and cultural life of the early Andalusi Caliphate, and his embassy inaugurated a period of good diplomatic relations between Catalonia and al-Andalus. The existence of a small cultural circle of so-called "Gotmar's followers," which included Atto of Vic, the count-bishop Miro Bonfill, and count Borrel II, has also been hypothesized. It has been suggested that by the end of the first half of the tenth century Arabic scientific writings could already have filtered into Catalonia through the channel opened by Gotmar's embassy.

Traces of Arabic influence can be detected in Gerbert's astronomical and mathematical works. Gerbert's teaching of astronomy at Rheims, as described by Richer, was based on the use of four demonstrational celestial spheres: one planetary sphere, one hemisphere, and two star spheres. The planetary sphere carried the circles of the planets suspended within the zodiacal armilla, and was used to show students apsides, altitudes, and the relative distances of the planets. A drawing of this sphere has been discovered in a Vatican manuscript, BAV, Pal. Lat. 1356 (fol. 113v). The hemisphere was equipped with sighting tubes (or fistulae) and it was used to familiarize the students with the classical five circles of the Aratean tradition (two arctic circles at 36° from the poles, two tropic circles at 30° from the arctic circles, and the circle of the equator located at 24° from the tropics). This hemisphere is described in detail in a letter, known as *De sphaera*, from Gerbert to his disciple, Constantine of Fleury. One of the star spheres featured a sighting tube (used to orient the sphere with the celestial pole), and had the stars and constellations outlined on it by iron and copper wires. The other star sphere displays an adjustable horizon ring that demarcates the visible and invisible constellations for any latitude desired, which was alien to the Latin astronomical tradition. However, the use of a horizon ring is well attested in all the surviving demonstrational celestial spheres of the Islamic tradition. Therefore Gerbert might have acquired knowledge of this technical element from Arabic sources. A number of twelfth- and thirteenth-century manuscripts credit Gerbert as the author of a treatise on the astrolabe, *De Utilitatibus Astrolabii* (with *incipit*: *Quicunque astronomicae discere*), but this attribution remains highly controversial. *De Utilitatibus Astrolabii* was certainly written by someone who not only had acquired knowledge of the astrolabe from Arabic sources but also had mastered other Latin astronomical sources. In particular, chapters XVIII and XIX of *De Utilitatibus Astrolabii* describe the Earth's subdivision into climatic bands (or *climata*) with their respective geographical locations, and these two chapters cannot be considered to have been derived from any Arabic source. It is noteworthy that Gerbert did show familiarity with the notion of climatic bands in a letter sent to a monk named Adam.

Gerbert is also said to have built a horologium for telling the time at night. His mathematical expertise ranged from knowledge of classical sources, *Boethius in particular, to the use of an innovative computing tool. In a letter to Constantine of Fleury he explains a difficult passage of Boethius's *De arithmetica* (II.1) on the

Unsigned painting of Gerbert of Aurillac during his reign as Pope Sylvester II (999–1003). (AKG Images)

changing of sesquiquartal numbers (an explanation known by the name *Saltus Gerberti*). According to Richer, Gerbert had manufactured a special abacus for his mathematical teaching at Rheims. This abacus was a board with twenty-seven columns that functioned with special counters or apices on which were carved special symbols. These symbols closely resemble Hindu-Arabic numeral notation. Gerbert also authored a small treatise, *Regulae de numerorum abaci rationibus*, to explain how to perform multiplication and division with the abacus.

Gerbert's works in geometry and music do not display any Arabic influence. Gerbert seems to have compiled sections of a *Geometria* and also wrote a letter to Adalbold of Utrecht (d. 1026) explaining the difference between arithmetical and geometrical procedures for calculating the area of a triangle. Evidence for Gerbert's expertise in music is mainly provided by two letters addressed to Constantine of Fleury explaining two passages of Boethius's *De musica*, and by descriptions of the organs he constructed. Among Gerbert's philosophical works, a brief logical treatise titled *De rationali et de ratione uti* is all that has been preserved.

See also **Astronomy, Islamic; Astronomy, Latin; Magic and the occult**

Bibliography

Bergmann, Werner. *Innovationen im Quadrivium des 10. und 11. Jahrhunderts*. Stuttgart: Franz Steiner Verlag Wiesbaden GmbH, 1985.

Bubnov, Nicolaus. *Gerberti postea Silvestri II Papae Opera Mathematica (972–1003)*. Berlin: R. Friedländer & Sohn, 1899.

Millás Vallicrosa, José. *Assaig d'història de les idees físiques i matemátiques a la Catalunya Medieval*. Barcelona: "Estudis Universitaris Catalans," Sèrie Monogràfica I, 1931.

Ordeig i Mata, Ramon. *Ató, bisbe i arquebisbe de Vic (957-971), antic arxiprest-ardiaca de Girona*. Studia Vicensia (1989) 1: 61–97.

Pratt Lattin, Harriett. *The Letters of Gerbert with his Papal Privileges as Sylvester II*. New York: Columbia University Press, 1961.

Riché, Pierre. *Gerbert d'Aurillac. Le Pape de l'An Mil*. Paris: Fayard, 1987.

MARCO ZUCCATO

GHAZALI, AL-

Abu Hamid Muhammad ibn Muhammad al-Ghazali was born in 1058 C.E. in Tus, a town near the modern-day Iranian city of Mashhad. Orphaned at an early age, he began his religious education in Tus, later moving to Nishapur where he studied jurisprudence (*fiqh*) and possibly philosophical theology (*kalam*) with the famous Ash'ari philosophical theologian al-Juwayni (1008–1085). Al-Juwayni had been appointed by the Seljuk vizier Nizam al-Mulk (1017–1092) to teach at the Nizamiyya religious college (*madrasa*), one of the several such newly established institutions he had endowed primarily for the teaching of Shafi'i jurisprudence. During the course of his studies here, al-Ghazali authored his earliest writings and was initiated into mystical Islam (*tasawwuf*).

After al-Juwayni's death, al-Ghazali joined Nizam al-Mulk's court, finally making his entry into Baghdad in 1091 where Nizam al-Mulk appointed him to teach jurisprudence at the Nizamiyya *madrasa* of Baghdad. In recognition of al-Ghazali's standing, Nizam honored him with the appellations "the ornament of the faith" (*zayn al-din*) and "the nobility of the leading scholars" (*sharaf al-a'imma*). But the political and social situation in Baghdad was in turmoil. Having wrested control of Baghdad from the Shi'i-leaning Buyids in 1055 the Seljuks had ushered in the period now known as the Sunni "revival." At the same time, they were engaged in fighting, literally and polemically, with the Christian Byzantines in Eastern Turkey, and the Shi'i Fatimid caliph in Cairo, as well as quelling internal opposition by the conservative Hanbalis who were striving to politically advance their conservative literalist position and to foment opposition against "heretical innovations" of Mu'tazili philosophical theology and sympathy towards the martyred mystic al-Hallaj (d. 992). In 1092, a year

after al-Ghazali's arrival in Baghdad, his benefactor Nizam al-Mulk was assassinated. A tumultuous series of events followed: the death of the Seljuk Sultan Malik Shah, a struggle of succession resulting finally in the appointment of Sultan Barkiyaruq in 1094, followed four days later by the death of the caliph al-Muqtafi culminating in the inauguration of his sixteen-year-old son al-Mustazhir as caliph, an event attended by al-Ghazali.

Al-Ghazali's years in Baghdad had been quite productive. He had, according to his *Autobiography*, engaged in an intensive study of religious truth ostensibly as result of skepticism. This initiated an intense examination of religious philosophy (*kalam*), Islamic Hellenistic philosophy (*falsafa*), the tenets of Ismailism, and possibly Islamic mysticism (*tasawwuf*). As a result, he composed several works, the most significant of these, with respect to his attitude towards science, are his *Maqasid al-falasifa* (*Aims of the Philosophers*), which is a summary of Islamic Hellenistic philosophy based on *Ibn Sina's Persian work *Danishnama-i 'Ala'i*, followed by his critique of this philosophy in his *Tahafut al-falasifa* (*Incoherence of the Philosophers*), then by his logical treatise *Mi'yar al-'ilm* (*Standard of Knowledge*), and then his treatise of religious philosophy, *Al-Iqtisad fi'l-i'tiqad* (*Moderation in Belief*). But his epistemological skepticism continued its ravages, and according to his *Autobiography*, resulted in a spiritual crisis, manifested in an inability to speak and thereby to teach. As a result, al-Ghazali quit Baghdad in November 1095 under the pretext of pilgrimage to Mecca.

Al-Ghazali went first to Damascus and then to Jerusalem, where he engaged in spiritual retreat and overcame his skepticism, finding certainty in mystical experience. He then commenced his influential magnum opus, *Ihya' 'ulum al-din* (*Revival of the Religious Sciences*), completed in 1105. The *Revival* is a reformulation of Islamic doctrine and practice grounded in the perspectives of mystical Islam instead of jurisprudential formalism.

After a sojourn of eleven years, al-Ghazali returned to retire in his hometown of Tus. Soon after, in 1106, he was persuaded by Nizam al-Mulk's son to return to teaching at Nizamiyya religious college of Nishapur. His *Autobiography* entitled *Munqidh min al-dalal* (*Deliverer from Error*) was written during this period as is his text on the principles of jurisprudence *al-Mustasfa fi 'ilm al-usul* (*Choice Elements Regarding the Principles of Religion*). He retired from teaching for a second time in 1109 and died in 1111. In total, over four hundred works have been attributed to him.

Attitude to Science

Customarily, historians of science concur with al-Ghazali's own classification, which derives from Ibn Sina, that "the sciences of the [Islamic Hellenistic] philosophers... consist of mathematics, logic, metaphysics, natural philosophy, and ethics" (*Autobiography*, 72). As such, the physical theory of the religious philosophers, namely their theories of matter, space, time, motion, and void, have no place in the discussion of the history of science in Islam. Al-Ghazali's familiarity with the atomistic physical theory of his teacher al-Juwayni is plainly evident in his works; however an examination of al-Ghazali's remarks reveals an ambivalent if not hostile attitude towards the atomism of the religious philosophers.

Al-Ghazali's early work *Aims of the Philosophers* is a summary of the logic, natural philosophy, and metaphysics of the Islamic Hellenistic philosophers and forms the basis of his familiarity with the Aristotelian cosmology that underlies their natural sciences. Ironically, as a result of the Latin translation of this work by *Domingo Gundisalvo in the twelfth-century, al-Ghazali or Algazel as he was known, came to be regarded as one of the Islamic Hellenistic philosophers. In the sequel to this work, *Incoherence of the Philosophers*, al-Ghazali's aim is "[refuting] the ancients, showing the incoherence of their beliefs and the contradiction of their doctrines with regards to metaphysics" (*Incoherence*, 3). In particular, his attacks are directed against Ibn Sina and al-Farabi. Al-Ghazali's critique is effective because it utilizes the conceptual vocabulary and methods of the Islamic Hellenistic philosophers. Hence the "incoherence" or perhaps even more apt, destruction or collapse of their doctrines as a result of incoherence, as is captured in the title of the Latin translation of this work, *Destructio Philosophorum*. Al-Ghazali charges the Islamic Hellenistic philosophers with heresy for their belief in the eternity of the world, God's lack of knowledge of particular events, and denial of physical resurrection, all of which are in opposition to the literal sense of the Qur'an. He also attacks some of their views on natural philosophy, particularly their theory of causality. While the attack is grounded in the occasionalism of the religious philosophers, al-Ghazali's argument is reminiscent of Hume's later critique of causality. However, one needs to bear in mind that the cosmology of the "scientists," that is to say the Islamic Hellenistic philosophers, not only claims that causation derives from the natural properties of objects, for example the property of fire to burn cotton, but moreover, as a result of their Neoplatonism, ascribes a causative role to celestial bodies, souls, and intellects which, via their emanations, influence and thereby participate in the causation of events in the terrestrial realm.

In his later works, particularly *Revival* and *Autobiography*, al-Ghazali discusses his perspective, as a legal scholar, on the utility of different kinds of knowledge with particular regards to preparing oneself for the next world. Knowledge is either religious, which is transmitted by prophets, or is secular and a result of the human intellect, observation, or social convention, for example arithmetic, medicine, or language. Some secular sciences have a utilitarian role insofar as they aid human beings preserve their health or society so that they may pursue what is truly important, which is to prepare for the next world. As such, the study of medicine or arithmetic is a collective obligation on societies. Yet, one should not engage too deeply in them for one may then lose sight of the real goal of human existence and waste precious time. Apart from medicine, the natural sciences have no utility and can, like *metaphysics, lead to heresy. However, *logic is a neutral tool for it consists of methods of proof and demonstration. It is also found in the religious disciplines albeit their terminology differs from that of Islamic Hellenistic philosophy. Al-Ghazali thereby devoted several works to logic. In his *al-Qistas al-mustaqim (Correct Balance)* he even claims a Qur'anic origin for logic. In the late text *al-Mustasfa*, which was composed during his return to teaching in Nishapur, al-Ghazali incorporated the Aristotelian logic of Islamic Hellenistic philosophy into the study of the principles of jurisprudence. However, Aristotelian logic is not a neutral and formal tool. It is grounded in the Aristotelian conceptual vocabulary of substance, form, accident and the Aristotelian categories. Al-Ghazali's action thereby had the consequence of embedding elements of Aristotelian *cosmology, ontology, and epistemology in that most Islamic of disciplines—the study of the principles of jurisprudence. Al-Ghazali's attitude towards religious philosophy, on the other hand, was less than enthusiastic. He endorsed its need, as being the same as medicine, namely that it may aid those who are beset by religious doubt and therefore is a collective obligation for Islamic societies. However, he did not endorse its claim to provide certain knowledge, although agreeing to its positions regarding God's omnipotence, omniscience, prophecy, occasionalism, and the lack of human free-will.

In the *Incoherence*, al-Ghazali had charged the Islamic Hellenistic philosophers with heresy. His conservative opponents, who were opposed to his engagement, critical though it was, with the Islamic Hellenistic philosophers, the Isma'ilis, and mystical Islam in turn laid the same charge against him. Al-Ghazali's response to them is found in his *Faysal al-tafriqa ma bayna al-islam wa al-zandaqa (Clear Criterion which Distinguishes between the Religion of Islam and Heresy)*, which was probably written during his first period of retirement in Tus. Al-Ghazali examined the juridical charge of heresy, noting that this charge had been hurled for sectarian purposes, by the Hanbalis against Ash'ari religious philosophers or by the Mu'tazilis against the Ash'aris. At this point in his career, al-Ghazali urged caution against hurling this charge injudiciously and proposed latitude of interpretation of the Qur'anic text within calibrated norms that respected the literal meaning of the text while allowing for metaphorical extension.

The influence of al-Ghazali's critique of Islamic Hellenistic philosophy during the medieval period may be gauged by its having stimulated a point by point rebuttal by the Andalusi Islamic philosopher *Ibn Rushd (1198). In modern times, the contemporary sociologist Toby Huff is the latest of a series of scholars who have regarded al-Ghazali's attitudes towards science as being extremely influential for its course in Islamic civilization. Huff argues that the decline of science in Islam is to be attributed primarily to the opposition of religious philosophy. This is exemplified by al-Ghazali's critical attitude towards the sciences, in particular by his critique of causality in the *Incoherence*. Huff's hypothesis has however been criticized by many reviewers. Some point to the corresponding critique of causality by David Hume in the seventeenth century as well as to the occasionalism of the followers of Descartes which suggest that since, by themselves, these attitudes failed to inhibit Western science in the seventeenth and eighteenth centuries, they cannot be held responsible for the decline of scientific activity in Islam. Perhaps more to the point is the observation that a case for documenting the influence of al-Ghazali's attitude remains to be made, particularly in the light of continuing scientific activity in Islamic lands four to five centuries after al-Ghazali's death.

See also Aristotelianism; God in Islam

Bibliography

Alon, I. Al-Ghazali's Theory of Causality. Journal of the American Oriental Society (1980) 100: 397–405.

Dallal, A. Ghazali and the Perils of Interpretation. Journal of the American Oriental Society (2002) 122: 773–787.

Frank, Richard. Al-Ghazali and the Ash'arite School. Durham, NC: Duke University Press, 1994.

Ghazali, Abu Hamid al-. "Autobiography." In Freedom and Fulfillment: An annotated translation of al-Ghazali's Munqidh min al-Dalal and other relevant works of al-Ghazali. Tr. R. McCarthy. Boston: Twayne, 1980, 61–143.

———. "The Clear Criterion for Distinguishing between Islam and Heresy." In Freedom and Fulfillment, 145–174.

———. "The Correct Balance." In Freedom and Fulfillment, 287–332.

———. The Book of Knowledge, being a Translation with Notes of the Kitab al-'ilm of al-Ghazali's Ihya 'ulum al-din. N. Faris, tr. Delhi: International Islamic Publishers, 1988.

———. The Incoherence of the Philosophers. Michael Marmura, tr. Provo, Utah: Brigham Young University Press, 1997.

Goldziher, Ignaz. "The Attitude of Orthodox Islam towards the 'Ancient Sciences.'" In Studies in Islam. M. Schwartz, tr. New York: Oxford University Press, 1981: 185–215.

Hourani, George. A Revised Chronology of Ghazali's writings. Journal of the American Oriental Society (1984) 104: 289–302.

Huff, Toby. The Rise of Early Modern Science: Islam, China, and the West. New York: Cambridge University Press, 1993.

Laoust, Henri. La Politique de Ghazali. Paris: Paul Geuthner, 1970.

Marmura, Michael. "Al-Ghazali's Attitude towards the Secular Sciences and Logic." In Essays on Islamic Philosophy and Science. G. Hourani, ed. Albany: State University of New York Press, 1975, 100–111.

———. Ghazali and Ash'arism Revisited. Arabic Sciences and Philosophy (2002) 12: 91–110.

ALNOOR DHANANI

GILBERTUS ANGLICUS

Gilbertus Anglicus (Gilbert the Englishman) was a physician and medical writer who lived in the early part of the thirteenth century. The earliest extant manuscript of his principal writing, the Compendium Medicine (Medical Compendium), refers to him as "Gilbertus de Aquila," which may suggest his identity with the Gilbert del Egle, priest and physician, who is documented in England between at least 1205 and 1214. He may have spent much of the rest of his career on the Continent. Although it is often speculated that he studied at *Salerno, all the Salernitan works he employs were readily available in England. The alleged connection to Montpellier cannot be disproven, but evidence also points to an association with Paris. It is thought that Gilbert died around 1250, but this is speculation.

Gilbert represents learned medicine at just the point when the "new" Arabic medicine was coming out of Spain. He is credited with two works: a commentary on the poem De urinis by the Salerno-trained physician *Gilles de Corbeil (d. 1224), and the Compendium medicine, a long general encyclopedia of medical practice composed c. 1230–1240. Working in the same encyclopedic tradition of Arabic writers such as *al-Majusi and Ibn al-Jazzar, and Salernitan predecessors such as *Johannes de Sancto Paulo, Gilbert arranged his Compendium in the common a capite ad calcem (head-to-toe) format. Gilbert went into considerable detail to define each condition, discussing its etiology and differential diagnoses (where he often employed his advanced knowledge of urinalysis). Gilbert's work is also distinctive in incorporating a considerable amount of surgery. Although Gilbert rarely names his sources, he clearly drew heavily on the writings of Johannes de Sancto Paulo, Roger de Baron, the Salernitan healer Trota, and the Italian surgeon *Roger Frugard. He also is one of the earliest to make use of Averroes (*Ibn Rushd), whose works had only recently started to impact Latin medicine.

Gilbert's Compendium was widely consulted and was reproduced in Paris by the pecia system as if it were a textbook. It was also employed near the end of the thirteenth century as the principal source for Ortolf von Baierland's Arzneibuch. Although soon superseded in academic instruction by *Ibn Sina's Canon and other works, copies of Gilbert's Compendium still appear in the fifteenth century among the books of practitioners from Spain to England, and it was still being used by compilers such as the Florentine physician Niccolò Falcucci (d. 1412) and the German translator Johannes Hartlieb (d. 1468). A selective English translation of the Compendium was made early in the fifteenth century and proved to be widely influential; the gynecological section circulated separately and became the most popular Middle English text in its field. A Hebrew translation of the Compendium is also known, as are selected translations into Irish, German, and Catalan. *Geoffrey Chaucer would list Gilbert as one of the authorities well known by the Doctor of Physick, though *Guy de Chauliac famously dismissed his work as being full of "fables," unproven empirical cures, and incantations.

See also Gynecology and midwifery; Medicine, practical; Trotula

Bibliography

Getz, Faye Marie. Healing and Society in Medieval England: A Middle English Translation of the Pharmaceutical Writings of Gilbertus Anglicus. Madison: University of Wisconsin Press, 1991.

Gilbertus Anglicus. *Compendium medicine Gilberti Anglici tam morborum universalium quam particularium nondum medicis sed et cyrurgis utilissimum.* Lyons: Jacobus Sacconus, 1510.

Green, Monica H., and Linne Mooney. "The Sickness of Women." In *Sex, Aging, and Death in a Medieval Medical Compendium: TCC R.14.52, Its Language, Scribe and Text.* Edited by M. Teresa Tavormina. Tempe: Arizona State University, 2005. (Edition of a modified version of the Middle English translation of Gilbert's gynecology.)

Riha, Ortrun. "Gilbertus Anglicus und sein 'Compendium medicinae': Arbeitstechnik und Wissensorganisation." Sudhoffs Archiv (1994) 78: 59–79.

MONICA H. GREEN

GILES OF ROME

Giles of Rome was an eminent theologian and commentator on the works of Aristotle in the second half of the thirteenth century. He was born very probably in Rome c. 1243–1247. He entered the Augustinian Order in Rome and then studied philosophy and theology in Paris, where he may have attended *Thomas Aquinas's lectures in the years 1269–1272. In any case, Aquinas had a very strong influence on Giles's philosophical and theological thought. In the years 1270–1277, as a bachelor of theology at the University of Paris, Giles lectured on the four books of the *Sentences* by *Peter Lombard and wrote most of his commentaries on Aristotle's works. In 1277 he was involved in the condemnation of heterodox *Aristotelianism by the Bishop of Paris, Etienne Tempier. One of the reasons for Giles's condemnation was his defense of the Thomist positions about the unity of the substantial form and the possibility of an eternal world. Another reason was the similarities between some of his views and those of the main targets of the condemnation, such as *Siger of Brabant. In reaction to the condemnation Giles wrote the polemic treatise *Contra gradus et pluralitatem formarum*, in which he maintained that the doctrine of the unity of substantial form is philosophically sound and not contrary to faith. After the condemnation Giles probably left Paris, but he returned in 1285 and was appointed master of theology. Between 1286 and 1291 he produced six *Quodlibeta* and several collections of *Quaestiones disputatae*. Following this academic period, Giles enjoyed a prominent ecclesiastical career. In 1292 he was elected Prior General of the Augustinian Order, and in 1295 he was appointed Archbishop of Bourges by Pope Boniface VIII. Giles of Rome died in Avignon on December 22, 1316.

Metaphysics

The distinction between essence and existence is a central topic of Giles's metaphysics. Although Giles finds this distinction in the writings of Aquinas, he gives a radical and controversial interpretation of it. Giles maintains that in every creature one needs to posit essence and existence as two distinct things. The essence of a creature is ontologically prior to its existence, and existence is a thing over and above the essence that a creature acquires when it passes from potential existence to actual existence. In Giles's account, the relation between essence and existence is very similar to the relation between substance and accident in Aristotle's metaphysics. As to the structure of a composite substance, Giles's final position in the debate about the unity or plurality of substantial forms is that there is only one substantial form in any composite with the exception of the human being: the question of humans, however, he leaves open because of theological concerns. Like Aquinas, Giles holds that the principle of individuation of a composite substance is matter endowed with a quantitative mode, which is prior to a substantial form and explains the multiplication of a substantial form, the so-called indefinite dimension (*dimensio indeterminata*).

Natural Philosophy

Giles's most extensive work in natural philosophy is his lengthy commentary on Aristotle's *Physics*, which became a standard reference for later commentators. In this work Giles not only gives a detailed explanation of Aristotle's text but also proposes original interpretations of a number of central issues of Aristotle's natural philosophy. For example, in his account of rarefaction and condensation, Giles introduces a distinction between the bodily dimensions, which do not remain the same when the body is condensed or rarefied, and the quantity of matter, which remains the same. This distinction is very similar to the modern distinction between volume and mass. In order to save Aristotle's claim that the place of a body is immobile, Giles modifies Aristotle's notion of place by distinguishing between material place and formal place. The material place of a body is the limit of the body containing it, that is, place in Aristotle's sense. The formal place of a body is an order (*ordo*) or distance (*distantia*) between the located body and the fixed points of the universe. When the containing body moves, the material place of a body at rest changes but its formal place stays the same and in this sense it is immobile. While a similar distinction is found in Aquinas, Giles's account is original because it makes material place and formal place two independent items and with two quite distinct roles. Material place is a principle of delimitation of the extension of a body, while formal place defines a frame of reference for describing the motion and rest of a body. As to Aristotle's theory of the continuum, Giles maintains that the extension of natural bodies is not infinitely divisible, but that it is composed of minimal parts, the so-called natural minima (*minima naturalia*). The existence of natural minima is due to the substantial form. For each substantial form there is a minimal extension in which that form can exist. Giles maintains that Aristotle's claim that time is continuous is not universally true, and admits the existence of a discrete time conceived of as a succession of instants without any intervening period of time. For example, Giles claims that the motion of a body in the void would not take place in an instant, as Aristotle and Averroes (*Ibn Rushd) maintain, but in a succession of instants, that is, in a discrete time. Giles also modifies

Aristotle's postulate of the unity of time by admitting the simultaneous existence of many temporal durations. On the debate about the eternity of the world, Giles's early position is very close to that of Aquinas. That is, he claims that Aristotle's and Averroes's arguments for an eternal world are not conclusive because they do not take into account types of production that do not involve physical change, but that it is theoretically possible that the world is eternal. After the *Condemnation of 1277, Giles takes the more careful position according to which it is theoretically possible to prove that the world had a temporal beginning, although adequate arguments for this claim have not yet been found.

See also **Elements and qualities; "Latin Averroists";
Hylomorphism**

Bibliography

Primary Sources
Giles of Rome (c. 1269–1273). *Quaestiones Metaphysicales.* Venice, 1501.
——— (c. 1271-3). *Super librum I Sententiarum.* Venice, 1521.
——— (c. 1274). *Super De generatione et corruptione.* Venice, 1505.
——— (c. 1274). *Quaestiones super librum I De generatione et corruptione.* Venice, 1505.
——— (c. 1274). *Theoremata de Corpore Christi.* Rome, 1554.
——— (c. 1274–1275). *Super Physicam.* Venice, 1502.
——— (1277-8). *Contra gradus et pluralitatem formarum.* Venice, 1500.
——— (1278-85). *Theoremata de esse et essentia.* Ed. E. Hocedez, Louvain: Museum Lessianum, 1930.
——— (c. 1286-7). *Quaestiones de esse et essentia.* Venice, 1503.
——— (1286-91). *Quodlibeta.* Louvain, 1646.

Secondary Sources
Donati, S. La dottrina di Egidio Romano sulla materia dei corpi celesti. Discussioni sulla natura dei corpi celesti alla fine del tredicesimo secolo. *Medioevo* (1986) 12: 229–280.
———. La dottrina delle dimensioni indeterminate in Egidio Romano. *Medioevo* (1988) 14: 149–233.
———. Studi per una cronologia delle opere di Egidio Romano. 1: Le opere prima del 1285. I commenti aristotelici. *Documenti e studi sulla tradizione filosofica medievale* (1990) 1.1: 1-112; (1991) 2.1: 1–74.
Eardley, P. Thomas Aquinas and Giles of Rome on the Will. *The Review of Metaphysics* (2003) 56A: 835–862.
Hocedez, E. Gilles de Rome et Henri de Gand sur la distinction réelle (1276–1287). *Gregorianum* (1927) 8: 358–384.
Nash, P. W. Giles of Rome on Boethius' *Diversum est esse et id quod est. Mediaeval Studies* (1950) 12: 57–91.
Pini, G. "Being and creation in Giles of Rome." In *Philosophie und Theologie an der Universitdt von Paris im letzen Viertel des 13. Jahrhunderts*, Edited by J. A. Aertsen, K. Emery, and A. Speer. New York: De Gruyter, 2000.
Porro, P. Ancora sulle polemiche tra Egidio Romano e Enrico di Gand: due questioni sul tempo angelico. *Medioevo* (1988) 14: 107–148.
Trifogli, C. La dottrina del luogo in Egidio Romano. *Medioevo* (1988) 14: 235–290.
———. *La dottrina del tempo in Egidio Romano. Documenti e studi sulla tradizione filosofica medievale* (1990) Ll: 247–276.
———. Giles of Rome on Natural Motion in the Void. *Mediaeval Studies* (1992) 54: 136–161.
———. Giles of Rome on the Instant of Change. *Synthese* (1993) 96.1: 93–114.

CECILIA TRIFOGLI

GILLES DE CORBEIL

The medical writer Gilles de Corbeil was born around 1140, presumably at Corbeil in the Île de France. He studied at *Salerno, and returned to Paris sometime between c. 1180 and 1194. There he probably taught medicine, and certainly composed his medical and satirical poetry. He died around 1124.

Of his four medical poems, two were widely copied, read and commented on, namely *De urinis* and *De pulsibus*. These are essentially versifications of two of the books of the *Articella anthology, Philaretus' *De pulsibus* and Theophilus' *De urinis* (to which Gilles adds additional material from *Isaac Judaeus). Indeed, in many *Articella* manuscripts Gilles' poems actually supplant Philaretus and Theophilus, and by 1270–1274 they were on the official reading list for the licentiate in medicine in Paris. Eminent masters such as *Gilbertus Anglicus and *Gentile da Foligno composed commentaries on them. They appeared in print in Padua in 1483, and went through eight subsequent Renaissance editions.

Gilles' poem on semiology, *De signis et symptomatibus egritudinum*, may also have been conceived as a substitute for, or supplement to, elements of the *Articella*, e.g., Hippocrates' *Prognosis*. After a brief overview of the signs indicating excess of one of the four humors, Gilles treats the symptoms of named diseases from head to foot, after the manner of a manual of therapeutics. Sections on gynecological disorders and on whole-body diseases such as arthritis, leprosy, and fevers follow. Gilles also discusses the causes of these ailments, as well as the symptoms, which reinforces the resemblance of this work to a *practica*. Despite this rational arrangement, *De signis* had a much more restricted circulation in the Middle Ages than did the pulse and urine poems. This is also the case with Gilles' fourth poem, *De laudibus et virtutibus compositorum medicaminum. De laudibus* is a verse compendium of Salernitan drug therapy, directly inspired by the *Antidotarium* of *Nicolas of Salerno (whose alphabetical order it adopts) and the commentaries on the *Antidotarium* by Platearius. Indeed, Gilles describes this work as a versification of Platearius' glosses. However, it concentrates on the powers of the individual drugs and considerations regarding their administration, rather than the recipes for compounding them.

Didactic poems such as these underscore the medieval teacher's role in producing summaries for his students (for example, Gilles reduces the hundred forty recipes of the *Antidotarium* to eighty), and in making large tracts of doctrine easy to digest and remember. Like the *Aphorisms* of Hippocrates (another constituent of the *Articella*), didactic poetry distilled medical learning into pithy axioms. Nonetheless, Gilles' poems are also replete with lively digressions. Some are mildly satirical in character, such as his aside on the erectile dysfunction that can be the unexpected result of overuse of the aphrodisiac diasatyrion, and the consequent vexation of the disappointed woman. Others are autobiographical and historical. In the epilogue of *De urinis*, the prologue to Book Three of *De pulsibus*, and above all in the prologues to the first two books of *De laudibus*, Gilles invokes the memory of his Salernitan teachers—archbishop Romuald II (d. 1181), the pre-eminent master Petrus Musandinus (student of *Bartholomaeus of Salerno), Salernus, Platearius, *Maurus, and *Urso—and asks Romuald's blessing on his own project to transplant Salernitan medical learning to the banks of the Seine. Gilles presents himself as the French kingdom's first teacher of academic medicine, and vaunts his Salerno training as a guarantee of intellectual excellence, particularly in comparison to the doctrines of Montpellier. He likewise castigates the "empirics" on the loose in the capital (including the chronicler Rigord) for their lack of knowledge of theoretical medicine. On the other hand, he praises Nicholas's *Antidotarium* as much for the experience it distills as for its instruction, and closes the *De laudibus* with a lengthy and impressive account of the physician's ethics and decorum. This balance of text-based medical theory and systematized practical medicine is typically Salernitan. Gilles himself was fiercely loyal to his old school, although he laments that standards have slipped, and of late students were graduating at a dangerously young age. In the prologue to Book Two of *De laudibus*, he also complains that the rising generation was rejecting the older Salernitan teaching.

Gilles de Corbeil was close to Peter the Chanter's reform circle in Paris, and supported its agenda in a scathing satire of the failures of the contemporary Church entitled *Hierapigra ad purgandos prelatos* ("A laxative to purge prelates"). Although medicine essentially plays an allegorical role in this poem—the spiritual remedy required for spiritual ills—Gilles occasionally resumes a more clinical voice: for example, he provides medical arguments to justify the reformers' critique of enforced clerical celibacy.

See also Constantine the African; Medicine, practical; Medicine, theoretical; Pharmacy; Universities

Bibliography

Primary Sources
Aegidius Corboliensis Carmina Medica. Edited by Ludwig Choulant. Leipzig: Voss, 1826.
Viaticus de signis et symptomatibus aegritudinum. Edited by Valentin Rose. Leipzig: Teubner, 1907.
Hierapigra ad purgandos prelatos. Extracts from Bibliothèque nationale MS nouv. acq. lat. 138 published in Vieillard, Essai (see below) pp. 360–410.

Secondary Sources
Ausécache, Mireille. Gilles de Corbeil ou le médecin péda-gogique au tournant des XIIe et XIIIe siècles. *Early Science*

and Medicine (1998) 3: 187–215.
Baldwin, J.W. *Masters, Merchants and Princes: the Social Views of Peter the Chanter and his Circle.* Princeton: Princeton University Press, 1970.
D'Irsay, Stephen. The Life and Works of Gilles de Corbeil. *Annals of Medical History* (1925) 7: 362-378.
Sudhoff, Karl. Salerno, Montpellier und Paris um 1200. *Archiv für Geschichte der Medizin* (1920) 20: 51–62.
Vieillard, C. L'urologie et les médecins urologues dans la médecine ancienne. *Gilles de Corbeil: sa vie, ses oeuvres, son poème des urines.* Paris: Librairie scientifique et littéraire, 1903.
Vieillard, C. *Essai sur la société médicale et religieuse au XIIe siècle, Gilles de Corbeil.* Paris: Honoré Champion, 1909.

FAITH WALLIS

GLASSMAKING

Most glass consists of minerals heated until they melt, then cooled at a rate that prevents them from resuming their crystalline structure. Regardless of its composition, glass behaves like a solid, but has the random structure of a liquid; it is less a material, therefore, than a state of matter. Glass exists in nature and it has been manufactured for more than four thousand years. Before 1500 C.E., glassmaking was restricted to Eurasia and North Africa, although elsewhere imported glass might be melted to make small objects. This entry deals exclusively with man-made glass and its focus is Europe and the "Central Islamic lands," which extended from Egypt to Iran. The entry discusses glass melting, forming, and finishing, and the role of glass in other technologies. The most glaring omission is glass in the Byzantine Empire, about which we know surprisingly little.

Glass Melting

Medieval glass was usually made from three ingredients: silica (the major constituent, usually in the form of sand), soda or potash (which acted as a flux), and calcium (which conferred stability). Depending on the time and place, the soda was usually either the mineral trona or ash derived from halophytic plants, although in Europe from the ninth century, potash, usually derived from beech leaves or ferns, replaced soda. The calcium was often introduced inadvertently as an impurity in the soda or silica. In parts of India, glass may have been made from a single ingredient: an earth containing silica, sodium, and calcium. Sometimes glassmakers in Europe and Western Asia produced lead silicate glasses, and in China some glasses had elevated quantities of lead and barium. In all these regions, the addition of selected oxides imparted color or decolorized the glass.

From the beginning, glassmaking (melting natural ingredients to produce "raw" glass) and glass working (transforming raw glass into objects) were independent activities, which required temperatures of approximately 1000–1100°C and 650–1020°C respectively, the latter depending on the technique employed. In pre-Roman times in the Mediterranean region and Western Asia, furnaces capable of attaining such temperatures were small and consequently only a few kilograms of glass could be produced in a single operation.

In the first century B.C.E., glass working was transformed by the discovery of glassblowing (see below), which enabled glass workers to produce a greater range of forms and to work more quickly than ever before. This accelerated production, and the corresponding increase in consumption that archeologists have noted throughout the Roman world, imply the ability to make raw glass on an unprecedented scale. The breakthrough that made this possible was the invention of the reverberatory tank furnace, where raw materials were fed into tanks capable of melting several tons at a time. The first known tank furnaces, in Egypt and the Levant, date from early Byzantine or Islamic times, but circumstantial evidence suggests that their invention may have taken place not long after the discovery of glassblowing. The presence of several tons of cullet (raw glass and broken vessels) on the underwater shipwreck at Serçe Limani, Turkey, indicate the large-scale trade in glass for recycling when the ship went down about 1026, while literary and archeological evidence shows that glassmakers at Tyre were exporting large quantities of raw glass both before and after the crusaders occupied the city in 1124.

We know little about medieval furnaces for glass working in the Central Islamic lands, but archeological excavations and literary sources (e.g., the twelfth-century writer Theophilus and a drawing of a workshop in a fifteenth-century manuscript of *Mandeville's Travels*) tell us something about workshops in Europe. Production was on a small scale and glass was both made and worked in the same place. Unless it was deliberately colored, most medieval European glass was light green or brown because of impurities in the raw materials. Beginning in the thirteenth century, however, glassmakers in some areas manufactured colorless glass: the forerunner of *cristallo* glass in Renaissance Venice. The medieval products were known as *Waldglas* (forest glass) because the workshops were usually located in forests that provided both fuel and potash.

Glass Forming and Finishing

The principal techniques of forming glass in the Mediterranean region and Western Asia in pre-Roman times were core forming, casting in molds, and slumping over forms. Core forming consisted of applying glass to a ceramic core, which was later removed mechanically. The labor-intensive technique was superseded very quickly by glass blowing. From time to time throughout the medieval period, various methods of casting and slumping were used in Eurasia and North Africa. In every region, however, the preferred method of forming glass vessels in the Middle Ages was blowing.

The word "glassblowing" is often used loosely to mean any kind of glass working: an indication of the extent to which glassblowing dominates the traditional repertoire of the glassworker. Strictly speaking, however, glassblowing is the term used to describe the process of gathering a mass of molten glass on the end of a blowpipe and inflating it by blowing through the other end.

The tools used by modern glassblowers are few and simple. In addition to the blowpipe, they include the marver (a smooth surface used to shape partly formed vessels), pontil (a metal rod used to support unfinished objects after removal from the blowpipe), jacks or pucellas (spring-loaded pincers used for shaping the glass), and molds. All these tools were used in the Roman world and we assume that they were universally available in the Middle Ages. Other traditional tools, which may or may not have been available, include blocks, shears, and the *soffietta* (puffer), which is used to inflate partly formed vessels when they are on the pontil.

During inflation, the mass of molten glass ("parison") was shaped in various ways, using some of the tools mentioned above. In addition to making vessels, the glassworker could blow the parison into a cylindrical form, which was cut open, flattened, and cut into window panes; or it could be spun into a disk to make circular "crown" panes. After modest beginnings, flat glass was produced on a prodigious scale in Europe in and after the twelfth century to satisfy the demand for large pictorial windows in churches.

Alternatively, the parison might be inflated in a decorated mold. Cup-shaped "dip" molds imparted patterns that remained in the glass regardless of the ultimate shape of the object, while "full-size" molds imparted both the pattern and the shape. Both types of mold were widely employed in the Islamic world, while in Europe dip molds were much more common than full-size molds. At the end of the forming process, all glass objects were allowed to cool slowly (a process known as annealing) to eliminate stresses, which could cause them to self-destruct.

At different times and in different places, glass workers in the Islamic world used a wide range of decorative techniques in addition to inflation in molds. While the object was still hot, they sometimes applied trails of molten glass, which could be left in relief or worked into the surface of the object by rolling it on a marver. They also produced repetitive ornament by pinching the object with decorated tongs. After objects had been annealed, they could be decorated by painting with vitreous enamels, gilding, or metallic stain, processes which required re-heating to fix the pigments permanently. An alternative technique, at which glass workers in the Central Islamic Lands excelled in the ninth and tenth centuries, was cutting, grinding, and polishing the surface with rotating wheels fed with an abrasive slurry.

Glassworkers in Europe used a smaller range of decorative techniques and, as far as we know, cutting was not practiced before the Renaissance and the use of staining was restricted to a limited quantity of late medieval window glass.

The Role of Glass in Other Technologies

Glass is everywhere and we tend to take it for granted. However, its role in the development of medieval science and technology was enormous. Glass vessels made possible medical diagnosis by uroscopy (inspection of urine samples), which began in the Islamic world, from which it spread to Europe. Glass apparatus was indispensable for scientific experiments. Beginning in the thirteenth century, Europeans had access to eyeglasses, which assisted everyone whose activities depended on close observation. In the words of Macfarlane and Martin "almost every great scientific advance needed glass at some stage."

See also **Eyeglasses; Mineralogy**

Bibliography

Baumgartner, Erwin and Ingeborg Krueger. *Phönix aus Sand und Asche: Glas des Mittelalters*. Munich: Klinkhardt & Biermann, 1988.

Brill, Robert H. and John H. Martin, ed. *Scientific Research in Early Chinese Glass*. Proceedings of The Archaeometry of Glass Sessions of the 1984 International Symposium on Glass, September 1984, Beijing. Corning: The Corning Museum of Glass, 1991.

Carboni, Stefano. *Glass from Islamic Lands*. New York: Thames & Hudson Inc., 2001.

Carboni, Stefano and David Whitehouse. *Glass of the Sultans*. New York: The Metropolitan Museum of Art, 2001.

Dell'Acqua, Francesca and Romano Silva, eds. *Il Colore nel Medioevo: Arte Simbolo Tecnica: La Vetrata in Occidente dal IV all'XI Secolo*. Papers presented at the third international conference on Color in the Middle Ages, September 1999, Lucca, Italy. Lucca: Istituto Storico Lucchese, Scuola Normale Superiore di Pisa, and Corpus Vitrearum Medii Aevi Italia, 2001.

Dodwell, C.R. *Theophilus, De Diuersis Artibus: Theophilus, The Various Arts*. London: Thomas Nelson and Sons Ltd., 1961.

Foy, Danièle and Geneviève Sennequier. *À travers le verre du moyen âge à la renaissance*. Rouen: Musées et Monuments départementaux de la Seine-Maritime, 1989.

Macfarlane, Alan and Gerry Martin. *Glass: A World History*. Chicago, The University of Chicago Press 2002.

Nenna, Marie-Dominique, ed. *La route du verre: ateliers primaires et secondaires du second millénaire av. J.-C. au Moyen Âge*. Lyon: Maison del'Orient Mediterranéen-Jean Pouilloux, 2000.

Raguin, Virginia Chieffo. *The History of Stained Glass: The Art of Light, Medieval to Contemporary*. New York: Thames & Hudson Inc., 2003.

Tait, Hugh, ed. *Five Thousand Years of Glass*. London: British Museum Press, 1991 (revised 1999).

Ward, Rachel, ed. *Gilded and Enamelled Glass from the Middle East*. London: British Museum Press, 1998.

DAVID WHITEHOUSE

GOD IN CHRISTIANITY

During the Middle Ages, God played practically no role in the mathematical, or exact, sciences of astronomy, optics, and mechanics, largely because there were no issues in the mathematical sciences that conflicted with Scripture or traditional theology. It was quite otherwise with the discipline of natural philosophy. The Biblical account of creation in Genesis guaranteed that the Christian God would play a significant role in the natural philosophy of the Latin Middle Ages. This was so primarily because of the works of Aristotle, whose numerous writings on natural philosophy were translated from Greek and Arabic into Latin during the twelfth and thirteenth centuries and thereafter formed the basis of all natural philosophy until the sixteenth century. Aristotle's treatises on natural philosophy, and the numerous commentaries on those works by his medieval followers, were concerned primarily with change and motion and the causes thereof. The domain of natural philosophy was therefore the entire physical world, which in Aristotle's interpretation meant both the celestial region (everything beyond the moon) and the terrestrial region (everything below the lunar sphere to the center of the earth).

Aristotle's views on a number of issues were contrary to Christian ideas about the world and its governance. His ideas about God were radically different. Aristotle's God did not create the world, which Aristotle regarded as eternal, without beginning or end; nor does he have anything to do with it. Indeed, he does not even know it exists. Aristotle thought of God as an immaterial, immobile substance located at the sphere of the fixed stars, the outermost sphere of our spherical cosmos. God thinks only of himself, because only he is an object of thought.

By contrast, the Christian God of Genesis is an all-powerful creator who created the world from nothing, requiring no prior material bodies or substances to do so. In creating the cosmos, God chose to make it a world of lawful regularity, although He could have made it otherwise, since He had infinite possibilities from which to draw. During the Middle Ages, theologians distinguished between God's ordained power (*potentia ordinata*) and His absolute power (*potentia absoluta*). By His ordained power, God chose the laws and entities He wished to include in the world. Once He had made his selections, it was generally believed that, apart from a miracle here and there, God would not intervene and alter the natural laws of the world He had created. That would imply a change of mind, which to theologians would have been unthinkable. The myriad of unrealized possibilities was now only hypothetically possible. It was, however, assumed that, by His absolute power, God could, if He wished, convert any of those hypothetical possibilities into reality, provided that such an act did not involve a logical contradiction.

Because it was believed that God had created a rational, lawfully operating universe, natural philosophers at the medieval universities, where almost all treatises on natural philosophy were written, found it unnecessary to intrude God into their discussions. Miracles were not regarded as part of natural philosophy. Nevertheless, for most of the thirteenth century, the Church and many conservative theologians were fearful that some of Aristotle's ideas and concepts about the world and its structure would subvert the faith. This was especially true at the University of Paris. In 1210, it was forbidden in Paris to read Aristotle's works on natural philosophy. This ban seems to have been ineffective, because by 1231 the

Church sought to purge the offensive errors from Aristotle's works and leave a sanitized version for scholars and students. The expurgation of Aristotle's texts was never carried out, and by 1255 all of Aristotle's works in natural philosophy were in use as textbooks in the arts curriculum at the University of Paris. By the late 1260s, a final assault was made. Rather than ban or expurgate Aristotle's works as had previously been attempted, the theologians now chose to issue public condemnations of ideas, many drawn from natural philosophy. The crisis came in 1277, when the bishop of Paris condemned two hundred and nineteen propositions or articles. Although the list was drawn up hastily, and was inconsistent and repetitious, many of the articles were relevant to natural philosophy and most were derived from the works of Aristotle.

Parisian theologians were deeply concerned about the restrictions Aristotle had inadvertently placed on God's absolute power. These limitations operated even in an area where Aristotle's theories and the Christian faith were in accord. If the creation account in Genesis strongly suggested a temporal beginning for the world, it also seemed to signify its uniqueness. Here, at least, Aristotle and Christianity seemed in agreement: there is only one world. This apparent unanimity was, however, deceptive. Although Aristotle's conclusion might be applauded, his derivation of it was offensive because he had argued that the existence of another world was impossible, or, as he put it, "there is not now a plurality of worlds, nor has there been, nor could there be" (De caelo 1.9. 279a. 7–11). To argue that creation of other worlds was absolutely impossible was viewed as a restriction on God's absolute power to do as He pleases. For this reason, article 34 condemned the idea that God could not create other worlds.

The *Condemnation of 1277 made it clear that what Aristotle regarded as "natural impossibilities" were not impossible for God, Who could make them realities if He so desired. Indeed, article 147 condemned those who believed "That the absolutely impossible cannot be done by God or another agent—An error, if impossible, is understood according to nature." Because of the condemnation, it became obligatory for all natural philosophers to concede that, by His absolute power, God could, if He wished, bring into existence any natural impossibility that Aristotle had identified. As a consequence, medieval natural philosophers and theologians conjured up hypothetical situations in which God was imagined to create other worlds that existed simultaneously; or that came into existence successively; and even worlds that existed simultaneously, one within another. In their conjectures, natural philosophers imagined that God created other worlds that were identical to ours, and then concluded that those worlds would be completely independent of each other with each operating by the same laws that governed our world. Although no one in the Middle Ages really believed that God had created other worlds of the kind described here, they did regard such worlds as supernaturally possible, whereas Aristotle considered them to be utterly impossible.

One of the condemned articles (article 49) held that God could not move the world with a rectilinear motion. Natural philosophers then argued that God could indeed do so, even though such a motion violated Aristotle's belief in an immobile cosmos and his concept of the way a body occupies a place or space.

Articles 34 and 49 both presupposed void spaces beyond our world. Some scholastic theologians assumed that an infinite void existed beyond our world, but that it was not a space created by God. Indeed, it was uncreated, because it was equated with God's infinite omnipresent immensity. Because God is an immaterial being without extension, English theologian *Thomas Bradwardine (c. 1290–1349) characterized Him as "infinitely extended without extension." By equating infinite void space with God's immensity, infinite space was regarded as real, though without extension. By being the first to introduce God into infinite space, medieval theologians influenced the spatial conceptions of seventeenth century scientists and philosophers, especially Samuel Clarke, Isaac Newton, Pierre Gassendi, and Thomas Hobbes.

Natural philosophers also assumed that, despite Aristotle's claim that a vacuum within our world is impossible, God could, if He wished, create vacua within our world. They imagined that God might do this by annihilating all or part of the matter that existed in our world. If He did, they then posed and answered questions such as: could material objects located within such a void space be capable of finite, rectilinear motion; or would their motions be instantaneous, as Aristotle argued? Would it be possible to measure distances in such void places? If people were located in such empty spaces, would they be capable of seeing and hearing each other? By such unusual and interesting questions, the concept of God's absolute power became an instrument for the introduction of subtle and imaginative questions, which were usually answered in terms of Aristotelian physics and cosmology, even though such "contrary to fact" conditions were impossible in Aristotle's natural philosophy. Although these novel questions and responses were subversive of Aristotle's natural philosophy, they did not cause the abandonment of the Aristotelian worldview. But they made many aware that things deemed impossible by Aristotle were indeed possible by God's supernatural power and, moreover, if God chose to enact all, or some, of them, they would be intelligible.

What God Can and Cannot Do

During the Middle Ages, only professional theologians were authorized to express themselves about God's attributes and powers. They usually did this in theological commentaries on the Sentences (Sententiae, or "opinions"), the basic theological textbook composed in the twelfth century by *Peter Lombard (c. 1095–1160), who divided his treatise into four books, the first of which was about God. Since medieval theologians were thoroughly trained in natural philosophy and logic, it became commonplace for them to inject both subjects into all sorts of theological questions, especially those concerned with God. It is no exaggeration to say that theologians transformed theology into a highly analytical subject that was heavily logico-mathematical and which was permeated by natural philosophy.

During the thirteenth and fourteenth centuries, theologians posed an amazing array of questions about God and His attributes and powers. They inquired about His knowledge; what He could or could not do; and what He had intended to do. In all these questions, it was axiomatically assumed that God could not produce simultaneous, contradictory actions. He could not, for example, make something exist and not exist at the same moment. Such an action was regarded as unintelligible. A primary concern was whether God could create an actual infinite magnitude or multitude. Some theologians were convinced that this would involve God in a contradiction, because if God created an actually infinite magnitude, He would be unable to create anything larger, since there is nothing larger than an infinite magnitude. Thus God's absolute power to do anything whatever would be restricted, which involves a contradiction.

There were theologians, however, who did not believe that a contradiction would be involved if God created an actually infinite magnitude or multitude. A major area of debate concerned the eternity of the world. Could God have created the world from eternity? St. Bonaventure (c. 1217–1274) drew what he regarded as a number of impossible consequences to demonstrate the absurdity of an eternal world and the necessity to believe in its creation. *St. Thomas Aquinas (c. 1224–1274), and others, however, rejected Bonaventure's arguments and insisted that neither the creation of the world nor its eternity was demonstrable. Thomas also proclaimed that no logical contradiction was involved in assuming that God could have created a world that existed from eternity, and which was therefore co-eternal with Himself.

Because God is an omnipresent, infinite being, theologians were strongly attracted to the infinite and found numerous occasions to discuss its different aspects. In the fourteenth century, a few of those who believed that God could create an actual infinite arrived at results about the nature of the infinite that were only rediscovered in the nineteenth century with the promulgation of infinite set theory by Georg Cantor. Gregory of Rimini (d. 1358) was convinced that God could produce three different kinds of infinites: an infinite magnitude, an infinite multitude, and an infinitely intense quality. Gregory showed that such terms as "part," "whole," "greater than," and "less than" were also applicable to infinites. In the course of his lengthy discussion, Gregory discovered the counter-intuitive idea that a part of an infinite can equal the whole infinite, which we can illustrate (although Gregory did not) by placing the even numbers into one-to-one correspondence with the natural numbers. Also in the fourteenth century, Henry of Harclay argued that one infinite can be greater than another, another idea that would be fully developed by Cantor in the nineteenth century.

Theologians also applied the concept of infinite divisibility to show what God could or could not do. By the use of proportional parts, they showed how God could make an infinite number of angels in an hour. They also conjured up examples to show how God's power might, under certain unusual circumstances, be indecisive. One theologian, Robert Holkot, imagined that in the last hour of his life, a man is meritorious in the first proportional part of the hour and unmeritorious in the second proportional part; he is again meritorious in the third proportional part, and unmeritorious in the fourth proportional part, and so on through an infinite series of decreasing proportional parts. Because the instant of death is not part of the infinite sequence of diminishing proportional parts, there can be no last instant in which the man can be either meritorious or sinful. Therefore God cannot judge him. Here again, the application of logico-mathematical techniques to God's powers led medieval theologians to strange conclusions.

Much of medieval theology devoted to God utilized natural philosophy and logico-mathematical analysis to explore God's powers and to determine what He could or could not do. Since it was assumed that God could do anything that did not involve a logical contradiction, much of the analysis of His powers to perform this or that action—for example, whether He could make a creature exist for only an instant—was an effort to determine whether a logical contradiction was involved in the performance of that action. Because of this extraordinary and distinctive concern, the Christian God of the Middle Ages in Western Europe differs dramatically from the Christian God of the modern world. This is immediately evident from the rather unusual questions medieval theologians proposed about God's powers, a number of which have already been mentioned:

Whether the foreknowledge of God is the cause of the future being the future.

Whether God could make the future not to be.

Whether God could do evil things.

Whether God could have made the world before He made it.

Whether God knew that He would create a world from eternity.

Whether without any change in Himself, God could not want something that at some (earlier) time He had wanted.

These, and numerous other, questions were largely answered by the application of logico-mathematical analysis that was regularly employed in natural philosophy.

See also **God in Islam; Religion and Science**

Bibliography

Courtenay, William J. John of Mirecourt and Gregory of Rimini on Whether God can Undo the Past. In *Recherches de théologie ancienne et médiévale* (1973) 40: 147–174. Reprinted in William J. Courtenay, *Covenant and Causality in Medieval Thought: Studies in Philosophy, Theology and Economic Practice*. London: Variorum Reprints, 1984, VIIIb.

———. *Capacity and Volition: a History of the Distinction of Absolute and Ordained Power*. Bergamo: Lubrina, 1990.

Funkenstein, Amos. *Theology and the Scientific Imagination from the Middle Ages to the Seventeenth Century.* Princeton: Princeton University Press, 1986.

Gilson, Etienne. *Reason and Revelation in the Middle Ages.* New York: Charles Scribner's Sons, 1938.

Grant, Edward. "God, Science, and Natural Philosophy in the Late Middle Ages." In Lodi Nauta and Arjo Vanderjagt, eds., *Between Demonstration and Imagination, Essays in the History of Science and Philosophy Presented to John D. North.* Edited by Lodi Nauta and Arjo Vanderjagt. Leiden: Brill, 1999, 243–267.

———. *God and Reason in the Middle Ages.* New York: Cambridge University Press, 2001.

Oakley, Francis. *Omnipotence, Covenant, and Order: an Excursion in the History of Ideas from Abelard to Leibniz.* Ithaca: Cornell University Press, 1984.

EDWARD GRANT

GOD IN ISLAM

In the Qur'an, the scriptural text of Islam, God is depicted as the Creator of the world, who created the world in six days, and then "sat" on His Throne. He hears, He sees, He creates directly by the command "Be!"; He is omnipotent, He "gives life and brings on death," He displays lightning, He brings on rain-clouds, He is the rain-maker, He makes crops grow, He is the agent who causes the embryo to grow and become fully grown, there is nothing that He has neglected in creation; He is omniscient, knowing "what goes into the earth and what emerges from it, what comes down from the sky and what rises up towards it" and He knows "your hidden secrets and apparent actions." God describes Himself with several attributes, Creator, Merciful, Knowing, Living, etc. The beings of creation continually praise and worship Him. The creation is full of signs of God; examples are the transformation of the dead land in spring, the creation of sexual pairs, the transformation of night into day, the use of constellations to guide man's travels, etc. Man needs to reflect on these signs and remember his Creator. Man will be resurrected and see his Creator on the Last Day when he will have to account for his actions.

Early Islamic discussions focused on the anthropomorphic and corporeal descriptions of God in the text of the Qur'an. Literalists asserted that problematic passages were to be accepted without question (literally "asking how"). But others who were opposed to literalism noted that these passages must be understood allegorically, for example, "God's Hand" represents His Power. The religious discipline of *kalam*, which is sometimes translated as "theology," emerged out of these discussions. In its classical form, formulated in the early tenth century, *kalam* asserted that God is completely different from Creation, which He created *ex nihilo*, God is the Omnipotent, nothing happens in the creation without God's power and knowledge; there is no natural causation as only God has, and in the view of one school of *kalam* human beings in a limited sense have the power of causal agency. God's freedom of action is absolute. Any notion that we have of uniformity in the working of nature is due to God's custom or habit of creating the same sequence of events, for example burning when fire and cotton are brought together. In fact, objects like fire and cotton are completely inert and have no properties which play a role in the burning when they are brought together. The conjunction of what are thought to be causes and effects are actually just concomitant events. Burning is, in fact, directly caused by God and is an intentional act, a free choice. The fact that God sometimes chooses to follow a different sequence of events is evident in those occurrences which we term "miracles."

The beginnings of Arabo-Islamic science are coterminous with the end of the process of the development of classical *kalam* (late eighth and ninth centuries C.E.). The pursuit of science started with the appropriation of the scientific knowledge of previous civilizations primarily via the movement to translate Greek and other scientific texts into Arabic. As such, the commitment of most scientists, during this period of the appropriation and subsequently naturalization of science in Arabic, was to the philosophical cosmology of a Neoplatonized Aristotelianism, known as *falsafa* (the Arabic transliteration of the Greek *philosophia*), which studied "the true nature of things." For Muslim scientist-philosophers, God was a Muslim version of the Neoplatonic Aristotelian God. *Falsafa* had definite positions regarding the nature of God as creator, the active engagement of God in the world, and the nature of God's knowledge. Uniquely, the early scientist-philosopher *al-Kindi (d. 870), argued that the world originated *ex nihilo* through God's direct act of creation. He supported this position by utilizing arguments which derive from the Christian philosopher-theologian Johannes Philoponus (fl. 6th century). Later scientist-philosophers such as *al-Farabi (d. 950), *Ibn Sina (d. 1037), and *Ibn Rushd (d. 1198) rejected al-Kindi's view and were committed to Aristotle's original position that the world is eternal, and the Neoplatonic view that the world is eternally emanating from God, and that emanation (or "overflowing") is the nature of Divinity. As such the question of whether God wills or chooses to emanate is meaningless. In fact the whole notion of whether we can have positive knowledge about God was raised, and many practitioners of *falsafa* asserted that we can only describe God through negative attributes. However, they agreed that God does not directly and intentionally intervene in the workings of the universe, but rather the events that occur in it are the result of natural causation, that is to say, the events are a result of the natural properties of objects and their receptivity to the "influences" of the emanations of celestial beings, that is to say celestial intellects and celestial souls. These natural properties and celestial influences therefore play a causal role in the events that occur in the world (which are thereby their effects). From the viewpoint of the concept of God, this is a completely deterministic world in which God's activity and role is limited to emanation. Moreover, this emanation is necessary and it follows therefore that God has no freedom of action. Yet, even though God is not directly engaged in the workings of the world, He is still the Aristotelian Unmoved Mover and the First Cause. On the basis of this view of Divine remoteness, and their notion of God's utter simplicity, the scientist-philosophers asserted that God's knowledge is universal and unchanging, and therefore confined to eternal, universal principles rather than knowledge of actual particular events and of particular individuals. As such, the *falsafa* concept of God represents a significant departure from the literalist reading of the Qur'an and the position of *kalam* and thereby demands an allegorical reading of revelation.

The religious thinker *al-Ghazali (d. 1111) criticized these views of the practitioners of *falsafa* in his *The Incoherence of the Philosopher*. Chief among these are the metaphysical views of the practitioners of *falsafa* regarding the eternity of the world, God's knowledge of particulars, their denial of physical resurrection, and their view on natural philosophy which claims that objects have natural properties which play a role in causation. On the basis of his detailed discussion of the first three of these views of the scientist-philosophers, al-Ghazali accuses them of unbelief. Therefore, in his view, the scientist-philosophers have placed themselves outside the normative beliefs of Islam. But in a later juridical work, *Clear Criterion*, which distinguishes between the religion of Islam and heresy, al-Ghazali offers a more nuanced discussion of the interpretive possibilities, particularly when the literal sense of the Qur'an conflicts with actual order of things, which in this case are the positions of *falsafa*'s philosophical cosmology. Al-Ghazali's *Incoherence* and *Clear* criterion were in turn criticized by the Andalusian scientist-philosopher Ibn Rushd in his *Incoherence of the Incoherence* and his *On the harmony between religion and philosophy*. In the later work, which is written from the perspective of his role as a jurist, Ibn Rushd utilizes the Qur'anic view of creation as containing the signs of God in his argument that the activity of science-philosophy (Ibn Rushd uses the term *hikma*, meaning wisdom, instead of *falsafa*!) is the study of existing things and reflecting on them as signs of their Maker. Therefore, the study of science-philosophy is not only sanctioned, but necessary from the perspective of Islamic Law. Ibn Rushd's position thus highlights the contentious position that its base, scientific activity, is a window to God's creation.

Following its decline in the thirteenth century, *falsafa* was, at least in many Sunni circles, incorporated into the discussions of *kalam*. This meant of course that the problematic *falsafa* views on creation *ex nihilo*, emanationism, natural causation, Divine knowledge, and God's lack of freedom of action had to be replaced by *kalam* views on these questions. Many scientists were now engaged in non-scientific professions which were affiliated with religious institutions of learning like the *madrasa* sometimes like law or Arabic grammar. Moreover, some mathematicians were employed by religious institutions, for example as official mosque time-keepers (*muwaqqit*). This then raises the question of whether they remained committed to the *falsafa* views on God and causation or the *kalam* views on these questions. As a result, A.I. Sabra suggests that they may have therefore held an instrumentalist view of knowledge. However, this thesis requires further research via an inquiry into the actual beliefs of the scientists of this period, and thereby their concept of God.

See also **Aristotelianism; God in Christianity**

Bibliography

al-Ghazalı, Abu Hamid. "The Clear Criterion for Distinguishing between Islam and Heresy." In *Freedom and Fulfillment: An Annotated Translation of al-Ghazali's Munqidh min al-Dalal and other relevant works of al-Ghazali*. Tr. R. McCarthy. Boston: Twayne, 1980, pp. 145–174.
———. *The Incoherence of the Philosophers*. Tr. Michael Marmura. Provo: Brigham Young University Press, 1997.
al-Kindı, Abu Ya'qub. *Al-Kindi's Metaphysics*. Tr. A. Ivry. Albany: State University of New York Press, 1974.
Ibn Rushd. *On the Harmony of Religion and Philosophy*. Tr. George Hourani. London: Luzac, 1967.
———. *The Incoherence of the Incoherence*. Tr. Simon van den Bergh. London: Luzac, 1978.
Rahman, Fazlur. *The Major Themes of the Qur'an*. Minneapolis: Bibliotheca Islamica, 1980.
Sabra, A.I. The appropriation and subsequent naturalization of Greek science in medieval Islam: A preliminary statement. *History of Science* (1987) 25: 223–243.

ALNOOR DHANANI

GROSSETESTE, ROBERT

Robert Grosseteste (c. 1170–1253), an influential philosopher and theologian, was born into a humble family in Suffolk, England. The first twenty years of his life are wanting in historical details. It is unclear how he was able to gain a basic education and eventually become so learned in the liberal arts. The earliest evidence places him in and around the diocese of Hereford where he was a member of the bishop's household from 1192 to 1198. That position was gained in part by a recommendation from Gerald of Wales who described the young Grosseteste as being learned in both canon law and medicine. The connection to Hereford may explain Grosseteste's initial exposure to medieval science, as it was a center for the study and dissemination of newly translated texts in natural philosophy. However, his two earliest works—one on the liberal arts in general (*De artibus liberalibus*), and another that advanced a theory of sound (*De generatione sonorum*)—reveal no influence of the new Arabic or Greek thought. After 1198 Grosseteste almost entirely disappears from the historical record until 1225, when he obtained an ecclesiastical benefice in the diocese of Lincoln. Four or five years later, the Franciscan convent at Oxford petitioned him to become its first lector in theology, a position he occupied until 1235, when the canons of Lincoln elected him bishop. Despite being responsible for the largest diocese in medieval England and being zealously committed to pastoral reform, Grosseteste was able to make time for theological and philosophical study. Most notably, he further developed

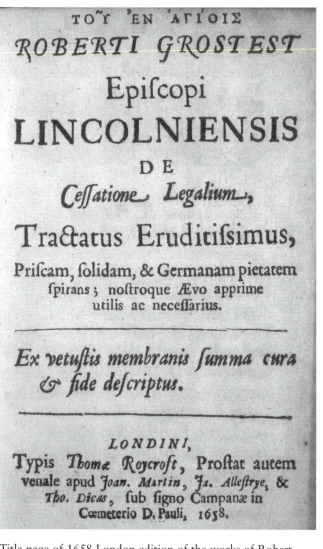

ΤΟΥ 'ΕΝ 'ΑΓΙΟΙΣ
ROBERTI GROSTEST

Epifcopi
LINCOLNIENSIS
D E
Ceffatione Legalium,

Tractatus Eruditiſsimus,

Priſcam, folidam, & Germanam pietatem
ſpirans; noſtroque Ævo apprime
utilis ac neceſſarius.

*Ex vetuſtis membranis ſumma cura
& fide defcriptus.*

LONDINI,
Typis *Thomæ Roycroft,* Proſtat autem
venale apud *Joan. Martin, Ja. Alleſtrye,* &
Tho. Dicas, ſub ſigno Campanæ in
Cœmeterio D. Pauli, 1658.

Title page of 1658 London edition of the works of Robert Grosseteste. (University of Pennsylvania Library/Edgar Fahs Smith Collection)

his ability to read Greek (which he had begun to learn while teaching the Oxford Franciscans), and began major translation projects including the corpus of Pseudo-Dionysius the Areopagite, the major works of John of Damascus, the first complete Latin rendering of the *Nicomachean Ethics,* a partial translation of Aristotle's *De caelo,* translations of some Greek commentators of Aristotle, and two other Pseudo-Aristotelian works (*De virtute* and *De lineis indivisibilibus*). Grosseteste died on October 9, 1253, leaving behind an impressive corpus of translation, commentary, and analysis.

Grosseteste's writings before 1220 are not very remarkable as they are more recapitulations of the Latin scientific tradition than original contributions. He makes consistent appeal to the teachings of the astrologers and alchemists, although he would unequivocally reject the validity of both after 1225. Among these early writings, however, is the notable *De sphaera* (c. 1215). Many scholars have speculated on the relationship between this text and *John of Sacrobosco's work of the same name. There is some evidence that Grosseteste may have had a copy of the latter as he wrote his own, and it may have been his attempt to put flesh on the bare bones of Sacrobosco's text. Even if a firm relationship between these two treatises cannot be established, later English readers of Sacrobosco's *De sphaera* employed Grosseteste's own text as a magisterial gloss.

After 1220, Grosseteste's scientific interests took an important turn. He began to integrate into his Neoplatonic worldview the writings of Aristotle, including newly translated texts and their Arabic commentaries. This amalgamation led to his major scientific and philosophical interest: the action of light. The reading of Aristotle had challenged Grosseteste to reconsider causation in the natural world. His exploration of meteorological phenomena (*De impressionibus elementorum*) included an account of how the rays of the Sun (and not Sun as a warm body itself) could account for the climatic differences between the various geographic regions. Hence it is the action of the reflection and condensation of rays that explains the warmth of valleys and the coldness of mountaintops. Heat caused by the Sun's rays also explains the appearance and disappearance of clouds as they moved through the three levels of the atmosphere. In his treatment of the cause of tides, Grosseteste is far more explicit on the causal nature of light. The explanation of change in the elements can be explained only in terms of rarefaction and condensation. This raises two fundamental premises: first, rarefaction is the motion of matter toward the periphery, and condensation is movement towards the center; second, since earth cannot be condensed any further and fire cannot be rarefied any more, the focus of elemental motion is on air and water. Having dealt with change in the air in a previous treatise, Grosseteste elects to examine motion in water, as exemplified in tidal movements. Despite the focus on one natural occurrence, he continues his discussion with a universal claim, namely that the efficient cause of elemental motion must be supralunary since an element cannot move itself nor can it be moved by another element. Grosseteste attaches the long-standing assertion that the Moon is the efficient cause of tides to a non-Aristotelian notion that the rays of light emitted by the Moon cause the waters to move. Light has become for him the medium by which heavenly bodies can influence the sublunary world.

Grosseteste developed his theory of light in two important ways in subsequent writings. The first was metaphysical as he claimed that light was the basis of all corporeal reality. "I consider the first corporeal form," Grosseteste writes in *De luce,* "which some call corporeity itself, to be light." This treatise is in part an attempt to resolve a quandary about the origins of corporeal bodies within a hylomorphic universe. Matter on its own has no extension, and requires a form to impress it to create a body. However, a form also has no extension since it is simple. Hence it would appear that something else is required to create a body with form and matter—unless there was a corporeal form that has its own capabilities of generating itself and could do so in a multidimensional way. The only created thing that can do this is light. Therefore, this light "multiplied itself by its very nature an infinite number of times on all sides and spread itself out uniformly in every direction. In this way it proceeded in the beginning of time to extend matter which it could not leave behind, by drawing it out along with itself into a mass the size of the material universe." The multiplication of light occurred until it reached its rarified maximum. The subsequent condensation produced the heavenly spheres and then the full condensation of light created the Earth. His "light metaphysics" would also lead Grosseteste to posit that color was light incorporated into a material body that could be seen by the human eye only when a greater light was diffused over it (*De colore*). This proposition in turn became the central metaphor for his theological account of truth, namely that each created thing contained truth in the same way a material body incorporated light as its color, but it required illumination by the uncreated light in order for the human mind to perceive the truth of a thing.

Secondly, the action of light demanded a more sophisticated account of rectilinear motion, and the only science that could adequately explain this was Euclidean geometry. While Grosseteste had begun to study the Greek and Arabic sources for Aristotle's *Optics* after 1220, it was not until the end of that decade and into the next that he had fully digested their principles. That full understanding of classical optics emerged in *De lineis, angulis et figuris* (c. 1228). It begins with a rather astounding assertion a for a medieval thinker: "All the causes of the natural *world* can be discovered in lines, angles, and figures, otherwise those causes could never be fully known." Grosseteste pursued one major example in his study of the rainbow (*De iride*), in which he notes that the *Physics* allows the enquirer to come to know the *quid* of the natural world, but it is the *Optics* that reveals the *propter quid*. This treatise also introduced a theory of refraction to explain the variation of color in a rainbow as well as its shape, in contradistinction to Aristotle who had used only reflection.

In addition to reading Aristotle for his own interests, Grosseteste also produced commentaries on the *Prior* and *Posterior Analytics*, the *Sophistici Elenchi*, *De caelo et mundo*, as well as notes on the *Physics* and the *Nicomachean Ethics*. John of Salisbury had commented a generation before that only mathematicians seemed to grasp the *Posterior Analytics*. Not surprisingly, then, Grosseteste's own commentary, the first in the Latin West (c. 1228–1230), adopts a Euclidian model where he regularly pauses to identify the "conclusions" that Aristotle had demonstrated—and this is in addition establishing the explicit connection between mathematics and Aristotle's own theory of scientific demonstration. Mathematics, for example, is presented as the ultimate example of knowledge of the universal, since the numerical objects are known consistently in one mode (in contrast to natural philosophy in which the frequency of things moves the mind towards the universal). And,

mathematics plays a pivotal role in articulating Aristotle's theory of subalternation, a construct that would solidify the relationship between geometry and optics. Grosseteste's *Notes on the Physics* were clearly a preparation for a major commentary that was never completed; nonetheless the notes began to circulate soon after he became bishop of Lincoln. While Aristotle greatly influenced his worldview and his own methodology, he never accepted all the tenets of the Stagirite. The doctrine of the eternity of the world he found in particular to be theologically and philosophically suspect. He first attacked the notion in a short treatise on eternal and temporal causality (*De finitate motus et temporis*), a topic that came directly out of his study of the *Physics*. He also addressed this same issue in a theological disputation on the eternal generation of the Son in the Trinity (*De ordine emanandi causatorum a Deo*). He then pursued the eternity of the world further in his commentary on the Genesis creation narrative (*Hexaëmeron*), where he attacked the philosophical assumptions that supported this doctrine.

While some historians have suggested that Grosseteste be counted among the fathers of modern science, his body of work does not suggest such a fundamental role in the history of science. Despite his assertion about the utility of mathematical analysis, he never considered quantitative analysis of the natural world to be necessarily superior to the qualitative. Moreover, while he continually referred to data obtained by experience (*experimento*), this was not a reference to any nascent empiricism. Rather, the phrase "experiential knowledge" (*scientia experimentalis*) could refer both to personal observation and repeatable (but not controlled) experiments, as well as to literary data found in the ancient texts. Grosseteste labored intensively on explaining the application of syllogistic logic in natural philosophy, but gave no account of how empirical evidence could be evaluated. He did adopt the Aristotelian *resolutio-compositio* method for exploring problems in natural philosophy, but this use did not require analysis of only observable data. Grosseteste's scientific writings had considerable influence on scholastics at Oxford, especially *Roger Bacon but also Richard Fishacre, Adam Marsh, and *Richard Rufus of Cornwall.

Although Grosseteste focused mainly on theological study after 1230, he never lost interest in the natural world. His inaugural lecture as a Master of the Sacred Page is an apology for how one can employ the quadrivium in biblical exegesis without impugning the superiority of the theological enterprise. His own exposition of Scripture betrays a continued fascination with creation: in addition to his exposition of Genesis, he exploited his scientific experience in his lectures on the Psalms and the book of Ecclesiasticus (partially surviving as *De operationibus solis*). His theological speculation was built on his experience with Euclidean and Aristotelian methodologies—although Grosseteste considered Aristotle's definition of science to be of limited value to a theologian since that science of demonstration focused primarily on the sublunary world.

At the heart of his theology was a theory of the unity of all creation that would eventually enjoy full union with its Creator, and he saw the Incarnation as the unifying force. That perception was clearly built on his earlier scientific study of the universe and his metaphysics of light.

See also **Agronomy; Aristotelianism; Optics and catoptrics; Scholasticism;** *Scientia*

Bibliography

Primary Sources

Baur, Ludwig, ed. *Die Philosophischen Werke des Robert Grosseteste, Bischofs von Lincoln.* Münster i. W.: Aschendorff, 1912.

Dales, R.C. The Text of Robert Grosseteste's *Questio de fluxu et refluxu maris* with an English Translation. *Isis* (1966) 57: 455–474.

Grosseteste, Robert. *Commentarius in Posteriorum Analyticorum libros.* Edited by Pietro Rossi. Firenze: L.S. Olschki, 1981.

———. *Commentarius in VIII libros physicorum Aristotelis.* Edited by R. C. Dales. Boulder, CO: University of Colorado Press, 1963.

———. *Hexaëmeron.* Edited by R.C Dales and S. Gieben. London: Published for the British Academy by the Oxford University Press, 1982.

McEvoy, James. The Sun as res and signum: Grosseteste's Commentary on Ecclesiasticus ch. 43, vv. 1–5. *Recherches de théologie ancienne et médiévale* (1974) 41: 38–91.

Panti, Cecilia. *Moti, virtù e motori celesti nella cosmologia di Roberto Grossatesta: studio e edizione dei trattati De sphera, De cometis, De motu supercelestium.* Florence: SISMEL, Edizioni del Galluzzo, 2001.

The Electronic Grosseteste. Edited by James R. Ginther. URL = <http://www.grosseteste.com>.

Secondary Sources

Crombie, A.C. *Robert Grosseteste and the Origins of Experimental Science 1100–1700.* Oxford: Oxford University Press, 1953.

Dales, R.C. Robert Grosseteste's Scientific Works. *Isis* (1961) 52: 381–402.

Editing Robert Grosseteste: papers given at the thirty-sixth annual Conference on Editorial Problems, University of Toronto, 3-4 November 2000. Edited by E.A. Mackie and J.Goering. Toronto: University of Toronto Press, 2003.

Ginther, J.R. Natural Philosophy and Theology at Oxford in the Early Thirteenth Century: An Edition and Study of Robert Grosseteste's Inception Sermon (Dictum 19). *Medieval Sermon Studies* (2000) 44: 108–134.

Laird, W.R. Robert Grosseteste on the Subalternate Sciences. *Traditio* (1987) 43: 147–169.

McEvoy, J. The Chronology of Robert Grosseteste's Writings on Nature and Natural Philosophy. *Speculum* (1983) 58: 614–655.

Southern R.W. *Robert Grosseteste: The Growth of an English Mind in Medieval Europe.* Oxford: Oxford University Press, 1986.

Thomson, S. Harrison. *The Writings of Robert Grosseteste, Bishop of Lincoln, 1235–1253.* New York: Cambridge University Press, 1940.

JAMES R. GINTHER

GUNDISALVO, DOMINGO

Domingo Gundisalvo (c. 1120-1184 C.E.), or in the Latin form of his name Dominicus Gondisalvus (also Gundissalinus), was one of the foremost of the Toledan translators. Working in the second half of the twelfth century, he became, in Knowles's phrase, "a kind of harbinger or sponsor of Arabian and Jewish thought, and helped make its introduction to the West a simple and natural process." He was a major figure in the movement of translation and dissemination of the "new" Arabic knowledge of the sciences that reenergized the schoolmen of the twelfth and thirteenth centuries. As well as a translator, he was an author (although the term must be used advisedly, for he was more of a cut-and-paste redactor) who became an authority for other medieval scholars.

Unfortunately, we possess little in the way of biography for any twelfth-century translator. With one notable exception, no contemporary seems to have written any account of the people involved in the important movement traditionally known as the Toledo School of Translators. More disappointing than this, though, is the fact that the raw materials for discovering biography do not exist in any abundance either; here we are dependent mostly on brief autobiographical allusions contained in the dedications of manuscripts. Only *Gerard of Cremona, the most prolific of all the translators, had anything like an attempt at biography written about him by his students. But, if we are willing to draw on a bit of speculation, we can present a brief biographical sketch of Gundisalvo.

First, Gundisalvo is attested as being from Cuéllar, a small town some nineteen miles (31 km) southwest of Toledo. Rivera has speculated about Gundisalvo's family of origin. Part of the village was given by Alfonso VII in 1140 to Juan, archdeacon of Segovia. In 1166, Juan became bishop of Osma and gave his portion of the village to his niece, Palencia, and her husband, Gonzalo Petri. If they had a son, his patronymic would have been González, Gundisalvus in Latin. Nearly contemporary with this, Domingo González is recorded as archdeacon of Cuéllar, residing in the chapter of Toledo and sometimes identified as the archdeacon of Segovia or of Toledo: it would appear that this is Gundisalvo the translator and author. If this is actually the case, then Gundisalvo would have come from a highly placed family from the frontier with royal connections; this would explain his level of education, knowledge of Arabic, and his entrée into the world of the church.

Second, Gundisalvo worked in Toledo in one of the most interesting periods in that city's history. Prior to the Christian Conquest of 1085, Toledo was one of the major centers of scientific and philosophical study in al-Andalus. This was primarily because of the patronage of the ruling family, the Banu Dhu'l-Nun. Yahya ibn Isma'il ibn Dhi'l-nun successfully built Toledo into a beautiful city and he was a patron of scholars and poets. *Sa'id al-Andalusi (d. 1065), who lived in that city, tells us that when the great library of the caliph at Córdoba, al-Hakam II, was being ransacked by the orthodox *ulama* (religious scholars) at al-Mansur's behest, many of the books were smuggled to Toledo. There scholars were welcomed; in particular, considerable numbers of Jews from the south moved to this "city of kings." In Christian hands, Toledo became a magnet for both Christians and Jews fleeing the Berber Muslim armies of the Almoravids. With its abundant libraries and numerous academics steeped in Islamic science and philosophy, Toledo in this period must have been an exciting environment for a scholar, especially for a translator.

Third, Gundisalvo was a churchman. Note that he is attested as an important member of the chapter of the cathedral, the archdeacon. This office was generally responsible for directing the educational functions of the chapter. His own writings have a theological bent, attempting to provide a rational basis for theology. Etienne Gilson has even credited him with being a pivotal figure who initiated a type of philosophical and theological reasoning which was to achieve its full realization with thirteenth-century scholars.

In older works (and even some modern ones) Gundisalvo is often cited as being a member of the "School of Translators" under the Archbishop Raymond. This is an unfortunate mistake which keeps being repeated, despite much scholarship to the contrary. As far as we can tell, there was no "school" in any sense of the word, something Charles Homer Haskins long ago recognized. Instead, what was in place was a system of patronage by highly placed churchmen (abbots and bishops) who commissioned translations and probably provided support for translators by appointing them to positions in cathedral chapters. This was clearly the case in Toledo, but it also was seen in other cities of newly reconquered northern Spain. More important for Gundisalvo, he is not attested in the chapter until after Raymond is dead. This is also true for the most prolific of all the translators, Gerard of Cremona. Therefore, the institutional context for the transfer of Arabic philosophical and scientific knowledge was not the product of an organized scholastic endeavor, but of the genius of individual scholars. This does not mean, however, that there was no direction of the process; on the contrary, it appears that the translators of Toledo were following much the same program as Andalusi Jewish and Islamic scholars did in learning science and philosophy. Considered in this respect, Gundisalvo's most important work was probably his *De Scientiis* (*On the Sciences*, his translation of *al-Farabi's Book of the Enumeration of the Sciences*), which appears to have guided translators as well as scholars in search of "the knowledge of the Arabs." This system of knowledge, based on the authentic texts of *Aristotle, stood in radical contrast to all earlier medieval classifications of knowledge, like that of *Hugh of St-Victor.

The work of Gundisalvo as a translator has been thoroughly studied. In the course of his career he produced the following: (1) *De Scientiis* (*On the Sciences*), a translation and adaptation of al-Farabi's *Kitab ihsa' al-Ulum* (*Enumeration of the Sciences*); (2) *Liber al-Kindi de Intellectu* (*Book of al-Kindi on Reason*); (3) Alexander of Aphrodisias, *De intellectu et intellecto* (*On Reason and Reasoning*); (4) *De intellectu* (*On Reason*), a translation of *Risalat fil-'aql* (*Letter on Reason*) of al-Farabi; (5) *Fontes Quaestionum*, probably a translation of the *Uyun al-masa'il* (*Source of Questions*) of al-Farabi; (6) *Liber exercitationis ad viam felicitatis* (*Reminder of the Way to Happiness*), a translation of al Farabi's *Tanbih asla sabil al-as'ada*; (7) *Liber de definitionibus* (*Book of Definitions*) of Ishaq al-Israeli; (8) *Liber introductorious in artem logicae demonstrationis*, attributed to the Ikwan as-safa'; (9) *Logica et philosophia algazelis*, a translation of the *Maqasid al-Falasifa* (*The Intentions of the Philosophers*) of al-Ghazali; (10) *Metaphysica Avicenna*, the metaphysics of the *Kitab al-Shifa* (*Book of Healing*) of Ibn Sina; (11) *De convenientia et differentia subiectorum de Avicenna*, an unknown work of Avicenna; (12) *Fons Vitae* (*Source of Life*) of Ibn Gabriol.

Gundisalvo's skill in Arabic is actually quite good. His method is anything but slavish, and he translates according to sense rather than word for word; in addition he adds or excises passages as he feels the necessity. In some of his translations he explicitly indicates that he worked with a co-translator; his collaborators were both Jews and Christians. Much has been written about this "dragoman" method of translating; as one might expect it was based in the reality of the social structure of Toledo, a city in which Arabic was the primary spoken language, where most scholars were multilingual, and between whom there was a lively intellectual exchange. Many of the translators working in Spain knew each other and often dedicated their works to each other.

Gundisalvo was also the author of five works that draw heavily on his translations. Scholars have described them variously as "mosaic" or "pastiche" works, yet they contain great originality. He is generally regarded as the first western Christian scholar to have been greatly influenced by Avicenna (*Ibn Sina). These books are: (1) *De divisione philosphiae* (*On the Divisions of Philosophy*); (2) *De Anima* (*On the Soul*); (3) *De Unitate* (*On Unity*); (4) *De Processione mundi* (*On the Procession of the World*); (5) *De Immortalitatae animae* (*On the Immortality of the Soul*).

In spite of being a somewhat uncreative author, it appears that Gundisalvo was aware of his central role in providing scholars the texts they needed in order to "know with certainty." He gave a glimpse of his intentions in the prologue to *De Anima* which addresses the need for new knowledge and the faith–reason dilemma which might accompany it:

"I have carefully collected all the rational propositions about the soul that I have found in the works of the philosophers. Thus, at any rate, a work hitherto unknown to Latin readers, since it was hidden in Greek and Arabic libraries, has now, by the grace of God and at the cost of immense labor, been made available to the Latin world so that the faithful, who toil assiduously for the good of their souls, may know what to think about it, no longer through faith alone but also through reason" (tr. Jean Jolivet, 142).

As it stands, this could have been written by any Jew, Muslim, or Christian who sought to be a philosopher.

The clear understanding is that understanding and reason are good for the soul of the believer.

The second text which indicated Gundisalvo's understanding of this problem is his translation of the very text which al-Farabi had written to justify the study of philosophy, the *Kitab al-Tanbih 'ala Sabil al-Sa'adah* or *Book of the Reminder of the Way to Happiness*. In this short work al-Farabi presented the thesis that the final goal of human life is happiness. He went on to say that by discretion a man can discover the attitudes and judgments that lead to happiness, and the only sure way to arrive at knowledge of good and evil is to learn philosophy. He then proceeded to show that by philosophy he really meant the acquisition of knowledge of the sciences. Thus, in these two translations Gundisalvo presented the Latin world with the rationale for the study of science—demonstrating the understanding that such study was transformative—and providing the handbook which told how the sciences should be arranged and studied so that one could reach that final goal of human life. Furthermore, such science was the only sure foundation for religious belief.

Gundisalvo's influence on medieval scholars was substantial, though often secondhand. From late in the twelfth century or early in the thirteenth there survives a curricular list of readings, probably from *Alexander Nequam. It indicates that he expected students to be reading the newly translated texts in the divisions as Gundisalvo had passed them on. *Robert Kilwardby wrote a text called "On the Rise of the Sciences," which is directly dependent on Gundisalvo's *On the Divisions of Philosophy*. Nearly contemporary with him, *Vincent of Beauvais copied almost all of "On the Sciences" into his *Speculum doctrinale*. This was one of the most widely read books of the Middle Ages. Slightly later, there are significant disputes in the new University of Paris about the way the sciences should be organized, learned, and taught. Masters of theology railed against the arts, beginning in the 1230s, and especially against the new divisions of knowledge in the arts' curriculum that put the newer, "secular" sciences up against their own specialty. The fact was that a new way organizing knowledge for teaching and learning was abroad in Europe: despite its detractors, it was never to be stopped.

See also Toledo; Translation norms and practice

Bibliography

Primary Sources
Baur, Ludwig, ed. "Dominicus Gundissalinus: De Divisione Philosophiae." *Beiträge zur Geschichte der Philosophie des Mittelalters*. Vol. 4. Münster: Aschendorf, 1903.

Grant, Edward and Marshall Clagett, translators. "Domingo Gundisalvo: Classifications of the Sciences." In Edward Grant, ed., *Sourcebook of Medieval Science*. Cambridge: Harvard University Press, 1974.

Secondary Sources
Alsono, M.M. Traducciones del Arcediano Domingo Gundisalvo. *Al-Andalus* (1947) 12: 295–338.

Burnett, Charles S. F. "The Institutional context of Arabic-Latin Translations of the Middle Ages: A Reassessment of the 'School of Toledo'." In Olga Weijers, ed. *Vocabulary of Teaching and Research between Middle Ages and Renaissance*. Turnhout: Brepohls, 1995.

Gilson, Etienne. *History of Christian Philosophy*. New York: Random House, 1955.

Haskins, Charles Homer. *Studies in the History of Science*. Cambridge: Harvard University Press, 1924.

Jolivet, Jean. "The Arabic Inheritance." In Peter Drinke, ed. *A History of Twelfth Century Philosophy*. New York: Cambridge University Press, 1988.

Knowles, David. *The Evolution of Medieval Thought*. London: Longman, 1963.

Rivera Recio, Juan F. *La Iglesia de Toledo*. Rome: Instituto Español de Historia Ecclesiástica, 1966.

MICHAEL C. WEBER

GUNPOWDER

Gunpowder and gunpowder weaponry were probably the most important technological innovations in all military history. Especially in Europe, gunpowder weapons revolutionized warfare, changed military strategy and tactics forever, destroyed old empires and created new ones, and challenged the privileged status of knights, nobles, and princes.

Origins in China

Nowadays it is of course common knowledge that gunpowder was invented in China, and it along with paper and the compass are very frequently listed among China's "gifts" to the world or at least the West's "debts" to China. But the priority of the Chinese invention of gunpowder has not always been affirmed; in the West it used to be widely believed that gunpowder had been invented by a fourteenth-century monk named Berthold the Black. Only at the beginning of the twentieth century did Gustav Schlegel establish Chinese priority in gunpowder invention, with much compelling evidence.

To this day, however, a persistent and widely circulated but incorrect cultural canard in the West holds that while the Chinese may have invented gunpowder, its first weaponized and military applications occurred in Europe. In reality, the Chinese were using and perfecting many varieties of gunpowder weaponry for the first time in world history between the tenth and fourteenth centuries Ironically, gunpowder was invented in China not by military men innovating more effective ways of destroying life but by alchemists who sought both the philosopher's stone and the mysterious and elusive elixir of immortality, a concoction or compound which, if ingested, would halt the natural aging process and prolong human life, perhaps even indefinitely. Chinese alchemists had been experimenting with brimstone (sulfur) since the Han dynasty (202 B.C.E.–220 C.E.). Sulfur especially had been used in many alchemical recipes for "potable gold" and "cyclically transformed gold elixir." Brimstone was of course highly volatile and toxic, so Chinese alchemists attempted to "subdue" its volatility by mixing it with saltpeter. The mixture of these two ingredients proved a key step towards the invention of gunpowder, but at the time it was hoped that compounds such as this might be used to turn molten lead into gold.

By 808 an alchemical work mentions a compound of six parts sulfur, six parts saltpeter, and one part birthwort herb (which would have contained enough carbon to make the compound combustible). This is probably the world's first crude formula for gunpowder. A mid-ninth-century Taoist alchemical work contains thirty-five elixir formulae which are listed as dangerous or improper; three of these contained saltpeter, and one was associated with a dire warning:

"Some have heated together sulfur, realgar (arsenic disulphide), and saltpeter with honey; smoke and flames result, so that their hands and faces have been burnt, and even the whole house where they were working burned down. Evidently this only brings Taoism into discredit, and Taoist alchemists are thus warned clearly not to do it."
This is a more refined formula for gunpowder. (The honey would have contained carbon.)

Around 1040 Zeng Gongliang (999–1078), the main compiler of *Wujing Zongyao*, a massive military compendium, published the world's first gunpowder formulae for three different varieties of weapons. These formulae contained sulfur and saltpeter as well as several other ingredients such as waxes, oils, roots, and resins. They bore little resemblance to the classic three-ingredient formula for gunpowder (seventy-five percent potassium nitrate, fifteen percent charcoal, and ten percent sulfur) familiar to schoolchildren today. They contained low nitrate levels and on ignition were deflagrative and incendiary rather than explosive or detonative in their effects.

Gunpowder Weaponry in China

Historically the Chinese have been no strangers to explosions and fireworks. As early as 200 B.C.E. the Chinese were heating sections of bamboo in fire until they exploded loudly. (Indeed, *baozhu*, a common term in Mandarin Chinese today for firecracker, literally means "exploding bamboo.") The Chinese thus had a fireworks tradition from very early times, and for several centuries they saw the properties of gunpowder deflagration and explosion as an extension of it.

But the Chinese did not always regard gunpowder as a mere fireworks novelty, and they were the first people in the world to make military use of gunpowder weapons. In the early tenth century they used a gunpowder fuse to ignite petroleum distillates in what might be thought of as a crude prototype of the modern flamethrower. The Chinese had long made extensive use of incendiary and inflammable oils and resins in warfare, but by the middle of the eleventh century truly explosive gunpowder bombs with a high percentage of saltpeter came on the scene. Known as "thunderclap bombs," these were ignited by fuse and then hurled by hand or catapult, and they terrified enemy troops and horses. By the early thirteenth century the Chinese were making deadly antipersonnel fragmentation bombs with metal casings that exploded into shrapnel. These "thunder-crash bombs" were used in 1232 against Mongol besiegers in northern China, and a contemporary account of their use is graphic:

"Among the weapons of the defenders there was the heaven-shaking thunder-crash bomb. It consisted of gunpowder put into an iron container; then when the fuse was lit and the projectile shot off there was a great explosion the noise whereof was like thunder, audible for more than a hundred *li* [tens of miles], and the vegetation was scorched and blasted by the heat over an area of more than half a *mou* [many acres]. When hit, even iron armor was quite pierced through."

The Chinese also used rockets and multiple-rocket launchers militarily, and by the end of the thirteenth century they were making and deploying gunpowder landmines complete with sophisticated triggering mechanisms. In addition, they used flares, grenades, and sea mines.

Despite a certain amount of popular wisdom to the contrary, the Chinese were also the first civilization to invent and use the true gun or cannon, or a tube containing and controlling an explosion which propelled a fairly tightly fitted projectile. Since the early tenth century they had been using "fire lances" or "flame-spewing spears," which were in effect lethal and long-burning Roman candles tied to long poles. Eventually fire lances evolved from bamboo tubes into metal tubes and emitted projectiles, although these were not true bullets because they were not tightly fitted into barrels. Needham dates the earliest known true gun in China to about 1280, while the first true gun appeared in Europe in c. 1326 or 1327. The lag time between the gun's first known existence in China and its appearance in Europe was thus remarkably short, and it may well have been that Chinese guns were carried to Europe and directly copied there. In the process, guns would have been introduced into the Islamic world as well, but, perplexingly, current evidence indicates that the first place outside of China where guns appeared was the Latin West. (The Arabs and Persians were already aware of a high-saltpeter recipe for gunpowder and its Chinese origins by the middle of the thirteenth century. Indeed, saltpeter was called "China snow" by the Arabs and "China salt" by the Persians.) It may have been that the Europeans, for whatever reason, were more immediately impressed with the military potential of the gun than the Muslims of the time were.

The Mongols and the thirteenth-century world empire they built probably made possible this pivotally important transfer of firearms technology and know-how from the East to the West. Nevertheless, the transfer of military technology that the Mongols fostered was by no means a one-way process. It is quite likely that the counterweighted trebuchet, a non-gunpowder siege engine which the Mongols found so useful for battering down the walls of fortified Chinese cities during the 1260s and 1270s, was introduced from the Mediterranean world to China during the second half of the thirteenth century.

Gunpowder in the West

Gunpowder became known in western Europe by the middle of the thirteenth century, but the particulars of how it arrived are not yet settled. Some scholars hold that it may have come through the Islamic lands to Byzantium or Spain and thence to western Europe. British Sinologist Sir Joseph Needham (1900–1995), the main editor and originator of the monumental, multivolume technological history *Science and Civilisation in China*, long held that the Franciscan friar William of Rubruck (c. 1220–c. 1293) likely brought back an important formula for gunpowder to Europe in 1256, when he returned from his travels to Mongolia, and gave it to his friend *Roger Bacon (1214–1294). Recent scholarship has strongly indicated that the Mongols and their armies during the thirteenth century did much to diffuse gunpowder and gunpowder weaponry throughout the Eurasian landmass.

Roger Bacon was clearly fascinated with gunpowder and seems to have written about its formula, at least initially, in anagrammatic secrecy. Perhaps he himself or some of his associates had been overawed by various experiments and experiences with the substance. At any rate, in his apparent description of gunpowder's effects in his *Opus majus* (published around 1267), one can almost hear, see, and smell the effects of the substance igniting:

"Certain inventions disturb the hearing to such a degree that if they are set off suddenly at night with sufficient skill, neither city nor army can endure them. No clap of thunder can compare with such noises. Some of them strike such terror to the sight that the thunders and lightnings of the clouds disturb it considerably less."

But for Bacon, the importance of gunpowder was beyond mere pyrotechnic spectacle; he had some inkling of its awesome destructive potential, and in one of his last works, *Opus Tertium* (published around 1268), he speculated on how it might be put to practical, if violent, use:

"By the flash and combustion of fires, and by the horror of sounds, wonders can be wrought, and at any distance that we wish—so that a man can hardly protect himself or endure it. There is a child's toy of sound and fire made in various parts of the world with powder of saltpetre, sulphur and charcoal of hazlewood. This powder is enclosed in an instrument of parchment the size of a finger, and since this can make such a noise that it seriously distresses the ears of men…. If the instrument were made of solid material the violence of the explosion would be much greater."

Following Bacon, other thirteenth-century European writers such as Albert the Great (*Albertus Magnus) and the pseudonymous Marcus Graecus, also wrote on the formulae for gunpowder. The exact proportions varied slightly, but all described a mixture of saltpeter, sulfur, and charcoal which, if ignited, produced powerful effects.

Gunpowder Weaponry in the West

The first gunpowder weapons in Western Europe were not bombs but large guns or cannon. References to the use of guns in western Europe during the late thirteenth and early fourteenth centuries are suspect and controversial. The first incontrovertible evidence of gun use in the Latin West dates to 1326. By the 1330s and 1340s there are many references to gunpowder weaponry in European materials, and they may have seen battlefield use by the middle of the fourteenth century. Toward the end of the fourteenth century, guns had become especially effective in siege warfare against the walls of castles, as in 1377 at the siege of Odruik, when Philip the Bold's cannons penetrated the castle's walls. Guns had a much smaller impact on late medieval battlefield fighting, and they only made gradual appearance on battlefields in the late fourteenth and early fifteenth centuries. (The problem was, of course, the heavy and unwieldy nature of the guns.) Smaller and more transportable guns were likely invented by the late fourteenth century. The first reference to a "hand gonne" dates to an English document written in 1388 during the reign of Richard II. By 1410 handheld guns were used by the dukes of Burgundy, and by the middle of the fifteenth century most battlefield encounters included at least some handheld guns.

Guns also were found on warships prior to the fifteenth century, and by the beginning of the century almost all warships, but especially English and Italian ones, carried at least some cannon. The first recorded sinking of a warship by cannon on another warship dates to 1499.

See also **Alchemy; Artillery and firearms; Catapults and trebuchets**

Bibliography

Allsen, Thomas T. "The Circulation of Military Technology in the Mongolian Empire." In Nicola di Cosmo, ed., *Warfare in Inner Asian History (500–1800)*. Leiden: E.J. Brill, 2002, pp. 265–293.

Buchanan, Brenda J., ed. *Gunpowder: The History of an International Technology*. Claverton Down, Bath: Bath University Press, 1996.

Chase, Kenneth Warren. *Firearms: A Global History to 1700*. New York: Cambridge University Press, 2003

Cocroft, Wayne D. *Dangerous Energy: The Archaeology of Gunpowder and Military Explosives Manufacture*. Swindon: English Heritage, 2000.

DeVries, Kelly. *A Cumulative Bibliography of Medieval Military History and Technology*. Leiden: E.J. Brill, 2002.

———. *Guns and Men in Medieval Europe, 1200–1500*. Burlington, Vermont: Ashgate Publishing Company, 2002.

———. *Medieval Military Technology*. Peterborough, Ontario: Broadview, 1992.

———. *Medieval Military Technology*. Second Edition. Peterborough, Ontario: Broadview, 2006.

DeVries, Kelly and Robert D. Smith. *The Artillery of the Valois Dukes of Burgundy, 1363–1477*. Woodbridge: Boydell, 2005.

Hall, Bert S. *Weapons and Warfare in Renaissance Europe: Gunpowder, Technology, and Tactics*. Baltimore: Johns Hopkins University Press, 1997.

Lewis, Archibald R. and Timothy J. Runyan. *Naval Power and Trade in the Mediterranean, A.D. 500–1100*. Princeton: Princeton University Press, 1985.

McNeil, William H. *The Pursuit of Power: Technology, Armed Force, and Society Since A.D. 1000*. Chicago: University of Chicago Press, 1982.

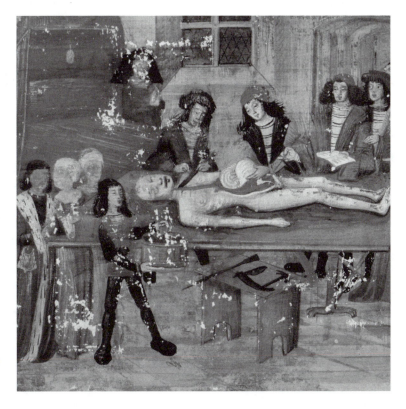

Illumination from a 1363 French manuscript of Guy de Chauliac's *Chirugia magna* depicting a postmortem at the Montpellier Faculty of Medicine. (Corbis/ Gianni Dagli Orti)

Needham, Joseph et al. *Science and Civilisation in China, Volume 5, Chemistry and Chemical Technology, Part 7: Military Technology; The Gunpowder Epic.* New York: Cambridge University Press, 1986.

Partington, J. R. *A History of Greek Fire and Gunpowder.* Cambridge: W. Heffer, 1960.

Sawyer, Ralph D. and Mei-chün Lee Sawyer. *Fire and Water: The Art of Incendiary and Aquatic Warfare in China.* Boulder: Westview, 2004.

Zhou, Jiahua. "Gunpowder and Firearms." In *Ancient China's Technology and Science*, compiled by the Institute of the History of Natural Sciences, Chinese Academy of Sciences. Beijing: Foreign Languages Press, 1983, pp. 184–191.

DAVID CURTIS WRIGHT

GUY DE CHAULIAC

The most famous name in medieval French surgery, Guy de Chauliac was born in Chaulhac in the south of France at the end of the thirteenth century. Legend has it that after he cured a noblewoman's fracture her wealthy family paid for his studies in medicine at the famous school of Montpellier. It is nevertheless established that he did receive the major part of his medical education at Montpellier. He himself states in his work that he studied under Raymond de Molieriis, who was chancellor of the University and taught there around 1335. Chauliac himself never taught at Montpellier, as was the custom for graduate masters, but instead went on to study in Bologna under Alberto de Zanchariis and Bertruccio. Although known mainly for his contribution to surgery, there is no evidence that he actually practiced as a surgeon. Guy de Chauliac first practiced medicine on a regular basis in Lyon where he was living in 1344. He later treated three successive popes—Clement VI, Innocent VI, and Urban V—dividing his time between Lyon and Avignon. Although he occasionally treated other high-ranking patients such as the Duke of Savoy in 1363, he appears to have been mainly attached to the Avignon papacy. In this cultural setting that has been described as "pre-humanistic," he had access to the palace's exceptional library and the possibility of practicing with colleagues from Montpellier, Bologna, Paris, and the Kingdom of Aragon. In the course of his life, he became a beneficiary of several canonical charges, Saint-Just in Lyon in 1344 and later Mende in 1367. He died in Lyon in July 1368.

His work, *Inventarium sive collectorium in parte chirurgicali medicinae*, stands out as a fundamental work for both medieval and early modern surgery, so much so that after its publication the tradition of learned surgery that had began with *Roger Frugard (Ruggiero Frugardi) appears to have come to an end. The *Inventarium* is an encyclopedia of surgical knowledge that gives precedence to ancient sources such as *Galen, who is cited eight hundred ninety times, and *Ibn Sina (Avicenna), to whom there are six hundred sixty-one references, and also uses material from more recent authors such as *Abu al-Qasim ibn Mahfuz (Albucasis) (one hundred seventy-five citations), and contemporaries such as *Henri de Mondeville (eighty-six), and all the Salernitan scholars, Frugard and his commentator Rolando of Parma (ninety-six), *Theodorico Borgognoni (eighty-five), Guglielmo de Saliceto (sixty-eight), and *Bruno Longoburgo (forty-six).

The book quickly became the standard text and was used, despite its highly scholastic content, as a vade mecum by most medieval surgeons. By the fifteenth century it had been translated into Middle French, Middle English, Italian, Catalan, Dutch, and Hebrew. The *Inventarium* or *Chirurgia Magna* was extensively copied in its Latin version and was first printed in 1490. It was published altogether twelve times in the course of the sixteenth century. Among the most complete editions of Chauliac's work is the annotated version of the Latin text published in 1579 by Montpellier doctor Laurent Joubert and the French edition published in 1890 by Edouard Nicaise. The introduction to this translation contains most of the biographical data concerning Guy de Chauliac. The Latin text of a Vatican manuscript dated 1373 was published in two volumes in 1997 with a commentary by Michael McVaugh. It provides the most comprehensive means of studying the text in its original form. One Middle English translation has been published by Margaret S. Ogden from a Parisian manuscript. The Middle French tradition has been studied by Sylvie Bazin-Tacchella, and several of her articles explain the importance of Chauliac's work in France.

The work itself lacks originality but its fundamental aim was to present the state of the discipline in Guy de Chauliac's time in the mid-fourteenth century. The *Inventarium* is in seven books, and starts with a chapter entitled *capitulum singulare* in which the author defines surgery and traces its history and filiation since ancient times. Having attributed its origins to *Hippocrates and *Galen, he continues by enumerating Arab sources such as *Haly Abbas, Albucasis, and *Al-Razi. The Salernitan masters and their Italian successors follow. Finally, he cites the influences of the school of Montpellier with *Henri de Mondeville and *Arnau de Vilanova, and in so doing shows that he was well aware of belonging to a long tradition of learning. This approach to the history of surgery from its origins to the Middle Ages is still valid today and is used, consciously or not, by most historians of medicine.

The content of Chauliac's work is profoundly marked by a Galenism stemming mainly from the translations from Arabic to Latin that were available at the end of the thirteenth century and were part of the learning program at Montpellier. However, Guy also had access to the works of Galen newly translated directly from the Greek by *Niccolò da Reggio at the papal court which he used extensively. The anatomical content of the work is therefore more original since it is based on a truer version of Galen's anatomical treatise *De usu partium* translated from the Greek rather than the faulty condensed version that was available in Latin before that.

One other interesting feature of the *Inventarium* is the vivid descriptions of the plague in France that can be found in the section devoted to apostemes. Guy was a witness to both outbreaks, those of 1348 and 1360. He even contracted the disease and cured himself. His distinction between bubonic and pneumonic plague has been called a model of clinical reporting.

The main contribution of the work is Guy's effort to assemble, collate, and present all the existing information on surgery and to integrate it with the medical scholastic discourse of the time. He also states his position on major doctrinal debates. For example, he disagrees with Theodoric and Henri de Mondeville's dry treatment of wounds. In addition, the *Inventarium* features notable original passages on tracheotomy, intubations, suturing methods, and accounts of a few interesting instruments such as the "pelican" for extracting teeth and a traction devise to treat fractures.

See also **Medicine, practical; Medicine, theoretical; Surgery**

Bibliography

Huard, Pierre, and Mirko D.Grmek. *Mille ans de chirurgie en Occident: Ve-XVe siècles*. Paris, Dacosta, 1966.
McVaugh, Michael. "Therapeutic strategies: surgery." In *Western Medical Thought from Antiquity to the Middle Ages*. Cambridge: Harvard University Press, 1998.
———. *Guigonis de Caulhaco Inventarium sive Chirurgia Magna*, vol. 1: *Text*. Leiden, E.J. Brill, 1997.
Nicaise, E. *La grande chirurgie de Guy de Chauliac*. Paris, Alcan, 1890.
Ogden, Margaret S. The Galenic Works Cited by Guy de Chauliac's Chirurgia Magna. *Journal of the History of Medicine* (1973) 28: 24–33.
Enselme, Jean. Biographie de Gui de Chauliac. *Revue Lyonnaise de la Médecine* (1969) 17: 697–710.

GENEVIÈVE DUMAS

GYNECOLOGY AND MIDWIFERY

Gynecology, the subfield of medicine that deals particularly with the diseases of the female reproductive organs, was not an area in which medieval practitioners specialized, but it was recognized as a distinct subject and, as such, often generated its own specialized literature when authors or compilers believed there existed a distinct audience for such works. In the Mediterranean context of Greco-Roman antiquity, female midwives or healers (*obstetrices* or *medicae*) were presumed to be responsible for everything we now put under both the headings "obstetrics" and "gynecology." By the end of the Middle Ages, at least in western Europe, midwives were often only responsible for attendance at normal births and, in some circumstances, for serving as manual assistants to male practitioners. Physicians were recognized as competent to diagnose and treat gynecological disorders, while surgeons increasingly were called on in cases of difficult births. This transition in the gendering of women's healthcare was not smooth, nor was it complete. Nevertheless, the question of whether women's healthcare was to be managed by laywomen themselves, by specialized female practitioners, or by male medical practitioners, constitutes a key issue in the development of the field over the course of the Middle Ages.

A variety of evidence—inscriptions, textual sources, sculpture, etc.—confirms female practitioners' responsibility for women's gynecological and obstetrical conditions in antiquity. Many of these women were literate, and Greek writers such as Soranus (first/second century C.E.) and *Galen addressed their works on women's diseases or anatomy to them. How long this situation persisted in the Byzantine world is not clear; a sixth-century text on gynecology is said to be the work of a female author, Metrodora, but the bulk of gynecological writing from the Byzantine period is only to be found in the works of male medical encyclopedists. The same is true of the Arabic-speaking world, where male physicians such as the Spaniard *al-Zahrawi or the Persian *Ibn Sina included significant sections on gynecology or obstetrics in their medical encyclopedias, but apparently had to give oral instruction to midwives to have their instructions carried out. Only three specialized works on women's medicine are known from the medieval Islamic world, all of them by male authors.

Western Europe is therefore distinctive, vis-à-vis Byzantium and the Islamic world, in having such a large tradition of independent gynecological writing. This sizable corpus (a total of more than one hundred and fifty texts or excerpts from larger works circulating separately between the fourth and fifteenth centuries) originated in late antiquity, in part when translators rendered Soranus's textbook, the *Gynecology*, into Latin several times. The most widely disseminated work was Muscio's, written probably in North Africa in the fifth or sixth century, which included a series of images of the fetus in utero. As in antiquity, most of these late antique texts were written for literate midwives; Muscio repeats Soranus's requirement that the good midwife be able to read and understand medical theory.

In the twelfth century, two new texts came out of the southern Italian town of *Salerno: *Conditions of Women*, which is a patchwork made primarily from other written texts (including a recent translation from the Arabic by *Constantine the African); and *Treatments for Women*, attributed to the female Salernitan practitioner Trota and distinguished by its rich therapeutical detail, extensive practical experience of the most intimate conditions of women's genitalia, and a broad conception of what the diseases of women actually are (everything from nuns' problems of maintaining their chastity to uterine prolapse and ano-vaginal fistula). No other text on women's medicine would match these qualities for several centuries.

The *Trotula (as these two Salernitan texts came to be called once they were linked with a third text on cosmetics) would quickly eclipse Muscio's *Gynecology* which, based on the Methodist theories of late ancient medicine, was no longer compatible with (or even intelligible to) the strongly Galenic environment after the twelfth century. Then, beginning in the early fourteenth century, a series of physicians associated with the medical school at Montpellier began to compose their own treatises on fertility. The earliest of these, by *Arnau de Vilanova, was quickly followed by at least six others, all of which to varying degrees, and with varying detail, drew on gynecological disease classifications and treatments to achieve the desired outcome of producing healthy progeny.

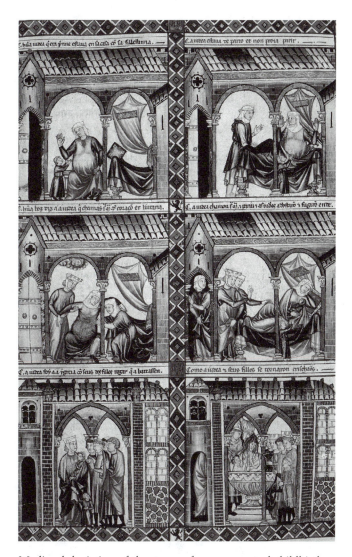

Medieval depiction of the stages of pregnancy and childbirth. (The Art Archive/Real biblioteca de lo Escorial)

In the fifteenth century, male medical writers turned yet another corner. They continued (as had male Salernitan writers and others throughout Europe after them) to compose medical encyclopedias organized in head-to-toe order, which situated gynecological and obstetrical conditions right after those of the male genitalia. Some of these sections became so big that they were circulated separately. Moreover, several writers composed entirely new texts on women's diseases. Thus, for example, a mid-fifteenth-century English writer took an earlier translation of *Gilbertus Anglicus's chapters on gynecology, rearranged them, and then added major new sections on childbirth (drawn from Muscio's text), on expelling the dead fetus, and various other conditions. Such works as these, in Latin as well as in several vernacular languages, greatly expanded the fund of gynecological knowledge available to average practitioners and, just as importantly, reflect how common male involvement with women's medicine had become.

Midwives and Other Female Practitioners

There is ample evidence that medieval women practiced in a variety of medical contexts besides midwifery; they were surgeons, apothecaries, barbers, and general healers. In fact, midwifery may have been the last of these fields to coalesce as a profession in the High Middle Ages. The environment that had supported the specialized (and literate) female midwives of antiquity had disappeared, and it is difficult to find evidence of any women taking on the formal title of "midwife" again prior to the latter half of the thirteenth century. In the interim (and even in many situations thereafter), it is likely that birth was managed by a network of female kin and neighbors, none of whom necessarily claimed to be more expert in handling childbirth than the others. In examining the range of possible audiences for gynecological texts, therefore, we must keep in mind that for most of the Middle Ages there was no predetermined "target audience" of literate specialist midwives to address. The first text on women's medicine that was specifically aimed at midwives was Michele Savonarola's *Regimen for the Ladies of Ferrara* (c. 1460), which actually addressed laywomen as well as midwives. The same was true of the two most famous midwifery manuals, the *Women's Handbook* (printed c. 1495), and the *Rosegarden for Pregnant Women and Midwives* (printed 1513), both published originally in German but later translated into a variety of different languages. Gynecological texts addressed generically to women, in contrast, can be found sporadically in several languages from the thirteenth to fifteenth centuries. The earliest are in French, with later ones in English and Dutch; all were probably composed by male authors or translators. The earliest of the English ones, called *The Knowing of Woman's Kind* [i.e., nature] *in Childing*, which dates from the late fourteenth or early fifteenth century, opens with a poignant claim that the text is meant to be shared among women so that they do not have to show their diseases to men. The upper-class women to whom such texts were addressed certainly do not represent the majority of medieval women, but such sentiments do reveal the tension caused by a social system that granted literacy and education to men—and so the possibility of engagement with formal medical theory—but only rarely to women.

See also **Magic and the occult; Medicine, practical; Salerno; Women in science**

Bibliography

Barkaï, Ron. *A History of Jewish Gynaecological Texts in the Middle Ages*. Leiden: Brill, 1998.

Green, Monica H. From 'Diseases of Women' to 'Secrets of Women': The Transformation of Gynecological Literature in the Later Middle Ages. *Journal of Medieval and Early Modern Studies* (2000) 30: 5–39.

———. *Women's Healthcare in the Medieval West: Texts and Contexts*. Aldershot: Ashgate, 2000.

Green, Monica H. and Linne R. Mooney. The Sickness of Women. In *Sex, Aging, and Death in a Medieval Medical Compendium: TCC R.14.52, Its Language, Scribe and Text*. Edited by M. Teresa Tavormina. Tempe: Arizona State University, 2005.

Musacchio, Jacqueline Marie. *The Art and Ritual of Childbirth in Renaissance Italy*. New Haven: Yale University Press, 1999.

Taglia, Kathryn. Delivering a Christian Identity: Midwives in Northern French Synodal Legislation, c. 1200-1500. In *Religion and Medicine in the Middle Ages*. Edited by Peter Biller and Joseph Ziegler. York: York Medieval Press, 2001, pp. 77–90.

MONICA H. GREEN

H

HENRI DE MONDEVILLE

Henri de Mondeville (c. 1260–1320) was a Norman surgeon, professor, and author who studied medicine and surgery at the universities of Paris and Montpellier. He claimed as his master Jean Pitard, who was court physician and battlefield surgeon to King Philip the Fair. Through his association with Pitard, Mondeville obtained a medical position in service to the king, and by 1301 was both a court physician and an army surgeon. He continued to serve in the same capacity Philip's successors, Charles of Valois, and Louis X. Mondeville also taught at the university, and by 1304 he was a lecturer at Montpellier in both medicine and *surgery. When teaching anatomy at Montpellier, Mondeville used fourteen illustrations to help his students visualize the hidden components of the body. These illustrations, while not accurate, were still an important step in standardizing the depiction of human anatomy; they were so influential that they were ultimately collected in a work entitled the *Anathomia*. From 1306 Mondeville taught and practiced anatomy and surgery at Paris, where he used full-sized versions of his previous anatomical illustrations to demonstrate human anatomy.

In addition to his illustrated guide to the human body, the *Anathomia*, Mondeville wrote a manual on the practice, craft, and art of surgery. This work, the *Chirurgia*, which appeared in both Latin and French, remained unfinished at his death. It was divided into five parts: anatomy, treatment of wounds, surgical pathology, treatment of fractures and dislocations, and pharmacology. Henri took as his sources *Galen, many of whose works were translated at Montpellier in the thirteenth century, and *Ibn Sina (Avicenna). Henri further incorporated the works of two of his near contemporaries, *Teodorico Borgognoni and Lanfranc, both of Lucca, and by both documenting and utilizing their surgical techniques contributed to the dissemination of Italian surgical practices in France. While Henri utilized the works of these authors as a foundation for his *Chirurgia*, he used them selectively in order to suit the needs of practical surgery.

He did not use the works of these authors systematically, and since he was less concerned with theory than with practice, he was able to move beyond them to create his own ideas.

In his *Chirurgia*, Henri outlined not only the particulars of practice but also the place of surgery in relation to the art of medicine. Traditionally surgery was considered

This illumination from a French fourteenth-century manuscript of Henri de Mondeville's *Chirurgia* depicts a dissection. (AKG Images/Bibliotheque Nationale, Paris)

a manual craft, and as such was viewed with disapprobation by learned physicians who had been trained in the theory of medicine at university. Mondeville argued that surgery was both art and craft, and therefore had a legitimate role in the medical curriculum of the university. As Simone C. Macdougall has shown, Mondeville sought not only to legitimate the practice of surgery but also to elevate it to a divine art. His *Chirurgia* illuminated the theoretical and practical elements of surgery as well as the financial and logistical aspects of practice necessary if one was to be successful in the field.

See also **Medicine, practical; Medicine, theoretical**

Bibliography

Primary Sources
Henri de Mondeville. *La chirurgie de maître Henri de Mondeville*. Edited by A. Bos. Paris: Firmin Didot, 1897.
———.*Chirurgie*. Translated [into French from Latin recension] by E. Nicaise. Paris: Alcan, 1893.

Secondary Sources
Bullough, Vern L. *The Development of Medicine as a Profession*. New York: Hafner Publishing, 1966.
Macdougall, Simone C. "The Surgeon and the Saints: Henri de Mondeville on Divine Healing." In *Journal of Medieval History*, Vol. 26, No. 3, 2000, pp. 253–267.
McVaugh, Michael. "The Nature and Limits of Medical Certitude at Early Fourteenth-Century Montpellier." In *Osiris*, 2nd Series, Vol. 6, Renaissance Medical Learning: Evolution of a Tradition, 1990, pp. 62–84.
Pouchelle, Marie-Christine. *The Body and Surgery in the Middle Ages*. Cambridge: Polity Press, 1990.

BRENDA GARDENOUR

HERBALS

The term "herbal" (*herbarium*) usually refers to early printed books of the fifteenth and sixteenth centuries on the therapeutic properties of plants used in medicine. However, it can be applied to earlier works dealing with the same topic, from their prototype, *De materia medica* (*MM*) by the Greek *Dioscorides (first century C.E.), to late-medieval compilations such as the early fourteenth-century *Liber de herbis*.

In their medieval canonical form, herbals usually consisted of a list of plants whose parts (roots, twigs, leaves, flowers, fruits, and seeds) were used as primary ingredients (that is, drugs) for the preparation of medicines, be they simple or composed. A chapter was devoted to each plant and all such chapters were ordered alphabetically by plant name. Each chapter normally contained the following: (a) The most commonly used Latin name of the plant and its synonyms; (b) A description of the plant; (c) The part or parts of the plant or plants to be used for therapeutic purposes (i.e., the drug or drugs), and their state (fresh or dry); (d) The preparation of the drug and, when appropriate, the proper ways to store it, that is, the type of container necessary for good conservation, without interaction between the drug and the substance of the container itself, and the maximum possible length of conservation without alteration of the drug and its properties; (e) The properties of the drug, usually expressed according to *Galen's system, that is, according to the four primary qualities (hot and cold; dry and humid) and their grade (on a scale of four degrees); (f) The disease or diseases for the treatment of which the drug was used; and (g) A drawing of the plant, more or less developed or schematic.

After the translation period and the assimilation of Arabic texts into Western medical sciences, the schema above was modified to include a list of synonyms that included the Greek and Arabic names of plants transliterated into the Latin alphabet and often adapted to Latin phonetics but which was deformed by mistakes of all kinds. The list of diseases was very often preceded by long quotations from previous authors' works. Such citations were attributed and ordered according to the probable chronological sequence of the authors, be they Greek (known through their Arabic versions themselves translated into Latin) or Arabic (in Latin translation). A further innovation was the inclusion of medieval commentaries on these authors; these might contain the text of the primary author, divided into thematic sections. Such commentaries tended to accumulate with the passage of time.

Byzantine and Arabic Precursors

In Byzantium, Dioscorides' *MM* rapidly became the standard work for the knowledge of herbal substances used for therapeutic purposes; it seems to have been preferred to Galen's works on the topic because of the Christianization of medicine. *MM* was widely spread from Egypt to Constantinople and from Rome to Syria. Its original text was rearranged several times, including the production of a herbal *stricto sensu*, first attested by the manuscript now in Vienna, Österreichische Nationalbibliothek, *medicus graecus* 1, c. 513 C.E. This herbal contained about three hundred plants and their representation in color illustrations, and was abundantly reproduced until 1453 and even later in the West. Eastern plants from the original version of *MM* were eliminated in this herbal, and not reintroduced until the eleventh century in the manuscript now Athos (Greece), Megistis Lavras, S 75.

The works of both Dioscorides and Galen were translated into Syriac during the sixth century. *MM* was translated into Arabic twice during the ninth century by *Hunayn ibn Ishaq working in Baghdad in collaboration with Istifan ibn Basil, and several other times later on. Plant representations in early Arabic copies of *MM* strongly recall their Greek models, and include other decorative elements suggesting natural habitats (with animals and environmental elements such as rivers and rocks, for instance) and human uses (with representations of physicians, for example). Their works contributed to the production of original Arabic herbals (or sections on herbal drugs in larger medical encyclopedias) such as the *Book on Medicinal Plants* of *al-Biruni and the *Canon* of

*Ibn Sina (Avicenna). The discursive genre of the herbal, such as represented by *MM* and reproduced among others by the above authors, was transformed by ibn Butlan (d. c. 1063) in the *Tables of Health*. He segmented textual information so as to present it in a tabular form where each column contains one single category of data: name, nature, degree, best variety, usefulness, toxicity, treatment of toxic action, property, usefulness according to patient's temperament and age, and to season and place.

Arabic herbalism attained its apogee in the Cordoban school, whose origin dates back to the Umayyad 'Abd al-Rahman I (756–788) and to his experiments of naturalization of Eastern plants. Local knowledge was enhanced during the tenth century thanks to a Greek copy of *MM* sent by the Byzantine emperor to the emir 'Abd al-Rahman III (929–961). During the twelfth and thirteenth centuries, al-Ghafiqi (first half of the twelfth century?), from Córdoba, and ibn al-Baytar (before 1204–1248), who was born in Málaga and traveled to the East, wrote the most comprehensive Arabic herbals, mainly following the *MM* model.

The West

Western herbals can be divided into three major chronological groups: (a) Late antiquity; (b) The translation period; and (c) The post-translation period.

(a) Late antiquity. Herbals of this period were mainly translations, adaptations, and compilations of previous or contemporary Greek and Latin works. They can be divided into two main sub-groups:

(a1) Translations and adaptations of Dioscorides' *MM*, and of books 20–27 of Pliny's *Natural History*, which are devoted to medicinal plants. These include (in probable chronological order): Gargilius Martialis (third century), Pseudo-Apuleius (fourth century?), *Medicina* and *Physica Plinii* (early fourth, and fifth/sixth century respectively), Theodorus Priscianus (fourth/fifth century), Vindicianus (fourth/fifth century) (now lost), Pseudo-Dioscorides, *De herbis feminis* (fifth century), Marcellus of Bordeaux (early fifth century), Serenus Sammonicus (of uncertain period, between second and fourth century), and *Isidore of Seville (bishop of Seville 600/601–636). Such works amalgamated local material, sometimes characterized by superstition and magic.

(a2) First medieval original syntheses, from the recipe book of Lorsch Abbey (Germany) (790 C.E.) to Hraban Maur (c. 780–856), Walahfrid Strabo (c. 808–849), and *Hildegard of Bingen (1098–1179). These works reflect the development of gardens of simples in the context of Western monastic institutions, and include the newly developed Christian approach to the medicinal powers of plants, characterized by prayers to the saints Cosmas and Damian which concentrate on God's creative power, and thus restrict speculation on the natural origin of the plant's therapeutic power, as well as materialist theories such as those of Galen.

(b) Translation period. Translation activity started in southern Italy, be it from Arabic into Greek or Latin (for the latter, *Salerno and *Monte Cassino, with *Constantine the African [d. after 1085]), and later pursued in Spain (*Toledo, among others with *Gerard of Cremona [c. 1114–187]), southern France (Montpellier), *Arnau de Vilanova, and Sicily under Manfred, King of Naples and Sicily (1258–1266). Translations included a wide range of works, from the classical *Canon* of Avicenna translated by Gerard of Cremona to the *Travelers' Medical Manual* of ibn al-Jazzar (d. 1004–1005) translated by Constantine as the *Viaticum*, and the *Tables of Health* of ibn Butlan translated in Sicily as the *Tacuinum sanitatis*, maybe by Faraj ibn Salim (thirteenth century). All such translations were widely spread in the West. Illustrations of *Tacuinum sanitatis* were particularly developed in northern Italy, with the creation of a new iconic genre: plants were inserted into scenes borrowing their elements from other scientific and non-scientific fields such as agriculture and the calendar.

(c) Post-translation period. The injection of Arabic texts into Western medicine fostered the writing of new herbals such as the *Regime of Health* (tenth/eleventh century), the *Dynamidios* perhaps of Gariopontus (late eleventh century), the herbal of Platearius commonly identified by its first words as *Circa instans* (twelfth century), the Salernitan secrets, and the early-fourteenth century *Book of Herbs*, with its French translation, the *Livre des simples médecines*. As the latter suggests, versions in the vernacular proliferated from then onward (even though they were not a novelty of that time), in Romance, Anglo-Saxon, and German languages. The illustrations of a copy of the *Liber de herbis*, the early fourteenth-century manuscript Egerton 747 now conserved at the British Library (London), have a realistic character that induced historians of art to think that they were made from nature directly, rather than reproducing previous models.

During the post-translation period, new translations of Greek works were made by such scholars as *Burgundio of Pisa, *Pietro d'Abano, and *Niccolò da Reggio. Characteristically, they included Galen's treatise *On the Mixtures and Properties of simple medicines* and tried to reintroduce Galen's herbalism, which was abandoned during the early Byzantine period. In Pietro d'Abano's pharmacological work, both Dioscorides' and Galen's texts are associated.

Into Print

The first printed herbal was the *Herbarius Maguntie impressus* (Mainz, 1484), followed by the *Herbarius Patavie impressus* (Passau,1485), and the herbal attributed to Arnau de Vilanova and Avicenna (Vicenza, 1491). In the same year came the *Ortus sanitatis* (Mains, 1491), immediately followed by the *De Plinii aliorumque in medicina erroribus* by Nicolao Leoniceno (1428–1524) published in 1492 (Ferrara), which put an end to the era of medieval herbals. The work suggested a return to Greek science (that is, to Dioscorides' *MM*) rather than using Pliny's *Natural History* or the Latin translations of Arabic medical treatises. No new herbal appeared before the *Herbarum vivae eicones* by Otto Brunfels (c.

1488–1534) in 1530 to be followed shortly by the *De historia stirpium commentarii* by Leonhart Fuchs (1501–1566).

See also **Botany; Magic and the occult; Pharmacology; Translation movements; Translation norms and practice**

Bibliography

Arber, Agnes. *Herbals. Their origin and evolution. A chapter in the history of botany, 1470–1670.* New York: Cambridge University Press, 1912.

Collins, Minta. *Medieval herbals. The Illustrative Traditions.* Toronto: University of Toronto Press, 2000.

Daems, Willem F. *Nomina simplicium medicinarum ex synonymariis Medii Aevi collecta. Semantische Untersuchungen zum Fachwortschatz hoch- und spätmittelalterlicher Drogenkunde.* Leiden: E.J. Brill, 1993.

Müller, Annette. *Krankheitsbilder im Liber de Plantis der Hildegard von Bingen (1098–1179) und im Speyerer Kräuterbuch (1456). Ein Beitrag zur medizinisch-pharmazeutischen Terminologie im Mittelalter.* 2 vols. Hürtgenwald: Guido Pressler Verlag, 1997.

Opsomer, Carmelia. *Index de la pharmacopée antique du Ier au Xe siècle.* 2 vols. Hildesheim: Olms-Weidmann, 1989.

Riddle, John M. *Dioscorides on pharmacy and medicine.* Austin: University of Texas Press, 1985.

Sadek, Mahmoud M. *The Arabic materia medica of Dioscorides.* St-Jean-Chrysostome: Les Editions du Sphinx, 1983.

Stannard, Jerry. *Herbs and herbalism in the Middle Ages and the Renaissance.* Aldershot: Ashgate, 1999.

———. *Pristina medicamenta. Ancient and medieval botany.* Aldershot: Ashgate, 1999.

Stirling, Iohannes. *Lexicon nominum herbarum, arborum fruticumque linguae latinae ex fontibus Latinitatis ante saeculum XXII scriptis.* Budapest: Encyclopaedia, 1995–1997.

ALAIN TOUWAIDE

HERMANN OF CARINTHIA

Hermann of Carinthia (fl. 1138–1143) was a translator from Arabic into Latin of texts on mathematics (including *astrology) and Islam, and the author of original works on astrology and *cosmology. The various epithets attached to his name—de Carinthia, Dalmata, Sclavus—indicate that he was a Slav from the northern Balkan region; and he himself refers to "Central Istria" as his homeland in his translation of *Abu Ma'shar's *Great Introduction*. He referred to himself as "Hermannus Secundus," perhaps in recognition that his scientific work was a continuation of that of Hermannus Contractus of Reichenau. Inspired by the example of *Thierry of Chartres, chancellor of Chartres cathedral, to whom he refers as "his most loving teacher" (*diligentissime preceptor*), he embarked on a program of translating mathematical works from Arabic, together with his colleague, Robert of Ketton, to improve the quality of the textbooks available for teaching the secular sciences (the seven liberal arts) in the Western schools. Many of the texts that they prepared have not survived, including their translation of *Ptolemy's *Almagest* from the Arabic, which was their ultimate aim and may never have been completed. But versions of astronomical tables, of *Euclid's *Elements* and Theodosius's *Spherics* have been attributed to them, and evidently formed part of their enterprise. In 1143 Hermann dedicated Ptolemy's *Planisphere* (on the mathematics of stereographic projection, on which the operation of the astrolabe is based) to Thierry. Robert and Hermann's project was interrupted in 1141 by a commission from Peter the Venerable of Cluny to translate the Qu'ran and a representative collection of texts on Islam, of which Hermann was responsible for *On the Generation of Muhammad* (on the transmission of a divine spirit from Adam to Muhammad), and *The Doctrine of Muhammad* (a simple exposition of Muslim belief). Hermann was particularly interested in establishing the scientific bases of astrology in Latin, by translating works (e.g., a work on general astrology by Sahl ibn Bishr, translated in León in 1138) and compiling manuals on specific topics (e.g., texts on weather forecasting and finding treasure and lost objects). He may have worked closely with *Hugh of Santalla in putting together *summae* of astrological judgments based on several Arabic authorities.

Principal Achievement

Hermann's most important contribution to astrology, however, was his translation of Abu Ma'shar's *Great Introduction to Astrology* (1140), which underpinned the whole field of astrological doctrine with rational arguments, several taken from Aristotle. Hermann used these doctrines and arguments in his original work *On the Essences* (1143), which was devoted to physics "whose first part" (in his own words) "considered the nature of the upper world, and second part, the nature of the lower world, these being respectively the formal causes and the material causes of all things" (from his preface to the *Planisphere*). The "essences" of the title are cause, movement, place, time, and "condition" (*habitudo*), and Hermann expertly weaves together doctrine from the Arabic and the Latin traditions to form a well-constructed synthesis on the constitution and operation of the cosmos, the formation of minerals, plants and animals, and finally the composition of man. Hermann was writing at a time when the subject matter of mathematics, physics, and metaphysics was still being established in the West. The section on "cause" in *On the Essences* is virtually an essay on metaphysics, while "movement" (the effect of the cause) involves discussion of physical principles, to which the astronomy of the *Almagest* is accommodated. The analogy of musical harmony is often invoked (e.g., in the comparison of the planets' diversification of the movement of the first cause to the production of different pitches issuing from a single breath being blown into pipes of different lengths), and the biological language of the mating of masculine and feminine elements, characteristic of alchemy, is used. Hermes and Plato are Hermann's most venerable authorities: the "Emerald Tablet" of Hermes—the alchemists' credo—is quoted (perhaps for the first time in Latin) and *Plato's *Timaeus* provides the model for the structure of the work, as well as for the principles of the Same and the Different which are the prerequisite for change. *On the Essences* was completed in Béziers, which is where we find Hermann's one known pupil, Rudolph of Bruges, composing a work on the use of the astrolabe in 1144. It is less likely that Hermann subsequently moved to Sicily and was responsible for a translation from Greek into Latin of the *Almagest*, which is attributed to him in one manuscript. Throughout his works Hermann is concerned with literary quality, and *On the Essences* is suffused with echoes of Latin poets and Classical mythology. The combination of myth and science, which was favored by the French Schools in the early twelfth century, was soon to be displaced by a drier scientific discourse, in which Aristotle's works were central. But Hermann's ideas lived on in extensive quotations of *On the Essences* in the work of the *Domingo Gundisalvo, while his translation of the *Great Introduction to Astrology* was printed three times in the Renaissance.

See also **Aristotelianism; Astrolabes and quadrants; Quadrivium**

Bibliography

Primary Sources
Abu Ma'shar. *Great Introduction*, translated by Hermann of Carinthia. In *Liber introductorii maioris ad scientiam judiciorum astrorum*. Edited by Richard Lemay, 9 vols. Naples: Istituto Universtario Orientale, 1995–1996, vol. VIII.
Hermann of Carinthia. *De essentiis*. Edited and translated by Charles Burnett. Leiden: E.J. Brill, 1982; Edited by Antun S. Kalenic. Pula: JAZU, 1990.
———. "The *Liber imbrium*, the *Fatidica*, and the *De indagatione cordis*." Edited by Shiela Low-Beer. Unpub. Doctoral Diss., City University of New York, 1979.
Euclid. *Elements*, translated by Hermann of Carinthia. Edited by H.L.L. Busard, Books I–VI. Leiden: E.J. Brill, 1968. Books VII–XII. Amsterdam: Mathematisch Centrum, 1977.
Ptolemy. *Planisphere*, translated by Hermann of Carinthia. Edited by Johan L. Heiberg. In *Ptolemaei opera astronomica minora*. Leipzig: Teubner, 1907, pp. 225–259.

Secondary Sources
Burnett, Charles. "Hermann of Carinthia." In *A History of Twelfth-Century Western Philosophy*. Peter Dronke, ed. New York: Cambridge University Press, 1988: 386–406.
———. Arabic into Latin in Twelfth-Century Spain: the Works of Hermann of Carinthia. *Mittellateinisches Jahrbuch* (1978) 13: 100–134.
———. "The Blend of Latin and Arabic Sources in the Metaphysics of Adelard of Bath, Hermann of Carinthia and Gundisalvus." In *Metaphysics in the Twelfth Century: On the Relationship among Philosophy, Science and Theology*. Matthias Lutz-Bachmann, Alexander Fidora and Andreas Niederberger, eds. Turnhout: Brepols, 2004: 41–65.
Dadic, Zarko. *Herman Dalmatin: Hermann of Dalmatia* (Croatian and English). Zagreb: Skolska Knjiga, 1996.
Haskins, Charles Homer. *Studies in the History of Mediaeval Science*. 2nd ed. Cambridge, MA: Harvard University Press, 1927: 67–81.

CHARLES BURNETT

HEYTESBURY, WILLIAM OF

William of Heytesbury (before 1313–1372/3) was a fellow of Merton College, Oxford, from 1330. With *Richard Swineshead, he belonged to the second generation of Mertonian "Calculators," building, in particular, on Richard Kilvington's *Sophismata* (1325) and *Thomas Bradwardine's *Insolubilia* and *Tractatus de Proportionibus* (1328). He develops his thought through logical puzzles, applying supposition theory, a form of semantic-logical analysis, to the explication of *sophismata* (problematic statements whose truth is at issue given certain assumptions). He is particularly noted, as was Kilvington, for his work on motion and the continuum. His work, though not itself empirical, helped to lay the conceptual groundwork for early modern science.

Heytesbury's most influential work was the *Rules for Solving Sophismata* (1335). It consists of six chapters. "On insoluble sentences" (*insolubilia*) concerns self-referential paradoxes. "On knowing and doubting" deals with reference in intensional contexts. "On relative terms" considers the reference of relative pronouns. "On beginning and ceasing" and "On maxima and minima" deal with continuum. "On the three categories" examines problems in velocity and acceleration in the three categories of place, quantity, and quality.

In "On beginning and ceasing," Heytesbury considers *sophismata* such as "some part of an object ceases to be seen by Socrates," given that the object is not now, but will be immediately after now, partly occluded by an object passing in front of it. He notes that this *sophisma* can be given two readings. It may be asserted that there is some one given part of the object that will, in every instant after this one, be entirely occluded. Given that reading, the sentence is false. Alternatively, it may be asserted that, at every moment after this present moment, there will be some part of the object entirely occluded at that moment (a different part for each moment). On that reading the sentence is true.

"On maxima and minima" concerns the limits of capacities, as measured on the range of actions a capacity can perform. Thus one might ask what the limit of a given person's capacity to run a distance in a given time is, measured on the continuous range of distances. In such a case there will be, it seems, either a greatest distance he can run, or a shortest he cannot, but not both, and one issue is to determine which of these options is correct in different cases. Heytesbury considers also the question when such a limit exists at all, and specifies that it will exist, for instance, as long as there is a distance that can be run in that time, and also a distance that cannot, and as long as any shorter distance can be run if a longer one can, and no longer distance can be run if a shorter cannot. In fact, this is true as long as distances form a compact continuum, but is not true if they are associated only with rational numbers, and not with irrational numbers such as the square root of two. Heytesbury's work here, although intended for an entirely different purpose, is conceptually related to the construction of *Real Numbers from Rationals* by Richard Dedekind in 1872.

The "Rules" was Heytesbury's most popular work, and remained important in Italy even after the Mertonians began to be ignored in Britain. It was made part of the curriculum at Padua in 1487, influencing the Paduan School and fifteenth-century Italian logicians such as Paul of Venice (d. 1429), and was used in Paris by the school of John Major in the early sixteenth century. With the rest of medieval logic, Heytesbury's work sank into obscurity after that. In addition to the "Rules" Heytesbury wrote two collections of *sophismata*, in one of which it was repeatedly argued that the respondent was a donkey, as well as some shorter works, for instance, "On the Compounded and Divided Senses," which dealt with scope ambiguities similar to that concerning the occluded object laid out above.

In the sixth chapter of the "Rules," Heytesbury states the mean-speed theorem for uniformly accelerated motion: a uniformly accelerated body will, over a given time, traverse a distance equal to the distance it would traverse if it moved continuously in the same period at its mean velocity (one half the sum of the initial and final velocities). Elsewhere, he points out, in a particular case, that a uniformly accelerated body will, in the second equal time interval, traverse three times the distance it does in the first. Domingo de Soto observed the applicability of the mean-speed theorem to free fall in 1555.

See also **Latitude of forms; Swineshead, Richard**

Bibliography

Heytesbury, William. *On Maxima and Minima: Chapter 5 of Rules for Solving Sophismata, with an anonymous four-teenth-century discussion*, translated with introduction and study by John Longeway. Dordrecht: D. Reidel, 1984.

———. *William of Heytesbury on "Insoluble" Sentences*, translated with notes by Paul Spade. Toronto: Pontifical Institute of Medieval Studies, 1979.

———. "The Compounded and Divided Senses," and "The Verbs 'Know' and 'Doubt'," translated by Norman Kretzmann and Eleonore Stump. In *The Cambridge Translations of Medieval Philosophical Texts*, Vol. 1: *Logic and Philosophy of Language*. New York: Cambridge University Press, 1988.

———. "On the three categories." Selections translated by E.A. Moody in Marshall Claggett, *The Science of Mechanics in the Middle Ages*. Madison, Wisconsin: University of Wisconsin Press, 1959. Reprinted in Edward Grant, *A Source Book in Medieval Science*. Cambridge: Harvard University Press, 1974.

Wilson, Curtis. *William Heytesbury: Medieval Logic and the Rise of Modern Physics*. Madison: University of Wisconsin Press, 1960.

JOHN LONGEWAY

HILDEGARD OF BINGEN

Hildegard of Bingen (1098–1179) led both a very conventional and a very unconventional life. Born into a well-connected family in the German Rhineland, at twelve she entered a Benedictine monastery. Seventy years later she died in a second Benedictine monastery no more than twenty miles from her birthplace. She took few trips, the longest only a few hundred miles from her monastery; her main supporters and friends were almost all relatives.

And yet Hildegard's life was remarkable. In her early forties she began to experience complex spiritual visions; by fifty she had completed her first book, *Scivias*, a grandiose illuminated text on the theological and sometimes the political implications of these visions. Two years later, despite her monastic vows, she left her first monastery and, taking most of its nuns with her, founded a new monastery at Bingen on the Rhine. Over the next thirty years she wrote many works, among them two other illuminated texts of theology, a musical drama (possibly the first in Europe), more than seventy liturgical pieces, a commentary on the Benedictine Rule, two saints' lives, and a glossary of a private language. By the end of her life she was well known, and her surviving letters include correspondence with most of the crowned heads of Europe, as well as numerous popes, archbishops, bishops, abbots, and abbesses.

Of greatest interest to historians of science, technology, and medicine are Hildegard's two medico-botanical works, *Physica* and *Causae et curae*. Her sources are still unknown. The texts imply that she was familiar with Galenism, folk practice, and the new Arabic medicine, and that she had gained practical knowledge of medicine as the infirmarian at her first monastery.

Physica is essentially a nine-book natural science encyclopedia (on plants, elements, trees, stones, fish, birds, animals, reptiles, and metals) in the tradition of Pliny the Elder (23–79) and *Isidore of Seville, as well as of *lapidaries, *bestiaries, and *herbals. The work consists of short passages on the medicinal properties of thousands of substances. Many of its observations are original, and even when presenting traditional information Hildegard is always idiosyncratic.

By contrast, the five-book *Causae et curae* is more of a manual of practical medicine, probably composed for the nun-infirmarian of Hildegard's new monastery at Bingen. Its first book summarizes natural science and cosmology; its second book presents an abbreviated human physiology; its third and fourth books provide medicinal recipes, and the fifth book has passages on prognostic techniques. Although sometimes confusing and still controversial, the text allows an unparalleled look at how one particular medieval practitioner assimilated the varied strands of medicine available—the Greco-Roman, the Christian, and the folk-oral.

For instance, Hildegard conflates three humoral ideas, while adding a few of her own. She takes a mainly Hippocratic view of the humors as bile, blood, melancholy, and phlegm, but sometimes assumes a rather more Galenic view, treating the humors as if they were identical with the qualities of hot and cold, wet and dry. At other times she treats "humor" as if it were the unique medicinal property of a plant—its sap—linguistically the original meaning of the Greek *chymos* (humor). None of this prevents her from also seeing humors idiosyncratically, as higher or lower, good or bad, in parallel with her concern with hierarchy and order. But it is Hildegard's concept of *viriditas* (greenness) that has provided scholars with their most important insights into the medieval body. *Viriditas* was originally a botanical concept signifying green sap, often used as a metaphor for the fertility of spiritual qualities. Although Hildegard does use *viriditas* in both these ways, she uniquely finds it also inside the body, and with hormone-like qualities. Thus her *viriditas* is a substance that circulates in the blood, is modified by food, and affects secondary sexual characteristics. This unique usage suggests that for her there was an implicit overlap between medieval doctor and gardener—just as the job of the gardener was to cultivate the *viriditas* of the plant, so the job of the physician was to nurture the *viriditas* of the patient.

Taken together, *Physica* and *Causae et curae* can provide the scholar with special insights into the medieval body. Long neglected, and then studied without reference to its context, Hildegard's work should instead be a reference point for many studies of medieval science, technology, and medicine—not just as "the woman's voice," or "the mystic's voice," or even "the genius's voice," but as the voice of an observant and pragmatic practitioner.

See also **Dioscorides; Encyclopedias; Galen; Gynecology and midwifery; Hippocrates; Hospitals; Illustration, medical; Medicine, practical; Medicine, theoretical; Microcosm/macrocosm; Natural history; Pharmaceutic handbooks; Pharmacology; Pharmacy;** *Regimen sanitatis*; **Salerno; Translation movements; Women in science**

Bibliography

Primary Sources

Hildegard of Bingen. *Holistic Healing.* Translated by Manfred Pawlik, translator of Latin text, Patrick Madigan, translator of German text, John Kulas, translator of foreword. Edited by Mary Palmquist and John Kulas. Collegeville: Liturgical Press, 1996.

Hildegard, Saint. *Hildegard's Healing Plants: From the Medieval Classic 'Physica.'* Translated by Bruce W. Hozeski. Boston: Beacon Press, 2001.

Kaiser, Paul, ed. *Hildegardis Cause et curae.* Leipzig: Teubner, 1903.

Migne, Jacques-Paul, ed. S. *Hildegardis Abbatissae Opera Omnia. Vol. 197, Patrologiae Cursus Completus. Series Latina.* Paris: Garnier, 1855.

Moulinier, Laurence, ed. *Beate Hildegardis Bingensis Causae et cure.* Vol. 1. Berlin: Akademie Verlag, 2003.

Patrologia Latina Database (CD-Rom). *Patrologiae Cursus Completus. Series Latina.* Alexandria, VA: Chadwick-Healey, Inc., 1995.

Throop, Priscilla. *Hildegard Von Bingen's Physica: The Complete English Translation of Her Classic Work on Health and Healing.* Rochester, VT:.Healing Arts Press, 1998.

Tombeur, Paul. "The Cetedoc Library of Christian Latin Texts: Cdrorn." Turnhout: Brepols, 2002.

Secondary Sources

Berger, Margret. *Hildegard of Bingen: On Natural Philosophy and Medicine.* Cambridge: D.S. Brewer, 1999.

Twentieth-century rendition of a thirteenth-century Lucca manuscript illustration of Hildegard of Bingen. (Lebrecht Music and Arts Picture Library/John Minnion)

Burnett, Charles and Peter Dronke, eds. *Hildegard of Bingen: The Context of Her Thought and Art.* London: Warburg Institute, 1998.

Flanagan, Sabina. *Hildegard of Bingen, 1098–1179: A Visionary Life.* 2nd ed. London: Routledge, 1998.

McInerney, Maud Burnett, ed. *Hildegard of Bingen: A Book of Essays.* London: Garland Press, 1998.

Newman, Barbara. *Sister of Wisdom: St. Hildegard's Theology of the Feminine.* Berkeley: University of California Press, 1997 (1987).

——— ed. *Voice of the Living Light: Hildegard of Bingen and Her World.* Berkeley: University of California Press, 1998.

Singer, Charles. "The Scientific Views and Visions of Saint Hildegard (1098–1179)." In *Studies in the History and Method of Science,* edited by Charles Singer, 155. Oxford: Clarendon Press, 1955.

Sweet, Victoria. "Hildegard of Bingen and the Greening of Medieval Medicine." *Bulletin of the History of Medicine* (1999) 73: 381–403.

———. "Body as Plant, Doctor as Gardener: Premodem Medicine in Hildegard of Bingen's Causes and Cures." Ph.D. dissertation, University of California San Francisco, 2003.

VICTORIA SWEET

HIPPOCRATES

A Greek physician, Hippocrates (460–between 375 and 351 B.C.E.) was born in the island of Kos (Aegean Sea) to a family of Asclepiads (descendants of Asclepiades, the mythological god of medicine). He practiced medicine in the north Aegean world (on the islands and the continent) in a pragmatical way (well summarized in the *Aphorisms*), with a special attention to the living conditions of the patients (see the treatise *Airs, waters, places*), physiological and pathological processes (including diagnosis and prognosis), alimentary diet and pharmacological therapy, and the interrelation between physicians and patients. On this basis, he has been traditionally credited with the development of scientific, viz., clinical medicine, free of superstition and supernatural processes (see, for instance, the treatise *Sacred disease*, in which the author denies that epilepsy results from supernatural causes). In the age of the Sophists, Hippocrates liked the professionalization of intellectual activities, and has been considered responsible for the transformation of the practice of medicine from a hereditary and exclusive privilege to a laicized and open profession. The Oath stipulated the conditions of the relationship of apprenticeship between a would-be physician and a practitioner-mentor. The relatives, disciples, and later followers of Hippocrates constituted the so-called School of Kos, inspired by the above principles and supposedly opposed to the School of Cnidus (on mainland Asia Minor, facing the island of Kos), characterized by a more rigid approach to medical examination and pharmacological therapy. Hippocrates' reputation as a successful physician is attested by *Plato.

Despite having lived in a period of development of written culture, Hippocrates does not seem to have written any medical treatise. However, some works that appeared later and circulated under his name might contain material dating back to him. Some sixty treatises of different medical and philosophical origins and periods (from the fifth century B.C.E. to the second C.E.) are attributed to him in manuscripts of the Byzantine period. They deal with physiology, the etiology, semiotics, diagnosis and prognosis of diseases, dietetics, pharmaceutical therapy and surgery, and the exercise and ethics of medicine. They seem to have been circulated in thematically coherent groups that then gradually became associated so as to form the so-called Corpus Hippocraticum of modern scholarship.

As early as Herophilus (330/320–260/250 B.C.E.), existing Hippocratic treatises were studied in the medical school of Alexandria. Hippocrates' approach to medicine, considered as of a dogmatic nature by empiricists from the Hellenistic period on, was reinvigorated and reinterpreted by *Galen. At the turn of the third century C.E., Hippocratic medicine met Christian faith, which denigrated the human body or promoted a discourse where physiological and pathological processes (of a material nature) were supplanted by a moral system of punishment and retribution (disease results from sin and healing from the grace of God). A compromise was soon reached: Hippocratic medicine was accepted provided its pagan components were eliminated. Between the fourth century and the sixth century, it was even absorbed into Christian faith, particularly with the cult of Saints Cosmas and Damianos, the so-called Anargyroi. Although these holy twins obtained their medical science directly from God (be it in pathology or therapeutics), they diagnosed and treated diseases in a typically Hippocratic way. Christianization of Hippocratic medical ethics is best represented by the layout of the Oath in Byzantine manuscripts, in the form of the Holy Cross.

In late antiquity, Hippocratic works were commented on in the Alexandria medical school by such teachers as Palladius (*Fractures*), Ioannes of Alexandria (*Nature of Child*, *Epidemics 6*), Stephanos of Athens (or of Alexandria) (*Aphorisms*, *Prognostics*), Asclepius (*Diseases of Women*) and the anonymous author of *Humors*. Their method followed a typical pattern: for each passage (lemma), the reading of the work was first discussed (with its possible variants); the general meaning of the lemma was then established; and the different interpretations proposed by previous authors and teachers were reviewed and discussed. Later Arabic sources have led to the postulation of the existence of a relatively rigid selection of twelve Hippocratic works studied in the Alexandrian school (the so-called Alexandrian Canon). Even though such an account should probably not be accepted too strictly, it is likely to reflect the state of affairs at the time of the takeover of Alexandria by the Arabs (642).

Translations

The Alexandrian method of teaching was reproduced in Ostrogothic Ravenna (sixth century). Some Hippocratic treatises were translated into Latin by Western teachers with a sufficient knowledge of Greek (*Aphorisms*; *Prognostic*; *Diseases of Women*; *Airs, waters, places*; *Nature of man*; *Weeks*; *Regimen*). These translations were made for practical rather than theoretical purposes, and seem to have also served as a basis for commentaries (instead of the Greek original text). Contrary to traditional historiography, the Lombard invasion of Italy (568) did not interrupt the tradition of the classical heritage. However, relations with the East were stronger under the Carolingians, and Hippocratic textual material arrived again from Byzantium before the eighth century as shown by the so-called Lorsch Arzneibuch (MS Bamberg, med. 1, from the abbey of Lorsch in Germany).

In the East, the twelve works of the supposedly Alexandrian Hippocratic canon were translated into Syriac by Sergius of Ra's al-'Ayn (d. 536). There was no Hippocratic Academy in Gundishabur, however, as claimed by a thirteenth-century historiographic tradition. Hippocratic treatises were known in the Arabic world from at least the ninth century. The *Aphorisms*, for example, served as a model for Masawayh's *Medical axioms*. They were translated into Arabic from Greek, principally by *Hunayn ibn Ishaq and a group of collaborators. Through these translations, Hippocratic medicine made its way into original works by Arab physicians.

Detail of a woodcut of 1511 depicting the three great medical authorities of the Middle Ages: (left to right) Galen, Avicenna (Ibn Sina), and Hippocrates. (Corbis/Bettmann)

Greek manuscripts of Hippocratic writings (be they of the entire corpus or of single works) circulated or were produced in southern Italy. They reproduced earlier manuscripts present in Italy, or new ones coming from the East (not necessarily Constantinople). From the eleventh century on (and maybe earlier), Arabic works were translated into Latin in the West in an enterprise best represented, though probably not initiated, by *Constantine the African. This movement was aimed at recovering Greek science and reintroduced Hippocratic texts into Western medicine. Constantine translated Galen's commentary on the *Aphorisms* and the *Prognostica*, and perhaps also the *Regimen in Acute Diseases*. *Gerard of Cremona (d. 1198) was responsible for the Latin version of Galen's commentary on the Hippocratic *Elements*. These texts were extremely popular from the twelfth to the fifteenth century as the high number of extant manuscripts currently inventoried suggests (*Aphorisms*: 137; *Regimen*: 203; *Prognostics*: 246) The so-called *Articella* that was thereby gradually constituted included the *Aphorisms*, the *Prognostics*, and the *Regimen in Acute Diseases*.

While pseudo-Hippocratic works proliferated in the West (Latin) and in the East (Greek), new Latin translations of Hippocratic or pseudo-Hippocratic works were made directly from Greek from the twelfth century on by, among others, *Burgundio of Pisa, Bartolomeo of Messina (fl. 1258–1266) (*Nature of Child*; *Nature of Man*), *Pietro d'Abano, *Arnau de Vilanova (*Law*), and *Niccolò da Reggio (*Regimen in Acute Diseases*; *Aphorisms*; *Oath*; *Law*; *Nutriment*).

At the end of the fifteenth century, Latin translations of Hippocratic treatises (be they medieval or new, viz., early humanistic ones) were printed together with the *Articella* or Arabic works: the *Aphorisms* (in the translation of Theodorus of Gaza [d. 1478]) in the 1476 edition of the *Articella*; *Airs, Waters, Places, Nature of Man*, and *Remedies* in the first printed edition (1481) of the Latin translation of al-Razi, *Liber ad Almansorem*; *The Oath* (Latin translation by Paolo Vergerio [1370–1444]) and *Nature of Man* (by Bartolomeo of Messina) in the 1483 edition of the *Articella*; and the Latin medieval translation of the *Aphorisms* in the 1489 edition of Maimonides' *Aphorisms*. At the same time, new humanistic translations were published independently: the *Art* by Andreas Brenta (c. 1460–c. 1485) in 1481; the *Oath* by Niccolò Perotti (fl. 1429/1430–1480/1490) in 1483; and the *Oath, Law, Nature of Man, Regimen*, and the *Art* by Andreas Brenta, in 1489–1490. Then, a new generation of Latin translations appeared, by among others Nicolao Leoniceno (1427–1524), Wilhelm Copp (c. 1460–1532) and Lorenzo Laurenziani (d. 1515). In 1524, such single translations were first published in a collective volume. The next year, a Latin translation of Hippocrates' *Eighty Volumes* was published by Marco Fabio Calvi (1440–1527), and, in 1526, the Greek text of Hippocrates' complete works was printed in Venice by Gian Francesco d'Asola (c. 1498–1557/1558), definitively putting an end to medieval Hippocratism and transforming Hippocrates into the Father of Medicine.

See also **Medicine, practical; Medicine, theoretical; Translation movements; Translation, norms and practice**

Bibliography

Primary Sources

Jouanna J. 1992. *Hippocrate*. Paris: Fayard (English translation: *Hippocrates*. Baltimore: Johns Hopkins University Press, 1999).

Hippocrates, Works. London: Heinemann, 8 vols., 1923–1994.

Secondary Sources

Aliotta G., D. Piomelli, A. Pollio, and A. Touwaide. *Le piante medicinali del «Corpus Hippocraticum»*. Milan: Guerini e Associati, 2003.

Kibre P. *Hippocrates latinus. Repertorium of Hippocratic writings in the Latin Middle Ages*. Revised edition. New York: Fordham University Press, 1985.

King H. 2002. "The Power of Paternity: the Father of Medicine meets the Prince of Physicians." In D. Cantor (ed.), *Reinventing Hippocrates*. Aldershot: Ashgate, 2002, pp. 21–36.

Maloney G. and R. Savoie. *Cinq cents ans de bibliographie hippocratique. 1473–1982*. St-Jean-Chrysostome, Quebec: Les Editions du Sphinx, 1982.

Mazzini I., and N. Palmieri. "Les écoles médicales à Rome. Programmes et mèthodes d'enseignement, langue, hommes." In P. Mudry, J. Piegeaud (eds.). *Les écoles médicales ‡ Rome*. Geneva: Droz, 1991, pp. 285–310.

Sezgin F. *Geschichte des arabischen Schrifttums, III. Medizin-Pharmazie-Zoologie- Tierheilkunde bis ca. 430 H.* Leiden: E.J. Brill, 1970, pp. 23–47.

Smith W. *The Hippocratic Tradition*. Ithaca: Cornell University Press, 1973.

Temkin O. *Hippocrates in a World of Pagans and Christians*. Baltimore: Johns Hopkins University Press, 1991.

Ullmann M. *Die Medizin im Islam*. Leiden: E.J. Brill, 1970, pp. 25–35.

ALAIN TOUWAIDE

HOSPITALS

The *Oxford English Dictionary* provides several definitions of the term hospital, including: "a house or hostel for the reception and entertainment of pilgrims, travelers, and strangers; a hospice," "a charitable institution for the housing and maintenance of the needy," "an asylum for the destitute, infirm, or aged," as well as our more modern definition of "an institution or establishment for the care of the sick or wounded, or of those who require medical treatment." An understanding of the development of the hospital as an institution, from its roots in Byzantium and the Dar al-Islam to its flowering in the medieval West, requires that we utilize these broader definitions of the structures, missions, and types of care provided by such institutions. While a majority of Byzantine and Islamic institutions provided advanced medical care administered by trained physicians, many early European medieval hostels and hospices did not. Such non-medicalized institutions are vital to the history of the hospital because they offered compassionate spiritual and physical care to the suffering, and this desire to alleviate pain is the fundamental mission behind the hospital as an institution, whether ancient, medieval, or modern.

Byzantine Hospitals

The first hospitals in Byzantium were modeled on Christian charitable institutions that had developed throughout the third and fourth centuries C.E. to house and feed the needy. *Xenones*, or hospices, provided food or shelter, while *nosokomeion*, or hospitals, provided medical care for the physically and mentally ill. St. Basil the Great founded one of the earliest hospitals at Caesarea, Cappadocia, c. 372 C.E. The *nosokomeion* and the surrounding complex, which became known as the Basileias, not only ministered to needy wayfarers as they passed through the province and provided spiritual care to those in crisis, but also offered therapeutic medical treatment delivered by trained physicians for those suffering in body and mind. The complex further contained areas dedicated to the care of the chronically ill, including the aged and the leprous.

St. Basil's was only one of the earliest in a long tradition of Byzantine hospitals. Healing institutions similar to those in Alexandria, Thessalonica, Ephesus, and Constantinople were opened throughout the empire, and continued to develop well into the Middle Ages. While both the Byzantine Church, through its network of metropolitans and bishops, and wealthy individuals founded hospitals, many more were established and funded by the imperial government. In 1136, Empress Irene Komnenos founded the hospital complex of the Pantocrator of Constantinople, the *typikon*, or charter, of which has survived. The Pantocrator contained specialized areas for surgery, a central hearth-altar, separate chambers for men and women, areas for the chronically ill, the mentally deranged, the aged, a leprosarium, a dormitory for hospital staff, a medical school, an outpatient area, and several chapels with elaborate mosaics. Staffing at the Pantocrator was hierarchical, with the *archiatros*, or head physician, acting as director of thirty-five physicians, several midwives, surgeons, and pharmacists, together with a sizeable nursing staff composed of men and women. The *archiatros* was also responsible for managing the non-medical staff of the hospital, including cooks, launderers, groundskeepers, and provisioners. The architecture of this hospital was based on that of the monastery at Meteora, and served to reinforce the theological assertion that every illness, whether physical or mental, was spiritual in origin; the healing process, therefore, began with a cleansing of the soul, administered primarily through contact with Christ and His Saints in the sacred space of the hospital.

Hospitals in the Dar al-Islam

The development of the hospital in Islam can be attributed to contact with Greek medical texts and institutions, the growing need for medical care in the rapidly developing cities of the Islamic empire, and the practice of charity and hospitality inherent in Islamic culture. The rise of Islam in the seventh century and its phenomenal expansion brought intellectuals into contact with the textual traditions of the West. By the sixth century, medical treatises had already been disseminated to the edges of the eastern Byzantine empire. Nestorian Christians, fleeing persecution by the Byzantine Church, brought libraries of medical texts eastward into Syria, and established centers of learning, such as the famed medical school at Gondeshapur. Muslim physicians not only made use of the Greek-to-Syriac translations produced at these centers, but also gathered Greek medical treatises from Byzantine cities, such as Alexandria, which had been absorbed into the Islamic Empire. Contact with Byzantine medical culture provided Islam with the institutional foundations for the development of the *bimaristan*, the Islamic hospital.

Islamic culture has at its core the fundamental belief that charity and hospitality are vital practices for both the individual and the community as a whole. Muhammad called on his people to care for widows, orphans, and the destitute. Since those suffering from illness were often incapacitated to the point where they could not support themselves, they were also to be provided for by the Muslim community. Individuals, through tithing and bequests (*zaqat* and *waqf*), contributed to the support of hospitals. Ultimately, the caliphs would found hospitals and their functioning would be supported and managed by the state. Islamic hospitals were predominantly secular in orientation, in contrast to those of Byzantium. Some of the most prominent *bimaristans* in the Islamic empire included the leprosarium at Damascus founded by the Umayyad caliph Ibn Walid, the hospital at Rayy at which *al-Razi practiced his art, the al-Baghdadi hospital founded by Harun al-Rashid and managed by the Bakhtishu family of Gundishapur, the Mansuria Hospital in Egypt, and the Egyptian Hospital of Ibn Tulun, the functioning of which is described in detail in the memoirs of Ibn Jubayr.

Islamic hospitals, although based on the institutions of Byzantium, were not mere reproductions of a received tradition; instead, Muslim physicians used Byzantine models to create distinctly Islamic institutions. Islamic hospitals were staffed by trained physicians and nurses under the guidance of a head physician; an individual appointed by the caliph oversaw the funding and management of non-medical aspects of the institution. Within the differentiated space of the Islamic hospital were areas for internal medicine, osteopathy, ophthalmology, and surgery, as well as separate wards for men, women, and the chronically ill. The hospital also contained a medical school, with a library and classrooms, a pharmacy, baths, an outpatient area, and a mosque. One significant contribution of Muslim physicians to the design of the hospital was a ward designated solely for the treatment of the mentally ill. These wards were open to the public, and allowed patients to continue to participate in the daily life of the community.

Hospitals in the Medieval Christian West

Roman hospitals of the third and fourth centuries were Christian charitable foundations established, primarily by bishops, to provide food, shelter, and basic care to the destitute. These foundations functioned as hospices, and while providing spiritual care and the alleviation of suffering, did not offer medical treatment. Unlike Byzantine institutions of the same period, which contained specialized rooms for different types of treatment, Roman hospices generally consisted of one room, an undifferentiated space within which the sick, the poor, and the transient co-existed. This sacred space might be imagined as a small chapel in which beds and pallets of straw were arranged. Throughout the sixth century, the pope exhorted bishops to continue to found hospices; Caesarius of Arles erected such a structure for the benefit of his flock. Many of these early foundations did not survive the urban decline of the seventh century and were left to decay. Charlemagne, in the ninth century, advocated the founding of hospices for the care of pilgrims and the infirm; however, many of these institutions were destroyed by subsequent barbarian invasions and political dissolution.

In addition to the Roman type of hospice was the monastic infirmary. The Rule of Saint Benedict called for the charitable care of the destitute and infirm. In response to this demand, Benedictine monasteries housed infirmaries for the care of sick inmates, and when necessary, people in the surrounding community. Both body and soul were treated simultaneously in the monastic infirmary. The infirmarian, acting as physician, utilized medicaments, such as salves and purgatives, as well as therapeutics, such as dietary regimens and massage, to treat bodily illness. The monastic community helped to heal the souls of the suffering through prayer, liturgy, and communion; the proximity of saintly relics also provided physical and spiritual benefits. In some cases music was allowed in the infirmary to help soothe the souls of the sick, thereby facilitating the healing process. The monastic infirmary was originally an undifferentiated space; however, by the ninth and tenth centuries a level of differentiation had been achieved, with the infirmary being divided into an area for the acutely ill, a pharmacy used for the concoction of medicines and blood-letting, a bath area, and a garden for growing medicinal herbs.

The medieval hospital advanced as a medical institution due to the reception of Eastern medical traditions via the translation of medical texts, as well as through contact with eastern hospitals during the Crusades. Early translations were made at the Benedictine monastery of *Monte Cassino, where *Constantine the African (fl. 1065–1085) rendered Arabic treatises, such as the *Pantegni* of *'Ali ibn al'Abbas al-Majusi, into Latin. In the twelfth century, scholars such as *Gerard of Cremona traveled to Spain in search of medical treatises, carrying them northward to monasteries, cathedral schools, and universities. The dissemination of medical texts, the development of the university, and a demand for medical care by the elite contributed to the development of the medical profession. By the thirteenth century, the physician was a recognizable member within the community. While private practice was predominant, physicians also donated their time for the sake of charity, and brought learned medical practice into the medieval hospital.

The Crusades brought Europeans into direct contact with Eastern hospitals, such as that of Saint John of Jerusalem. The structure of Saint John's Hospital was Byzantine, with differentiated areas for specialized activities. It was staffed by trained physicians and nurses who cared for the inmates. In 1125, the Knights of Saint John's Hospital, or the Hospitallers, were recognized as an official order, and were placed in charge of Saint John's. As the order expanded, the Hospitallers founded and staffed hospitals throughout the Mediterranean and Europe.

The Hospitallers were only the most prominent of a myriad of orders dedicated to the care of the sick. Religious confraternities and lay brotherhoods, particularly the Augustinian Canons, offered their services both by running hospices and by nursing in hospitals. This desire to care for the destitute and the suffering came in response to the needs produced by the rapid urbanization of the twelfth century; overcrowding, poverty, and unsanitary conditions combined to create an environment rife with disease. In the twelfth century, there was not only a physical and social need for hospital care, but also a spiritual desire to offer health care as a form of charity. During this period, Christ's humanity, and the suffering of His flesh, became powerful religious concepts. As Christians meditated on the suffering of Christ, they were called to alleviate the suffering of their fellow Christians. In response, people not only supported hospitals through almsgiving, but also by performing the arduous tasks involved in nursing. In the thirteenth century, the Beguines of the Lowland countries were vital suppliers of nurses for urban hospitals.

Late-period Problems

The fourteenth century marked a period of decline for the medieval hospital. Increased urban poverty taxed funding institutions beyond their means. And while hospitals continued to function, the quality of care offered in them was compromised not only by the high demand for trained physicians outside the hospital, especially during the Black Death, but also by the waning of pious charity among the general population. Ultimately, hospitals would fall under secular control and offer far lower amounts of compassionate care than institutions of the twelfth century. Specialized facilities, such as those for the housing of orphans, the aged, and the insane, came to dominate. In general, the inmates of these facilities were neither incorporated into the broader Christian community nor treated as objects of compassion. Instead they were categorized as "the sick," and thus sequestered from the "healthy" for the protection of society.

See also **Medicine, practical; Medicine, theoretical; Surgery**

Bibliography

Brodman, James. *Charity and Welfare: Hospitals and the Poor in Medieval Catalonia*. Pittsburgh: University of Pennsylvania Press, 1998.

Byrd, Jessalynn. "Medicine for Body and Soul." In *Religion and Medicine in the Middle Ages*. Edited by Peter Biller and Joseph Ziegler. Leeds: Leeds University Press, 2001.

Foucault, Michel. *The Birth of the Clinic: An Archaeology of Medical Perception*. Translated by A. M. Sheridan Smith. New York: Pantheon Books, 1973.

Grmek, Mirko, ed. *Western Medical thought from Antiquity to the Middle Ages*. Translated by Antony Shugaar. Cambridge, MA: Harvard University Press, 1998.

Gutas, Dimitri. *Greek Thought, Arab Culture: The Graeco-Arabic Translation Movement in Baghdad and Early Abbasid Society*. London: Routledge, 1998.

Horden, Peregrine. "Music in Medieval Hospitals." In *Religion and Medicine in the Middle Ages*. Edited by Peter Biller and Joseph Ziegler. Leeds: Leeds University Press, 2001.

Lindberg, David. *The Beginnings of Western Science: The European Scientific Tradition in Philosophical, Religious, and Institutional Context, 600 B.C. to A.D. 1450*. Chicago: Chicago University Press, 1992.

Miller, Timothy S. *The Birth of the Hospital in the Byzantine Empire*. Baltimore: Johns Hopkins University Press, 1985.

Miller, Timothy S. The Knights of Saint John and the Hospitals of the Latin West. *Speculum* (1978) 53: 709–733.

Numbers, Ronald and Daryl Amundsen, eds. *Caring and Curing*. Baltimore, Maryland: Johns Hopkins University Press, 1998.

Rawcliffe, Carole. *Medicine for the Soul: The Life, Death, and Resurrection of an English Medieval Hospital*. Gloucester: Sutton Publishing, 1999.

Risse, Guenter. *Mending Bodies, Saving Souls: A History of Hospitals*. Oxford: Oxford University Press, 1999.

BRENDA GARDENOUR

HOUSE BUILDING, HOUSING

The first-century-C.E. Roman historian Tacitus described in his work *Germania* the living conditions and communities of a tribe of people living to the north of Rome: the Germans. Included in *Germania* are examples of different types of German houses. Two of these houses would become popular throughout Europe and endure throughout most of the Middle Ages. The first was the sunken hut. This consisted of a pit, approximately three feet (0.9 m) deep and covered with a roof of animal dung or a mixture of leaves, twigs, and mud. These houses were typically small, with an area of approximately thirty square feet (2.8 sq m) and were used for many purposes, including storage, living space, and as workshops.

Tacitus also described the timber-framed house. This type of dwelling was much more common than the sunken hut, and gradually replaced it. It had an important architectural feature, known as a cruck, which allowed for high ceilings. A cruck consists of a tree trunk and its lowest branch: the wood was split horizontally and the halves were placed opposite each other, forming a type of arch. The trunk served as part of the wall frame and the branch as part of the roof frame. A beam ran horizontally along the top of the cruck arch to form the peak of the roof. The vertical tree trunks were squared off and placed into post holes dug in the earth, which allowed for a snug fit between the wall and the ground and provided greater protection from the elements. In addition, the beams were portable and often were reused in the construction of new houses. Over time, stone pads were

placed at the bottom of the post holes to allow the frame of the house to rest on a solid base; such stability proved very important in the rainy climate of northern Europe.

Medieval timber-framed houses ranged in size from as little as approximately two hundred square feet (18.6 sq m) to more than twelve hundred square feet (111.5 sq m). House size was often described by indicating the number of bays a house possessed; a bay is the space between the vertical beams. A small cottage would have one bay, while a larger house would have as many as three or four. Bays were laid on a single axis, producing very narrow buildings: consequently, the largest houses are often referred to as long houses (*longa domus*) and are perhaps the most famous type of medieval house. Long houses are also called mixed houses, as domesticated animals were often allowed to inhabit a portion of the dwelling: the animals were usually separated from the human occupants by a partition. Despite their size, the typical long house rarely contained more than one or two rooms.

The walls of timber-framed houses were made either of cob or of wattle and daub. Cob is a combination of mud, straw, and chalk that dries extremely hard. Because it is not baked, however, it is very susceptible to water, which causes it to erode. Wattle and daub is a woven mat of twigs and branches covered with mud. Neither cob nor wattle and daub are very durable, and medieval timber-framed houses were not built to last. Their building materials guaranteed their impermanence, and houses often became uninhabitable after less than twenty years. In addition, wattle and daub walls were so weak that the crime of housebreaking—entering a house through the wall itself—was not uncommon.

The roof of a timber-framed house was usually thatched with reeds, sticks, or straw. A hole was cut into the roof to provide ventilation for the stone hearth in the house; to avoid fires, the hole was often surrounded by tiles. Roof material was not only very susceptible to fire, but also rotted in the rain and provided a breeding ground for insects, birds, and rats; the latter were especially dangerous in a society where plague was common.

Regional varieties existed throughout Europe. In Italy, for example, the poor lived in similar one-room cob houses with thatched roofs. Wealthier farmers, however, used brick or stone for walls, and roofs were made with clay tiles. These houses were larger than timber-framed houses, and often were divided into several rooms. In Spain, the poorer people living in Muslim kingdoms inhabited what later Christian settlers called *casas moriscas*. The walls were of cob or tabby (Spanish, *tapia*: earth mixed either with pebbles or some other aggregate, with straw as a binding agent) packed down in a mold and built up in courses. *Casas moriscas* had two stories: the lower story contained a bedroom or living room along with a kitchen and a corral, and the upper story usually served as a storehouse agricultural products.

By the end of the Middle Ages better building material was increasingly available, and village houses frequently had masonry foundations, were larger, and were built on stronger frames.

Cities

The bulk of medieval urban housing was also of the timber-frame variety, although stone houses were much more common in cities than they were in the countryside. Stone and brick were usually reserved for the wealthy, however, and the houses of the poor were typically constructed from cob and had thatched roofs. Urban houses possessed multiple stories. The size of these houses often caused their frames to sag and lean as they grew older. It was not uncommon for poorer families to inhabit a single room in a house, or for a house to have several families residing in it. The wealthier were able to afford an entire house.

The first floor of a wealthy house usually served as a place of business, and a staircase in the back led up to the family domain. The second floor was dominated by the solar, a large open dining and living room. Connected to the rear of the solar was the kitchen, and the two rooms shared a large, common fireplace. The third stories and above served as bedrooms.

The windows of these houses were covered with oiled parchment, *paper, or fabric, as glass was not a readily available commodity; shutters were often an added protection from the elements. Consequently, these houses could be quite dark, and candles, lamps, and the hearth provided most of the light.

See also **Stone masonry**

Bibliography

Duby, Georges, ed. *A History of Private Life*. Vol. II: *Revelations of the Medieval World*. Cambridge, MA: Harvard University Press, 1988.

Gies, Joseph and Frances Gies. *Life in a Medieval City*. New York: Harper Collins, 1981.

———. *Life in a Medieval Village*. New York: Harper and Row, 1990.

Glick, Thomas F. *From Muslim Fortress to Christian Castle: Social and Cultural Change in Medieval Spain*. Manchester: Manchester University Press, 1995.

Hanawalt, Barbara A. *The Ties that Bound: Peasant Families in Medieval England*. New York: Oxford University Press, 1986.

ANDREW DONNELLY

HUGH OF SAINT-VICTOR

Hugh of Saint-Victor (d. 1141) was born in Saxony, perhaps c. 1096, and initially educated at Hammersleben, in the diocese of Halberstadt. In 1115, Hugh traveled to France in the company of his uncle, the archdeacon of Halberstadt, ending up at the newly founded abbey of Saint-Victor in Paris. This abbey, initially established in 1108–1109 as a community of Augustinian canons by William of Champeaux (d. 1122), quickly became a major stimulus for reform of the church in France under its first abbot, Gilduin. Hugh of Saint-Victor soon emerged as the abbey's leading teacher, making Saint-Victor famous as a center of intellectual and spiritual life, rivaling the schools of Notre-Dame and Sainte-Geneviève.

Hugh of Saint-Victor. Unattributed engraving in *Vrais portraits et vies des hommes illustre*s (1584) by André Thevet (c. 1516–1592). (Mary Evans Picture Library)

Hugh was always fascinated by the relationship between the material world and the spiritual life. One of Hugh's earliest major writings is *De tribus diebus*, a meditation on how physical creation manifests the power, wisdom, and benignity of God, thus leading humanity to reflect on the trinitarian nature of God as Father, Son, and Holy Spirit. Because *Peter Abelard argued that the three persons of the Trinity were names given to signify these three divine attributes in the *Theologia 'Summi boni'* (c. 1120), it has traditionally been assumed that Hugh must have drawn on the work in *De tribus diebus*. Reversing this view, Dominique Poirel has argued that Hugh may have written *De tribus diebus* before Abelard's first discussion of the Trinity, perhaps c. 1118–1119. Whatever the exact relationship between these two writings, Hugh was much more interested than Abelard in the physical attributes of the sensible world, which he describes as being like a book through which God's power, wisdom, and benignity are revealed. He was more interested in the tradition of Plato's *Timaeus* than in the writings of Aristotle about language.

Probably in the early part of his teaching career, Hugh completed a series of introductions to the liberal arts. His treatise *De grammatica* was largely dependent on Donatus and *Isidore of Seville, and did not develop any speculative issues about the meaning of words, such as fascinated William of Champeaux and Peter Abelard. Instead, he transferred his attention to questions relating to the visible world. In his treatise on the practice of geometry (*Practica Geometriae*), Hugh investigates measuring height (*altimetria*), measuring distance (*planimetria*), and measuring the size of the cosmos (*cosmimetria*). Hugh does not claim to advance new ideas in this treatise, only to bring together scattered ideas of great thinkers of the past. He draws in particular on the *Geometria* attributed to *Gerbert of Aurillac, and above all on the commentary of *Macrobius on *The Dream of Scipio*, to reflect on a range of practical issues, above all the relationship between the diameter of the Earth and the diameter of the Sun, and the role of a curved horizon. We do not know if Hugh ever completed the treatise he promised at the end of the *Practica Geometria*, about the movements of the heavens, perhaps also inspired by Macrobius. Hugh did complete, however, a treatise *De mappa mundi*, in which he uses a physical image of the world to draw out a spiritual theme about the true Jerusalem.

Hugh was also very original in the way he integrated mechanical arts into his vision of philosophy. In his *Epitome Dindimi in philosophiam*, he expands the traditional three-fold division of *logica*, *physica*, and *ethica* (attributed to Plato by Augustine in *De civitate Dei* VIII.4), into a four-fold system by dividing *physica* into *theorica* and *mechanica*. This imitated an Aristotelian distinction between the theoretical and the practical, transmitted by *Boethius in the first version of his commentary on Porphyry. Drawing on a statement in Boethius's *De trinitate*, Hugh further divides *theorica* into *mathematica*, *physica*, and *theologia*, while *mechanica* he defines as fabric-making, tool-making (*armatura*, sometimes mistranslated as "armament"), commerce, agriculture, hunting, medicine, and theatrics. While Isidore had identified *mechanica* as one of seven branches of *physica* (alongside arithmetic, geometry, music, astronomy, astrology, and medicine), no previous writer had related practical skills to philosophy in such detail. Hugh argues that as human actions have a moderating wisdom, without which they cannot accept form, they should not be considered completely apart from philosophy (*Epitome*, ed. Baron, p. 196).

Hugh expands this system in greater detail in *Didascalicon*, written perhaps c. 1127 as a manual explaining how all the liberal arts relate to philosophy. Here he explains that *logica* was the last of the arts to be discovered, and leaves this to the end of his treatise. He gives attention first to the theoretical or speculative arts, namely theology and *mathematica*, dealing with abstract quantity and embracing the *quadrivium (arithmetic, music, geometry, and astronomy), and then to the various crafts that come under *mechanica*. Hugh's account is remarkable for the absence of negative remarks about all of these practical skills, including professions such as commerce, medicine, and theater, which were elsewhere often regarded as inferior because of their worldly nature.

Hugh is aware of the works of the major pagan authors on each of these skills, but does not go into detail. His larger theme is to compare their practical wisdom to the sacred wisdom of Holy Scripture, which needs to be studied both at a historical and tropological level.

After writing the *Didascalicon*, Hugh seems to have devoted his attention to theological issues. While he had written extensively on the meaning of the books of the Old Testament, it is only in his *De sacramentis*, written in the 1130s, that he developed the theological synthesis for which he became famous. Hugh's major theme was that the history of salvation is one of creation and restoration. The process of restoration is achieved through the notion of sacrament, understood as a material symbol becoming charged with sacred significance, and thus leading humanity back to God. While there were the equivalent of sacraments before Christ, it is only with the incarnation that God has become fully accessible to humanity.

See also Scientia

Bibliography

Primary Sources

Gautier-Dalché, Patrick, ed. La 'Descriptio mappe mundi' de Hugues de Saint-Victor: texte inédit avec introduction et commentaire. Paris: Etudes augustiniennes, 1988.

Hugh of Saint-Victor. Hugonis de Sancto Victore Opera Propaedeutica. Edited by Roger Baron. Notre Dame: University of Notre Dame Press, 1966. [Practica geometriae, De grammatica, Epitome Dindimi in philosophiam]

Hugh of Saint-Victor. Practical geometry. Practica geometriae. Translated with notes by Frederick A. Homann. Milwaukee: Marquette University Press, 1991.

Sicard, Patrice, ed. Hugues de Saint-Victor et son école. Turnhout: Brepols, 1991.

The Didascalicon of Hugh of St. Victor: a medieval guide to the arts. Translated with notes by Jerome Taylor. New York: Columbia University Press, 1961.

Secondary Sources

Allard, Guy H. "Les arts mécaniques aux yeux de l'idéologie médiévale." In Les arts mécanique au moyen âge, ed. G. H. Allard and S. Lusignan. Montréal-Paris: Bellarmin-Vrin, 1982. pp. 13–31.

Baron, Roger. Sur l'introduction en Occident des termes geometria, theorica et practica. Revue d'histoire des sciences (1955) 8: 298–302.

Coolman, Boyd Taylor. Pulchrum Esse: The Beauty of Scripture, the Beauty of the Soul, and the Art of Exegesis in Hugh of St. Victor. Traditio (2003) 58: 175–200.

Poirel, Dominique. Hugues de Saint-Victor. Paris: Cerf, 1998.

Vallin, Pierre. 'Mechanica' et 'Philosophia' selon Hugues de Saint-Victor. Revue d'histoire de la spiritualité (1973) 49: 257–288.

Vermeirre, André. "La navigation d'après Hugues de Saint-Victor et d'après la pratique du XIe siècle." in Les arts mécaniques au moyen âge, pp. 51–61.

Whitney, Elspeth. "The Artes Mechanicae, Craftmanship and Moral Value of Technology." In Design and Production in Medieval and Early Modern Europe: Essays in Honor of Bradford Blaine, ed. Nancy van Deusen. Ottawa: Institute of Mediaeval Music, 1998. pp. 75–87.

CONSTANT J. MEWS

HUGH OF SANTALLA

Hugh of Santalla was a translator of texts on astronomy, *astrology, and magic, who lived in Tarazona in the mid-twelfth century. "Santalla" is a common place name in the northwest of Spain, especially in Galicia. Hugh is attested in 1145 as a "magister" in the entourage of Michael, bishop of Tarazona from 1119 until 1151, to whom he dedicated all those translations that have dedications. He may have still been alive in 1179, if he can be identified with a "magister Ugo" who attested a document of one of Michael's successors in that year (Juan Frontín, bishop of Tarazona, on January 20, 1179). He benefited from the presence of the library of the last Muslim rulers of Saragossa in the neighboring stronghold of Rueda Jalón, in the "inner recesses" of which his bishop found a commentary on astronomical tables. This fortress was ceded by Sayf al-Dawla to Alfonso VII of Castile in 1140–1141, but it is not clear whether the manuscripts came into Michael's hands at this time, or were already available before, thanks to the friendly relations between the Castilian and Saragossan monarchs. Hugh's prefaces to his translations, which tell us a lot about his attitude and methodology, give the impression that he is discovering sciences among the Arabs that have hitherto been kept secret from the Latins. These include the methods of shoulder-blade divination and sand divination (called by him "geomancy"), the first giving instructions on how to "read" various marks on the shoulder blade of a sheep from which the flesh has been removed by boiling, the second involving constructing and interpreting three-tier figures of one or two dots each, created by randomly drawing lines of dots. He was the first to reveal the sacred credo of the alchemists—the *Emerald Tablet* of Hermes—which was destined to have a long and illustrious history. The *Emerald Tablet* is reproduced at the end of Hugh's translation of Pseudo-Apollonius's *On the Secrets of Nature*. Apollonius claims to have discovered both this book and the tablet in the hands of Hermes in an underground cavern. The *Secrets of Nature* provides a *cosmology and an account of animals, vegetables, and minerals, in which alchemical principles of male and female, generation, and bonds between the constituents of the universe predominate. Hugh also came across a bibliography of more than two hundred books on astrology whose essence had been distilled in a large work attributed to Aristotle: the *Book of Aristotle Containing the Totality of All Questions, both Genethlialogical and Revolutionary, drawn from the 255 Volumes of the Indians*. This book, which he translated, is apparently a version of a lost Arabic text by *Masha'allah, which would have been one of the earliest Arabic compendia on astrology and is based on both Greek (Rhetorius, Vettius Valens, *Ptolemy, and Dorotheus) and Middle Persian (Andarzaghar) sources. Hugh's most ambitious project appears to have been to select and translate from Arabic the works of ten leading authorities on judicial astrology. It is presumably from these translations that the compendia known as the *Book of the Three Judges* and the *Book of the Nine Judges* were compiled, perhaps with the aid of his fellow translator, *Hermann of Carinthia. His astrological works, including the *Book of the Nine Judges*, were copied together in a series of twelfth-century manuscripts once belonging to St. Augustine's Abbey, Canterbury, and subsequently copied into Oxford, Bodleian Library, Savile 15. The *Book of the Nine Judges* was translated into French, and was printed in 1509, but Hugh's most influential work was on weather forecasting—a translation of a text attributed to Hermes, and "abbreviated" by "Jafar Indus"—which exploits the division of the sky into twenty-eight lunar mansions rather than the twelve signs of the zodiac, and which has survived in more than thirty manuscripts and two printed editions (Peter Liechtenstein, Venice 1507, and Jacques Kerver, Paris 1540).

See also **Alchemy; Translation movements**

Bibliography

Primary Sources

The Liber Aristotilis *of Hugo of Santalla*. C. Burnett and D. Pingree, eds. London: Warburg Institute, 1997.

Jafar Indus. In C. Burnett, Lunar Astrology: The Varieties of Texts Using Lunar Mansions, with Emphasis on *Jafar Indus*. Micrologus, (2004), 12:. 43–133 (on pp. 86–116).

El comentario de Ibn al-Mutanna a las Tablas Astronómicas de al-Jwarizmi. E. Millás Vendrell, ed. Madrid-Barcelona: Consejo Superior de Investigaciones Científicas, 1963.

Liber Amblaudii et Hermetis de spatula. C. Burnett, ed. In Hermes Trismegistus, *Astrologia et divinatoria*. P. Lucentini et al., eds. Turnhout: Brepols, 2001: 265–272.

Ps.-Apollonius de Tyane (Balinus). *De secretis naturæ (Kitab sirr al-haliqa)*. F. Hudry, ed. *Chrysopœia*, (1997–1999) 6: 1–154.

Secondary Sources

C. H. Haskins, *Studies in the History of Mediaeval Science*. 2nd ed. Cambridge, Mass.: Harvard University Press, 1927: 67–81.

Burnett, C. "The Establishment of Medieval Hermeticism." In *The Medieval World*. P. Linehan and J. L. Nelson, eds. London and New York: Routledge, 2001: 111–130.

———. "A Hermetic Programme of Astrology and Divination in mid-Twelfth Century Aragon: The Hidden Preface in the *Liber novem iudicum*." In *Magic and the Classical Tradition*. C. Burnett and W. F. Ryan, eds. London: Warburg Institute, 2005.

CHARLES BURNETT

HUNAYN IBN ISHAQ

Hunayn ibn Ishaq (808–873) was born at Hira, near Najaf (part of modern Iraq). Trained in medicine, which he occasionally practiced, he is best known as a translator of Greek medical texts, especially works of *Galen, into Syriac and Arabic. Medieval biobibliographical sources report that his father, an apothecary by profession, was a 'Ibadi, a member of one of the Arab tribes that had embraced Christianity. It is likely that his family origins would have made him at least bilingual (Arabic and Syriac), with probably some knowledge of liturgical Greek.

As a young man, Hunayn journeyed to Baghdad, the Abbasid capital, where he attended the *majlis* (salon) of Abu Zakariyya' Yahunna ibn Masawayh, court physician to caliphs al-Ma'mun, al-Mu'tasim, al-Wathiq, and al-Mutawakkil. One day, irritated at the young man's persistence in seeking answers, Yahunna is reported to have ejected him from the company, saying: "What connection do people from Hira have with medicine...? Go change money in the streets." Yahunna, from Gundishapur, the old Nestorian center of medical learning, may have regarded Hunayn as an interloper ambitious to acquire knowledge that would help him to usurp positions traditionally held by another socio-political group. Moreover, there are reports that Yahunna had been commissioned by al-Ma'mun to organize and lead translation activity in Baghdad. Considerable money and prestige could be earned from such pursuits, and he may have regarded his precocious student as a serious rival. Thus rebuffed, Hunayn set off for Byzantium, where he stayed for several years, during which he developed a considerable facility in Greek. On his return, Yahunna was forced to recognize his abilities and eventually apologized. It was Hunayn's first, but not his last, encounter with competition for court patronage and jealous colleagues. Such competition fueled the translation movement in Arabic for several generations.

Hunayn made his first translation at about the age of seventeen, preparing a Syriac version of *Galen's *De facultatibus naturalibus* for Jibril ibn Bakhtishtu', a powerful court figure. It was Jibril's son, Bakhtishtu', who later conspired against Hunayn, perhaps feeling threatened by Hunayn's increasing prestige in the court of al-Mutawakkil, and engineered his fall from grace. Hunayn was imprisoned and his library sequestered. Although later restored to his position following his medical intervention on behalf of the caliph, the episode again illustrates the deep rivalries for patronage and power that beset the Abbasid court and influenced the transmission of Greek learning into Islamic culture.

It was during this fall from favor that Hunayn wrote, in 856, to 'Ali ibn Yahya, another powerful courtier, beseeching assistance. In his letter, he mentions one hundred twenty-nine works of Galen with which he was familiar, describes their basic contents, and notes various translations into Syriac and Arabic which he had either made himself or which he had supervised or corrected. That he could write in such detail, relying solely on memory, indicates a thorough familiarity with the Galenic corpus, both in Greek and in its various translations.

The often-cited description of the translation process given by al-Safadi (d. 1363), differentiates two basic techniques: (1) A literal, *ad verbum*, style in which the translator replaces each successive term in the original with an equivalent term in the new language; and (2) A less literal, *ad sensum*, style in which the translator attempts to understand the meaning of a phrase or sentence in the original and then renders that meaning into the new language. The former technique has often been criticized for producing a stilted and awkward translation at best and a completely incomprehensible document at worst, while the second, if properly done, yields a true and comprehensible rendition of the author's intention. Al-Safadi explicitly associates the second technique with the work of Hunayn. Although too simplistic to be of much use to historians, this neat dichotomy does serve to explicate Hunayn's goal as translator. Frequently, this *ad sensum* translation required the development of new technical *vocabulary and terminology. Hunayn's "scientific" procedure also involved collecting several manuscripts of a text and collating them in order to arrive at a text which would then serve as the basis for translation.

Hunayn trained a number of younger scholars to assist him in his translation of the Galenic medicine. Among them were his son, Ishaq ibn Hunayn, and his nephew, Hubaysh ibn al-Hasan al-A'sam. Because the members of this "school" of translators adhere to much the same general principles and often edited one another's work, the contributions of each may be distinguished only through detailed philological study. The problem has been compounded by later copyists who have attributed works to Hunayn, as the leader of the school. The name of Hubaysh, for example, is very similar in Arabic orthography to that of Hunayn. Evidence indicates that later copyists have tended to "correct" the name of the nephew and thus ascribe to Hunayn the work of the younger man. In a somewhat similar vein, the name of Hunayn has come to be attached to several manuscripts of Ishaq's Arabic version of Euclid's *Elements*. Whether Hunayn actually assisted Ishaq in creating this translation is not yet known, but the preponderance of evidence ascribes the basic effort to Ishaq, rather than to Hunayn.

Some of Hunayn's translations of Galenic works found their way into the Latin tradition. Among those who translated them was *Gerard of Cremona, who produced Latin versions of the *Expositiones super librum Ypocratis de regimine acutarum egritudinem* and *De expositione libri Ypocratis in prognosticatione*, as well as the Pseudo-Galen *De secretis*. Most important was his translation of the *Tegne* (or *Ars Parva*), which Gerard knew in the form of a commentary by 'Ali ibn Ridwan. Hunayn's translation of Galen's *De tactu pulsus* was translated by *Mark of Toledo. These became part of the basis for the Galenic character of Latin medieval medicine.

Hunayn also wrote several original medical treatises of his own. His approach was largely based on Greek, and especially Galenic, sources. Perhaps the best known was *al-Masa'il fi'l-Tibb* (*Questions concerning Medicine*), a summary of key ideas of the Galen on health and medical science in the form of questions and answers. It was one of the earliest Arabic works to enter Latin, as the *Isagoge Iohanitii ad Tegni Galeni* (*Constantine the African). It was later translated (Mark of Toledo) as *Liber isagogorum* and yet again (Rufus of Alexandria) as *Liber questionum medicalium discentium in medicina*. Its influence on the practice of medicine in the Latin West, as well as in the Islamic world, is difficult to overestimate. It was one of the first works to divide medicine into theoretical and practical aspects. This distinction helped medicine to move beyond its former place in the practical arts, but

A twelfth-century manuscript copied from the original ninth-century text of Hunayn's *al-'Ashar Maqalat fi'l-'Ayn* (*Ten Treatises on the Eye*). (Science Museum Library)

also tended to discourage experiment and innovation. His *al-'Ashar Maqalat fi'l-'Ayn* (*Ten Treatises on the Eye*) discusses both the theoretical and practical medical aspects of ophthalmology. It entered Latin under two different, and confusing, titles: *Galeni liber de oculis translatus a Demetrio* and *Liber de oculis Constantini Africani*, and continued to influence Western thought, at least indirectly, until the sixteenth century. Thus Hunayn played an important role in two different *translation movements. Although many of his translations of Galenic works did not reach the Latin West, those that did played a significant role in establishing the study of medicine.

See also **Medicine, practical; Medicine theoretical; Patronage of science; Translation norms and practices**

Bibliography

Bergsträsser, G. *Hunain ibn Ishak und seine Schule*. Leiden: E.J. Brill, 1913.

De Young, G. Ishaq ibn Hunayn, Hunayn ibn Ishaq, and the Third Arabic Translation of Euclid's *Elements*. *Historia Mathematica* (1992) 19: 188–199.

Ghalioungui, P. *Questions on Medicine for Scholars by Hunayn ibn Ishaq*. Cairo: Al-Ahram Center for Scientific Translation, 1980.

Gutas, D. *Greek Thought, Arabic Culture: The Greco-Arabic Translation Movement in Baghdad and Early 'Abbasid Society*. London: Routledge, 1998.

Jacquart, D. "Les traductiones médicales de Gérard de Crémone." In P. Pizzamiglio, ed., *Gerardo da Cremona*. Cremona: Biblioteca statale e libraria civica di Cremona, 1992, pp. 45–56.

Lindberg, D. *Theories of Vision from al-Kindi to Kepler*. Chicago: University of Chicago Press, 1976.

Maurach, G. *Johanicius: Isagoge and Techne Galenieni. Sudhoffs Archiv* (1978) 62: 148–179.

Meyerhof, M. *The Book of the Ten Treatises on the Eye Ascribed to Hunain ibn Ishaq*. Cairo: Government Press, 1928.

———. New Light on Hunain ibn Ishak and his Period. *Isis* (1928) 8: 685–724.

Saliba, G. Competition and the Transmission of the Foreign Sciences: Hunayn at the Abbasid Court. *Bulletin of the Royal Institute for Inter-Faith Studies* (2000) 2: 85–101.

GREGG DE YOUNG

HYLOMORPHISM

During the Middle Ages most of the theories of matter that proliferated in *universities and other locales of learned culture depended on the concept of hylomorphism. Medieval hylomorphism derived from Aristotle's writings; the term refers to the concept that substances are composites of matter and form. While the precise meanings of matter and form were debated, acceptance of these principles entailed the rejection of atomistic positions which held that substances are composed of discrete indivisible particles separated by empty spaces or voids, and that the differences in the qualities of substances depend only on the position, shape, and motion of these particles. Rather, substances are composed of a matter, continuous and potentially divisible throughout, that acts as a substrate for substantial forms that define the essence of the substance and for accidental qualities that explain the non-essential characteristics of a given substance. Both the essential forms and the accidental qualities inhere to the matter. While there were notable exceptions, such as the *mutakallimun* in the Islamic world, almost all of medieval learned culture subscribed to one or another version of hylomorphism, and rejected atomism and the existence of voids.

Aristotle's hylomorphism accounts for the composition of substances as well as the metaphysics of change, whereby change comprised both the alteration of qualities and the transformations into a new substance. In the *Physics*, Aristotle used the principles of matter, form, and privation to explain change. Matter is the underlying substrate that persists when a substance goes from not having a given quality or form (privation) to having this quality or form. Using Aristotle's example of a marble statue, the marble, or the matter, persists while it begins as a chunk of stone, not having a defined form, and, in the end, the marble takes on the shape or form of Hermes. Matter and form can also be considered in terms of potency and act. According to this framework, matter, or what persists through change, can potentially, while it is unformed, receive suitable forms. Thus the block of marble, or some other substance with a suitable disposition, is potentially a statue, and after the sculptor has chipped away at it, in actuality it is a statue. Form and matter are mutually dependent; they are not separable. Neither can exist without the other, as Aristotle rejected not only *Plato's contention that forms were eternal substances in themselves that can exist independently of matter but also the idea that formless matter could exist.

Interpreters of Aristotle, from late antiquity to well past the Middle Ages, understood hylomorphism in terms of a continuum from prime matter to pure form. Prime matter was thought to be the most basic underlying substrate of all corporeal substances; it was without any form or quality, and equivalent to pure potency. Pure form was considered analogous to pure actuality and was frequently considered to be equivalent to God. Accordingly, every substance is a composite of prime matter and a substantial form that defines its essence.

Two major problems that faced proponents of hylomorphism and interpreters of Aristotle were the question of precisely which substances are composites of matter and form and which are not, and the question of how the disposition of matter relates to the acceptance of a substantial form. Debates over these questions primarily are found not only in medieval commentaries and questions on Aristotle's *Physics*, *Metaphysics*, *De caelo*, *Meteorologica*, and *De generatione et corruptione*, but also in some quodlibetal questions, commentaries on Genesis, and commentaries on *Peter Lombard's Sentences*. Typically these works were written in conjunction with lectures given at universities.

Sublunary, Celestial, and Incorporeal Substances

What limits Aristotle set on hylomorphism were unclear to medieval thinkers; we find three representative positions among *Ibn Sina (Avicenna), an eleventh-century Persian, *Ibn Rushd (Averroes), a twelfth-century Andalusi, and *Ibn Gabirol (Avicebron), a twelfth-century Jew who lived in Islamic Spain. Their three stances were key to framing subsequent debates on the issue. Avicenna maintained that all corporeal and only corporeal substances are composites of matter and form. Thus among hylomorphic composites he included celestial bodies, but excluded spiritual substances. In *On the Substance of the Orbs*, Averroes argued directly against Avicenna, claiming that only sublunary bodies are composite. Emphasizing the role of matter as a substrate for change, he interpreted matter as being a potentiality with respect to a substantial form. Thus he believed that matter existed only in bodies that are capable of changing into a new substance. Or in other words, matter only exists in substances subject to generation and corruption. As a result he denied that celestial bodies were composites of matter and form because they only undergo change with respect to place, or locomotion, an accidental not substantial change. Avicebron, in his *Fons vitae*, promoted a position that is sometimes called universal hylomorphism, whereby all created substances, inclusive of intelligences, spiritual beings, and both celestial and sublunary bodies are composites of matter and form. Avicebron's position holds some affinities with Augustine's doctrine of seminal reasons. According to this doctrine, during the creation of the world, God introduced the forms of all natural beings that would eventually develop after creation into matter, which was in a state of unshaped chaos before creation. In this manner God sowed the seeds of all created beings that would eventually come into existence. By shifting the meaning of potency from meaning possibility to power or virtue, Avicebron saw matter as endowed with an active potency that would lead to the realization of the undeveloped form, or inchoate form, with which it was endowed by God. Since each substance has its identity, or eventual substantial form, imprinted in its matter, matter and form become universal principles for all created substances. While Avicebron's views influenced many within the Franciscan tradition, such as Bonaventure, other scholars in the Latin West, such as *Albertus Magnus, *Thomas Aquinas, and *Giles of Rome, criticized the concepts of active potency of matter and inchoate form, claiming that proponents of these doctrines confused the ideas of matter as a substrate and as a potency. Thus, harking back to the views of Averroes and Avicenna, they concluded that matter is not the same for corruptible and incorruptible bodies, and that these terms are used only in an equivocal or homonymous sense.

Substantial Transformation and Mixture

The second major issue surrounding hylomorphism regards the relation of matter to substantial form. According to the typical medieval interpretation of Aristotle there exists in the sublunary region a hierarchy of matter and form, from the most simple substances to the more complex ones. Thus it is possible to understand the various levels of matter and form to be comprised of: prime matter, the prime qualities (hot, cold, wet, dry), the four elements (earth, water, air, fire), homeomerous or homogeneous mixtures of the elements (metal, rock, blood, flesh), anhomeomerous or heterogeneous natural parts or organs (liver, root, heart, etc.), and finally full organisms. The hierarchy functions so that the lower level substances become the matter for the higher ones. Thus the prime qualities are the matter of the elements, which in turn are the matter for mixtures, which in turn are the matter for the organs, and so on. The problem which arises is to reconcile the view that argues that mixtures are composed of the elements, and the view that all mixtures are a composite between a substantial form of the mixture (forma mixti) and prime matter. A true mixture, according to Aristotelian doctrine, is the union of different substances into a new substance. A mixture differs from what has been called a chemical combination, or mixtum ad sensum (mixture according to sense), in which the various substances appear to be mixed but in reality are divided into small parts that are juxtaposed. The precise question that was frequently raised was: what happens to the substantial forms of the elements when

they become part of a mixture? Again the debate depended in part on the concept of potency, because the Aristotelian text demanded that the elements that formed the new substance remain potentially in the newly formed substance.

Three views are representative of debates over this question during the years 1000 to 1600; in this case the positions are those of Avicenna, Averroes, and Thomas Aquinas. Avicenna contended that the substantial forms of the elements remain unchanged in a mixture. Rather their qualities undergo a remission. This remission of the qualities created what Latin scholars dubbed a complexio or temperament, which had a significant role not only in medieval natural philosophy but also in medical theory. This temperament composed of reduced qualities was thus prepared to receive the new substantial form of the mixture, which was given directly from God, in this case called dator formae (giver of form). As a result, the new substantial form supervenes over the substantial forms of the elements, which remain in the new substance although with their powers blunted. Directly attacking Avicenna, Averroes argued that not only the qualities of the elements undergo a remission but also their substantial forms are weakened. The broken-down or diminished forms then unite to create the new substantial form. Averroes's position provoked much criticism among scholars in the Latin West. In particular they attacked the view that substantial forms could undergo remission. While it was widely held that qualities could change with respect to degree, as was developed and broadly applied in the doctrine of the *latitude of forms, substantial forms could not. A diminished substantial form would result in the impossible existence of a form that was neither substantial nor accidental but somewhere in the middle. Thomas Aquinas offered an alternative to both Avicenna's and Averroes's views. Thomas argued that the substantial forms of the elements are destroyed. However, the elements remain potentially in the substance because their virtues—that is their active and passive qualities, combined in a new proportion—remain in the new mixture and are subordinate to the new substantial form of the mixture. Versions of Thomas's position were common throughout the late Middle Ages including in the work of *Duns Scotus.

The composite of matter and form remained the framework for defining substances and explaining change, at least for bodies in the sublunary world, well into the sixteenth and seventeenth centuries when atomism became a viable alternative. Nevertheless even many of the early matter theories that relied on the motion and position of small particles to explain the characteristics of matter relied on hylomorphism, as they maintained that even the minute corpuscles that composed the world were composites of matter and form.

See also **Aristotelianism; God in Christianity; God in Islam**

Bibliography

Des Chene, Dennis. *Physiologia: Natural Philosophy in Late Aristotelian and Cartesian Thought.* Ithaca: Cornell University Press, 1996.

Emerton, Norma E. *The Scientific Reinterpretation of Form*. Ithaca: Cornell University Press, 1984.

Gill, Mary Louise. *Aristotle on Substance: The Paradox of Unity*. Princeton: Princeton University Press, 1989.

Lüthy, Christoph and William R. Newman, eds. The Fate of Hylomorphism: 'Matter' and 'Form' in Early Modern Science. Special issue of *Early Science and Medicine* (1997) 2: 215–352.

Lüthy, Christoph, William R. Newman, and John E. Murdoch, eds. *Late Medieval and Early Modern Corpuscular Matter Theories*. Leiden: E.J. Brill, 2001.

McMullin, Ernan, ed. *The Concept of Matter in Greek and Medieval Philosophy*. Notre Dame: Notre Dame University Press, 1965.

Maier, Analiese. *On the Threshold of Exact Science*. Edited and translated by Steven D. Sargent. Philadelphia: University of Pennsylvania Press, 1982.

CRAIG MARTIN

I

IBN AL-HAYTHAM

Abu 'Ali al-Hasan Ibn al-Hasan Ibn al-Haytham al-Basri al-Misri, known in Latin as Alhazen, was born in Basra in 965 C.E. and died in Cairo c. 1040 C.E. The principal historical bio-bibliographic sources regarding his life and works were preserved in *Ta'rikh al-hukama'* by Ibn al-Qifti (d. 1248), and *Tabaqat al-attibba'* by Ibn Abi Usaybi'a (d. 1270), albeit their accounts were at times disharmonious.

It is claimed that Ibn al-Haytham started his career as a civil servant in Basra under the Buwayhids (Buyids). However, in developing a scholarly penchant, and growing frustrated with the perfunctory restrictions of his office, it is reported that he feigned insanity to relinquish his secretarial post, and to immerse himself in his scientific pursuits. Having excelled in scholarship and associated speculations about the technological applicability of theoretical knowledge, he was invited by the Fatimid Caliph al-Hakim bi-Amr Allah to design a dam in Egypt that would regulate the seasonal flood of the Nile. Once in Cairo, Ibn al-Haytham accepted al-Hakim's offer to appoint him as chief engineer of the Fatimid court, and subsequently led an expeditionary mission to Upper Egypt (*sa'id misr*) to survey potential sites on the banks of the Nile for the construction of the proposed dam. Following thorough inspections of an optimal gorge known as al-Janadil (The Cataracts), which is located to the south of Aswan, Ibn al-Haytham became aware that his project was unfeasible given the restrictive conditions of the riverbanks, and the unrealizable specifications of workmanship, budget, and available building techniques. It is furthermore recounted that he had doubts from the outset about the achievability of this initiative, given that a dam had never been built by the ancient Egyptians, whom he admired for their mathematical and construction skills. Following this unsuccessful field mission, Ibn al-Haytham returned to Cairo with his engineering team and confessed to his patron that the design objectives were unachievable. Disappointed with the technological acumen of his chief engineer, al-Hakim decommissioned

Ibn al-Haytham from his scientific office, and apportioned him an administrative function so that he could retain his stipend. Becoming increasingly concerned for his personal safety, and worried by his patron's capriciousness, Ibn al-Haytham feigned madness and remained confined to his dwelling until the Caliph's death in 1021. After this period of internment, Ibn al-Haytham lived in the vicinity of al-Azhar, and earned a livelihood from copying manuscripts of classical texts, including *Euclid's Elements and *Ptolemy's *Almagest*.

Ibn al-Haytham advanced compelling investigations in mathematics. For instance, he assessed Apollonius of Perga's *Conica* in his *Maqala fi tamam kitab al-makhrutat* (*On the Completeness of the Conics*), and in his *Shakl Banu Musa* (*The Proposition of Banu Musa*; namely, making reference here to the erudite sons of Musa Ibn Shakir, fl. c. 850–870 in Baghdad). Moreover, his geometric *Lemmas* (*muqaddamat*), which came to be known among seventeenth-century European scholars as "Alhazen's Problem," became a classic in the history of science in describing a solution to the question: "How, from any two points opposite a reflecting surface (plane, spherical or cylindrical), can we find a point on that surface at which the light from one of these two points reflects unto the other?" Ibn al-Haytham attempted also to solve Euclid's fifth postulate, and composed a commentary on the premises of the *Elements* (*Sharh musadarat kitab Uqlidis*). He furthermore dedicated two tracts to "the quadrature of crescent figures/lunes" (*al-ashkal al-hilaliyya*), and examined the application of motion to geometric demonstrations (namely, what some describe as being a "cinematographic" process in geometry). He also systematized analytical geometry, by deploying algebra in geometric constructions, and furthered the field of infinitesimal mathematics. In the domain of number theory he built on the works of *Thabit ibn Qurra (d. 901), and on the findings of the latter's grandson, Ibrahim Ibn Sinan (d. 946 C.E.), by investigating amicable numbers (*a'dad mutahabba*; namely a pair of numbers, such as 220 and 284, each of which equals the sum of the other's aliquot parts), and

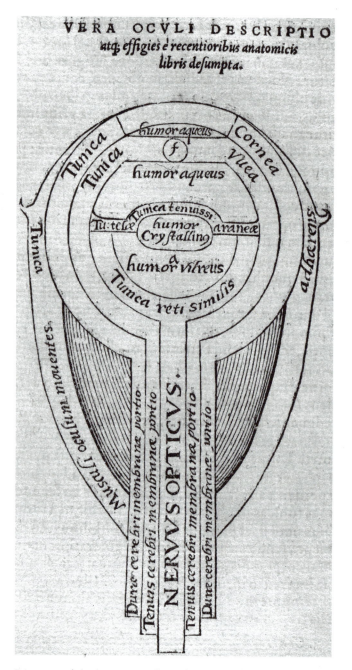

VERA OCVLI DESCRIPTIO
atq; effigies è recentioribus anatomicis
libris desumpta.

Diagram of the human eye from the 1572 Latin edition of Ibn al-Haytham's *Kitab al-manazir* (*Optics*) in Friedrich Risner's *Opticae Thesaurus*. (Science Museum Library)

the atmosphere, the nature of the eclipse (*Maqala fi surat al-kusuf*), the twilight and moonlight (*Risala fi daw' al-qamar*, *Treatise on Moonlight*).

Moreover, he inquired about the first law of motion in mechanics according to which it was observed that a body would move perpetually unless arrested by an external agent. And, in his elucidation of phenomena associated with the attraction between masses, he made observations regarding the magnitude of acceleration, which resulted from a principle crudely analogous to a force of gravity.

It is also worth noting that, in most of his inquiries, he tended to combine mathematics with physics, and to substantiate theoretical knowledge with experimental verification and controlled testing (*al-i'tibar*), including the design and use of scientific instruments and installations, such as *al-bayt al-muzlim* (camera obscura).

Ibn al-Haytham's most influential accomplishment as a polymath was principally embodied in his *Kitab al-manazir* (*The Optics*, composed in the second quarter of the eleventh century). This monumental work was translated into Latin as *De aspectibus* or *Perspectiva*, sometime in the twelfth century, and was later recollected in Friedrich Risner's *Opticae Thesaurus* in Basel around 1572. This opus was divided into seven books which were grouped under three principal parts: Books I–III dealt with the problems of rectilinear vision, Books IV–VI investigated reflection, and Book VII examined refraction. The transmission of this text to Europe had a major impact on the course of development and maturation of the *perspectiva* traditions in medieval science and Renaissance art. Ibn al-Haytham's legacy in optics left a profound impression on the works of medieval scholars including *Roger Bacon, *John Pecham, and *Witelo, and found conceptual prolongations and creative applications in the works of Renaissance artists and theorists such as Leon Battista Alberti, Lorenzo Ghiberti, and Egnazio Danti. While his *Optics* was widely disseminated, carefully studied, and integrated within European scholarship, up to the times of René Descartes and Christiaan Huygens its circulation in medieval Islamic civilization was marginal. The principal adaptation of his theories of vision and light in the context of the history of scientific ideas in Islam took its serious turn with the *Tanqih al-manazir* (*Revision of the Optics*) by Kamal al-Din al-Farisi (d. 1320), who completed his studies at the Maragha observatory-cum-school under the direction of the astronomer Qutb al-Din al-Shirazi (d. 1311). Eventually, Kamal al-Din expanded Ibn al-Haytham's findings in the *Optics* in terms of a theory explicating the occurrence of the rainbow (*qaws quzah*) based on refractions on rain droplets, a phenomenon that he simulated in an experimental model consisting of a transparent spherical glass vessel filled with water (to represent a single rain drop), which was subjected to a controlled light-beam passing through an aperture, while being located within a camera obscura. There were no comparable breakthroughs in the subsequent history of optics in Islam, and the last tract in that domain that might have been of scholarly significance was composed as a commentary on Kamal al-Din's

perfect numbers (*a'dad tamma*, namely a numeral whose positive divisors, excluding it, add up to itself. For instance, 6 is a perfect number, since 6 = 1 + 2 + 3).

In addition, Ibn al-Haytham conducted studies in astronomy, such as those included in *al-Shukuk 'ala Batlamiyus* (*Dubitationes in Ptolemaeum*, a critique directed at Ptolemy's *Almagest*, *Planetary Hypotheses*, and *Optics*), *Fi ru'yat al-kawakib* (*On the Appearance of the Stars*), or *Maqala fi adwa' al-kawakib* (*Treatise on the Lights of the Stars*). He also investigated the density of

Tanqih by Taqi al-Din Muhammad Ibn Ma'ruf (d. 1585), the Syrian astronomer at the Ottoman court.

It is no exaggeration to state that Ibn al-Haytham's theories of vision and light constituted the most remarkable accomplishment in optics from the times of *Ptolemy (d. c. 165 C.E.) to those of Johannes Kepler (d. 1630). Being dissatisfied with the disputes of the ancient Greeks over the nature of vision and the comportment of light, Ibn al-Haytham embarked on composing his *Kitab al-manazir*, which aimed partly at completing the work initiated by Ptolemy by way of novel methods of inquiry. Ibn al-Haytham's inventiveness built on the views of the Greek physicists (*tabi'iyyin*), who endorsed intromission theories of vision according to which the form of a visible object is introduced into the eye, and he interpretively appealed to the optical models of the Greek mathematicians (*ashab al-ta'alim*), who upheld emission theories of light according to which visible objects get lit by way of light-rays (or a non-consuming gentle fire) emitted from the eyes in the shape of a cone or pyramid. While the emission mathematical models offered Ibn al-Haytham geometric descriptions of the propagation of light-rays from the eyes in the form of a cone of vision, the physical theories of intromission assisted him in explicating how the form of a visible object is received by the eyes. Reassessing these findings, Ibn al-Haytham rejected the claim that vision occurs by way of the emission of a light-ray from the eye, and systematized the intromission theory by way of showing that sight resulted from the introduction of light (or the luminous forms of visible objects) into the eye through rectilinear radial propagations across transparent media in the shape of a virtual geometric cone of vision (*makhrut al-shu'a'*).

Ibn al-Haytham distinguished the conditions of sight from those of light, and he complemented his theoretical results with a thorough anatomical examination of the structure of the eye, and a comprehensive explication of the conditions of binocular vision (both respectively treated in chapters five and six of Book I of *Kitab al-manazir*), along with an investigation of the errors of direct sight (*aghlat al-basar*, Book III of *Kitab al-manazir*). His models were furthermore supported by a theory of visual perception that combined geometry with physiology and *psychology. For instance, Ibn al-Haytham distinguished the immediate mode of perception by way of glancing from contemplative vision, which, in some instances, is accompanied by prior knowledge. In examining the perception of particular visible properties (*al-ma'ani al-mubsara*), of which he enumerated twenty-two aspects (in contrast with Ptolemy's seven), inclusive of distance, position, solidity, shape, size, opacity, beauty, etc., he also distinguished pure sensation (*mujarrad al-hiss*), which perceives light qua light and color qua color, from recognition (*ma'rifa*), discernment (*tamyiz*), and comparative inference (*qiyas*) that get aided by the workings of imagination (*takhayyul*) and memory (*dhikr*). Ibn al-Haytham also argued that sensation was ultimately effected by the last sentient (*al-hass al-akhir*; *sentiens ultimum*), which is located in the anterior part of the brain (*muqaddam al-dimagh*), and not by the eyes alone. Moreover, he

explicated phenomena associated with binary vision by showing that two images of the single form of a visible object are received in each of the crystalline of the eyes, passing then via the vitreous to the hollow nerves as sensations, and ultimately being unified in the cavity of the common nerve, by virtue of which they reach the last sentient as an ordered single form of a sensible object. Furthermore, in delineating the optimal conditions of vision, Ibn al-Haytham stressed that the viewed object must be bright and should be positioned at a moderate distance from the perceiver's eyes that comprises a transparent medium (*shafif*). Moreover, the visible object must be in a plane with the eyes, and its body should have a proper volume, as well as allow for the trapping of some light rays, given that a completely transparent body is virtually invisible. In addition, the observer should have sufficient time to see the object with two healthy eyes that are able to perform effective concentrations in scrutiny and contemplation. Ibn al-Haytham also noted that when sight perceives individuals of the same species repeatedly and continually, a universal form (*sura kulliya*; *forma universalis*) of that species takes shape in the imagination and gets recollected in recognition, while consequently assisting in the grasping of the quiddity (*mahiyya*, essence) of a corresponding visible object and its inspected properties.

Ibn al-Haytham's theory of light in *Kitab al-manazir* was supplemented by a synoptic study entitled *Risala fi al-daw'* (*Treatise on Light*), which examined the essence of light and inquired about its propagation through variegated transparent media. He also explored catoptrics, using finely polished surfaces, including parabolic and spherical burning mirrors, as well as studied the effects of lenses and visual magnifications. His optical theories were also associated with meteorological explorations of refraction and reflection in accounting for phenomena such as the halo and the rainbow (*Maqala fi al-hala wa qaws quzah*), and the "Moon illusion" (namely when the Moon appears to be larger at the horizon than at the culmination or zenith).

In view of establishing an abstract domain for geometry, and as a result of his investigation of mathematical analysis and synthesis (*Fi al-tahlil wa al-tarkib*) and knowable entities (*Fi al-ma'lumat*), Ibn al-Haytham composed a tract entitled *Qawl fi al-makan* (*A Treatise on Place*). In this work he advanced a thorough critique of the conception of *topos* as noted in *Book Delta* of Aristotle's *Physics*. Combining geometrical demonstrations with everyday observations, Ibn al-Haytham rejected the definition of place as a two-dimensional boundary of a containing body that is at rest and is in contact with what it contains. In contrast, he attempted to show that place (*al-makan*) is an imagined three-dimensional void (*khala' mutakhayyal*) between the inner surfaces of the containing body. Consequently, he posited place as being analogous to a room or space, in a manner that echoed the corollaries of John Philoponus (sixth century C.E.), and anticipated the seventeenth-century conceptions of *extensio*. Ibn al-Haytham's definition of *al-makan* attracted a bold critique in defense of

Aristotle's physical definition of *topos* by the philosopher 'Abd al-Latif al-Baghdadi (d. c.1231) in the epistle *Fi al-radd 'ala Ibn al-Haytham fi al-makan* (*A Refutation of Ibn al-Haytham's Place*). Ultimately, Ibn al-Haytham's geometrical conception of *al-makan* accorded well with his affirmation of the visibility of depth (*al-'umq*) and distance (*al-bu'd*) in *Kitab al-manazir*, which carried tacit phenomenological imports in its potential surpassing of the epistemic limitations of what centuries later was advocated in the immaterialist doctrine of George Berkeley, who polemically negated the visibility of space.

See also **Aristotelianism; Optics and catoptrics**

Bibliography

Primary Sources
Ibn al-Haytham. *Kitab al-manazir*, ed. A.I. Sabra, Kuwait (1983, 2002).
———. *The Optics of Ibn al-Haytham, Books I–III, On Direct Vision*, trans. A. I. Sabra, London (1989).
———. *Majmu' al-rasa'il*. Hayderabad (1938)

Secondary Sources
El-Bizri, N. La perception de la profondeur: Alhazen, Berkeley et Merleau-Ponty. *Oriens-Occidens: Cahiers du centre d'histoire des sciences et des philosophies arabes et médiévales*, CNRS (2004) 5: 171–184.
Lindberg, David C. Alhazen's Theory of Vision and its Reception in the West. *Isis* (1967) 58: 321–341.
———. *Theories of Vision from al-Kindi to Kepler*. Chicago: University of Chicago Press, 1976.
Omar, Saleh Beshara. *Ibn al-Haytham's Optics: A Study of the Origins of Experimental Science*. Minneapolis: Bibliotheca Islamica, 1977.
Raynaud, D. Ibn al-Haytham sur la vision binoculaire: Un précurseur de l'optique physiologique. *Arabic Sciences and Philosophy* (2003) 13: 79–99.
Sabra, A. I. "The Physical and the Mathematical in Ibn al-Haytham's Theory of Light and Vision." In *The Commemoration Volume of Biruni International Congress in Tehran*. Tehran, 1976.
———. "Sensation and Inference in Alhazen's Theory of Visual Perception." In *Studies in Perception: Interrelations in the History of Philosophy and Science*. Edited by Peter K. Machamer and Robert G. Turnbull. Columbus: Ohio State University Press, 1978.
———. Ibn al-Haytham's Lemmas in Solving 'Alhazen's problem. *Archive for History of Exact Sciences* (1982) 26: 299–324.
Vescovini, G.F. La fortune de l'*Optique* d'Ibn al-Haitham: Le livre *De aspectibus* (*Kitab al-manazir*) dans le moyen âge latin. *Archives internationales d'histoire des sciences* (1990) 40: 220–238.

NADER EL-BIZRI

IBN AL-SAFFAR

Abu l-Qasim Ahmad ibn 'Abd Allah ibn 'Umar al-Gafiqi al-Andalusi, better known as Ibn al-Saffar ("son of the coppersmith"), was a great astronomer in al-Andalus, and one of the most important members of the school of *Maslama of Madrid (d. 1007). Ibn al-Saffar lived in his native city, Córdoba, where he taught sciences, since he was an expert in arithmetic, geometry, and astronomy. Nevertheless, the political situation of al-Andalus at that time (the beginning of the eleventh century) became unstable on account of the *fitna* (civil war). These were the times of the fall of the Umayyad caliphate and the inauguration of a new order, that of the small kingdoms or *taifas*. Ibn al-Saffar moved to Denia, on the east coast of the Iberian Peninsula, a kingdom ruled by the slave Mujahid al-'Amiri (r. 1012–1045). Ahmad ibn al-Saffar died there in 1035. His brother, Muhammad, who also retired in Denia, was a celebrated constructor of astronomical instruments. Two astrolabes and a plate, at least, are preserved today (in the Royal Scottish Museum in Edinburgh, Scotland, the Westdeutsche Bibliothek in Marburg, Germany, and the Museo Nazionale in Palermo, Italy, respectively).

Ahmad ibn al-Saffar's disciples in Córdoba included Ibn Bargut, al-Wasiti, Ibn Shahr, al-Qurashi, and Ibn al-'Attar.

*Al-Khwarizmi's *Sindhind*—the original text of which is lost—reached al-Andalus and was adapted by Ibn al-Saffar and his teacher Maslama of Madrid. *Ibn al-Samh and Ibn al-Saffar also made two recensions. The Arabic text of the version of Maslama and Ibn al-Saffar is lost, but there are several Latin translations of it. One is by *Adelard of Bath (fl. 1116–1142); another is attributed to the Spanish Jew *Pedro Alfonso (fl. late eleventh/early twelfth century). It is difficult to establish which data were taken from al-Khwarizmi or which were provided by the Andalusian astronomers, because materials from the Indo-Iranian, Greco-Arabic, and Hispanic traditions are found. Nevertheless, it seems clear that certain tables that use the meridian of Córdoba or refer to the Hispanic era (HE) are due to Maslama and his disciples.

Ibn al-Saffar's most popular work is a treatise on the use of the astrolabe, a book that was still used in European scientific settings during the fifteenth century. In the opinion of *Sa'id al-Andalusi, the treatise was clear, simple and comprehensible. *John of Seville and Plato of Tivoli (fl. first half of twelfth century, Barcelona) translated it into Latin. The Latin translation by John of Seville—edited by Millás in 1955—wrongly attributed to Maslama was, in fact, the translation of Ibn al-Saffar's treatise on the astrolabe except for the last chapter, which is probably a fragment taken from the Maslama's *zij* (table). This would explain why later scholars thought that the authorship of the whole manuscript belonged to the teacher, Maslama. The translation by Plato of Tivoli—edited by Lorch, Brey, Kirschner and Shöner in 1994—has an introduction in which Plato offers his work to a certain Johannes David and states that this is the best Arabic treatise that he has ever read. There is also a Hebrew version by *Profatius Judaeus and another in Old Spanish and into Spanish in Hebrew characters. Finally, *Alfonso X the Wise's astronomers used the work several times. In the book, Ibn al-Saffar describes all the usual information contained in a treatise of this kind. One of the topics analysed is the determination of the *qibla* (or direction to Mecca): the text gives a value of 30° south of east for the *samt* of the *qibla* at Córdoba, which corresponds to the azimuth of the rising Sun at the winter solstice. In this work, Ibn al-Saffar refers to Ptolemy's *Geography*, a mention which shows that Andalusian astronomers were interested in other works apart from the Sindhind. The Arabic text was edited by Millás (who also translated it into Catalan) in 1955.

Ibn al-Saffar designed the oldest surviving Islamic sundial, made in about 1000 in Córdoba (preserved in the Museo Arqueológico Provincial of Córdoba, Spain). On the fragment of the sundial preserved, it is possible to observe the curve for the midday (*zuhr*) prayer but, presumably, the original instrument had that of the afternoon (*asr*) prayer. In spite of the fact that it is explicitly attributed to Ibn al-Saffar, the errors on the sundial could not have been made by a careful astronomer, so perhaps the instrument was only "in the manner of" Ibn al-Saffar.

See also **Arithmetic; Astrolabes and quadrants; Astrology; Astronomy, Islamic; Commercial arithmetic; Geometry; Religion and science**

Bibliography

Primary Source
Sa'id al-Andalusi. *Kitab tabaqat al-umam*, ed. Cheikho, Beirut, 1912, 70 (see also two other editions: Hayat Bu 'Alwan, Dar al-Tali'a li-l-Tiba'a wa-l-Nashr. Beirut, 1985; Djulamrida Djamshidnizad-i Awwal, Tehran, 1415/1995); trad. R. Blachère, *Livre des catégories des nations*, Paris, 1935, pp. 130–131.

Secondary Sources
Castells, Margarita and Julio Samsó. Seven Chapters of Ibn al-Saffar's lost zij. *Archives Internationales d'Histoire des Sciences* (1995) 45: 229–262.
Lorch, Richard, G. Brey, S. Kirschner, and Chr. Schöner. "Ibn as-Saffar's Traktat über das Astrolab in der Übersetzung von Plato von Tivoli." In *Cosmographica et Geographica. Festschrift für Heribert M. Nobis zum 70. Geburstag (= Algorismus 13)*. Edited by B. Fritscher and G. Brey. I: 125–180.
Lorch, Richard. "The Treatise on the Astrolabe by Rudolf of Bruges." In *Between Demonstration and Imagination. Essays in the History of Science and Philosophy presented to John D. North*. Edited by Lodi Nauta and Arjo Vanderjagt. Leiden: E.J. Brill, 1999.
Millás Vallicrosa, José María. Sobre un "Tratado de astrolabio" atribuido a Abraham b. 'Ezra. *Sefarad* (1944) 4: 31–38.

MONICA RIUS

IBN AL-SAMH

Ibn al-Samh was born in Córdoba (979) and died in Granada (1035). He grew up in a learned milieu: he was a disciple of *Maslama of Madrid (d. 1007), and became a prominent astronomer and mathematician in his school, one of the most important centers for the study of the exact sciences in al-Andalus. Soon after the beginning of the *fitna* (the civil war that brought down the Umayyad caliphate), Ibn al-Samh moved to Granada, where he worked in the service of the local chief, the Berber Habus ibn Maksan (1019–1038) whose Jewish minister, Samuel ibn Nagrella, was also interested in mathematics and astronomy. No other biographical information is given by Arabic sources.

Abu Marwan Sulayman ibn Muhammad ibn 'Isa ibn al-Nashi, the most important of Ibn al-Samh's disciples, was also a geometer and mathematician and gives a list of nine books written by his teacher. According to Ibn al-Khatib, Ibn al-Samh wrote an essay on history, but there is no evidence of it. In fact, Ibn al-Samh was a specialist in scientific fields such as astronomy, mathematics and, probably, medicine.

Although Ibn Khaldun (*Muqaddimah*, ed. Beirut, 1961, 906) states that Ibn al-Samh wrote an abstract of the *Almagest*, no other source gives this information. On the other hand, like Maslama of Madrid and *Ibn al-Saffar, Ibn al-Samh composed a version of a table (*zij*) based on the *Sindhind* by *al-Khwarizmi (fl. 800–847), but it has not survived either.

Ibn al-Samh composed a treatise on the construction of the astrolabe (which is partially extant in ms. Escorial, Arabe, 972, 29r–29v) and another on its use, *Kitab al-'amal bi'l-asturlab* (complete text preserved in ms. British Museum, Arab, 405). The book was the most complete tract written in the Iberian peninsula during the Middle Ages (one hundred twenty-nine chapters on the use of the instrument). Although Ibn al-Saffar's treatise was more popular, the text is especially interesting because it deals with questions not usually analysed in works of this kind (such as the visibility of the Moon or its latitude and longitude). In his *Kitab al-'amal* he quotes Habash al-Hasib (fl. 835), clear evidence that the eastern astronomer was known in al-Andalus at the end of the tenth century. The text also shows that the school of Maslama knew and used the works of *al-Battani (Albategnius). This book was the source of a treatise on the use of the spherical astrolabe composed at the court of *Alfonso X the Wise. Since the king's astronomers did not have an Arabic text on the spherical astrolabe from which to make the Castilian translation, they took Ibn al-Samh's treatise and made an adaptation of it.

A new instrument conceived in al-Andalus for the first time and later developed in Latin Europe, the equatorium, is another of Ibn al-Samh's great contributions to astronomy. Indeed, his treatise on this instrument is the first known text of this type, followed by works by Azarquiel (*Ibn al-Zarqalluh) and Abu'l-Salt of Denia (c. 1067–1134). The instrument described by Ibn al-Samh is a hybrid astrolabe-equatorium and his treatise is preserved in the Alfonsine translation included in the *Libros del Saber de Astronomia*. Ibn al-Samh gives the numerical parameters necessary for the construction of the instrument. He uses al-Battani's values for the longitudes of the apogees of the planets, al-Khwarizmi and Maslama's values for the ascending nodes of the planets and, finally, the eccentricities and ratios of the epicycles of the planets from the *Almagest*. The equatorium has eight plates (one for the Sun, six for the deferents of the Moon and the five planets, and one for the planetary epicycles) carefully explained and placed within the mater of an astrolabe. This instrument helped to determine the longitude of a planet and saved astronomers a great deal of time, especially if one bears in mind that their main aim was to cast horoscopes.

*Sa'id al-Andalusi states that Ibn al-Samh (like Maslama of Madrid and *al-Zahrawi) wrote several books on *commercial arithmetic. Ibn al-Samh composed two works on calculation, al-Kitab al-Kafi fi'l-hisab al-hawa'i (probably ms. Escorial Arabe 973, 1–30; Berlin Ar. 6010, 1–23) and al-Kitab al-kamil fi'l-hisab al-hawa'i, and two other books on numbers, Kitab Thimar al-'adad al-ma'ruf bi'l-mu'amalat (usually known as al-Mu'amalat) and Kitab Tabi'at al-'adad. On geometry, Ibn al-Samh wrote Kitab al-Madkhal ilaa' l-handasa fi tafsir Kitab Uqlidis (a commentary on the Book of *Euclid) and al-Kitab al-kabir fi' l-handasa. This last text is partially extant in a Hebrew translation by Qalonymos ibn Qalonymos (fourteenth century).

See also Arithmetic; Astrology; Astronomy, Islamic

Bibliography

Millás Vallicrosa, José María. Estudios sobre Azarquiel. Madrid-Granada: Consejo Superior de Investigaciones Científicas, 1943–1950.

———. Los primeros tratados de astrolabio en la España árabe. Revista del Instituto Egipcio de Estudios Islámicos (1955) 3: 35–49 (reprinted in Nuevos estudios sobre historia de la ciencia española, Barcelona, 1960, 61–78).

Rashed, Roshdi. Les mathématiques infinitésimales du IXe au XIe siècles. Fondateurs et commentateurs. Vol 1 : Banu Musa, Ibn Qurra, Ibn Sinan, al-Khazin, al-Quhi, Ibn al-Samh, Ibn Hud. London: Al-Furqan, 1996.

Samsó, Julio. Las ciencias de los antiguos en al-Andalus. Madrid: Mapfre, 1992.

Sánchez Pérez, J. Biografías de matemáticos árabes que florecieron en España. Madrid: E. Maestre, 1921.

Sezgin, Fuad. Geschichte der Arabischen Schriftums. 12 vols. Leiden, 1978, 6: 249.

Vernet, Juan and Julio Samsó. "The Development of Arabic Science in Andalusia." In Encyclopedia of the History of Arabic Science. Edited by Roshdi Rashed. New York: Routledge, 1996.

MONICA RIUS

IBN AL-ZARQALLUH

Abu Ishaq Ibrahim ibn Yayha al-Naqqash (d. 1100), known as Ibn al-Zarqalluh or Ibn al-Zarqiyal (whence the Spanish Azarquiel), was the most important astronomer of the Middle Ages in the Iberian Peninsula. He worked in Toledo under king al-Ma'mun (1037–1074). Ibn al-Zarqalluh left Toledo and went to Córdoba, which belonged, then, to the Abbadi kingdom of Seville, either at the beginning of the reign of al-Qadir (1081–1085) or when Alfonso VI conquered the city in 1085. In Córdoba he was protected by al-Mu'tamid ibn 'Abbad (1069–1091). He died in that city on October 15, 1100.

According to the Yesod 'Olam of Isaac Judaeus (fourteenth century), al-Zarqalluh started his career as an instrument maker who worked for the Toledan team of astronomers led by qadi *Sa'id al-Andalusi (1029–1070). His interest in designing new astronomical instruments appears very early: in 1048–1049 he dedicated a treatise on the azafea (al-safiha) to the Abbadi prince of Seville al-Mu'ayyad bi-Nasir Allah who was then only eight or nine years old and later became king al-Mu'tamid. The azafea, like the astrolabe, is an analog computer used to solve graphically problems of spherical astronomy and astrology, but while the astrolabe needs a specific plate for each latitude, the azafea is a universal instrument which can be used for any latitude. His description on the construction and use of the instrument is extant both in Arabic and in the Spanish Alfonsine translation (Libro de la Açafeha). At a later date, he seems to have dedicated a simplified version of the same instrument to the same al-Mu'tamid: this variant became very popular in Medieval Europe through Latin and Hebrew translations of the treatise on its use. He also dedicated to al-Mu'tamid a treatise on the use of the equatorium (extant in Arabic), another analog computer the purpose of which is to calculate planetary longitudes. The complexity of the Ptolemaic Mercury model led him to represent Mercury's deferent not as a circle but as an ellipse, which he identified as such: this is the first known instance of the use of conic sections in astronomy. His descriptions of the construction of such an instrument (c. 1080–1081) and of an armillary sphere are known to us only through Alfonsine translations (Libros de las láminas de los siete planetas, Libro de las Armellas). The thirteenth-century Egyptian astronomer Abu'l-Hasan 'Ali al-Marrakushi attributes to Ibn al-Zarqalluh a sine quadrant (another one appears on the back of the earliest variant of the safiha) with movable cursor in the line of the quadrans vetustissimus, known in Latin Europe since the end of the tenth century.

Ibn al-Zarqalluh's collaboration with qadi Sa'id and his team must have awakened his interest in observations, astronomical tables and astronomical theory. His solar observations must have begun between 1050 and 1055 at the latest: the aforementioned al-Marrakushi states that he was observing in Toledo in 1061. Although no details are extant, these observations are confirmed in al-Zij al-Kamil fi'l-Ta'alim ("The perfect set of astronomical tables based on mathematics") by Ibn al-Ha'im al-Ishbili (c. 1205) who attributes to Ibn al-Zarqalluh not only the usual twenty-five years of solar observations but also thirty-seven years of observations of the Moon (both in Toledo and in Córdoba). According to an anonymous Toledan contemporary, author of a Kitab al-Hay'a ("Book on Cosmology"), he appears to have used a large sized instrument. As a result of his lunar observations, he introduced a modification in Ptolemy's lunar model. His solar observations were incorporated to the solar mean motion tables extant in the Toledan Tables as well as to the solar tables of his perpetual Almanac.

The Toledan Tables, known through a Latin translation, seem to be the result of an adaptation of the best available astronomical material (*al-Khwarizmi, *al-Battani) to the coordinates of *Toledo made by a team led by Saʻid and in which Ibn al-Zarqalluh seems to have had an outstanding position. They also include a set of "trepidation tables" (used to calculate the value of the precession of the equinoxes—considered, then, to be variable—for a given date), apparently related to the work of Ibn al-Zarqalluh for he wrote, c. 1085, an important *Treatise on the Motion of the Fixed Stars* (extant in a Hebrew translation) in which he designed three different geometrical trepidation models and tried to obtain with them results which would fit the observations made by Hipparchus (147 B.C.E.) and Ptolemy (139 C.E.), as well as those used by *Thabit ibn Qurra (831 C.E.) and, finally, al-Battani (883 C.E.) and Ibn al-Zarqalluh's own observations (c. 1075). The same kind of historical preoccupations appear in his book on the Sun, written between 1075 and 1080 and known only through indirect sources. Its title was either *On the Solar Year* or *A Comprehensive Epistle on the Sun*. In it Ibn al-Zarqalluh improved enormously on the corrections made, c. 830, by the astronomers of the Abbasid Caliph al-Maʼmun, in Baghdad and Damascus, on Ptolemy's solar model, and established, very accurately, that the solar apogee has a characteristic motion of 1∞ in every two hundred seventy-nine solar years. Furthermore, a study of the different values of the solar eccentricity established by the aforementioned Hipparchus, Thabit, al-Battani and himself led him to design a solar model with variable eccentricity which became extremely influential in later Andalusi and Maghribi astronomy and reached Europe where it was mentioned by Copernicus. We also have an indirect reference to another theoretical work of him in which he criticized Ptolemy's method to obtain the eccentricity of Mercury.

Ibn al-Zarqalluh compiled also a perpetual *Almanac*, preserved in Arabic, Latin and in an Alfonsine translation. It is based on a Greek work computed by a certain Awmatiyus in the third or fourth century C.E.—although, as we have seen, the solar tables seem the result of the Toledan observations—and its purpose is to simplify the computation of planetary longitudes: for that purpose Babylonian planetary cycles ("goal years") are used. After the completion of one of these cycles the true longitudes of a given planet will be the same on the same dates of the year as at the beginning of the cycle. Perpetual *almanacs seem to be characteristic of Andalusian astronomy and they were also used in the Maghrib and in Medieval Spain.

See also **Astrolabes and quadrants; Astronomy, Islamic; Planetary tables**

Bibliography

Comes, M. *Ecuatorios andalusíes*. Barcelona: Instituto Millás-Vallicrosa de Historia de la Ciencia Arabe, 1991.
Millás Vallicrosa, J.M. *Estudios sobre Azarquiel*. Madrid-Granada: Consejo Superior de Investigaciones Científicas, 1943–1950.
Pedersen, Fritz S. *The Toledan Tables. A review of the manuscripts and the textual versions with an edition.*
Historisk-filosofiske Skrifter 24: 1–4. Copenhagen: Det Kongelige Danske Videnskabernes Selskab, 2002.
Puig, R. Al-Zarqalluh's Graphical Method for Finding Lunar Distances. *Centaurus* (1989) 32: 294–309.
Richter-Bernburg, L. "Saʻid, the Toledan Tables, and Andalusi Science." In *From Deferent to Equant: a volume of studies in the history of science in the ancient and medieval Near East in honor of E.S. Kennedy*, edited by D.A. King and G. Saliba. New York: New York Academy of Sciences, 1987, pp. 373-401.
Samsó, J. *Las ciencias de los antiguos en al-Andalus*. Madrid: Mapfre, 1992, pp. 147–152, 166–240.
———. "Trepidation in al-Andalus in the 11th Century." In Samsó, *Islamic Astronomy and Medieval Spain*. Aldershot: Variorum, 1994, no. VIII.
Samsó, J. and H. Mielgo. Ibn al-Zarqalluh on Mercury. *Journal for the History of Astronomy* (1994) 25: 289–296.
Toomer, G.J. The Solar Theory of az-Zarqal. A History of Errors. *Centaurus* (1969) 14: 306–336.
———. "The Solar Theory of az-Zarqal. An Epilogue." In *From Deferent to Equant (op. cit.)*, pp. 513–519.

J. SAMSÓ

IBN BAJJA

Ibn Bajja (Avempace), born c. 1070, in Saragossa, al-Andalus, died in 1139 in Fez, Morocco. One of the most outstanding philosophers of al-Andalus, he was a commentator on Aristotle and a multifaceted scholar who mastered medicine, mathematics, astronomy, biology, music and poetry.

Life, Education, and Intellectual Career

At the time of ibn Bajja's birth Saragossa was the chief city of a kingdom ruled by one of the most learned dynasties in the history of al-Andalus, the Banu Hud. The kings al-Muqtadir ibn Hud (1046–1081/2) and al-Muʼtaman ibn Hud (1081/2–1085, credited with having written the most important Andalusi mathematical treatise, *Kitab al-Istikmal* (*The Book of Perfection*), made their court a focus of learning, particularly philosophy and mathematics. Ibn Bajja must have been trained in this ambience although we lack concrete information about his early years. We can presume that he studied a wide range of scientific and philosophical disciplines, particularly logic and mathematics, together with the religious and linguistic and literary lore that was common to any learned men of the time. We have direct evidence of his proficiency in logic during his first epoch in Saragossa and about his commitment to learning, because he moved to Seville in order to find the best teachers in astronomy. He also learned geometry from the Valencian mathematician Ibn Sayyid al-Kalbi, possibly indirectly. His works on astronomy, mathematics, music, and logic might have been written in this first period of his life. When the Almoravids (the North African dynasty that ruled al-Andalus during the first half of the twelfth century) seized Saragossa in 1110, Ibn Bajja became minister of the new governor Ibn Tifalwit. Preferment by the Almoravids provided him with a comfortable position that aroused (together with Ibn Bajja's haughty personality) the envy of most of his contemporaries. His reputation for religious heterodoxy might reflect such rivalries, although there might well be sound reasons for it, particularly if we bear in mind that the rule of the Almoravids was characterized by a strict religiosity. After the death of his patron in 1117, his life changed dramatically. He travelled to many cities of the Almoravid kingdom and spent reasonably long periods in some of them: Xàtiva, where he was imprisoned (perhaps for religious reasons), Granada, Seville, Almería, Oran, and Fez. Some sources tell that during that period he served as minister of the Almoravid ruler Abu Bakr Yahya b. Yusuf b. Tashfin for some twenty years in the Maghrib, but this information is not completely reliable. Official patronage aside, Ibn Bajja supported himself as a physician and devoted much of his time to studying and writing. During this period, his principal disciple and friend, Ibn al-Imam, to whom some of his works are dedicated, seems to have played an important role in his life. In the work done in this second period of his life, two epochs can be distinguished: that devoted to commentaries on Aristotelian treatises and another in which he wrote his most personal works such as *The Rule of the Solitary* and *Man's Contact with the Intellect*.

Philosophy and Science

One of the main topics in Ibn Bajja's philosophy is the theory of knowledge, which he treats under the influence of the Neoplatonized thought of the philosopher *al-Farabi. He attaches great importance to scientific knowledge, and therefore to Aristotelian scientific method. On the one hand, he tackles the subject in his commentaries (actually, a collection of notes arranged quite haphazardly known as *Ta'aliq Kitab al-Burhan*, (that is, notes on al-Farabi's commentary on Aristotle's *Posterior Analytics*, *Kitab al-Burhan* [*Book of Demonstration*], which is the name given to both the Arabic translation of Aristotle's treatise and al-Farabi's commentary). In addition, he studies scientific method in some of his Aristotelian commentaries, particularly those on the *Physics* and *Parts of Animals*, the first chapters of which are important sources for Aristotle's conception of scientific method. At a third level, he considers the problems that Aristotle's deductive method suggest for each science, particularly mathematics, astronomy, biology, and medicine. He pays great attention to the acquisition of first, indemonstrable, premises which are the basis of the scientific syllogism, and he stresses the importance of using it correctly, in order to attain real scientific knowledge. His speculations in that domain reached the philosopher and physician *Ibn Rushd and to some extent influenced, in the second half of the twelfth century, the search for ways to accommodate agreement with Aristotelian tenets in astronomy and medicine. As a commentator of Aristotle, Ibn Bajja is characterized by his original developments, but is not always easy to grasp due to his sketchy style.

Mathematics and Astronomy

As a mathematician, Ibn Bajja is known because of his transmission of the geometry of an Andalusi mathematician of the eleventh century, Ibn Sayyid, which has only come down to us in an account by Ibn Bajja himself referring to his mentor's studies of Apollonius's *Conics*. It seems that Ibn Sayyid had reworked this treatise on the basis of some new definitions which were equivalent, although not identical, to the ones given in the original. By doing this, he was able to avoid difficult propositions and posit new ones. He studied curves greater than the second degree generated by the intersection of conical and non-conical surfaces, which might have been the subject of an algebraic analysis rather than a geometrical one. He also addressed two classical problems: the trisection of the angle and the determination of two mean proportionals. Ibn Bajja states that he completed those works while adding some new problems to them, and that he had planned to write a book on this subject.

Ibn Bajja was not an astronomer proper, although he himself recounts that he had performed astronomical observations. In any case, he was knowledgeable enough in the theory of this science to judge the work of contemporary astronomers. In this regard, Ibn Bajja was aware of the innovations in, and corrections to, the planetary models in *Ptolemy's *Almagest* propounded by mathematical astronomers of the eleventh century, such as the Andalusi *Ibn al-Zarqalluh (d. 1100 in Córdoba) and the Egyptian natural philosopher *Ibn al-Haytham. In an epistle, he criticizes both for some amendments to Ptolemy, thus showing his preference for the latter. At least one of his criticisms (Ibn al-Haytham's model of Mercury) has proved to be right. The only treatise on astronomy by Ibn Bajja that has come down to us, *Kalam fi'l-Hay'a* (*Discourse on Astronomy*), contains a critique of the mathematical astronomers and of the *Almagest* in which he argues that their planetary models do not fit the tenets of Aristotelian scientific method. This kind of reasoning is echoed by Ibn Rushd in his only extant astronomical work, *Mukhtasar al-Majisti* (*Abridgement of the Almagest*). In this context, we can examine Ibn Bajja's role in the movement known as "the revolt against Ptolemy," in which Ibn Rushd was involved, whose main objection to Ptolemy was his use of eccentrics and epicycles that implied planetary motions not centred on the Earth and which contradicted Aristotelian tenets. The Jewish philosopher *Maimonides stated in his *Guide of the Perplexed* that Ibn Bajja accepted eccentrics while rejecting epicycles, but the truth is that in many instances he in fact accepted epicycles (namely in his commentary on the *Physics*). Consequently, his position on this point should be regarded as that of a predecessor, inasmuch as he contributed to the lessening of Ptolemy's authority by hinting at his methodological inconsistencies, thus paving the way for reformists such as the astronomer *al-Bitruji.

Ibn Bajja, who wrote a commentary on Aristotle's *Physics* (*Sharh Kitab al-Sama' al-Tabi'i*), generally adheres to Aristotelian tenets. Notwithstanding this, he adopts some Neoplatonic ideas on dynamics based on his partial acquaintance with John Philoponus. Following Aristotle, he divides motion into natural and non-natural, but, against Aristotle, he considers the existence of a kind of fatigue (in Arabic, *kalal*, cf. Lettink, *Aristotle's Physics and its Reception in the Arabic World*, 22 and *passim*) in non-natural motion (a Neoplatonic assumption) due to both the mover and the resistance exerted by the moved. This fatigue is not present in natural motion but he proposes a case in which fatigue appears in this kind of motion: the falling of a body along an inclined plane. More relevant for the development of dynamics is his positing of motion in a void. Although Ibn Bajja's commentaries were not known in European tradition, quotations by Ibn Rushd transmitted some of his ideas to medieval Latin scholars such as *Aquinas and *Duns Scotus. It has been claimed that Ibn Bajja's influence reached the young Galileo Galilei through the scholastics and also the physicists of the Renaissance (Benedetti and Borro), and inspired his famous experiment at the tower of Pisa. Recent research and greater acquaintance with Ibn Bajja's commentary on the *Physics* has revised this position. Ibn Bajja followed John Philoponus' doctrines about falling bodies. Arguing against the existence of a void, Aristotle had objected that the time a body takes to cover a certain distance is proportional to the density of the medium. His "law of motion for falling bodies" can be expressed, accordingly, in terms of weight (W, which is the moving force) and density or resistance of the medium (D): $V = W/D$. The absence of a medium would thus entail an instantaneous movement, which is not possible. Philoponus, followed by Ibn Bajja, objected that a medium is not necessary, and adduced the planetary motions, which have finite velocities in the absence of resistance to a medium. The time taken by such motion must be due to the space to be covered. Therefore, the Aristotelian formula could be rewritten as $V = W - D$, from which the paradox of instantaneous movement would not follow and motion could only depend on weight. In accordance with this argument, Ibn Bajja states that, when moving in a medium, a body would experience some retardation due to the density or viscosity of that medium. This retardation might be understood as a loss in velocity, therefore $Vm = Vo - K \cdot Dm$ (where Vm is velocity in medium, Vo velocity in void, K a constant and Dm the density or viscosity of the medium and $K \cdot Dm$, the loss in velocity). Another possible interpretation, according to Aquinas, is that the retardation meant here consists of some further time to travel in a medium added to the time in the void, which can be expressed as $V = W/Ro + Dm$ (where W is the weight that impels the body and Ro the resistance of the medium). Galileo, in *De Motu*, also assumes the retardation proposed by Philoponus and Ibn Bajja, but the formula that he employs in order to express it cannot be derived from Ibn Bajja. It is also worth noting that these commentaries applied physical concepts of the sublunary world to planetary motion, thus foreshadowing al-Bitruji's proposals.

Another salient contribution in the disciplines that nowadays pertain to physics might be found in Ibn Bajja's view on the Milky Way, extant in his commentary of Aristotle's *Meteorology*, a treatise that he knew in the distorted version of Yahya al-Bitriq (d. c. 830). Aristotle's opinion (the Milky Way results from the ignition by the motion of the heaven of dry and hot exhalations that fill the upper part of the atmosphere, in regions in which the stars are particularly large, dense and close together) had been emended in al-Bitriq's version (the light we see is actually the light of the stars, not that of the ignited material, which would cause us to see the Milky Way merely as a continuous patch). Ibn Bajja perfects al-Bitriq's view by determining the role of the ignited material taken in that process: it is responsible for the refraction of the light of the stars that causes them to be seen as a continuous patch. This view was echoed in Ibn Rushd's commentaries to *Meteorology*.

Biology

Ibn Bajja wrote two main treatises on biology: first, a commentary on Aristotle's zoological works mainly focused on *Generation of Animals* and *Parts of Animals* (titled in a recent edition, *Kitab al-Hayawan* [*The Book of Animals*], which is also the name given to Aristotle's zoological work); and, second, a short commentary on the pseudo-Aristotelian *De Plantis*, actually written by Nicolaus Damascenus (*Kalam fi'l-Nabat*, *The Discourse on Plants*). Both works share common features: the commentary restricted to those fragments of the original that interest the author in order to complement them; concern with the scientific method; and an apparent recourse to personal observations. In his *Kitab al-Hayawan*, he divides zoology into four parts according to a personal synthesis of the first book of *History of Animals* (the first tackles issues related to the perceptible parts; the second to the reason why animals have organs; the third to the parts they have in common; the last to the parts that differ). He collates dispersed passages from Aristotle on the reproduction of insects, and produces a coherent description that contains some data furnished by his observations. He discusses the controversial issue of the contribution of male and female to generation, adopting, against Galen, the Aristotelian opinion that while the female does not contribute semen to generation, she may produce some semen-like fluid during copulation. *Ibn Sina and Ibn Rushd (the latter probably influenced by Ibn Bajja) were also of the same opinion. As for Ibn Bajja's *Kalam fi'l-Nabat*, it is worth noting his attempt to follow, in botany, the guidelines found in Aristotles's zoology by studying, first, the characteristics common to all plants and, second, their essential differences. Accordingly, he sketches a classification that somewhat differs from that of Nicolaus Damascenus, which begins with the pair of *differentiae* rooted/rootless and proceeds with a wide range of opposite pairs, most of them related to habitat. This classification, by no means systematic, is illustrated with a wealth of examples. The genera and species thus defined are explained and studied according to Aristotelian tenets, even though the issues under discussion are not always fully developed. Water plants deserve a longer study (a short treatise on the water lily has been preserved). He also treats the problem of boundaries in the animal and vegetal kingdoms: animals such as sponges, apes and ostriches lead him to question a strict division among various groups. However, in no way does he propound any kind of solution foreshadowing the theory of evolution, as we can find in other Arab authors. He provides an interesting discussion of the existence of gender in plants, denied by Aristotle but known to an Arab who observed that the palm tree has both male and female flowers. Discussing this example and that of the fig-tree, Ibn Bajja acknowledges a sort of sexual reproduction that somewhat corrects Aristotle's opinion.

Medicine and Pharmacology

Only a small part of Ibn Bajja's medical treatises have survived. We know that he abridged one of the most famous Arabic manuals, *al-Razi's Hawi (Kitab Ikhtisar al-Hawi li'l-Razi)* and that, together with a certain Abu Sufyan al-Andalusi, he wrote a treatise on the work of one the most outstanding pharmacologists of eleventh-century al-Andalus, Ibn Wafid (*Kitab al-tajribatayn 'ala adwiyat Ibn Wafid* [*Book on the Two Experiments concerning Ibn Wafid's Drugs*]). This latter treatise has been the object of a partial reconstruction on the basis of the quotations found in the work of later pharmacologist and botanist, Ibn al-Baytar (d. 1248). Related works by Ibn Bajja remain unpublished in ms. Berlin 5060 WE 87 and have not been studied. Their titles are *Fi'l-mizaj* (*On Temperament*), *Ta'aliq fi'l-Adwiya al-Mufrada* (*Notes on Simples [according to Galen]*), *Maqala fi'l-Hummayat* (*Chapter on Fevers*), and *Sharh fi'l-Fusul* (*Commentary On [Hippocrates's] Aphorisms*). The last and longest of them shows once again his concern for methodology and can be seen as an antecedent of Ibn Rushd's *Kitab al-Kulliyyat* (*Book of Generalities*): Ibn Bajja starts with the same threefold division of medicine into a part devoted to the knowledge of objects (bodily organs and members), another to the knowledge of medical aims (the preservation of health) and a third to the means that support the aims. Both treatises deal with the necessary principles that a physician should know. Nevertheless, Ibn Bajja tackles only theoretical issues, describing medicine as an art in which many sciences intervene, the role that syllogism plays in it, and the dialectic between deduction and practice.

See also **Astronomy, Islamic; Botany; Logic; Medicine, theoretical; Pharmacology; Zoology**

Bibliography

Primary Sources
Ta'aliq Kitab al-Burhan. Edited by M. Fakhri. In *Al-Farabi, Kitab al-Burhan wa-Shara'it al-Yaqin ma'a Ta'aliq Ibn Bajja 'ala l-Burhan*. Beirut: Dar al-Mashriq, 1987.
Kalam fi l-Hay'a. Partial edition by S. Yafut. "Ibn Bajja wa-'ilm al-falak al-batlimusi." In *Dirasat fi ta'rikh al-'ulum wa-l-ibistimulujiya*. Rabat, 1996.
Rasa'il falsafiyya li-Abi Bakr ibn Bajja. Edited by J. al-D. al-'Alawi. Beirut-Casablanca, 1983: 84–87 (see epistles 1 and 4 for astronomy, 3 and 4 for mathematics).
Kitab al-Kawn wa-l-Fasad. Edited and translated into Spanish by J. Puig. Madrid: Consejo Superior de Investigaciones Científicas, 1995.
Sharh al-Athar al-'Ulwiyya. Edited and translated into English by P. Lettinck in *Aristotle's Meteorology and its Reception in the Arab World*. Leiden: E.J. Brill, 1999.
Sharh al-Samac al-Tabi'i. Edited by M. Ziyada. Beirut: Dar al-Kindi, 1978.
Kalam fi'l-Nabat. Edited and translated into Spanish by M. Asín Palacios. *Avempace Botánico. Al-Andalus* (1940) 5: 255–299.
Kitab al-Hayawin. Edited by J. 'Amarati. Casablanca: Al-Markaz al-Thaqafi al-'Arabi, 2002.
Kalam fi'l-Nilufar. Jamal al-Din al-'Alawi ed. *Rasa'il Falsafiyya*, first part, epistle 7.

Secondary Sources
Cabo, A. Aproximación descriptiva del Kitab al-Tajribatayn de Avempace y Sufyan al-Andalusi. *Anaquel de Estudios Árabes* (2004) 15: 45–56.
Djebbar, A. "Deux mathématiciens peu connus d'al-Andalus." In *Vestigia Mathematica. Studies in Medieval and Early Modern Mathematics in Honour of H.L.L.Busard*. Edited by M. Folkerts and J. P. Hogendijk. Amsterdam-Atlanta: Rodopi, 1993.
Endress, G. "Mathematics and Philosophy in Early Islam." In *The Enterprise of Science. New Perspectives*. Edited by J.P. Hogendijk and A.I. Sabra. Cambridge: MIT Press, 2003.
Forcada, M. "La ciencia en Averroes." In *Averroes y los averroísmos. Actas del III Congreso Nacional de Filosofía Medieval*. Edited by J. Ayala. Saragossa: Sociedad de Filosofía Medieval, 1999.
Goodmann, L.E. "Ibn Bajjah." In *History of Islamic Philosophy*. Edited by S. H. Nasr and O. Leaman. New York: Routledge, 1996.
Kruk, R. "Ibn Bajja. Commentary on Aristotle's *De Animalibus*." In *The Ancient Tradition in Christian and Islamic Hellenism*. Edited by G. Endress and R. Kruk. Leiden: Research School CNWS, 1997.
Lettinck, P. *Aristotle's Physics and its Reception in the Arabic World with an Edition of the Unpublished parts of Ibn Bajja's Commentary on the Physics*. Leiden: E.J. Brill, 1994.
Lomba, J. *Avempace*. Zaragoza: Diputación General de Aragón, 1989.
Pines, Shlomo "La dynamique d'Ibn Bajja." In *L'aventure de la science*. Mélanges Alexandre Koyré. 2 vols. Paris: Hermann, 1964.
Samsó, J. Sobre Ibn Bajja y la astronomía. *Sharq al-Andalus* (1993–1994) 10–11: 669–682.
Yafut, S. *Nahnu wa-l-'ilm. Dirasat fi tarikh 'ilm al-falak bi-l-garb al-islami*. Rabat: Dar al-Talica li-l-Tibaca wa-l-Nashr, 1995.

MIQUEL FORCADA

IBN BUKLARISH

Ibn Buklarish (or Biklarish) (fl. 1085–1110) was a Jew who served as physician to the Hudid emir of Saragossa, al-Musta'in for whom he composed a pharmacological treatise, the *Kitab al-Musta'ini*, named after the emir.

The *Materia Medica* of *Dioscorides had been translated from Greek into Arabic by Istifan ibn Basil and corrected by *Hunayn ibn Ishaq. The Arabic version was widely disseminated through the Islamic world, mainly in versions with the entries arranged in alphabetical order. The text was then regionalized. A separate translation from the Greek was produced in al-Andalus (Islamic Spain) by physicians under the direction of the Jewish vizier, Hasday ibn Shaprut, whereby local plant names (both Romance and Berber) were intercalated appropriately. This group included Ibn Juljul, who wrote a book on simples not mentioned by Dioscorides.

In his book, Ibn Buklarish provides a theoretical introduction to *pharmacology and then lists some seven hundred substances in tabular form. The first column contains the name of the substance in alphabetical order; the second, its Galenic grade; the third, synonyms in other languages; fourth, effects of the treatment; fifth, properties and method of administration.

Ibn Buklarish adopted the norms of mathematical pharmacology established by *al-Kindi. *Galen had held that each medicinal substance was composed of the four elements in different proportions, whose strength can be characterized by varying strengths of the four qualities: hot, cold, wet, and dry. When the humors are in imbalance, a medicine is administered that is equal in strength but opposite in quality to the imbalance (McVaugh, 1975: 4). Al-Kindi proposed that there was a relationship between the quantity of a medicinal substance and its quality. According to this abstruse system, as the intensity of the medicine's effect (its grade) increases arithmetically, the ratio between the opposing qualities, which determines the effect of the medicine, increases geometrically. With compound medicines the issue was whether each simple retains its original quality or whether it the compound had a single, new "complexion." Galen, supporting the latter concept, illustrated it by the example of what happens when hot water and ice are mixed together. Ibn Buklarish (Labarta, 1980: 206) gives the same example, without alluding to Galen, in order to introduce practical problems of measuring out amounts of simples of varying degrees of heat and cold, always using al-Kindi's ratios.

The rationale of the system is to aid the pharmacist in determining the degree of a given compound and of preparing a compound of a given intensity. (McVaugh, 1967: 58). The pharmacist actually does this by weighing the simples forming the compound. The usefulness of the system, according to Ibn Buklarish, is that lacking a simple of the right grade, two simples can be mixed together to achieve it, if the laws of proportion are followed. He follows this rather abstract account with examples of hot and cold medicines of each grade, one through four. Thus mustard displays the fourth grade of heat, mercury the fourth of cold.

When the physician makes a diagnosis he first must determine in what grade and in which direction the patient has suffered an imbalance. He then explains that it is difficult for the physician to select the proper medicine, especially if he does not know how the ancient sages had determined the grades in the first place. In practice, this is determined by touch. The first grade of heat must be established through experience. In the second grade the heat is apparent, but does not cause irritation. The third grade causes irritation, without burning; the fourth causes burning. The reverse criteria hold for the degrees of cold. He goes on to say that the rules apply to how one mixes simples of varying grade. The formula says nothing of the effects of the medicine which one knows either from experience or by recourse to a book such as his.

Although *Gerard of Cremona translated al-Kindi's book into Latin (it is known by its *incipit*, *Quia primos*) al-Kindi's system had scant following in Europe, although *Arnau de Vilanova, in his *Aphorismi de gradibus*, followed him quite literally. Therefore, Ibn Buklarish's almost cursory recapitulation of al-Kindi's rules seems to attest to their routinization in Arab pharmacology. *Ibn Rushd attempted, without success, to replace al-Kindi's rules by proposing that the ratio between the opposing qualities increases arithmetically, not geometrically. Ibn Rushd's proposal, which suggested that a medicine could exert an effect even if compounded with a greater amount of its opposite ran contrary to the logic of medieval medical pharmacology.

See also **Medicine, practical; Translation norms and practice**

Bibliography

Dubler, César E. and Elias Terés, eds. La *"Materia Medica" de Dioscorides*. 6 vols. Barcelona and Tetuan, 1952–1957.

Labarta, Ana. "La farmacología de ibn Buklaris: sus fuentes." In *Actas del IV Coloquio Hispano-Tunecino*. Madrid: Instituto Hispano-Árabe de Cultura, 1983, pp. 163–174.

———. "El prólogo de al-Kitab al-Mustacini de Ibn Buklaris." In Juan Vernet, ed. Estudios sobre historia de la ciencia árabe. Barcelona: Consejo Superior de Investigaciones Científicas, 1980, pp. 181–316.

Levey, M. and S.S. Souryal. The Introduction to the *Kitab al-Musta'ini* of Ibn Biklarish (fl. 1106). *Janus* (1968) 55: 134–166.

McVaugh, Michael R. Arnald of Villanova and Bradwardine's Law. *Isis* (1967) 58: 56–64.

THOMAS F. GLICK

IBN EZRA, ABRAHAM

Abraham Ibn Ezra's (c. 1089–c. 1167) main contribution to the history of science lies in the composition of a voluminous, significant, but little known scientific corpus. His scientific and literary output was not produced in Muslim Spain, where he was born and grew up and received his secular education in the best tradition of Arabic-Andalusian science. His first works date precisely from the time he departed from al-Andalus and arrived at Rome in 1140, when he was probably already fifty years old. Thereafter he led the life of an intellectual wanderer, roaming through Italy, France, and England, teaching and writing prolifically on a wide variety of subjects.

Ibn Ezra wrote almost exclusively in Hebrew, in itself a landmark innovation, and the organization and scope of his literary and scientific production are typical of his times. His scientific contribution emerges as the very embodiment of the twelfth-century Jewish passage from Arabic to Hebrew and the rise of medieval Hebrew science. On a broader European stage, his output may be understood as one of the multiple expressions of the twelfth-century scientific renaissance. Ibn Ezra, however, is exceptional: instead of the scholar coming from the Christian North to the Iberian Peninsula to initiate a translation enterprise, the usual course of events, his is the opposite case of an intellectual imbued with Arabic culture who quits al-Andalus, roams around the Christian countries, and in the course of his wanderings imparts the scientific and cultural knowledge that he amassed during his youth in Iberia.

Homogeneous Body of Learning

Ibn Ezra's scientific corpus is composed of approximately thirty works. This large number, however, includes multiple versions of his treatises. Writing was Ibn Ezra's main means of subsistence, and he was required to satisfy a demand that increased during his wanderings in Latin Europe. He probably produced a new version of his work every time he came to a new town. If the multiple versions are excluded from his oeuvre, there remain seventeen distinct treatises, including one translation from Arabic into Hebrew. Although still a large number, they may well be regarded as a rather homogeneous body of knowledge devoted to teaching, with a clear encyclopedic approach, the *hokhmat ha-mazzalot* ("wisdom related to the zodiacal signs"). This multivalent term was coined by Ibn Ezra himself to denote astronomy and mathematics, the study of the *calendar, and *astrology. These are his key subjects, and his treatment of them is internally interconnected by a network of cross-references, thus reinforcing the impression that the works are not separate but parts of a unified whole. Ibn Ezra's scientific works were designed mainly as textbooks or reference books, aimed chiefly at conveying conventional scientific knowledge to the layman. As such, they are naturally infused with a clear didactic character and do not make any pretension to innovation.

Ibn Ezra rose to fame principally because of his outstanding Hebrew biblical exegesis. Perhaps the main reason for his success and popularity is the fact that in his biblical commentaries he introduced essential elements derived from his scientific corpus. Biblical exegesis for Ibn Ezra, however, was not simply a way to popularize ideas presented more systematically in his scientific work; it was itself an enterprise even more significant than the independent scientific treatises. This is especially noticeable in his exegetical excursus, an independent article in which he departed from rigorous reference to the words of the biblical text, combining rich scientific contents to enlarge the scope and discuss controversial exegetical issues.

Ibn Ezra's scientific corpus may be divided into four genres: mathematics and astronomy; the Jewish calendar; the astrological encyclopedia, and translations from Arabic into Hebrew.

1. Mathematics, Astronomy, Scientific Instruments, and Tools

Sefer ha-mispar (*Book of the Number*), an arithmetic textbook, Ibn Ezra's first scientific work, was written in Italy, possibly in the city of Lucca, in about 1146 or earlier. It is divided into seven chapters, dealing with multiplication, division, addition, subtraction, fractions, proportions, and square roots. *Sefer ha-mispar* also presents and explains in its introductory chapter the decimal positional system. It is one of the first works to introduce the arithmetic of *al-Khwarizmi, including the decimal positional system, into Latin Europe, contemporaneously with a Latin version entitled *Algorismus*.

Ibn Ezra wrote explanatory canons to astronomical tables in four versions: two in Hebrew (Lucca, c. 1146; Narbonne c. 1148), which are entitled *Sefer ta'amei ha-luhot* (*Book of the Reasons behind Astronomical Tables*); and two in Latin (Pisa, c. 1146, and France, 1154), which are both entitled *Liber de rationibus tabularum*. Several manuscripts survive of one of the Latin versions, but only a few excerpts from the Hebrew versions are extant in Ibn Ezra's biblical exegesis as well as in the work of one his medieval super-commentators. Comparison reveals that the Hebrew and Latin versions were similar in certain details but quite different in other significant parts. Although Ibn Ezra knew Latin, it would be safer to assume that he wrote the versions in that language with the help of a disciple. The extant Latin version begins by delineating the astronomical and astrological features of each of the seven planets, and deals at length with the Sun and the Moon. It continues with a trigonometric chapter, and ends with specific astronomical problems, such as establishing the Moon's latitude, the latitude of cities, the seasonal hours, the twelve astrological houses or the first visibility of the lunar crescent. Ibn Ezra refers explicitly to Hipparchus, *Ptolemy, Dorotheus of Sidon, and Hermes; Hindu astronomical tables are referred to as *tabulas indorum*; he mentions the names of notable Arabic scientists such as al-Khwarizmi, *al-Battani, al-Sufi, *Ibn Sina, *Thabit ibn Qurra, al-Nayrizi, Ibn Yunus, Banu Sakir, *Masha'allah, and *Abu Ma'shar. There are also references to Andalusi scientists such as Ibn al-Muthanna, *Maslama of Madrid, *Ibn al-Saffar, and *Ibn al-Zarqalluh.

Ibn Ezra composed *Sefer keli ha-nehoshet* (*Book of the Instrument of Brass*) to describe the physical configuration of the astrolabe and impart information about its astronomical and astrological uses. The treatise was written in three different Hebrew versions (Northern Italy and Provence in the 1146–1148 period), as well as in a single Latin version, composed with the aid of a disciple. A common characteristic is that, although the astrolabe is known as an instrument mainly intended for astronomical use, an important portion of all four versions is devoted to typically astrological procedures.

Sefer ha-ehad (*Book on the Unit*), composed prior to 1148, is the first Hebrew work dealing with the attributes of numbers. It qualifies as an outstanding mathematical treatise precisely because it is concerned with pure mathematics, and unlike *Sefer ha-mispar* makes no pretence of serving as an auxiliary or practical tool for related subjects. Ibn Ezra divided *Sefer ha-'ehad* into nine short chapters, each of which deals with the characteristics of one of the nine numerals, explained by employing various elements belonging to arithmetical, geometrical, and combinatorial analysis, as well as astrology and theology.

2. The Jewish Calendar

Ibn Ezra wrote *Sefer ha-'ibbur* (*Book of Intercalation*), designed to describe and explain central aspects of the Jewish calendar, in two different versions (Verona, 1146; Narbonne, 1148). The second version is lost, and the first version, although ostensibly divided into three chapters, appears in the printed edition as well as in most of the manuscripts without the third chapter. Fortunately, a fragment of the third chapter has recently been found in the Vatican MS. Ebr. Urbinati 48. The first part provides, in a rhyming poem, four methods for calculating the beginning of the lunar months of the Jewish calendar. The second chapter discusses, inter alia, the mean conjunction of the Sun and Moon, the determination of the length of the lunar month, the controversy about the length of the solar year; the mean motion of the Moon and the visibility of the new crescent. The fragment of the third chapter deals with cords and arcs, and includes a discussion of the degrees of the numbers and of the decimal positional system, which is similar to that in *Sefer ha-mispar*.

Three *responsa* related to the Jewish calendar were composed by Ibn Ezra in Provence between 1148 and 1154 in answer to questions posed by a certain David Ben Joseph of Narbonne. After discussing in the first *responsum* the value and usefulness of a special calendrical table covering two hundred and forty-seven years and including thirteen cycles of nineteen years, Ibn Ezra presented in the second *responsum* the diverse opinions of Indian, Persian, Greek, and Islamic astronomers about the length of the solar year in order to explain why a gap of four weeks occurred in 1139 between the Jewish Passover and the Christian Easter. In the third *responsum* Ibn Ezra referred to a controversy dividing Jewish calendar scholars regarding the chronology of the world's creation. In this framework, Ibn Ezra unleashed an attack on an unnamed commentator, who, under closer scrutiny, turns out to be *Abraham Bar Hiyya.

Ibn Ezra wrote *Igeret ha-shabbat* (*The Epistle on the Sabbath*) in December 1158 in one of the cities of England. Ibn Ezra starts the epistle with an intriguing literary fiction: a messenger appears to him in a dream with a letter complaining that Ibn Ezra's students brought books containing a commentary on Genesis 1:5, in which they were exhorted to violate the Sabbath. A reader confining himself to the opening paragraphs would hardly have guessed that the epistle in its main parts is basically a scientific treatise about the Jewish calendar. In fact, the epistle has three chapters, each with a separate discussion about the beginning of the three chief periods

of cyclical time: the year, the month, and the day. At the end of the epistle, Ibn Ezra introduced a third, new commentary on Genesis 1:5, in which he retracted the opinion he had expounded in his previous two commentaries on the Pentateuch.

3. The Astrological Encyclopedia

Fourteen of Ibn Ezra's thirty treatises deal with the four main systems of Arabic astrology: nativities, elections, interrogations, and universal astrology. Although apparently separate, there are compelling reasons for regarding them as parts of a single encyclopedia. They are interrelated by an intricate net of cross- references, which refer the reader to relevant data in the other books, and most of them are products of a steady and concentrated effort carried out in the 1148–1149 period in a single location, the city of Béziers in Provence.

Abraham Ibn Ezra completed *Reshit hokhmah* (*Beginning of Wisdom*), his chief astrological work, in June 1148 as the first link in a continuous and concentrated effort that produced seven treatises covering the various branches of astrology. *Reshit hokhmah*, a textbook explaining the most basic tenets of the various branches of astrology, was divided by Ibn Ezra into ten chapters, dealing with three main subjects: (a) A general description of the fixed stars, the zodiac constellations and their astrological characteristics (chapters i, ii, and iii); (b) A general description of the astrological characteristics of the planets, and their interrelations (chapters iv, v, vi, and vii); and (c) A general discussion of miscellaneous astrological concepts, such as the lots, aspects, and some elements of general astrology (chapters viii, ix, and x). *Reshit hokhmah* was translated after Ibn Ezra's death into various European languages.

Immediately afterward Ibn Ezra composed *Sefer ha-te'amim* (*Book of Reasons*), in which he tried to expound the astrological reasons for the concepts mentioned in *Reshit Hokhmah*. As such, the first version of *Sefer ha-te'amim* closely follows the structure and organization of *Reshit hokhmah*, and explains the reasons for astrological concepts in precisely the order in which they appear in the latter. A second version of *Sefer ha-te'amim*, written at an unspecified place and time, is also extant. In this version, however, the division into ten chapters, as well as the sequence of the topics as adopted in *Reshit hokhmah*, completely disappear.

Ibn Ezra continued in the same year of 1148 with the composition of *Sefer ha-moladot* (*Book of Nativities*), a "nativity" being a horoscope cast for the date (and hour) of the subject's birth. Ibn Ezra makes numerous references to *Sefer ha-moladot* in his other writings, and it is thus clear that he regarded it as one of his most central astrological works. *Sefer ha-moladot* begins with a brilliant introduction intended to demonstrate, via eight examples, that, in the matter of astrological judgments, the universal overrides the particular. The central and major part of the treatise is divided into twelve chapters, each dealing with one of the twelve astrological houses and the techniques for interpreting their astrological characteristics. Ibn Ezra concluded the treatise with a discussion of the so-called *tequfat ha-shanim* (*revolutiones annorum* in Latin or *tahawil al-sinin* in Arabic), that is, the calculation of the years, or fraction of years, that have passed since the birth of an individual. A second version of *Sefer ha-moladot*, written c.1154 and entitled *Liber Abraham Iude de nativitatibus*, is extant in the Latin translation undertaken by Henry Bate, as well as other translations of Ibn Ezra's works into Latin and French, about one hundred years after Ibn Ezra's death.

Next, Ibn Ezra wrote two new treatises: *Sefer ha-mivharim* (*Book of Elections*) and *Sefer ha-she'elot* (*Book of Interrogations*). The first deals with an astrological system designed for choosing the most auspicious moment to perform a specific act, by the expedient of casting the horoscope and observing the place of the Moon in the astrological houses. The second treatise deals with an astrological system designed to reply to questions addressed to the astrologer and relating to common incidents of daily life, such as matters concerning someone who goes missing, discovering a thief or recovering a lost item. Both treatises were composed by Abraham Ibn Ezra in two different versions, the first in 1148, and the second at a later date that is very difficult to establish. Afterwards, Ibn Ezra composed *Sefer ha-me'orot* (*Book of Luminaries*), apparently in two versions of which only one is currently extant. This treatise is concerned with medical astrology, i.e., with the influence that the Moon exerts on human health.

The last component of the astrological encyclopedia is *Sefer ha-'olam* (*Book of the World*), which was composed, like the other parts, in two versions. This treatise is concerned with general astrology, that is, the branch of astrology dealing with the collective fate of humankind, by means of astrological forecasts as well as astrological analysis of past history. Both versions, although they plainly differ in several aspects, follow similar sources, notably Ptolemy's *Tetrabiblos* regarding eclipses, and Abu Ma'shar's *Kitab al-qiranat* (*De magnis conjunctionibus annorum revolutionibus ac eorum profectionibus*) regarding the three periodic conjunctions of Saturn and Jupiter (great: 960 years; middle: 240 years; and lesser conjunction: 20 years). Possibly in northern France, in the 1153–1156 period, Ibn Ezra composed *Mishpetei ha-mazzalot* (*Book of the Judgments of the Zodiacal Signs*), an astrological textbook introducing general tenets and topics. As such, it can be considered as a second version of *Reshit hokhmah*, although it was conceived as separate from the astrological encyclopedia. *Mishpetei ha-mazzalot* was organized as a series of discussions of various astrological subjects: the zodiacal constellations and their astrological characteristics; the astrological houses and the differences of opinion about their proper arrangement; the planets and their astrological characteristics; the astrological aspects; the astrological lots. Into this clearly astrological milieu Ibn Ezra embedded interesting astronomical observations, related mainly to the elongation of the planets in relation to the Sun.

4. Translations from Arabic into Hebrew

Although many translations of Arabic scientific treatises into Hebrew are ascribed to Ibn Ezra, only in one case may we safely assert that Ibn Ezra was actually the translator: one of the two extant Hebrew translations of Ibn al-Muthanna's commentary on the astronomical tables of al-Khwarizmi. Not only does Ibn Ezra identify himself in this translation, but he also applies an idiosyncratic strategy: he consistently uses some old biblical Hebrew words, which in his opinion express central scientific concepts, and obstinately avoids the use of cognate or loan words stemming from the Arabic language, particularly in cases where, in his view, original scientific Hebrew terms were available in the biblical text.

See also **Arithmetic; Cosmology; Encyclopedias; Translation movements; Translation norms and practice; Planetary tables**

Bibliography

Goldstein, B.R. Astronomy and Astrology in the Works of Abraham Ibn Ezra. *Arabic Sciences and Philosophy* (1996) 6: 9–21.

Langerman, Y.T. "Some Astrological Themes in the Thought of Abraham Ibn Ezra." In *Rabbi Abraham Ibn Ezra: Studies in the Writings of a Twelfth-Century Jewish Polymath*. Cambridge: Harvard University Center for Jewish Studies, 1993, pp. 28–85.

Millás Vallicrosa, José M. "El magisterio astronómico de Abraham Ibn Ezra en la Europa latina." In *Estudios sobre historia de la ciencia española*. Barcelona, 1949, pp. 289–347.

Sela, S. Abraham Ibn Ezra's Scientific Corpus—Basic Constituents and General Characterization. *Arabic Sciences and Philosophy* (2001) 10: 91–149.

———. Abraham Ibn Ezra's Special Strategy in the Creation of a Hebrew Scientific Terminology. *Micrologus, Nature, Sciences and Medieval Societies* (2001) 9: 65–87.

———. *Abraham Ibn Ezra and the Rise of Medieval Hebrew Science*. Leiden: E.J. Brill, 2003.

SHLOMO SELA

IBN GABIROL, SOLOMON BEN JUDAH (AVICEBRON)

Solomon ben Judah ibn Gabirol (Abu Ayyub Sulayman ibn Yahya ibn Gabirul) was born in Málaga c. 1020 and lived in Spain mostly in Saragossa until 1054/1058. His Hebrew poems (they number five hundred and twenty-eight in the latest edition), both religious and secular, brought him great fame during his lifetime although his constant quarrelling with the wealthy patrons on whom he depended was a cause of his difficult circumstances and of his wanderings. Ibn Gabirol boasted of having written twenty books but only two of those that are extant are certainly his, and both were written in Arabic. The first is metaphysical and lacks specifically Jewish content and terminology; the original text of the *Mekhor Hayyim* (*Source of Life*), a philosophical dialogue, is no longer extant but some short passages and a book of systematic extracts have been translated to Hebrew; however they had few echoes in later Jewish philosophy. On the contrary, the mid-twelfth Latin translation *Fons vitae* had a profound influence on some Christian thinkers, especially on thirteenth-century Fransciscans. *Thomas Aquinas mentions the book or its author almost forty times. In the Christian West, Avicebron—or Avencebrol or Avemcebron—was considered as a Muslim or a Christian until 1846, when S. Munk identified the Hebrew extracts with the *Fons vitae*.

In Ibn Gabirol's neoplatonic philosophy, theoretical knowledge is the purpose of human existence; it starts from the knowledge of matter and form in this world, progresses with the science of purer and purer matters and forms, and culminates in knowledge of the divine Will, considered as separate from matter and form and thus entirely pure and divine. The highest principle is the First Essence—God—and is above reach; next is the divine Will, then universal substance and form, then the simple substances—intellect, soul, and nature—and finally the material world. The entire universe, spiritual as well as material, is composed of matter and form only: both are one and multiple, similar and different; they are found at every level of the hierarchy of beings. Beings are first diversified by their forms, material and spiritual, while matter is one and universal; however, elsewhere, Ibn Gabirol writes that the cause of the diversity of beings is not form, for form is one and purely spiritual, but matter which can be perfect and fine, or coarse and heavy. To understand how universal matter and form are produced by the Will, that they are at the same time different beings, subsisting by themselves, having only one essence and nonetheless cannot subsist without each other, even for a single moment, one must examine the composite spiritual beings, which are called simple; for a being is called simple in relation to what is inferior to it, and composite in relation to what is superior. Thus the entirety of existing beings is organized along a line that starts with universal matter and form. The further one departs from this source, the more composite a being is in relation to that which precedes it and simple in relation to that which follows it; but however far one may be from the first source, the inferior is in a way the image of the superior, as man himself is an image of the whole world. When the human soul has understood the fabric of the universe and how it flows from the Will, it has attached itself to the Will and has reached the Source of Life, deliverance from death and ultimate felicity.

Ibn Gabirol's second book is ethical: the *Kitab Islah al-Akhlaq* (*The Improvement of Moral Qualities*) was translated into Hebrew in 1167 as *Sefer Tikkun midot ha-nefesh* and discusses the parallel between the universe (the macrocosm) and man (the microcosm). The description of the virtues and vices which is tied to the five senses and linked to the four material elements and the four corporeal humors (air/blood, water/phlegm, earth/black gall, fire/yellow bile). Thus, for example, sight is related to pride, humility, modesty, and impudence. A diagram tabulates these twenty ethical traits which are to be improved by constant self-discipline starting from youth, helped by Scripture's admonitions and sentences from the Sages. This arithmetical ethics applies to the "animal" soul and is illustrated by many biblical verses. Other allegorical explanations from the Bible are quoted in the much-studied biblical commentary by *Abraham ibn Ezra (1089–1164) making Ibn Gabirol the first well-known philosopher in the West to use philosophical commentary for revealed text.

Ibn Gabirol's Hebrew poems are not devoid of scientific and philosophical content, especially the long one called *Keter Malkhut* (*The Royal Crown*), which is a kind of religious rendering of the *Source of Life*. It weaves a Ptolemaic Muslim cosmology with an emotional longing of the human soul to go back to its original source and a profound feeling of humans' frailty and God's greatness. The first strophes praise God's transcendence and the mystery of his existence. In the following ones, the whole cosmos is described, beginning as does the human soul from the sublunary world. Each strophe deals with one of the spheres or its motion: Earth and its four elements; the Moon, its positions and eclipses; Mercury, Venus, the Sun and its annual movements; the relative positions of the Sun and the Moon, Mars, Jupiter, Saturn; the fixed stars of the Zodiac; the twelve zodiacal mansions of the planets; the ninth sphere; the tenth sphere of the intelligence, its being the source of the souls and of the angels; and, beyond the outer sphere, the Throne of Glory with, beneath it, the place for the souls of the departed righteous, the providential sources of nature, and finally the human soul which originated from the divine Glory but having been made the guardian of a body has to begin its return back to the heavens. More strophes paint this journey and the confessions of sin, petitions, and thanksgivings. This last part of the poem explains why it is part of the liturgy for the Day of Atonement in many Sephardic communities and is printed in a number of prayers books.

See also **Elements and qualities**

Bibliography

Avencebrolis (Ibn Gebirol). *Fons vitae ex arabico in latinum translatus ab Iohanne Hispano et Dominico Gundissalino* ed. Clemens Baeumker, Münster, 1892, 1895.

Ibn Gabirol, Solomon. *Selected Religious Poems*, ed. by Israel Davidson, transl. into English verse by Israel Zangwill. New York: Arno Press, 1973.

Loewe, Raphael. *Ibn Gabirol* (with a bilingual ed. of *The Royal Crown*). New York: Grove Weidenfeld, 1990.

Munk, Salomon. *Extraits de la Source de Vie de Salomon Ibn-Gebirol traduits de l'arabe en hébreu par Schem-Tob fils de Joseph ibn Falaquéra in Mélanges de philosophie juive et arabe.* Paris: Vrin 1857–1859; reprint ed., 2003.

Wise, Stephen S. *The Improvement of The Moral Qualities; an ethical treatise of the eleventh century by Solomon ibn Gabirol, printed from an unique Arabic manuscript, together with a translation, and an essay on the place of Gabirol in the history of the development of Jewish ethics.* New York: Columbia University Press, 1902.

COLETTE SIRAT

IBN MAJID, AHMAD

Ahmad Ibn Majid was an Arab cosmographer and navigator of the fifteenth century. He was born in the central highlands of Arabia, the son and grandson of navigators, around 1430 and died sometime after 1500. He wrote more than forty works, most of them on navigation and mainly written in verse. Learned in navigational astronomy, he was familiar with *Ptolemy's *Almagest*; the *zijat* (astronomical tables) of *al-Tusi and *al-Battani, and the geographies of Yaqut and Ibn Hawqal, among others: "We have corrected their works where they were in error…," he wrote, "and pointed out the errors in their works which have caused the destruction of many ships."

In his major navigational treatise, *Kitab al-Fawa'id* (*Book of Lessons on the Foundations of the Sea and Navigation*), Ibn Majid justifies navigation by saying that without it you cannot establish the *qibla*, the canonical direction of Mecca required for Muslim prayer. The book contains detailed sailing instructions for the Indian Ocean, including Ceylon, the Bay of Bengal, and the Siamese coast, together with various islands of the East Indies, such as Sumatra and Java, plus Madagascar and Zanzibar off the east coast of Africa. His sailing directions for the Red Sea were novel and definitive in Arab seamanship.

In the book, Ibn Majid describes three kinds of routes: (1) *dirat al-mul* (mainland routes), always in sight of land; (2) *dirat al-matlaq* (set courses), which rely on fixed bearings; and (3) *dirat al-iqtida'* (conclusive courses), where the ship sets out from one known place and ends in another.

The practical principles of navigation involve twelve rubrics that Ibn Majid enumerates: (1) the lunar mansions; (2) rhumbs of the compass; (3) routes; (4) east-west distances between points at the same attitude on two opposite coasts); (5) variation of the altitude of the Pole Star; (6) measurements for latitude by observing stellar altitude (always taken at night; Arab navigators did not shoot the Sun); (7) visible signs (water color, tides); (8) revolutions of the Sun and the Moon; (9) winds; (10) seasons; (11) instruments carried on shipboard; and (12) captain-crew reactions. He describes sea snakes, reefs, kinds of birds, and sea coasts, that is, the information a captain would use for dead reckoning. However, he also describes in some detail the use of the magnetic compass.

The earliest mention of the compass in Arabic dates from 1282 and describes a floating needle, which is taken as indicative of Chinese origin. Usually, however, the dry form of magnetization—the lodestone—was used. First, the compass box has to be placed correctly, according to Ibn Majid, or it is impossible to sail a true course. Then the needle has to be magnetized: "As for our recounting navigational science, on the passing of the lodestone over the compass box, we have made a great rule about this which has never been set down in a book: the Pole Star can only be in opposition to its south point." Magnetic variation was noticed but thought to be a defect in the process of magnetizing the needle. In practice, the compass was used to navigate by dividing the horizon or the ship itself (that is, the deck or the gunwales) into thirty-two divisions for taking sights which corresponded to rhumbs on the compass card (*bayt al-ibra*, house of the needle). The course (*majra*) was charted along rhumb lines. If the destination did not lie along the rhumb, the captain could sail due east or west until he reached a new bearing. Ibn Majid describes a method of sailing between two rhumbs. If the Pole Star was not visible, the navigator used the *qiyas* (analogy) method: he took the altitude of another star at a known time and deduced from this the position of the Pole Star, or of Ursa Minor (Arabic, *Farqadan*) in southern latitudes. In the Indian Ocean shooting the Pole Star was the equivalent of the Mediterranean and Atlantic method of taking the noon altitude of the Sun. In tropical latitudes, the Sun's altitude at noon is always high and the Pole Star close to horizon (the reverse of the Mediterranean).

Ibn Majid had followed the Portuguese attempts to reach the Indian Ocean via the Cape of Good Hope where, he thought, there was a channel (Arabic, *madkhal*) connecting the Atlantic and Indian oceans. He believed Africa to be much shorter than it really it is and the distance around the Cape to the Magrib accordingly not very far. The terra incognita believed to lie to the south was thought barren and unappealing commercially, which made the Arabs uninterested in exploring there. Ibn Majid was known in Europe only as the navigator who guided Vasco da Gama from east Africa to the western coast of India in 1495. He appears in Portuguese sources as Malemo Canaqua (= *mu'alim kanaka* = ship captain of celestial navigation). The fifteenth-century historian Qutb al-Din al-Nahrwali mentions ibn Majid by name in the same context and calls Da Gama *al-amilandi* (admiral) of the Franks.

The work of Ibn Majid had considerable influence on subsequent Islamic navigation. In his book *'Umdat al-Mahriyya fi dabt al-'ilm al-bahriya* (*Mahri's Principles of Accuracy in Navigational Science*), Sulaiman al-Mahri, a South Arabian navigator who may possibly have been trained by Ibn Majid, produced in prose what can be seen as a simplification of Ibn Majid's often complex theorization. Then the Turkish captain and navigator, Sidi 'Ali Re'is (c. 1500–1562, also known as Katibi or Çelebi) continued the tradition is his *Kitab al-muhit* (*Book of the Ocean*), which was based on the writings of ibn Majid and al-Mahri.

See also Navigation

Bibliography

Tibbetts, Gerald R. *Arab Navigation in the Indian Ocean before the Coming of the Portuguese being a translation of the Kitab al-Fawa'id fi usul al-bahr wa'l-qawa'id of Ahmad b. Majid al-Najdi*. London: Royal Asiatic Society/Luzac, 1971.

———. *A Study of the Arabic Texts Containing Material on South-East Asia*. Leiden: E.J. Brill, 1979.

THOMAS F. GLICK

IBN RUSHD

Abu'l-Walid Muhammad ibn Ahmad ibn Muhammad ibn Rushd al-Hafid, known as Averroes in the European tradition, was born in Córdoba, al-Andalus, in 1125, and died in Marrakech (Morocco) in 1198. He is the most important philosopher of al-Andalus, the medieval commentator on Aristotle par excellence, a physician of note, and also knowledgeable in astronomy, biology, and other sciences.

Life, Education, and Intellectual Career

Raised in the bosom of an outstanding family of Muslim religious scholars and jurists, Ibn Rushd reached high positions within the legal administration of the Almohads, the North African dynasty that ruled al-Andalus and North Africa from the middle of the twelfth century until of the beginning of the thirteenth in al-Andalus, and until the end of the second third of this century in their last North African dominions. At the same time, he undertook another career focused on the study of philosophy and other sciences of Greek tradition, also under the patronage of the Almohads. During his youth in Córdoba he studied medicine with Ibn Jurrayul. His studies of astronomy with a certain Abu Ishaq ibn Wadi' might also date from this period. We are informed that in Seville he became the disciple of Abu Ja'far ibn Harun al-Tarjalli, a court physician from whom he learned philosophy and mathematical sciences. He also met in Seville the most influential physician of his time, *Ibn Zuhr, with whom he had a fruitful relationship that probably contributed to his medical training. The physician and philosopher Ibn Tufayl might also have been a relevant influence in those years. As early as 1153, he was in the service of the Almohads. The caliphs Abu Ya'qub Yusuf (1163–1184) and al-Mansur (1184–1199) bestowed their favor on him and named him to important posts such as judge in Seville and Córdoba, chief judge of Córdoba, and chief physician. Political and religious reasons underlie this, since the Almohads professed a particular religious doctrine that had a rationalistic side to which Ibn Rushd and other philosophers contributed as theologians. In particular Abu Ya'qub Yusuf, a learned sovereign interested in philosophy, astronomy and medicine, fueled philosophic and scientific activity in the court. The sources claim that it was at his request—conveyed through Ibn Tufayl, who had introduced Ibn Rushd to the caliph around 1169 or earlier—that Ibn Rushd undertook his full commentary on Aristotle. Al-Mansur changed his mind, however, due to political reasons and Ibn Rushd, together with other philosophers and scientists, fell into disgrace for a short period of time. Philosophy was publicly condemned and Ibn Rushd banished to Lucena, although he was later rehabilitated.

Philosopher and Scientist

Ibn Rushd's scientific contribution is strongly linked to his philosophical thought, insofar as the main work of his life, the profound study of Aristotle's works, provided him with an epistemological framework in which he tried to harmonize other sciences. He followed in this the path opened some decades before by *Ibn Bajja, who influenced his early writings.

Astronomy

Ibn Rushd was acquainted with the fundamentals of astronomy and he himself reports some personal observations, but refused to become an astronomer (he often complained about the long time celestial observations take). However, in his first period, characterized by the influence of *Ibn Bajja's doctrines in several fields, he wrote his *Mukhtasar al-Majisti* (summary of the *Almagest*), preserved in a Hebrew translation as yet unpublished. It consists of a critical account in the light of the achievements of some antecedent mathematical astronomers, which emended some of Ptolemy's models. The sources he considers are the following: *Islah al-Majiti* (corrections to the *Almagest*) by the Andalusi astronomer Jabir ibn Aflah (flourished in the first half of the twelfth century); the treatises by the Andalusi astronomer *Ibn al-Zarqalluh (d. 1100) on the motion of the fixed stars and on the sun; the *Kitab fi Hay'at al-'Alam* (*Book on the Configuration of the World*) and *Shukuk 'ala Batlamys* (*Doubts about Ptolemy*) by Egyptian natural philosopher *Ibn al-Haytham (born in Basra, 965, died in Cairo, 1039, although recently his authorship of *Hay'at al-'Alam* has been called into question). Most of the alternatives and criticisms to Ptolemy propounded in these treatises are accepted (e.g., Ibn al-Haytham's physical configuration of the heavenly spheres, Ibn al-Zarqalluh's alternative models for the sun which include his discovery of the motion of the solar apogee, etc.), while he rejected others (e.g., the order of planets given by Jabir). In general, he seems to agree with Ptolemy's paradigm, even if he poses some methodological objections perhaps under the influence of Ibn Bajja (e.g., the rejection of the epicycle) and claims to redefine the whole system. The short commentaries (*jawami'*) to Aristotle's works written about the same epoch, reflect the hesitant opinions expressed in the *Mukhtasar al-Majisti*, as well the authors mentioned in this treatise. This can be seen in his commentary on *Metaphysics* XII.8, where Aristotle describes planetary motions: Ibn Rushd's number of spheres seems to correspond to the numbers given in Ibn al-Haytham's *Hay'at al-'alam*. Lacking consistent alternatives, Ptolemy's paradigm is provisionally accepted, except in specific cases such as the existence of a ninth sphere (cause of the diurnal motion of the stars), which contradicts Aristotelian tenets. To argue this, he does not object in astronomical terms but on the basis of the metaphor of the "universal animal" found in Ptolemy's *Planetary Hypothesis* and also echoed in Ibn Tufayl's *Risalat Hayy Ibn Yaqzan*, that symbolizes the existence of planetary motions in opposite directions, which is one of the main problems to be solved by an author wishing a profound reform of Ptolemy, as we will see. As he proceeds in his Aristotelian commentaries, his opinions evolved towards a stricter Aristotelianism. In the

Middle and, particularly, the Long commentaries, appear the opinions linking him to the so-called "Andalusi revolt against Ptolemy." The very bases of that movement were the rejection of eccentrics and epicycles insofar as they contradict the necessity of circular and uniform motions around the Earth—i.e., the center of the universe—for the planets. It is worth noting that, apart from a certain influence of Ibn Bajja, Ibn Tufayl might have directly inspired Ibn Rushd inasmuch as, according to *al-Bitruji, Ibn Tufayl created a cosmology that ignored these geometrical devices, but did not explain it to anyone. The most important texts by Ibn Rushd on this question can be found in his commentary to *Metaphysics* XII.8, in which Aristotle refers to planetary motion according to the models of Eudoxus and Calippus that Ibn Rushd ignored. In order to find alternatives to Ptolemy, Ibn Rushd, aware of the necessity of long-term astronomical observations that exceeded his capacity, restricts himself to positing the existence of a spiral or helicoidal movement (*lawlabi*) that accounts for both daily motion and motion in longitude. This intuitive idea, based on the observation of the Sun, has some precedents in Plato and Theo of Alexandria, but in Ibn Rushd it might have sprung from a misreading of Aristotle when dealing with the unrolling spheres of the system of Eudoxus and Calippus. Ibn Rushd's interpretation of the *lawlabi* motion is related, however, to the Platonic vision of the problem: the fixed stars, for example, are affected by the daily motion (360° in 24 hours from East to West), but these stars have also a slow motion on the plane of the ecliptic and from West to East, which might be interpreted as the result of trepidation, a theory defended by Ibn al-Zarqalluh and other Andalusi astronomers of the eleventh century. The combination of these two motions gives as a result a *lawlab* (spiral). The suggestion of this motion links Ibn Rushd's theories with the geometrical models created by al-Bitruji (flourished in the second half of the twelfth century), the Andalusi astronomer that met the requirements of both Ibn Tufayl and Ibn Rushd and probably belonged to their intellectual circle. Al-Bitruji, as recent research has shown, reconstructed the fundamentals of Eudoxian astronomy (e.g., the hippopede) on the basis of Ibn al-Zarqalluh's models.

Medicine

A significant part of Ibn Rushd's medical works consists of commentaries (eight treatises by Galen and *Ibn Sina's didactic poem on medicine entitled *Urjuza fi'l-tibb*). In his Galenic commentaries (actually abridged paraphrases with notes), Ibn Rushd treats Galen in much the same way as he treated Ptolemy, explaining and correcting here and there. Aristotelian natural philosophy and biology, as well as methodological correction, underlie most of his additions, although Galen's opinions seem to be more authoritative for him than those of Ptolemy, and the Hippocratic-Galenic medical paradigm is never called into question. Sometimes Galen's opinion is corrected to conform with Aristotle, but we can see also attempts at harmonization such as in the case of breathing, which is voluntary according to Aristotle while involuntary in Galen: Ibn Rushd, referring to his own experience, admits some influence of conscious will.

His original work can be divided into a set of monographic treatises of a practical bias that tackle a wide range of subjects (theriac, poison, preservation of health, fevers, etc.), and an important manual, *Kitab al-Kulliyyat fi'l-Tibb* (*Book of Generalities about Medicine*). This latter treatise, known in Latin translation as the *Colliget*, brought the author wide renown in Latin medical circles. Ibn Rushd wrote it following a request from the caliph in which Ibn Tufayl might have played some role, as in the case of the Aristotelian commentaries. A first version of the book, which apparently is the Arabic text that has come down to us, was possibly written between 1162 and 1169. A revision that might be dated around 1194 seems to be the basis for the Latin translation. The general purpose of the book consists of presenting the theoretical bases of medicine that a physician should know. Consequently, the book had to be complemented with a practical treatise that Ibn Rushd ought to have written but never did. Aware of the difficulty of such a treatise, but also of its necessity, Ibn Rushd seems to have relied on a therapeutic manual by the most important physician of his time, Abu Marwan ibn Zuhr, the *Kitab al-Taysir fi'l-Mudawat wa'l-Tadbir* (*Practical Manual of Treatments and Diets*). This treatise had also been written under royal command, but the palace had rejected it because of its difficulty. The quotations from Ibn Zuhr found in the *Kulliyyat* bear witness to the deep influence of this pragmatic approach to medicine. Taken together, the *Kulliyyat* and the *Taysir* may be considered the Andalusi counterpart to Ibn Sina's *Canon*, the most influential medical manual of Islamic science. Whatever the case, the purpose of Ibn Rushd's *Kulliyyat* agrees with that enunciated in the first book of Ibn Sina's *Canon*, although the two treatises differ. Ibn Rushd restructures medicine according to an Aristotelian pattern and, in this regard, some influence of Ibn Bajja's medical writings seems to have operated, although its extent has not been studied yet. Ibn Rushd, like Ibn Bajja, starts with a conception of medicine as a practical science that can be divided into three parts: the study of a part devoted to the knowledge of the objects (i.e., bodily organs and members), another to the knowledge of aims (preservation of health) and a third to the means that lead to the aims (healing). This division is then inserted into the framework of Aristotle's theory of causes (material, formal, efficient, and final). After this, medical matters are developed in seven books that correspond to the above mentioned divisions: book I, on anatomy, material cause; book II, on physiology, and book III, on pathology, formal cause; book IV, on symptoms, book V, on pharmacology and diet, efficient cause; book VI on hygiene and book VII on therapy, final cause. In his expositions Ibn Rushd appeals fairly frequently to his experience and personal observation of the facts described. The treatment of anatomy in *Kulliyyat* has been considered one of Ibn Rushd's most original contributions, since he sets aside the classical head-to-toe order and shifts the Galenic description of a living body to the study of a passive body, just as if he was examining a corpse. His reasons, however, have nothing to do with dissection, as has been suggested as a result of his appeals to experience, but, once again, are due to his *Aristotelianism. Ibn Rushd considers here the opposition between substance, the body, and accident, the movement of human body. Consequently, we see for the first time the study of anatomy separated from that of physiology. Apart from a general exposition, the anatomical descriptions are not original, because he mostly relies on antecedent manuals such as al-Razi's *Hawi*. Ibn Rushd, however, is able to correct on occasion some mistakes of his sources by accurate reasoning or observation. For example, with regard to the muscles, he anticipates later scientific trends in that his approach can be portrayed as an attempt to separate the organ from its function, thus escaping from the traditional teleology of Galen. The exposition of physiology also follows an Aristotelian pattern according to *Physics* I, 184a: scientific knowledge of a thing means the knowledge of its principles (the four elements as a substrate), causes (the four causes linked with the functions of the organs), and elements (the doctrine of matter and form applied to the relationship between organs). In developing these issues, Aristotle's influence can also be noted, as in the case of digestion, in which the heart plays a more important part than does the liver, against Galen's assumptions. The book on pharmacology and diet contains some salient features that spring from his combination of observation and experience with deductive science. One of them is the interesting material he gives on diet in al-Andalus; another is its correction to *al-Kindi's law for determining the degree of a compound drug, which was very controversial among the medieval European physicians owing to a faulty reading. In this context, it should be noted that, although the Latin translation of his work has been the source of some misunderstandings (such as the question of whether he discovered retinal sensitivity or not—he did not), the truth is that it contributed to the development of medicine. For instance, Ibn Rushd's opinions on fevers stimulated constructive debate and medieval physicians could find in the *Colliget* an emphasis on medical experience that accounted for its high standing in the field of scholarly medicine.

Sciences of Natural World: Physics and Zoology

Ibn Rushd wrote several commentaries on the Aristotelian treatises on natural philosophy and science. In these works he was plainly under the influence of previous authors of the Greek tradition (e.g., Alexander of Aphrodisias, Themistius, and Philoponus) and the Arabic (al-Farabi) and Andalusi (Ibn Bajja) traditions. The influence of the last named is remarkable in Ibn Rushd's early commentaries, particularly in the field of dynamics. Notwithstanding this, Ibn Rushd tended to avoid great innovations in the Aristotelian tenets (e.g., his rejection of motion in a void, accepted by Ibn Bajja on the grounds of Philoponus' thought).

He also wrote a commentary on Aristotle's zoological works, which has come down to us only in Latin and Hebrew translations. Unfortunately, this commentary has no critical edition and is virtually unstudied. This notwithstanding, it is worth noting that his profound reading of original texts led him to study concrete aspects in the light of the whole Aristotelian corpus, thus positing some new solutions such as the greater importance accorded to celestial bodies in the generation of beings. In this as in many other instances, Ibn Rushd only felt that he was uncovering the true sense of Aristotle's work.

See also **Astronomy, Islamic; Medicine, theoretical; Zoology**

Bibliography

Primary Sources

Averrois Commentaria Magna in Aristotelem. De Celo et Mundo. F. J. Carmody, ed. 2 vols. Leuven: Peeters, 2003.

García Sánchez, E. Un opúsculo inédito de Averroes sobre higiene individual: Fi hifz al-sihha (ms. árabe 884 de El Escorial). *Dynamis* (1984) 4: 247–263.

Kitab al-Kulliyyat fi'l-Tibb. Edited by J. M. Fórneas Besteiro and C. Álvarez de Morales. 2 vols. Madrid: Consejo Superior de Investigaciones Científicas, 1987.

Kitab al-Sama' al-Tabi'i. Ed. Puig, J. Madrid: Instituto Hispano-Arabe de Cultura-Consejo Superior de Investigaciones Científicas, 1983.

Rasa'il Ibn Rushd al-Tibbiyya. Edited by G. Anawati and S. Zayid. Cairo: Al-Hay'a al-Misriyya al-'Ammah li'l-Kitab, 1987.

Sharh al-Sama' wa'l-'Alam. Facsimile ed. with introduction by G. Endress. Frankfurt: Institut für Geschichte des Arabische Islamischen Wissenschaften, 1994.

Secondary Sources

Anawati, Georges C. Le traité d'Averroès sur la thériaque et ses antécédents grecs et arabes. *Quaderni di studi arabi* (1987–1988) 5–6: 26–48.

Carmody, F.J. The Planetary Theory of Ibn Rushd. *Osiris* (1952) 10: 556–586.

Cruz Hernández, M. *Abu'l-Walid Ibn Rushd (Averroes). Vida, obra, pensamiento e influencia.* Córdoba: Caja Sur, 1997.

El Otmani, S. and D. Moussaoui. Système nerveux et neuropsychiatrie chez Ibn Rochd (Averroes) et Ibn Zohr (Avenzoar). *Histoire des sciences médicales* (1992) 26: 281–286.

Endress, G. Averroes' *De Caelo.* Ibn Rushd's Cosmology in his Commentaries on Aristotle's *On the Heavens. Arabic Sciences and Philosophy* (1995) 5: 9–49.

———. "Mathematics and Philosophy in Early Islam." In *The Enterprise of Science. New Perspectives.* Edited by J.P. Hogendijk and A.I. Sabra. Cambridge: MIT Press, 2003.

Forcada, M. "La ciencia en Averroes." In *Averroes y los averroísmos. Actas del III Congreso Nacional de Filosofía Medieval.* Edited by J. Ayala. Saragossa: Sociedad de Filosofía Medieval, 1999.

Freudenthal, G. The Medieval Astrologization of Aristotle's Biology: Averroes on the Role of the Celestial Bodies in the Generation of Animate Beings. *Arabic Sciences and Philosophy* (2002) 12: 111–127.

Gätje, H. Probleme der Colliget-Forschung. *Zeitschrift der Deutschen Morgenländischen Gesellschaft* (1980) 130: 278–303.

———. Zur Lehre von den Temperamenten bei Averroes. *Zeitschrift der Deutschen Morgenländischen Gesellschaft* (1982) 132: 243–268.

———. Die Vorworte zum Colliget des Averroes. *Zeitschrift der Deutschen Morgenländischen Gesellschaft* (1986) 136: 402–427.

Hastenteufel, Hermann and Wirmer, David. "Averroes-Database." http://uni-koeln.de/phil-fak/thomasinst/averroes

Hugonnard-Roche, H. L'Épitomé du De Caelo d'Aristote par Averroès: questions de méthode et de doctrine. *Archives d'Histoire Doctrinale et Littéraire de Moyen Age* (1985) 52: 7–73.

Jacquart, D. and Micheau, F. *La médecine arabe et l'occident médiéval*. París: Maisonneuve & Larose, 1990.

Lay, Juliane. L'Abregé de l'Almageste: un inédit d'Averroès en version hebraïque. *Arabic Sciences and Philosophy* (1996) 6: 23–61.

Leaman, O. *Averroes and His Philosophy*. Oxford: Clarendon Press, 1988 (2nd ed., Richmond: Curzon, 1997).

Lettinck, P. *Aristotle's Physics and its Reception in the Arabic World with an Edition of the Unpublished parts of Ibn Bajja's Commentary on the Physics*. Leiden: E.J. Brill, 1994.

———. *Aristotle's Meteorology and its Reception in the Arab World*. Leiden: E.J. Brill, 1999.

Lindberg, D.C. Did Averroes Discover Retinal Sensitivity? *Bulletin of the History of Medicine* (1975) 49: 273–278. Reprinted in Lindberg, *Studies in the History of Medieval Optics*. Aldershot: Ashgate, 1983.

Mazliak, P. *Avicenne et Averroès: Médecine et biologie dans la civilisation de l'Islam*. Paris: Vuivert, 2004.

Samsó, Julio. *Las Ciencias de los Antiguos en al-Andalus*. Madrid: Mapfre, 1992.

Torre, E. *Averroes y la Ciencia Médica. La Doctrina Anatomofuncional del Colliget*. Madrid: Ediciones del Centro, 1974.

MIQUEL FORCADA

IBN SINA

Abu 'Ali al-Husayn ibn 'Abd Allah ibn Sina—often known in the West as Avicenna, following a common style of Latinizing Arab names—was the greatest philosopher, scientist, and writer on medicine of the Middle Ages. An ethnic Persian, he was born in Kharmaithen, near Bukhara, in 980 C.E. He was a precocious genius, and acquired much of his early learning from his father, a local government official. By the age of ten the boy had learned the Qur'an by heart, knew the grammar of Arabic and was familiar with some of its poetry. He soon became interested in medicine, and while still in his teens he successfully treated the Samanid ruler Nuh ibn Mansur for an unspecified illness. The sultan in gratitude granted Ibn Sina access to the extensive royal library, where the youth steeped himself in works on law, then medicine, and finally metaphysics. By the millennium Ibn Sina had engaged in correspondence with *al-Biruni: the great scholar sent the young man a list of questions, ten on Aristotle's *De Caelo*, and a further eight on discursive matters; Ibn Sina answered them all. At the age of twenty Ibn Sina had acquired a wide reputation as a polymath, and was much in demand as a physician and an administrator.

Meanwhile, personal and public events conspired to alter the course of Ibn Sina's life. His father died, and the Samanid dynasty was overthrown by Turkish forces under the command of Nuh ibn Mansur's son, Mahmud. Bereaved, disempowered, and denied accustomed access to scholarly work, Ibn Sina left Bukhara, moving first to Rayy and then to Qazvin: he earned his living the while as a medical practitioner. Later he settled in Hamadan, where he first became physician at the court of the Buyid prince Shams al-Dawlah and was subsequently twice appointed vizier. On the ruler's death in 1022, Ibn Sina was forced to flee to the court of Ala' ad-Dawlah in Esfahan. There he spent the next fourteen years, the most tranquil and productive period of his life. He died in Hamadan in 1037.

Writings

Ibn Sina wrote approximately four hundred fifty works, about half of which are currently extant. Of the latter, one hundred fifty are on philosophy, and forty on medicine. The two most influential were the *Kitab al-Shifa* (*The Book of Healing*) and *al-Qanun fi'l-tibb* (*The Canon of Medicine*). The *Kitab* was an astoundingly ambitious attempt to provide a comprehensive account of all human knowledge. Often said to be the longest book ever written by a single author, it was both theoretical and practical, setting out not only to describe and to elucidate, but also to categorize. It is divided into four main parts, on logic, physics, mathematics, and metaphysics. Within those broad categories the *Kitab* also deals with numerous other subjects: the only significant omissions are detailed examinations of ethics and politics. Logic encompasses rhetoric and poetics; physics includes psychology, plants, and animals. Mathematics is divided into four branches: one is music, and the other three—arithmetic, astronomy, and geometry—are subdivided into further categories. Arithmetic contains algebra and Indian addition and subtraction; astronomy features astronomical tables, geographical tables, and the *calendar; geometry is subdivided into geodesy, statics, kinematics, hydrostatics, and optics. From astronomical observations made at Hamadan and Esfahan Ibn Sina formulated several theories, perhaps the most important of which was that Venus is closer to the Earth than the Sun.

The *Kitab al-Shifa* is strongly influenced by the ancient Greeks. The parts of the work that treat logic reveal an author who is steeped in Aristotle, but not awed by him. In his *Autobiography*, Ibn Sina admitted or claimed that he had not understood Aristotle's *Metaphysics* before reading the commentary on it by *al-Farabi. However that may be, the *Kitab* demonstrates a mastery of the subject, and one of Ibn Sina's aims in the work is to reconcile Hellenic Neoplatonism with the rigors of Islam.

Illustration from Michael Maier's 1617 *Symbola Aureae Mensae* showing Avicenna practicing alchemy. The symbolism represents the volatization of the fixed, and the fixation of the volatile. (Topham/Charles Walker)

Similarly, Ibn Sina's section on mathematics features a *summa* of *Euclid's *Elements* and a digest of *Ptolemy's *Almagest*. The former includes, inter alia, lines, angles, planes, parallels, triangles, the use of rulers and compasses, the areas of triangles and parallelograms, the properties of circles, and the volumes of polyhedra and spheres. This material is presented axiomatically rather than analytically, but Ibn Sina does attempt a proof of Euclid's fifth postualte in another of his works.

Ibn Sina's *Canon* is based on the work of *Galen, and preserves the Greek author's division of all matter into four elements (air, water, fire, and earth) and four humors (blood, black bile, yellow bile, and phlegm). Yet the *Canon* goes beyond anything in *On the Art of Healing*: it includes all the medical and pharmacological knowledge of the time, and deals with general principles of medicine, simple drugs, diseases of specific parts of the body, diseases spreading over large areas of the body (such as fevers), and medicines. The work's *materia medica* considers some seven hundred sixty drugs, with comments on their application and effectiveness. The *Canon* also records the work of Roman physicians, and derives material from other Arabic books on the subject; it is furthermore an account of the author's own experience as a practicing physician, although these parts of the work are written from memory, since Ibn Sina lost his clinical notes during his travels.

The *Canon* distinguishes mediastinitis from pleurisy and recognizes the contagious nature of phthisis (tuberculosis); it attests the spread of disease by water and soil; it gives a scientific diagnosis of ankylostomiasis and attributes the condition to an intestinal worm. Ibn Sina stresses the importance of dietetics, the influence of climate and environment on health, and the benefits of anesthetic in surgery. Ibn Sina advised surgeons to treat cancer in its earliest stages, ensuring the removal of all the diseased tissue, and counsels experimentation on animals before humans.

Moreover, the *Canon* is distinguished by the arrangement of its material, and it was the clarity of Ibn Sina's work as much as its comprehensiveness that made it influential throughout the Middle Ages, not only in the Muslim world but also in the West. Although there was no school of Avicenna, as there was of Averroes (*Ibn Rushd), it may reasonably be asserted that Ibn Sina had a greater impact on medieval thought than any other author.

Influence

Ibn Sina was the leader and the inspiration of Muslim Aristotelians, but his thought was not circumscribed by Hellenism, and in his later years he attempted to formulate an original "Oriental philosophy" (*al-hikmat al-mashriqiyah*). His principal aim was to alter perception of *kalam*—which during his lifetime was regarded as an adjunct of politics—so that it would be treated as a branch of metaphysics, a demonstrative science. Although most of his works on this subject are currently lost, the available material reveals an incipient mystical theosophy that profoundly influenced the subsequent development of Islamic philosophy, particularly in Persia.

Ibn Sina's two main works reached the West during the twelfth century. Archbishop John of *Toledo became aware of the importance of the *Kitab al-Shifa*: the work may have been introduced to him by Avendauth. By 1200 there were partial Latin translations of the *Kitab al-Shifa* by *Gundisalvo, John of Spain, and *Alfred of Sareschel; there was also a complete Latin version of the *Canon*. Ibn Sina's ideas were widely assimilated into European thought. The religious and philosophical material in the *Kitab* became synthesized with the work of St. Augustine to form one of the foundation stones of *Scholasticism. The *Canon* was the most important work of its kind and continued to influence the theory and practice of medicine until the seventeenth century: as a medical authority Ibn Sina was unsurpassed, and equalled only by *Hippocrates and Galen.

See also **Agronomy; Albertus Magnus; Alchemy; Alderotti, Taddeo; Alum; Anatomy; Aquinas, Thomas; Aristotelianism; Arnau de Vilanova; Astrology; Bacon, Roger; Bartholomaeus of Bruges; Bartolomeo da Varignana; Benzi, Ugo; Bernard de Gordon; Borgognoni, Teodorico; Botany; Bredon, Simon; Buridan, John;** *Consilia;* **Despars, Jacques; Elements and qualities; Frederick II; Gentile da Foligno; Gerard of Cremona; Ghazali, al-; Gilbertus Anglicus; Gundisalvo, Domingo; Guy de Chauliac; Gynecology and midwifery; Henri de Mondeville; Herbals; Hylomorphism; Ibn Bajja; Ibn Ezra, Abraham; Ibn Zuhr; Illustration, scientific; Impetus; Jacopo da Forlì; John of Gaddesden; John of Saint-Amand; Khayyam, 'Umar al-; Lanfranco of Milan; Lapidaries; "Latin Averroists"; Liuzzi, Mondino de';** **Logic; Majusi, al-; Medicine, practical; Medicine, theoretical; Metaphysics; Meteorology; Microcosm/macrocosm; Mineralogy; Music theory; Nature: diverse medieval interpretations; Patronage of science; Petrus Hispanus; Pharmacology; Plague tractates; Pseudo-Aristotle; Psychology; Razi, al-;** *Regimen sanitatis;* **Richard of Middleton; Richard Rufus of Cornwall;** *Scientia;* **Siger of Brabant; Surgery;** *Tacuinum sanitatis;* **Torrigiano de' Torrigiani; Translation movements; Translation norms and practice; Universities; Witelo**

Bibliography

Arberry, Arthur J. *Avicenna on Theology*. Westport: Hyperion Press, 1979.

Avicenna. *A Treatise on the Canon of Medicine of Avicenna, incorporating a translation of the first book*, by O. Cameron Gruner. London, Luzac & Co., 1930.

———. *Avicennae Arabvm medicorvm principis*. Venetiis, apud Iuntas, 1595.

———. *Avicennae De congelatione et conglutinatione lapidum; being sections of the Kitab al-shifa. The Latin and Arabic texts, edited with an English translation of the latter and with critical notes by E. J. Holmyard and D. C. Mandeville*. Paris, P. Guethner, 1927.

———. *Avicennae medicorum arabum principus, Liber canonis, de medicinis cordialibvs, et Cantica*. Basilae, per Ioannes Heruagios, 1556.

———. *Avicennae philosophi praeclarissimi ac medicorum principis Compendium de anima. De mahad. i. de dispositione, seu loco, ad quem revertitur homo, vel anima eius post morte. Aphorismi de anima. De diffinitionibus, & quaesitis. De divisione scientiarum*. Farnborough, Gregg, 1969.

———. *Avicenna's Treatise on Logic. (A concise philosophical encyclopaedia) and autobiography*. Ed. and translated from the original Persian by Farhang Zabeeh. The Hague: Nijhoff, 1971.

———. *Les causes de la production des lettres/Avicenne, Abu Ali al Husayn ibn Sina; traduction et commentaire Nebil Radhouane*. Carthage: Académie tunisienne des sciences, des lettres et des arts "Beit al-Hikma," 2002.

———. *Liber canonis*. Hildesheim: G. Olms, 1964.

———. *Opera philosophica*. Venise, 1508. Latin and French Selections. Louvain: Édition de la bibliothèque S.J., 1961.

———. *The Propositional Logic of Avicenna*. Translated from the Arabic, with introduction, commentary and glossary by Nabil Shehaby. Boston: Reidel, 1973.

Benzi, Ugo. *Expositio super quarta fen primi canonis Avicennae*. Venice, Andreas Calabrensis (Papiensis), 1485.

Corbin, Henry. *Avicenna and the Visionary Recital*, tr. by Willard R. Trask (1961; reprint, Princeton: Princeton University Press 1990) [translation of *Avicenne et le récit visionnaire*, 1954].

Dahiyat, Ismail M. *Avicenna's Commentary on the Poetics of Aristotle: A Critical Study with an Annotated Translation of the Text*. Leiden: E.J. Brill, 1974.

Davidson, Herbert A. *Alfarabi, Avicenna, and Averroes on Intellect: Their Cosmologies, Theories of the Active Intellect, and Theories of Human Intellect*. New York: Oxford University Press, 1992.

Durrany, K. S. Ibn Sina's Concept of Man. *Studies in the History of Medicine* 6 (1982).

Fakhry, Majid. *Ethical Theories in Islam*, 2d ed. Leiden: E.J. Brill 1994.

Gohlman, William E. *The Life of Ibn Sina: A Critical Edition and Annotated Translation*. English & Arabic. Albany: State University of New York Press, 1974.

Goodman, Lenn E. *Avicenna*. New York: Routledge 1992.

Gutas, Dimitri. *Avicenna and the Aristotelian Tradition: Introduction to Reading Avicenna's Philosophical Works*. Leiden: E.J. Brill, 1988.

Hall, Robert E. A Decisive Example of the Influence of Psychological Doctrines in Islamic Science and Culture: Some Relationships between Ibn Sina's Psychology, Other Branches of His Thought, and Islamic Teachings. *Journal of the History of Arabic Science* (1979) 3.

Heath, Peter. *Allegory and Philosophy in Avicenna (Ibn Sina): with a Translation of the Book of the Prophet Muhammad's Ascent to Heaven*. Philadelphia: University of Pennsylvania Press, 1992.

Janssens, Jules L. *An Annotated Bibliography on Ibn Sina (1970–1989), Including Arabic and Persian Publications and Turkish and Russian References*. Louvain: University of Leuven Press, 1991.

Kemal, Salim. *The Poetics of Alfarabi and Avicenna*. Leiden: E.J. Brill, 1988.

Krueger, Haven C. *Avicenna's Poem on Medicine*. Springfield: Thomas, 1963.

Marmura, Michael E. Plotting the Course of Avicenna's Thought. *Journal of the American Oriental Society* (1991) 111.

———. Some Aspects of Avicenna's Theory of God's Knowledge and Particulars. *Journal of the American Oriental Society* (1962) 82.

———. *The Metaphysics of The Healing*. Provo: Brigham Young University Press, 2004.

Morewedge, Parviz. Philosophical Analysis and Ibn Sina's Essence-Existence Distinction. *Journal of the American Oriental Society* (1972) 92.

———. *The Metaphysica of Avicenna (Ibn Sina): A Critical Translation-Commentary and Analysis of the Fundamental Arguments in Avicenna's Metaphysica in the Danish nama-i 'Ala'i (The Book of Scientific Knowledge)*. New York: Columbia University Press, 1973.

Nasr, Seyyed Hossein. *Three Muslim Sages: Avicenna/ Suhrawardi/Ibn Arabi*. 1964; reprint, New York: Caravan Books, 1976.

Nasr, Seyyed Hossein, and Oliver Leaman, eds. *History of Islamic Philosophy*, 2 vols. New York: Routledge, 1996.

Rahman, F. *Avicenna's Psychology: An English Translation of Kitab al-najat, book II, chapter VI, with historico-philosophical notes and textual improvements on the Cairo edition*. Westport: Hyperion Press, 1981.

———. Essence and Existence in Avicenna. *Medieval and Renaissance Studies* (1958) 4.

Rescher, Nicholas. Avicenna on the Logic of Conditional Propositions. *Medieval and Renaissance Studies* (1963) 4.

Shah, Mazhar H. *The General Principles of Avicenna's Canon of Medicine*. Karachi, Naveed Clinic, 1966.

JACOB PRIMLEY

IBN ZUHR

Known in the medieval Latin medical tradition as Avenzoar, Abhomeron Abinçoar or Abymeron Avenzohar, Abu Marwan ibn Zuhr was born in Seville around 1091 and died in his native city in 1162. He belonged to a family which produced prominent physicians over several centuries in al-Andalus (medieval Muslim Spain), and was also renowed for its political influence and literary contributions. In addition to an education in Islamic law, theology and literature as befitted someone of his social and intellectual status, Ibn Zuhr began his medical training and practice early in life under his father, Abu'l-'Ala' ibn Zuhr. The parent quickly introduced the child to the study of Galenic and Hippocratic writings, although Ibn Zuhr must also have become familiar with a number of medical treatises by earlier Eastern Islamic physicians, partially transcribed in some of his father's works. According to his own account, when he still was a young boy, his father made him swear the Hippocratic Oath and allowed him to work as his assistant or even his substitute. Ibn Zuhr became court physician to the Almoravid dynasty in Seville, and although his native city remained his base, he also lived for periods in the North African city of Marrakech (Morocco). A number of aspects of his biography remain obscure, such as the reasons why he—and his father—fell out of favor with the Almoravid ruler 'Ali ibn Yusuf ibn Tasufin. This situation forced him to flee and abandon his family and Seville for a long time, during which he was seriously ill. Eventually, around the year 1130, Ibn Zuhr was jailed in Marrakesh, although he continued to practice medicine and even attended relatives and dignatories of the Almoravid court. He was released either shortly before or after 'Ali ibn Yusuf's death in 1143, and remained for some time in the North African city, conquered by the Almohad dynasty in 1147. On his return to Seville, he devoted himself to medical practice and teaching, as well as to the composition of books under the patronage of the Almohad caliph 'Abd al-Mu'min. He died in Seville in 1162 as the result of a *nagla* (epithelioma).

Medical Works and Achievements

Unlike his more versatile Islamic colleagues, Ibn Zuhr devoted himself exclusively to medicine, and in his practice he seems to have observed strictly the precepts of the Islamic religion. He was a convinced Galenist, although his interest focused on practical rather than theoretical or speculative issues. As he himself admitted, he was very keen on pharmacology, and paid special attention to the improvement of recipes, particularly on efforts to disguise their bad smell or taste. He is traditionally attributed with the first descriptions of mediastinal tumors, abscess of the pericardium, and intestinal erosion. He is also said to have introduced, or at least improved, artificial feeding through the gullet or through the rectum, and to have identified the *sarcoptes scabiei* as the cause of scabies. Likewise, he is known for having recommended tracheotomy, a procedure which when young he performed only once on a goat. Such discoveries and therapeutic advice—which, in general, still require a critical assessment—appear in his most renowned medical treatise, the *Kitab al-Taysir fi-mudawat wa'l-tadbir (Book to Facilitate Therapeutics and Regimen)*. This work on pathology and therapy was translated into Hebrew, and also into Latin in 1281 by John of Capua. The Latin version, reprinted at least ten times between 1490 and 1576, was employed as a textbook in European universities along with works by *al-Razi (865–925) and *Ibn Sina (980–1037). The *Kitab al-Taysir* is believed to have been written at the request of the Cordoban philosopher and physician *Ibn Rushd (1126–1198), whose ambiguous statement regarding this is not backed up by the Sevillian physician. According to the prologue of Ibn Zuhr's book, it is more likely that the *Taysir* was composed at the request of the caliph 'Abd al-Mu'min. As the book was written under the supervision of someone who found the treatise excessively scientific, Ibn Zuhr added a short treatise on compound drugs known as *Kitab al-Jami'*. These two texts were usually printed along with the *Kitab al-Kulliyat fi'l-tibb (Book on the Generalities of Medicine)* by Ibn Rushd, because they complemented each other forming a basic body of medical theory and practice. Ibn Zuhr also wrote a book on dietetics (*Kitab al-Aghdhiya*), and several essays on a variety of topics, such as skin diseases (*Risala fi'l-baras*), disorders of the kidneys (*Maqala fi 'ilal al-kulà*), the superiority of honey over sugar (*Risala fi tafdil al-'asal 'ala'l-sukkar*), and a short treatise entitled *Kitab al-Qanun (Book of the Norm)*. The only work by Ibn Zuhr known to have been written for the Almoravid dynasty is his *Kitab al-Iqtisad fi islah al-anfus wa-l-ajsad (Book of the Golden Mean Regarding the Treatment of Souls and Bodies)*, written in his youth and dedicated to the governor of Seville, Ibrahim ibn Yusuf ibn Tashufin— 'Ali ibn Yusuf's son—in 1121. Identified with the

Avenzoar. From the 1493 *Liber chronicarum mundi*
(Nuremburg Chronicle) by Hartmann Schedel. (Topham/
Ann Ronan Picture Library/HIP)

Kitab al-Zina (*Book on Cosmetics*) believed to be lost,
the *Kitab al-Iqtisad*, although devoted to therapy, is one
of the few medieval Islamic treatises dealing extensively
with cosmetics. In this work, Ibn Zuhr went far beyond
the usual topics advocated by his predecessors, that is, the
use of perfumes, ointments, collyria, skin and hair treatments, or dental and sexual norms to improve a person's
external appearance. He also proposed surgical operations to remedy congenital or acquired features which
affect physical beauty, such as a large nose, extremely
thick lips or lips which do not cover teeth when smiling,
crooked teeth, tears in the earlobes caused by adorn-
ments, or malformations of the thorax. It is unlikely that
Ibn Zuhr ever performed any of the surgical procedures
he described, since in his *Taysir* he admitted that the sight
of blood caused him to vomit and even to faint. However,
the *Kitab al-Iqtisad* constitutes an interesting piece within medieval Islamic medical literature, as the author's
interest is not simply restricted to improving the functioning of the diverse parts of the body or to enhancing
its attractiveness as a means of promoting human reproduction. Beauty and physical embellishment are
subordinated to an aesthetic ideal which the author considered to be a prime objective of medicine and a
necessary instrument to serve God.

See also **Galen; Hippocrates; Medicine, practical;
Medicine, theoretical**

Bibliography

Primary Sources

Ibn Zuhr. *Kitab al-Aghdhiya* (*Book on Foodstuffs*), also
known as *K. al-Aghdhiya wa-l-adwiya* (*Book on Foodstuffs
and Drugs*). Arabic edition, Spanish translation and study
by Expiración García Sánchez. Madrid: CSIC, AECI, 1992.

———. *Kitab al-Qanun* (*Book of the Norm*). Partial edition
by M.A. al-Jattabi. *Al-Tibb wa-l-atibba, fi-l-Andalus al-
islamiyya.* 2 vols. Beirut: Dar al-Gharb al-Islami, 1988, I,
304–308.

———. *Kitab al-Taysir fi mudawat wa-l-tadbir* (*Book to
Facilitate Therapeutics and Regimen*). Ed. by Mishil Khuri.
Dimashq: Dar al-Fikr, 1983.

———. *Risala fi tafdil al-ʿasal ʿalà l-sukkar* (*Epistle on the
superiority of honey over sugar*). Partial edition by M.A. al-
Jattabi. *Al-Tibb wa-l-atibbaʾ fi-l-Andalus al-islamiyya.* 2
vols. Beirut: Dar al-Gharb al-Islami, 1988, I, 310–317.

Secondary Sources

Álvarez Millán, Cristina. Actualización del corpus médico-lit-
erario de los Banu Zuhr. *Al-Qantara* (1995) 16: 173–180.

Azar, Henry A. *Ibn Zuhr (Avenzoar) "Supreme in the Science
of Medicine since Galen."* Ph. D. Dissertation, University of
North Carolina at Chapel Hill. Ann Arbor: U.M.I.
Dissertation Information Service, 1998.

Colin, Gabriel. *Avenzoar, sa vie et ses oeuvres.* Paris: E.
Leroux, 1911 (reprinted in *Abu ʾl ʿAlaʾ Ibn Zuhr (d.
525/1130) and his son Abu Marwan ibn Zuhr (d.
557/1161). Texts and Studies.* Collected and reprinted by
F. Sezgin in collaboration with M. Amawi, C. Ehrig-Eggert,
E. Neubauer. Frankfurt am Main: Institute for the History
of Arabic-Islamic Science at the Johann Wolfgang Goethe
University, 1996.

De La Puente, Cristina. *Avenzoar, Averroes, Ibn al-Jatib.
Médicos de al-Ándalus. Perfumes, ungüentos y jarabes.*
Madrid: Nívola, 2003.

Gayangos, P. de. *The History of the Mohammedan Dynasties
in Spain.* 2 vols. London: Oriental Translation Fund,
1840–1843.

Kuhne Brabant, Rosa. *El Kitab al-Iqtisad de Avenzoar, según
el ms. nº 834 de la Biblioteca del Real Monasterio de El
Escorial.* Extracto de Tesis Doctoral. Madrid: Facultad de
Filosofía y Letras, Universidad Complutense, 1971.

———. "Avenzoar y la cosmética." In *Orientalia Hispánica
sive studia F.M. Pareja octogenario dicata.* 2 vols. Ed. by
J.M. Barral. Leiden: E.J. Brill, 1974. I, 428–437.

———. "Aportaciones para esclarecer alguno de los puntos
oscuros en la biografía de Avenzoar." In *Actas del XII
Congreso de la Unión Europea de Arabistas e Islamólogos
(Málaga, 1984).* Madrid: s.n., 1986, pp. 433–446.

———. "Abu Marwan b. Zuhr: un professionel de la médicine
en plein XIIème siècle." In *Le Patrimoine Andalous dans la
Culture Arabe et Espagnole.* Tunis: C.E.R.E.S., 1991, pp.
129–141.

———. "Reflexiones sobre un tratadito dietético práctica-
mente desconocido: el *Tafdil al-ʿasal ʿalà l-sukkar* de Abu
Marwan b. Zuhr." In *Homenaje al Profesor José Mª
Fórneas Besteiro.* 2 vols. Granada: Universidad de Granada,
1994, II: 1057–1144.

———. *Zina e islah.* Reflexiones para entender la medicina
estética del joven Abu Marwan b. Zuhr. *Al-Andalus–
Magreb* (1996) 4: 281–298.

———. "La medicina estética, una hermana menor de la medicina científica." In C. Alvarez de Morales, ed. *La Medicina en
al-Ándalus.* Granada: El Legado Andalusí, 1999, pp. 197–207.

Peña Muñoz, Carmen. Capítulo del bazo en el *Kitab al-Taysir* de Avenzoar. *Awraq* (1981) 4: 131–142.

Peña Muñoz, Carmen and Giron Irueste, Fernando. Aspectos inéditos en la obra médica de Avenzoar: el prólogo del *Kitab al-Taysir*. *Miscelánea de Estudios Árabes y Hebraicos* (1977) 26: 103–116.

Renaud, Henri-Paul-Joseph. Trois études d'histoire de la médicine en Occident. II: Nouveaux manuscrits d'Avenzoar. *Hesperis-Tamuda* (1931) 12: 91–105 (reprinted in *Abu 'l 'Ala' Ibn Zuhr (d. 525/1130) and his son Abu Marwan ibn Zuhr (d. 557/1161). Texts and Studies*. Collected and reprinted by F. Sezgin in collaboration with M. Amawi, C. Ehrig-Eggert, E. Neubauer. Frankfurt am Main: Institute for the History of Arabic-Islamic Science at the Johann Wolfgang Goethe University, 1996.

CRISTINA ÁLVAREZ MILLÁN

IDRISI, AL-

Abu 'Abdallah Muhammad ibn Muhammad ibn Idris, called al-Sharif al-Idrisi (1100–1165) was born in Sabta (Ceuta) into a family that claimed rights to the caliphate. His immediate ancestors, the Hammudids, had ruled in Málaga from where they immigrated to Northern Africa after they had lost their power. Al-Idrisi was educated in Córdoba and traveled widely in North Africa, Europe and Anatolia. In about 1138, the Norman king of Sicily, Roger II (1097–1154), invited al-Idrisi to his court, supposedly to protect him from his enemies. Some scholars, however, have proposed that after having engaged in a major campaign of conquering Northern Africa and al-Andalus, Roger was more interested in acquiring a possible pretender and potential puppet ruler.

Roger never used al-Idrisi in this way. He rather made him share with him his vast experiences as a traveler. He asked him to construct a map that would represent the entire contemporary world and inform him about its inhabitants, their countries, their economies, taxes, habits and languages, mountains, seas, and the distances. Roger told al-Idrisi to comment on the map and to supplement its information in a separate text. While the map is lost, the text is extant in thirteen manuscripts, five of which contain the full texts and eight of which include maps. These maps are mostly regional maps. Several manuscripts also contain a small world map, which recently has been found in a thirteenth-century copy of an eleventh-century Fatimid manuscript on curiosities of the world. Johns and Savage-Smith concluded that this particular world map is not the product of al-Idrisi's work. Whether a world map engraved on silver was al-Idrisi's own work is highly doubtful too. Al-Idrisi himself ascribed all the work to Roger, who supposedly collected and evaluated all geographical information, transferred it to a drawing board and then engraved the map on the silver disk with his own hands. Al-Idrisi also confirms that the entire project was one of cooperation with other scholars of the Norman court, scholars invited from elsewhere and experienced travelers.

The maps that are found in the manuscripts of al-Idrisi's commentary on the engraved map are sectional maps. The Hammudid prince chose an innovative scheme for arranging the flood of information in a rectangular world map by dividing it first into the seven standard climates and by then subdividing each climate into ten sections. While the extant maps focus mainly on towns, seas, lakes, rivers, and mountains, the text entitled *Nuzhat al-mushtaq fi khtiraq al-afaq* (*The Book of Pleasant Journeys into Faraway Lands*) indicates their distances and directions and describes physical, economic and cultural properties. According to Ahmad, al-Idrisi's work "is the most exhaustive medieval work in the field of physical, descriptive, cultural and political geography."

In addition to the *Nuzhat*, another geographical text by al-Idrisi called either *Uns al-muhaj wa-rawd al-faraj* (*Intimacy of Souls and Gardens of Pleasure*) or *Rawd al-faraj wa-nuzhat al-muhaj* (*Gardens of Pleasure and Recreation of the Souls*) exists in three manuscripts. It contains seventy-two sectional maps, which differ in content and outline from those in the manuscripts of the *Nuzhat*. As a rule, they are simpler and less well organized. Scholars disagree as to whether this text is an abbreviation of the *Nuzhat* or another text mentioned by an Arab Sicilian poet.

Al-Idrisi's work combines the cartographic traditions created during the Abbasid caliphate, e.g., the works of translators, mathematicians, astronomers, and philosophers at the court of the caliph al-Ma'mun, which in turn were based on *Ptolemy's *Geography* and *Almagest*, and the works of philosophers, geographers, administrators, and travelers in Iran and Syria, which drew on Sasanian geographical concepts and tools. The sectional maps in the manuscripts of the *Nuzhat* show a marked improvement in geographical and cartographic knowledge compared to earlier Arabic and Persian maps. This is particularly true for North Africa, Europe and Western Asia.

Al-Idrisi's *Nuzhat* inspired several later Arabic and Iranian geographers and historians. It also served as a major tool for Italian, Dutch, and French mapmakers from the late sixteenth to the mid-eighteenth century.

See also **Cartography; Geography, chorography; Navigation**

Bibliography

Ahmad, S. Maqbul. "Cartography of al-Sharif al-Idrisi." In *The History of Cartography*, Vol. Two, Book One. *Cartography in the Traditional Islamic and South Asian Societies*, J. B. Harley and David Woodward, eds. Chicago: University of Chicago Press, 1992, pp. 156–172.

Johns, Jeremy and Emilie Savage-Smith. *The Book of Curiosities*: A Newly Discovered Series of Islamic Maps. *Imago Mundi* (2003) 55: 7–24.

SONJA BRENTJES

ILLUMINATION

Manuscript copies of scientific texts contained in many instances polychrome or monochrome illuminations (not to be confused with diagrammatic presentation of data in works of mathematics and logic), which might date back to classical antiquity (see for example the diagrams in the biological treatises by Aristotle) and also included authors' portraits. In papyrus rolls illustrations were placed within the columns of text. When a book was transformed from roll to codex, they were integrated into the text. They then covered all the page or a portion of it. The flat surface of the page in codices made it possible to frame pictures and to add a background (in plain color or illustrative).

In the tradition of many texts, illuminations have not always been preserved in the original language (particularly Greek), but in translation in different and not necessarily related cultures (Latin, Arabic, Georgian, Armenian, Coptic or Slavic, for example), a fact suggesting that they were originally present in the common source (Greek). Their disappearance might result from different factors, from the Christianization of science in late antiquity (for instance the elimination of scenes representing the mythological creation of medicinal plants) to Iconoclasm.

Illuminations are present in the manuscripts of several scientific disciplines: medicine, with anatomy and physiology, diagnosis (flasks of urine, the color of which was used for diagnostic purposes), surgery and surgical instruments, orthopedics and bandages, materia medica and therapeutics, medication (with different techniques, from bleeding to clysters); astronomy (representations of constellations) and astrology (zodiacal signs); cosmography, geography, and cartography; natural sciences, with encyclopedias, specialized treatises and also travelogues; zoology (including ichthyology and ornithology) and hunting; *mineralogy and *alchemy; pneumatics and automata; poliorcetic and military sciences.

A crucial question is that of realism and first-hand observation. While it is generally believed that classical scientific pictures were realistic and were gradually transformed over time (just like texts), it might be the opposite: the most ancient pictures were schematic and represented only the main features of the realities dealt with, in an analytical way and without a synthetic perception. Realism would be a later reinterpretation of such pictures, consisting mainly in introducing proportions and more detailed representations of the elements, with or without observation of nature. In the West, observation of nature was supposedly introduced into scientific illustrations around 1300 C.E. In printed books, it did not appear until 1530 and the Herbarum vivae eicones of Otto Brunfels (c. 1489–1534).

In Byzantium, scientific illustrations seem to have been rather rare. In botany, only *Dioscorides' De materia medica was illustrated (and not *Galen or any other similar work), and plants were represented extracted from their natural environment, in a way characterized as essentialist. In some cases, such pictures gave rise to large and expensive deluxe copies, particularly in the early Byzantine period and the so-called Macedonian and Palaiologan Renaissances (tenth and fourteenth centuries respectively). Arabic scientists and artists replaced Greek personages and mythological topics with Arabic ones (for

example in astronomy), suggested the natural context of plants and animals (maybe by transferring elements between scientific fields), and incorporated natural elements into their human context (particularly for medicines and pharmacy, also by transferring pictures from literary texts to scientific ones). During the period preceding the translation enterprise from Arabic into Latin, classical illustrations were better preserved in the West than in Byzantium. Successively, it was influenced by the Arabic model, particularly in such a genre as the Tacuinum sanitatis (especially in fourteenth-century northern Italy), where plants used for medicinal purposes were included in highly artistic miniatures whose elements were borrowed from different iconic fields (from chivalry literature to calendars). Conversely, scientific motifs were transferred to manuscripts of non-scientific fields.

See also Bestiaries; Herbals; Illustration, medical; Medicine, practical; Medicine, theoretical

Bibliography

Backhouse, Janet. Medieval Birds in the Sherbone Missal. Toronto: University of Toronto Press, 2001.
Brandenburg, Dietrich. Islamic Miniature Painting in Medical Manuscripts. Basel: Roche Editiones, 1982.
Brown, Michelle P. Understanding Illuminated Manuscripts. A Guide to Technical Terms. London: The British Library, 1994.
Collins, Minta. Medieval Herbals. Toronto: University of Toronto Press, 2000.
Cogliati Arano, Luisa. The Medieval Health Handbook. Tacuinum sanitatis. New York: George Braziller, 1976.
De Hamel, Christopher. Medieval Craftsmen. Scribes and Illuminators. Toronto: University of Toronto Press, 1994.
———. The British Library Guide to Manuscript Illumination. History and techniques. London: The British Library, 2001.
Hein, W.-H. and D.A. Wittop Koning. Die Apotheke in der Buchmalerei. Frankfurt: Govei-Verlag, 1981.
Jones, Peter Murray. Medieval Medicine in Illuminated Manuscripts. London: The British Library, 1998.
Mackinney, Loren. Medical Illustrations in Medieval Manuscripts. London: Wellcome Historical Medical Library, 1965.
Page, Sophie. Astrology in Medieval Manuscripts. Toronto: University of Toronto Press, 2002.
Stückelberger, Alfred. Das illustrierte Fachbuch in der antiken Naturwisenschaft, Medizin und Technik. Mainz: Philipp von Zabern, 1994.
Weitzmann, Kurt. Studies in Classical and Byzantine Manuscript Illumination. Chicago: Chicago University Press, 1971.

ALAIN TOUWAIDE

ILLUSTRATION, MEDICAL

Medical books from the Middle Ages often contain images as well as texts. This applies to academic medical texts as much as to remedybooks, and there is, surprisingly, considerable overlap between the illustrations found in both kinds. Drawings of a zodiac man showing the parts of the body ruled by the signs of the zodiac are sometimes highly finished works of the illuminator's art, but sometimes very crude sketches by the scribe himself or herself. The same applies to vein men showing the places on the body from which to let blood for particular ailments, and to urine glasses in which the color and contents of urine are distinguished for diagnostic purposes. All of these types of illustration are common from the thirteenth century onward, and late medieval medical manuscripts are more likely to be illustrated than their earlier counterparts.

Motivations

Categorizing medieval medical illustration poses problems of definition. Medical illustration in modern printed books or electronic media is commissioned to illustrate a textbook or an article. This was not the case so far as we can tell for the vast majority of medieval images. The author was very seldom in a position to specify what illustration he wanted for his text. There are some special cases in which we know this happened—for instance with the illustrations to the works of *John of Arderne, in which the text itself calls for illustrations to be placed at certain points. Surgery is the one form of medical writing in which such a procedure was envisaged, and written surgeries were a genre invented in the western Middle Ages. As *anatomy fell within the purview of the surgeons, we might expect this to lend itself above all other medical subjects to illustration, but apart from the occasional bone man, illustrating the skeletal structure of the human form, anatomical images are not found at all frequently. Surgical operations were much more popular subjects for illustration. This may have had to do as much with their potential for dramatic narrative art as with their instructional value, to judge from the illustrated copies of the first author of a western surgery, *Roger Frugard. In those exceptional copies of his *Chirurgia* the surgeon and the patient are envisaged as engaged in a kind of courtly dance enlivened with surgical instruments, leading us to conclude that the illustrations can hardly have functioned as contributing parts in a technical manual of instruction.

If the medieval medical author was not generally commissioning pictures to illustrate his works, then we must expect the impulse to illustrate to come from elsewhere. Delighting the eye of the wealthy owner is evidently one common motive. The program of illustrations to a text such as the *Li livres dou sante* of Aldobrandino of Siena, which gives health advice to royal and noble patrons, typifies this motivation. The various foods, drinks, and *materia medica* illustrated are not passing on medical information but adorning the manuscript at significant breaks in the text with elegant pictures. Academic medical texts commissioned for teachers, but not those for students, were similarly adorned from the thirteenth century onward with historiated initials. As for example in the famous Dresden codex of Galen these images give a miniaturized glimpse of the world of medicine. The illuminator, who was not a specialist illustrator of medical books, but a professional artist working on commission to illustrate a variety of religious and secular texts, commonly seizes on a subject suggested by a phrase or word in the first few sentences of the chapter of text. Then he will illustrate that phrase or word by painting the initial letter in the first word of the chapter. Most medical manuscripts with illustrations were in fact copies of existing exemplars, which meant that the illustrator had only to copy the illustrations found in the manuscript he was copying, not to devise a program of illustrations from scratch.

At the other end of the spectrum from the illuminated manuscript is the copy made by a medical practitioner for him or herself of a text needed for practical purposes. In such a case the practitioner might or might not choose to take the trouble to try to copy images, depending on the trouble required and the practical value of the image. The zodiac man, vein man, and urine glasses mentioned above are all images with a value in diagnosis, prognosis or therapy. This no doubt accounts for their ubiquity in otherwise unillustrated and unpretentious manuscripts. The zodiac man figure tells the practitioner how to avoid surgery or medication while the Moon is in the sign of the body that influences the part to be operated on or medicated. The vein man tells which vein must be opened to purge humors that cause the ailment in a particular organ or disease of the whole body. The urine glasses enable the practitioner to make a diagnosis built on the particular qualities of the urine sample, most notably its color. Relatively crude copies of such illustrations may be found in manuscripts clearly used by practitioners. It is not simply the case, however, that the more closely related to medical practice an image is, the cruder its execution. A number of physicians' calendars produced in England and France in the fourteenth and fifteenth centuries were clearly intended to be worn at the belt of the practitioner, since their parchment membranes were sewed together into folded sections tied to a strap. Yet in some of them we find quite elaborately illuminated pictures of the vein man, the zodiac man, urine glasses as well as tables of eclipses.

Classical Traditions

The western Middle Ages inherited a body of images of medicine from the ancient world. We know from the discussion in Pliny and elsewhere that the practical value of illustrations of *materia medica* was a matter of lively debate in the early centuries C.E., and in the early sixth century Juliana Anicia codex in Vienna we have a survivor of what is evidently an already well-established tradition of botanical pictures. The pictures suggest that observation from nature played a greater part in illustration in the earlier period than it was to do before the fifteenth century Italian *herbals. But the inheritance of images from classical medicine extended to images of anatomy and of surgery, as well as to *materia medica*. The dress and attitudes found in figural art in early medieval medical manuscripts indicates an origin in the late classical or early Byzantine period. One series of early surgical pictures of operations for couching of cataract, extirpation of nasal polyps, and excision of hemorrhoids is first met in the twelfth century, but undoubtedly descends from prototypes in the early centuries C.E. Similarly a series of illustrations of cautery points on the human body at which the hot iron is to be applied shows in the handling of naked figures and the surgeon's dress that it may have come from images first used in the Alexandrian medical schools. The oldest attested tradition of anatomical illustration in the Middle Ages is actually obstetrical. In a ninth-century manuscript in the Royal Library in Brussels are thirteen drawings of the fetus in different positions within a flask-shaped womb. The illustrations usually accompany a text of Moschion's *Gynaecia* written originally in the sixth century, but probably itself based on the writings of Soranus of Ephesus, who practiced in Rome about 100 C.E. They continued to be copied in the West up until the fifteenth century.

One of the features of the older traditions of medical illustration is that the relationship between text and image is much looser than modern preconceptions allow. Sometimes with the early images there are no texts, quite possibly because text and image have gone separate ways. This is presumably the case with an image of seated physician taking the pulse of a woman patient found in a German medical manuscript of the thirteenth century (British Library, Arundel MS 295, fol.256), which must have accompanied a text on pulse once, but now survives only as an image. Moreover, even when text and image are found together in a manuscript it is not always clear that they accompanied each other originally. The fetal illustrations to Moschion are more normally found in manuscripts accompanying a section of text from the thirteenth-century author *Gilbertus Anglicus's Compendium medicinae*. This is sometimes found independently in Middle English translation as "The Sekeness of Wymmen," still accompanied by the thirteen images. Nor does text always take priority over illustration, despite the logocentric character of university medical learning in the Middle Ages. Sometimes the texts are simply inscriptions within the images, as with the captions to the cautery images, or the instructions accompanying vein men which tell the viewer where to let blood for particular ailments. In these cases the text explains how to interpret the image, rather than the image illustrating the text.

Healing Images

Finally we should consider images insofar as they were supposed to carry healing properties in themselves. Of course there were images that were instrumental in calculation for diagnosis and prognosis, like the volvelles that showed how to find the day of the Moon for a particular solar day, or the sphere of Pythagoras that predicted the outcome of illnesses by turning the patient's name into numbers and subjecting them to simple arithmetical manipulation. But some images were designed to act amuletically, to protect the wearer against illness or to give the weare relief. There are several kinds of images that fit this model, for instance altarpieces or frescoes in *hospitals on which the patients might gaze, and devotional images of the Virgin or the saints that might be found in books or hung on the wall, whose inscriptions suggest that they carry healing power. More personally there are pilgrim badges, rings or jewels that might be worn for protection, for instance the image of the shrine of St. Thomas at Canterbury consisting of the saint's head This was one of the commonest pilgrim badges, and sometimes comes with an inscription stating that "St. Thomas is my medicine." Like the wax agnus dei obtained in Rome and made from paschal candles, images like this were sacralized by contact with the shrine or by being made from sacramental material. Once sacralized they conferred protection on the wearer against specific diseases or the onset of pestilence or sudden death.

See also **Alchemy; Astrology; Illustration, scientific; Instruments, medical; Surgery; Medicine, practical; Medicine, theoretical**

Bibliography

Collins, Minta. *Medieval Herbals: the illustrative traditions.* London: British Library, 2000.
Herrlinger, Robert. *History of Medical Illustration from Antiquity to AD 1600.* London: Pitman Medical, 1970.
Hunt, Tony. *The Medieval Surgery.* Woodbridge: Boydell Press, 1992.
Jones, Peter M. *Medieval Medicine in Illuminated Manuscripts.* London: British Library and Centre Tibaldi, 1998.
McKinney, Loren C. *Medical Illustrations in Medieval Manuscripts.* London: Wellcome Historical Medical Library, 1965.
Murdoch, John E. *Album of Science: Antiquity and the Middle Ages.* New York: Scribner, 1984.

PETER MURRAY JONES

ILLUSTRATION, SCIENTIFIC

The use of images and other graphical devices in scientific and technical literature, although limited in extent and variety, was already well established in antiquity, as can be inferred from textual references and extrapolation from extant Byzantine manuscript copies of ancient works. Notable genres of Hellenistic illustrated texts include *herbals and treatises on mechanical devices, most famously those of *Dioscorides and Hero of Alexandria, respectively. Greek illustrated scientific texts that were translated into Arabic in the eighth and ninth centuries C.E.—and more generally all those that followed a specific visual format—strongly influenced the medieval traditions of scientific illustration and visual communication. By the late Middle Ages, in Islam as well as in Europe, these traditions reached a remarkable level of diversity, scope, and sophistication.

Modern historians of science have come to appreciate the importance of issues dealing with representation and visualization, the interplay of art and science, and the nonverbal aspects of cognition and scientific communication. Scholarship on these topics for early-modern and modern science has become substantial, but this cannot be said of the current historiography of science in pre-modern societies. Traditionally, a widespread tacit assumption denied pictures any special epistemological significance: cognitive authority was conferred primarily to linguistic representations. But pictures and graphics are more than mere auxiliary devices of elementary didactic value. A result of recent scholarship on the use of pictures in science is that "we ought to abandon our artistic prejudice that some graphics are noble whereas others are purely instrumental" (Massironi 2002).

Taken in a restrictive sense, the term "scientific illustration" refers solely to pictorial depictions of the natural world. Illustrations of this kind are commonly encountered in works of *botany, *pharmacology, *zoology, *anatomy, *mineralogy, and cosmography. In addition, several types of non-pictorial graphics also played an important role in pre-modern science. A widely diverse array of visual devices—schemata, tables, and diagrams—served to convey information effectively and to facilitate memorization and learning. Some of them actually performed a mapping of abstract concepts in visual form. Geometrical diagrams were an indispensable part of the mathematicians' and astronomers' toolbox. Theoretical writings on music contained diagrams representing ratios, intervals, and modes. Technical drawings of machines and scientific instruments also have a distinguished tradition throughout the medieval period. In the following, we will briefly describe the development of scientific illustrations in the Islamic world, and then in the Latin Middle Ages. A final section will examine the practice and semantic of technical diagrams in both geographical areas more closely.

The Islamic World

Two important factors contributed to the shaping of the Islamic tradition of scientific illustration: the Muslims' intimate acquaintance with the art and learning of Sassanid Persia and of the Near Eastern Hellenistic world, and, more specifically, the import of Byzantine scientific, medical, and philosophical illustrated manuscripts in early Abbasid Iraq (eighth to tenth centuries). Although the dates of the earliest known copies of Arabic illustrated versions of classical texts are rarely before the twelfth or thirteenth centuries, there is no doubt that the tradition must have begun earlier. The oldest extant example of scientific illustrations—actually the earliest surviving illustrated Islamic manuscript—is located in the Bodleian Library, Oxford (MS. Marsh 144), and contains the famous *Book of the Constellation Figures*, which 'Abd al-Rahman al-Sufi wrote in Rayy (near modern Tehran) around 965 C.E. at the request of the Buyid Sultan 'Adud al-Dawla. It was copied in 1009 by al-Sufi's own son from the author's original

Illustration of a water clock from the 1354 transcription of al-Jazari's *Comprehensive Work on the Theory and Practice of the Mechanical Arts*. (Corbis/Burstein Collection)

autograph. Its delicate drawings of the constellation figures reveal a reinterpretation of classical iconography with a perceivably Islamic outlook. The linear style of the figures may betray their being copied from, or inspired by, the engravings on celestial globes. The fact that late copies of this treatise follow the same stylistic tradition confirms the peculiar conservatism, even sometimes archaism, of scientific illustrations.

Another remarkable illustrated treatise was composed around 1200 by Isma'il ibn al-Razzaz al-Jazari, an engineer active at the court of the local Turkish dynasty of the Artuqids in Amid (modern Diyarbakır in Turkey). His *Comprehensive Work on the Theory and Practice of the Mechanical Arts*, which survives in fifteen copies, describes fifty mechanical devices of various kinds (water-clocks and candle-clocks, dispensers, fountains, musical automata, water-raising machines, etc.), and features one full-page illustration for each model and several smaller diagrams of individual components, with a total of one hundred seventy-two illustrations. Its miniatures have long been appreciated for their beauty by art historians and collectors, but they also have intrinsic value as documents of the history of technology. Such technical drawings display an admirable clarity and expressiveness and carry information that can hardly be recovered from the text alone. It would be a mistake to see them as mere decorative but useless embellishments, as some art historians have claimed in the past.

Contrary to common belief among non-Muslims, the Qu'ran does not formally forbid the representation of humans and animals. Numerous prophetic traditions, however, were interpreted by theologians in a sense that made such practices condemnable. Yet, very often their admonitions were simply ignored, especially in Persia, Central Asia, Mughal India, and Ottoman Turkey. In religious contexts, pictorial depictions of living beings were indeed generally considered inappropriate and non-pious, but when their purpose was secular they were seldom problematic. In a civilization where the written word occupies a central place, it is not surprising that the calligraphic properties of the Arabic script are frequently used in illustrations and diagrams to augment their visual semantic. For instance, in geographical maps by al-Istakhri the Arabic script not only serves to label certain areas, but also, through extension of the baseline of the script, to draw borders between adjacent regions of the map.

Medieval Europe

Icons have always played a central role in ancient and medieval Christianity, and it is not surprising that we find a much greater profusion of figurative images in medieval Latin scientific manuscripts than in Arabic ones. Since the history of learning in Western Europe had direct roots in late Roman antiquity, ancient traditions of illustrating books, in particular didactic ones, never really ceased. Several Carolingian manuscripts contain illustrated versions of works by classical or early medieval authors such as Pliny, *Boethius, *Macrobius, *Martianus Capella and *Isidore of Seville. Some of these illustrations became even more famous than the text they originally accompanied and were independently reproduced in later manuscripts.

After the massive arrival of new translations of Arabic and (to a lesser extant) Greek sources in the twelfth century and the creation of universities, European scholarship was also infused with new conventions of visual communication in technical disciplines, such as astronomy, astrology, *alchemy or geomancy. Encyclopedic works flourished in the thirteenth century, and several of these were illustrated with natural historical topics. At the same time, classical texts such as Pliny's *Historia naturalis* or Aristotle's *De animalibus* were occasionally illustrated.

There were several reasons why an author or, more often, a copyist, might choose to add illustrations to a text. Buoncompagni da Signa, a master in Bologna in the early thirteenth century, praised the didactic virtues of images to facilitate the memorization and internalization of concepts. While more lavishly illustrated codices were in general commissioned by wealthy patrons, a substantial number of textbooks containing graphical material were indeed produced for school or university consumption. In this context, pictures often have a mnemonic function. Figures were also frequently employed to summarize an argument, thus easing a student's assimilation of arduous material.

Technical Diagrams

Diagrams obey specific rules. In pre-modern times, these rules obviously differed from those formulated by modern authorities on graphic communication, but they are surprisingly close to their essential principles. Ancient and medieval diagrams and graphics—though typologically far remote from our pie charts, histograms, and flowcharts—are nevertheless non-trivial, coherent and efficient means of conveying information in the most economical and schematic manner.

Diagrams are indispensable in several mathematical disciplines. In an epistolary exchange dealing with subtle questions of Aristotelian natural philosophy, *al-Biruni reminded his younger colleague *Ibn Sina that diagrams were an imperative necessity of scientific discourse and reasoning: "When you come to discuss the reflection [of solar rays on mirrors], you should make a diagram of it, because only through a drawing does your formulation make sense; (otherwise) how can one check what you say?" (al-Biruni and Ibn Sina 1995, p. 54).

The characteristics of geometrical diagrams typical of Greek mathematics are actually true for all mathematical sciences until the modern period: such diagrams are not auxiliary devices, as they convey independent cognitive statements. Moreover, they cannot be completely recovered from the text alone. In ancient and medieval astronomy, the use of graphical tools was not restricted to plane geometrical diagrams. Several problems of mathematical astronomy are associated with the configurations of the celestial sphere and require the use of spherical trigonometry. There also existed several alternative graphical methods that allowed one to solve spherical problems in two dimensions in a more expedient way and made possible the derivation of complex formulae without recourse to spherical trigonometry. Graphics thus have an important heuristic power. Further developments in "graphical calculus" occurred in the context of instrument-making, especially in the Near East.

Tridimensional figures were often problematic and were avoided whenever possible. When representing circles in perspective, medieval illustrators systematically showed them with the shape of almonds, but this may be viewed as a pure convention. The representation of spherical configurations obeyed the specific rule that all elements, even those that would be invisible if drawn on a solid sphere, should be represented as though the sphere were "flattened out" or "squashed." A similar phenomenon occurs with the "distorted" representation of the regular polyhedra in all manuscript and early printed copies of *Euclid's *Elements*. Such diagrams may appear strange to us, unused to visualize spherical configurations in this manner. Yet, they follow precise conventions that were perfectly understood by educated medieval readers.

See also **Astrology; Astronomy, Islamic; Astronomy, Latin; Botany; Cartography; Dioscurides; Herbals; Illumination; Illustration, medical; Music theory; Natural history; Printing; Zoology**

Bibliography

Armstrong, Lilian. The Illustration of Pliny's *Historia Naturalis*: Manuscripts before 1430. *Journal of the Warburg and Courtauld Institutes* (1983) 46: 19–39.

al-Biruni and Ibn Sina. *al-As'ilah wa'l-ajwibah (Questions and answers): including the further answers of al-Biruni and al-Ma'sumi's defense of Ibn Sina.* Edited by Seyyed Hossein Nasr and Mehdi Mohaghegh. Kuala Lumpur: International Institute of Islamic Thought and Civilization, 1995.

Carboni, Stefano. *Following the Stars: Images of the Zodiac in Islamic Art.* New York: Metropolitan Museum of Art, 1997.

Charette, François. *Mathematical Instrumentation in Fourteenth-Century Egypt and Syria: The Illustrated Treatise of Najm al-Din al-Misri.* Leiden: E.J. Brill, 2003.

Eastwood, Bruce. *Astronomy and Optics from Pliny to Descartes: Texts, Diagrams and Conceptual Structures.* London: Variorum, 1989.

King, David. *A Survey of the Scientific Manuscripts in the Egyptian National Library.* Winona Lake: Eisenbrauns, 1986.

———. "Some Illustrations in Islamic Scientific Manuscripts and Their Secrets." In *The Book in the Islamic World: The Written Word and Communication in the Middle East.* Edited by George N. Atiyeh. Albany: State University of New York Press, 1995, pp. 149–177.

Le Berrurier, Diane. *The Pictorial Sources of Mythological and Scientific Illustration in Hrabanus Maurus'* De rerum naturis. New York: Garland, 1978.

Massironi, Manfredo. *The Psychology of Graphic Images: Seeing, Drawing, Communicating.* Translated by Nicola Bruno. Mahwah: Erlbaum, 2002.

Mazzolini, Renato, ed. *Non-verbal Communication in Science prior to 1900.* Florence: Olschki, 1993.

Murdoch, John. *Album of Science: Antiquity and the Middle Ages.* New York: Scribner's, 1984.

Obrist, Barbara. Wind Diagrams and Medieval Cosmology. *Speculum* (1997) 72: 33–84.

Saxl, Fritz. Illustrated Medieval Encyclopedias. *Journal of the Warburg and Courtauld Institutes* (1957) 5: 82–142.

Weizmann, Kurt. "The Greek Sources of Islamic Scientific Illustrations." In idem, *Studies in Classical and Byzantine Manuscript Illumination.* Chicago: University of Chicago Press, 1971, pp. 20–44.

Wellesz, E. An Early al-Sufi MS in the Bodleian Library in Oxford. *Ars Orientalis* (1959) 3: 1–26.

FRANÇOIS CHARETTE

IMPETUS

The motion of projectiles is one of the problems which the Aristotelian theory of motion does not satisfactorily explain. In his *Physics*, Aristotle offers two explanations for the continuation of motion after the original mover has lost contact with the moved body: the theory of mutual replacement—which he seems to reject—and the layer theory, according to which the layers or parts of the air are not only moved by the original mover but also receive the power to act themselves as a mover. The obvious alternative was to assume a force impressed to the *mobile*, a *virtus impressa* or impetus. This solution had already been proposed by the sixth century philosopher Johannes Philoponus, then recurred in Arabic sources, was probably "rediscovered" in the thirteenth and fourteenth centuries, and was referred to even in the technical literature of the seventeenth century. Nevertheless, there is no coherent theory or even "physics" of the *virtus impressa* or impetus, rather, the concepts change from author to author. Despite serious challenges to the Aristotelian theory of motion resulting from its assumption, it remained an ad hoc solution for a puzzling problem.

It is central for an understanding of these discussions that there is a fundamental difference between Aristotelian and classical physics: whereas in the latter—following from the principle of inertia—one has to explain why motion stops, for Aristotle every motion and its continuation need a cause. In Book Seven of the *Physics*, Aristotle formulates two principles concerning the cause of motion: firstly, that "anything involved in a process is necessarily brought into operation by some agency," and, secondly, that "a 'proximate' mover… is correlative to what it moves." Thus, motion or change requires an ontologically distinct mover which continuously has to be in contact with the thing moved.

Aristotle deals with projectile motion in Book Eight of the *Physics*. His two solutions are obviously advanced to save the two principles. The theory of mutual replacement (*antiperistasis*), according to which the air comes around behind to push the mobile forward (as later explained by Simplicius), is only touched on, and it is the layer theory which is Aristotle's own solution. It comprises a double kind of transmission: the original mover conveys to the first layer of the air not only the faculty to move the projectile but also the faculty to transmit this to the next layer. When this transmission ceases, the next layer only moves the body itself, and then the projectile falls down.

Many later authors were not satisfied with either solution. In his commentary on the *Physics*, Johannes Philoponus rejected the role of the air as a decisive factor because for him the air rather resists. He proposed an incorporeal force that the original mover impresses into the moved body (*dynamis endotheisa*) which functions as the immediate cause according to the two Aristotelian principles. This is spent by resistance, and thus the projectile motion finally comes to an end. Philoponus also used his concept to explain natural motions and the motion of the heavens: gravity and levity are nothing else than forces impressed by the Creator, and in creation God also impressed an incorporeal force in the spheres of the heavens moving them ever since.

Philoponus mentioned his theories only in passing; he did not create a new natural philosophy. His commentary on the *Physics* only partially survives and was probably translated into Latin only in the sixteenth century. But the Arabic commentators of Aristotle probably knew at least of Philoponus's remarks in Book Four. *Al-Farabi had already used the term *mail qasri* or violent inclination as an Arabic substitute for impressed force. At the beginning of the eleventh century, Avicenna (*Ibn Sina) in his *Kitab al-Shifa* not only rejected both Aristotelian theories but also those of Philoponus. His own solution was that the moved body receives an inclination (*mail*) from the mover, which is not a force itself, but an instrument of the force of the mover to communicate its action to the thing moved. Like Philoponus, he extended this concept to natural motions, too. The *mail* is the not self-exhausting, but a destructible, immediate cause of the movement, persisting if there were no resistance—as when operating in a void. On the contrary, for Abu'l-Barakat projectile motion in a void would come to an end after the *mail* had exhausted itself.

Neither the ideas of Johannes Philoponus nor the different Arabic concepts of *mail* may have reached the Latin West. But impetus probably was something like a "natural solution" for the earlier scholastics, at least outside the "doctrinal context" of philosophy, that is, outside commentaries on Aristotle. For example, *Richard Rufus of Cornwall (c. 1236) observes that projectiles sharing the same medium may pass one another in contrary directions, and hence Aristotle's explanation cannot suffice. Instead, Rufus suggests that the projector makes an "impression" on the projectile proportional to the weight of the object. *Thomas Aquinas closely followed the Aristotelian explanation of projectile motion in his *Physics* and *De Caelo*, but in his *Quaestiones disputatae*, he discussed the influence of an agent acting by an instrument and compared it to the motion of an arrow which will continue until the force impressed by the agent expires. At the end of the thirteenth century, Petrus Johannes Olivi quoted the theory of a "similitude" or "impression" of the mover flowing in the *mobile*, but in another text he explicitly rejected this theory. Finally, it was in the theological context of the instrumentality of the sacraments that there was the first positive assumption of an intrinsic principle in violent motions. In his commentary on the *Sentences* (c. 1320), Franciscus de Marchia used projectile motion as an illustration for the continued action of the sacraments. For him, the original mover "leaves" a force in the projectile (a *virtus derelicta*) which expires by itself after some time. Therefore, when discussing celestial motions, he had to retain angels or intelligences which move the heavens using the impetus as a kind of instrument.

Probably this solution was known to *John Buridan and *Albert of Saxony, who concluded that projectiles are moved by a force impressed by the original mover and inferred that if there is more matter *ceteris paribus*, a greater force can be impressed. In Buridan's *ultima lectura* on Aristotle's *Physics*, impetus became a technical term defined as a not self-expending quality which can

only be diminished by resistance. When God created the universe, He impressed an impetus into the celestial bodies which has moved them ever since, and the acceleration in the fall of heavy bodies results from an additional impetus which is acquired by the heavy body itself. Their concept of impetus thus had far-reaching implications, touching on both violent and natural or terrestrial and celestial motions. Nevertheless, the Aristotelian foundation remained intact, the concepts of impetus being rather an effort to find an explanation of projectile motion fitting the two principles of motion.

This theory of impetus was a characteristic of the Parisian "school," although for *Nicole Oresme and *Marsilius of Inghen the impressed force exhausts itself. Their commentaries spread at the central European universities, in Poland, Italy, and Scotland; sometimes they even became obligatory reading. Italian authors such as Biagio Pelacani and Paolo Nicoletti accepted an impressed force as cause of the continuation of projectile motion—though rather hesitatingly—and Nicolaus Cusanus used his own concept of impetus in his *De ludo globi*. In the sixteenth century, the concepts of impetus became a kind of "official" scholastic doctrine. Domingo de Soto, in his commentary on the *Physics* (1545), decided in favour of an impressed force, quoting Thomas's *Quaestiones disputatae*, and one of Galileo's Pisan professors, Francesco Buonamici, attributed the concept of impetus to Philoponus, Albert of Saxony, and Thomas.

It was during this process that the terms "impetus" and *"virtus impressa"* gradually lost their original meanings. In *De Motu antiquiora*, Galileo decided in favor of an impressed force in natural and violent motions, leaving aside its Aristotelian context. A pragmatic use of impetus occurred in the mechanical literature of the sixteenth and seventeenth centuries, for example in Niccolò Tartaglia, who explained the motion of a cannonball by the assumption of an impressed force. In 1696, James Moxon and Venturus Mandey published their *Mechanick Powers: or, the Mistery of Nature and Art unvail'd*, in which they used their concept of impetus to explain the continuity of projectile motion and the acceleration of falling bodies. For them, it is related to the quantity of motion so that it is rather like the impulse in modern physics: not the cause of motion, rather its effect. The same holds true for a treatise of Leibniz on the use of the concept of impetus in machines.

For the Aristotelian natural philosophy taken as a whole, the problem of projectile motion is in fact no more than marginal. Nevertheless the concept(s) of impetus put key doctrines of Aristotle into question: the essential difference of natural and violent motions or that of celestial and elementary motion. Thus, certain elements of Aristotle's theory of motion were in danger of losing their original function, and in the end it may have become easier to replace the whole system. The different concepts of impetus finally contributed to the climate of intellectual change in the latter part of the fifteenth century.

See also **Aristotelianism; Nature: diverse medieval interpretations**

Bibliography

Primary Sources
Clagett, Marshall. *The Science of Mechanics in the Middle Ages.* (Publications in Medieval Science, 4) Madison: University of Wisconsin Press, 1959.
Francesco de Marchia, Giovanni Buridano, Alberto di Sassonia, Marsilio d'Inghen. La Teoria dell'impeto. Testi latini di filosofia medievale. (Testi universitari) Torino: G. Giappichelli, 1969.

Secondary Sources
Drake, Stillman. A further reappraisal of impetus theory: Buridan, Benedetti, and Galileo. *Studies in History and Philosophy of Science* (1976) 7: 319–336.
Duhem, Pierre. *Le Système du Monde. Histoire des doctrines cosmologiques de Platon à Copernic.* 10 volumes. Paris : Librairie Scientifique Hermann, 1913–1959. vol. VIII: La physique Parisienne au XIVe siècle (suite).
Funkenstein, Amos. Some remarks on the concept of impetus and the determination of simple motion. *Viator. Medieval and Renaissance Studies* (1971) 2: 329–348.
Giannetto, E. and G. D. Maccarone, S. Pappalardo, A. Tinè. Impulsus and Impetus in the Liber Jordani de Ratione Ponderis. *Mediaeval Studies* (1992) 54: 162–185.
Maier, Anneliese. *Zwei Grundprobleme der scholastischen Naturphilosophie. Das Problem der intensiven Größe. Die Impetustheorie.* (Studien zur Naturphilosophie der Spätscholastik II—Storia e Letteratura 37) 3rd ed. Roma: Edizioni di storia e letteratura, 1968.
———. *Zwischen Philosophie und Mechanik* (Studien zur Naturphilosophie der Spätscholastik V—Storia e letteratura 69) Roma: Edizioni di storia e letteratura, 1958.
Pines, Shlomo. Les précurseurs musulmans de la théorie de l'impetus. *Archeion* (1938) 21: 298–306.
———. Un précurseur Bagdadien de la théorie de l'impetus. *Isis* (1953) 44: 247–251.
Sarnowsky, Jürgen. *Die aristotelisch-scholastische Theorie der Bewegung. Studien zum Kommentar Alberts von Sachsen zur Physik des Aristoteles.* (Beiträge zur Geschichte der Philosophie und Theologie des Mittelalters, N.F., 32) Münster i. W.: Aschendorff, 1989.
Wolff, Michael. *Fallgesetz und Massebegriff. Zwei wissenschaftshistorische Untersuchungen zur Kosmologie des Johannes Philoponus.* (Quellen und Studien zur Philosophie, 2) Berlin: de Gruyter, 1971.
———. *Geschichte der Impetustheorie. Untersuchungen zum Ursprung der klassischen Mechanik.* Frankfurt a. M.: Suhrkamp, 1978.
Zimmermann, Fritz. "Philoponus's impetus theory in the Arabic tradition." In *Philoponus and the Rejection of Aristotelian Science.* Edited by Richard Sorabji. Ithaca, N.Y.: Cornell University Press, 1987. pp. 121–129.
JÜRGEN SARNOWSKY

INSTRUMENTS, AGRICULTURAL

Agricultural tools, because they are generic in nature, defy any easy or logical scheme of classification. Functionality produces generic lists, while morphological typologies do not necessarily reflect historical continuity.

Creswell used the paddles of traditional horizontal *watermills to show that one can classify a traditional tool morphologically without thereby gaining any insight at all into the historical sequence in which the types have originated or diffused. Over time, tools might change for economic or cultural reasons, or reflect changes in the material to which the tool is applied, or its shape and function might change in response to some exogenous factor: the use of iron-dependent tools could be expanded or changed in consonance with the nature of the local iron-founding technology. A generic tool may not be represented by any generic terminology. Parts of tools (blade, shank, etc.) may well have more stable terminologies than the tool itself. The name of a tool in an inventory may well not suffice to identify what is meant. It is also difficult to read generic tools (such as hoes, spades, sickles, forks, and rakes) for their social content in societies where people of all classes owned the same tools.

Cultivating Tools

The Roman or scratch plow (Latin *aratrum*; generically called an ard) had a symmetrical share and it deposited earth on both sides. Some had "ears" attached to the share to facilitate clearing the clods. It did not turn over the soil; therefore the field had to be cross-plowed or else worked with a spade occasionally. The heavy plow (Latin *carruca*; French *charrue*) is a mainly wooden instrument consisting of a long plow beam to which the team was hitched. Beneath the plow beam hung a share-beam. On its front end was a wrought-iron cap called the share which broke up the sod on impact. A few inches in front of the share a knife, or coulter, was driven through the plow beam to slice the earth horizontally before the share broke it into pieces. Behind the share, on the right side of the plow was a wooden mold-board which pushed the earth to the right to make furrows. Two stilts were fitted to the rear of the plow as a guide for the plowman. If the machine had wheels, they were attached to the forward end of the plow-beam. The two plow types existed contemporaneously in Carolingian times. Both *aratrum* and *carruca* turn up in charters but it not always clear which tool is intended (since *aratrum* was the classical Latin for plow generally) or whether it had a mold-board or not, the critical distinction.

The heavy plow could not be used without adequate harnessing which according to Duby (109) was an eleventh-century phenomenon and included the padded shoulder collar for horses, the frontal yoke for oxen, and shoes for both. In France, the horse did not begin to replace the ox as a plow beast until the twelfth century and not commonly till thirteenth. The replacement was by no means universal: horses required expensive shoeing and oats to eat. Whether they plowed with horse or oxen, larger estates began to increase the number of draught animals in the twelfth century and the supply of fodder required to feed them.

The bimodal categorization of plow types, while convenient for medieval Europe, is less useful for a comparative approach because plow types are notably varied and mold-boards can be found on ards as well as wheeled plows. Thus a Berber ard with small, symmetrical moldboards was introduced in southern Spain under Muslim rule and survived there after the conquest of Granada in 1492. The precise configuration of a plow type was determined by local ecological characteristics, such as soil type and topography (hillside tillage required an oblique orientation of the share, level fields, a horizontal orientation) in addition to specific mechanical desiderata such as how steady the farmer wanted the motion of the implement to be (this affects whether stilts are used or not, how the stilts are attached, and whether the stilts are designed to control depth of plowing as well as the straightness of the course).

The moldboard is present in China by the ninth century and is described, along with other components, in a short treatise called "Classic of the Plow" (*Lei-ssu ching*, c. 880 C.E.): "The plough has eleven parts altogether, counting both wood and metal. The soil thrown up by the plough is called the ridge… and the part which throws up this ridge is called the ploughshare; the part which inverts the ridge is the moldboard. Weeds will always spring up on the ridge [after ploughing] unless their roots are cut by inverting the soil" (Bray, 229). Bray (235) argues that the Chinese plow could not have been the antecedent of the medieval European heavy plough. The Chinese had moldboards from the first century C.E., but always made of metal, not wood as in Europe. In China, the share was always symmetrical and the moldboard, either symmetrical or asymmetrical, placed above it vertically. In the European heavy plow, the moldboard was always asymmetrical and mounted longitudinally behind the share. Coulters, moreover, were very uncommon in China. Nor is the Chinese moldboard plow heavy; it weighs a bit more than an ard, is not wheeled and can be pulled by one animal.

Harvesting Tools

Sickles and scythes are both ancient instruments that were universally diffused in the Middle Ages. Sickles used a slicing or chopping motion to cut the stalks of virtually any crop, while scythes required a long, swinging stroke to cut herbaceous stalks for hay, whether near the ground or at mid-height depending on the length of scythe handle and whether the blade is horizontal or tilted. The short-handled scythe was of ancient vintage and was used in the Middle Ages, particularly models with two short bars mounted on the shaft for ease of handling. In the thirteenth century, new forging techniques made it possible to make a scythe with its blade tilted to twenty-five degrees, allowing it to be used to harvest barley and oats. A short-handled scythe called the Flemish hook was developed around the same time; it was twice as efficient as the sickle and replaced it in some areas.

Threshing, the process whereby the grain is separated from the straw, was performed in medieval Europe consistent with the antecedent Roman practice. The wheat or rye was carried to a threshing floor (a circular area with a compact earthen surface; Latin *area*, Spanish,

era). Then a threshing sledge (Latin *tribulum*; Spanish, *trillo*), a wooden sled with flint teeth mounted on its lower surface, was dragged over it. The operation could be done by hand, with a flail, but it was extremely tedious to perform.

The Importance of Iron

Other instruments such as hoes, spades, harrows, scythes, sickles, and pitchforks were known by generic names that concealed wide stylistic variations. By the later Middle Ages, there were more iron tools: two-pronged iron pitchforks, iron-tipped shovels, wheeled plows made mainly of wood, with iron shares. Two iron pieces dependent on advances in metallurgy were important new elements in mature medieval agricultural in northern Europe. The lengthening of the plowshare in the eleventh and twelfth centuries that new forging techniques made possible produced a two- to four-fold increase in the weight of the share from around ten ounces to one pound one ounce (0.3–0.5 kg), which in turn changed the way fields were plowed. Myrdal speculates that the heavier, longer, share (documented for Sweden) was designed to break fallow and may have been used on specialized fallow-breaking ards along with a plow or ard for cultivating. The second piece was the iron-shod spade, the earliest examples of which date to the tenth and eleventh centuries. This made it easier to dig stubborn roots out of compacted soil, and therefore was used along with, and as a complement to, plowing. It also vastly eased the digging of ditches, with the result that ditching fields for drainage (first archeological evidence in Sweden is from the eleventh century) became a commonplace.

In other respects, the spade, like the hoe, was a generic instrument.

See also **Agriculture**

Bibliography

Bray, Francesca. The Evolution of the Mouldbord Plow in China. *Tools and Tillage* (1976) 3: 227–239.

Comet, Georges. "Technology and Agricultural Expansion in the Middle Ages: The Example of France North of the Loire." In G. Astill and J. Langdon, eds. *Medieval Farming and Technology: The Impact of Agricultural Change in Northwest Europe*. Leiden: E.J. Brill, 1977, pp. 11–39.

Creswell, Robert. "Of Mills and Waterwheels: The Hidden Parameters of Technological Choice." In P. Lemonnier, ed., *Technological Choices Transformation in Material Cultures since the Neolithic*. New York; Routledge, 1993: 181–213.

David, Johan. *L'Outil*. Tournhout: Brepols, 1997.

Duby, Georges. *Rural Economy and Country Life in the Medieval West*. London: Edward Arnold, 1968.

Myrdal, Janken. "The Agricultural Transformation of Sweden, 1000–1300." In Astill and Langdon, *Medieval Farming and Technology*, pp. 147–171.

Raepsaet, Georges. "The Development of Farming Implements between the Seine and the Rhine for the Second to the Twelfth Centuries." In Astill and Langdon, *Medieval Farming and Technology*, pp. 41–68.

Sach, Frantisek. Proposal for the Classification of Pre-Industrial Tilling Implements. *Tools and Tillage* (1968) 1: 3–27.

White, K. D. *Roman Farming*. Ithaca: Cornell University Press, 1970.

THOMAS F. GLICK

INSTRUMENTS, MEDICAL

For the surgeon *Lanfranco of Milan in the thirteenth century, instruments were a source of tension. On the one hand, they were a means to achieving the surgeon's three primary goals: enter the closed body, repair what was sundered, and remove what was in excess, all manual activities. Without doubt, instruments were critical to the functioning of a surgeon, who needed scalpel, probe, and cautery. Indeed, Lanfranco could be quite broad in his definition of a surgical instrument, including leeches, for example. On the other hand, such instruments betokened manual activity. For the elite physician, such manual associations implied menial status, rather than the elevated status of the learned, textualist physician. Lanfranco thus often also used medicinals as a way of achieving the same end. The medieval relationship with medical instruments was thus a complex one and often inflected with multiple social meanings. To better understand this relationship, we will use a textualist's tool as a guide—the Aristotelian four causes of a thing (material, formal, efficient, and final)—in order to understand medieval medical instruments.

Medical instruments were made out of brass, bronze, copper, iron, lead, steel, tin, and rarely silver or gold. Some were made of wood, ivory or bone, as in Viking forceps. The overall prevalence of any material is very uncertain, given the ravages of time, but bronze is most common in surviving forceps. The composition of the instrument clearly altered its properties. Probes made of copper or lead, for example, could be bent to follow serpentine tracts. Brass or copper bowls, used for mixing pharmaceuticals, as in the Anglo-Saxon leechbooks, were dictated by the recipe, and may have played an important chemical role in the drug's efficacy. Cupric salts, for example, are released into a liquid mixture when heated in such bowls; these salts have verifiable antibacterial properties in the modern laboratory. Other materials clearly had more magical functions, as the use of red matter for the curing of diseases of the blood. Innovations in metallurgy and smithing also impacted on medical instruments. With the shift, in the fourteenth century, away from hammer-welding toward iron shaping and casting, smiths entered "the age of the blacksmith, locksmith, and armorer," and were able to demand higher prices. Nonferrous metalsmiths by and large had few changes in their practices, particularly in making copper cups for dry and wet cupping or vessel fashioning.

The range of "typical" forms of medieval medical instruments probably included: scalpels, probes for examining wounds and fistulae, sounds, dilators, mallets, trephines, hooks, catheters, chisels, saws, clamps, forceps, cups, bowls, cauteries, the mohel's knife, and a variety of other shapes. Fine distinctions in form could be quite important; surgeons distinguished between the shapes of needles—rounded or flat, for example, to be used for different wounds and suturing needs. The form was usually closely associated with the procedure being undertaken—repair from hemorrhoid, fistula, cancer, cataract, amputation, nasal polyp, bladder stone, depilation, tooth extraction, fracture setting or trauma each took different instruments. In addition, preparers of pharmaceuticals used bowls/pestles, mortars, spatulae, and scales. Sometimes, the last named became mechanisms of regulation, as for example in Paris from the fourteenth century onward, when new systems of weights and measures became expected and legislated. As with metalworking tools themselves, until the late Middle Ages very few formal changes probably occurred in common surgical instruments. Indeed, for some instruments, the medieval form probably mirrored the simplest of Roman designs, although they became increasingly complex by the end of the Middle Ages. The images in innovative texts such as those of Albucasis (*al-Zahrawi), probably had few practical incarnations.

Intellectually, for the West, the most innovative event for the development of surgical instruments was the translation of Albucasis' *Al-Tasrif li man ajaz an-il-talif*, probably by *Gerard of Cremona in the twelfth century. Subsequently, it was important to the work of surgical authors such as *Guy de Chauliac in his magisterial *Chirurgia magna* and went through a number of vernacular translations throughout Europe. Albucasis' work was very influential in conveying textual imagery of surgical instruments. Not surprisingly, the less practically oriented copyists of his Latin translations often misunderstood the images and diagrams of instruments for decorative imagery. Their own illuminations left out the intended meanings.

Practicing surgical authors, such as *Henri de Mondeville, Guy de Chauliac, and ultimately Ambroise Paré innovated in instrument design by necessity; by the early modern period, inventive German instrument makers coincided with a renewed interest in older and contemporary surgical texts, provoking new illustrations in early printed books of instruments, such as the wound men and the implemental images of Hieronymus Brunschwig's *Dis ist das Buch der Chirurgia* (1497).

Yet medical instruments may be considered more broadly in their form and function, as Lanfranco did. The eyeglass, for example, was one of the most significant generalized inventions of the Middle Ages. Probably first appearing in the late thirteenth century in Italy, *eyeglasses extended the useful working life of the presbyopic learned or manually skilled figure far beyond the early fourth decade when the desiccating lens of the eye typically made close work such as manuscript production or metal work nearly impossible.

In its most general, functional sense, the medical instrument may be considered to include textual technologies. Dating to Quintilian, at least, *instrumentum* could refer to a document. But its technological implication also rose in the Middle Ages, as exemplified by the medical concordance, invented in late-thirteenth-century Paris. In a cognate fashion, the *instrumentum novum* of the Middle Ages was the New Testament, the increased use of which inspired the invention of the concordance. Another such instrument used in practice was the *vade mecum*, which allowed healers to carry with them condensed information in a highly accessible format. In addition, the growing tools of mathematics became instruments for intellectual investigation and prediction. Predictive mathematical formulae for pharmaceutical compounds, for example, leapt forward in the early fourteenth century with the work of *Arnau de Vilanova.

At the level of scholastic discourse, Michael McVaugh has also described a medical "instrumentalism" that was progressively espoused in the thirteenth and fourteenth centuries. This intellectual approach allowed empiricism to define justifiable knowledge in the face of traditional Aristotelian philosophy; to some extent "theories" became tools for the empiric. Practical experience interpreted with the "New Galen" of the medical universities and translations of Avicenna gave primacy to medical explanations over philosophical ones, as in the roles of the four principal members as "instruments" of the body.

Finally, the functional distinction between the "scientific" and the "medical" instrument was not always a clear one. Medieval medicine had a profound dependence on *astrology, for example. Thus the astrolabe could be considered a medical instrument every bit as powerful as the scalpel.

Essentially, the medical instrument, whatever its material, formal or efficient cause, had as its final cause the alteration of the world around the medieval medical thinker or practitioner. Ultimately, those instruments also shaped their users. Whether the surgeon using a scalpel identified as a manual practitioner or the regent master altering his interpretation of Galen because of associative terms in a concordance, and so becoming a medical "instrumentalist," the reciprocal relationship between instruments and their users during the Middle Ages was both rich and complex.

See also **Medicine, practical; Medicine, theoretical; Surgery**

Bibliography

Primary Sources

Albucasis. On Surgery and Instruments: A Definitive Edition of the Arabic Text with English Translation and Commentary. Translated by M. S. Spink and G. L. Lewis. London: Wellcome Institute of the History of Medicine, 1973.

Hieronymus Brunschwig. *Dis ist das Buch der Chirurgia.* Strasbourg: Johann Grüninger, 1497.

Lanfranco da Milan. *Ars completa totius cyrurgie.* Printed with the Cyrurgia of Guy de Chauliac. Venice, 1498.

Secondary Sources

Baker, Patricia. Roman Medical Instruments: Archaeological Interpretations of Their Possible "Non-functional" Uses. *Social History of Medicine* (2004) 17: 3–21.

Milne, John Stewart. *Surgical Instruments in Greek and Roman Times.* Oxford: Clarendon Press, 1907.

McVaugh, Michael. The Nature and Limits of Medical Certitude at Early Fourteenth-century Montpellier. *Osiris* (1990) 6: 62–84.

———. "Therapeutic Strategies: Surgery." In *Western Medical Thought from Antiquity to the Middle Ages.* Edited by Mirko D. Grmek and translated by Antony Shugaar. Cambridge: Harvard University Press, 1998, pp. 273–290.

Perrot, Raoul. Les blessures et leur traitement au Moyen-Age d'apres les textes medicaux anciens et les vestiges osseux. Thèse. Lyon: Universite Claude Bernard, 1982.

Trotter, David. Les manuscrits latins de la Chirurgia d'Albucasis et la lexicographie du latin médiéval. *Bulletin du Cange* (2001) 59: 127–202.

Møller-Christensen, Vilhelm. *The History of the Forceps: An Investigation on the Occurrence, Evolution and Use of the Forceps from Prehistoric Times to the Present Day.* Copenhagen: Levin & Munksgaard; London: Humphrey Milford at the Oxford University Press, 1938.

Vollmuth, Ralf. *Traumatologie und Feldchirurgie an der Wende vom Mittelalter zur Neuzeit.* Stuttgart: Franz Steiner, 2001.

WALTON O. SCHALICK, III

IRRIGATION AND DRAINAGE

Irrigation and drainage are related systems of engineered water flow. Irrigation is the human-made supply of water to agricultural or horticultural crops, usually under conditions of aridity or semiaridity (seasonal drought). Drainage refers to the removal of excess water from agricultural fields. Particularly in semiarid areas, they frequently appear conjoined, as arterial (irrigation) and venal (drainage) canals (sometimes with the two types of water differentiated symbolically as "live" and "dead" water—Spanish *aguas vivas* and *aguas muertas*). Both can be considered "common pool resources" (Ostrom), with the signs changed. Irrigation subtracts water from a common pool and therefore requires rules for its allocation. In medieval Holland, the resource managed by *waaterschappen* (Water Boards that administered dikes and drainage canals) was the wherewithal to remove enough water from fields to permit cultivation. Rules are required, not for the allocation of water, but for the smooth functioning of procedures for its removal. Both agricultural irrigation and drainage systems usually are components of integrated water systems: irrigation systems have to have a drainage component to carry off excess water. In this context, the irrigation and drainage components of an integrated hydraulic system have been compared to arterial and venal functions. In addition, water mills were frequently mounted within irrigation or drainage systems. Because of the typically integrated nature of hydraulic systems, "irrigation and drainage" are frequently found under the same rubric in standard histories of technologies. Moreover, because of the complexity and scale of such systems, the institutions that various societies have developed to administer them also have several common features.

Water systems involve both physical structures (*canals, diversion dams, sluices, lifting devices, and so forth) and institutional ones (operating procedures whereby water is allocated or otherwise subjected to principles of management). Both are properly "technological." Water could not be allocated lacking either physical or institutional components. Technology is, in this context, as much a mental as a material process.

Hydraulic Societies

Wittfogel (1957) focused attention on the relationship between control of water and authoritarian political regimes. Like Marx and Hegel before him, he recognized an obvious relationship between water control and the wealth and administrative reach of ancient empires of Nile, Tigris–Euphrates, Indus, and Yellow River valleys. The relationship holds only on large rivers, however, where flood control is also an issue, and under conditions of full aridity. In semi-arid conditions, the social and cultural responses to irrigation are richly varied. There were no large-scale irrigation systems run by the agro-managerial bureaucracies of centralized states of the type envisioned by Wittfogel either in the medieval Islamic world or in Europe. The Abbasids tried to keep the Sasanian irrigation system functioning, but when the Nahrawan Canal was breached in 935 to halt an advancing army, the system was never repaired. In Europe, the fragmentation of political authority that was characteristic of feudal society worked against any such large-scale effort. The Acequia Real del Júcar, the largest irrigation canal built in Christian Spain (begun by James I of Aragon) enjoyed royal patronage, but was administered as an autonomous irrigation community with substantial irrigator control.

Inasmuch as irrigation was practiced continuously from antiquity into the Middle Ages in arid areas of the Middle East and North Africa, and in the successor states of the Roman Empire, wherever the Romans themselves had irrigated, there has typically been confusion in national historical schools regarding the cultural paternity of irrigating systems. "Popular diffusionism" which attributes, e.g., Roman or Arab paternity to any old-looking artifact has also muddied the waters. Historiographical battles in Spain over the Roman or Arab paternity of different irrigation systems has been typified by the inability of historians to distinguish between the physical structures (in particular, canals) and the institutions of water allocation; the latter bear more intelligible cultural markers than do the former which, in general, cannot be "read" for ethnicity. Only since the 1980s have medieval archeologists taken an interest in water systems, with a subsequent boom in the study of medieval water systems.

All water allocation systems involve some principle of proportionality. In general water is distributed in proportion to the amount of surface irrigated. The proportions are embodied in water rights assigned to individual irrigators or groups of irrigators (in tribal systems) and these proportional rights are given material form in various physical appurtenances of irrigation networks that ensure proportional division of the water. In Valencia, Spain, the debit of irrigation canals was successively subdivided generally through structures called *partidors* ("divisors") which would divide the flow into carefully calibrated equal parts (most divisors being 1:1, but others are 2:1, depending on the lay of the land.). In Elche, there were movable divisors, called *mahimones*, which allow the canal officials to vary the proportions of flow between two channels depending on the allocation of water downstream on a particular day. Proportionality is expressed in various ways through the objectives of autonomous communities of irrigators, typically those irrigating from a single canal. Virtually all such systems embody a principle of equity (that is, equal allocation of water per unit of right) enforced through institutions of local control via tribal or communal monitoring procedures.

Medieval Irrigation

Many medieval Italian towns (e.g., Salerno, Saluzzo, Viterbo) had irrigated market-garden districts on their peripheries. The Po valley was the site of large irrigation projects, always drawn from tributaries of the Po. In Milan, the Naviglio Grande was built in the late twelfth century, originally to supply water from the Ticino River to the city's moat. It was then enlarged and used both for navigation and irrigation. In the later Middle Ages, outlets of fixed dimension supplied secondary canals, replacing haphazardly placed diversion dams that impeded navigation.

In Spain, although the Romans had irrigated there, the irrigation systems in place when the Christian forces conquered Islamic Spain, had generally been built and organized by tribal irrigators, either Arab or Berber. Place-name evidence slows this to be true both for the small mountain communities, as well as for the large, peri-urban huertas surrounding such cities as Valencia and Murcia. In Valencia, where the water table of the huerta is very high, Muslim tribal groups irrigated from springs. As settlement grew denser and the spaces in between settlements gradually were brought under irrigation, the water table was lowered at the same time as the system grew more and more integrated until, at some point before the Christian conquest of 1238, the canals were linked up and water diverted from the Guadalaviar (modern Turia) River, replacing the system of springs. The history of the Valencian huerta is further complicated by the fact that some decades before the Christian conquest, a huge flood carved out an entirely new river bed between the city and the sea, making the early Muslim-built system even harder to reconstruct. The division of water among the eight canals of the huerta, moreover, also seems to reflect a Muslim-inspired allocation principle: it replicates the allocation of water among the canals of the Ghuta or huerta of Damascus, where the water at each stage of the river is reckoned as holding twenty-four units (qirats, in Damascus, filas, or "threads" of water, in Valencia), apparently representing an original division by hours.

In the oases of the Islamic world, irrigation developed a distinctive cultural style. Date palms required irrigation and also a system of canals designed so that the parcels could be laid out regularly. Ibn Hawqal describes the palm grove of Basra (Iraq) and a complex network of channels drawn from the Obolla canal, as an integrated hydraulic system: "At high tide, water flows into each canal, irrigates the palm groves and, upon passing the walls surrounding them, it is distributed through the network of secondary canals without any need to measure it." In the Saharan oases, some of which (like Gafsa) also had palm groves, water was typically distributed by time units measured with inflow or outflow clepsydras.

Medieval irrigation systems have been studied archeologically, especially small-scale, tribally based systems of Islamic Spain. One of the advantages of this kind of analysis is that it covers long extensions of time, across cultural frontiers (the Christian conquest and continuation of relict Muslim systems) and therefore reflects, in a particularly vivid manner, episodes of intensification (early Islamic period) and abatement (post-conquest feudal period in particular). As Arabs migrated westward across North Africa and continued, along with North African Berbers, into Islamic Spain they introduced the former practices of their homelands in a literal fashion, although the tool kit admitted flexibility of approaches to varying topographies and water sources with different hydraulic characteristics. For example, filtration galleries or qanats, originally a Persian technique whereby tunnels were built skimming the surface of water tables, were diffused westward and were used on all scales, from monumental *qanats* in the Sierra de Guadarrama that supplied Madrid with drinking water, to tiny galleries a few meters long that tapped small springs for small-scale irrigation in mountain valleys.

Medieval irrigation was not confined to arid areas or to field crops. Meadows were irrigated to increase their productivity. The large-scale irrigation of meadows was practiced in medieval Lombardy, making it possible to sustain more farm animals over the winter. And in Valais, Switzerland, a microclimate that is relatively warm and dry, expansion of meadow irrigation began in the early fourteenth century as a strategy for agricultural growth under conditions where the arable was pretty much totally developed. A further extension in the fifteenth century was tied to a considerable increase in the grazing of cows (Reynard).

Mediterranean Drainage

The Romans had undertaken some successful drainage schemes, particularly in the Po Valley. Fields were crisscrossed with trenches running transversely to field furrows and which emptied into drainage canals. Roman law required collective maintenance of dikes and trenches forming a common drainage system. Between the eleventh and thirteenth centuries there was considerable diking and drainage canal construction in the Po Valley. Cistercians, in particular, were prominent in monastic drainage projects in Tuscan wetlands particularly in the twelfth century, and towns such as Pistoia, Prato, and Siena reclaimed their marshy plains by drainage in the thirteenth century.

Littoral marshlands of the Mediterranean presented different opportunities. Historically there have been four distinct strategies for the use of littoral wetlands. The first is hunting and gathering as an activity complementary to agriculture. This is the origin of the Valencian paella, all of whose ingredients (rice, rabbit, and shellfish) come from littoral wetlands. Second are local extensions of productive activities at the edges of wetlands, such as creating pasture with local dikes. The third is conversion to rice paddies or huerta (by extending already existing canal systems). The fourth is to open towards the sea and create small harbors or sea channels (Horden and Purcell, 188–189). In medieval Valencia, all four strategies were deployed simultaneously. Trenches were dug into the marshlands (*marjals*) east of the city to drain them. Then irrigation canals were extended from the already irrigated areas close to the city. Water flowing in surface channels, however, had the effect of raising the water table with the result that the channels would disintegrate unless constantly maintained. The *marjals* were reclaimed from around 1386 when the bishop reduced tithes on property there to entice settlement. The fields there, he said, had become marshy and barren due to the ruin and canals and drainage ditches owing to the low density of population. The project was successful until the drought of 1412–1415, when settlement retreated again. The net short-term result of such projects was the extension of marsh, because an abandoned marsh with irrigation canals leading into it is marshier than in its natural state.

Drainage Systems of Medieval Holland

There were three stages in the development of drainage in lowland Holland. In the late tenth century peasants began draining peat bogs by widening and straightening natural bog streams and digging ditches. In the Rijnland the water drained into the Old Rhine River. In the second stage, flood control had become an issue, and dikes and dams were built. By the end of the twelfth century a considerable area had been reclaimed for settlement and agriculture. Around 1160 the Old Rhine silted up, flooding both its banks as a result of which fifteen villages jointly built a dam, the Zwammerdam, to stop the flow of water, which had the result of causing flooding upstream. Finally in 1226 the count of Holland recognized the existing structures of village cooperation which later was known as the Rijnland Drainage Authority (Hoogheemraadschap van Rijnland). By 1250 dikes had built along all the major rivers and the Zuider Zee. In 1286 the count merged the offices of bailiff, the count's highest administrative officer in the Rijnland, with the water board's head, the Dike-reeve, essentially fusing feudal and drainage administration. The water board coordinated and inspected the drainage networks of its member communities, who paid a tax called *morgengeld* to the Board for the upkeep of those dikes and dams it maintained. Local drainage ditches were the responsibility of villages. Disputes were heard by trustees of the Drainage Authority who made regular court appearances in the villages. Other drained areas, such as Delfland and Schieland, had similar institutions

The third stage was polderization, a response to peat subsidence and formation of inland lakes. Polders were fields surrounded by embankment and individually drained. When polders finally sank below the level where they could be drained by gravity flow, the drainage windmill was used to pump the water. *Windmills, the first of which was built in 1408, required permission of the Water Board because they added more water to the already overtaxed system (TeBrake, 2000, 2002)

In the fifteenth century massive, chamber-type sluices were built of wood, thirteen feet (four meters) high and wide by sixty-five feet (twenty meters) long, with a gate at each end. Sluices served mainly to control the inflow and outflow of water at a dam, although some could also function as ship locks. Most sluices however were more modest and used for drainage only. Gates, which were the effective controlling mechanisms of drainage, varied in design. Where the water level on each side varied little, hand-operated, guillotine gates were used, with as many as eight men required to lift the gate, using ropes and winches. Other gates had hinged doors, some turning on a vertical axis, others on a horizontal one. All such turning gates functioned automatically and were used where the outside water level changed frequently: at low tide the fresh water pushed the gate open, high tide closed it. Such hinged gates are very old and specimens found in culverts on the Maas River have been dated archeologically from the first century B.C.E. to the second century C.E. In the fifteenth century, a new style of large turning was introduced, large with copper fittings to reduce wear. To increase capacity, sets of double gates were sometimes used. These evolved by the sixteenth century into the mitered gate which formed an angle facing the sea when closed, so that pressure from sea water closed them tighter than was possible with flat gates (Van Dam).

The English Fens

The medieval Fenland of England was a marshy woodland that saw much reclamation in the thirteenth century. A 1223 document records how there was no habitation in Widenhale, "all being then waste and in the nature of a fen. But afterwards the inhabitants of that place… came; and with draining and banking, won as much thereof by their industry as they could." Twenty-five years later Matthew of Paris recorded in his *Chronica Maiora* (1256): "Concerning this marsh a wonder as happened in our time; for in years past, beyond living memory, these places were accessible neighed for man nor for beast, affording only deep mud with sedge and reeds, and inhabited by birds, indeed more likely by devils as appears form the life of St. Guthlac who began to live there and found it a place of horror and solitude. This is now changed into delightful meadows and also arable ground." Drainage was one of the two most significant

modalities of agricultural expansion in medieval Europe, along with forest clearance.

See also **Agriculture; Canals; Clepsydra; Noria**

Bibliography

Darby, H. C. *The Medieval Fenland*. Newton Abbot: David & Charles, 1974.
Glick, Thomas F. *Irrigation and Society in Medieval Valencia*. Cambridge: Harvard University Press, 1970.
Glick, Thomas F. and Helena Kirchner. "Hydraulic systems and Technologies of Islamic Spain: History and Archeology." In P. Squatriti, ed., *Working with Water in Medieval Europe: Technology and Resource-Use*. Leiden: E.J. Brill, 2000, pp. 267–329.
Horden, Peregrine and Nicholas Purcell. *The Corrupting Sea*. Oxford: Blackwell, 2000.
Ibn Hawqal. *La configuration de la terre (Kitab surat al-ard)*. J. H. Kramers and G. I. Wiet, eds. 2 vols. Beirut: 1964: I, 229.
Ostrom, Elinor. *Governing the Commons*. New York: Cambridge University Press, 1990.
Reynard, Denise. *Histoires d'eau. Bisses et irrigation en Valais au XVe siècle*. Lausanne: Université de Lausanne, 2002.
Squatriti, Paolo. *Water and Society in Early Medieval Italy, AD 400–1000*. New York: Cambridge University Press.
TeBrake, William. "Hydraulic Engineering in the Netherlands during the Middle Ages." In P. Squatriti, ed., *Working with Water in Medieval Europe: Technology and Resource-Use*. Leiden: E.J. Brill, 2000, pp. 101–127.
———. Taming the Waterwolf. Hydraulic Engineering and Water Management in the Netherlands During the Middle Ages. *Technology and Culture* (2002) 43: 475–499.
Van Dam, Petra J. E. M. Ecological Challenges, Technological Innovations: The Modernization of Sluice-Building in Holland, 1300–1600. *Technology and Culture* (2002) 43: 500–520.
Wittfogel, Karl A. *Oriental Despotism*. New Haven: Yale University Press, 1957.

THOMAS F. GLICK

ISAAC JUDAEUS

Ishaq ibn Sulayman al-Isra'ili (the Latin name forms are Isaac Judaeus or Isaac Israeli) was an important author of medical and philosophical treatises which were appreciated by medieval scholars in Islamic territories as well as in Europe. Born in about the middle of the ninth century C.E. into a Jewish family in Egypt, he started his medical career as an oculist in Cairo. Between 905 and 909 he emigrated to Kairouan and became court physician of the last Aglabid ruler Ziyadat Allah III. In 909 the founder of the Fatimid dynasty, 'Ubayd Allah al-Mahdi, captured Kairouan and Isaac changed into the services of the new rulers. He died about 932 reputedly over one hundred years old. Thirteenth-century historians of the Fatimids (Ibn Hammad, Ibn al-Athir and Ibn Hallikan) place him in the context of Fatimid rulers after 'Ubayd Allah al-Mahdi but these accounts are purely anecdotal. Isaac remained unmarried and childless; he is supposed to have said that he had no children but that his work would keep his memory alive. During his time in Kairouan he instructed two disciples: Ibn al-Gazzar who became famous in Europe as the author of a medical treatise for travellers (*Zad al-musafir/Viaticum*) and Dunas ibn Tamim who followed his master as court physician in Kairouan. The most important biography of Isaac is given by Ibn Abi Usaybi'a (d. 1270) in his famous collection of three hundred eighty biographies of physicians.

Isaac's works, all written in Arabic, are essentially based on the ancient Greek sciences but in the medical field he gives largely therapeutical instructions which he had tested as a practicing physician. A list with his medical and philosophical writings is given by Ibn Abi Usaybi'a. Isaac compiled the most important book on the subject of "fevers" (*Kitab al-hummayat/Liber febrium*) written in Arabic. The book is divided into five parts: "the nature of fever," "one day (ephemera) fever," "hectic fever (tuberculosis)," "acute fever," and "putrid fever." According to Ibn Abi Usaybi'a, Isaac himself considered his Book of Fevers as his most significant work. Also important is his treatise on urines (*Kitab al-baul/Liber urinarum*), a diagnostic guidance for the physician which explains the nature of the urine, its different colors and its various residua. Perhaps the most extensive book on dietetics written in Arabic is Isaac's *Kitab al-agdiya/Dietae universales et particulares*. It is divided into a general part on the nature of dietetics and a special part on the different kinds of food. All these medical treatises were translated into Latin by *Constantine the African and played a crucial role in the medical teaching of the Middle Ages, especially before 1400. Often Isaac's medical treatises are found in close context with *Articella*-manuscripts.

Ibn Abi Usaybi'a mentions three further medical writings of Isaac which are not yet identified: an introduction into the art of medicine (*Kitab al-mudhal ila sina'at at-tibb*), a book on the pulse (*Kitab fi'l-nabd*), and a book on the all-round remedy Theriac (*Kitab fi'l-tiryaq*). Furthermore a manuscript conserved today in Aleppo lists a treatise on antimony (*Maqala fi'l-kuhl*) under Isaac's authorship. According to Steinschneider there may exist summaries of the Book of Fevers, the Book of urines, and the Book on the pulse. Maybe Isaac is also the author of a treatise on the ethics of the physician which is preserved in a Hebrew translation (*Musar harofe'im*).

As for his philosophical work Isaac is considered as the father of Jewish Neoplatonism. *Maimonides, however, appreciated his medical writings higher than his philosophical efforts. Isaac's philosophical treatises show his strong dependence on *al-Kindi and on a pseudo-Aristotelian neoplatonic source. Isaac's Book on Definitions and Descriptions (*Kitab al-hudud wa'l-rusum/De definitionibus*) was known in two Latin versions, one by *Gerard of Cremona, and one anonymous. His most extensive work on philosophical matters is the *Book on the Elements* (*Kitab al-ustuqussat/De elementis*), which was read in Europe in the Latin translation of Gerard of Cremona. There is also a "Chapter on Elements" in a Hebrew manuscript which goes back to

Isaac. The *Book on Substances* (*Kitab al-gawahir*) has survived merely in fragments while the *Book on Spirit and Soul* (*Kitab fi r-ruh wa-n-nafs*) is extant only in Hebrew. Steinschneider ascribes two more philosophical treatises and one commentary on the Genesis to Isaac but this remains unproved. Jewish scholars, too, widely discussed and translated Isaac's work already in the Middle Ages.

See also **Aristotelianism; Galen; Hippocrates; Medicine, practical; Medicine, theoretical; Pseudo-Aristotle; Salerno; Universities**

Bibliography

Primary sources
Altmann, Alexander and Samuel M. Stern. *Isaac Israeli, a Neoplatonic philosopher of the early tenth century. His Works translated with comments and an outline of his Philosophy* (Scripta Judaica 1). Oxford: University Press, 1958, reprinted Westport, Conn: Greenwood Press, 1979.
Ibn Abi Usaybi'a. *'Uyun al-anba fi tabaqat al-atibba'/Sources d'informations sur les classes des médecins*. Edited by Jahier, Henri and Noureddine, Abdelkader. Algier: Librairie Ferraris, 1958, pp. 6–9.
The Latin versions of Isaac's work are printed in: *Omnia opera ysaac*. Lyons, 1515.
The edition of the Hebrew translation of the Book of Fevers is prepared by Lola Ferre Cano (Universidad de Granada).

Secondary Sources
Altmann, Alexander. Isaac Judaeus/Israeli. In *Encyclopaedia Judaica IX*. Jerusalem: Encyclopaedia Judaica (and others), 1971, pp. 1063–1065.
Jacquart, Danielle and Françoise Micheau. *La médecine arabe et l'occident médiéval*. Paris: Maisonneuve et Larose, 1990, pp. 107–118 and 167–203.
Sezgin, Fuat. Geschichte des Arabischen Schrifttums III: *Medizin, Pharmazie, Zoologie, Tierheilkunde*. Leiden: E.J. Brill, 1970, pp. 295–297.
Steinschneider, Moritz. *Die arabische Literatur der Juden*. Frankfurt am Main, 1902, reprinted Hildesheim: Olms, 1964 and 1986, pp. 39–45.
Ullmann, Manfred. *Die Medizin im Islam* (Handbuch der Orientalistik. Erste Abteilung (Der Nahe und der Mittlere Osten), Ergänzungsband VI). Leiden: E.J. Brill, 1970, pp. 137–138.
Veit, Raphaela. *Das Buch der Fieber des Isaac Israeli und seine Bedeutung im lateinischen Westen - Ein Beitrag zur Rezeption arabischer Wissenschaft im Abendland* (Sudhoffs Archiv Beihefte 51). Stuttgart: Franz Steiner Verlag, 2003, pp. 319–320.

RAPHAELA VEIT

ISIDORE OF SEVILLE

Isidore of Seville (Isidorus Hispalensis) was born between 560 and 570, possibly in Cartagena or Seville, and died on April 4, 636, in Seville. He was a scholar who mastered the entire knowledge of his time, collating it from sources of ancient civilization and communicating it to the Middle Ages. He was the first of the great medieval encyclopedists, and he inspired and influenced the activities of many subsequent generations in this field. He came from a prominent family, members of which held important positions in the Church. Following the early death of his parents he spent his childhood in the care of his oldest brother, Leander, Archbishop of Seville, at whose court he received an education of the highest quality. He was allowed to spend his time in the tranquil study of Greek, Latin, and Hebrew manuscripts in the prelate's library, and to concentrate on literary work. After Leander's death Isidore was chosen in the year 600 to succeed his brother as archbishop, a position he held until his own death almost forty years later. At that time the Church represented the only sanctuary for literary creation in Latin. Isidore made full use of this opportunity. His extensive literary works stimulated the hitherto passive environment of the Spanish Catholic Church into more lively literary production and proved to be the forerunner of the seventh-century golden age of Latin literature in Spain. Isidore contributed greatly to the revival of literary creativity in the field of theological, apologetic, and exegetic literature. Among his major works was *De ecclesiasticis officiis* (*Church Offices*), a basic history of the liturgy and the development of the Church as an institution. Isidore's most important work of exegesis, concerning interpretations of the Bible and the reading of Latin Church fathers, is *Mysticorum expositiones sacramentorum* (*Interpretations of Mystical Secrets*). Another important work by Isidore is *Contra Iudaeos de fide Christiana* (Concerning the Christian Faith against the Jews). Isidore also wrote on the natural sciences; his work *De natura rerum* (*On the Nature of Things*), sometimes known as *Liber rotarum* (*Book of Circles*), describes chiefly astronomical and meteorological phenomena.

Differentiae (*Differences*) lies on the boundary between natural science and linguistics. Of the traditional genres of ancient literature, only historiography was cultivated during Isidore's youth. Isidore wrote a history of the world, *Chronica* (*Chronicle*): like all his work it is written in a dry and stereotypical style and the content is not original; he draws exclusively on the work of his predecessors in this field. Nevertheless, by this volume Isidore influenced all medieval historiography up to the beginning of the Renaissance. Shorter versions of the chronicle became part of his most celebrated and widely read work, *Etymologiae* (*Etymologies*).

Isidore's extraordinarily extensive literary creation was for him only a preparation for the *Etymologiae*, the concluding work of his life, on which he labored for decades. Whereas he immediately published the other works that he produced during these years, he held this work—also entitled *Origines*—back from his readers. Only in around 633, and for reasons of ill health, did he unwillingly and resignedly entrust completion and final correction of the work to his pupil and friend Braulio of Saragossa (Braulio Saragossensis, d. 651, Bishop of Saragossa from 631). The encyclopedic *Etymologiae* comprises twenty books, although its organization into different books is not Isidore's work but the result of

Isidore of Seville. From *The Lives of the Fathers, Martyrs and Other Principal Saints* (1928) by Alban Butler. (Topham/Charles Walker)

Braulio's later intervention. The encyclopedia obtained its name from the fact that each item begins with an explanation of its origin. For many terms Isidore tries to define their origin (*origo*) and their original, undistorted meaning (*etymon*). Isidore did not provide the work with a prologue in which he would seek to outline the principles and objectives of his work; nevertheless it is evident that the etymological approach was not designed purely for linguistic and pedagogic reasons—i.e., to master the vocabulary of Latin (which also contains more than 1,500 Spanish words, as well as terms from other languages)—but also had gnoseological (epistemological) purposes: he wanted to reveal the meaning of the facts to which the words referred. This approach was derived from the ancient belief in the secret unity of the word and the object that it describes. The author's task certainly also comprised an attempt to provide the enormous volume of collated information with a certain unifying element, order, and system. The work remained unsurpassed until the thirteenth century and was regarded as the summary of all knowledge. It became an essential part of European medieval culture. Soon after the invention of typography it appeared many times in print. It is an enormous collection, a compendium of information and definitions, a compilation in which the author, according to the customs of his time, often does not state his sources or does so unreliably (despite this, more than one hundred ancient sources have been identified in the work). The method of mechanical compilation is here chosen as an expression of humility before the extent of the material collected by previous ages. The following is a schematic survey of the content of *Etymologiae*. Books I–III: seven liberal arts (*septem artes liberales*), namely, the trivium—grammar, rhetoric, and dialectics—and the *quadrivium—*arithmetic, geometry, music, and astronomy—based especially on Cassiodorus and *Boethius. Book IV: medicine (based on Caelius Aurelianus). Book V: rudiments of Roman law; chronology; an abbreviated version of the *Chronica*, recounting history from the creation of the world to Isidore's own time, i.e., to the year 615. Events chiefly from Greek and Roman history are set against a biblical background. Book VI: introduction to a study of the Bible; explanation of the *calendar, including the means of calculating the date of Easter; the book ends with an exposition of the bases of the Christian liturgy. Book VII: basic terms of Christian doctrine, including a list of ecclesiastic ranks. Book VIII: opponents of the Christian Church, sects, heresies, and paganism, including an explanation of the names of the Greek and Roman gods. Book IX: languages and peoples of the world; family, marriage; the Roman state, its organization, army, law. Book X: alphabetical *vocabulary of roughly six hundred lesser-known Latin expressions with explanations of their etymology and meanings. Book XI: the human body, the stages of human life; description of mythological monsters and several famous metamorphoses of mythological figures into animals (based on Lactantius). Book XII: *zoology (based on Pliny and Solinus, as were the two following books). Book XIII: meteorological phenomena; parts of the world. Book XIV: fundamentals of the *geography of the world known to Isidore. Book XV: *architecture and town planning. Book XVI: *mineralogy. Book XVII: *agriculture. Book XVIII: varied mixture of martial art and weaponry, sport, theater, gladiatorial games, and games of chance. Book XIX: house building and road building, cloth production, making of jewelry. Book XX: food, beverages, home fittings (furniture), gardening and agricultural tools.

See also **Astronomy, Latin; Encyclopedias; Medicine, theoretical; Meteorology; Music theory**

Bibliography

Primary Sources

Isidore de Séville. *De differentiis*. Livre I. Par C. Codoner (in Spanish). Paris, France: Les Belles Lettres 1992.
———. *De natura rerum*. Edited by G. Becker. Amsterdam: Hakkert 1967.
———. *De natura rerum* (Traitè de la nature). Edited by J. Fontaine (with French transl.). Bordeaux, France: Féret, 1960.
———. *Étymologies*. Paris, France: Les Belles Lettres 1981– .
Isidori Hispalensis episcopi Etymologiarum sive Originum libri XX. I-II. Edited by W. M. Lindsay. Oxford: Clarendon Press, 1911.
Sancti Isidori, Hispalensis episcopi, Opera omnia. I-VII. Edited by Faustinus Arevalo. 7 volumes. Rome: typis A. Fvlgonii 1797–1803. Reprint: J. P. Migne, *Patrologiae cursus completus, series Latina* [PL]. 221 volumes in 223. Paris, France: Apud Garnieri Fratres 1844–1891. vols. 81-84.

Secondary Sources

Brunhölzl, F. *Geschichte der lateinischen Literatur des Mittelalters*. I. München: W. Finck 1975.
McCluskey, Stephen C. *Astronomies and Cultures in Early Medieval Europe*. New York: Cambridge University Press 1998, pp. 123–126, 145–147.
Díaz y Díaz, M. C. *Isidoriana; colección de estudios sobre Isidoro de Sevilla*. León, Spain: Centro de Estudios 'San Isidro', 1961.
———. *San Isidoro de Sevilla. Etimologías. Edicion bilingüe. Introduccion general*. Madrid, Spain: Editorial Católica, 1982.
Diesner, Hans-Joachim. *Isidor von Sevilla und seine Zeit*. Stuttgart, Germany: Calwer 1973.
Dressler, Heinrich. *De Isidori originum fontibus*. Turin, Italy: V. Bona, 1874.
Duhem, Pierre. *Le système du monde*. Paris, France: Librairie Scientifique Hermann, 1913–1959. (Isidore of Seville: III. Paris 1958, pp. 1–12.)
Fontaine, Jacques. *Isidore de Séville et la culture classique dans l'Espagne wisigothique*, 2 volumes. Paris, France: Études Augustiniennes 1959; second edition, 3 volumes. Paris, 1983.
Göbel, Gabriele M. *Weisser, weisser Isidor*. Düsseldorf, Germany: Schwann 1987.
Hillgarth, J. N. The Position of Isidorian Studies: A Critical Review of the Literature 1936–1975. Studi medievali (1983) 24: 817–896.
Lear, F. S. St. Isidore and Mediaeval Science. *Rice Institute Pamphlets* (1936) 23: 75–105.
Pérez de Urbel, Justo. *Isidor von Sevilla. Sein Leben, sein Werk, seine Zeit*. Köln, Germany: J.P. Bachem, 1962.
Sharpe, William D. *Isidore of Seville: The Medical Writings*. Philadelphia: American Philosophical Society 1964 (transl. of *Etymologiae* IV and XI).

PETR HADRAVA AND ALENA HADRAVA

J

JABIR IBN HAYYAN (GEBER)

Traditionally, the Muslim polymath and alchemist Jabir ibn Hayyan (c. 721–815 C.E.) is believed to have been born in the town of Tus, just outside the city of Khurasan (modern-day Mashhad) in northeast Iran. He was soon orphaned after his father, a pharmaceutical chemist from Kufa, was arrested and executed for having advocated the Abbasid usurpation of the Umayyad family during the internal struggle for power. After the Abbasid family seized the Caliphate, in 748 C.E., Jabir is claimed to have befriended the sixth Shi'ite Imam, Ja'far al-Sadiq (700–765 C.E.), who exclusively taught him among other things the art of *alchemy, and thereafter became a compiler. However, even though there are numerous instances where Jabir cites the name of Ja'far al-Sadiq in the invocation *wa haqqi sayyidi* ("By my Master"), some historians and scholars have maintained that, because there appears to be no mention of a disciple named Jabir in Shi'ite literature, the relationship between Jabir and Ja'far al-Sadiq should be dismissed as legend. Moreover, as early as the tenth century, the identity and legitimacy of Jabir appear to have been convoluted.

In the earliest extant biobibliographic reference to Jabir, documented and compiled in 987 C.E. by the Arabic bookseller Ibn al-Nadim (d. 995 C.E.), the *Kitab al-Fihrist* (*Book of the Index*) recorded that Shi'is claimed that Jabir was one of their *abwab* (spiritual leaders) who was a companion to Ja'far al-Sadiq. Subsequently, Ibn al-Nadim mentioned a group of philosophers who claimed Jabir was a colleague who wrote on logic and philosophy. In another section of the *Fihrist*, it states that a group of scholars and *warraqun* (stationer-copyists) maintained that if Jabir existed, the only writing that can be ascribed to him is *Kitab al-Rahmah al-Kabir* (*The Large Book of Mercy*); since all other writings were composed by individuals who intentionally falsified the authorship of their work by ascribing it to Jabir. Whereupon Ibn al-Nadim responded that Jabir was authentic and adamantly refuted the assertion that Jabir never existed; and, thus, concluded by offering a list of various treatises on Shi'i doctrine, owned by Jabir, as well as numerous treatises on the sciences written by Jabir. In the end, Ibn al-Nadim quoted Jabir, using his *kunya* (honorific) Abu Musa, as having claimed to have composed over three thousand six hundred books and three hundred leaves on a variety of subjects.

The Jabirian Corpus

The Jabirian corpus is generally presented as having consisted of major theoretical and applicable scientific treatises on alchemy, astrology, medicine, instruments of war, mechanics, etc., and smaller commentaries, paraphrases, supplementary explanations, and refutations that cover such diverse disciplines as languages, philosophy, logic, mathematics, sermons, occultism, cosmology, music, charms, poetry, etc. Due to the sheer magnitude and diversity found in the Jabirian corpus, as well as numerous Greek scientific and philosophical paraphrases, some historians and scholars have maintained that the writings were not solely the work of Jabir. Rather, it has been argued that, beginning in the second half of the ninth century, the Isma'ili movement emerged from a form of proto-Shi'i gnosis; and subsequently attempted to influence religious, philosophical, ideological, and political mediums through a propagandistic compilation and presentation of the known sciences. In particular, it has been alleged that it was the Qarmati-Isma'ili movement that was directly responsible for employing technical terms in most of the these scientific writings; and, sometime between the tenth or early eleventh century, the multi-generational literary endeavor reached its final form in a Corpus Jabirianum. It should be noted, however, that the origins of the Isma'ili movement are fragmentary until the middle of the ninth century, and ongoing hypotheses continue to be debated by historians and scholars.

The Geber Corpus

It appears from extant manuscripts that during the twelfth and thirteenth century the Latin West was introduced to five alchemic texts by the alchemist "Yeber" or

"Gebir filius Hegen ezahufy" (that is, Jabir ibn Hayyan al-Sufi). Subsequent centuries would come to know the alchemist as Ieber, Jeber, Geber Abinhaen or Geber ebn Haen (Jabir ibn Hayyan), Giaber, Gebri Arabis philosophi ("the Arab philosopher Geber"), etc.; until, eventually, the Latin name became standardized as Geber. It should be noted, however, that some historians and scholars who have addressed the "Jabir-Geber problem" do not believe that that the Latin Geber was de facto the ninth century Jabir ibn Hayyan, but rather a twelfth- or thirteenth-century Latin "pseudo-Geber." The position is maintained, in part, due to the absence of any original extant Arabic works prior to the twelfth or thirteenth century which correspond directly to the Latin Geber corpus. Indeed, according to the thesis, the only extant Arabic work of possible authenticity ascribed to Jabir is the *Kitab al-Rahmah al-Kabir*. Another proposition that has been asserted, to uphold the claim of a Latin pseudo-Geber, is that the materials and processes mentioned in the Geber corpus (e.g., *aqua regia*, *alumen plumae*, *alumen roccae*, *sal petrae*, *sal tartari*, etc.) were only available during the thirteenth and fourteenth centuries. However, it has been suggested that an etymological corruption or mistranslation of these and similar words might account for the historical exclusivity; in addition, it has been asserted that many authentic Arabic-Islamic expressions appear throughout the Geber corpus. Conversely, counterarguments have maintained that not only was the scholastic Latin used in the Geber corpus inadequate to translate such equivalent Arabic texts, but such an etymological corruption has not been conclusively established; furthermore, similar to the practice of forgeries in Greek and Muslim alchemical literature, the imitation and incorporation of authentic Arabic-Islamic phrases was simply used in the Geber corpus to intentionally promote a sense of authentication. Nevertheless, it should be noted that only a mere fraction of Latin alchemical literature, as well early Greek alchemic texts via Syriac and Arabic translations, has been made available in scholarly editions; but it is not unusual for original versions of translated manuscripts to be permanently lost to natural decomposition or human destruction. In short, the authenticity of the Geber corpus remains uncertain and is presently a matter of conjecture.

Single Volume

The Geber corpus was generally presented to the Latin West in a single volume and consisted of five alchemic treatises: *Summa perfectionis magisterii* (*The Sum of Perfection*), *De investigatione perfectionis* (*The Investigation of Perfection*), *De inventione veritatis* (*The Invention of Verity*), *Liber fornacum* (*Book of Furnaces*), and *Testamentum* (*Testament*). Of the five treatises, *Summa perfectionis magisterii* is perhaps the most important work. It is divided into two parts. The first discusses (1) The problems involved in the preparation and processes of an elixir; (2) Refutations against the sceptics of the art of alchemy; (3) The natural properties of metals (i.e., gold, silver, lead, tin, copper, and iron) and the division of arsenic, mercury, and sulphur; (4) The method and observation involved in the calcinations, crystallization, distillation, reduction, and sublimation of ores, minerals, solutions, spirits, etc. The second part examines: (1) The importance of understanding the nature of spirits in relation to gold, silver, lead, tin, copper, iron, arsenic, mercury, and metallic sulphide; (2) The properties and preparations for making different medicines; and (3) The laboratory apparatuses and processes involved in the art of alchemy, followed by a summary.

It has been noted by historians and scholars that Jabirian science incorporated the Pythagorean theory of cosmic harmony (a theory derived from qualitative or symbolic properties of numbers). In particular, according to Jabirian science, *jawhar* (substance) consisted of the four elements *harr* (hot), *bard* (cold), *balla* (moist), and *yubs* (dry), which could all be arranged in altering proportions of the numbers 1, 3, 5, and 8, but would always result in the universal constant of 17. Thus, when these four elements are perfectly combined with "sulfur" (i.e., a metaphor for active masculinity) and "mercury" (i.e., a metaphor for passive femininity), gold is produced; and the process is generally referred to as the Jabirian "sulfur-mercury theory." In addition, it has been suggested that the numerical postulate of the action of drugs, ascribed to *Galen, was also incorporated into the framework of Jabirian science. Whereupon each of the four elements (i.e., hot, cold, moist, and dry) used in curing by contraries, was associated with seven grades of intensity, with each grade possessing four degrees of strength, yielding the total number of permutations and combinations in the formula *4 x (7 x 4) = 112.* The computation was probably derived from early Arabic translations of Galen carried out by the Nestorian Christian mediator and translator *Hunayn ibn Ishaq al-'Ibadi (808–873 C.E.). In an epistle of 856 C.E., Hunayn claimed to have translated one hundred four works of Galen (out of a total of one hundred twenty-nine titles) into Syriac and Arabic; and it appears that the Jabirian science not only incorporated parts of these translations in its writings, but also adopted some examples of the proto-Arabic scientific terminology introduced by Hunayn.

Therefore, it appears that Jabirian science attempted to develop a theoretical premise, based on the theory of the reconfiguration of qualities in accordance to their universal position; and, essentially, presented a systematic and rigorous schematic methodology that would be applicable to the transmutation of base metals into gold, the preparation of medicines, and all other processes of the universe. Thus, by the fourteenth and fifteenth century, the Jabir-Geber corpus influenced both scientific and mystical circles; and by the sixteenth and seventeenth centuries, the republication of the collected works seems to have contributed to a revival in alchemy and alchemical medicine.

See also **Fihrist**; **Music theory**

Bibliography

Berthelot, Marcellin. *Introduction a l'étude de la chimie, des anciens et du Moyen Age*. Paris: G. Steinheil, 1889.

Haq, Syed Nomanul. *Names, Natures, and Things: The Alchemist Jabir ibn Hayyan and his Kitab al-Ahjir (Book of Stones)*. Dordrecht and Boston: Kluwer, 1994.

Ibn al-Nadim, Muhammad ibn Ishaq. *The Fihrist of Al-Nadim; a Tenth-Century Survey of Muslim Culture*. Bayard Dodge, ed. New York: Columbia University Press, 1970.

Kraus, Paul. *Jabar ibn Hayyan: Contribution a l'histoire des idées scientifiques dans l'islam*. Hildesheim and New York: Georg Olms, 1989.

Newman, William R. *The Summa Perfectionis of Pseudo-Geber: A Critical Edition, Translation and Study*. Leiden: E.J. Brill, 1991.

Russell, Richard. *The Alchemical Works of Geber*. York Beach: S. Weiser, 1994.

TOD BRABNER

JACOPO DA FORLÌ

A doctor in the Arts and Medicine and a teacher, Giacomo della Torre is best known as Giacomo (or Jacopo) da Forlì, from the name of his natal town in current Emilia-Romagna. He was born c. 1360 to a wealthy family, and died in Padua on February 12, 1414.

Jacopo da Forlì spent all his life in northern Italy, teaching different branches of the medical and natural sciences in several universities. His career seems to have been turbulent and was characterized by frequent moves, the refusal of a position, and breaches of commitments. He first taught natural philosophy (1383–1385), *astrology and grammar (1384–1385), and medicine and philosophy (1385–1400) at the University of Bologna. In 1388 (while still in Bologna), he was offered a lectureship in natural and moral philosophy in Florence, but declined the offer. In 1400, he moved from Bologna to Padua, at the university of which he taught medicine (1400–1402), as he did also at the universities of Ferrara (1402–1404), and Siena (1404). In the latter, he was offered and accepted a renewal, but he did not respect his commitments. After three years (1407), he resumed teaching at the university of Padua, where he held the chair of ordinary medicine. In 1412, he agreed to lecture at the university of Parma, but again did not fulfill his commitment. He pursued his teaching activity at the university of Padua until the end of his life.

As a university teacher of medicine, Jacopo da Forlì commented on two major works of the post-Salernitan period, the Hippocratic *Aphorismi* and *Galen, *Ars parva* (known as *Tegni* or *Microtegni*), which were included in the so-called *Articella*. To them he added the *Canon* of Avicenna (*Ibn Sina). The Latin translations of the Greek texts date back to such translators as *Constantine the African (d. after 1085), and to *Gerard of Cremona (c. 1114–c. 1187) for Avicenna. Jacopo da Forlì returned neither to the original Greek text—as *Pietro d'Abano (1257–c. 1315) already had before him—nor to possible new Latin translations made from the Greek. He produced (in chronological order) commentaries on Avicenna's chapter *De generatione embrionis* from the *Canon* (Padua, 1400); the Hippocratic *Aphorismi*, 2 (Ferrara, 1403); Galen, *Ars parva* (Padua, 1407), and Avicenna, *Canon*, 1.1–2 (Padua, 1413–1414). His commentary on Galen became a textbook for the teaching of the third-year course of theoretical medicine in Padua, and replaced the work of *Torregiano de' Torregiani (c. 1270–c. 1350) used previously. His commentary on Avicenna was widely used later as a university textbook.

The importance of Jacopo da Forlì in medical university teaching during the late Middle Ages is well illustrated by the several manuscripts of his commentaries, and their many printed editions during the late-fifteenth and early-sixteenth centuries: the commentary on Hippocrates was printed as early as 1473 and reprinted several times: 1477 (Padua), before 1480 (Padua), 1495 (Venice), 1501 (Pavia), 1502 and 1508 (Venice), 1512 (Pavia), 1519, and 1520 (Venice); the commentary on Avicenna, *De generatione embrionis*, was printed in 1479 (Pavia) and reprinted in 1485 (Siena), and 1489 and 1502 (Venice); the *Expositio super tres libros Tegni Galieni* was first printed in 1475 (Padua) and reprinted c. 1477 (Padua), 1487 (Pavia), 1491 and 1495 (Venice), 1501 (Pavia), 1508 (Venice); the commentary on Avicenna, *Canon*, was first printed c. 1474 (Milan) and reprinted in 1479 (Venice), 1484–1487 and 1488 (Pavia), 1508, 1518, 1520 (Venice).

Besides such teaching texts, he also wrote a *Questio de intensione et remissione formarum* (1381–1384), which was printed in Treviso before 1480 and reprinted in Venice in 1496, as well as other works known only in manuscripts, such as *Commentarii super Aristotelis Physicorum libris I-IV* and discourses. Other works are known only by title.

His commentaries (particularly on Avicenna) rely heavily on previous works, especially the *Conciliator* of Pietro d'Abano, the commentaries on Avicenna, *Canon*, by Dino del Garbo (d. 327), and the *Anathomia* of *Mondino de' Liuzzi (d. 1326).

Already in his time, Jacopo da Forlì was held in high esteem and considered the most learned and greatest physician of his age. As such he followed Marsiglio de Santa Sofia (d. 1405?) and was followed by *Ugo Benzi (1376–1439), with whom he was in contact. He is credited with a significant contribution to the formation of the Averroist interpretation of Aristotle's philosophy at the University of Padua. Unquestionably a highly talented teacher, from his turbulent career he seems to have had a similar level of self-esteem.

See also **Aristotelianism; Hippocrates; Medicine, theoretical**

Bibliography

Lockwood, D.P. *Ugo Benzi: Medieval philosopher and Physician, 1376–1439*. Chicago: University of Chicago Press, 1951.

Pesenti, Tiziana. *Professori e promotori di medicina nello Studio di Padova dal 1405 al 1509. Repertorio Bio-Bibliografico*. Padua: Edizioni Lint 1984, pp. 103–112.

Randall, John Herman. *The School of Padua and the emergence of modern science*. Padua: Editrice Antenore, 1961.

Siraisi Nancy. *Avicenna in Renaissance Italy. The Canon and Medical Teaching in Italian Universities after 1500.* Princeton: Princeton University Press, 1987.

———. *Medicine and the Italian Universities, 1250–1600.* Leiden: E.J. Brill, 2001.

ALAIN TOUWAIDE

JAMES OF VENICE

Although James of Venice (fl. c. 1136–1150) was a prolific translator and commentator of Aristotle, little can be said with any certainty about the details of his life. He referred to himself as "Veneticus Grecus," which might mean either that he was a Greek born in Venice, a Venetian born and educated in Greece, or an expatriate Venetian who adopted Greece as his second home. There is some circumstantial evidence that John of Salisbury (c. 1115/1120–1180) was acquainted with James, and Minio-Paluello speculated that he might have been the Italo-Greek translator from Sancta Severina in Calabria whom John met in southern Italy about 1148–1153. Whatever the case may be, we know that he was in Constantinople in April 1136, where he heard a theological debate between Anselm of Havelberg (d. 1158) and the archbishop of Nicomedia. In 1148, he provided legal advice to the archbishop of Ravenna and may have been present at the council at Cremona in July of that year. Although referred to as "*clericus*," he may never have been ordained a priest.

James's translations of Aristotle include the so-called "vulgate" version of the *Posterior Analytics*, the "*vetus translatio*" of the *Physics*, the *Metaphysica vetustissima*, and translations of *De anima* and large portions of the *Parva naturalia* (*De longitudine et brevitate vitae, De iuventute et senectute, De resperatione, De morte et vita, De memoria et reminiscentia*). Fragments of his translation of *De sophisticis elenchis* survive, as do portions of his translation of a Greek commentary on that work and the *Posterior Analytics* by "Alexander," while translations of the *Topics* and *Prior Analytics* attributed to him have not been found. In addition to the legal opinion conveyed in the letter to Archbishop Moses of Vercelli, he was also the author of commentaries on *De sophisticis elenchis, Topics,* and the *Prior* and *Posterior Analytics*, produced perhaps about 1130. And if the "Jacobus grecus" mentioned by Cerbano in his *Translatio mirifici martyris Ysidori* is the translator "Jacobus Veneticus," it would seem that James had put his hand to writing a historical account of a voyage of the Venetians east to Constantinople.

Both his letter to the archbishop of Ravenna and his surviving translations indicate that James's preferred translation style was literal, a technique derived not always from linguistic inadequacies but rather the goal of reflecting accurately difficult and unfamiliar material in the twelfth century. His syntax frequently reflects that found in the Greek text which he was translating, and when no exact equivalent can be found in Latin James provides the Greek term first, then a Latin correspondent, which has now acquired a novel definition. As a result, at least in some circles James's translations were criticized as obscure, although John of Salisbury defended his translation of the *Posterior Analytics* and attributed the problems encountered by French masters to the difficulty of the work, not the translator's skill. On the other hand, John also recognized the limitations of James's linguistic skills, at least in comparison with those of other translators; while he seems to have regarded him as eloquent, his knowledge of Latin was less than perfect.

The success of James's translations may be measured by the numbers of surviving copies in manuscript. The "vulgate" *Posterior Analytics* is extant in two hundred and seventy-five manuscripts; the three other translations of the text combined can be found in only eight manuscripts. Likewise, his translations of the *Physics* and *De anima* remained the dominant versions until displaced by the newer translations of *William of Moerbeke more than a century later. These early translations were a principal means by which Aristotle's ideas were assimilated in western Europe.

See also **Aristotelianism; Translation movements; Translation, norms and practices; William of Moerbeke**

Bibliography

Brams, Josef. "James of Venice, Translator of Aristotle's *Physics*." In *Praktika Pagkosmiou Synedriou Aristoteles, Thessalonike, 7–14 Augoustou 1978 = Proceedings of the World Congress on Aristotle, Thessaloniki, August 7–14, 1978.* Edited by Ioannes Nikolaou Theodorakopoulos. 4 volumes. Athens: Ekdosis Ypourgeiou Politismou & Epistemon, 1981–1983. vol. 2, pp. 188–191.

Ebbesen, Sten. Jacobus Veneticus on the *Posterior Analytics* and some early 13th-century Oxford masters. *Cahiers de l'Institut du Moyen-âge Grec et Latin* (1977) 21: 1–9.

Gutman, Oliver. James of Venice's Prolegomenon to Aristotle's *Physics: De intelligentia. Medioevo. Rivista di Storia della Filosofia Medievale* (2002) 27: 111–140.

Minio-Paluello, Lorenzo. Jacobus Veneticus Grecus: canonist and translator of Aristotle. *Traditio* (1952) 8: 265–304.

Pertusi, Agostino. "Cultura Greco-Bizantina nel tardo medioevo nelle Venezie e suoi echi in Dante." In *Dante e la cultura Veneta. Atti del Convegno di Studi (Venezia, Padova, Verona, 30 marzo–5 aprile 1966).* Edited by Vittore Branca and Giorgio Padoan. Florence: Olschki, 1966, pp. 157–197.

STEVEN J. LIVESEY

JEAN DE MEURS

Jean de Meurs (Johannes de Muris) was born in Normandy in the diocese of Lisieux in the 1290s; a more accurate birthdate cannot be given. His first writing, a critique of the ecclesiastical computation of the calendar, dates from 1317. A noticeable feature of this treatise of 1317 is that it employs the Tables of Toulouse, not the *Alfonsine Tables*. In 1321 Jean became a master of arts in Paris and wrote among other things *Expositio tabularum Alfonsi regis*. In 1323, at the Sorbonne in Paris, he wrote the *Musica speculativa secundum boetium*, an abbreviation of *De musica* of *Boethius, and in 1324 the

Fractiones magistri J. de Muris, a synoptic table of his *Arithmetica speculativa*, contained in MS Paris, BnF lat. 16621, fol. 62v–64r. Very probably in this period Jean wrote his *Arithmetica speculativa*. In the same year (1324) Jean completed a *Figura maris aenei Salomonis*, i.e., a demonstration of the quantity and figure of the bronze basin in the temple of Salomon. Between 1338 and 1342 he was among the clerks of Philippe III d'Évreux, king of Navarre, and in 1344 he was canon of Mezières-en-Brenne, in the diocese of Bourges. According to the *explicit* of MS Paris, BnF lat. 14736, Jean completed his *Quadripartitum numerorum* on November 13, 1343. In a letter dated September 25, 1344, Jean de Meurs was summoned to Avignon by Pope Clement VI for a conference on calendar reform. According to Gushee it may be assumed that Jean left for Avignon shortly after receipt of Pope Clement's letter, i.e., in October 1344.

In another treatise, which goes by the name *De arte mensurandi* from the incipit "*Quamvis plures de arte mensurandi*," Jean refers to the *Quadripartitum numerorum* as follows:

(1) Book V, Part 2, Prop. 17: *per artem quam in quadripartito numerorum alias explanavi* (by the art which I have explained elsewhere in the *Quadripartitum numerorum*).

(2) Book V, Part 3, Prop. 8: *per artem quam in quadripartito numerorum alias ordinavi* (by the art which I have set in order elsewhere in the *Quadripartitum numerorum*).

(3) Book X, Prop. 2: *Et hanc artem in quadripartito numerorum alias ordinavi* (and this art I have set in order elsewhere in the *Quadripartitum numerorum*).

From these references we may conclude that Jean wrote *De arte mensurandi* after the *Quadripartitum numerorum*, and very likely before his departure to Avignon in 1344.

The epistolary treatise, which Jean and Firminus de Bellavalle composed to transmit their findings and recommendations concerning calendar reform, is dated 1345. No later date for his activity has been established. Besides the works mentioned above Jean wrote a series of tracts on music and astronomy. In the remainder of this entry, we discuss only his mathematical works.

Quadripartitum numerorum

Jean's main mathematical work, the *Quadripartitum numerorum*, which takes its name from its division into four books, consists of a metrical and a prose part. According to L'Huillier the text in verse is written at the end of the work before the last tract of Book IV entitled *De arte delendi*. The prose portion of the *Quadripartitum* is divided into four books and a *semiliber* interpolated between books III and IV. Book I, containing a prologue and twenty-four chapters, is devoted to arithmetic and based on the *Arithmetica* of Boethius and *Euclid's *Elements*. In Book II, containing twenty-seven chapters, Jean treats the multiplication and division of integers and introduces fractions. His sources are an unedited arithmetical tract contained in MS Paris, BnF lat. 15461 and

Jean de Lignères's *Algorismus minutiarum*. Book III, containing twenty chapters and forty-five questions, is devoted to algebra. His source is *al-Khwarizmi's *De iebra et almucabala* (*Algebra*), translated by *Gerard of Cremona. After having written the twenty chapters of Book III, Jean became acquainted with the *Liber abaci* (*Book of the Abacus*) of *Leonardo Fibonacci. He has used this work for his *Semiliber* and the forty-five questions in this order. Book IV is devoted to practical applications of arithmetic and includes five tracts: the first two concern mechanics (*De moventibus et motis* and *De ponderibus et metallis*), the third is entitled *De monetis, scilicet de arte consolandi*, and the fourth, *De sonis musicis*, is lost or was never written. The last tract, *De arte delendi*, is an elaboration of the fifth part of Chapter Twelve of Fibonacci's *Liber abaci*. Of the thirty-two chapters in Tract I, Grant (1971, 361–377) has published an English translation of chapters 12–14, 21–26, and 28, and Clagett (1978, 7f.) has translated Chapter Thirty-One. As appears from this last chapter, Jean apparently was acquainted with *On Spiral Lines* of Archimedes. The text of the second tract was translated by Clagett (1959, 113–120). (For an English translation of the definitions and postulates see Moody/Clagett 1960, 41, 43.)

The codex Plimpton 188 of New York's Columbia University, containing inter alia the *Quadripartitum numerorum*, belonged to *Regiomontanus (1436–1476). Although not written by him, he abundantly annotated it. L'Huillier (1980) has reported on the contents of his notes. As can be deduced from Regiomontanus's *Tradelist*, he intended to publish the work.

The codex New York, Columbia University, Plimpton 173 (a. 1424) contains a work entitled *Aggregatorium sive compendium artis arismetrice* written by Rolandus Ulysbonensis (Roland l'Ecrivain). Roland plagiarizes here, for his work resembles the *Quadripartitum numerorum* as contained in the MS Paris, BnF lat. 14736 (Charmasson, 1978).

De arte mensurandi

The subject of *De arte mensurandi* is practical geometry. One can distinguish two principal parts. Interrupted by death, it seems, the author of the first part did not complete the work. There was a Continuator who took up his work in Chapter V, Part 1, Prop. 9. The identity of the original author of the first part is unknown, but the Continuator was Johannes de Muris. In the proem of the work the original author outlines its scope and objectives. While he intended to complete his work in eleven chapters, in reality the work consists of twelve chapters. Jean utilized the following Archimedean works, translated by *Moerbeke in 1269: *On Spiral Lines*, *On the Measurement of the Circle*, *On the Sphere and the Cylinder*, *On Conoids and Spheroids*, and Eutocius' *Commentary on the Sphere and the Cylinder*. He displays a modest knowledge of Archimedean semiregular polyhedra (Chapter XI) and in Chapter XII, Prop. 30 he says that the volume of a torus is equal to the product of the area of the describing circle and half of the length of the path of its center instead of the length of the path of its center. At the end of Chapter XI, Prop. 5, Jean tells us that a stonecutter has made for him in his presence models of regular and semiregular polyhedra. As far as we know, Jean was the first in the Latin Middle Ages to occupy himself with this subject. Jean inserted the hybrid *Circuli quadratura* of 1340 in Chapter VIII. It consists of two unequal parts. The first comprises thirteen propositions and seven definitions, all drawn from Moerbeke's translation of *On Spiral Lines*. The second part consists of one proposition, the fourteenth, which is taken from the Moerbeke translation of *On the Measurement of the Circle*. Clagett (1978) has published an English translation and commentary of propositions 1–14. Jean has added a fifteenth proposition: "Given a square to construct a circle equal to the given square." In addition, Clagett (1978) has published an English translation and commentary of Chapter 6, Prop. 26–29 (pp. 1323–1325), Chapter 7, Prop. 16 (pp. 27–29), Chapter 8, Prop. 1 (pp. 40–43), and Chapter 10 (pp. 105–121).

The autograph Paris, BnF lat. 7380 was in possession of *Nicole Oresme's nephew, Henri Oresme, and of Oronce Finé (1494–1555), who made use of it in his *Protomathesis*. The *Commensurator*, a tract long attributed to Regiomontanus, consists of a collection of propositions (without their proofs) borrowed from *De arte mensurandi*. In his *Underweysung der Messung mit dem zirckel und richtscheyt* (Nuremberg, 1525) Albrecht Dürer (1471–1528) translated into German the treatment of the problem of finding two proportional means between two given quantities that appears in the *De arte mensurandi*, Chapter 7, Prop. 16.

Arithmetica speculativa

The *Arithmetica speculativa*, an abridgement of the *Arithmetica* of Boethius, was very popular for a long time, as appears from the thirty-four manuscripts which are known. The work was also printed twice: in Vienna 1515 in a mathematical collection containing *Arithmetica communis* (of Jean); *Proportiones breves*; *De latitudinibus formarum*; *Algorithmus* M. Georgii Peurbachii *in integris*; *Algorithmus* Magistri Joanis de Gmunden *de minuciis phicisis*. In 1538, it was printed a second time in Mainz under the title of *Arithmetica speculativa*.

See also **Algebra; Archimedes; Arithmetic; Peuerbach, Georg; William of Moerbeke**

Bibliography

Boncompagni, Baldassarre. *Scritti di Leonardo Pisano, matematico del secolo decimoterzo*. 2 volumes. Rome: Tipografia delle scienze matematiche e fisiche, 1857–1862.

Busard, Hubert L.L. *Het rekenen met breuken in de middeleeuwen, in het bijzonder bij Johannes de Lineriis*. Mededelingen van de koninklijke vlaamse academie voor wetenschappen, letteren en schoone kunsten van belgie. Brussel: Paleis der Academiën, 1968, nr.7.

———. Die "Arithmetica Speculativa" des Johannes de Muris. *Scientiarum Historia* (1971) 13: 116–132.

———. *Johannes de Muris, De arte mensurandi. A Geometrical Handbook of the Fourteenth Century*. Stuttgart: Franz Steiner Verlag, 1998.

Charmasson, Thérèse. L'*Arithmétique* de Roland l'Ecrivain et le *Quadripartitum numerorum* de Jean de Murs. *Revue d'Histoire des Sciences* (1978) 31: 173–176.

Clagett, Marshall. *The Science of Mechanics in the Middle Ages*. Madison: University of Wisconsin Press, 1959.

———. *Archimedes in the Middle Ages*, Vol. III. Philadelphia: American Philosophical Society, 1978.

Grant, Edward. *Nicole Oresme and the Kinematics of Circular Motion*. Madison: University of Wisconsin Press, 1971.

Gushee, Lawrence. New Sources for the Biography of Johannes de Muris. *Journal of the American Musicological Society* (1969) 22: 3–26.

L'Huillier, Ghislaine. Regiomontanus et le *Quadripartitum numerorum* de Jean de Murs. *Revue d'Histoire des Sciences* (1980) 33: 193–214.

———. Aspects nouveaux de la biographie de Jean de Murs. *Archives d'Histoire Doctrinale et Littéraire du Moyen Age* (1981) 47: 272–276.

———. Le Quadripartitum numerorum *de Jean de Murs, Introduction et Edition critique*. Genève: Librairie Droz, 1990.

Libri, Guillaume. *Histoire des sciences mathématiques en Italie*. 4 vols. Paris: J. Renouard, 1838–1841. I: 253–297. (Reprint Hildesheim: Georg Olms, 1967).

Moody, Ernest A. and Marshall Clagett. *The Medieval Science of Weights*. Madison: University of Wisconsin Press, 1960.

Poulle, Emmanuel. Jean de Murs et les Tables alphonsines. *Archives d'Histoire Doctrinale et Littéraire du Moyen Age* (1981) 47: 241–271.

Saby, Marie-Madeleine. Mathématique et métrologie parisiennes au début du XIVe siècle: Le calcul du volume de la mer d'airain, de Jean de Murs. *Archives d'Histoire Doctrinale et Littéraire du Moyen Age* (1991) 66: 197–213.

H.L.L. BUSARD

JOHANNES DE GLOGOVIA

Born about 1445, Johannes (John) of Glogovia was one of the most important philosophers and professors at the University of Kraków when Nicholas Copernicus (1473–1543) was there between 1491 and 1495. It is virtually certain that John or some of his students taught Copernicus the liberal arts.

Glogovia is located in Lower Silesia in western Poland about fifty miles (80 km) northwest of Wroclaw. Descended from the Schelling family of merchants, John received his elementary education at local schools, and entered the University of Kraków in the spring of 1462, obtaining a bachelor's degree in arts in 1465, and a master's degree in 1468. In the same year he became a lecturer in the faculty of arts, remaining in this capacity except for a brief interruption until his death in 1507. During his long career he taught nearly every subject in the faculty of arts, wrote dozens of commentaries and collections of questions, and published several works that continued to be used by scholars at the university until the 1530s.

John's most important works are on *logic, natural philosophy, and *metaphysics. As a typical scholastic philosopher, he lectured and wrote his works under the influence of Aristotle, but he also relied on the ideas of *Ibn Rushd (Averroes) and Averroists such as Paul of Venice, John of Jandun, and *Pietro d'Abano. He cited *Giles of Rome, *Thomas Aquinas, *Albertus Magnus, John Versor, and followers of *Johannes Duns Scotus extensively. As these influences suggest, John was an eclectic thinker who summarized opposing arguments, and attempted to reconcile them.

Perhaps his most innovative work was in logic. He commented on the major logical works of Aristotle and on the handbooks of *Petrus Hispanus. He adopted an interpretation of the logic of consequences that Copernicus may have encountered directly or indirectly through John's students. Although it was not a completely innovative view, John argued forcefully for the idea that in evaluating the logical validity of a conditional proposition or argument, we should consider the relevance of the antecedent to the consequent. In logic, such a criterion leads to rejection of the paradoxes of strict implication, namely, that from an impossible proposition anything follows, and that a necessary proposition follows from anything. John expressed his rejection of the paradoxes clearly and decisively. Perhaps Copernicus had such a criterion in mind in his dedicatory letter to Pope Paul III in De revolutionibus, where he criticized Ptolemaic astronomers for having omitted something essential or having admitted something extraneous and irrelevant as part of their method. Copernicus may have been relying for this criticism on the views of logicians such as John of Glogovia who argued for relevance as a criterion of validity.

In natural philosophy, John tended to reject the nominalistic views of his predecessors at Kraków, and reintroduced the views of thirteenth-century philosophers and their fifteenth-century followers such as John Versor. The mid-century revival of thirteenth-century commentaries and the influence of Thomism was followed in the third quarter of the century by a more historically oriented *Aristotelianism under the influence of Italian humanists. In his Questions on Aristotle's Physics (c. 1484–1487), John acquainted his students with the interpretations of ancient and medieval Aristotelians as well as with the nominalist and Parisian traditions. Accordingly, late fifteenth-century students learned not only about the doctrines of Aristotle but also how medieval authors had modified Aristotelian doctrines. Such adaptations contributed to a variety of "Aristotelian" interpretations, which in turn led to a variety of non-Aristotelian and even anti-Aristotelian conclusions. Some of the departures from Aristotle's views were typical of Christian readers, for example, the denial of the eternity of the world, but others were more controversial. Several Kraków natural philosophers argued that extracosmic void space is actually infinite and that it can serve as a receptacle for bodies. Some asserted that celestial matter and terrestrial matter are essentially the same or, at least, belong to the same genus, and some of them adopted the *impetus theory in several forms to account for projectile motion. John of Glogovia did not always share these views, but he reported them to his students in his commentary and attempted to reconcile different opinions. Copernicus's discussion of natural philosophy, especially the motions of Earth, adapted the Aristotelian principle of natural motion to a heliocentric system, reinterpreting Aristotle's explicit assertions to the contrary as dialectical exercises and not as decisive arguments against the natural circular motion of the spherical Earth.

John's work in astronomy and geography exemplifies the extent to which the University of Kraków emphasized mathematics. Even theoreticians such as John learned to use observational instruments, made measurements, constructed tables and astrological calendars, adapted astronomical tables to the Kraków meridian, explained the motions of the Sun, Moon, and planets from a geocentric perspective, and became familiar with the geographical discoveries of the New World. John understood the details of the Ptolemaic models, as demonstrated by his comments about the way that the motions of the planets are linked to the motion of the Sun, a fact that Copernicus thought needed explanation. Teachers such as John trained students in mathematics, and inspired them to undertake serious mathematical studies. It is likely that Copernicus's teachers in Kraków introduced him to these subjects and stimulated him to make a closer examination of Ptolemaic models. Both Albert of Brudzewo and John of Glogovia emphasized the Averroistic critique of Ptolemaic models and the inadequacy of Ptolemy's lunar model to account for the observed size of the moon at quadrature. The first observation that Copernicus made as Domenico Maria Novara's assistant at Bologna in 1496 was of an occultation of the star Aldebaran by the Moon. He used this occurrence to test the adequacy of the Ptolemaic lunar model, and later cited it to confirm the superiority of his lunar model.

Despite the importance of John of Glogovia's works, many of them remain unedited to this day.

See also **Albert of Saxony; Astronomy, Latin; Geography, chorography; John of Sacrobosco; "Latin Averroists"; Marsilius of Inghen; Oresme, Nicole; Planetary tables; Ptolemy; Peuerbach, Georg; Quadrivium; Regiomontanus, Johannes; *Theorica planetarum*; Universities**

Bibliography

Boh, Ivan. "John of Glogovia's Rejection of Paradoxical Entailment Rules." In *Die Philosophie im 14. und 15. Jahrhundert*. Edited by Olaf Pluta. Bochumer Studien zur Philosophie, 10. Amsterdam: B. R. Grüner, 1988, pp. 373–383.

Glogovia, Johannes de. *Commentarius in "Metaphysicam" Aristotelis*. Edited by Ryszard Tatarzylski. Opera philosophorum medii aevi, 7. Warsaw: Academy of Catholic Theology, 1984.

Goddu, André. Consequences and Conditional Propositions in John of Glogovia's and Michael of Biestrzykowa's Commentaries on Peter of Spain and Their Possible Influence on Nicholas Copernicus. *Archives d'histoire doctrinale et littéraire du moyen âge* (1995) 62: 137–188.

———. The Logic of Copernicus's Arguments and·His Education in Logic at Cracow. *Early Science and Medicine* (1996) 1: 28–68.

Knoll, Paul W. "The Arts Faculty at the University of Cracow at the End of the Fifteenth Century." In *The Copernican Achievement*. Edited by Robert S. Westman. Berkeley: University of California Press, 1975, pp. 137–156.

Zwiercan, Marian. "Jan of Glogów." In *The Cracow Circle of Nicholas Copernicus*. Edited by Józef Buszko. Copernicana cracoviensia, 3. Kraków: Jagiellonian University Press, 1973, pp. 95–118.

ANDRÉ GODDU

JOHANNES DE SANCTO PAULO

Johannes de Sancto Paulo (John of Saint Paul) was a twelfth- and early thirteenth-century medical writer associated with the famous medical "school" of *Salerno. Little is known about him other than what can be gleaned from his writings. He studied under Romuald, archbishop of Salerno (d. 1181). He was thus a contemporary of three of Salerno's most accomplished theorists, *Maurus of Salerno, *Gilles de Corbeil, and *Urso of Calabria. Johannes mentions in passing that one Raynerius copied out a draft of his oral teachings, and in at least two of his treatises he makes reference to his *socios* (students). Johannes thus attained some kind of status as a medical master, even though his work focuses on the practical rather than the theoretical side of medicine. A suggestion that he was a Benedictine monk from the monastery of Saint Paul in Rome (d. 1214–1215) remains to be verified. Since he refers in one of his works to a term that "our Salernitans" (*nostri Salernitani*) use for a kind of pustule, he seems to acknowledge both his residence in the city and his sense that his own identity lies elsewhere.

Johannes is credited with at least four works: the *Breviarium medicine* (*Breviary of Medicine*); *De simplicium medicinarum virtutibus* (*On the Virtues [or Powers] of Simple Medicines*), also known as *De conferentibus et nocentibus diversis medicinis* (*On the Beneficial and Harmful Effects of Different Medicines*); *Flores dietarum* (*The Flowers of Diets*); and a treatise on critical days. Other works are attributed to him, notably a commentary on some pharmaceutical tables (*Commentarium Tabulae Richardi*) and *De carnibus*, but these have yet to be confirmed. The treatise on critical days must have been one of Johannes's earlier works since he cites it in the *Breviary*; the latter must have also been rather early since it was written while Romuald was still alive (hence, before 1181).

Johannes divides the *Breviary*, a general medical compendium, into five books: the first on "general" diseases that afflict the whole body (such as swellings, wounds) or its surface (including all skin conditions); the second on the vital organs and respiratory system; the third on the digestive organs; the fourth on the genitalia, joints, hands, and feet; and the fifth on fevers. The *Breviary* is distinguished from earlier twelfth-century encyclopedic works by Salernitan masters such as those by Copho, Johannes Platearius, and *Bartholomaeus of Salerno by Johannes's heavy reliance on the *Viaticum* of Ibn al-Jazzar, one of the Arabic works translated by *Constantine the African in the late eleventh century, and by its more extensive scope. Indeed, the *Breviary* is the first Salernitan composition to attempt to match the *Viaticum*'s nosological and therapeutic detail. Johannes's stated aim is a systematic explanation of the signs and causes as well as the treatments for diseases; in fact, however, he sometimes describes the diseases without offering any cures at all. The work's ambitious scope and clear exposition of humoral theory led to a wide circulation throughout Europe until it was superseded in the mid-thirteenth-century by the work of *Gilbertus Anglicus, who used Johannes as one of his sources.

Johannes' works on simples (natural medicinal substances used by themselves without being compounded with other active ingredients) and the medical properties of foodstuffs also enjoyed considerable popularity well into the fifteenth century because they were so straightforward and handy for basic reference. Johannes says that he wrote his work on simples because the major pharmaceutical work then circulating under *Galen's name had been hopelessly corrupted over the generations by careless scribes. Johannes lists the basic substances used in Salernitan *materia medica*, dividing them into categories such as herbs, seeds, flowers, gums, etc. *The Flowers of Diets* is a complementary text, explaining the elemental makeup (i.e., hot, cold, dry, wet) of basic foodstuffs such as grains and beans, and how these foods contribute to dissolving or generating the various humors of the body. It draws heavily on the work on diets by *Isaac Judaeus, whose writings had also been latinized by Constantine the African.

In the context of other Salernitan writings, Johannes's work would have considerable influence. However, Johannes seems not to have developed any unique concepts in medical theory, therapy, or the organization of medical knowledge. He is rarely cited by subsequent authors—notable exceptions being *Gentile da Foligno and *John of Arderne—possibly because his works often circulated under the names of other writers such as Mesue and *Bernard of Gordon, and aside from two German dissertations in the early twentieth century he has not been studied by modern scholars other than as a source of information on medieval foods.

See also **Medicine, practical; Pharmaceutic handbooks**

Bibliography

Kroemer, Georg Heinrich, ed. *Johanns von Sancto Paulo, "Liber de simplicium medicinarum virtutibus" und ein anderer Salernitaner Traktat, "Quae medicinae pro quibus morbis donandae sunt" nach dem Breslauer Codex herausgegeben*. Borna-Leipzig: Druck von Robert Noske, 1920.

Ostermuth, Hermann Johannes, ed. *"Flores diaetarum": eine salernitanische Nahrungsmitteldiätetik aus dem XII. Jahrhundert*. Borna-Leipzig: R. Noske, 1919.

MONICA H. GREEN

Illustration of a proctology procedure in a fourteenth-century manuscript of John of Arderne's *Practica*. (National Library of Medicine)

JOHN OF ARDERNE

Born in 1307, John of Arderne, an English surgeon who practiced first in the East Midlands town of Newark and then later in London, is best known for authoring an influential *Practica* on the subject of fistula-in-ano. Written in Latin in the 1370s, the *Practica* was subsequently translated into several English versions and continued to be copied in both languages up until the end of the sixteenth century.

The surgical *practica* was a genre generally composed by academic surgeons for the purposes of teaching, but Arderne cannot be shown to have attended any of the great continental schools of surgery. Indeed, Arderne differentiates himself from his predecessors by replacing the head-to-toe order typical of scholastic surgeries with an extended, and highly remarkable, concentration on the anus and its surrounding area. He is also unusual in beginning his *Practica* with an extensive list of professional anecdotes, some of which refer either by name or by title to such affluent patients as the mayor of Northampton, the treasurer of the Black Prince's household, and several senior ecclesiastics. The presence in this company of Sir Adam Everingham, a well-regarded knight in the retinue of Henry, Earl of Derby, along with occasional references to Henry's campaigns in Gascony and Spain, suggests that Arderne might have served in the future Duke of Lancaster's entourage. This, however, has yet to be proven.

Although Arderne describes his treatment for fistula-in-ano as a radical improvement over existing operations, he in fact combines two well-established methods, ligature and incision, that derive ultimately from Greco-Roman authorities. The influential Arabic surgeon Albucasis (*al-Zahrawi), influenced by Paul of Ægina, recommends either incision or cautery of the afflicted area, but only if the operator can avoid damage to the sphincter. Alternatively, the surgeon can thread a ligature through the fistula and out the anus and then gradually tighten it, a safer yet more excruciating means to cut the intervening flesh. In the thirteenth century, the Italian surgeons Bruno Longoburgo and *Teodorico Borgognoni, students of Ugo da Lucca, proposed the novel use of ligature as a means to secure the flesh to facilitate the faster and more practical method of cutting with a razor. John of Arderne, for his part, revises this latter operation by employing a peg that allows him to tighten the ligature at will, thereby controlling the speed and intensity of the resulting incision. An impressive program of illustrations accompanies the text and clarifies immensely the highly involved procedure it describes. Some modern practitioners regard Arderne's innovations as unnecessarily cumbersome. Indeed, his impressive rate of success could well have been the result not of the treatment itself, but of a conservative post-operative strategy that emphasized bed-rest while at the same time downplaying the medieval surgical commonplace that ulcers and other wounds require frequent reopening.

Besides the *Practica*, John of Arderne is also responsible for a number of shorter treatises on various aspects of medicine that appear together in manuscripts as the *Liber medicinalium*. This collection includes notes on medicinal herbs, a short treatise on hemorrhoids, and discussions of a number of topics ranging from gynecology to afflictions of the eye. Indeed, his authorship of *De cura oculorum* in 1377 is the latest record we have of his life; he presumably died not long thereafter.

See also **Medicine, practical**

Bibliography

McVaugh, Michael. "Therapeutic Strategies: Surgery." In *Western Medical Thought from Antiquity to the Middle Ages*, ed. Mirko D. Grmek, trans. Antony Shugaar. Cambridge: Harvard University Press, 1998.

Murray Jones, Peter. "Four Middle English Translations of John Arderne." In *Latin and Vernacular*, ed. A.J. Minnis. Cambridge: D.S. Brewer, 1989, pp. 61-89

———. "John of Arderne and the Mediterranean tradition of scholastic surgery." In *Practical Medicine from Salerno to the Black Death*, eds. Luis Garcia-Ballester, Roger French, Jon Arrizabalaga, and Andrew Cunningham. New York: Cambridge University Press, 1994, pp. 289–321.

JEREMY CITROME

JOHN OF GADDESDEN

John (of) Gaddesden (d. 1348/9) is the first prominent English physician to be educated solely in England, and is best known for his medical compendium, the *Rosa anglica* (*English Rose*). Originating from Hertfordshire, Gaddesden first appears as a fellow at Merton College, Oxford, in 1305. He would eventually earn master's degrees in both arts and medicine, and a bachelor's in theology. He entered royal service in 1332 and remained in service to the king until his death, perhaps from the plague.

According to his own testimony, he compiled the *Rosa anglica* in his seventh year after incepting as a master of arts, probably c. 1313. As a work of his early career, it is not surprising that it is more a compilation of the teachings of others than an original synthesis. The *Rosa* is distinguished from the encyclopedic work of his predecessor, *Gilbertus Anglicus (d. c. 1250), by its heavier reliance on Arabic sources: Mesue, Rhazes (*al-Razi), Avicenna (*Ibn Sina), Averroes (*Ibn Rushd), and Serapion. While Gaddesden also makes frequent use of *Constantine the African, he generally eschews Salernitan authorities for Montpellierain masters such as *Bernard de Gordon. His work thus captures the state of scholastic medicine in the early fourteenth century.

Like his model Bernard de Gordon, Gaddesden consistently divides each heading into subsections on causes, symptoms, prognosis, and treatments. Despite his heavy reliance on the work of others, Gaddesden also incorporates his own cures, most famously, a treatment for smallpox that he employed on one of the young princes that involved wrapping the patient in red cloths. Gaddesden also reported a variety of charms and other alternative practices.

Of the nearly twenty extant copies of the *Rosa anglica*, half are now housed in British libraries. It was heavily employed by later fourteenth- and fifteenth-century medical writers in England, such as John Mirfeld who used it as the basis for his *Breviarium Bartholomei*, a medical handbook for the hospital of St. Bartholomew in London. It was similarly employed by the author of a lengthy gynecological text that expands on Gaddesden's several chapters on women's diseases by fusing them with a variety of excerpts from other texts, including the *Trotula. Portions of the *Rosa anglica* were translated into English, while a nearly complete Irish translation was made in the late fourteenth or fifteenth century; it was also the basis for a composite health regimen composed in Gaelic by Cormac Mac Duinnshleibhe (fl. c.

1459). More surprising (since there is no evidence that Gaddesden himself ever traveled outside of England) is the *Rosa anglica*'s popularity on the continent as well. Manuscripts are now found from Germany to Spain, and the first printed edition appeared in Pavia in 1492. The *Rosa* was reprinted three more times thereafter.

In addition to the *Rosa anglica*, Gaddesden is credited with authorship of several smaller texts, including a treatise on "the pestilence" which circulated in both Latin and English. This must have been his last work, since he seems to have himself died of the plague.

See also **Medicine, practical**

Bibliography

Carlin, Martha. "Gaddesden, John (d. 1348/9)." In *Oxford Dictionary of National Biography*. Oxford: Oxford University Press, 2004.

Cholmeley, H.P. *John of Gaddesden and the 'Rosa medicinae'*. Oxford: Clarendon Press, 1912.

John of Gaddesden. *Rosa anglica practica medicinae*. Pavia: Franciscus Girardengus and Joannes Antonius Birreta, 1492.

Olsan, Lea T. Charms and Prayers in Medieval Medical Theory and Practice. *Social History of Medicine* (2003) 16:3: 343–366.

Voigts, Linda Ehrsam, and Patricia Deery Kurtz, eds. *Scientific and Medical Writings in Old and Middle English: An Electronic Reference*. Society for Early English and Norse Electronic Texts. Ann Arbor: University of Michigan Press, 2000. (CD-ROM.)

Wulff, Winifred, ed. *Rosa anglica sev Rosa medicinæ Johannis Anglici: An Early Modern Irish Translation of a Section of the Mediaeval Medical Text-book of John of Gaddesden*. Irish Texts Society, v. 25. London: Simpkin, Marshall, 1929.

MONICA H. GREEN

JOHN OF GMUNDEN

John of Gmunden was born 1380/1384 in Gmunden am Traunsee, Austria, the son of a tailor, whose presumed family name was Kraft. After matriculating in arts at the University of Vienna in 1400 he became a bachelor in 1402 and a master in 1406. Although his first known lecture in 1406 in Vienna was focused on "*Theoricae (planetarum)*," during the first phase of his career (1406–1416) his other lectures mainly dealt with non-mathematical subjects. In 1409 he became *magister stipendiatus* which brought him regular income from the Collegium Ducale. In 1415 he became a bachelor of theology, which obligated him to give two appropriate lectures until 1416. In 1417 he was ordained as priest.

His main scientific activities lay in astronomy, mathematics, and to a lesser degree in theology. From 1416 to 1425 he lectured exclusively on mathematical applications to astronomy, thus becoming the first specialized professor in this field. He was dean of the faculty of arts in 1413 and 1423 and held several administrative positions as well (e.g., treasurer). This was his most productive scientific period: he wrote a booklet on the art of calculating with sexagesimal fractions and produced various tables of proportions and a treatise on the sine-function in relation to arcs and chords, well within the knowledge boundaries of Arabic geometry, showing that he was acquainted with the works of *Jean de Meurs. In astronomy, his collaboration with Johann Andreas Schindel (who had left Prague University) led to the knowledge at Vienna of the writings of Richard of Wallingford concerning the *albion*, an instrument that calculated planetary positions. His application of this instrument to determination of an eclipse provided a useful tool in the teaching of astronomy at Vienna. His description of the equatorium (which he called *instrumentum solempne* after *Campanus de Novara) was greatly esteemed by *Peuerbach and subsequently by *Regiomontanus. He gave hints that the *torquetum* could be used for establishing longitude differences. His main efforts, however, lay in the construction and handling of the astrolabe joined with a star catalogue (1425) as well as the use of the (new) quadrant devised by Robert of England. Construction plans for an ivory quadrant for the German Emperor Frederick III (1438) show his connection to court artisans. While there is no documentation of observation activity by John himself, his pupils were good observers, and his influence on the astronomically interested prior of the monastery of Klosterneuburg (close to Vienna), Georg Müstinger, was especially strong.

In his third period of activity (1425–1431), he withdrew from the Collegium Ducale, became vice-chancellor of the university and canon of the Episcopal church of St.-Stephen. During this period he produced astronomical tables and *volvelles* (analogue paper computers) and lectured on the astrolabe, obviously dependent on a treatise of Christiannus de Prachatiz.

In his last period (1431–1442), he became *plebanus* (vicar) of St.-Vitus in Laa (an der Thaya), a rich parish that belonged to the University and provided a handsome income. Besides being renowned for his calendrical calculations, in his will he bequeathed his book collection, together with globes and instruments, to the faculty of arts, materials that provided an intellectual legacy at Vienna. While he certainly was no astrologer, he left astrological books to the library but imposed heavy restrictions on their circulation among students. John of Gmunden died on February 23, 1442, in Vienna and was buried in the crypt of St.-Stephen's cathedral. A typical scholastic, he did not invent anything personally but prepared many texts in an easily understandable form that established Vienna subsequently as a center of astronomical learning.

See also **Astrolabes and quadrants; Astronomy, Latin**

Bibliography

Firneis, Maria G. "Johannes von Gmunden—der Astronom." In *Der Weg der Naturwissenschaft von Johannes von Gmunden zu Johannes Kepler*. Edited by G. Hamann and H. Grössing. Vienna: Verlag der Österreichischen Akademie der Wissenschaften, 1988, pp. 65–84.

Hadrava, Petr and Alena Hadravová. "John of Gmunden as a Predecessor of Georg of Peuerbach." In *Peuerbach-Symposium 2004*. Edited by Franz Pichler. Linz, Austria: Rudolf Trauner, 2004, pp. 1–8.

North, John D. *Richard of Wallingford: An edition of his writings*. 3 volumes. Oxford: Clarendon Press, 1976.

Vienna, Österreichische Nationalbibliothek, Cod. 2332, 2440, 5268, 5412, 5418.

MARIA G. FIRNEIS

JOHN OF SACROBOSCO

Not much is known about Sacrobosco apart from his writings. The meaning of his name is unclear. "Sacrobosco" translates the common place-name Holywood. It may well refer to Holywood, in Nithsdale, Scotland (near Dumfries), site of a Premonstratensian abbey, where he may have served for a few years. He probably attended the University of Oxford. About 1221 he went to the University of Paris, where he lectured in the arts faculty on mathematical topics. A cryptic verse added to the end of his *Computus* refers to 1244 or 1256 as a significant date, most likely the year of his death. His tombstone at the monastery of Saint-Mathurin in Paris was destroyed long ago, but it is known to have been engraved with an astronomical instrument, in honor of his work on astronomy, and an epitaph calling him a *computista*, that is, a practitioner of the art of *computus* or time-reckoning.

Sacrobosco's significance to the history of science lies in his composition of elementary mathematical and astronomical textbooks. The *Algorismus*, a textbook on *arithmetic using *Arabic numerals, enjoyed a fair level of popularity and survives in a number of manuscripts and early printed editions. Another work usually ascribed to Sacrobosco, the *Tractatus de quadrante*, explained the manufacture and use of a kind of quadrant, an astronomical instrument. It is significant as an early set of Latin instructions for this instrument, but the small number of manuscripts (only eighteen have been identified) suggests it was superseded by better texts in the fourteenth century. His most influential works were the *Computus* and the *Tractatus de sphaera*.

The *Computus* contains two main parts corresponding to Sacrobosco's two divisions of time-reckoning: the motion of the Sun, which determines the civil calendar, and the motion of the Moon, which determines the ecclesiastical calendar. Thus, while an astronomer studies all the celestial objects, the *computista* is concerned only with the two luminaries. Sacrobosco added nothing significantly new in his textbook on *computus*, a discipline that had reached maturity centuries earlier. However, he was among the first to publish a proposal for reform of the Julian calendar.

Sacrobosco wrote one of a number of elementary textbooks on astronomy with the title *Sphaera*; in popularity his surpassed all others. The "sphere" of the title refers to the aetherial sphere of the heavens, itself divided into several planetary spheres; the elementary sphere comprising the four Aristotelian elements; and the armillary

Frontispiece of a fourteenth-century edition of John of Sacrobosco's *Sphaera*. (Topham/RHR)

course of reading in mathematics at medieval universities. The situation changed with the advent of printing. Sacrobosco's *Sphaera* was among the first scientific works to be printed in the fifteenth century, and it remained in print and readily available into the seventeenth century, but it almost never appears with his other works. Instead, it is found alone—perhaps with a commentary—or else with one or more other astronomical works, frequently a *theorica*. New commentaries were written. Some, like the commentary of the Jesuit Christopher Clavius, stretched to hundreds of pages in length and dwarfed Sacrobosco's little book. The total number of printed editions of the *Sphaera* is in the hundreds. The *Computus*, on the other hand, only went through about thirty-five editions, nearly half of them from a single city: Wittenberg. The disparity in the fortunes of these two textbooks reflects the contrast between the flourishing of astronomy in the Renaissance and the gradual disappearance of computus.

See also **Arithmetic; Astronomy, Latin; Elements and qualities; Quadrivium**

Bibliography

Knorr, Wilbur R. Sacrobosco's *Quadrans*: Date and Sources. *Journal for the History of Astronomy* (1997) 28: 187–222.

Lattis, James L. *Between Copernicus and Galileo: Christopher Clavius and the Collapse of Ptolemaic Cosmology*. Chicago: University of Chicago Press, 1994.

Pedersen, Olaf. In Quest of Sacrobosco. *Journal for the History of Astronomy* (1985) 16: 175–221.

Thorndike, Lynn. The *"Sphere"* of Sacrobosco and Its *Commentators*. Chicago: University of Chicago Press, 1949.

KATHERINE A. TREDWELL

sphere, an instrument used to represent the heavens and earth schematically. The book begins with basic Aristotelian *cosmology: the Earth is a sphere resting immobile at the center of the world, surrounded by the celestial sphere which revolves every twenty-four hours. Next comes a discussion of the armillary sphere and the celestial circles it represents. The longest section explains the risings and settings of celestial bodies that result from the daily rotation of the heavens. A brief survey of planetary theories and eclipses concludes the book.

Sacrobosco's textbooks are characterized by a narrative style laying out the facts of mathematics and astronomy for the reader. They avoid both the demonstrative approach of Ptolemy and the *quaestio* method of debate then popular at Paris. Numerous classical references and quotations give his works a humanistic air. Yet his frequent citation of al-Farghani illustrates the importance of Arabic sources in the medieval western encounter with *Ptolemy.

The *Algorismus*, *Sphaera*, and *Computus* appear together in a number of manuscripts of the thirteenth and fourteenth centuries, typically with more advanced astronomical texts such as a set of *planetary tables and a *theorica planetarum*. Such collections demonstrate that Sacrobosco's textbooks formed the core of a standard

JOHN OF SAINT-AMAND

A French author, physician, and cleric, John of Saint-Amand was one of the three most important medical authors of the late thirteenth century (along with *Taddeo Alderotti and *Arnau de Vilanova) in adapting Arabic and Ancient medical texts and ideas into Latin. He helped to formulate the "New Galen" at the turn of the fourteenth century.

Born c. 1230, probably in Saint-Amand en Pouelle, John's early life is largely unknown. He undoubtedly studied the liberal arts and medicine at the University of Paris, and was probably also a regent master at the Paris Medical Faculty. Besides his likely academic position, John held more than five ecclesiastical positions, all within nine miles (14 km) of Saint-Amand, including the canonacy of the cathedral of Notre-Dame de Tournai. As a physician, he saw patients, including women and children, and potentates such as Bishop Gautier de Croix. John died between March 14 and May 7, 1303, and was memorialized in Tournai Cathedral.

John's Latin medical works number more than twenty. His two principal texts are *Revocativum*, comprised of *Concordanciae*, *Areolae*, and *Abbreviationes librorum*

Galeni, and *Expositio super Antidotarium Nicolai*. The *Concordanciae* is an alphabetized listing of keywords in the works of *Galen, *Hippocrates, Avicenna (*Ibn Sina) and others; it is also a very early adaptation of the textual device invented in contemporary Paris for biblical interpretation. *Abbreviationes* summarizes seventeen mostly Galenic and some Hippocratic treatises. *Areolae* is a consideration of simple medicines as well as brief *discursi* on compounds and laxatives, and survives in at least thirty-two manuscripts.

The *Expositio*, a commentary on the *Antidotary Nicholai*, is John's most engaging work. He wrote it sometime between 1290 and 1303. The *Antidotary* was written by an unknown figure in Salerno and circulated widely among apothecaries and physicians. John's commentary exists in at least forty-six manuscripts in its entirety and at least twenty-four manuscripts in excerpt or fragment, from the thirteenth to the sixteenth centuries; it was printed in editions from 1494 to 1623. In Paris *Expositio* became the lynchpin for regulation of apothecaries' stock by the French Crown and the Medical Faculty. Consequently, it was closely kept and corrected by the Faculty.

John was the first Latin academic to comment on the medical work of Avicenna, and one of the earliest to refer to Serapion's texts. In common with many of his near contemporaries, John wrote scholastic treatises: nine commentaries on medical texts in the stipulated or pending medical curriculum: *Quaestiones supra tertiam fen primi Canonis Avicenni*; *Commentarius in Avicennam, liber quartus*; *Super Dietas Isaaci*; *Super Febrium Isaaci*; *Glosule in Isagogas Iohannitii*; *Scripta super Librum pulsuum Philareti*; *Scripta super Librum urinarum Theophili*; *Commentum super Librum de regimine acutorum*; and *Additiones Mesue*. These commentaries were joined by others on more pharmacological and pharmaceutical texts: *Breviarium de Antidotario*; *Super Dietas Isaaci*; and *Additiones ad Tacuinum de regimine sanitatis* as well as *De modis medendi*, *De remediis*; and uncertainly *Liber in medicacione cirurgie*. Various *receptae*, *excerptae*, and marginalia also survive. Two texts linked to his name now appear to be lost: *De conservatione sanitatis et tardatione senectutis* and *De viribus plantarum*. Several texts descend to us under separate titles, but are originally parts of his longer works, attesting to their popularity and specific use.

His corpus is relatively standard in its breadth, but unique in its depth of pharmacological examination. Simply put, he represented a second stage in the advancement beyond the Salernitan transmission of *Gilles de Corbeil. His gross interests, pharmacy and medical educational codification, were the same, but his subject and manner of addressing those themes were more elaborate and subtle. From poetry to concordancing, from pharmaceutical listing to pharmaceutical theorizing and standardizing, John advanced over Gilles in codifying Parisian academic medicine. Yet John went beyond mere bridging. His interest in Galen exceeded curricula during his lifetime. His choice of texts fits in more closely with that of Montpellier more than forty years later. However, John's commentaries also suggest his association with the earlier University of Paris curriculum. Thus John was an innovative figure in the scholastic assimilation of the work of Galen, at once working within the Articellan system of his educational youth and yet anticipating later didactic precepts. Additionally his impact was felt beyond the academy. The elite surgeon Henri de Mondeville used John's system of citation and phrasing, suggesting he read the work closely.

John's pharmacologic ideas were also highly integrative and original; simultaneously, they were particularly philosophical compared to the rest of the faculty. John addressed a controversy in pharmacology head-on—how do simple drugs behave when compounded (i.e., is the sum of the parts less than the whole?), suggesting that the measures of the key characteristic (radix) of a drug could be quantified, weight or measured. He also argued that a process of fermentation occurred in the mixing of simples, creating a new formulation in the compound, following along an Avicennan model.

Arguably, until *Jacques Despars in the fifteenth century, John cast the most far-ranging synthetic and theoretical shadow on the University of Paris medical faculty at a time when it was becoming the model for all European universities.

See also **Pharmaceutic handbooks; Pharmacology; Universities**

Bibliography

Primary Sources
Jean de Saint-Amand. *Expositio super Antidotarium Nicholai in Mesue et omnia quae cum eo imprimi...* (Venetiis: Iuntas, 1549), fo. 230v–72r.
Pagel, Julius Leopold. *Die Areolae des Johannes de Sancto Amando (13.Jahrhundert)*. Berlin: Georg Reimer, 1893.
———. *Die Concordanciae des Johannes de Sancto Amando*. Berlin: Georg Reimer, 1894.

Secondary Sources
Arnau de Vilanova. *Aphorismi de gradibus*. Edited by Michael R. McVaugh, Arnaldi de Villanova Opera Medical Omnia, t. II. Granada and Barcelona: Universidad de Barcelona, 1975.
García Ballester, Luis. "The New Galen: A Challenge to Latin Galenism in Thirteenth-century Montpellier." In *Text and Tradition: Studies in Ancient Medicine and its Transmission: Presented to Jutta Kollesch*. Leiden: E.J. Brill, 1998, pp. 55–83.
Jacquart, Danielle. "L'oeuvre de Jean de Saint-Amand et les méthodes d'enseignement à la Faculté de Médecine de Paris à la fin du XIIIe siècle" dans Jacqueline Hamesse, éd., *Manuels, programmes de cours et techniques d'enseignement dans les universités médiévales*. Louvain-la-Neuve: Université Catholique de Louvain, 1994, pp. 257–275.
Schalick, Walton O. Add One Part Pharmacy to One Part Surgery and One Part Medicine: Jean de Saint-Amand and the Development of Medical Pharmacology in Paris, c. 1230–1303. Johns Hopkins University, Ph.D., 1997. University Microfilms: Ann Arbor, 1997.

WALTON O. SCHALICK, III

JOHN OF SAXONY

John of Saxony (Jean de Saxe, Iohannes de Saxonia, John Dank, Danco, Danekow) was probably born in Germany, perhaps in Magdeburg. His scholarly work is believed to date from the end of the thirteenth century. However, his presence in Paris can only be proven from 1327 to 1335. John of Saxony is quoted in medieval manuscripts as well as in contemporary literature as the author of various astronomical or astrological treatises, although his authorship is questionable in some of these cases. We shall deal here with three works originating from his hand. A *computus, preserved in manuscript form only and dated to the year 1297, is attributed to John of Saxony. In the manuscript itself, Iohannes Alemanus is given as the author. Also mentioned are the geographical longitudes of Paris and Magdeburg, which is considered to be John of Saxony's birthplace. These and other facts prove beyond almost any doubt that John of Saxony is the author of this computus. He is certainly the author of the commentary to the astrological treatise *Liber introductorius ad magisterium iudiciorum astrorum* written by al-Qabisi (Alcabitius), the Arab scholar of the second half of the tenth century. The Alcabitius treatise, which was also known as the *Liber isagogicus*, was translated into Latin by Iohannes Hispalensis in the twelfth century. The commentary by John of Saxony is preserved in many dozens of manuscripts, several incunabulae and old prints, the latest of which dates from the middle of the sixteenth century.

The most important works by John of Saxony are his *Canons on the Alfonsine Tables* (*Tabule Alfoncii*) from 1327. The aim of this treatise was to enable students at the University of Paris to use astronomical tables. In medieval science, such tables were a useful means by which to make astronomical calculations, chiefly of planetary positions. They were used to derive ecliptic longitudes of planets for any chosen time and observer's position, lunar phases, lunar and solar eclipses, as well as calendar data, etc. The *Alfonsine Tables*, which are the best known of the preserved tables, became the most widely used astronomical tables in late-medieval Europe. They were completed in the Spanish city of *Toledo around the year 1272 on the order of the Castilian king *Alfonso X the Wise (r. 1252–1284). Like the eleventh-century *Toledan Tables* from which they were developed, the *Alfonsine Tables* were based on the geocentric model of the planetary system as described in *Ptolemy's *Almagest*. Although the *Alfonsine Tables* were originally written in Castilian, they were soon disseminated in Latin translation all over Europe. The first printed edition was published in 1483, and further editions followed quickly one after the other. Around 1320, the Alfonsine Tables became known in Paris, where the astronomers Jean de Lignères (Iohannes de Lineriis), his pupil John of Saxony, and later also *Jean de Meurs (Iohannes de Muris) recalculated them and supplemented them with canons, i.e., explanations, instructions, and rules for their use. We do not know how much the original version of the tables in Castilian was changed because this has not been preserved. We do know, however, that the calculation of all mean movements of the planets was consistently transformed into sexagesimal form in Paris. It was supplemented by tables for interpolation into individual days and their parts, while the original tables in Castilian provided the values for the calculation of mean planetary motions in twenty-year periods. Tables were also harmonized with the local Parisian meridian and modified and supplemented in other respects. The *Alfonsine Tables* were disseminated from Paris to other parts of Europe (in tandem with the establishment of new universities) and were modified in order to conform to the corresponding local meridians. In Central Europe they were commonly used, for example, at the universities of Prague and Kraków, as is evident from the manuscripts preserved there. The so-called *Tabulae resolutae* (*Resolved Tables*) usually tabulated planetary positions for certain latitudes and years. John of Saxony's canons were published in print for the first time by Erhard Ratdolt in Venice in 1483, together with the first edition of the *Alfonsine Tables*. The canons by John of Lignères and Jean de Meurs have been never published in print.

See also **Universities**

Bibliography

Primary Source
Les tables alphonsines, avec les canons de Jean de Saxe. Édition, traduction et commentaire par Emmanuel Poulle. Sources d'Histoire Médièvale. Paris: Éditions du Centre national de la Recherche 1984.

Secondary Sources
Chabás, José. The Diffusion of the Alfonsine Tables: The Case of the Tabulae Resolutae. *Perspectives on Science* (2002) 10: 168–178.
Duhem, Pierre. *Le système du monde.* Paris: Librairie Scientifique Hermann, 1914–1959. (John of Saxony: IV. Paris 1916, pp. 76–90.)
Porres de Mateo, Beatriz. "Astronomy between Prague and Vienna in the 15th Century: the Case of John Sindel and John of Gmunden." In *Tycho Brahe and Prague: Crossroads of European Science.* Edited by J. R. Christianson, A. Hadravová, P. Hadrava, and M. Solc. Acta Historica Astronomiae, vol. 16. Frankfurt am Main: Harri Deutsch Verlag 2002, pp. 248–255.
Porres, Beatriz and José Chabás. John of Murs's "Tabulae permanentes" for finding true syzygies. *Journal for the History of Astronomy* 32: 63–72.
Poulle, Emmanuel. Jean de Murs et les tables alphonsines. *Archives d'Histoire doctrinale et litteraire du Moyen Age* (1980) 47: 241–271.

PETR HADRAVA AND ALENA HADRAVA

JOHN OF SEVILLE

There has been much controversy concerning the identity of John of Seville ("Iohannes Hispalensis"), and whether he is a different person from several other "Johns" who were active in the field of Arabic science at approximately the same time. One can isolate a group of texts translated by the same scholar, whose name appears as "Iohannes Hispalensis" (usually with the addition of "et Limiensis/Lunensis"): the regimen of health from *Pseudo-Aristotle; *The Secret of Secrets* (addressed to Tarasia, the queen of the Portuguese from 1112–1228); Qusta ibn Luqa (Costa ben Luca) *On the Difference Between the Spirit and the Soul* (a brief treatise giving medical writers' descriptions of the corporeal spirit and Aristotle's and Plato's definitions of the soul, addressed to Raymond de La Sauvetat, archbishop of Toledo 1125–1152); al-Farghani (Alpharganus) *Book on the Science of the Stars* (an introduction to Ptolemaic astronomy, in thirty chapters, completed in Limia on March 11, 1135); and several works on the branches of astrology: al-Qabisi (Alcabitius), *The Introduction to Astrology* (possibly 19 March 19, 1135), Umar ibn al-Farrukhan al-Tabari (Omar), *On Nativities*, *Abu Ma'shar (Albumasar), *The Great Introduction to Astrology* (probably translated in 1133), *Masha'allah *On Questions* and *On the Matter of Eclipses*, and *Thabit ibn Qurra *On Talismans* (a text on astrological magic, translated in Limia). In addition, works on the construction and use of the astrolabe are attributed to the same author, which may not be translations. Moreover, manuscript affiliation and similarity of style suggest that three further astrological works by Albumasar, all concerning general and historical astrology, should be included: *The Book of Experiments*, *The Flowers* and *On the Great Conjunctions*. These texts indicate that John of Seville was active in northern Portugal (possibly in Ponte do Lima), in the 1120s and 1130s, and may have moved to *Toledo, if his dedication of a text to the archbishop of that city indicates patronage. He may thus be the "John of Toledo" who translated *al-Majusi's *On Nativities* in July 1152 or 1153. It remains to be proved whether he is the "John of Spain" (Iohannes Hispanus) or "magister Iohannes," who was definitely established in Toledo later in the twelfth century, collaborating with *Domingo Gundisalvo on translating *al-Ghazali's *Aims of the Philosophers* and *Ibn Gabirol's *Fount of Life*, and writing sophisticated works on astronomical tables (*On the Differences between Astronomical Tables*, written for two Englishmen, Gauco and William), on Indian arithmetic (*The Book of Alchorismi on the Practice of Arithmetic*, based on *al-Khwarizmi's lost book on Indian arithmetic), and possibly on business arithmetic (*The Book of Mahameleth*). The last two works occur together in a manuscript (Paris, Bibliothèque nationale de France, lat. 15461) whose other work is a calendar written for Toledo in or just after 1159. He also may be different from the "Iohannes Hispalensis" who, in 1142, wrote a work on the four main branches of astrology, prefaced by an introduction (the *Ysagoge* and *Book of the Four Parts,* or *Epitome of the Whole of Astrology*), since the subject matter and terminology of this work are much closer to those of the astrological works of *Abraham ibn Ezra which were written in Tuscany and Béziers in the 1140s. A "John David" was the dedicatee of a text on the astrolabe written in Béziers by Rudolph of Bruges in 1144, and is described as "most skilled in the

four disciplines of mathematics... most zealous in the science of the stars—nay rather in every science committed to script," in a dedication of another text on the astrolabe, translated by Plato of Tivoli in Barcelona. A "master John David of Toledo" achieved legendary status as the originator of a prediction of cataclysmic events resulting from a "great conjunction" of all the planets in Libra in 1229. Identification of "John of Seville" with Avendauth (= "Son of David" in Hebrew) would, however, seem impossible, since Avendauth, another collaborator of Gundisalvo, is more likely to be the Jewish scholar, Abraham ibn Daud, the outlines of whose biography are reasonably clear.

John of Seville's translation of *On the Difference between the Spirit and the Soul* was incorporated into the curriculum of natural philosophy in the medieval universities (as occasionally was his translation of the *Secret of Secrets*), and was frequently glossed and commented on, whilst his astrological translations—especially those of Alcabitius's *Introduction* and Albumasar's *Great Introduction* and *Great Conjunctions*—were central texts for the study of astrology and were printed in the Renaissance.

See also **Astrolabes and quadrants; Toledo**

Bibliography

Primary Sources
Albumasar. *Liber introductorii maioris*, translated by John of Seville. In Abu Ma'sar al-Balhi, *Liber introductorii maioris ad scientiam judiciorum astrorum.* Edited by Richard Lemay, 9 vols. Naples: Istituto universitaria orientale, 1995–1996, vol. V.
———. *De magnis coniunctionibus.* In Abu Ma'sar, *On Historical Astrology.* Ed. Keiji Yamamoto and Charles Burnett, 2 vols. Leiden: E.J. Brill, 2000.
Alcabitius, *Introductorius.* In Al-Qabisi (Alcabitius): The Introduction to Astrology. Ed. Charles Burnett, Keiji Yamamoto and Michio Yano. London and Turin: Warburg Institute and Nino Aragno, 2004.
Liber Alchorismi de practica aritmetice. In Muaammad ibn Musi al-Khwarizmi, *Le Calcul Indien (Algorismus).* Ed. André Allard. Paris: Blanchard, 1992, pp. 62–224.
Johannes Hispalensis. *Epitome totius astrologiae.* Nürnberg: in officina Ioannis Montani et Ulrici Neuber, 1548.

Secondary Sources
Burnett, Charles. "Magister Iohannes Hispalensis et Limiensis" and Qusta ibn Luqa's *De differentia spiritus et animae*: a Portuguese Contribution to the Arts Curriculum? *Mediaevalia, Textos e Estudos* (1995) 7–8: 221–267.
———. John of Seville and John of Spain: a *mise au point*. *Bulletin de philosophie médiévale* (2003) 44: 59–78.
D'Alverny, Marie-Thérèse. "Avendauth?" In *Homenaje a Millás-Vallicrosa.* 2 vols. Barcelona: Consejo Superior de Investigaciones Científicas, 1954–1956, I, pp. 19–43.
Thorndike, Lynn. John of Seville. *Speculum* (1959) 34: 20–38.
Williams, Steven J. *The Secret of Secrets. The Scholarly Career of a Pseudo-Aristotelian Text in the Latin Middle Ages.* Ann Arbor: University of Michigan Press, 2003.

CHARLES BURNETT

JORDANUS DE NEMORE

Although little is known of the life of Jordanus de Nemore (fl. c. 1220), twelve treatises are attributed to him in a library catalogue of the works of Richard de Fournival, compiled between 1246 and 1260. It is therefore likely that he lived and wrote during the first half of the thirteenth century. The works ascribed to Jordanus are concerned with mechanics and mathematics. He appears to be the author of at least six works. The name of Jordanus is most intimately associated with the medieval "science of weights" (scientia de ponderibus), or statics, to which he contributed more than any of his contemporaries. As testimony to his stature, commentators on his works on statics sometimes attributed their own contributions to him. However, thus far only one work in statics can be definitively assigned to Jordanus: The Elements of Jordanus on the Demonstration of Weights (Elementa Jordani super demonstrationem ponderum). Another work, The Book of Jordanus de Nemore on the Theory of Weight (Liber Jordani de ratione ponderis), is probably by Jordanus.

Of these two treatises, the Theory of Weight is the more important, but taken together they represent the most significant works in medieval statics. In them, Jordanus introduces into statics the idea of component forces by means of a concept he called gravitas secundum situm ("positional gravity"). Jordanus applied positional gravity to both rectilinear and arcal paths. Although it does not yield correct results when applied to an arcal path, when Jordanus applied it to rectilinear paths he achieved brilliant accuracy. He also presented a proof of the law of the lever by means of the principle of work, which was previously a vague concept. In the Theory of Weight (Book I, Proposition 10), Jordanus again employs the principle of work in a proof of the inclined plane, demonstrating that "If two weights descend along diversely inclined planes, then, if the inclinations are directly proportional to the weights, they will be of equal force in descending."

Jordanus advanced statics by combining the dynamical and philosophical approach characteristic of Aristotelian physics with the mathematical physics of *Archimedes. He derived rigorous proofs within a mathematical format based on Archimedean statics and Euclidean geometry. Jordanus's treatises gave rise to an extensive commentary literature from the thirteenth to the sixteenth centuries. With the advent of printing, Jordanus's ideas were widely disseminated and influenced leading scholars of the sixteenth and seventeenth centuries, including Galileo Galilei.

Jordanus seems to have been as talented in mathematics as in mechanics. Treatises on geometry, proportions, algebra, and theoretical and practical arithmetic are attributed to him. His Liber Philotegni de triangulis (The Book of the Philotechnist on Triangles) was medieval geometry of the highest order. In the fourth book, Jordanus presents the most sophisticated proofs, including the trisection of an angle, as well as a proposition on how to square the circle in which Jordanus gives a proof that differed from that given by Archimedes in his famous treatise, Measurement of the Circle.

Theoretical arithmetic in the Middle Ages was greatly influenced by Jordanus's Arithmetica (Arithmetic). The work is divided into ten books in which Jordanus presents more than four hundred propositions. These proceed by way of definitions, postulates, and axioms after the arithmetic books of *Euclid's Elements, and thus depart from the earlier tradition of *Boethius's Arithmetic, which was rather informal and often philosophical. Many of Jordanus's propositions had counterparts in Euclid's Elements, but some did not. One that was independent of Euclid is Book I, Proposition 9, where the enunciation of the proposition reads: "The [total sum or] result of multiplication of any number by however many numbers you please is equal to the result of the multiplication of the same number by the number composed of all the others." In modern notation, Jordanus proves that if $AB = D$, and $AC = E$, then $D + E = A (B + C)$. Jordanus also composed an algorism (Demonstratio Jordani de algorismo) in which he described the basic arithmetic operations and extraction of roots.

Algebraic treatises in the Middle Ages were often practical texts for the instruction of lawyers and merchants. Jordanus, however, proceeds in the manner characteristic of Greek mathematicians of the caliber of Euclid, Diophantus, and Pappus. In his treatise De numeris datis (On Given Numbers), Jordanus made algebra an analytic discipline more than three centuries before François Viète, who wrote his Introduction to the Analytical Art in 1591. Although Jordanus was probably familiar with Arabic works on algebra and perhaps also with the Liber abaci by *Fibonacci, On Given Numbers is nonetheless an original treatise. It was widely used in the fifteenth and sixteenth centuries and *Regiomontanus (1436–1476) planned to publish it, but died before he could do so. Jordanus incorporated three distinct elements into every proposition: (1) Formal enunciation of the proposition; (2) The proof; and (3) A numerical example. Although the treatise is wholly rhetorical, Jordanus did use letters of the alphabet to represent numbers.

Jordanus composed a treatise on the planisphere (De plana spera) in which he sought to represent on a plane surface the points and circles on a sphere—in other words, stereographic projection. Projections of this kind were usually applied to astrolabes, but Jordanus does not mention those instruments in his treatise. Jordanus's Planisphere was the most important, and most widely disseminated, treatise on stereographic projection in the Middle Ages.

A treatise on treating fractions (Liber de minutiis) has also been attributed to Jordanus, as well as a brief work on proportions (Liber de proportionibus), the propositions of which strongly resemble those in the fifth book of Euclid's Elements. For the high level and range of his mathematical and mechanical ideas and proofs, Jordanus de Nemore had no equal in the Latin Middle Ages.

See also **Algebra; Arithmetic; Weights, science of**

Bibliography

Busard, H.L.L., ed. *Jordanus de Nemore, De elementis arithmetice artis: a medieval treatise on number theory.* Stuttgart: F. Steiner, 1991.

Høyrup, Jens. Jordanus de Nemore, 13th century mathematical innovator: An essay on intellectual context, achievement, and failure. *Archive for History of Exact Sciences* (1988) 38: 307–363.

Hughes, Barnabas Bernard, ed., and tr. *Jordanus de Nemore: "De numeris datis." A critical edition and translation.* Berkeley: University of California Press, 1981.

Moody, Ernest A. and Marshall Clagett, ed and tr. *The Medieval Science of Weights (Scientia de ponderibus): Treatises Ascribed to Euclid, Archimedes, Thabit ibn Qurra, Jordanus de Nemore and Blasius of Parma.* Edited with Introductions, English Translations, and Notes. Madison: University of Wisconsin Press, 1952, 119–227.

Thomson, Ron B., ed. Jordanus de Nemore: Opera. *Medieval Studies* (1976) 38: 97–144.

———, ed. *Jordanus de Nemore and the mathematics of astrolabes: De plana spera.* [Studies and texts, 39] Toronto: Pontifical Institute of Medieval Studies 1978.

EDWARD GRANT

K

KHAYYAM, 'UMAR AL-

Although today most renowned for his poetry (especially the quatrains collectively known as *The Rubaiyat*), 'Umar al-Khayyam was foremost a mathematician, astronomer, and philosopher. His work on the solutions of cubic equations, the parallel postulate and other issues in Euclidean geometry, and solar *calendar reform each advanced discipline boundaries significantly, and in some cases re-invented them.

Born in Nishapur around 1048 shortly after the Seljuk Turks conquered the area, Khayyam was often beset with political difficulties. He began the life of a scholar at an early age. By 1070, when he received the support of chief justice Abu Tahir of Samarkand, he had already written treatises on *algebra, *arithmetic, and music. At Samarkand he completed his most important work, the *Treatise on the Proofs and Problems of Algebra*, in which he deals particularly with the solutions of cubic equations. Methods to solve quadratics had been known for millennia; in particular, *al-Khwarizmi's famous *Algebra* dealt extensively with them. Without a theory of negative numbers, the equations $x^2 = mx + n$ and $x^2 + mx = n$ (for example) must be dealt with separately; al-Khwarizmi had established a classification of the different "species" of linear and quadratic equations that can arise. Khayyam extended this to cubics, arriving at twenty-five different types. For the thirteen cubics that cannot be reduced immediately to equations of lower order, Khayyam applies geometric techniques: he treats the parameters as line segments, and constructs various conic curves from them. Appropriate intersections of these conics produce line segments that satisfy the given equations. Four of the irreducible cubics had been solved by previous authors; in the *Algebra*, solutions are given to all thirteen. Khayyam also searched for numeric solutions: as he says, "We have tried to express these roots by algebra but have failed. It may be, however, that men who come after us will succeed"—foreshadowing the work of sixteenth-century Italian mathematicians, especially Gerolamo Cardano. Khayyam's time at Samarkand also produced *Difficult Problems of Arithmetic*, in which

"Hindu methods" of finding square and cube roots are extended to roots of arbitrary order. This work is now lost, but evidence of later writers suggests that Khayyam used the binomial expansion $(a + b)^n = a^n + na^{n-1}b + \ldots nab^{n-1} + b^n$ to develop his procedure.

In 1074, with the invitation of the Seljuk sultan Malikshah and his vizier Nizam al-Mulk, Khayyam traveled to Isfahan to supervise its new observatory and to establish an astronomical program geared to reforming the calendar for agricultural and economic purposes. Although he was viewed with suspicion for his supposed atheist tendencies, his time at Isfahan was one of the most peaceful and productive periods of his life. Khayyam's proposed calendar, never implemented, is actually a better fit to the true solar year than the Gregorian calendar. He also supervised the construction of the *Zij Malikshah*, an astronomical handbook of which only a fragment, a small star catalogue, survives. Khayyam's major mathematical work composed in Esfahan, the *Difficulties in the Postulates of Euclid*, contains two major contributions. The first is his treatment of *Euclid's parallel postulate, the assertion that if two lines cross a given line segment so that the interior angles are less than two right angles, they must eventually meet on that side of the given segment. Many attempts to prove this postulate were made from Greek times up to the discovery of non-Euclidean geometry. Khayyam's analysis avoids the common trap of assuming implicitly some other statement that turns out to be equivalent to the parallel postulate itself. Instead, he forms what was eventually to be called the "Saccheri quadrilateral," which is constructed by drawing two equal line segments perpendicularly to either end of a straight line, and connecting the other ends. He appeals to a principle in a (now lost) work of Aristotle, namely, that two convergent lines must meet, to demonstrate that the quadrilateral in fact must be a rectangle. The second contribution in *Difficulties* was a twofold improvement to the theory of ratios expounded in Euclid's *Elements* Book V. Muslim scientists had been dissatisfied with Euclid's definition of the equality of ratios, and had proposed an alternate approach known as the anthyphairetic definition. Khayyam demonstrates that this is logically equivalent to Euclid, and thus Book V does not have to be rewritten to take into account the substituted definition. Khayyam also worked with the definition of compound ratios, leading to a consideration of ratios of magnitudes as a new kind of number, thus foreshadowing the emergence of irrational numbers and the real number continuum.

The deaths of both of Khayyam's patrons made it difficult for him to continue his work after 1092. His fall from grace led to the withdrawal of funding for the observatory, and he spent some effort trying to convince the Seljuk court to restore it. He eventually left Esfahan for Merv, the site of the new Seljuk capital in 1118, where he wrote a number of works on topics including algebra, mechanics, astronomy, and geography. He died around 1131, and was buried according to his request in Esfahan, where his tomb still exists today.

In addition to his scientific and poetic writings Khayyam wrote several philosophical treatises, influenced strongly by *Ibn Sina (Avicenna). They include discussions on the subject of a universal science and on questions of the universality of existence. It is difficult to determine Khayyam's own perspective on these and other philosophical questions, since the authenticity of many of the existing poetic writings is in doubt and the philosophical treatises may have been influenced by Khayyam's patrons. However, his astronomical and especially his mathematical writings are an enduring testament to a powerful scholar who pursued both foundational questions and the frontiers of science.

See also **Astronomy, Islamic; Geography, chorography; Music theory; Planetary tables**

Bibliography

Rashed, Roshdi and Bijan Vahabzadeh. *Omar Khayyam the Mathematician*. New York: Bibliotheca Persica Press, 2000.

Sayili, Aydin. *The Observatory in Islam and its Place in the General History of the Observatory*. New York: Arno Press, 1981 (reprint of 1960 edition).

Vahabzadeh, Bijan. Al-Khayyam's Conception of Ratio and Proportionality. *Arabic Sciences and Philosophy* (1997) 7: 247–263.

GLEN VAN BRUMMELEN AND JULIA XENAKIS

KHWARIZMI, AL-

Abu Ja'far Muhammad ibn Musa al-Khwarizmi is remembered as the founder of *algebra; however, he was a scholar with interests and writings ranging across most of the ancient mathematical sciences. As his name indicates, he was probably of central Asian origin, although little else is known of his early life. From the dedications of his works, it is clear that he wrote for the Abbasid Caliph al-Ma'mun (813–833 C.E.) and was an active member of the circle of scholars in ninth century Baghdad, associated with the *Bayt al-hikma. These scholars worked for many patrons of the highest political

and social circles—including caliphs and viziers—and produced a body of knowledge in Arabic that became the basis for advances in Islamic philosophy, medicine, mathematics, and engineering (Gutas). Before he died, sometime in the middle of the century, al-Khwarizmi's fame was established on the basis of his written works.

Early in his reign, al-Ma'mun expressed a desire for practical *astrology and the mathematics required to support its application. Al-Khwarizmi filled this bill and more. His most famous text was the *Handbook for Calculation by Completing and Balancing (Kitab al-muktasar fi hisab al-jabr wa'l-muqabalah)*. As the title indicates, the book demonstrates two main processes for solving equations. While he may have found both methods in Diophanes' *Arithmetic* and probably derived some of his terminology from Indian mathematical practice, it was al-Khwarizmi who brought these elements together. He shows that solvable equations take one of six standard forms. The remainder of the book deals with the practical applications of algebra to problems of inheritance, trade, and legacies, and he uses geometrical figures to explain equations. Confusing and ironic as it may be, al-Khwarizmi did not use any kind of numerical symbols or algebraic notation—all problems were discussed in words. This work became the foundational text of algebra, even within his lifetime. The Latin translation of this text was one of the crucial elements in the so-called Twelfth-Century Renaissance.

Also important to the history of mathematics, al-Khwarizmi wrote a small work on *Calculation with Hindu Numerals*. This book was clearly written after the *Algebra*, to which it refers. Like the *Algebra*, it appears to be the first work of its kind, treating the Hindu numbers and place-value notation as derived from Indian mathematics. It teaches the use of the numerals, the basic arithmetical operations, fractions, and the extraction of square roots. This work was not of great consequence in the Arabic-speaking world and the Arabic original has not survived. However, it had a revolutionary impact in Europe, in its Latin translation titled *Algoritmi de numero Indorum (Khwarizmi on Indian Numbers)*, the deformation of his name yielding the modern mathematical term, algorithm. His third major work was his astronomical tables, or *Zij al-Sindhind*. This book described the positions of the planets, the Moon, and the Sun, based in a calendar and a specific location. It then included the tables and the instructions for computations of the positions of the heavenly bodies. Like the mathematical works, this was based on a Sanskrit original, known as *Siddhanta*. His tables indicate familiarity with Greek and Persian tables, as well as the Indian text; as in his other works, he was attempting a synthesis of the knowledge from the legacy of sources created in earlier civilizations. Surprisingly, none of the tables was correlated with observation, even though contemporary Baghdadi astronomers had already found more accurate values for some astronomical phenomena. Perhaps most surprising, the original text was based on the Yazdigird III calendar rather than the Hijra calendar. Because of its practical importance, this work had wide diffusion, appearing in Muslim Spain within his lifetime. Here, his original tables were studied by *Maslama of Madrid and his pupils whose adaptation, more accurate than the original, adjusted the tables to make them useful to astronomers in the West. This version was then translated by *Adelard of Bath and *Pedro Alfonso, and it is only this Latin version that survives complete whereas in Arabic only selections from the original survive.

Al-Khwarizmi's two other surviving works are the *Geography* and the *Extraction of the Jewish Calendar*. It appears that the *Geography* represents an important advance over *Ptolemy's work of the same name. It has been speculated that al-Khwarizmi's work was based on a world map constructed by a collection of scholars for al-Ma'mun; the *Geography* represents superior knowledge of the Islamic lands and the areas visited by Muslim traders and merchants. The work on the Jewish calendar is curious. He says that he wrote it because an explanation of that calendar was necessary for those who happen to use it. Its occasion or purpose remains obscure; perhaps it was used by historians and writers trying to reconcile the differences between the Islamic and Christian calculations of the *annus mundi*.

Al-Khwarizmi wrote several other books which do not seem to have survived: a *Book on the Construction of the Astrolabe*, a *Book on the Use of the Astrolabe*, a *Book of the Sundial*, and a *Chronicle* which is frequently quoted by later historians.

Al-Khwarizmi is one of the most influential medieval mathematicians and astronomers. While his creativity was inspired by borrowing, the developments, especially of algebra, were his own. Even though he was only one of a circle of savants working in al-Ma'mun's Baghdad, he is the only one who created a branch of knowledge and gave his name to a process: algebra and algorithm. Because he brought disparate elements together in a new structure of scientific knowledge, others were able to advance the science beyond his foundations. It is fair to characterize his work as more "practical" than "theoretical": his algebra, his astronomical tables, his geography, and his lost works all fulfill useful purposes. But precisely for this reason his works endured, especially in Western Europe.

See also **Astronomy, Islamic; Commercial arithmetic; Geography, chorography; Planetary tables**

Bibliography

Al-Khwarizmi. *The Astronomical Tables of al-Khwarizmi.* Edited by Otto Neugebauer. Copenhagen: Royal Danish Academy of Sciences and Letters, 1962.

Gutas, Dimitri. *Greek Thought, Arabic Culture.* London: Routledge, 1998.

Kennedy, E.S. "Al-Khwarizmi on the Jewish Calendar." *Scripta Mathematica* (1964) 27: 55–59.

———. *A Survey of Islamic Astronomical Tables.* Philadelphia: American Philosophical Society, 1956.

Pingree, David. "Indian Astronomy in Medieval Spain." In *From Baghdad to Barcelona*, 2 vols. Edited by Julio Samso and Josep Casulleras. I: 39–48 Barcelona: Anuari de Filologia XIX, 1996.

Roshdi, Rashid. "Al-Khwarizmi's Concept of Algebra." In *Arab Civilization: Challenges and Response.* Edited by G.N. Atiyeh and I.M. Oweiss. 98–111. Albany: SUNY Press, 1988.

Van Dalen, Benno. "Al-Khwarismi's Astronomical Tables Revisited." In Samso and Casulleras, I: 195–252.

MICHAEL C. WEBER

KILWARDBY, ROBERT

Robert Kilwardby died at the papal court in Viterbo, Italy, on September 11, 1279. Although aspects of his career as an intellectual and churchman are known, nothing is really known about his early life except that he studied at Paris. It would be nice to know if he studied with the natural philosopher Richard Fishacre at Oxford in the early 1240s, for instance: it is possible and some of their ideas are similar. He was teaching in the arts faculty of the University of Paris in the late 1240s but left sometime around 1250 to begin the study of theology. This switch is of great significance when trying to understand his central role in the *Condemnation of 1277. As a member of the arts faculty in the 1240s Kilwardby could not teach theology or touch on theological issues. His reputation as one of the most able commentators on Aristotle during this period still stands: no mean accomplishment for it was only just at this moment that Aristotle was really being read and taught in Christian Europe. Kilwardby would later come to be highly regarded as a theologian and this reputation, combined with his elevation in 1273 to the office of Archbishop of Canterbury, made him a powerful churchman. As a churchman he appears to have been extremely conscientious in his duties—and that was not universally true in the Middle Ages—and known for his piety. He went on a pastoral visitation of his province, for example, despite the invariable hardships of sustained travel in those days.

Among Kilwardby's most important works are *De ortu scientiarum* (1250); his *Sentences*-commentary (1252); and his *Letter to Peter Conflans* (1277). Perhaps the common theme of these works is an interest in harmonizing oppositions. For example, in a short metaphysical work, *De natura relationis*, Robert tries to show that a substance can also be a relation. While this claim would confound anyone who had read Aristotle's *Categories*, any reader of his *Metaphysics* would likewise be amazed at Kilwardby's argument in his *Sentences*-commentary that one and the same thing (*res*) can be genus, species, and individual substances. However, it must not be thought that Kilwardby was dismissive of Aristotle or that he had some perverse cast of metaphysical mind. In fact, intense scrutiny of Aristotle and radical reworkings of his categories of thinking were pretty much the bread and butter of philosophers and theologians in the second half of the thirteenth century. Henry of Ghent and *Johannes Duns Scotus are the most famous of Aristotle's transformers, of course, but like Kilwardby they brought a fundamentally theological vision to bear on Aristotle and alter his categories of thought for deep, thoroughly worked out, theological reasons. Henry and

Robert Kilwardby (left) performs the Archbishop of Canterbury's traditional ceremonial duty at the coronation of Edward I (r. 1272–1307) as king of England at Westminster Abbey in August 1274. (Color lithograph c. 1910.) (Mary Evans Picture Library)

Scotus were thoroughgoing metaphysicans but Robert often tried to justify his transformations of Aristotle by appealing to biology.

Although Robert Kilwardby had yet to study theology when he wrote his famous work on the origin and order of the sciences, *De ortu scientiarum* is nevertheless a remarkable presentation of Christian Platonism, a profoundly theological metaphysics, and this despite the fact that Aristotle's *Metaphysics* is the most cited work within it and second most cited is the *Posterior Analytics*. But this is of a piece with Robert's interest in reconciliation. Although Robert's cosmology was thoroughly Platonic, his use of Aristotle was not mere window-dressing. Like Bonaventure, Robert argued that the inner reality of the physical world was music but unlike Bonaventure he wanted Aristotle as one of his authorities for his opinions. Thus Robert was the first to define music, a science that was taught as part of the *quadrivium in the arts faculty, as *numerus harmonicus*. He derived the idea of music as a mathematical science from Aristotle's position in the *Posterior Analytics* that music is a subordinate science to *arithmetic, and so one of the *scientiae mediae*, sitting between mathematics and physics in the hierarchy of the sciences. Robert's definition became a source for later medieval musical theorists who like him espoused a strongly Platonic cosmology: and it was a fairly common position in the Middle Ages to defend Platonism by the idea that music as a structuring principle of the natural order sat close to the core of reality.

Robert's commitment to Platonism never left him and was certainly reinforced by his reading of Augustine and taking him as a mentor in theology after 1250. This theologico-philosophical position is the backdrop for Robert's well-known, and much-debated, intervention in the academic affairs of the University of Oxford. There, in 1277, he condemned a number of propositions ranging from issues in grammar to natural philosophy. Among

the issues condemned, and by far the most significant and wide-ranging, was the thesis that there is a single substantial form in man. Robert was a defender of the common position in the Middle Ages that the human being is made up of a plurality of substantial forms. This position was a commonplace in medical literature until the seventeenth century. His 1277 *Letter to Peter Conflans* is a defense of this thesis almost exclusively in terms of medicine and biology, albeit with a strong metaphysical accent. Defending the plurality thesis in this way, with reasoning drawn from embryology, comparative anatomy, and physiology was quite common. Famously, it was not the position held by *Thomas Aquinas, nor did Thomas draw on biology for his defense of the unicity thesis. Although there is debate about this, a consensus does exist that Robert did take a swipe at his Dominican confrere in 1277 when condemning the unicity thesis. However that may be, what is crucial here is that the plurality position suited Augustinian Platonism and a theology in which a powerful contrast exists between humans as divided in substance and God as utterly one in being. Robert had elaborate theological and scientific reasons for handing down his 1277 condemnations and his action cannot merely be cast as some "conservative backlash" against, or fear of, Arabo-Aristotelian scientism: and sadly, one reads such opinions in a fair chunk of the literature on Robert and 1277.

See also **Aristotelianism; Music theory; Plato**

Bibliography

Primary Sources
Robert Kilwardby. *De ortu scientiarum*. Albert G. Judy, ed. London: British Academy, 1976.
———. *On Time and Imagination*. O. Lewry, ed. Oxford: Oxford University Press, 1987.
———. *Quaestiones in libros I-IV Sententiarum*. Ed. Johannes

Scheider (I); Gerhard Leibold (II); E. Gössmann, G. Leibold (III); Gerd Haverling (IV). Munich: Bayerisches Akademie der Wissenschaften, 1986–1995.

Secondary Sources

Judy, A.G. "Introduction." In *De ortu scientiarum*. London: British Academy, 1976.

McAleer, G.J. The Science of Music: A Platonic Application of the *Posterior Analytics* in Robert Kilwardby, *De ortu scientiarum*. *Acta Philosophica* (2003) 12: 323–335.

———. The Presence of Averroes in the Natural Philosophy of Robert Kilwardby. *Archiv für Geschichte der Philosophie* (1999) 81: 33–54.

Sharp, D. E. The 1277 Condemnation of Kilwardby. *New Scholasticism* (1934) 8: 306–318.

———. The Philosophy of Richard Fishacre. *New Scholasticism* (1933) 7: 283–297.

Sommer-Seckendorff, Ellen Mary Frances. *Studies in the Life of Robert Kilwardby*. Rome: Istituto Storico Domenicano, 1937.

G.J. McAleer

KINDI, AL-

Very little is known of the life of Abu Yusuf Ya'qub ibn Ishaq al-Kindi, called "The Philosopher of the Arabs": descended from the south-Arabic tribe of Kinda (hence his name). He was born in Kufa (first capital of the Abbasid empire) in Iraq, around 800. He got his intellectual education first in Basra, of which his father was governor, then in Baghdad, where he carried on his scientific career and where he died, after 866. He was a member of a group of philosophers in the circle of the caliph al-Ma'mun (813–883) and the *Bayt al-Hikma* and made some of the early translations of Aristotle, Proclus, and Plotinus from Greek, all of them now lost. Al-Ma'mun's successor, al-Mu'tasim, appointed al-Kindi as the tutor of his son Ahmad. Somehow out of favor during the reign of al-Wathiq, al-Kindi regained some favor with al-Mutawakkil before falling into disgrace due to the intrigues of other scientists (the Banu Musa or Abu Ma'shar) who were also his rivals.

Al-Kindi then divided his activities between Kufa, Basra and Baghdad, the three most prestigious cities of the Abbassid empire, centers during the ninth century of an intense intellectual activity, supported by political power: the passage under the Arab domination of non-Arabic-speaking nations, heirs of rich intellectual traditions, induced a fertile cultural and social mixing. Contemporary to the studies of grammar, linguistics and hermeneutics in the schools of Kufa and Basra, the religious speculation, stirred by controversies arousing of the confrontation with believers of other religions (Christians, Jews, Zoroastrians…) became more dialectical. At the same time the Arabo-Islamic culture appropriated and developed for its own account scientific and philosophical elements elaborated in Persia, India, and and also Greece: the massive movement of translation of the Hellenistic heritage coincided with the first scientific researches. This century is one of the most brilliant of the universal history.

Al-Kindi is a good example of an encyclopedic thinker, nurtured on Greek thought and, at the same time, involved in the religious controversies of the time, he is the author of a very vast work, of which unfortunately very little is left: while the biobibliographer Ibn al-Nadim (writing approximately one hundred fifteen years after al-Kindi's death) ascribes to him in his *Fihrist* more than two hundred seventy works, no more than thirty have survived. Al-Kindi's interests embraced almost all sciences, to which he developed, starting from the premises of Greek science, a personal and original interpretation. He is in particular the author of the most substantial work on optics since late antiquity.

Philosophy

Al-Kindi's philosophy was especially indebted to *Plato and Aristotle, who for him had intrinsically the same doctrine (we recognize here one of the syncretistic aspects of late Greek thought). His philosophy integrates problems and concepts originating in various currents of Neoplatonism (Proclus, Plotinus). His thought is also closely related to *kalam*, or rational Islamic theology; in particular its *mu'tazilite* branch, which played an important role in the introduction of elements of Greek philosophy into the Islamic thought, as well as some of the key subjects he studies, such as the unicity of God, man's free will, and the thesis of the "created" Qu'ran.

Al-Kindi, relying on the principle that reason is an attribute specific to mankind, considers that philosophy has to explain by its own methods the truths expounded in the Qu'ran in a condensed form. Inasmuch as for him, philosophical truth accords on the whole with revealed truth, there is no conflict between reason and religious faith. He develops this thesis in several works, including his *First Philosophy* and the epistle *On the Number of Aristotle's Books*. The central theme is that prophetic science and human science have the same content, the only difference being that the first one is instantaneous, gained without effort or prior knowledge, because it comes from God. *First Philosophy* contains a violent criticism of those who, under cover of religion, denigrate philosophical speculation.

Most of al-Kindi's works are epistles (*risala*), rather short texts, rigorously organized, dealing with well defined subjects (this style of writing will become afterwards rather common amongst philosophers writing in Arabic). Al-Kindi devotes, inter alia, several epistles to the proof of the finitude of the world in time and in space and to the fact that the infinite exists only potentially (a problem already tackled in his *First Philosophy*), thus breaking with Aristotle's cosmology and incorporating some Neoplatonic concepts (such as those found in the *Theology* of Pseudo-Aristotle or in Proclus' book on *The Pure Good*).

Optics

Al-Kindi's work in the field of optics is double-faceted: while it is directly indebted to Hellenistic optics—most of the Greco-Hellenistic texts on the subject were translated into Arabic early, as far back as the ninth century—it is nevertheless forward-looking and opens several new fields of research.

In antiquity, Optics was, strictly speaking, a geometry of the perception of space and optical illusions (as in *Euclid's *Optica*); it was based on the doctrine of the emission by the eye of a visual ray, the nature of which is only geometric. This ray is just a segment of a straight line joining two points, referring neither to the physical nature of light nor to the physiology of the eye. The theory of the "visual ray," often criticized by philosophers, is the theory espoused by the supporters of geometrical optics, except when they study burning-mirrors (a set-piece of ancient science whose subject is the reflection of solar rays).

Al-Kindi supports the theory of the visual ray, but for him vision is due to a radiant power issuing from the eye and forming the air into straight lines. This now endows the visual ray with a physical reality: it becomes "a light power which impresses a luminosity in all the air it comes across... such as a living limb by which the pupil feels all the bodies it touches." With al-Kindi, optics becomes a field falling within the province both of geometry and physics. This physical conception of the visual ray leads al-Kindi to take into account the duality of light versus vision and to study, not only the way the objects are seen, but also the propagation of luminous rays and the physical properties of light. These multiform links forged between light and vision created a dilemma that was only resolved a century and a half later by *Ibn al-Haytham who, definitively giving up the theory of the visual ray, developed the hypothesis that light rays, entering the eye, are the true cause of vision.

Al-Kindi's *On Solar Rays*, at the cusp of late antiquity and the nascent Arabic tradition, is the first Arabic text to deal with burning-mirrors. His purpose in this treatise was to remedy the inadequacies in Anthemius of Tralles' study and to complete it. The optical works of al-Kindi influenced his successors, particularly Ibn al-Haytham.

See also **Archimedes; Aristotelianism; God in Islam; Optics and catoptrics; Pseudo-Aristotle; Ptolemy; Thabit ibn Qurra**

Bibliography

D'Ancona Costa, C. *Aristotele e Plotino nelle dottrina di al-Kindi sul primo principio. Documenti e studi sulla tradizione filosofica medievale* 1993.

Guerrero, Rafael and Emilio Tornero. *Obras filosóficas de al-Kindi*. Madrid: Coloquio, 1986.

Ivry, A. L. *Al-Kindi's Metaphysics. A Translation of Ya'qub ibn Ishaq al-Kindi's Treatise "On First Philosophy"* with introduction and commentary. Albany: State University of New York Press, 1974.

Jolivet, Jean. *L'intellect selon al-Kindi*. Leiden: E.J. Brill, 1971.

Rashed R., and J. Jolivet. *Oeuvres philosophiques et scientifiques d'al-Kindi*, vol. 1 *L'optique et la catoptrique*, vol. 2 *Métaphysique et cosmologie*. Leiden: E.J. Brill, 1997–1998.

HÉLÈNE BELLOSTA

KOSMAS INDIKOPLEUSTÊS

A Greek merchant in the first half of the sixth century, Kosmas traveled from Alexandria to Eastern Africa and Arabia and supposedly sailed also to India and Sri Lanka (hence his qualification of *Indikopleustês*, that is, *Sailor to India*). He has been identified as the person to whom the physician Alexander of Tralles (sixth century) dedicated his treatise *On fevers*. If so, Kosmas was the son of the physician who taught medicine to Alexander at an unspecified place (perhaps Tralleis rather than Alexandria, as recently suggested). In contact with Alexander since his youth, he remained a life-long friend, even though he moved abroad, according to Alexander's own words. In his old age, he became a monk at the Rhaitu monastery in the Sinai.

Kosmas is best known for his work *Christianikê topographia* (*Christian Topography*), comprising twelve books in which he proposed a Christian conception of the universe. The program was not new, but dated back to the Fathers of the Church. During Kosmas' life, however, Christianization of society, science and culture was enforced, particularly under the Byzantine emperor Justinian I (b. c. 482, emperor 527, d. 565): when the philosophical school of Athens—where classical, viz., pagan, philosophy was taught—was closed in 529, some teachers, who moved from Athens to Alexandria, were later called to Constantinople by the Emperor, and medicine, for example, was transformed by means of the development of the cult of Kosmas and Damianos (martyred in the late-third century). In this context, the conceptions of the Earth and the universe inherited from antiquity were to be replaced by a new one, compatible with the Old Testament and the account of the creation of the world. The topic was the object of a philosophico-scientific polemic illustrated by such philosophers as Proclus (410 or 412–485) and John Philoponus (c. 490–after 567). It opposed not only Christians and pagans according to a traditional interpretation, but also Christian heterodox groups (among others the Nestorians) and Christian orthodoxy. Kosmas refuted the Aristotelico-Ptolemaic cosmology and proposed a literalist interpretation of the biblical text, following the Syro-Antiochean tradition of biblical exegesis, traditionally opposed to the Alexandrian school. In this view, the Earth is a rectangular plate of four hundred travel days from west to east, and two hundred from north to south, surrounded by the Ocean. At the northern end of the Earth, a cone-shaped mountain rises up, which hides the Sun during the night. The firmament is a two-story vault like Moses' tabernacle, which is built on vertical walls: the first story is perishable, and the second divine and eternal.

The scientific interest of the *Topography* is not limited to illustrating the creation of a new cosmography and geography, but resides also in the wealth of information of all kinds (not only natural history, but also ethnography and history of religions, for example) that Kosmas gathered on the basis of personal observation or hearsay. Among other things, he described the life of the Near East, not only the expansion and rituals of Christian Church(es), but also trade activity, including the rivalry between the Persian and the Byzantine empires, the natural environment with the plants and animals of India, such as pepper and coconut, or unicorn, buffalo, giraffe, and hippopotamus, and he even made a copy of a Greek inscription in Adulis from the so-called Monumentum Adulitanum.

The work is known in more than thirty Byzantine manuscripts, three of which are illustrated (Vaticanus graecus 699, ninth century; Florentinus, Mediceus Laurentianus, 9.28, eleventh century; Sinaiticus graecus 1186). It was translated into Slavonic between the twelfth and thirteenth century and was influential in Kievan Rus, as well as in the Nestorian Near East, and in popular medieval geography. Fragments of the *Topography* were published in the seventeenth century, and the full text in 1707 by Bernard de Montfaucon in his *Collectio nova patrum et scriptorum graecorum*.

See also **Geography, chorography; Travel and exploration**

Bibliography

Anastasos, M.V. The Alexandrian Origin of the Christian Topography. *Dumbarton Oaks Papers* (1946) 3: 73–80.

Pigulevskaia, N. V. *Byzanz auf den Wegen nach Indien. Aus der Geschichte der byzantinischen Handels mit dem Orient vom 4.-6. Jh.* Berlin and Amsterdam: Hakkert, 1969.

Wolska-Conus, W. *La Topographie chrétienne de Cosmas Indicopleustès, théologie et science au VIe siècle.* Paris: Presses Universitaires de France, 1962.

———. *Cosmas Indicopleustes, Topographie chrétienne. Introduction, texte critique, illustration, traduction et notes.* 3 vols. Paris: Éditions du Cerf, 1968.

———. La «Topographie Chrétienne» de Cosmas Indicopleustès. Hypothèses sur quelque thèmes de son illustration. *Revue des Etudes Byzantines* (1990) 48: 155–191.

ALAIN TOUWAIDE

L

LANFRANCO OF MILAN

Lanfranco was born in Pisa in the first third of the thirteenth century and died in Paris c. 1306. The details of his life are made hazy by the intervening centuries. We know he learned medicine at the University of Bologna; we know he studied under Guglielmo da Saliceto and that he practiced surgery in Milan; and we know that the Guelph-Ghibelline civil war forced him to flee c. 1290 first to Lyon, where he completed his *Chirurgia parva*, then to Paris by 1295. His *Chirurgia magna* (*Great Surgery*) (1296) was largely written in France, probably in Paris, and dedicated to King Philip IV (the Fair).

Philip the Fair and his court increasingly regulated the medical marketplace and displayed an affinity for Italian medicine. A foreigner in domestically inspissated Paris, Lanfranco's dedication surely was intended to curry favor, but the text also suggests how isolated he felt in his exile. Having students may have mitigated that personal and professional isolation. It is likely that Lanfranco taught or at least inspired the royal surgeon and author *Henri de Mondeville at this time. We know that Jan Ypermann, the Flemish surgeon of the early fourteenth century, described Lanfranco as his teacher and summarized his ideas.

While the details of Lanfranco's life are hazy, the impact of his work is clearer. He joined his master, Guglielmo da Saliceto, as well as *Teodorico Borgognoni, Henri de Mondeville, and *Guy de Chauliac in distinguishing learned *surgery from its purely manualist origins. In a time of market-based maneuvering, such actions were necessary for the ambitious surgical practitioner and teacher. Thus Lanfranco appears to have resonated with the proto-professionalizing forces around him. The introductory tone of *Chirurgia magna*, for example, suggests a scholastic influence, and his clinical vignettes rail against the unlettered healer, *laicus*, rather than inveighing against the depredations of the learned physician.

Chirurgia magna is divided into five parts, describing: (1) The boundaries of surgery, stressing deontology, anatomy and general surgical conditions; (2) Wound surgery from head to toe; (3) Specific surgical conditions from the dermatologic to varieties of cancer, roughly from head to toe; (4) Fractures and dislocations; and (5) An antidotary. The first four divisions fell strictly into the style of the new Italian surgery advanced by Guglielmo da Saliceto, embracing anatomy and a textual tradition with authoritative authors (largely *Galen and *Ibn Sina), buttressed by a display of clinical experience and reference to his master. Lanfranco is thus secure as the primary conduit of Italian surgery to northern Europe, although the importance of Henri de Mondeville is only slightly less in this regard.

Woodcut showing the treatment of head injuries. From 1528 German edition of Lanfranco's works. (National Library of Medicine)

The body of the text of *Chirurgia magna* offers standard therapeutic fare, although Lanfranco follows his master in arguing for a moderate approach to wound healing. As famously recounted by Henri de Mondeville, three schools of thought existed. One advocated a strict diet and extensive wound manipulation to generate an abscess, the so-called "laudable pus." A second argued for a less strict diet and cleansing the wound, which Henri himself favored. The middle ground between the two extremes was staked out by Lanfranco and Saliceto.

Bringing Surgery into Medicine

Lanfranco also introduced an antidotary at the end of his great work. Classically, therapeutics had been divided into regimen, drugs, and surgery. The first two interventions were the province of the physician, the last that of the surgeon. Michael McVaugh has suggested that Lanfranco's pharmaceutical addition may have been another attempt to bring surgery closer to the elite status of the physician. This same device was embraced by Mondeville after him.

Translated into Middle English, French, and Spanish in the Middle Ages, *Chirurgia magna* had an enduring influence on the development of lay surgical traditions after the peak of high medieval learned surgery. *Chirurgia parva* was also translated into French and German and printed frequently in the sixteenth century.

See also **Medicine, practical; Medicine, theoretical**

Bibliography

Primary Source
Lanfranco da Milan. *Ars completa totius cyrurgie*. Printed with the Cyrurgia of Guy de Chauliac. Venice, 1498.

Secondary Sources
Agrimi, Jole and Crisciani, Chiara. The Science and Practice of Medicine in the Thirteenth Century according to Guglielmo da Saliceto, Italian Surgeon. In *Practical Medicine from Salerno to the Black Death*. Edited by Luis García-Ballester, Roger French, Jon Arrizabalaga, and Andrew Cunningham. New York: Cambridge University Press, 1994, pp. 60–87.
De Tovar, Claude. Les versions françaises de la "Chirurgia parva" de Lanfranc de Milan: Étude de la tradition manuscrite. *Revue d'Histoire des Textes* (1982–1983) 12–13: 195–262.
Keil, Gundolf. "Lanfranks 'Chirurgia parva' in böhmischer Textgestaltung des Spämittlelalters: Ein Vergleich mit knodurrierenden Textendwürfen anderer deutscher Sprachlandschaften." In *Aspekte der Textgestaltung: Referate der Internationalen Germanistischen Konferenz, Ostrava*. Ostrava: Universität, Philsophische Fakultät, 2001: 55–67.
McVaugh, Michael. "Therapeutic Strategies: Surgery." In *Western Medical Thought from Antiquity to the Middle Ages*. Edited by Mirko D. Grmek and translated by Antony Shugaar. Cambridge: Harvard University Press, 1998: pp. 273–290.
Rosenman, Leonard D., tr. *The Surgery of Lanfranchi of Milan*. Philadelphia: Xlibris, 2003.

WALTON O. SCHALICK, III

LAPIDARIES

Lapidaries are books of information about the properties and virtues of precious and semi-precious stones. Each entry in a lapidary usually tells of the color and origins of the stone, as well as its medicinal, magical, moral, and protective properties. Lapidaries are sometimes independent works and sometimes form part of more wide-ranging encyclopedic compilations. In both cases lapidaries are often found in close proximity to herbals because, as is commonly claimed, God has given virtues to herbs, to stones, and to words. Lapidaries were very popular throughout the Middle Ages, especially in the fourteenth and fifteenth centuries, and they appear in hundreds of medieval and early modern manuscripts. As late as the seventeenth century, lapidaries containing both traditional lore and newer information from world exploration continued to be printed and widely copied in manuscript form.

The origins of the medieval lapidary are in classical writings, Arabic writings, and biblical exegesis. Most prominent among the classical works is Book 37 of the *Natural History* compiled by Pliny the Elder (23–79 C.E.), which was an authoritative source of information about stones throughout the Middle Ages. Pliny was the major influence on two other well-known compilations that had a great influence on later medieval lapidaries, the first-century *Wonders of the World* (*Collectanea Rerum Memorabilium*) by Solinus, and the sixth-century *Etymologies* of *Isidore of Seville. From the medical tradition of the classical world, the most important lapidary is the *Damigeron* (named for its alleged author), a first-century Greek work translated into Latin, probably in the fifth century. It was the basis for the *De Lapidibus* of Marbode of Rennes (d. 1123), which has a predominant influence on later medieval lapidaries. From the Arabic tradition the most important sources are Latin translations of two eleventh-century works, *De congelatione et conglutinatione lapidum*, originally the work of *Ibn Sina (Avicenna), and *Secretum secretorum*, which was translated into Latin twice and then into the vernacular languages. The exegetical sources are commentaries on the lists of jewels found in scripture: the breastplate of Aaron (Exodus 28: 17–20, 39: 10–14), the lamentation of the King of Tyre (Ezekiel 28: 13), and the foundations of the New Jerusalem (Revelation 21: 19–20).

Marbode's lapidary initiates a flowering of the lapidary tradition, both in Latin and in the vernacular languages. Four encyclopedic works of the thirteenth century incorporate lapidaries, all of them indebted to Pliny, Isidore, and Marbode, and are major contributions to the tradition: *The Purposes of Things* (*De finibus rerum*) by Arnold of Saxony, *The Properties of Things* (*De proprietatibus rerum*) by *Bartholomaeus Anglicus, *The Nature of Things* (*De natura rerum*) by *Thomas of Cantimpré, and *The Great Mirror* (*Speculum maius*) by *Vincent of Beauvais. In the same century the renowned scholar *Albertus Magnus compiled *The Book of Minerals*, for which he borrowed material from the lapidaries of Thomas, Arnold, and Marbode.

Vernacular lapidaries also begin to flourish in the thirteenth century. However, a work from outside this tradition, the *Old English Lapidary*, compiled between 950 and 1050, is certainly the earliest vernacular lapidary. Spanish and French versions of Marbode are extant in manuscripts of the twelfth century, and versions in those languages and in Italian circulate regularly from the thirteenth century onwards. *Alfonso X the Wise, king of Castile and Leon (1250–1284), encouraged production of numerous lapidaries, the best known of which organizes stones under the twelve signs of the zodiac. Still other French lapidaries are produced in significant numbers in the thirteenth and fourteenth centuries, and several were, in turn, translated into English. Among the most interesting is a late-thirteenth-century lapidary produced for a King Philip, probably Philip IV the Fair (1285–1314), which treats the stones in Aaron's breastplate and in Revelation. It circulated widely, to judge by the eleven known manuscripts, and was twice translated into English in the fourteenth and fifteenth centuries. It is related to a lapidary found in the French *Sidrac*, a late-thirteenth-century encyclopedic work that also enjoyed a wide circulation. Both Bartholomaeus Anglicus's encyclopedia and the *Secretum Secretorum* were translated into numerous European vernaculars, which assured a wide audience for their information about stones.

The dissemination of information about stones is evident in a variety of medieval writings. In romances the heroine almost unfailingly presents a ring to the hero as he is about to set off on his adventures. In that ring is a magical jewel, usually of unspecified nature, which protects the hero in battle. In Wolfram von Eschenbach's *Parzival*, Gahmuret, father of the hero, dies because goat's milk is poured on his helmet of adamant, causing it to become as soft as a sponge. In the romances of Alexander the Great, his victory over the forces of Darius put him in possession of a land strewn with precious stones. In some versions Alexander finds the tomb of Ninus, the Assyrian king, which is carved from a single amethyst. In the Middle English *Prose Alexander*, after burying Darius, Alexander ascends to the throne of Cyrus by means of seven stairs, five of them made of precious stones, the properties of which are set forth in great detail, just as they appear in lapidaries. English medical treatises sometimes incorporate information about stones for their medicinal and other values; often these are simply entries taken from any of the popular lapidaries. A popular item concerns the use of jet: when placed in bed with a sleeping woman, the stone forces her to reveal her secrets to her husband. Household inventories show the value placed on the virtues of stones, particularly those that can indicate the presence of poison in foods. A particularly interesting archeological discovery is the fifteenth-century Middleham Jewel, found in 1985 after having been buried for centuries near Middleham Castle in Yorkshire, England. It consists of a sapphire set into a lozenge-shaped container for a holy relic. This container, inscribed with liturgical verses and two names for God commonly used as charms, unites the virtues of stones and the virtue of words with imagery of the Nativity of Jesus and of the Trinity. The Middleham Jewel provides an excellent context in which to understand the influence of the lapidary, which reveals to mankind useful mysteries of the Creator's creation.

See also **Magic and the occult; Mineralogy**

Bibliography

Albertus Magnus. *Book of Minerals*. Translated by Dorothy Wyckoff. Oxford: Clarendon Press, 1967.

Bahler, Ingrid and Katherine Gyékényesi Gatto, eds. *The Lapidary of King Alfonso X the Learned*. New Orleans: University Press of the South, 1997.

Evans, Joan. *Magical Jewels of the Middle Ages and the Renaissance Particularly in England*. Oxford: Clarendon Press, 1922.

Fery-Hue, Françoise. La tradition manuscrite du Lapidaire du roi Philippe. *Scriptorium* (2000) 54: 91–192.

Jones, Peter Murray, and Lea T. Olsan. Middleham Jewel: Ritual, Power, and Devotion. *Viator* (2000) 31: 249–290.

Kitson, Peter. Lapidary Traditions in Anglo-Saxon England: Part I, the Background; the Old English Lapidary. *Anglo-Saxon England* (1978) 7: 9–60.

———. Lapidary Traditions in Anglo-Saxon England: Part II, Bede's Explanatio Apocalypsis and Related Works. *Anglo-Saxon England* (1983) 12: 73–123.

Marbode of Rennes. *De lapidibus*. Edited by John M. Riddle. Wiesbaden: Franz Steiner Verlag, 1977.

Riddle, John M. Geology. In *Medieval Latin: An Introduction and Bibliographical Guide*. Edited by F. A. C. Mantello and A. G. Rigg, 406–410. Washington, D.C.: Catholic University of America Press, 1966.

GEORGE KEISER

"LATIN AVERROISTS"

Latin Averroism is a historiographical category that originated in the foundational work of the nineteenth-century French scholar Ernest Renan. Also sometimes known as radical or secular *Aristotelianism, it refers to the outlook of certain medieval and Renaissance natural philosophers who were inspired by the works of Averroes (*Ibn Rushd), a twelfth-century Islamic legist, physician, and philosopher from al-Andalus who wrote numerous commentaries on Aristotle. In the traditional account that stems from Renan's work, Averroists are defined by their support for monopsychism, a term coined by Gottfried Wilhelm Leibniz, the eighteenth-century German philosopher, that refers to the belief that the human intellect is separate and numerically one, that the world is eternal, and that philosophical truths are independent of theological truths (the so-called doctrine of double truth). These positions were regarded as controversial because of their incompatibility with ecclesiastical positions and were at times censured, as for example in the *condemnation of 1277. Nevertheless, Averroes' commentaries continued to be a prominent source for those interested in Aristotle until the mid-seventeenth century. The broad influence of his commentaries in the Latin West gave rise to his moniker "The Commentator."

Accounts of Latin Averroism have emphasized its prominence at the end of the thirteenth century in Paris, where scholars such as *Siger of Brabant and *Boethius of Dacia discussed Averroes' works and at times adopted or adapted his positions, and in fifteenth-century Bologna and Padua, where prominent professors of philosophy such as Nicoletto Vernia, Gaetano of Thiene, and Agostino Nifo grappled with his works. While these individuals identified themselves with some aspects of the Averroist tradition, they by no means represent its entire scope. The use of Averroes' works as a guide to Aristotle was widespread from the time of their initial translation into Latin in approximately 1230 until 1630. The thorough expositions of his long commentaries and the conciseness of his middle commentaries and epitomes, which rendered a large number of Aristotle's writings more intelligible, recommended his works to scholars. Furthermore, his stated goal of revealing the literal intent and mind of Aristotle was admired and emulated by his proponents. Nevertheless, his writings provoked scorn among others throughout Europe during the same period. *Thomas Aquinas, Ramon Llull, and Petrarch were among the scholars who wrote polemics against Averroes or Averroists.

While Averroes maintained a readership throughout the late Middle Ages and into the Renaissance, the translation of his commentaries came in two waves. The first wave took place in the first half of the thirteenth century and is associated with the work of *Michael Scot, William of Luna, and Hermann the German, who translated some fifteen commentaries on logic, ethics, and natural philosophy from Arabic into Latin. The Arabic versions of many of Averroes' commentaries were no longer available soon after his death. Thus the second wave of Latin translations, which were printed a number of times by the Venetian Giunta press, used earlier Hebrew translations as the source for nineteen new Latin translations.

Perhaps the most notable position of Averroes and Latin Averroists was the contention that the active and passive parts of the rational soul were numerically one. This was based on interpretations of Aristotle's writings about *psychology, in particular of passages in *De anima III*, which maintained that the intellective part of the soul was composed of two parts: one passive, the other active, sometimes referred to as the potential and the agent intellects. The agent intellect creates knowledge in the potential intellect by imprinting forms. Arguing against Avicenna (*Ibn Sina), who claimed that a separate single agent intellect illuminated each individual's potential intellect, Averroes contended that all of humanity shared the same potential intellect, to which it was linked to through sensation. Thus, in Averroes' view, the number of intellects is one and is not identical to the total number of human souls. The negative consequences of this argument for Christian teachings on personal immortality are significant and provoked numerous responses among defenders of ecclesiastical stances. Despite the controversial prominence of this position, it should be noted that the adoption of Averroes' arguments and the use of his commentaries were not limited to this particular issue. His works were used as a guide to large portions of the Aristotelian corpus, much of which stirred little controversy while it served as a foundation for philosophy in the Middle Ages and Renaissance.

See also **Aristotelianism**

Bibliography

Endress, Gerhard and Jan A. Aertsen, eds. *Averroes and the Aristotelian Tradition*. Leiden: E.J. Brill, 1999.

Renan, Ernest. *Averroès et l'averroïsme*. Paris: Maisonneuve & Larose, 2002.

Wolfson, Harry A. The Twice-revealed Averroes. *Speculum* (1961) 36: 373–392.

CRAIG MARTIN

LATITUDE OF FORMS

In medieval natural philosophy and theology, the "latitude of forms" is the dimension of qualities in intensity. In a common example, heat's intensity is called its latitude. The Latin word *latitudo*, which appears many times in the Vulgate translation of the Bible, primarily means "breadth," as when a field is said to have length and breadth or a box is said to have length, breadth, and depth. The word can, however, also mean variability or range of variation. In ancient Greek medicine, health was thought to correspond to a balance or temperament of the bodily humors or fluids, whereas sickness was thought to correspond to an imbalance, meaning that the person or animal was too hot, cold, moist or dry. Deviations from the ideal balance or temperate state were classified into four degrees, with the first degree being moderate or even imperceptible, while the fourth degree would cause death. To be healthy, however, it was not necessary for the humors to be in a state of perfect balance; one could deviate from the ideal within an interval or latitude and still be healthy. Thus health, on this theory, has a latitude or corresponds to a range of conditions. In a related usage, it could be said in medieval economic or ethical theory that the just price for an item has a latitude: traders can agree on higher or lower prices within a certain range without their trade being considered unjust or unfair.

In medieval theology, the latitude of forms typically appeared in commentaries on *Peter Lombard's *Book of Sentences*, Book I, distinction 17, in discussions of the Holy Spirit, grace, charity or love. In this context, grace, charity or love were considered to be habits of the human soul (understood as qualities of a substance, as heat may be a quality of a body). Charity or grace, freely given to humans by God, is what enables a human being to love or to do good works. Some humans have more charity or grace than others, so that there is a latitude of charity.

In scholastic natural philosophy and theology, the theory of the latitude of forms, sometimes known as the theory of the intension and remission or forms, was frequently deployed to address problems of many kinds.

It is difficult to say whether the primary locus for the development of the theory was in theology or in natural philosophy. In any case, elaborations of theories of the latitude of forms in theology had repercussions on natural philosophy and vice versa. Aristotle had classified motions into three basic kinds: motion in place or locomotion, motion in quantity or augmentation and diminution, and motion in quality or alteration. He argued that motions in all three categories are continuous, insofar as what is gained in each motion is continuous. In medieval Aristotelian terms, the latitude of form gained in alteration is analogous to the distance gained in locomotion. But just as one part of a rotating body may traverse space faster or cover more space in a given time than another part, so one part of a body being heated may become hotter more quickly than another part. As the medium closer to a light source is brighter than a part of the medium farther away, so the part of a body closer to a heat source gains a greater latitude of heat than a part farther away. Hotness in a body could thus be said to have a "longitude" in the sense of an extension in the body (actually three extensions in the three dimensions of the body) and at the same time a latitude in intensity, which could vary from one part of the body to another. On the other hand, charity in a human soul has only intensity or latitude, because the soul is not corporeal and so is not extended in place.

In the later Middle Ages, two theories of the relation of degrees to latitudes of qualities were predominant. In one theory, which might be associated more or less closely with *Thomas Aquinas and which was often held by Dominicans, degrees of quality are indivisible and are related to latitudes as points are related to lines. In the other theory, associated with *Duns Scotus and often held by Franciscans, degrees of quality are not indivisible but are related to latitudes as shorter lines are related to longer lines. When degrees are considered indivisible, alteration may be said to occur by a "succession of forms," a theory held by Gottfried of Fontaines and Walter Burley, among others. When degrees are considered as smaller continua, alteration may be said to occur by the addition of part to part, a theory expounded by Duns Scotus and widely held by later numerous natural philosophers.

The French natural philosopher and theologian *Nicole Oresme is famous for having proposed geometrical or graphical representations of latitudes of forms, sometimes called "configurations of qualities," according to which the extension of the form in a body is represented by one line, on which perpendicular lines can be erected representing the intensities of form at each point. Then the area of the figure produced by such a scheme is said to represent the "quantity of quality." When such a scheme is applied to the case of locomotion, the "extension" of the motion can be taken to be the time elapsed, the "intensity" of the motion at any instant is the velocity, and then the "quantity of the local motion," or the area of the figure, is the distance traversed. Basing himself on work done earlier at Oxford, Oresme showed graphically that a uniformly accelerated body will traverse the same distance as a body that moves for an equal interval

of time with the degree of velocity had at the middle instant of the accelerated motion. Theories of the latitude of forms were a part of the curriculum at late medieval and early modern universities, represented, for instance, by writings on the intension and remission of forms by Blasius of Parma and *Jacopo da Forlì. The theory of the latitude of forms was thus part of the intellectual tradition available to early modern scientists if they chose to use it.

See also **Heytesbury, William of; Swineshead, Richard**

Bibliography
Clagett, Marshall. *The Science of Mechanics in the Middle Ages.* Madison: University of Wisconsin Press, 1959.
———. *Nicole Oresme and the Medieval Geometry of Qualities and Motions. A Treatise on the Uniformity and Difformity of Intensities Known as Tractatus de configurationibus qualitatum et motuum.* Madison: University of Wisconsin Press, 1968.
Kaye, Joel. *Economy and Nature in the Fourteenth Century. Money, Market Exchange, and the Emergence of Scientific Thought.* New York: Cambridge University Press, 1998.
Maier, Anneliese. *Zwei Grundprobleme der Scholastischen Naturphilosophie. Das Problem der Intensiven Grösse. Die Impetustheorie.* 3rd. ed. Rome: Edizioni di Storia e Letteratura, 1968.
Murdoch, John, and Edith Sylla. "The Science of Motion." In *Science in the Middle Ages.* Edited by David Lindberg. Chicago: University of Chicago Press, 1978.
Sylla, Edith. Medieval Concepts of the Latitude of Forms: The Oxford Calculators. *Archives d'histoire doctrinale et littéraire du moyen-âge* (1973) 40: 223–283.

EDITH DUDLEY SYLLA

LEATHER PRODUCTION

Leather is a material produced from the skin of any vertebrate, whether mammal, bird, fish or reptile, by a series of processes that renders it non-putrescible under warm, moist conditions. A true leather will retain this property despite repeated wetting and drying. Other skin products, such as rawhide, parchment, and alum-tawed pelts, lose this resistance to microbiological attack when wet.

The use of hides and skins is thought to date from before the evolution of *Homo sapiens*, and the majority of cultures throughout the world have developed more or less complex skin-working techniques. By the pre-dynastic period in Egypt the three major types of tannage had already evolved, as follows:

(a) Treating the skins with fatty materials, such as brains and marrow, often in conjunction with a smoking stage. Fish oils were employed in medieval and later times for producing buff and chamois leathers;

(b) The use of *alum and salt together with various fatty lubricating materials. This technique seems to have been associated particularly with Middle Eastern and Mediterranean cultures;

(c) The vegetable tanning process in which prepared hides and skins are steeped in infusions of specific twigs, leaves, barks, or roots. This appears to have been the most widespread method employed for the production of heavier leathers in Europe in medieval times. Vegetable tanned leathers, however, do not seem to have been manufactured in Northern Europe in the earliest medieval period. Indeed the process seems to have been abandoned in Britain at the end of the Roman period and only reintroduced some centuries later.

The leathermaking crafts were divided into the "heavy" trades of the tanners and curriers and the "light" trades of the fellmongers, whittawyers, glovers, leather dressers, and skinners (fur dressers). The tanners and curriers processed thicker hides using the vegetable tanning process, whereas the light leather processors dealt with sheep, goat, and deer skins as well as those of dogs and other animals. The skinners processed the pelts of a wide range of animals, from cats and rabbits to ermines and squirrels.

The leathermaking processes fall into three groups: the pretanning operations where the skins are cleaned and their structure opened up; the tanning processes where the skin structure is stabilized chemically, and the post-tanning stages which give the desired characteristics to the final product.

In the pretanning operations, the hides were first washed to remove dirt, blood, and dung. They were then treated to loosen the hair, either by leaving them in warm, damp conditions until incipient putrefaction set in or by the action of alkalis such as wood ash or lime. When the hides were judged to be in the correct condition they were spread over a curved beam and the hair was scraped off using a blunt two-handled knife. After further alkali treatment the flesh (the subcutaneous membrane together with fat, muscle and other tissues) was cut off with a sharpened, two-handled knife. It was then cleansed further using enzymes produced either by fermenting barley or from warm suspensions of dog or pigeon dung. It was only after these operations, which could have taken up to three months, that the hides were ready for tanning.

With the vegetable tanning process the hides were first handled into and out of pits containing weak, previously used tanning liquors. The hides were then piled flat in pits with layers of ground vegetable tanning material spread between them. In England extracts of oak bark were employed but the material used depended on what was available locally. When the pit was full, strong, fresh extracts of tanning material were poured onto the hides and they were left for a year or more until the active ingredients had penetrated completely and reacted with the skin structure.

With the alum tawing process the pretanned pelts were thrown into wooden tubs containing a paste made from flour, salt, alum, and water together with lubricating materials such as egg yolk, butter, or olive oil. The paste was worked into the skins by trampling them underfoot. This process was repeated a number of times.

Oil tanning consisted of working marine oils into the pelt in a similar manner and then allowing the oil to oxidize. Cod, herring, seal and porpoise oils were used, and the operation was repeated until the leather was judged to be properly tanned. By the late medieval period fulling stocks similar to those employed in the wool textile industry were widely used to work the oil into the pelts.

Some leathers appear to have been prepared using a combination of alum and oil tannages, and some commentators have suggested that the renowned Cordoban leathers were made using a combination of alum and vegetable tannages.

In the case of heavy vegetable tanned leathers, the post-tanning operations were carried out by a separate group of craftsmen, called curriers. This separation of tanners from curriers appears to have been widespread throughout Europe and was a feature of the quality-control system imposed by the craft guilds. The currier shaved the hides to the required thickness with a specially shaped knife, impregnated them with a mixture of oils and fats, softened them mechanically and, where required, imparted a polished surface finish.

The strict division of tanning and post-tanning operations imposed by the heavy leather guilds was not found among light leather producers. These leathers, whether they were tanned by the oil, alum, vegetable, or combination process, were dyed using a range of natural dyestuffs, dried, softened mechanically and given the desired surface finish. Fur skins were washed, had the subcutaneous membrane cut off and processed in a similar manner to dehaired skins with oil, alum or, occasionally, vegetable tannins. After tanning, the skins were softened and the fur treated to give a rich sheen.

See also **Paints, pigments, and dyes**

Bibliography

Cameron, E. *Sheaths and Scabbards in England A.D. 400–1100*. British Archeological Report 301, Oxford, 2000.

Thomson. R. Tanning—Man's First Manufacturing Process? *Transactions of the Newcomen Society* (1981) 53: 139.

Thomson, R. "Leather Working Processes" in Esther Cameron, ed. *Leather and Fur: Aspects of Early Medieval Trade and Technology*. London: Archetype Publications (for the Archeological Leather Group), 1998.

Veale, E. *The English Fur Trade in the Late Middle Ages*. Oxford: Oxford University Press, 1956.

Waterer, J.W. *Leather in Life, Art and Industry*. London: Faber & Faber, 1946.

ROY THOMSON AND QUITA MOULD

LIUZZI, MONDINO DE'

Born c. 1270 in Bologna into a respected medical family of Florentine origin, Mondino de' Liuzzi is the best known anatomical writer of late medieval Europe. His father was an apothecary, and, after studying medicine at the university of Bologna with *Taddeo Alderotti, Mondino followed in the footsteps of his uncle Liuzzo, entering into what would be a lifelong career teaching in the faculty of arts and medicine in Bologna, where he died in 1326. He is most famous for his *Anothomia* (*Anatomy*), which he probably composed over a number of years, completing it at the earliest in 1316. This textbook aimed to teach the subject through human dissection. After a brief introduction, Mondino discussed the different regions of the body in what came to be the canonical order of dissection: the abdominal organs, the genitals, the organs of the thorax, the organs of the head, and the bones and extremities. In an age that lacked adequate provisions for refrigeration, this order was determined by the need to dissect the parts of the body most prone to corruption first.

Although his *Anothomia* is renowned for its description of human dissection, Mondino did not initiate this practice, which was referred to in passing by his teacher, Alderotti, as early as 1275. Nor should his work been understood as aiming to replace the authority of texts with that of firsthand observation, or at discovering new truths about the inside of the human body and correcting previous errors. Rather, it was intended to help students visualize and assimilate the anatomical information contained in older texts. Mondino relied on a variety of Greek and Arabic medical writers, including most notably *Galen (including the *De juvamentis membrorum*, or *On the Uses of the Members*, attributed erroneously to him) and *Ibn Sina (Avicenna). His use of transliterated Arabic terms, such as *mirach* (peritoneum) and *zirbus* (omentum), testifies to the central place of Arabic medical writing in the teaching of anatomy, as in late medieval learned medicine as a whole. Many of his descriptions, including that of, for example, the purported seven cells of the human uterus, reflect earlier textual tradition, supplemented and shaped by the dissection of animals.

For two hundred years after its composition, Mondino's treatise was enormously influential, especially in Italy, which was the only area of Europe in which dissection became a standard, if infrequent, part of university medical instruction. It survives in at least twenty-five manuscripts and was printed numerous times beginning in 1478, including in Italian and French translation, until it was superseded by Andreas Vesalius' *De humani corporis fabrica* (*On the Fabric of the Human Body*) in 1543. Although Mondino's later fame rested almost entirely on his *Anothomia*, he wrote numerous other medical works on practical and theoretical topics, of which the most widely copied were his *Consilia (medical opinions on individual cases) and his commentaries on works of *Hippocrates, Galen, and Avicenna, which reflect the curriculum at the university of Bologna at the time.

See also **Anatomy; Medicine, practical; Medicine, theoretical; Universities**

Bibliography

Primary sources
Mondino de' Liuzzi. *Anothomia di Mondino de' Liuzzi da Bologna, XIV secolo*. Edited by Piero P. Giorgi and Gian Franco Pasini. Bologna: Istituto per la Storia dell'Università di Bologna, 1992.

———. *Expositio super capitulum de generatione embrionis Canonis Avicennae cum quibusdam quaestionibus*. Edited by Romana Martorelli Vico. Rome: Istituto Storico Italian per il Medio Evo, 1992.

Secondary Sources
Giorgi, Piero P. and Gian Franco Pasini, Introduction and biographical notes. In *Anothomia di Mondino de' Liuzzi da Bologna, XIV secolo*. Edited by Piero P. Giorgi and Gian Franco Pasini. Bologna: Istituto per la Storia dell'Università di Bologna, 1992.
Mondino de' Liuzzi, *Anothomia*, trans. Michael McVaugh. In *A Source Book of Medieval Science*. Edited by Edward Grant. Cambridge: Harvard University Press, 1974. (Partial translation.)
Siraisi, Nancy G. *Taddeo Alderotti and His Pupils*. Princeton: Princeton University Press, 1981.

KATHARINE PARK

LOGIC

Since medieval scientific culture is based mainly on the study of (authoritative) writings on the one hand and on oral disputations on the other, logic is the fundamental science providing the equipment for both coherent interpretation of texts and consistent argumentation in discussions. First, parts of the logical corpus of Aristotle (*Organon*, "Tool"), viz., *On Interpretation* and *Categories*, Porphyry's *Isagoge* ("Introduction," viz., to the *Categories*), pertinent writings by *Boethius, and entries in early *encyclopedias constituted the basis for the study of logic. In and after the twelfth century, the four parts of the *Organon* on arguments (*Prior* and *Posterior Analytics*, *Topics*, *Sophistical Refutations*) together with other sources such as Greek and Arabic commentaries, also became available in Latin. The complete corpus is known as the *logica antiquorum* ("Logic of the Ancients"), and consists of the *logica vetus* ("Old Logic"), i.e. the theory of terms and sentences, and the *logica nova* ("New Logic"), i.e., the theory of arguments. The new wealth of sources soon pushed Latin scholasticism to produce original contributions to Aristotelian logic as supplements (*logica modernorum*, "Logic of the Moderns"), viz., on the properties of terms, consequences (as a comprehensive theory comprising syllogistics and topics), insolubles, and obligations. Besides these important new translations of sources, the rise of the *universities especially had a significant impact on the history of logic. Every student of the higher faculties of law, medicine, and theology (where also disputations were held) had solid training in logic. The predominance of philosophy and logic at the faculty of arts, however, gave also rise to conflicts with theology, as is shown, for example, by the famous Parisian *Condemnation of 1277 and later discussions.

According to the dominant view of the Middle Ages, logic is the science of the valid argument. Since the validity of an argument depends on the truth-values of the sentences of which it is composed, and the truth-values of the sentences depend on the terms of which they are composed, medieval logic has the following structure: doctrine of terms, of sentences, and of consequences or arguments. The scientific status of logic is discussed within an Aristotelian framework, viz., whether it is a skill (*ars*) or a science (**scientia*), and whether it is a practical or theoretical (speculative) science. The answers to these questions (already discussed in antiquity) depend on the respective definitions of those concepts. In this connection, the distinction between *logica utens* ("using logic") and *logica docens* ("teaching logic") was introduced as the distinction between the use *of* arguments (practical) and the reflection *on* arguments (theoretical). Generally, logic was construed as a practical attitude of the understanding whose immediate end is not pure knowledge, but good acting in the course of arguing and of acquiring knowledge. Insofar as logic is the necessary presupposition of all other sciences, it was called "*scientia scientiarum*" or "*ars artium*" or also a "tool" (Greek *organon*, Latin *instrumentum, adminiculum*). It was then further discussed, whether the field of logic is language (*sermo*) or reason (*ratio*: the Greek *logos* may mean both), what is reflected in the designations "*scientia sermocinalis*" vs. "*rationalis*." As a science of reason, logic deals (according to **Ibn Sina*) with concepts of a second level (*intentiones secundae*, such as the predicables) which are often construed as mere beings of thought (*entia rationis* in contrast to *entia realia*). From a modern point of view, the medieval concept of logic is quite large, insofar as it comprises or touches such disciplines as ontology, semantics, epistemology, philosophy of science, in addition to formal logic.

Terms (*Termini*)

Since logic is interested in the truth-values of sentences and arguments, terms (i.e., words and ideas or concepts in the sense of uncombined signs of the public and mental language) are the ultimate elements of analysis. Following Aristotle, a distinction between three levels of language is made and accordingly a distinction between written, spoken and mental terms. Such terms are either categorematic, i.e., meaningful in themselves, or syncategorematic, i.e., functional only without proper meaning. Categorematic terms with their definite meaning (*significatio*) are either on the level of an object language or on that of a metalanguage (*primae* vs. *secundae intentionis/ impositionis*). As terms of an object language they must belong to one of the ten Aristotelian categories. The framework of the object language can be described by means of the five terms of the metalanguage of Porphyry's *Isagoge* (and Aristotle's *Topics*) thus: every category divides into individuals, species and genera, and a species embraces a genus and a specific difference. These internal relations of the categories are necessary and essential and they are the basis for Aristotelian definitions by genus and difference. Relations between categories, however, are contingent. Medieval realism holds that Aristotelian species and genera have existence independently of thought and language and accordingly it holds also that *objects* (and not only words or concepts) are predicated;

finally, it sees the categories as a classification of reality. These very points are rejected by the opposite party of nominalism or conceptualism.

Syncategorematic terms build sentences out of categorematic terms (as the *copula*, the verb "is" connects subject and predicate), quantify those sentences (*signa distributiva*, such as "every" or "some"), or negate them, or build more complex sentences out of them ("and," "or," "if").

Properties of Terms (*Proprietates Terminorum*)

As soon as categorematic terms enter a sentence, they acquire "properties" or functions conditioned by the context. Disregarding any of these functions may cause fallacies, and the theory was first developed also in this connection. The variable list of such properties comprises mainly *suppositio, copulatio, appellatio, ampliatio,* and *restrictio*. At first, supposition was regarded as the property of subjects (logically) or substantives (grammatically), and copulation as the property of predicates or adjectives and verbs, but that distinction was soon neglected, so that supposition then was construed as the property of subjects as well as predicates, both of which counted as nouns in a large sense. Thus, supposition became the most important property of terms: it served as a classification of that *for which* a term in the context of a sentence stands, and *in which manner* it does so. The first function generated three main species of supposition. A general term in the context of a sentence may stand for: (1) The individuals to which it applies; (2) The universal; (3) Itself or a similar term. Case (1) is known as "personal supposition," e.g., "A man walks"; case (2) "simple supposition," e.g., "Man is a species"; case (3) "material supposition," e.g., "Man is a noun." First, these examples show that in all three of these cases it is the same (type of) term "man" which supposits in the different ways respectively, and that the cases are *not* distinguished by *different* terms. Second, they show that ontology (the debate over universals) plays a role here: nominalists interpreted the signification of a general term as the extensional reference to the individuals to which it applies, realists saw it as the intensional meaning of the corresponding universal (*res universalis, forma* or *natura communis*). Accordingly, personal supposition for the nominalists is significative (i.e., corresponding to the original signification) and primary, whereas simple supposition as reference to the universal in the sense of a mental concept is nonsignificative ("man" is not true of the concept of man) and secondary. For the realists, on the contrary, since the intension of a term fixes its extension, simple supposition has semantic primacy. The debate between **William of Ockham* and Walter Burley in the fourteenth century is a good example of differences in semantics and ontology.

According to the respective quantity and quality of the sentence, a term in personal supposition refers to its extension differently. The subdivision of personal supposition is carried out with the concepts of *descent under* and of *ascent to* a general term. Singular terms supposit discretely, general terms supposit commonly, and that in different ways: In the sentence "Some man walks," e.g., the descent under the subject term "man" leads to a disjunction of singular sentences, "This man walks," or "that man walks," etc., and from each part of the disjunction one can assent to the original general sentence. This mode of common personal supposition is called "determinate."

In the early period of "modern" logic, the property of appellation meant the reference of a general term to *existent* individuals. Later on it was used with regard to intensional, temporal and modal contexts. For example, in the sentence "A white thing was black," the predicate "black" has appellation in the sense that it must have been predicable truly at some past time of the thing referred to by the subject. But the subject term "a white thing" has the property of ampliation in the sense that being black was true of something which is *or was* white.

Sentences (*Propositiones*)

Sentences are expressions (*orationes*) of a special kind, in which a predicate is said (affirmatively or negatively) of a subject, making such expressions true or false. The structure of simple sentences is generally conceived as tripartite (subject + *copula* + predicate); because of the Aristotelian primacy of the "first" (i.e., individual) substances as the ultimate subjects of predication, the canonical form of an atomic sentence is thus: singular term + *copula* + general term. The categorematic constituents of a sentence are called its "matter," the syncategorematic ones are the "form of the sentence." The matter of sentences is "natural" when the predicate belongs necessarily to the subject, and "contingent" when the predicate may belong to the subject; it is "remote" when it is impossible for the predicate to belong to the subject. Sentences having the structure subject—*copula*—predicate are called "categorical," compounds of several sentences are called "hypothetical." Categorical sentences differ according to quantity (singular vs. general, i.e., indefinite, particular, universal) and quality (affirmative vs. negative). If the *copula* is not modally determined, the sentence is assertoric (*de simplici inesse/inhaerentia*), if it is modally determined, the sentence is a modal one (*de inhaerentia modificata*), e.g., "Socrates is necessarily an animal." This example is a case of a modal sentence in the "divided" sense and corresponds to the modern notion of a *de re* modality. There is also a "composite" sense, if the modal operator does not refer to the *copula*, but to the complete that-clause ("*de dicto*"), e.g., "It is necessary that Socrates is an animal." The truth-conditions (*causae veritatis*) for all these sorts of sentences are stated in the pertinent treatises. A philosophical matter of dispute, especially in the fourteenth century, is the signification of sentences, viz., whether they signify things in the Aristotelian categories or states of affairs in addition to such things.

Consequences (*Consequentiae*)

Consequences are hypothetical sentences consisting of (at least) two categorical sentences as antecedent and consequent, together with a sign of consequence (*nota consequentiae*), viz., an "if" in front of the antecedent, or a "therefore" in front of the consequent. The definition of a valid consequence as truth-preserving (if the antecedent is true, the consequent cannot be false) is problematic for the scholastics, because it is related to sentences which are ephemeral lingual or mental beings. For that reason it is sometimes defined in terms of the *signification* of the antecedent and consequent.

Consequences are either formal or material: formal consequences hold in virtue of their form alone (i.e., in virtue of their syncategorematic constituents in a certain arrangement), whereas in material consequences the validity also depends on the matter (the categorematic terms). Material consequences are further divided into simply valid ones (*simpliciter*), and conditionally valid ones, viz., only valid right now (*ut nunc*): "A man walks, therefore an animal walks" is simply valid, because the relation of species to genus is necessary. On the other hand, "Buridan walks, therefore a professor walks" is only valid for the time when Buridan is actually a professor (in other words, the relation of substance to accident is contingent).

The most important kind of formal consequences is the syllogism, as it is laid down by Aristotle in the *Prior Analytics*. The antecedent there consists of (the conjunction of) two sentences, the major and minor premises, and three terms, major, middle, and minor term. The consequent is the conclusion drawn from these premises, in which the middle term no longer occurs. The arrangement of the three terms in the two premises yields four syllogistic figures (of which the fourth is a matter of dispute). Together with the quantity and quality of the sentences, there are then different modes (of which nineteen are generally held to be valid) for which the scholastics coined the names "Barbara," "Celarent," etc., which can be easily remembered. Only syllogisms of the first figure are complete, in the sense of evident, whereas the other figures require proofs that consist in making reductions to the first figure with the help of other inferences, such as conversion. There are several kinds of syllogisms, according to the different kinds of terms (finite vs. infinite, nominative vs. oblique case) and sentences (categorical vs. hypothetical, assertoric vs. modal). Lists of rules were carefully stated for all of these. Important medieval contributions to syllogistics concern expository syllogisms (which have a singular premise) and modal syllogisms.

Insolubles (*Insolubilia*)

Insolubles were defined as sentences whose solution is difficult, in the sense that it is hard to determine their truth-values. This was especially true of semantic paradoxes of self-reference. The Liar Paradox has been the classical example since antiquity. Self-referential paradoxes were dealt with in many variants, e.g., "This sentence is false"; the problem is whether this sentence is true or false. Among the most prominent medieval solutions of this paradox (besides the Aristotelian theory of fallacies) were the following: the theory of *cassatio*, which held that such a sentence is meaningless, because nothing is asserted in it, and therefore is neither true nor false. The theory of *restrictio* simply forbade self-reference altogether, but usually no satisfying criterion for distinguishing between acceptable and vicious self-reference was given. A variant of this is the theory of *transcasus*, which is based on the intuition that sentences can change their truth-value over the course of time; in principle, it is denied again that the semantic predicate "false" may apply to the very sentence whose part it is. Finally, there is the theory of a twofold signification of sentences: direct signification is due to the predicate, indirect signification is due to the *copula* by which the sentence is asserted to be true. Therefore, the insoluble in question is false, because it signifies itself to be both true and false. A comprehensive list of fifteen solutions is given by Paul of Venice (d. 1429) in his *Logica magna*. Many other insolubles and sophisms are discussed by the scholastics with great subtlety, e.g., regarding the concepts of beginning and ceasing, exception and exclusion, part and whole, etc.

Obligations (*Obligationes, Ars Obligatoria*)

Closely related to consequences and insolubles, both in theory and in teaching, is the theory of obligations. This is the most peculiar medieval contribution to the history of logic. Its purpose was presumably the training of students in consistent argumentation. The name "obligation" is derived from the fact that of two disputants, the "*respondens*" is obliged to react according to certain rules to a sentence (*positum*) put forward by the "*opponens*." Within the scope of these rules, the opponent tries to drive the respondent into making contradictions, and the latter tries to resist these attempts. In the case of the species of obligation called "position," a contingently false sentence is usually put forward, e.g., "You are in Rome" when the disputation is held at Paris. The respondent admits the *positum* which then becomes the "*obligatum*." The opponent then puts forth further sentences, to which the respondent can reply in three different ways: "I concede this," "I deny this," "I doubt this." These possibilities of replying depend on the logical relation which the new *propositum* bears to the original *positum*, viz., whether it follows from it (*pertinens sequens*), contradicts it (*pertinens repugnans*), or is logically independent of it (*impertinens*). If the logical relation of a new *propositum* is only to the first *positum*, the obligational game follows the lines of the so-called "New Response," if it is to the previous entire game, it follows the "Old Response." The main rules according to which the respondent has to reply to new *proposita* are the following: everything that follows has to be conceded; everything that contradicts has to be denied; everything that is logically independent has to be conceded, if it is known to be true, or denied, if it is known to be false, or doubted, if it is neither, i.e., uncertain. Insolubles and sophisms then serve to show that all possibilities of the respondent lead to offenses against the rules, once a vicious positum has been admitted. The solutions which are given in the relevant treatises point out the deficiencies of such an obligational dispute.

See also **Abelard, Peter; Albert of Saxony; Aristotelianism; Boethius; Bradwardine, Thomas; Buridan, John; Heytesbury, William of; Kilwardby, Robert; Marsilius of Inghen; Metaphysics; Nature: diverse medieval interpretations; Petrus Hispanus; Pierre d'Ailly; Translation movements**

Bibliography

Primary Sources
Buridan, John. *Summulae de dialectica*. Translated by Gyula Klima. New Haven: Yale University Press, 2001.
Burley, Walter. *On the Purity of the Art of Logic. The Shorter and the Longer Treatises*. Translated by Paul Vincent Spade. New Haven: Yale University Press, 2000.
Kretzmann, Norman and Eleonore Stump, ed. *The Cambridge Translations of Medieval Philosophical Texts*. Vol. 1. *Logic and the Philosophy of Language*. New York: Cambridge University Press, 1988.
Marsilius of Inghen. *Treatises on the Properties of Terms*. Edited and translated by Egbert P. Bos. Dordrecht: Reidel, 1983.
Paulus Venetus (Paul of Venice). *Logica magna*. Oxford: Oxford University Press, 1978–1991.
(Petrus Hispanus. *Tractatus* called afterwards *Summule logicales*.) Peter of Spain. *Language in Dispute*. Translated by Francis P. Dinneen. Amsterdam: Benjamins, 1990.
(William of Ockham.) *Ockham's Theory of Terms*. Part I of the *Summa logicae*. Translated by Michael J. Loux. Notre Dame: University of Notre Dame Press, 1974.
(———.) *Ockham's Theory of Propositions*. Part II of the *Summa logicae*. Translated by Alfred J. Freddoso and Henry Schuurman. Notre Dame: University of Notre Dame Press, 1980.
William of Sherwood. *Introduction to Logic*. Translated by Norman Kretzmann. Minneapolis: Minnesota University Press, 1966.

Secondary Sources
Ashworth, E. J. *Language and Logic in the Post-Medieval Period*. Dordrecht: Reidel, 1974.
Biard, Joël. *Logique et théorie du signe au XIVe siècle*. Paris: Vrin, 1989.
Broadie, Alexander. *Introduction to Medieval Logic*. 2nd Edition. Oxford: Clarendon Press, 1993.
Grass, Rainer. *Schlußfolgerungslehre in Erfurter Schulen des 14. Jahrhunderts. Eine Untersuchung der Konsequentientraktate von Thomas Maulfelt und Albert von Sachsen in Gegenüberstellung mit einer zeitgenössischen Position*. Philadelphia: Grüner, 2003.
Green-Pedersen, Niels J. *The Tradition of the Topics in the Middle Ages*. Munich: Philosophia, 1984.
Jacobi, Klaus, ed. *Argumentationstheorie. Scholastische Forschungen zu den logischen und semantischen Regeln korrekten Folgerns*. Leiden: E.J. Brill, 1993.
Kann, Christoph. *Die Eigenschaften der Termini. Eine Untersuchung zur Perutilis logica Alberts von Sachsen*. Leiden: E.J. Brill, 1994. (Includes a Latin edition of Treatise II of Albert of Saxony's *Logica*.)
Keffer, Hajo. *De obligationibus. Rekonstruktion einer spätmittelalterlichen Disputationstheorie*. Leiden: E.J. Brill, 2001.
Kretzmann, Norman, Anthony Kenny and Jan Pinborg, ed. *The Cambridge History of Later Medieval Philosophy*. New York: Cambridge University Press, 1982.
Lagerlund, Henrik. *Modal Syllogistics in the Middle Ages*. Leiden: E.J. Brill, 2000.

Nuchelmans, Gabriel. *Theories of the Proposition. Ancient and Medieval Conceptions of the Bearers of Truth and Falsity.* Amsterdam: North-Holland, 1973.

Pironet, Fabienne. *The Tradition of Medieval Logic and Speculative Grammar. A Bibliography (1977–1994).* Turnhout: Brepols, 1997. (A continuation of E. J. Ashworth's bibliography, Toronto: Pontifical Institute of Mediaeval Studies, 1978.)

Read, Stephen, ed. *Sophisms in Medieval Logic and Grammar. Acts of the Ninth European Symposium for Medieval Logic and Semantics, held at St Andrews, June 1990.* Dordrecht: Kluwer, 1993.

Rijk, L. M. de. *Logica Modernorum. A Contribution to the History of Early Terminist Logic.* Two volumes in three parts. Assen: Van Gorcum, 1962 and 1967.

Shank, Michael H. *"Unless You Believe, You Shall Not Understand." Logic, University, and Society in Late Medieval Vienna.* Princeton: Princeton University Press, 1988.

Thom, Paul. *The Syllogism.* Munich: Philosophia, 1981.

———. *Medieval Modal Systems. Problems and Concepts.* Aldershot: Ashgate, 2003.

Yrjönsuuri, Mikko. *Obligationes. 14th Century Logic of Disputational Duties.* Helsinki: Societas Philosophica Fennica, 1994.

———, ed. *Medieval Formal Logic. Obligations, Insolubles and Consequences.* Dordrecht: Kluwer, 2001.

Paul V. Spade. Medieval Logic and Philosophy. May 23, 2004. URL = <http://www.pvspade.com/Logic/>

Gyula Klima. Society for Medieval Logic and Metaphysics. February 19, 2005. URL = <http://www.fordham.edu/gsas/phil/klima/SMLM/>

Edward N. Zalta, ed. The Stanford Encyclopedia of Philosophy. (Spring 2005 Edition). URL = < http://plato.stanford.edu/>

HARALD BERGER

LOMBARD, PETER

Born in the environs of Novara toward the end of the eleventh century, Peter Lombard's early life is virtually unknown until his migration north of the Alps to study at the cathedral school of Rheims, about 1134. By 1136, he had moved on to Paris, where he probably was an external student at the school of St. Victor, under the celebrated master, *Hugh. By 1144/1145, he had become a canon of Notre Dame, itself an accomplishment for a foreigner among the closed French, privileged chapter of the cathedral; Peter's advancement there speaks to his academic accomplishments during the previous decade. As he advanced in the ecclesiastical ranks, he continued to teach in the cathedral school, his lectures the genesis of works in theology and hermeneutics. In 1159, he became bishop of Paris but died scarcely a year later, on July 21 or 22, 1160.

Peter's works include slightly more than thirty sermons that have survived, a commentary on the Psalms completed before 1138 and commentaries on the Pauline epistles (known collectively as the *Collectanea*) composed between 1139 and 1141 and revised between 1155 and 1158. Recent scholarship suggests that Peter glossed virtually the entire Bible, a work that he probably bequeathed to the chapter, but which now appears to have been lost. But without question, the most significant of his works was the *Sententiae in IV libri distinctae*, the result of his course in systematic theology taught at Paris for two decades and published in its final form between 1155 and 1157.

The Lombard's *Sentences* are emblematic of a movement beginning in the late eleventh century to develop a systematic theology as a science in its own right. Prior to 1150—and even after the composition of the *Sentences*—there were many attempts to collect and organize the central tenets of Western Christian doctrine but, as Marcia Colish has shown, they were inferior to Peter's version in organization, comprehensiveness, coherence, use of source materials, and pedagogical utility. After a brief prologue, in which he professes to limit personal speculation while remaining close to the positions of the Fathers [*Sicubi vero parum vox nostra insonuit, non a paternis dicessit limitibus*], Peter divides his work into four books, each progressing farther into the historical and doctrinal positions of Christianity. Book I focuses on the existence, trinity, and attributes of God; Book II covers the creation, man, sin, liberty, and grace; Book III is devoted to Christology, redemption, virtues, and commandments; Book IV concludes with the sacraments and eschatology.

While the *Sentences* did not receive immediate and unanimous acceptance—in his own century, the Lombard's positions on Christology and the Trinity were attacked, and in the thirteenth century readers such as *Robert Grosseteste and *Roger Bacon worried that the work threatened to displace the Scriptures in the theological curriculum—several early developments helped ensure its eventual canonical position within theological faculties and religious schools across Europe. First, Peter himself seems to have formatted the text for pedagogical use, employing rubrics to indicate patristic citations and parts of the text. Beginning in the twelfth century, the text was glossed according to the medieval technique of *accessus ad auctores*, indicating that Peter was already esteemed as a significant authority. By about 1222, the Franciscan Alexander of Hales (c. 1180/1190–1245) had begun using it as the text for his theological course at Paris; its subsequent adoption throughout the university and the preeminence of Paris gave the *Sentences* enormous prestige elsewhere. And finally, Alexander modified the text by devising distinctiones to facilitate precise citations of passages from the *Sentences*, emulating a technique already adopted by users of Gratian's *Decretum* and later adapted to Aristotle's works. As a result, the *Sentences* acquired the intellectual cachet invested in these other works, and together they became the significant pedagogical tools of the legal, theological, and arts faculties of nascent universities.

Aside from its role in the theological curriculum, the *Sentences* also offered opportunities to develop extra-theological, including scientific, issues. Part of the reason for this derives from the educational course followed by students in the late Middle Ages. Whether in arts faculties or schools of religious orders, students lectured on the

Sentences following a previous exposure to the philosophical curriculum, chiefly the works of Aristotle. Moreover, the text of the *Sentences* itself displays Peter's tendency, like that of many of his contemporaries, to formulate positions using Aristotelian terminology and concepts. Consequently, the Lombard's discussion of particular topics in the *Sentences* became a traditional locus for elaboration and expansion of scientific positions.

One such occurs at the very beginning of the work itself. The opening line of Book I, chapter 1, "*Omnis doctrina est de rebus vel de signis*," although quoting Augustine's *De doctrina christiana*, echoed the incipit to the *Posterior Analytics* ["*Omnis doctrina et omnis disciplina intellectiva fit ex praeexistenti cognitione...*"]; readers of both texts drew inspiration from speculative grammar investigations of the relationship between signs and reality. Moreover, twelfth-century prologues to commentaries addressed questions about the author's intentions, the *materia* of the work, the branch of knowledge to which it belonged, and its *modus tractandi*, among other things. This gradually evolved into an "Aristotelian" prologue focused on the four causes: the subject matter, the formal mode of treatment, the authorship, and the final cause or purpose of the work. Throughout the thirteenth century, and extending into the early fourteenth century, commentators on the *Sentences* devoted considerable space in their prologues to questions regarding the very nature of theology as a potentially scientific discipline along the lines of Aristotle's emerging views and, by extension, to discussions of the nature of science, the relationships between human and divine science, and theoretical foundations of scientific disciplines.

A second instance occurs near the end of Book I, where Peter Lombard takes up the question of whether God can do better or different than He does. This was one of the most contentious issues of the twelfth century, and already before Peter addressed it, *Peter Abelard had responded negatively, collapsing God's power and will and arguing that what God wills, He must do necessarily. Although he was not the only one to do so, Peter Lombard vigorously opposed this position, and while he never actually used the terms *potentia ordinata* and *potentia absoluta*, much of his discussion hinges on this distinction that bore considerable fruit later when applied to the inviolability of Aristotle's discussions of nature. As a result, Book I, d. 44 became a frequent site for such questions as "Whether God could make a better world than this world?"

Finally, in taking up sacramental theology in Book IV, Peter examines the status of accidental properties of bread and wine that remain after the sacramental change in the Eucharist. One position that he raises but dismisses is the incomplete change of the elements, so that the accidental properties might inhere in what remains of the bread and wine. The alternative, with which he is clearly not satisfied, is that the substance of bread and wine is totally annihilated and the "accidents remain, subsisting by themselves" [IV, d. 12. c. 1]. Not only did this invite continued discussion of hylomorphic aspects of

Fifteenth-century drawing of Peter Lombard. (Corbis)

Eucharistic doctrine, but by the early fourteenth century, issues of motion and the nature of impetus as a causal mechanism came to be applied to sacramental discussions as well.

See also **Aristotelianism; Hylomorphism; Scholasticism;** *Scientia*; **Vocabulary**

Bibliography

Brown, Stephen F. "The Reception and Use of Aristotle's Works in the Commentaries on Book I of the Sentences by the Friar Preachers in the Early Years of Oxford University." In *Aristotle in Britain during the Middle Ages: Proceedings of the International Conference at Cambridge, 8-11 April 1994 organised by the Société Internationale pour l'Etude de la Philosophie Médiévale*. Edited by John Marenbon. Turnhout: Brepols, 1996, pp. 351–369.

Colish, Marcia L. *Peter Lombard*. 2 volumes. Leiden: E.J. Brill, 1994.

Lombard, Peter. *Sententiae in IV libris distinctae*. 3rd edn. Edited by I. Brady. Grottaferrata: Collegio S. Bonaventura, 1971–1981.

Medieval Commentaries on the Sentences of Peter Lombard. Current Research. Volume 1. Edited by G. R. Evans. Leiden: E.J. Brill, 2002.

Murdoch, John E. "From Social into Intellectual Factors: An Aspect of the Unitary Character of Late Medieval Learning." In *The Cultural Context of Medieval Learning*. Edited by John E. Murdoch and Edith D. Sylla. Dordrecht, Holland; Boston: D. Reidel, 1975, pp. 271–348.

Stegmüller, Friedrich. *Repertorium commentariorum in Sententias Petri Lombardi*. 2 volumes. Würzburg: Schoningh, 1947; V. Doucet. Supplément. Florence: Coll. S. Bonaventurae, 1954.

Sylla, Edith D. "Autonomous and Handmaiden science: St. Thomas Aquinas and William of Ockham on the Physics of the Eucharist." In *The Cultural Context of Medieval Learning*. Edited by John E. Murdoch and Edith D. Sylla. Dordrecht, Holland; Boston: D. Reidel Pub. Co., 1975, pp. 349–391.

STEVEN J. LIVESEY

M

MACROBIUS

Ambrosius Theodosius Macrobius was a high-ranking official of the later Roman Empire, quite possibly a pagan, whose three surviving works are the *Saturnalia*, which describes a symposium set in 384 C.E.; a treatise comparing Greek and Latin verbs, and the *Commentary* composed in the early fifth century on Cicero's *Dream of Scipio*. This last work was an important source of Neoplatonic cosmology and philosophy in the Middle Ages. It expounds the last chapter of Cicero's *Republic*, in which Scipio the Younger is taken in a dream by his adoptive grandfather up to the stars to look back on the Earth and to contemplate the heavenly destiny of those who serve the state. Macrobius ranged widely over scientific topics in his *Commentary*: the nature of number and its presence in the cosmos and human life, astronomy, geography, and the harmony of the spheres. He wrote at a fairly basic level, not always accurately, and provided some illustrative diagrams of the spheres, rainfall, and celestial and terrestrial zones. Despite not fitting neatly into the categories of the *quadrivium, his work became a useful medieval school text, surviving in more than two hundred manuscripts, of which nearly half were copied in the twelfth century.

Interest in the *Commentary* was shown in the Carolingian Renaissance of the ninth and tenth centuries, during which it provided astronomical background to the study of the *computus, and arithmetical theory for the study of the abacus and music. *John Scottus Eriugena and Abbo of Fleury incorporated Macrobius's cosmology into their philosophical works, and *Gerbert of Aurillac drew on his discussion of geometrical solids. By the twelfth century, the *Commentary* had become a standard liberal arts text, and continuous commentaries were composed. One of these is by *William of Conches, who also used Macrobius as a source for his work. *Adelard of Bath used cosmological material from the *Commentary*, and Macrobius's work influenced the poetry of *Bernard Silvestre and Alain de Lille. But access to superior Arabic science made Macrobius's astronomy and treatment of number seem out of date. Thirteenth-

century encyclopedists such as *Bartholomaeus Anglicus and *Vincent of Beauvais cited Macrobius as an authority but the *Commentary* was no longer at the forefront of scientific debate.

There were four main areas of medieval scientific interest in Macrobius's *Commentary*: number, astronomy, music, and geography. Macrobius examines the qualities and significance of the numbers two to eight, focusing particularly on seven and its presence in the planets, the lunar month, the pre- and post-natal life of humans, and their bodily structure. Medieval computists corrected Macrobius's rough calculations, and when sources such as *Constantine the African became known, they could illuminate Macrobius's remarks on the *elements and human physiology. The mathematics and geometry of the *Commentary* were basic, and *Boethius and later *Euclid were more important authorities. However, Macrobius's exposition of the numerical proportions in the structure of the World Soul (the animating principle of the universe in Neoplatonic thought) prompted William of Conches to explore its geometrical aspects in some depth in his own commentary on the text.

Macrobius's *Commentary* is full of astronomical descriptions, and it was a basic source for medieval treatment of the celestial circles, the Milky Way, the ecliptic, the zodiac (divided into twelve by the Egyptians, according to Macrobius, using a *clepsydra), the order of the planets, and the measurement of the Sun. All of these were the focus of interest and controversy to his medieval readers. For example, Macrobius notes the disagreement between the Platonists, who argue that the Sun is directly above the Moon, and the "Chaldeans," who place it above the Moon, Mercury, and Venus. He says that this dispute arose because Mercury and Venus appear sometimes above and sometimes below the Sun. He was probably alluding to some sort of epicyclic theory, and his medieval readers speculated, using diagrams, as to what he meant. The standard solution became three intersecting circles of orbit. The measurement of the Sun offered a set exercise in calculation, to make Macrobius's rough estimates more precise. They involved calculating with

Arab astronomers measure the angles between objects in space and on land. Woodcut from 1513 Venice edition of Macrobius' Commentary on Cicero's *Dream of Scipio*. (Mary Evans Picture Library)

fractions (probably using an abacus) the Earth's diameter and its shadow, the Sun's orbit, and its circumference.

Macrobius described how Scipio the Younger heard the harmony of the spheres in his dream, and this provided the opportunity for some basic Pythagorean *music theory in the *Commentary*. He defines the musical intervals and their mathematical relationships, of which the most complex was the semitone. Because the ratio of the full tone, 9:8, has no rational square root, it cannot be equally divided. The semitone, Macrobius states, has the ratio 256:243. Medieval commentators were able to demonstrate how this ratio is derived, again using fractions. The harmony of the spheres raised for them a question of acoustics: what were the moving and colliding objects which produced sound? The Earth and the celestial sphere were considered to be stationary, and William of Conches, at least, thought that the planetary spheres did not touch each other. He also considered the question of the pitch of the sounds made by the spheres, making in effect the necessary distinction between absolute and angular speed.

Toward the end of his dream Scipio the Younger is shown how small is the inhabited area of the Earth, and Macrobius offers some geographical comment. He describes the two temperate zones, divided by an impassible hot belt and capped by icy polar regions. He argues that the temperate zone in the southern hemisphere must logically be inhabited. But there were theological reasons for disputing the existence of the antipodes, for, as St. Augustine pointed out, if they were cut off by the hot belt, their inhabitants could not be descended from Adam, nor could they be saved. In the late eleventh century, Manegold of Lautenbach condemned Macrobius's theory as heretical.

Macrobius's *Commentary* transmitted classical scientific lore in a reasonably simple if not very systematic way. It could be a stimulus to scientific thought, through its controversies and occasional vagueness. The setting of its exploration of cosmology within one of the great literary masterpieces of the ancient world gave it depth and attractiveness for the medieval world.

See also **Astronomy; Cosmology; Geography, chorography; Magic and the occult**

Bibliography

Hüttig, A. *Macrobius im Mittelalter: Ein Beitrag zur Rezeptionsgeschichte der Commentarii in Somnium Scipionis.* Frankfurt-am-Main: P. Lang, 1990.

McCluskey, Stephen C. *Astronomies and Cultures in Early Medieval Europe.* New York: Cambridge University Press, 1998.

Peden, Alison. "Music in Medieval Commentaries on Macrobius." In *Musik und die Geschichte der Philosphie und Naturwissenschaften im Mittelalter.* Edited by F. Hentschel. Leiden: E.J. Brill, 1998.

———. The Medieval Antipodes. *History Today* (1995) 45: 27–33.

Stahl, William H, ed. *Macrobius. Commentary on the Dream of Scipio. Translated with an Introduction and notes.* New York: Columbia University Press, 1952.

Willis, James, ed. *Ambrosii Theodosii Macrobii Commentarii in Somnium Scipionis.* Leipzig: Teubner, 1970.

ALISON PEDEN

MAGIC AND THE OCCULT

While in the modern world belief in magic is often held to be opposed to and incompatible with scientific rationalism, in medieval Europe conceptions of magic developed and were held in harmony with contemporary scientific, that is, theological and natural philosophical, thought. By the later Middle Ages, some aspects of magic became fields of academic or quasi-academic study. Certainly educated elites regarded many common magical practices as foolish and irrational. They did not maintain, however, that such practices were necessarily ineffective, only that uneducated people performed them without proper understanding of the means by which they operated. Authorities themselves were convinced that they could understand the workings of magical operations in essentially logical and coherent ways. Most typically Christian authorities explained supposed magical effects by means of demonic forces. In fact perhaps the most basic aspect of authoritative medieval conceptions of magic was that magical rites invoked demons, as opposed to prayer and legitimate church ceremonies that drew on divine power for their effect. Yet some authorities, particularly in the later Middle Ages, also allowed for a variety of magic that relied on natural but occult forces inherent in the physical world.

Forms and Functions of Medieval Magic

Magic as a general category would only have been discussed by educated elites in the Middle Ages, employing the Latin terms *magia* or *ars magica*. Common people would have spoken, in various vernaculars, of specific practices—spells, charms, incantations, the carrying of tokens or amulets, the observation of signs or omens. Or they would have referred to the desired ends these acts were believed to achieve—divination, healing, or protection, among many others. There is little way to determine to what extent, if any, ordinary people conceived of such varied practices as related to or representative of a single category of action that might broadly be described as magic. Nevertheless, such actions were often grouped together by authorities. Early Christian authors, seeking not just to supplant the cults of the classical world but to subsume them into an entirely Christian universe, argued that the myriad rites of pagan antiquity were essentially related in that they all secretly called on and expressed reverence for Christian demons. This reliance on demonic power became essential to medieval conceptions of magic.

Demonic connections aside, early-medieval authorities inherited most of their conceptions of magic, along with most of their systems of knowledge, from the ancient world. In his *Etymologies*, *Isidore of Seville (c. 560–636) provided an encyclopedic summary of various kinds of magic, based on ancient categories. Geomancers, aeromancers, hydromancers, and pyromancers were those who, supposedly following systems first developed by the ancient Persians, divined the future by the four elements. Augurs foretold the future based on the flights of birds, a highly developed practice in the Roman world. *Mathematici* made predictions based on the positions of the stars. Divination in general figured heavily in Isidore's discussion of magic, as it had among many of the early church fathers, including the great Augustine of Hippo (354–430), who wrote a work specifically *On the Divination of Demons*. Isidore joined Augustine in condemning all magic as relying on demonic power.

Beyond the categories of learned authorities, a wide variety of magical practices existed in medieval Europe, employed by all levels of society. Such practices served an equally wide variety of purposes. They often entailed divination in some form, but perhaps their most common functions were protective and medicinal—to heal injury or disease, or to ward off illness, accident, or misfortune. People spoke ritualized spells or incantations, often incorporating elements of official prayers or blessings. They also carried certain items or objects as protective amulets, or they could inscribe a spell or blessing on some object to fashion a curative or protective talisman. Herbs and other plants might be administered to the sick, but here too more magical elements were often incorporated. A particular root might be gathered at a certain time of night or under a certain astrological sign, or it might be prepared as a medicine while reciting some spell or blessing. Harmful effects were also possible. Spells were widely believed to be able to cause illness and injury, to impede fertility and sexual activity, or to prevent crops from growing, and the use of poisons was typically regarded as an aspect of harmful magic.

The Rise of Learned Magic

In the early Middle Ages, authorities tended to link magic primarily to paganism and the supposed survival of pagan practices in predominantly Christian Europe. Although they might inveigh strongly against such practices, they typically did not treat them with great intellectual seriousness. Rather they associated these practices with simple, uneducated folk who had been led into error by demonic deceptions. They still held that magic was real, in that magical rites induced demons to act, but they regarded most supposedly magical effects as illusions caused by demons. Educated people, they maintained, would be able to see through such deceits. As one early-tenth-century document declared about certain common magical beliefs: "Truly, who is so stupid and obtuse as to believe that all these things that happen only in spirit actually occur in the flesh." Magic was largely a matter of common credulity and demonic trickery, and did not need to be investigated more deeply. By the twelfth century, however, this view was changing.

During the intellectual revival broadly labeled the "Renaissance of the Twelfth Century," intellectual and scholarly activity increased across Europe. *Cathedral schools formed in major urban centers, and by the end of the twelfth century the first *universities emerged. The rise of schools led to a rediscovery of ancient sources long neglected in Europe, and soon drew an influx of other ancient sources either unknown or lost to the West from the Byzantine East and from the Muslim world, which had preserved and expanded the classical intellectual tradition far more effectively than had medieval Europe. Among these texts were some that treated aspects of magic with great seriousness and intellectual precision, and brought to this subject the intellectual weight of antiquity. Magic never became a fully accepted subject of study at medieval schools and universities, but some scholars began to dabble in areas of magic, and a few such as *Michael Scot (c. 1175–1235) and *Albertus Magnus (c. 1190–1280) developed (usually false) reputations as great magicians. Another major scholar associated with magic was *Gerbert of Aurillac (c. 940–1003). He was one of the earliest scholars to pursue learning in Spain, a major location of Muslim-Christian intellectual interaction. He then returned to northern Europe and eventually became Pope Sylvester II. By the late eleventh century his rise to power was being explained as the result of magical skills he had learned in his youth. Clearly magic was no longer being conceived as the province primarily of the lowly and uneducated.

The principal branch of new, learned magic in later-medieval Europe was *astrology. Of course, some astrology had existed in early-medieval Europe too, but now with fuller access to the writings of classical authorities such as *Ptolemy and Arab authorities such as *al-Kindi and *Abu Ma'shar, more systematic and learned forms of astrology emerged, as did various forms of astral magic in which certain materials, inscriptions, or incantations were used to draw down and manipulate the power of heavenly bodies. Again Arab treatises, such as Ghayat al Hakim (Aim of the Wise), or Picatrix as it became known in Europe, provided important and authoritative sources. *Alchemy was another major area of learned magic, and again much alchemical knowledge derived from the Arab world, for example from the writings of *Jabir ibn Hayyan, known in Europe as Geber. Above all, European scholars sought to understand the operations of magic in terms of the natural philosophy of Aristotle, which increasingly dominated their understanding of the physical world.

Demonology and Demonic Magic

The rise of learned magic caused some authorities to question the longstanding Christian position that most, if not all, aspects of magic relied on demonic power. Astrologers, astral magicians, and alchemists claimed that they were manipulating entirely natural although hidden or occult forces in the physical world, and arguments about the potential extent of such natural magic continued into the Renaissance. The influx of new learning beginning in the twelfth century, however, also served to reinforce the belief that much magic was dangerously demonic. In the thirteenth century, the great theologian *Thomas Aquinas (c. 1225–1274) argued strenuously that astral magicians, insofar as they employed invocations clearly directed at some intelligence, were engaging with demons and not simply the natural power of the stars. Moreover, a form of learned magic developed in these years that openly relied on demonic forces. Practitioners of necromancy, as this art was called, claimed that they commanded demons by means of complex and powerful rituals, but church authorities maintained that these rites masked the secret worship of demons in exchange for magical services.

Learned authorities of the thirteenth, fourteenth, and fifteenth centuries devoted much attention to the exact range and extent of demonic powers, mainly seeking to explain demonic actions in terms of Aristotelian physics. They argued, for example, that although demons were spiritual beings, they might mimic physical forms by condensing the air around them, and by similar means they could produce illusions and other magical effects. Famously, Aquinas and other authorities developed a rationale by which demons might impregnate women although they could not themselves generate semen. First the demons took female form and seduced human men. Having thus gained human seed, they then took male form and used it to impregnate women. Precisely because conceptions of demonic power and aspects of magic were tied to other areas of theological and natural philosophical thought, as such thought became more advanced in the later medieval period, concern over magic escalated rather than declined.

Common magical practices also persisted throughout this period, of course, and these too were increasingly demonized in the minds of concerned authorities. By the early fifteenth century, the notion of diabolical witchcraft developed. Practitioners of common forms of harmful magic believed to cause illness, wither crops, or impede fertility were now cast as members of conspiratorial, diabolical cults. Although the emergence of witchcraft in late-medieval Europe and the ensuing witch-hunts primarily in the early modern period are typically viewed as irrational by modern observers, the concept of witchcraft took hold precisely because it made sense in terms of larger theories of magic, demonic power, and the natural world that developed during the Middle Ages.

See also **Aristotelianism; Bacon, Roger; Gynecology and midwifery; Herbals; Lapidaries; Macrobius; Medicine, practical; Miracle**

Bibliography

Ankarloo, Bengt, and Stuart Clark, eds. Witchcraft and Magic in Europe: The Middle Ages. Philadelphia: University of Pennsylvania Press, 2002.

Burnett, Charles. Magic and Divination in the Middle Ages: Texts and Techniques in the Islamic and Christian Worlds. Aldershot: Variorum, 1996.

Cohn, Norman. Europe's Inner Demons: The Demonization of Christians in Medieval Christendom, rev. ed. Chicago: University of Chicago Press, 2000.

Fanger, Claire, ed. Conjuring Spirits: Texts and Traditions of Medieval Ritual Magic. University Park: Pennsylvania State University Press, 1998.

Flint, Valerie I.J. The Rise of Magic in Early Medieval Europe. Princeton: Princeton University Press, 1991.

Kieckhefer, Richard. European Witch Trials: Their Foundations in Popular and Learned Culture, 1300–1500. Berkeley: University of California Press, 1976.

———. Magic in the Middle Ages. New York: Cambridge University Press, 1989.

———. Forbidden Rites: A Necromancer's Manual of the Fifteenth Century. University Park: Pennsylvania State University Press, 1998.

Peters, Edward. The Magician, the Witch, and the Law. Philadelphia: University of Pennsylvania Press, 1978.

Stephens, Walter. Demons Lovers: Witchcraft, Sex, and the Crisis of Belief. Chicago: University of Chicago Press, 2002.

Thorndike, Lynn. A History of Magic and Experimental Science, 8 vols. New York: Columbia University Press, 1923–1958.

MICHAEL D. BAILEY

MAGNET AND MAGNETISM

Some aspects of magnetic behavior were already known to the Chinese and to some in the ancient Greco-Roman world. Magnetic declination was mentioned in a Chinese work by Shen Kua, composed around 1088. The phenomenon of magnetic repulsion was mentioned in the ancient world by the Roman poet Lucretius (c. 95–c. 55 B.C.E.), although he was ignorant of magnetic polarity. In his widely read *Natural History*, Pliny (c. 23–79 C.E.), the Roman historian, devotes a section to the magnet, mentioning that iron is attracted and drawn to a magnet and that a magnet attracts other magnets.

By the thirteenth century, *Bartholomaeus Anglicus (fl. 1220–1250) mentions the magnet in his encyclopedic treatise, *De proprietatibus rerum* (*On the Properties of Things*). After explaining that a magnet can move iron, Bartholomew attributes various fantastic curative powers to magnets. Toward the end of the thirteenth century, Henry Bate (1246–1317) included a substantial discussion of magnetism in his comprehensive treatise *Speculum divinorum et quorundam naturalium* (*Mirror of Divine Things and of Some Natural Ones*). Bate derived his basic ideas about magnetism from the Aristotelian scholastic tradition, but may have personally performed a few experiments with magnets.

The first detailed description of magnetism, however, was written in 1269 by *Peter Peregrinus (fl. 1269). Peter entitled his treatise *Epistola de magnete* (*Letter on the Magnet*) which, he tells us at the end of his work, was completed on August 8, 1269, at the siege of Lucera in southern Italy, where he was apparently a military engineer in the service of Charles of Anjou, King of Sicily. *Roger Bacon had the highest regard for Peter Peregrinus, whom he described as *magister experimentorum* ("master of experiments"). Peter's description of magnetism is the first known account of the properties of magnets and also the first account of magnetic polarity in which the north and south poles are distinguished. Peter observed that if a magnet were broken into two parts, each part would function as a magnet with north and south poles, and that if the opposite poles of the two parts were brought together, they would seek to reunite into a single magnet. Indeed, he explains that if the two magnets were somehow glued together at their point of contact, they would form a single magnet with north and south poles, just like the original magnet. Although the ancients had been aware of magnetic attraction and repulsion, they had not associated it with polarity—the attraction of like poles, and the repulsion of unlike poles—as Peter Peregrinus did.

Peregrinus recognized that a magnet could magnetize an iron needle by contact. If, after contact, an iron needle is placed on a piece of wood or straw that floats on water, the end of the needle that was touched by the north pole of the magnet orients itself toward the southern part of the heavens, and the part touched by the south pole of the magnet turns toward the north celestial pole. Since the needle is polarized like a magnet, it takes on the properties of a magnet. Peregrinus was also aware that the needle's magnetized poles could be reversed when the same poles of magnet and needle are brought into contact. Thus, if the north pole of a magnet were brought into contact with the north pole of a magnetized iron needle, the north pole of the needle would be converted to a south pole.

Peregrinus mistakenly believed that the poles of a magnet received their magnetic power or virtue from the celestial poles. It was William Gilbert who, in his famous work *On the Magnet*, published in 1600, hit on the fruitful idea that the Earth was a large spherical magnet.

Because Peter Peregrinus believed that the ultimate source of magnetic power was the entire celestial sphere from which magnetic power streamed down incessantly, he concluded that if a spherical magnet were constructed with fixed pivots at its poles that enabled the magnet to rotate freely, it would do so perpetually. In his *Letter on the Magnet*, Peregrinus includes a chapter entitled "The Art of Making a Wheel of Perpetual Motion" (Chapter Three of Part Two). Peregrinus was not the first to propose a perpetual motion machine—Villard de Honnecourt (fl. 1225–1250) did so earlier in the thirteenth century. Although late medieval natural philosophers rejected the idea of perpetual motion, arguing that inexhaustible forces did not exist in nature, many individuals in succeeding centuries found merit in the idea, including the great philosopher Gottfried Leibniz (1646–1716).

Peter also devised a magnetic compass, which he describes in his *Letter on the Magnet* as a dry, pivoted compass, which is placed in a circular box made of wood or brass. "By means of this instrument," Peter explains, "you can direct your course towards cities and islands and any other place wherever you may wish to go by land or sea, provided the latitude and longitude of the places are known to you."

Pivoted Compass

Somewhere in Italy shortly after 1300, perhaps in Amalfi, the dry pivoted compass was made easier to use by fixing to the pivoting needle a card with the compass points marked on it. By use of this compass card, helmsmen could steer their ships much more easily. This was a mere refinement, however. The real contribution was the dry-pivoted compass itself, which Peter Peregrinus seems to have been the first to announce. His *Letter on the Magnet* is probably the first treatise devoted exclusively to that object. Not only did he distinguish between north and south poles, and provide a rule for the attraction and repulsion of those poles, but he also applied this knowledge to the development of a magnetic compass. Peter Peregrinus may rightly be said to have founded a science of magnetism.

See also **Bacon, Roger; Nature: diverse medieval interpretations; Nature; the structure of the physical world; Navigation**

Bibliography

Grant, Edward, ed. *A Source Book in Medieval Science.* Cambridge: Harvard University Press, 1974, pp. 367–376.

Harradon, H.D. Some Early Contributions to the History of Geomagnetism-I. *Terrestrial Magnetism and Atmospheric Electricity* (now the *Journal of Geophysical Research*) (1943) 48: 3–17.

Peregrinus, Peter. *The Letter of Petrus Peregrinus On the Magnet, A.D. 1269.* Translated by Brother Arnold (Joseph Charles Mertens) with Introductory Notice by Brother Potamian (M.F. O'Reilly). New York: McGraw, 1904.

Thorndike, Lynn. John of St. Amand on the Magnet. *Isis* (1945) 36: 156–157.

EDWARD GRANT

MAIMONIDES

The Judaeo-Arabic author Moses Maimonides (in Arabic Abu 'Imran Musa ibn 'Ubayd Allah ibn Maymun al-Qurtubi, in Hebrew Mosheh ben Maymon, also known by the acronym "RaMBaM") was born in Córdoba in 1138 and died in Fustat (Cairo) in 1204. He was a leading figure in medieval Jewish culture not only as a jurist, a theologian, and a philosopher, but also as a physician. His interest in medical art seems to have begun rather early (in 1160–1165), while he was in Morocco; but he practiced and taught medicine during the last thirty years of his life, while he lived in Fustat. In this later period, he rose to a high rank as a court physician—first, of the vizir of the Egyptian sultan Saladin al-Qadi al-Fadil, and then of Saladin's son and successor, al-Malik al-Afdal. His reputation as a practitioner of medicine seems to have been questioned by some of his contemporaries; in any case, medieval sources describe him as a good medical theoretician. As a matter of fact, he wrote a number of medical treatises, following the example of Isaac Israeli (*Isaac Judaeus); these texts, mostly depending on Greek and Arabo-Islamic sources, played a role in spreading the knowledge of ancient and medieval medicine among Jews during the Middle Ages.

Maimonides also displayed a highly-refined knowledge in other fields of science, particularly *astronomy. He appears to have learned astronomy in his youth, while he was still in Spain, by reading the works of such local Arabo-Islamic scholars as *Ibn Bajja and Jabir ibn Aflah, whose pupils he allegedly met; he seems to have given this science a primary role in his own "order of studies." No Maimonidean treatise specifically devoted to astronomy is extant, but a few treatments of some specific astronomical questions are found in some of his philosophical and theological works. Mathematical and even zoological writings have also been ascribed to Maimonides, but the authorship of most of them is still undecided.

Historical Significance

In science and the history of science, Maimonides' relevance is not due to the fact that he elaborated and diffused new doctrines of his own: as far as can be concluded from what is currently known about his extant works, as a rule he discussed questions typical of twelfth-century Andalusi Muslim scientists, and in a number of cases he was probably inclined to follow the solutions proposed by those scholars. Only in some circumscribed cases does he give original interpretations of old doctrines. Maimonides' relevance is rather due to his "canonization" of the study of sciences (the exact sciences in particular) in medieval Jewish culture. First, he gave science a role as a step in the process which should be followed by a Jew for reaching what Maimonides regards as the utmost point of human knowledge—namely, the knowledge of God and of His creation. Second, it should be stressed that Maimonides had a clear philosophical approach to the sciences. In his opinion, they should be generally based on solid logical demonstration, close to Aristotle's methods, and not only on empirical observation. They progress in a cumulative way, through the continuous correction and refinement of data already acquired by the ancients. In many cases, he departs from the treatment of a scientific subject by drawing conclusions which are relevant for some fields of Aristotelian philosophy (*metaphysics, ethics, human *psychology). In this way, he gave an important stimulus to the development of Jewish science in Middle Ages, and in medieval Europe in particular, in the way traced by such other Spanish Jewish scholars as *Abraham bar Hiyya and *Abraham ibn Ezra.

Maimonides as a Physician

Ten medical treatises at least, in the Arabic language, are commonly ascribed to Maimonides, and most of them were written in consequence of the author's personal connections to some members of the Egyptian elite. The minor ones are short monographs on specific illnesses: the *Treatise on Asthma*, the *Epistle on Hemorrhoids* (written around 1187), and the *Book on Coitus* (written in 1190 or 1191). Some others are systematic treatises of diet, hygiene, and *pharmacology (poisons and drugs): the treatise *On the Regimen of Health* and the *Treatise on the Causes of Symptoms*, both written at the request of al-Malik al-Afdal from 1198 onwards; the *Book on Poisons and the Protection against Fatal Drugs*; and the *Commentary on the Names of Drugs*. Most of Maimonides' major medical writings are commentaries on, or reworkings of, famous works of ancient Greek medicine: a compendium of some of *Galen's writings (in particular, of the *Art of Curing* and other texts), written before 1190; a commentary on *Hippocrates' *Medical Aphorisms*; a series of "medical aphorisms," apparently his own, but in reality mostly inspired by Galen's works (the so-called *Medical Aphorisms of Moses*, written between 1185 and 1190). Apart from the Galenic compendium (which is still unpublished and has been only partially translated into English) and the work on the names of drugs (first edited by Max Meyerhof in 1940), all these works won some success in late medieval European medicine through their various Latin and Hebrew versions of the thirteenth and fourteenth centuries. In the twentieth century, Süssman Muntner first published some of these Hebrew versions, and Fred Rosner rendered them into English.

The dependence of Maimonides' medical works on ancient and medieval Arabo-Islamic sources, in particular Galen, has been stressed by many scholars, but personal achievements in medicine by Maimonides himself, if any, have not yet been made objects of detailed studies. However, it appears that Maimonides dealt with some medical themes owing to their philosophical significance. An example of this is given by the preventive role played by a good medical regimen (*regimen sanitatis*) in preserving human health—an idea which was regarded as so important by the author that he specifically devoted to it not only the above-mentioned work, but even some chapters of his Jewish law code, written in Hebrew, the *Mishneh Torah* (in the book devoted to the *Ethical Laws*, the *Hilkot De'ot*). According to Maimonides, there must be no conflict among the various regimens regulating aspects of man's life, namely, the rules which govern personal hygiene (i.e., medicine), the regulations concerning social and familiar relationships (i.e., politics), and the system of injunctions and prohibitions which limit involvement in worldly pursuits, so permitting a stronger involvement in intellectual and spiritual activity (i.e., religion and philosophy). This idea of the close connection between medicine and philosophy could have come to Maimonides from Galen, who supported it in some of his works. Maimonides' reliance on Galen as physician did not prevent him from developing a harsh critique of some of Galen's philosophical views in Chapter Twenty-five of his *Medical Aphorisms*. However, this critique is due to ideological reasons: Galen had a low reputation in medieval Arabic philosophy because of his religious agnosticism and his critique of the Judaic and Christian concept of prophecy.

Of course, the philosophical importance Maimonides gave to some aspects of medicine did not prevent him from acknowledging the role played in this science by empirical data. He seems to have accepted the idea—already found in the work of *al-Farabi—that medicine was primarily an "art," that is, a practical science with a logic of its own. According to him, a physician should be able to follow a particular way of reasoning, typical of medicine, whose rules are not always completely identical to those valid in mathematical sciences; in some particular cases, a medical treatment should be regarded as valid, even though no theoretical explanation of its validity can be found, provided that repeated observations, under the control of more than one physician, show that it really works.

Maimonides as an Astronomer

Maimonides' contribution to *astronomy, although more limited than that to medicine, has aroused considerable interest, and has been examined by scholars in greater detail. The importance given to astronomy by Maimonides is due to the idea, typical of medieval Jewish and Islamic Aristotelianism, that there is a close connection between knowledge of the nature and structure of the celestial spheres (the main subject of medieval astronomy) and the knowledge of metaphysics, which was

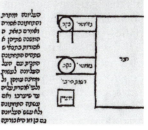

Page from an edition of the Mishnah with Maimonides' commentary. The diagrams are designed to clarify complicated points. Printed by Joshua Soncino and Joseph ibn Peso in Naples (1492). (Topham/RHR)

regarded as "divine science," focused on the emanated intellects which rule those spheres.

Most of Maimonides' extant treatments of astronomical subjects are found both in the *Mishneh Torah* and in his masterpiece, the philosophic-theological work *The Guide of the Perplexed* (written in 1180–1190). In both cases, as is usual in Maimonides, discussions concerning exact sciences are meant to give an answer to religious or philosophical questions.

The reason why Maimonides devoted a number of chapters of his law code (in the section about the "sanctification of the new moon," the *Hilkot qiddush ha-hodesh*) to a very precise astronomical question—namely, how to calculate if the lunar crescent can be seen on the eve of the thirtieth day of each Hebrew lunar month, or not—is strictly bound to a Jewish religious demand. To reply to this question, Maimonides elaborates his own method for calculating what he calls the "arc of vision," namely the sum of the difference between the real positions of the Moon and the Sun, and two-thirds of the latitude of the Moon. This method is based on Arabic astronomical sources, but Maimonides seems to have simplified it. Some data about the structure of the heavens and the dimensions of some stars and planets are found also in the general description of the cosmos according to Aristotelian physics given in the first part of the *Mishneh Torah* (the *Basic Principles of the Law*, in Hebrew *Hilkot yesodei ha-Torah*), but these data contain nothing really new.

The other, and best known, Maimonidean passage concerning astronomy is Chapter Twenty-four of Part II of the *Guide of the Perplexed*. In this passage the author discusses a well-known question debated by twelfth-century Andalusi astronomers, in particular by Jabir ibn Aflah: the problems raised by the contradiction between the principles of Aristotelian physics (according to which the heavenly motions should be circular and uniform) and the doctrines of the epicycles, as found in Ptolemaic astronomy, and of the eccentric spheres. Maimonides reports the two different solutions to these problems proposed by Ibn Bajja in his *Treatise on Astronomy* (apparently lost), and by *Thabit ibn Qurra. However, he seems to choose neither of them, nor does he explicitly propose any definitive solution of his own. In any case, his discussion is not aimed at reaching a purely scientific conclusion about this question, but has an evident philosophical aim: to show that some conclusions of Aristotelian cosmology can be questioned, as in the case of creation from nothing (*creatio ex nihilo*)—which, according to him, can be accepted, although it is at variance with Aristotle's doctrine of world's eternity.

Another passage in the *Guide* concerning an important astronomical subject is Chapter Nine of Part II, in which Maimonides shortly discusses two questions: first, whether Venus and Mercury are placed below the Sun, as affirmed by *Ptolemy, or above it, as supported by "the ancients" and ibn Aflah, and as accepted by himself; second, the number of the celestial spheres. According to Maimonides, the spheres bearing stars are four (one for the fixed stars, one for the five planets, one for the Sun, and one for the Moon). Maimonides apparently adopts this well-known solution for a philosophic-theological purpose: to give a scientific explanation of the cosmological doctrine of the fourfold structure of the heavens which, according to him, was already found in some Biblical texts.

One of the most quoted Maimonidean writings is his *Letter to the Sages of Montpellier about Astrology*. Although it does not contain a discussion of an astronomical question, it is well known because of its explicit repudiation of *astrology, due to philosophical reasons. Maimonides simply could not accept the view that stars emanate any non-corporeal force—a view which, although agreed on by a number of medieval Jewish scholars, he reputed to be at variance with the principles of Aristotelian philosophy.

Maimonides on Mathematics and Zoology)

According to some medieval Arabic sources, Maimonides wrote and edited a number of texts on mathematics. In particular, he allegedly composed a mathematical treatise, which strictly depended on a well-known Spanish Arabic work on mathematics, the *Book of Perfection* (in Arabic, *Kitab al-istikmal*) by al-Mu'taman Ibn Hud (king of Saragossa, 1082–1085). As a matter of fact, however, no mathematical writing explicitly ascribed to Maimonides has been found, apart from a collection of glosses on Apollonius of Perga's *Conical Sections*, which has been recently identified. This does not mean that Maimonides was not concerned with mathematics: on the contrary, his interest can be seen in references to mathematical subjects found in his extant works (the *Guide of the Perplexed*, the *Commentary* on the *Mishnah*, the *Mishneh Torah*). However, his approach to mathematics also appears to have been mainly a philosophical one. In the dedication letter of the *Guide*, he alludes to mathematical studies made together with his pupil, Joseph ben Judah; and in Part I, Chapter Seventy-three, of this work he refers to a passage of Apollonius in order to give a philosophical interpretation of the doctrine of the two asymptotic lines—a passage which seems to have stimulated the translation and diffusion in the Latin and Hebrew Middle Ages (from 1200 onwards) of an anonymous Arabic tract on this very subject. In any case, it seems that Maimonides did not agree with the foundations of the Pythagorean doctrine of numbers, which was going to become one of the main bases of the Kabbalah.

The manuscript tradition also ascribes to Maimonides a work on *zoology: this is the *Tract Comprising Excerpts from Aristotle's Book of Animals*, first published in 1966. It consists of a series of excerpts, most of which are taken from a medieval Arabic translation of Aristotle's zoological works, plus some short observations by the author himself. Due to the apparent philosophical insignificance of this text, its Maimonidean authorship has been often questioned. However, there is a possibility that it is really a mutilated collection of notes on zoological themes, made by Maimonides for personal use.

See also **Aristotelianism; Medicine, practical; Medicine, theoretical; Religion and science**

Bibliography

Primary Sources

Bos, Gerrit, ed. and tr. *The Medical Works of Moses Maimonides*. Provo, Utah: Brigham Young University Press, 2002–2004.

Pines, Shlomo, tr. *The Guide of the Perplexed*, 2 vols. Chicago: University of Chicago Press, 1963.

Rosner, Fred, ed. and tr. *Maimonides' Medical Writings*, 7 vols. Haifa: Maimonides Research Institute, 1987–1995.

Secondary Sources

Bos, Gerrit. "The Reception of Galen in Maimonides' Medical Aphorisms." In Vivian Nutton, ed., *The Unknown Galen*. London: Institute of Classical Studies, University of London, 2002.

Cohen, Robert S. and Hillel Levine, eds. *Maimonides and the Sciences*. Boston: Kluwer Academic Publishers, 2000.

Kraemer, Joel L. "Maimonides on Aristotle and the Scientific Method." In Eric L. Ormsby ed., *Moses Maimonides and His Time*. Washington: Catholic University of America Press, 1989.

Langermann, Y. Tzvi. The Mathematical Works of Moses Maimonides. *Jewish Quarterly Review* (1984) 75: 57–65.

———. "Maimonides and the Sciences." In *The Cambridge*

Companion to Medieval Jewish Philosophy, edited by Daniel H. Frank and Oliver Leaman. New York: Cambridge University Press, 2003.

Lévy, Tony and Roshdi Rashed, eds. *Maïmonide philosophe et savant (1138–1204)*. Leuven: Peeters, 2004.

Rosner, Fred and Samuel Kottek, eds. *Moses Maimonides: Physician, Scientist, and Philosopher*. Northvale, N.J.: Jason Aronson, 1993.

Stroumsa, Sarah. Al-Farabi and Maimonides on Medicine as a Science. *Arabic Sciences and Philosophy* (1993) 3: 235–249.

Zonta, Mauro. "Maimonides as Zoologist?—Some Remarks About a Summary of Aristotle's Zoology Ascribed to Maimonides." In Görge K. Hasselhoff and Otfried Freisse, eds. *Moses Maimonides (1138-1204)*. *His Religious, Scientific, and Philosophical Wirkungsgeschichte in Different Cultural Contexts*. Würzburg: Ergon Verlag, 2004.
MAURO ZONTA

MAJUSI, AL-

'Ali ibn al-'Abbas al-Majusi, known to the West as Haly Abbas, is ranked among the top three of most eminent Arab doctors from the Middle Ages, surpassed only by al-*Razi and Avicenna (*Ibn Sina). Highly regarded as a surgeon and especially well known for his description of the action of the heart, he died in 994. He was a Zoroastrian, or at least came from a family of Zoroastrians, and was Persian by birth. He flourished between 940 and 980, especially at the Caliphate of Baghdad. This Caliphate was a remarkable cultural phenomenon and included the collaboration of Muslims, Jews, and Christians in and around the royal library, called *Bayt al-hikma. It was the director of this institution, the Christian Hunayn ibn Ishaq al-'Ibadi (Johannitius [d. 873]), who collated the texts of the *Articella. Largely a collation of works by *Hippocrates and *Galen, the *Articella* became the basic text of the medical curriculum in the Latin Middle Ages. Haly Abbas's fame in the Christian West rested in large part on his reputation as a commentator on Galen and his work was appended to the *Articella* sometime around 1250. The *Articella*'s texts were translated into Latin by *Constantine the African and *Gerard of Cremona, while Haly Abbas's *Pantegni* was translated by Constantine. However, the *Pantegni* began exerting influence in the Latin West at least as early as *William of Conches (1080–c. 1154). A strong influence on John of Salisbury, William is associated with the School of Chartres, the dominant school of natural philosophy in the twelfth century.

His seminal work is the *Kitab al-maliki*, or *The Royal Book of All Medicine*—so named for its encyclopedic quality and because it was written for a prince of Shiraz. Typical of most medical works of the period, it is divided into two basic divisions, one theoretical, the other practical. Amongst practical concerns are issues of diet, al-Majusi being a great believer in limited intervention, with prevention the primary goal and interventions only to be made when truly necessary. In medical theory, he famously gave a vivid description of how the arteries draw air and blood from the heart during the diastolic phase, whilst during the systolic phase they empty themselves of the same. His advice to surgeons respecting cancer is no different from modern practice: remove the cancer and surrounding tissue, as well as flushing any infected blood, in hopes of forestalling its spread.

Although al-Majusi's work, like that of all the Arab physicians, rests on ancient Greek medicine, Hippocrates and Galen in particular, his reputation in the West was enormous and very much tied to the success and dominance of the *Articella*. This text remained the basis of the medical curriculum at Padua, Europe's most prestigious school of medicine boasting the likes of *Pietro d'Abano as an alumnus, until 1465 despite the enormous influence and repute of the medical contributions of Aristotle, Averroes (*Ibn Rushd) and, of course, Avicenna. The importance of this text, and thus of Haly Abbas, cannot be underestimated for many medieval libraries had multiple copies with some non-university libraries even having as many as eight! Although Haly Abbas's *Pantegni* or *Super Tegni* was very much seen as a commentary on Galen, the Latin version of al-Majusi reveals an extremely systematic mind, and a mind with a definite philosophical interest, that adds a real cogency to Galen's prolix writings. With this said, it will surprise no one who knows the Latin medievals that they would find Haly Abbas a very congenial mind. Their debt to physician-thinkers such as Haly Abbas is enormous, even though Western medicine did make its own serious innovations during the High Middle Ages. For example, you do not find in the works of Haly Abbas the extensive comparative biology (anatomy and physiology) typical of Western medical literature, a manner of investigation they drew from Aristotle's books on animals.

There is a question as to how welcome the works of the Arab physicians were in the West since the texts arrived there outside of any Christian framework. Some have thought the texts were unwelcome and viewed as subversive of good morals, especially regarding sexuality. Such thoughts are hardly convincing when it is remembered that the Arabic texts of authors such as al-Majusi formed the curriculum of the Latin medical schools for hundreds of years and, on one crucial point at least, the medical literature did serve a central theological end. Medicine was granted a large degree of autonomy in the Latin Middle Ages, as were all the sciences, in large part because of the theological dictum made famous by Thomas Aquinas that grace perfects nature. Medicine was not only granted a certain autonomous standing on account of theology but it in turn supplied a crucial characterization of nature. The most contested issue in the Latin West from the introduction of Aristotle until the seventeenth century was whether man was a composite of many substances or only one substance. Conceiving of the human as a more or less fragile plurality of substances, forms, and things served the desire to preserve the transcendence of God. The Greek and Arab physicians provided an account of anatomy and physiology rooted in a pluralist conception of the human body. Indeed, Galen identified the root of the need for medicine

Illumination from 1356 manuscript of *The Book of John Mandeville*, otherwise known as *Mandeville's Travels*. (Lebrecht Music & Arts Photo Library).

in this metaphysical fragility. The rigor and systematicity of Haly Abbas's *Pantegni* ought to be regarded as an original contribution to pluralist medical theory, for his formulations of the issues cannot be found in the Latin translations of Galen. In this regard, the influence of Haly Abbas is especially evident in the fifteenth-century philosopher Paul of Venice, a member of the influential Augustinian Order of Friars and a teacher at Padua. Formulations of the plurality thesis about man's composition akin to those of Haly Abbas and Paul of Venice find their way into the work of Baroque physicians in the seventeenth century, as well as Descartes' famed dualism and, in an extreme formulation, Gassendi's atomism. It is sufficient to say that the figure of al-Majusi cast a long shadow over the development of Western thought.

See also **Medicine, practical; Medicine, theoretical; Surgery**

Bibliography

Burnett, C. and D. Jacquart, eds. *Constantine the African and 'Ali Ibn Al-'Abbas Al-Magusi: The Pantegni and Related Texts*. Leiden: E.J. Brill, 1994.

Jordan, M. D. *The Invention of Sodomy in Christian Theology*. Chicago: University of Chicago Press, 1997.
McAleer, G. J. Was Medical Theory Heterodox in the Latin Middle Ages? The Plurality Theses of Paul of Venice and the Medical Authorities, Galen, Haly Abbas and Averroes. *Recherches de Théologie et Philosophie médiévales* (2001) 68: 349–370.
Siraisi, N.G. *Arts and Sciences at Padua: the Studium of Padua before 1350*. Toronto: Pontifical Institute of Mediaeval Studies, 1973.

G. J. MCALEER

MANDEVILLE, JOHN

The Book of John Mandeville, although its narrator claims to have been an English knight born at St. Albans around 1300, is a compilation of a variety of materials "overwritten" by a narrative voice presenting the information as its own. The author was probably French, possibly a cleric, his identity "encrypted" in the narrative mélange. The book draws on *De sphaera* of *John of Sacrobosco for astronomical information. The geographical information on Egypt and Palestine is indebted to

William of Boldensele's *Liber de quibusdan ultramarinis partibus* (*Book of Certain Overseas Regions*, 1336), those on China and India to Odoric of Pordenone's *Relatio* of 1330. Material on human and natural marvels lifted from the work of *Vincent of Beauvais appears throughout his narrative. Mandeville presents a geometrized globe, with an expectation of symmetry in the disposition of land and people in the face of the Earth. He reflects to a certain degree the fourteenth-century preoccupation with quantification and measurement. Although he claims to have taken sights with an astrolabe in both northern and southern hemispheres, he includes latitudes of places in Europe only. Both Mandeville and *Marco Polo knew that the Pole Star was too low in the Indian Ocean to be used for navigation. Oderic, who had been there in 1316–1318, also knew this. Mandeville says the "Antarctic" star was used instead, but there is no such star. Canopus is probably meant.

The cosmographical information conveyed can be summarized as follows: there are two fixed stars, the Pole Star in the northern hemisphere, and Antarctic in the southern, which can be observed only in the respective hemisphere of each; the Earth is round and circumnavigation possible; all parts of the Earth are habitable, and the seas passable; societies in the southern hemisphere are "foot against foot" (that is, antipodal) to ours; his calculation of the Earth's circumference as 31,500 miles (50,692 km) is larger than the figure of 20,425 miles (32,870 km) that he attributes to the "ancient sages." Mandeville claimed to have sailed as far north as 62° and as far south as 33°46'.

Mandeville's story of the mariner who circumnavigated the globe in both directions was known to *Columbus and played a role in the latter's planning for a westward voyage to India. Because of the roundness of the Earth, "men may environ all the earth of all the world... and turn again to his country that had company and shipping and conduct." To prove this point he recounts the story of a man who sailed east until he came to an island where he heard his own language spoken; then he sailed west and reached his home again. Years later, while in Norway, he recognized the island he had previously visited. He had thus circumnavigated the globe in both directions. He also dismissed the commonly held notions that the torrid zone or equatorial regions of the Earth were impassable, and that if a ship sailed to the southern hemisphere it could not get "back up" again. Around the time Mandeville was supposed to have lived, *John Buridan lectured at the University of Paris on whether the torrid zone was habitable. Columbus was interested in both these points, and the Portuguese were reluctant to sail past Cape Bojador, on the west African coast, for the very fears that Mandeville addressed. His description of the terrestrial paradise, closed off by a wall of fire and the raging torrents of four rivers also set an image in the mind of Columbus, who thought that the mouth of the Orinoco River confirmed this picture.

See also **Astrolabes and quadrants; Geography, chorography**

Bibliography
Primary Sources
Moseley, C.W.R.D., trans. *The Travels of Sir John Mandeville*. Harmondsworth: Penguin, 1983.
Seymour, M.C., ed. *Mandeville's Travels*. Oxford: Clarendon Press, 1967.

Secondary Sources
Bennett, Josephine Waters. *The Rediscovery of Sir John Mandeville*. New York: MLA, 1954.
Campbell, Mary B. *The Witness and the Other World: Exotic European Travel Writing, 400–1600*. Ithaca: Cornell University Press, 1988.
Higgins, Iain Macleod. *Writing East: The "Travels of Sir John Mandeville."* Philadelphia: University of Pennsylvania Press, 1997.
Moody, E. A. John Buridan on the Habilitability of the Earth. *Speculum* (1941) 16: 415–425.

THOMAS F. GLICK

MARK OF TOLEDO

Mark of Toledo was a significant mediator between the cultures of the Almohad Islamic dynasty and Christians of Castile in the early thirteenth century. He is attested as a deacon and/or canon at the cathedral of Toledo in documents dating between March 16, 1193, and March 17, 1216. His father came from Old Castile, but Mark was brought up in Toledo and had sufficient command of Arabic to explore the libraries of the Arabs (*armaria Arabum*) for texts that would be useful for the Latins. These comprised on the one hand medical texts, on the other hand texts concerning the Islamic religion. He had studied medicine, first from "Arabic books," then at a "studium" (perhaps Montpellier), and his aim seems to have been to improve the standard Latin curriculum in medicine of his time, that known as the *Articella*, compiled in *Salerno in the late eleventh century. Thus he substituted for the first text of the *Articella*—the *Isagoge* ("Introduction") written by *Hunayn ibn Ishaq but thought to derive from Greek—a fuller version of the Arabic text, which preserved the question and answer format, and for the relevant text on pulses (by Philaretus), two texts written by *Galen. D'Alverny identifies as Mark's translation of the *Isagoge* the anonymous Latin version in Vat. Pal. Lat. 1098. The other medical texts are firmly attributed to Mark, and follow each other in the manuscripts, being preceded by a general preface: Galen, *On Pulses*, *On the Usefulness of Pulses*, and *On Liquid Movements* or *On Obvious and Hidden Movements* (a text lost in Greek concerning muscular movements, such as that of the tongue, the diaphragm, respiration, swallowing, the role of the nerves proceeding from the brain, and voluntary movements). In making these translations Mark was attempting to find the "doctrine of Galen and others... which the Arabs had led off from the stream of the Greeks." Another translation of Galen's *On Pulses* had been made contemporaneously by *Burgundio of Pisa, but, as often happens, the Arabic-Latin version is easier to read than the over-literal Greek version. While Mark prepared the medical translations on the insistence of the masters and students of the medical college he attended, his other contribution to knowledge resulted from the initiative of his own archbishop, Rodrigo Jiménez de Rada (archbishop of Toledo 1209–1247) and Mauritius, an archdeacon of the cathedral. This was the translation of the Qu'ran, accompanied by the principal texts of the Mahdi (religious leader/prophet) of the Almohads, Ibn Tumart. The earlier translation of Robert of Ketton was evidently unknown in Toledo. Mark's translation is very faithful to the Arabic text, and served archbishop Rodrigo for his own *Historia Arabum*. In his preface Mark shows that he knew other Arabic texts concerning Muhammad, and is remarkably objective (for his time) in the way he discusses the Muslim faith. Ibn Tumart belonged to the school of *al-Ghazzali (as Mark acknowledged), and Mark sees his Creed ('*Aqida*) as providing valuable philosophical arguments for the unity of God. His translation is the earliest specimen of Islamic theology in Latin. Mark completed his translation of the Qu'ran between July 1209 and June 1210, and of the *Creed* and two shorter *Spiritual Guides* and *Laudations* by Ibn Tumart on June 1, 1213, just after Mauritius's election to the bishopric of Bruges. A translation of an invective against Islam written by a Christian Arab in Toledo—the *Contrarietas Alpholica*—which immediately follows Mark's version of the Qu'ran in a late manuscript, is probably not by Mark.

While writing a highly literary Latin in his prefaces, with several allusions to Classical works, in his translations he follows the *verbum de verbo* technique, to such an extent that he often reproduces the rhythm of the Arabic phrases, while his terminology sometimes coincides with that of an Arabic-Latin/Latin-Arabic dictionary written in Spain in the thirteenth century (the so-called "*Vocabulista in arabico*," ed. C. Schiaparelli, Florence 1871).

The translations of the three treatises by Galen were included in a *Corpus Galenicum* that was used widely in the medical schools from the second half of the thirteenth century onward, and the last two were printed in several of the *Opera omnia* of Galen in the Renaissance. While the Qu'ran was copied a few times, the works of Ibn Tumart survive in only one manuscript (Paris, Bibliothèque Mazarine, 780, copied in 1400), but there is evidence that they accompanied Mark's translation of the Qu'ran in a manuscript belonging to the popes in Avignon in 1369.

See also **Medicine, practical; Medicine, theoretical; Toledo; Translation movements;**

Bibliography

Corpus Galenicum. Ed. G. Fichtner. Tübingen: Institut für Geschichte der Medizin, 1992 (see items 61, 32 and 278).

Burman, Thomas E. Exclusion or Concealment: Approaches to Traditional Arabic Exegesis in Medieval Latin Translations of the Qu'ran. *Scripta Mediterranea* (1998–1999) 19–20: 181–197.

———. *Tafsir* and Translation: Traditional Arabic Qu'ran Exegesis and the Latin Qu'ran's or Robert of Chester and Mark of Toledo. *Speculum* (1998) 73: 703–732.

D'Alverny, Marie-Thérèse. *La Connaissance de l'Islam dans l'Occident medieval*. Aldershot: Variorum Reprints 1994, articles I (Deux traductions latines du Coran au Moyan Age), II (Marc de Tolède, traducteur d'Ibn Tumart) and VII (Marc de Tolède).

CHARLES BURNETT

MARSILIUS OF INGHEN

Marsilius of Inghen was one of the leading thinkers of the late medieval period. His works were read at many *universities in France, Italy, and Germany, and were occasionally even part of the regular curriculum. Together with *John Buridan, *Nicole Oresme, and *Albert of Saxony he belonged to the so-called "Parisian School" of natural philosophy, which contributed substantially to the development of the theory of motion in the Middle Ages. It was through the writings of Marsilius that many ideas of the "Parisian School" spread across Germany in the fifteenth century (Heidelberg, Erfurt, Basel, Kraków).

Central to his thinking was the belief that the natural philosopher (*philosophus naturalis*) should describe the world without reference to any miracles, basing himself exclusively on principles which every human being could affirm to be necessary. However, while he accepted the consequence that human reason, relying on its own principles, may come to conclusions which differ from those of faith, this did not mean that he questioned faith. For he remained convinced that faith revealed truth and was therefore necessary as a source in the search for truth. But as a natural philosopher he wished to argue solely within the limits of human reason, bracketing revelation. Using this methodology, he foreshadowed the principles of modern natural science.

Life and Writings

As is the case with many medieval authors, the early life of Marsilius of Inghen remains obscure. In all probability, he was born around 1340 in the city of Nijmegen, where he most likely also received his early education. In any case, many of his later students came from Nijmegen and during the latter stage of his career he had further contacts with the city.

In 1362 he became Master at the Arts Faculty in Paris. He was a colleague of Geert Groote, the initiator of the *Devotio Moderna*, with whom he shared the opinion that there was a tension between faith and natural reason. Unlike Marsilius, however, Geert Groote later left academic life, urging Marsilius to do the same, albeit unsuccessfully. At the University of Paris Marsilius had a flourishing career. His lectures attracted many students and he held several administrative posts, including the rectorship of the university. He left Paris for an unknown destination in 1379, probably due to problems caused by the Great Schism. In 1386 he became the first rector of the University of Heidelberg, which he had helped to found. Here he was again Master of Arts and held numerous administrative offices, acting as rector of the university no fewer than nine times. In Heidelberg he also finished his study of theology, which he had begun in Paris, and was the first theologian to be promoted at this university. He died at Heidelberg on August 20, 1396. His colleague Nicholas Prowin made the funeral oration, characterizing him as a devout man. The text of this speech was published in 1499 by masters of the University of Heidelberg, along with humanist epigrams on Marsilius and a defense of nominalism which they attributed to him.

Marsilius left a great number of academic writings, which have survived in manuscripts and printed versions of the fifteenth and sixteenth centuries. A small part of them is available in modern critical editions. His writings are the fruit of his teachings at Paris and Heidelberg, which consisted mainly of commentaries on the works of Aristotle, Scripture, and the *Sentences* of *Peter Lombard. They are modeled according to the format of the late medieval scholastic *quaestio* (question), in which each step of the argument is summarized in a separate *propositio* or *conclusio* (statement).

Marsilius's writings cover a wide range of the subjects that were taught at the medieval universities. He wrote treatises on logic, natural philosophy, metaphysics, ethics, and theology, some of which have come down to us in different versions. A number of treatises bear in the title the word "*abbreviatio*" (summary). These are no summaries of the regular commentaries, however, but independent treatises, characterized by a condensed style of reasoning. The identification of his writings is sometimes difficult, since the questions discussed and the wording of many *conclusiones* (statements) are often similar to those found in the works of John Buridan and Nicole Oresme.

Basic Ideas

In the medieval period, Marsilius was regarded as a nominalist. Although he did not label himself as such, not long after his death he became depicted as a *nominalis* (nominalist) and a *modernus* (modern). This happened in the context of the debates between the old way (*via antiqua*) and the modern way (*via moderna*)—a discussion about the correct interpretation of Aristotle, which took place at many universities in Germany. The defenders of the new way considered the writings of Marsilius their model, even identifying the new method with the way Marsilius had commented on the writings of Aristotle (*via marsiliana*).

The key notion of Marsilius's nominalism is his theory of universals, which is similar to that of John Buridan. According to Marsilius, universals are products of human thinking. No universals exist outside the human mind, for in reality there are only individuals. Even universals, considered as concepts in the human mind, are individuals. The universal concept "man" is a singular concept, which signifies universally; that is, it refers to every individual man outside the human mind.

If the natural philosopher draws the conclusion "all fire is hot," he does so not because there is a universal nature "fire" existing in all singular instances of fire, but because of empirical observation, which shows every instance of fire to be hot. Such repeated observations, if they cannot be questioned, urge the human intellect to form the universal proposition "all fire is hot," even though it has not seen all possible instances of fire. Marsilius accepts the Aristotelian notion that scientific knowledge must be universally true. Since there are no universals in physical reality, the immediate object of natural science cannot be the singular thing as such, but only the proposition. Natural science according to Marsilius is therefore the description of singular physical things by means of propositions which the human mind accepts as being universally true.

Among the basic principles of natural philosophy, Marsilius counts the theorem "nothing comes from nothing." According to him this principle is based on sense perception and the judgment of the human intellect that universally "all things come from other things." Natural philosophers cannot deny this principle without contradicting themselves. If this principle is accepted, however, it is impossible to hold that the universe is created from nothing, that time and motion have a beginning, and that God is almighty—statements which are accepted by faith. The underpinning of these articles of faith by *natural philosophy is therefore impossible, Marsilius argued, both in his philosophical and theological writings, even if according to faith and truth (*secundum fidem et veritatem*) God has created the world from nothing indeed.

Marsilius solved this seeming contradiction between faith and reason by pointing out that man in his earthly life has only partial access to truth, since man, being dependent on sense perception, has only a limited number of principles on which to base his arguments. Only faith can show whether or not natural reasoning has any value when touching on issues beyond the realm of physical reality, such as creation. Physically, one can prove that there is a singular first cause of reality, which has intellect and will. But that this first cause can freely resurrect dead bodies is impossible to show by means of natural arguments. According to Marsilius, therefore, the discussion of these issues should be avoided in natural philosophy and limited to theology only (*dubitatio theologicalis non spectat ad praesens negotium*).

This notwithstanding, sometimes Marsilius does adduce evidence from faith as an argument in his physical writings. But he does this only when faith does not contradict the arguments put forward by the natural philosopher. A good example is the way in which he defends the theory of *impetus. According to this theory, the movement of a body is not caused by one or more bodies pushing on it, as Aristotle had claimed, but by a power, or impetus, which has been transmitted to that body by the initial agent. In support of this theory, Marsilius puts forward many empirical observations, such as that of a ball falling down and bouncing back from the floor. The bouncing could not be accounted for by Aristotle's theory, because the air which initially pushed the ball downward would keep it on the floor, but was perfectly comprehensible according to the theory of impetus. That his opinion contradicted Aristotle's, Marsilius countered by stating that he did not feel himself bound to Aristotle where Aristotle held views which according to natural reason were not true. In a different way, he considered an argument from faith, taken from the *Condemnation of 1277, that God could move the whole universe in one straight line. Marsilius used this argument as evidence for the theory of impetus. He felt no hesitation about doing this in his physical writings because, as he remarked, it confirmed what all empirical data (*omnes apparentiae*) about impetus had shown and because as a statement from faith it was true, although the statement itself could not be proven by human reason.

In his theological works, however, Marsilius accepted revelation as an extra source of information which, independent of confirmation by natural arguments, could be used in theological reasoning. As in his other writings, here he also showed that natural reasoning could not prove basic tenets of faith. To counterbalance this lack of natural proof, he referred to evidence from Scripture, which he considered to be undeniably true, and from tradition, which he broadly interpreted, including the Fathers, the Councils, Canon Law, and theologians such as *Aquinas whose writings were accepted as trustworthy. This gives his theology an undertone of eclecticism; however, to denounce his theology as such would miss the point, since it is indeed the consequence of his methodology: where natural reason fails, faith as revealed in Scripture, as accepted by the Church, and as explained by *theologi approbati* (approved theologians) must count as evidence.

See also **Aristotelianism; Miracle; Scholasticism**

Bibliography

Primary Sources
Abbreviationes super octo libros Physicorum Aristotelis. Venice, 1521.
Quaestiones super libros Priorum Analyticorum. Venice, 1516. Reprint Frankfurt am Main: Minerva, 1968.
Quaestiones super quattor libros Sententiarum. Mainz, 1501. Reprint Frankfurt am Main: Minerva, 1966.
Quaestiones super quattuor libros Sententiarum, 2 vols., ed. Manuel Santos Noya. Leiden: E.J. Brill, 2000.
Treatises on the Properties of Terms, ed. Egbert P. Bos. Dordrecht: D. Reidell, 1983.

Secondary Sources
Caroti, Stefano and Pierre Souffrin, eds. *La nouvelle physique du XIVe siècle*. Firenze: Olschki, 1997.
Hoenen, Maarten J.F.M. *Marsilius of Inghen, Divine Knowledge in Late Medieval Thought*. Leiden: E.J. Brill, 1993.
Marshall, P. Parisian Psychology in the Mid-Fourteenth Century. *Archives d'histoire doctrinale et littéraire du moyen âge* (1983) 50: 101–193.
Reina, Maria E. *Hoc hic et nunc. Buridano, Marsilio di Inghen e la conoscenza del singolare*. Firenze: Olschki, 2002.
Ritter, Gerhard. *Studien zur Spätscholastik I: Marsilius von Inghen und die okkamistische Schule in Deutschland*. Heidelberg: Carl Winter, 1921.

MAARTEN J.F.M. HOENEN

MARTIANUS CAPELLA

Martianus Capella is known from only one work: *De nuptiis Philologiae et Mercurii*, a handbook of ancient knowledge embellished by the tale of the marriage of Mercury and Philology. Martianus was probably born in Carthage. His work, which cannot be dated more precisely than sometime in the fifth century, is divided into nine books: the first two deal with the narrative of Mercury's and Philology's wedding; the following seven are dedicated to the seven liberal arts, which present themselves as bridesmaids and explain their own functions. Books Three, Four, and Five are introductions to the arts of the trivium: *Grammatica*, *Dialectica*, and *Rhetorica*; Books Six to Nine deal with the arts of the *quadrivium: Geometria*, *Mathematica*, *Astronomia*, and *Harmonia* (or *Musica*). In modern scholarship the book has long been scorned, especially because Martianus summarizes the ancient knowledge of the seven liberal arts in such a way that he sometimes betrays insufficient knowledge of the subject matter. It has been regarded as a flawed collage, written in a style so embellished that it has become impenetrable.

Despite its undoubted shortcomings, the work is important for several reasons. Firstly, *De nuptiis* is probably the best source of knowledge of Varro's work on the mathematical disciplines. Martianus explicitly but not exclusively bases his books on the mathematical arts on Varro's works, and forms a starting point for a reconstruction of the ancient Roman mathematical disciplines. Secondly, it is considered a crucial work for the foundation of the medieval curriculum. With his limitation of the arts to seven, and his deliberate division of these arts into three language-related arts, and four number-related arts, Martianus was the earliest authority for the canonization of the seven liberal arts. His example was widely followed throughout the Middle Ages and beyond. Thirdly, *De nuptiis* appears to have been the most popular textbook on secular knowledge in the Middle Ages, especially in the Carolingian period. Its popularity is attested by the overwhelming number of manuscripts and commentaries on the text. Both the production of manuscripts and the compilation of commentaries began early in the ninth century. The commentaries form the earliest sources for the reception of ancient learning on several of the liberal arts. The work also had a profound influence on medieval treatises on the arts.

The books on the arts of the quadrivium open with *Geometria*, the art of measurement. The book contains, as expected, a short digest of Euclidean geometry, but, due to the applicability of geometry to land surveying, it actually devotes more pages to a geographical description of the Earth. Martianus bases his work mainly on Pliny the Elder's *Natural History*, and Solinus's *Collectanea*. For Book Seven, dedicated to *Arithmetica*, the art of mathematics, Martianus used Nicomachos's *Introduction to Arithmetic*, and *Euclid's *Elements*, or, more likely, Latin primers based on these works. It contains classifications and definitions of the kinds of number, series of numbers, different kinds of calculations (multiplication, division, etc.), and classifications of the ratios of numbers. Rather simple examples are given, which do not exceed the level of elementary *arithmetic. Martianus also includes a translation and illustration of many Euclidean propositions.

Book Eight is devoted to the *ars astronomia*, and describes the celestial sphere, the (eccentric) circular orbits of the planets, the constellations of the stars, and the planets themselves. The account is far from systematic. For example, Martianus states that there are eleven constellations in the zodiac, but adds that it is not necessary to list the zodiacal signs. He gives the lengths of days and nights at the solstices, but does not locate them at a specific latitude. Of particular importance in Martianus's planetary theory is his assertion that five of the seven planets circle around the Earth, the center of the universe, but the other two, Mercury and Venus, orbit the Sun. This element of circumsolarity was picked up by Carolingian scholars (notably *John Scottus Eriugena, who explored this subject in his *Periphyseon*), who studied Martianus next to Pliny, *Macrobius, Calcidius, *Isidore of Seville and *Bede. In the commentaries the planetary doctrines of these writers were compared to each other or, at times, used to interpret each other.

In Book Nine, *De Harmonia*, the study of music is approached as a technical discipline which is essentially Pythagorean in nature, explaining music in terms of mathematical ratios. Martianus introduces the main concepts of the discipline, and treats seven subjects separately: *soni* (pitches), *spatia* (intervals), *systemata* (systems), *genera* (modes of tetrachord division), *modi* (various modes: Dorian, Lydian, Phrygian, etc.), *commutatio* (modulation), and *modulatio* (melodic composition). Finally the subject of quantative verse is treated. In the mythological narrative in Books One and Two, and in the introduction to Book Nine, the subject of harmony is given greater prominence: in line with Platonic and Pythagorean traditions music is revealed to contain truths about the order of the cosmos. The subject of music, the scientific measurement of ratios, and the mathematical harmony of consonance can equally be applied to the divine order of the cosmos, which uses the same principles.

In the earlier Middle Ages, Martianus's books on arithmetic and music were fundamental, surpassed only, perhaps, by *Boethius's manuals on these subjects. Martianus's book on astronomy remained important throughout the Middle Ages. More importantly, however, *De nuptiis* offered a perspective on classical learning which was full of pagan, (Neo-) Pythagorean and (Neo-) Platonic elements, but which was nevertheless easy to adopt in a Christian society. The allegory, in which the elevation of man through knowledge and learning is illustrated, is as much a defense of the classical tradition of the seven liberal arts as a successful plea for their place in the ideal Christian education.

See also **Astronomy, Latin; Music theory**

Bibliography

Primary Sources
Martianus Capella. *De nuptiis Philologiae et Mercurii.* Ed. Willis, J., Leipzig, Germany: Teubner, 1983.

Trans. and intr. by Stahl, W.H. and Johnson, R. *Martianus Capella and the Seven Liberal Arts.* 2 vols. New York: Columbia University Press, 1971.

Secondary Sources
Eastwood, B.S. "The astronomies of Pliny, Martianus Capella and Isidore of Seville." In *Science in Western and Eastern Civilization in Carolingian Times.* Eds. P.L. Butzer and D. Lohrmann. Boston: Birkhäuser Verlag, 1993, pp. 161–180.
———. Astronomical Images and Planetary Theory in Carolingian Studies of Martianus Capella. *Journal for the History of Astronomy* (2000) 31: 1–28.
Guillaumin, J.-Y. *Martianus Capella, Les noces de Philology et de Mercure. Livre VII: L'aritmétique.* Paris: Belles Lettres, 2003.
Leonardi, C. I codici di Marziano Capella, parts I–II. *Aevum* (1959) 33: 443–489, and *Aevum* (1960), 34: 1–99 and 411–524.
Lozovsky, N. *"The earth is our book": geographical knowledge in the Latin West, ca. 400–1000.* Ann Arbor: University of Michigan Press, 2000.
Lutz, C.E. "Martianus Capella." In *Catalogus Translationum et Commentatorium. Mediaeval and Renaissance Latin Translations and Commentaries. Annotated Lists and Guides.* Eds. Cranz, F.E., Kristeller, P.O., et alii. Vol. II, Washington D.C.: The Catholic University of America Press, 1971, 367–381. "Addenda et corrigenda," Vol. III (1976), 449–452 and Vol. VI (1986), 185–186.
Teeuwen, M.J. *Harmony and the Music of the Spheres. The ars musica in ninth-century commentaries on Martianus Capella.* Leiden: E.J. Brill, 2002.

MARIKEN TEEUWEN

MASHA'ALLAH

Masha'allah ibn Athari, or Ibn Sariya, was a Jewish astrologer of Persian origin, from Basra (Iraq), although he is sometimes considered Egyptian due to the easy confusion, in Arabic script, between *misri* (Egyptian) and *basri* (Basrian). He was active in Iraq between the caliphate of al-Mansur (754–775) and that of al-Ma'mun (813–833) but the last secure date in his life is 809, for his work *Fi qiyam al-khulafa'* shows his knowledge of the date of the death of Harun al-Rashid (786–809).

Together with Nawbakht, 'Umar ibn Farrukhan al-Tabari and al-Fazari, he cast the horoscope to establish the propitious moment for the foundation of Baghdad on July 30, 762. The planetary positions of this horoscope were computed using the Pahlavi text of the *Zij al-Shah*, called in Persian *Zij-i Shahriyaran*, "The Royal Astronomical Tables," which were translated into Arabic c. 790. The *Zij al-Shah* was also used by Masha'allah to compute the sixteen horoscopes preserved by Ibn Hibinta (fl. Baghdad 929) in his abridgement of Masha'allah's *Fi'l-qiranat wa'l-adyan wa'l-milal* ("On conjunctions, religions and doctrines"). These horoscopes have been used by Kennedy and Pingree to establish the parameters of the mean motions of Saturn, Jupiter, and the lunar nodes according to the *Zij al-Shah*. This is a clear example of how important astronomical information can be gathered from astrological sources.

Masha'allah represents an early stage in the introduction of foreign sciences in Arabic culture and he is the author of one of the first syntheses of Iranian, Indian, and Greek traditions. Thus, he is one of the channels through which Iranian astrological ideas were introduced in Abbasid Baghdad: these ideas, as shown in *Fi'l-qiranat*, were based, on the one hand, on the Sassanian doctrine which explains great changes in human history using Saturn–Jupiter conjunctions which take place approximately every twenty years. To this Masha'allah adds the Zoroastrian doctrine of the thousands, by ascribing one thousand years to each planet from the moment of the creation of the world (8291 B.C.E.). The cycle ends in 3709 C.E., twelve thousand years later. This kind of astrological history was officially supported by the Abbasid Caliphate because it presented its dominion as the result of a scheme governed by the stars and as the legitimate continuation of the great empires of Mesopotamia and Iran.

According to Masha'allah a millenium governed by Mars began in year 709 C.E., forty-one years before the accession to power of the Abbasids (750) who were protected, therefore, by the beginning of a cycle. On the other hand, a conjunction of Saturn and Jupiter in 749 announced, according to him, the victory of the dynasty.

Masha'allah's sources were also Indian and Greek. He may have had access to the former through the Indian astronomer who arrived to Baghdad in 771 or 773 with an Indian embassy, and worked with al-Fazari in an Arabic translation of a Sanskrit astronomical text. As for his Greek sources, he could have used Sasanian translations or very early Arabic versions of Syriac texts. Both a Latin text (*Hugh of Santalla's *Liber Aristotilis*) and a Byzantine Greek one preserve a bibliography, compiled by Masha'allah, of some one hundred twenty-five books on astrology written by twelve authorities including Aristotle, Hermes, *Ptolemy, Dorotheus of Sidon, Democritus, *Plato, and Vettius Valens. The influence of Dorotheus, whose work was accessible in a Persian translation, is clear in Masha'allah's *Kitab al-mawalid* ("Book on nativities") and in another work of his extant in a Latin translation (*Super significationibus plantarum in nativitate*). Another remarkable influence is that of Aristotle: like *Abu Ma'shar (787–886) after him, he was interested in Aristotelian Physics—available to him in Syriac sources—which he summarized in chapters one to seven of his *De scientia motus orbis*, known in *Gerard of Cremona's translation.

Masha'allah wrote on all branches of astrology. Pingree has collected information on twenty-eight works of his related to astrological history, nativities and anniversaries, astrometeorology, projection of rays, interrogations and elections etc. Apart from the aforementioned *Fi'l-qiranat*, his interest in astrological history led him to compile *Fi qiyam al-khulafa' wa ma'rifat qiyam kull malik* ("On the accession of the caliphs and the knowledge of the accession of every king"), which includes the horoscopes of the spring equinoxes of the years in which the Prophet Muhammad and eighteen caliphs (from Abu Bakr to Harun al-Rashid)

acceded to power. He also studied questions related to the prediction of rains and winds (*Kitab al-amtar wa'l-riyah*): his disciple Abu 'Ali al-Khayyat probably wrote a recension of this work which was the source of the *Liber novem iudicum* compiled in the court of *Frederick II of Sicily. A Moroccan astrologer of the early fifteenth century, Abu 'Abd Allah al-Baqqar, quotes texts of his related to the prediction of the oscillation of the prices of olive oil. Eclipses were another topic dealt with by Masha'allah in a work which is only extant in Latin and Hebrew translations. This text contains a curious reference to magnetism, also found in Indian sources, which compares the influence of heavenly bodies in the sublunar world to the attraction of iron by a magnet. This is another example of an attempt, which we find mainly in Abu Ma'shar, of justifying astrology with physical arguments.

He does not seem to have felt a great interest in pure astronomy although biographical sources ascribe to him a non-extant book on the armillary sphere as well as another one on the construction and use of the astrolabe. The latter was considered to be the Arabic original of two extremely popular Latin texts on these two topics which were the main source used by the authors of the first treatises on this instrument in Spanish (*Alfonso X), English (*Geoffrey Chaucer), and French (Pelerin de Prusse). Kunitzsch has proved that the aforementioned Latin treatises are unrelated to Masha'allah and that their Arabic source is a work by the Andalusi astronomer Maslama al-Majriti (*Maslama of Madrid) (d. 1007). Finally, his *De scientia motus orbis* contains an introduction to astronomy (chapters 8–24) in which Ptolemy and Theon of Alexandria are mentioned, although the planetary models described are pre-ptolemaic and seem to be influenced by Indian sources.

See also **Astrolabes and quadrants; Astronomy, Islamic; Planetary tables**

Bibliography

Burnett, Charles and David Pingree. *The Liber Aristotilis of Hugo of Santalla*. London: The Warburg Institute, 1997.

Goldstein, B.R. "The Book on Eclipses by Masha'allah." *Physis* (1964) 6: 205–213.

Gutas, Dmitri. *Greek Thought, Arabic Culture*. New York: Routledge, 1998.

Kennedy, Edward S., and David Pingree. *The Astrological History of Masha'allah*. Cambridge: Harvard University Press, 1971.

Kunitzsch, Paul. *On the Authenticity of the Treatise on the Composition and Use of the Astrolabe Ascribed to Messahalla. Archives Internationales d'Histoire des Sciences* (1981) 106: 42–62. Reprint in Kunitzsch, *The Arabs and the Stars*. Northampton: Variorum Reprints, 1989.

Levi della Vida, G. Un opuscolo astrologico di Masha'allah. *Rivista degli Studi Orientali* (1933–1934) 14: 270–281.

Pingree, David. "Masha'allah: some Sasanian and Syriac sources." In *Essays in Islamic Philosophy and Science*, edited by G.F. Hourani. Albany: State University New York Press, 1975, pp. 5–14.

———. Classical and Byzantine Astrology in Sasanian Persia. *Dumbarton Oaks Papers* (1989) 43: 227–239.

Thorndike, L. The Latin Translations of the Astrological Works by Messahalla. *Osiris* (1956) 12: 49–72.

JULIO SAMSÓ

MASLAMA OF MADRID

The founder of distinctive schools of mathematics and astronomy in Islamic Spain (al-Andalus), Maslama of Madrid (Abu'l-Qasim Maslama ibn Ahmad al-Faradi al-Majriti) was born in the mid-tenth century C.E., and died in 1007.

Very little is known about Maslama's life. His place of birth is uncertain, but it was probably Madrid, which at that time was nothing more than a fortified frontier post. He spent most of his life in Córdoba: there he was educated, taught most of his students, and there he died. *Sa'id al-Andalusi does not mention Maslama's age at his death, but says that it occurred just before the caliphate began to fall into disorder. Maslama should not be confused with the alchemist Abu Maslama of Madrid, who clearly lived in the latter part of the eleventh century and whose work was reviled by the historian Ibn Khaldun (1332–1406).

While Maslama is mentioned as a mathemetician by his contemporary Ibn Hazm (who thought al-Andalus was not particularly advanced in this field, a judgment shared by modern scholars), the primary source for his life is Sa'id al-Andalusi in his *Book of the Categories of the Nations*. Sa'id says that "He was the chief mathematician in al-Andalus during his time and better than all the astronomers who came before him" (*Categories*, 64). He is reported to have been the student of Abu Ayyub ibn 'Abd al-Ghafir ibn Muhammad and Abu 'Abs ibn 'Abd al-Rahman ibn al-Hayrith al-Ansari. He was part of a circle of learned men who associated together in Córdoba during the reign of the caliph al-Hakam II (c. 943 C.E.). These scholars worked with the active encouragement of the caliph, who is reported to have procured books for his scholars from Baghdad and the other intellectual centers of the East. Maslama also is reported to have educated a sizable group of students, who have been characterized as an "important mathematical and astronomical school" (Samsó, 953). Among them were *Ibn al-Samh, *Ibn al-Saffar, al-Kirmani, and an Ibn Khaldun, an ancestor of the celebrated historian.

Maslama's works include mathematics and astronomy and the majority are no longer extant in Arabic. His mathematical work was typical of Andalusi scholars: *The Fruits of the Science of Numbers* (*Thimat 'ilm al-'adad*) was a treatise on *mu'amalat*, the practical mathematics of commercial transactions. His real importance, though, was in astronomy. Sa'id tells us that he was "fond of studying and understanding" the *Almagest* (*Categories*, 64). There is also a tradition that he was one of the first to introduce the *Epistles of the Brethren of Purity* (*Rasa'il Ikhwan al-Safa*) into al-Andalus; whether this is so or not, it was certainly his pupil, al-Kirmani, who introduced the *Rasa'il* to Andalusi intellectuals beyond Córdoba. Like many astronomers, Maslama was the author of a treatise on the use and construction of the astrolabe which has survived (Vernet and Catalá, 18–19). He is credited with providing a summary of *al-Battani's work on the motion of the planets, notes on the Theorem of Menelaus, a translation of the *Planisphere* of *Ptolemy, and with the translation and adaptation of the shorter of two versions of *al-Khwarizmi's astronomical tables (the *Zij al-Sindhind*). This work was his lasting contribution to medieval science. Al-Khwarizmi's tables had come into al-Andalus in the time of 'Abd al-Rahman II, and Maslama is credited with two useful modifications of them: first, he changed al-Khwarizmi's dates from the Persian to the Hijra calendar and, second, he adapted of some of the tables to the geographical coordinates of Córdoba. In some cases, these modifications improved the accuracy of the Tables considerably (Samsó, 961). He probably also introduced certain Andalusi elements into the Tables, as well as some Ptolemaic material. Since neither al-Khwarizmi's nor Maslama's tables are extant in their original Arabic, it is hard to say for certain. Maslama's revision of al-Khwarizmi's tables became influential in Europe when they were translated by *Adelard of Bath and *Pedro Alfonso in the twelfth century. It is only in this Latin version that his work survives complete.

Maslama and his pupils appear to have combined the Ptolemaic and Indian astronomical traditions but had not completely integrated them with observational data. Sa'id al-Andalusi reports that he himself had written a book pointing out the places where Maslama was in error in this regard. One of Maslama's pupils, *Ibn al-Zarqalluh, combined his scholarly tradition with the astronomical observations of Sa'id's circle, resulting in "a new kind of Andalusi astronomy" which was highly significant in the development of both Islamic and medieval European astronomy (Samso, 960–968).

See also **Astrolabes and quadrants; Astronomy, Islamic; Astronomy, Latin**

Bibliography

Kennedy, E. S. *A Survey of Islamic Astronomical Tables.* Philadelphia: American Philosophical Society, 1956.

al-Khwarizmi. The Astronomical Table of al-Khwarizmi. Edited by Otto Neugebauer. Copenhagen: Royal Danish Academy of Sciences and Letters, 1962.

Mercier, R. "Astronomical Tables in the Twelfth Century." In *Adelard of Bath: An English Scientist and Arabist of the Twelfth Century*. Edited by C. Burnett. London: Warburg Institute, 1987, pp. 87–118.

Sa'id al-Andalusi. *Book of the Categories of the Nations.* Tr. and ed. in S. Salem and A. Kumar. *Science in the Medieval World*. Austin: University of Texas Press, 1991.

Samsó, Julio. "The Exact Sciences in al-Andalus." In *Legacy of Muslim Spain*. Edited by S. K. Jayyusi. Leiden: E.J. Brill, 1994, pp. 952–973.

Vernet, Juan and M.A. Catalá. Las Obras matematicas de Maslama de Madrid. *Al-Andalus* (1965) 30: 15–47. Includes an edition and translation of Maslama's Treatise on the Astrolabe.

MICHAEL C. WEBER

MAURUS OF SALERNO

The medical writer and teacher Maurus of Salerno was born into a well-connected family in southern Italy c. 1130. His student *Gilles de Corbeil in his De laudibus compositorum medicaminum addresses Maurus as the concives of *Urso of Calabria, which suggests, albeit obliquely, that Maurus hailed from Calabria. He studied at *Salerno c. 1150–1160 under Matthaeus Platearius and Petrus Musandinus, the student and successor of *Bartholomaeus of Salerno, and taught medicine at Salerno himself from about 1165 to about 1200. Gilles implies that his was a strong personality, one that commanded the respect of court circles. By his wife Theodora (d. 1239) he had two sons, Matthew and John, both also magistri in physica. Maurus's death is recorded in the necrology of the confraternity of San Matteo, Salerno, in 1214.

With his contemporary Urso of Calabria, Maurus developed Salernitan medical education in the direction of greater theoretical sophistication, a more formalized curriculum, and a more rigorous pedagogical approach, notably through the use of the quaestio. He was a very prolific author, devoting much of his attention to questions of medical semiotics, an area that straddles the boundary between theoretical medicine and practical medicine. His most significant contributions to medical *scientia were mediated through his commentaries on the entire *Articella in the six-book version popularized by Bartholomaeus of Salerno. This suite of commentaries is preserved in MS Paris, Bibliothèque nationale lat. 18499. While drawing on the standard Salernitan corpus of writings, whose core was the oeuvre of *Constantine the African, and on previous Articella commentaries, particularly that of Archimatthaeus, Maurus also made use of new resources such as the prose *Salernitan Questions (notably in his commentary on the Isagoge of *Hunayn ibn Ishaq), the Greco-Latin translations of Aristotle's works on natural philosophy, especially De generatione et corruptione. His and Urso's role in launching the Aristotelian libri naturales into the academic milieu of Europe is attested by quotations in the works of *Alexander Nequam and in the commentary by Ralph of Longchamp on Alain de Lille's Anticlaudianus. Maurus also wrote a number of works on uroscopy: De urinis or Regulae urinarum (including Quoniam de urinarum scientis tractaturi earum notitiam…), De symptomatibus urinarum (including Notandum in principio quod urine in principio egritudinis…), and Urinae abbreviatae (including Urina pallida vel subpallida…). His treatise on bloodletting, De flebotomia, also contains an important discussion of haematoscopy, or diagnosis from the condition of blood. This constitutes something of an innovation in the medieval diagnostics, and Maurus' work dominated haematoscopy well into the early modern period. Also ascribed to his pen are an Anatomia, a brief work intended as a script to accompany the dissection of a pig. Like the Anatomy ascribed to Copho and the "Second Salernitan Demonstration," Maurus's anatomy begins by defining anatomy and justifying the use of a pig as a surrogate for the human body, before proceeding to a description of the organs in the order in which they are seen during a dissection. Maurus is also credited with a Practica, a treatise on fevers (De febribus compositis), and a work on veterinary medicine entitled Doctrina (or De curatione) equorum. His reputation is attested by laudatory epithets such as "optimus physicus" (in the necrology mentioned above) and "Galenienus Salernitanus" (in Paris, Bibliothèque nationale lat. 8654B, a manuscript of De flebotomia). De urinis in particular enjoyed enormous popularity, and was translated into Italian. Gilles de Corbeil also contributed to its diffusion by citing its doctrine in his own poem on uroscopy. A number of Maurus's works were also translated into Hebrew, and he is the most frequently cited Salernitan author in *Vincent of Beauvais' Speculum maius.

Maurus's work is essentially practical, but he displays a deep engagement with the philosophical foundations of medicine and the use of logical argumentation, notably in his Isagoge commentary. Topics that particularly attracted him were the nature of the *elements and qualities, the notion of mixture and complexion, and the biological phenomena that derive from these concepts. Maurus shared with Urso of Calabria an interest in the notion of the elementatum (the "elemented," or the element as it exists in the real world, rather than in a pure state), a topic much discussed in the School of Chartres. The scope and diffusion of his writings played an important role in acclimatizing Salernitan medicine to the Scholastic and Aristotelian milieu of the nascent universities.

See also **Aristotelianism; Medicine, practical; Medicine, theoretical**

Bibliography

Primary Sources

Benedict, K.H. "Die Demonstratio anatomica corporis animalis." Ph.D. dissertation, Universität Leipzig, 1920.

Buerschapper, Rudolf. "Ein bisher unbekannter Aderlasstraktät des Salernitaner Arztes Maurus." Ph.D. dissertation, Universität Leipzig,, 1919.

[Commentary on Aphorisms of Hippocrates]. Edited by Salvatore De Renzi, Collectio salernitana 4. 513–557. Naples: Tipografia del Filiatre-Sebezio, 1852–1859.

Maurus of Salerno, Twelfth-century 'Optimus Physicus' with his Commentary on the Prognostics of Hippocrates. Edited and translated by Morris Harold Saffron. Transactions of the American Philosophical Society n.s. vol. 69, pt. 1. Philadelphia: American Philosophical Society, 1972.

Morpurgo, Piero. Il commento al de pulsibus Philareti de Mauro Salernitano. Introduzione ed editione critica dal ms. Parisinus Latinus 18499. Dynamis (1987–1988) 7–8: 307–346.

Ploss, Werner Ludwig Heinrich. "Anatomia Mauri, eine bisher unbekannte salernitaner Skizze vom Bau des Menschen auf Grundlage einer Zergliederung des Tierkörpers." Ph.D. dissertation, Universität Leipzig, 1921.

Regulae urinarum (De urinis). Edited by De Renzi, Collectio salernitana 3.2–51 (1854).

Sudhoff, K. "Weitere Texte der Anatomia Mauri." Archiv für Geschichte der Medizin (1923) 14: 56–58.

Secondary Sources

Lenhardt, Friedrich. *Blutschau: Untersuchungen zur Entwicklung der Hämatoscopie.* Würzburger medizinhistorische Forschungen 22. Pattensen: H. Wellm, 1980.

Jacquart, Danielle. "Aristotelian Thought in Salerno." In *A History of Twelfth-Century Philosophy*, edited by Peter Dronke. New York: Cambridge University Press, 1988, pp. 407–428.

Morpurgo, Piero. "Il capitulo sugli elementi di Mauro Salernitano: 'Elementa' e 'elementata.' Un also aspetto della polemica tra Gerardo da Cremona e i 'philosophi salernitani.' In *Platonismo e Aristotelismo nel Mezzogiorno d'Italia (secc. XIV–XVI)*. Edited by Giuseppe Roccaro. Palermo: Officina di Studi Medievali, 1989, pp. 211–228.

Sudhoff, Karl. Constantin, der erste Vermittler muslimischer Wissenschaft ins Abendland und die beiden Salernitaner Frühscholastiker Maurus und Urso, als Exponenten dieser Vermittlung. *Archeion* (1932) 14: 359–369.

FAITH WALLIS

MEDICINE, PRACTICAL

The division of medicine into theory and practice, while not unknown in the early Middle Ages, was of limited interest in a period when medical education was largely informal. By contrast, the conceptual bedrock of Scholastic medicine is the distinction between *medicina practica* and *medicina theorica*, and the subordination of the former to the latter. (The article *Medicine, theoretical outlines some of the main trends of thought on this issue.) *Galen's *Tegni* supported the concept of practical medicine as the conservation and restoration of health, i.e., hygiene and therapeutics. Practice, in this sense, was defined by the goal of preventing or curing *mala complexio* or disrupted humoral balance. The main instrument of hygiene was regimen, which aimed to adjust or mitigate the "non-naturals" (environmental or behavioral factors such as climate, diet, etc.). Regimen was also, in principle at least, the initial stage in therapy: since the body's humors shared elemental qualities of heat, cold, moisture, and dryness with the natural world, they could be augmented or diminished by foods of particular qualities, or by activity such as exercise. In preventive regimen, the body's *complexio* was supported by providing it with food etc., which matched its temperament *similia similibus* ("like with like"). Used as therapy, however, regimen cured by counteracting dominant qualities in order to restore balance *contraria contrariis* ("contraries with contraries"). In the words of the thirteenth-century physician *Taddeo Alderotti, "all conservation is by similarity, all cure by contrary."

If efforts to rectify humoral disequilibrium through regimen failed, the next step was drugs. Drug therapy was conceived in two ways: either the drug was a more intense and concentrated form of diet therapy designed to produce effects of a generic nature (e.g., a carminative drug expelled flatulence) or on a particular organ (e.g., "cordials" strengthened the heart); or the drug was a means of evacuating corrupt humors from the body through vomiting or purgation. The literature on drug therapy ranged from theoretical consideration of the nature of drug action to more practically oriented manuals of *materia medica* and instructions for compound remedies.

Should the use of drugs fail to rectify or eliminate corrupt humors, the physician would then prescribe "surgery," i.e., evacuation by opening a vein (phlebotomy or blood-letting), by cautery, or by cupping (the application of heated cups to the skin in order to draw diseased matter from the interior of the body to its surface). Evacuative surgery formed part of the wider field of surgery, which also encompassed the repair of trauma (*solutio continuitatis*).

Choice and management of therapy were in principle the prerogatives of the learned physician, who possessed knowledge of the hidden causes of complexional disease, could interpret its signs, and on this basis predict its outcome. University-trained physicians aimed to distinguish their cognitive activity of clinical judgment and prescription from the manual work of drug preparation or surgery. These were to be delegated to subordinate apothecaries and surgeons or barbers. This hierarchy defined practice not with reference to its object, but with reference to its epistemological status as a intellective act, not mere "operation." It underpinned the more or less successful attempts by learned physicians to control other kinds of practitioners, and to qualify learned "practice" as uniquely rational and safe, especially with respect to diseases inside the body. The concern with professional boundaries of practice was often proportional to the economic and social stakes. Apothecaries were warned that they should only dispense, not prescribe; surgeons were admonished that they dealt only with the surface of the body: neither were to act without the physician's direction. Midwives attracted less attention, although assisting during normal birth might easily glide into the physician's domain if the midwife treated gynecological disorders or advised on the regimen of the pregnant woman. Finally, the medical care given to the sick poor in *hospitals by nursing sisters and brothers, even when it involved administration of drugs, was never the target of physicians. Doctors might serve hospitals for motives of piety, or be called in as consultants, but they had neither the opportunity nor the motivation to control the activities of charitable medicine.

Genres of Literature on *Medicina Practica*

The literature of medical practice is highly various in audience, format, and language. Scholastic classroom genres include glosses on Galen's treatises on diseases, symptoms, and treatment, or commentaries on the relevant portions of the great Arabic synopses, e.g., the section on fevers from *Ibn Sina's *Canon*, or books nine to twelve of *al-Razi's *Liber ad Almansorem*. At the "bedside" end is the physician's folding girdle-almanac, containing calendars, astrological information, blood-letting indications, and also perhaps a colored chart of urine types.

Manuals of general *practica* normally arranged diseases according to the body part affected, from head to toe (*a capite ad calcem*), with additional sections on fever and conditions such as paralysis that affected the whole body. *Bernard of Gordon's *Lilium medicinae*, a typical *practica* by an academic physician, adopts a systematic analytical grid for each disease, comprising definition, etiology, symptoms, prognosis, treatment, and *clarificatio* (related issues and controversies). Besides general *practica*, medical writers composed treatises on particular disease categories including fevers, individual diseases such as gout, and disorders of particular organs (e.g., the uterus). While *practica* are prescriptive rather the descriptive, the author's experience is often invoked to illustrate and val date the principles derived from Galen and the Arab medical authorities: the *ars* of medicine followed its *scientia*. But the literature of practical medicine also encompassed genres which thrust experience into the foreground. *Experimenta* are collections of tried-and-true remedies, devoid of theoretical explanation, but elevated above mere empiricism by the status of the author (e.g., *Arnau de Vilanova), and even the status of the patient who received the treatment. *Consilia* were letters or reports of advice to individuals which diagnosed an ailment and prescribed regimen and adjuvant drug therapy: professor-practitioners often collected their *consilia* for teaching purposes. Customized *regimina* for individuals, such as Arnau's *Regimen sanitatis ad regem Aragonum*, or for classes of people (soldiers on campaign, pregnant women, etc.) could also serve as instructional material.

Texts on medical practice, and particularly pharmacy and surgery, were also of interest to those practitioners who operated outside the ranks of the academically trained; this is increasingly the case in the later Middle Ages. Translations helped to disseminate *practica* to this wider audience. For example, the Latin *Compendium medicinae* of *Gilbertus Anglicus was translated into English, and condensed in the process through omission of theoretical material. The *Antidotarium* of *Nicholas of Salerno, a standard school text, was also translated and adapted for the working apothecary. Recipe collections are particularly widespread in both Latin and the vernacular, and seem to have interested every level of literate medieval society. Scholastic encyclopedias of surgery, such as the *Inventarium* of *Guy de Chauliac, were translated into various vernacular languages; indeed, *Henri de Mondeville composed his surgical treatise in both Latin and French versions. This is also the case with more modest productions, such as technical manuals on bloodletting. The dissemination of information on practical medicine was also allied to charity. Clerical authors bulk large in this sub-genre, such as *Petrus Hispanus (author of the *Thesaurus pauperum*, a handbook of cheap and simple treatments for the poor, or rather, for the parish priest to whom they turned for assistance), and John Mirfield (author of the *Breviarium Bartholomei*). The angelical conjunction of religion and medicine assumed a rather exceptional form in the writings of *Hildegard of Bingen.

See also Botany; Calendar; Elements and qualities; Gynecology and midwifery; Herbals; Instruments, medical; Medicine, theoretical; Pharmaceutic handbooks; Pharmacy; Pharmacology; *Regimen sanitatis*; Surgery

Bibliography

Agrimi, Jole and Chiara Crisciani. *Les consilia médicaux. Typologie des sources du moyen âge occidental*, 69. Turnhout: Brepols, 1994.

Demaitre, Luke. Scholasticism in Compendia of Practical Medicine, 1250–1450. *Manuscripta* (1976) 20: 81–95.

———. Theory and Practice in Medical Education at the University of Montpellier in the Thirteenth and Fourteenth Centuries. *Journal of the History of Medicine and Allied Sciences* (1975) 30: 103–119.

García-Ballester, Luis, Roger French, Jon Arrizabalaga and Andrew Cunningham, eds. *Practical Medicine from Salerno to the Black Death*. New York: Cambridge University Press, 1994.

Getz, Faye Marie. Charity, Translation, and the Language of Medical Learning in Medieval England. *Bulletin of the History of Medicine* (1990) 64: 1–17.

———, ed. and trans. *Healing and Society in Medieval England: a Middle English Translation of the Pharmaceutical Writings of Gilbertus Anglicus*. Madison: University of Wisconsin Press, 1991.

Jacquart, Danielle. "'Theorica' et 'practica' dans l'enseignement de la médecine à Salerne au XIIe siècle." In *Vocabulaire des écoles et des méthodes d'enseignement au moyen âge*, edited by Olga Weijers. Études sur le vocabulaire intellectuel du moyen âge 5. Turnhout: Brepols, 1992, pp. 102–110.

Jacquart, Danielle. "La pratique dans les oeuvres médicales de la fin du moyen âge." *Colloque international d'histoire de la médecine médiévale. Orléans, 4 et 5 mai 1985*. Orléans: Société orléanaise d'histoire de la médecine—Centre Jeanne d'Arc, 1985. Vol.1, pp. 55–63.

———. Theory, Everyday Practice, and Three Fifteenth-Century Physicians. *Osiris* (1990) 2nd ser., 6: 140–160.

McVaugh, Michael R. *Medicine Before the Plague. Practitioners and their Patients in the Crown of Aragon, 1285–1345*. New York: Cambridge University Press, 1993.

———. Arnald de Vilanova's *Regimen Almarie* (*Regimen castra sequentium*) and Medieval Military Medicine. *Viator* 23 (1992): 201–213.

———. The *Experimenta* of Arnald of Villanova. *Journal of Medieval and Renaissance Studies* (1971) 1: 107–118.

———. Quantified Medical Theory and Practice at Fourteenth Century Montpellier. *Bulletin of the History of Medicine* (1969) 43: 397–413.

Riddle, John M. Theory and Practice in Medieval Medicine. *Viator* (1974) 5: 157–170.

Voigts, Linda E. and Michael R. McVaugh. *A Latin Technical Phlebotomy and its Middle English Translation*. Transactions of the American Philosophical Society 74, 2. Philadelphia: American Philosophical Society, 1984.

FAITH WALLIS

MEDICINE, THEORETICAL

In the Hellenistic period, Aristotle's division of philosophy into theory (knowledge pursued as an end in itself) and practice (knowledge directed toward action) was applied to medicine. Herophilus of Calcedon divided medicine into three parts, corresponding to three epistemic objects: health, disease, and "neutral things" or factors capable of changing health into disease and vice versa. He called the category "health," comprising the study of the human body, its parts and processes, *to logikon*, or the "rational part" of medicine. His contemporary Erasistratus of Ceos distinguished the study of the body and of the causes of disease from the activities of diagnosis and therapy: the former he termed *to epistemikon* ("what is known with certainty"), the latter *to stochastikon* ("what is probable"). In his *Art of Medicine* (known to medieval readers as the *Tegni*), *Galen merged and refined these two schemes. Medicine is "the science which considers health, disease and the neutral state," but with respect to three things: (1) Body (broadly comprising the modern categories of anatomy and physiology); (2) Signs (medical semiology): and (3) Causes (disease etiology). The Arabic medical encyclopedists, notably *Hunayn ibn Ishaq, influenced by Aristotle, identified this triad as the theory of medicine. The practice of medicine comprised hygiene or preventive medicine (the regulation of the "neutrals"), and therapeutics. Philosophically oriented physicians such as *Ibn Sina (Avicenna), on the other hand, defined practice in epistemological terms: the practice of medicine is not the physician's action, but rather the knowledge which enables him to "form an opinion," that is, to decide on a plan of treatment (*Canon of Medicine* 1, fen 1, doctrine 1). Avicenna's formulation allowed western academic physicians to claim that practical medicine, while less epistemologically certain (being "opinion") than theory, was nonetheless a cognitive category, and therefore within the domain of philosophy.

Medieval Galenic Medical Theory

Early medieval medicine was rich in practical literature, but like the medicine of late antiquity apparently indifferent to or reserved about theory. Some theoretical texts of the Alexandrian curriculum were translated into Latin in or near *Ravenna in the sixth century, but they account for no more than a small percentage of surviving medical writings. In the Carolingian period, however, scholars speculating on the division of knowledge and the nature of the arts tentatively identified theoretical knowledge associated with medicine, particularly physiology, with natural philosophy (*physica*). Interest in medicine as *physica* intensified at the end of the tenth century. The historian Richer of Reims wrote a famous account of his own efforts to locate and study the *logica*—that is, the medical theory—of *Hippocrates. In the last decades of the eleventh century, *Constantine the African translated into Latin (and significantly adapted) the *Mas'il fit-tibb*, a schematic introduction to fundamental concepts of Galenic medical theory by *Hunayn ibn Ishaq, known in the West as Johannitius. This *Isagoge* (purportedly an "introduction" to Galen's *Tegni*) became the prefatory text of the *Articella*, and was studied by generations of medieval medical students. Its introduction into the Western canon of medicine, along with the first part of the *Kitab Kamil as-sin'a at-tibbya* (*Complete [or Perfect] Book of the Medical Art*) of *'Ali ibn al-Abbas al-Majusi (Haly Abbas), also translated by Constantine, signals a "theoretical turn" associated with the writings of Salernitan masters. The *Isagoge* is therefore an influential guide to the basic concepts and terms of medical theory, and the discussion of theory which follows here is largely based on it.

Medicine comprises the "naturals," i.e., the body and its parts; the "non-naturals," i.e., environmental or behavioral factors affecting the body for good or ill; and the "contra- naturals," i.e., disease conditions. The seven naturals represent a spectrum from the most material to the most "subtle" components of the body. They are: (1) the elements of the world (earth, air, fire, water); (2) their qualities (hot, cold, wet, dry); (3) their microcosmic cognates, the four bodily humors (blood, red bile, black bile, phlegm); (4) the solid members of the body formed from those humors; (5) the body's energies; (6) its operations; and (7) the "spirits" which control vital functions. To these, Johannitius adds the "accidental" factors of age, color, bodily shape, and sex.

The body is a macrocosm of the physical universe, and its life cycle replicates the seasons. This system of correspondences is held together by the elemental qualities: hot and wet (air, blood, childhood, spring), hot and dry (fire, red bile, youth, summer), cold and dry (earth, black bile, maturity, fall) and cold and wet (water, phlegm, old age, winter). Nonetheless, life is primarily sustained by heat and moisture (an idea borrowed from Aristotle's biology). Aging, for example, is understood as the gradual, natural qualitative change from hot and moist to cold and dry. Death is the extinction of the body's congenital quantum of innate heat and "radical moisture."

The humors combine to form the "homogeneous members," i.e., solid tissues such as bones and muscle, and liquids such as blood (the blood in the veins being a mixture of the humors). The homogeneous members combine to form heterogeneous members, i.e., organs such as the stomach or the hand.

The "principal" members are lodged in the three main cavities of the body: the brain within the skull, the heart (with its auxiliary member, the lungs) in the chest, and the liver (with digestive and reproductive members) in the abdomen. The principal members are the seats of the spirits (*spiritus*: subtle yet material entities which direct the functions of life) which manifest specific energies (*virtutes*). The liver is the instrument of the natural spirit (*spiritus naturalis*), whose action is the natural energy (*virtus naturalis*) that accomplishes nutrition, growth, and reproduction. Blood is manufactured in the liver from food, and distributed through the veins, from which it is taken up as nutriment by the various parts of the body at need. Digestion is a multi-stage process of transforming food into body, and at each stage, waste products are produced: feces from the first digestion in the stomach, urine from the second digestion in the liver during the process of blood production, and various material extrusions such as hair and earwax from the third digestion in the veins, and the fourth in the members (women, being naturally colder and wetter than men, and hence incapable of complete digestion, also produce a residue of menstrual blood). This entire process is conceptualized as "coction" or cooking. The body's actions in gaining mastery over corrupt or excessive humors, or in repairing a wound, are also understood as a kind of digestion, which produces waste products such as pus. The heat required for coction is furnished by the vital spirit (*vitalis spiritus*), whose seat is the heart. Air drawn in by the lungs is transformed by the heat and vital spirit in the heart into inspirited air, which is distributed to the body through the arteries, mixed with blood. On reaching the brain, this inspirited air is transformed into "animal spirit" (*spiritus animalis*, i.e., the spirit responsible for *anima*, the functions of sensation, motion, and cognition) and conveyed by the nerves (conceived as hollow vessels) to the members.

The organs of the body also possess "faculties" (*operationes, facultates*). For Galen, the faculties were the *pneumata* or spirits, as manifest in their workings or effects. Arab writers connected four of these to the general physiological model through a pair of qualities: the "appetitive faculty" is hot and dry, the "digestive faculty" hot and moist, the "retentive faculty" cold and dry, and the "expulsive faculty" cold and moist. For example, the uterus is understood to draw in semen through its "appetitive faculty" in order to conceive; its "retentive faculty" allows it to contain the growing fetus, while its "expulsive faculty" is activated during birth. The arteries throb because the vital spirit endows them with a "pulsatile faculty."

Health is the proper balance (*complexio* or *temperamentum*, translating the Greek *krasis*) of the qualities, and the proper symmetry (*compositio*) of the heterogeneous members. Strictly speaking, *complexio* is the balance of qualities, but most medical writers (especially Avicenna) thought of it as a balance of humors. Balanced *complexio* is relative and individual, leading to the notion of "latitude of health." Medieval writers speak of individual temperament not as absolutely balanced, but as "justly" balanced (*ad iustitiam*), and often compare it to a well-governed kingdom. Hence, rather than thinking in terms of "the normal" they prefer to speak of what is "natural" to the individual, age group or sex. Finally, the different parts of the body have their proper *complexiones*: e.g., the brain is cold and moist. Soft organs are usually identified as wet, hard organs (such as the sinewy heart) as dry.

Galen's phrase for "non-naturals" is "necessary (i.e., unavoidable) things." This is the third of his three categories of "corruption," the first two being natural and unavoidable qualitative change (i.e., aging) and accidental and avoidable change (poison, wounds, etc.). The only area over which medicine claims some control is the third category of "accidental, unavoidable things," the non-naturals. The first aim of medicine is therefore to prevent illness and maintain health.

The non-naturals are environmental and behavioral factors influencing health and disease: air, food and drink, elimination and retention, exercise and rest, sleep and wakefulness, psychological states (Johannitius adds sexual activity to this list). The science of the non-naturals belongs to medical theory; precepts based on this science are conveyed through *regimina sanitatis*.

In manuals of theory such as the *Isagoge*, the contranaturals or disease states are classified into three broad categories: (1) *Mala complexio* or disorders of temperament (humoral balance); (2) *Mala compositio* or congenital defect; and (3) *Solutio continuitatis*, "breach of continuity" or trauma. Thus disease was not precisely an entity in Galenic medicine, but an event ("accident") or state. Drawing on Aristotelian *hylomorphism, doctors defined health and disease as "forms determining matter"; hence medieval physicians regarded as disease what a modern doctor would term clinical presentation or symptom. Such disease specificity as exists in medieval medical theory lies closer to the modern concept of the syndrome: hence, a *morbus* was a disease of *mala complexio* with a proper name designating a particular cluster of symptoms (e.g., gout, leprosy, migraine). Ontologically, this was a fairly weak concept, because a *morbus* could manifest differently in patients of different complexion, and one *morbus* could change into another. Leprosy presented an interesting challenge to this model. Particularly in the fourteenth and fifteenth centuries, and apparently in response to increasing demands on the medical profession for expert opinion in accusations of leprosy, authors such as *Gilbertus Anglicus and Jordanus de Turre concentrated on cataloguing the features of leprosy that were definitive and invariable. The Black Death posed a different type of problem, for its universal scope defied the Hippocratic model of an "epidemic" as a local outbreak of acute and virulent disease. Learned commentators invoked cosmological and astrological explanations based on the notion of a global *infectio* or tainting of the atmosphere, with consequent poisoning of the soil, water, foodstuffs, etc., over wide regions. Although plague might be caused by environmental factors, it was understood to spread through contact (*contagio*).

All *morbi* are diseases of *mala complexio* or humoral imbalance leading to the "putrefaction" or "corruption" of the humors. The Hippocratic root of this image seems to be a septic wound, which not only looks and smells like rotting meat, but is also accompanied by swelling and heat. Hence fever and swellings ("apostemes") are the two basic genera of *morbi*, a fever being the expression of an internal humoral putrefaction.

Diagnosis rested on the decoding of signs which revealed the body's state, and identified the disease-event. The physician laid great store on inspection of the patient's excreta, especially the urine, since waste products of digestion indicated the state of the natural spirit. Of equal importance was the pulse, seen as the direct action of the vital spirit in the arteries. Supplementing these were a wide array of signals which could be read in the face, eyes, posture, comportment, and skin color of the patient, as well as in the presence or absence of clinical events such as sweating and seizures. While the *Isagoge* of Johannitius provided the overall conceptual framework of semiology, the other books in the *Articella*—Hippocrates' *Aphorisms* and *Prognostics*, *On Pulses* by Philaretus, and *On Urine* by Theophilus—furnished its substance. The Scholastic physician's concern to rationalize prognosis focused increased attention on mathematical techniques, such as calculating the "critical days" when the disease would take a turn for better or worse. In the later Middle Ages, universities, especially in Italy, promoted medical *astrology as a technique for more precise and reliable diagnosis and prognosis.

Diagnostic classification of fevers according to their seat was a very important part of medieval pathology, as it affected both prognosis and therapy. An "ephemeral fever" was located in one of the three principal spirits discussed above; a "putrid fever" was caused by the corruption of one of the four humors; a "hectic fever" was seated in the solid members. Putrid fevers in turn were classified according to the humor affected, which was revealed by the fever's periodicity: corrupt blood produces continued fever (*synochus*); red bile produces tertian fever (paroxysm every three days, counting inclusively); phlegm produces quotidian fever (i.e., recurring every day); and melancholy produces quartan fever (recurring every four days).

"Swellings" covers inflammation, as well as tumors or boils. These are classified according to the responsible humor; cancer, for example, is an aposteme caused by burnt or "adust" melancholy.

Other classification schemes allowed physicians to nuance the idea of disease localization. A "similar" disease is a condition which can occur in any member, e.g., "aching." A "universal" disease affects the whole body, e.g., paralysis. An "official" disease acts on a specific member, e.g., gout. Johannitius's subdivision of official diseases shows how this schema cuts across the distinctions of *mala complexio*, *mala compositio*, and *solutio continuitatis*. He distinguishes official diseases according to the following criteria: (1) shape, including what we would consider normal variations in shape, e.g., a long head, or flat feet, as well as pathological conditions, e.g. "roughness of the trachea or bronchi"; (2) size; (3) number, defined as any abnormality of augmentation or diminution, e.g., polydactylism, but also worms and warts; (4) position, i.e., removal of a member from its proper place or some defect in relation to neighboring parts (e.g., hare lip).

The Literature of Theorical Medicine

Western scholars took their first steps towards original thinking on medical theory in the twelfth century by composing commentaries on the *Articella* texts. The earliest are anonymous, but after mid-century they are signed by authors including *Bartholomaeus of Salerno, *Maurus of Salerno, *Urso of Calabria, and later *Petrus Hispanus. The thirteenth century saw the expansion of the canon of medical theory. The principal works studied and commented on in the universities were now the first book of *Canon* of Ibn Sina, and a number of newly available texts by Galen, including *On Accident and Illness* (*De accidenti et morbo*), *On Complexions* (*De complexionibus*), *On Illness of Diverse Complexion* (*De malicia complexionis diverse*), *Distinguishing Fevers* (*De differentiis febrium*), *Critical Days* (*De diebus criticis*), *On Affected Parts* (*De locis affectis*, known in the Middle Ages as *De interioribus*), and an adapted version of *The*

Usefulness of Parts entitled *De iuvamentis membrorum*. The last two works were important in the development of academic anatomy based on human dissection; *Mondino de' Liuzzi structured his dissection lessons as "material commentaries" on these treatises.

Commentary, together with its offshoot, the *quaestio*, was a principle genre of Scholastic writing on medical theory. A commentary on the *Isagoge*, one on the first book of the *Tegni*, another on books One and Two of the *Canon*, and perhaps one on the *Aphorisms* of Hippocrates were *de rigueur* for academic physicians. By the end of the medieval period, theory was taught and debated not only through these primary texts, but in the light of authoritative commentaries by *Taddeo Alderotti, Tommaso del Garbo, *Torregiano de' Torregiani, *Gentile da Foligno, Jacopo da Forlì, and Jacques Despars. There was, however, a parallel stream of reflection on physiology associated with the study of Aristotle's natural philosophy, particularly the biological writings, *De anima*, and the *Problemata*. Aristotle's attention to medical issues attracted philosophers to medical theory, and physicians to Peripatetic philosophy. One of the best-known medieval analyses of conception and embryogenesis is by the theologian *Giles of Rome, while in the Italian universities, where arts and medicine were taught in the same faculty, physician-philosophers such as *Pietro d'Abano found fertile ground for speculation in the *Problemata*.

Issues in Theoretical Medicine

Aristotle's influence also determined which questions connected with medical theory attracted sustained interest. Perhaps the most important was the nature of medicine and medical knowledge itself. Although properly speaking a debate on epistemology or method rather than theory, this question functioned typically as an opportunity to define and defend medicine's identity as theory, and to clarify its relationship with *physica*. The question itself is invariably formulated in Aristotelian terms. Is medicine a *scientia*? If so, is it a speculative *scientia*, or a practical one? Or is medicine an *ars*, i.e., an intellectual skill employed in doing or making something? What medicine *was* had implications for how it should be *taught*, its *doctrina*. Galen in the *Tegni* seems to state that medicine's *doctrina* comprises *resolutio* and *compositio*, terms which he himself does not clearly define, but which were interpreted as equivalent to Aristotelian induction and deduction. Ibn Sina likewise reduced the "naturals" and "non-naturals" to Aristotle's four-fold schema of causation. Commentaries on the *Tegni* and the opening chapter of the *Canon* were therefore the classic occasions for addressing this issue.

The second zone of debate encompassed issues where Aristotle's views of the body and its processes seemed to conflict with those of Galen and the Arab medical writers. The primacy of the heart in Aristotelian physiology apparently conflicted with Galen's Hellenistic model of three principal members; similarly, Galen's understanding of conception as the union of male and female seed was impossible to reconcile with Aristotle's doctrine that the male contributed form alone, and the female only matter to the act of generation. Although somewhat atypical, the *Conciliator* of Pietro d'Abano stands as an eloquent symbol of the intense dialogue of Aristotle and Galen in the medical faculties.

See also **Anatomy, human; Aristotelianism;** *Articella;* **Elements and qualities; Galen; Hippocrates; Medicine, practical; Nature: the structure of the physical world; Plague tractates; Psychology;** *Regimen sanitatis;* **Salerno; Scholasticism; Universities**

Bibliography

Bono, James J. Medical Spirits and the Medieval Language of Life. *Traditio* (1984) 40: 91–130.

Bylebyl, Jerome J. The Medical Meaning of *Physica. Osiris* (1990) 2nd ser. 6: 16–41.

Cadden, Joan. "Albertus Magnus' Universal Physiology: the Example of Nutrition." In *Albertus Magnus and the Sciences: Commemorative Essays.* Edited by James Weisheipl. Toronto: Pontifical Institute of Mediaeval Studies, 1980.

Campbell, Anna. *The Black Death and Men of Learning.* New York: AMS, 1966. Reprint of 1931 ed.

Demaitre, Luke. The Description and Diagnosis of Leprosy by Fourteenth-Century Physicians. *Bulletin of the History of Medicine* (1985) 59: 327–344.

French, Roger. De iuvamenis membrorum and the Reception of Galenic Physiological Anatomy. *Isis* (1979) 70: 96–109.

Jacquart, Danielle. "Medical Scholasticism." In *Western Medical Thought from Antiquity to the Middle Ages.* Edited by Mirko D. Grmek. Cambridge, Mass: Harvard University Press, 1998.

———. La médecine médiévale dans le cadre parisien. Paris: Fayard, 1998.

———. "La question disputée dans les Facultés de médecine." In *Les questions disputées dans les Facultés de Théologie, de Droit, et de Médecine.* Edited by B.C. Bazàn, G. Fransen, D. Jacquart and J.W. Wippel. Typologie des sources du moyen âge occidental, 44–45. Turnhout: Brepols, 1985.

Jacquart, Danielle and Françoise Micheau. *La médecine arabe et l'Occident médiévale.* Paris: Maisonneuve et Larose, 1990.

Jordan, Mark D. Medicine as Science in the Early Commentaries on 'Johannitius'. *Traditio* (1987) 43: 121–145.

Lawn, Brian. *The Rise and Decline of the Scholastic 'Quaestio Disputata' with Special Emphasis on its Use in the Teaching of Medicine and Science.* Leiden: E.J. Brill, 1993.

McVaugh, Michael. The Humidum Radicale in Thirteenth Century Medicine. *Traditio* (1974) 30: 259–283.

Ottosson, P.-G. *Scholastic Medicine and Philosophy. A Study of Commentaries on Galen's "Tegni" (ca. 1300–1450).* Naples: Bibliopolis, 1984.

Rather, L.J. The 'Six Things Non-Natural': a Note on the Origins and Fate of a Doctrine and a Phrase. *Clio Medica* (1968) 3: 337–347.

Schöner, E. *Das Vierschema in der antiken Humoralpathologie.* Sudhoffs Archiv, Beiheft 4. Wiesbaden: Steiner, 1964.

Siraisi, Nancy G. *Medieval and Early Renaissance Medicine. An Introduction to Knowledge and Practice.* Chicago: University of Chicago Press, 1990.

FAITH WALLIS

METAPHYSICS

To the medieval mind, metaphysics was that science or body of learning which stood at the head of all other branches of human knowledge because it was the source of their ordering principles. The term was first used by early editors of the works of Aristotle to designate the books that came after the books on nature—literally *meta ta physika* ("after the physics"). Later thinkers, perhaps influenced by Neoplatonism, read much more into it than that. Since Aristotle speaks of metaphysics as the investigation of the ultimate causes of things and as the "science of first principles," it made sense to think of it as prior to the other, more specialized sciences, as the source of their principles, and therefore, as constituting the highest form of human wisdom. By late antiquity, the concept of metaphysics as the ordinatrix, or active ordering principle, of all other knowledge was already well established.

Metaphysics is a theory about what ultimately exists. This was important for medieval scientists because it told them the kinds of things that could figure in the explanation of natural phenomena. Metaphysics also provided the rationale for dividing the special sciences into an orderly system reflecting the rationality and goodness of its creator: physics, for example, is concerned with bodies insofar as they move; its subaltern or derivative science of psychology with movement insofar as it is animate. This tended to favor teleological explanations, since most thinkers subscribed to the principle that at least in its normal operations, which are what God has ordained for the world, Nature never acts *frustra* (without a purpose). Of course, unexplained deficiencies in the natural order could implicate God's goodness, or omnipotence, or both, so their working assumption was that our failure to understand a phenomenon must be due to individual human ignorance, or fallibility, or both.

Universals and Particulars

Because they believed that the existence of absolutely everything other than God depends on God's having freely chosen to create it, medieval philosophers were much more interested than their Greek and Roman counterparts in determining the nature of being. At issue here was not only the nature of God's necessary being as opposed to the contingent being of creatures, but also the question of whether the categories we use to classify created beings have any reality over and above our concepts of them. Surely if it is true to say that my dog and my house are both brown, they must have something in common, some real nature or quality that makes them so? Porphyry (c. 232–304) was the first to raise the question of the ontological status of the concepts of genus, species, difference, necessary attribute, and accident in his *Isagoge* or introduction to Aristotle's *Categories*, although he sets it aside as too difficult for his audience. Two centuries later, *Boethius reexamined the question in his commentaries on Aristotle and Porphyry, developing what has become known as the moderate realist view that universals are real without being entities or things. His treatment determined the agenda of the medieval debate, which waxed and waned for the next thousand years in a wide variety of contexts and disciplines.

The debate was complicated by the fact that its participants did not always distinguish clearly between the linguistic question of the function of universal predicates (e.g., the notion "is brown"), which Aristotle had discussed in *De interpretatione*, from the metaphysical question of the nature of universal attributes, which is what Porphyry and Boethius had added to the mix. Sometimes this led to an author advancing two theories. *Peter Abelard, for example, seems to have a nominalist account of universal names or terms (i.e., universals "name" only particular things, such as particular dogs and houses), and a realist account of universal attributes (i.e., things having the same color share the status, e.g., the status of being brown, without having anything in common). These theories tended to be very sophisticated and went far beyond similar discussions in antiquity. It is worth noting that *Plato's theory of exemplar universals, according to which universals have an eternal mode of existence that transcends the things of this world, was known but widely rejected, again because it clashed with the assumption that everything in the universe, from mud to angels, depends for its existence on God's creative act.

From a scientific point of view, what was at stake in the debate over universals was the status of scientific knowledge. The nominalist who claims that universals are merely linguistic or conceptual categories can avoid the embarrassment of having to posit real entities that do not really exist, which is what the defender of real attributes seems committed to. No one has met brownness all by itself, apart from brown dogs and brown houses. But nominalism has its own embarrassments. In the absence of real causal relations, for example, a strict nominalist would have no way of explaining how one thing could be the cause of another, since every instance of cause and effect would be a unique event. In the fourteenth century, *John Buridan argued that common concepts are based on the fact that particular things just naturally resemble each other, and that although our intellects are capable of recognizing such similarities, we are not acquainted with anything in the particulars that justifies this. Here it was customary to cite a passage from the *Liber Sex Principiorum* (*Book of Six Principles*, referring to the last six of Aristotle's ten categories) of Gilbert of Poitiers (1076–1154): "Nature operates in a hidden fashion [*occulte*] with regard to universals." Buridan tries to anticipate skeptical worries by arguing that it is not possible to achieve absolute certainty in this life, and that, in the absence of compelling reasons to think otherwise, our empirical judgments are reliable enough to justify our claim to have knowledge of the external world.

By the mid-fourteenth century, nominalism—or what is more accurately called conceptualism—had become the default position of most philosophers who thought about these questions, so that in the later medieval period it is more accurate to think of nominalism as a parsimonious way of doing philosophy than as a doctrine denying the existence of real universals. The manifesto of later medieval nominalism has come down to us in the form of "Ockham's razor," which states that "entities are not to be multiplied beyond necessity" (*entia non sunt multiplicanda praeter necessitatem*). Of course, nominalists disagreed about how many entities one must posit. *William of Ockham, for example, believed that everything can be explained with the categories of substance and quality, but Buridan rejects this, claiming one also needs the category of quantity, since it is not possible to "qualify" quantity.

Metaphysics was completely transformed in the Latin West by the recovery of Aristotle's *Metaphysics* in the middle of the eleventh century. Along with this important text came translations of commentaries on Aristotle's works from the Islamic intellectual tradition. Medieval philosophers relied extensively on commentators such as *Ibn Sina (Avicenna) and later, *Ibn Rushd (Averroes), to make sense of Aristotle's difficult remarks. Together, these new sources provided metaphysicians with a whole new range of analytical tools that could assist them in their study of the natural world. The most influential of these were the distinctions between form and matter, substance and accident, and essence and existence. Aristotle's four "causes" or principles of explanation were also appropriated, which allowed them to distinguish between inquiries into the matter or "stuff" of which something is made (material cause); its form or pattern (formal cause); its maker or agent source (efficient cause); and its end or purpose (final cause). Although Aristotle seems to have regarded final cause as a local principle, concerned with the particular ends of living things (apple seeds tend to become apple trees), medieval thinkers read it globally as well, in terms of the orderly structure of a natural world which they saw as filled with signs of divine providence. The application of these concepts can be seen in the Five Ways of *Aquinas, which seek to demonstrate the existence of God using the notions of efficient, formal, and final cause.

By the fourteenth century, however, explanations in terms of efficient causes came to dominate natural philosophy, whereas teleological explanations were viewed with suspicion (except in accounts of human action, which seemed obviously purposive). This was due in part to the popularity of nominalist methods in natural philosophy. For Ockham, Buridan, and *Nicole Oresme, teleological argumentation moves in the wrong direction, beginning with the assumption (mistaken, in their minds) that we have special access to the seminal reasons God used to create the world. They could not square this with the fact that the world we encounter is everywhere filled with particular things whose structure and relationships can only be surmised from experience—an experience that is also limited and fallible. Accordingly, they argued that the principles of natural science must originate from the things whose operations they seek to explain, even if this means we can no longer view them as self-evident. This subtle shift in orientation helped set the stage for modern empirical science.

See also **Aristotelianism; Reason**

Bibliography

Primary Sources

Bosley, Richard, and Martin Tweedale (eds.). *Basic Issues in Medieval Philosophy*. Peterborough, Ont.: Broadview Press, 1997.

Frank, William A., and Allan B. Wolter, ed. & tr. *Duns Scotus: Metaphysician*. West Lafayette: Purdue University Press, 1995.

Hyman, Arthur, and James J. Walsh, eds. *Philosophy in the Middle Ages: The Christian, Islamic, and Jewish Traditions*. Second Edition. Indianapolis: Hackett, 1987.

Spade, Paul V., ed. and tr. *Five Texts on the Mediaeval Problem of Universals: Porphyry, Boethius, Abelard, Duns Scotus, Ockham*. Indianapolis: Hackett, 1994.

Tweedale, Martin. *Scotus vs. Ockham: A Medieval Dispute over Universals*. Texts Translated into English with Commentary. 2 vols. Lewiston: Edwin Mellen Press, 1999.

Secondary Sources

Adams, Marilyn McCord. *William Ockham*. 2 vols. Notre Dame: University of Notre Dame Press, 1987.

Henninger, Mark. *Relations: Medieval Theories, 1250–1325*. Oxford: Clarendon Press, 1989.

Jordan, Mark D. *Ordering Wisdom: The Hierarchy of Philosophical Discourses in Aquinas*. Notre Dame: University of Notre Dame Press, 1986.

King, Peter. "Abelard on Metaphysics." In *The Cambridge Companion to Abelard*. Edited by Jeffrey Brower and Kevin Guilfoy. New York: Cambridge University Press, 2004, pp. 65–125.

Zupko, Jack. *John Buridan: Portrait of a Fourteenth-Century Arts Master*. Notre Dame: University of Notre Dame Press, 2003.

JACK ZUPKO

METEOROLOGY

During the Middle Ages meteorology was typically considered to be the science of material change in the sublunary region, which comprises the Earth and the area between the Earth and the Moon. This subject was far more inclusive than it is in modern times and included not just the weather, but also all atmospheric phenomena, including phenomena such as comets and the Milky Way, which we no longer consider to be atmospheric, earthquakes, volcanoes, and the motions of the sea and rivers, such as tides and flooding. From antiquity and throughout the medieval period, meteorology was a standard part of the study of *natural philosophy. As a result, a large number of the most widely read natural philosophers wrote specific treatises on meteorology or included discussions of this subject in encyclopedic works or handbooks. Unlike today's meteorology, the field was not dedicated primarily to prediction but rather to causation and explanation. Some authors, however, investigated how future weather phenomena could be inferred from signs; one prominent method, astrometeorology, used observations of celestial bodies as a means for forecasting the weather. While frequently derivative of Aristotle's writings, especially in the Islamic world and the later Middle Ages in Christian Western Europe, meteorological works showed a wide range of approaches and utilized a variety of sources. Since it was believed that the cause of weather phenomena was connected to the motions of celestial bodies and because of the weather's manifest connections to human health, astronomy, *astrology, and medicine were often closely tied to meteorology.

Ancient Sources

Medieval meteorology was heavily influenced by ancient writings. Which ancient authors were most influential depended on place, time, and linguistic and philosophical culture. The first three books of Aristotle's *Meteorology* provided the framework for many treatments of meteorology. Additionally, it was a subject for commentaries and university lectures. Other influential ancient texts included Seneca's *Natural Questions*, which had particular currency during the early Middle Ages in the Latin West, the Hippocratic *Airs, Waters, Places*, which explained how changes in weather and climate affect health, and the Aristotelian *Problemata*.

Aristotle's *Meteorology* was known and transmitted through translations. In the ninth century, Yayha ibn al-Bitriq translated into Arabic a paraphrase of this work that was subsequently circulated throughout the Islamic world. Several new translations were made during the thirteenth century, when Samuel ibn Tibbon rendered the work into Hebrew and *Gerard of Cremona made a Latin translation from the Arabic version. In the 1260s, Gerard's version was superseded by *William of Moerbeke's translation composed directly from the Greek. This version remained the standard for centuries. Alexander of Aphrodisias's commentary, written in the second century C.E., was also known in the Islamic world and in the Christian West after William of Moerbeke's translation of it, again in the 1260s. Mahieu le Vilain translated the work into French vernacular around the end of the thirteenth century.

General Framework

By and large, medieval accounts of meteorology were informed by Aristotelian, Ptolemaic, and Neoplatonic understandings of geocentric *cosmology. It was held that the cosmos could be conceptually and spatially divided; the Earth and the space below the sphere of the Moon, the sublunary region, is the center of the universe and characterized by physical instability and perpetual change. All substances in this region are compounds of the four elements: earth, water, air, and fire. Under the influence of the active primary qualities, the hot and the cold, these elements transform into each other. Meteorology is the science of these transformations. For Aristotle, unlike other kinds of knowledge regarding nature, meteorological explanations had little recourse to teleology or formal causes. Rather, material and efficient causation accounts for meteorological change. The Sun is the efficient or moving cause that acts on matter, composed out of the four elements. Precisely how the Sun affects the sublunary region, whether from heat generated by motion or transmission of heat rays, remained a subject of debate from antiquity throughout the Middle Ages. In any case, the Sun causes the elements to form into two exhalations, one moist and similar to vapor, the other dry and smoky. These exhalations circulate from the surface of the Earth to sphere of the Moon. Their motions and mutual transformations result in weather phenomena, such as clouds, precipitation, lightning, and thunder, as well as meteor showers, comets, the Milky Way, and other "fires" in the sky. The irregular nature of these phenomena confirms their sublunary status. Analogous exhalations move underneath the surface of the Earth and are responsible for earthquakes, volcanic eruptions, hot springs, the formation of metals, and other subterranean and what we would describe as seismic events. While the exhalations are the unifying causes of change in the sublunary region, geometrical explanations are given for the rainbow. As a result, Aristotle's text became a key source for those who desired to apply mathematical optics to the natural world.

For Aristotle, the knowledge of meteorology is imperfect. Because of the irregularity of happenings in the sky and the difficulty in observing them accurately, Aristotle presented his explanations with caution and noted the inconclusiveness of his theories. In general Aristotelian concepts were prominent in medieval writings on meteorology, although they were frequently adapted, altered, and transformed. In both antiquity and the Middle Ages, naturalistic explanations for the weather were favored. As a result, the idea that lightning and thunder had divine origins was widely rejected or ignored.

Early Latin Medieval Meteorology (Pre-1200)

Because of the centrality of meteorology to natural philosophy, a large number of authors addressed these issues from antiquity onwards. In the early Middle Ages many prominent authors took up these questions. *Isidore of Seville's *Etymologies*, *Bede's *On the Nature of Things*, Pseudo-Bede's *On the Constitution of the Heavenly and Terrestrial Worlds*, the *Salernitan Questions*, *William of Conches' *On Philosophy*, and *Adelard of Bath's *Natural Questions* either defined or explained meteorological issues, such as winds, thunder, lightning, tides, flooding, and the division of the world into climatic zones. It was most commonly held that the world was divided into five zones, a middle zone that was excessively hot, two temperate inhabited zones, and two zones of extreme cold. These authors theorized without the benefit of direct access to Aristotle's writings, rather informing themselves by late-Roman writings, Calcidius's abbreviated version of *Plato's *Timaeus*, and perhaps some Arabic sources.

Islamic Meteorology

Practitioners of *falsafa*, a form of Islamic philosophy inspired by the Greek tradition, wrote numerous works on meteorology. Some of the most heralded Islamic philosophers took up this field. The fifth book of the *Kitab al-Shifa* by *Ibn Sina (Avicenna), the *Short and Middle Commentaries on the Meteorology* of *Ibn Rushd (Averroes), and the *Commentary on the Meteorology* of *Ibn Bajja (Avempace) should be counted among these. Islamic authors developed interpretations found not only in al-Bitriq's paraphrase of Aristotle, but also in a compendium by *Hunayn ibn Ishaq, a paraphrase of Olympiodorus's *Commentary on the Meteorology* written in Greek in the sixth century C.E., and a version of Alexander of Aphrodisias's *Commentary on the Meteorology*. These works had different approaches and goals. For example, Ibn Rushd tried to reconcile Alexander and Aristotle, while Ibn Sina's approach was more critical and included additional explanations and appeals to experience not found in ancient texts. Both of their works were translated into Latin and had significant influence on medieval Christian authors.

Latin Meteorology in the Later Middle Ages

Soon after the translation of Aristotle's *Meteorology* into Latin in the first part of the thirteenth century, an Englishman, *Alfred of Sareschel, wrote the first Latin commentary on this work. By the end of the century, Aristotle's work had found a fixed place in university curricula. Public lectures and disputations on this text proliferated, as is evidenced by the more than one hundred known authors who commented on this text between 1200 and 1500. Following *al-Farabi, many medieval scholars considered meteorology to follow thematically the abstract discussions of the elements and qualities as found in *On Generation and Corruption* and to lead to treatments of biology and the soul. *John Buridan labeled the subject of this work "imperfect mixtures," meaning compounds of elements that had not received a substantial form and thus were easily subject to *generation and corruption. Buridan's label stuck, and commentators, even as late as the seventeenth century, described the book's contents in a similar fashion. Among the other more influential commentators on this work were: *Albertus Magnus, *Thomas Aquinas, Peter of Auvergne, *Nicole Oresme, Themo of Judea, Walter Burley, *Pierre D'Ailly, and Blasius of Parma. While Aristotelian commentary literature dominated the field, meteorological questions were also treated in encyclopedic works, such as *Vincent of Beauvais's *Speculum maior*, hexaemeral literature, and commentaries on *Peter Lombard's *Sentences*.

Astrometeorology and Medicine

The field of astrometeorology, while existing in antiquity, was renewed in the medieval Islamic world. Many Christian scholars appropriated and added to this Islamic intellectual tradition. Intimately tied to astrology, the premise of astrometeorology is that because of connections between astral bodies and sublunary substances, it is possible to prognosticate the weather on the basis of the position of the Sun, the Moon, the planets, and the stars. While the effects of the Moon and especially the

Sun on the terrestrial region seem obvious, the powers of planets and stars were attested to in theoretically sophisticated writings, such as those by Avicenna and *Abu Ma'shar al-Balkhi (Albumashar), who explained how celestial intelligences and emanations affected and created terrestrial substances. *Al-Kindi's *On Rains*, which directly addressed prognostication, continued to be widely circulated in Latin during the fifteenth century, as did *Robert Grosseteste's *De impressionibus aeris* (*On Things Seen in the Air*). Grosseteste also authored a work that explained the tides as being caused by lunar influences. While astrometeorology was potentially a field with practical applications, for instance for agriculture or military campaigns, the audience for these treatises was most likely professional scholars.

Meteorological studies were extremely pertinent to medical sciences. Because the dominant humoral theory of disease was based on the premise that health was the result of balance of four humors (blood, yellow bile, black bile, phlegm) that were characterized and affected by the sensible qualities of hot, cold, wet, and dry, the understood effects of weather and climate on health were legion. Following Hunayn ibn Ishaq's *Isagoge* (*Introduction to Medicine*), air was widely considered to be one of the non-naturals, that is, something external to the body that affects health. Thus changes in the temperature and quality of air were seen to be major determinants of disease and part of the larger notion of *regimen sanitatis*, whereby patients altered their patterns of eating, drinking, sleeping, in order to secure better health. Portions of the Aristotelian *Problemata* also deal with the relation between health and weather. Most notably the Italian physician *Pietro D'Abano wrote a lengthy commentary on this work that discussed this issue in detail.

See also **Aristotelianism; Elements and qualities; Medicine, practical; Medicine, theoretical; Universities**

Bibliography

Boyer, Carl B. *The Rainbow from Myth to Mathematics.* Princeton: Princeton University Press, 1987.
Ducos, Joëlle. *La météorologie en français au Moyen Age (XIIe-XIVe siècles).* Paris: Honoré Champion, 1998.
Jenks, Stuart. Astrometeorology in the Middle Ages. *Isis* (1983) 74: 185–210.
Lettinck, Paul. *Aristotle's Meteorology and Its Reception in the Arab World.* Leiden: E.J. Brill, 1999.
Taub, Liba. *Ancient Meteorology.* New York: Routledge, 2003.

CRAIG MARTIN

MICHAEL SCOT

Michael Scot evidently was from Scotland. Our earliest knowledge of him, however, is as a *magister* in the entourage of Rodrigo Jiménez de Rada, archbishop of Toledo, at the Fourth Lateran Council in 1215. On August 18, 1217, he completed a translation of *al-Bitruji's *On

the Movements of the Heavens, with the help of a certain "Abuteus Iudeus." Before 1220 he had translated in *Toledo the nineteen Arabic books of Aristotle's *De animalibus* (*On Animals*), which consisted of the Description of Animals, Parts of Animals, and Generation of Animals. In the 1220s we find him in Bologna (1220) and winning the support of Popes Honorius III (1224–1225), who praised him for his "singular learning" (*singularis scientia*), and Gregory IX (1227), who credited him with knowing Hebrew, Arabic, and Latin. Both popes obtained for him benefices in England and Scotland (he refused the archbishopric of Cashel in Tipperary on the

Unidentified man sitting on a throne with a book. From late-twelfth/early-thirteenth century manuscript of a work by Scottish magician Michael Scot. (Topham/The British Library/HIP)

grounds that he did not know Irish). He dedicated a translation of Averroes' (*Ibn Rushd's) Large Commentary on Aristotle's *On the Heavens* to Stephen of Provins, who, in 1231, had been appointed by Pope Gregory IX to head a commission for purging the newly translated works of Aristotle from statements incompatible with Christian belief.

By the late 1220s Michael Scot was in the court of *Frederick II of Sicily and describes himself as the "astrologer" (*astrologus*) of the Emperor. He dedicated to Frederick a translation of *Ibn Sina's *Summary concerning Animals* (*Abbreviatio Avicenne de animalibus*), and wrote his sprawling three-part *Introduction to Astrology* (*Liber introductorius ad astrologiam*) for him. It is also likely that he continued to translate the Large Commentaries of Averroes on Aristotle's works on natural science, and Averroes' *On the Substance of the World*, although only the commentaries *On the Heavens* and *On the Soul* (among the works on natural science) are specifically attributed to him directly in the manuscripts. Other attributions include works on urines, and on alchemy. He also maintained close contacts with other leading scholars of the time, such as *Fibonacci, who dedicated the second edition of his *Liber abaci* to him (1228), and Jacob Anatoli, a translator of philosophical works into Hebrew, who was "bound to" Michael Scot for a while in Naples in the early 1230s, and who records discussions with Michael and the Emperor concerning passages in *Maimonides' *Guide of the Perplexed*. A visit to Paris is mentioned by *Roger Bacon, and this may have been the occasion for him writing a commentary on a popular work of cosmology: the *Sphaera* of *John of Sacrobosco. According to Henry of Avranches, writing in 1236, Michael Scot was already dead by then, but a reference to "the time of Pope Honorius IV" (1243–1254) in the title of the *Liber particularis* in some manuscripts (if it is not a later addition) would suggest that he lived longer.

Michael's avowed aim was to make scientific and philosophical doctrine comprehensible even to a beginner by writing in a "vernacular" form of Latin (*vulgariter in grammatica*). In the case of the *Introduction to Astrology* this meant writing a kind of Latin which was very close in syntax and vocabulary to Italian. In the translations from Arabic it meant slightly departing from a literal translation in order to make the Latin readily intelligible. Even so, his original writings differ considerably in style from the translations attributed to him, which may be due to the fact that he relied on interpreters to help him translate (as he explicitly states in the case of the translation of al-Bitruji). The *Introduction to Astrology* draws on a remarkably wide range of sources, both original Latin texts and the full range of translations from Arabic from the tenth-century Alchandreana to texts of Averroes and Maimonides. It includes within its three books a physiognomy (the last book), a set of questions posed by Frederick II, and texts on the constellations, the planetary system according to the Ptolemaic model, on the astrolabe, on the soul, on music, and wonders of the world. Other topics dealt with in passing are definitions of philosophy, angels, demons, divination from thunder, how to

produce the most healthy and successful children and the therapeutic qualities of various hot springs. Michael's innovation lies in adapting the doctrine of Arabic astrological texts to a Christian and Imperial society, his imaginative elaboration of received material, and a lavish use of illustrations and technical diagrams. His illustrated catalogue of the constellations was frequently copied, and his *Book on Physiognomy* was printed several times already before 1500. Of more fundamental influence, however, were his translations: Aristotle's *On Animals*, and the Large Commentaries of Averroes, which became essential texts within the curriculum in natural sciences in medieval universities.

See also **Aristotelianism; Magic and the occult**

Bibliography

Primary Sources
Al-Bitruji, *De motibus caelorum*. Edited by Francis J. Carmody. Berkeley and Los Angeles: University of California Press, 1952.
Averroes, *De caelo et mundo*. Edited by Francis J. Carmody and Rüdiger Arnzen. 2 vols. Leuven: Peeters, 2003.
Michael Scot, *Ars Alchemie*. Edited by S. H. Thomson. *Osiris* (1938) 5: 523–559.

Secondary Sources
Ackermann, Silke. "Habent sua fata libelli." In *Wissen an Höfen und Universiten: Rezeption, Transformation, Innovation. Akten der Tagung in Frankfurt am Main, 5.-6. Oktober 2001*. Frankfurt: 2005.
Burnett, Charles. Michael Scot and the Transmission of Scientific Culture from Toledo to Bologna via the Court of Frederick II Hohenstaufen. *Micrologus* (1994), 2: 101–126.
Edwards, Glenn M. The Two Redactions of Michael Scot's Liber Introductorius. *Traditio* (1985), 41: 329–340.
Thorndike, Lynn. *Michael Scot*. London and Edinburgh: Thomas Nelson, 1965.
———. *The Sphere of Sacrobosco and its Commentators*. Chicago: University of Chicago Press, 1949.

CHARLES BURNETT

MICROCOSM/MACROCOSM

The doctrine of "microcosm/macrocosm" implies the existence of a close relationship between the world as a whole (macrocosm) and part of it, usually man (microcosm), in their structure and contents, as well as of a strong influence of the former on the latter and vice versa, due to a sort of "universal sympathy." Therefore, in the Middle Ages it was usually employed, both in Europe and the Near East, in many fields of science: *alchemy, *astrology, medicine, and magic. It was also found in Medieval Hermetic religious writings. However, "macrocosm" and "microcosm" are primarily philosophical terms related to *cosmology, and systematic treatments of them are found in some works of medieval Latin and in those of Arabic and Hebrew philosophers that tackle anthropological and cosmological themes. According to most of these treatments, the various corporeal and spiritual parts and characteristics of man have a precise correspondence in the world, usually in mathematical terms: e.g., the two eyes correspond to the Sun and the Moon, the four humors (blood, phlegm, red bile, black bile) correspond to the four cosmic elements (fire, air, water, earth), the twelve orifices of the human body correspond to the twelve zodiacal signs, etc. Of course, part of this doctrine is based on the Pythagorean idea that the world and its parts are made and ruled according to a numerological system. One of the main consequences of the doctrine of "microcosm/macrocosm" is that the world has—like man, life, soul, and intellect—an organicist vision of the cosmos which connects such doctrine to one of the most successful trends of medieval philosophy in Europe and in the Near East: Neoplatonism. However, the medieval theory of "microcosm/macrocosm" has independent origins in different geographical and cultural areas, and reflects different sources. Some of them are Greek: Empedocles, *Plato's *Timaeus* and *Philebus*, Stoicism, Plotinus, and Gnosis; traces of "microcosm/macrocosm" are found in Aristotle's physics too, where this doctrine is usually rejected. Other sources are ancient Indian (the *Rig Veda*), which influenced Persian thought on "microcosm/macrocosm" during the Sasanid era (from the third to the seventh century), especially through the main religions of that area: Manicheism and Mazdaism.

Syriac, Arabic, Hebrew, and Latin cultures

In the early medieval Syriac literature from the Persian area (Mesopotamia and Iran), some traces of the doctrine of "microcosm/macrocosm" are found in such authors as Ahudhemmeh (sixth century), Theodor Bar Koni (c. 900 C.E.), and the writer of *The Syriac Book of Medicine*. However, the first systematic treatment of this doctrine in the Near East is found in the philosophical-scientific encyclopedia of the Brethren of Purity (*Ikhwan al-safa'*), written in tenth-century Iraq. In the twenty-sixth and thirty-fourth epistles of this work, bearing the respective titles of *Man as a Little World* and *World as a Big Man*, the doctrine of "microcosm/macrocosm" is explicitly defended and explained, and innumerable and detailed particulars about the correspondences between man and the world, mostly in numerological terms, are given. According to the Brethren of Purity, the world is a sort of immense animal having a general soul, and whose body consists of the heavens; and this doctrine permeates the whole text of their encyclopedia. Of course, significant signs of knowledge of this doctrine appear also in later Arabic authors: astrologers such as *Abu Ma'shar al-Balkhi (Albumasar), and physicians such as *'Ali ibn al-Abbas al-Majusi (Haly Abbas), who hints at it in his *Pantegni*.

The doctrine of "microcosm/macrocosm," possibly through the interpretation given to it by the Brethren of Purity, strongly influenced many aspects of medieval Hebrew thought. Traces of it are found in a number of texts, bound to the Jewish religious tradition and written in various parts of the Mediterranean: in commentaries on the *Sefer Yezirah* by Saadiah Gaon (Mesopotamia, first half of the tenth century) and Shabbetai Donnolo

(Italy, mid-tenth century), and in the theological works by Bahya Ibn Paquda (Spain, second half of the eleventh century) and Judah Halevi (Andalusia and Near East, first half of the twelfth century). Further significant signs of the doctrine appear in the works of Jewish philosophers pertaining to Neoplatonism. In the *Book of Definitions* by Isaac Israeli (*Isaac Judaeus), philosophy is defined as a form of self-knowledge, since all is known through the knowledge of man; *Ibn Gabirol's *Fons Vitae* examines the parallelism of spiritual and material worlds, leading to the new doctrines of the "spiritual matter" and of the "categories of the spiritual world." The Hebrew fortune of the doctrine of "microcosm/macrocosm" culminates in the *Book of the Microcosm* by Joseph Ibn Zaddik (Spain, first half of the twelfth century), in which not only the idea of man as a replica of both the corporeal and the spiritual worlds is explained, but also detailed lists of comparisons between man and the world are given.

After 1150, although *Maimonides admitted the existence of an elaborate analogy between the whole of the being and man in Chapter Seventy-two of Part I of his *Guide of the Perplexed*, the influence of the doctrine on Hebrew culture decreased. Consistent traces of it survived only in authors and works still influenced by Neoplatonism, e.g., in Natanael Ibn al-Fayyumi (Yemen, second half of the twelfth century), and in late-medieval Kabbalah as well.

In the Latin Middle Ages, a Christian version of the doctrine developed. It was based on the key role of man in the world according to Christian anthropology: according to it, man (and Jesus Christ as a man) epitomizes the entire scale of beings, spiritual and material ones, due to his superiority and dignity. Of course, the first two chapters of the Genesis were seen as one of the main sources of this doctrine.

The most significant period when the doctrine of "microcosm/macrocosm" spread in Medieval Latin culture was the twelfth century, and this should be connected both to the diffusion of Neoplatonism in France and elsewhere, and to the influence of Arabic medicine through *Constantine the African and the school of *Salerno. In this period, a good knowledge of this doctrine is witnessed by many authors: *Hildegard of Bingen and Godefroy of Sanct Victor (died 1194) in their religious writings, *Bernard Silvester in his cosmological treatise bearing the significant title *De mundi universitate sive megacosmus et microcosmus*, the *Philosophia* of Daniel of Morley (an Englishman who studied in Toledo), and Alain de Lille (active in England or in Paris) in his *De planctu naturae*. Later on, in the thirteenth century some traces of it are found even in *Robert Grosseteste's cosmological and cosmogonical works.

See also **Aristotelianism; Medicine, theoretical**

Bibliography

Conger, George P. *Theories of Macrocosms and Microcosms in the History of Philosophy*. New York: Columbia University Press, 1922.

Allers, Rudolph. Microcosmus. From Anaximandros to Paracelsus. *Traditio* (1944) 2: 319–407.

Finckh, Ruth. *Minor mundus homo. Studien zur Mikrokosmos-Idee in der mittelalterlichen Literatur.* Göttingen: Vandenhoeck Ruprecht, 1999.

Schipperges, Heinrich. "Einflüsse Arabischer Medizin auf die Mikrokosmosliteratur des 12. Jahrhunderts." In *Antike und Orient im Mittelalter*, edited by Paul Wilpert and Willehad P. Eckert. Berlin: Walter de Gruyter, 1962.

Philippe Gignoux. "Microcosm and Macrocosm." http://www.iranica.com/articles/ot_grp5/ot_ microcosm_20040616.html (2004).

MAURO ZONTA

MILITARY ARCHITECTURE

Man has always needed to defend himself by keeping his attackers out of his domain, and thus both the need for societal protection and the building of walls to provide this protection predate the Middle Ages. This meant choosing a site that was in the first place geographically and physically difficult to reach and then improving those hindrances with the addition of man-made barriers. General historical studies have established an incredibly lengthy chronology for the study of fortifications. Walls, such as those found around Jericho, Troy, Duras Europas, Tyre, Rome, and elsewhere in the ancient world, were famous for sustaining defenses, and sometimes ultimately failing, against often overwhelming numbers of determined attackers.

The Roman Empire's peace and stability depended on its defenses, a fact well understood by its leaders, and perhaps no other civilization has ever devoted so much effort or money to the construction and upkeep of its defenses. By the second century C.E., the very extensive Roman empire was nearly surrounded by fortifications. Fortresses were built along the Danube, Rhine, and Euphrates rivers, and lengthy walls were built in Scotland, Numidia, and Germany. These were supplemented with watchtowers, outpost forts, and signal towers. Within these borders were walled towns—some surrounding as much as 500 acres (about 200 hectares)—and fortified garrisons. All of these fit into the grand military strategy of the Roman Empire, one that by the second century was less interested in outside conquest than in preserving internal peace and prosperity.

This peace of the Roman Empire, the *pax romana*, was to be short-lived, however, as the third century brought invasions from outside and civil war from inside the Empire. Not only in Europe, but everywhere, the borders began to fail. The problem with the border fortifications was not that they were too few or too weak. They had never been built to withstand invasions, merely to impede the progress of invading armies until the legions garrisoned behind them could respond. When Roman legions did not respond, either because of their lack of numbers or because of the enormity and frequency of these invasions, the fortifications failed to keep out the enemy invaders; during the fourth and fifth centuries, "barbarian" invaders almost completely overran the Empire.

Still, Roman fortifications remained the primary defensive strongholds of Europe during the early Middle Ages. There were several reasons for this. They were well constructed—built 10–14 feet (about 3–4.3 m) thick of cut facing stone over earth and stone rubble, and held together by concrete. New fortifications were expensive to build, and, perhaps most important, although least considered, the walls surrounding most of the Roman cities had actually protected their citizens quite well. Despite possessing what should have been adequate siege technology, the barbarians suffered some spectacular failures in attempting to take the towns of the Empire.

Most barbarian leaders refused to destroy the walls of a captured town unless they feared that the walls might harbor later resistance against them. The Goths, Lombards, Franks, and other barbarian occupiers of the western Empire did not add any town walls of their own. They did keep the existing walls in good repair. What the barbarian conquerors of the western Empire added instead of new town walls were rural fortifications, precursors of medieval castles. Details about these early castles are at best limited. There is not even any way of determining exactly how many were built in the early Middle Ages. They were largely earth-and-wood fortifications, sometimes referred to simply as ring-works; and because there was little stone construction involved, few archeological remains survive. They also did not often rely on walls or towers for their protection, but on the inaccessibility of their location. Many were built on high places, some on rocky promontories or isolated buttes. At other times, their defense was aided by a wall or rampart. Only rarely was this a stone wall; more frequently it was an earthen rampart crowned by stacked stones and wood. These castles also stood apart, and in some instances quite a distance apart, from the urban areas already defended by town walls, making them in effect the protectors of the rural regions of western Europe. Several were constructed to protect agricultural and economic centers, serving as refuges for farmers and other agricultural workers during times of war. Others were sanctuaries or ecclesiastical centers. However, many castles were built and controlled by wealthy individuals, and in these cases served as proto-feudal manors, both as residences for these "nobles" and as defenses for the people who worked on their nearby agricultural lands.

Motte and Bailey

These castles were especially important in the face of raiding forces, such as the Vikings or Hungarians, especially as these raiders were often not numerous or serious enough to undertake the effort to attack or besiege such a fortress. Alfred the Great thus found in his earth-and-wood *burhs* safety from Vikings invading his kingdom, while German and French marcher lords secured their borders from similar invasions with similar fortifications. Eventually these earth-and-wood fortifications were replaced by the motte-and-bailey castles. In its simplest form, the motte part of the motte-and-bailey castle was little more than a tall earthen mound topped by a superstructure of wood. The bailey was an enclosed yard, often quite large, surrounding the motte and separated from it by a ditch. As such, the motte-and-bailey castle provided protection to its inhabitants and potential refugees from the size of the bailey, the depth and width of the ditch and from the height of the mound. They were also not expensive to build, although the amount of labor needed to construct one would have been significant.

It was the Crusades that introduced European leaders and fortification builders to the styles, techniques, and uses of precipitous terrain as added defense that would become the characteristics of all high and late medieval fortifications. While by the time of the First Crusade Europeans had already been constructing castles in stone, William the Conqueror's White Tower and Colchester Castle being two of the most famous of these structures, the paucity of wood in the Middle East necessitated that all Crusader fortifications be constructed in stone. Additionally, as so few Crusaders remained in their captured "kingdoms" after their initial conquests, with perhaps as many as one-half to two-thirds of those still alive at the fall of Jerusalem—estimated to be fewer than 25,000—returning to Europe, and few newer Crusading recruits taking their place, numerous fortifications needed to be built there. Scholars have been unable to put a definitive total on the number of castles that were built during the time of the Crusaders' Middle Eastern occupation. However, it is clear that the number lies above one hundred, if not two hundred.

In deference to those fortifications being built in Europe at the same time, Crusader castles built in the countryside used the harshness and inaccessibility of the Middle Eastern terrain to add to the defensibility of the structures. These castles were built on the summits of precipitous crags or next to steep ravines. The Crusaders even fortified caves. Most castles had thick walls—usually more than 16 feet (5 m) in width—faced with large stones and intricate, well-defended entryways. They were also incredibly large, essentially castle complexes, able to shelter and provide all of the necessities of life for a large number of people for a long time. Because their inhabitants anticipated long sieges that might last until reinforcements could arrive from Europe, the castles were provided with reservoirs for water supply and large cellars for food storage. For example, at the castle of Margat it is estimated that there were sufficient food and water supplies to feed a garrison of one thousand men for five years.

It seems logical, although this logic can also be confirmed by empirical, archeological, and written evidence, that soldiers returning from the Crusades were deeply impressed by the security provided by the fortifications there, for only at the end of the Crusades, from the middle of the thirteenth century on, were these castles even threatened by enemy troops. Indeed, most Crusader castles withstood almost all attempts to attack or besiege them, with many surrendering only when the numbers of defenders inside fell so low as to make abandonment more prudent than resistance. These returning soldiers then transferred this fortification construction knowledge to Europe where it influenced the building of castles and urban fortifications for the remainder of the Middle Ages, especially during the twelfth and thirteenth centuries, the so-called "golden age" of medieval fortifications.

The construction of any medieval fortification was extremely expensive. Whether it was an earth-and-wood construction built using only the expense of forced labor, a large stone castle complex that served both as royal residence and fortification, or a town wall to extend around the urban area of even a small town, let alone a city the size of Bruges, Ghent, Milan, Florence, Naples, Paris, or Constantinople, such a construction was a major economic endeavor. Sometimes the cost of a medieval fortification is known, for example, the cost of Caernarvon Castle, built by Edward I in Wales at the end of the thirteenth century, is recorded as having cost the English king £20,000, with a total for all of his castle construction projects in Wales costing between £62,000 and £80,000. At other times, the expense can be seen from a more indirect means, such as the punishment so often levied by conquering generals of having the urban fortifications of a defeated town pulled down, the cost of rebuilding a perceptible deterrent against disputes with the conqueror.

These medieval fortifications, with their straight, tall stone walls, also did not fall easily. If those inside a fortification, whether a castle or a town, wanted to withstand an attacking army they generally did, and little could dissuade them from this determination. Attacking the walls of such fortresses was costly in terms of men and was generally only accomplished with the use of large numbers of artillery pieces and other siege machines, and generally also if there was no army friendly to the besieged that could bring relief. Thus time in these situations was very important; the army with time on its side usually won or lost the siege. Time also allowed conquest more frequently by the old means of mining, starvation, negotiation, or treachery. This meant that almost all sieges took a very long time to accomplish, if they were accomplished at all: Rome took ten years to fall in 410; Château Gaillard was besieged for more than a year in 1203–1204; Calais took nearly the same amount of time in 1346–1347; and Constantinople held out for almost a year in 1453; while Neuss did not fall after more than a year's siege in 1474–1475. Additionally, despite the contrary thought prevailing, gunpowder weaponry did not alter this situation decisively, as the siege of Neuss, among others, proved.

Although castles continued to be built throughout the end of the Middle Ages, fortification builders began more and more to disregard the defensive aspects of the structure and to emphasize comfort and luxury in their place. A late medieval castle, now better described as a fortified residence, had to be architecturally beautiful. No longer would a simple, plain keep or a castle complex hidden behind huge and ugly walls suffice to meet the aesthetic demands of its owner. Defense was not entirely forgotten, however. Rural fortified residences often continued to be built in inaccessible places, and walls were still large, crenellated, and lined with towers.

Nevertheless, most of these late medieval fortresses were no more than small-scale imitations of earlier fortifications, and even those meant to withstand foreign attack or to inhibit civil war could not compare with the castles built in the twelfth and thirteenth centuries. Fortified residences were also built in towns, where wealthy individuals, both noble and non-noble, desired a security for their families and possessions similar to that of the rural castle.

Yet fortified residences were not the primary fortification construction of the late Middle Ages. This was instead the town wall. Before the fourteenth and fifteenth centuries, few new town walls had been constructed. Even Paris, the largest and most populated town of western Europe, went without a complete enclosure until the mid-fourteenth century. By then, however, town governments had begun to recognize the need for new fortifications. Local violence, civil war, and foreign invasion all threatened the security and prosperity of those living within their boundaries. The solution to the problem was to build new walls surrounding the towns. Indeed, during the late Middle Ages so many towns built protective walls around their boundaries that by the end of the fifteenth century few notable population centers were without a sizeable fortification surrounding them.

See also **Arms and armor; Catapults and trebuchets; Water supplies and sewerage**

Bibliography

Bradbury, Jim. *The Medieval Siege*. Woodbridge: Boydell Press, 1992.

Brown, R. Allen. *English Castles*. 3rd ed. London: B.T. Batsford, 1976.

Bur, Michel. *Le château*. Typologie des sources du moyen âge occidental, 79. Turnhout: Brepols, 1999.

Coulson, Charles. *Castles in Medieval Society: Fortresses in England, France, and Ireland in the Central Middle Ages*. Oxford: Oxford University Press, 2003.

DeVries, Kelly. *A Cumulative Bibliography of Medieval Military History and Technology*. Leiden: E.J. Brill, 2002; update, 2004.

———. *Medieval Military Technology*. Peterborough: Broadview Press, 1992.

Higham, Robert and Philip Barker. *Timber Castles*. Mechanicsburg: Stackpole Books, 1995.

Kennedy, Hugh. *Crusader Castles*. New York: Cambridge University Press, 1994.

Kenyon, John R. *Medieval Fortifications*. New York: St. Martin's Press, 1990.

Pounds, N.J.G. *The Medieval Castle in England and Wales: A Social and Political History*. New York: Cambridge University Press, 1990.

Taylor, Arnold. *The Welsh Castles of Edward I*. London: Hambledon Press, 1986.

Thompson, M.W. *The Decline of the Castle*. New York: Cambridge University Press, 1987.

Thompson, M.W. *The Rise of the Castle*. New York: Cambridge University Press, 1991.

Toy, Sydney. *A History of Fortification from 3000 BC to AD 1700*. London: W. Heinemann, 1955.

KELLY DEVRIES

MINERALOGY

Mineralogy is usually believed to have begun in the early modern period, and the medieval study of minerals is often regarded as a "proto-mineralogy," an unscientific discipline about the supposed properties of minerals, which included notions of petrography, crystallography, and metallurgy, as well as the study of such non-minerals as pearls, acids, and alcals. As a matter of fact, in the Middle Ages mineralogy was both descriptive and theoretical. Descriptive mineralogy consisted mostly of *lapidaries, lists of precious stones and metals with supposed medical or magical properties; moreover, descriptions of minerals were inserted into various *encyclopedias or *pharmaceutic handbooks. Theoretical mineralogy was mainly devoted to the geological question of the origin of minerals, and connected with mining, metallurgy, and *alchemy. Medieval accounts of the formation of minerals were usually given in organic terms, according to which minerals were fossil bodies, grown within the body of the Earth; their generation was ascribed to a sort of sexual process of fusion between two different substances. In medieval mineralogy extensive use was made of Greek and Latin sources: a key role was played by Book Five, Chapter Six of Aristotle's *Meteorology*, according to which minerals are produced from earth and water in the subsoil through the action of two different exhalations, a dry one for stones and a moist one for metals. Other sources were Theophrastus's and Xenocrates of Ephesos's treatises on stones, Book Five of *Dioscorides' *Materia Medica*, and books Thirty-three to Thirty-seven of Pliny the Elder's *Natural History*.

Mineralogy in the Near East

In the early Middle Ages, mineralogy aroused the interest of Near Eastern Christian scholars. Descriptions of stones and metals, in which the question of their formation was discussed according to Aristotle's doctrine, are found in Syriac encyclopedic works such as James of Edessa's *Hexaemeron* (seventh century) and Job of Edessa's *Book of Treasures* (817 C.E.). *Pseudo-Aristotle's *De Lapidibus*, a lapidary that won great success in medieval Arabic, Latin, and Hebrew literature, was probably composed in a Christian Arabic milieu in the ninth century.

Mineralogy was deeply studied in medieval Arabo-Islamic culture. Of course, many lapidaries were written dealing with gemmology and the use of precious stones in practical medicine and in magic, and special sections of medical and cosmographical encyclopedias were devoted to mineralogy (e.g. al-Qazwani's treatment of stones in the thirteenth century); but there were also numerous writings dealing with minerals from a theoretical point of view.

Epistle Nineteen of the philosophical-scientific encyclopedia of the Brethren of Purity (*Ikhwan al-Safa'*), written in tenth-century Iraq, is probably the first systematic medieval Arabic treatise of mineralogy. According to it, Nature is the efficient cause, and planets are the formal causes of minerals. The Brethren divide minerals into two categories: those generated in the soil (sulfur and salts) or in the seabed (pearls and corals) in a short time (approximately one year), and metals, which are generated in several years in the bowels of the Earth, as a result of the fusion of mercury and sulfur. This doctrine, which is found also in thirteenth-century Hebrew science, was based on *Jabir ibn Hayyan's and *al-Razi's alchemical works, where "stones" and "bodies" (namely metals) were classified among minerals together with "spirits" (mercury, ammoniac, sulfur, etc.), vitriols, borax, and salts.

In eleventh-century Arabic literature, a detailed, often original, description of minerals is found in *al-Biruni's *Book of the Knowledge of Precious Stones*, which also contains a table of their specific heights. Another important contribution to medieval Arabic mineralogy was made by *Ibn Sina, who devoted chapter five of the section On Meteorology and Minerals of his encyclopedia, *The Cure*, to the formation and classification of minerals. According to Ibn Sina, who re-elaborated the doctrine of Aristotle, minerals derive from different mixtures of water and earth: the strongest mixture, resulting from the action of dryness, produces "stones"; a less strong mixture, resulting from the action of heat and cold, produces "fusible substances," namely metals; weak mixtures of water and earth produce either oily minerals, which are not easily soluble—i.e., "sulfurs"—or salty minerals, which are easily soluble—i.e., "salts." Ibn Sina explains the formation of metals as a result of the fusion, in the bowels of the Earth, of two basic constituents, mercury and sulfur, having various degrees of purity and combustiveness. His work had great success: it was the key source for mineralogical treatments by the Arabic followers of Ibn Sina, as well as by the Syriac philosopher Gregory Bar Hebraeus (thirteenth century); in around 1200 it was translated into Latin with a commentary by *Alfred of Sareschel, and was added to the medieval Latin translation of Book Four of Aristotle's *Meteorology*, thus being regarded as an unofficial Aristotelian treatment of mineralogy. Ibn Sina's mineralogy seems to have had had no rival in later medieval Arabic philosophy.

Mineralogy in Europe

In Europe, a systematic theoretical study of minerals began mainly as a result of the translation and diffusion of Arabic mineralogical and alchemical works after 1200; but many lapidaries, in various languages including Latin, French, and Old English, existed long before this date. The most successful of them was that by Marbode of Rennes (eleventh century). Special sections about stones, where some reflections concerning the formation of minerals are found, were included in *Hildegard of Bingen's *Book of the Different Natures of Creatures* (in which minerals are credited with medical and religious properties, even with life), as well as in twelfth- and thirteenth-century encyclopedic cosmologies by *Alexander Nequam, *Bartholomaeus Anglicus, and *Vincent of Beauvais. However, the most systematic treatment of mineralogy in the Latin Middle Ages, where the philosophical methods of *Scholasticism were

applied, was *Albertus Magnus's *Book of Minerals*. This work, based on Ibn Sina's doctrine as interpreted in the light of Albertus's personal reflection and experience, is divided into five books: Book One describes the general characteristics of "stones"; Book Two includes a traditional lapidary; Book Three deals with metals in general, while Book Four describes each of them; Book Five is devoted to what Albertus calls "middle bodies" (salts, vitriol, sulfurs, etc.). What is more significant in Albertus's work is the application of the Aristotelian doctrine of causes to mineralogy: according to him, minerals should be studied by looking for their material, efficient, and formal causes, which he identifies in water and earth, heat and moisture, and what he calls the "mineral virtue," respectively.

See also **Alchemy; Aristotelianism; Lapidaries**

Bibliography

Goltz, Dietlinde. *Studien zur Geschichte der Mineralnamen in Pharmazie, Chemie und Medizin von den Anfängen bis Paracelsus*. Wiesbaden: Steiner, 1972.

Holmyard, Eric J. and David C. Mandeville. *Avicenna, De congelatione et conglutinatione lapidum, being sections of the Kitab al-Shifa'*. Paris: Geuthner, 1927.

Mieleitner, Karl. Zur Geschichte der Mineralogie im Altertum und im Mittelalter. *Fortschritte der Mineralogie, Kristallographie und Petrographie* (1922) 7: 427–480.

Nobis, Heribert M. "Der Ursprung der Steine: zur Beziehung zwischen Alchemie und Mineralogie im Mittelalter." In *Toward a History of Mineralogy, Petrology, and Geochemistry*, edited by Bernhard Fritscher and Fergus Henderson. München: Institut für Geschichte der Naturwissenschaften, 1998.

Wyckoff, Dorothy. *Albertus Magnus' Book of Minerals*. Oxford: Oxford University Press, 1967.

Zonta, Mauro. Mineralogy, Botany and Zoology in Medieval Hebrew Encyclopaedias. *Arabic Sciences and Philosophy* (1996) 6: 263–315.

MAURO ZONTA

MONSTERS

For medieval writers, the word "monster" (*monstrum* and its cognates) referred in the first instance to a human being or animal that deviated significantly from the form usual for its kind. Monsters included creatures with extra or missing parts, as well as conjoined twins, people of ambiguous sex, and beings that appeared to straddle the boundary between two animal species—between human and pig, for example, or between goat and ox. By extension, monsters also included human races of unfamiliar physiognomy, such as pygmies, people with dog's heads, people with no head or one enormous foot, who where thought to inhabit Africa and Asia, on the fringes of what was for Europeans the known world. A third category of "monster" comprised dangerous species of animals, some of them apparent hybrids, such as the whale or the basilisk (a creature halfway between a rooster and a snake). What all these creatures had in common was their menacing nature; not only were they unusual and unfamiliar, but they were also objects of well-deserved fear. Pygmies were hostile to outsiders, while whales could swallow men alive, like Jonah, and the basilisk could kill a person with a glance.

The most frightening monsters of all, however, were animals and humans of unusual conformation, now commonly described in terms of "birth defects." Understood as signs of God's anger at sinful human behavior, these were interpreted as terrifying omens of his impending vengeance, presaging epidemics and devastating wars. Thus monsters were associated with the broader category of divine prodigies, inherited from Greek and Roman religion, which also included comets, earthquakes, celestial apparitions, and rains of blood. For centuries, medieval European chroniclers, moralists, and theologians were content to record the birth of such creatures for the edification and eventual reformation of their readers, as divine (or sometimes demonic) interventions in the natural order.

Beginning in the twelfth and thirteenth centuries, however, European natural philosophers began to focus on secondary causes—chains of natural cause and effect—as part of the revival of Greek ideas concerning the natural world. Instead of attributing the existence of monstrous races, species, or even individuals to divine will or demonic action, they began to use principles from the works of *Galen and Aristotle, particularly their theories of *generation, to offer natural explanations for unusual creatures. Thus, for example, some argued that beings of intermediate sex (also known as "hermaphrodites") should not be seen as judgments on human sinfulness; rather, they resulted when an animal's internal complexion fell midway between hot (male) and cold (female), or when the father's seed did not succeed in "mastering" the seed or matter contributed by the mother. Similarly, conjoined twins were born when the maternal matter was more than enough for one fetus but not enough for two. At the same time, they debated the theological status of the so-called monstrous human races, concluding for the most part that they lacked fully rational human souls.

The most difficult types of monster to explain were apparent hybrids between different animal species or between humans and animals; these were generally interpreted as the products of interspecies sex—a contravention of the natural order itself seen as deserving of divine punishment. In *On the Generation of Animals*, Aristotle had denied the possibility of such hybrids, arguing that crosses between significantly dissimilar species were naturally impossible, because their gestation periods were too unlike; thus creatures that appeared to be hybrids must spring from some other cause. *Albertus Magnus was the first medieval writer to explore this and other problems concerning the generation of monsters in detail. Like Aristotle, he argued that hybrids did not arise from mixing two kinds of seed, but were produced when the father's seed was too weak to shape the matter supplied by the mother. Instead, like an arrow that missed its target, it might produce a child that did not resemble

its father at all. In some cases, he argued, the influence of an animal constellation, such as Taurus or Pisces, might substitute for the formative power missing from the father's seed, producing the effect of bull or fish.

Not everyone was convinced by this explanation, however, and other accounts of such hybrids were proposed. In the second half of the fourteenth century, for example, *Nicole Oresme proposed a variant on Albertus's theory, rejecting the astrological explanation and substituting for it a causal account based on the order of the formation of the fetus. According to Aristotle (in an early version of the phylogenetic principle), this developed sequentially in the course of gestation, progressing from inanimate mass to plant to animal to human status. Oresme speculated that the fetus might also progress by smaller steps through all the species of animal. Thus if the father's seed was too weak to push the entire body of the fetus to the appropriate stage for its species, the offspring might resemble a lower animal in whole or in part; in this way, for example, a sow might give birth to something that looked partly like a dog. Later natural philosophers continued to refine these kinds of explanations to produce ever more nuanced natural explanations of unusual births.

These late medieval attempts to demystify monsters formed part of a broader philosophical movement to rethink the physical world in terms of natural regularities, if not yet in terms of natural laws. These regularities, instilled by God in His Creation, made the world at least in part predictable and amenable to scientific exploration. This permitted authors such as Albertus Magnus and Oresme to distinguish phenomena with natural causes from demonic interventions and divine miracles. Although natural philosophers and theologians continued to debate the exact location of the boundary between these two realms, the result was dramatically to expand the former. Rather than being the frighteningly unpredictable product of daily intervention by God and other supernatural intelligences, monsters, like most other natural phenomena, reflected causal regularities that were subject to human understanding if not human control.

See also **Aristotelianism; Miracle; Religion and science; Zoology**

Bibliography

Primary Sources
Albertus Magnus. *On Animals: A Medieval Summa Zoologica*. Translated and annotated by Kenneth F. Kitchell, Jr. and Irven Michael Resnick. Baltimore: Johns Hopkins University Press, 1999.
Gerald of Wales. *History and Topography of Ireland*. Translated by John J. O'Meara. Harmondsworth: Penguin, 1982.
Liber monstrorum. Edited and translated into Italian by Franco Porsia. Bari: Dedalo, 1976.
Oresme, Nicole. "*De causis mirabilium*." In Bert Hansen, *Nicole Oresme and the Marvels of Nature: A Study of his De causis mirabilium with Critical Edition, Translation, and Commentary*. Toronto: Pontifical Institute of Medieval Studies, 1985.

The Benedictine abbey at the summit of the 1,703 feet (519 m) Monte Cassino in central Italy. (Corbis/Bettmann)

Secondary Sources

Céard, Jean. *La nature et les prodiges: L'insolite au XVIe siècle*. Geneva: Droz, 1977.

Daston, Lorraine and Katharine Park. *Wonders and the Order of Nature 1150–1750*. New York: Zone, 1998.

Friedman, John Block. *The Monstrous Races in Medieval Art and Thought*. Cambridge: Harvard University Press, 1981.

Rousset Paul. Le sens du merveilleux à l'époque féodale. *Le Moyen Age* (1956) 62: 25–37.

Wittkower, Rudolf. Marvels of the East: A Study in the History of Monsters. *Journal of the Warburg and Courtauld Institutes* (1942) 5: 159–197.

KATHARINE PARK

MONTE CASSINO

Around 529 C.E., the abbey of Monte Cassino was founded by St. Benedict of Nursia on a craggy hilltop overlooking the valley of the Garigliano near Naples. The importance of this foundation for medieval religious history is enormous but beyond our purview. However, the role of Monte Cassino in intellectual history is grounded in the religious life of the monastery.

Benedict's own life was typical for a late antique nobleman: he studied the *liberalia studia*: grammar, rhetoric, and law. Like Gregory the Great and Caeserius of Arles, Benedict was ambivalent about secular studies; he knew he needed a certain amount of study to be able to devote himself to his true goal, the *lectio divina*, as it came to be called. Each monk, following Benedict's foundational rule, was required to read one codex each Lenten season. Consequently, the monastery had to possess books—at least one for each monk present—and the monks needed to know how to write them and to read them. Because of this provision, Monte Cassino became an intellectual center with school, *scriptorium* and library. At the same time, in the Roman world outside the monastery, intellectual life was moribund if not in serious decline. As Reynolds and Wilson put it: "It was the monastic centers which were destined, often in spite of themselves, to play the major part in preserving and transmitting what remained of pagan antiquity." While Monte Cassino itself was of only limited importance for the copying and preserving of pagan literature, it inaugurated this important practice, required by its rule, which led other monasteries to follow its example.

In spite of this tradition, very few manuscripts of scientific interest survive from the early Middle Ages: from the sixth century we have only remnants of the *Natural History* of Pliny. Some other texts, most notably Macrobius's *Somnun Scipionis*, must have been preserved, but we do not know where or by whom they were copied. Despite this lack of surviving texts, there is evidence that Monte Cassino has been a center of medical practice in the sixth century utilizing pagan medical texts. Monte Cassino was itself in an oft-contested area and was destroyed in 580 and 883 C.E. After both destructions, the monastery was abandoned for long periods.

However, as Reynolds and Wilson have stated: "The most dramatice single event in the history of Latin scholarship in the eleventh century was the phenomenal revival of Monte Cassino." The resurgence of Monte Cassino seems to have begun in 1058: at the start of that year its former abbot, Frederick, was Pope, Desiderius became the new abbot, and in the second half of the year the Norman rulers of south Italy extended their power over the abbey and its lands, Robert Guiscard becoming its protector. Guiscard's benefactions greatly enriched the abbey, allowing it to become the premier monastic house in all of Italy: his generosity to the abbey was eighteen times the amount he proffered to the Papacy! With this level of support, the monastery was able to support a wide range of scholarly activities. Under the abbacy of Desiderius (1058–1087), the most important figure in the history of science at Monte Cassino flourished: *Constantine the African. Like the translators who later worked in Norman Sicily, Constantine introduced his own versions of Arabic science to the Latin West. A native of North Africa (one tradition suggests Tunis), Constantine, who was probably a convert from Islam, became aware of the paucity of medical texts in the Norman lands. His contribution to Western medicine has been characterized by McVaugh as "the most extensive and important group of texts... which for the first time communicated the expanded Arabic medical tradition." This group of texts included his own works as well as translations of *Galen, *Hippocrates, Haly Abbas (*Ali ibn al-Abbas), *Hunayn ibn Ishaq, and others. His translating was not woodenly literal, as much of the medical corpus was, but instead was filled with explanatory expansions to aid those unfamiliar with the Arabic tradition. His influence was felt not only at Monte Cassino and nearby *Salerno where there was a circle of scholars related to him, but also in Sicily, Spain, and at Montpellier.

After this high point the monastery declined in the twelfth century as serious and talented monks began to join more austere and reformist orders. As a consequence, Monte Cassino did not become a beacon of medical study as Salerno and Montpellier did.

See also **Medicine, practical**

Bibliography

Bloch, Herbert. *Montecassino in the Middle Ages.* 3 vols. Cambridge: Harvard University Press, 1986.

Cowdrey, H.E.J. *The Age of the Abbot Desiderius: Montecassino, the Papacy, and the Normans in the Eleventh and early Twelfth Centuries.* Oxford: Clarendon Press, 1983.

Lecercq, Jean. *The Love of Learning and the Desire for God.* New York: Fordham University Press, 1961.

Lindberg, David L. *The Beginnings of Western Science.* Chicago: University of Chicago Press, 1992.

Loud, G.A. *Robert Guiscard: Southern Italy and the Norman Conquest.* London: Longman, 2000.

Newton, Francis. *The Scriptorium and Library of Monte Cassino, 1058–1105.* New York: Cambridge University Press, 1999.

Reynolds, L.D. and N.G. Wilson. *Scribes and Scholars: A Guide to the Transmission of Greek and Latin Literature.* Oxford: Oxford University Press, 1968.

MICHAEL C. WEBER

MUSIC THEORY

In the Middle Ages, the term *musica* chiefly referred to the theoretical exploration of music rather than to the object itself. Basically, there were two ways of exploring music, only one of which can be said to have been part of the history of sciences. On the one hand, music theory introduced the practice of music (*musica practica*). On the other hand, music theory developed as a mathematical discipline (*musica theorica* or *musica speculativa*). Both variants had their origin in antiquity, but with *Boethius's *De musica* the standard text for the medieval *musica theorica* had been established.

Boethius was the first author to assign music theory to an ensemble of mathematical sciences that he named the *quadrivium, and which encompassed *arithmetic, music theory, geometry, and astronomy. The concept was pedagogically motivated and influenced by Pythagorean and Platonic ideas. While geometry and astronomy dealt with continuous quantity (either immobile or mobile), arithmetic and music dealt with discrete quantity, i.e., number, either per se or as related to another number (ratios).

Referring to a string as a unit, any interval could be expressed through numerical ratios. The octave (2:1), for example, resounds if one hits the half in relation to the whole string. The *Tetraktys*—the numbers 1 2 3 4 or 6 8 9 12, that represented octave, fifth, fourth, and whole tone—was taken as an axiomatic point of departure (illustrated by the Pythagoras legend) from which all other intervals were deduced exclusively through arithmetical principles: whole numbers, addition and subtraction. The relationship between number and sound was vague. It is clear, however, that numbers were not simply understood as a theoretical means that would help to explain nature. The whole tone, for example, could not be divided into two equal halves because this division could not be expressed through arithmetical means.

Musica theorica was not subject to any significant changes during the first centuries of the Middle Ages. Instead, music theorists concentrated on the explanation of musica practica, i.e., plainchant and organum. With the reception of Aristotelian *logic, however, the subject of music theory was reconsidered. Indeed, the discussion started within the commentaries on Aristotle's *Analytica Posteriora* by *Robert Grosseteste (1170–1253) and *Robert Kilwardby (1215–1279). Only now, a consistent subject was to be constructed.

At this time the quadrivium, while still an oft-used term, was dissolving into a much more complex network of sciences (for example represented by the arts faculties of the early *universities). Within the actual lectures, music theory obviously played a marginal role, although there exists some evidence that it was taught. The subject of music theory as well as its place within the system of sciences was now described referring to the related concepts of either *subalternatio* (Grosseteste and Kilwardby) or *scientia media* (*Thomas Aquinas). These concepts described the position of the music-theoretical subject between arithmetic and physics confirming its subordination to arithmetic. They led to a more precise definition of the subject which was now called *numerus sonorous* or *numerus relatus ad sonum*.

Acoustics

Soon after the articulation and definition of the *numerus sonorus* (most comprehensively by Jacques de Liège c. 1330), however, authors such as *Thomas Bradwardine and Johannes Boen (d. 1367) questioned the fundamental decision about this subject. They could not understand why the whole tone could not be divided into two equal halves since sound was a continuum. For them, numerical ratios apparently were a means to explain natural phenomena; their concept of the subject of music was fundamentally different and could have yielded a quantitative acoustics had it been applied consequently. However, it was only Marin Mersenne (1588–1648) who scrutinized the Pythagoras legend, discovering that the deduction of the ratios from the weight of hammers would not work acoustically.

Yet, there was an acoustics in the Middle Ages, and it formed part of natural philosophy. In a highly abbreviated way, Boethius had absorbed many elements of classical acoustics and even went beyond that. He defined sound as "vibration [*percussio*] of air which is unresolved up to the ear," and considered the relationship between the tension of a string, its speed of reverberation, and the height of the resulting sound. This observation seemed to be the basis of his music theory, for, he argued, one could relate one sound to another (higher or lower) sound using numerical ratios because of those vibrations. However, the way his treatise developed did not follow this idea but preferred the simpler model of the monochord. It was not until the twelfth-century "Renaissance" in France and Italy put new life into natural philosophy that acoustical questions were resumed. Authors including *Adelard of Bath, Bernard of Chartres, *William of Conches, and the anonymous writer of the Salernitan Questions dealt with phenomena such as echo, sound's penetration of walls or the behavior of bells. Often acoustic theories depended on the theory of visual rays. In the early thirteenth century, Grosseteste developed his highly original theory of sound in which he described it as "encapsulated light."

Meanwhile John Blund (c. 1175–1248) had initiated the tradition of *De anima*-commentaries. Despite its originality, his interpretation (which considered psychological factors of consonance perception) was not continued by later authors. However, a framework was established within which acoustical theories began to unfold. Elaborating on Aristotelian thought, including its Arabic interpretations by *Ibn Sina and *Ibn Rushd, they developed mostly within commentaries on *De anima* as well as *De sensu et sensato*, *De caelo*, and the spurious *Problemata*. These commentaries (by, among others, *Albertus Magnus, Thomas Aquinas, *Giles of Rome (Aegidius Romanus), and *John Buridan) discussed the generation of sound, its medium, its ontological status, its reception (focusing on *multiplicatio specierum*, a theory about the distribution of sense objects), whether celestial bodies can produce sound and so on (the physiology of the ears only later being considered). With the formation of the universities, this tradition persisted well into the fourteenth and fifteenth centuries. It can be observed that its regional center shifted from Oxford and Paris to Bologna and Padua in the second half of the fourteenth century. *Pietro d'Abano's commentary on the *Problemata* can be considered as an important source foreshadowing this shift.

Thus, acoustical theories were hardly developed in texts that would be considered as music theory. Of course, a certain influence can be detected in the works of *Jean de Meurs, Jacques de Liège and others. Most original in that sense were the *Questiones musice* from late-fourteenth-century Italy, which were only received by Ugolino de Orvieto (1380–1452) in the fifteenth century. The separation between music theory and acoustics became plausible by a comparison of music theory and optics. Only music theory was part of the quadrivium. Thus, Kilwardby asked why optics was not considered a fifth mathematical discipline. He emphasized the relation of its subjects (eye, visual rays, and the visible) to natural philosophy rather than mathematics. Although optics is in some sense subordinate to geometry, this *subalternatio* differs from that of music to arithmetic. While music theory considers number as such, optics does not consider the straight line as such but as the representation of a physical entity only. Thus, while optics included geometrical methods in order to explain natural phenomena, music theory referred to natural phenomena in order to apply arithmetical facts. Music theory does principally exclude natural phenomena which are not related to arithmetic. These elements were subjects of acoustics. Thus, the sciences dealing with sound fell into two disciplines: music theory and acoustics (as a subdiscipline of natural philosophy).

In spite of this separation yet another form of acoustics developed within musical writings, first of English, then of Italian origin. It obviously developed from musical practice and considered intervals that did not fit the Pythagorean tuning. The earliest source describing this phenomenon is the treatise of Theinred of Dover (twelfth century). In the late thirteenth or early fourteenth century Walter Odington (c. 1260–1346) explained that some singers used the ratios 5:4 and 6:5 for the major and minor thirds respectively. These are the first signs of the emergence of a discourse on interval ratios that were designed to find tunings which helped to avoid the practical shortcomings of the Pythagorean. Only in the fifteenth century were new tunings, temperaments, and interval divisions proposed at greater length. Unlike the authors of *musica theorica*, most authors of this tradition were also composers. They included Ugolino de Orvieto, Ramis de Pareia, and Franchinus Gaffurio. Thanks to these and other authors, practical acoustics had become an advanced topic of music theory in its broader sense. However, it must not be seen as a further stage of *musica theorica* but rather as another discipline. Hence the first sources of an acoustics in the modern sense can be found precisely beyond the scientific borders of *musica theorica*.

Influence of Exact Sciences on Music Theory

By the thirteenth century *musica practica* embraced in addition to the theory of plainchant a rather complex theory of rhythm and notation (*musica mensurabilis*) as well as a theory of counterpoint. These, of course, were practical disciplines. However, they deserve mention here as they were influenced by Aristotelian concepts of time and motion. This impact was very strong on authors such as Jean de Meurs and Jacques de Liège. Indeed, it has not only been suggested that Jean's theory of rhythm needs to be interpreted along the lines of *scientia media* but also that he was influenced by the mathematicians of Merton College, Oxford.

Such intersections are not surprising. Most of the theoretical musical treatises of the thirteenth and fourteenth centuries are either anonymous or can be related to persons about whom hardly anything is known. However, there is at least some biographical evidence about two authors whose writing included *musica theorica*. Both reveal strong ties to scientific research in other fields. Walter Odington was also astronomer and especially known for his alchemical treatise *Icocedron*, and Jean de Meurs was just as important in the fields of geometry and astronomy as in music theory. Also, investigation of the scientific network in which Jean de Meurs was embedded has revealed connections with *Nicole Oresme.

There was also influence toward the opposite direction. It has been claimed that music theory influenced structures of philosophical and scientific argumentation. What is more, music theory took the place of an ideal of order. Indeed, the purpose of *musica theorica* can be seen in its function to demonstrate the idea of cosmos, harmony, and order that was essential also for natural philosophy, epistemology, and metaphysics. Jacques de Liège's *Musica coelestis* described the harmony of Aristotle's categories, and Thomas Aquinas referred to ideas of harmony when explaining the possibility of experience. Hence the importance of *musica mundana*.

See also **Aristotelianism; Arithmetic; Astronomy, Islamic; Astronomy, Latin; Logic; Nature: diverse medieval interpretations; Optics and catoptrics;** *Scientia*

Bibliography

Crombie, Alistair C. *Science, Optics and Music in Medieval and Early Modern Thought*. London, Ronceverte: Hambledon Press, 1990.

Della Seta, Fabrizio. "Utrum musica tempore mensuretur continuo, an discreto." Premesse filosofiche ad una controversia del gusto musicale. *Studi musicali* (1984) 13: 169–219.

Goddu, André. "Music as Art and Science in the Fourteenth Century." In *Scientia und ars im Hoch und Spätmittelalter* (Miscellanea Medievalia 22). Edited by I. Craemer-Ruegenberg and A. Speer. New York: Walter de Gruyter, 1994, pp. 1023–1045.

———. Music, Philosophy, and Natural Science in the Middle Ages. *Studies in Medieval Thought (Kyoto)* (1998) 40: 1–18.

Haas, Max. "Musik zwischen Mathematik und Physik: Zur Bedeutung der Notation in der 'Notitia artis musicae' des Johannes de Muris (1321)." In *Festschrift für Arno Volk*. Cologne, Germany: Musikverlag Gerig, 1974, 31–46.

———. Studien zur mittelalterlichen Musiklehre I: Eine Übersicht über die Musiklehre im Kontext der Philosophie des 13. und frühen 14. Jahrhunderts. *Forum musicologicum* (1982) 3: 323–456.

Hentschel, Frank, ed. *Musik, und die Geschichte der Philosophie und Naturwissenschaften im Mittelalter*. Boston: E.J. Brill, 1998.

———. *Sinnlichkeit und Vernunft in der mittelalterlichen Musiktheorie*. Stuttgart, Germany: Franz Steiner, 2000.

Lindley, Mark. Fifteenth-century Evidence for Meantone Temperament. *Proceedings of the Royal Musical Association* (1975/6) 102: 37.

———. "Stimmung und Temperatur." In *Geschichte der Musiktheorie*, vol. 6: *Hören und Messen in der frühen Neuzeit*. Edited by Frieder Zaminer. Darmstadt, Germany: Wissenschaftliche Buchgesellschaft, 1987.

Münxelhaus, Barbara. *Pythagoras Musicus: Zur Rezeption der pythagoreischen Musiktheorie als quadrivialer Wissenschaft im lateinischen Mittelalter*. Bonn-Bad Godesberg, Germany: Verlag für systematische Musikwissenschaft, 1976.

Panti, Cecilia. La scienza musicale nella prospettiva 'occamista' di un anonimo Magister artium del tardo Medioevo. *Studi musicali* (1990) 19: 3–32.

———. The First 'Quaestio' of ms Paris, B.N. lat. 7372: 'Utrum musica sit scientia'. *Studi Medievali Serie Terza* (1992) 33: 265–313.

Sachs, Klaus-Jürgen. *Mensura Fistularum. Die Mensurierung der Orgelpfeifen im Mittelalter*. 2 vols. Murrhardt: Musikwissenschaftliche Verlags-Gesellschaft, 1970–1980.

———. *Der Contrapunctus im 14. und 15. Jahrhundert. Untersuchungen zum Terminus, zur Lehre und zu den Quellen*. Wiesbaden, Germany: Franz Steiner, 1974.

Tanay, Dorit Esther. *Noting Music, Marking Culture: The Intellectual Context of Rhythmic Notation, 1250-1400*. Holzgerlingen: American Institute of Musicology; Hänssler Verlag, 1999.

Taschow, Ulrich. Die Bedeutung der Musik als Modell für Nicole Oresmes Theorie. *Early Science and Medicine* (1999) 4: 37–90.

Wittmann, Michael. Vox atque Sonus. Studien zur Rezeption der Aristotelischen Schrift "De anima" und ihre Bedeutung für die Musiktheorie. 2 vols. Pfaffenweiler: Centaurus-Verlagsgesellschaft, 1987.

FRANK HENTSCHEL

N

NATURAL HISTORY

Most medieval writings on this subject are influenced by Pliny, whose encyclopedia of the first century C.E., *Historia naturalis* (*Natural History*), became the model for the genre and the principal source of similar works of late antiquity, including those of Aelian and Solinus. Pliny's massive survey of the lands and peoples of the empire, of which around two hundred manuscripts survive, was a seemingly inexhaustible source of data about animals, plants, and minerals. The origin of properly medieval writing on nature can be traced to the "hexaemeral literature," a group of commentaries on the biblical narrative of the six days of creation. Written by Patristic authors including Basil and Ambrose, and incorporated into the commentaries on Genesis by Augustine and *Bede, these works contain information on living creatures, plants, and animals taken from Greco-Roman sources. In his *On Christian Doctrine*, Augustine (d. 430) envisaged two complementary intellectual programs regarding the study of nature in the context of Biblical exegesis. On the one hand, he enjoined believers to write about animals, trees, herbs, and stones that could be of help in the interpretation of those passages in the Bible in which these things are mentioned. On the other hand, he discussed the broader question of the *allegoria in factis* ("allegory of things"), by which he meant that not only the words but also the natural creatures mentioned in scripture are themselves signs and as such susceptible of being interpreted. These two projects were actually fulfilled with the development of the medieval encyclopedias. A substantial part of all of them is concerned with natural history. Of the twenty books of *Isidore of Seville's *Etymologies*—a vastly influential encyclopedia of the seventh century—four deal with beasts, geography, plants, and minerals.

Late twelfth- and thirteenth-century encyclopedias such as *Alexander Nequam's *On the nature of things*, *Bartholomaeus Anglicus's *On the properties of things*, and cognate works in the Dominican tradition such as *Vincent of Beauvais' *Speculum naturale* (*Mirror of Nature*) and *Thomas of Cantimpré's *On the Nature of Things* were mainly devoted to natural knowledge. Insofar as these works drew on Pliny, Solinus, and Seneca—besides many ancient and early medieval works in Latin and Arabic—they embodied the closest approximation to what can be considered as a medieval natural history. It should, however, be borne in mind that the aims and structure of these works were very different from those of their Roman models. For one thing, these medieval treatises were conceived with an explicit religious goal in view. Nature was not the pagan deity of antiquity, nor even the handmaiden of God in His creation (as was the case in the twelfth-century Platonic works on nature), but "the nature of a thing," expressing that which makes a particular kind of being what it is as the result of having been created by God. The proclaimed purpose of the treatises on the nature of things was to deploy the programs formulated by Augustine. In most cases, minerals, plants, and animals were listed alphabetically within sections which mirrored the medieval taxonomy of natural creatures. For example, Thomas of Cantimpré's *On the Nature of Things* has six books on animals (quadrupeds, birds, sea monsters, fish, serpents, and *vermes* [worms]), two books on plants (trees, aromatic trees, herbs), and two on minerals (stones and metals). Such classifications, indebted to folk taxonomy and Biblical lore on nature, are quite representative of other works of the same kind. Many of the short chapters devoted to animals end with one or more allegorical interpretations of the beast or bird; the chapters on plants are mainly concerned with their medical uses. In the late thirteenth and the fourteenth century, these works gave way to moralized encyclopedias and collections of exempla. These were explicitly conceived as tools for preaching, and purported to provide interesting stories taken from allegorized properties of animals and plants which could be used to enliven sermons and for moral edification.

Animals, Plants, and Stones

Discourse on natural history, considered as the sum of texts on animals, plants, and minerals, was fragmented in a variety of genres of writing, each of which expressed a particular attitude to knowledge. All this literature, ultimately derived from antiquity and with roots in popular lore and theological and literary traditions, constituted a complex and fluid system of textual borrowings.

In the case of animals, the most representative genre was perhaps that of the *bestiaries. An important difference between bestiaries and works on the nature of things was that in the former what is said about a given animal is in great part determined by the moral and religious teaching which is the main purpose of the work, while in the latter there is a neat distinction between the account of the animal and its interpretation. Technical works on animals comprised the books on hunting—such as *The Hunting Book* of Gaston Phébus (fourteenth century)—and the rich literature on hawking, with the outstanding example of *Frederick II's *On the art of falconry*. There were also texts on animal medicine, either of accipiters or of horses (examples of the latter are the treatises by Jordanus Rufus, Lorenzo Rusio, and *Teodorico Borgognoni). Non-European animals were outstanding characters in the literature of travels to the Far East. Some of these works were accounts of real voyages, such as those of *Marco Polo and the Franciscans William of Rubruquis and John of Plano Carpini, while others were imaginary, like the *Travels* of *John Mandeville. Fantastic beasts inhabited the literature on exotic lands, including the Latin and vernacular Alexander romances and associated texts. Purely literary works, such as collections of fables and fabliaux, also contributed to medieval lore on animals.

Knowledge about the vegetable world was mainly transmitted through the *herbals, which focused on the healing virtues of a given plant and contained instructions for its collection, preparation, and dosage. Although medieval *pharmacy was for the most part herbalistic, it did not exclude animal and mineral substances. The early medieval Sixtus Placitus's *Book on quadrupeds*, for instance, was a treatise on animal drugs and *Hildegard of Bingen's *Physica* is a treatise that recapitulates in its nine books the healing properties of minerals, stones, trees, plants, quadrupeds, and fish. One of the first incunabula, the *Hortus sanitatis* (*Garden of Health*) (Mainz, 1491), although usually considered a herbal, amounts in fact to an illustrated natural history, with more than one thousand small woodcuts of minerals, plants and animals. As was the case with animals, there is also technical literature on plants, particularly on gardening and *agriculture, such as the treatise of Petrus Crescentius which also has books on animal husbandry, veterinary and hunting.

With respect to the mineral world, the characteristic genre was the *lapidaries, mostly dealing with precious and semi-precious stones.

The medieval menagerie, as represented in texts, pictures, and sculptures, was populated with many wondrous and some monstrous beings. For a number of reasons, animals were more the vehicle of legend and imagination than plants. This is explained by the fact that bestiaries relied on allegory, while herbals served a practical purpose (although the technical literature of hawking and hunting is quite sober in this respect). Many of the manuscripts containing texts on natural creatures were illustrated. In the thirteenth century, visual images of birds, beasts, and plants in manuscript illuminations and sculpture became more "naturalistic" through the growing development of techniques of "realistic" depiction.

Natural History and Natural Philosophy

Besides the literary genres mentioned so far, it should be noted that the Aristotelian and pseudo-Aristotelian works on animals and plants gave rise to a strong tradition of commentary. *Albertus Magnus (Albert the Great) commented on Aristotle's books on animals and wrote original works on minerals and plants (the pseudo-Aristotelian *On Plants* was translated and commented on by *Alfred of Sareschel). One of the remarkable aspects of Albert's work is that he incorporated into his Aristotelian commentaries works which pertained to other genres of writing: a lapidary, a herbal, and a dictionary of animals. Taken as a whole and with his short treatise on geography, this set of books constitutes an attempt to deal with the three kingdoms of nature from the point of view of natural philosophy. In order to include an inventory of created beings into his Aristotelian project, Albert tailored and modified his materials. While he claimed that these things were not properly philosophical, nonetheless he used them to enrich the Aristotelian commentaries with a concern for particular species. During the thirteenth century the Dominican friars became engaged in a common and energetic inquiry into nature. It has been argued that the ultimate goal of this activity was to provide stabilized meanings to the interpretation of nature attuned to the orthodox teachings of the Christian church. The resulting works cover a wide spectrum: from the encyclopedia of Thomas of Cantimpré, akin to natural history, to the natural philosophical commentaries of Albertus Magnus.

See also **Agriculture; Aristotelianism; Bestiaries; Botany; Encyclopedias; Geography, chorography; Illustration, scientific; Mineralogy; Nature: the structure of the physical world; Pharmaceutic handbooks; Religion and science; Travel and exploration**

Bibliography

Abeele, Badouin van den. Bestiaires encyclopédiques moralisés. Quelques succédanés de Thomas de Cantimpré et de Barthélemy l'Anglais. *Reinardus* (1994) 7: 209–228.

Asúa, Miguel de. El De animalibus de Alberto Magno y la organización del discurso sobre los animales en el siglo XIII. *Patristica et Mediaevalia* (1994) 15: 3–26.

Cummins, John. *The Hound and the Hawk. The Art of Medieval Hunting*. London: Weidenfeld and Nicolson, 1988.

French, Roger K. Putting animals on the map: the natural history of the Hereford Mappa Mundi. *Archives of Natural History* (1994) 21: 289–308.

French, Roger K. and Andrew Cunningham. *Before Science. The Invention of the Friar's Natural Philosophy*. Aldershot: Scolar Press, 1996.

Herdson, Noel, ed. *An Early English Version of Hortus sanitatis*. London: B. Quaritch, 1954.

Nauert, Charles G., Jr. Humanists, Scientists and Pliny: Changing Approaches to a Classical Author. *American Historical Review* (1979) 84: 72–85.

Stannard, Jerry. "Natural History." In *Science in the Middle Ages*. Edited by David C. Lindberg. Chicago: University of Chicago Press, 1978.

Steel, Carlos, Guy Guldentops and Pieter Beullens. *Aristotle's Animals in the Middle Ages*. Leuven: Leuven University Press, 1999.

Yapp, William B. *Birds in Medieval Manuscripts*. London: The British Library, 1981.

MIGUEL DE ASÚA

NATURE: DIVERSE MEDIEVAL INTERPRETATIONS

The concept of Nature is Greek in origin. The word for Nature is *Physis*. There is considerable debate about the meaning of this word. For Aristotle, its original meaning seems to have been the coming to be of growing things. Aristotle himself provides a more detailed definition of the word in his account of the fundamental concepts of *Physics*. The Latin term *Natura* as a translation of *Physis* signifies "to be born," or birth. And after about 1255 Aristotle would be institutionalized in the university learning of the day as the "authority" in philosophy: *Philosophus*. Earlier Neo-Platonic interpretations of Nature would be overshadowed for the academic philosophers but would persist and be revived by Marsilio Ficino in the fifteenth century. In the early fourteenth century, Petrarch in *The Ascent of Mont Ventoux* would present a more naturalistic and humanistic perception of nature.

To read modern philosophical commentary, however, the reader is left with the impression that the Middle Ages lacked a concept of Nature. Heidegger holds that the Latin translation of the Greek word "*Physis*" as "*Natura*" led to a loss of meaning. Pierre Hadot holds that the Middle Ages witnessed a divorce between philosophical discourse and a way of life. Thus, even Platonism and *Aristotelianism "were reduced to the status of mere conceptual material which could be used in theological controversies." Philosophy is represented as the servant or even the slave of a superior theology or wisdom. Moreover, in *Nature and Man in the Middle Ages*, Alexander Murray argues that, despite the literature on this concept, there was no concept of nature in the Middle Ages.

If this is all that can or should be said about the concept of Nature in the Middle Ages, perhaps one ought to close the book on the subject. There are problems here, however. First, translation is not just the story of fundamental loss of meaning. Second, among the significant Philosophers as distinct from what *Roger Bacon calls the "common students" of philosophy, there was a keen sense for the Greek and Latin meanings of the word "Nature."

Is there a kernel of truth in the views of Heidegger and Hadot? Yes, there is. For Augustine, who is a major source for medieval thought, and for René Descartes who is commonly seen as the "authority" or founder of modern philosophy, philosophy itself is primarily concerned with the following subject-matter: God and the Soul. In such a view of things, Nature as such, as a primary principle of change and motion, disappears out of view or at least becomes a matter of secondary consideration. God is the truly creative principle and created things are caused or produced by God.

This curtailment of the pagan Greek and Latin scope of the word "Nature" can be seen in the apologetics of Latin writers such as Prudentius, Lactantius, and Ambrose. For Prudentius, Nature is the servant of God's handiwork. Nature is both a pro-creator and a sustainer of humanity. She assists in the creativity of God. Nature herself does not have a "moral authority"; she can only serve, not judge. In Lactantius, one notices the contrast between the art/intelligence of the divine creator and what is created, namely, Heaven and Earth. For Ambrose, nature is the work of God, is subordinate to God, but is also the pro-creator of the birth of natural things. Natural things follow a Law of Nature which has been ordained by God.

Personification

Still, the thinkers of the Middle Ages did not quite forget Nature (*Natura*). And rather than being the "servant" or "slave" of a superior wisdom, as Hadot implies, Nature (*Natura*) as the personification of that wisdom had the status of a Goddess. Hence, if Nature is a servant, she is no mere subordinate. She will have to be Pro- or Co-Creator. Nevertheless, with the institutionalization of Aristotle in the thirteenth century, this aspect of Nature as divine would gradually give way to a more "secular" and scientific understanding. And much of the later Francis Baconian masculine birth of time will be prefigured in this philosophical Aristotelian understanding of nature in Latin philosophy. In this world, nature as feminine has been abolished as an important concern to philosophy.

To understand the concept of Nature in the Middle Ages, it is important to understand the origins and uses of this concept. Four thinkers are fundamentally important for the development of the concept. They are Augustine, *Boethius, Pseudo-Dionysius, and *John Scottus Eriugena. They were supplemented by various texts having a Platonic or Stoic background.

Even Augustine did not altogether exclude Nature. In his important *De doctrina christiana*, he retains a strong distinction between natural and conventional meaning. Nature is something to be explored and understood by means of "number, weight, and measure." To gain a sense of the Greek meaning of Nature as understood in the early Middle Ages, however, one needs to turn to Boethius, Pseudo-Dionysius, and Eriugena.

Boethius presents his definition of Nature in *Contra Eutychen*: "Nature, then, may be affirmed either of bodies alone or of substances alone, that is, of corporeals or incorporeals, or of everything that is in any way capable of affirmation." Since, then, nature can be affirmed in three ways, it must obviously be defined in three ways. For if you choose to affirm nature of the totality of things, the definition will be of such a kind as to include all things that are. It will accordingly be something of this kind: "Nature belongs to those things which, since they exist, can in some measure be apprehended by the mind." This definition, then, includes both accidents and substances, for they can be apprehended by the mind. The phrase "in some measure" is included because God and matter cannot be apprehended by the mind, be it so whole or perfect, but they still are apprehended in a measure through the removal of accidents. The reason for adding the words, "since they exist" is that the mere word "nothing" denotes something, although it does not denote nature. For it denotes, indeed, not anything that is, but rather non-existence, but every nature exists. And if we choose to affirm "nature" of the totality of things, the definition will be as we have given it above.

In Book Four of the *Consolation of Philosophy* Boethius presents his account of the place and role of Nature in the ordering of the universe. This account will be foundational for much philosophical poetry and prose in the Middle Ages. *Philosophia* begins her account with the assertion that the generation and process of all of mutable nature in terms of its cause, order and form are derived from the divine Mind. The origination of these is called *Providence*. The procession of this order in time is called *Fate*. As he puts it, "this order of fate proceeds from the simplicity of Providence." Fate is the instrument of this Providence, and is aided in this by all powers, heavenly and earthly.

The personification of Nature as a "Goddess" has to be taken seriously. It is a reflection of two separate traditions. First, it reflects the tradition of the Greek thought of a cosmic goddess of infinite life. This poetic tradition will receive new life in twelfth-century works such as the *De mundi universitate* of *Bernard Silvester and Alain de Lille's *De planctu naturae* and *Anti-Claudianus*.

Pseudo-Dionysius is important in that he leads medieval thinkers to think of nature as "being" or what is, and of God as "super-essential," that is, beyond being. God is the transcendent ineffable One; being, or what is, is subject to the examination of reason.

It is with Eriugena that one finds a philosophical synthesis of Augustine, Boethius, and Pseudo-Dionysius. In this sense, he is a foundational source for the thinking about nature in the Middle Ages. The very title of Eriugena's major work, *Peri Physeon (De divisione naturae)* echoes Greek concerns with Nature as such. For him, nature does not mean just "this or that" thing, but Nature as a whole including God. John O'Meara's paraphrase of this division provides a useful summary:

"The first and fundamental division of all things which can be grasped by the mind or lie beyond its grasp is into those things that are and those things that are not. Nature is the term we apply to all things, to those that are and to those that are not. Nature is a genus that is divided into four species: that which creates and is not created, that which is created and also creates, that which is created but does not create, and that which neither creates nor is created.

The third species is the contrary of the first, as the fourth is of the second. The fourth species is classed among the impossibles, since it is of its essence that it cannot be. The first species is the Cause of all things that are and that are not, that is, God; the second is the primordial causes; and the third those things that become manifest through coming into being in times and places."

In this way, Nature is worked into a Christian-Platonic understanding of the world. The first and fourth division is God as Source and End. The second is the Primordial Causes as creative, and the third is "created natures" including the human being. Elsewhere, Eriugena presents the human being as "the workshop" of nature in which the human intelligence re-creates nature on its way back to the One. This broad philosophical concept of Nature would provide the background for much poetry and philosophy at least up until the burning of Eriugena's book in Paris in 1210, and would continue to have a lasting influence on the "greater philosophers" including Aquinas, Eckhart, and Nicholas of Cusa, not to mention the great Latin poets of the Middle Ages.

It is in the twelfth century, however, that one witnesses a re-birth of a concern with Nature in Poetry and in Philosophy. This re-birth is commonly associated with the Neo-Platonism of the School of Chartres. This re-birth reintroduced ideas of nature from Latin pagan writers such as Macrobius, Chalcidius, Martianus and others.

This "Chartrian" notion of nature presents the world as a *macrocosmos* and the human being as a *microcosmos*. The study of the *macrocosmos* will reveal the nature of the *microcosmos*, the human being. Hence it is not surprising that early reviewers of the *De mundi universitate* of Bernard Silvester accused that work of paganism. In this allegorical fable (*integementum*), Bernard provides a synthesis of pagan and Christian worlds. Still, the Neoplatonic influence is evident throughout the poem. Nature is described as "maker" (*artifex*). She is the one who provides bodies for the souls that derive from *Noys* (the divine mind). Nature is an intermediary between the supra-lunary world of the heavens with the divine mind and the created bodies in this world. This notion of nature as the mediator between the heavens and bodies, and between souls and bodies will have a long influence. Even the introduction of the more "naturalistic" *Aristotelianism of the schools in the thirteenth century will not deflect its influence. It will simply be absorbed by it. Further, this Neoplatonic vision of nature will be revived in the later Renaissance by the greatest Platonist of the age, Marsilio Ficino. The application of this idea to nature will become very evident in his work, *De vita libri tres*.

It is a common claim that Alain de Lille made "the single most significant contribution to the history of the goddess Natura in medieval literature" (George D. Economou). In the *De planctu naturae*, modeled after Boethius's *Consolation of Philosophy*, the goddess *Natura* appears to the poet in a vision. Again, as in the tradition mentioned above, her task is to give order and structure to the production of mutable things. She is the vice-regent of God, responsible for the generation of things. The very costume of *Natura* details her heavenly origin and her regency over the created world where she is responsible for the generation of the human being as the image of the macrocosm. She is the vicar of God. The Law of Nature, thus, reflects the eternal law of God. Hence, she advocates marriage as the proper end of human generation, and condemns man's subversion of her laws in sodomy.

The task of the *Anti-Claudianus* is to set out the creation of a new human being who by means of an imitation of Christ will re-create nature and return it to its end, God as fulfillment. This work involves a cosmic journey, the normal human struggles for moral perfection, and man's place in the universe. This debate on nature and sexual love is of course expressed with great skill in Jean de Meun's *Roman de la Rose*. Indeed, it closely parallels the poems of Alain de Lille. Nature is again seen as the vicar of God, the one responsible for implementing the order of nature. This tradition of the "Goddess Nature" will later be depicted in *Chaucer's Parlement of Fowles.

Yet soon after the work of Bernard Silvester and Alain de Lille, a new approach to nature presented itself to Latin readers. With the translation into Latin of works on *astronomy and *astrology such as the *Introduction to Astronomy* by *Abu Ma'Shar (Albumasar), Latin readers now found that advances in cosmology had been achieved in the Islamic world. And yet the reference to a divine source of order is not absent from these works. These works would become an integral part of the twelfth- and thirteenth-century translations of Aristotle.

The introduction of Aristotle to the curriculum of the medieval university took place between 1150 and 1260. By 1255, candidates for the M.A. degree at Paris were required to read the texts of the Stagarite. And by 1267 *Roger Bacon in his *Communia naturalium* will boast that natural philosophers no longer believe in "the world-soul" or such mythological belief. This marked a profound change in the approach to the concept of Nature. Nature is no longer seen as a "goddess." Nature is now a structure with rational properties that can be scientifically understood. And with the use of instruments, the human being can examine all of the heavens and the Earth. Nature is a stable present order subject to investigation by reason and will of human action. This new Aristotelian concept of Nature has very distinctive characteristics.

Nature in the Aristotelian sense is defined in reference to two other concepts, Art (*techne*) and Chance (*tuche*). These two concepts continued to influence the understanding of nature throughout the Middle Ages. In certain respects, the issue of Art versus Nature referred back to fundamental issues in Greek Philosophy. Gregory Vlastos in *Plato's Universe* outlines the manner in which, for Plato, Art triumphs over Nature as a principle of change. And yet the recovery of Aristotle in the thirteenth century and later helped recover elements of the importance of Nature as a principle of motion and rest. Yet this would have to be integrated with Augustine's interpretation of divine ideas, where Art came to be fundamentally identified with the creative primordial causes. Hence, due to Art, Nature was the expression of the divine plan.

Following on the recovery of Aristotle, the word Nature had multiple meanings. These meanings are tied to the technical uses of the term *physis/natura* in Aristotle. He acknowledges that *phusis* with a long *u* signifies the growth or coming to be of things. From the observation of living things, nature came to be used as the active principle of growing things. This meaning was extended to become the technical term, nature, as the source of movement or the active principle of movement in all natural things. But Aristotle also identifies nature with the matter involved in growth, that out of which natural things come. Again, nature came to be applied to the structure/form and composition of natural things. Aristotle's criticism of the pre-Socratics, much echoed in the texts of medieval natural philosophers, attacked their reduction of form to matter. Again, the term nature was extended to mean every essence. Nevertheless, despite the multiple meanings, the medieval thinkers are very precise about the use of the term. Hence, whereas the modern meaning of the term Nature is very loose, possibly signifying the sum total of things, a manifold, the medieval connotations of the term, like the ancient connotations, are varied.

One must not forget, however, that the concept of Nature that medieval Latins received is filtered through the commentaries of Islamic philosophers, in particular those of Avicenna (*Ibn Sina) and Averroes (*Ibn Rushd). This interpretation lends a strongly necessitarian and deterministic reading of the order of nature in the light of the executive will of God. And as in *Abu'Mashar, the reference to a feminine role in the development of nature is not absent.

What then is the fundamental shift of meaning from the Platonism of the twelfth century to the Aristotelianism of the thirteenth century with respect to the Concept of Nature? James Weisheipl puts the matter succinctly:

"The fundamental assumption in the Aristotelian conception of nature is that natural phenomena, that is, those arising from neither Art nor Chance, are intelligible; there is a regularity, a determined rationality, about these phenomena which can be grasped.... Therefore, we must admit that in each physical reality there is something given in experience, which is none other than the spontaneous manifestation of its characteristics and proper activities. There is nothing 'behind' this spontaneity, as far as the body is concerned; it is just 'given' in experience. Thus, it will follow that Nature will have active and passive principles."

Following on this will be the fundamental distinction between natural agency/ bodies and artificial agency/ bodies. But even here, qualifications are called for. Through various sources, especially Augustine, Stoic doctrines of matter as having an active element were integrated with the Aristotelian doctrine of matter so that matter was not seen by all natural philosophers in the Middle Ages as a purely passive principle. This is especially the case for the Franciscan tradition.

It would appear now that what had previously been reserved to creative divine ideas or art, is now seen as also the prerogative of the human being. Artificial production is the result of the idea in the mind of the human being even though the idea has its ultimate source in the mind of God. Finally, nature as matter signifies not only pure passivity but all the passive powers in nature. Nature as form was the principle of spontaneous activity.

This division of nature would have significant consequences for the male/female distinction and for issues of gender throughout the Middle Ages. It would influence all assumptions about the internal powers of male and female. Prudence Allen has studied this issue carefully. She begins her account with one of the earliest teachers of natural philosophy, Roger Bacon. He is seen as a representative of the position of sex-neutrality. Both men and women share the same rationality. Further, he states that he is following the example of *Robert Grosseteste in not simply accepting what Aristotle said as the truth. Aristotle is a wise man "but nevertheless, he did not reach the limit of wisdom...." In his theory of generation, Bacon offers a scientific explanation, and emphasizes the role of the heavenly bodies. Unlike Bacon, the main tradition of Paris, based on *Albertus Magnus, and represented by *Thomas Aquinas and *Giles of Rome, stresses the polarity of the sexes. Allen acknowledges the central role that the texts of Giles played even in the Faculty of Medicine.

The Aristotelian revolution brought about a more diversified concept of nature. This had very significant impact on various scientific fields from the study of the elements to sensation to human knowledge. And yet it is significant that the sex neutrality position of a Roger Bacon gave way over time to the more popular view of sex polarity. As Allen puts it, Aristotle's views on nature and generation influenced all levels of education and practice in the Middle Ages.

One major consequence of this Aristotelian definition of nature was the gradual disappearance of the sex complementarity view associated with twelfth-century women writers such as Roswitha, Héloïse, and Herrad. In brief, something as seemingly abstract as the Concept of Nature had fundamental practical implications for even the most intimate details of life and the organization of human education and relations.

One also witnesses a new concern with the "manipulation" of nature on the part of some philosophers and scientists such as Roger Bacon and Pierre de Maricourt (*Peter Peregrinus) c. 1267. Emphasis is placed on the work of the hand in the construction of a compass, the uses of magnets, the calculation of distances with instruments, and the building of optical means for extending vision. Alongside this new concern with the "manipulation" of nature, one notices a new concern with setting out the boundaries of an Art and Science of Nature. In other words, just as Logic provides the rules for correct argumentation, the experimentalist will have need of a practical logic or method. The function of this logic will be to distinguish the art and science of Nature from Magic, and also from other human pursuits such as morals and religion. While there is evidence in both Roger Bacon and Pierre de Maricourt of actual experimentation and the construction of artificial experiments,

one must be cautious about general claims concerning flying machines and submarines. These latter belong to the utopian realm of fiction, and are not original with Roger Bacon. Still, it is clear that in the mid-thirteenth century, influenced by actual contacts with the world of Islam, the Latin West came to have a sense that natural science was a pursuit that would require the mastery of the problems presented to it by two of the great scientists of the ancient world, Aristotle and Ptolemy. Indeed, they already see that Islamic scientists such as *Ibn al-Haytham decisively advance the study of vision and light, and present them with new models for scientific advancement.

While it is true that Petrarch introduces a new humanistic concern with nature, it is clear also that the medieval image of Nature as feminine "Goddess," as the personification of divine Wisdom, and as the one responsible for the production of things through generation continues to have an influence into the late Renaissance. Katherine Park has demonstrated that a new image of Nature, one quite distinct from the medieval image, begins to appear in the 1470s at Naples. It was the result of a collaboration between the Roman scholar Luciano Fosforo and the miniaturist Gaspare Romano in the illustrations of a manuscript copy of Pliny's *Natural History* for Cardinal John of Aragon. This new image "of Nature as a lactating woman, partly or completely naked, or as a woman endowed with many breasts" would have a marked influence on Renaissance perceptions of Nature and would in part replace the medieval image of Nature as divine "Goddess," organizer of the production of generated things.

We have seen that many influences, both pagan and Christian, go into the making of the medieval concept of Nature. This concept in its many forms had a longlasting influence into the Renaissance and even into modernity.

See also **Microcosm/macrocosm; Nature: the structure of the physical world**

Bibliography

Allen, Prudence. *The Concept of Woman: The Aristotelian Revolution, 750 B.C.–A.D. 1250*. Grand Rapids, Michigan: William B. Eeerdmans Publishing Company, 1985.

Boethius. *Theological Tractates; The Consolation of Philosophy, with an English Translation of "I. T.," Revised by H.F. Stewart*. Edited by H.F. Stewart and E.K. Rand. Cambridge: Harvard University Press, 1968.

Chenu, M.D. *Nature, Man and Society in the Twelfth Century*. Selected, edited, and translated by Jerome Taylor and Lester K. Little. Chicago: University of Chicago Press, 1968.

Dronke, Peter, ed. *A History of Twelfth-Century Western Philosophy*. New York: Cambridge University Press, 1988.

Economou, George D. *The Goddess Natura in Medieval Literature*. Cambridge: Harvard University Press, 1972.

Hackett, Jeremiah, ed. *Roger Bacon and the Sciences: Commemorative Essays*. Leiden: E. J. Brill, 1997.

Jeauneau, Edouard. *"Lectio philosophorum": Recherches sur l'Ecole de Chartres*. Amsterdam: Hakkert, 1973.

Mensching, Günther. "Metaphysik und Naturbeherrschung im

Denken Roger Bacons." In Lothar Schäfer und Elizabeth Ströker, eds. *Naturauffassungen in Philosophie, Wissenschaft, Technik* [Band 1: Antike und Mittelalter]. Freiburg/München: Verlag Karl Alber, 1993.

Modersohn, Mechthild. *Natura als Gottin im Mittelalter: Ikonographische Studien zu Darstellungen der personifizierten Natur.* Berlin: Akademie Verlag, 1997.

Murray, Alexander. "Nature and Man in the Middle Ages." In John Torrance, ed., *The Concept of Nature [The Herbert Spencer Lectures].* Oxford: Clarendon Press, 1992.

O'Meara, John J. *Eriugena.* Oxford: Clarendon Press, 1988.

Park, Katherine. "Nature in Person: Medieval and Renaissance Allegories and Emblems." In Lorraine Daston and Fernando Vidal, eds., *The Moral Authority of Nature.* Chicago: University of Chicago Press, 2004.

Roberts, Lawrence D., ed. *Approaches to Nature in the Middle Ages.* Binghamton, New York: Medieval & Renaissance Texts & Studies, 1982.

Vlastos, Gregory. *Plato's Universe.* Seattle: University of Washington Press, 1975.

James A. Weisheipl, O.P. *Nature and Motion in the Middle Ages.* Edited by William E. Carroll. Washington, D.C.: The Catholic University of America Press, 1985.

JEREMIAH HACKETT

NATURE: THE STRUCTURE OF THE PHYSICAL WORLD

In the literature of the Middle Ages, the goddess Natura was the personification of Nature. She ruled over social relations and was the inspiration for right living according to reason. But the goddess Nature played no role in understanding the workings of nature from the standpoint of science and natural philosophy. The means of understanding nature's operations in the physical world came to the Middle Ages with the translation of Aristotle's works on natural philosophy in the twelfth and thirteenth centuries. Aristotle's ideas about nature and the "natural" appear in almost all of his non-logical works, including those on ethics and politics, where he has much to say about human nature. His views on the role of nature in the material cosmos of our physical world, however, are revealed largely in those treatises commonly known as "the natural books," namely *Physics, On the Heavens, On Generation and Corruption, On the Soul,* and *Meteorology,* along with his biological treatises. During the late Middle Ages, almost all scholars accepted Aristotle's understanding of nature.

Aristotle divided the world into two radically different regions: the celestial and the terrestrial. Together, these regions comprised the whole of nature. They were assumed to form a "ladder" (the so-called "ladder of nature"), a concept based on the idea that there is a gradation of perfection and virtue in the universe ranging from the center of the Earth, the least perfect region, to the outermost sphere of the universe, the most perfect. The farther things are from the Earth, the nobler and more perfect they are. The two regions are separated at the concave surface of the lunar sphere: everything beyond forms the celestial region, everything below, the terrestrial region.

The Celestial Region

The celestial region is composed of, and everywhere filled with, an incorruptible ether. The planets and stars are made of it, as are the spheres in which they are embedded, and which carry them around perpetually with a uniform, circular motion. The only change that occurs in the celestial region is the change of position experienced by celestial bodies as they are carried round by their espective orbs. Because it was generally regarded as fitting that a nobler being should influence a less noble being, it was universally believed that the essentially incorruptible and unchanging celestial region necessarily influences and dominates the incessantly changing terrestrial region.

The Terrestrial Region

In contrast to the celestial region, the terrestrial region, which lies below the lunar sphere, consists of bodies in a perpetual state of change. These bodies are either one of the four elements—fire, air, water, and earth—or compounds composed of two or more of those elements. Every animate and inanimate body in the terrestrial region is composed of matter and form, where the matter serves as a substratum in which the form inheres. For Aristotle the form of a thing or body is expressed in its defining characteristics—the properties that make it what it is. In the terrestrial realm, nature is a collective term for all the bodies contained therein, each of which consists of matter and form. If unimpeded, each of these bodies acts in accordance with its natural potentialities. In so doing, it is capable of acting on other bodies—that is, it is capable of causing effects on them. Thus did Aristotle allow for secondary causation. He believed that every effect was produced by four causes acting simultaneously, namely a material cause, which is the thing from which something is made; a formal cause, which produces the defining characteristics of a thing; an efficient cause, which is the agent of an action; and the final cause, or the purpose for which the action is undertaken. These four causes are capable of producing four kinds of change or motion: substantial change occurs when something comes into being or passes out of existence; qualitative change is the alteration of something, as when its color changes, or it becomes harder or softer; quantitative change involves an increase or decrease in size or weight; and change of place is motion from one place to another.

In the Middle Ages, natural philosophers regarded the domain of nature as essentially that which embraced all motion and rest with respect to a body's natural place. The concept of natural place was fundamental to their idea of nature and the key to Aristotle's idea of what makes the natural world what it is. Aristotle believed that the terrestrial region—that is, the part of the world that lay below the concave surface of the lunar sphere and extended all the way to the center of our spherical Earth at the center of the world—was naturally divided into four concentric layers, each of which was the natural place of one of the four elements. The outermost concentric ring is that of fire; the next is that of air, beneath which is the concentric ring of water and then, at the center of the world, the sphere of Earth, the center of which coincides with the geometric center of the universe. If a body is removed from its natural place it will, if unimpeded, seek to move back to it. Thus a piece of the element earth, or a compound body in which earth is predominant, will move naturally downward toward the Earth's center and come to rest naturally on the Earth's surface. Similarly, a fiery body, or a compound that is primarily fire, will always, if unimpeded, rise upward toward the natural place of fire. Air and water are intermediate elements. That is, an airy body will rise upward when in earth or water and descend when in the concentric region of fire; similarly, water, or a compound body in which water is predominant, will rise when in the earth, but descend when in the natural places of fire or air.

Nature embraces the totality of things that have an innate capacity for motion. Moreover, Nature always acts for a purpose in order to achieve some goal or end. For example, a heavy body that falls to Earth does so in order to come to rest in its natural place on the Earth's surface. By their very natures, animate and inanimate bodies always act to acquire their respective defining forms, that is, to become in actuality what they had previously been only potentially, as when a child grows into an adult or a seed develops into a plant. Aristotle regarded such natural transformations as substantial changes.

Nature does not act with a conscious purpose. No God or Divine Mind causes the changes in nature. All things that change have an innate capacity for reaching their goals or ends. This was acceptable to Christians, who assumed that God had created the world and ordained Nature with the powers and capacities to act in the manner that Aristotle had described. Although God could, and did, create miracles that are contrary to the natural order, He rarely did so. The Aristotelian concept of cosmic nature, with its two radically different parts that were held together by a "ladder" rising from the least noble and perfect beings to the most noble and perfect, was abandoned with the rejection of scholastic natural philosophy in the seventeenth century.

The scholastic natural philosophers who described and investigated nature did so largely by abstract, non-empirical means, and with preconceived ideas about the way the universe ought to operate. Although, like Aristotle, they emphasized the empirical foundations of knowledge, their analyses and interpretations were not based on careful observations. Theirs was an "empiricism without observation," and ultimately a "natural philosophy without nature." By the seventeenth century, natural philosophers abandoned this approach, seeking instead actually to observe the operations of the real, physical world.

See also **Aristotelianism; Cosmology; Nature: diverse medieval interpretations**

Bibliography

Cadden, Joan. "Trouble in the Earthly Paradise: The Regime of Nature in Late Medieval Christian Culture." In Lorraine Daston and Fernando Vidal, eds. *The Moral Authority of Nature*. Chicago: University of Chicago Press, 2004, pp. 207–231.

Dales, Richard C. The De-animation of the Heavens in the Middle Ages. *Journal of the History of Ideas* (1980) 41: 531–550.

Grant, Edward. Medieval and Renaissance Scholastic Conceptions of the Influence of the Celestial Region on the Terrestrial. *Journal of Medieval and Renaissance Studies* (1987) 17: 1–23.

———. *Planets, Stars, and Orbs: The Medieval Cosmos 1200–1687*. New York: Cambridge University Press, 1994.

———. "Medieval Natural Philosophy: Empiricism Without Observation." In Cees Leijenhorst, Christoph Lüthy, Johannes M. M. H. Thijssen, eds. *The Dynamics of Aristotelian Natural Philosophy from Antiquity to the Seventeenth Century*. Leiden: E.J. Brill, 2002, pp. 141–168.

Murdoch, John E. "The Analytic Character of Late Medieval Learning: Natural Philosophy Without Nature." In Lawrence D. Roberts, ed., *Approaches to Nature in the Middle Ages*. Binghampton, NY: Center for Medieval and Early Renaissance Studies, 1982, pp. 171–213.

EDWARD GRANT

NAVIGATION (ARAB)

The Arabian Peninsula, surrounded by the Red Sea, the Indian Ocean, and the Arabian (or Persian) Gulf, had a geostrategic position in relations between East and West. Before the beginning of Islam in 622 the Arabs had had some nautical experience which was reflected in the Qur'an (VI, 97: "It is He who created for you the stars, so that they may guide you in the darkness of land and sea"; XIV, 32: "He drives the ships which by His leave sail the ocean in your service"; XVI, 14: "It is He who has subjected to you the ocean so that you may eat of its fresh fish and you bring up from it ornaments with which to adorn your persons. Behold the ships plowing their course through it.") and in ancient poetry (some verses of the poets Tarafa, al-A'sha', 'Amr Ibn Kulthum, and others). Arabs used the sea for transporting goods from or to the next coasts and for the exploitation of its resources (fish, pearls, and coral). However, their experience in maritime matters was limited due to the very rugged coastline of Arabia with its many reefs and was limited to people living on the coast. Because they lacked iron, Arab shipwrights did not use nails, but rather secured the timbers with string made from palm tree thread, caulked them with oakum from palm trees, and covered them with shark fat. This system provided the ships with the necessary flexibility to avoid the numerous reefs. The Andalusi Ibn Jubayr and the Magribi Ibn Battuta confirm these practices in the accounts of their travels that brought them to this area in the thirteenth and fourteenth centuries, respectively. Ibn Battuta also notes that in the Red Sea people used to sail only from sunrise to sunset and by night they brought the ships ashore because of the reefs. The captain, called the *rubban*, always stood at the bow to warn the helmsman of reefs.

The regularity of the trade winds, as well as the eastward expansion of Islam, brought the Arabs into the commercial world of the Indian Ocean, an experience that was reflected in a genre of literature which mixes reality and fantasy. Typical are the stories found in the *Akhbar al-Sin wa-l-Hind* (*News of China and India*) and *'Aja'ib al-Hind* (*Wonders of India*), as well as the tales of Sinbad the Sailor from the popular *One Thousand and One Nights*. But medieval navigation was also reflected in the works of the pilots such as *Ahmad Ibn Majid (whose book on navigation has been translated into English) and Sulayman al-Mahri.

In the Mediterranean Sea

The conquests by the Arabs of Syria and Egypt in the seventh century gave them access to the Mediterranean, which they called *Bahr al-Rum* (Byzantine Sea) or *Bahr al-Sham* (Syrian Sea). Nautical conditions were very different in this sea: irregular but moderate winds, no heavy swells, and a mountainous coastline that provided ample visual guides for the sailors on days with good visibility. The Arabs took advantage of the pre-existing nautical traditions of the Mediterranean peoples they defeated. In addition, we have evidence for the migration of Persian craftsmen to the Syrian coast to work in ship building, just as, later on, some Egyptian craftsmen worked in Tunisian shipyards.

The Arab conquests of the Iberian Peninsula (al-Andalus) and islands such as Sicily, Crete, and Cyprus set off a struggle between Christian and Muslim powers for control of the Mediterranean for trade, travel, and communications in general. Different Arab states exercised naval domination of the Mediterranean, especially during the tenth century. According to the historian Ibn Khaldun, warships were commanded by a *qa'id*, who was in charge of military matters, armaments, and soldiers, and a technical chief, the *ra'is*, responsible for purely naval tasks. As the Arabs developed commercial traffic in Mediterranean waters, they developed a body of maritime law which was codified in the *Kitab Akriyat al-sufun* (*The Book of Chartering Ships*). From the end of the tenth century and throughout the eleventh, Muslim naval power gradually began to lose its superiority.

In navigation technique, the compass reached al-Andalus by the eleventh century, permitting mariners to chart courses with directions added to the distances of the ancient voyages. The next step was the drawing of navigational charts which were common by the end of the thirteenth century. Ibn Khaldun states that the Mediterranean coasts were drawn on sheets called *kunbas*, used by the sailors as guides because the winds and the routes were indicated on them.

In the Atlantic Ocean

The Atlantic coasts of Europe and Africa, despite their marginal situation with respect to the known world at that time, had an active maritime life. The Arabs usually called this Ocean *al-Bahr al-Muhit* ("the Encircling or Surrounding Sea"), sometimes *al-Bahr al-Azam* ("the Biggest Sea"), *al-Bahr al-Akhdar* ("the Green Sea") or *al-Bahr al-Garbi* ("the Western Sea") and at other times *al-Bahr al-Muzlim* ("the Gloomy Sea") or *Bahr al-Zulumat* ("Sea of Darkness"), because of its numerous banks and its propensity for fog and storms. Few sailors navigated in the open Atlantic, preferring to sail without losing sight of the coast. The geographer *al-Idrisi in the middle of the twelfth century informs us so: "Nobody knows what there is in that sea, nor can ascertain it, because of the difficulties that deep fogs, the height of the waves, the frequent storms, the innumerable monsters that dwell there, and strong winds offer to navigation. In this sea, however, there are many islands, both peopled and uninhabited. No mariners dare sail the high seas; they limit themselves to coasting, always in sight of land." Other geographers, including Yaqut and al-Himyari, mention this short-haul, cabotage style of navigation. Yaqut observes that, on the other side of the world, in the faraway lands of China, people did not sail across the sea either. And al-Himyari specifies that the Atlantic coasts are sailed from the "country of the black people" north to Brittany. In the fourteenth century, Ibn Khaldun attributed the reluctance of sailors to penetrate the Ocean to the inexistence of nautical charts with indications of the winds and their directions that could be used to guide pilots, as Mediterranean charts did. Nevertheless, Arab authors describe some maritime adventurers who did embark on voyages of exploration.

Fluvial Navigation

Only on the great rivers such as the Tigris, the Euphrates, the Nile and, in the West, the Guadalquivir was there significant navigation. It was common to establish ports in the estuaries of rivers to make use of the banks to protect the ships.

Nautical Innovations

Two important innovations used by the Arabs in medieval period are worthy of mention: the triangular lateen sail (also called staysail), and the sternpost rudder. The lateen sail made it possible to sail into the wind and was widely adopted in the Mediterranean Sea, in view of its irregular winds. The Eastern geographer Ibn Hawqal, in the tenth century, described seeing vessels in the Nile River that were sailing in opposite directions even though they were propelled by the same wind. To mount only one rudder in the sternpost which could be operated only by one person proved vastly more efficient that the two traditional lateral oars it replaced. Although some researchers assert that this type of rudder originated in Scandinavia and then diffused to the Mediterranean Sea, eventually reaching the Arabs, it is most likely a Chinese invention which, thanks to the Arabs, reached the Mediterranean.

Toward Astronomical Navigation

The Arabs made great strides in astronomical navigation in the medieval period. With the help of astronomical tables and calendars, Arab sailors could ascertain solar longitude at a given moment and, after calculating the Sun's altitude as it comes through the Meridian with an astrolabe or a simple quadrant, they could know the latitude of the place they were in. At night, they navigated by the altitude of the Pole Star. For this operation Arab sailors in the Indian Ocean used a simple wooden block with a knotted string called the *kamal* which was used to take celestial altitudes. They also knew how to correct Pole Star observations to find the true North. Ibn Majid, for example, made this correction with the help of the constellation called *Farqadan*, which can only be seen in equatorial seas.

The determination of the longitude was a problem without a practical solution until the invention of the chronometer in the eighteenth century. Arab sailors probably may have used a sand clock to measure time, because they knew how to produce a type of glass that was not affected by weather conditions. So they could estimate the distance that the ship had already covered, even though speed could not be accurately determined. The navigational time unit used was called *majra*, which the geographer Abu l-Fida' defines as "the distance that the ship covers in a day and a night with a following wind," a nautical day that it is the rough equivalent of one hundred miles.

See also **Columbus, Christopher; Fishing; Shipbuilding; Transportation; Travel and exploration**

Bibliography

Fahmy, Aly Mohamed. *Muslim Naval Organisation in the Eastern Mediterranean from the Seventh to the Tenth Century A.D.* 2 vols. Cairo: General Egyptian Book Organisation, 1980.

Lewis, Archibald Ross. *Naval Power and Trade in the Mediterranean, A. D. 500–1000.* Princeton: Princeton University Press, 1951.

Lirola Delgado, Jorge. *El poder naval de Al-Andalus en la época del Califato Omeya.* Granada: Universidad de Granada, 1993.

Picard, Christophe. *La mer et les musulmans d'Occident au Moyen Age. VIIIe-XIIIe siècle.* Paris: Presses Universitaires de France, 1997.

Pryor, John H. *Geography, Technology and War. Studies in the Maritime History of the Mediterranean, 649–1571.* New York: Cambridge University Press, 1988.

Tibbetts, G. R. *Arab Navigation in the Indian Ocean before the Coming of the Portuguese being a translation of* Kitab al-Fawa'id fi usul al-bahr wa'l-qawa'id *of Ahmad b. Majid al-Najdi.* London: Royal Asiatic Society, 1971 .

JORGE LIROLA

NEQUAM, ALEXANDER

Alexander Nequam (also known as Neckam or Neckham) (1157–1217) was born and brought up in St. Albans, England. He studied in Paris at the school of the Petit Pont, c. 1175–1182, before returning to England in 1183. He then taught for a year at Dunstable and then at St. Albans before teaching at Oxford from c. 1190.

Sometime between 1197 and 1202 he became a canon at the Augustinian abbey of Cirencester. While Nequam never wrote any formal treatise on natural science, his writings are informed by a strong sense of observation of the natural world. His *De nominibus utensilium*, a list of words intended to teach vocabulary to schoolchildren, was modelled on the *Phale totum* or *De utensilibus* of Adam of Petit Pont. It uses everyday examples, such as household utensils, food, houses and furniture, cooking, parts of a castle, and the farm. Among his references to ships is the earliest known reference to a compass with a magnetized needle that revolved until it pointed north. Nequam's work provides a vivid insight into everyday life in the late twelfth century.

Much of Nequam's writing is concerned with grammatical and moral issues. His most widely copied work, the *Corrogationes Promethei*, deals with figures of speech and literary constructions, updating the instruction provided by Donatus and Priscian. A second section deals with difficult words in the Bible. His *Sacerdos ad altare* is similar to *De nominibus utensilium* in form, but deals with clerical matters. It draws on a wide range of classical works, including the *Bucolics* and *Georgics* of Virgil, and the epigrams of Martial, which were not widely read in the twelfth century. Nequam uses edifying stories to preach against any false sense of moral superiority.

His interest in scientific matters is evident in his *De naturis rerum et in Ecclesiasten*. He is one of the first known scholars to show awareness of scientific texts newly translated from both Arabic and Greek. He incorporates quotations from pseudo-Avicenna, *De caelo et mundo*, as well as from Aristotle's *Ethica*, and the *Liber XXIV philosophorum* and *Liber de causis*, translated by *Gerard of Cremona. He seems to have derived his knowledge of these texts not from his studies in Paris in the 1170s, but from his contacts at Oxford, perhaps from Englishmen such as Daniel of Morley and *Alfred of Sareschel, who had travelled in Spain. Alexander makes use of medical writings from *Salerno, especially *De commixtionibus elementorum* by *Urso of Calabria, the *Tegni* of *Galen, the *De dietis universalibus* of Isaac, the *Pantegni* of Constantine the African, and the *Quaestiones naturales* of *Adelard of Bath. Like Gerald of Wales (1175–1204), another source of information about animals, Alexander Nequam draws his natural science both from ancient authors such as Isidore, Solinus, and Cassiodorus, and from his own observation. In the *De naturis rerum* and the *Laus sapientiae divinae*, a metrical version of the same treatise, Alexander develops the theme that examining the works of nature leads to the love of God. The *Laus sapientiae divinae* deals with the stars, the rivers of Europe, the theory of the elements, and the three parts of the world. In the *Suppletio defectuum*, a supplement to the *Laus sapientiae divinae*, he describes birds, trees, herbs, birds, and animals, giving each of them a moral significance. In a second section, he deals with creation as a whole, then with the problems of man and the human soul, the Sun, Moon, and planets. Only in the final section does he deal with theology and the seven liberal arts.

Besides scriptural commentaries, Alexander wrote a major synthesis of theology, the *Speculum speculationum*, which was more conjectural than the *Sentences* of *Peter Lombard and in keeping with the philosophical reflections of St. Anselm (c. 1033–1109). Nequam frames his treatise as an attack on the false argument of the Cathars, "illiterate heretics" who distinguish between a good God and the creator of a corrupt world. His theme throughout the four books of his treatise is that God is the source of all good things, and that evil has no separate source, but rather has to be understood as the absence of good.

See also **Nature: diverse medieval interpretations; Translation movements**

Bibliography

Primary Sources

Alexander Nequam, De naturis rerum libri duo: with the poem of the same author, De laudibus divinæ sapientiae. Edited by Thomas Wright. Rerum britannicarum medii aevi scriptores 34. London: Longman, 1863.

———. "*De nominibus utensilium.*" In Anthony B. Hunt, *Teaching and Learning Latin in Thirteenth-Century England*, 3 vols. Woodbridge, Suffolk: Brewer, 1991, 1: 177–190.

———. Speculum speculationum. Edited by Rodney M. Thomson. Auctores Britannici medii aevi 11. New York: Oxford University Press, 1988.

Secondary Sources

Holmes, Urban T. *Daily living in the twelfth century; based on the observations of Alexander Neckham in London and Paris.* Westport: Greenwood Press, 1980.

Hunt, Richard W. *The schools and the cloister: the life and writings of Alexander Nequam (1157–1217).* Oxford: Clarendon Press, 1984.

O'Donnell, J. Reginald, "The liberal arts in the twelfth century with special reference to Alexander Nequam (1157-1217)." In *Arts libéraux et philosophie au Moyen Age: IVe Congrès international de philosophie médiévale Montréal 1967.* Paris: Vrin 1969, pp. 583–591.

Viarre, Simone. "*A propos de l'origine égyptienne des arts libéraux: Alexandre Neckam et Cassiodore.*" Arts libéraux et philosophie au Moyen Age: IVe Congrès international de philosophie médiévale, Montréal 1967. Paris: Vrin, 1969, pp. 583–591.

CONSTANT J. MEWS

NICCOLÒ DA REGGIO

A Greek and Latin bilingual scholar born in Calabria, Niccolò da Deoprepio da Reggio is known as a professional translator working at the Angevin court in Naples during the period 1308–1345 (if not later). Biographical data are scant: his year of birth is unknown, but should have been sometime around 1280. Unknown also is the place where he earned a medical degree, although Bologna and Padua have been suggested. The year of his death, no better attested, is likely to have been around 1350.

The first mention of a payment for the translation of a medical text made for Charles II of Anjou (1254–1309) dates back to 1308. Niccolò then pursued his activity at the Angevin court under Robert (b. 1275, king 1309, d. 1343) and Joanna I (b. 1326, queen 1343, d. 1381). Judging from his translation of *Galen, *De utilitate particularum*, dated 1317, Niccolò also worked for private physicians. In 1319, he was presented to the Naples Studium for a doctorate and a teaching licence. In 1322, he traveled to the papal court of Avignon under John XXII (b. 1249, pope 1316, d. 1334) as king Robert's physician, and in 1331 he was sent to Constantinople by the king on a diplomatic mission to the Byzantine emperor Andronicus III Palaiologos (b. 1297, emperor 1328, d. 1341), from whom Robert later received a Greek Galen manuscript as a gift.

At the Angevin court, Niccolò was not the only translator, but he was the most productive. He specialized in translating Galenic treatises from Greek into Latin, with more than sixty translations. They covered many fields of Galen's production: commentaries on Hippocratic works (*Commentarii in Hippocratis Aphorismos*, 1314); philosophy, epistemology, and logic (e.g., *De praecognitione*, perhaps translated from the manuscript offered by Andronicus III; *De historia philosophorum* and *De subfiguratione empirica*, both dated 1341; *De causis procatarticis*, and *De substantia virtutum naturalium*, which is a part of *De propriis placitis*); anatomy (e.g., *Anatomia matricis, Anatomia oculorum*, and *De utilitate particularum*, dated 1317); physiology (e.g., *De utilitate respirationis*, translated before 1309, and *De causis respirationis*); pathology (e.g., *De passionibus uniuscuisque particule*, made in 1335 or 1336 from the manuscript received by Robert from the Byzantine emperor; *De temporibus paroxismorum seu periodorum, De temporibus totius egritudinis*, and *De tumoribus*); diagnosis and prognosis (e.g., *De pronosticatione*); surgical therapeutic methods (e.g., *De flebotomia*, translated before 1309); pharmaceutical therapy (e.g., *De compositione medicamentorum secundum locos*, in 1335 or 1336; *Sex ultimi [libri] de simplici medicina; De virtute centauree; De tyriaca*); and diet (*De subtiliante diaeta*).

Niccolò's program aimed at revising and achieving the program of assimilation of ancient medicine, particularly Greek, previously carried out by such previous translators as *Constantine the African (d. after 1085) at *Monte Cassino, *Burgundio of Pisa (c. 1110–1193), *Gerard of Cremona (c. 1114–1187) in *Toledo, *Pietro d'Abano (c. 1257–c. 1315), and *Arnau de Vilanova (c. 1240–1311) in Montpellier. To this end, Niccolò translated neither Arabic works, nor Arabic versions of Greek texts (as did Constantine the African, Gerard of Cremona, and Arnau de Vilanova, for instance), but the original Greek texts (as Burgundio of Pisa and Pietro d'Abano already did). Not only did he complete translations left incomplete by such translators as Pietro d'Abano, but also he translated anew Galenic treatises previously translated, and he rendered into Latin works that had not been translated before. He also translated some Greek non-medical texts.

Niccolo da Reggio's translation technique consisted in proceeding "*de verbo ad verbum, nichil addens, minuens vel permutans.*" It has been differently appreciated. D'Alverny, stressing that such method was that of all previous translators from Greek, considered that it led him to literally follow the original text and to adopt Greek technical terms (by transliterating rather than translating them) when he found them adequate. Furthermore, on the basis of his prefaces, she thought that he was a mediocre Latinist. Editors of Galen's Greek works translated by Niccolò, such as for example V. Nutton, concluded that Niccolò "developed an accurate method and technical vocabulary whereby to express even the smallest features of the Greek original." It seems, however, that such a method did not always produce understandable texts for non-Greek speakers.

Niccolò strongly contributed to the reintroduction, diffusion, and assimilation of Galenic writings and medicine into Western medicine, as the manuscript tradition of his translations indicates. His translations probably reached southern France: according to Montpellier physician *Guy de Chauliac (c. 1290–c. 1367/1370), Niccolò sent some of his translations to the papal Curia in Avignon (*Inventarium sive Chirurgia magna, capitulum singulare*). In the Renaissance, some of Niccolò's translations were printed as early as 1490 in the Venice edition of Galen. Several editions appeared during the sixteenth century.

See also **Translation movements; Translation norms and practice**

Bibliography

Calvanico, R. *Fonti per la storia della medicina e della chirurgia per il regno di Napoli nel periodo Angioino.* Naples: L'Arte tip., 1962, p. 128.

D'Alverny, M.-Th. Pietro d'Abano traducteur de Galien. *Medioevo* (1985) 11: 19–64, pp. 41–46.

Deichgräber, K. *Die griechische Empirikerschule.* Berlin: Weidmann, 1965, pp. 7–11.

Dürling, R.J. A chronological census of Renaissance editions and translations of Galen. *Journal of the Warburg and Courtauld Institutes* (1961) 24: 229–305.

———. Corrigenda and addenda to Diels' Galenica. *Traditio* (1967) 23: 461–476.

Larrain, C. J. Galen, De motibus dubiis: die lateinisch Übersetzung des Niccolò da Reggio. *Traditio* (1994) 49: 171–233.

Lo Parco, F. Niccolò da Reggio, antesignano del risorgimento dell'antichità ellenica nel secolo XIV, da codici delle biblioteche italiane e straniere e da documenti e stampe rare. *Atti della Reale Accademia di Archeologia, Lettere e Belle Arti di Napoli* (1910) 5.11: 243–317.

Nutton, V. *Galen, On prognosis.* Berlin: Akademie-Verlag, 1979, pp. 23–34.

———. *Galen, On my own opinions.* Berlin: Akademie Verlag, 1999, pp. 33–37.

Pezzi, G. "La vita e l'opera di maestro Nicolao da Reggio." In *Atti della IX Biennale della Marca e dello studio Firmano per la storia dell'arte medica.* Fermo: Benedetti e Pauri, 1971, pp. 229–233.

Russo, P.F. *Medici e veterinari calabresi.* Naples: s.n., 1962, pp. 71–102.

Thorndike, L. Translations of works of Galen from the Greek by Niccolo da Reggio (c. 1308–1345). *Byzantina Metabyzantina* (1946) 1: 213–235.

Weiss, R. The translators from Greek of the Angevin court of Naples. *Rinascimento* (1950) 1: 195–226.

Wille, I. Ueberlieferung und Uebsersetzsung. Zur Uebersetzungtechnik des Nikolaus von Rhegium in Galen's Schrift De temoribus morborum. *Helikon* (1963) 3: 259–272.

ALAIN TOUWAIDE

NICHOLAS OF SALERNO

Very little is known about the physician and teacher Nicholas of Salerno (fl. c. 1150), but his putative authorship of the *Antidotarium Nicolai*, one of the most influential *pharmaceutical handbooks produced in the medieval West, makes him a convenient point of reference for a broader discussion of the complex traditions of Salernitan drug lore. The *Antidotarium* has also been ascribed to Nicholas of Aversa, to the Byzantine writer Nicholas Myrepsos (fl. c. 1300), to Nicholas Prepositus, and to one Nicolaus Alexandrinus: however, the inclusion in the *Antidotarium* of a recipe for *vomitus noster* ("our emetic"), which apparently corresponds to the *vomitus Nicolai* cited by Master Salernus in his *Compendium* (c. 1155–1160) argues for the existence of Nicholas of Salerno, and his authorship of the *Antidotarium*.

The *Antidotarium Nicolai* is an alphabetically organized manual containing recipes for compound remedies, based on an eleventh-century Salernitan compendium, the *Antidotarius magnus*. The *Antidotarius magnus* had a number of drawbacks: it was unwieldy (more than one thousand entries), and the recipes, drawn from a variety of ancient, early medieval, and early Salernitan sources, often appeared in numerous variant forms. Taking his cue from the anonymous commentary in the *Antidotarius* entitled *Liber iste*, Nicolas selected about one hundred ten to one hundred fifteen of the most commonly used and useful compounds (he refers to them in the preface as the *usuales medicinae*), to which he added a few original preparations of his own, e.g., the *vomitus noster*. Later versions expanded the number of recipes to about one hundred seventy-five. He laid out the entries in a broadly standardized manner: an explanation of the name of the drug is followed by its therapeutic indication, ingredients, mode of preparation, dosage, and form of administration. Nicholas equipped his manual with an index of *synonyma*, which contributed to rationalizing the nomenclature of *materia medica*, and added information on preserving drug substances. Above all, he clarified and standardized the system of apothecary measures used in the *Antidotarius magnus*, notably by introducing the "grain" (*granum*, the weight of a grain of wheat, or one-twentieth of a scruple), a small unit which allowed the recipes to be made up with precision, but in modest quantities suitable for an individual physician's practice or apothecary's shop. All these innovations made the *Antidotarium Nicolai* the foundation document of medieval practical pharmacy.

In his preface, Nicolas indicates that his target audience is physicians: he is concerned to give them the tools to make up standard medicines at an affordable cost, and to dispense them with confidence. Its virtues were immediately appreciated: Salernitan writers on practical medicine, such as the author of the "First Salernitan Gloss" on the surgery of *Roger Frugard, were already citing the *Antidotarium* by the 1190s. The book's potential as a teaching tool inspired a commentary composed probably in the third quarter of the twelfth century by the Salernitan Matthaeus Platearius. Scholastic glosses continued to be produced to the end of the medieval period, e.g., by *John of Saint-Amand, and a course on the *Antidotarium* was obligatory for medical students at Paris by 1270–1274. Encyclopedists such as *Vincent of Beauvais (c. 1244) referred to it. At the same time, the *Antidotarium* began to assume the status of a standard pharmacopoeia: for example, *Frederick II of Sicily's Constitutions of Melfi enjoined apothecaries to compound their drugs in accordance with "the antidotary," and the apothecary ordinances of Ypres (1292–1310) named the *Antidotarium* as the official formulary.

It is difficult to exaggerate the long-term influence of the *Antidotarium Nicolai*. Extensively translated and excerpted in vernacular remedy collections (English, French, German, Dutch, Italian, Spanish, Hebrew, and even Arabic), the Latin text enjoyed a vigorous career in printed form from 1471 onward, and it continued to be issued and used down to the eighteenth century. The history of its diffusion is closely bound up with that of its logical companion-text, the *Circa instans*, a twelfth-century Salernitan manual of "simples" or drugs based on one (usually botanical) substance. The two are often found together in medieval manuscripts. Like the *Antidotarium*, *Circa instans* underwent considerable elaboration, and was also frequently translated. The *Antidotarium Nicolai* and *Circa instans* together bear witness to Salerno's talent for rationalizing the subject matter of practical medicine, hence securing its domain within the Scholastic ideology of medical *scientia*.

See also Herbals; Medicine, Practical; Pharmacy; Pharmacology; Salerno; Universities; Weights and measures

Bibliography

Primary sources

Eene middelnederlandsche vertaling van het Antidotarium Nicolai met den latijnschen tekst der eerste gedrukte uitgave van het Antidotarium Nicolai. Edited by W.S. van den Berg. Leiden: E.J. Brill, 1917.

L'Antidotaire Nicolas: deux traductions françaises de l'Antidotarium Nicolai, l'une du XIV. siècle… l'autre du XV. siècle…. Edited by Paul Dorveaux. Paris: Welter, 1896.

Nicolas of Salerno. *Antidotarium…* Venice: Nicholas Jenson, 1471. Facsimile edition in Goltz (see below); transcription (with variant readings) in van den Berg (see below).

Un volgarizzamento tardo duecentesco fiorentino dell'Antidotarium Nicolai. Montreal, Bibliotheca Osleriana 7628. Edited by Lucia Fontanella. Alessandria: Edizioni dell'Orso, 2000.

Secondary Sources

Braekman, Willy and Gundolf Keil. Fünf mittelniederländische Übersetzungen des 'Antidotarium Nicolai.' Untersuchungen zum pharmazeutischen Fachschriftum der mittelalterlichen Niederlande. *Sudhoffs Archiv* (1971) 55: 257–320.

Goltz, Dietlinde. *Mittelalterliche Pharmazie und Medizin: dargestellt an Geschichte und Inhalt des Antidotarium Nicolai: mit einem Nachdruck der Druckfassung von 1471.* Veröffentlichungen der Internationalen Gesellschaft für Pharmazie, n.F, 44. Stuttgart: Wissenschaftliche Verlagsgesellschaft, 1976.

Keil, Gundolf. Zur Datierung des Antidotarium Nicolai. *Sudhoffs Archiv* (1978) 62: 190–196.

Lebede, Kurt-Heinz. "Das Antidotarium des Nicolaus von Salerno und sein Einfluss auf Entwicklung des deutschen Arzneiwesens. Text und Kommentar von zwei Handschriften der Berliner Staatsbibliothek." Berlin: Diss, 1939.

Lutz, A. "Der verschollene frühsalernitanische Antidotarius magnus in einer Basler Handschrift aus dem 12. Jahrhundert und das Antidotarium Nicholai." In *Die Vorträge der Hauptsammlung der Internationalen Gesellschaft für Geschichte der Pharmazie* XVI, Stuttgart: Wissenschaftliche Verlagsgesellschaft, 1960.

———. "Aus der Geschichte der mittelalterlichen Antidotarien." In *Die Schelenz-Stiftung II 1954–1972.* Veröffentlichungen der Internationalen Gesellschaft für Geschichte der Pharmazie n.F. 40. Stuttgart: Wissenachaftliche Verlagsgesellschaft, 1973, pp. 115–121.

FAITH WALLIS

NORIA

Noria is a generic term for a water-lifting wheel, from Arabic, *na'ura*, "to groan" (from the distinctive noise made by a current-wheel revolving on its axle). There were two kinds of hydraulic wheels. The first is the current wheel, compartmented or with a rim of pots, moved by the force of the water alone, which lifted water from large rivers or irrigation canals. These wheels were mechanically simple, typically very large in size, and required no gearing. Celebrated examples are the great noria of Islamic *Toledo, driven by water from an aqueduct over the Tagus River, and the wheel at La Ñora, Murcia, driven by the current of Aljufia irrigation canal. The current-driven noria occupies a unique role in the history of technology: the first self-acting machine.

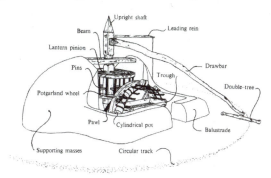

Diagram of an animal-drawn typical noria. (Thorkild Schioler)

Norias on the Orontes River at Hama, Syria. (Corbis/Charles & Josette Lenars)

The second wheel is the short-shafted, geared wheel moved by animal power. It was constructed from around two hundred separate parts, all of them wood, and so could be kept in repair by the farmer himself or a local carpenter. The animal, usually a donkey, walks along a circular track, hitched to a shaft which moved a horizontal lantern wheel which engaged teeth set in a vertical wheel which, in turn, raised the water by means of an endless chain of pots affixed to its rim with a continuous rope. The Andalusi agronomical writers mentioned this noria and suggested practical measures whereby the farmer could enhance the efficiency and longevity of his machine. Thus Abu'l-Khayr and Ibn al-'Awwam recommended the use of hardwoods (such as olive), most likely for the teeth of the potgarland wheel, inasmuch as softwoods were usually employed for the lantern wheel. Abu'l-Khayr prescribes the arrangement of five pots to every cubit of rope, while Ibn al-'Awwam recommended that the pots be supplied with an air vent to prevent breakage as the force of the water pushed each pot against the wall of the well or into the pot behind it. Ibn al-'Awwam also noted that the longer the shaft, the less force required of the animal to move the wheel; the track diameter could vary from sixteen to twenty-three feet (five to seven meters), depending on the force required.

The water raised by the noria either flowed directly into canals irrigating a field, or was stored in a tank until the farmer needed it. The tank or small reservoir (Arabic, *birka*; Spanish, *alberca*) also served to regulate the flow of water from the noria to the field. These were made of earth and were triangular in shape, with an approximate surface of 20 x 16 x 16 feet (6 x 5 x 5 m).

Both wheels have sometimes been called, generically, Persian wheels. The name was coined by English travelers in Persia who surmised that the device had diffused from Persia to India. But the term has no ancient or medieval authority. There is no evidence for any mechanical water-lifting device in the Mediterranean world before the third century B.C.E., except for the swape (*shaduf*). The earliest literary reference to a wheel with bucket chain used for irrigation is Philo of Byzantium (late third century B.C.E.). According to Oleson, all mechanical water-lifting devices were associated with Hellenistic Egypt and none was more ancient except for the *shaduf*.

The animal-drivern noria was ubiquitous in the Islamic world, and it made it possible for a single family to produce a surplus for the market. The cultivated belts around many towns from Spain to India owed their prosperity to its introduction. In areas where it was common, it contributed to substantial economic growth on the regional level. One proof of the noria revolution is that in an area of La Mancha in the province of Toledo, Spain, archeological surveys reveal that an original Roman irrigation system based on dams and canals was abandoned and replaced by another system based on wells and norias in the Islamic period.

Numerous thirteenth-century Spanish documents—for example, the *Repartimientos* of Murcia and Valencia—refer to wheels drawing water from irrigation canals. Christian documents of this era use the terms *noria* and *aceña* (from *saniya*, originally a long-shafted, geared wheel) interchangeably. Both the wheel itself and the pots seem related to Syrian prototypes, according to comparative ethnological research carried out by Schiøler. Andalusis introduced the Syrian-style wheel in Morocco, and the Christians of northern Spain acquired the technique through the migration of Mozarab farmers and, later, by conquest. In the later Middle Ages the *sènia* (from *saniya*, but in this case a short-shafted, animal-driven wheel) diffused northward from Valencia and Tortosa and became widespread in Catalonia proper.

See also **Agriculture**

Bibliography

Glick, Thomas F. *From Muslim Fortress to Christian Castle.* Manchester: Manchester University Press, 1995.

Oleson, John Peter. *Greek and Roman Mechanical Water-Lifting Devices: The History of a Technology.* Toronto: University of Toronto Press, 1984.

Schiøler, Thorkild. *Roman and Islamic Water-Lifting Wheels.* Copenhagen: Odense University Press, 1973.

Smith, Norman. *Man and Water: A History of Hydro-Technology.* New York: Scribner's, 1975.

THOMAS F. GLICK

O

OPTICS AND CATOPTRICS

The science of optics (or *perspectiva*, as it was known during the Middle Ages) had its origin in Greek antiquity, in the mathematical analyses of *Euclid and *Ptolemy, the physical theories of Aristotle and the Atomists, and the anatomical and physiological endeavors of *Galen. All three traditions were transmitted eastward into central Asia and subsequently translated into Arabic in the eighth and ninth centuries. In the twelfth and thirteenth centuries, these same materials, now accompanied by a large collection of original writings by Islamic scholars, were again translated, this time from both Arabic (mainly) and Greek (to a minor degree) into Latin.

Vision

The central problem of ancient and medieval optics was to understand how we see. Everyone who approached the question of vision agreed that some form of contact must be established between the eye and the visible object. On the extramission theory, visual power emanates from the seeing eye to the seen object; on the intromission theory, something travels from the visible object to the eye. The first objective was to determine which of these two theories is correct, and to identify the nature of the entity that passes from observer to object or from object to observer. The ancient atomists were perhaps the earliest to address this question, arguing that convoys of atoms representing the visible object in shape and color flowed from object to observer, thereby accounting for the facts of visual perception. Aristotle shared the intromissionism of the atomists but refused to accept the notion that anything like the atomists' convoy of atoms will do. In short, he denied the possibility of a flow of material from object to observer. Rather, he maintained, a stationary medium undergoes an instantaneous qualitative transformation, provoked by light or color and received instantaneously by the eye. Thus light (such as that of the Sun as it peeks over the horizon) transforms a transparent medium, such as air or water or glass, from potential transparency to actual transparency. Once the medium is actually transparent, colored objects situated within it or on its periphery produce further qualitative change in the medium—a red object colors the medium (in some undefined sense) red, right up to and including the interior humors of the eye. This is sufficient to cause perception of the object as red.

The extramission theory of vision was defended by Euclid, who revealed little or no interest in the physical nature of the messenger and dealt almost exclusively with the geometry of sight. A cone of rays, he argued, emanates from the observer's eye, and anything in the visual field encountered by one or more of these rays is seen. The advantages of this theory were perspectival: the size of an object was judged by the angle between visual rays terminating on its extreme points. Move the object closer, and it appears larger because the rays now encountering its extremes are separated by a larger angle. If an object appears in the upper left of the observer's visual field, that is because it intercepted a ray in the upper left of the visual cone. And if an object falls between adjacent rays, it is not seen at all.

The astronomer Ptolemy defended Euclid's extramission theory in his *Optica*, while arguing that the rays were physical things—visual flux—rather than purely mathematical entities. He insisted that the visual cone is a continuous body of visual flux, rather than radiation proceeding along discrete geometrical lines, separated by spaces. Colored objects, he argued, produce a modification in the visual flux, which is read by the eye and brain as color. Ptolemy also developed a geometrical analysis of binocular vision.

Finally, Galen described the gross anatomy of the eye in terms closely resembling modern knowledge. As for the act of vision, he argued that visual power flowing down the optic nerves and out of the eyes transforms the surrounding transparent medium (the air), endowing it with the power of sight and rendering it capable of perceiving whatever it touches.

The first Islamic author to take up visual theory was the philosopher *al-Kindi (d. c. 870), whose goal was to extend and defend Euclid's extramission theory, including his cone of visual rays. But al-Kindi insisted, with Ptolemy, that the cone must be a continuous body rather than a collection of discrete rays. He also proposed, in what would turn out to be a revolutionary suggestion, that radiation departing from the eye does not go forth as a single visual cone, but rather as an infinity of discrete cones emanating in all directions from each point on the surface of the eye, thereby differentially "illuminating" the medium. Al-Kindi's purpose in this argument was to explain why objects located near the central axis of the eye are seen with greater clarity. Some one hundred fifty years later, *Ibn al-Haytham would put al-Kindi's argument to use for a quite different purpose.

Al-Kindi lived and worked in Baghdad, the home of the 'Abbasid court, which boasted a rich intellectual life. Ibn al-Haytham (d. c. 1039) was born in Basra, on the Persian Gulf, but apparently spent most of his productive scholarly life in Cairo. A towering mathematician, Ibn al-Haytham produced a synthesis of ancient theories, which managed to draw the useful elements from each of the ancient rivals. Although firmly committed to the intromission theory, Ibn al-Haytham sought to adopt the visual cone of the extramissionists for the sake of its mathematical contributions. He did this by arguing that although the "forms" of light or color issue in all directions from every point of a visible object (here borrowing al-Kindi's revolutionary idea and putting it to use for a different purpose), only one ray from each point falls perpendicularly on both the cornea and front surface of the crystalline lens (concentric surfaces) and enters the sensitive organ of the eye (the crystalline lens) without refraction. All other rays are weakened by refraction sufficiently to be ignored. Those unrefracted rays form a visual cone and endow the intromission theory (until then looked on purely as a non-mathematical theory about the physical nature of the vision-causing entity) with all of the mathematical capabilities of the extramission theories of Euclid and Ptolemy. As for that other major problem—identifying the agents of vision that emanate from the visible object to the eye—Ibn al-Haytham identified them as the "forms" (a very Aristotelian conception) of light and color. Finally, Ibn al-Haytham introduced Galen's anatomical discoveries into his theory, tracing radiation as it passes through the eyes and optic nerves to their junction, where forms passing through the two eyes are united and judged by the "final sentient power."

Ibn al-Haytham's great Optica was translated into Latin near the beginning of the thirteenth century, thus joining previously translated texts by Aristotle, Ptolemy, Euclid, al-Kindi, and *Hunayn ibn Ishaq's summary of Galen. The first scholar in Christendom to master the whole of this Greek and Islamic legacy appears to have been Franciscan friar *Roger Bacon (d. c. 1292). With Ibn al-Haytham (known to Bacon as Alhacen) as his primary guide, but also taking account of all the other ancient and medieval authorities on the subject, Bacon produced a synthesis of his own, developing at great length his theory of the "multiplication of species" (multiplicatio specierum, better translated as the "propagation of images") to explain the agency that bore visual information from the observed object to the observer.

The other problem that Bacon needed to address was that of the direction of radiation, on which his authorities were evenly divided. Bacon perceived that Alhacen had not disproved the existence of extramitted visual rays, but only that if they existed they were incapable of accounting for visual perception. Bacon therefore invented a new function for them, namely, to prepare the medium for receiving the vision-producing intromitted rays. Thus everybody had a piece of the truth. Vision was caused by intromitted rays, but extramitted rays existed and performed an auxiliary function.

Bacon's ideas were spread by his own publications, but also by a younger Franciscan brother, the future Archbishop of Canterbury *John Pecham, who presented an abbreviated version of the Baconian synthesis in his Perspectiva communis, which became the standard text on the subject in the medieval universities as late as the end of the sixteenth century. Through their influence, and that of an enormous tome by the Silesian *Witelo (also influenced by Bacon), the optical theories of Alhacen and Bacon came to dominate philosophical thought on problems of sensation and cognition to the end of the Middle Ages.

Reflection and Refraction

Vision was the central problem of medieval perspectiva, but it was not the only one. In Catoptrica, Euclid dealt with the phenomena of reflection and refraction and formulated laws of reflection, which we still accept. The two most basic principles were: (1) That angles of incidence and reflection at a plane or curved reflecting surface are equal; and (2) That the image of an object seen by reflection is located where the rectilinear extension of the ray issuing from the eye (entering the eye for an intromissionist) intersects the cathetus (the perpendicular running from the observer's eye to the reflecting surface). Building on this foundation, Euclid proceeded to prove a collection of relatively sophisticated propositions.

Ptolemy rearticulated much that he found in Euclid's Catoptrica, but added an empirical approach, experimentally confirming the law of equal angles. Ptolemy proceeded to a geometrical analysis of reflection in concave spherical and convex spherical mirrors, especially sophisticated in the former case, involving claims about image shape and clarity—again, offering experimental confirmation of his results. The latter part of Ptolemy's Optica is lost, but in the existing portion of his fifth book he undertook a brief analysis of refraction, going well beyond anything achieved by his predecessors. He revealed a full non-numerical understanding of the qualitative geometry of refraction, which he applied to concave and convex spherical surfaces as well as to plane surfaces. And he made a famous effort to discover a quantitative law of refraction by experimental means, arriving at an interesting geometrical series but falling short of discovering the modern law.

When Ibn al-Haytham wrote his great Optica in the eleventh century, he had at his disposal all the principal Greek works on optical subjects. Drawing inspiration from Ptolemy's *Optica*, he prepared an exhaustive geometrical (but non-numerical) analysis of image formation owing to reflection and refraction in reflecting or refracting surfaces of plane, spherically concave or convex, and cylindrically concave or convex form. His analysis included attention to the number, location, size, and shape of the images. The approach was empirical—he replicated Ptolemy's experimental apparatus for demonstrating the rules of refraction but omitted Ptolemy's numerical results. His approach was also causal—a search for the physical behavior that would explain the phenomena of reflection and refraction, by the use of mechanical analogies. Ibn al-Haytham's *Optica* was not to be equaled for mathematical sophistication until the seventeenth century.

Ibn al-Haytham's *Optica* (translated into Latin as Alhacen's *De aspectibus*) powerfully shaped the optical writings of Bacon, Pecham, and Witelo—the former two of whom offered abbreviated versions of Ibn al-Haytham's analysis, while the verbose Witelo managed to expand on Ibn al-Haytham (and all the other sources at his disposal). Borrowing from a short treatise by Ibn al-Haytham that circulated in Latin translation, entitled *De speculis comburentibus* (*On Burning-Mirrors*), Witelo also dealt with the focusing properties of paraboloidal mirrors.

Late Medieval Developments

The colors of the rainbow were among the most striking optical phenomena and, inevitably, led to causal speculation. Aristotle had attributed the rainbow to the reflection of sunlight in a cloud. That theory was dismissed by *Robert Grosseteste (c. 1169–1253), who doubted that reflection in a cloud could explain the rainbow's shape. His alternative was to attribute the rainbow to multiple refractions in a cloud, but he provided no detail on how this might come about. Bacon, well-informed on Grosseteste's theory, was not persuaded. Committed to an empirical approach to the question, he examined rainbows observable in artificial sprays or those accompanying a waterfall. In the case of rainbows in the sky, he noticed that the rainbow moved as the observer moved and must therefore be produced in a different set of droplets for every different position of the observer. It followed, he argued, that the rainbow was the product of reflections not from the cloud as a whole, but from its individual droplets of moisture. One more Baconian discovery was measurement of the maximum elevation of the rainbow as forty-two degrees (a correct value proposed by no earlier author, doubtless obtained by use of an astrolabe).

Finally, early in the fourteenth century, the Dominican Theodoric of Freiberg (d. c. 1310) undertook a remarkable experimental investigation, projecting rays of light through water-filled glass globes, which were meant to simulate the individual raindrop in a cloud. These experiments taught him that the primary rainbow was the result of two refractions (as light entered and departed from the individual raindrops), along with a total internal reflection at the rear surface of the drop; the secondary rainbow from the same two refractions combined with two internal reflections—essentially the modern theory of the rainbow.

A final phenomenon is worthy of mention because of the interest it attracted during the Middle Ages. Ever since Aristotle, close observers had noticed that the light issuing from a spherical object, such as the Sun, passing through a non-circular aperture, projected an image that imitated the shape of the Sun rather than of the aperture—a problem made interesting because it seemed to hint that light was not being rectilinearly propagated. Ibn al-Haytham took up this puzzle and solved it satisfactorily, but in a treatise that was not available to Latin-speaking scholars. Roger Bacon tackled the problem without help from earlier sources, struggling intelligently through three different versions, managing in the end to retain rectilinear propagation, but paying the price elsewhere in his argument. A successful solution in the West, which recognized the problem as one of scale, would have to wait for Kepler in the seventeenth century.

A substantial tradition of commentary on optical topics continued through the later Middle Ages. Much of this was motivated by debates over sensation and cognition, to which both the Aristotelian and Baconian traditions had made contributions. Debates over the number of colors in the rainbow provided additional motivation. The geometrical side of *perspectiva* also attracted continuing interest, as *perspectiva* came to serve, in many universities, as a stand-in for geometry in the arts curriculum. Kepler's establishment of optics on a modern foundation early in the seventeenth century, including his successful theory of the retinal image and a convincing analysis of the problem of radiation through small apertures, represented correction and fulfillment, rather than repudiation of the medieval syntheses of Ibn al-Haytham and Roger Bacon.

See also **Aristotelianism**

Bibliography

Crombie, Alistair C. *Robert Grosseteste and the Origins of Experimental Science 1100–1700.* Oxford: Clarendon Press, 1953.

Eastwood, Bruce S. *Astronomy and Optics from Pliny to Descartes.* London: Variorum, 1989.

Grant, Edward and John E. Murdoch, eds. *Mathematics and its Applications to Science and Natural Philosophy in the Middle Ages: Essays in Honor of Marshall Clagett.* New York: Cambridge University Press, 1987.

Lindberg, David C., ed. & trans. *John Pecham and the Science of Optics: Perspectiva communis.* Madison: University of Wisconsin Press, 1970.

————. *Roger Bacon and the Origin of Perspectiva in the Middle Ages: A Critical Edition and English Translation of Bacon's Perspectiva, with Introduction and Notes.* Oxford: Clarendon Press, 1996.

————. "Roger Bacon on Light, Vision, and the Universal Emanation of Force." In *Roger Bacon and the Sciences: Commemorative Essays.* Edited by Jeremiah Hackett. Leiden: E.J. Brill, 1997, pp. 243–275.

————. *Roger Bacon's Philosophy of Nature: A Critical Edition, with English Translation, Introduction, and Notes, of De multiplicatione and De speculis comburentibus.* Oxford: Clarendon Press, 1983.

_____. *Studies in the History of Medieval Optics*. London: Variorum, 1983.

_____. *Theories of Vision from al-Kindi to Kepler*. Chicago: University of Chicago Press, 1976.

Rashed, Roshdi, ed and tr. *Oeuvres philosophiques et scientifiques d'Al-Kindi*, vol. 1: *L'optique et la catoptrique*. Leiden: E.J. Brill, 1997.

_____. *Optique et mathématiques*. London: Variorum, 1992.

Sabra, A. I. *Optics, Astronomy and Logic*. London: Variorum, 1994.

_____, ed and tr. *The Optics of Ibn al-Haytham: Books I-III On Direct Vision*. 2 vols. London: The Warburg Institute, 1989.

_____. "Sensation and Inference in Alhazen's Theory of Visual Perception." In *Studies in Perception: Interrelations in the History of Philosophy and Science*. Edited by Peter K. Machamer and Robert G. Turnbull. Columbus: Ohio State University Press, 1978, pp. 160–185.

Smith, A. Mark, ed and tr. *Alhacen's Theory of Visual Perception: A Critical Edition, with English Translation and Commentary, of the First Three Books of Alhacen's De aspectibus*. 2 vols. Philadelphia: American Philosophical Society, 2001.

_____. Getting the Big Picture in Perspectivist Optics. *Isis* (1981) 72: 568–589.

_____, tr. *Ptolemy's Theory of Visual Perception: An English Translation of the Optics, with Introduction and Commentary*. Philadelphia: American Philosophical Society, 1996.

Tachau, Katherine H. *Vision and Certitude in the Age of Ockham: Optics, Epistemology and the Foundations of Semantics, 1250-1345*. Leiden: E.J. Brill, 1988.

DAVID C. LINDBERG

ORESME, NICOLE

Nicole Oresme (c. 1320–1382) was born in Normandy, near Caen. Virtually nothing is known of his early life. He studied at the University of Paris where he was a master of arts by the academic year 1341–1342. He studied theology at Navarre, where in 1356 he became a doctor of theology and grand master of the college. After holding a number of church offices, he was made bishop of Lisieux in 1377, partly no doubt because he had the powerful backing of King Charles V, who ruled France from 1364 to 1380. He remained bishop until his death in 1382.

Oresme's relations with Charles V and the royal court were significant. He first came into contact with Charles's father, King John II, who used Oresme's knowledge of finance to aid the state. Using this experience, Oresme wrote a *Treatise on Money* in both Latin and French versions. Overall, his treatise had a significant influence. At the royal court Oresme came to know the heir apparent, and when Charles V succeeded to the throne he asked Oresme to translate from Latin into French four of *Aristotle's treatises, three of which were directly relevant to government, namely the *Nicomachean Ethics*, *Politics*, and *Economics*. The fourth treatise, *On the Heavens*, may have been included because it was Aristotle's great work on cosmology. Perhaps Charles hoped that it would give his courtiers a cosmic background for their lessons in statecraft. Oresme accompanied his translation of *On the Heavens* with a detailed French commentary on the text. It was his last known work, completed in 1377, and one of his most important.

Oresme was perhaps the most original-minded, innovative natural philosopher and mathematician of the Middle Ages. The range of his written works is truly impressive, embracing politics, monetary policy, economics, theology, magic, and treatises on the dangers of *astrology. His primary interests, however, were natural philosophy and the application of mathematics to natural philosophy. Using the scholastic format of *quaestiones*, Oresme left commentaries on all of Aristotle's books on natural philosophy, and also wrote treatises on various major themes in natural philosophy, often emphasizing the mathematical aspects of the subjects he considered. Although Oresme had great respect for Aristotle, he frequently disagreed with him.

Oresme's Scientific Ideas and Contributions

Oresme's approach to nature provides an important insight into his ideas about the physical world. He was convinced that nature operated in a regular manner and that a given natural cause would invariably produce its natural effect. He was strongly opposed to those who invoked magical and supernatural explanations for phenomena that he regarded as wholly natural. But Oresme was equally convinced that human ability to acquire certain knowledge of nature's workings was limited, and often uncertain, which led him to proclaim that many propositions about the natural world required as much of an act of faith to accept their truth, as did the truths of revelation. This attitude probably explains why Oresme, more than occasionally, presented equally plausible alternatives for some important problems in natural philosophy.

One such problem concerned the status of the Earth at the geometric center of the world: was it stationary at the center of the world while the celestial bodies made a daily rotation around it, as Aristotle and his followers believed; or did it rotate once daily on its axis, while the heavens remained stationary? Oresme presents a series of impressive arguments in favor of the Earth's axial rotation, most of which were repeated almost two centuries later by Nicholas Copernicus in his momentous treatise *On the Revolution of the Heavenly Orbs* (1543). Oresme concluded that physical and astronomical phenomena could be equally well explained in either of the two rival hypotheses. No evidence could decide the issue. In light of this stalemate, Oresme opted, on biblical grounds, for the traditional Aristotelian opinion that the Earth was stationary at the center of the world. A second significant issue involved Aristotle's claim that the existence of more than one world is impossible. Oresme argued, as did many in the Middle Ages, that God could create other worlds if He wished; hence, it was certainly possible that other worlds could exist. Moreover, if God did create other worlds, they would coexist with ours. Each world would have its own center and circumference, and would be a self-contained entity independently of the other worlds. Content to demonstrate the possibility of other worlds and convinced that no scientific arguments could decide the issue, Oresme again chose to adopt the universally held traditional view that there is only one world.

Perhaps more than anyone else, Oresme applied mathematics to a variety of problems in natural philosophy. He gave a mathematical foundation to the ideas first proposed by *Thomas Bradwardine in his *Treatise on Ratios* (1328). In a treatise entitled *De proportionibus proportionum* (On Ratios of Ratios), Oresme first presented certain elements of the mathematical theory of proportionality, relying on the fifth and tenth books of Euclid's *Elements*. A "ratio of ratios" is actually an exponent that relates two ratios. For example, in the proportional relationship $A/B = (C/D)^{p/q}$, the ratio p/q is a "ratio of ratios" because it relates the two ratios A/B and C/D. Oresme gives examples in which p/q is either rational, forming a "rational ratio of ratios," or irrational, forming an "irrational ratio of ratios." In effect, Oresme had arrived at the concept of an irrational exponent, perhaps for the first time. He also introduced probability considerations into his treatises. Taking one hundred rational ratios from 2/1 to 101/1, he demonstrates that any two proposed unknown ratios are probably incommensurable, as, for example, 3/1 and 2/1, where 3/1 does not equal $(2/1)^{p/q}$ (that is, p/q is irrational). On this assumption, he showed that the odds were 197 to 1 that any "ratio of ratios" chosen at random from this group of one hundred rational ratios would be related by an irrational ratio, that is, by an irrational exponent.

Oresme applied his mathematical ideas on "ratios of ratios" to the motion of bodies, rejecting, as had Bradwardine earlier, Aristotle's mathematical representation of motions involving motive forces and mobile bodies. In his *Treatise on the Commensurability or Incommensurability of the Celestial Motions*, Oresme extended his ideas, arguing for the probability that any two celestial motions are probably incommensurable. From this conclusion, Oresme inferred that precise astrological prediction would be impossible. Throughout most of his career, Oresme was a strong opponent of astrology and wrote treatises against it. One of his desired objectives was to weaken Charles V's belief in astrological prognostication, an objective that was not realized.

Medieval scholars were interested in what they called "the intension and remission of qualities," a study of the way qualities varied in intensity or in which they lost intensity (remission). At Merton College, Oxford, scholars used a numerical approach to measure the variations, but Oresme used geometrical figures, as we discover in his lengthy treatise titled *On the Configurations of Qualities and Motions*. Oresme's significant move was to assume that qualitative intensities were like continuous magnitudes and therefore representable by lines and surfaces, that is, by geometric figures. Qualities were imagined to increase or decrease their intensities uniformly or non-uniformly. All sorts of qualitative intensities were measured: pains, joys, music, colors, and many more. In a two-dimensional figure, the base, or horizontal line, represented the

A prince mints coins. Illumination from a fifteenth-century manuscript of Nicole Oresme's *Treatise on Money*. (AKG Images)

extension of a quality in a subject; the perpendiculars erected on that base represented the intensity of the quality at that point. A right triangle, for example, could represent any quality that was assumed to increase uniformly from zero degree to any maximum intensity.

Not only were variations in qualities represented in the intension and remission of forms, but uniform and non-uniform velocities were similarly treated. Within this context, scholars at Merton enunciated the mean speed theorem, but it was Oresme who first proved it geometrically. The mean speed theorem is usually represented as $s = 1/2at^2$, where s is the distance traversed, a represents uniform acceleration, and t is the time of acceleration. Oresme thus anticipated Galileo's proof of the same theorem in *The Two New Sciences* (1638). Oresme also anticipated a significant corollary that Galileo drew from the mean speed theorem.

Oresme, it is important to recognize, was really mathematizing fictional qualities and their imaginary intensities. He was not applying mathematics to the real world, but was rather engaged in an intellectual exercise that, in medieval terms, was "according to the imagination" (*secundum imaginationem*). It remained for Galileo to apply these important theorems and definitions about motion to the motion of real bodies and thereby establish a new science of mechanics. This should not, however, diminish Oresme's great mathematical accomplishments and his profound use of the imagination. Arriving at some of the basic concepts of the new mechanics—even if applied only to imaginary conditions—is a considerable contribution and achievement.

In *On Seeing the Stars*, Oresme rightly rejected the traditional idea that the refraction of light can only occur at a single interface between two media of differing densities. In place of this interpretation, which had been held by Ptolemy, Alhacen (*Ibn al-Haytham, the great Islamic author on geometrical optics), and many others, Oresme insisted that light is refracted along a curved path when it is traveling through a single medium of uniformly varying density. To arrive at the curved path, Oresme used his knowledge of convergent infinite series. That is, the successive refractions produced successive line segments, which formed a curved line as they increased to infinity. This important interpretation of the refraction of light was always thought to have originated with Robert Hooke and Isaac Newton. In fact, it was Oresme who, without proof, first proclaimed the concept, while Hooke and Newton were apparently the first to demonstrate its truth.

Although Oresme did not furnish experimental evidence for some of his most important scientific ideas, he deserves high praise for having enunciated the ideas described here long before they were independently rediscovered in the seventeenth century by such eminent scientists as Galileo and Newton.

See also **Astrology; Cosmology; Latitude of forms; Optics and catoptrics**

Bibliography

Primary Sources

Oresme, Nicole. *Nicole Oresme: Le Livre du ciel et du monde.* Edited by Albert D. Menut and Alexander J. Denomy. Translated with an Introduction by Albert D. Menut. Madison: University of Wisconsin Press, 1968.

———. *De proportionibus proportionum and Ad pauca respicientes.* Edited by Edward Grant. Madison: University of Wisconsin Press, 1966.

———. *Maistre Nicole Oresme: La Livre de Yconomique d'Aristote. Critical Edition of the French Text from the Avranches Manuscript with the original Latin version.* Introduction and English translation by A. D. Menut. Transactions of the American Philosophical Society, New Series 47, pt. 5. Philadelphia: American Philosophical Society, 1957.

———. Nicole Oresme and the Kinematics of Circular Motion: "*Tractatus de commensurabilitate vel incommensurabilitate motuum celi.*" Edited with an Introduction, English Translation, and Commentary by Edward Grant. Madison: University of Wisconsin Press, 1971.

———. *Quaestiones super De generatione et corruptione.* Edited by Stefano Caroti. Munich, Germany: Verlag der Bayerischen Akademie der Wissenschaften, 1996.

———. *The De moneta of Nicholas Oresme and English Mint Documents.* Edited by Charles Johnson. New York: Nelson, 1956.

Secondary Sources

Caroti, Stefano. Quaestio contra divinatores horoscopios. *Archives d'histoire doctrinale et littéraire du moyen âge* (1976) 43: 201–310.

Courtenay, William J. The Early Career of Nicole Oresme. *Isis* (2000) 91: 542–548.

Grant, Edward. Jean Buridan and Nicole Oresme on Natural Knowledge. *Vivarium* (1993) 31: 84–105.

———. "Nicole Oresme, Aristotle's *On the Heavens*, and the Court of Charles V." In *Texts and Contexts in Ancient and Medieval Science: Studies on the Occasion of John E. Murdoch's Seventieth Birthday.* Edited by Edith Sylla and Michael McVaugh. Leiden: E.J. Brill, 1997, pp. 187–207.

Kaye, Joel. *Economy and Nature in the Fourteenth Century. Money, Market Exchange, and the Emergence of Scientific Thought.* New York: Cambridge University Press, 1998. Chapter 7.

Kirschner, Stefan, Oresme on Intension and Remission of Qualities in His Commentary on Aristotle's *Physics*. *Vivarium* (2000) 38: 255–274.

EDWARD GRANT

P

PAINTS, PIGMENTS, DYES

Many dyes and pigments used in earlier centuries and referred to by Greek and Roman authors, including *Dioscorides, Pliny the Elder, and Vitruvius, continued to be employed throughout the medieval period and well beyond 1500. Many, such as saffron, kermes and lead white, had applications in medicine and cooking. Between the fifth and fifteenth centuries, the use of some coloring matters declined, notably the costly shellfish purple dye used around the Mediterranean. Some new materials were introduced, such as the pigment lead-tin yellow, which derived from the glass and *pottery industries and appeared in the fourteenth century, and several dyestuffs from Central and South America after 1492.

Dyes were extracted from plant and animal sources and used in solution on cloth, leather, and other materials. In general, they were not suitable for use as pigments without modification to render them insoluble. Many medieval collections of technological and medical recipes, from the Mappae Clavicula collection (the earliest extant text of which dates from about 800) onward, contain recipes to prepare pigments from red and yellow dyestuffs on aluminum- or calcium-containing substrates.

Cloth could be dyed as a piece; thread or yarn could also be dyed before weaving or, in the case of wool, fleece could be dyed before spinning. The majority of dyes required the textile to be mordanted, using *alum or, for blacks, iron salts. The dye molecules then bond with the metal ion of the mordant attached to the textile. Some, such as the yellow dye saffron and the lichen dyes, could be dyed directly, dissolving the colorant in hot water or, for the lichen purples, an ammoniacal solution (urine). Indigo blue and shellfish purple are vat dyes, so called after the wooden vats used by medieval woad dyers. These are present in the plant or shellfish in the form of soluble precursors. Treatment of the source material (or of solid indigo) in a warm, alkaline solution gave a greenish-yellow liquid, into which the textile was placed. On removing the textile and exposing it to light, the yellowish-green color deposited on the fibers was oxidized to insoluble blue (indigotin)or purple (dibromoindigotin) respectively. This was repeated to give a darker color.

Shellfish purple (Tyrian purple) was obtained from the hypobranchial gland of muricid sea snails *Bolinus brandaris* (Linnaeus, 1758) and related species. The industry suffered in the disorder following the collapse of the Roman empire and Arabic advances westward: the dye was still produced in a few Eastern Mediterranean centers for prestigious textiles and parchment for books, but with the loss of Constantinople, the last major purple-dyeing center, to the Turks in 1453, its use ceased. A purple color was obtained more economically using lichen dyes. The lichens used included orchil, *Roccella tinctoria* DC, and related species in Mediterranean regions, and parelle, *Ochrolechia parella* (L.) Massal and cudbear, *O. tartarea* (L.) Massal in cooler areas. This or a similar species was an important item of Norwegian trade by the fourteenth century and textiles dyed with lichen purple dating from several centuries earlier have been found in Anglo-Saxon and Viking sites in Norway, Denmark, England, and Ireland.

Purples were also obtained using indigo and a red mordant dye, such as madder, kermes, or brasil. This required two dyeings: blue in the indigo vat, then, after mordanting in alum solution, red (or the other way round). Different shades could be obtained depending on the depth of the indigo dyeing.

Woad, *Isatis tinctoria* L., and the indigo plant, *Indigofera tinctoria* L., and related species, are the source of indigo, which was used almost exclusively to dye blue. Until the sixteenth century, woad was the principal European source; notable centers for its cultivation include Languedoc in France, Thuringia in Germany, and Tuscany in Italy. It was generally traded as dried balls of the crushed, fermented leaves; further fermentation was necessary before the woad was used for dyeing. Because the dyeing method was different to that used for the red and yellow mordant dyes, blue dyers were often organized separately in city guild structures. Oriental indigo was imported as dark blue lumps of the extracted dyestuff, certainly by the twelfth century. It was widely used as a pigment. Oxidized dye floating on the surface of the woad vat was also skimmed off for use as a pigment: "flower of woad" or "florey."

Madder is one of the most ancient and most permanent red dyes. The madder group of plants includes dyer's madder, *Rubia tinctorum* L., wild madder, *R. pergegrina* L., and the bedstraws, *Galium* spp. Dyer's madder was cultivated in parts of France, Lombardy, Sicily, and Spain and reached other countries, such as Britain, through trade: it has been identified in dyebath waste in ninth-century York. It was an important crop in the Netherlands. The dyestuff is obtained from the root and contains many anthraquinone constituents including alizarin and pseudopurpurin, gradually converted to purpurin on exposure to air. By varying dyeing conditions and using plants of different ages, a wide range of pinks, reds, oranges, and browns could be obtained. Madder was also much used in combination with other dyestuffs.

Sappanwood, *Caesalpinia sappan* L.—brasil or brexilium—was described by *Marco Polo (1254–1324) growing at Quilon, on the west coast of India, in Sri Lanka (Ceylon), and in Malaysia (Lobak), and was imported into Europe from these regions. The dyestuff is not lightfast, but was widely used for its brilliant, rich red color, in spite of the many regulations forbidding or strictly controlling it. It was an important coloring matter in manuscript *illumination, and as a red ink. South American species, including *C. echinata* Lamarck (pernambuco wood) were imported into Spain shortly after the arrival of *Christopher Columbus in the New World. The discovery of other rich sources of the wood culminated in the discovery of Brazil itself, named after the wood, by Portuguese navigator Pedro Alvares Cabral.

Use of Insects

The most expensive red dyes were obtained from species of scale insect. Kermes, *Kermes vermilio* Planchon—the medieval "grain" in English—is parasitic on the kermes oak, *Quercus coccifera* L., found in scrubland around the Mediterranean. The dyestuff (principally kermesic acid with a small proportion of flavokermesic acid) was obtained from the female insects, which were gathered in late spring or early summer, preferably just before the eggs hatched. Kermes was used to dye scarlet red on the highest quality wool and silk; in the Low Countries, England, and France, the name "scarlet" came to be applied, by transference, to the widest, closely woven wool fabrics which were of a quality to be dyed "in grain." From the thirteenth century, cities such as Montpellier in France, and Lucca, Venice, Genoa, and Florence in Italy were centers for kermes dyeing The dyestuff has been identified on royal and other expensive textiles dating from the fifth century onwards. In 1464 Pope Paul II decreed that kermes was to be used for the robes of cardinals, replacing shellfish purple.

A purplish-crimson dye was obtained from scale insects in which the principal constituent is carminic acid. Polish cochineal, *Porphyrophora polonica* L., is parasitic on the roots of the perennial knawel, *Scleranthus perennis* L., and other plants. It was found in areas of light sandy soil extending from northwestern Europe to Kazakhstan. Armenian or Ararat cochineal, *Porphyrophora hameli* Brandt, is found on the underground stems of grasses in saline sandy soils, typically in the plain of the Arax river. Polish cochineal was of great importance in northern and eastern Europe, particularly after the Arab conquest of the Mediterranean regions rendered the export of kermes difficult. Both Polish and Armenian cochineals were imported into Italy, perhaps from the very late fourteenth century onward, where they were used principally on silks. The discovery of the Mexican cochineal insect, *Dactylopius coccus* Costa, which contains far more dye (carminic acid) than the Old World species, and its import firstly into Spain (from 1523) and subsequently into the rest of Europe caused the decline of all the Old World scale insects

The lac insect, *Kerria lacca* (Kerr, 1782), and related species, found across India south-east Asia and southern China, form colonies on the twigs of *Butea monosperma* (Lam.) Taubert and other trees. The insects secrete a brownish, resin-like protective coating, so substantial that it envelops the insects and encrusts the twig. The dyestuff (principally laccaic acids) gives a color similar to that obtained from the cochineals and was used for dyeing in the eastern Mediterranean, notably in those areas under Islamic influence. It was little used for textiles in other parts of Europe, where kermes and the Old World cochineals were available, but it has been identified on leather book bindings. The use of this and other red dyes in pigment making is discussed below.

Sources of Yellow

Many plants were used as sources of yellow dyestuff, for dyeing and also for pigment-making. Most were mordant dyes, although saffron, obtained from the stigmas of the saffron crocus, *Crocus sativus* L., is a direct dye. Its use was also mentioned in manuscript illumination recipes. The mordant dyes were usually based on flavonoid dyestuffs, found widely in plants. Many species were probably used locally for dyeing, such as heathers (*Calluna vulgaris* [L.] Hull) and the skins of the onion (*Allium cepa* L.). However, over Europe as as whole, weld, *Reseda luteola* L., was probably the most important source of yellow dye. Seeds have been found in dyestuff waste in cities such as York (the ninth to the eleventh centuries) and Perth, Scotland (twelfth century) and it was cultivated and exported from regions such as Cyprus and the Italian Marches. It was used to give a range of yellows and particularly greens, for which its slightly lemon hue was particularly suitable: there was no suitable naturally occurring green dye. For this it was used before or after dyeing with indigo. The principal dyestuff constituent is luteolin, also present in another widely used plant, dyer's broom, *Genista tinctoria* L. Recipes from the thirteenth century onward indicate that both weld and dyer's broom were used for yellow pigments, often made by the addition of potash alum and chalk to the dyestuff solution. Other important sources of luteolin-containing yellow dyes include saw-wort, *Serratula tinctoria* L., used in Italy, and the southern Mediterranean trentanel, *Daphne gnidium* L., which is mentioned in Spanish Arabic texts of the eleventh and twelfth centuries.

Golden yellows on silk were given by the wood of young fustic, *Cotinus coggygria* Scop., which contains the flavonoid fisetin. The shrub grows widely in central and southern Europe and Turkey, and was also used for tanning leather.

The principal flavonoid constituent in onion skins is quercetin, which gives a more golden yellow than luteolin, but is less stable to light. This, with other constituents, is found in the berries of buckthorn, *Rhamnus* spp. The unripe berries give a golden yellow, perhaps more important for dyeing after the medieval period. The dyestuff was also used to prepare a yellow pigment, and the juice of the ripe berries was used to prepare sap green, which was used in manuscript illumination; locally the ripe berries of other shrubs may have been used similarly.

Paint usually consists of a solid powdered pigment, ground with a medium serving to bind the pigment particles together into a coherent film and to attach them to the support. Paint could be applied to walls (stone, wood or brick); sculpture (stone, wood, ivory); wooden panels; fabric (linen, silk or other textiles); *paper, parchment, and ivory.

For wall painting, the pigments might be mixed with water (or lime water) and applied to fresh plaster: as the plaster set, the pigments were bound into it. This is true fresco—*buon fresco*—and its use continued in Tuscany and other parts of Italy beyond 1500. This method was unsuitable for alkali-sensitive pigments, which were applied to the dry surface bound in a solution of animal skin glue, casein or egg. In northern Europe drying oils (linseed and occasionally walnut) were widely used for wall painting from the twelfth century and probably earlier; glue (distemper) was also used. Drying oils, egg tempera, and glue were also used to paint sculpture and on panel and canvas supports. In any particular medium, the effects obtained could be varied according to the opacity of the pigments and the number and color of the layers in which the paint was applied (usually at least two).

In general the range of pigments suitable for use in manuscripts was wider than for other forms of painting: colored plant juices could be used directly. Juices were obtained from flowers, such as blue cornflowers, by pressing the petals; small pieces of clean linen—clothlets—were then soaked in the juice and allowed to dry. When required, the clothlet was soaked in water, releasing the color. Blue berries, such as the bilberry, found in rocky or montainous regions of Europe, and other similar berries, and lichen dyes, were used to give blues or purples.

Mineral-Derived Pigments

Many pigments were insoluble minerals, ground, washed and levigated until suitable for use, but some had been manufactured from Roman times: lead white, red lead

and verdigris, for example. Blue was of particular significance in Christian art and the best blue pigments were also the most costly. Ultramarine blue, extracted from lapis lazuli, was the most prestigious and expensive of all pigments, partly because it was difficult to obtain and its availability was variable. Lapis lazuli was imported from Badakhshan, northern Afghanistan; Marco Polo describes the stones originating in a vein in the mountains. The blue mineral itself is lazurite, a complex, sulfur-containing sodium aluminum silicate; lapis lazuli also contains calcite and gold-colored flecks of pyrite (iron sulfide). Merely grinding the mineral gives a rather pale blue. During the thirteenth century, an elaborate extraction method, involving kneading the ground mineral in a paste made of oil, wax and resin, under water, was devised: the blue lazurite particles were released into the water while the impurities were retained in the greasy mass. Ultramarine has been identified in works of art across Europe, including twelfth-century English wall paintings, thirteenth-century Norwegian altar frontals, and Italian paintings of the thirteenth to the fifteenth centuries. It has also been identified in Anglo-Saxon manuscripts as early as the tenth century, although indigo was more generally used until c. 1000 C.E.

The other important blue pigment was azurite, a basic copper carbonate mineral, usually found in association with the related green mineral, malachite. Both were found in regions of Europe where copper was mined, including France, Germany, and Bohemia. The color varies from an almost pure blue to greenish blue; the reddish mineral cuprite, often present as an impurity, also influences the color. The best grades were the most expensive, rivalling ultramarine in price. The pigment is not stable in alkaline conditions, sometimes turning green owing to the formation of basic copper chlorides. In England and Scandinavia, azurite was used frequently from the thirteenth century, largely replacing ultramarine and suggesting an interruption in its supply; in Italy, Mediterranean trade and the importance of Venice as a trading center ensured that both pigments remained available. Other blue pigments were indigo and, in the fifteenth century, the blue glass pigment, smalt (containing cobalt), more important in later centuries. In addition, many recipes for the preparation of blue pigments, almost always copper salts, occur in European written sources from the eighth century onwards.

There was no purple pigment, other than shellfish purple, very occasionally used in manuscript illumination. Purple colors were obtained either by mixing blue and red pigments or, more commonly, by applying a blue or red translucent pigment over an underpaint of red or blue pigments, often mixed with white, or a mixture of all three. In fresco dark reddish-purple iron oxides, containing a very pure variety of haematite, could be used.

The red pigment vermilion, red mercuric sulfide, was available as the ground mineral, cinnabar; Almadén, Spain, was an important source. However, the method of making vermilion from its constituent elements of mercury and sulfur was known from about 800 C.E. Because mercuric sulfide was itself the source of mercury and sulfur, and the process was of interest to alchemists, many recipes for its production appear in technological documentary sources from this time onward. This opaque, brilliant pigment was used in all forms of painting throughout the medieval period, although with some local variations: it seems not to have been much used in Anglo-Saxon or Northern French manuscript illumination before about 1000 C.E., red lead being used instead.

More translucent, crimson reds were provided by pigments made from red dyestuffs. These pigments, often identified in northern European sources by names such as sinoper, cynople and variants, were often the most expensive after ultramarine and azurite, particularly those prepared from the scale insect dyestuffs. Study of pigment recipes from about the ninth century onward suggests that lac was an important source of dyestuff for pigment preparation: the raw material was treated with alkali to dissolve the dyestuff and alum was added, giving a purplish-red precipitate of the pigment. Lac and its dye were known as *lacca* in Latin, and the name was also given to these dark red pigments in general. The color is similar to that of shellfish purple and perhaps *lacca* was a useful substitute in manuscript illumination. From the fourteenth century until the seventeenth, pigments from the expensive kermes and cochineal dyestuffs dyes were made from textile shearings (the Italian *lacca di cimatura*) rather than from the insects directly, extracting the dyestuff using alkali and precipitating the pigment by the addition of alum. It is probable that the more orange-toned madder lakes were also frequently made in this way. Lake pigments were widely used in easel paintings, polychromed sculpture and wallpaintings, applied in oil and other media; since they are alkali-sensitive they were not used in fresco.

Red lead or minium was known as a product of the smelting of lead ore from Classical times, although in medieval times it was generally prepared by heating lead white (basic lead carbonate) in air. It was widely available, inexpensive, opaque, and a brilliant orange color; it also encouraged the drying of the oils used in painting. It has been identified in illuminated manuscripts from the eighth century onward and in easel painting of all periods, from all over Europe. Like other pigments unstable in alkaline conditions it was not suitable for use in fresco or with fresh lime wash, although it was widely used in northern European wall painting in oil or other media, particularly from the thirteeenth century. Here areas painted with the pigment have frequently changed to dark brown/black or occasionally white, depending on the humidity and other conditions.

The cheapest and most widely available red pigments were the red ochres, earths containing hematite, perhaps with other iron oxides, and various clay minerals. These and the related yellow ochres (containing goethite and other minerals) are found in deposits all over Europe. Their stability made them suitable for use in all forms of painting. Some varieties, containing a high proportion of clay minerals, could be polished and were particularly suitable for use as a bole for laying and burnishing gold leaf. Iron oxide pigments were often used in wall painting for drawing the design on the plaster before painting. In true fresco the design was drawn on the penultimate layer of plaster, usually in a red iron oxide: this is known as the sinopia in Italian. It was then covered with the fresh plaster to which the pigments were applied. The same name was often used for the iron oxide itself (not to be confused with the names for red lakes).

The glistening mineral orpiment, yellow arsenic trisulfide, was found in mountainous or volcanic regions of Europe, including Austria, Germany, Italy, and France; it was also synthesized in later medieval times. Its tendency to react with pigments containing lead or copper limited its use, and it was not suitable for use in fresco. It is rarely found in wall painting, but was used for polychromed sculpture and easel painting, and probably most widely in manuscript illumination. It was also mixed with indigo to make greens, found in manuscript illumination from the ninth century and occasionally in easel painting.

Until the fourteenth century, yellow ochre, orpiment, and pigments prepared from yellow dyestuffs such as weld were the only yellow pigments. Yellow lead monoxide, like red lead, could be prepared by heating lead white, but its rapid darkening made it a poor pigment. During the fourteenth century, pale yellow pigments made from lead and tin became available. The use of lead-tin oxides as opacifiers for glass was already known and one of the two forms of the pigment, known as lead-tin yellow type II, is associated with the glass industry. It contains some silicon and free tin oxide and appeared first in Bohemian and Italian painting. The other, more common, form, lead-tin yellow type I, is associated with the ceramic industry and was made by fusing lead and tin oxides. Both were very stable and came to be used in all forms of painting.

The green mineral pigments used included green earth, the copper-containing malachite, found in association with azurite, and copper hydroxychloride minerals such as atacamite and paratacamite. Green earth contains iron-rich clay minerals, usually glauconite or celadonite. Sources of green earth occur widely across Europe, but vary considerably in color, some being blue-grey, while others are olive green. Green earth was often used as an underpaint for flesh tones in both easel painting and wall paintings, most typically seen in Florentine panels of the fourteenth century. The copper-containing green pigments are all rather similar in colour and properties. They include malachite, found in association with azurite, and basic copper chlorides, such as atacamite. Green copper-containing pigments were also prepared synthetically. Verdigris (blue-green basic copper acetates) was prepared by the action of vinegar fumes on copper plates; from late medieval times Montpellier in southern France was noted for its preparation. In some recipes, it was suggested that the plates were spread with honey and salt, giving a product containing basic copper chlorides. Verdigris was used in oil painting and in manuscript illumination, often with a yellow such as saffron. Over time it dissolved in the oil medium, giving a brilliant green glaze.

Lead white, basic lead carbonate, was the most important white pigment. It was prepared by suspending lead over vinegar fumes in a warm environment, a method known from Classical times. It was opaque in oil and egg tempera media and was used throughout the medieval period, in most forms of painting; in manuscript illumination and true fresco, chalk or other calcium carbonate whites, which are too translucent to serve as white pigments in oil paint, were used. Calcium carbonate and calcium sulfate (gypsum) were also used as preparatory or ground layers in easel painting and for polychromed sculpture. Black pigments were usually based on carbon (charcoal and other burnt plant matter); certain black minerals were also occasionally used locally.

See also **Alchemy; Alum; Cloth production; Leather production; Medicine, practical; Mineralogy**

Bibliography

Balfour-Paul, Jenny. *Indigo*. London: British Museum Press, 1998.

Bomford, David, Jill Dunkerton, Dillian Gordon, Ashok Roy and Jo Kirby. *Art in the Making: Italian Painting before 1400*. London: National Gallery Company Ltd, 1989.

Brunello, Franco. *The Art of Dyeing in the History of Mankind*. Translated by Bernard Hickey. Vicenza: Neri Pozza Editore, 1973.

Cennino d'Andrea Cennini. *Il libro dell'arte*. Edited by Daniel V. Thompson, Jr. 2 vols. New Haven: Yale Univerity Press, vol. I. Italian text 1932, vol. II. English text 1933. (English text reprinted as *The Craftsman's Handbook: the Italian Il libro dell'arte*. New York: Dover, 1956.)

Clarke, Mark. *The Art of All Colours*. London: Archetype Publications Ltd., 2001.

Clarke, Mark. Anglo-Saxon manuscript pigments. *Studies in Conservation* (2004) 49: 231–244.

Dyes in History and Archaeology (1989) 7 onwards (formerly *Dyes on Historical and Archaeological Textiles* (1982–1988) 1–6). Issues 7–15 (1989–1997) York: Textile Research Associates; issues 16/17 (2001) onward. London: Archetype Publications Ltd.

Gage, John. *Colour and Culture: Practice and Meaning from Antiquity to Abstraction*. London: Thames & Hudson, 1993.

Howard, Helen. *Pigments of English Medieval Wall Painting*. London: Archetype Publications Ltd., 2003.

Rosetti, Gioanventura. *The Plictho of Gioanventura Rosetti*. Translation of the first edition of 1548 by Sidney M. Edelstein and Hector C. Borghetty. Cambridge: M.I.T. Press, 1969.

Theophilus. *De Diversis Artibus—The Various Arts*. Edited and translated by C.R. Dodwell. Oxford: Clarendon Press, 1986.

JO KIRBY

PAPER

The origins of paper-making are traditionally associated with the bureaucrat Ts'ai Lun in China around 105 C.E., although paper archeology shows its presence there at least two centuries earlier. Paper soon spread to Japan and Central Asia. Transference of the craft into Islamic hands has been credited to the capture of Chinese prisoners at the Battle of Talas in 751, but that is doubtless a legend covering a process of gradual diffusion. Paper was soon being manufactured at great centers such as Baghdad (794), Damascus, and Cairo, and then generalized in Islamic markets. The court official al-Fadl ibn Yahya in the Abbasid caliphate promoted and popularized its use in the 790s, unless this story conceals a transference process appropriated by propagandists for the Barmakid family. Paper use spread rapidly through the 800s in Islam until it dominated over parchment and especially over papyrus by 950. By 1050 it was widely employed throughout the Maghrib (North Africa and Spain).

Various kinds and qualities of linen-rag-based paper were then a commonplace in Spain as elsewhere in Islam. Ibn 'Abdun in his market regulations (*hisba*) for Seville, and Peter the Venerable's mockery of rag material in Islamic Spain bear witness to its ordinary manufacture in the twelfth century, while both *al-Idrisi and Yaqut record that Islamic Játiva in Mediterranean Spain exported a world-famous product. Christian Spain had no paper manufacture until it overran the Islamic centers in the mid-thirteenth century. Even then the Christian role was to supervise the *Mudejar* or subject Muslims who continued their valuable enterprise, particularly at Játiva. César Dubler, Oriol Valls i Subirà, and others have proposed a twelfth-century Christian manufacture in hydraulic mills because fugitives from Almoravid or Almohad Spain brought the craft north. Valls even argues for a plethora of Christian paper mills from the Pyrenees to Tarragona, appearing from 1113 to 1244. This bizarre thesis remains influential. Josep Madurell i Marimón defends the existence of a paper mill at Copons in Catalonia in 1193, but that claim rests on a manuscript misreading.

Technology and Hydraulics

There were two processes of medieval paper-making—a hand craft in small domestic shops, and hydraulic mills powered by overshot or undershot vertical watermills with beating trip-hammers. Both systems required great quantities of water; both were noisome and therefore tended to be removed from population centers; and both used rags as raw material. Instead of flax fibers, the process in both systems commonly drew on rags from the linen clothing that was increasingly fashionable.

A description of the domestic craft, flawed in some details, has come down to us from the Zirid sultan al-Mu'izz ibn Badis (1007–1061 C.E.) The fibers were released by repeated soakings and rubbing; a twenty-four-hour cycle of such soaking leached out the quicklime; pounding with stone mortars and more soaking yielded the essential pulp; the pulp went into wooden molds, was pressed in sheets, sized with chalk or starch, and glazed with a smooth stone. The pulp could be held in the mold by horizontal laid-lines or pontillons and vertical chain-lines or corondells that left an imprint. The wet sheets were couched on felt as alternating pages in a press. Maghribian and Christian Spanish paper showed zigzag or hash marks. These resulted from folding the sheet, rather than as an imitation of the tanner's knife.

Despite the almost universal supposition that the Islamic manufactories were proper mills, the evidence indicates that they were small handcraft workshops traditional in Islamic industries. The oft-cited four hundred mills at Fez and the large plant with twenty workers near Játiva in 1050 under one "Abu Mescufa" are mere fantasies. Thus the three *wiraqat* or paper manufactories at Damascus were installed not as mills on the Barada River but at a nearby *'ayn* or spring, though other mills and querns were common there. Johannes Pederson cites al-Maqrizi for a papermaking "*khan* with a mill" at Cairo; but the Arabic text has a marketing warehouse (*khan al-wiraqah*) without a mill. Muslim authors in general call any paper manufactory a *wiraqah* rather than a mill (*tahun*).

An exhaustive survey of mills in Islamic Spain for every conceivable type of mill from the ninth to the fifteenth century has not a single paper mill. A citation of hydraulic paper mills floating on the Tigris River in tenth-century Baghdad is now widely discredited. Donald Hill, however, has found an ambiguous description from *al-Biruni in eleventh-century Samarkand that may possibly be an Islamic hydraulic exception. When Christians conquered Mediterranean Spain they inherited many kinds of Islamic mills (*molendina*) but for paper manufacture only paper presses (*almaxera papiri*). Other Christian manufactories, such as the contract places at Genoa in 1235 and 1255, seem to have been small domestic affairs. Actual paper mills were a Christian innovation, the earliest apparently at Játiva in 1282. Further research may clarify the vexed question of Islamic paper "mills" and claims about the first paper mill in Christendom.

Fabriano near the Adriatic port of Ancona in Italy holds a hallowed place in paper history as the first hydraulic paper mill in the west. This claim too disappears on close examination. The unanimity on the claim is marred by the broad range of dates proposed for its beginning, from 1268 as the most commonly received (Tsien) to 1276 (Lynn White), to "prior to 1283" (Geoffrey Glaister), to "the last thirty years of the thirteenth century" or "possibly before then" or "perhaps" in the eleventh century. The Fabriano claim rests on two manuscripts, one of 1276, the other of 1278, still accessible at the Silvestrine monastery at Montefano in Italy. Close examination reveals that the claim is based on a misreading of the Latin *carcer* (prison or enclosure) as Italian *cartiera* (paper mill). An ambiguous notice of 1283 removes seven *cartarii* from the town to avoid polluting the water. There is no 1268 mill. By the mid-fourteenth century however, the jurist Bartolo da Sassoferrato (1313–1357) was describing an established paper industry at Fabriano in which each craftsman had his own watermark.

Paper manufactories as mills multiplied during the late thirteenth and early fourteenth centuries in Italy. Evidence can be flimsy but a current survey has suggested: Prato (1285), Aquilea and Colonica (1288), Amalfi (1289), Modena (1292), Bologna and Cividale (1293), Colle del Val d'Elsa (1317), La Tana (1318), Padua (1339), Treviso (1340), Borgo di San Giacomo (1349), Nespolo (1356), Forli (1370), Fermignano (1375), Toscolano, Pignerolo and Nocera (1381), and Caselle Torinese (1392).

Southern France has no such mills before the fifteenth century; the rest of France has claims for Troyes (1348) and Essonnes (1355), as well as for Beaujeu (1383), Vedènes (1390), and Besançon (1392). German claims include Nurnberg (1389), Ravensburg (1393), and Chemnitz (1398). Flanders has a claim at Houplines (1389). The Catalan statesman Ramon Muntaner (1265–1336) complained that a list of the crimes committed by Barcelona's commercial rival Genoa would fill "all the amount of paper manufactured in the town of Játiva." Antoni Aragó Cabañas and Josep Trenchs have traced acceptance of paper from Valencia–Catalonia through Provence and down the curve of northern Italy, especially in notarial books, with parchment still strong at Rome and southern Italy and influencing France, Portugal, and England.

Marketing and Regulation

Long before Europeans made paper, they purchased it from Islamic sources. Early tariff lists show it moving through Christian ports as at Barcelona in 1222. It traveled up the Ebro River from Tortosa to Tudela. When the Spaniards conquered the Islamic Valencian regions, they inventoried their conquests in great detail in *repartimientos* (distributions) on imported paper, including expensive *nasri* paper. Paper was still a luxury item in Europe at the beginning of the thirteenth century, but toward the end of that century had become a general commodity mass produced by mills. It was bought in quantity for bureaucratic accounts, for the ubiquitous notaries in their paper volumes, for military business, and famously for the massive registers that filled the chancery of the Arago-Catalan realms. The literate merchant culture flourishing around the western Mediterranean created in turn a lively market for rags and for this "parchment of rags." New technologies such as eyeglasses (1280s) helped this evolution. The invention of the headle-treadle loom (1190s) and the spinning wheel (Speyer around 1280), as well as the popularity of linen clothing fed into the movement. The Holy Roman Emperor around 1231 discouraged the use of paper for serious records, and also ordered paper from cotton (*charta bombacyna*) to be discontinued in public documentation. Rivalry, especially between Italy and Spain, gave rise to improvements such as watermarks as brand names, better glue and vegetable sizing, shorter and more flexible fibers, and sturdier frames.

Governmental regulation of paper manufacturing and sales can be seen in detail in crown documents concerning the community of paper craftsmen at Játiva. King James the Conqueror progressively assimilated Játiva during the years 1244 into the late 1250s. In 1261 he assigned an annual pension to the Muslim governor (*qadi*) of Játiva from "Our revenues and profits from the press for paper which the said Saracens make." The king similarly assigned a pension of a thousand sous in 1276 to Abu Bakr the vizier of Murcia, to be taken "out of Our revenues and profits from paper of the town of Játiva." In 1274 James assured the aljama or community of Játiva's Muslims forever "that on the paper you make henceforth in Játiva you are not to give any tax except three Valencian pennies" for each ream. No mill or hydraulic device appears until an episode in 1282, when James's heir and successor Pere the Great caused a mill to be erected at Játiva but then retreated from imposing its use on the unwilling Játiva craftsmen. His privilege assured them that "any of you may keep in his own home and in other places wherever you choose, both inside and outside the Moorish quarter of Játiva, whatever stones for making paper, and may keep the paper itself, and may sell it" to any persons. This is the first real paper mill we have record of in Europe (the Fabriano claim falling short, as shown above), and as a Mudejar-operated enterprise the first paper mill also in the Islamic cosmos.

Other crown privileges guaranteed the Játiva craftsmen's lodgings for business in Valencia city (1282), a monopoly on any paper making in the kingdom (1292), reasonable taxes (1282), and protection against thieves who took paper or pulp (1286, 1300). Around 1340 and again around 1352 the crown instituted angry reforms in the quality and size of Játiva's paper and imposed teams of inspectors on the "masters of paper." In the fourteenth century the dislocations of war came close to crippling the Játiva industry, although the crown was regularly collecting taxes on it in the late fifteenth century. Prices and schedules meanwhile fluctuated so much as to be anarchic; in a 1284 list, five hundred sheets made a ream and ten or twelve reams a bale. Measurements also varied, controlled by the market.

By 1280 paper was six times cheaper than parchment at Bologna, and prices fell throughout the fourteenth century. One paper usage count in southern France has a ratio of one paper to forty-one parchment items in the thirteenth century falling to one to seven in the fourteenth. A radical shift in the market occurred at the opening of the fifteenth century when Islamic industries collapsed due to political turmoil, leading to widespread export of paper and general goods from Europe into Islam. Another major shift came when Johann Gutenberg's movable type introduced mechanical writing or printing into Europe in the 1440s.

The phenomenon of paper transformed the administrative, scholarly, and social life of the Islamic world, as it later did that of the Christian West. In both venues it also facilitated commercial and religious life. More than kings or wars it altered the human landscape. Above all, paper helped transform Europe from an oral to a written culture.

See also **Printing; Technological Diffusion; Watermills**

Bibliography

al-Hassan, Ahmad and Donald R. Hill. *Islamic Technology. An Illustrated History*. New York: Cambridge University Press, 1986.

Basanoff, Anne. *Itinerario della carta dall'oriente all'occidente e sua diffusione in Europa*. Documenti sulle arti del libro, 4. Milan: Edizioni Il Polifilo, 1965.

Bloom, Jonathan M. *Paper Before Print: The History and Impact of Paper in the Islamic World*. New Haven: Yale University Press, 2001.

Briquet, Charles-Moïse. *Les filigranes: dictionnaire historique des marques du papier des leur apparition vers 1282 jusqu'en 1600*. Amsterdam: Paper Publications Society, [1907] 1968.

Burns, Robert I. The Paper Revolution in Europe: Crusader Valencia's Paper Industry—a Technological and Behavioral Breakthrough. *Pacific Historical Review* (1981) 50: 1–30.

———. *Society and Documentation in Crusader Valencia*. Diplomatarium of the Crusader Kingdom of Valencia, 1, introduction. Princeton: Princeton University Press, 1985.

———. "Paper Comes to the West, 800–1400." In *Europäische Technik im Mittelalter 800 bis 1400: Tradition und Innovation*. Edited by Uta Lindgren. Berlin: Gebracht Mann Verlag, 1994.

———. "Paper," *Medieval Iberia, an Encyclopedia*. Edited by E. Michael Gerli. New York: Routledge, 2003.

Hunter, Dard. *Papermaking: The History and Technique of an Ancient Craft*. New York: Dover, [1947] 1978.

Ibn Badis, al-Mu'izz. *Medieval Arabic Bookmaking and its Relation to Early Chemistry and Pharmacology*. Edited by Martin Levey. Philadelphia: American Philosophical Society, *Transactions*, n.s. 52, pt. 4., 1962. pp. 3–79.

Madurell i Marimón, Josep. *El paper a les terres catalanes: contribució a la seva història*. 2 vols. Barcelona: Fundació Salvador Vives Casajuana, 1972.

Pedersen, Johannes. *The Arabic Book*. Princeton: Princeton University Press, [1946] 1984.

Polastron, Lucien. *Le papier: 2000 ans d'histoire et de savoirefaire*. Paris: Imprimerie Nationale, 1992.

Tsien Tsuen-Hsuin. *Paper and Printing*. Science and Civilization in China, 6. Edited by Joseph Needham. New York: Cambridge University Press, 1985.

Valls i Subirà, Oriol. Paper and Watermarks in Catalonia. 2 vols. Amsterdam: Paper Publications Society, 1970.

———. *La historia del papel en España, siglos X–XIV*. 3 vols. Empresa Nacional de Celulosas, 1978–1932.

ROBERT I. BURNS, S.J.

PATRONAGE OF SCIENCE

The Middle Ages did not exhibit a "system" of patronage, but "the action of a patron in supporting, encouraging, or countenancing a person, institution, work, art, etc.," (*Oxford English Dictionary*) certainly existed. Medieval records of patronage reflect a relationship based on: (a) Acceptance of reciprocal obligations; (b) Recognition of intellectual and sensible affinities between individuals, and (c) Acknowledgement of the sponsoring authority. Hand in hand with outright employment, this relationship led to the support of intellectual and productive activity. Medieval nobility became patrons in order to surround themselves with learning and luxury. Few medieval European economies were viable enough to provide even the basics to everyone; production was largely the result of commission. What evolved during the Middle Ages as a practice of offering to a chosen few sponsored

Medieval manuscript illustration depicting the death of Louis IX in Tunis. The French king was one of the outstanding patrons of medieval science. (Corbis/Archivo Iconografico, S.A.)

opportunities to speculate, reflect, and create original work in university or court settings, only thereafter flourished into an actual patronage system, in which persons of means supported and encouraged intellectuals and artists to pursue a life of scholarly or artistic expression for the patron's reflected glory.

Patronage of *Scientia* and Scholars

Patronage of *scientia* touched all knowledge and learning; it enveloped medieval patronage of science. The greatest medieval sponsor of the academic search for knowledge was the Roman Christian Church, the sustaining force behind the new medieval university. The church demanded that the patronized institution reflect well on its patron. The university had thus to be a haven of consensus around true *scientia*, and the place where that *scientia* was explored. The degree and title of university master became for the church a stamp of the patronage of *scientia* as well as a symbolic acknowledgement of its proprietary rights, and those of the university, as patrons, over the fruits of a student's subsequent labors.

The debates of *Scholasticism developed a sophisticated means to the end of harmonious agreement on what constituted *scientia*. They were not, however, to represent academe, and thus, when disputes arose over, for example, interpretations of Aristotle, rather than suffer disharmonious evolution toward a new academic paradigm of *scientia*, the patron church denounced them through

declarations, such as the *Condemnation of 1277. The coincidence between Christian theology and the predominantly Aristotelian scientific endeavor of the medieval university, between *religion and science, was fortuitous. It led to the many material expressions of patronage which allowed for the ethos and the physical presence of universities to flourish. It also afforded students two important sources of financial support. The more lucrative of these came in the form of parish church benefices from posts held in absentia by students as clerics and scholars. The other was the college fellowship; *Bartholmaeus of Bruges, Master of Arts, was probably among those who received a bursary from the college de Sorbonne while he studied medicine and theology in Paris.

Patronage of the Sciences and Scientists

In the Middle Ages, the patronage of *scientia* was as important as, if not more important than, the patronage of specific sciences and scientists. Some of the greatest medieval intellectuals—*Albertus Magnus, *Al-Biruni, *Ibn Sina (Avicenna), and *Ibn al-Haytham (Alhacen), all products of university or court sponsorship—personified curiosity and mastery of *scientia* as much as command of any particular science. Financial support for medieval *translation movements, a strategy to recover a "wiser past," was also patronage of *scientia*. Nonetheless, specific sciences and scientists were also recipients of medieval patronage. Virtually every branch of knowledge benefited, but those, theoretical and/or practical, most frequently identified with sponsorship were *alchemy and *astronomy, music, *zoology, *agriculture, *surgery and *anatomy, and *astrology and *medicine.

Medieval people were not naïve about the fruits of patronage. From reading the historical record, *Sa'id al-Andalusi, eleventh-century author of *Tabaqat al-'Umam* (*Book of the Categories of Nations*), saw an enlightened political leader as key to the scientific achievements of past cultures. A few medieval monarchs might have met his criteria: *Alfonso X the Wise, king of Castille and Leon (1221–1284), *Frederick II, King of the Germans and Holy Roman Emperor (1194–1250), or Hülegü, Khan of the Mongols (1217–1265). Alfonso the Wise commissioned astronomical works: *Libro del saber de astronomia* (*Book of Astronomical Knowledge*) and the *Alfonsine Tables*. Frederick II presaged Renaissance patrons' *Kunstkammer* collections with his menagerie of exotic animals. His *De arte venandi cum avibus* (*On the Art of Hunting with Birds*) (1244–1250), a compilation of over nine hundred images and descriptions of birds of prey, exemplified medieval patronage of scientific observation and illustration. Hülegü Khan, patron of the observatory at Maragha (northwestern Iran), enabled astronomers to compile the *Zij I Il-khani*, a Persian collection of astronomical tables (1272).

Medieval aristocrats patronized all types of architecture, ecclesiastical and secular. French King Louis IX erected the Sainte Chapelle; Jean, Duke of Berry, constructed territorial castles and was so enamored of their *stone masonry that he commissioned their depiction in beautiful *illumination in *Les Très Riches Heures*, a book of hours. Cathedrals, and astronomical *observatories, *bridges, *water supply and sewage routes, *irrigation and drainage, *navigation, *canals, *road building and all styles of medieval *military architecture derived from patronage. *Hospitals are another interesting case in point. Kings patronized charities that cared not only for the sick and lepers, but also for the poor and aged; by extension they frequently supported the premises used for such care. However, the pattern of medieval royal patronage for such houses diverted them from their scientific purpose: they became "royal retirement homes" rather than medical hospitals.

Financial support had a significant impact on contemporary technology, particularly on *agriculture, *cartography, *coinage, engineering, *printing, and *shipbuilding. Specific artifacts could even be singled out as having evolved because of medieval patronage: the *calendar, aspects of military technology (*arms and armor, *artillery and fire arms, *catapults and trebuchets, and the *stirrup), agricultural, astronomical, navigational, medical, and optical instruments, *norias (waterwheels), *watermills, *windmills, and virtually anything produced with the aid of a mill, such as the refined raw materials for the textiles in *cloth production.

Among the more famous medieval scientists who received patronage are *Ibn al-Haytham, *al-Biruni, and *Ibn Sina. From 833 on, according to Sa'id al-Andalusi, "There has always been a select group of scientists, Muslims and others, who were attached to Banu 'Abbas as well as other Muslim rulers and who worked in astronomy, geometry, medicine, and other ancient sciences." Many of the foremost Muslim intellectuals had the support of royal patronage. They were not primarily teachers, but in the absence of strong protection these natural philosophers were subjected to attacks from influential religious leaders who were offended by scientific rationality and some Aristotelian natural philosophical doctrines.

Idealized medieval accounts of the relationship between patron and beneficiary represent the patronized as an equal, admired and well paid, but the record is somewhat different. Careers of numerous beneficiaries were fundamentally based on a patron's desire for clerical or princely power. Drawn to Milan by Duke Francesco Sforza (1401–1466), Antonio Averlino (c. 1400–c. 1462) supervised the realization of numerous buildings, but his patron's power occasioned objections to his work from local guildsmen. Two very well-known recipients of power patronage were *Christopher Columbus and *Marco Polo. Patronized achievements in certain sciences and technologies fit particularly well as expressions of power, notably in anatomy, geography, manufacturing, and *travel and exploration.

On the one hand, medieval patronage of science affords an examination of the identity of natural science within contemporary socioeconomic and intellectual culture. On the other, however, medieval power patronage blurred distinctions between science, technology, and art. In both ecclesiastical and secular patronage of clockwork, for example, fostering of science and technology occurred under the patronage of art. Considered more abstractly, respect for needed concrete results was transferred to the more general field. Particular technological skills acquired enough cultural significance that written accounts of them qualified as adequate gifts to a patron. Patronage and the use of science, technology, and art for the display and legitimization of political power helped create the science-technology-art fusion about which Aristotle had written centuries earlier in the *Politics*: "In all the arts and sciences both the end and the means should be within our control."

See also **Instruments, optical**

Bibliography

Primary Source

Sa'id al-Andalusi. *Science in the Medieval World "Book of the Categories of Nations."* Translated by Sema'an I. Salem and Alok Kumar. Austin: University of Texas, 1991.

Secondary Sources

Shank, Michael M., ed. *The Scientific Enterprise in Antiquity and the Middle Ages*. Chicago: University of Chicago Press, 2000.

Wilkins, David G. and Rebecca L., eds. *The Search for a Patron in the Middle Ages and the Renaissance*. Lewiston, NY: The Edwin Mellen Press, 1996 Medieval and Renaissance Studies, Volume 12.

B.B. PRICE

PECHAM, JOHN

An Englishman educated at the universities of Oxford and Paris, John Pecham entered the Franciscan order in the 1240s or the 1250s. Later he returned to Paris, where he earned a theological doctorate in 1269 and served as regent master in theology for the next two years. During this Parisian period, Pecham wrote a number of biblical commentaries, a work on *Peter Lombard's Sentences, and a treatise on the soul. Pecham's theology was mainstream Franciscan—he was an Augustinian, and he opposed the philosophical novelties (including Thomistic ones) then popular in Paris. Pecham returned to England in the early 1270s to take up a position in the Oxford theological faculty. He left that post in 1275 for the provincial ministership of the Franciscan Order. In 1277 he was appointed master of theology at the papal court, and in 1278 he became Archbishop of Canterbury, a post that he held until his death in 1292. Pecham's work was clearly influenced by that of *Robert Grosseteste and *Roger Bacon.

Although highly educated in natural philosophy and the mathematical sciences, Pecham is important not for original contributions but for his achievements as a science educator. Pecham wrote a number of scientific treatises, apparently elementary textbooks intended to instruct his Franciscan brothers. These include a Tractatus de sphera and probably a Theorica planetarum—cosmological works based primarily on Aristotle's On the Heavens, *Sacrobosco's Sphere, and al-Farghani's Elements of Astronomy. He also wrote a Treatise on Number, and Questions on the Eternity of the World.

On the science of optics, Pecham wrote a Tractatus de perspectiva and Perspectiva communis. The latter was the only one of his works to acquire a wide circulation. It was noteworthy not for its original conclusions (although Pecham does dispute Bacon's theory of the rainbow), but as a popular distillation, accessible to non-specialists, of the optical writings of *Ibn al-Haytham, Roger Bacon, and others. The difference between Pecham's Tractatus de perspectiva and his Perspectiva communis is striking. The former has significant religious content and was apparently intended as a devotional aid. The latter deals exclusively with optics, and reveals neither biblical nor theological influence. This treatise is still extant in sixty-seven manuscript copies (quite a large number for a medieval scientific treatise). It was printed twelve times between 1482 and 1665, including a 1593 Italian translation. It became the standard late-medieval elementary textbook on perspectiva, spreading optical knowledge among innumerable European scholars. It was cited as late as the seventeenth century by Johannes Kepler and Giambattista Riccioli.

See also Optics and catoptrics

Bibliography

Lindberg, David C. A Catalogue of Medieval and Renaissance Optical Manuscripts. Toronto: Pontifical Institute of Mediaeval Studies, 1975.

Lindberg, David C., ed. John Pecham and the Science of Optics: Perspectiva communis, with an Introduction, English Translation, and Critical Notes. Madison: University of Wisconsin Press, 1970.

MacLaren, Bruce R. "A Critical Edition and Translation, with Commentary, of John Pecham's Tractatus de sphera." Ph.D. dissertation, University of Wisconsin, Madison, 1978.

Pecham, John. Questions Concerning the Eternity of the World. Trans. by Vincent G. Potter, S.J. New York: Fordham University Press, 1993.

Sharp, D. E. Franciscan Philosophy at Oxford in the Thirteenth Century. Oxford: Clarendon Press, 1930; reprt. New York: Russell & Russell, 1964.

DAVID C. LINDBERG

PETER PEREGRINUS

Virtually nothing is known about the life of Peter Peregrinus, other than what can be deduced from a concluding note in only one of the nearly forty manuscripts of his work on magnetism: "Finished in the camp at the siege of Lucera, in the year of our Lord 1269, on the eighth day of August." If this statement is valid, Peter was part of the army of Charles of Anjou, king of Sicily, besieging Lucera that year. There is no indication of why he received the honorific title Peregrinus (Pilgrim): it may have been either because he had actually made a pilgrimage, or because he had participated in papally sanctioned campaigns.

Manuscripts also refer to him as Petrus de Maharncuria, which would make his home town Maricourt in Picardy. All other biographical "information" about him is pure speculation.

Peter appears to be cited by *Roger Bacon as a "perfect mathematician," and as one who valued experience over argument, but this identification appears to stem from marginal glosses in only a few of the Bacon manuscripts, rather than from Bacon himself.

The first of Peter's two surviving works is a "letter" on magnetism—Epistula de Magnete—in thirteen chapters, found in forty manuscripts as well as several translations into vernacular languages and two early printed editions. The first part—ten chapters—describes the physical properties and effects of the lodestone (Peter does not deal with the occult properties elsewhere ascribed to magnets). He describes the physical characteristics of lodestones; their polarity and how to determine where the poles are and which pole is which; the repulsion and attraction of like and opposite poles; the attraction of iron by lodestones; the magnetization of iron by lodestones, and the ability to reverse the polarity in such an induced magnet; and the source of the magnetism (the celestial, rather than the terrestrial, poles).

The second part of the work consists of three chapters and describes three magnetic devices. The first two are a "wet" or floating compass and a "dry" compass. The third is a perpetual motion machine which operates by having a toothed wheel pass near a lodestone so that the teeth are alternately attracted by one pole and repulsed by the other.

The *Nova Compositio Astrolabii Particularis* (found in four manuscripts) describes the construction of a universal astrolabe which could be used at a variety of latitudes without changing the plates. Unlike *Ibn al-Zarqalluh's more famous universal astrolabe in which vertical halves of the heavens were projected onto a plane through the poles, Peter projected both the northern and southern hemispheres onto a plane through the equator (which was also the limit of projection). There are no known surviving astrolabes based on this treatise. The use of such an astrolabe is very complicated, and since it is probable that most sophisticated users were not frequent travelers, they were probably happier with the traditional (and simpler) stereographic astrolabe.

The influence of Peter Peregrinus's astrolabe was virtually nil. His reputation derives mainly from his work on magnetism which was much copied in the centuries after he wrote it.

See also **Astronomy; Magnet and magnetism**

Bibliography

Petrus Peregrinus de Maricourt. *Opera*, edited by Loris Sturlese and Ron B. Thomson. Pisa, Italy: Scuola Normale Superiore, 1995.

Tabarroni, Giorgio. "Le lettre di Pietro di Mariecourt sul magnete (agosto 1269) e il suo destinatario, Sigieri di Foucancourt." *Atti dell'Accademia dell'Istituto delle scienze di Bologna* (1984–1985) 73: 45–50.

RON B. THOMSON

PETRUS HISPANUS

From the end of the thirteenth century the *Summulae logicales* or *Tractatus*, written by Petrus Hispanus, came to be adopted throughout European *universities, with the exception of England, as a key textbook in the study of *logic. Until the end of the sixteenth century, it was copied hundreds of times and printed in more than two hundred editions, meriting commentaries by important philosophers, yet during this period little or no interest was dedicated to the author himself. At the same time, the *Thesaurus pauperum*, a medical prescription book also attributed to Petrus Hispanus, circulated extensively in manuscript form or in print throughout Europe among lettered medical practitioners, but mainly outside the university milieu. In the manuscripts there are no indications that these two works had been written by the same author. Ricobaldus of Ferrara includes in his *Historia Universalis* (completed in 1297) a brief note about Pope John XXI, "called master Petrus Hispanus," to whom he attributes the *Tractatus* but makes no reference to other works. In his *Historia Ecclesiastica Nova* (c. 1313–1316), Bartholomew of Lucca shows little esteem for the personality of Pope John XXI, whom he calls "dominus Petrus Hispanus," and a Portuguese known as "Petrus Iuliani," yet he praises his science and indicates that the Pope was an expert in medicine, having written a book called *Thesaurus pauperum* and *Problemata* following

Aristotle's style, but he says nothing of the logic work. This distinct identification of Petrus Hispanus with Pope John XXI is found later in some manuscripts and printed editions, but it is only in 1554 that Conrad Gesner in *Bibliotheca Universalis* attributes both works, the *Summulae* and the *Thesaurus*, to the same Petrus Hispanus, identified again as Pope John XXI, by this time more frequently described by bibliographers and ecclesiastical historians as a man of science. Gesner's combined attribution became authoritative, and the association with the pope was subsequently broadened by the inclusion of other works attributed to "Petrus Hispanus," especially in the twentieth century by Martin Grabmann. The traditional list of these works comprises about forty titles, in more than eight hundred manuscripts, including texts on logic, *natural philosophy, *zoology, medicine (theoretical and practical), theology, and *alchemy. But neither their content nor what is known of the lives of the future pontiff or other thirteenth-century Peters of Spain justify the attribution of these works to the one and same author. In the final section to this entry, consideration will be given to possible identifications of various authors associated with works attributed to Petrus Hispanus, but before doing so, a brief census of the more important works within this corpus will be made.

Logical and Philosophical Works

The *Tractatus* (or *Summulae logicales*) is the first of two works on logic by Petrus Hispanus. The twelve treatises subsumed under this work are divided into two parts. The first part reformulates the presentation of the *logica antiquorum* on modalities, propositions, syllogisms and topics, based on the works of Aristotle, Porphyry, and *Boethius. Following the introduction, Treatise II concerns Predicables, III Categories, IV Syllogisms, V Topics, and VII Fallacies. The second part of the *Summulae* introduces the medieval innovation of the *logica modernorum* on the properties of terms, primarily signification and supposition, that establish a theory of reference (*suppositio*), carefully classified into its variants, where the author expresses a moderate realism; Treatise VI discusses Suppositions, VIII Relatives, IX Amplifications, X Appelations, XI Restrictions, and XII Distributions. The successful combination of ancient and modern logic in the same textbook conferred on the work an important role in the dissemination of Scholastic approaches to discussion, argumentation and proof, and for this reason the *Summulae* became an essential textbook in the logical training of young students. Among many others, *John Buridan, *Marsilius of Inghen, Dante, John Versor, Luther, and Copernicus bear direct or indirect witness to the methodological influence of this work. *Syncategoreumata*, Peter of Spain's other logic work, is less well-known but nevertheless was adopted and commented on in some university courses. The logical rules for using syncategorematic words (such as "only," "alone," "unless," "but," etc.) that cause truth or falsity in a proposition are discussed through sophisms or linguistic puzzles. According to L.M. de Rijk, the two works were written in Northern Spain between 1230 and 1240 (although their dissemination is not known before 1270). An old theory suggests that the author could have been a Spanish Dominican, although attempts to identify him have thus far been fruitless [D'Ors (1997), (2001), (2003), whose suggestions have been discussed by Tugwell (1999)].

However, there are no traces of these logical texts in the other works attributed to Petrus Hispanus, even when they discuss logical matters, as is in the case of the *Sententia cum questionibus in libros De anima I–II Aristotelis*. Explicitly ignoring theological arguments, the author of the *Sententia* defends a natural discussion of man marked by anthropological dualism, where the body plays a merely instrumental role. The only acceptable origin of knowledge is sensible experience, from which intellect abstracts the intelligible species that actualizes the conformity between mind and things. According to Gauthier (1984), the commentary was written before 1250 by a master of arts in Toulouse, but none of the author's texts on embryology, cosmology or physics cited internally in the *Sententia* are known. The *Scientia libri de anima* is a completely different work, an extensive systematic treatise on man composed by a "Petrus Hispanus Portugalensis" probably before 1240. Existence, life, nourishment, sensation, feeling, knowledge, action, are all explained under the strong influence of *Ibn Sina and medical-physiological doctrines. Asserting that illumination and the intuition of forms are the ultimate grounds for truthful knowledge, the faculties of the soul are presented in spiritual ascension, culminating in the mystical fulfilment of man in the contemplation of the Creator. This author also wrote a *Tractatus bonus de longitudine et brevitate vitae*.

Two different commentaries on *De animalibus* by Aristotle are attributed to Petrus Hispanus, but they could not both have been written by the same author. Their positions on the mind distinguish each from the other and from the works discussed previously. The "Florence version" has the form of *sententiae cum questionibus*, with one thousand three hundred fourteen questions, while the "Madrid version" has a sequence of eight hundred fourteen questions. Apart from methodological and zoological problems, controversies between medical practitioners and philosophers are discussed in the same commentary, which includes problems related to the location, hierarchy and function of organs, and many other medical issues like illnesses, reproduction or growth and organic morphology. In these cases, the author turns to medical sources like *Galen or *Hippocrates. The *Problemata* are one hundred twenty-seven short questions and answers mainly on zoological particularities extracted from the "Madrid commentary" of *De animalibus*.

Medical Works

The medical works attributed to Petrus Hispanus can be divided into two main genres: prescription books and commentaries. The practical prescription books are focused on curative medicine and probably written in the second half of the thirteenth century. The author insists on the importance of sanitary habits, especially dietary ones, in conserving health and prolonging life. These books include the *Thesaurus pauperum*, which proposes cures for all ills from head to foot, *De febribus* which generally completes the former, *De oculo* which assembles three practical compilations on ophthalmology and eye diseases and the short *De phlebotomia* on the most favourable days for the surgical practice of bleeding. The three opuscules of the *Liber de conservanda sanitate* and the *Tractatus dietarum totius anni ad utilitatem humani corporis* are included in the *regimen sanitatis literature. The *Diete super cyrurgia* deals with the healing of the wounded.

The medical commentaries attributed to Petrus Hispanus cover a large part of the texts of the medical university curriculum. They form an extended version of the *Articella, in some ways expanding the commentaries by *Bartholomaeus of Salerno. There is good reason to believe that these works were composed by the "magister Petrus Hispanus medicus" who practiced medicine in Siena and taught at the city's studium between 1245 and 1250. It is also believed that this master was in some way connected to the court of emperor *Frederick II, as mentioned in *Diete super cyrurgia*. Containing nearly three thousand *quaestiones*, the commentaries include separate works on *Constantine the African's *Viaticum*, Galen's *Tegni* and *De crisi et super de diebus decretoriis*, Hippocrates's *Prognostica*, *Regimen acutorum* and *Aphorisma*, *Hunayn ibn Ishaq's *Isagoge in Artem parvam Galeni*, and finally three works by *Isaac Judaeus: *De dietis particularibus*, *De dietis universalibus*, *De urinis*.

There are profound differences between the practical compilations of pharmacological, surgical, astrological or superstitious prescriptions that had wide-spread popular dissemination and the scholastic commentaries known in academic circles, which are technically argued and which, through the discussion of authorities, are clearly intended to establish medicine as a *scientia, offering a thorough characterization of diagnostic, prognostic and therapeutic medical procedures. The influence and dissemination these two groups of works make them an important part of the process of medicalization and professionalization of health care that marks the end of the Middle Ages.

The Several Petri Hispani

The diversity of contexts of composition and dissemination and the lack of a theoretical continuity between these works justifies their distribution among several authors of the thirteenth century: "Petrus Hispanus logicus," "Petrus Hispanus Portugalensis," and "Petrus Hispanus medicus Senensis," who may be someone other than "Petrus Hispanus medicus compilator." The commentary on *De anima* and the *Sententia* on *De animalibus* may have been written by anonymous authors. Still other works attributed to Petrus Hispanus—for example, the theological *Expositio librorum beati Dionisii* and the *Sermones*—may belong to a monk or mendicant. A further mention must be made of a "Petrus Hispanus grammaticus," the twelfth- or thirteenth-century author of the *Summa "Absoluta cuiuslibet"* on syntax, and of two or three "Petri Hispani" who were Bolognese masters during the thirteenth century and authors of commentaries and compilations on canonical law. Finally, the set of alchemical works (*Liber de famulatu philosophie, Liber naturalis de rebus principalibus naturarum, Operatio ad congelandum mercurium in veram lunam, Veni Mecum, Verba secreta in arte Alkimie*) are almost certainly by a Petrus Hispanus from the second half or end of the fourteenth century. Bearing in mind the documented career and life of Petrus Juliani, the future Pope John XXI, authorship of none of the works mentioned in this article can be attributed to him. The pope had merely an indirect connection with the Parisian doctrinal *Condemnation of 1277 by the Bishop of Paris, a condemnation that was to shape several subsequent philosophical and scientific discussions.

See also **Medicine, practical; Medicine, theoretical; Scholasticism**

Bibliography

Primary Sources

Commentarium super librum dietarum particularium Isaaci (in *Omnia opera Ysaac*. Lugduni: Bartholomeus Trot in officina Johannis de Platea 1515, vol. I, fol. CIII–CLVI).

Commentarium super librum dietarum universalium Isaaci (in *Omnia opera Ysaac*. Lugduni: Bartholomeus Trot in officina Johannis de Platea 1515, vol. I, fol. XI-CIII).

Commentarium super librum urinarum Isaaci (in *Omnia opera Ysaac*. Lugduni: Bartholomeus Trot in officina Johannis de Platea 1515, vol. I, fol. CLVI–CCIII).

De dieta (Pseudo) Hippocratis per singulos menses anni observanda or *De regimine sanitatis* (ed. Pereira 1971, pp. 414–419).

De phlebotomia (ed. P. Gil-Sotres. *Scripta Minora de flebotomia en la tradición médica del siglo XIII*, Santander-Pamplona: Universidad de Cantabria 1986, p. 84).

Dietae super chirurgia (ed. K. Südhoff. "Eine Kurze Diätetik für Verwundete von Petrus Compostellanus [Petrus Hispanus]." In idem, *Beiträge zur Geschichte der Chirurgie im Mittelalter*. Leipzig: J.A. Barth 1918, vol. II, pp. 395–398).

Expositio librorum Beati Dionysii, (ed. M. Alonso. *Exposição sobre os livros do Beato Dionísio Areopagita*. Lisbon: Instituto de Alta Cultura, 1957).

Glosae super Tegni Galeni (ms. Madrid, BN, 1877, fol. 48ra–109ra; titles of the 485 questions in Salmón 1998, pp. 17–36).

Glosae supra Pronostica Hippocratis (ms. Madrid, BN, 1877, fol. 124ra–141vb; titles of the questions in Salmón 1998, pp. 49–62).

Liber de morte et vita et de causis longitudinis et brevitatis vite (ed. M. Alonso. *Pedro Hispano, Obras Filosóficas* III. Madrid: Consejo Superior de Investigaciones Científicas 1952, pp. 403–490).

Liber de oculo (ed.-trad. A.M. Berger. *Die ophtalmologie (liber de oculo) des Petrus Hispanus (Petrus von Lissabon, später Papst Johannes XXI)*. München: J.F. Lehmann, 1899.

Liber naturalis de rebus principalibus naturarum, frag., (ed.

*Manuel Alonso. *Pedro Hispano, Obras Filosóficas* III. Madrid: Consejo Superior de Investigaciones Científicas 1952, pp. 491–502).

Notulae super Isagoge Iohannicii in Artem parvam Galeni (ms. Madrid B.N. 1877, fol. 24ra–47vb; titles of the 287 questions in Salmón 1998, pp. 7–17).

Notulae super Regimine acutorum Hippocratis (ms. Madrid, BN, 1877, fol. 110ra–123va; titles of the 331 questions in Salmón 1998, pp. 36–49).

Problemata (ed. in de Asúa 1991, pp. 359–403).

Questiones et sententia super libro De animalibus Aristotelis (ms. Firenze, BNC, Conv. soppr., G. 4.853, fol. 79ra–187rb; titles of the questions in de Asúa 1991, pp. 291–358).

Questiones super libro De animalibus Aristotelis (ms. Madrid, BN, 1877, ff. 256r–290v; titles of the questions in Asúa 1991, pp. 244–290).

Questiones supra Viaticum Constantini (partial ed. in Mary Frances Wack. *Lovesickness in the Middle Ages. The Viaticum and Its Commentaries*. Philadelphia: University of Pennsylvania Press, 1990, pp. 83–108, 232–251, 305–310., pp. 230–251, 305–310; the Version A is in fact anonymous).

Sententia cum questionibus in libros De anima I-II Aristotelis (ed. M. Alonso. *Comentário al de anima de Aristóteles*. Madrid: Bolaños y Aguilar, 1944).

Scientia libri de anima (ed. M. Alonso. Madrid: Bolaños y Aguilar 1941; 2nd ed. Barcelona: J. Flors, 1961).

Sermones (cfr. Schneyer, J.-B. *Repertorium der Lateinischen Sermones des Mittelalters, für die Zeit von 1150-1350*, Münster i. Westfalen: Aschendorffsche Verlagsbuchhandlung 1969–1990; vol. 4: Autoren L–P, 1972, pp. 652–663).

Summa de conservanda sanitate (ed. Pereira 1973, pp. 444–491).

Syncategoremata (ed. de Rijk 1992).

Thesaurus pauperum and *De febribus* (ed. Pereira 1973, pp. 76–408).

Tractatus (ed. de Rijk 1972; Engl. transl.: Dinneen, F.P. *Peter of Spain, Language in Dispute*. Amsterdam: John Benjamins, 1990).

Secondary Sources

de Asúa, Miguel J.C. "The Organization of Discourse on Animals in the Thirteenth Century. Peter of Spain, Albert the Great, and the Commentaries on 'De animalibus'." Ph.D. Dissertation, University of Notre Dame (Indiana), 1991.

———. "The Relationships Between Medicine and Philosophy in Peter of Spain's Commentary on *Articella*." In *Papers of the Articella Project Meeting. Cambridge, December 1995*. Cambridge–Barcelona: Cambridge Wellcome Unit for the History of Medicine–CSIC 1998, pp. 13–27.

García y García, Antonio. *Estudios sobre la canonistica portuguesa medieval*. Madrid: Fundación Universitaria Española, 1976.

Gauthier, René-Antoine. "Préface." In *Sancti Thomae de Aquino Sententia libri de anima*. (Opera Omnia t. XLI*1). Rome–Paris: Commissio Leonina; J. Vrin, 1984, cfr. pp. 236*–242*.

Grabmann, Martin. *Mittelalterliche lateinische Aristotelesübersetzungen und Aristoteleskommentare in Handschriften spanischer Bibliotheken*. München: Bayerische Akademie der Wissenschaften, 1928, cfr. pp. 63–65, 98–113 (reimpr.: idem, *Gesamelte*

Akademieabhandlungen. Paderborn: F. Schöningh, 1979, I, pp. 383–495).

Hasse, Dag N. *Avicenna's* De Anima *in the Latin West: The Formation of a Peripatetic Philosophy of the Soul 1160–1300.* London–Torino: Warbourg Institute, 2000, pp. 55–60.

Kneepkens, C.H. *Het "Iudicium Constructionis." Het Leerstuk van de constructio in de 2de Helft van de 12de Eeuw.* Nijmegen: Ingenium Publisher, 1987.

Köhler, Theodor W. *Der philosophisch-antropologische Diskurs im dreizehnten Jahrhundert. Die Erkenntnisbemühungen um den Menschen im zeitgenössischen Verständnis.* Leiden: E.J. Brill, 2000 (passim).

Maierù, Alfonso. *University Training in Medieval Europe.* Leiden: E.J. Brill, 1994.

Meirinhos, J.F. "Giovanni XXI." In *Enciclopedia dei Papi.* Roma: Istituto della Enciclopedia italiana, 2000, vol. II, pp. 427–436.

Morpurgo, Piero. *L'idea di natura nell'Italia Normannosveva.* Bologna: CLUEB 1993, pp. 109–146.

Nagel, Silvia. Antropologia e medicina nei *Problemata* di Pietro Ispano. *Medioevo* (1991) 17: 231–248.

Nardi, Paolo. *L'insegnamento superiore a Siena nei secoli XI-XIV. Tentativi e realizzazioni dalle origini alla fondazione dello Studio generale.* Milano: Giuffrè, 1996, pp. 56–63.

d'Ors, Angel. Petrus Hispanus O.P., *Auctor Summularum.* *Vivarium* (1997) 35: 21–71; (II): Further Documents and Problems. *Vivarium* (2001) 39: 209–254; (III) Petrus Alphonsi or Petrus Ferrandi? *Vivarium* (2001) 41: 249–303.

Pereira, Maria Helena da Rocha. *Obras Médicas de Pedro Hispano.* Coimbra: Acta Universitatis Conimbrigensis, 1973.

de Rijk, Lambert M., ed. *Peter of Spain (Petrus Hispanus Portugalensis) Tractatus, Called Afterwards Summulae logicales, First Critical Edition from the Manuscripts with an Introduction.* Assen: Van Gorcum, 1972.

——, ed. *Peter of Spain (Petrus Hispanus Portugalensis) Syncategoreumata. First Critical Edition with an Introduction and Indexes, with an English Translation by J. Spruyt.* Leiden: E.J. Brill, 1992.

Salmón, Fernando. *Medical Classroom Practice: Petrus Hispanus' Questions on Isagoge, Tegni, Regimen Acutorum and Prognostica (c. 1245–50) (MS Madrid B.N. 1877, fols 24rb–141vb).* Cambridge-Barcelona: Cambridge Wellcome Unit for the History of Medicine-CSIC, 1998.

Tugwell, Simon. Petrus Hispanus: Comments on Some Proposed Identifications. *Vivarium* (1999) 37: 103–113.

Thijssen, J.M.M. Hans. *Censure and Heresy at the University of Paris 1200–1400.* Philadelphia: University of Pennsylvania Press, 1998, pp. 43–46.

JOSÉ FRANCISCO MEIRINHOS

PEUERBACH, GEORG

Georg Peuerbach (or Peuerbach) was a prominent fifteenth-century astronomer and astrologer. He was originally named Georg Aunpeckh, from Peuerbach, Austria, where he was born sometime after 1421. (The standard birth date of May 30, 1423, has no firmer basis than a mid-sixteenth-century horoscope.) Peuerbach matriculated at the university in Vienna in 1446, earning his B.A. degree in 1448. Between 1448 and 1451 he traveled in Italy, where he impressed the likes of Nicholas of Cusa and lectured on astronomy in Padua. On returning to Vienna, he received his master of arts degree in 1453 and lectured on classical Latin poetry (including Virgil and Juvenal) at the university. His own literary aspirations appear in Latin love poems addressed to a young Carthusian novice who later became a priest, and in two letters preserved in a collection of model epistles.

Peuerbach's acquaintance with Johann Nihil, the astrologer of Emperor Frederick III of Hapsburg, and his renown in mathematics and astronomy brought him into association with several courts as an astrologer. Among his first patrons was the emperor's nephew, the young King Ladislaus V Posthumus, who ruled Lower Austria, Bohemia, and Hungary until his premature death in 1457. Thereafter Peuerbach served the emperor himself, who held court in Wiener Neustadt, near Vienna. Peuerbach's chief associate was his disciple and colleague *Regiomontanus (Johannes Müller of Königsberg), with whom he collaborated on these and other projects, including observations of eclipses and comets (including that of 1456, now known as Halley's Comet).

Peuerbach is most renowned for his *New Theories of the Planets* (*Theoricae novae planetarum*), on which he lectured at the Viennese Citizens' School (*Bürgerschule*) in 1454. Regiomontanus, who copied one of the earliest manuscripts of the work at the time, would also issue the *editio princeps* in Nuremberg c. 1472, initiating a lively printing history. Erhard Ratdolt included it in the elementary astronomical compendia he published in Venice (1482 and 1485), which were widely imitated. The *Theoricae novae* became an influential university sixteenth-century textbook of planetary theory, displacing the widely used anonymous thirteenth-century *Theorica planetarum communis*. By the mid-seventeenth century, Peuerbach's *Theoricae novae* had appeared in more than fifty Latin, Hebrew, and vernacular editions. It also spawned a handful of commentaries that testify to its reception in university circles. It introduced many students (including Copernicus, Galileo, and Kepler) to a simplified, but also updated and more physical, version of *Ptolemy's *Almagest*. Although Peuerbach says almost nothing about the planetary spheres themselves, the illustrations in the manuscripts and in Regiomontanus's first printed edition (c. 1472) depict eccentric planetary models embedded within spherical shells with inner and outer surfaces concentric to the Earth. These models resemble those described in the writings of *Roger Bacon and *Ibn al-Haytham, and in Ptolemy's *Planetary Hypotheses*, which was known in the Middle East but not in Europe.

Peuerbach computed an influential set of eclipse tables, *Tabulae eclipsium* (c. 1459). Based on the thirteenth-century *Alfonsine Tables*, they eased the computational difficulties with an innovative, labor-saving organization. The eclipse tables circulated widely in manuscript before the first Viennese edition of 1514. Peuerbach also composed several smaller treatises, still in manuscript, devoted to elementary arithmetic, more accurate sine tables, the construction of astronomical instruments (the gnomon, the astrolabe, the quadrant), and calculating devices.

Peuerbach not only wrote about instruments; he was also a skilled craftsman who designed and built them. He invented a hinged, portable sundial with a compass whose dial for the first time showed the difference between magnetic and true north. Of his handiwork, five exemplars of the sundial survive (including one of gilded brass probably destined for Emperor Frederick III), as well as one astrolabe.

At the urging of the visiting Greek cardinal Bessarion, Peuerbach in 1460 began an *Epitome* of Ptolemy's *Almagest*. He had completed only the first six (of thirteen) books when he died in Vienna the following year, not yet forty years old. Peuerbach's contribution to the *Epitome* follows closely the thirteenth-century *Almagestum minor*. Regiomontanus eventually revised and completed the *Epitome* (c. 1462), raising the work to new critical heights. The *Epitome of the Almagest* circulated in manuscript until the first printed edition appeared in Venice in 1496. Copernicus owned a copy, which introduced him to the complexities of Ptolemy.

At his death, Peuerbach was reportedly working on a mysterious "new theory" that Johannes Angelus (Vienna) claimed to have used to produce an almanac (1510–1512) with non-Alphonsine planetary positions.

See also **Astrolabes and quadrants; Astronomy; Ptolemy; *Theorica planetarum*; Regiomontanus, Johannes**

Bibliography

Aiton, Eric J. Peurbach's *Theoricae novae planetarum*: A Translation with Commentary. *Osiris*, 2nd series (1987), 3: 4–43.

Dobrzycki, Jerzy and Richard L. Kremer. Peurbach and Maragha Astronomy? The Ephemerides of Johannes Angelus and their Implications. *Journal for the History of Astronomy* (1996) 27: 187–237.

Grössing, Helmuth. *Humanistische Naturwissenschaft: Zur Geschichte der Wiener mathematischen Schulen des 15. und 16. Jahrhunderts*. Baden-Baden: Verlag Valentin Koerner, 1983.

Lerner, Michel-Pierre. *Le Monde des sphères*. 2 vol. Paris: Les Belles Lettres, 1996–1997.

Zinner, Ernst. *Leben und Wirken des Joh. Müller von Königsberg genannt Regiomontanus*. 2nd ed. Osnabrück: Otto Zeller Verlag, 1968. Translated by Ezra Brown, *Regiomontanus: His Life and Work*. Amsterdam: North Holland, 1990.

MICHAEL H. SHANK

PHARMACEUTIC HANDBOOKS

At the end of antiquity, pharmaceutical literature included six major types of manuals, as follows:

(a) Treatises of *materia medica* dealing with the substances from the three natural realms (plant, animal, mineral) used in the preparation of medicines, that is, drugs. The field was dominated by the most finished work of antiquity on this matter, *De materia medica* (*MM*) by the Greek *Dioscorides. *MM* mainly contained the following: description of the drugs, therapeutic

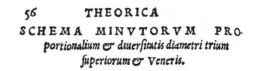

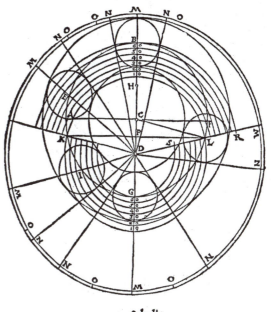

properties, and medical uses. Spread across the entire Mediterranean world, it was translated into Latin (sixth century [?]), Syriac (sixth century), and Arabic (several versions from the ninth century onward). Its content was rearranged several times in Byzantium, for among other reasons to produce a herbal, and excerpted in several early medieval booklets, from Gargilius Martialis (third century) to the Pseudo-Dioscorides' *De herbis feminis* (fifth century). Many of these books included color representations of the plants, animals and minerals.

(b) Treatises of medicines arranged according to their pharmaceutical types, or by diseases and affected organs. The prototype of such genres was, for the former, *On Medicines by Genres* by *Galen and, for the latter, *On Remedies Easily to Procure*, attributed to Dioscorides, and the *On Medicines by Places* of Galen. In the latter and other similar treatises, each chapter deals with the treatment of one disease and all chapters are classified on the principle of *a capite ad calcem* (from head to toe), that is, the topography of diseases, from the pathologies of any kind of the head to the lower members, passing through the heart and vascular system, the digestive system, the urinary tract, gynecology, and the arms and legs.

(c) Treatises on compound medicines. Further to the development of this therapeutic strategy from the early first century B.C.E. onward and their fashion in the Roman empire, not only compound medicines flourished, but also manuals that gradually accumulated their formulas. Their prototype was *On Antidotes* by Galen. Formulas were listed under the name of their creator, their main therapeutic property, or their principal ingredient(s), accordingly.

(d) Treatises on venoms and poisons. Treatises on poisons very often followed larger works on *materia medica*, so as to complement them by studying the toxic action of substances whose therapeutic action is analyzed in the foregoing material. Treatises on venomous animals often accompanied the former, so as to constitute a complete treatment of toxicology. Both types of works feature inventories of the toxic agents (plants and minerals for poisons; snakes, scorpions, venomous fishes, and some other terrestrial animals supposedly venomous such as the salamander, for the venoms), described their action on human physiology, and listed therapies. In some cases, such treatises were autonomous works as the most ancient currently known, by Nicander (second century B.C.E. [?]).

(e) Lists of products of substitution. Since drug availability could vary according to the season, the place, and trade, drugs with a determined action could be replaced by other ones with an identical or similar action. Such products of substitution were enumerated in lists made of two columns: the left column contained the drugs originally required, and the right one their substitutes. The prototype of such work is a treatise *On Substitution Products* ascribed to Galen. In the Latin West, such treatises were entitled *quid pro quo*.

(f) Tables of pharmaceutical weights and measures, according to local systems, sometimes including tables of conversion of different systems.

Such classical types were fundamentally reproduced in Byzantium, the Arabic world, and the West. Over time, however, they underwent a similar general evolution: the data of the first four types were often amalgamated so as to form a unique work, called *iatrosophion* in Byzantium, *aqrabadhin* in the Arabic world (a deformation of the Greek word *grafidion*, meaning "notebook"), and *receptarium* or *antidotarium* in the West. This was all the more so because Greek works were translated into Arabic, and such Arabic translations, together with new Arabic works were translated in turn into Latin. Such manuals were often associated in the same book to works of the last two types above, so as to form complete handy reference works. Whatever their contents, such manuals were very often used as notebooks by physicians who annotated texts in the margins, also reporting the results of their personal practice of medicine. As a consequence, texts in this kind of handbooks were fluid and changing. Their evolution was not determined by the accumulation of mistakes gradually introduced by successive generations of copyists contrary to a generally admitted opinion.

Two main new pharmaceutical genres were developed during the Middle Ages:

(g) In the Arabic world, Ibn Butlan (d. 1063 [?]) transformed the presentation of *materia medica* data in his *Tables of Health*: instead of using a discursive presentation, he segmented textual information so as to present it in a tabular form. Each column contained a single category of data, among others: name, nature, degree, best variety, usefulness and toxicity of drugs. This kind of presentation was transmitted to the West under the title of **Tacuinum sanitatis* and the fourteenth-century North-Italian manuscripts containing such text were illustrated with full page paintings where plants were inserted into their natural and human context.

(h) In Byzantium and the West, after the period of translation of Arabic medical works into Greek and Latin respectively, bilingual dictionaries of medical technical terms (especially, but not exclusively, the names of plants) were compiled. Such terms resulted from the nature of translation: very often, technical terms were not properly translated, but simply reproduced from Arabic and transliterated into Greek and Latin accordingly. Bilingual dictionaries aimed at compensating for this shortcoming of translation method: they provided the Arabic transliterated term in the column on the left and its mere translation(s) in the column on the right or, at least, a short explanation of the Arabic transliterated term in order to clarify its meaning. In the West, such genre was particularly illustrated by the *Synonyma* of Simon of Genoa, and by the *Opus pandectarum* of Matthaeus Silvaticus, both of which were compiled in the first half of the fourteenth century.

See also **Pharmacology; Pharmacy and *materia medica*; Translation norms and practice**

Bibliography

Delatte, Armand. *Anecdota Atheniensia et alia 2*. Paris: Les Belles Lettres, 1939.

Dioscorides: Pedanii Dioscuridis Anazarbei. De materia medica libri quinque. Edidit M. Wellmann. 3 vols. Berlin: Weidmann, 1906–1914 (reprinted 1958 and 1999).

Hultsch, Friedrich. *Scriptores metrologici*. Stuttgart: Teubner, 1864.

ibn Butlan. *Le Taqwim al-Sihha (Tacuini Sanitatis) d'Ibn Butlan: un traité médical du XIe siècle. Histoire du texte, édition critique, traduction, commentaire*. By H. Elkhadem. Louvain: Peeters, 1990.

Kästner H. Pseudo-Dioscoridis De herbis feminis. *Hermes* (1896) 31: 578–636 and (1897) 32: 160.

Matthaeus Silvaticus. *Opus Pandectarum*. Venice: Simon de Luere, 1507.

Simon Genuensis. *Clavis sanationis*. Venice: Simon de Luere, 1507.

ALAIN TOUWAIDE

PHARMACOLOGY

In the history of therapeutics the term pharmacology, which was created in nineteenth-century Germany, usually refers to the laboratory analysis of the therapeutic action of medicines independently from their administration to a patient. Scholars interested in the history of ancient pharmacy have recently used such term in a different meaning, however, of etymological nature: the science of *pharmaka*, that is, of the substances of natural origin introduced into—or applied on—the body to restore its normal state when it is disturbed by disease. For such scholars, pharmacology has an even more limited meaning and principally deals with the theoretical fundament of pharmaco-therapy.

The Classical Heritage

The Roman period (particularly the early empire) transmitted to later ages two major theoretical systems to describe and account for the action of *pharmaka*: holism and reductionism, best represented respectively by the *De materia medica* of *Dioscorides c. 20–70 C.E.) and the *De simplicium medicamentorum temperamentis et facultatibus* of *Galen (129–post 216 [?] C.E.)

In the holistic system, natural substances with therapeutic properties (called drugs or simple medicines), whatever their nature (plant, animal, mineral), exert a unique action resulting from their link to the cosmos, be it their coming to being during a phase of world creation (i.e., cosmogony), their geographical distribution in the actual world, and any other peculiarity of geographico-cosmic nature. For example, substances linked with the first of the Five Ages of Humankind in mythology warm up the body and, as a consequence, eliminate all excesses of humidity, as do also substances coming from the edges of the known world, that is, from the reign of the Sun. On the basis of patients' examination, physicians chose a property to be administered according to the principle of *contraria contrariis*: the *pharmakon* had to compensate for the deficiencies in the equilibrium of body function as analyzed in physiology. The selected *materia medica* reintroduced into the body the deficient qualities and thus restored the natural equilibrium previously disturbed by illness.

In the reductionist system, substances used as medicines associated different therapeutic qualities (in fact, opposite ones: hot and cold, dry and wet), which could be objectively measured on a four degrees scale, whose zero was not the absence of a quality (mathematical zero), but the equilibrium of the two opposites. As a consequence, a degree of one quality according to such system was not its distance from zero, but its quantitative difference when compared with its opposite. Reductionist pharmacology also included a materialistic theory of matter, in fact an atomism derived from Asklepiades of Bithynia (first century B.C.E.). Such atomism, harshly opposed by Galen even though it was partially integrated by him in his pharmacological system, did not correspond to Democritus' atomism, but was of a specific nature: according to Asklepiades, indeed, the body and medicines are made of particles that can be transferred from medicines to the body (and conversely) and interact. In Galen's reorganization, no reference was made to atoms, but only to parts (*merê*), which have different shapes and physical qualities (thin or thick, heavy or light, for

example) and can be absorbed more or less easily and quickly into the matter of the body.

In both systems, the action of drugs and medicines was defined as a *dunamis*, that is, a power (*virtus* in medieval medical Latin). Potentially present in the drug and the medicine, such power becomes active only in determined circumstances, in fact the physiological conditions of the body. Such definition was created as early as the mid- or late fourth century B.C.E., perhaps in the milieu of Aristotle (384–322), particularly with Diocles of Carystus (fourth/third century B.C.E.). The action of poisons and venoms, which is more clearly perceivable, was used as a prototype to build a model that was further transferred to drugs and medicines.

During the period mid-first century to the second century C.E., a third system was created on the basis of Asclepiades' atomism: methodism. According to it, the many states of the body could be reduced to three only: dense (*status strictus*), relaxed (*status laxus*), and intermediary (*status medius*). Such states resulted from the move of bodily particles within the body, with a higher concentration in one point and, as a consequence, a deficiency in another one. Therapy consisted in restoring the natural distribution of particles within the body by moving them. Such system had a minor place in medicine, particularly because it was harshly opposed by Galen.

From the early first century B.C.E. to the middle of the first century C.E., a new trend developed in pharmacology: compound medicines. Their principle consisted in associating different drugs in a unique medicine, so as to theoretically make it possible to treat a broad spectrum of diseases with only one medicine. Such approach probably originated in the context of toxicology in the second century B.C.E. in Asia Minor, and was further transferred to Rome and extended to other sectors of pathology. It reached its maximum with Andromachos, physician to the Roman emperor Nero (54–68 C.E.), who improved a previous formula and associated up to eighty ingredients. In the second century C.E. many formulas existed, which bore the name of their creator, of their supposed action, and of their main ingredient, for instance. Galen listed and exposed them in his treatise *On antidotes*.

Reception

In Byzantium, the authors of medical encyclopedias of the early period, Oribasius (fourth century), Aetius (sixth century), and Paul of Ægina (seventh century), associated holism and reductionism in different ways. Later on (from the tenth century onward), this was no longer the case: Dioscorides' holism seems to have been preferred over Galen's reductionism. This might be the result of a transformation of pharmacology and, more generally, of medicine and science, which had happened in the meantime. Pharmacology was Christianized, particularly with the so-called Anargyri, that is, the twin brothers Kosmas and Damianos (third century). According to the legend, they received a Christian education from their mother Theodora. Provided with medical knowledge directly from God, they cured sick people for free (hence their qualification of Anargyri). They suffered martyrdom during the reign of Diocletian (284–305), and were venerated by Christians as holy healers. They then performed posthumous therapeutic miracles. Their cult seem to have been well established in Constantinople in the sixth century at least. The medicines used by the Anargyri were the same as those of lay learned physicians; however, their meaning was different: they did not work because of any special intrinsic quality of matter, but only thanks to the action of God. As a consequence, theoretical speculation was eliminated from the field of pharmacology, asit was from pathology and physiology, with the Christian anthropology developed by the Fathers of the Church, Basil of Caesarea (c. 329–379), Gregory of Nazianzos (329/330–c. 390), Gregory of Nyssa (between 335 and 340–after 394), and John Chrysostom (between 340 and 350–407), and authors as Nemesius of Emesa (fourth century) and Meletius, of uncertain period (between the seventh and thirteenth centuries).

From Byzantium, the classical heritage was transmitted first to the Syriac world (sixth century), then to the Arabic one (ninth century onward). Both Dioscorides' holism and Galen's reductionism were received in the Arabic world, as was also the strategy of compound medicines. The latter posed theoretical problems that were extensively studied. One dealt with the actual nature of their therapeutic property. Was it identical to the sum of the properties of the ingredients or another one? If the latter, another problem consisted in identifying the new property of compound drugs. Did it result from the interaction of the ingredients on each other? If so, what was it? Two main conceptual systems were created to answer such questions: a mathematical one by *al-Kindi and a philosophical one by *Ibn Sina. The former relied on Galen's theory of degrees of drug properties, and proposed a mathematical formula to determine the final property of compound medicines, while the latter suggested that the property of compound medicines cannot be theoretically evaluated, but needed to be tested on patients to be known. Such position lead to a total relativism: individual reactions to medicines could change from one patient to another, and even for the same patient, according to his temporarily bodily conditions. As a consequence, no action of any medicine could be predicted. Medicines had to be repeatedly tested, not only from one patient to another, but also on the same patient.

In the West, methodism was somehow perpetuated with the Latin translation of the treatises of pathology and therapeutic of Soranos (first/second century C.E.) by Caelius Aurelianus (active c. 400). It was also present in the therapeutic manual of Theodorus Priscianus (fourth/fifth century), and introduced into the sixth-century Latin translation of Oribasius, and the Ravenna commentaries on Galen's treatises *On medical schools* by Agnellus (active c. 600 C.E.).

Transformation

As in the Byzantine world, pharmacology was transformed by Christianization, particularly (but not only) the Anargyri. Transferred from the East, their cult arrived as early as the end of the eighth century, if not earlier, for it is attested in the recipe book of Lorsch Abbey (Germany), of 790 C.E. According to Christian theological pharmacology, the therapeutic action of plants resulted from the direct action of God during Creation, in fact, His Mercy for Humankind and His Willingness to provide Humankind with a relief for physical sufferance. On this basis of therapeutic mysticism developed, best illustrated by *Hildegard of Bingen (1098–1179).

After translations into Latin introduced Arabic medical works into Western science, first in southern Italy (particularly at *Salerno and *Monte Cassino, with Constantine the African [d. after 1085]), then in Spain (*Toledo, with *Gerard of Cremona [c. 1114–1187]) and finally in southern France (Montpellier, with *Arnau de Vilanova [c. 1240–1311]), compound medicines were more and more frequently present in pharmacology. The theoretical problems posed in the Arabic world were repeated in the West, especially the evaluation of the therapeutic property of compound medicines according to a mathematical formulas in the way of al-Kindi, with works entitled Book on the degrees of medicines by such authors as Constantine the African (d. after 1085) and Arnau de Vilanova, among others.

A first return to Greek pharmacology was made by *Pietro d'Abano (1257–c. 1315), who traveled to Constantinople. In his pharmacological work, he associated Dioscorides' holism and Galen's reductionism in the way of early Byzantine medical encyclopedists. Even though such work was printed as early as 1478 (Colle, Tuscany), it was not before Nicolao Leoniceno (1428–1524) that Greek pharmacology was fully reintroduced into Western medical science. Not only in *De Plinii aliorumque in medicina erroribus* (*On the Mistakes of Pliny and Many Other Authors on Medicine*) first published in 1492 (Ferrara), but also in his similar subsequent works, did Leoniceno foster a return to a pharmacology relying mainly, if not exclusively, on simples, particularly Dioscorides' *MM*, whose Greek text he might have edited for the first printed version by Aldo Manuzio (Venice, 1499). With this work, Leoniceno ended medieval pharmacology, be it Arabic speculation on the property of compound medicines, Christian theological explanation of the origin of the therapeutic properties of simple drugs, or the use of compound medicines.

See also **Medicine, practical; Medicine, theoretical; Pharmacy** and *materia medica*

Bibliography

Primary Sources
Dioscorides: Pedanii Dioscuridis Anazarbei. De materia medica libri quinque. Edidit M. Wellmann. 3 vols. Berlin: Weidmann, 1906–1914 (reprinted 1958 and 1999).

Gunther, Robert T. *The Greek herbal of Dioscorides. Illustrated by a Byzantine A.D. 512, Englished by John Goodyer A.D. 1655, edited and first printed A.D. 1933.* Oxford: Oxford University Press, 1934.

Raeder Johannes. *Oribasii Collectionum medicarum reliquiae,* 4 vols. Leipzig: Teubner, 1928–1933.

Secondary Sources

Debru, Armelle, ed. *Galen on Pharmacology. Philosophy, History and Medicine.* Leiden: E.J. Brill, 1997.

Durling, Richard. *A Dictionary of Medical Terms in Galen.* Leiden: E.J. Brill, 1993.

García Ballester, Luis. Galen and Galenism. *Theory and Medical Practice from Antiquity to the European Renaissance.* Aldershot: Ashgate/Variorum, 2002.

Levey, Martin. *Early Arabic Pharmacology.* Leiden: E.J. Brill, 1973.

Schmitz, Rudolf. *Geschichte der Pharmazie I. Von den Anfänge bis zum Ausgang des Mittelalters.* Eschborn: Govi-Verlag, 1998.

Stannard, Jerry. *Herbs and Herbalism in the Middle Ages and the Renaissance.* Aldershot: Ashgate, 1999.

———. *Pristina medicamenta. Ancient and Medieval Botany.* Aldershot: Ashgate, 1999.

Touwaide A. "Strategie terapeutiche: i farmaci." In *Storia del pensiero medico occidentale. I: Antichità e medioevo.* Edited by M.D. Grmek. Rome and Bari: Laterza, 1993: 349–369 (English translation: "Therapeutic strategies: drugs." In *Western Medical Thought from Antiquity to the Middle Ages.* Edited by M.D. Grmek. Cambridge: Harvard University Press, 1998, pp. 259–272 and 390–394).

———. "The Aristotelian School and the Birth of Theoretical Pharmacology in Ancient Greece." In *The Pharmacy. Windows on History.* Basel: Editiones Roche, 1996, pp. 11–22.

Vallance, John T. *The Lost Theory of Asclepias of Bithynia.* Oxford: Clarendon Press, 1990.

Watson, Gilbert. *Theriac and Mithridatum. A Study in Therapeutics.* London: The Wellcome Historical Medical Library, 1966.

ALAIN TOUWAIDE

PHARMACY AND *MATERIA MEDICA*

Pharmacy was defined until recent times as the branch of medical sciences devoted to the preparation, conservation, and administration of medicines (*pharmaka*). *Materia medica*, which was often confused with medical botany, defined (whether distinguished from pharmacy or not) the gathering of natural substances from the three realms (plant, animal, and mineral) to be used as the primary ingredients (drugs) for the preparation of medicines. From the nineteenth century onward, *materia medica* also included the chemical analysis of the active principles contained in the plants and other products (whether natural or not) provided to pharmacists by wholesalers. While the above definition of pharmacy can be used without anachronism to describe ancient and medieval activity, that of *materia medica* has to be taken in the limited sense of gathering natural substances, selecting their parts to be used (that is, the drugs), and trading such materials.

The Classical Heritage

The spectrum of operations contributing to medieval pharmaceutical activity was rooted in the classical tradition gradually shaped from *Hippocrates and the Hippocratic corpus to the end of antiquity and the dawn of the Middle Ages.

In an early epoch, the Hippocratic itinerant physician relied mainly on local natural resources to get ingredients for medicines. He was also responsible (perhaps with the help of a disciple) for the transformation of such substances into drugs, the preparation of medicines, and also their administration to the patients. Medicines were administered in different ways, with a limited number of forms, however: ingestion, particularly in the form of soups; inhalation, by burning the therapeutic substances; fumigation and injection, especially in gynecology; external applications, for post-surgery medication, and the treatment of wounds and skin diseases.

The military expedition of Alexander the Great (356–323 B.C.E.) to the Near East and India expanded the range of materia medica, all the more because scientists (among others, botanists) accompanied the troops to observe and describe the regions they crossed, their physical geography, and their fauna and flora, as well as their inhabitants and their habits. In so doing, scientists also collected plant specimens and drugs that they brought back to Greece. They acclimated non-native living plants, introduced new or not well-known therapeutic products into Greek drug lore, and either opened the way to or strongly reactivated the trade of Oriental drugs. Such trade gradually expanded and even reached Italy after the Eastern Mediterranean was absorbed into the Roman sphere, mainly by Pompey (106–48 B.C.E.). Oriental drugs became fashionable and were actively traded in the early Roman empire.

The development of science fostered by Alexander, possibly on the basis of his education by Aristotle, the creation of the Library and the Museum in Alexandria, the rivalry between the libraries of Alexandria and Pergamon, and the scientific emulation among the kingdoms that arose in Asia Minor after Alexander's death and the division of his empire, are all factors that contributed to create a scientific analysis of *materia medica* and pharmacy. Such analysis dealt with the inventory and systematic description of materia medica and drugs, their therapeutic properties and applications, and the techniques to prepare and administer medicines. Study was not necessarily conducted in a particular place at a particular time, but rather resulted from the gradual accumulation of data obtained in different places and by means of different methods.

A program of systematic description of *materia medica* and drug description, though not attested by any explicit information, can be inferred by comparing Hippocratic pharmacy and Theophrastean botany, on the one hand, with, on the other, their first-century equivalents, particularly *De materia medica* by the Greek *Dioscorides (first century C.E.). While Hippocrates' practice relied on circumstantial resources, and Theophrastean botany described plants in an often inconsistent way, the work of Dioscorides inventoried all substances used for therapeutic purposes known to him, described plants according to a regular pattern partially inspired by Theophrastus' method, and classified drugs in an organized, viz., hierarchical, way. Such a procedure is characteristic of the Alexandrian scientific program. If so, scientific study of pharmacy could have originated in the milieu of Herophilos (330/320–260/250 B.C.E.) and his later followers. The Aristotelian school in Athens could also have contributed to such a new development, particularly with Diocles of Carystus (fourth/third century C.E.), credited in modern scholarship with the redaction of the first herbal.

The therapeutic properties and applications of drugs seem to have been analyzed in different contexts characterized by specific methods. Speculating on the pathological processes of diseases, Aristotelian physicians hypothesized that medicines should antagonize them according to the general principle of *contraria contrariis* used in ancient therapy. This way of reasoning, already present in the *Problemata* of the Aristotelian school, was qualified as dogmatic by its opponents, the empiricists. The empiricists proceeded by experiments guided by the principle of transfer: medicines efficaciously used in the treatment of one disease could be transferred to the treatment of another, similar disease. Although empiricists refused to speculate on unknown entities, they implicitly assumed that externally similar symptoms resulted from identical internal causes and could thus be treated by the same agents. An apparently more empirical approach was taken by the sovereigns of the Hellenistic kingdoms of Asia Minor. They had a strong interest in *pharmacology and pharmacy, particularly the Attalids of Pergamon (from 269 to 133 B.C.E.) and Mithridates king of Pontos (130–64 B.C.E.), best attested by the poems *On venoms* and *On poisons* by Nicander of Colophon (second century B.C.E. [?]). These sovereigns tried drugs, poisons, and venoms on themselves or on guinea pigs, observed their actions, and created new pharmaceutical techniques and forms, including such new principles as the gradual buildup of tolerance to poisons in order to create a reaction of immunity, and compound medicines associating a high number of components so as to offer a wide spectrum of action, including protection against venoms and poisons.

Finally, the techniques to prepare and administer medicines were probably investigated in the different contexts above, and also in such other minor centers as the school of pharmacology supposedly active at Tarsus (Asia Minor) at the beginning of the Common Era. One of its disciples and heirs could be Dioscorides, author of the most comprehensive manual of *materia medica* of antiquity where all the results of the different streams above were associated, contributing to its deep influence on the pharmaceutical practice of all subsequent periods, Byzantium, the Syriac and Arabic worlds, and the Middle Ages.

Professionalism, Techniques, and Instruments

The expansion and specialization of drug trade in the Roman empire contributed to a certain independence of pharmaceutical activities from the medical profession. Providers were distinguished according to the nature of the products that they marketed, from raw drugs (be they Oriental or local) to final products (themselves differentiated according to their forms and uses). Drug trade fluctuated according to seasons (including annual variations) and places. To compensate for possibly insufficient availability, it included the technique of substitution: a drug with a determined property could be replaced by another with the same or an equivalent property. Raw drugs and those medicines that could be conserved required different types of recipients according to their nature: Leaves and perfumed substances had to be conserved in wooden boxes; seeds in sheets of papyrus or plant leaves; liquid drugs (plant juices) in receptacles made of silver, glass, horn, ceramics or box-wood; liquid ophthalmic medicines, and preparations containing vinegar, pitch and resin in bronze vases; medicines including animal fat in tin containers. Some drugs (particularly the mineral ones) were traded in the form of dry tablets marked with a seal that indicated their origin (for example, Lemnos ocher). Drug and medicine prices were fixed by such imperial price edicts such that of Diocletian in 301.

The expansion and diversification of medicine use required a wide range of administration techniques, differentiated for simple and compound medicines. Simple medicines aimed at internal use were of two main types: a liquid produced by decoction in a hot medium (principally water) or by dilution in a cold liquid (often wine); a solid or half-solid product made by amalgamating the therapeutic substance to a more or less therapeutically inactive binder such as bread. Simple medicines for external use were creams of different kinds associating the active matter to others, fat, mucilaginous plants, liquids (such as vinegar) or mineral products. Compound medicines contained a high number of components (sometimes more than eighty) and were tablets made of such substances amalgamated by means of one or more binding products, theoretically inactive from a therapeutic point of view. Such medicines were often named according to their supposed creator, their main property or use, or a reference to the nature and number of their ingredients. Dry medicines were often inscribed with seals mentioning the name of the pharmacist, of the preparation or some other.

The preparation of medicines required a vast set of instruments including knives with different sizes and kinds of blade, scrapers, filters, sieves, vases of all kinds in ceramic (often new ones, not to be impregnated with other substances, with their internal side made impermeable with pitch) or other matters (above), ladles and spoons of several shapes and dimensions, mortars in different matters and pestle, as well as balances of precision or for higher quantities, and containers of all sizes and matters. The local for drug and medicine preparation needed to be well ventilated and equipped with water, one or more sink(s), and a source of heat. A shady, dry, ventilated and large place was required for the dessication of fresh plants, which hung on a thread. A shelf in a similar place (the *apotheke*) was necessary to store drugs and prepared medicines. Their period of validity was known.

This body of elements was transmitted to the subsequent periods, be they Byzantine, the Syriac, and the Arabic worlds, or the West, where they underwent three major modifications:

(a) In the early Middle Ages, the preparation of drugs and medicines, and the administration of the latter shifted from individual providers (specialized or not, and dealing with drugs or medicines) or a secondary activity of physicians in the Roman empire to the monastic institution. An important step in this transformation was the creation of monastic gardens of medicinal plants attested as early as the end of the eighth century (the book of remedies of the Lorsch Abbey, in Germany). They resulted from the Christianization of therapeutic and transformed the pharmaceutical profession, which became institutional and sedentary.

(b) In the Arabic world, new pharmaceutical forms were created thanks to the production of two new substances: sugar and alcohol. The former made it possible to better amalgamate active substances and to produce medicines not easily exposed to moisture and degradation, and the latter to extract the active principles of drugs by the process of distillation. Pharmaceutical apparatus was modified and included alembics. Furthermore, the creation and development of the technique of glazed ceramic led to the production of drug containers of a new kind: the vase called albarello in Italian Renaissance. Due to its glazed cover, its wall did not interact with the drugs in the vase and thus ensured a better conservation of drugs and medicines, without any alterations.

(c) In the post-Salernitan Middle Ages, the exercise of pharmaceutical activity was regulated and officially separated from the practice of medicine. Such legislation is traditionally attributed to *Frederick II of Hohenstaufen (1212–1250), emperor and king of Sicily, in the so-called Constitution of Melfi (Italy), dated 1231/1241. They prohibited to physicians to exercise an activity of pharmacist, and even to have a pharmaceutical activity in common with pharmacists, so as to avoid monopolistic practices. On the other hand, pharmacists were submitted to inspections by state officers, particularly to verify the authenticity and quality of the drugs they were using for the preparation of medicines, and pharmacists had to prepare medicines under the supervision of physicians to avoid not only possible fatal mistakes, but also falsifications in the preparation of medicines. Such a control over pharmacists was repeated at the eve of the Renaissance, with the so-called *Ricettario Fiorentino* of 1498, which is traditionally considered as the first pharmacopoeia, that is, a collection of remedies whose composition was determined by a college of physicians commissioned by the civil authority, which thus guaranteed the efficacy of such remedies if they were properly prepared.

See also **Medicine, practical; Medicine, theoretical**

Bibliography

Aliotta, Gianni, Antonino Pollio, Daniele Piomelli and Alain Touwaide. *Le piante medicinali del "Corpus Hippocraticum."* Milan: Guerini e Associati, 2003.

Debru, Armelle, ed. *Galen on Pharmacology, Philosophy, History and Medicine.* Leiden: E.J. Brill, 1997.

Durling, Richard. *A Dictionary of Medical Terms in Galen.* Leiden: E.J. Brill, 1993.

Kartunnen, Klaus. *India and the Hellenistic World.* Helsinki: Finnish Oriental Society, 1997.

Korpela, Jukka. "Aromatarii, pharmacopolae, thurarii et ceteri. Zur Sozialgeschichte Roms." In *Ancient Medicine in its Socio-Cultural Context.* Edited by Ph. J. van der Eijk, H.F.J. Horstmanshoff and P.H. Schrijvers. Amsterdam: Rodopi, 1995, pp. 101–118.

Levey, Martin. *Early Arabic Pharmacology. An Introduction based on Ancient and Medieval Sources.* Leiden: E.J. Brill, 1973.

Opsomer, Carmelia. *Index de la pharmacopée antique du Ier au Xe siècle.* 2 vols. Hildesheim: Olms-Weidmann, 1989.

Riddle, John M. *Dioscorides on Pharmacy and Medicine.* Austin: University of Texas Press, 1985.

———. *Quid pro quo: Studies in the History of Drugs.* Hampshire: Variorum, 1992.

Sadek, Mahmoud M. *The Arabic materia medica of Dioscorides.* St-Jean-Chrysostome: Les Editions du Sphinx, 1983.

Schmitz, Rudolf. *Geschichte der Pharmazie I. Von den Anfänge bis zum Ausgang des Mittelalters.* Eschborn: Govi-Verlag, 1998.

Schulze, Christian. *Die pharmazeutisch Fachliteratur in der Antike. Eine Einführung.* Göttingen: Duehrkop & Radicke, 2002.

Stannard, Jerry. *Herbs and Herbalism in the Middle Ages and the Renaissance.* Aldershot: Ashgate, 1999.

———. *Pristina medicamenta. Ancient and Medieval Botany.* Aldershot: Ashgate, 1999.

Touwaide, Alain. "Strategie terapeutiche: i farmaci." In *Storia del pensiero medico occidentale. I: Antichità e medioevo.* Edited by M.D. Grmek. Rome and Bari: Laterza, 1993, pp. 349–369 (English translation: "Therapeutic strategies: drugs." In *Western Medical Thought from Antiquity to the Middle Ages.* Edited by M.D. Grmek. Cambridge: Harvard University Press, 1998, pp. 259–272 and 390–394).

———. "The Aristotelian School and the Birth of Theoretical Pharmacology in Ancient Greece." In *The Pharmacy. Windows on History.* Basel: Editiones Roche, 1996, pp. 11–22.

Watson, Gilbert. *Theriac and Mithridatum. A Study in Therapeutics.* London: The Wellcome Historical Medical Library, 1966.

ALAIN TOUWAIDE

PHYSIOGNOMY

The English word physiognomy is derived from the Greek *phusis* (nature) and *gnomon* (interpreter) or gnome (indicator). Late medieval physiognomic texts linked the word to *onoma* (name) or *nomos* (law). It is the art of judging a person's character and potential behavior by the external appearance of his or her bodily organs on the basis of an analysis of their size, proportion, shape, color, and texture. In classical Greece it also involved the study of motion, gestures, and the voice. The origins of Latin physiognomy were partly in the Hippocratic corpus and in the works of the doctor-physiognomist Loxus. Hippocrates was credited with founding the discipline;

the first appearance of the verb "physiognomize" is in the Hippocratic *Epidemics*. It was *Galen who, in *De complexionibus* II 6 (*On Temperaments*) and *Quod animi mores* 7–8 (*That the Faculties of the Soul Follow the Mixtures of the Body*), building on Aristotle and Hippocrates, was to provide for physiognomy the causal footing of humoral theory. He tied together the threads in Aristotle and the Hippocratic corpus in order to provide a medical framework for physiognomy, and he appears to have endorsed its basic principles. However, he criticized the "physiognomists" for failing to address the issue of causation.

The ancient texts of learned physiognomy, which were unknown throughout the earlier part of the Middle Ages, started to be available again for Latin readership in the twelfth and particularly in the thirteenth century, and then stimulated original medieval contributions to that science. These contributions included scholastic debates, commentaries (on the physiognomy attributed to Aristotle or on other medieval physiognomic texts), and new compilations of physiognomic knowledge systematically ordered and accompanied by detailed causal explanations. Some of the knowledge was drawn directly from the Greek texts, but part of it was introduced to the Latin West through Arabic sources, which transmitted the Greek knowledge or occasionally produced original contributions.

The following are the main scientific sources (Greek and Arabic) for the rise of medieval physiognomic thought which gradually became available to Latin readership in the twelfth and thirteenth centuries.

1. Polemon's *De physiognomonia liber*, possibly written in Greek around 133–136 C.E., preserved in a ninth-century Arabic translation, and available today in a modern Latin translation based on a 1356 Arabic manuscript made in Damascus, in a Greek paraphrastic epitome by Adamantius the Sophist, and in an anonymous fourth-century Latin treatise known as *Anonymus latinus*.

2. The fourth-century physiognomic compilation known as *Anonymus latinus*, which uses Pseudo-Aristotle's *Physiognomonics*, but in particular Polemon's physiognomy and the now-lost text of a certain Loxus, who appears also to have been a Hellenistic physician. The earliest manuscript of *Anonymus latinus* is from the early twelfth century.

3. *Al-Razi's *Liber almansoris* (or *regalis*, or *ad regem almansorem*), Book II (from the early tenth century; available in Latin in the translation of *Gerard of Cremona, from the 1180s), which of all early physiognomic texts was responsible for the medicinalization of physiognomy.

4. *Secretum secretorum*, Book 8 (or Book 10 in the Arabic tradition), an eighth-century Arabic translation of pseudo-Aristotelian epistles from the Hellenistic or Roman era, a school epitome of Aristotle's *Nichomachean Ethics* and a gnomological collection combined with Arabic sources. In c. 850–900 the base text was taken up by an unknown compiler who turned it into a Mirror for Princes; by 1100 it reached its full development and became available in partial Latin translations from c. 1125 by *John of Seville, and in a complete Latin

translation from c. 1230 by Philip of Tripoli on the basis of an Arabic manuscript he found in Antioch.

5. *Physiognomonics*, a treatise believed throughout the Middle Ages to be Aristotelian but consigned by modern research to the ranks of "Pseudo-Aristotle." Although Pliny clearly believed that Aristotle had written a physiognomical treatise, it has long been generally accepted that this is an epitome of the work of two Peripatetic authors of the third century B.C.E. following up Aristotle's interests. It became available in Latin in the 1260s in the translation from Greek by Bartolomeo da Messina who was active at Manfred's court in Palermo.

In both the rediscovery of Classical physiognomic texts and their assimilation, as well as in the original medieval contributions to that science, the Hohenstaufen courts played a significant role. It was at *Frederick II's court that the earliest versions of Philip of Tripoli's translations of the *Secretum secretorum* started to circulate, as well as possibly early versions of Pseudo-Aristotle's *Physiognomonics*. And it was at Manfred's court in the 1260s that Bartolomeo da Messina produced his translation of Pseudo-Aristotle's *Physiognomonics*, which quickly became the starting-point for scholastic debate. The first original medieval contribution to physiognomy was made by Michael Scotus (*Michael Scot) during his stay at the court of Frederick II between 1228 and c. 1235.

In addition to the rediscovery and propagation of the classical texts in numerous manuscripts, medieval natural philosophers and physicians assembled various physiognomic compilations, which they normally dedicated to men of power. These included:

1. Michael Scotus, *Liber Physiognomiae* for Frederick II, c. 1230.

2. Aldobrandino da Siena, *Regimen sanitatis*, pt. 4, for Beatrice of Savoy, Duchess of Provence, c. 1257.

3. An anonymous author may have compiled a short treatise on physiognomy for King Vàclav (Wenceslas) II of Bohemia (ruled 1283–1305).

4. *Pietro d'Abano, *Liber compilationis phisonomie* for Bardellone de Bonacossi the lord (*capitaneus generalis*) of Mantua (1292–1299); c. 1295.

5. Roland l'Ecrivain (Rolandus Scriptoris) *Reductorium phisonomie* for John, Duke of Bedford, the regent of England during the infancy of Henry VI; c. 1430.

6. Michele Savonarola, *Speculum phisonomie* for Leonello d'Este, Marquis of Ferrara (1441–1450); c. 1445.

7. Bartolomeo della Rocca Cocles, *Chiromantie ac physionomie anastasis* for Alessandro Bentivoglio, son of Giovanni Bentivoglio, dictator of Bologna; 1504.

Furthermore, natural philosophers composed a corpus of commentaries on Pseudo-Aristotle's *Physiognomonics*. William of Aragon (before 1310), *John Buridan, and Guilelmus de Mirica—whose work was dedicated to Pope Clement VI (1342–1352)—were all arts masters who were active both as students and as teachers at the faculty of philosophy in Paris. Commentaries on Aristotle's *Books of Animals* also included extensive physiognomic data such as those by *Albertus Magnus (1250s) and *Petrus Hispanus (1260s?). In the same way the genre of natural philosophical questions and problems is an important source of material for those interested in medieval physiognomic thought.

Not surprisingly many of the contributors to what became recognized in the second third of the thirteenth century as the science of physiognomy had some medical background. Medical practice and physiognomy have been linked since the beginning of human history because both revolve around the semiotics of the body. The physiognomer has always used the same analytical categories (color, movement, shape, texture) as those that help physicians to decipher pathologic conditions and reach diagnostic determinations.

What was the unique medieval contribution to the ancient science of physiognomy in addition to the above-mentioned new physiognomic compilations? In short, the answer is medicinalization and causal explanation. Medicine and physiognomy came to share a common theoretical framework, which compelled learned theoreticians of physiognomy to present their science by quoting from medical books and using concepts taken directly from medical theory and anatomy. Michael Scot (who was heavily indebted to al-Razi's *Liber almansoris* book II) was the first to introduce to Western medieval physiognomic discourse the concept of complexion. He provided no explanation for the particular physiognomic signs, and continued in this respect the classical physiognomic tradition that had disappointed so many, including *Galen. However, by starting his *Liber Physiognomiae* with a detailed and systematic discussion of generation and complexion, Scot located the physiognomic discourse within the broader natural philosophical context. The novelty of this approach was that a physiognomic treatise included an explanation of how some external bodily signs emerge, and how one can, with the correct knowledge, regulate them, at least partially.

Almost two centuries would elapse before physiognomic theory (in the work of the academic physician Rolandus Scriptoris in the 1430s) fully embraced the concept of complexion to explain the physiognomic signs themselves and to tie physiognomy firmly to humoral theory and to medicine. Rolandus's singular contribution was his attempt to go beyond the usual lament that physiognomic discourse lacked causal explanations and actually to provide reasons for the physiognomic signs. In this respect he was the first to provide a comprehensive theoretical framework to physiognomic thought, an enterprise which was independently developed less than fifteen years later by another medical man, Michele Savonarola in his *Speculum phisonomie*. These fifteenth-century physicians were not satisfied with simple repetition of the traditional lists of signs and their meanings. They were after an ordered theory that would enable them to structure physiognomy on a firm basis of cause and effect. Temperamental humorology provided this theoretical basis, on which the traditional set of signs and their significance could peacefully rest and consequently safely and validly be employed by those who possessed the requisite knowledge.

In a world where every natural phenomenon was regarded as a sign of spiritual, transcendental reality, such an instrumental use of the body posed no problem. Materialistic though it was, it was clear to everyone that physiognomy deciphered inclinations and did not impose deterministic behavioral traits. A biologically determined inclination did not free the person from the moral responsibility to suppress, curb and control, when necessary, such an inclination.

A thorough inspection of the parts of the heavens together with a full understanding of the diversity of the body's particulars are the key for identifying the varieties of human character, habits and actions. Here the fundamental analytical term, which Rolandus attributes to Galen and to other "teachers of medicine," is an innate formative spirit mixed with frothy moisture that from its passive agent—blood—forms the heart and consequently the other organs and is responsible for their shape. The diversity of the spirit and blood involved in this primary activity at the stage of fetal formation affects character traits and not only the external shape of the body.

Another medieval innovation to the science of physiognomy is its treatment of the female body. In particular, physiognomy's role as the decoder of sexual behavior and tastes turned women into an object of physiognomic gaze in a way never envisaged in classical physiognomy. The classical physiognomer spoke to men and targeted the male body. He was interested in the female body only as a deviation from the male norm. Consequently, little attention was given in classical physiognomic texts to the female body. When Michael Scot surveys the body's organs and presents the catalog of physiognomic signs and their significance in the third part of his *Liber Physiognomiae* (and after having devoted much space in previous chapters to the woman's contribution to the shape and form of the embryo), he specifically says that this section contains specific items related to the body of both sexes. However his user-friendly and well ordered (from head to toe) catalog of physiognomic signs applies mostly to men, and only indirectly to women, the judgment of whom is more difficult and problematic since the female complexion is so distant from the male complexion which is the standard against which everything is measured. But in dedicating in the first part of the book such an important role to women's influence on the shape of the child and by suggesting that the physiognomic signs apply to both sexes, Scot opens the way to the inclusion of the female body (or at least the uniquely feminine organs) in the physiognomic scheme. By around 1300 learned physiognomy came to include chapters devoted to the physiognomy of the sexual organs, both male and female, and to the female breasts.

The Practice of Physiognomy

The physiognomic examination was performed on a naked subject and in many respects was similar to a medical checkup. If an examination in the nude was not possible, one could still perform a valid physiognomic analysis from the shoulders upwards, postponing examination of the other organs to a later opportunity. It was important to include an oral examination, namely to hear the examinee talking, since the way of talking and the enunciation of words were clearly indicative of a person's character (every physiognomic treatise included a chapter on the voice). An examination of the texture, color, quantity, and shape of the hair opened the physiognomic check-up. Then, stroking the head one should examine its composition, shape, and the proportions of the neck. Next the forehead was checked, followed by an examination of the quality, color, and position of the eyes. Both these organs are indicative of intellective power, which is represented in the frontal part. The movement of the eyes as well as the gait of the whole body is necessary for a proper physiognomic examination. Judgment on the basis of one sign is unreasonable. Comparison of a variety of signs, together with the ordering of signs according to their varied importance (the eyes, as "windows of the soul," are charged with many more physiognomic signs than any other bodily organ) are necessary for a valid determination of significance. This is to be followed by a check of signs related to the hands (the mother of all organs, *organum organorum*), chest, shoulders, legs and feet, belly and buttocks, bearing in mind that only a comparative approach which regards the quality and the context not the quantity of signs, can assure a proper judgment. In this process signs, which are the result of environmental conditions (climate, regional variations, and air quality), age, or habits have an inferior physiognomic meaning, if any at all.

Physiognomy's traditional role as a rhetorical tool, namely, that of defaming one's political opponents was maintained in the Middle Ages, but its main role was to enable people in positions of power (within the family, profession or ordinary social relationships, business, school, monastery, army, court or state) to make the right choice of associates, friends, councilors, and partners. Other uses of this knowledge included the detection of alcoholics, of inclination to domestic violence, of sexual behavior, appetite, and taste; the prediction of life expectancy, of professional, intellectual and academic inclinations and capacities; and the proneness to piety and religiosity, to virginity and chastity. The physiognomic gaze helped physicians to determine the complexion of individual organs or of the whole body, exposed pathological liars and played a role in selecting soldiers for combat and for detecting signs of madness.

For the Latin physiognomer of the Middle Ages the ideal physiognomic type (characterized by a perfectly balanced complexion as attested by a perfectly proportioned body, hence perfect character and behavior) was neither an individual belonging to a specific ethnic group, nor a model of perfect beauty. Beauty plays no role in learned physiognomic discourse. It was Jesus Christ—a super-national second Adam representative of mankind in general. Medieval physiognomy was thus generally non-ethnic. The basic unit of all analysis was man (*homo*); consequently the physiognomic texts of the Middle Ages are essentially humanistic and universalistic in their approach.

See also **Medicine, practical; Medicine, theoretical**

Bibliography

Primary Sources

Anonyme Latin. *Traité de physiognomonie*, edited by Jacques André. Paris: Les Belles Lettres, 1981.

Bartolomeo della Rocca Cocles. *Bartholomei Coclitis Chiromantie ac physionomie anastasis cum approbatione magistri Alexandri de Achillinis*. Bologna, 1504.

Förster, Richard, ed. *Scriptores physiognomonici graeci et latini*, 2 vols. Leipzig: Teubner, 1893.

Michael Scotus. *Liber physonomie*. Venice, 1477.

Pietro d'Abano. *Liber compilationis physonomie*. Padua, 1474.

Secondary Sources

Agrimi, Jole. *Ingeniosa scientia nature: Studi sulla fisiognomica medievale*. Firenze: Sismel, 2002.

Jacquart, Danielle. La physiognomonie à l'époque de Frédéric II: Le traité de Michel Scot. *Micrologus* 2 (1994), pp. 19–37.

Thomann, Johannes. *Studien zum "Speculum physiomomie" des Michele Savonarola*. Zurich: Copy Quick, 1997. (PhD thesis, Universität Zürich, 1992).

Williams, Steven J. *The Secret of Secrets: The Scholarly Career of a Pseudo-Aristotelian Text in the Latin Middle Ages*. Ann Arbor: University of Michigan Press, 2003.

Ziegler, Joseph. "Text and Context: On the Rise of Physiognomic Thought in the Later Middle Ages." In *De Sion Exibit Lex et Verbum Domini de Hierusalem. Essays on Medieval Law, Liturgy and Literature in honour of Amnon Linder*, edited by Y. Hen. Turnhout: Brepols, 2001, pp. 159–182.

——. Médecine et physiognomie du XIVe au début du XVIe siècle. *Médiévales* (2004) 46: 87–105.

——. The Physiognomist's Kidney in the Fifteenth Century. *Journal of Nephrology* (2004) 17.4, 1–5.

——. "The Beginning of Medieval Physiognomy: The Case of Michael Scotus." In *Wissen an Höfen und Universitäten: Rezeption, Transformation, Innovation*, edited by Johannes Fried, (=Wissenskultur und gesellschaftlicher Wandel Bd. X). Berlin: Akademie Verlag, 2005.

JOSEPH ZIEGLER

PIERRE D'AILLY

Pierre d'Ailly was born in Compiègne in 1350, the child of prosperous bourgeois parents. He was sent to Paris in 1364 to study at the University as *socius* of the College of Navarre. Master of arts in 1368, he became doctor of theology in 1381, grand maître of the College of Navarre in 1384, chaplain to French king Charles VI, and chancellor of the University of Paris in 1389, bishop of Le Puy in 1395, bishop of Cambrai in 1397, and cardinal in 1411. He died in Avignon in 1420.

During his brilliant ecclesiastical and political career, Pierre wrote some one hundred seventy-four treatises and opuscules on theology, philosophy, devotion, politics, poetry, and science. But he seems to have been very much helped by a small research team, composed notably by his nephew Raoul Le Prestre and by an anonymous colleague, more competent than he in scientific fields.

It was with this help that Pierre compiled more than twenty scientific texts. The most important and famous is the *Imago mundi*, completed in 1410. Inspired mainly by *John of Sacrobosco's *De sphaera*, *Roger Bacon's *Opus maius*, and the *Traité de l'espere* (*Treatise on the Sphere*) (c. 1356–1365) by *Nicole Oresme, d'Ailly's predecessor as the head of the College of Navarre, the *Imago mundi* is a clear and didactic cosmographical compilation. But there is almost nothing new in this work, which may even be regarded in some ways as a regression in comparison with Oresme, and which was superseded by Jacopo d'Angelo's Greco-Latin translation (1406–1409) of *Ptolemy's *Cosmographia*, a version used only later (c. 1415–1416) by d'Ailly in his *Compendium cosmographie*.

Pierre d'Ailly's *Imago mundi*, however, was influential for two reasons: first, it was copied with most of his other scientific treatises in his personal *scriptorium* and widely diffused after his death by Raoul Le Prestre, his executor; second, it was printed by John of Westphalie in Louvain, c. 1480–1483, with fifteen other treatises by d'Ailly and five by Gerson, and the most famous owner of this edition was *Christopher Colombus, who annotated the whole volume, c. 1490. It was in the eighth chapter of the *Imago mundi* that Colombus found a confirmation of his geographic intuition: "Aristotle says that a small sea lies between the end of the western side of Spain and the beginning of the eastern part of India." Colombus interpreted this sentence thus: "Aristotle. Between the end of Spain and the beginning of India there is a small sea navigable in a few days." One knows how it turned out, but this does not imply that Pierre d'Ailly was "the spiritual father of America," as stated by Edmond Buron in 1930. Columbus chose in fact the data that best suited him, and we could say paradoxically that a great step in the history of humanity may have been partly the result of a scientific regression.

John of Westphalie's edition of Pierre d'Ailly's scientific works contained two other cosmographical treatises: the *Epilogus mappe mundi* (1410) and the *Compendium cosmographie* (c. 1415–1416), five texts and tables related to a program of calendar reform presented in 1411 to John XXIII, the pope recently elected in Pisa, and seven treatises about historical astrology. In the first of these treatises, the *Tractatus de legibus et sectis contra superstitiosos astronomos* (*On the laws and the sects, against the superstitious astrologers*), finished in 1410, d'Ailly followed Roger Bacon in associating each of six principal religions with the conjunction of Jupiter and another planet, but he found Bacon guilty of superstitious error when he tried to show that astrology had foretold the rise of Christianity: for d'Ailly, the sects of the Chaldeans, the Egyptians, the Muslims, and the sect of the Antichrist were subject to celestial causality, but the Mosaic law and the Christian religion were supernatural and exempt from astrological causation. He developed this in greater detail in a trilogy of texts composed in 1414, the *Vigintiloquium de concordia astronomice veritatis cum theologia*, the *De concordia astronomice veritatis et narrationis historice*, and the *Elucidarium astronomice concordie cum theologia et historica veritate*, of which the best edition is Erhard Ratdolt's (Augsburg, 1490). In these three treatises, founded more directly on *Abu Ma'shar's *On Great Conjunctions*, d'Ailly tried to write an astrological history, showing the concordance of astrology (as a "natural theology"), Christian theology, and history. This trilogy showed an evolution in his conception, in comparison with his youth, when he believed that the end of the world was imminent: as Laura Ackerman Smoller has shown, his better knowledge of conjunctionism and the historical evolution of the period, dominated by the Great Schism, led him to "the postponement of the end." With the help of his anonymous colleague, he calculated the dates of past and future conjunctions of Saturn and Jupiter, drew up the horoscope of Christ (hesitating to put His ascendant in Virgo or in Libra), and observed, among many other computations, that a cycle of ten revolutions of Saturn will be closed in 1789, and that the Antichrist might appear around this year. It is for that reason that Pierre d'Ailly has sometimes been considered a prophet of the French Revolution.

See also **Astrology; Calendar**

Pierre d'Ailly. From *Les vrais portraits et vies des hommes illustres* (1584) by French engraver André Thevet. (Mary Evans Picture Library)

Bibliography

Boudet, Jean-Patrice. "Un prélat et son équipe de travail à la fin du Moyen Âge: remarques sur l'œuvre scientifique de Pierre d'Ailly." In Marcotte, Didier ed., *Humanisme et culture géographique à l'époque du Concile de Constance. Autour de Guillaume Fillastre* (Actes du colloque de l'Université de Reims, 18–19 novembre 1999). Turnhout: Brepols, 2002, pp. 127–150.

Buron, Edmond. *Ymago mundi de Pierre d'Ailly. Texte latin et traduction française des quatres traités cosmographiques de d'Ailly et des notes marginales de Christophe Colomb. Étude sur les sources de l'auteur*, 3 vol. Paris: Maisonneuve, 1930.

Guenée, Bernard. *Between Church and State: The Lives of Four French Prelates in the Late Middle Ages*, translated by Arthur Goldhammer. Chicago: University of Chicago Press, 1987. Chapter 3: "Pierre d'Ailly (1351–1420)."

Smoller, Laura Ackerman. *History, Prophecy and the Stars. The Christian Astrology of Pierre d'Ailly, 1350–1420*. Princeton: Princeton University Press, 1994.

JEAN-PATRICE BOUDET

PIETRO D'ABANO

Pietro d'Abano (Petrus de Abano, Petrus Aponensis, Petrus Paduanus) was a physician and philosopher born in Abano, Italy (near Padua), c. 1250. He was in Paris for most of the last decade of the thirteenth century, where he almost certainly taught at the university. He then returned to his native Padua by at least 1307 where he taught medicine and philosophy until his death in 1315 or 1316. At some point he traveled to Constantinople in order to learn Greek. His scholarly output is unusual, including no commentaries on the standard scholastic texts in medicine or philosophy, which adds difficulty to assessing the stages of his career. Pietro's work was nevertheless influential in establishing the framework for future inquiry in *natural philosophy, and continued to arouse interest for centuries after his death, as evidenced by frequent citations and multiple printings of his books. However his career was not without controversy. He tells us that while in Paris he was accused by an inquisition led by the Dominicans of Saint Jacques of promulgating fifty-five errors, including the doctrine that the human soul derives from the potency of matter, but was rescued by the intervention of the Pope. He was brought to trial twice more after his return to Padua. Due in part to his trials for heresy, he acquired a posthumous reputation as a magus, with several works on *magic and the occult being falsely attributed to him and (probably) apocryphal details added to his biography, including the claim that his bones were disinterred and burned. His alleged role in the transferral of Latin Averroism from Paris to Padua continues to be a topic of discussion.

Works and Doctrine

Pietro's works include original treatises in medicine and *astrology, commentaries and additions, and translations. His diverse interests in natural philosophy are best shown in his *Conciliator litium medicine* (1303, revised 1310), an encyclopedic medical work of two hundred ten *differentiae* (differences) which deliberates about the conflicting opinions of medical and philosophical authorities. Like most of his contemporaries, Pietro divided medicine into theory and practice. Medical theory is most like *scientia*: certain knowledge of the principles of nature and the effects derived from these principles; practice includes the guidance of the patient's regimen, ideally in view of medical theory. Pietro's explanations rely most on the theory of complexion, which posits that four qualitative forces of hot, cold, wet, and dry are the principles of change in every material being, including the human body. This system of *elements and qualities was a hybrid of the thought of Aristotle and *Galen, much elaborated on by Arabic philosophers. Beyond the elemental qualities, nature is imbued at every level with "virtues" or forces, most notably astrological influences, to which he devoted considerable attention. These forces both predispose all matter to certain activities and are a continual source of alteration and instability. The role of the physician is to be the "minister of nature," understanding nature's workings, so that everything does not appear to happen by fortune or divine impulse, as the ignorant and superstitious believe. There is a moral current throughout Pietro's thought as well: because of the close connection between body and soul, he argues that as psychological as well as physical wellbeing are achieved in correspondence with the multifarious natural virtues.

Pietro's synthesis of medicine and philosophy extended to the methodologies of these disciplines, for which he has been credited for his contribution to the development of scientific method. In the *Conciliator*, he combines Galen's methods of medical doctrine with Aristotle's modes of scientific knowledge. His goal was to ensure both the validity of the creation of universal scientific knowledge and the application of this knowledge in particular situations, the latter a problem of special concern to medicine. Although the scientific character of his medicine has been most emphasized in modern scholarship, Pietro nevertheless acknowledges that medicine must often be satisfied with probable solutions.

Pietro's inclination toward solving controversial problems is also evident in his extensive *Commentary on the [pseudo]-Aristotelian Problems* (1310), a collection of questions on various topics in natural philosophy. Again, he relies heavily on qualitative physiology to interpret these problems. This commentary was the first of its kind in Latin, and soon became the standard commentary on the text in the West, used and adapted by other authors, and translated in part into French by Evrart de Conty (c. 1380).

Pietro's estimation of the importance of astrology (or *astronomy—he used the terms interchangeably) is seen in several independent treatises on the subject. His *Lucidator* (1310, but probably unfinished) consists of six *differentiae* on the nature of astrology, the movement of the universe, the spheres, eccentrics and epicycles, the movement of planets, and the position of the Sun. His *On the Motion of the Eighth Sphere* (*De motu octavae* *spherae*) (1310) and *Imagines* (a.k.a. *Astrolabium Planum*), focus on more specific issues.

Pietro wrote a few other practical works in addition to the practical portion of the *Conciliator*. His *Compilatio Physionomiae* (1295) catalogues predispositions of the body and soul, as signified by variations in the parts of the body. It differs from other contemporary physiognomies in its emphasis on astrology. *On Poisons* (*De venenis*) (c. 1316) classifies poisons and cures along with their effects on the body. His *Addition to Mesue* (*Additio ad Mesue*) adds information about diseases of the heart to the *Universal Canons* of Johannes Mesue the younger. Pietro also wrote a gloss on *Dioscorides' *De materia medica*.

In his writing, Pietro refers to several of his own translations, yet it has been suggested that he did not publish them, but rather made them for his personal use. It is generally accepted that Pietro completed *Burgundio of Pisa's translations of Galen's *De sectis* and *Therapeutica* (or *De methodi medendi*), and manuscripts also state his authorship of several others translations of Galen. A translation of the *Problems* of pseudo-Alexander of Aphrodisias is also attributed to Pietro. There seems, however, little ground for the widely held opinion that he made an integral translation of the [pseudo]-Aristotelian *Problems*. Finally, Pietro is said to have translated pseudo-Hippocrates' *De medicorum astrologia*, and translated French versions of astrological treatises by *Abraham ibn Ezra into Latin.

See also **Alderotti, Taddeo; Aristotelianism; "Latin Averroists"; Medicine, practical; Medicine, theoretical; Translation movements**

Bibliography

Primary Sources
Federici Vescovini, Graziela, ed. Pietro d'Abano. *Trattati di Astronomia. Lucidator dubitabilium astronomiae, De motu octavae sphaerae e altre opere* (Il mito e la storia). Padova: Editoriale Programma, 1992.
Riondato, Ezio and Luigi Olivieri, ed. *Pietro d'Abano, Conciliator. Ristampa fotomeccanica dell'edizione Venetiis apud Iuntas 1565* (I Filosofi Veneti. Sezione II–Ristampe 1). Padova: Editrice Antenore, 1985.

Secondary Sources
Alessio, Franco. "Filosofia e Scienza. Pietro da Abano." In *Storia della cultura veneta, II: Il trecento*. Dir. da G. Arnaldi e M. Pastore Stocchi. Vicenza: Pozza, 1976, pp. 171–206.
Cadden, Joan. "Nothing Natural is Shameful": Vestiges of a Debate about Sex and Science in a Group of Late-medieval MSS. *Speculum* (2001) 76: 66–89.
D'Alverny, Marie-Thérèse. "Pietro d'Abano et les 'naturalistes' à l'époque de Dante." In *Dante e la cultura veneta: atti del Convegno di studi organizzato dalle Fondazione "Giorgio Cini," Venezia, Padova, Verona, 30 marzo–5 aprile 1966*. Edited by V. Branca and G. Padoan. Florence: Olschki, 1966, pp. 207–219.
De Leemans, Pieter and Michèle Goyens, ed. *Aristotle's Problemata in Different Times and Tongues* (Mediaevalia Lovaniensia). Leuven: Leuven University Press, 2005.
Federici Vescovini, Graziella. "La médicine synthèse d'art et de science selon Pierre d'Abano." *Les Doctrines de la science de l'antiquité à l'âge classique*. Edited by Roshdi Rashed and Joel Biard. Leuven: Peeters, 1999, pp. 238–255.
———. "Peter of Abano and Astrology." In *Astrology, Science and Society: Historical Essays*. Edited by P. Curry. Woodbridge: Boydell and Brewer, 1987, pp. 19–41.
Hasse, Dag Nikolaus. "Pietro d'Abano's 'Conciliator' and the Theory of the Soul in Paris." In *Nach der Verurteilung von 1277. Philosophie und Theologie an der Universität von Paris im letzten Viertel des 13. Jahrhunderts. Studien und Texte*. Edited by Jan A. Aertsen, Kent Emery, Jr., and Andreas Speer. New York: Walter de Gruyter, 2001, pp. 635–653.
Jacquart, Danielle. "L'influence des astres sur le corps humain chez Pietro d'Abano." In *Le corps et ses énigmes au Moyen âge: Actes du colloque, Orléans, 15–16 mai 1992*. Edited by B. Ribémont. Caen: Paradigme, 1993, pp. 73–86.
Medioevo: Rivista di storia della filosofía medievale (1985) 11 (= special issue entirely devoted to Pietro d'Abano), includes the English article by Nancy Siraisi, "Pietro d'Abano and Taddeo Alderotti: Two Models of Medical Culture," among others.
Nardi, Bruno. "Intorno alle dottrine filosofiche di Pietro d'Abano." In his *Saggi sull'aristotelismo padovano dal secolo xiv al xvi*. Firenze: Sansoni, 1958, pp. 19–74.
Olivieri, Luigi. *Pietro d'Abano e il pensiero neolatino: filosofia, scienza e ricerca dell'Aristotele Greco tra i secoli XIII e XIV* (Saggi e Testi 23). Padova: Antenore, 1988.
Paschetto, Eugenia. *Pietro d'Abano: medico e filosofo*. Firenze: Nuovedizioni Enrico Vallecchi, 1984.
Randall Jr., J.H. The Development of Scientific Method in the School of Padua. *Journal of the History of Ideas* (1940) 1: 177–206.
Siraisi, Nancy. *Arts and Sciences at Padua: The studium of Padua before 1350* (Pontifical Institute of Mediaeval Studies. Studies and texts 25). Toronto: Pontifical Institute of Mediaeval Studies, 1973.
———. The Expositio Problematum Aristotelis of Peter of Abano. *Isis* (1970) 61: 321–339.
Thorndike, Lynn. *A History of Magic and Experimental Science*. 8 Vols. New York: Macmillan (vols. 1–2) and Columbia University Press, 1923–1958, II, pp. 874–947.
Wallace, William. Circularity and the Paduan *Regressus*: From Pietro d'Abano to Galileo Galilei. *Vivarium* (1995) 33: 76–97.

MATTHEW KLEMM AND PIETER DE LEEMANS

PLAGUE TRACTATES

For the greater part of the twentieth century the history of plague was written according to the modern medical conceptualization of this condition. Yet from the 1980s onward a growing contest against this "official story" developed from at least two sides. On the one hand, some historians of epidemics have questioned in clinical and epidemiological terms the identification of the Black Death and the subsequent late medieval and early modern plagues with modern bubonic plague. On the other, the radical historicity of plague—as with any other disease label—as well as the incommensurability between modern and pre-modern plagues because of their corresponding to entirely disparate defining criteria have been emphasized in the "new cultural" history of disease. Thus the condition nowadays labeled as bubonic plague should be distinguished from the diseases known as "plague" and "pestilence" in the past. While the former is a nineteenth-century medical construction and, in particular, a product of the germ theory, the latter is to be applied to most high-mortality epidemics in the Middle Ages and, to a great extent, during all pre-bacteriological times.

Plague Tractates: A Medical Literary Genre?

Under the conventional name of "plague tractates" is grouped a large and rather heterogeneous set of medical works in which learned practitioners projected their perceptions of and reactions to catastrophic disease in the Middle Ages. Among the authors were practitioners belonging to Islam, Christianity, and Judaism, the three great monotheistic religions of Europe and the Middle East at that time.

Most plague tractates share a practical and temporary condition, although they were written in various languages and formats in accordance with their disparity of addressees and purposes. In Europe, the earliest tractates appeared on the occasion of the 1348 Black Death, but their number increased over the next hundred and fifty years and even later, while plague and pestilences were still an important health issue. The wastefulness of this literary genre in the Middle Ages is attested by the fact that nearly three hundred manuscript works in Latin and various vernacular languages from the period 1348–1500 were inventoried at different European libraries during the first quarter of the twentieth century, as well as no fewer than one hundred and thirty editions of plague tractates which had issued from the printing presses by 1500.

Plague tractates have been usually grouped within the larger genre of *regimina sanitatis*—the dominant expression of hygiene before the eighteenth century whose purpose was to maintain and/or improve individual health by means of conveniently regulating almost every aspect of daily life through the six non-naturals (*sex res non naturales*). Although most life regimes were addressed to privileged individuals (kings, popes, and civil and ecclesiastical noblemen), some of them were generically intended either for a general readership or for the specific needs of different occupations, activities, age groups, localities or diseases. Yet this grouping ignores the fact that a proportion of the plague tractates that appeared during the period also included a curative regime along with the traditional preventive one. Nevertheless, it would not be possible to ascribe them to any other more clinical and therapeutically orientated genre of medieval and early modern medical literature such as the *consilia or the tractatus because—again, due to the unlike condition of their potential addressees— some plague tractates were written in a very personal and specific way while others were more doctrinal and generical by focusing on describing the causes, the signs, and the preventive and curative treatment of this condition.

Most medieval plague tractates were primarily intended for other medical practitioners though they had additional readers among theologians, natural philosophers and other members of the cultivated elites. Yet, from the mid-fourteenth-century Black Death, some of them were mainly addressed to common people through different mediations, namely the municipal authorities—e.g., the *Regiment de preservació de pestilència* (1348) that Jacme d'Agramont, a medical lecturer at the university of Lleida (Crown of Aragon), wrote at request of the municipal authorities; the monarchy—e.g., the *Compendium de epidimia* (1348) written by the college of masters of the medical faculty of Paris at request of King Charles VI of France—or the medical corporations—e.g., the *Consilium contra pestilentiam* (1348) written by *Gentile da Foligno, a medical lecturer at the Italian university of Perugia, at request of the local college of physicians which, according to his recommendations, "should advise landlords to designate some good men to meet with physicians, and to follow their instructions in order to make the necessary arrangements for preserving the health of people in the city." Such a diversity of potential addressees for the medieval plague tractates makes evident the capacity of scholastic medicine to answer to the social and health challenge that catastrophic disease posed on disparate geographical areas.

Some plague tractates, like those of the Paris masters and Agramont, also allow us to estimate the degree of social acceptance and prestige that university medicine had attained in Latin Europe by mid fourteenth century. In their Compendium, the Paris masters responded as an expert collective to the French king's request of information about plague, its causes and its remedies. On the other hand, Agramont's report to Lleida's town councillors with a whole set of practical knowledge that could be implemented to keep its population free from the menacing epidemic, represented an outstanding effort to spread beyond the restricted limits of learned people, the new knowledge of scholastic medicine and *natural philosophy. This sort of popularizing work—quite unusual in 1348—implied not only translating that new knowledge from Latin into a vernacular language, but also decoding a conceptual and formally complex jargon of abstruse technical terms into the simple and direct language of common people.

Medicalizing A Social Calamity

The fact that Jacme d'Agramont, Gentile da Foligno, and so many other practitioners died in 1348, presumably as victims of plague, did not impede that the plague tractates underwent a great profusion as a response to the subsequent epidemic crises that ravaged Europe until well into the eighteenth century. Thus, it can be claimed that university medicine not only survived to the challenge posed by catastrophic disease, but it came out reinforced from that proof. Indeed, from the mid-fourteenth-century epidemic outbreak of Black Death onwards, this social calamity underwent a gradual "medicalization" in terms of the specific care university practitioners gave to its victims, as well as of their interpretations of its nature and causes. While the medical image of plague experienced noticeable changes during the subsequent four hundred years, mostly in accordance with whatever intellectual trends were dominating medicine in each place and at each moment, yet the theoretical model which guided university medical responses remained essentially constant during the whole period.

How did medical practitioners perceive plague in the Middle Ages? Generally speaking, they tackled it as a medical problem, and did so with the help of three intellectual and technical resources, namely their university training, which was based on the medical system of Latin Galenism; their previous medical experience, both their own and that of other practitioners, when confronted by deadly epidemic diseases; and the authoritative knowledge of the particular ancient and medieval physicians, particularly *Ibn Sina's peculiar interpretation of Galenic doctrine.

By "plague" or "pestilence" most physicians understood a universal condition of the air that was attributable to "celestial causes," although the emphasis on this kind of causes varied according to time and place. According to the Christian vision of the cosmos—a view which was unquestionable in Europe until well into the eighteenth century, and was also shared by the two other great monotheist religions in the Mediterranean—God's Will was the first cause of plague as well as of everything else in His Creation. However, after Christian scholastic natural philosophers had constructed idea of a natural world autonomously run by natural laws except for the unusual circumstances of miracles, Christian medical practitioners were assigned competence on secondary causes of human health and disease, while theologians kept their intellectual and professional monopoly on the *Primum Movens*. Apart from that, *Abu Ma'shar's constellation theory was their main point of reference to interpret the ways by which (allegedly) the macrocosm continuously influenced the microcosm; and Aristotle's concepts of generation and corruption—the two basic movements in the sublunar world—were the core of all their interpretations concerning the ways in which plague broke out and spread.

Sometimes, along with celestial causes (influences from the planets, zodiacal signs and comets, among others), university practitioners made "terrestrial causes" (exhalations from the earth and waters) play a role in the generation of plague. This resort was particularly handy when they needed to explain the appearance of a plague circumscribed to a more restricted area. Last but not least, the feasibility of causing plague by means of human artifice was also considered; and accusations against the Jewish minority were indeed circulating among Montpellier physicians as early as 1348. This idea, which allows a society to project the social anxiety caused by the presence of a deadly epidemic onto particular scapegoats, was then politically instrumental to foster the stigmatization of certain social groupings (religious minorities, prostitutes, lepers).

The universal condition of the air that was defined as plague or pestilence indicated a change "against nature" in the substance of this primary element, that is, its corruption. Given that air was considered as the most essential element, the effects of this alleged corruption should be almost infallibly massive; otherwise, it should not be considered as a "true plague." Thus, rather than a disease in itself, plague was the cause of numerous and diverse effects deriving from the massive corruption of living things in the sublunar world, among which there were many disease conditions. For instance, when faced with the mid-fourteenth-century Black Death, Jacme d'Agramont stated that plague (*pestilència*) successively involved all the beings of the "three degrees of life" (trees and plants, animals, and human beings) through the food chain. Among its effects he pointed out "corruptions, sudden deaths and various disease conditions."

From 1348 university medical practitioners were also concerned about establishing noticeable signs in the physical environment that would allow them either to forecast the outbreak of plague or to detect its actual presence at any place. Generally speaking, they used rare natural phenomena, referring to air and meteors, to plants and animals, and to the local pattern of diseases. Along with such signs, they constantly and unequivocally associated the bad smell of air with the presence of corruption in this element—which indeed warned them about the risk or actual presence of plague. As we will see later, this association would have a wide impact on the setting up of preventive measures, whose purpose was eliminating any stink and, even more so, perfuming the atmosphere on the assumption that this would reinforce its resistance to corruption.

Although the outbreak of plague was essentially unpredictable because it depended, in the last resort, upon macrocosmic and microcosmic powers out of human control, its potential of spreading was directly related to the amount of air involved in the corruption process. Thus, in these circumstances the accumulation of organic matter multiplied the chance of propagation of plague. Some natural meteors, like winds, could accelerate its diffusion. At the same time, most disease conditions which were held to be the effects or accidents of plague, were allegedly transmissible through interpersonal contagion by different ways—breath, skin exhalations, sight, personal objects, closeness—the nature of which was subject to medical debate.

We have seen that most university medical practitioners agreed that air was the vehicle of plague spreading. Yet, since 1348 some of them began to wonder why each plague had some specific signs and not others. To Gentile da Foligno, when the corrupted air of pestilence penetrated a body unable to resist corruption, then a "poisonous matter" was generated close to the lungs and heart. This matter did not act by means of the properties derived from its humoural mixture (*complexio*), but by means of its "poisonness," that is, as a result of its specific property of being poisonous. Gentile claimed that, because of its power of self-multiplication, even very small amounts of this poisonous matter could infect the whole body, corrupt all the bodily members (including the heart), and eventually cause the death of the person infected. In turn, "poisonous vapors" that were exhaled by the bodies of those infected enabled pestilence to be passed from one person to another, and from one place to another. Quite significantly, at this point Gentile da Foligno echoed a well-known paragraph from *De differentiis febrium* in which *Galen referred to "certain seeds of pestilence" that were thrown out by any pestilent body into the surrounding air.

At all events, Gentile's views implying a vague notion of causal specificity were barely accepted in 1348. However, over the course of the subsequent centuries they had an increasing impact on university practitioners' views on the causes of plague. If they had hitherto used to think that in the plague times individuals got sick because corrupted air fell on bodies whose complexion was unbalanced as a result of an unsuitable life regime, during the fifteenth and early sixteenth centuries they gradually accepted that people could also suffer from plague as a consequence of a direct action on their bodies by the poisonous matter of this condition.

The rapid and wide acceptance of Girolamo Fracastoro's systematic reformulation of Galen's views on contagion (1546) means that the notion that individuals only suffered from an infectious condition—either epidemic or not—when they came into contact with its peculiar morbid matter, had gained many supporters among university medical practitioners by the mid-sixteenth century. Anyhow, this poisonous matter was not assumed to be a sufficient cause of plague until infectious conditions and their causality were reformulated in the context of late nineteenth-century germ theory.

The notion of contagion was alien neither to Galen nor to late medieval and renaissance Latin Galenism. Fracastoro's merit was not so much the supposed originality of his theory as his success in systematizing Galen's ideas on contagion and in consciously adapting them—always within the framework of humanist Galenism—to the specific demands of his historico-cultural context. To medieval medical practitioners, spreading air and contagion were but two different and successive stages in the process of plague diffusion, and by no means alternative and exclusive ways for its dissemination. Thus, the pestilential poison was in the air and could enter the human bodies through ways such as mouth, nose, skin pores and, according to some practitioners, even sight.

Preventive Measures during the Black Death

Thus, confronted by the 1348 Black Death, university practitioners usually prescribed preventive measures pointing toward three major, complementary goals. First, they tried to avoid or stop the process of air corruption by keeping rooms, houses, and cities well ventilated and free of rubbish, particularly manure and animal entrails, because of their alleged great facility to give rise to corruption, and they also strove to eliminate the bad smell by means of burning aromatic herbs and of vinegar fumigations, in order to purify the air and reinforce its resistance to corruption. Second, they tried to keep individuals resistant to plague by means of a regimen

most suitable to neutralize the natural proclivity of the patient's complexion to humoral corruption, with the supplementary help of some specific antidotes of proved efficacy against this condition. Finally, once the epidemic had broken out, they recommended their patients to avoid any occasion of interpersonal transmission of plague, by means of practical measures that went from avoiding crowds to following the popular advice—caricatured ad nauseam—of *fugere cito, longe, et tarde reverti* ("escape early and far away and turn back as late as possible"). Any further modification of these measures that might have been introduced on the outbreak of further epidemics during the next four hundred years or so merely showed a quantitative development of these guidelines—albeit always in with growing sophistication.

When preventive measures failed to prevent the individual from falling ill, the resource to a curative treatment of plague still remained. Then, led by their Galenist views, practitioners intended to reinforce the patient's natural virtues in order to hold the effects of pestilential poison as well as to facilitate its elimination before this poison produced a functional failure of the main members that led to individual's death. To a great extent, the curative measures were interchangeable with those preventive ones, for they mainly consisted of setting a suitable life regime and of prescribing drugs intended to diverse purposes, mostly purgatives, cordials and antidotes.

Yet, these measures used to be complemented by small surgical interventions such as bloodletting and cauteries. Allegedly, bloodletting allowed the evacuation of poisonous matter gathered at any member. To localize the member or members "injured" by the poison, practitioners were guided by the *apostemata*—swellings of purulent matter that could appear in different places of the bodily surface. Since it was assumed that they revealed the emunctories (*emunctoria*) through which the superfluities from the injured members were evacuated, their localization determined the precise vein from which a particular patient should be bled. The three most worrying localizations of the *apostemata* were under the left armpit, behind the ears, and in the right groin, for they were linked with injuries of the three main bodily members, namely heart, brain, and liver, respectively. Practitioners also used to prescribe direct intervention on the *apostemata* with the purpose of breaking them, and of attracting, solving, and evacuating the poisonous matter collected there, by means of several procedures: deep escharification and application of cupping-glasses; or cauterization—"actual" (with incandescent iron) or "potential" (with caustic medicines)—and the application of poultices.

Although the simple *apostema* was the accident which the plague tractate writers earlier and most often referred to, they also dealt with the specific treatment of those considered malignant *apostemata* such as the "anthrax"—gathering of *apostemata* with points of suppuration—and the "carbuncle"—black *apostema* produced by thick and viscous blood.

Last but not least, the curative regime in some plague tractates included medicines explicitly intended for different social strata. Gentile da Foligno, for instance, recommended to those "rich and wealthy enough" a potion consisting of barley water which had to be boiled with a gold straw before use in various recipes.

See also **Aristotelianism; Astrology; Cosmology; Elements and qualities; God in Christianity; Medicine, practical; Medicine, theoretical; Microcosm/macrocosm; Miracle; Religion and science;** *Regimen sanitatis;* **Scholasticism; Surgery; Universities**

Bibliography

Agrimi, Jole and Chiara Crisciani. *Typologie des sources du Moyen ge Occidental. A-V.D.3: Les consilia médicaux.* Turnhout: Brepols, 1994.

Arrizabalaga, Jon. "Facing the Black Death: Perceptions and Reactions of University Medical Practitioners." In *Practical Medicine from Salerno to the Black Death.* Edited by Luis García-Ballester, Roger French, Jon Arrizabalaga, and Andrew Cunningham. New York: Cambridge University Press, 1994, pp. 237–288.

Barkai, Ron. "Jewish Treatises on the Black Death (1350–1500)." In *Medicine from the Black Death to the French Disease.* Edited by Roger French, Jon Arrizabalaga, Andrew Cunningham and Luis García-Ballester. Aldershot: Ashgate, 1998, pp. 6–25.

Biraben, Jean-Nöel. *Les hommes et la peste en France et dans les pays européens et mediterranées.* 2 vols., Paris–The Hague: Mouton, 1975–1976.

Cohn, Samuel K., Jr. *The Black Death Transformed. Disease and Culture in Early Renaissance Europe.* London: Arnold, 2002.

Cunningham, Andrew. "Transforming Plague: The Laboratory and the Identity of Infectious Disease." In *The Laboratory Revolution in Medicine.* Edited by Andrew Cunningham and Perry Williams. New York: Cambridge University Press, 1992, pp. 209–244.

Dols, Michael W. *The Black Death in the Middle East.* Princeton: Princeton University Press, 1977.

Guerchberg S. "The Controversy over the Alleged Sowers of the Black Death in the Contemporary Treatises on Plague." In *Change in Medieval Society. Europe North of the Alps, 1050–1500.* Edited by Sylvia L. Thrupp. London: Owen, 1965, pp. 208–224].

Hirst, L. Fabian. *The Conquest of Plague. A Study of the Evolution of Epidemiology.* Oxford: Clarendon Press, 1953.

Klebs, Arnold C. and Eugénie Droz. *Remèdes contre la peste: facsimilés, notes et liste bibliographique des incunables sur la peste.* Paris: E. Droz, 1925.

Laín Entralgo, Pedro. *Historia de la Medicina.* Barcelona: Salvat, 1978.

Martin, A. Lynn. *Plague? Jesuit Accounts of Epidemic Disease in the 16th Century.* Kirksville: Sixteenth Century Journal Publishers, 1996.

Nutton, Vivian. The Seeds of Disease: An Explanation of Contagion and Infection from the Greeks to the Renaissance. *Medical History* (1983) 27/1: 1–34.

Nutton, Vivian. The Reception of Fracastoro's Theory of Contagion: The Seed That Fell Among Thorns? *Osiris* (1990) 6: 196–234.

Scott, Susan and Christopher J. Duncan. *Biology of Plagues. Evidence from Historical Populations.* New York: Cambridge University Press, 2001.

Twigg, Graham. *The Black Death: A Biological Reappraisal.* London: Batsford, 1984.

JON ARRIZABALAGA

PLANETARY TABLES

We shall refer here to sets of astronomical tables, whether or not associated with the planets, and in particular to those sets that became part of the astronomical tradition. Therefore, it also includes tables used to solve trigonometric problems, tables for syzygies (new and full moons), solar and lunar eclipses, star tables, geographical tables, and so on. On the other hand, this article does not deal with special sets of tables known as ephemerides and *almanacs.

In his treatises known as the *Almagest* and the *Handy Tables,* *Ptolemy (c. 100–175 C.E.) inserted many tables to help the practitioner of astronomy calculate the positions of the Sun, the Moon, the five planets, and related matters. Among these tables some could be used to compute directly celestial phenomena such as rising-times, conjunctions, and oppositions of the two luminaries to determine the values of intermediate variables involved in astronomical calculations, such as chords, parallaxes, the solar declination, or planetary mean motions, equations, and latitudes.

During the Middle Ages scientists in the Islamic world introduced a specific genre in astronomy, that of the *zij* (plural, *zijat*), or astronomical handbooks, where each one consists of a collection of tables and a text explaining their use. These *zijat* had a two-fold purpose: to provide users with a handy tool to compute both the positions of celestial bodies and the times of celestial phenomena, sometimes for astrological purposes, and to transmit the mathematical models and parameters on which these tables were based. Some of these sets of tables included the results of observations carried out over long periods of time, while others were just adaptations of previous *zijat* updated to a new time period or adjusted to the local coordinates of the potential user. In 1956 E.S. Kennedy published a seminal survey of Islamic *zijat,* and in 2001 D.A. King and J. Samsó presented an overview of the current state of research on medieval Islamic astronomical *zijat.* Usually a *zij* contains tables for chronology and conversions between various calendars; trigonometric functions (such as the sine function, which had replaced Ptolemy's chord function); spherical astronomy (such as tables to determine the length of daylight for any geographical latitude); the equation of time (i.e., the difference between apparent and mean time); Sun, Moon and the planets (mean motions, equations, and celestial latitudes); planetary stations, retrogradations, and visibility (including lunar visibility); parallax and eclipses; geographical coordinates; star tables; astrology (such as tables for the equations of the astrological houses, the projection of the rays or the excess of revolution). Of course, other tables not falling into any of the above categories are found here and there in the many different sets computed by medieval astronomers.

Among the Islamic *zijat* it is possible to distinguish two lines of transmission: the Indo-Iranian and the Ptolemaic traditions. The first tradition has its roots in Indian astronomy and depends on Greek material prior to Ptolemy. Two of the *zijat* commonly ascribed to this tradition are the *Sindhind*—a set of tables that seems to have been based on the Sanskrit *Brahmasphutasiddhanta*, composed by Brahmagupta in 629, and introduced in Baghdad at the end of the eighth century—and the *zij* of *al-Khwarizmi (c. 825) whose starting point (epoch) is the beginning of the era of Yazdegird, or Persian era: June 16, 632 (JDN 1952063). This tradition soon lost its vigor in the Middle East but flourished in the Western Islamic world, for al-Khwarizmi's *zij* was adapted at least twice in al-Andalus (the Muslim part of the Iberian Peninsula at the time), by Maslama al-Majriti (d. 1007) and *Ibn al-Saffar in the eleventh century. These revisions and their comments were partially translated into Latin and Hebrew in the twelfth century in the Iberian Peninsula.

However, the mainstream tradition is that based on Ptolemaic models. It was transmitted to the West primarily by *al-Battani (c. 900). His tables were compiled for the latitude of Raqqa, now in Syria, and used two calendars, that of the Hijra era (epoch: July 15, 622 C.E.) and that of the Seleucid era (epoch: October 1, 312 B.C.E.). Following his predecessors in Baghdad and Damascus, Yahya ibn Abi Mansur (fl. c. 828–833) and Habash al-Hasib (d. c. 864–874) who had also compiled their own *zijat*, al-Battani modified certain parameters found in Ptolemy's works, but maintained the models underlying them. For instance, he chose 1.59.10° as the maximum equation for the Sun and 1.59° for Venus, whereas Ptolemy had used 2.23° for both celestial bodies, and the value for precession ascribed to al-Battani is 1° in sixty-six years, in contrast to Ptolemy's value of 1° in one hundred years. As was the case with other compilers of *zijat*, al-Battani also adapted the values of some crucial variables to his time rather than Ptolemy's. Thus, for the obliquity of the ecliptic he used 23.35° (Ptolemy: 23.51.20°) and for the position of the solar apogee, 82.17° (Ptolemy: 65.30°). The text accompanying al-Battani's tables was translated into Latin, Hebrew, and Castilian in the Iberian Peninsula during the twelfth and the thirteenth centuries.

Within the same tradition the Eastern Islamic world produced a wealth of *zijat* throughout the Middle Ages, always preserving the essential characteristics of Ptolemaic astronomy. Among many others we may cite *al-Qanun al-Mas'udi* by *al-Biruni (c. 1025), the *Zij-i Ilkhani* attributed to *Nasir al-Din al-Tusi (1201–1274), and the *Zij-i Sultani* (c. 1440) of Ulugh Beg.

In the Western world, both the Indo-Iranian and the Ptolemaic traditions survived in al-Andalus and the Maghrib (North Africa), and most Muslim astronomers compiled tables mixing materials from the two basic sources. The most successful *zij* was that known as the Toldedan Tables, and it became the main vehicle of transmission of Arabic astronomy to scholars in the Latin world. Most of the latitude-dependent tables in this collection were computed for *Toledo not long before the city fell under Christian rule (1085). It has been argued that these tables were the result of the work of a team of astronomers directed by *qadi* *Sa'id al-Andalusi (d. 1070) which included the celebrated *Ibn al-Zarqalluh (Azarquiel). The Arabic original is not extant but hundreds of copies of the Latin version, mainly from the thirteenth and fourteenth centuries, have survived. As F.S. Pedersen (2002) has extensively shown, "Toledan Tables" is a term covering a complex reality because there are three texts associated with this *zij*, as well as a multiplicity of tables, not always fully consistent with each other. To follow the examples of parameters mentioned above, for the obliquity of the ecliptic the Toledan Tables present two different values: 23.51° (a rounding of Ptolemy's value) and 23.33.30° (a value associated with Azarquiel, but probably already used by ninth-century Muslim astronomers). Note that both values differ from al-Battani's. On the other hand, the Toledan Tables reproduce al-Battani's tables for the equations of the Sun and Venus (maximum values of 1.59.10° and 1.59°, respectively). Besides being translated into Latin, the Toledan Tables were soon adapted to the Christian calendar and some of the tables were recomputed for localities other than Toledo, such as Toulouse, Marseilles, and Novara, giving rise to sets of tables slightly different from each other.

In al-Andalus and the Maghrib, various astronomers continued producing *zijat* in the tradition of Azarquiel, introducing new parameters, giving new presentations to old tables, and compiling new ones, but hardly deviating from the essential features established by their predecessors. Among these astronomers were Ibn al-Kammad (c. 1100), Ibn al-Ha'im (c. 1200), Ibn Ishaq al-Tunisi (c. 1193–1222), Ibn al-Banna' (1256–1321), Ibn al-Raqqam (d. 1315), and Ibn 'Azzuz al-Qusantini (d. 1354), and even in the Christian part of the Iberian Peninsula we find a set of astronomical tables in the same tradition. Indeed, the Tables of Barcelona, compiled by the astronomers in the service of Peter IV of Aragon (r. 1336–1387), mainly depend on those of Ibn al-Kammad.

The Alfonsine Tables

About two hundred years after the compilation of the Toledan Tables, another set of tables was produced in Toledo: the Alfonsine Tables. They were composed under the patronage of Alfonso X, king of Castile and León (r. 1252–1284) by two scholars, Isaac ben Sid and Judah ben Moses ha-Cohen. This book consisted of a set of astronomical tables computed for the city of Toledo and a text explaining their use. The tables had January 1, 1252 as epoch, corresponding to the year of the king's accession. The text has been preserved in a unique manuscript in Castilian, but unfortunately the tables have not survived. On the original tables, only conjectures can be offered based on the numerous indications found in the text, but they seem to form a coherent set of tables much in the style of previous Arabic *zijat*. Moreover, the Toledan Tables were probably a direct source for the Alfonsine astronomers. The Alfonsine Tables, in a Latin version, had an immense success and became the most useful computing tool for Latin astronomers until the end of the sixteenth century.

The Castilian Alfonsine Tables arrived in Paris in the early fourteenth century and they began to spread throughout Europe after they were recast by the Parisian astronomers. Among them, John Vimond (c. 1320) constructed tables based on the Alfonsine Tables, although more limited in scope, incorporating parameters of Castilian origin and undoubtedly reflecting tabular material at hand in the Iberian Peninsula. Vimond used 2.10° for the maximum solar equation, and 4.56° for the maximum lunar equation. Vimond's contemporaries in Paris, *Jean de Meurs, John of Lignères, and *John of Saxony, among others, compiled various sets of tables—mostly using Vimond's parameters—and wrote canons explaining their use and praising Alfonso's achievements in astronomy. The result of the efforts and ingenuity developed by the Parisian astronomers of the early fourteenth century in recasting the Castilian Alfonsine Tables is known as the Parisian Alfonsine Tables. Among its characteristics is the use of the coordinates of Toledo for the tables that depend on geographical latitude, dividing the circle into six signs of 60° (rather than into twelve signs of 30°), and the presentation of the tables for the mean motions of the Sun, the Moon, and the planets as multiplication tables of their respective daily mean motions, even though these features can (separately) be traced back to earlier astronomers.

During the fourteenth century, the Parisian Alfonsine Tables reached England (where the Oxford Tables of 1348 ascribed to William Batecombe introduced double argument tables to compute the positions of the planets), Italy, the Greek world of Byzantium, and came back to Spain, giving rise to a variety of tables that preserve the basic parameters of Alfonsine astronomy but differ in presentation.

At the same time the Hebrew astronomical tradition developed in the Iberian Peninsula and southern France, beginning with Abraham Bar Hiyya of Barcelona in the twelfth century. Although the authors of the Castilian canons of the Alfonsine Tables were Jews, the community of Jewish astronomers did not follow Alfonsine astronomy. As far as we know, this is the case of the *zij* of Isaac Israeli (*Isaac Judaeus), working in Toledo at the end of the thirteenth century, and the tables produced by Levi ben Gerson (d. 1344), one of the few medieval astronomers who constructed tables based on his own observations and departing from Ptolemy's models and parameters. Other tables, quite different from those available to Christian scholars, were those called *Six Wings* by Immanuel Bonfils (c. 1360), the tables by Jacob ben David Bonjorn (1361), a follower of Levi ben Gerson, the tables compiled by Judah ben Asher II of Burgos (d. 1391), and the tables by Isaac al-Hadib (1391), a refugee from Spain in Sicily.

After 1400, the Parisian Alfonsine Tables reached all practitioners of astronomy and all centers of learning in Europe, and gradually superseded the Latin versions of the Toledan Tables. Many astronomers adapted these tables to the coordinates of their cities, others constructed new tables to give solutions to specific problems, which is the case for Nicholaus de Heybech of Erfurt (c. 1400) who addressed the problem of finding the time between mean and true syzygies, and still others recast tables making them more user-friendly. But none of these "innovators" changed a single parameter of the tables or challenged the Ptolemaic models underlying them. This is why all these individual tables, as well as sets of them, ultimately based on Alfonsine astronomy, belong to a category that has been called the "Alfonsine Corpus." Within this large corpus we may cite the *Tabulae resolutae*, a form of presentation of the Parisian Alfonsine Tables that was quite popular in central Europe and Poland in the middle years of the fifteenth century; the tables of Giovanni Bianchini, active in Ferrara c. 1460, whose extensive set of tables was first published by S. Beuilaqua in Venice in 1495; the tables of *Abraham Zacuto of Salamanca, originally contained in his *ha-Hibbur ha-gadol*—a synthesis of the Hebrew and the Alfonsine traditions—and popularized as the *Almanach perpetuum*, published in Leiria, Portugal, in 1496; and the *Tabule astronomice Elisabeth Regine*, produced by Alfonso de Córdoba to honor the queen of Castile and Aragon, Isabella I (d. 1504) and first published by P. Liechtenstein in Venice in 1503. The *editio princeps* of the Parisian Alfonsine Tables themselves was published by E. Ratdolt in Venice in 1483, becoming the standard form of the Alfonsine Tables, and a second edition, with much the same pattern, was due to L. Santritter, also in Venice, in 1492. It seems clear that the Venetian publishers took advantage of the Alfonsine Corpus to produce a series of bestsellers.

The publication of Copernicus's *De revolutionibus* (Nuremberg, 1543) began to undermine the dominance of the Alfonsine Tables in the field of astronomical computation. Although Copernicus copied and adapted many tables in the Alfonsine Corpus and continued to use models that were essentially Ptolemaic, heliocentrism introduced quite a number of changes. The tables in *De revolutionbus* were later modified and integrated into a new set of tables, the *Prutenic Tables*, compiled by Erasmus Reinhold and dedicated to Albert, Duke of Prussia. These tables were first published by Petreius in Nuremberg in 1551, but did not completely displace the Alfonsine Tables. This occurred in 1627, with the publication of the *Rudolphine Tables*, a set of tables based on Johannes Kepler's elliptical orbits and completed by him. The *Rudolphine Tables* opened a new era for astronomical computation and, together with the introduction of telescopic observations, freed European astronomy from dependence on the Ptolemaic tradition.

See also **Astronomy, Islamic; Astronomy, Latin**

Bibliography

Chabás, J. and B. R. Goldstein. *The Alfonsine Tables of Toledo.* Dordrecht-Boston: Archimedes, New Studies in the History and Philosophy of Science and Technology, 2003.

———. *Astronomy in the Iberian Peninsula: Abraham Zacut and the Transition from Manuscript to Print.* Philadelphia:

American Philosophical Society, 2000. Transactions, vol. 90, part 2.

Goldstein, B. R. *The Astronomical Tables of Levi ben Gerson.* Hamden, Ct.: Archon Books, 1974.

Kennedy, E. S. *A Survey of Islamic Astronomical Tables.* Philadelphia American Philosophical Society, 1956. Transactions vol. 46, part 2.

King, D.A. and J. Samsó (with a contribution by B. R. Goldstein). Astronomical Handbooks and Tables from the Islamic World (750–1900): An Interim Report. *Suhayl* (2001) 2: 9–105.

Nallino, C. A. *Al-Battani sive Albatenii Opus Astronomicum,* 2 vols. Milan, 1903–1907.

Neugebauer, O. *The Astronomical Tables of al-Khwarizmi.* Copenhagen: Munksgaard, 1962.

Pedersen, F. S. *The Toledan Tables: A Review of the Manuscripts and the Textual Versions with an Edition.* Copenhagen: Munksgaard, 2002.

Ratdolt, E. *Tabulae astronomice illustrissimi Alfontij regis castelle.* Venice, 1483.

Swerdlow, N. M. and O. Neugebauer. *Mathematical Astronomy in Copernicus's De Revolutionibus.* New York: Springer-Verlag, 1984.

JOSÉ CHABÁS

PLATO

Throughout the Latin Middle Ages Plato was mainly known through the *Timaeus* in the partial (17A-53C) translation made by Calcidius in the fourth century C.E. There was also a considerable indirect tradition of Platonic doctrines through Latin authors such as Augustine, *Macrobius, *Martianus Capella and *Boethius, and through the translated Aristotle. This indirect transmission is of great importance for metaphysical doctrines such as the theory of ideas, participation, the account of knowledge and science, and the nature of the soul. But Plato's contribution to the development of science in the Middle Ages came almost solely through the *Timaeus* and the accompanying commentary of Calcidius. This commentary with its long digressions made the difficult poetic text of Plato more accessible to scholars, which was the objective of the translator. But Calcidius confronted his readers with new problems of interpretation, in particular because he had integrated in his exposition much material from Middle and Neoplatonic sources (in particular Porphyry). The Calcidius edition of the *Timaeus* was immensely popular in the Middle Ages. About one hundred sixty-five copies of the text survive, many of them with glosses. There are also dozens of independent glosses and commentaries on the text. The way Calcidius shaped the medieval understanding of the *Timaeus* was so pervasive that scholars did not always distinguish between his exposition and the original views of Plato. What they quote as an opinion of Plato is often only Calcidius' view.

In the *Timaeus* Plato offers a "likely account" of the generation of the world. This world is a living organism created by a divine Maker as an image of an eternal intelligible paradigm, which is itself a great organism encompassing the forms of all living beings. The divine Demiurge made this world as perfect as a copy might be which is formed after an eternal model. The copy is produced in a "receptacle" which has the function of both space and substance. Calcidius identified it with the Aristotelian "matter." The world is thus the product of intelligent design (coming from its divine Maker) and necessity due to matter, whereby intelligence dominates and uses necessity for the best possible outcome. The Demiurge created the bodily structure of the whole universe and the soul governing it. As for the production of the particular human animals within this world, he delegated this task to the celestial gods, after having made himself the immortal rational soul. The inferior demiurges (who came to be identified with the celestial planetary gods) framed the human body and located in it the different parts of the mortal soul with their respective desires and passions.

In this remarkable account of creation Plato mixes a mythical narrative with a rational explanation, integrating all information available from the sciences of his time, cosmology, astronomy, mathematics (in its three branches: arithmetic, geometry, and harmony), anatomy and physiology, physics, optics, chemistry (the analysis of the different sorts of elements and their qualities; the discussion of colors), and medicine. The important final section on the causes of the diseases of body and soul and on their treatment through exercise, diet, and medicine is unfortunately lacking in Calcidius. It would have greatly interested his medieval readers! Missing also is the section on the geometrical construction of the elementary bodies out of triangles, which offers a wonderful example of mathematical physics. In the Middle Ages this original Platonic doctrine was only indirectly known through the detailed criticism of Aristotle in *De Caelo* III. One has to wait until the Renaissance to see the influence of this speculative mathematical physics on the new attempts of a physical explanation of the world, in Galileo and Kepler. There was, however, in the section of the *Timaeus* translated and explained by Calcidius, sufficient material to provoke further scientific investigation.

In his commentary Calcidius offers an explanation of the different factors playing a role in the mythical narrative. Thus he clarifies the status of the Good (which he understands as the ineffable first God), Providence, the demiurge, the Forms, the world soul, matter, and necessity. He insists more than Plato does on the correspondence between the *macrocosmos* and the *microcosmos*, which is the human animal composed out of the same elements as the world. The treatment of some important problems gives rise to long digressions, for example on the nature of the soul, on fate and providence, on the celestial gods and the demons, which were much read by later scholars. The longest section of the commentary is devoted to a systematic treatment of the nature of matter ("*tractatus de silva*"), including a historical survey of various doctrines. Matter is neither corporeal nor incorporeal, but in potency all things; it is without form, without quantities or qualities, without change, yet the substrate of all things in change.

In his explanation of the views on time and eternity expressed in the *Timaeus*, Calcidius inserts a most interesting survey of different astronomical hypotheses to explain the movements of the planets and of the heaven of the fixed stars. Translating and adapting a long section of Theo of Smyrna (a Platonic mathematician of the second century C.E.) he explains the difference between a mathematical and a physical study of celestial movements, he deals with the eccentric movements and epicycles and refers to the hypothesis of Heraclides of Pontus (fourth century B.C.E.) on the revolutions of Venus and Mercury as satellites around the Sun. This astronomical section had a far-reaching influence. Through Calcidius (who is the only source), the original hypothesis of Heraclides continued to fascinate astronomers throughout the Middle Ages and may even have inspired Tycho Brahe. When discussing the location of the world soul, Calcidius emphasizes the importance of the Sun as the center of life, from where a *vitalis vigor* or life-giving force stretches throughout the universe. The *Timaeus* analysis of the geometrical proportion existing between the four elements and Plato's explanation of the division of the soul into harmonic intervals gave Calcidius the opportunity for a long section on harmony. The section on the "world soul" brought about a heated discussions in the twelfth century.

Read and interpreted together with the works of other Latin authors from late antiquity, Martianus Capella and Macrobius, the *Timaeus* of Calcidius became the most authoritative text on cosmology and the sciences of the *quadrivium in the early Middle Ages, until it was replaced by the growing influx of translations of Arabic scientific treatises and of Aristotle's works. *Gerbert of Aurillac (tenth century), for example, uses Calcidius in his mathematical writings, though complementing him with Arabic sources. He considers Plato together with Pythagoras as an authority in *arithmetic. Plato also had a great reputation as an authority on music (a reputation he also owes to the influence of Boethius' treatise *De institutione musica*).

The *Timaeus* enjoyed its greatest popularity in the eleventh and twelfth centuries. In the newly developing *cathedral schools the study of the *Timaeus* was the obligatory starting point for a explanation of the universe through its natural causes ("*lectio physica*") seen as an alternative and a complement to a symbolic interpretation of nature (based on the biblical and patristic tradition. The "*Glossae super Platonem*" of William of Conches and Bernard of Chartres constitute the first attempts in the Middle Ages to establish a "*scientia naturalis*" wherein a purely rational explanation of physical phenomena is given. The fact that Plato presented his explanation of the physical world as an account of the creation of the world by a divine Father, who is motivated only by goodness, made it easy to reconcile this new naturalistic explanation of the world with the Christian understanding of the creation (deriving from Genesis). Thus, in his explanation of the first days of creation ("*de sex dierum operibus*") *Thierry of Chartres promises to explain the genesis of the world "*secundum phisicam et ad litteram*" and "*secundum ordinem naturalem*" in contrast to the "*allegorica and moralis lectio*," which had been sufficiently developed by the fathers. *Timaeus* insisted that "nothing comes to be without a cause" ("*legitima causa et ratio*" [28A]), and offered a wide range of causes, from the most proximate (immanent in the natural process) to the ultimate first divine cause: matter, generated forms in matter; the elements with their particular qualitative forces; nature; necessity; world soul; providence; paradigmatic forms; and the Creator of the world. As *William of Conches put it in his *Cosmographia* (c. 1248): "Regarding the causes of things the opinion of Plato prevails" ("*in causas rerum sentit Plato*").

By the middle of the twelfth century Plato was generally considered as the great master in Physics, whereas Aristotle was appreciated as the authority in matters of logic. This evaluation changed radically at the turn of the thirteenth century with the discovery of the Aristotle's books on natural philosophy. Those books became the basic texts for teaching and research on natural philosophy for the following centuries. Nevertheless the *Timaeus* kept attracting new readers, even outside the scholastic curriculum.

Although the study of the *Timaeus* offered an extraordinary impetus for a scientific investigation of natures, the natural philosophy inspired by Plato remained speculative and metaphysical, with the main ambition of reconciling a rational explanation with the biblical understanding of creation. It did not lead to exploration of new areas of study, except with those authors who made also use of the new Arabic material.

Besides the influence of the *Timaeus*, Plato is also known in the later Middle Ages for his views on occult sciences, *magic, and *alchemy, because of some treatises circulating under his name, such as the "*Liber vaccae*" (*Book of the Cow*) and the "*Liber quartorum*," translated from the Arabic. The *Book of the Cow* describes magical experiments for the artificial generation of animals and different recipes for producing miraculous effects and illusions. More influential was (and still is in esoteric circles) the alchemical treatise "*Liber quartorum*." It has the literary structure of a commentary on a text of "Plato" ("*Summa Platonis*"). The unknown author of this "text" gives a cosmological explanation in the tradition of the *Timaeus* with a particular attention for the different properties of the elements. The correspondence between *macrocosmos* and the *microcosmos* offers an evident foundation for the alchemical praxis. The treatise gained great authority in sixteenth-century alchemical literature. The fact that Plato's name was also associated with a chapter of the "*Turba philosophorum*" also contributed to his fame as alchemist.

See also **Aristotelianism; Astronomy; God in Christianity; Microcosm/macrocosm; Optics and catoptrics**

Bibliography

Duhem, P. *Le système du Monde. Histoire des doctrines cosmologiques de Platon a Copernic*, Tome III. Paris: Hermann, 1958.

Dutton, P.E. *The "Glosae super Platonem" of Bernard of Chartres*. Toronto: Pontifical Institute of Medieval Studies, 1991.

The three Polos—Niccoló, his brother Maffeo, and his son Marco—at an audience with Kublai Khan. From *Les Livres du Graunt Caam*, c. 1400. (Topham/Bodleian Library)

Speer, A. *Die entdeckte Natur. Untersuchungen zu Begründungsversuchen einer 'scientia naturalis' im 12. Jahrhundert*. Leiden: E.J. Brill, 1995.

Waszink, H., ed. *Timaeus a Calcidio translatus commentarioque instructus*. Leiden: E.J. Brill, 1962.

CARLOS STEEL

POLO, MARCO

Marco Polo was born in Venice in 1254, the same year in which his father Niccoló and uncle Maffeo set out first for Constantinople, and then to China. In 1271, the brothers set out for China again, with Marco in tow. Along the way, Polo learned to speak Persian, the language of commerce in Asia. They remained in China until 1290, in the court circle of Kublai Khan. Polo returned to Venice in 1295 at the age of forty-one or forty-two. He apparently had a draft of his memoir with him when around 1296 he was captured and held prisoner by the Genoese. In Genoa he met a writer of Arthurian-style adventure stories named Rustichello of Pisa who molded Polo's narrative into a text called *Devisement du monde*. Today Polo's narrative is usually titled *Travels of Marco Polo*. He died in 1324.

There are numerous versions of Polo's *Travels*, the one most commented being the so-called "F Text," a copy written in an Italianate French, ostensibly the one closest to Rustichello's original. Most medieval copies were of Francesco Pipino's Latin translation. Polo's book is composed of two hundred thirty-three chapters. The account begins with details about the Polos' journey and relationship with Kublai Khan; then, a description of the Near East, including Asia Minor, Armenia, Georgia, northern Iraq, and Persia, interlaced with fantastic stories; an odd itinerary into China through Kashmir, Samarqand, and the desert—none of this known to Europeans; the geography and customs of the Mongol heartland; Northern China and Khanbalikh (Beijing), capital city of the Great Khan, together with economic information that Polo knew from experience; an imaginary trip from Khanbalikh west to Burma; an account of South China (Mangi); then Japan, Indochina, Java and Sumatra, India, the Indian Ocean, and East Africa. The book ends with an account of the Ilkhanate, the Golden Horde, and wars among the Tartar princes, which may have been a late addition to the original corpus of the text.

Although Polo provided, for the first time, detailed information about the places where spices long familiar to Europeans had originated, his book was not meant to be a guide for merchants, because he supplies little of practical use for them. It is a work of geography quite possibly drawn up on the basis of documents, such as relay itineraries, used in normal Mongol administration. He says he will describe what he personally had observed and relies, especially for the non-Chinese material, on the charts, maps, and writing of mariners familiar with the Indies.

Polo and Science

In the Z text, an abbreviated Latin version derived from F, Polo gives an account of astrological activities in the Khan's court. He says that they involve five thousand people—Christians, Muslims, and Chinese—all supported by the emperor:

"They have their astrolabes, upon which are described the planetary signs, the hours and their several aspects for the whole year. The astrologers of each distinct sect annually proceed to the examination of their respective tables, in order to ascertain the course of the heavenly bodies, and their relative positions."

Later in the same passage he remarks on the twelve-year cycle of the Tartar calendar. The passage, while exaggerated, reflects Kublai's establishment in 1271 of a Western Astronomical Office, staffed with Arab and Persian astronomers, which was separate from an office of Chinese astronomers. Kublai's idea was to maintain two complete staffs working under different cosmological theories, and to check the results of their observations against each other. The Z text also contains an interesting and seemingly accurate description of the Egyptian sugar refining industry.

When in Sumatra, Polo observed a "star" (actually a comet visible in China in 1293) which had a sack-like form, and which he later observed again toward the south. Back in Italy sometime before 1303, he described the comet to *Pietro de Abano who reproduced both the observation and Polo's drawing of it in his *Conciliator controversiarum*. He also bolstered Abano's opinion that the "torrid zone" was habitable.

Polo's geographic knowledge of China is filtered through the lens of Persian, the lingua franca of Westerners in the Khanate. He did not know Chinese and was indifferent to many aspects of Chinese culture. His Persianization of Chinese place-names suggests that he might have had a map of China drawn by the Persian cosmographer *al-Tusi, who served the Mongol Ilkhanate of Hulagu around the time when the Polos first arrived in China.

Polo's Influence

Polo's geographical information was reflected on four-teenth-century maps, most spectacularly Abraham Cresques' "Catalan Atlas" of 1375, a world map constructed on the model of a portolan chart, where the continental mass of Asia first appears in a form recognizable to us. The more recent material in the Atlas is embodied in a central strip across Asia which, when disentangled and interpreted, is more or less the itinerary of Nicolo and Maffeo Polo in their first trip across Asia. Indeed the two brothers are depicted in one of the map's panels. *Christopher Columbus mined Polo's *Travels* for information about Asia; his annotated copy survives.

Polo is not mentioned in any Chinese documents insofar as is known, most likely because he held no official position in the government administration. He was a courtier, sent on extraordinary missions by Kublai,

to whom he personally reported. Marco's account of his assignment, along with his father and uncle, to deliver a Mongol princess to in Persia in the spring of 1290 is confirmed by the account of Rashid al-Din, the Persian historian. So Frances Wood's attempt to disprove Polo's presence in China has been amply refuted by Igor de Rachewitz and J. Jensen.

See also **Travel and exploration**

Bibliography

Critchley, John. *Marco Polo's Book*. Aldershot: Variorum, 1992.

Jensen, J. "The World's Most Diligent Observer." *Asiatische Studien. Etudes Asiatiques* (1997) 51: 719–726.

Larner, John. *Marco Polo and the Discovery of the World*. New Haven: Yale University Press, 1999.

Olschiki, Leonardo. *Marco Polo's Asia*. Berkeley: University of California Press, 1960.

Rachewitz, Igor de. "Marco Polo Went to China." *Zentralasiatische Studien* (1997) 27: 34–92.

Wood, Frances. *Did Marco Polo Go to China?* London: Secker & Warburg, 1995.

Yule, Henry. *The Book of Ser Marco Polo*. London: John Murray, 1875.

THOMAS F. GLICK

POTTERY

Pottery making involves a technical process that begins with the selection and treatment of clays, continues with body preparation, drying, decorating where carried out, and finally firing in a kiln. Most techniques used in the Middle Ages in each of these pottery-production phases were already known in antiquity. Instruments such as the potter's wheel driven by foot-pedal and the built kiln with firebox and chamber were not at all new, since they had been widely used in the great Roman pottery-making workshops. In fact, we can talk of a "regression" in the technical area of pottery-making after the more or less abrupt disappearance of these industrialized Roman production centers. Until the early thirteenth century, and then only for certain production, we do not encounter mass-produced standardized pottery, marketed and distributed on a large scale over a wide geographical area, similar to that of the Roman period. The social conditions of this production, and the methods of distribution and use, would also be completely different. After the seventh century and the disappearance of the patterns of distribution and use that made this standardized, large-scale production possible, the workshops disappeared and, together with so many other forms of the production of manufactured goods, pottery production became a far more modest affair, with a distribution capacity that was also more limited. They were mainly replaced by very local artisanal production and even by household production whose technical process was simplified and reduced to the strictly necessary. The technical reversal in pottery manufacture needs to be seen in the context of the general situation regarding techniques for the manufacture of objects and for building construction. It is not simply a case of lost technical skills, but rather the disappearance of the State and the conditions of production that made technical sophistication and its associated craft infrastructure unnecessary. In the case of construction techniques, for example, we see a return to dwellings built from perishable materials, the re-use of ancient buildings or of their construction materials; stone quarrying and cutting techniques disappear until at least the eleventh century in most of Europe or somewhat earlier in very exceptional cases. The State that promoted the commerce and urban life indispensable for conditions of standardized production had disappeared. Wealthy, urban social sectors able to acquire these wares had also disappeared in many regions of Europe. Only in areas where certain vitality still remained during the eighth century, whether urban (Italy) or commercial (the most northern part of Frankish Gaul), more elaborate techniques of pottery production endured in specialized workshops, with limited regional distribution. Examples are the red-painted fine ware in Italy or Merovingian gray and black wares. Neither the geographical diffusion of these wares nor the quantities produced was ever similar to the magnitudes of Roman pottery production.

Thus, the production of pottery between the eighth and the ninth/tenth centuries is, very often, household-type production, carried out within the domestic unit and for self-sufficiency, or at most in small workshops, possibly of seasonal activity, run by craftsmen with very little specialization who manufactured modest quantities of objects and marketed them at a very local level. The acquisition and use of pottery would also be limited to the most irreplaceable functions, the cooking of food or storage for example, leaving aside less urgent functions such as tableware. In these conditions of production, distribution, and use—the three fundamental aspects that need to be considered in the study of pottery—the technical level of manufacture consists basically of hand-building or using a turntable (slow-wheel), with open firing or in very rudimentary kilns.

Various hand-building techniques are known: pinching, which consists of squeezing clay between fingers and thumb, with the walls of the vessel being thinned and increased in height by repeating this action rhythmically. The forms that can be obtained are very basic, with round bases and more or less open walls: coiling, which consists of placing rolls or coils around the circumference and gradually increasing the height, producing a ridged and grooved surface, which is evened by scraping and smoothing; slab building, which consists of forming flat slabs of clay, with the edges being joined by pressing or smearing, suitable for forming rectangular shapes or very large vessels; and drawing, which consists of the potter opening a lump of clay by forcing his fist into it; the walls are then refined by squeezing the clay between the hands while simultaneously stretching it upwards, obtainable shapes being somewhat more closed. In all these techniques, the possibilities for varying shapes are very few.

The slow wheel consists of a disk-shaped support for the clay, which can be turned on another fixed support, sometimes in the form of an axle. The rotating movement is performed either by the potter's own hands, with the artifact being formed while turning takes place, or by those of an assistant. Throwing performance depends on the speed of rotation and the time the rotating movement lasts. In the case of the slow wheel, this level of performance is low in comparison with the kickwheel. In contrast to hand modeling, the turntable involves kinetic energy in addition to the potter's muscular energy, thereby allowing vessels to be better finished and somewhat more complex shapes to be produced than the simple vessels obtained by hand modeling. However, the very low and uneven rotation speed of the slow wheel also limit the possibilities of complexity of vessel shape in comparison with what can be produced using the pedal wheel. Pottery manufactured on a slow wheel is characterised by its asymmetry, thick walls (these being difficult to make thin), irregular throwing rings, and abundance of finger marks not eliminated during the forming process. Indeed, it is often difficult to determine whether a vessel has been made by hand or with the help of a slow wheel. The forerunner to the slow wheel may have been a heavy stone support made to turn on the floor while the vessel was formed.

This production procedure does not allow for a wide range of forms, and the known repertoires are basically limited to cooking vessels and a few larger storage jars. In the latter case, the vessels are formed in parts that, when already in an advanced stage of dryness, are joined together by sticking with slurry or slip (clay that has been made watery but is still dense enough to remain viscous), and the joints reinforced with clay coils. In addition, such production is not standardized, i.e., the various pieces of the same form made by the same potter are not all exactly the same: they have defects or small details that differentiate them from one another, such as wall thickness, size, rim inclination, etc., which ensure that each vessel has its own small but particular characteristics. This throwing procedure, and the low level of specialization of potters, also prevented large quantities of pieces from being manufactured. They are therefore repertoires (this term refers here to the whole range of vessel shapes produced in one or various workshops) with little variety in form and with only a limited amount of vessels, acquired and used as household ceramic furnishing (referring here to the set of vessels acquired and used in a domestic unit), which consist of a small number of vessels having basic functions.

The kinds of decoration for this type of production also tend to be very simple: carved, incised, and impressed decoration performed with simple tools (punches, ropes, fingernails, fingers, etc.), applied decoration, where coils or nipple shapes molded separately are stuck to the body, and which usually have some kind of function such as for reinforcing the joints between parts of the vessel that have been independently thrown. Less frequently seen are examples of painted decoration, usually very simple motifs—lines, geometrical shapes, or spots made using the fingers—and the use of oxides, such as iron and manganese, to give a reddish or blackish coloration. Finally, techniques such as burnishing and polishing—rubbing the already dried surface of the piece with a hard instrument—which partly eliminates porosity and can produce a burnished effect, or slips, sometimes tinted, which also have the function of reducing porosity. These decoration techniques are applied before firing, onto the still-soft clay (for applied, incised and impressed decoration and slips) or onto the already-dried clay (for burnishing and painting).

The usual firing method for household production must basically have been that of open firing. The simplest form consists of stacking pieces of pottery in direct contact with the glowing fuel. This gives a very uneven firing that took place at a low temperature. Somewhat more elaborate is open firing in a single-chambered kiln, in which the vessels are also in direct contact with the fuel, but are stacked in a shallow pit on top of it and are also covered over with fuel and some form of lid made of clay, earth or manure with flue holes that allow the necessary draught for burning. Firing is also very slow and uneven. After the cooling process, which is particularly lengthy, the kiln is dismantled to remove the pieces of pottery. Each firing therefore involves the construction and destruction of this small infrastructure. The volume of vessels fired in each firing is very limited, and would in no case permit mass production. In addition, the unevenness of the firing, and the low temperatures attained, produce large quantities of firing waste.

As long as there was no minimally consolidated urban and commercial structure that would permit the existence of specialized pottery production, these production methods, associated with rudimentary techniques such as the turntable and open firing, continued to survive. In the High Middle Ages, the organization of periodic rural markets assured the existence of contacts and exchange that would otherwise have been excessively random. This type of market enabled the circulation of goods on a local and regional level. Frequenting such meeting-points eventually led to the emergence of specialists. Some of these markets came to connect networks of regional markets, thereby diversifying exchange. The centers of these networks were initially rural settlements, largely inhabited by peasants. As the network became denser, in the centers where the highest level of exchange was concentrated, the proportion of inhabitants living on commercial activity was more significant. These centers would become the towns that were to spring up again at the height of the Middle Ages.

The Emergence of Specialization

It is not therefore until the tenth/eleventh century at least, or a little earlier in exceptional cases, that we begin to see the appearance of these centers of urban exchange concentrating specialists in craft work and those related to commercial activity. Potters were to be one of these specialist groups, now working in workshops that were becoming increasingly stable, and where forming and firing techniques, such as the kickwheel and two-chamber kilns, began to be readopted, together with more sophisticated decorating and surface-treatment techniques, such as glazes. The recovery of these techniques allowed increasingly standardized production to be carried out, more varied in shape and produced in greater quantities, although without reaching the levels of the Roman period. Distribution methods also changed, although they continued at regional levels, with long-distance movements still being very exceptional; when this did occur, it was not on a large scale and only affected very specific vessels or production, such as the first luxury tableware sets. The pottery production of these specialists would gradually come to replace entirely the non-specialized domestic production.

The kickwheel has a much higher level of performance than the turntable, due to its faster and more even rotation. The potter's hands are completely free and are exclusively given over to throwing, while his feet can adjust the spin speed, keeping it stable or speeding it up as required. The spinning support is fixed to an axle that, in turn, is secured to a platform acting as a pedal. The evenness of rotation and its higher speed allow throwing vessels with thinner walls, of more regular size and attributes. Lifting rings, where not entirely eliminated, are more regular and parallel. The vessels are therefore better finished, more pieces can be produced in the same time and, finally, the variety of shapes can also be increased, since these forming conditions enable greater difference of detail to be added to the basic structure of each shape. The possibility of varying shape is reflected in the repertoires produced, and in the household ceramic furnishing acquired and used, with more shapes now being seen than those strictly necessary for cooking and storing. There is, for example, the appearance of tableware.

The kilns associated with these production conditions are stable, double chamber structures—one for the fuel and the other for stacking the pieces. The most widely used double-chamber kiln in medieval Europe was that known as the updraft kiln. This kiln consists of a lower combustion chamber (firebox), sometimes underground and fitted with a stokehole through which fuel is inserted. The upper or firing chamber is situated above the firebox, having a floor with flues through which the heat, gases, ash and flames pass. Draught is ensured by the holes in the firing chamber's vaulted cover. Firing is produced due to heat spread by conduction and convection, whereas the open or single chamber kiln relied on conduction alone. Temperatures of up to 1,100° C are attained. Firing is therefore more efficient and even. The downdraft kiln has the two chambers, for combustion and firing, side by side. The firing-kiln cover has no holes and draught is ensured by a chimney situated at the back of the firing chamber. However, this type of kiln was not used in Europe until modern times, though it was known in China in the T'ang and Sung dynasties. The downdraft kiln gives a much higher thermic performance than the updraft kiln since the heat spread inside the kiln is produced by conduction, convection, and irradiation. The chamber's closed vaulting irradiates heat onto the pieces. Temperatures of up to 1,300° C are achieved. This type of kiln is needed for kaolinic clays such as those used to produce porcelain. However, the clays used in the West in medieval times could not support such high temperatures and melt down occurred at around 1,000° C. The updraft kiln was therefore better adapted to this type of clay, since it did not reach such high temperatures.

As regards decoration and coating techniques, particularly noteworthy was the diffusion of glaze coatings from the end of the thirteenth century onwards in the Western world, in certain workshops in the Christian kingdoms of the Iberian Peninsula and in Italy. This type of covering, with associated decorative motifs, had already been in regular use in Andalusi workshops since the tenth century, although glazed pottery has been documented in al-Andalus in the ninth century. The main glaze compound is silica in the form of quartz, to which other minerals are added. Transparent lead glazes were the most common. These could also be of tin. Tin oxide creates an opaqueness that eliminates the covering's transparent nature. Coloring substances could be added to this base: iron oxide, which provided a tonality ranging from yellow to brown; copper oxide, which gave green or bluish colorings; cobalt oxide, which gave blues, with browns and blacks provided by manganese oxide. These substances could also be used to create decorative motifs. Such coverings and decorations were usually applied to previously fired vessels. After application, in order to obtain the glazed effect, the pieces would be fired for a second time. As in the case of the clay body, glaze tonalities would depend on the oxides used and the conditions of the firing process, i.e., within a reducing or oxidizing atmosphere.

Glazed pottery in the West is a characteristic feature of low medieval production from the thirteenth century onwards. Production methods are characteristic of highly specialized workshops generating a substantial quantity of pieces, with highly standardized repertoires that also contain a wide variety of shapes. Distribution is characterized by regional and long-distance commercialization, as with other types of manufacturing. A distinction should also be made between luxury production and production intended for a more common use, although these might be equally diverse in terms of forms, and may have been produced under the same production conditions. Pottery acquisition and use in the Low Middle Ages, like that of other manufactured goods, was general throughout all social levels. Only luxury wares had more restricted customers.

In al-Andalus, production, distribution, and use follow a similar process of evolution, but the chronologies are different. The consolidation of commercial networks around towns seems to have occurred rather earlier, especially in the areas closest to Córdoba, where from the tenth century production in specialized workshops, using the pedal wheel, glazes, and varied standardized forms, was already a reality. Nevertheless, in al-Andalus as a whole, these conditions would not develop until the end of the tenth and the start of the eleventh century.

In conclusion therefore, the technical development that can be observed in medieval pottery production is not the result of one or several channels of diffusion, although some production may have been derived from imitating techniques in other workshops. This occurred for instance in the medieval workshops of the Christian kingdoms that conquered al-Andalus, where glazing techniques learned from the Andalusi potters were developed. Yet, even in this case, the adoption of more sophisticated forming, decorating and firing techniques is closely linked to very specific forms of the production, distribution and use of pottery and manufactured goods in general, in an urban and commercial context which is sufficiently developed for production to be carried out under highly specialized craftwork conditions.

Bibliography

Cuomo di Caprio, N. *La ceramica in archeologia. Antiche tecniche di lavorazione e moderni metodi di indagine.* Roma: L'Erma di Bretschneider, 1985.

Kirchner, H. "Las técnicas y los conjuntos documentales. La cerámica." In Barceló, Miquel et al. *Arqueología Medieval. En las afueras del medievalismo.* Barcelona: Editorial Crítica, 1988: 88–133.

Orton, C., P. Tyers, and A. Vince. *Pottery in Archaeology.* New York: Cambridge University Press, 1993.

Rye, O. S. *Pottery Technology. Principles and Reconstruction.* Washington: Taraxacum, 1988.

Wickham, C. "Overview: Production, Distribution and Demand." In R. Hodges, and W. Bowden, eds. *The Sixth Century. Production, Distribution and Demand.* Leiden: E.J. Brill, 1998, pp. 279–292.

Wickham, Chris. "Overview: Production, Distribution and Demand, II." In I.L. Hansen and C. Wickham, eds. *The Long Eight Century. Production, Distribution and Demand.* Leiden: E.J. Brill, 2000, pp. 345–378.

HELENA KIRCHNER

PRINTING

The development of pictographs, hieroglyphs, syllabaries, alphabets, and other symbolic representations of language, written or inscribed on any number of surfaces (papyrus, clay tablets, wax tablets, palm leaves, etc.), is the process that separates what we conventionally think of as history from prehistory. Prior to the mid-fifteenth century, each piece of writing, whatever its alphabet or other system, whatever its tools, whatever its surface or medium, was an individually made object. If one copy of a text existed, and a second was wanted, the latter would have to be made again by a fresh stint of handwork. Then about 1450 in Europe, a new invention, typographic printing, was developed, by which texts could be multiplied in notionally identical copies, all within a single process of production. Within twenty to twenty-five years, this invention radically changed the tempo and scale of bookmaking, which in turn radically changed the systems of book distribution, the prices of books, readers' expectations for books, and so on.

About Johann Gutenberg, the inventor of European printing, there are some thirty documentary records from 1430 to his death in early 1468. Yet none of these, or almost none, can be said to reveal a living personality or temperament that speaks to us. Gutenberg was born in Mainz in the patrician family of Gensfleisch. In 1430 Johann Gutenberg and other Mainz patricians were in exile, but a peace organized by the archbishop allowed them to return. Gutenberg was probably then residing in the Rhine metropolis of Strassburg. That, at any rate, is where he is found in 1434, and where he seems to have lived, perhaps not continuously, for the next decade. The nature of Gutenberg's work in Strassburg has been the subject of generations-old discussion and controversy. In one of several partnerships Gutenberg formed in the late 1430s, he taught gemstone polishing, *stein bollieren.* Another was concerned with the making of "mirrors." A partner in this venture, Andreas Dritzehn, died suddenly at Christmastide 1438, and his brothers made claims against Gutenberg. One of their witnesses swore that when Andreas died he had in his house a press and other related equipment; and that Gutenberg asked Andreas's brother Claus to take apart the pieces lying in the press, so that no one should understand their function. Another witness, a goldsmith, said that about three years earlier Gutenberg had paid him one hundred florins "only for that relating to printing" (*alleine daz czu den trucken gehöret*).

Most commentators have assumed that the Strassburg documents of 1439 refer in obscure terms to early typographic experiments. However, the most careful scholar, Kurt Köster, argued that the press and other equipment mentioned in the documents related directly to the "mirror" project—the manufacture of reflective badges which were supposed to be able to capture the virtuous emanations of the saintly relics when they were publicly displayed. In Köster's view, to assume that the words "press" and "printing" in themselves indicate proto-typographical experiments is anachronistic. It may be possible, nonetheless, that among "all Gutenberg's arts and projects" in Strassburg (*alle sin künste und afentur*), there were experiments in typography. The papal secretary Mattia Palmieri of Pisa compiled annals during his years in Rome from 1450 onward. Among his records was an entry that "Johann Gutenberg zum Jungen, patrician of Mainz on the Rhine, with great genius invented in 1440 a means of printing books." It is conceivable, though unprovable, that this is based on an authentic statement from Gutenberg, transmitted to Palmieri via the early German printers in Rome.

In any case, by late 1448 Gutenberg had returned to Mainz, and sometime in the following years we first find physical survivals of early printing experiments: a small fragment of the *Sibyllenbuch*, and similar fragments of several editions of the Latin grammar of Donatus. These are plausibly earlier, perhaps even several years earlier, than the first precisely datable piece of Mainz printing: the thirty-one-line Cyprus Indulgence, of which copies were distributed no later than October 1454.

From the earliest Mainz fragments onward there is good evidence that Gutenberg's printing system was conceptually and materially identical to subsequent European (and eventually extra-European) printing as it

was practiced for centuries to come. Its basis was the use of movable metal types—it would be better to call them recycling types—each bearing on its face in relief a distinctive letter or character in reverse image; a viscous, oil-based ink strikingly denser and darker than scribal inks ("not common ink," as Peter Schoeffer put it in one of his colophons); and a levered, screw-action press, whose plate produced a powerful, even impression when brought down over a piece of paper or vellum laid on top of an inked page of the composed types. After the required number of impressions was printed of a particular page, the types were recycled: cleaned, taken out of the composed page, and returned to the correct boxes of their typecase. Because of this recycling, a relatively small supply of type—say, enough to compose three or four pages of text without running out of any necessary characters—was sufficient for printing texts of any length and in as many copies as were wanted.

An important consequence is that in almost all early printed books of more than a few pages, impressions from the same pieces of type will appear recurrently, in different places on different pages from beginning to end; but never, of course, twice on the same page. If the types of a given letter are essentially identical—if they are all, for instance, correctly cast from the same mold and are in fresh condition—this recurrence of single types on different pages will be invisible. But if some of the types are deformed or otherwise damaged in ways that change the face of their characters, they become distinctive, and can be traced from one page to another.

The common opinion of the last hundred years and more has been that from Gutenberg onward, types were cast in stable, long-lived molds, so that hundreds of essentially identical a's, b's, c's, and so on, could be cast from their respective molds. It was believed that each letter or character was engraved on the end of an individual hard-metal punch, and that the punches were hammered into blanks of softer metal to create stable matrices. Certainly it seems to be true that by 1500, and probably by 1480 or a few years before, that is how most founts of type were made, and continued to be made for hundreds of years.

But the earliest types are different. Recent typographic investigations have considerably revised our picture of how Gutenberg and the other printers of the first generation made their types. Detailed digital photography of early printing, and mathematical comparisons of the sizes, shapes, and angles of the individual type impressions have shown that in these books, on any given page, no two impressions of any given character are identical. The angles of strokes, and other measurements, are different—sometimes strikingly different—from one impression to another of what by the received opinion ought to be virtually identical types. The variations go beyond the slight fluctuations that might be explained by differences in inking and impression. We are led to conclude that these earliest European types do not derive from stable metal matrices struck by individual letter-punches. They were made by some other process, by which the shapes of an "a" (b, c, etc.) were individually

Engraving of 1520 showing a printing press.
(Corbis/Bettmann)

constructed in matrices of some plastic medium such as fine sand. These "ad hoc" matrices could be cast into only once, then had to be refashioned for every subsequent casting of a letter.

The hypothesis of sandcasting or its equivalent for making the earliest types is not new; it was suggested in 1853 by Auguste Bernard. However, the proponents of sandcasting assumed that the forms pressed into the sand to create temporary molds consisted of complete, finished letter shapes. These recent investigations indicate rather that each such mold was an individual construction, with its letter form shaped by the impression of a variety of smaller elements to create the shafts, curves, oblique strokes, and terminal lozenges. To the best of our present knowledge this form of typemaking—"cuneiform typography," in the phrase of its investigators—was the system used for all the European typefonts, and hence of all the first printers, up to about 1470. The time and stages of transition to "conventional" punch-matrix typography remain to be discovered. The most that can be said at the moment is that by the later 1470s a scattering of Italian printing-trade documents, most notably the 1480 will of Nicolas Jenson, begin to refer clearly to punches and matrixes as the sources for type.

The small variations in letter shapes inevitable in cuneiform typography went unnoticed by the first readers of printed books, just as they did by even the keenest eyes of later incunabulists. In such a book as the Gutenberg Bible, the effect of the printed page was one of striking sharpness and regularity. When Aeneas Silvius, the future Pope Pius II, saw sample sheets of the Gutenberg Bible at the Imperial diet in Frankfurt in October 1454, he reported to his friend Cardinal Carvajal in Rome that the sheets were "exceedingly clean and correct in their script, and without error, such as Your Excellency could read effortlessly without glasses."

The grand achievement of the Gutenberg Bible (1455) did not mark the end of Gutenberg's typographic experiments. Two more major experiments were carried out in the early Mainz years, one of which was certainly

Gutenberg's, the other of which possibly involved him, or possibly was carried out entirely by Johann Fust and his son-in-law Peter Schoeffer after the breakup of their partnership with Gutenberg. This latter experiment was color printing, whereby not just the black letter of text, but also the red and blue of initial letters (including decorative work for major initials), such as were usually added later by rubricators, were printed in a single press operation. This was a particularly complex undertaking, and only a few books were produced by means of it. The earliest was the Mainz Psalter of 1457, which was conspicuously signed by the new partnership of Johann Fust and Peter Schoeffer. Whether Gutenberg himself participated in the three-color experiments cannot be clearly determined. There is at least a hint that he did: a variant of one of the versal initials of the 1457 Psalter later shows up in Gutenberg's stock.

The second experiment was a more interesting one, and can be securely attributed to Gutenberg: the invention of a system for, so to speak, freezing typographic compositions. As noted above, the central idea of Gutenberg's first invention was that types recycle continuously, from page to page, so that a relatively small type supply, perhaps a few dozen kilos of typemetal in the simplest case, could in principle suffice for producing any book. But this beautifully "minimalist" conception also carried a drawback: every composed page of type had only a brief lifespan, as it went through the press to print a fixed number of impressions. If even a few days later you wanted to print that page again, you had to reset it from the beginning.

Facilitating Subsequent Editions

At the end of the 1450s Gutenberg developed a solution. Recycling types were composed into lines of text in the usual way. But instead of being locked up in type pages and sent to press, these lines were gathered in pairs, and impressed into a plastic medium such as had been used to make the single types themselves, thus creating a temporary mold containing the complete image of two text lines. Thin typemetal strips were cast into these secondary molds, and these, assembled into pages, made up the printing surface from which the books in question were printed. After being printed from, the strips were disassembled and stored, probably page for page. They could be quickly reassembled in the future, whenever (or if ever) a new edition of that text was called for.

Three books—two brief religious pamphlets, and the giant Latin dictionary of Giovanni Balbi, the *Catholicon*—were printed by this system, c. 1459–1460. The strips for these three books were retained, and after Gutenberg's death were used again to print new impressions. These new impressions are textually identical to the original impressions, except in subtle ways that for long were overlooked by bibliographers: they are on different paper supplies from the earlier ones; they embody a few minor accidents to the pairs of lines; and the pairs shift slightly in position from one impression to the next. The Catholicon shop—it printed an Indulgence

broadside as late as 1464—is our last evidence for Gutenberg's activity as a printer. In 1465, he was taken into the retinue of the archbishop of Mainz, on terms which must have been essentially a pension; and by the beginning of 1468 he had died.

This last invention of Gutenberg's was perhaps not a financial success. The paired-line technology reached a dead end, whereas the movable-type technology flourished astonishingly. But both inventions deserve our admiration for the clarity of their underlying ideas. Many later generations of printers saw the advantages that could result from not having to reset every new piece of printing. A wide variety of inventions of later centuries solved or tried to solve the same problem in different ways: by means of stereotype (conceptually identical to Gutenberg's two-line strips), Monotype and Linotype composition, and photographic offset printing, to name only some of the chief stages.

Printing may be thought of under two aspects: as a specific technology or group of technologies; and as an idea that can be brought, or could have been brought, into being by any of various different technologies. As the history of Far Eastern books shows, the mechanical multiplication of texts goes back centuries before Gutenberg lived. Techniques such as those used for the striking of coins and seals could have been modified to produce multiplied texts even in the pre-Christian era of the West. The introduction of paper into Europe has often been mentioned as one of the enabling events for typography, but printing could have been done with equal facility on papyrus and parchment. The primary but lacking requirement for many centuries before the fifteenth had been not a specific technique—a specific form of metalworking—but rather the idea itself. It may well be that toward the middle of the fifteenth century the general idea of multiplying texts had presented itself to others beside Gutenberg. Perhaps the most suggestive hints that this was the case lie in two documents of the 1440s. In Venice, 1447, a document referred to "*alcune forme da stanpar donadi et salteri*": Donatuses and Psalters. Similarly, but hundreds of miles distant, the abbot of Cambrai, Jean Le Robert, recorded in 1446 and 1451 having bought in Bruges and Valenciennes copies of the *Doctrinale* of Alexander de Villa Dei which had been "*jettez en moule.*" In neither case can we connect the suggestive words with any physical survivals, but it is surely significant that all the texts involved were schoolbooks, just as the largest single group of earliest Mainz printing is represented by fragments of various editions of the Donatus *Ars minor.* The techniques that lay behind these Venetian and Flemish references to lost books can only be guessed at.

In its first fifteen years the new invention spread slowly. Before 1465, only a handful of towns saw printing shops within their walls, and only Mainz had produced a substantial number of printed works. In the following decade, roughly 1465–1475, the diffusion was broader and notably more rapid. About seventy new towns over a wide expanse of Europe gave homes to printing shops: as far north as Lübeck, and as far south as Reggio di Calabria; as far east as Kraków and Budapest, and as far west as Segovia. By 1475 some two thousand printed editions had been produced and distributed in hundreds of thousands of copies. It is essentially in this quarter-century that the interrelated trades of printing and printed-book publishing were born, and had come to involve several hundred or more people, scarcely any of whose names we know. Some shops were entirely anonymous in their output. But even where we have the name of the owner or chief figure of a shop—say, Johann Mentelin, first printer in Strasbourg—we scarcely ever know the names of the shop personnel, let alone of those who transmitted sheets of printed books from one town to another. Yet it is through the mostly undocumented movements of those workers that the printing trade dispersed and expanded, and that their products came into the hands of readers.

A realistic measure of the spread of printing must bring into account many related factors: geographical spread; number of shops; number of editions; sizes of the books produced, sizes of paper, and varying formats; numbers of copies printed. It must also take into account the failures of shops, which in most cases was presumably a failure in the marketing of their editions. For many of these factors, the available data are few or almost non-existent: quantification is not possible. And in the end all this is only groundwork or background for still more detailed analysis of what is perhaps the fundamental, but widely neglected question: precisely what texts were printed, and for whom?

By 1475, the printed book had become a common object of European literate culture, especially of Latin-language culture. Hand copying of texts still continued, but by this date there were hundreds of central texts that could now in principle be supplied by the printed-book market. These included the majority of the most commonly used works of Latin learning, from the elements of the language to classical letters; and on to technical works of Aristotelian thought, of civil and canon law, of Bibles and theology. The printed supply of even more specialized literature in printed form, such as medical writings, was just getting under way, as also of Breviaries and Missals. By the close of the next quarter century, 1500, the techniques developed by Gutenberg had spread across Europe and the printed book had become not just common, but, in a real sense, standard; not just for Latin writings, but also for classical Greek and for the major vernacular literatures of Europe.

See also **Paper**

Bibliography

Davies, Martin. *The Gutenberg Bible*. London: British Library, 1996.

Ing, Janet T. *Johann Gutenberg and his Bible: A Historical Study*. New York: Typophiles, 1988.

Köster, Kurt. *Gutenberg in Straßburg: Das Aachenspiegel-Unternehmen und die unbekannte afentur und kunst*. Mainz: Gutenberg-Gesellschaft, 1973.

Needham, Paul. Johann Gutenberg and the Catholicon Press.

Papers of the Bibliographical Society of America (1982) 76: 395–456.

——. The Paper Supply of the Gutenberg Bible. *Papers of the Bibliographical Society of America* (1985) 79: 303–374.

——. "The Text of the Gutenberg Bible." In *Trasmissione dei Testi a Stampa nel Periodo Moderno*, edited by Giovanni Crapulli. 2 vols. Rome: Ateneo: 1985–1987: II: 43–84.

——. Haec sancta ars: Gutenbergs Invention as a Divine Gift. *Grolier Club Gazette* (1990) 42: 101–120.

Hans Widmann, ed. *Der gegenwärtige Stand der Gutenberg-Forschung*. Stuttgart: A. Hiersemann, 1972.

PAUL NEEDHAM

PROFATIUS JUDAEUS

Jacob ben Makhir Ibn Tibbon was an astronomer and translator active in southern France in the late thirteenth century. He was probably born in Marseilles c. 1236, and he died in Montpellier in 1304. He is also known by his Provençal name, Don Profiat Tibbon, as well as by the Latinized form for it, Profatius (or Prophatius) Judaeus. He was a member of the Ibn Tibbon family, a group of physicians and translators of science books who lived in southern France in the twelfth and thirteenth centuries, including Samuel ben Judah Ibn Tibbon (d. 1232) and his son Moses ben Samuel Ibn Tibbon (d. 1283), Jacob's uncle.

Jacob was educated in Lunel and spent most of his working life in Montpellier where he studied medicine. His efforts were mainly devoted to translations from Arabic into Hebrew, and among the authors whose works he translated we find some Greek scientists but mostly astronomers from the Middle East or al-Andalus, the Muslim part of the Iberian peninsula. All but one of his translations dealt with astronomy, namely, Averroes' commentary on Aristotle's *History of Animals*. The first text he translated (c. 1255) seems to have been the Arabic version of *Euclid's *Elements*, soon followed by the treatise of Qusta ibn Luqa (ninth century) on the use of a spherical astrolabe. Jacob translated into Hebrew a treatise on a special type of astrolabe, the *Azafea*, by the eleventh-century Toledan astronomer *Ibn al-Zarqalluh (Azarquiel), and in 1263 he collaborated with John of Brescia in translating it into Latin, as we are informed by the *explicit* of the Latin version: *Profatius gentis hebreorum uulgarizante et Johanne Brixiensi in latinum reducente*. That was about the same time as this book by Azarquiel was translated into Castilian at the court of *Alfonso X of Castile, and about three decades later than Judah ben Moses ha-Cohen, a Jew in the service of the Castilian king, translated the *Azafea* into Latin with the help of a Christian. We note that both Judah ben Moses and Jacob ben Makhir collaborated with a Christian to translate an Arabic text into Latin, using an intermediary vernacular language.

Jacob ben Makhir is credited with other translations from Arabic into Hebrew: the Arabic version of Euclid's *Data* by Ishaq ibn Hunayn (ninth century), and the Arabic versions of the *Spherics* by Menelaus of Alexandria and of *On the Moving Sphere* by Autolycus of Pitane. In 1271 or 1275 Jacob rendered into Hebrew *On the Configuration of the World* by Ibn al-Haytham, known in the West as Alhazen (d. c. 1040). Finally, at unknown dates, Jacob translated two other treatises written by Andalusi astronomers: the *Islah al-Majisti* (*Correction of the Almagest*) by Jabir ibn Aflah of Seville (twelfth century), a severe critic of *Ptolemy's astronomy; and a treatise on the use of the astrolabe by Ahmad ibn al-Saffar (eleventh century), probably from Córdoba.

Besides these and possibly other translations that have been attributed to him, Profatius Judaeus is the author of at least two original works, both devoted to astronomy. The first is a treatise in Hebrew written between 1288 and 1293 on a quadrant of his own invention: an astronomical instrument designed to measure the altitude of celestial bodies. Jacob devised a new type of quadrant and called it "quadrant of Israel," but it was soon known as *quadrans novus* (new quadrant), as opposed to the *quadrans vetus* (old quadrant), a traditional type of quadrant the description of which is attributed to Guillelmus Anglicus in 1231, and the tenth-century *quadrans vetustissimus*. The *quadrans novus* is known today as the astrolabe quadrant and it is indeed a planispheric astrolabe presented in a quarter of a circle. Jacob wrote an expanded version of his treatise in 1301 which is only extant in Latin. The first version was translated into Latin in 1299 by Armengaud Blaise with the help of Jacob himself, and the second by Peter of Saint Omer c. 1309.

Another treatise on an astronomical instrument has been attributed to Profatius. This work is entitled *De armillis* and consists of instructions to construct an equatorium (a device for representing planetary models that allows the user to determine planetary positions without recourse to computations), but this attribution is still controversial.

The *Almanach perpetuum*

The work that gave Jacob most renown is a particular set of astronomical tables called *Almanach perpetuum*. It is extant in various Hebrew codices, and its translation into Latin is preserved in many manuscripts. The Latin incipit of the canons reads: *Quia omnes homines naturaliter scire desiderant*. In 1323 Andalò di Negro wrote a new set of canons to Jacob's almanac, adapting them to his city, Genoa. Jacob's almanac is also known as the almanac of Dante Alighieri (d. 1321), for the Florentine poet owned a copy and used it in his writings. The entries in the tables in the almanac were calculated for the meridian of Montpellier on the basis of the Toledan Tables and were aimed at providing the positions of the Sun, the Moon, and the five planets, directly, without any additional computations. The tables for the daily positions of the Sun begin on March 1, 1301, and those for the planets on various days in March 1300. The almanac also contains tables for the computation of eclipses and several tables for purposes of interpolation. Profatius's *Almanach perpetuum* was highly regarded by subsequent astronomers, and it was mentioned and praised by outstanding astronomers such as *Abraham Zacuto in the fifteenth century, Copernicus and Reinhold in the sixteenth century, and Johannes Kepler in the seventeenth century.

See also **Almanacs; Astrolabes and quadrants; Elements and qualities**

Bibliography

Boffito, J. and C. Melzi d'Eril. *Almanach Dantis Aligherii sive Profhacii Judaei Montispessulani Almanach Perpetuum ad annum 1300 inchoatum*. Florence: L. S. Olschki, 1908.

Millás Vallicrosa, J. M. *Don Profeit Tibbon. Tractat de l'assafea d'Azarquiel*. Barcelona: Arts Gràfiques, 1933.

Toomer, G. J. Prophatius Judaeus and the Toledan Tables, *Centaurus* (1973) 64: 351–355.

JOSÉ CHABÁS

PSEUDO-ARISTOTLE

Throughout the Middle Ages works falsely ascribed to Aristotle played a significant role in the transmission and assimilation of his philosophy. Well over one hundred pseudo-Aristotelian treatises circulated in the period. They can be divided into three groups on the basis of their original language: Latin, Greek, or Arabic.

Latin Works

Very few Latin works were attributed to Aristotle. Two typical examples are *De tempestatum presagiis*, a section of Pliny the Elder's *Natural History* (XVIII. 342–365) on weather prediction, and the *Ars notaria*, a treatise on shorthand written in the late twelfth century by the English monk John of Tilbury. In both cases the misattribution seemingly occurred through an accident of manuscript transmission. It is easier to see why Aristotle was thought to be the author of *De sex principiis*. This logical tract, dating from the twelfth century, was intended as a supplement to the *Categories*, and regularly featured as an appendix in manuscripts of the *Organon*. It was later assigned, also wrongly, to the twelfth-century scholar Gilbert of Poitiers.

Greek Works

Several Greek pseudo-Aristotelian texts, mostly coming from the Peripatetic school, were translated into Latin in the thirteenth century. *Robert Grosseteste, in addition to translating the *Nicomachean Ethics* and the first two books of *De caelo*, produced a Latin version of *De lineis indivisibilibus*, a treatise on the indivisibility of lines, which was later paraphrased by *Albertus Magnus. *Thomas Aquinas reported, however, that some assigned the tract to Aristotle's successor Theophrastus—an attribution which goes back to antiquity.

The most prolific medieval translator of Greek pseudo-Aristotelian treatises was Bartholomaeus of Messina. We know from manuscript colophons that, at the behest of

Manfred, King of Sicily from 1258 to 1266, he produced Latin versions of the *Problemata*, *De mirabilibus auscultationibus*, *De principiis*, *De signis*, and the *Magna moralia*, all of which he regarded as genuine works of Aristotle. Bartholomaeus is also credited, on stylistic grounds, with the translations of *De coloribus*, most likely by Theophrastus, and *De mundo*, a cosmological tract probably dating from the first century B.C.E. or C.E. The latter treatise, which is preceded by a letter from Aristotle to Alexander the Great, was translated into Arabic in the ninth century, from a sixth-century Syriac version of the Greek text, and became closely associated in the Islamic world with the Alexander romance.

In 1295 Durandus de Alvernia revised an earlier anonymous Latin version of the *Oeconomica*, a pseudo-Aristotelian treatise on household management, the third book of which no longer survives in Greek. There is a complete extant Greek text of *De plantis* or *De vegetabilibus*, a botanical treatise preserved in one hundred fifty-nine manuscripts. It was produced, however, by a thirteenth-century Byzantine scholar from *Alfred of Sareschel's late twelfth-century Latin version of an Arabic translation made around 900, via a ninth-century Syriac intermediary, of a lost Greek work written by Nicholas of Damascus in the first century C.E. While the Greek *De plantis* still appears in modern editions of Aristotle, *De inundatione Nili*, a tract on the flooding of the Nile, which has a good claim to authenticity and which survives in a frequently copied thirteenth-century Latin translation, has been excluded from the Aristotelian canon on the grounds that no Greek exemplar has ever been identified.

Arabic Works

The majority of Arabic pseudo-Aristotelian works, many of which were translated into Latin in the Middle Ages, deal with occult subjects: *astrology, physiognomy, *alchemy, and chiromancy. Others contain Greek philosophical material, though more often Platonic and Neoplatonic than Aristotelian. The *Theology*, for instance, was compiled in the ninth or tenth century, probably in Syria, and derives mainly from Books IV–VI of Plotinus's *Enneads*. Immensely influential among Muslim philosophers, it was unknown in the West until the early sixteenth century. By contrast, the *Liber de causis*, a ninth-century work from Baghdad, which was adapted from Proclus's *Elements of Theology*, made little impact on the Arabic world but survives in over two hundred copies in the twelfth-century Latin translation by *Gerard of Cremona. Usually seen as a complement to the *Metaphysics*, it became part of the Aristotelian curriculum at the University of Paris in 1255 and attracted commentaries by, among others, *Roger Bacon, *Siger of Brabant, and Albertus Magnus. But in his commentary of 1272, Thomas Aquinas, who had read *William of Moerbeke's 1268 Latin translation of the *Elements of Theology*, correctly surmised that the *Liber de causis* was put together by an Arab scholar using excerpts from Proclus's treatise. The *Liber de pomo*, a

tenth-century Arabic work modeled on *Plato's *Phaedo*, portrays Aristotle's death-bed conversation with his pupils, during which the philosopher keeps himself alive long enough to assert his belief in the immortality of the soul and the creation of the world by smelling the life-giving fragrance of an apple. Translated into Hebrew around 1235, and then from Hebrew into Latin, purportedly by King Manfred of Sicily, it exists in some one hundred manuscripts, often together with genuine works, and provided support for the claim that Aristotle's philosophy was compatible with Christianity.

De causis proprietatum elementorum, a treatise on the properties of elements, was translated by Gerard of Cremona from a lost ninth-century Arabic original. Although there are one hundred twenty-seven extant manuscripts, there is only one commentary on it, by Albertus Magnus. *De mineralibus*, a brief extract on minerals from the *Kitab ash-shifa* (*Book of Healing*) by *Ibn Sina (Avicenna), was translated into Latin by Alfred of Sareschel, who appended it to Book IV of the *Meteorology*. Although usually regarded as an authentic part of Aristotle's treatise, some scholastics, including Roger Bacon and Albertus Magnus, recognized its Arabic origins.

By far the most successful pseudo-Aristotelian work was the *Secret of Secrets*, which was more widely diffused than any genuine treatise of Aristotle. According to the proem, it was first translated from Greek into Syriac and then from Syriac into Arabic in the ninth century. No Greek original has been found, however, and the earliest Arabic fragments date from the mid-tenth century. The core of the treatise is a lengthy letter from Aristotle to Alexander containing political and moral advice. Through the accretion of miscellaneous information on magic, astrology, alchemy, and physiognomy, the letter grew into an encyclopedic work. A partial Latin version from the middle of the twelfth century, probably by *John of Seville, survives in one hundred fifty manuscripts, while a complete translation by Philip of Tripoli, dating from the first half of the thirteenth century, exists in some three hundred fifty copies. Despite this extensive dissemination, it did not usually accompany authentic works of Aristotle, and was never printed in an edition of his works. Roger Bacon was the only medieval philosopher to write a commentary on it. The *Secret of Secrets* was also translated from Arabic into Hebrew in the late thirteenth or early fourteenth century and from Hebrew into Russian. The two Latin translations spawned versions in many European vernaculars—nine in English alone, plus others in German, French, Catalan, Portuguese, and Italian—making this pseudo-Aristotelian treatise one of the most popular books of the Middle Ages.

See also **Aristotelianism; Translation movements**

Bibliography

Aristotle, Pseudo-. *The Apple or Aristotle's Death (De pomo sive De morte Aristotilis)*. Translated by Mary F. Rousseau. Milwaukee: Marquette University Press, 1968.

———. *Secretum secretorum: Nine English Versions.* Vol. I: *Text.* Edited by M. A. Manzalaoui. Oxford: Oxford University Press, 1977.

———. *The Liber de causis.* Translated by D. J. Brand. Milwaukee: Marquette University Press, 1984.

Kraye, Jill. *Classical Traditions in Renaissance Philosophy.* Variorum Collected Studies Series CS 743. Aldershot: Ashgate, 2002. Articles IX–XV: "The Aristotelian Canon."

Kraye, Jill, W. F. Ryan and C. B. Schmitt, eds. *Pseudo-Aristotle in the Middle Ages: The Theology and Other Texts.* Warburg Institute Surveys and Texts XI. London: The Warburg Institute, 1986.

Ryan, W. F. and Charles B. Schmitt, eds. *Pseudo-Aristotle, The Secret of Secrets: Sources and Influences.* Warburg Institute Surveys and Texts IX. London: The Warburg Institute, 1982.

Schmitt, Charles B. and Dilwyn Knox. *Pseudo-Aristoteles Latinus: A Guide to Latin Works Falsely Attributed to Aristotle before 1500.* Warburg Institute Surveys and Texts XII. London: The Warburg Institute, 1985.

Williams, Steven J. *The Secret of Secrets: The Scholarly Career of a Pseudo-Aristotelian Text in the Latin Middle Ages.* Ann Arbor: University of Michigan Press, 2003.

JILL KRAYE

PSYCHOLOGY

The modern term "psychology" arises from the ancient distinction between the body and the soul; its subject is the non-bodily, "mental" or "spiritual" aspect of a living human character. Its medieval equivalent would have been the study of the soul and its functions, and the debate on the nature of the soul was central to both religious and secular learned traditions.

Discussions of the human soul have, broadly speaking, a threefold origin: in religion, philosophy, and medicine. From about the twelfth century there was a widely accepted consensus, especially in medicine, about the nature of the soul, but in earlier periods there had always been differing views, and the terminology was frequently difficult and at times ambiguous.

Religion and Philosophy

Both Christianity and Islam posited an immortal human soul, separable from the body, and destined after death for a divine judgment by which it would be assigned, depending on the conduct of the human being in life, to eternal punishment or reward. St. Paul stressed the conflict between the immortal destiny of the soul and the immediate and pressing demands and desires of the body in Galatians 5:17: "The flesh lusteth against the spirit; and the spirit against the flesh"; Christians were exhorted to exercise bodily self-discipline and restraint in order to liberate the soul from concerns for the transient life in this world; religious discussion of the soul was generally focused on its moral capacities.

Religious views on the soul were heavily influenced by the thought of the ancient Greek philosophers, especially *Plato and Aristotle. Both thinkers were deeply interested in the nature of man, and Aristotle conducted detailed research into the natural world. They held that the human capacity for reason and thought was unique among all other known organisms. A fundamental premise of Greek philosophy was that everything is made up of "matter," the shapeless stuff which provides the substance of all physical things, and "form," the pattern or shape by which that matter is organized into a particular thing. Thus a human body is made up of matter, the four elements, and is a human by virtue of a "form" which makes that matter a human, not a lion or a lettuce. Without the presence of a form, the elements dissolve again into their constituent parts, as a mortal body decays after death. Plato and Aristotle argued that the human intellect learned by discovering how to grasp the non-material "ideas" or "forms" from the multiplicity of experience: by seeing individual chairs, the mind comes to a sense of what "chair" means, abstracted from any individual characteristic. In grasping abstractions, the mind is able to generate principles and engage in reasoning general rules. This purely human capability led the two philosophers to argue for some sort of immortality for the human soul.

Aristotle's *On the Soul* provided a detailed discussion of the various forms of life, which the author viewed as an increasingly sophisticated series of forms: plants, animals, and humans, as things having life, are first distinguished from inanimate matter, and are then discussed in terms of their increasing complexity and capacities. The forms of animate beings are seen as "souls": The lettuce has a form that enables it to feed and grow; the lion's form endows the creature with all the powers of the plant, but adds the five senses and the ability to move; the human form confers the additional power of reason. In each case, the form is the creature's "soul," but only in the human soul is there something more than the realizing of the powers of the body. In a famously obscure passage (*On the Soul*, III 5), Aristotle hints that, since reason has no organ, the soul is not entirely dependent on its bodily organism in the way that an animal's is.

One crucial difference between Plato and Aristotle, however, was that Plato believed that the "ideas" of things had an existence independent of matter, and could be grasped in contemplation by the trained human mind. Aristotle held that the forms had existence only when embodied in matter, and that human minds always needed particular examples in order to grasp them. Plato held that the soul had a pre-existing memory of ideas, and that it could gradually learn to escape from its dependence on the body; Aristotle held that the soul was a "blank slate," and always needed the aid of bodily powers to enable it to think. In later medieval summaries, Plato was said to have held that a human was a soul using or wearing, or even imprisoned, in a body; Aristotle believed that man was a being made up of soul and body, and that consequently neither a separated soul nor a corpse could properly be described as a human.

The views of Plato and Aristotle were enormously influential on Christianity. The works of Plato were mostly not directly available to the Latin Middle Ages, but the church father Augustine of Hippo was deeply impressed by the similarity of Plato's views to those of St. Paul, and handed on in his writings a profoundly Platonic portrayal of the soul, with its innate knowledge of God and goodness, at odds with the mortal prison in which it finds itself in this world. Augustine's views provide a continuous current within Christian thought.

Medicine

In the medical tradition the distinction between soul and body was chiefly apparent in the fundamental mandate of the physician: physicians were charged with keeping people alive, and preserving whatever it is that distinguishes a living body from a dead one. The soul for them was essentially life, the "breath of life" or "spirit of life" which keeps the heart beating and the lungs breathing. The soul of the philosophers, the intellectual powers or the mind, also concerned medical practitioners: it was immediately apparent that, however non-material thought may be, it could still be powerfully impeded by damage to the material organ of the brain. If reason had no organ, as the philosophers argued, how could it be affected by damage to part of the body? Physicians found a solution to this problem by positing a third term, the "bodily spirit," as a medium between the immaterial soul and the physical body. (They derived this idea ultimately from Stoic philosophy: The Stoics believed that everything was made up of matter, although some matter was too subtle for our senses to perceive.) Physicians envisaged the bodily spirit as the subtlest kind of matter in the universe below the Moon: like a kind of gas, it could not be perceived by the senses, but it was nonetheless material, and its departure from the body broke the link between body and soul, form and matter, and constituted death. The second-century physician *Galen handed on a unified medical synthesis, combining Greek philosophy, Hippocratic medical theory, and the Stoic conception of the pneuma or spirit, which dominated all medical ideas until the sixteenth century.

The idea of bodily spirit is confusing, both because it was the Stoic equivalent of "soul," and because St. Paul uses the word "spirit" where the philosophers use "soul." A small treatise which carefully points out the distinction between the soul and the bodily spirit, written by the Syrian philosopher-physician Costa ben Luca (d. c. 912), addressed the need to clarify the point. It was translated into Latin and widely read. Costa stresses that the soul is incorporeal, but that the spirit is a material body; the spirit is contained within the body, but the soul is not; the spirit, when separated from the body, perishes, but the soul does not.

Later Medieval Medical Theory of Bodily Spirit

Galen's medical theories were translated into Arabic, and summarized and synthesized by the great Arabian physicians, many of whom, such as Avicenna (*Ibn Sina), were philosophers as well as physicians. Their works, clarifying and elaborating on Galen and Aristotle, passed into the Latin west during the twelfth century, and provided the foundation of medical theory for at least the next four hundred years. This medical theory harmonized with philosophical and religious views.

The human soul, strictly speaking, fell outside the bounds of medicine, since it was held to be immortal and immaterial. Its existence, however, is presupposed by all medieval theorists, and the bodily spirit, through which it communicates with the body, was entirely within the physician's territory. The soul was defined as having various powers, which were classified as the three kinds of soul in the Aristotelian system. The "nutritive" or "vegetable" powers of nutrition, growth and reproduction corresponded to the plants; the "sensitive" powers of the five senses, the power of voluntary motion, and hence powers of imagination and memory to guide that motion, corresponded to the soul of the higher animals; all of these powers were effected within the body by the bodily spirits. The third kind of soul, the "rational" power, belonged to man (and angels), and its connection with the bodily spirits was debatable. Sometimes these three souls were envisaged diagrammatically as a triangle contained inside a square contained inside a circle.

Medically speaking, the system worked very elegantly. Every living human baby was born with a supply of vital spirit in the heart which was derived from the seed of its parents. The vital spirit, material but imperceptible to the senses, kept the human soul and body together. It was continually fed with the best blood of the heart, and supplemented with air drawn into the heart from the lungs. Some of this vital spirit was conveyed with the blood through the veins to the liver, where it effected the nutritive powers: it organized the nourishment of the body by creating blood from the food. Another part of the vital spirit, the finest and subtlest, made its way from the heart via the arteries to the base of the brain, where it was further refined in the *rete mirabile*, a "marvellous net" of arteries (now known to be mythical), and further augmented by air drawn in by the nostrils. This refined spirit, now called "animal spirit," was then drawn up to the series of interconnected cavities in the brain, the "brain ventricles," from which arose the nerves, hollow tubes which conveyed the animal spirit to all parts of the body. The nerves from the five senses met in the foremost ventricle, and conveyed all the sense impressions there; damage to the front ventricle was held to be the cause of hallucinations and disorders of perception. The spirit in the next ventricle effected some sort of judgment on the sense-impressions presented to it: In animals this was the instinct by which the lamb perceives the wolf, and "judges" it to be dangerous. This judgment then compels voluntary motion, and the lamb runs away. The spirit in the third ventricle at the back of the brain operated the power of memory, by which even animals could learn from their perceptions and remember associations. Man is complicated because in addition to these "sensitive" powers he had the power of reason, which, strictly speaking, had no organ. In the Aristotelian system, even reason needed the impressions from the senses to provide the raw material for thought, so if the ventricles, or the spirit within them, were damaged, thought became impossible. The rational soul was not itself subject to medicine, but its tools (the brain, the animal spirit, and the nerves), all of which were material things, were subject to medical intervention. What made man different from the animals were the power of rational choice, abstract thought, and the ability to overrule instinct.

The doctrine of the animal spirit in the brain accounted for a good deal of what we might call psychology: Its qualities explained the different kinds of perception. If, for instance, the spirit in the foremost ventricle were afflicted by excess coldness and dryness, it would be more receptive to images associated with melancholy; the sufferer would dream of dark and frightening things, and all perceptions would be tinged with the gloomy qualities of the spirit. Rational or instinctive judgment and memory could be affected by a moist and heated spirit, the kind generated by consumption of alcohol, because it would be unstable and unsuitable for serious thought; women and children were held to be intellectually inferior because their physical make-up rendered their brains unsuited to the steady labor of abstract thought. Memory varied according to the quality of the hindmost ventricle and the spirit within it.

Another area which would come under the modern idea of psychology may also be accounted for by the theory of bodily spirits: The vital spirit in the heart caused the psychological phenomena which we call the emotions. Medieval physicians—for example, Haly Abbas (*al-Majusi) in *Liber Regius* IV v–viii—considered the emotions to be "passions," physical effects suffered when the vital spirit is impacted by some external stimulus. Thus they explained that when an external occasion of joy was received by the human organism, the spirit in the heart was heated and expanded, and rushed out to all the extremities, warming and brightening the whole being. Conversely, sorrow or grief caused the spirit in the heart to contract and shrink inwards, causing a physical sensation of cold. The emotions are "passions" in the sense that the vital spirit was "passive" in regard to them: it suffered and responded to them. There are still expressions in the English language that reflect this theory: People may be "in high spirits" or "low spirited" or depressed; rage is "hot-spirited," and "sprightly" means cheerful. There had always to be a supply of spirits in the heart to maintain life, which medieval physicians seem to have regarded as analogous to a candle-flame. They knew that one could die of joy: the spirits rush out of the heart so enthusiastically that the flame goes out, like a candle in the wind. In death by sorrow the spirits huddle together and burn out like a dying wick. The theory of bodily spirits explained why we need air and nourishment to survive, and why death occurs with our "last breath": when we "expire" the spirits are finally breathed out of the body. For the scientist or physician, the theory of the bodily spirit provided a very satisfactory explanation of the psychophysical phenomena of human life, and left the subject of immortal soul and its moral choices to the moralist.

See also **Aristotelianism; Elements and qualities**

Bibliography

Aristotle. *De Anima*. Edited with introduction and commentary by Sir David Ross. Oxford: Clarendon Press, 1961.

Bartholomaeus Anglicus. *On the Properties of Things*. Translated by John Trevisa; edited by M.C. Seymour and others. Oxford: Clarendon Press, 1975.

Costa ben Luca [also known as Qusta ibn Luqa]. De differentia animae et spiritus. In *Excerpta e libro Alfredi Anglici De motu cordis*, edited by Carl Sigmund Barach. Innsbruck: 1878. An English translation may be found in John W. Livingston, Qusta ibn Luqa's Psycho-Physiological Treatise On the Difference Between the Soul and the Spirit. *Scripta Mediterranea* (1981) 2: 53–77.

Gruner, O. Cameron. *A Treatise on the Canon of Medicine of Avicenna*. London: Luzac & Co., 1930.

Harvey, E. Ruth. *The Inward Wits*. London: The Warburg Institute, 1975.

Wack, Mary Frances. *Lovesickness in the Middle Ages: The Viaticum and Its Commentaries*. Philadelphia: University of Pennsylvania Press, 1990.

Wolfson, Harry A. The Internal Senses in Latin, Arabic and Hebrew Philosophical Texts. *Harvard Theological Review* (1935) 28: 69–133.

RUTH HARVEY

PTOLEMY

Little is known about Ptolemy's life except for the scanty information contained in his own works. According to these, Claudius Ptolemaeus lived and worked in Alexandria in Egypt between about 100 and 175 C.E. In particular, he made astronomical observations during the years 127–141, as indicated in one of his earliest works, the *Almagest*. Ptolemy was a Roman citizen writing in Greek, descended from Hellenized ancestors. His name seems to a mixture of Greco-Egyptian ("Ptolemaeus") and Roman ("Claudius"). Many of his works are addressed to "Syros," who is otherwise unknown.

An inscription (now called the *Canobic Inscription*) engraved on a stele, now lost, erected in Canopus, about twelve miles (20 km) east of Alexandria in 149/150 C.E. contains a list of parameters for the planetary motions, in agreement for the most part with those in the *Almagest*. Written after the *Canobic Inscription* in about 150 C.E., the *Almagest*, Ptolemy's first major work, was entitled in Greek *Mathematike Syntaxis* (*Mathematical Composition*) and was later known as *Megiste Syntaxis* (*The Greatest Composition*). This title was rendered in Arabic as *Kitab al-majasti* and, after its translation from Arabic into Latin in the twelfth century, it was referred to as *Almagestum*. Ptolemy's fame rests mainly on the *Almagest*, a treatise arranged in thirteen books and, according to Toomer, "a masterpiece of clarity and method, superior to any ancient scientific textbook and with few peers from any period. But it is much more than that...."

After a general description of an Earth-centered universe, Book I explains the trigonometrical tools needed to follow the arguments in the rest of the *Almagest*. In particular, Ptolemy defined the chord function (Crd), closely related to the modern sine function: sin α = (Crd 2α)/120, and compiled a table of chords at 0;30° intervals. In Book II Ptolemy then focused on various problems of spherical trigonometry such as the determination of the obliquity of the ecliptic and the calculation of right and oblique ascensions, among others.

In Book III Ptolemy explained his solar theory. First he compared his own observations of equinoxes with those of Hipparchus (second century B.C.E.) and Meton (fifth century B.C.E.), and then fixed the length of the tropical year as 365;14,48 days, which was also Hipparchus's value. Starting from this parameter, Ptolemy derived the values for the mean motion of the Sun and the lengths of the seasons and, in order to explain the variation of the solar velocity, he constructed a geometrical model where the Sun moves with uniform angular velocity on a circle whose center is not the Earth.

Books IV and V are devoted to lunar theory. From various observations made by Babylonian astronomers, transmitted via Hipparchus, and his own, Ptolemy deduced the durations of different periods of lunar motion and determined the numerical values of the parameters to be used in his lunar model. Ptolemy improved Hipparchus's simple epicyclic model and, by comparing his observations with the computed positions of the Moon, he developed a much more refined lunar model. Ptolemy then analyzed the distances and apparent

Illuminated initial from the 1482 Ulm edition of Ptolemy's *Geography* showing the author holding an armillary sphere . (Corbis/Gianni Dagli Orti)

diameters of the Moon and the Sun as well as lunar parallax, all of which are needed in the computation of lunar and solar eclipses.

The theory of eclipses is explained in Book VI: Ptolemy presents tables and gives precise rules to calculate the circumstances of eclipses (times, limits, duration, magnitude, etc.) for any given place.

The fixed stars are the subject of Books VII and VIII. Ptolemy compares his own observations with those of Hipparchus and other astronomers, such as Aristyllos and Timocharis, and explains that the distances of the stars with respect to each other stay the same over time, although the whole starry sphere moves at a constant rate of precession of 1° in one hundred years. He then displayed a star catalogue of one thousand and twenty-two different stars and nebulae, distributed in forty-eight constellations, and for each star he gave its name or description, its longitude, latitude, and magnitude (ranging from one to six).

In Book IX Ptolemy ordered the planetary spheres, including the Sun and the Moon, with respect to the Earth as follows: Moon, Mercury, Venus, Sun, Mars, Jupiter, and Saturn. Using planetary periods of Babylonian origin, Ptolemy deduced the mean motions of the five planets and then proceeded to construct geometrical models for each of them, making the planets move with uniform angular velocity on a circle about a point (later called "equant") symmetrically placed on the opposite side of the center of the circle from the Earth on the apsidal line. The determination, based on a small number of observations, of the parameters of the five planets is found in Book IX (Mercury), Book X (Venus and Mars), and Book XI (Jupiter and Saturn). Finally, Books XII and XIII deal with two problems of remarkable difficulty: planetary retrogradation and stations, and planetary latitudes, respectively.

Written after the *Almagest*, The *Handy Tables* is another major work on astronomy, where Ptolemy gathered all the tables in the *Almagest*, revising and expanding them, and included an introductory text explaining their use. In the *Handy Tables* Ptolemy introduced a number of modifications and additions with respect to the *Almagest*. In addition to some improvements in the parameters embedded in various tables, a basic change has to do with the epoch of the tables: the era of Philip (noon, November 12, 324 B.C.E.) in the *Handy Tables*, instead of the era of Nabonassar (noon, February 26, 747 B.C.E.) used in the *Almagest*. The *Handy Tables* have survived through a text composed by Theon of Alexandria (fl. 360 C.E.).

Ptolemy wrote the *Planetary Hypotheses* in two books some time after the *Almagest* and the *Handy Tables*. This treatise is thus considered as Ptolemy's last thoughts on astronomy. It is partially preserved in Greek, but there exists an Arabic translation of the complete text. In the *Planetary Hypotheses*, Ptolemy made several changes in the parameters and the models, adding a "physical" approach to the geometrical models presented in the *Almagest* and a detailed arrangement of the planetary spheres according to their distances from the Earth. In the

Middle Ages, this cosmological system of nested spheres was known as the "Ptolemaic system."

The *Tetrabiblos*, meaning a treatise in four books, is concerned with the influences of the celestial bodies on terrestrial events. Ptolemy considered this work on *astrology as a natural complement to his textbook on mathematical astronomy, the *Almagest*, as he himself explicitly indicates in the introduction to Book I. The *Tetrabiblos*, also known as the *Quadripartitum* in its Latin translation, was regarded as the highest authority among practitioners of astrology during the Middle Ages and the early modern period.

Ptolemy's *Geography*

Ptolemy's treatise on cartography is arranged in eight books and bears the title *Geography*. It is based on a similar work by Marinos of Tyre (fl. 110 C.E.) and lists about eight thousand localities for which Ptolemy gave geographical coordinates (longitude and latitude). As presented by Ptolemy, the known world (the *oikoumene*) extended 180° in longitude, from the prime meridian through the Fortunate Isles (Canary Islands), and 90° in latitude, from 16;25° south to 63° north of the equator. The *Geography* also addresses the difficult problem of mapping the world. To represent the inhabited world on a plane surface, Ptolemy proposed two projections: the first is a conic projection resulting from mapping the sphere onto a cone tangent to it such that distances are preserved along meridians and along the parallel of Rhodes (36°N), whereas the second is a variant of it such that distances are preserved along meridians and the parallels through Thule (63°N), Syene (modern Aswan in Egypt) (23;50°N), and the parallel on the opposite side of the equator at the same southern latitude as Meroe's latitude is to the north of the equator (16;25°S). As most of the data available at the time concerned only the Roman Empire, and even those were far from accurate, it is no surprise that Ptolemy's mapping led inevitably to severe distortions, such as the oversized length attributed to the Mediterranean Sea.

Written in five books, the *Optics* is not extant in Greek and survives only in a Latin version based on the lost Arabic translation. In this work Ptolemy explained a general theory of vision; discussed the role of light and color in vision; enunciated three laws of reflection, also demonstrated by experiment; and presented his experiments on refraction, the results of which turn out to be quite close to those obtained by Snell's law of refraction (seventeenth century).

Apart from these major works, Ptolemy is the author of other treatises where he applies mathematics to different domains. The *Phases of the Fixed Stars*, in two books, is concerned with the heliacal risings and settings of bright stars and the prognostications associated with them. The *Analemma*, known only through its Latin translation, deals with the problem of the determination of the angles required to construct sundials. The *Planisphaerium* is extant only in Arabic translation, and its main object is the study of the projection of the celestial sphere onto a plane, nowadays called stereographic projection. The three books of the *Harmonica* present Ptolemy's *music theory.

Works of Dubious Authorship

Other works have been attributed to Ptolemy. Among them are a philosophical text entitled *On the Faculties of Judgment and Command*; a set of one hundred aphorisms on astrology, widely used during the Middle Ages and better known by its Latin translation, *Centiloquium*; and still others, on mechanics and geometry, but in all cases these attributions have been disputed.

Ptolemy was certainly one of the most influential astronomers of antiquity. The "Ptolemaic System" laid down in his *Almagest*, a handbook repeatedly translated into Arabic and Latin, as well as other languages, dominated mathematical astronomy during the Middle Ages up to the sixteenth century and was rarely contested throughout this long period. It has been said that a great deal of intellectual effort was expended by astronomers during more than a thousand years after Ptolemy trying to understand and, in some cases simplify, the contents of the *Almagest*.

See also **Astronomy; Geography, chorography; Planetary tables**

Bibliography

Neugebauer, O. *A History of Ancient Mathematical Astronomy*. New York: Springer Verlag, 1975.

Toomer, G. J. *Ptolemy's Almagest*. London: Duckworth 1984; new ed., Princeton: Princeton University Press, 1998.

JOSÉ CHABÁS

Q

QUADRIVIUM

In his *Nine Books on Disciplines*, Varro (first century B.C.E.) identified a canon of nine liberal arts considered essential for Roman education. Later abbreviated to the seven liberal arts (grammar, rhetoric, *logic, *arithmetic, geometry, music, and *astronomy), the first three came to be known as the trivium, the last four as the quadrivium. It seems that *Boethius (d. 524 C.E.) was the first to attach this term to the four mathematical disciplines; in the first chapter of his *De institutione arithmetica* he states that among the Greeks, and with Pythagoras in particular, "it was manifestly established that scarcely anyone could scale the summit of perfection in philosophical disciplines who did not pursue such nobility of prudence by a sort of quadruvium (scil. fourfold way)...." While Boethius' *Arithmetica* itself and the "quadruvium" (the earliest manuscripts uniformly preserve this orthography, which gave way to the more familiar form in the tenth and eleventh centuries) were based on the Greek tradition of Nicomachus of Gerasa (fl. c. 100 C.E.), who refers to "four methods," the term and the conception that the four mathematical disciplines are propaedeutic to philosophy seems Boethian.

Although Boethius also wrote handbooks translated and adapted from Greek sources on several of the liberal arts, in the high Middle Ages the preferred texts for the quadrivium were Boethius' *Arithmetica* and *Musica*, *Euclid's *Elements* (usually in the shortened form *Adelard II*, now believed to be the work of Robert of Chester (fl. 1141–1150)), and the *Sphaera* of *John of Sacrobosco. If one looks only at university statutes, it would seem that study of the quadrivial disciplines was given comparatively scant attention in the curriculum: generally students were obliged to hear these mathematical works for only a few days or weeks, in contrast to lectures on logic or *natural philosophy, which often comprised a full term and were repeated several times during the student's academic training. On the other hand, there were both inside and outside the universities medieval scholars whose facility with mathematics belied the curricular neglect. This suggests that, in addition to internal venues, mathematical

Surrounding these cloisters at the University of Salamanca are the halls in which medieval students studied the quadrivium. (Corbis/Dusko Despotovic)

training in the quadrivial arts was accomplished informally, outside the university structure.

The quadrivial disciplines were pursued for a variety of reasons. Astronomy and its related field, *computus*, were useful for calendrical purposes and because they were considered necessary for proper medical diagnosis and treatment. But Boethius' assertion that the quadrivium was a foundation for higher studies was frequently a powerful motivation. In the twelfth century there was an interest in developing theology *more geometrico*, as a discipline with definitions, axioms, postulates, and derived conclusions. One of the most compelling motivations was Aristotle. Drawing on Aristotle's discussion in the *Categories*, Boethius himself had provided the structural organization of the quadrivium, in which arithmetic and geometry dealt with discrete and continuous quantity, respectively, and music and astronomy considered those genera of quantity as they were seen in proportion and in the motions of the heavens. The mathematical disciplines also folded back on the study of Aristotle: there is a strong tradition, noted by *Roger Bacon and *Thomas Bradwardine among others, that the study of geometry was useful in reading Aristotle, who frequently used geometrical or mathematical examples to illustrate philosophical issues and methods.

See also Aristotelianism; Arithmetic; Astronomy, Latin; Boethius; Music theory

Bibliography

Beaujouan, Guy. "The Transformation of the Quadrivium." In *Renaissance and Renewal in the Twelfth Century*. Edited by Robert Louis Benson, Giles Constable and Carol Lanham. Cambridge, MA: Harvard University Press, 1982, pp. 463–487.

Boethius. *De Institutione Arithmetica*. G. Friedlein, ed. Leipzig: Teubner, 1867; translated by M. Masi, *Boethian Number Theory: A Translation of the De Institutione Arithmetica*. Amsterdam: Rodopi, 1983.

Burnett, Charles. The Instruments which are the Proper Delights of the Quadrivium: Rhythmomachy and Chess in the Teaching of Arithmetic in 12th-century England. *Viator* (1997) 28: 175–201.

Evans, Gillian Rosemary. The Influence of Quadrivium Studies in the Eleventh and Twelfth-Century Schools. *Journal of Medieval History* (1975) 1: 151–164.

Kibre, Pearl. "The Quadrivium in the Thirteenth Century Universities (with special reference to Paris)." In *Arts Libéraux et philosophie au moyen âge. Actes du IVe congrès international de philosophie médiévale, Université de Montreal, 27 août–2 septembre 1967*. Paris: J. Vrin, 1969, pp. 175–191.

Molland, A. George. "The Quadrivium in the Universities: Four Questions." In *Scientia und ars im Hoch- und Spätmittelalter. Albert Zimmermann zum 65. Geburtstag*. Edited by Ingrid Craemer-Ruegenberg. [Miscellanea mediaevalia 22] Berlin: de Gruyter, 1994, pp. 66–78.

North, John. "The Quadrivium." In *A History of the University in Europe. Volume 1: Universities in the Middle Ages*. Edited by Hilda de Ridder-Symoens. New York: Cambridge University Press, 1992, pp. 409–441.

White, Alison. "Boethius in the Medieval Quadrivium." In *Boethius. His Life, Thought and Influence*. Edited by Margaret Templeton Gibson. Oxford: Blackwell, 1981, pp. 162–205.

STEVEN J. LIVESEY

R

RAVENNA

Ravenna, on the Adriatic coast of Italy, was an Etruscan foundation that obtained the status of Roman *municipium* in 49 B.C.E. The capital of the province of Flaminia and Picenum, it was the center of a prosperous economic activity, and the base of the Roman Adriatic fleet from the time of Augustus onward. In 402, it was preferred to Milan by the Western emperor Honorius (b. 384, emperor 393, d. 423) as the seat of his court because of its natural defenses and its access to the sea. After a period of strong development, Ravenna declined, particularly during the years preceding the deposition of the Roman emperor (476). It then became the capital of Italy with Odoacer (b. c. 433, king 476, d. 493) and the Ostrogoth kings, from Theodoric (c. 454–526) on. The city gained political importance and attracted a wealthy class of senators and scholars, among whom were *Boethius (c. 480–c. 524) and Cassiodorus (c. 487–c. 580). It was embellished with new construction and became an important and productive cultural center. In 540, Belisarios (c. 505–565) took the city for the Byzantine emperor Justinian I (b. c. 482, emperor 527; d. 565). An increased number of officials and soldiers then arrived in the city, particularly from the East. After the Lombard invasion of 568, Ravenna was transformed into a militarized place (the so-called Exarchate), where Latin elements became increasingly present. Social, religious, and fiscal turmoil in the city during the sixth and seventh centuries, as well as the expansion of the Lombards in Italy, and tensions between Constantinople and the papacy led to several seditious movements from the end of the seventh century on. After the revolt against Constantinople in 727 and the occupation of the city by the Lombards in 732, Ravenna was recovered by Byzantium. In 751, it was definitively conquered by the Lombards, and was then transferred to the papacy. It rapidly declined, even though it remained the seat of an important archbishopric.

The seat of imperial schools of grammar and rhetoric in the sixth century, Ravenna had also a school of medicine that was identified in the early nineteenth century and was further investigated from the late 1870s on. Its activity and production began to be brought to light as early as the 1930s with H. Mørland and A. Beccaria, and has been the object of extensive research during recent decades by philologists, historians of medicine, and paleographers. It seems that the school reproduced the model of the school of Alexandria, dating back to the first Ptolemies and still active in late antiquity.

Latin translations of Greek classical texts were available by that time or were made in Ravenna from the sixth century on or, as has been proposed by E.M. Vázquez Bujan, in Southern Italy. The corpus traditionally attributed to Ravenna expressed a strong preference for Hippocratic literature with such treatises as the *Aphorismi* (a sort of encyclopedia of medical theory and practice), *De aeris, aquis et locis* (dealing with the influence of environmental circumstances on human health), *De hebdomadibus* (a philosophical work on the relationship between Man and the universe, and the importance of the number seven), *De mulierum affectis* (gynecological pathology), *Prognosticon* (semiotics and prognosis of diseases), and *De victus ratione* (diet). Nevertheless, other Greek works were translated into Latin: the early-Byzantine encyclopedia of Oribasius (fourth century), the treatise of Rufus of Ephesus (first–second century C.E.), the introductory works to medicine of *Galen (129–after 216 [?] B.C.E.), Alexander of Tralles (sixth century), and the third book of the encyclopedia of Paul of Ægina (seventh century). The selection of treatises, particularly Hippocratic, shows a tendency toward a reduction of theory and a decanonization of texts typical of Western medicine until the recovery and reassimilation of Greek medicine through the translation into Latin of Arabic works relying on Greek treatises.

Ravenna teachers known by name are Agnellus, Gessius, and Ioannes Alexandrinus. They were called *iatrosophistae*, according the Greek term, and do not seem to have been the authors of the translations above. They commented on classical Greek texts probably translated into Latin, and not on their original Greek versions. They seem to have preferred Galen (contrary to what happened for the translations), even though the Hippocratic *Aphorismi* were included in their program. Galen's works commented on included *De sectis* (an introductory presentation of the different medical schools at Galen's time), *Ars medica* (a short work on pathology that summarizes Galen's other and more important treatises on the topic), *De pulsibus ad tirones* (an introduction to sphygmology), and the *Therapeutica ad Glauconem* (a brief introduction to the nature of fevers and their treatment). Significantly, such works correspond to the first part of the so-called Alexandrian canon (the introductory corpus), a fact suggesting that the Ravenna medical program was shaped by the model of Alexandria and repeated its philosophical orientation. Commentaries, though made by possibly Greek-speaking teachers, seem to have been Latin autonomous works rather than translations from Greek. Commentaries include Hellenisms and transliterations from Greek, contrary to the translations.

See also **Hippocrates; Medicine, theoretical; Translation movements**

Bibliography

Agnellus of Ravenna. *Lectures on Galen's De sectis*. Buffalo: Dept. of Classics, State University of New York at Buffalo, 1981.

Beccaria, A. *I codici di medicina del periodo presalernitano (secoli IX, X, XI)*. Rome: Edizioni di Storia e letteratura, 1956.

———. Sulle tracce di un antico canone latino di Ippocrate e Galeno. *Italia Medioevale e Umanistica* (1959) 2: 1–56; (1961) 4: 1–75; (1971) 14: 1–24.

Cavallo, G. "La scrittura scritta tra antichità tarda e medioevo." In *Storia di Ravenna*. Edited by A. Carile. 2 vols. Venice: Marsilio, 1992, II. 2, pp. 79–125.

Mazzini, I. "Caratteri comuni a tutto l'Ippocrate latino tardo-antico e conseguenti considerazioni su alcuni emendamenti al testo." In *I testi di medicina latini antichi. Problemi filologici e storici*. Edited by I. Mazzini and F. Fuso. Rome: G. Bretschneider, 1985, pp. 63–74.

Mazzini, I. and N. Palmieri. "L'école médicale de Ravenne. Programmes et méthodes d'enseignement, langue, hommes." In *Les écoles médicales à Rome*. Edited by P. Mudry and J. Pigeaud. Geneva and Nantes: Librairie Droz, 1991, pp. 285–310.

Mørland, H. Die lateinischen Oribasiusübersetzungen. *Symbolae Osloenses* (1932) suppl. 5: 43–51.

Müller-Rohlfsen, I. *Die lateinische ravennatische Übersetzung der hippokratischen Aphorismen aus dem 5/6. Jahrhundert n. Chr. Textkonstitution auf der Basis der Übersetzungscodices*. Hamburg: Lüdke, 1980.

Palmieri, N. Un antico commento a Galeno della scuola medica di Ravenna. *Physis* (1981) 23: 204–211.

———. *L'antica versione latina del «De Sectis» di Galeno*. Pisa: ETS, 1989.

———. "Il commento latino-ravennate all'Ars medica di Galeno e la tradizione alessandrina." In *Tradición e innovación de la medicina latina de la Antigüedad y de la Alta Edad Media*. Edited by M.E. Vázques Buján. Santiago de Compostela: Servicio de Publicacións e Intercambio Científico da Universidade de Santiago de Compostela, 1994, pp. 57–75.

Vázques Buján, M. E. Problemas generales de la antiguas traducciones médicas latinas. *Studi Medievali* (1984) 25: 641–680.

Wallis, F. "The experience of the book: manuscripts, texts, and the role of epistemology in early medieval medicine." In *Knowledge and the Scholarly Medical Traditions*, ed. D. Bates. New York: Cambridge University Press, 1995, pp. 101–126.

ALAIN TOUWAIDE

RAZI, AL-

According to *al-Biruni, Abu Bakr Muhammad Ibn Zakariyya al-Razi (Rhazes) was born in Rayy (near modern Tehran) in 865 C.E. He may have first focused on alchemy and done experiments, which affected his eyesight, and then moved to medicine, in which he excelled. He directed the Rayy hospital and died there in 925, although this date is disputed.

He was well known as a freethinker, who claimed that revelation to a particular people at a particular time would be contrary to God's justice, which he wanted to uphold. Some dubbed him "The Heretic," but he was highly respected by al-Mansur, the governor of Rayy. His great model was *Galen, who wrote *The Best Doctor is also a Philosopher*, and like him he saw himself as the complete physician, i.e., physician of the body through medicine, and physician of the soul through philosophy and reformation of character in particular. For instance, in the introduction to his *Spiritual Physick* he explains that al-Mansur asked him to write it as a companion to the *Liber Almansoris*, a previous textbook on bodily medicine he had dedicated to al-Mansur.

Al-Razi's own intellectual autobiography-cum-bibliography and apology for his right to be called a true philosopher emphasizes his consideration of medicine as philosophy, which we now deem to be two totally distinct disciplines, as two sides of the same coin. Although officially taking Socrates as his master, al-Razi is in fact following the footsteps of Galen, whose works he knew well, since most of them were translated into Arabic, the Arabic translation being in some cases the only surviving version. In 2003 Stephen Menn showed the importance of Galen's own numerous and extended biobibliographical passages in his various works as the origin of a biobibliographical genre leading to al-Razi's text, as well as to intellectual autobiographies of Avicenna (*Ibn Sina) and *al-Ghazali, indeed right up to Descartes. In this brief but fascinating text written at the end of his life, al-Razi not only defends his character and his medico-philosophical endeavor but also offers an interesting normative ethic derived from God's three basic attributes of intelligence, justice, and compassion. As he believes in transmigration he argues for vegetarianism and develops an environmental ethic.

Just as Galen freely criticized his predecessors, whether Empirics or Methodics or Epicurean and Stoic philosophers, al-Razi did not hesitate to criticize his own predecessors including Galen. In his *Doubts on Galen* written at the end of his life, al-Razi brings up "doubts" or, more accurately, criticisms relating both to Galen's medicine and philosophy. These "doubts" are organized according to various works of Galen: (1) On demonstration; (2) On the views of Hippocrates and Plato; (3) On the elements according to Hippocrates; (4) On the Commentary on Hippocrates' nature of the human being; (5) On mixtures; (6) On "al-Mayamir" (which deals with compound drugs); (7) On healing methods; (8) On painful members; (9) On causes and accidents; (10) A brief treatise on the art of medicine; (11) On aphorisms; (12) On the preservation of health; (13) On acute illnesses; and (14) An advanced treatise on the pulse. In the course of this enterprise he refers to many other works of Galen.

In his *Spiritual Physick* al-Razi bitterly criticizes Galen for affirming that the soul is mortal, and indicates that his favorite philosopher is Plato. Again, faithfully following Galen who had written a *Commentary on the Medical Statements in the "Timaeus"* in no fewer than four books, al-Razi might have written a commentary on Plato's *Timaeus*, which he certainly knew at least through its Galenic summary that survived only in Arabic.

Galen had insisted on the importance of logic and al-Razi, always keen to highlight the parallel between medicine and philosophy, entitled an introductory book to medicine *Isagoge* as a match to Porphyry's *Isagoge* to Aristotle's *Logic*, which introduced the philosophy curriculum in both the Greek and the Arabic traditions.

As Galen had written several medical texts for beginners, al-Razi did not limit himself to his *Isagoge* but also penned a *Kitab al-Murshid aw al-Fusul* (*Guide-book or Aphorisms*), published by Iskandar in 1961 and translated into French as *Guide du médecin nomade* in 1980.

Original Contributions

Al-Razi's main medical works show his originality and explain his fame, mainly as a physician in the East and in the West during Middle Ages. Under the name of Rhazes he makes an appearance in *Chaucer's *The Canterbury Tales*. Besides his medical textbook dedicated to al-Mansur in 903, translated into Latin by *Gerard of Cremona between 1150 and 1180, which enjoyed several Renaissance editions, we have his *al-Hawi* or *Comprehensive Book on Medicine*, a diary, which Faraj ben Salim, a Jewish physician, translated into Latin in 1279 in Naples under the title *Continens*. Iskandar describes it as "merely a commonplace book, an aide-mémoire, and a private record of the author's comments and reflections on case histories of his patients and on medical books written from the time of Hippocrates down to his own time." Such a description underrates its value as one of the first extensive studies in clinical medicine which al-Razi mined to prepare some of his published treatises. He even records clinical observations about his own illnesses. According to Iskandar, these medical files might have been arranged "in accordance with the accepted method of writing medical books, beginning with the head and working downwards to the toes." This collection of notes was left to his sister and edited posthumously by his students. It should be distinguished from the *Kitab al-Hawi* in four books which al-Razi himself published shortly before his death.

His *Treatise on the Small-pox and Measles* remained of great importance up to the eighteenth century when it was twice translated into Latin and into Greek by the Byzantine Symeon Beth probably in the eleventh century.

This very incomplete listing is rather impressive but in his autobiographical *The Book of the Philosophic Life*, in which al-Razi refers to a few other medical texts, he proudly speaks of his large *Summary* or *al-Jami' al-Kabir*, a medical encyclopedia, and the sacrifices he endured for it: "With respect to the latter, none of the people of the kingdom has surpassed me nor has anyone yet followed along in my steps or copied me.... In working on the large Summary, I spent fifteen years working night and day so weakening my eyesight and ruining the muscles in my hand that at this moment I am prevented from reading and writing. Though my situation is thus, I exert myself as much as I can not to abandon them and always have recourse to someone to read and write for me."

In one of its parts, *Kitab Saydalat al-tibb*, or *Pharmacology*, al-Razi argues that pharmacy is simply an auxiliary of medicine, once again following Galen who distinguished physicians from pharmacists. According to al-Razi, pharmacists should be mainly concerned with purchasing pure kinds of drugs, storing them safely, and keeping them unadulterated. His work on pharmacology is completed with two *Aqrabadhin* or *Formularies*, i.e., recipes and advices on how to compound drugs, the *al-Adwiya al-murakkaba* and its summary, the *Aqrabadhin*.

Most of these works were also translated into Hebrew but at times from the Latin version.

Al-Razi saw himself as the new Galen in considering spiritual medicine or philosophy and bodily medicine as two branches of one and the same discipline as well as in his spirit of independence and dedication to scholarship.

See also **Medicine, practical; Medicine, theoretical**

Bibliography

Primary Sources
Kitab al-Shukuk 'Ala Jailinus. Edited by Mehdi Mohaghegh. Teheran: International Institute of Islamic Thought and Civilization of Kuala Lumpur, 1993.
Libro de la introducción al arte de la medicina o "Isagoge" (Kitab al-madkhal ila sina'at al-tibb). María de la Concepción Vásquez de Benito, ed. and trans. Salamanca: Instituto Hispano-Arabe de Cultura, 1979.
The Spiritual Physick of Razes. Translated by Arthur J. Arberry. London: John Murray, 1950.
La médecine spirituelle. Translated by Rémi Brague. Paris: Flammarion, 2003.
The Book of the Philosophic Life. Translated by Charles E. Butterworth. *Interpretation* (1993) 20: 227–236.
Guide du médecin nomade. Translated by El-Arbi Moubachir. Paris: Sindbad, 1980.

Secondary Sources
Druart, Thérèse-Anne. The Ethics of al-Razi (865–925). *Medieval Philosophy and Theology* (1997) 6: 47–71.
Iskandar, Albert Z. "The Medical Bibliography of al-Razi." In *Essays in Islamic Philosophy and Science*. Edited by George F. Hourani. Albany: State University of New York Press, 1975: pp. 41–46.

Menn, Stephen. "The *Discourse on the Method* and the Tradition of Intellectual Autobiography." In *Hellenistic and Early Modern Philosophy*. Edited by Jon Miller and Brad Inwood. New York: Cambridge University Press, 2003, pp. 141–191.

Stroumsa, Sarah. *Freethinkers of Medieval Islam: Ibn al-Rawandi, Abu Bakr al-Razi, and Their Impact on Islamic Thought*. Leiden: E.J. Brill, 1999.

THÉRÈSE-ANNE DRUART

REASON

Reason is used here in the sense of argument for preferring one option to another, especially with respect to claims about the universe and physical nature. In the Middle Ages the relation between religious faith and reason produced a dynamic tension that contributed to some of the most spectacular achievements of medieval culture.

In the Byzantine tradition scholars attempted to integrate Greek philosophy into their religious perspective by interpreting Greek philosophy as derived from prophetic wisdom, and *Plato as Moses translated into Greek. Byzantine philosophy was based on Neoplatonic metaphysics, which influenced interpretations of logic and mathematics. Scholars trace the origins of the *quadrivium to the Pythagoreans and the traditional list of the seven liberal arts back to the first century B.C.E., a scheme that was transmitted to the West by Cicero, Augustine, and *Boethius among others. As part of the liberal arts, mathematics was viewed as the branch most worthy of a free human being, and as the discipline that prepared students for metaphysics and theology.

After the Islamic conquests of the seventh and eighth centuries C.E., Muslim scholars undertook a major program of translation that preserved and transmitted the great scientific and philosophical achievements of the Greeks. The ideal of Islamic education, however, was religious, leading to a division between religious sciences and their tools (linguistic sciences) and rational sciences (mathematics and philosophy). There was strong opposition in some circles to the study of philosophy, but in Spain there developed a vigorous program in defense of philosophy and its constructive relation to religion. *Ibn Rushd (Averroes) in the twelfth century represents the high point of this effort. His commentaries on Aristotle influenced Latin scholastics so pervasively that they referred to him routinely as "the Commentator."

Scholars attribute the rise of Jewish philosophy—with the exception of Philo of Alexandria (c. 20 B.C.E.–c. 40 C.E.)—to the cultural revival of the tenth century in the Islamic East. For the next three hundred years Jewish philosophers wrote in Arabic. As Islamic centers in Europe declined, Hebrew became the principal language of philosophy and the sciences. Through contacts with Latin scholastic authors they enriched their earlier ideas, influencing Christian authors in turn and making original contributions to the mathematical disciplines. Students were introduced to higher philosophical studies after their elementary religious education. *Maimonides, for example, addressed his *Guide for the Perplexed* to religious believers. Rationalistic interpretations of religion in Jewish contexts served the practical purpose of supporting political and social customs and institutions.

Medieval scholars recognized the importance of logical reasoning. Arising out of the Hellenistic context in which Christianity was born, orthodox theologians tried to come to grips with the mysteries of the faith so as to defend belief from charges of irrationalism. Because revelation requires language, and language requires explication, most theologians recognized the need for philosophical training to safeguard fundamental doctrines from heretical interpretations. Medieval scholars shared the belief that humans are under an obligation to evaluate the arguments and evidence on which their conclusions are based. Underlying such a belief are assumptions that humans can discover and articulate rational grounds for their conclusions, and that the universe is ordered in a way that corresponds with the human mind. As most medieval thinkers in the Christian tradition conceived it, even faith involves intellectual assent to a proposition. The contrast between faith and reason rested, not on a difference between separate faculties, but on the difference between the evidence that moves the intellect to assent in an act of faith and the evidence that moves it to a strictly rational assent. Scholars who found this account unsatisfactory resorted to a theory of illumination, divine and natural, to explain the difference, and still others constructed an account that distinguished between revelation, reason, and experience as different sources of certain knowledge.

With respect to theories of perception, medieval scholars, for the most part, followed Aristotelian doctrine. The Aristotelian account is broadly reliabilist, believing that the senses provide correct qualitative information and that the most important deceptions and illusions are easily recognized and corrected. At the level of ordinary experience the Aristotelian exposition is a commonsense account, rejecting by virtue of its assumptions any possibility that the qualities that we perceive in our experience are partly the product of other hidden and more fundamental things. The Aristotelian account also regards mathematics as a valuable tool but one that abstracts from physical reality and is subject to logical and ontological constraints. For example, Aristotle maintained that circular and rectilinear motions are incomparable because "circular" and "rectilinear" belong to different kinds of things, just as the sharpness of a pencil and the sharpness of a musical tone are incomparable. Medieval scholars discussed and sometimes criticized Aristotle's assumptions and conclusions, but they never entirely escaped the commonsense view, thus often underestimating the need for precise, quantitative descriptions of complex phenomena such as the motions of bodies. Common sense suggested that weight and resistance are factors in the motion of a falling body. Medieval critics of Aristotle's laws of motion merely produced a more sophisticated mathematical analysis without any more quantified empirical data. The result, however much rooted in common sense and ordinary experience, was a decidedly rationalistic account of the physical universe. Natural philosophy defined its task as the understanding of nature based on a knowledge of causes, rarely relating the causal analysis to any precise empirical investigation. The Neoplatonic and Stoic traditions also reinforced the deeply held conviction that the universe is a harmonious order reflecting the wisdom, omniscience, and beneficence of its divine creator.

With respect to the theoretical bias of ancient *cosmology, there are exceptions, and these are instructive. The medical tradition was more empirical, criticizing the generalizations of philosophers that were based on few observations. In fact, Aristotle was careful to survey the opinions of his predecessors, believing that their views contained valuable insights which required critical assessment. In his biological works Aristotle also undertook his own empirical investigations. In other words, Aristotle himself was not as rationalistic as he became when commentators tended to use his treatises as authoritative textbooks.

In areas such as optics, *pharmacology, astronomy, statics, and kinematics there were important advances in mathematical and empirical analysis, though not always together. In optics, a mathematical-experimental analysis emerged in the fourteenth century that is attributable to the Greco-Arabic tradition and the philosophical interest in problems related to vision, optical illusions, and striking optical phenomena such as rainbows. In pharmacology, analysis of the relation between a geometric increase of a quality and an arithmetic increase in its effect may have contributed to understanding qualitative changes in a quantifiable way, the motion of a uniformly accelerated body, and other conceptual developments related to mass, momentum, and force. Probably because of the real difficulty in producing precise measurable data, however, such considerations remained theoretical. In astronomy, by the fifteenth century more and more experts became aware of several problems with Ptolemaic models and the accuracy of observational data. The fact that medieval scholars used mathematics to try to understand the subjects that they treated, whether physical phenomena or spiritual virtues, confirms their commitments to the power of rational analysis and to the conviction that reality at all levels, though dependent on God's will, is intrinsically rational.

Aside from developments related to the university, there are many examples in the general culture of the medieval period that have a rationalistic character. The technologies of windpower and waterpower; the dramatic improvements in agricultural technology; spectacular achievements in architecture, painting, and sculpture; the networks of commercial fairs and towns; the maintenance of transportation routes; improvements in shipbuilding, canals, and horse transport; the gradual transition from a barter to a money economy along with the development of banking and insurance; all of the efforts at quantification and the maintaining of records and statistics—all attest the development of an ever more complex society accompanied by the creation of bureaucratic, educational, and legal institutions. In areas where theory and practice went hand in hand—for example, in medicine, music, architecture, and the like—we find increasingly sophisticated efforts to establish practice on sound rational, often mathematical, principles.

The superiority of theology and faith as directed toward salvation did not suppress other objects of study, each of which was seen to have a method appropriate to the investigation of that object. Theology was regarded as the queen of the sciences because it was thought to possess the greatest dignity, but the conclusions of other sciences cannot be extrapolated from the principles of theology nor from texts of the Bible. Whatever misgivings medieval scholars may have had about natural curiosity, they generally recognized the legitimacy of other disciplines and the practical need for education. The institutions that they created demonstrate their commitment to professional standards and competence, as well as to examination of competing and conflicting ideas and their reconciliation. In the disciplines of philosophy, theology, law, and medicine, medieval scholars developed and applied rigorous methods of analysis, and thereby contributed to both empirical and rationalistic approaches to nature, necessary conditions for the emergence of modern science.

See also **Arabic numerals; Arnau de Vilanova; Astronomy, Islamic; Astronomy, Latin; Bradwardine, Thomas; Cathedral schools; Commercial arithmetic; Condemnation of 1277; Elements and qualities; Experiment, experimenta; Heytesbury, William of; God in Christianity; God in Islam; Latitude of forms; Logic; Nature: the structure of the physical world; Optics and catoptrics; Quadrivium; Religion and science; Scholasticism;** *Scientia;* **Swineshead, Richard; Translation movements; Universities**

Bibliography

Arts libéraux et philosophie au moyen âge. Actes du quatrième congrès international de philosophie médiévale, Montreal, 1967. Montreal: Institut d'Études Médiévales; Paris: J. Vrin, 1969.

Berman, Harold J. *Law and Revolution: The Formation of the Western Legal Tradition.* Cambridge, MA: Harvard University Press, 1983.

Drake, Stillman. Medieval ratio Theory vs. compound Medicines in the Origins of Bradwardine's Rule. *Isis* (1973) 64: 67–77.

Fakhry, Majid. *Averroes (Ibn Rushd), His Life, Works, and Influence.* Oxford: Oneworld, 2001.

Funkenstein, Amos. *Theology and the Scientific Imagination From the Middle Ages to the Seventeenth Century.* Princeton: Princeton University Press, 1986.

Gilson, Étienne. *Reason and Revelation in the Middle Ages.* New York: Charles Scribner's Sons, 1938.

Grant, Edward. *God and Reason in the Middle Ages.* New York: Cambridge University Press, 2001.

Lindberg, David C. *Theories of Vision from al-Kindi to Kepler.* Chicago: University of Chicago Press, 1976.

McVaugh, Michael. Arnald of Villanova and Bradwardine's Law. *Isis* (1967) 58: 56–64.

Murdoch, John E. "The Analytic Character of Late Medieval Learning: Natural Philosophy Without Nature." In

Approaches to Nature in the Middle Ages. Edited by Lawrence D. Roberts. Binghamton: Center for Medieval and Early Renaissance Studies, 1982, pp. 171–213.

Wallace, William A. *Causality and Scientific Explanation*. 2 vols. Ann Arbor: University of Michigan Press, 1972–1974.

ANDRÉ GODDU

REGIMEN SANITATIS

The *regimen sanitatis* (regimen of health) was a popular genre of medical literature in late-medieval Europe that advised readers how to maintain and regain their health through a lifestyle of moderation. It was rooted in the ancient Greek medical theories of *Hippocrates and *Galen, according to which health was the result of a harmonious balance of the four humors (bodily fluids) blood, phlegm, yellow bile, and black bile. In order to keep these humors in check, six areas, known as the *sex res non naturales* or six non-naturals, were considered of particular importance:

1. *Aer* (Air)
Topics discussed under this heading usually included the geographic and climatic conditions, air quality, the seasons, winds, location of a person's house, change of location through travel, clothes, and perfumes, but also the air as a carrier of disease, such as the plague.

2. *Cibus et Potus* (Food and Drink)
Always regarded as the most important non-natural, advice on diet could range from general guidelines on nutrition regarding appetite, quantity, quality, order, and time of food consumption to dietetic lists of foodstuffs and their humoral qualities, as well as culinary recipes. Of the beverages, water and wine were the most prominent.

3. *Motus et Quies* (Exercise and Rest)
Covered under this heading were aspects such as the type, quality, quantity, speed, and intensity of physical activity, the effects of excessive and moderate exercise on the body, and the rhythm of physical activity and rest periods. Physical activity was understood to encompass not only work (e.g., hunting, fishing, sailing, construction, carpentry work, sewing), and sports (e.g., riding, running, wrestling), but also activities such as playing musical instruments or board games.

4. *Somnus et Vigilia* (Sleeping and Waking)
The rhythm of sleep and waking periods, their ideal lengths, and their relation to food consumption, digestion, and emotional well-being are some of the typical topics subsumed under this heading.

5. *Repletio et Evacuatio* (Repletion and Excretion)
Considered to be of equal importance to regulating the intake of food and drink was the proper management of the various excretions from urine and feces to winds, saliva, mucus, vomit, menstrual blood, and semen. Purging and bloodletting (phlebotomy) were also sometimes included in the list, as were coitus, baths, and massages.

6. *Accidentia Animi* (Emotions)
Seen as both physical and psychic phenomena, the emotions usually discussed under this heading were joy, anger, anxiety, fear, sadness, and shame. As in all other areas, moderation was the guiding principle when it came to emotions.

Early medieval regimens of health such as the *Diaeta Theodori* dealt mainly with food and drink; some, such as Anthimus's *De observatione ciborum*, were addressed to rulers. Loosely grouped around the six non-naturals were the dietetic rules in the popular *Secretum secretorum*, and the *Regimen sanitatis Salernitanum*. Despite its claim of being a letter written by Aristotle to his famous pupil Alexander the Great, the *Secretum* was probably an Arab compilation from c. 1000 C.E. The *Regimen sanitatis Salernitanum*, written in verse, and containing material from the *Secretum secretorum*, was a later compilation, possibly from the thirteenth century, that may or may not have originated in *Salerno, Italy, seat of medieval Europe's oldest medical school. By far the most popular European regimen, the *Regimen sanitatis Salernitanum* grew between the fourteenth and the nineteenth century from three hundred sixty-four hexameter verses to over three thousand five hundred. It was translated into many European languages, including French, German, English, and Italian, and appeared in more than two hundred fifty printed editions, at least forty of which were incunabula. Medieval school medicine as taught in Salerno, Montpellier, Paris and elsewhere, was based on regimen literature that applied the structure of the six non-naturals much more rigidly. The texts used at Salerno were Latin translations of Arab-Islamic regimens contained, for instance, in the *Isagoge* of Johannitius (*Hunayn ibn Ishaq), and the *Liber pantegni*, an adaptation of the *Kitab al-Malaki* (*Royal Book*) of *Ali ibn Abbas al-Majusi (Haly Abbas) made by *Constantine the African in the eleventh century. The regimens in the *Liber de medicina ad Almansorem* of Rhazes, and the *Canon medicinae* of *Ibn Sina (Avicenna), translated by *Gerard of Cremona in *Toledo in the twelfth century, were part of the curriculum at the medical school of Montpellier. Other important Arab regimens that circulated in Europe in the later Middle Ages in Latin translation were Avicenna's *Cantica*, the regimen in the *Colliget* of *Ibn Rushd (Averroes), the *Regimen sanitatis* of *Moses Maimonides, and Ibn Butlan's *Tacuinum sanitatis*. Beginning in the thirteenth century, European physicians compiled their own regimens from these Arab texts. Most of them were written in Latin and later translated into the vernacular. Among the best known were the *Régime du corps* of Aldobrandino da Siena (1256), the *Summa conservationis et curationis* of William of Saliceto (1275), the *Liber de conservatione vitae humanae* of *Bernard de Gordon (1308), the *Regimen sanitatis ad inclytum regem Aragonum* of *Arnau de Vilanova (1308), the *Sanitatis conservator* of Konrad von Eichstätt, the *Regimen sanitatis* of Magninus Mediolanensis (fourteenth century), and the fifteenth-century regimens *De regimine sanitatis* of *Ugo Benzi, the *Libellus de sex rebus non naturalibus* of Michele Savonarola, the *Regimen* of Heinrich von Laufenberg, the *De Regimine Sanitatis Ad Laurentium Medicem* of Antonio Benivieni, and the *De triplici vita* of Marsilio Ficino. Konrad von Eichstätt's text, in particular, influenced a number of Latin and German regimens of the fourteenth and fifteenth centuries, including the *Tractatus de regimine sanitatis* of Arnold von Bamberg, the *Ordnung der Gesundheit*, the *Regimen vite* of (Pseudo-) Ortolf von Baierland, the *Regel der Gesundheit* of (Pseudo-) Arnau de Vilanova, and the *Büchlein der Gesundheit*.

In addition to the general regimens for healthy adults, physicians compiled special regimens for people thought to belong to the neutral state between sickness and health, such as pregnant and lactating women, infants, the elderly, and convalescents. *Consilia* were regimens written for a specific, usually high-ranking personality. Other related genres of dietetic literature were regimens for the months of the year (*regimen duodecim mensium*) and the four seasons, and the prophylactic plague regimens. The impact of the *regimen sanitatis* on late-medieval medical practice and the lifestyles of millions of Europeans cannot be overestimated, as it extended the physicians' sphere of influence from the sick to the healthy.

See also **Medicine, practical; Medicine, theoretical**

Bibliography

Albala, Ken. *Eating Right in the Renaissance*. Berkeley: University of California Press, 2002.

Bylebyl, Jerome J. "Galen on the Non-Natural Causes of Variation in the Pulse." *Bulletin of History of Medicine* (1971) 45: 482–485.

Braekman, W. L. *Studies on Alchemy, Diet, Medicine and Prognostication in Middle English*. Brussels: Omirel UFSAL, 1986.

Collectio Salernitana: ossia documenti inediti e trattati di medicina appartenenti alla scuola medica salernitana. Edited by Salvatore de Renzi. 5 vols. Naples, 1852–1859. Reprint, Bologna: Forni Editore, 1967.

Copland, Robert, trans. *Aristotle: Secretum secretorum*. English. Amsterdam: Theatrum Orbis Terrarum, 1970.

Cummins, Patricia Willet. *A Critical Edition of Le Regime Tresutile et Tresproufitable pour Conserver et Garder la Santé du Corps Humain*. Chapel Hill: North Carolina Studies in the Romance Languages and Literatures, 1976.

Dols, Michael. *Medieval Islamic Medicine: Ibn Ridwan's Treatise "On the Prevention of Bodily Ills in Egypt."* Berkeley: University of California Press, 1984.

Ficino, Marsilio. *Three Books on Life*. Edited and translated by Carol V. Kaske and John R. Clark. Binghamton: Medieval and Renaissance Texts and Studies in conjunction with the Renaissance Society of America, 1989.

García Ballester, Luis. "On the Origin of the 'six non-natural things' in Galen." In *Galen und das hellenistische Erbe. Verhandlungen des IV. Internationalen Galen-Symposions veranstaltet vom Institut für Geschichte der Medizin am Bereich Medizin (Charité) der Humboldt-Universität zu Berlin, 18-20 September 1989*. Edited by Jutta Kollesch and Diethard Nickel. Beihefte zu Sudhoffs Archiv. Zeitschrift für Wissenschaftsgeschichte. Stuttgart: Franz Steiner, 1993, 105–115.

Grant, Mark. *Galen on Food and Diet*. London: Routledge, 2000.

Green, Robert Montraville. *A Translation of Galen's Hygiene (De Sanitate Tuenda)*. Springfield, Ill.: Charles C. Thomas, 1951.

Hagenmeyer, Christa. *Das Regimen Sanitatis Konrads von Eichstätt: Quellen-Texte-Wirkungsgeschichte*. Stuttgart: Franz Steiner Verlag, 1995.

Harington, Sir John. *The School of Salernum: Regimen Sanitatis Salerni, The English Version*. Salerno: Ente Provinciale Per Il Turismo, 1959.

Heikki, Mikkeli. *Hygiene in the Early Modern Medical Tradition*. Helsinki: Academia Scientarum Fennica, 1999.

Jansen-Sieben, Ria and Frank Daelemans. *Voeding en geneeskunde / Alimentation et médicine*. Brussels: Archief en Bibliotheekwezen in Belgie, 1993.

Jarcho, Saul. Galen's Six Non-Naturals: A Bibliographic Note and Translation. *Bulletin of the History of Medicine* (1970) 44: 372–377.

Krueger, Haven C. *Avicenna's Poem on Medicine*. Springfield: Charles C. Thomas, 1963.

Liechtenhan, E., ed. and trans. *Anthimi De observatione ciborum ad Theodoricum regem Francorum epistula*. Berlin: Akademie-Verlag, 1963.

Maimonides, Moses. *Regimen sanitatis oder Diätetik für die Seele und den Körper*. Edited and translated by Süssmann Muntner. Basel: Karger, 1966.

Milham, Mary Ella, ed. *Platina: On Right Pleasure and Good Health: A Critical Edition and Translation of De honesta voluptate et valetudine*. Tempe: Medieval and Renaissance Texts and Studies, 1998.

Niebyl, Peter H. The Non-Naturals. *Bulletin of the History of Medicine* (1971) 45: 486–492.

Rather, Lelland J. The 'Six Things Non-Natural': A Note on the Origins and Fate of a Doctrine and a Phrase. *Clio Medica* (1968) 3: 337–347.

Weber, Shirley Howard, ed. *Anthimus: De observatione ciborum*. Leiden: E.J. Brill, 1924.

Weiss-Adamson, Melitta. *Medieval Dietetics: Food and Drink in Regimen Sanitatis Literature from 800 to 1400*. Frankfurt am Main: Peter Lang, 1995.

MELITTA WEISS-ADAMSON

REGIOMONTANUS, JOHANNES

Johannes Regiomontanus, also known as Johannes Müller of Königsberg, was born on June 6, 1436, in Königsberg (Franconia, Germany). He first emerges in the historical record as *Joannes molitoris*, "John of the miller." The familiar version of his name derives from the Latin form of Königsberg. This miller's son became the foremost mathematician and mathematical astronomer of fifteenth-century Europe, a sought-after astrologer, and an early printer specializing in the mathematical sciences.

After attending university in Leipzig for two years, Regiomontanus matriculated at Vienna at the age of thirteen. By this time, he had already computed a set of astronomical tables. During his Viennese years (1450–1461), he completed his M.A. degree, collaborated with his mentor *Georg Peuerbach on several astronomical

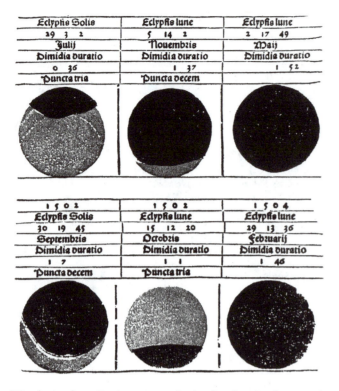

Eclypßis Solis	Eclypßis lune	Eclypßis lune
29 3 2	5 14 2	2 17 49
Julij	Nouembris	Maij
Dimidia duratio	Dimidia duratio	Dimidia duratio
0 36	1 37	1 52
Puncta tria	Puncta decem	

1 5 0 2	1 5 0 2	1 5 0 4
Eclypßis Solis	Eclypßis lune	Eclypßis lune
30 19 45	15 12 20	29 13 36
Septembris	Octobris	Februarij
Dimidia duratio	Dimidia duratio	Dimidia duratio
1 7	1 1	1 46
Puncta decem	Puncta tria	

Woodprint from Regiomontanus' calendar showing lunar and solar eclipses for the years 1497 to 1504. Printed by Ratdolt in Venice. (Topham/Charles Walker)

and astrological projects, including observations of eclipses and comets (notably the one known today as Halley's Comet), the construction of instruments, and the casting of horoscopes for the nearby court of Emperor Frederick III of Hapsburg.

During a diplomatic visit to Vienna (1460–1461), the Greek cardinal Bessarion encouraged Peuerbach to write an *Epitome* of *Ptolemy's *Almagest* that would correct the problems he saw in George of Trebizond's 1450 translation of and commentary on this work. At Peuerbach's premature death in 1461, the work was only half finished.

Regiomontanus left Vienna for Italy with Bessarion, to whose extended household he belonged during his Italian years (1461–1465/1467?). Under this prominent patron, Regiomontanus completed the *Epitome of the Almagest* by 1462. In his hands, the *Epitome* became not only a summary, but also a critical examination of the *Almagest* and one of the best introductions to Ptolemy's mathematical astronomy. In particular, Regiomontanus demonstrated the possibility of an eccentric alternative to the models for Mercury and Venus in Book Twelve of the *Almagest*. This alternative model—impossible according to Ptolemy—lies behind Nicholas Copernicus's earliest notes about the arrangement and distances of the planetary spheres around the mean position of the Sun.

While in Bessarion's entourage, Regiomontanus perfected his Greek, lectured on al-Farghani's astronomy at the University of Padua, and read widely in his patron's Greek library. He also joined Bessarion's longstanding feud with the anti-Platonic rhetorician George of Trebizond. This controversy prompted Regiomontanus to write his longest expository work, the *Defense of Theon against George of Trebizond*, a book-by-book attack on Trebizond's commentary on Ptolemy's *Almagest*. The dispute was so acrimonious that, a generation later, Regiomontanus was (falsely) rumored to have been poisoned by Trebizond's sons.

Contribution to Mathematics

Regiomontanus mastered medieval mathematics and went beyond it. His contributions include the formalization of trigonometry (*On Triangles*, later printed in Nuremberg in 1533) and the discovery of Diophantus's work (unknown in Europe). In addition to his work in plane and spherical trigonometry and geometry, Regiomontanus's correspondence shows interest in, among other things, perfect numbers, the five regular solids, and quadratic, cubic, and higher equations.

Regiomontanus was a painstaking critic of problems in contemporary astronomy, from the teaching of the subject to fundamental matters of theory and observation. In his *Disputationes contra deliramenta cremonensia*, he attacked a widely used university text, the thirteenth-century *Theorica planetarum communis* attributed to *Gerard of Cremona. In its stead, he promoted Peuerbach's *Theoricae novae planetarum*. In astronomical theory, he criticized the mismatch between theory and observation in predictions of planetary position and size (e.g., lunar diameter). In addition, he hoped to reform astronomy so that its models would both be physically coherent and predict planetary positions successfully. Although he admired Ptolemy's *Almagest*, Regiomontanus saw it as a work relying on two-dimensional devices that reflected the Greek astronomer's concern for predictions and his neglect of physical considerations. Regiomontanus claimed that a proper astronomy should compromise neither predictions nor physical coherence. For him this meant a mathematical astronomy based on concentric spheres rather than the eccentrics and epicycles of Ptolemy's *Almagest*. Despite the problems with this project (e.g., concentric spheres do not allow variation in planetary distance), Regiomontanus continued to hope that he could find a concentric physical astronomy that would match or exceed the predictive power of Ptolemy's work. While he sketched concentric-sphere models only for the Sun and Moon in 1460, his hopes for a full-scale astronomy along these lines still reverberate in the manuscript of his *Defense of Theon against George of Trebizond*, which he was revising in the 1470s.

From 1467 to 1471 Regiomontanus served as astrologer to the court of King Matthias Corvinus in Buda, Hungary. In 1471 he moved to Nuremberg, where he established an instrument shop and a printing press. He announced plans to print forty-five classical, medieval, and contemporary books primarily in mathematics, astronomy, optics, music, and astrology. His printing advertisement included works ranging from

Euclid's *Elements* to his own *Defense of Theon*. Only nine editions appeared, including Peuerbach's *New Theories of the Planets* (c. 1472), his own four-hundred-page *Ephemerides* (the first tables of daily planetary positions), and his German and Latin calendars, which included small, moveable, brass arms. Beyond their new content, these works solved the technical problems involved in, and inaugurated, the printing of astronomical diagrams and tables of numbers. Regiomontanus's concern for the authentic meaning of texts inspired him to emend the manuscripts that he expected to print, laying the groundwork for many later fifteenth- and sixteenth-century editions. He continued to make celestial observations with the Nuremberg patrician Bernhard Walther.

Clearly, Regiomontanus was skilled with his hands and in the use of materials. He had made an astrolabe for Bessarion in 1462, and his Nuremberg workshop was preparing an *astrarium* (astronomical clock) c. 1474. Neither this instrument nor his full printing program would come to fruition, but his technical skills fueled the legend according to which he had built, like Archytas, a mechanical fly. In 1475, for consultations about calendar reform, Regiomontanus traveled to Rome, where he died at age forty, probably of plague, on July 6, 1476.

Regiomontanus's unfinished printing program lived on in the output of other presses, most notably those of Erhard Ratdolt (Venice and Augsburg) in the 1480s, and of Johannes Schöner (Vienna) and Petreius (Nuremberg) in the early sixteenth century.

See also **Astronomy, Latin;** *Theorica planetarum*

Bibliography

Hughes, Barnabas. *Regiomontanus on Triangles*. Madison: University of Wisconsin Press, 1967.
Rose, Paul L. *The Italian Renaissance of Mathematics from Petrarch to Galileo*. Geneva: Droz, 1973.
Shank, Michael H. Regiomontanus on Ptolemy, Physical Orbs, and Astronomical Fictionalism: Goldsteinian Themes in the "Defense of Theon against George of Trebizond." *Perspectives on Science* (2002) 10: 179–207.
Swerdlow, Noel. "Regiomontanus on the Critical Problems of Astronomy." In *Nature, Experiment and the Sciences*. Edited by Trevor Levere and William Shea. Boston/Dordrecht: Kluwer, 1990, pp. 165–195.
———. Science and Humanism in the Renaissance: Regiomontanus's Oration on the Dignity and Utility of the Mathematical Sciences. In *World Changes: Thomas Kuhn and the Nature of Science*. Edited by Paul Horwich. Cambridge: MIT Press, 1993, pp. 131–168.
———. "Astronomy in the Renaissance." In *Astronomy Before the Telescope*. Edited by Christopher Walker. New York: St. Martin's Press, 1996, pp. 187–230.
———. Regiomontanus's Concentric-Sphere Models for the Sun and Moon. *Journal for the History of Astronomy* (1999) 30: 1–23.
Zinner, Ernst. *Leben und Wirken des Joh. Müller von Königsberg genannt Regiomontanus*. 2nd ed. Osnabrück: Otto Zeller Verlag, 1968. Translated by Ezra Brown, *Regiomontanus: His Life and Work*. Amsterdam: North Holland, 1990.

MICHAEL H. SHANK

RELIGION AND SCIENCE

The historical relationship between religion and science is surely obscure. For all that, it has been highly, sometimes acrimoniously, debated. As the twenty-first century begins, the United States has witnessed a furious political row over the theory of evolution and what is sometimes advanced as its alternative, creationism. The question comes down to who has the right to decide what appears in textbooks for public-schools. On one side stand education professionals and most biologists, speaking on behalf of "science"; on the other fundamentalist Christian churches and defenders of "family values," speaking for "religion" and ultimately in the name of God. In this spectacle, science and religion find themselves directly opposed, contesting the authority to determine "truth" and thus dictate what children learn.

Although many observers, both scholars and laity, would protest that the antithesis in the American standoff is overdrawn, perhaps even factitious—the result of a category mistake pitting religion against science as two varieties of a uniform genus of knowledge simply conceived—much the same oppositional view is in fact enshrined in the standard historical narrative of the rise of modern natural science. Here Galileo plays the archetypal role of "scientist," champion of a truth set free from revelation, while the Roman inquisitors do duty for partisans of the other side, insisting on the unrestricted right of "religion" to set the set the terms for education and cognition—in this case, of course, "religion" as mediated by the church. By this account, "science" as we know it in the modern world—and which most of the story's tellers take as the model for knowledge of the truth—appeared only when the competing claims of "religion" were beaten back, tamed by intrepid seekers of truth who took Galileo's censuring not as cause for silence but instead heroic resistance. In a Manichaean universe such as this, science and religion can coexist only when one accepts the epistemic hegemony of the other.

It is a pity that such a vision so dominates both popular and learned discourse in our world. Examined without prejudice, the history of science and religion in the Middle Ages has a vastly more complex, at times even entirely antithetical, story to tell. We can take steps toward a modest survey of this history by agreeing at the outset that there are two fundamental questions to be asked to get the relation between religion and science straight. The first is: how has religion affected the shape or content of science? The second reverses the terms: how has science exercised an influence on religion?

Religion in the Middle Ages can be said to have exercised an influence on scientific knowledge either materially, affecting its content and extent, or more formally, shaping the way it was viewed and approached. In the early Middle Ages, for example, especially in the golden years of monasticism from the eighth to the tenth century, religion provided the material grounds for much of what we would take as the scientific components of Latin learning. By creating the need for an accurate grasp of the lunar calendar, the round of monastic liturgy promoted an interest in astronomy and considerable application to the mathematics required to calculate the motions of heavenly bodies and thus establish precise dates and times, a discipline referred to in Latin revealingly as "*computus*." The biblical commentator and church historian of eighth-century England, *Bede, was by no means exceptional for having authored important studies on chronology and the determination of dates. Much later in the Middle Ages, university theologians' interests in puzzles about potentially quantifiable qualities such as "grace" or "virtue" opened the door in their work for technical discussions again of a highly mathematical nature about numerical progressions and the measurement of continuities, subjects of investigation medievalists recognize under the heading "intension and remission of forms." Although in this latter case theologians may not deserve primary credit for sustaining innovative thought—for arts masters were interested as well—they nonetheless made great material contributions to it. Negatively speaking, on the other hand, it would seem that the time and intellectual energy devoted to matters of liturgy, religious devotion and biblical commentary in the monastic regime—for long stretches of the Middle Ages the principal locus of learned activity—precluded any serious attention to subjects and activities we would consider scientific. The stereotype of medieval religion crowding out scientific concerns must surely derive from this apparent grain of truth.

On the formal side of the ledger, religion can likewise be pictured as bearing on science in both positive and negative ways. Contrary to widespread current assumptions, religious thought through most of the high Middle Ages, once monasticism had lost its near monopoly in intellectual affairs, encouraged what we would take to be independent and self-sustaining currents of scientific inquiry. The humanism of twelfth-century theology—which the historian Chenu associated with a revitalizing "light from the East"—inspired a more general naturalism, an interest in "nature" as an object of study in itself, that underlay the considerable achievements of thinkers of that time in cosmology and much of natural philosophy. Likewise the demands of thirteenth-century *Scholasticism drew even masters of theology into realms of speculation that we would consider more scientific than religious, again most often fields corresponding to modern physics, biology, and chemistry. From the "*Hexaëmeron*" commentaries of Robert Grosseteste to the encyclopedic compendia of *Albertus Magnus, much work produced by high-medieval theologians appears fundamentally scientific to modern eyes. Yet intellectual sensibilities derived from religious sentiment could also inhibit scientific inquiry, especially when regarded as done for science's sake alone. Thirteenth-century warnings against "vain curiosity," issued periodically by theologians from the first decades to the last, set limits within university walls on science conducted with a sense of autonomy or even internal coherency of plan. In fourteenth-century Italy, humanists such as Petrarch inveighed against the worthless natural philosophy engendered by scholastic theological disputes, prioritizing instead both moral and devotional speculation.

The almost anti-scientific humor historians have sometimes detected in early Renaissance thought would seem in this light a sign of religion's power to narrow the bounds of the intellectual world.

Even more purely formal was the apparent power of religious thinking to determine the way science was pursued or understood. Returning to twelfth-century theological preoccupation with creation as manifested in "nature," or advancing to fifteenth-century humanists' fascination with the legacy of classical and Hellenistic Greece as evident in the Florentine Marsilio Ficino—surely part of a greatly religious if non-scholastic cultural milieu—we see the repeated emergence of an intellectual idealism affecting more arenas of learning than religion alone. The so-called "Platonism" of twelfth-century natural science can thus be viewed in large part as a "scientific" effect of religious intellectual commitments, and so, too, the Platonizing mathematicism of the fifteenth and sixteenth centuries, an outgrowth of Florentine humanism Thomas Kuhn put forth as formative on Copernicus and Copernican science.

Less formal but equally determinative would be the impact of religion on science proposed in the now legendary thesis of Pierre Duhem. In this account, late-thirteenth-century *Aristotelianism was stopped in its tracks by theological concerns about divine omnipotence, creation, and the nature of the soul, eventuating in the famous Parisian *Condemnation of 1277. The unintended result was a turn among those interested in science to new lines of speculation free of Aristotle's commitments to the absolute character of place, for instance, or the cosmic hierarchizing of the laws of motion. For those agreeing with Duhem, the seeds of a modern universe, where the Earth need not be at the center and all bodies need not move towards a natural place, were planted by this religious, emphatically non-scientific, act of from the high Middle Ages. Almost as if by accident, religion should thereby be credited with having deflected the course of science.

But what about the alternative question: how might science have affected religion? To be sure, modern sensibilities, and thus historians' investigations, have been less inclined to consider the relationship from this perspective. Yet medievalists have sometimes found it to be a productive approach. Here, the formal link between science and religion has attracted the greater attention. Late medieval debates about whether theology constituted a science, and especially thirteenth-century efforts to fashion a scholastic theology that was truly scientific, are pointed to again and again as examples of how modes of thinking that originated in the natural sciences spilled over into the religious arena, particularly among the very learned. It is now standard to affirm that as the prestige of Aristotle's writings grew in the late twelfth and early thirteenth centuries, scholars at the newly emergent *universities fell increasingly under the influence of an Aristotelianizing epistemology anchored to an apodictic model of science. So far as natural science was concerned, masters in the schools of arts appealed to this model as methodological endorsement for efforts to work from

Aristotle's foundations to fill in the substance of the fields already delineated in his corpus of scientific works. Eventually, theologians, too, felt pressured to conform to the same cognitive ideal. The result was, if not theology as science—though many in theology at mid-thirteenth century believed that this was what they ought to produce—at least theology expounded according to the terms of scientific discussion. The product was Scholasticism in paradigmatic form, the sort epitomized in the great *summa* of Thomas Aquinas or that attributed to Alexander of Hales. In this view, theology was what it was in the high Middle Ages because of the allure of Aristotle's view of the natural sciences.

The material influence of science on religion, if less spectacular, has nevertheless not been overlooked. Again, the high Middle Ages are seen as providing the most fertile ground. Indeed, the rise of a scholastic theology in the thirteenth century would appear to constitute the enabling condition. For if religious speculation was to be held to the discursive standards of natural philosophy, perhaps the natural sciences would themselves have to furnish crucial elements for a theologian's explication of the realities entailed by Christian faith. Formal doctrines such as transubstantiation of the host, originating in the thirteenth century, are perhaps best understood as theological expressions of the natural scientific learning of the day.

In the end, however, after all consideration of deep functional connections between religion and science as evidenced in the historical development of both, it is hard not to return to where we began, with a simple intuition that, when all is said and done, religion tends to stand in science's way. Hence the perennial attraction of the example of Galileo. In a cultural world where both science and religion can lay claim to authority, is it not likely that knowledge generated in one sphere will, on occasion, be seen as substantively in conflict with knowledge generated in the other? And if so, will not one sphere be forced to give way, science to religion in Galileo's case, religion to science during the eighteenth-century Enlightenment? Scientific thinkers, in both the medieval and the modern world, have often been led by such reasoning to worry about the autonomy of speculation in their field. Echoing Duhem, we can note, for example, attempts in the thirteenth century by theologians—as in the Condemnation of 1277—to impose limits on questions of natural philosophy, such as the eternity of the world, as debated in the schools of arts.

At this point, one is tempted to reflect once more on the late-medieval run-up to modern science. Among historians it is common to say that calls for a scientific theology in the thirteenth century, followed by conflicts surrounding the condemnations at century's end, led to a progressive distancing of the intellectual domains of theology and natural science in the fourteenth century. In the eyes of some interpreters, the upshot was a liberation of science. Thus the speculations of *John Buridan and *Nicole Oresme on geocentrism or the nature of motion, both in some way laying the groundwork for modern science. For others, however, there finally resulted an estrangement of theology from science so great that theologians no longer felt compelled to accommodate the ideas of contemporary scientists at all. The almost inevitable outcome, from this perspective, was Galileo's conviction for heresy. So far, advocates of the two approaches have found little common ground. Perhaps that will remain the case until we develop more subtle understandings of the sociology of knowledge.

See also **God in Christianity; Lombard, Peter; Reason; Scholasticism;** *Scientia*

Bibliography

Chenu, Marie-Dominique. *La théologie au douzième siècle.* 2nd edition. Paris: J. Vrin, 1966. (Partial translation: *Nature, Man, and Society in the Twelfth Century.* Chicago: University of Chicago Press, 1968.)

Eastwood, Bruce S. Medieval Empiricism. The Case of Grosseteste's Optics. *Speculum* (1968) 43: 306–321.

Funkenstein, Amos. *Theology and the Scientific Imagination from the Middle Ages to the Seventeenth Century.* Princeton: Princeton University Press, 1986.

Grant, Edward. "Science and Theology in the Middle Ages." In *God and Nature. Historical Essays.* Edited by David C. Lindberg and R.L. Numbers. Berkeley: University of California Press, 1986.

Kuhn, Thomas S. *The Copernican Revolution.* Cambridge, Mass.: Harvard University Press, 1957.

Marrone, Steven P. *The Light of Thy Countenance. Science and Knowledge of God in the Thirteenth Century.* 2 vols. Leiden: Brill, 2001.

Murdoch, John E. "Pierre Duhem and the History of Late Medieval Science and Philosophy in the Latin West." In *Gli studi di filosofia medievale fra otto e novecento.* Rome: Edizioni di Storia e Letteratura, 1991.

Tambiah, Stanley J. *Magic, Science, Religion, and the Scope of Rationality.* New York: Cambridge University Press, 1990.
STEVEN P. MARRONE

RICHARD OF MIDDLETON

A Franciscan theologian probably of English origin (c. 1249–1302), Richard of Middleton (Richardus de Mediavilla) studied at Paris, where he was regent master (professor) of the Franciscan School from 1284 to 1287. His most important works, contained in many manuscripts and printed in the sixteenth century, are a commentary on the *Sentences* by *Peter Lombard and eighty *Quodlibetal Questions.* Most of his *Disputed Questions* are still unpublished. Richard enjoyed great fame in schools for centuries.

Historians basically agree on Richard of Middleton's doctrinal position: he is rooted in the Franciscan tradition (especially the work of Bonaventure), although his views on philosophical and theological matters are closer to those of *Thomas Aquinas and Henry of Ghent, and he appears to have considerably assimilated *Aristotle's thought. In matters regarding physics and *cosmology, to safeguard divine almightiness and inspired to some degree by the *Condemnation of 1277, Richard made various corrections to the peripatetic view. Although his contribution to medieval thought is important, it is generally agreed to have had less significance than that attributed to it by Pierre Duhem (1861–1916), who described Richard as a forerunner of fourteenth-century or even of modern science.

Richard showed great interest in subjects taken from experience, particularly matters of natural philosophy. Discussing the epistemological foundations of theology, he certainly did not put forward an original theory of *scientia, in the Aristotelian meaning of the term. However, what is innovative and methodologically important in his work is the recognition that even some qualities, such as charity, can increase and decrease and therefore are measurable as a continuum: Although they have no mass quantity, they have a force quantity (*latitude of forms). Also various substantial forms, such as the *elements, "receive the more and the less."

Richard's interest in the quantitative aspects of scientific knowledge is confirmed by the attention he devoted to the question of the infinite. In his opinion, any mathematical quantity can be divided endlessly, but a physical quantity can be divided endlessly only by God: no created power could maintain in being parts of fire or air which are so small that they cannot act. However, even the result of any division performed by God would only be potentially infinite: any actual infinity is excluded in creatures.

Richard's argument, like Bonaventure's, was against the possibility of creation ab aeterno. However, this does not invalidate the possibility, completely excluded by the Aristotelian cosmology, of empty space, provided that it is finite: God could produce a vacuum by destroying any creature between the heaven and the earth. In defense of that view, Richard explicitly referred to the syllabus of Parisian bishop Stephen Tempier, and he did so again when he defended, against Aristotle (De coelo) and *Plato (Timaeus), the possibility that God may produce other worlds, by "world" meaning not the totality of creatures, but the things as a whole contained below a surface which is not contained in other surfaces. To explain the movement, he therefore combined the theory of natural places with an acknowledgement of the role of distance: Any body consisting of earth would naturally tend not to the center of its world but to the center of the world in which it was placed.

Richard showed greater interest than many theologians of his time in several matters of biology and theoretical medicine. However, while the zoological corpus and the Parva naturalia of Aristotle are used through precise quotations, his references to various medical theories of the tradition influenced by *Hippocrates and *Galen (spirits, humors, complexions, etc.) seem rather generic. In quite a few quodlibetal questions (on the imagination's capacity to change the body, on the premonitory value of dreams, and on the possibility of suggestion and telepathic communication), a widely used source is the De anima of Avicenna (*Ibn Sina), although it was in part contested by Richard since it goes against faith.

Once again, Richard's attitude toward Aristotelian doctrine appears ambivalent. He approved of the embryological theory of the gradual hominization in support of the theory of the plurality of forms in man, championed by Richard against Thomas Aquinas (treatise De gradu formarum). On the contrary, as regards the principles of human *generation, which is an important issue in the Sentences for the doctrine of the hereditary sin and for Christology, Richard corrected the Philosopher, interpreting him in the light of Avicenna's theory (De animalibus): in accordance with the point of view of physicians, a certain active role is also assigned to the "female seed" in the generative process.

See also **Medicine, theoretical; Religion and science**

Bibliography

Primary Sources

Richardus de Mediavilla. *Super quatuor Libros Sententiarum Petri Lombardi quaestiones subtilissimae (Questions on the Four Books of Peter Lombard's Sentences), Quodlibeta quaestiones octuaginta (Eighty Quodlibetal Questions).* 4 vols. Brescia, 1591; repr. Frankfurt am Main: Minerva, 1963.

——. *Quaestio de gradu formarum (A Question on the Hierarchy of Forms),* ed. R. Zavalloni, *Richard de Mediavilla et la controverse sur la pluralité des formes. Textes inédits et étude critique.* Louvain: Éditions de l'Institut Supérieur de Philosophie, 1951, 35–169.

Secondary Sources

Cova, Luciano. *Originale peccatum e concupiscentia in Riccardo di Mediavilla: vizio ereditario e sessualità nell'antropologia teologica del XIII secolo.* Rome: Edizioni dell'Ateneo, 1984.

Cross, Richard. "Richard of Middleton." In *A Companion to Philosophy in the Middle Ages.* Edited by Jorge J. E. Gracia and Timoth Noone. Oxford: Blackwell, 2003, 573–578.

Duhem, Pierre. *Le Système du monde. Histoire des doctrines cosmologiques de Platon à Copernic.* 10 vols. Paris: Hermann, 1913–1959.

Hocedez, Edgar. *Richard de Middleton: sa vie, ses oeuvres, sa doctrine.* Louvain: Spicilegium Sacrum Lovaniense, and Paris: Librairie Ancienne Honoré Champion, Édouard Champion, 1925.

LUCIANO COVA

RICHARD RUFUS OF CORNWALL

According to his younger contemporary *Roger Bacon, Richard Rufus of Cornwall was a favorite of the "foolish multitude," considered mad by the wise and censured at Paris when he lectured on theology there toward the end of his life. According to the Franciscan chronicler Thomas of Eccleston, the same Parisian lectures earned Rufus the renown of a "great and admirable philosopher."

Richard entered the Franciscan Order in 1238 as a Parisian master of arts. As a bachelor of theology, he lectured at Oxford around 1250 and in Paris around 1253, becoming that university's fifth Franciscan regent master of theology about three years later. He probably died not long after November 1259, when he inherited a habit and a copy of the canonical epistles.

As a Parisian master of arts before 1238 Rufus was one of the first to teach the scientific works of Aristotle, an established part of the undergraduate curriculum by 1255 but at the time still the object of suspicion and the subject of a ban on instruction at the university of Paris as late as 1231. His commentaries on Aristotle's *Metaphysics*, *Physics*, *De generatione et corruptione*, and *De anima* derived at least in part from his classroom lectures, are among the earliest works of this kind to survive from the Latin West. At Oxford, Rufus was the first bachelor of theology to lecture on *Peter Lombard's *Sentences*, following Richard Fishacre who lectured on Lombard as a master of theology.

As a student of Aristotelian natural philosophy Rufus was in the first instance a commentator on Aristotelian texts, examining and resolving doubts raised by the texts at hand.

For Rufus following Aristotle, "science" (*scientia*) was knowledge derived from logical demonstration. Aristotle was an eminently logical writer, and the elucidation of the deductive part of his thought was no small part of the commentator's task. At the same time, however, Rufus was fully prepared to compare his reading of Aristotle with the testimony of experience, as with the demands of Christian belief, and willing, where necessary, to revise Aristotle's claims, taking a questioning, critical approach which set an agenda for his successors.

Physics

Rufus's treatment of the problem of projectile motion in Book Eight of the *Physics* offers a good example of his intellectual methods, as well as one which was to be influential in the later development of medieval impetus theory. According to Aristotle's understanding, motion involves contact between a moving body and something that moves it; physical bodies do not move in the absence of a distinct motor moving them. Yet a ball continues to move in the direction it is thrown after it leaves the hand of the thrower, and an arrow in the direction it is shot after it leaves the bow: what, then, accounts for this motion? On Aristotle's own account, as Rufus presents it—following the interpretation of Aristotle's great Arabic commentator Averroes (*Ibn Rushd)—it is the medium, the air or water through which the projectile passes, which moves it along. Because of their flexibility and divisibility, air and water have the special property of being able to pass on the motion they have received from the initial mover even when they themselves have ceased to be moved, albeit with gradually decreasing force as one part of air or water moves the next.

For Rufus, however, this is a piece of special pleading consistent neither with Aristotelian principles nor with the observable phenomena. To the extent that this solution simply displaces the problem of finding a mover from the projectile to the medium, Rufus is able to defend (or interpret) Aristotle by means of an appeal to another

Aristotelian fundamental, the composition of all natural bodies by form and matter. A projector throwing a ball divides the air in an unnatural or violent way by his motion, separating and expanding its parts to a greater extent than is compatible with the form of air (which governs, among other things, the density and internal distribution of its matter). The separated parts do not return initially to their proper position but are more condensed than is compatible with their form. Each successive compression and expansion of the parts of the air distend it less until the parts come to rest at their proper place. The successive motion of the parts before they come to rest in the proper position produces a motion that is transmitted to the ball without the need to postulate an additional mover. It is, Rufus says, "as we see in the string of a lyre pulled out of its place."

Still, Rufus goes on to point out, this cannot be a sufficient explanation—even if, as he also notes, it may have been enough for Aristotle's immediate purposes. Two projectiles can pass one another in the same medium going in different directions, and a stone is more easily thrown than a ball of feathers of the same size; something other than the medium and its motion, therefore, must be responsible for these different results. This Rufus characterizes as an "impression" made by the thrower on the thing thrown, rearranging its parts in a way similar to the rearrangement of the parts of the medium already described. Heavier things receive a stronger impression because they offer greater resistance, having a greater natural inclination to be elsewhere (that is, to fall downward), and violence, by definition, is proportional to resistance.

Psychology

In his commentary on Aristotle's *De anima* Rufus does not pursue this account, although its elements can be found: there are impressions received (2.12.Q4), effects caused by rearrangement of parts (2.10.Q1), and the persistence of motion in compressed media (3.12.E2). Whereas in the *Physics* Rufus sought to supplement Aristotle's account, in his psychology Rufus eventually departs deliberately from Aristotle's explanation of apprehension. Rufus prefers Augustine's account of how species in our organs of perception produce sensation in the soul. Rather than acting directly on the soul, such species excite the soul, which responds to that stimulation by considering within itself a similitude of that species (2.12.Q2). In his *De anima* commentary, Rufus seeks to support this account of excitation by reference to the Aristotle's analogy between sensation and the impression made on wax by a signet ring: nothing material is transmitted. In his *Contra Averroem 1*, Rufus makes it explicit that the species received are not efficient causes of sensation, and in his last lectures on Aristotelian natural philosophy, he not only explicitly accepts Augustine's account but also asks whether Aristotle's claim that sensible objects move the soul is deceptive or can be salvaged.

On the whole, however, Rufus taught his students Aristotelian psychology: species of colors and other sensible qualities found in external objects are received by our five particular external senses, which are linked to what Aristotelians call a "common sense" that apprehends motion, rest, and other common sensibles. Our ability to receive, retain, and reproduce sensible images or phantasms is a function of imagination or memory. Within the intellect, the "possible intellect" that responds to sensation is distinguished from the "agent intellect" that abstracts sensible forms making them accessible to the "possible intellect." Absent from Rufus's account is the estimative faculty postulated by Avicenna (*Ibn Sina) and Arab psychologists to account for flight or pursuit responses.

Chemistry

For Rufus and other medieval Aristotelians everything in the external world is ultimately comprised of four elements—earth, water, air, and fire. Even the simple body fire contains within it the other three elements subsisting in essential potential. When the elements combine and mix with each other to produce complex substances, the substantial change is incomplete, since the ingredients from which they are made persist in accidental (proximate) potential, rather than essential (remote) potential.

Mixture is the process that combines ingredients. We call the product of elemental mixture "mixts" (from the Latin *mixtum*) rather than "mixtures" to distinguish product from process.

The elements combine to produce like parted substances or homoeomeries. Animated homoeomeries or mixts such as flesh, blood, bone, and bile are combined to produce organs such as the head, heart, and liver, the hetereomerous parts of plants and animals; inanimate homoeomeries such as sulfur and mercury combine in various proportions to produce different metals.

Rufus explains substantial change as a function of form and ultimate matter. Ultimate matter includes not only prime matter but also contrary forms existing in potential (*Phys.* 2.2.1). In the case of elemental change from fire to air, air to water, and so on, the underlying matter is informed only by the most general form. The matter underlying homoeomerous parts, such as bone, blood or bile, are the elements themselves. More complex mixtures combine ingredients that are themselves mixts. Silver and gold, for example, are produced when their substantial form actualizes matter having the correct proportions of mercury and sulfur. Animals are characterized by two kinds of forms, their substantial form—humanity, for example—and the form of the body that informs the four elements in mixts such as flesh or blood (*Phys.* 2.5.2).

Since the elements in a primary mixt persist in proximate potential, such that only their combination with elements having contrary qualities prevents them from actualizing their distinctive elemental qualities, they can reemerge from the mixt when it breaks down. The possibility that elements can be recovered from a mixt is one of six criteria for an Aristotelian mixture. In addition, to (1) Recoverability, the others are as follows: (2) Uniformity: Every part of a mixt is the same; it has the same ingredients in the same proportion; (3) Potentiality: Ingredients exist potentially in the mixt; (4) Equilibrium: The powers of the mixable bodies balance each other; (5) Alteration: Mixture involves the alteration of the qualities of the ingredients over time. Since their interaction is reciprocal, ingredients must share the same kind of matter; (6) Incompleteness: The change involved in mixture is not total.

These criteria serve to distinguish mixture from generation and corruption, juxtaposition, augmentation, and alteration.

Rufus's distinctive contribution to the theory of Aristotelian mixture is his account of the state of the elements within the mixt: the claim that they are in accidental or proximate potential. Rufus refers to embedded forms in accidental potential as matter's active potentials. He describes matter that includes an active potential to emerge into actuality in the right conditions of heat and humidity as a "necessity."

Nutrition is another form of incomplete change, in which food flows in and becomes flesh—or bone, or bile, etc.—as it is absorbed, but also deteriorates and flows out and is eliminated. Aristotle characterizes nutrition by three criteria. It must be the result of the addition of something external; the internal flesh which is nourished must persist through the change, and every part of flesh must be nourished. These criteria serve to distinguish nutrition from qualitative change, generation, and corruption.

The problem with these criteria is that jointly they seem to imply one of the following: that there is a void into which food flows as it is absorbed; that food and flesh must coexist in the same place, or that only some parts of the flesh grow. Aristotle's solution is to distinguish between flesh by species and flesh by matter. Rufus accepts this distinction but rejects what he takes to be Aristotle's deployment of his distinction to solve the problem. Instead Rufus solves this problem by suggesting that after the food loses its form, its matter is subsumed under flesh by matter, so that they both occupy the same place. Flesh by species together with flesh by matter including active potentials that enable it to grow inform the advening matter of the food to produce new flesh. Since the unity thus achieved is imperfect, and the matter of the food that has become flesh retains its non-fleshy potentials, the fleshy mixture partly breaks down, and some of the matter absorbed from food is eliminated and flows out.

Conclusion

Richard Rufus taught physics, psychology, and chemistry from Aristotelian texts and responded critically and creatively to problems in Aristotelian science. As a theologian, he continued to address many of the same problems—including, for example, a discussion of nutrition in answering the question what is true humanity. The excitement of his approach helps to explain the rapid introduction of Aristotelian natural philosophy into the curriculum. He was deeply indebted to Averroes from whom he took not only an interpretative approach to

Aristotle but also a set of important issues. By contrast, Rufus seems deliberately to have avoided positions stated by Avicenna, which may account in part for Roger Bacon's hostility since Bacon was committed to defending Avicenna as the greatest authority on Aristotelian philosophy.

Like Bacon, Rufus was strongly influenced by *Robert Grosseteste and concerned about the consistency of Aristotelian natural philosophy with Christian theology. Unlike Bacon, however, Rufus adopted from Grosseteste not only a special regard for knowledge acquired by experience, but also a willingness to reject Aristotle's views. Rufus took this step decades before Bacon was willing to do so, so the lectures they gave at Paris before 1250 are quite different even if often closely related. Those lectures exercised considerable influence on the subsequent commentary tradition; the difference in their approach explains in part the richness of the scholastic tradition.

See also Cosmology; Elements and qualities; Hylomorphism; Impetus; Nature: diverse medieval interpretations; Psychology; Scholasticism; *Scientia*; Universities

Bibliography

Primary Sources

Brewer, J. S., ed. *Monumenta franciscana; scilicet, I. Thomas de Eccleston de adventu fratrum minorum in Angliam; II. Adae de Marisco epistolae; III. Registrum fratrum minorum Londoniae. Rerum britannicarum medii aevi scriptores, or Chronicles and Memorials of Great Britain and Ireland during the Middle Ages (Rolls Series)*, vol. 4. London: Longman, Brown, Green, Longmans, and Roberts, 1858.

Denifle, Henricus, and Aemilius Chatelain, eds. *Chartularium universitatis parisiensis*. Vol. 1, *Ab anno MCC usque ad annum MCCLXXXVI*. Paris: Ex typis fratrum Delalain, 1889.

Richard Rufus of Cornwall. [Pseudo-Peter of Spain]. Expositio libri De anima. In *Pedro Hispano, Obras filos—ficas*, vol. 3. Edited by Manuel Alonso. Instituto de Filosofía "Luis Vives," Serie A, no. 4. Madrid: Consejo Superior de Investigaciones Cient'ficas, 1952.

———. *In Physicam Aristotelis*. Edited by Rega Wood. Auctores britannici medii aevi, no. 16. Oxford: For the British Academy, by Oxford University Press, 2003.

Roger Bacon. *Compendium of the Study of Theology*. Edited and translated by Thomas S. Maloney. Studien und Texte zur Geistesgeschichte des Mittelalters, ed. Albert Zimmermann, vol. 20. New York: E. J. Brill, 1988.

Thomas of Eccleston. *Tractatus de adventu fratrum minorum in Angliam*. Edited by A. G. Little. Tout Memorial Publication Fund. Manchester, England: Manchester University Press, 1951.

Secondary Sources

Little, A. G. The Franciscan School at Oxford in the Thirteenth Century. Archivum franciscanum historicum (1926) 19: 803–874.

Raedts, Peter. *Richard Rufus of Cornwall and the Tradition of Oxford Theology*. Oxford Historical Monographs. Oxford: Clarendon Press, 1987.

Weisberg, Michael, and Rega Wood. Richard Rufus's Theory of Mixture: A Medieval Explanation of Chemical Combination. In *Chemical Explanation: Characteristics, Development, Autonomy*, ed. Joseph E. Earley, Sr. Annals of the New York Academy of Sciences, vol. 988. New York: New York Academy of Sciences, 2003, 282-292.

Wood, Rega. Richard Rufus of Cornwall and Aristotle's Physics. Franciscan Studies (1992) 52: 247–281.

———. Richard Rufus of Cornwall on Creation: The Reception of Aristotelian Physics in the West. *Medieval Philosophy and Theology* (1992) 2: 1–30.

———. Richard Rufus: Physics at Paris before 1240. *Documenti e studi sulla tradizione filosofica medievale* (1994) 5: 87–127.

———. Roger Bacon: Richard Rufus' Successor as a Parisian Physics Professor. *Vivarium* (1997) 35: 222–250.

———. Richard Rufus's De anima Commentary: The Earliest Known, Surviving, Western De anima Commentary. *Medieval Philosophy and Theology* (2001) 10: 119–156.

REGA WOOD AND JENNIFER OTTMAN

ROADS

Transportation by water was so much cheaper than overland transport that new roads were rarely built in the Middle Ages and efforts to improve communications were focused instead on *bridges. Upgrading a river crossing from ford to bridge was more cost-effective than building a new road. Thus, road construction cannot be described as an organized engineering activity in the medieval world. Rather, it is appropriate to speak of strategies or responses that medieval societies adopted to deal with a defined category of infrastructure. Wherever Roman roads survived, they often continued in use, to the point at which there are many instances of modern trunk highways reflecting continuity in use since Roman times. In eastern Spain, the Via Augusta is marked by place names in Romance and Romance Arabisms, such as Llosa and Albalat, both meaning paving stones and, by extension, highway (the town of al-Balat in northern Syria is likewise adjacent to a Roman road).

The basic medieval sense of road (*via*) was an unobstructed right of way. In the early Middle Ages, such rural roads as existed were generally unsuitable for wheeled vehicles, so the right of way had be broadly interpreted. Thus, in 972 the abbot of the monastery of Cardeña secured a royal privilege to take a cart "through whatever place it might go: if there were no direct highway we give you license to pass through pastures, through cultivated fields and vineyards, and to break boundaries along the way taken in order to proceed by cart, or horses, or loaded mules."

Practically no building of new roads was done. Causeways of considerable extension were built in marshes or in connection with drainage, but technically they had more in common with bridges, using similar construction techniques. Other than such infrequent projects, the most one finds are major repairs as when, in 1353, King Edward III of England ordered the resurfacing of the road from Temple Bar to Winchester: landowners on each side of the road were responsible for clearing a footpath seven feet (2.1 m) wide, with a paved central strip.

The Arco de Bara over the Via Augusta near Tarragona in eastern Spain. Paved by the Romans, this 1,700-mile (2,735 km) road between Rome and Cádiz was maintained more or less unaltered throughout the Middle Ages. (Corbis/Archivo Iconografico, S.A.)

Work gangs from towns, originally recruited to work on city walls, were also used for road work. In the course of the transition from Roman to feudal modes of governance the responsibility for maintaining roads, whether rural or urban, typically shifted from public authorities to private proprietors on whose parcels such roads bounded. Both town and royal ordinances make this clear.

City Streets

Roman paving was not usually a factor in medieval towns. The constant rebuilding of urban space tended to raised the street level over time to the point where, in formerly Roman towns as separate as Canterbury (England) and Barcelona (Spain), the Roman street level is between thirteen and nineteen feet (4–6 m) below the current level.

Medieval town officials were constantly at pains to keep the streets clean and in repair. The main problems were dumping household and trade refuse into the streets or otherwise unlawfully blocking free passage. Such problems can be appreciated from fourteenth-century dispositions of the town council of London, recorded in pipe-rolls (1326) "That all streets and lanes of the City and suburbs be cleansed and delivered of rubbish, timber and other hindrances, and that pentices and jetties be so high that man may ride beneath without hindrances, and that if any be ruinous and dangerous, they be removed."

Routine street cleaning was handled independently be each ward, which hired *rakyeres* (rakers) to clear the rubbish. Citizens were responsible for the condition of the street in front of their houses or shops. In 1362 the aldermen proclaimed "that each one keep his street clean according to the ordinance thereon made; that no one cast water or anything else out of window but bring it down and put it in the kennel." Large cities had public works bureaus charged with maintenance of walls, moats, and streets. In Valencia, royal roads within the municipal bounds of the city of Valencia (which included the surrounding agricultural district or huerta) and the ditches draining them were under the supervision of the municipal office of walls and sewers (*Fabrica de Murs i Valls*). Their maintenance therefore fell within the jurisdiction of the town council, which on occasion would name a road inspector (*visitador dels camins*) to make the round of the royal roads once or twice a month to enforce its rulings. Failure to comply with road regulations was the subject of a communication from Prince John of Navarre to the bailiff general of Valencia in 1450. The municipal officials had informed the Prince that the roads of the huerta were totally ruined as a result of the inattention of the residents, especially in flooding the roads. They suggested that the treasurer (*racional*) of the city be given charge of enforcing the road regulations. That royal justice has to be invoked in routine maintenance of roads suggests the intractability of the problem.

In Europe, it might be said with respect to communications that bridges, not roads, were the crucial elements. Bridges were a necessity and were regarded as both utilitarian and aesthetically pleasing, prestigious works that could be paid for by tolls and other capitalization strategies. Masons and carpenters were plentiful. Conversely, roads presented too many problems for a society segmented into multiple jurisdictions.

In the Islamic world, wheeled vehicles disappeared in the early Middle Ages because camels proved to be an economically more efficient means of transport. As a result, the pattern of regularly laid-out streets in former Roman cities was gradually subverted. Without wheeled vehicles, there was no need to keep them up. Streets were nothing more than the places left over between buildings, which accounts for the often sinuous nature of urban street trajectories in Muslim towns. Streets followed the natural pitches of local topography, although clearly municipal authorities were charged with a certain level of upkeep, and certain conventions of design were obeyed, such as cambering streets in such a way that sewage and run-off ran down the middle of the street, sometimes guided by paving stones.

See also **Bridges; Technological diffusion; Transportation**

Bibliography

Bulliet, Richard. *The Camel and the Wheel.* New York: Columbia University Press, 1990.

Hindle, Brian Paul. *Medieval Roads.* Aylesbury: Shire Publications, 1982.

Hindley, Geoffrey. *A History of Roads.* Secaucus, N.J: Citadel, 1972.

Menéndez Pidal, Gonzalo. *Los caminos en la historia de España.* Madrid: Cultura Hispánica, 1951.

Rubiera, María Jesús. *Villena en las calzadas romana y árabe.* Alicante: Universidad de Alicante, 1985.

THOMAS F. GLICK

S

SALERNITAN QUESTIONS

The term "Salerntian Questions" refers to a collection of twenty-nine or thirty to three hundred thirty-two (and even as few as seven in one manuscript) Latin questions and answers on natural philosophy (*Questiones phisicales*), probably compiled c. 1200 (if not somewhat earlier) by an English scholar perhaps in the circle of Hereford known for its translations of Arabic mathematical treatises into Latin.

The date of the collection is estimated on the basis of the quotations, the absence of material resulting from the so-called "new Aristotle," and the reduced use of Latin translations of Arabic works by *Gerard of Cremona (c. 1114–1187).

The text, which includes later interpolations, is formed of different groups of questions from various sources, all of which cannot necessarily be well identified. The original compiler seems to have been a non-clerical master in a faculty of arts (since he refers to sexual matters without the reticence that might be expected from religious or monastic teachers), who was trained in *physica* at *Salerno or another place not well identified (Montpellier or Paris) where Salernitan teaching had arrived prior to 1200. His audience probably was students of medicine, and his teaching activity is likely to have dealt with *physica* (including medicine). Some theological content is present in the collection, a fact that does not necessarily imply that the later masters who contributed to the collection taught in religious schools; some of them might have had clerical status.

The core of the collection comes almost certainly from the School of Salerno (there is an explicit reference to Salerno in two questions), and is influenced by the teaching of such Salernitan masters as Urso and Maurus of Salerno. The sources include classical material such as the Hippocratic *Aphorisms* in the translation attributed to *Constantine the African (d. after 1085); the *Tegni* (or *Microtegni*, or *Ars parva*) of Galen in the *versio antiqua*, which seems to have been made from the Greek text and not from an Arabic version; inauthentic Galenic treatises (*De oculis*, *De spermate*, and *De compagine membrorum sive de natura humana*); some classical poets (Lucretius, Juvenal, Ovid, and Virgil); Latin encyclopedias (principally Pliny and *Isidore of Seville) and philosophers (Seneca); and Dioscorides, *De materia medica*. Late antique works are present with Vindicianus, the *Gynaecia* of Caelius Aurelianus, the *Epistola de observatione ciborum* of Anthimus, and the *De viribus herbarum* of Macer. Among the Salernitan and post-Salernitan works, one can quote the *Pantegni theorica* and other treatises of Constantine the African, the *Anatomia* of Copho, the *Aphorismi*, *De coloribus*, and *De commixtionibus elementorum* by Urso of Salerno, the *Super Isagogen Ioannitii*, as well as the *Regulae urinarum* by Maurus of Salerno, the *De febribus* of Garioponto, the *Flos Medicinae* of Salerno, the *Anatomia Nicolai* (c. 1170), the *Circa instans* of Mattheus Platearius, and the *Liber Dietarum universalium* by Isaac Israeli (*Isaac Judaeus). Among the texts by English authors there is the *Dragmaticon* of *William of Conches, and the *Topographia Hibernie* by Giraldus Cambrensis (c. 1185).

The genre of the *questiones* dates back to the *Problemata* of the Aristotelian school and was particularly productive in the Middle Ages, especially as a support for teaching. It remained in use during the Renaissance: for instance, the *Speculator* by Theodoricus Ulstenius (c. 1460–1508) used material from the Salernitan questions.

See also **Aristotelianism**; *Articella*; **Medicine, theoretical**; **Scholasticism**

Bibliography

Lawn, Brian. *The Salernitan Questions. An Introduction to the History of Medieval and Renaissance Problem Literature*. Oxford: Clarendon Press, 1963.
———. *The Prose Salernitan Questions edited from a Bodleian manuscript (Auct. F. 3. 10)*. London and Oxford: The British Academy and Oxford University Press, 1979.

ALAIN TOUWAIDE

SALERNO

Salerno is a city in southern Italy along the coast of the Tyrrhenian Sea, south of Naples. Founded as a Roman colony in antiquity, it was essentially refounded by the Lombards in the eighth century, later serving as the capital of the Norman Principality of Salerno until Count Roger II, in creating himself King of Sicily, moved the capital to Palermo in 1130. Salerno, still known today as the *Civitas Hippocratica* ("Hippocratic State"), is famous in the history of science primarily for its medical school, the reputation of which extended throughout Europe, despite the fact that in the twelfth century it was no more than an informal gathering of masters and pupils. Its importance declined in the thirteenth century with the rise of rival medical centers in Bologna, Montpellier, and Paris. Nevertheless, its contribution to medical learning in western Europe was profound, for it was here that the highly philosophical Galenic medicine of the Arabic world first made its entrance into medieval western Europe.

Salerno's medical history is often divided into three periods: early Salerno, when it was distinguished primarily by the empirical skills of its practitioners; "high" Salerno, essentially the twelfth century, when the most important Salernitan medical texts were compiled; and late Salerno, the thirteenth century and on, when Salerno continued to be a medical center of local importance but had faded from international prominence.

Most of the tales of early Salerno concern skilled individual practitioners. For example, the Norman historian Orderic Vitalis (1075–c. 1142) tells of a monk who traveled in the mid-eleventh century to France and Italy in order to educate himself. Already erudite by the time he reached Salerno, he nevertheless found himself bested in medical knowledge by a learned woman (*sapiens matrona*). The city's doctors were always seeking ways to improve clinical medicine. In the mid-eleventh-century a Salernitan named Gariopontus revised and restructured a body of medical writings that had been circulating in Europe since late antiquity. His *Passionarius* was then commented on by students using textual exegesis similar to that which would characterize *Scholasticism. The same technique would later be used to analyze a body of introductory texts that came to be known as the *Articella* and served as the foundation for medical teaching throughout western Europe.

In the twelfth century, dozens of other medical works were composed in Salerno, only some of which have identifiable authors. They included writings on medical theory (including three tracts on pigs, whose *anatomy was studied in lieu of human dissections); diagnosis and therapeutics (including general medicine, fevers, uroscopy, and *gynecology); and major *pharmaceutic handbooks (including the two most influential in all medieval Europe, the *Circa instans* and the *Antidotarium Nicolai*). There was also work on medical ethics. Only *surgery seems to have remained underdeveloped among the medical subdisciplines at Salerno.

While empirical concerns with effective therapy never diminished, Salernitan practitioners increasingly tied their practices to an understanding of how medical theory explained the causes of disease and the effects of drugs. Practitioners moved from calling themselves simply *medici* (healers) to *medici et phisici* (healers and persons learned in natural science), hence the origin of the term still used in English today for medical doctor, "physician." Perhaps influenced by the Muslims who still populated Sicily at the time, in 1140 King Roger II instituted a regulation that obliged prospective physicians to present themselves to his officials and judges for an examination of their skill and basic knowledge.

Salerno's fortunes declined after the city was sacked by in 1194 by the Holy Roman Emperor Henry VI. Although some of the most accomplished theoretical work came from scholars active around 1200—including *Urso of Calabria, *Maurus, and *Gilles of Corbeil—the absence of any major figures in the thirteenth century suggests a marked disruption in intellectual life. Outside Salerno, Salernitan texts, or works influenced by the perspectives of the Salernitan school (such as a series of natural science interrogations known simply as the *Salernitan Questions) were widely circulated, becoming particularly popular in England.

Despite Salerno's importance in the general history of medicine, research into the period has progressed little since the Salernitan scholar Salvatore De Renzi published his monumental but flawed five-volume study of the school in the mid-nineteenth century. Small theses on individual texts appeared regularly from students of Karl Sudhoff in Leipzig early in the twentieth century and isolated researches by modern scholars continue, but these have yet to assess all that the medical practitioners and writers of medieval Salerno achieved.

See also **Constantine the African; Galen; Gilles de Corbeil; Johannes de Sancto Paulo; Medicine, practical; Medicine, theoretical; Trotula; Universities**

Bibliography

Amarotta, Arcangelo R. *Salerno romana e medievale: Dinamica di un insediamento*. Società Salernitana di Storia Patria, Collana di Studi Storici Salernitani, 2. Salerno: Pietro Laveglia, 1989.

Chiarelli, Leonard C. A Preliminary Study on the Origins of Medical Licensing in the Medieval Mediterranean. *Al-Masaq: Islam and the Medieval Mediterranean* (1998) 10: 1–11.

Cuna, Andrea. *Per una bibliografia della Scuola medica Salernitana (secoli XI-XIII)*. Milan: Guerini e Associati, 1993.

Glaze, Florence Eliza. "The Perforated Wall: The Ownership and Circulation of Medical Books in Medieval Europe, c. 800–1200." Ph.D. Dissertation, Duke University, 1999.

Jordan, Mark D. The Construction of a Philosophical Medicine: Exegesis and Argument in Salernitan Teaching on the Soul. *Osiris*, 2d ser. (1990) 6: 42–61.

Kristeller, Paul Oskar. *Studi sulla Scuola medica Salernitana*. Naples: Istituto Italiano per gli Studi Filosofici, 1986.

Renzi, Salvatore De (ed.). *Collectio Salernitana ossia documenti inediti, e trattati di medicina appartenenti alla scuola medica salernitana*. 5 vols. Naples: Filiatre-Sebezio, 1852–1859; repr. Bologna: Forni, 1967.

Skinner, Patricia. *Health and Medicine in Early Medieval Southern Italy.* The Medieval Mediterranean, 11. Leiden: E.J. Brill, 1997.

MONICA H. GREEN

SCHOLASTICISM

The term "scholasticism" generally refers to both a historical movement and a systematic method that arose during the Middle Ages and (notwithstanding the derogatory views of Renaissance humanists, who first coined the term) exerted enormous influence on the intellectual culture of the period.

Perhaps the most fundamental issue concerned with the history of Scholasticism is its origin. Early scholars contended that elements of scholastic method and the culture of Scholasticism go all the way back to antiquity and Aristotle in particular. But while it is certainly the case that there were ancient schools, that Aristotle discussed a dialectical procedure in his writings, and that medieval scholars drew on those discussions in formulating their scholastic method, the causal connection is at best remote rather than proximate. Early scholars, such as Endres and Grabmann, pointed instead to a confluence of related developments in different disciplines. As Europe emerged from the tenth-century invasions and the consequent social and political instabilities they produced, both the Church and emerging states sought to collect and compile legal codes, a movement that was assisted by the recovery of Roman law. But it is instructive to note that when Roman law came to light in Italy at the end of the eleventh century, it was the Digest—a compilation of the legal opinions of Roman jurists—and not the Code or the Novels that attracted the greatest interest. Earlier in the century, both Burchard of Worms (d. 1025) and Ivo of Chartres (c. 1040–1115) compiled large collections of rules governing all manner of Christian behavior. At the same time, the Church came to recognize that doctrinal pronouncements by the Fathers and the popes were in an equal state of disorganization, and frequently contradiction, as *Peter Abelard (1079–1142) observed in his *Sic et non.* Grabmann and others observed that some of the earliest examples of scholastic method arise in the contexts of assimilating and reconciling discordant legal and doctrinal pronouncements, as Gratian did for canon law in his *Decretum* (1140) and *Peter Lombard (1095/1100–1160) did for theology in the *Sentences* (written 1155–1157).

While Grabmann recognized that Abelard could not be the father of this movement or method (both because the technique was already in place before his time and because the *Sic et non* failed to adopt the various methodological rules he set forth in the prologue), he generally considered Scholasticism a Western creation, with some influence from Byzantine writers such as Photius (820–897). In reaction to this general consensus, George Makdisi argued that the Scholastic movement and method could be seen in earlier Islamic legal developments. Most instructive for

Makdisi was the fact that the technique of *al-khilaf*, what he referred to as the "sic-et-non method," was central to the Islamic process for determining orthodoxy. In his view, Islam had to depend on consensus (*ijma*) to define orthodoxy because it had no councils or synods; *al-khilaf* provided the technique for assessing consensus. As he put it, "the development of this method [*viz., sic et non*] in Christianity could very well not have happened at all, whereas without it, Islam could not have remained Islamic." Leaving aside the formal discrepancies between the techniques employed by Ibn 'Aqil, the eleventh-century legal scholar in whose works Makdisi found the use of *al-khilaf*, and the scholastic works of *Thomas Aquinas (c. 1224–1274), this characterization misconstrues the Latin connections between Scholastic culture and synodical or conciliar declarations. For it was almost always the case that doctrinal positions were promulgated by synods and councils after protracted and often intense debate and disagreement in the very Scholastic documents and procedures that Makdisi considered incidental to Christian culture. Seen from this perspective, however much transmission may have occurred, the incentives for scholastic techniques seem to have been equally present in both Islamic and Christian cultures.

The Nature of Scholasticism

At its core, Scholasticism refers to the pedagogical technique of the schools. Indeed, the term itself is derived from the *magister scholasticus*, the schoolmaster or head of instruction in the studia of monasteries, religious houses, or cathedrals. The central focus of scholastic education was the authoritative text, whether legal, philosophical, medical or theological. The prominence of the text can be seen in each of the two main pedagogical techniques of medieval education, the lecture and the disputation.

Unlike its modern namesake, the medieval lecture (*lectura*, literally a reading) was a sequential introduction to the text that defined the course. Within the university setting, lectures were distinguished by both the content and the time of day in which they were given. In the morning, fully qualified masters gave their detailed and comprehensive "ordinary" lectures on the core texts of the curriculum. These were followed in the afternoon by "extraordinary" or "cursory" lectures delivered by bachelors—that is, apprentice scholars whose lectures were part of their training for the degree—over the same books (essentially providing the medieval equivalent to the modern review session) or over secondary books in the curriculum. The lecture itself followed a formal pattern. First, the act of reading the base text sometimes provided a copy of the work itself; the frequent complaints of students that the reading proceeded too quickly and the countervailing injunctions of university authorities against reading too slowly suggest that transmission of the text *viva voce* did occur. Second, the lecturer "established the text," that is, provided corrections to errors within circulating copies, thereby ensuring that all students in the class were using the same text. Third, he noted the hierarchical divisions of the text, which in surviving student copies often appear as gibbet-like symbols. Fourth, the master explained linguistic, terminological difficulties, as well as the positions adopted by previous authoritative commentators on the text, both as preliminaries to his own more extended analysis. Finally, important questions or issues within the section of text under discussion that day were analyzed in greater detail.

In short, the lecture provided a relatively economical technique for the transmission of an authoritative textual tradition, one that emphasized both order and recollection of detail. By contrast, the second pedagogical technique, the disputation, assumed the assimilation of this tradition and encouraged the creative juxtaposition of elements from the texts to resolve problems. The centrality of this exercise can be seen in its presence throughout the scholar's life: part of the bachelor's training involved attendance at his master's disputations, and in time he was obliged to "respond" (responsiones) in a private mock dispute with his master or other students; magisterial careers included the expectation of engaging regularly in disputations, either the ordinary kind, in which positions were carefully proposed and prepared in advance, or de quolibet, in which the master would debate any question with any person. Such an exercise was an academic tour de force, in which students and masters alike could display their intellectual prowess, but they also were a means of expanding and extending the tradition of the text.

Although the lecture predated the disputation in the pedagogical development of the early university, one can also see how the disputed question evolved from the lecture. As masters prepared their lectures, certain parts of the text proved problematic and necessitated prolonged resolution. In the prologue to his Sic et non, Abelard articulated several possible explanations for apparent contradictions within the text, including the variability of language and meaning, false attributions of authorship, corruptions in the text itself, and retractions within the writings of authorities. In response, Abelard noted that "consistent or frequent questioning is defined as the first key to wisdom," and then immediately observed that "Aristotle, the most clear-sighted of all philosophers, urges us to grasp this wholeheartedly." By themselves, these questions raised within the context of the lecture did not constitute disputations, but it appears that by the time of Simon de Tournai (c. 1130–c. 1203), that is, by the opening years of the thirteenth century, a repertoire of such questions had been detached from the lecture and formed autonomous exercises in their own right. This process was aided by the masters' growing recognition that education involved active engagement of the text, the creation of several compendia of "sentences"—the opinions of authoritative authors—and the growing assimilation of the new logic of Aristotle, especially the two Analytics, the Topics, and the Sophistical Refutations.

While the precise formulation of the disputed question both varied across European universities and evolved through the High Middle Ages, a central format can be seen within the genre. First, the question, appropriately formulated and answerable either in the affirmative or the negative, is enunciated. Following this, in support of one response—generally the one that is ultimately rejected—the author presents several "principal arguments." In the Sed contra, the author observes the contrary position, generally supported by an authoritative quotation. Following this, the author presents his extended discussion of the issue (the responsio) in a format that displayed considerable variation throughout the Middle Ages. By the fourteenth century, for example, it was not uncommon for authors to present multiple opinions expressed by previous scholars and arguments against those opinions as well as subsidiary conclusions and doubts that serve as preliminaries to the author's ultimate resolution of the question. Finally, the author returns to the "principal arguments" and replies to each, often drawing on the distinctions and conclusions developed in the responsio.

Transcription and Dissemination

Although the lecture and the disputation were oral exercises in the university, both came to be disseminated in written format through reportationes, that is, a transcription prepared during the oral session by someone else, a reportator. Beyond these "live" sessions, works that were originally delivered orally and transcribed were also revised by master himself and "published" as ordinationes. As a result, scholastic materials survive in a complex array of formats, from occasional notes used by masters in the oral sessions, to private student notes, more authoritative reportationes and subsequently ordinationes, and finally derivatives of these materials, often abbreviations that permitted rapid scanning of results without the more tendentious details.

Other forms of scholastic literature often reflect the techniques developed in the lecture and disputation. The systematic and comprehensive Summae, in which both law and theology were organized with rigor and precision, reflect in their constituent parts the questions that lay at the heart of the disputation. The scholastic commentary on authoritative texts adopted techniques from both the lecture and the disputation, depending on whether the commentary was structured as a literal exposition or a topical series of questions. But beyond these products of lecture and disputation, a collection of ancillary literatures grew up to help scholastic authors in the preparation of their works. Chief among these was the florilegium, a collection of extracts taken from authoritative authors. Florilegia that focused on the bible or the Fathers were extremely popular among sermon writers and theologians, but philosophical florilegia, such as the Auctoritates Aristotelis or the Propositiones Aristotelis, were mined for the commentary literature, both in the arts and theology. Union lists of books and catalogues of libraries, arranged alphabetically and thematically, appeared in the thirteenth century and proved to be enormously valuable in the search for materials on which to base lectures and commentaries. Handbooks of logical technique, such as *William of Heytesbury's Rules for *solving sophisms*, were aimed at the undergraduate market as guides in training young scholars in the art of disputation. And finally, in the service of those preparing for examinations, compendia of questions and responses such as those found in Barcelona, Archivio de la Corona de Aragón, Ripoll 109, served as convenient (if frequently misleading) study aids to overburdened students of the scholastic curriculum.

See also **Aristotelianism; Cathedral schools; Encyclopedias; Universities; Vocabulary**

Bibliography

Baldwin, John W. *The Scholastic Culture of the Middle Ages, 1000–1300.* Lexington: Heath, 1971.

Bazàn, Bernardo C. *Les Questions disputées et les questions quodlibétiques dans les facultés de théologie, de droit et de médecine.* Turnhout: Brepols, 1985.

Del Punta, Francesco. "The Genre of Commentaries in the Middle Ages and its Relation to the Nature and Originality of Medieval Thought." In *Was ist Philosophie im Mittelalter?* [Miscellanea mediaevalia 26] Edited by Jan A. Aertsen, Andreas Speer. Berlin: W. de Gruyter, 1998, pp. 138–151.

Endres, Joseph Anton. Über des Ursprung und die Entwicklung der scholastischen Lehrmethode. *Philosophisches Jahrbuch* (1889) 2: 52–59.

L'enseignement des disciplines à la Faculté des arts, Paris et Oxford, XIIIe-XVe siècles: actes du colloque international. Edited by Olga Weijers and Louis Holtz. Turnhout: Brepols, 1997.

Les Genres littéraires dans les sources théologiques et philosophiques médiévales: définition, critique et exploitation. Actes du Colloque international de Louvain-la-Neuve, 25-27 mai 1981. Louvain-la-Neuve: Université catholique de Louvain, 1982.

Giusberti, Franco. *Materials for a Study on Twelfth Century Scholasticism.* Napoli: Bibliopolis, 1982.

Grabmann, Martin. *Die Geschichte der scholastischen Methode nach den gedruckten und ungedruckten Quellen.* 2 vols. Freiburg im Breisgau: Herdersche Verlagshandlung, 1909–1911.

Hamesse, Jacqueline. "The Scholastic Model of Reading." In *A History of Reading in the West.* Edited by Guglielmo Cavallo, Roger Chartier, Lydia G Cochrane. Amherst: University of Massachusetts Press, 1999, pp. 103–119.

Lawn, Brian. *The Rise and Decline of the Scholastic 'Quaestio Disputata' With Special Emphasis on its Use in the Teaching of Medicine and Science.* Leiden: E.J. Brill, 1993.

Makdisi, George. The Scholastic Method in Medieval Education: An Inquiry into its Origins in Law and Theology. *Speculum* (1974) 49: 640–661.

Medieval Literary Theory and Criticism, c. 1100-c. 1375: the commentary-tradition. Edited by A. J. Minnis and A. B. Scott. Oxford: Clarendon Press, 1988.

Panofsky, Erwin. *Gothic Architecture and Scholasticism.* New York: Meridian Books, 1957.

Radding, Charles and William W. Clark. *Medieval Architecture, Medieval Learning: Builders and Masters in the Age of Romanesque and Gothic.* New Haven: Yale University Press, 1992.

Weijers, Olga. *La 'disputatio' dans les Facultés des arts au moyen âge.* Turnhout: Brepols, 2002.

STEVEN J. LIVESEY

SCIENTIA

Despite the etymological connections, *scientia* in the Middle Ages designated an intellectual condition or state that was both broader and narrower than the modern term derived from it. While a full treatment of the subject goes well beyond the limitations of this entry, the goal here will be to provide some measure of the complexity of *scientia* and its applications in the Latin Middle Ages.

From its beginnings, Christianity displayed an ambivalent and cautious attitude toward *scientia*. It was, after all, the tree of the knowledge of good and evil (*lignum scientiae boni et mali*) that occasioned the fall of humanity from its pristine state, but also necessitated the incarnation and redemption of Christ. In a widely-cited passage, Saint Paul observed in 1 Corinthians 8:1 that "knowledge puffs up, but love builds up" (*scientia inflat, charitas vero aedificat*). Yet four chapters later (12:8), in his discussion of the gifts of the Spirit, Paul noted that some within the body of Christ are given the "word of knowledge" (*sermo scientiae*) by the Spirit. Through these and other passages, readers were warned that the value of *scientia* depended on both its source and purpose.

Like the scriptures on which they based their positions, the Fathers offered a broad spectrum of positions about the value of *scientia*. As has often been observed, Tertullian (c. 155–c. 230) and others of his persuasion considered secular philosophy at best irrelevant, and possibly distracting or corrupting influences in the Christian life. Far more accommodating were members of the Alexandrian school, such as Clement (d. 211–215), whose typological interpretation of the story of Abraham and his sons born of Sarah and Haggar came to prefigure the proper Christian use of secular knowledge: the useful parts of philosophy were to be employed to the advantage of the spiritual, as a handmaid (*ancilla*) of theology. In a particularly telling passage of *City of God*, Augustine (d. 430) sought to link the authority of scripture with the authority of secular knowledge: "As in the case of visible objects which we have not seen, we trust those who have (and likewise with all sensible objects), so in the case of things which are perceived by the mind and spirit, i.e. which are remote from our own interior sense, it behooves us to trust those who have seen them set in that incorporeal light..." (*De civ. Dei* xi.3). Both faith and *scientia* depend ultimately on the same indirect first principles that must be accepted, not proved, a perspective that had a long trajectory in Latin medieval intellectual circles.

The other principal influence on medieval understanding of *scientia* was the classical tradition, and the positions of Aristotle in particular, according to which *scientia* was strictly distinguished from belief or opinion. *Scientia* begins with experience, the repeated applications of which produce intuition or insight into the universal condition. As a result, this side of Aristotle's method resembles an inductive process; but Aristotle was also emphatic that real *scientia* is not produced until it is rigorously demonstrated through a deductive process beginning with first principles and definitions. According to Aristotle, the demonstrated propositions must satisfy three criteria: they must be universally true; they must contain terms that are essential to one another, thereby ensuring the necessity of the propositions; and they must be formed in such a way that the predicate is true of the subject strictly speaking, and not by virtue of some wider domain. Particularly in view of this third criterion, Aristotle considered scientific disciplines largely autonomous entities, each with its own subject domain, principles, and propositions. As a result, the invocation of principles from one discipline in the demonstrations of another, which Aristotle referred to as *metabasis*, was strictly forbidden, because such boundary infractions could introduce ambiguities, or worse still, errors into the demonstrative process. The only exception admitted by Aristotle belonged to a relatively small class of disciplines, known as the subalternated sciences, in which the principles of one science depend on the propositions of another, as for example, the principles of geometrical optics rely on the results of geometry.

Closely related to these issues was the distinction between *scientia quia* (that is, knowledge of the fact) and *scientia propter quid* (that is, knowledge through the cause). In a purely formal sense, *scientia* for Aristotle was the search for the middle terms of syllogisms. As he observed in the *Posterior Analytics*, one can demonstrate that the Moon is spherical by observing that the shadow cast on the Moon is circular, but such demonstrations do not arise from the cause of sphericity, but merely the observed effect of sphericity. By changing the middle term of the syllogism—making sphericity the cause through which the Moon's waxing and waning arises—one obtains a qualitatively stronger result: because, as Aristotle asserted in the opening chapter of the *Physics*, we truly know things when we know their causes, the more conclusive form of demonstration (which the Middle Ages came to call *demonstratio potissima*) is that which is based on the ultimate principles of things, their causes. This, and only this, produces *scientia propter quid*.

Because the medieval understandings of *scientia* rested in large measure on the transmission of Aristotle's works, the early Middle Ages came to view *scientia* as a matter of textual analysis, drawing on *Boethius's translations of the *Categories*, *De interpretatione*, and Porphyry's *Isagoge*. In the sacred sphere, this fit conveniently into the prevailing emphasis on theology as exegesis, in which Augustine's discussions of method combined with the remnants of classical culture to tease meaning from the scripture. At the same time, several early medieval scholars, including Boethius, Cassiodorus (c. 480–c. 575), *Martianus Capella (fl. 410–439?), *Isidore of Seville (c. 560–636), and *Bede (d. 735) continued the ancient handbook tradition that preserved a remnant of classical scientific work. Often two or three times removed from the original sources, their goal was to summarize the details of those sources without the substantiating arguments, in the process obscuring or misconstruing the systematic structure of the material. Thus, for example, their treatments of mathematics are little more than statements of definitions and theorems without proofs, and Isidore of Seville's discussion of matter theory in Book

XIII of the *Etymologies* places Aristotle's hylomorphic theory adjacent to the atomist theory, without discussing or even observing their incompatibility.

Under these conditions, theoretical discussions of *scientia* consisted largely of perfunctory classifications of the sciences, themselves resting on handbook restatements of the Aristotelian tripartite division of theoretical philosophy into metaphysics, mathematics, and physics, or the Stoic division of philosophy into ethics, logic, and physics, without further discussion of the incompatibility of these classifications or the methodological issues on which they rested. In particular, disciplines were distinguished primarily by the objects on which they focused, not always the methods that they employed. Physics, for example, focuses on the forms of bodies as they exist in matter; mathematics the forms of those bodies as they exist apart from matter; and metaphysics being that can exist of itself and apart from matter. While this was accompanied by some reference to the intellectual processes by which each discipline operates, it did not investigate the logical or syllogistic intricacies of *scientia*.

Medieval Developments

All of this began to change in the course of the twelfth century, when though a variety of channels classical materials and materials from the Islamic tradition entered western Europe. Now in possession of the so-called New Logic (the *Prior* and *Posterior Analytics*, the *Topics*, and the *Sophistical Refutations*), European scholars became acquainted with Aristotle's more elaborate discussions of *scientia*, demonstration, subalternation, and *metabasis*. As Aristotle's other works—especially *Physica*, *De anima*, *De caelo*, *Ethica Nicomachea*, *Metaphysica*—and the works of Islamic scholars filtered into Europe, Latin scholars possessed the content necessary to both complete the theoretical discussions of *scientia* and augment the simple classifications of the sciences carried over from the early Middle Ages. All of these new works were assimilated within a receptive new institution, the university. The product of this assimilation was a reconceptualization of the *scientiae* in Western culture.

A singularly important influence in this process was the introduction of Aristotle with his Islamic commentators. Largely because of the way that Aristotle had been received into Islamic culture, as an encyclopedic corpus of natural knowledge with the methodological prescriptions of the *Posterior Analytics*, there was a related perspective that became known as both Aristotle and his commentators were brought into Western Europe. This is perhaps most pronounced in the work of Averroes (*Ibn Rushd), the Commentator as he was known in Latin circles, but it can already be seen in the influence of Avicenna (*Ibn Sina) a century earlier. Avicenna's *Qanun* (*Canon*) enjoyed a special place within the medical community of the Western Middle Ages, and because the medical community seems to have had a central role in the early introduction of Aristotle in the twelfth century, Avicenna's readings of Aristotle and their application to medicine were especially formative. Antiquity in general and Aristotle in particular had viewed medicine in very distinct senses, as both an art and a science, a practice that depended on both the empirical observations of patients by doctors and the traditions learned at the hands of senior practitioners, and a theoretical discipline that had its own principles, just like natural philosophy. Avicenna's emphasis was placed on the latter sense of medicine as the consideration of the human body insofar as it is healthy or sick, and therefore in his view, the physician must know the causes of health and sickness, including both symptoms and the principles of being.

In some quarters, medicine was considered a science subordinate to psychology, the basic text of which was Aristotle's *De anima*. As a result, introductory lectures and formal prologues to *De anima*—and to the basic texts of medical faculties at universities—focused on three issues: whether medicine was a science, the most appropriate method of teaching medicine, and the particular subject matter of medicine. Many if not most of these long and detailed introductions adopted the Aristotelian perspective, augmented by Avicenna, of the nature of *scientia* and discussed the relationship between empirical medicine and scientific medicine in much the same way that Aristotle had delineated *scientia quia* and *scientia propter quid*.

A second influential development arose from a Latin source, the comments of *Robert Grosseteste (c. 1168–1253). As a translator of the *Nicomachean Ethics* and one of the earliest commentators on the *Physics* and the *Posterior Analytics*, Grosseteste's positions were cited repeatedly by subsequent readers of Aristotle's works. Especially in the area of the subalternate sciences and the interrelationship of disciplines, his comments added two crucial elements to the medieval position. First, in his commentary on the *Physics*, Grosseteste argued that in subalternate sciences such as astronomy, natural accidents were added over and above (*superadditur*) the subjects of pure mathematics, thereby making a composite subject of the new discipline. In his commentary on the *Posterior Analytics*, while agreeing with Aristotle that the subalternate, inferior discipline provides *scientia quia* and the subalternating, superior discipline *scientia propter quid*, Grosseteste observes that in astronomy or optics, neither geometry nor natural philosophy as subalternating sciences can provide the complete cause of phenomena: geometry provides the formal cause, natural philosophy the efficient and material cause. As a result, complete *propter quid* demonstrations must include both, and so astronomy and optics are partially subalternated to two (or more) disciplines.

Much the same kind of development can be seen in another important application of *scientia*, namely in the scholastic discussions of theology as a science. Over the course of the twelfth century, the older descriptive and exegetical senses of theology came to be augmented and in some quarters replaced by an analytic, systematic theology. Once again, as in the case of medicine, the introductory lectures on or prologues to theological texts began to explore the scientific nature of theology, drawing on Clement's imagery of the *ancilla*. While more conservative commentators emphasized that *ancilla* must be taken in the sense of *famulatus* (that is, a servant), more philosophically astute writers drew the parallel of the ancillary relationship of philosophy and theology and Aristotle's discussion of subalternation. Their discussions followed two paths. Some, such as *Thomas Aquinas (c. 1224–1274), asked whether Aristotle's account of *scientia* and the first principles on which it was based shed light on the foundations of theology: is theology scientific because it proceeds from principles known in a superior *scientia*, viz. the knowledge of God and the blessed? In other words, as subsequent readers of Thomas rendered his position, "our theology is a subalternated science to the science of the blessed" (*Summa Theologiae* I, 1, 2; John of Reading [1989] 102). The other path focused instead on the relationship between theology and the human sciences; as Henry of Ghent (d. 1293) argued, theology subordinates other sciences to itself because scripture speaks *propter quid*, through causes, about those things that the human sciences speak only *quia* and by experience.

While these kinds of speculations about the relationships between theology and the human sciences had a residual effect beyond the Middle Ages—consider, for example, Galileo's arguments in his *Letter to Christina* about the proper understanding of the preeminence of theology—for a variety of reasons such discussions seem to have been eclipsed by the third or fourth decade of the fourteenth century. First, prologues to commentaries on the *Sentences* (the chief locus for such speculations) diminished in size and all but disappeared by 1340. More to the point, scholars seem to have exhausted the traditional questions of the scientific status of theology and moved on to epistemological questions about the sources and certainty of *scientia*.

The strands of those developments are numerous, complex, and not always disentangled. One focused on the psychological states by which *scientia* was acquired and retained. Drawing on an account in Aristotle's *Categories* (VIII 8b28–34), scholastic authors considered *scientia* a mental state, or *habitus*, that was permanent or at least difficult to change. Beginning in the late thirteenth century and extending through the next century, scholars debated the relationship between those mental states and the particular elements of scientific knowledge humans possess. Some, including Peter Aureol (d. 1322), argued that there was a single overarching *habitus* that governed each discipline, conferring an essential unity recognizable in the discipline's content and method. *William of Ockham (c. 1285–1347) and others argued that this did not suffice to explain how humans acquired discrete parts of disciplinary understanding, and so proposed that each discipline was governed by multiple mental habits, each corresponding to a proposition or even a part of a proposition within the discipline. Essential unity of scientific disciplines was therefore sacrificed for a conventional unity that permitted more flexible alterations of their contents.

Another important element of this development concerned the sufficiency of the criteria for *scientia*.

Although the standard criteria involved the evidence of both reason and experience, increasingly in the fourteenth century there were doubts about the possibility of one or the other, or in some cases, both. Many of the novel positions of fourteenth-century natural philosophy were developed *secundum imaginationem*, that is, hypothetically and not categorically. Thus, in a famous passage from his *Livre du ciel et du monde*, *Nicole Oresme argued that neither experience nor rational proof was capable of establishing the cause for diurnal phenomena. His objective in the discussion was to provide a "means of refuting and checking those who would like to impugn our faith by argument." By the end of the fourteenth century, scholars at the new university in Vienna expressed doubts about the sufficiency of Aristotelian syllogistic in proving or even expressing core theological positions like the Trinity. There are perhaps several interrelated developments that were responsible for these shifts. First, the condemnations at Paris and elsewhere in the late thirteenth century, combined with an emphasis on voluntarist theology at the same time, encouraged subsequent scholars to include possible divine interventions in the natural world, and consequently all demonstrative or inductive proofs were subject to cancellation by divine omnipotence. Second, while Aristotle had distinguished sharply between dialectical and demonstrative proofs, later medieval scholars came to blur the distinctions between these modes of argument. Third, many of the natural speculations of the late Middle Ages arose in *quaestiones disputatae*, and especially *quaestiones de sophismatibus*, in which the goal of the participant in debate was not demonstration of universal truth, but agility in the disputation. And finally, Joel Kaye has argued that hypothetical currents of the fourteenth century arose from the economic theories of money and value that emphasized relative rather than absolute measures.

On occasion, these currents merged in the late Middle Ages. In 1342/1343, the Augustinian Hermit Gregory of Rimini (d. 1358) argued in his commentary on the *Sentences* that God could preserve the habit of perspective in the intellect, while not preserving the habit of geometry. In such an intellect, perspective would be a subalternate science, even though it would have no understanding of its own principles, but rather only faith. In this hypothetical example, fueled by the emphasis on divine omnipotence, only those parts of perspective that were acquired before the loss of geometric knowledge would retain their scientific status; conclusions derived subsequently would fail to be scientific. Subsequent commentators, such as the Cistercian James of Eltville (d. 1393), even argued that evidence is not necessary for *scientia*: a collection of propositions would be scientific by virtue of the fact that it conforms to the rules of *consequentiae*, even though by divine omnipotence it has no subjective referent. Extreme though these examples may be, they suggest the extensive deviations between late medieval understandings of *scientia* and the Aristotelian sources on which they were grounded.

See also **Condemnation of 1277; Logic; Medicine, theoretical; Reason; Religion and science; Universities**

Bibliography

Brown, Stephen F. "Late Thirteenth Century Theology. 'Scientia' pushed to its Limits." In *'Scientia' und 'Disciplina.' Wissenstheorie und Wissenschaftspraxis im 12. und 13. Jahrhundert*. Edited by Rainer Berndt, Matthias Lutz-Bachmann, Ralf M. W. Stammberger. Berlin: Akademie Verlag, 2002, pp. 249–260.

Chenu, M.-D. *La Théologie comme science au XIIIe siècle*. Paris: J. Vrin, 1969.

Crombie, Alistair. *Styles of Scientific Thinking in the European Tradition: The History of Argument and Explanation Especially in the Mathematical and Biomedical Sciences and Arts*. 3 vols. London: Duckworth, 1994.

Funkenstein, Amos. *Theology and the Scientific Imagination from the Middle Ages to the Seventeenth Century*. Princeton: Princeton University Press, 1986.

Hintikka, Jaakko. On the Ingredients of an Aristotelian Science. *Nous* (1972) 6: 55–69.

Kaye, Joel. *Economy and Nature in the Fourteenth Century: Money, Market Exchange, and the Emergence of Scientific Thought*. New York: Cambridge University Press, 1998.

Livesey, Steven J. "Scientific Writing in the Latin Middle Ages." In *Scientific Books, Libraries and Collectors*. Edited by Andrew Hunter. 4th edition. Aldershot: Ashgate, 2000, pp. 72–98.

———. *Theology and Science in the Fourteenth Century: Three Questions on the Unity and Subalternation of the Sciences from John of Reading's Commentary on the Sentences*, edition and critical commentary. Leiden: E. J. Brill, 1989.

McKirahan, Richard D., Jr. Aristotle's Subordinate Sciences. *British Journal for the History of Science* (1978) 11: 197–220.

Murdoch, John. "The Analytic Character of Late Medieval Learning: Natural Philosophy without Nature." In *Approaches to Nature in the Middle Ages*. Edited by Lawrence Roberts. Binghamton, NY: Center for Medieval & Early Renaissance Studies, 1984, pp. 171–213.

———. "From Social into Intellectual Factors: An Aspect of the Unitary Character of Late Medieval Learning." *The Cultural Context of Medieval Learning*. Edited by John Murdoch and Edith Sylla. Dordrecht, Holland: D. Reidel Publishing Co., 1975, pp. 271–348.

Oresme, Nicole. *Le Livre du ciel et du monde*. Edited by A. D. Menut and A. J. Denomy. Madison, Wisconsin: University of Wisconsin Press, 1968.

Scientia und ars im Hoch- und Spätmittelalter. Edited by Ingrid Craemer-Ruegenberg and Andreas Speer. [Miscellanea mediaevalia 22/1-2] Berlin: Walter de Gruyter, 1994.

Weisheipl, James A. Classifications of the Sciences in Medieval Thought. *Mediaeval Studies* (1965) 27: 54–90.

STEVEN J. LIVESEY

SHIPBUILDING

Early medieval Europeans received from their predecessors two broad ranges of wooden shipbuilding traditions, one in the Mediterranean and the other in the northern seas. At the same time Chinese shipwrights had already developed the central features of the design of the junk. Its watertight compartments, adjustable keel, and highly flexible number of masts each carrying a lug sail with battens, made the junk a highly versatile and reliable seagoing ship. Junks by the year 1000 were much larger than any ships in Europe or in the great oceanic area where a Malaysian shipbuilding tradition predominated. There, ocean-going rafts with outriggers or twin hulls and rigged with, at first, bipole masts ranged much more widely than vessels from any other part of the world carrying the designs and building practices across the Indian Ocean to Madagascar and around the Pacific Ocean to the islands of Polynesia. Along the shores of the Arabian Sea shipbuilders constructed dhows, relatively shallow cargo vessels rigged with a single triangular or lateen sail. The planks of the hulls were typically sewn together with pieces of rope, a loose system which made the hull flexible, and so able to handle rough seas, but not very watertight. There were also serious limitations on how big such hulls could be built, unlike junks where vessels of one thousand tons and more seem to have been feasible.

Mediterranean Practice

Roman shipbuilders followed Greek practices in building their hulls with mortise and tenon joints. Wedges or tenons were placed in cavities or mortises gouged out of the planks and held in place by wooden nails passed through the hull planks and the tenons. In the Roman Empire the methods of fastening predominated on all parts of ships, including the decks, and the tenons were very close to each other. The resulting hull was extremely strong, heavy, and sturdy so the internal framing was minimal. The hull was also very watertight but even so the surface was often covered with wax or even copper sheathing to protect it from attack by shipworm (*Teredo navalis*). Propulsion came from a single square sail stepped near the middle of the ship. Often the mainsail was supplemented with a small square sail slung under the bowsprit. Roman shipbuilders produced vessels of two general categories, round ships with length-to-breadth ratios of about 3:1 propelled entirely by sails, and galleys with length-to-breadth ratios of about 5:1 propelled both by the standard rig and by oars. Although it was possible to have multiple banks of rowers, in the Roman Empire there was typically only one, with each rower handling a single oar. Shipbuilders gave all those vessels at least one but often two side rudders for control.

As the economy declined in the early Middle Ages and the supply of skilled labor was reduced, the quality of shipbuilding deteriorated. The distance between mortise and tenon joints increased, and on the upper parts of hulls such joints disappeared entirely with planks merely pinned to internal frames. The trend led by the end of the first millennium C.E. to a new form of hull construction. Instead of relying on the exterior hull for strength, shipbuilders transferred the task of maintaining the integrity of the vessel to the internal frame. The process of ship construction as a result reversed, with the internal ribs set up first and then the hull planks added. The planks were still fitted end-to-end as with the old method but now to maintain watertightness they needed to be caulked more extensively and more regularly. The internal frames gave shape to the hull so their design became much more important. The designer of those frames in turn took on a significantly higher status, the hewers of the planks a lesser position. The new type of skeleton-first construction made for a lighter and more flexible ship which was easier to build, needed less wood, but required more maintenance. Increasing the scale of the ship or changing the shape of the hull was now easier. Builders used the new kind of construction both on large sailing round ships and oared galleys.

In the course of the early Middle Ages Mediterranean vessels went through a change in rigging as well. Triangular lateen sails were in use in classical Greece and Rome for small vessels. As big ships disappeared with the decline of the Roman Empire and economy the lateen sail came to dominate and square sails all but disappeared. Lateen sails had the advantage of making it possible to sail closer to the wind. Lateen sails had the disadvantage that when coming about, that is changing course by something of the order of ninety degrees, the yard from which the sail was hung had to be moved to the other side of the mast. In order to do that the yard had to be carried

Thirteenth-century Arabic manuscript depiction of a dhow. (Corbis/Arne Hodalic)

over the top of the mast, which was a clumsy, complex, and manpower-hungry operation. There was a limitation then on the size of sails and thus on the size of ships. It was possible to add a second mast, which shipbuilders often did both on galleys and on round ships since that was the only way to increase total sail area.

Northern European Practice

Shipbuilders around the Baltic and North Seas in the early Middle Ages produced a variety of different types of vessels which were the ancestors of a range of craft that melded together over the years to create one principal kind of sailing ship. The rowing barge was a simple vessel with overlapping planking. The planks could be held fast by ropes but over time shipbuilders turned to wooden nails or iron rivets for the purpose. That type of lapstrake construction for hulls meant that internal ribs were of little importance in strengthening the hull. At first shipwrights used long planks running from bow to stern but they discovered that by scarfing shorter pieces together not only did they eliminate a constraint on the length of their vessels but they also increased the flexibility of the hulls. At some point, probably in the eighth century, the rowing barge got a real keel and also a single square sail on a single mast stepped in the middle of the ship. The new type, with both ends looking much the same, was an effective open ocean sailor. Scandinavian shipbuilders produced broadly two versions of what can be called the Viking ship after its most famous users. One version was low, and fitted with oars and a mast that could be taken down or put up quickly and with a length-to-breadth ratio of 5:1 or 6:1. The other version had a fixed mast, few if any oars at the bow and stern which were there just to help in difficult circumstances, and a length-to-breadth ratio of around 3:1. Both types had a single side rudder which apparently gave a high degree of control. The Viking ship evolved into a versatile cargo ship which was also effective as a military transport and warship. Often called a keel because of one of the features which allowed it to take to the open ocean, it was produced in variations throughout northern Europe and along the Atlantic front as far south as Iberia.

The other types that came from early medieval northern shipyards were more limited in size and complexity. The hulk had a very simple system of planking which gave way over time to lapstrake construction. The hull had the form of a banana and there was no keel so it proved effective in use on rivers and in estuaries. The hull planks, because of the shape of the hull, met at the bow in a unique way and were often held in place by tying them together. Rigging was a single square sail on a single mast which could be, in the case of vessels designed for river travel, set well forward. The cog had a very different form from the hulk. While the planks on the sides overlapped there was a sharp angle between those side planks and the ones on the bottom. Those bottom planks were placed end-to-end and the floor was virtually flat. With posts at either end almost vertical the hull was somewhat box-like. The type was suited to use on tidal flats where it could rest squarely on the bottom when the tide was out, be unloaded and loaded, and then float off when the tide came in. There was a single square sail on a single mast placed in the middle of the ship. The design certainly had Celtic origins but it was transformed by shipwrights in the High Middle Ages to make it into the dominant cargo and military vessel of the North.

Shipbuilders, possibly in the Low Countries, gave the cog a keel. In doing that they also made changes in the form of the hull, overlapping the bottom planks and modifying the sharp angles between the bottom and side planks. The result was a still box-like hull which had greater carrying capacity per unit length than keels. The cog could also be built higher than its predecessors but that meant passing heavy squared timbers through from one side to the other high in the ship to keep the sides in place. Shipbuilders fitted the hull planks into the heavy posts at the bow and stern and also fixed a rudder to the sternpost which was more stable than a side rudder. In the long run it would prove more efficient as well. Cogs could be and were made much larger than other contemporary vessels. Greater size meant a need for a larger sail and a larger crew to raise it. To get more sail area sailors added a bonnet, an extra rectangular piece of canvas that could be temporarily sewn to the bottom of the sail. That gave the mariners greater flexibility in deploying canvas without increasing manning requirements. Riding higher in the water and able to carry larger numbers of men than other contemporary types cogs became the standard vessels of northern naval forces, doubling as cargo ships in peacetime.

While the two shipbuilding traditions of the Mediterranean and northern Europe remained largely isolated through the early and High Middle Ages, from the late thirteenth century both benefited from extensive contact and borrowing of designs and building methods. Sailors in southern Europe used the cog certainly by the beginning of the fourteenth century and probably earlier. Shipwrights in the Mediterranean appreciated the advantages of greater carrying capacity but they were also conscious of the limitations set by the simple rig. They added a second mast near the stern and fitted it with a lateen sail. They also changed the form of hull construction, going over to skeleton-first building. The result was the carrack, in use by the late fourteenth century. It was easier to build, probably lighter than a cog of the same size, and could be built bigger. Most of all the two masts and the presence of a triangular sail gave mariners greater control over their vessels and made it possible for them to sail closer to the wind. The next logical step, taken sometime around the end of the fourteenth century, was to add a third small mast near the bow to balance the one at the stern. The driving sail and principal source of propulsion was still the mainsail on the mainmast but the combination or full-rig made ships more maneuverable and able to sail in a greater variety of conditions. While older forms of ships, such as the keel or the cog or the lateen-rigged cargo ship of the Mediterranean, did not by any means disappear, the full-rigged ship came to dominate exchange over longer distances, especially in the form of the full-rigged carrack travelling between southern and northern Europe. Northern Europeans were slow to adapt to skeleton-first hull construction, in some cases even combining old methods with the new one. By the end of the fifteenth century the full-rigged ship was the preferred vessel for many intra-European trades, in part because of its handling qualities, in part because of its versatility, and in part because its crew size could be reduced per ton of goods carried compared to other types. The greater range also led to its replacing, for example, the simpler, lower, lateen-rigged caravel in Portuguese voyages of exploration along the west coast of Africa. Full-rigged ships in daily use were the choice for voyages of exploration and became in the Renaissance the vehicles for European domination of the ocean seas and for the resulting international trading connections and colonization.

See also **Navigation; Travel and exploration**

Bibliography

Bass, George, ed. *A History of Seafaring Based on Underwater Archaeology*. London: Thames and Hudson, 1972.

Friel, Ian. *The Good Ship: Ships, Shipbuilding and Technology in England, 1200–1520*. London: British Museum Press, 1995.

Gardiner, Robert, ed. *The Earliest Ships: the Evolution of Boats into Ships*. London: Conway Maritime Press, 1996.

———, ed. *Cogs, Caravels and Galleons The Sailing Ship 1000–1650*. London: Conway Maritime Press, 1994.

Hattendorf, John B., ed. *Maritime History in the Age of Discovery: An Introduction*. Malabar, Florida: Krieger, 1995.

Hutchinson, Gillian. *Medieval Ships and Shipping*. Rutherford: Fairleigh Dickinson University Press, 1994.

Lane, Frederic C. *Venetian Ships and Shipbuilders of the Renaissance*. Baltimore: Johns Hopkins Press, 1934.

Lewis, Archibald R. and Timothy J. Runyan. *European Naval and Maritime History, 300–1500*. Bloomington: Indiana University Press, 1985.

McGrail, Seán. *Boats of the World from the Stone Age to Medieval Times*. Oxford: Oxford University Press, 2001.

Pryor, J. H. *Geography, Technology and War: Studies in the Maritime History of the Mediterranean 649–1571*. New York: Cambridge University Press, 1988.

Unger, Richard W. *The Ship in the Medieval Economy, 600–1600*. London: Croom-Helm Ltd., 1980.

RICHARD W. UNGER

SIGER OF BRABANT

Siger of Brabant (c. 1240–c. 1282/1284) has long held a prominent position in thirteenth-century philosophy. He was involved in several doctrinal controversies, became the target of two condemnations, was placed in Paradise by Dante, and had an impact on the interpretation of Aristotle's philosophical *psychology until the fifteenth century. Siger was a native of the French-speaking part of the duchy of Brabant. His geographical origin put him into the Picard Nation when he started his studies at the arts faculty of the University of Paris, around 1255–1257. He became a regent master in that faculty in the 1260s, certainly by 1266, and never transferred to any of the other faculties (law, medicine, or theology). Siger's study at the arts faculty coincided more or less with the legislation of 1255 that integrated the entire known corpus of Aristotle's writings, translated into Latin, into the curriculum at Paris. Masters of arts were required to lecture on Aristotle's works, and students of arts were thus exposed to Aristotelian philosophy during classes, at disputations, and at exams. An important tool in the appropriation of Aristotle's thought was the commentaries by Averroes (*Ibn Rushd), which had also been translated into Latin. The project of the study of Aristotle and Averroes runs like a red thread through Siger's career. Most of Siger's surviving works are the result of his teaching at the arts faculty. They are either commentaries on Aristotle's works or hark back to disputations and exercises. Many of them are transcripts from his lectures (*reportationes*), some of which were later revised by Siger. His works started to circulate between 1265 and 1274–1276. Toward the end of 1276, Siger held an ecclesiastical office as a canon at St. Paul's in Liège.

Two areas of Siger's philosophical activities are particularly relevant for medieval science: his views on the eternity of the world and his philosophical psychology. The latter field was based on his reading of Aristotle's *De anima*, which at the time was considered a branch of natural philosophy or science (*philosophia naturalis*; *physica*), namely the branch that dealt with living nature.

In a separate question written before 1270, Siger claims that it is contradictory to deny the eternity of the human species, and thus, by implication, advocates the eternity of the universe. For reasons set out below, he became more cautious after 1270. In his treatise *De aeternitate mundi* (*The Eternity of the Universe*), dated c. 1272, he diligently notes the philosophical arguments, such as those by Aristotle, in favor of an eternal, i.e., beginningless, universe. He himself agrees, however, on the basis of faith, that the world has been created in time, and thus had a beginning. Siger denies that this view can be demonstrated by philosophical arguments.

Siger is best known for his views on the nature of the intellect and on immortality. Before 1270, he embraced Averroes' position that there is one unique intellect, common to all human beings, the theory of the unicity of the human intellect. Between this intellect and human beings exists an operational unity in that the latter provide images (from sense perception), from which the former abstracts the intelligible forms. This position came under attack in *Thomas Aquinas's *The Unity of the Soul* (*De unitate intellectus*, 1270). Particularly worrisome about the unicity of the intellect from a Christian perspective is the rejection of personal survival and immortailty and the denial of reward and punishment in accord with the behavior of each human being in this life. As a result of Aquinas's philosophical criticism, Siger revised his position in later treatises, and eventually even rejected Averroes' position. In particular, he came to distinguish more clearly his own view from the views of the philosophers he was examining: Aristotle, Averroes, Avicenna (*Ibn Sina), Algalzel, Themistius.

Siger's views on the eternity of the universe and the unicity of the human intellect provoked a reaction from Bishop Etienne Tempier. In 1270 Tempier included them in his thirteen theses that were prohibited in the arts faculty. In the *Condemnation of 1277, Siger became one of the main targets, together with his contemporary *Boethius of Dacia, in the much larger prohibition of two hundred nineteen theses. Siger's works bring to the surface the tensions that existed between some of Aristotle's and Averroes' views, and certain truths of faith. For Siger, truth rested on the side of faith, but at the same time, he established the autonomy of philosophical inquiry, based on reason and experience and also aimed at the truth, even though at times a truth limited in scope. He thus prepared the ground for a scientific attitude.

See also **Aristotelianism; "Latin Averroists"; Nature: diverse medieval interpretations; Religion and science**

Bibliography

Primary Sources
Bazán, Bernard, ed. *Siger de Brabant.Quaestiones in Tertium De anima, De anima intellectiva, De aeternitate mundi.* Louvain: Publications universitaires, 1972.
———. *Siger de Brabant. Écrits de logique, de morale et de physique.* Louvain: Publications universitaires, 1974.

Secondary Sources
Van Steenberghen, Fernand. *Maître Siger de Brabant.* Louvain: Publications universitaires, 1977.
Wippel, John F. *Mediaeval Reactions to the Encounter Between Faith and Reason.* Milwaukee: Marquette University Press, 1995.

JOHANNES M.M.H. THIJSSEN

SOUTH-CENTRAL ASIAN SCIENCE

South-central Asia, particularly India, is famous for its rich tradition in religion and philosophy, but less renowned for its scientific culture. However, evidence suggests that scientific activity was extensive in India in the Middle Ages, and the Indian scientific corpus of the period has been estimated at around three million manuscripts, the majority of which remain unexamined by modern historians of science. Among the areas in which scientific activity was carried out were natural science, technology, medicine, architecture, astronomy, and mathematics. This article focuses on an important subset of Indian science, the so-called "exact" sciences, or in Sanskrit *jyotihsastra* (astral science). Included in *jyotihsastra* are mathematics, astronomy, and various divinatory procedures.

In the Indian context, where both astronomy and astrology belong to *jyotihsastra*, no substantial difference was perceived between an astronomer and an astrologer. Mathematical astronomy was a tool for the calculation of planetary positions, and knowledge of planetary positions was necessary for astrological predictions. Many Indian astronomical treatises introduce concepts which have no deeper astronomical purpose, but which play a role in astrology.

The development of *jyotihsastra* in India during the medieval period was a combination of indigenous activity as well as the importation of foreign scientific ideas, most notably from Greece, and, in the later medieval period, from Islamic Western Asia. Mathematics was, for a large part, a tool utilized and developed by astronomers for their astronomical models and computations, but it also became important in its own right, especially in economics, geometry, conversions of *weights and measures, number theory, *algebra, and trigonometry.

One of the most striking features of medieval Indian scientific works is their format. Like almost all Sanskrit literary works, the *jyotihsastra* texts were composed in verse. This was partly to aid memorization as the texts were transmitted orally, but also to challenge the students: some authors, it seems, deliberately made their verses obscure in order to test their pupils. This scientific "poetry" greatly contrasted with the written documents that provided the basis of most other sciences in the rest of the world at that time. In order for the material to fit these metrical patterns, a flexible vocabulary was needed, and authors could always make up their own synonyms rather than use a specifically correct term. As a result Indian science always lacked a rigid or standard nomenclature like that of, for example, the ancient Greeks.

The poetic form also entailed a certain degree of obscurity as scientists sought to convey complicated expressions in a restricted space: form influenced the treatment of the subject matter. In order to facilitate the daunting task of memorizing large amounts of technical material, the scientists developed many strategies to make the verses more memorable. A frequent problem was representing long strings of numbers, and several ingenious ways were developed to overcome it. For example, the *bhutasankhya* system was used extensively, in which common objects associated with an amount through everyday or mythological connections were substituted for the number itself (for example, "nails" represented the number twenty and "Vedas," the quartet of Hindu sacred books, stood for the number four). Another method was the South Indian *katapayadi* system, in which each syllable of the Indian script was associated with a different number, and combinations of numbers were ingeniously arranged to spell words representing larger numbers.

In addition, symbols representing numerals in a base ten system were used. *Al-Biruni, a Muslim scholar who accompanied Mahmud of Ghazni during his conquest of India and wrote a famous work on India, observed that Indian scientists did not use letters of their alphabet for numerical notation in the way that their Islamic counterparts used Arabic letters, but rather used numerals in a base ten system.

The obscurity of the verses of the major works was remedied by accompanying commentaries, written for the most part in prose, which sought to elucidate the texts.

The commentators did this in many ways, for example by explaining the grammar, paraphrasing the verse, providing synonyms or definitions, or by giving worked examples. The commentaries are often most helpful in deciphering the mathematical rules contained in the verses of the original work. It was not uncommon for authors to write commentaries on their own work.

The Indian Astronomical Model

Indian astronomers used a geocentric astronomical model in which the planets each have two epicycles, one known as *manda* (Sanskrit: slow), the other as *sighra* (fast). Both revolve around the deferent, the circular path of the planet in its orbit around the Earth. This concept helps to explain the "wobble" that is sometimes observable in planets. The Sun and the Moon have only one epicycle, the *manda*, and hence do not appear to oscillate. The true position of the planet is found by calculating the mean of the two epicycles. From the modern heliocentric point of view, one can think of the *manda* as accounting for the fact that the orbit of a planet around the Earth is not circular, and the sighra for the fact that the Earth is orbiting the Sun. It is certain that the Indian planetary model was based on a Greek prototype which adhered to an Aristotelian idea of concentricity, namely that all complex motion is a product of smaller and simpler circular, uniform motion.

In the Indian conception of time, 4,320,000 years is known as a *mahayuga*. This period is subdivided into four smaller periods, known as *yugas*, namely *krta*, *treta*, *dvapara*, and *kali*. One thousand *mahayugas* make up one *kalpa*, and at the end of the *kalpa* there is a partial destruction of the universe. This conception formed the basis of Indian astronomy. The astronomers would provide the number of revolutions of each planet during the span of a *kalpa*, or during a *mahayuga*. From these numbers, together with other parameters (radii of epicycles, positions of apogees and nodes, etc.), as well as knowledge of how much of the *kalpa* had passed, could be computed the mean position of the planets at any given time. This methodology spread to Islamic Western Asia. In particular, the Arab astrologer Abu Ma'shar (b. 787) wrote a work entitled *Zij al-hazarat* in which the mean motions of the planets are calculated in this way, from the number of revolutions in a *yuga*.

From the time of the introduction of Greek geometrical models of astronomy in India until the adoption of Islamic astronomy in the fifteenth century, the model remained essentially the same. The Indian astronomical milieu was not one of careful observation followed by revisions of the model or the constants utilized in it, but rather one in which changes occured as the mathematical formulae were investigated and refined. Some formulae were simplified for increased ease of practical use; others were elaborated and made theoretically more correct, but they tended to be the ones that had the least practical application.

Other techniques employed by the Indian astronomers were analemmas, two-dimensional planar representations of the celestial sphere, in which calculations concerning arcs and angles on the sphere can be treated as plane triangles, and linked to this, ratios derived from similar triangles, known in Sanskrit as *trairasika* (the rule of three). In trigonometry, Indians used the sine function as well the versed sine (versine) function. The traditional approach was to tabulate the sine function for certain values of the angle and then compute a given sine using linear interpolation or second-order differences, but algebraic expressions for computing the sine of a given angle were also given. There were many different values used for R (the radius of the circle in which the angle is measured), including 3438, 150, 120, and 60. Observational equipment was never very sophisticated, which is perhaps an indication of the significance of observation to the working astronomer in terms of improving and refining parameters.

The Indian astronomical tradition is divided into a number of schools, the so-called *paksas*. In terms of fundamental presuppositions the paksas differ little. They share the same basic astronomical model as that outlined above, but employ different values of planetary revolutions per *kalpa*, radii of epicycles, etc.

The oldest of the *paksas* is the *brahmapaksa*, which originated around the beginning of the fifth century, when Greek material was transmitted into India. This school gave the existing material a distinctly Indian form, presenting it as the revelation of the god Brahma. The brahmapaksa flourished in western and northwestern India. In this system, the epoch begins at sunrise at Lanka, an imagined equatorial city on the Indian prime meridian through Ujjain (23°11'N 75°46'E). Other *paksas* and their chief features are discussed below.

Early cosmological accounts, established in various Indian sacred texts, depict a flat Earth at the center of which is a huge mountain, Meru, whose peak points toward the polestar. Above the Earth, centered on the axis of Meru, is a series of wheels on which the luminaries and the planets, suspended from the tail of a large fish, revolve in the cosmic winds. The order varies, but the most common is: Sun, Moon, Mercury, Venus, Mars, Jupiter, Saturn, the *naksatras* (twenty-seven or twenty-eight constellations in the path of the Moon), and the *saptarsis* (Ursa Major).

The traditional cosmology was prevalent in society at large as well as among most learned people in medieval India, but with the introduction of foreign scientific ideas, a more theoretically based model was adopted by the astronomers. This was the geometrical model outlined above and based on Greek ideas in which the planets revolve around a centrally placed spherical Earth (the earliest works reflecting this interpretation date from the fifth and sixth centuries C.E.).

Due to its sacred nature and the popular credence attached to it, astronomers could not entirely disregard the older cosmology. In a sense, the attempt to create a synthesis of the two cosmologies is as old in India as the introduction of geometrical models. The astronomers placed Mount Meru at the North Pole (a place suited for this purpose for a number of reasons) and relegated other curiosities of the older cosmology to the southern hemisphere. Later, a whole literary genre evolved to attempt to reconcile the two cosmologies, an enterprise which is, in fact, still going on today.

Relating to this conception of time, Indian astronomical treatises are of several kinds: these include *siddhantas*, *tantras*, *karanas*, *kosthakas*, and *yantras*. A *siddhanta* is a fully fledged treatise, based on the beginning of the *kalpa*. A *tantra* simplifies matters by taking the beginning of the present *kaliyuga* as an epoch, and a *karana*, which generally contains approximate formulae meant for easy use, utilizes an epoch close to the time of its author. A *kosthaka* is a text which includes tables and accompanying explanation. A *yantra* is a text on instruments.

Notable Astronomers and Mathematicians

Aryabhata (born 476 C.E.), who lived in Pataliputra (modern Patna in Bihar), founded two of the astronomical *paksas*: the *aryapaksa*, whose system is expounded in his treatise the *Aryabhatiya*, and the *ardharatrikapaksa* (in which the epoch begins at midnight, rather than at sunrise) which he expounded in c. 500 C.E. in a now lost work. Aryabhata sought to simplify the astronomical system, not through actual observations of the heavens (as is illustrated by the fact that he does not talk about the stars in the *Aryabhatiya* and that the position of the ascending nodes of the planets and the Sun at the beginning of the present *kaliyuga* form an arithmetical progression), but through mathematical manipulation. In his system, a *kalpa* consists of one thousand eight *mahayugas* each of which is divided into four equal *yugas*, and a mean conjunction occurs at the beginning of each *mahayuga*, a fact that allows him to operate within the shorter span of a *mahayuga* rather than the longer *kalpa*. In the mathematical section of the *Aryabhatiya*, Ayabhata deals with arithmetic, algebra (for example a method of finding integer solutions of the equation $ax \pm c = by$), and trigonometry. He also gives a value of π correct to eight decimal places:

$$\pi = \frac{62832}{20000}$$

(although in his works, for practical purposes, he uses the traditional approximation $\pi = \sqrt{10}$).

Three centuries later another school appeared which sought to apply Aryabhata's astronomical parameters while adhering to the traditional division of the *kalpa* and the *yugas*. This is the so-called *saurapaksa*. In order to utilize Aryabhata parameters within the framework of the traditional division of the *kalpa*, the expounders of the *saurapaksa* postulate a period of 17,064,000 years at the beginning of the creation during which the planets remain motionless. Authors adhering to this *pakda* include Jnanaraja (fl. 1503).

Almost immediately after Aryabhata, the famous astronomer Brahmagupta (b. 598 C.E.), who was to become Aryabhata's most outspoken rival, wrote two important astronomical works following the tradition of the *brahmapaksa*, in which he often adopted a critical attitude towards Aryabhata. The first, the *Brahmasphutasiddhanta*, was written when Brahmagupta

was thirty years old. This work contains material ranging from planetary theory, eclipse theory, mathematics, including rules for cyclic quadrilaterals (although Brahmagupta never mentions the applicability of these quadrilaterals to a circle, there can be no doubt that this is what he intended), and the so-called *bija* (algebraic) calculations), instruments, and mathematical tables. In this work, Brahmagupta pursues mathematics for the sake of mathematics and not exclusively as an aid to astronomy. His second work, the *Khandakhadyaka* (with an epoch of Sunday, March 15, 665 C.E.), was a response to Aryabhata's *Ardharatrikapaksa*. Both works were known in Sanskrit to al-Biruni, who quotes many passages, especially in his works *India* and in *al-Qanun al-Mas'udi*. The legacy of Aryabhata and Brahmagupta was far-reaching, and many works written thereafter are simply are based on their achievements.

A later astronomer who wrote both important original works and commentaries on older texts is Bhaskara II (b. 1114). Bhaskara II was celebrated for his achievements by his contemporaries: An inscription dating from 1207 records that funding was given to form an educational institution dedicated to the study of the his works. The *Siddhantasiromani* and the *Karanakutuhala* (a *siddhanta* and a *karana* respectively) and the *Bijaganita* and the *Lilavati* (mathematical works) are his most important achievements. To the latter work, the *Lilavati*, tradition has attached a charming story, found in many variants, of a beautiful young woman named Lilavati, to whom many of the mathematical problems in this work are addressed. According to one, Bhaskara II had calculated that Lilavati, his daughter, had to be married at a certain time to save her future husband from a premature death. To effect this, he constructed a waterclock that would indicate the auspicious time. However, Lilavati had her curiosity aroused and, while looking at the waterclock, a pearl from one of her ornaments fell into it, causing the water to flow at a slower rate. Lilavati thus became a widow as a young woman; to console her, her father taught her mathematics and wrote a mathematical treatise, naming it in her honor. As similar stories exist in other contexts, this is presumably a pre-existing story that got attached to the Lilavati.

Among the mathematical problems studied by Bhaskara II are arithmetic, plane and solid geometry, and the solution of certain indeterminate equations. In particular, following the mathematician Jayadeva (c. 1050 C.E.), he expounds a method for the solution of what is now known as Pell's equation, i.e., integer solutions to the equation $ax^2 + 1 = y^2$ where a is a given integer, giving solutions to specific examples that were not solved in Europe until centuries later.

Influence from Islamic astronomy can be seen in India as early as the tenth century in the work of Munjala and Sripati, which seem to contain traces of Islamic concepts. However, it is not until the latter half of the fourteenth century that a direct transmission can be confirmed, most notably in the work of the Jain astronomer Mahendra Suri (fl. 1370). He wrote the first Indian treatise on the astrolabe, called the *Yantraraja* (1370), which contains a

Sine table with R = 3,600, an Islamic value for the obliquity of the ecliptic (Σ = 23.35), and listed the latitudes of various cities, including Mecca, Nishapur, and Samarkand.

Narayana (fl. 1356), one of the most famous Indian mathematicians of the medieval period, wrote the *Ganitakaumudi* (1356), a work devoted to mathematical operations concerning numbers. Particularly ingenious are his square root approximation, his work on number sequences and series, and magic squares which explore the properties of combinations and permutations.

At around the same time in the south of India, Madhava (c. 1340–1425), founder of the Keralese mathematical school, flourished. Some of his works on astronomy survive, but none of his mathematical works are extant. His mathematical results were, however, preserved in later works in his school. Madhava is most famous for his value of π (π = 3.14159265359), correct to eleven places, as well as his expressions for the series expansions of the sine, cosine, and arc-tangent functions, which were not discovered in Europe until two centuries later.

As seen earlier, one of the consequences of the oral scientific tradition was that preservation of existing information was more important than scientific development. Scientists were much more concerned with borrowing parameters and tinkering with mathematical formulae than with improving parameters through frequent and extended observations. Most Indian astronomers mention the need for agreement between computed and observed phenomena, but they lacked the practical techniques to make observations that were accurate enough for their purposes. In fact, many of the procedures concerning observations mentioned in the texts simply cannot be carried out practically.

It is not until the fourteenth century, with the work of the Keralese astronomer Paramesvara (c. 1380), that a deliberate list of observations is included within a work. These observations, which comprise thirteen eclipses, both solar and lunar, ranging from 1393 until 1432, are recorded in his work the *Siddhantadipika*. However, despite this conscious inclusion, the extent to which these observations actually affected Paramesvara's parameters is undetermined.

Paramesvara wrote three other works on eclipse theory of varying length and detail. As well as several other original texts, including the *Drgganita* (1431) and the *Goladipika*, he wrote commentaries on astronomical texts that were dominant in Kerala at the time. Most of the works are preserved in Malayalam, a South Indian Dravidian language.

Paramesvara's style of astronomy, including his emphasis on observation, was passed down, through his son Damodara, to the famous astronomer Nilakantha (b. 1444). Nilakantha developed the efforts begun by Paramesvara for placing more emphasis on observation in astronomy. He not only asserted the importance that astronomy be based on experimentation and observation and that calculations should reflect reality (as many previous astronomers had done), but gave details and examples of how this was to be achieved. Nilakantha declared that eclipse observations were the most convenient and useful

means to achieve this. Nilakantha is also an important source of information about Madhava.

See also **Astronomy, Islamic**

Bibliography

Datta, B. and A. N. Singh. *History of Hindu Mathematics, A Source Book*, Parts 1 and 2 (single volume). Bombay: Asia Publishing House, 1962.

Pingree, D. E. *Jyotihsastra: Astral and Mathematical Literature*. Wiesbaden: Harrassowitz 1981.

Sarasvati Amma, T. A. *Geometry in Ancient and Medieval India*. Second revised edition. New Delhi: Motilal Banarsidass, 1999.

Subbarayappa, B. V. and K. V. Sarma. *Indian Astronomy: A Source-Book*. Bombay: Nehru Centre, 1985.

CLEMENCY WILLIAMS AND TOKE KNUDSEN

SURGERY

During the Middle Ages, surgery gained new status within the European healthcare system. There were surgeons in antique Rome and in the Arab world but they were never as well organized or as recognized as surgeons were to become in western Europe during the Middle Ages. Surgeons are mentioned in a variety of sources throughout Europe as early as the eighth century but surgery did not attain a state of institutional stability until the thirteenth century. Several factors made possible this emergence of surgery as a recognized profession at this time. First of all, numerous translations of Arabic medical sources played an essential role in the establishment of European surgery. Meanwhile, the rise of urban living led to the creation of new settings for the transmission of medical knowledge such as the university and the corporation with its accompanying apprenticeship system. Of course, surgery, defined as a manual intervention on the body, was considered a fairly radical medical strategy. Such a strategy fell far behind diet and medication in the scheme of Galenic medicine and was mainly centered on the relief of external ailments such as wounds and apostemes (abscesses) but also on more internal ailments such as cancer.

The rise in the status of surgeons seems to have paralleled that of the barbers with whom they banded together in many European towns. Barbers had traditionally performed bleeding, one of surgery's most ancient functions, and for that reason they closely associated with the generally more learned surgeons. As surgeons added book learning to their practical training, they positioned themselves halfway between the manual branch and the learned branch of medical practice. Excluded from most of the universities, surgeons managed to acquire academic knowledge through the use of books, first in Latin and later in vernacular languages. The thirteenth-century Parisian surgeon *Henri de Mondeville, who lobbied for the inclusion of surgery in academic curricula, divided the art of surgery into two indispensable branches: *magisterium* (mastering the theory), and *ministerium* (mastering the practice). Learned surgeons tended to adopt this model but they were outnumbered by the less learned city surgeons. Nevertheless, by the late Middle Ages, mastering the theory of surgery had been facilitated by the increased availability of a Mediterranean learned tradition of scholastic surgery, consisting of ancient sources and modern authorities.

Ancient Sources

Like other parts of medical theory, surgery is deeply embedded in Hippocratic medicine. Some works of the Hippocratic Corpus (c. 500 B.C.E.) on the subject bear witness to the high level of technical mastery Greek surgery had attained. After that, little is known of surgery before Celsus in the first century but the few surgical passages in his *De Medicina* show remarkable progress in the field of operative surgery and anatomy. Between these two eras lay the Hellenistic period and the Alexandrian school with its known concern for anatomy represented by doctors such as Herophilus and Eratistratus. *Galen, who attended that school and whose influence on medieval medicine was profound, paid attention to surgery especially through his interest in anatomy. He agreed with *Hippocrates in classifying surgery as a third way of intervention and was basically a generalist, but the position he held as a physician for gladiators in Pergamum had given him considerable expertise in field surgery. In any case, the main contributor to late antique surgery is Paul of Ægina, whose seven-book compilation of known ancient medical writings is set out in such a way that it became a practical manual for doctors. Book Six deals extensively with surgery and treats the surgical ailments one by one from head to toe.

Arabic Sources

While Greco-Roman surgery constituted the primary source of knowledge, ancient surgical writings reached medieval Europe through a very limited number of compilations and fragments. Oribasius, Paul of Ægina, and Aetius of Amida only became known in Western Europe through *al-Zahrawi (Albucasis). It is therefore clear that medieval surgery was born out of Arabic medicine. Aside from Albucasis, *Ibn Sina (Avicenna), *al-Razi, and *Ali ibn al-Abbas al-Majusi (Haly Abbas) were the main external sources of surgical knowledge before the Renaissance.

Albucasis, a Cordoban surgeon of the eleventh century, wrote a surgical treatise entitled *Kitab al-Tasrif*, a complete encyclopedia of everything needed by surgeons to perform their art, from Hippocratic humoral theory to descriptions of surgical procedures including drawings of some two hundred surgical instruments. This massive work inspired most subsequent medieval surgical writings thanks to its translation into Latin in the late 1100s by *Gerard of Cremona in *Toledo. Translation and assimilation of Arabic and antique science took place not only in Spain but also in Italy, especially in *Salerno, which became an important center of knowledge. *Constantine the African and his assistants made numerous translations from Arabic to Latin, notably of two of the most important texts for the transmission of antique medicine: the *Isagoge* by *Hunayn ibn Ishaq, and the *Pantegni* by *Ali Abbas al-Majusi. Both works were practical digests of Galenic lore and served as introductions to humoral theory until more of Galen's works were made available in Latin and until Avicenna's convenient synthesis became the preferred source of medical knowledge. In particular, the *Pantegni* contained a section devoted to surgery that closely followed that of Paul of Aegina. This book was for long the most readily available source of ancient surgical knowledge in the West. The only exclusively surgical text produced in this period is the Bamberg surgery, a rather erratic compilation of existing texts and techniques taken mainly from the *Pantegni*.

The Salernitan Period

Around 1200, Salerno became a center of learning providing regular courses in medicine: regimen, uroscopy, and therapy were its main themes. Despite the fact that surgery was not an essential part of the cursus at Salerno, that important southern Italian center of learning saw the emergence of a new genre that would determine the path taken by surgery in the next century: the Anatomies, brief treatises based on the dissection of pigs. The first of these works, attributed to Cophon, is devoid of Arabic influence but the second, entitled *Second Demonstration of Anatomy*, uses the *Pantegni* extensively.

The school of Salerno played an important role in establishing surgery as an independent part of medicine. This tendency is made clear in *Roger Frugard's *Chirurgia*, otherwise known as the *Rogerina*. One can identify many sources in the *Rogerina*, which was the predominant Greco-Latin influence on Paul of Aegina and Oribasisus as well as on Arabic sources, mainly those translated by Constantine. This earliest surgical work of the Middle Ages set the standard for scholastic surgical discourse and gave rise to numerous commentaries. The most popular of these was Roland of Parma's *Rolandina*, two treatises which, together with the commentaries on Frugard made by the "Four Masters," constitute the basis of later European surgery.

Surgery in Northern Italy

From Salerno, learned surgery spread to northern Italy, where it acquired adepts in Padua and Bologna. Bruno de Longoburgo composed his *Chirurgia magna* in Padua around 1252. His work introduced a more systematic use of Albcassis's surgery, indicating that Spanish translations were becoming more widely available. Ugo de Borgognoni, a veteran of crusades in Syria and a pensioner of the city of Bologna, was another contributor, although his work is known only through his disciple, *Teodorico Borgognoni. The most important contribution to the northern Italian movement came later from

Guglielmo of Saliceto with his *Treatise on Surgery*, the first work to include a chapter on anatomy. The author's clinical experience is made clear by his reference to autopsies, but his main contribution is his stated conviction—which he shared with other northern Italian surgeons—that surgery cannot be practiced or understood without medical theory. This necessary connection between medicine and surgery gave rise to a new trend of Mediterranean scholastic surgery.

*Taddeo Alderotti was a famous teacher at Bologna and around him gathered several scholars who were interested in anatomy. One of Thaddeo's disciples, *Mondino de' Liuzzi, performed the first documented dissection in 1326, and related the deed in his *Anatomia*. Historians today recognize this event to be quite an arbitrary stepping-stone since dissections had already been performed throughout Italy and southern France, but it is cited as a turning point in the history of medicine. Its impact was felt more in academic teaching than in the practice of surgery. Another student of Taddeo, Dino del Garbo, the son of a Bolognese surgeon, was the author of a commentary on the surgical parts of Avicenna's *Canon*.

Surgery in France and England

The spread of surgical knowledge from Italy to France was largely the result of the peregrinations of *Lanfranco of Milan, a disciple of Guglielmo of Saliceto after his exile from Milan in 1290. The prologue of his *Chirurgia magna* or *Practica* is a tribute to the city of Paris where he was well received and treated. His sojourn in Paris is believed to have added new vitality to the movement for learned surgery. It follows closely the first statutes on surgery in the provost's *Livre des métiers* in 1268. We also know that the king of France pensioned a number of surgeons during this time. One of them was Jean Pitard, who contributed to the establishment of surgery as a Parisian craft. His disciple Henri de Mondeville gave us the first *Chirurgia* written in France but the work was never finished due to Mondeville's fragile state of health. Henri de Mondeville gave anatomy lessons at Montpellier in 1304 of which an Occitan account has survived. His work was partly translated in 1314 but did not have a determining effect on the evolution of surgery. Mondeville is cited several times by his successor, *Guy de Chauliac, with regard to his dry treatment of wounds, a procedure that was abandoned by later medieval surgeons and thus initiated a doctrinal controversy in the fourteenth century.

Probably the most learned surgeon of the Middle Ages, Guy de Chauliac studied medicine at Montpellier around 1335 and later became a member of the Pope's retinue at Avignon. His *Inventarium sive collectorium in parte chirurgicali medicinae* became a fundamental text for medieval and modern surgery. The *Inventarium* is an encyclopedia of surgical knowledge that is mainly derived from ancient sources such as Galen—whom he cites eight hundred ninety times—and Avicenna but also uses material from more contemporary authors such as Albucasis, Henri de Mondeville and all the Salernitan

scholars and surgeons. The book was used by most medieval surgeons and was translated into Middle French, Middle English, Italian, Catalan, Dutch, and Hebrew before the end of the fourteenth century. Its content was also adapted in excerpts, abridged versions, and questions that are still extent in libraries and archives.

The work of *John of Arderne, a fourteenth-century English surgeon, embodies another kind of medieval surgery. Although he had no formal education in medicine, he played an important role in the promotion of learned surgery. He was self-educated, teaching himself Latin which he avowedly wrote very badly, as well as the elements of learned medicine. His most famous work is the *Treatises of the Fistula in Ano, Hemorrhoids, and Clysters*, in which he presents some of his techniques for curing such conditions. Since John of Arderne did not have any academic training, it has been widely believed that his career was spent largely on the battlefields. However, a closer look at his writings reveals nothing of the sort, and the first part of the *Treatises* offers remarkable insights into the practice of surgery in England at the turn of the fourteenth century.

Surgery and Health Care

The evolution of learned surgery bore little relation to the experience of most city surgeons. Most of these practitioners were trained by apprenticeship and never read Latin. Fortunately, most of the surgical literature became available in vernacular languages as early as the beginning of the fourteenth century. Nevertheless, the little we know of the content of the master's exams, in France for example, seems to suggest that basic knowledge of the veins, anatomy, and some elements of the humoral theory were the only requirements for practice. In Spain, Italy, and the south of France, surgeons were heavily involved in public health care, employed by city councils on a yearly basis as resident doctors or hired specially in times of plague. Some surgeons were also involved in the judicial system, and may have performed the very first autopsies. Their manual skills made them popular with health care practitioners and useful assistants to more theoretically oriented doctors. Their often cheaper rates assured them of regular work, especially in rural communities.

See also **Medicine, practical; Medicine, theoretical**

Bibliography

D'Arcy Power. *John Arderne, Treatises of fistula in ano, Haemorroids and Clysters*. London: Kegan Paul, Trench, Trübner & Co., 1910.

Grmek, Mirko D. *Mille ans de chirurgie en Occident, Ve–XVe siècles*. Paris: Dacosta, 1966.

Jones, Peter Murray. "John Arderne and the Mediterranean Tradition of Scolastic Surgery." In *Practical Medicine from Salerno to the Black Death*, edited by Luis Garcia-Ballester et al. New York, Cambridge University Press, 1994.

Kristeller, Paul Oscar: The School of Salerno, its Development and its Contribution to the History of Medicine. *Bulletin of the History of Medicine* (1945) 17: 138–194.

McVaugh, Michael. *Guigonis de Caulhiaco: Inventarium sive chirurgia magna*, vol. I, text. Leiden: E.J. Brill, 1997.
Nicaise, Edouard. *Guy de Chauliac: La grande chirurgie*. Paris: Alcan, 1890.
———. *Henri de Mondeville: La chirurgie*. Paris: Alcan, 1893.

GENEVIÈVE DUMAS

SWINESHEAD, RICHARD

Richard Swineshead, "the Calculator," a fellow of Merton College, Oxford, from 1344, wrote the *Book of Calculations* (*Liber Calculationum*) in the 1340s, as well as the short works *On Change* and *On Local Motion*. He became famous chiefly because Leibniz, who was familiar with his work, identified him as the first to apply mathematics to natural science in Scholastic philosophy.

In his book, Swineshead presupposes an Aristotelian/Neoplatonic physics, and searches for a logically adequate, mathematically precise account of it, with the evident intention, unlike *William of Heytesbury, of giving a complete account of the field. He considers imaginary, physically impossible cases as long as they are not logically contradictory, so one might conclude that this is mathematics and logic, not physics. He surely also thinks, however, that this conceptual investigation advances physics by clarifying our view of first principles, which are known through themselves, not through observational evidence. He believed physical processes occurred through the reproduction of qualities in things suited to receive them. He attempts to give this Aristotelian view mathematical expression, assuming qualities to be measurable. Why? Most probably he saw that qualities do vary in degree, and that a complete physics would explain why a quality of a given degree is produced in a given situation. Most qualities were not measurable in practice (the instrumentation for measuring temperature, for instance, was not yet developed), but Richard might have pursued empirical investigations in local motion, as Galileo was to demonstrate. If he did not, it is because Richard thought rational intuition sufficient to work the thing out, despite its implicit empirical content, and perhaps saw clearing the field of plain contradictions as a prior task.

The *Book of Calculations* begins with the intension and remission of forms, that is, the degrees of qualities such as heat or whiteness. What degree is assigned to a body with different degrees in different parts, and to mixed bodies, such as a mixture of fire and earth? Richard's mathematics allows him to treat only those bodies which have parts of different constant intensions, as in a body half white and half black, and those in which the intension varies uniformly in space from one degree to another.

Swineshead then turns to rarity and density. A difficulty rooted in *Thomas Bradwardine's rule is resolved: if we define rarity as a proportion of quantity of matter to volume, then twice the rarity is the proportion "added to" itself, i.e., the square of the proportion. So one pound of stuff occupying twice the space would be four times as rare. Swineshead specifies that rarity and density are proportional to the space occupied by a constant quantity of matter. Thus "twice as rare" will mean "same amount of matter in twice the volume." He then applies the results already obtained for qualities to difform densities.

Powers are next. When one body acts on another, he thinks, its power of action has a coordinate power of reception or resistance in the other body. How is a power to be measured, given this Aristotelian view? Swineshead rejects the position, later assumed by *Nicole Oresme, that the active power of a body is the product of the intension of the quality and the volume of stuff it qualifies. On this view, the intension of a quality in a body will increase as the body condenses, unless it loses some of its quality. Swineshead holds that a contracting body maintains the same intension and the same "multitude of form," its form becoming more dense, but not more intense. Richard then examines the power to receive an action, and the maximum and minimum of a power, which is treated as in William of Heytesbury.

Richard then considers a heavy body moving through the center of the world, its natural place. He argues that once part of it is past the center, it will begin to counteract the downward motion of the rest. As he works out the mathematics, the body will move more and more slowly, never actually reaching the center of the universe.

Next, he turns to light, with an eye to *Robert Grosseteste, and the power of a light source to act on a medium with a given resistance. Here he depends on simple geometrical visualization, without the complex argumentation of the earlier treatises.

After that, Richard takes up local motion, drawing on Bradwardine's *De Proportionibus* and his rule relating force, resistance and velocity. He states the mean-speed theorem, and finally considers a non-resisting medium and the increase of a resistance or power to the maximum degree.

See also **Latitude of forms**

Bibliography

Primary Source
Swineshead, Richard. *Liber Calculationum*. Padua: s.p. 1477 and Venice: O. Scoti, 1520.

Secondary Sources
Claggett, M. Richard Swineshead and late medieval physics. *Osiris* (1950) 9: 131–161.
Hoskin, M.A. and A.G. Molland. Swineshead on Falling Bodies: An Example of Fourteenth Century Physics. *British Journal for the History of Science* (1966) 3: 150–182.
Molland, A.G. "Richard Swineshead and Continuously Varying Quantities." In *Actes du XIIe Congrès international d'histoire des sciences*. 12 volumes in 15. Paris: Albert Blanchard, 1970–1971. vol 3A, pp. 127–130.
Sylla, Edith D. *The Oxford Calculators and the Mathematics of Motion, 1320–1350: Physics and Measurements by Latitudes*. New York: Garland Publishing, 1991, pp. 626–714.

JOHN LONGEWAY

T

TACUINUM SANITATIS

This practical handbook of preventive medicine was put together by the Arab physician Ibn Butlan. A native of Baghdad, where he studied and taught medicine and philosophy, Ibn Butlan traveled widely in the Middle East. In Aleppo the Christian physician and theologian practiced medicine. Among the other places he visited were Jaffa, Cairo, Constantinople, and Antioch, where he entered a monastery and died around 1066 C.E. His best-known work was the *Taqwim al-sihha* (*Tables of Health*), a *regimen sanitatis* in chart form for quick reference, of which nine Arabic manuscripts have survived. It was translated into Latin in the second half of the thirteenth century by an anonymous translator, probably at the court of Manfred of Sicily in Palermo. Under the title *Tacuinum sanitatis* it quickly gained popularity across Europe. Some seventeen manuscripts of the Latin version have come down to us, of which the earliest dates back to the thirteenth century. In 1531 the Latin *Tacuinum* was first printed in Strasbourg, and in 1533 a German translation by the Strasbourg physician Michael Herr followed under the title *Schachtafelen der Gesundheyt*, that alluded to the arrangement of the charts in the form of a chessboard. Both the Latin and German printed versions contain woodcuts by Hans Weiditz the Younger.

In the *Tacuinum sanitatis*, the content is divided into forty *tacuini* or tables of seven objects each that are arranged vertically. Horizontally, fifteen *domus* or criteria, such as the nature, benefit, or harm of a given item, are listed for each of the two hundred eighty objects. General dietetic information on food and drink from a sixteenth *domus* precedes the forty tables. In the introduction, Ibn Butlan names the *sex res non naturales* or six non-natural causes of sickness and health, traditionally part of *Regimen sanitatis* literature, in the following order: (1) Air; (2) Food and drink; (3) Exercise and rest; (4) Sleeping and waking; (5) Repletion and excretion; and (6) Emotional well-being. Ibn Butlan touches on all of them (albeit in a different order), but does not afford them equal prominence in the book. The first thirty *tacuini*, three-quarters of the work, are devoted to foodstuffs, and between one and four *tacuini* each to the remaining five non-naturals. The foodstuffs include fruits, grains, legumes, various types of bread, vegetables, herbs, milk, dairy products, eggs, the meat of domestic and wild animals, birds, fish, and other seafood, animal parts, and some prepared foods. Different types of water, wine, flowers, and desserts conclude the food section. Somewhat surprisingly, the *Tacuinum* continues with the emotions that normally form the end of a medieval *regimen*. Discussed are joy, shame, anger, fear, anxiety, and sadness, but also music and dance. The section on the filling and emptying of the body is combined with sleeping and waking, and includes items such as drunkenness, constipation, vomiting, purgation, sex, dreams, and storytelling. As part of exercise are listed riding, hunting, fishing, wrestling, jumping, walking, and ball games, but also clapping hands, playing the lute, and crushing grapes with one's feet, singing, whistling, bathing and grooming, chess, and rolling dice. Clothing, fragrant substances, syrups, and fruit juices lead into the last section on air, in which the focus is on air quality, temperature, humidity, seasons, winds, geographic location, proximity to mountains and oceans, and soil conditions.

In the fourteenth and fifteenth centuries a number of much abbreviated and richly illuminated versions of the *Tacuinum* were produced that became desired showpieces of princely libraries. No longer in tabular form, these luxurious manuscripts typically discussed just over two hundred items each, one per page, with pride of place being given to the images, genre-scenes of daily life in late fourteenth-century Italy; the text was severely reduced. Rooted in the tradition of the illustrated herbal, this type of *Tacuinum* has survived in at least nine manuscripts, including one in Italian translation. Five manuscripts (Liège, Paris, Vienna, Casanatense, and Rouen) are believed to be closely related and to have originated in the workshops of the artist Giovannino dei Grassi in the valley of the Po River in Lombardy. A concordance of the five slightly different texts reveals that together they list a total of two hundred eighty-six different items. This is more than the two hundred eighty of the complete tabular version. The name of the author, Ibn Butlan, appears in a variety of spellings in the manuscripts (*Albullasem, Albulkasem, Ellbochasim,* or *Ububchasym*). Although *Hippocrates, *Galen, *Dioscorides, Oribasius, Rhazes (*al-Razi), Johannitius (*Hunayn ibn Ishaq), and other physicians are mentioned in some manuscripts, Ibn Butlan shows stronger affinities to his contemporaries Haly Abbas (*'Ali ibn al' Abbas al Majusi) and Avicenna (*Ibn Sina).

See also **Medicine, practical; Medicine, theoretical**

Bibliography

Adamson, Melitta Weiss. "Ibn Butlan. *Tacuinum sanitatis.*" In idem. *Medieval Dietetics: Food and Drink in Regimen Sanitatis Literature from 800 to 1400.* Frankfurt am Main: Peter Lang, 1995, 83–91.

Arano, Luisa Cogliati. *The Medieval Health Handbook TACUINUM SANITATIS.* Translated and adapted by Oscar Ratti and Adele Westbrook. New York: George Braziller, 1976.

Conrad, Lawrence I. "Scholarship and Social Context: A Medical Case from the Eleventh-century Near East." In *Knowledge and the Scholarly Medical Traditions.* Edited by Don Bates. New York: Cambridge University Press, 1995, pp. 84–100.

Elkhadem, Hosam. *Le "Taqwim al-sihha" (Tacuini sanitatis) d'Ibn Butlan: un traité médical du XIe siècle. Histoire du texte, édition critique, traduction, commentaire.* Académie royale de Belgique, classe des lettres, Fonds René Draguet, vol. 7. Leuven, Belgium: Aedibus Peeters, 1990.

Herbarium: Natural Remedies from a Medieval Manuscript. Texts by Adalberto Pazzini and Emma Pirani. Original Captions by Ubuchasym de Baldach. Translated by Michael Langley. New York: Rizzoli, 1980.

Ibn Butlan. *The Physicians' Dinner Party.* Edited from Arabic manuscripts and with an introduction by Felix Klein-Franke. Wiesbaden: Harrassowitz, 1985.

Opsomer, Carmélia. *L'art de vivre en santé. Images et recettes du moyen âge. Le Tacuinum Sanitatis (manuscrit 1041) de la Bibliothèque de l'Université de Liège.* Liège: Édition du Perron, 1991.

Pacht, Otto. Early Italian Nature Studies and the Early Calendar Landscape. *Journal of the Warburg and Courtauld Institutes* (1950) 13: 13–47.

———. Eine wiedergefundene Tacuinum-Sanitatis Handschrift. *Münchner Jahrbuch der bildenden Kunst,* 3. F. (1952/53) 3/4: 171–180.

Schacht, J. Ibn Butlan. In *Encyclopedia of Islam.* Vol. III. 2nd edition. Edited by B. Lewis, V. L. Ménage, Ch. Pellat and †J. Schacht. Leiden: E.J. Brill, 1971.

Sigler, Lora Ann. The Genre of Gender: Images of Working Women in the *Tacuina sanitatis.* Ph.D. dissertation, University of California, Los Angeles, 1992.

Spencer, Judith, trans. *The Four Seasons of the House of Cerruti.* New York: Facts on File, 1984.

Tomas de Cantimpré, Santo, De natura rerum (lib. IV–XII). Tacuinum sanitatis Ibn Butlan. Códice C-67 de la Biblioteca Universitaria de Granada. Facsimile edition, Commentaries, Preliminary Studies, Transcription, Castilian and English Translation under the Direction of Luis García Ballester. Granada: Universidad, 1975.

Ullmann, Manfred. *Islamic Medicine.* Translated by Jean Watt. Edinburgh: Edinburgh University Press, 1978.

Wickersheimer, E. Les Tacuini Sanitatis et leur traduction allemande par Michael Herr. In *Bibliothèque d'Humanisme et Renaissance.* Vol. XII. Geneva: 1950, 85–97.

Zotter, Hans. *Das Buch vom gesunden Leben: die Gesundheitstabellen des Ibn Butlan in der illustrierten ‹bertragung des Michael Herr, nach der bei Hans Schott erschienenen Ausgabe Straßburg 1533; mit 32 getreuen Farbwiedergaben aus dem Tacuinum sanitatis Codex Vindobonensis 2396.* Graz, Austria: Akademische Druck- und Verlagsanstalt, 1988.

MELITTA WEISS-ADAMSON

TECHNOLOGICAL DIFFUSION

The diffusion of technology from East to West was a movement that united the medieval world from China to England into a vast area of shared know-how. Within the broad geographical compass of the Eurasian continental mass, we can of course detect more specific patterns of technical innovation that can be described in more geographically circumscribed terms. Diffusion was one of the main motors of technological innovation and is associated with a variety of other factors, such as the migration of artisans, the patterns of long-distance trade, the development of urban markets, and the need for agricultural production to adjust to rising population, among others. In this movement, the Islamic conquests of the eighth–tenth centuries were crucial because they created a vast zone of cultural interaction stretching from Spain to northern India which was a propitious medium for the spread of ideas. As Needham (I, 220–223) observed, the Islamic world was focal with respect to science; choices were made there that resulted in the acceptance and propagation of Indian and Greek science, for example, but not Chinese. On the other, that filter was not applied with respect to technology.

Westward Movement

There is some convergence of ideas among historians on what Arnold Toynbee (*Study of History,* 3) called the "cultural conductivity of nomadism" that one finds also in Needham, White, and Allsen. For White, techniques associated with the agricultural revolution of the early Middle Ages diffused westward across the steppes of central Asia through the chain of nomadic societies. So the heavy plow reached the Goths from the Slavs, perhaps by the early sixth century (53), while the stirrup spread "across the great plains of Asia to the region north of Black Sea" (20). Hence it reached Byzantium via the Avars, Bulgars or Magyars. For Toynbee, the reason nomadic groups display cultural conductivity is their very mobility; for Allsen, because nomads are cultural generalists with few developed technical specialties, when they come into control of states (as in the case of the Mongols) they require the acquisition of exogenous ideas and techniques. The Mongols institutionalized cultural borrowing, as in the Office of Western (i.e., Arabic) Astronomy (1263 C.E.). The focality of the Islamic

Illumination from a thirteenth-century manuscript of the *Book of Games* by Alfonso X, King of Spain. (Corbis/Gianni Dagli Orti)

empire in East-to-West technological diffusion also depended on the control of states; yet the Arabs, of course, manifested the characteristic nomadic openness to new techniques when they ended up in control of a vast empire.

Harnessing

Andre Haudricort (1948) argued on linguistic evidence that the modern horse-collar originated in central Asia and reached eastern and northern Europe from the East around 800 C.E. Part of the argument concerning the rigid horse-collar has to be with the relationship between it and elements of the camel saddle and packs. Although the details are confusing and the origins and diffusion of specific components unclear, the social context of the evolution of the collar is the relationship between camel-riding nomads and sedentary farmers. Harnessing technology is an interesting vehicle for the study of technological diffusion and comparative history of technology because it has a limited number of components (breast or withers strap, whipple-tree, shafts joined by a crossbar, and collar) found in various configurations. Bulliet's solution (204–205) is that the collar reached Europe through the chain of central Asian nomads, while the breast strap arrived from North Africa. He further identifies, also on the basis of linguistic evidence, two families of harnesses in southern Europe: a Mediterranean sphere encompassing North Africa, Spain, Italy, and the western Mediterranean islands, with Sicily and Spain providing the channels of transmission between North Africa and Europe, and a French-Provencal sphere.

Chess

The game of chess originated in India and was then cultivated in Persia: these regions were the immediate sources of the Arabic game, which became known as *al-Sitranj*. Thus chess followed the same path of diffusion westward as did Indian astronomy and mathematics, and possibly was played by merchants along the Silk Route. The first technical treatises in Arabic appeared in the ninth century.

Paper and Sugar Manufacture

In the manufacture of *paper and sugar, related techniques tended to diffuse in discrete packages. The vertical watermill traveled from east to west as the organizing element in a distinctive package of Chinese techniques that included the processing of oil, paper, sugar, indigo, lac, and tea, all by means of vertical, trip-hammer mills, wherein hammers attached to the axis of the water-wheel pounded the product to the point where the process could be continued manually (Daniels). It is possible to trace the diffusion of paper and sugar manufacture across the Arabic-speaking world by noting the appearance of the surnames al-Warraq (paper-maker) or al-Sukkari (sugar-maker) in the ninth century. It is likely, therefore, that paper and sugar processing arrived at the western terminus of diffusion, Islamic Spain, simultaneously, along with the vertical wheel and trip-hammer assembly, which could also be used for the fulling (pounding) of woolen cloth and for rice husking. The prototype of the common tilt-hammer fulling mill was the Chinese rice-husking mill, which was vertical and undershot.

Indian Agriculture

The same holds true for a distinctive package of crops and agricultural techniques that the Arabs called *filaha hindiyya*—Indian *agriculture. A cluster of crops grown in India under monsoon conditions (sugar cane, rice, citrus trees, watermelon) could only be grown under irrigation the Mediterranean region, with its summer droughts. So they diffused along with Persian and Arab irrigation techniques (such as the qanat or filtration gallery and the *noria), which formed part of a flexible "tool kit" that tribal irrigators could deploy in a variety of microclimates with different topographical and hydrological conditions.

West-to-East Diffusion

Techniques diffused in the opposite direction too, of course. A simplified astrolabe or saphea invented by *al-Zarqalluh in eleventh-century *Toledo became known in the Near East. Ibn al-Qifti (d. 1248) says: "Al-Zarqalluh invented the saphea on which, in spite of its small size, are conjoined the most ephemeral details of the science of the movements of the celestial spheres. When the scholars of the East learned of this apparatus there were incapable of understanding it until God helped them" (Vernet, 564).

See also **Astrolabes and quadrants; Irrigation and drainage; Watermills**

Bibliography

Allsen, Thomas T. *Culture and Conquest in Mongol Eurasia.* New York: Cambridge University Press, 2001.

Bulliet, Richard W. *The Camel and the Wheel.* Cambridge: Harvard University Press, 1975.

Daniels, Christian. Agro-Industries: Sugarcane Technology. In Joseph Needham, *Science and Civilisation in China*, vol. 6, part 3. New York: Cambridge University Press, 1996, pp. 1–539.

Needham, Joseph. *Science and Civilisation in China. Vol. I. Introductory Orientations.* New York: Cambridge University Press, 1954.

Vernet, Juan. La ciencia en el Islam y Occidente. In *Occidente e l'Islam nell'alto medioevo*, 2 vols. Spoleto: Centro Italiano di Studi sull'Alto Medioevo, 1965, II: 537–572.

White, Lynn, Jr. *Medieval Technology and Social Change.* Oxford: Clarendon Press, 1962.

THOMAS F. GLICK

THABIT IBN QURRA

Thabit ibn Qurrah Abu'l Hasan ibn Zahrun al-Harrani (known as Thebit Ben Corah in the Latin West), was one of the most highly accomplished scholars in the Arabic world, especially in the field of mathematics. He was born in Harran in northern Mesopotamia, probably in 824 C.E., and died in Baghdad on February 19, 901. He owed to his origins in Harran his knowledge of Syriac (his native tongue), and his experience of the star-worshipping sect of the Sabaeans, whom he is said to have represented in Baghdad. Having settled in Baghdad at an early age, under the tutelage of the three brothers and mathematicians called the Banu Musa, he soon became the leading figure of his time in the translation of Greek mathematical works, which he interpreted and supplemented with innumerable works of his own. He was supported by the caliphs, and worked closely with *Hunayn ibn Ishaq, several of whose translations he revised. Nearly two hundred works are attributed to him, mostly in Arabic, but a few in Syriac. Among the numerous Greek works he translated, or of which he improved an earlier translation of, are Epaphroditus's commentary on Aristotle's *Meteorology*, several works of *Archimedes, books V–VII of Apollonius of Perga's *Conica* (the Greek original of which is lost), *Euclid's *Elements*, *Data*, and *Optics*, Nicomachus of Gerasa's *Introduction to Arithmetic*, Pappus's Commentary on *Ptolemy's *Planisphere*, Theodosius's *Spherics*, Autolycus' *On the Moving Sphere*, and Ptolemy's *Almagest*, *Planetary Hypotheses*, and *Geography*. Of many more works he made synopses or abridgements (especially in respect to Aristotle's logical works, *Galen's medical works and Ptolemy's astrological handbook, the *Tetrabiblos*) and commentaries (e.g., of the *Almagest*, and of *Plato's *Republic*). His original writings cover the fields of the divisions of science, natural science, music, medicine, and mechanics. Especially important and influential are his works on *arithmetic and geometry, astronomy and on astrological images (talismans). He showed how algebraic and geometrical proofs related to each other, and developed theorems for measuring cones, paraboloids and spheroids which were independent of Greek precedents. The theorem that he discovered for generating "amicable numbers" (i.e., pairs of numbers in which the sum of the factors of one is equal to the other), still goes under his name. In astronomy the two focuses of his attention were the mathematical paradigms whose model was provided in the *Almagest*, the culmination of Greek mathematical astronomy, and the data in the *Zij al-Mumtahan*, the astronomical tables commissioned by the caliph al-Ma'mun in about 830, which represented the most rigorous combination of mathematical learning and observation up to that date. Thabit did not follow his Greek predecessors uncritically. He was well known for advocating the non-Ptolemaic astronomical theory of "trepidation"—the forward and backward movement of the sphere of the fixed stars. It may be no coincidence that, in this, he follows a theory that Theon of Alexandria attributes to ancient makers of talismans (*hoi palaioi ton apotelesmatikon*). For he wrote on manipulating astrological and other natural forces by means of manufactured talismans—even using the "sympathetic" relations of amicable numbers for empowering talismans of love. This interest, which sets him apart from his contemporary mathematicians in Baghdad, may be related to his involvement with the Harranian Sabaeans, on whose beliefs he wrote several texts on Syriac. Several of Thabit's translations or revisions were in turn translated into Latin, but his name was no longer associated with these texts. Thabit's European reputation rests rather on: (1) The small collection of original astronomical texts that were translated into Latin, mainly by *Gerard of Cremona in the third quarter of the twelfth century; and (2) His work on talismans, versions of which were translated by *Adelard of Bath and *John of Seville, again in the twelfth century. The Arabic original of the Latin text on trepidation attributed to him—*De motu octave sphere*—has not been identified, and doubt has been cast on his authorship, but it served to make the theory canonical among several generations of Western astronomers through being adopted in Gerard of Cremona's *Theorica planetarum*.

See also **Astronomy, Islamic; Translation norms and practice**

Bibliography

Carmody, F.J. *The Astronomical Works of Thabit b. Qurra*. Berkeley: University of California Press, 1960.
Roshdi Rashed. *Les mathématiques infinitésimales du IXe au XIe siècle*, I. London: al-Furqan Islamic Heritage Foundation, 1996, pp. 139–673.
Thabit ibn Qurra. *Oeuvres d'astronomie*. Ed. Régis Morelon. Paris: Les Belles Lettres, 1987.

CHARLES BURNETT

THEODORIC OF FREIBERG

Theodoric (Theodoricus Teutonicus de Vriberch, maister Dietreich, Dietrich) was born at Freiberg in Germany between 1240 and 1250. He joined the Dominican order before studying in Cologne and Paris and before teaching in Trier and Paris. From 1293 to 1296 he was provincial prior of Germany and from 1294 to 1296 vicar general, too. In 1296 he received the degree of master of theology in Paris, where he had been teaching for two years. In 1310 he was appointed vicar provincial again. He died probably between 1318 and 1320.

Theodoric was unquestionably one of the most important philosophers, theologians, and natural scientists of the Middle Ages. This is revealed both by his university career—Theodoric was the only German other than *Albertus Magnus to earn the title of magister in *theologia* at Paris in the thirteenth century—and by his writings. Apart from a few *Quaestiones* and *Epistulae*, these were not huge *summae*, but rather *tractatus* (treatises), which were always devoted to carefully selected problems. These works manifest a clearly theoretical intention, for Theodoric wished to take a stand on the most significant and, frequently, the most difficult philosophical, theological, and natural scientific questions of his time. The treatise form allowed him to handle such questions methodically and proximately within a general horizon in order to recommend specific solutions.

Theodoric's principal aim was to destroy common misconceptions in *metaphysics and theology. It was *Thomas Aquinas who was mostly criticized by Theodoric. While Aquinas considered the intellect to be a passive faculty of the human soul, Theodoric took the view that it is an active power of the soul having a constitutive function with respect to the quiddity of natural things and to what they are in themselves, because it is acting as an efficient cause. The agent intellect has three objects: being as being; God as its intellectual principle, and its own essence. Aquinas, however, spoke of the abstractive function of the agent intellect and ignored the fact that Aristotle and Albertus Magnus had taught that the agent intellect is able to reflect on itself and to understand itself as its own object. Other Thomistic theories rejected by Theodoric were the real difference between essence and existence, and the possibility of separating accidental forms from their substance. The latter, according to Theodoric, was a wholly non-Aristotelian opinion put forward by Aquinas in order to defend the theory of transubstantiation which, however, is untenable from a philosophical point of view.

As a natural scientist Theodoric devoted important treatises to the study of the nature of the continuum, of that of contrariety, and of the optical phenomenon of the rainbow. A continuum consists of connected parts which make it countable, and two extreme points which allow it to be measured. Such a continuum actually exists as a whole, as in dimensions, or is a successive process like motion from one place to another or like time. But for time it is significant that it exists in the soul without having any extra-mental being. Time is an effect of the speculative intellect which is the efficient cause of the extension between a before and an afterwards limiting the process of motion. Time is nothing in the real world of *generation and corruption, but something caused by the intellect giving it existence. Thus Theodoric combined elements of the theories developed by Aristotle, Augustine, and *Ibn Rushd, while his own theory was adopted by Nicholas of Strasbourg.

In the realm of natural generation, qualitative dispositions are necessary as instruments of natural agents. The structure of these instruments is based on natural contrariety. Aristotle had a wide notion of contrariety. According to Theodoric perfect natural contrariety occurs in the third species of quality only which contains passive qualities and affections. In Aristotle's philosophy perfect contrariety can be found in the field of four categories; according to Theodoric, however, it is restricted to one category and within this category to one particular species. Evidently, it was Theodoric's methodical aim to establish a well-founded science by reducing natural principles.

Theodoric's particular place in the history of science is assured by his theory of the rainbow that was to be perfected only centuries later by Descartes and Newton. Theodoric was not content merely to observe nature but attempted to duplicate nature's operation by isolating the component factors of that operation in a way that permitted their study at close range. Since most of Theodoric's predecessors compared the colors of the rainbow with the spectrum resulting from the Sun's rays passing through a spherical flask of water, they tended to equate the flask with a cloud or with a collection of drops. Theodoric, however, saw that the individual dewdrop played a significant role. He was the first to trace correctly the path of the light ray through the drop and to see that this involved two refractions: one at the surface of the drop nearer the observer, and one internal reflection at the surface farther from him. After this explanation of the primary, or lower, rainbow, Theodoric went on to explicate the mechanism for the production of the secondary, or upper, rainbow. He discovered that the light ray, in this case, follows a path quite different from that in the production of the lower rainbow, involving as it does two refractions at the surface of the drop nearer the observer and two internal reflections at the surface farther from him. Thus it was possible for Theodoric to give adequate reasons for the inversion of the colors in the secondary rainbow. But Theodoric was not content with his optical-geometrical expositions. He forced his empirical investigations and, without giving any reasons, he spoke of the empirical fact that the four colors of the lower rainbow are arranged in their specific order and inverted in the upper bow. Thus the theories of the *perspectivi*, especially *Ibn al-Haytham's theory, were undoubtedly repudiated by Theodoric in the last period of his natural philosophy, but his own empirical initiatives did not make any impact on natural scientists at the end of the Middle Ages.

See also **Metaphysics; Optics and catoptrics**

Bibliography

Primary Sources

Theodoric of Freiberg (Dietrich von Freiberg) (c. 1280–1320). *Opera Omnia*, vol. 1, ed. B. Mojsisch. Hamburg: Felix Meiner, 1977; vol. 2, ed. R. Imbach, M.R. Pagnoni-Sturlese, H. Steffan and L. Sturlese. Hamburg: Felix Meiner, 1980; vol. 3, ed. J.-D. Cavigioli, R. Imbach, B. Mojsisch, M.R. Pagnoni-Sturlese, R. Rehn and L. Sturlese. Hamburg: Felix Meiner, 1983; vol. 4, ed. M.R. Pagnoni-Sturlese, R. Rehn, L. Sturlese and W.A. Wallace. Hamburg: Felix Meiner, 1985.

——— (1293). *Treatise on the Intellect and the Intelligible (Tractatus de intellectu et intelligibili)*, transl. from the Latin, with an Introduction and Notes by M.L. Führer. Milwaukee, WIS: Marquette University Press, 1992.

Secondary Sources

Flasch, Kurt, ed. *Von Meister Dietrich zu Meister Eckhart.* Hamburg, Germany: Felix Meiner, 1984.

Imbach, R. "Gravis iactura verae doctrinae." Prolegomena zu einer Interpretation der Schrift De ente et essentia Dietrichs von Freiberg. *Freiburger Zeitschrift für Philosophie und Theologie* (1979) 26: 369–425.

Kandler, Karl-Hermann, Burkhard Mojsisch, and Franz-Bernhard Stammkötter, ed. *Dietrich von Freiberg. Neue Perspektiven seiner Philosophie, Theologie und Naturwissenschaft. Freiberger Symposion: 10–13. März 1997,* Bochumer Studien zur Philosophie 28. Amsterdam and Philadelphia: B.R. Grüner, 1999.

Libera, Alain de. *Introduction à la mystique Rhénane. D'Albert le Grand à Maître Eckhart.* Paris: O.E.I.L., 1984.

Maurer, A.A. The De quidditatibus entium of Dietrich of Freiberg and its Criticism of Thomistic Metaphysics. *Mediaeval Studies* (1956) 18: 173–203.

Mojsisch, Burkhard. "Die Theorie des Intellekts bei Dietrich von Freiberg." Ph.D. Dissertation, Hamburg: Felix Meiner, 1977.

Sturlese, Loris. *Storia della filosofia tedesca nel Medioevo. Il secolo XIII.* Accademia Toscana di Scienze e Lettere "La Colombaria," Studi, 149. Florence: Leo S. Olschki, 1996.

Wallace, William A. *The Scientific Methodology of Theodoric of Freiberg. A Case Study of the Relationship between Science and Philosophy.* Studia Friburgensia, New Series, 26. Fribourg: University Press, 1959.

BURKHARD MOJSISCH

THEORICA PLANETARUM

Theorica planetarum is the name given to a group of textbooks on astronomy in use from the twelfth to the seventeenth centuries. The term *theorica* is derived from a medieval division of astronomy into two parts: a *pars theorica* on computational astronomy, and a *pars practica* on *astrology. A *theorica* explains the planetary models of *Ptolemy in sufficient detail to enable the student to understand and use *planetary tables, but without introducing advanced material, such as the derivation of models from observation, for which students would have to refer to Ptolemy's *Almagest* itself.

A *theorica planetarum* covers only the more complicated motions of each planet and of the sphere of fixed stars. It says nothing about the motion of rising and setting shared by all celestial objects, which in geocentric systems is held to be caused by their daily rotation around the Earth. This was known as the "first motion," to distinguish it from the "second motions" of the planets. Before reading a *theorica planetarum*, the student studied a more elementary type of astronomical textbook on the daily rotation known as a *sphaera* or "sphere," most likely the *Tractatus de sphaera* written by *John of Sacrobosco in the thirteenth century.

Medieval *Theoricae*

Several minor *theoricae planetarum* are known from the Middle Ages. However, two medieval *theoricae* clearly dominated the genre. The first and more popular of these was probably written by *Gerard of Cremona. His name certainly appears on many early printed editions, but since the majority of manuscripts are anonymous texts, authorship has been contested. In support of the tenuous medieval tradition of authorship, Richard Lemay has drawn attention to a manuscript of the *theorica* collected with works translated by Gerard. Perhaps it is safest to regard Gerard as the only serious candidate, which would place the composition of the *theorica* in the second half of the twelfth century. Otherwise it may be a thirteenth-century work. In the nineteenth century Boncompagni proposed Gerard of Sabbionetta as the true author of this *theorica*. Since no medieval manuscript makes this attribution and no other evidence supports it, Boncompagni's theory has fallen out of favor, but the reader may find Gerard of Sabbionetta named as the author in some older studies.

The *theorica planetarum* ascribed to Gerard treats Ptolemaic planetary theory in eight chapters on the Sun, the Moon, the motions of the lunar nodes used to predict eclipses (called Dragon's Head and Dragon's Tail), the three superior planets (Mars, Jupiter, and Saturn), the inferior planets (Mercury and Venus), eclipses and epicyclic phenomena (i.e., stations and retrogradations), latitude theory (a chapter which also contains material on the precession of the equinoxes and other subjects), and astrological aspects (significant positioning of the planets with respect to each other). An overview of the chapter on solar theory will serve to illustrate the character of the text as a whole. The Sun moves around the Earth on a circle which is eccentric, meaning that its center is actually at a slight distance from the center of the world. (This is the deferent circle of Ptolemaic astronomy.) Consequently, even though the Sun's motion is perfectly uniform, it appears to speed up and slow down as it approaches and recedes from us. The main purpose of the chapter—and of the book as a whole—was to provide a glossary for planetary tables, which employed specialized words for the circles, lines, and points used to compute the Sun's position. Like the *Almagest*, this *theorica* presents the motions of the planets in terms of geometrical circles. It says nothing about converting the models into systems of nesting orbs, although a method of conversion was used in medieval *cosmology.

The *theorica* strays from the *Almagest* in minor respects. For instance, Ptolemy did not include the lunar nodes as discrete concepts; the importance of the Dragon's Head and Tail was a development of medieval astronomy. Neither did he discuss aspects in the *Almagest*, which did not cover astrology. The material on latitude theory in the *theorica* includes a method of calculation originating in India, a sign of the interconnections between medieval Latin, Islamic, and Hindu astronomy. Minor changes such as these do not detract from the importance of the *theorica* as a textbook. Despite being terse, sometimes to the point of obscurity, the book satisfied the need to provide students with an introduction to the recently rediscovered astronomy of the ancients.

Olaf Pedersen, author of a series of articles on the *theorica*, identified over two hundred manuscripts. It was also frequently printed in the fifteenth and sixteenth centuries. In either form, it is often bound with Sacrobosco's *Sphaera* and sometimes a set of tables or other astronomical texts. Medieval and Renaissance statutes from the universities of Paris and Oxford confirm that arts students satisfied the requirements of the *quadrivium in part by reading a *sphaera* at the bachelor's level and a *theorica planetarum* at the master's. We can be sure that many read "Gerard's" *theorica*.

The other principal *theorica* was by *Campanus de Novara, who gave instructions on the manufacture of a set of astronomical instruments known as equatoria. An equatorium represents the motion of a planet by a series of rotating disks. It may be used for crude but rapid calculations or for teaching purposes. What makes this theorica more accessible than purely geometrical representations of planetary models is its likening of disks to cross-sections of three-dimensional orbs. In the same book, Campanus calculated the size of each planet and its minimum and maximum distances from Earth in miles, based on parameters from an astronomical textbook by al-Farghani (ninth century). Campanus's *theorica* and his system of planetary distances were popular in the fifteenth century, but interest in them declined rapidly after the Middle Ages. It was not printed before modern times.

Theoricae in the Renaissance

In 1454 the humanist and astronomer *Georg Peuerbach began to use a *theorica* of his own composition for his lectures in astronomy. One of his students, *Johannes Regiomontanus, became both a celebrated mathematician in his own right and one of the first scientific publishers. In 1472 he printed Peuerbach's lectures. They were reprinted many times through the seventeenth century under some variation of the title *Theoricae novae planetarum*. He also printed a short work of his own composition, the *Disputationes contra deliramenta Cremonensia*, attacking the old *theorica* and implicitly promoting the new.

The *Theoricae novae* covers essentially the same material as its competitor, although the arrangement of material is slightly altered. For instance, precession and latitude theory each has its own chapter. Peuerbach explains each model in a detailed and comprehensible manner, presenting them as sets of orbs, unlike the popular medieval *theorica*, which had treated them as combinations of circles.

The fate of the *theorica* genre is intimately tied to the rediscovery of Ptolemy in the Latin West. Before its appearance, planetary astronomy could be learned only from rudimentary handbooks. Even early *theoricae* represent a great advance in the teaching of astronomy. The *theoricae* of Campanus and Peuerbach are progressively more sophisticated and take the reader closer to the technical level of the *Almagest*. It is no coincidence that Regiomontanus, Nicolas Copernicus, and other leading figures of the Renaissance learned astronomy from Peuerbach's *Theoricae novae*. But by the seventeenth century the *theorica* had outlived its usefulness.

See also **Astrolabes and quadrants; Astronomy, Latin**

Bibliography

Aiton, E. J. Peurbach's Theoricae novae planetarum: A Translation with Commentary. *Osiris*, 2nd series (1987) 3: 5–44.

Benjamin, Jr., Francis S., and G. J. Toomer. *Campanus of Novara and Medieval Planetary Theory: "Theorica Planetarum."* Madison: University of Wisconsin Press, 1971.

Pedersen, Olaf. Theorica: A Study in Language and Civilization. *Classica et Mediaevalia* (1961) 22: 151–166.

———. "The Decline and Fall of the Theorica Planetarum: Renaissance Astronomy and The Art of Printing." In *Science and History: Studies in Honor of Edward Rosen.* Wroclaw: Polish Academy of Sciences Press, 1978. Studia Copernicana 16, 157–185.

KATHERINE A. TREDWELL

THIERRY OF CHARTRES

Thierry of Chartres was one of the most important twelfth-century cathedral school masters. He was a philosopher and extraordinary teacher of natural science, and members of his circle also became important teachers and translators of Arabic scientific and mathematical texts. He is often seen as the major figure of "Chartrian Platonism."

Thierry was born around 1100, probably in Brittany. Tradition identifies him as the younger brother of Bernard of Chartres, master and chancellor of that school. This school was renowned in the twelfth century, producing not only these two brothers but also *William of Conches, Gilbert of Poitiers, Clarembald of Arras, and John of Salisbury. The school reached its apogee during Thierry's tenure there. He is first recorded as the *magister scholarum* in 1121. Like many scholars, he was also appointed an archdeacon of Dreaux nearby. His career progressed to teaching in Paris by 1134, where among his pupils were Adalbert of Mainz, Peter of Poitiers, Ivo of Chartres, and William of Tyre. He is particularly noted at this time for his teaching of the ancient classification of the trivium: grammar, rhetoric, and dialectic. In 1141 he succeeded Gilbert of Poitiers as chancellor of Chartres. He appears to have died before 1155. In the latter part of his career he seems to have taught only more advanced students, having lost patience with "the ignorant mob and the mish-mash of the schools." His advanced students, though, were full of effusive praise for him, calling him "Aristotle's worthy successor," "the foremost philosopher in the whole of Europe," "the most learned of explorers of the liberal arts," and "the soul of Plato granted once again by heaven to mortals."

Thierry's scholarly work falls into three categories: works on the trivium, most notably his commentaries on ancient rhetorical treatises, his interpretive tract "On the Works of the Six Days," and his massive *Heptateuchon*. For medieval science especially the latter two are significant. In the *Heptateuchon* Thierry laid out a curriculum for the whole of the liberal arts, hence the name. This book not only had his introductions, but the texts of the authors he felt needed to be studied. It reveals that Thierry was one of the first scholars to use the "new" texts of Aristotle's *Organon* for the study of dialectic but it also contained the astronomical tables attributed to *Ptolemy and *al-Khwarizmi (recently translated in Spain), and texts of a mathematical tradition going back to and including those of *Gerbert of Aurillac. It has been claimed that Thierry introduced the use of the zero and decimal notation to European mathematics in an opusculum at the end of the geometry section of the *Heptateuchon* (Haring, 340; Clerval, 236). He believed that the quadrivial sciences (arithmetic, geometry, music, and astronomy) offered the knowledge of the reality that then had to be interpreted and expressed by the interpretive skills learned in the trivium. This is significant for it turned the ancient evaluations of these two groups of sciences on their head: what had been considered the lesser group (the trivium) became the key to human understanding.

Because philosophical and theological knowledge were inseparable for Thierry, philosophical sciences are the pathway to wisdom which is knowledge of God. It is in this sense that he is a Platonist: the matter of this world reveals the Ideas of God. This method is best seen in his work on creation, *On the Works of the Six Days*: eschewing the common medieval moral or allegorical methods of interpretation, the creation account of Genesis is first explained by findings of natural science and philosophical explanation. The biblical text here is taken as demonstrating the natural, physical laws of the universe that scholars have discovered. Only after this demonstration are theological points drawn. This approach has been called "the first systematic attempt to withdraw cosmology from the realm of the miraculous" (Klibansky, 8). As Dronke has put it, granting divine creation a priori "he accepted empirical principles pervasively, not selectively." In his Aristotelian analysis, God is the effective cause but the four elements studied by natural science are the material causes of the universe. As he understands the universe, while it has been created by God, it can be explicated (unfolded) by mathematical (i.e., astronomical) understanding.

Thierry was a pivotal figure: one of the first intellectuals to value the study of the natural world though he ultimately utilized that study to understand God.

See also **Aristotelianism**

Bibliography

Clerval, A. *Les écoles de Chartres au Moyen-âge (du Ve au XVIe siècle)*. Paris: A. Picard et fils, 1895.

Dronke, Peter. "Thierry of Chartres." In Peter Dronke, ed., *A History of Twelfth-Century Western Philosophy*. New York: Cambridge University Press, 1988, pp. 358–385.

Fredborg, K.M. *The Latin Rhetorical Commentaries by Thierry of Chartres*. Toronto: Pontifical Institute of Mediaeval Studies, 1988.

Häring, N.M. *Commentaries on Boethius by Thierry of Chartres and His School*. Toronto: Pontifical Institute of Mediaeval Studies, 1971.

———. "Chartres and Paris Revisited." In J. Reginald O'Donnell, ed., *Essays in Honour of Anton Charles Pegis*. Toronto: Pontifical Institute of Mediaeval Studies, 1974, pp. 268–329.

Jeauneau, Edouard. *"Lectio Philosophorum": Recherches sur l'Ecole de Chartres*. Amsterdam: A.M. Hakkert, 1973.

Klibansky, Raymond. "The School of Chartres." In M. Clagett, ed., *Twelfth-Century Europe and the Foundations of Modern Society*. Madison: University of Wisconsin Press, 1961.

Southern, R. W. "Humanism and the School of Chartres." In R. W. Southern, ed., *Medieval Humanism*. Oxford: B. Blackwell, 1970, pp. 61–85.

MICHAEL C. WEBER

THOMAS OF CANTIMPRÉ

Thomas of Cantimpré (de Chantimpré, de Brabant, van Bellenghem, or DeMonte) was born in Bellingen, Brabant, Flanders, in 1200/02, and died in Louvain in 1263/72.

According to his own writings and secondary sources based on those writings (absent archival documents), Thomas (possibly his monastic name), was the son of a nobleman, DuMont, who traveled to the Holy Land and served King Richard I of England (Richard Coeur de Lion). Thomas was educated from a very young age for a life in the Roman Church, as insurance for his father's spiritual welfare. His early years from the age of about five were spent in school, probably in Cambrai. In 1216/17, profoundly influenced by Jacques de Vitry, he became a canon regular in the Augustinian brotherhood at Cantimpré, where he remained for fifteen years. In 1231/32 he joined the Dominican preaching order in Louvain (founded 1228), to which he remained attached for the rest of his life. He spent 1237–1240 in Paris studying, and after 1248 went to Cologne, where he became a disciple (auditor) and probably collaborator of *Albertus Magnus for several years, when *Thomas Aquinas was Albertus's student.

Thomas of Cantimpré's output is divided between hagiographical works (four lives of saints and a supplement to another) and two major works ostensibly devoted to the natural world. The unifying impetus for all was a concern with preaching: to offer preachers and educators mnemonically striking material which would remain with an audience and provide *exempla* for moral behavior. To this end also, early in his career he chose to memorialize intensely lived saints' lives, although later his interest transferred to lives representing spiritual development. The lives he penned were: *Vita Ioannis Abbatis primi Monasterii Cantimpratensis et eius Ecclesiae fundatoris* (Prologue 1223/8; last chapter at the end of his life); *Supplementum* to deVitry's *Vita Mariae Oigniacensis in Namurcensi Belgii Dioecesi* (c. 1230); *Vita Cristinae Virginis cognomento Mirabilis* (1232); *Vita B. Margaretae Iprensis* (1240); and *Vita Piae Lutgardis* (c. 1248).

The two works which concern us here are *De natura rerum* and *Bonum universale de apibus*. *De natura rerum* (c. 1225–1240) is the first of the great thirteenth-century *encyclopedias to deal with the natural world. It occurs fragmentarily or complete, anonymously or attributed to others (including Albertus), in upward of one hundred sixty manuscripts, forty-four of which Boese collated for a modern edition of the text (without apparatus). Thomas identifies himself as its author in the preface to *Bonum de apibus*. The twenty books deal with human anatomy, the soul, monstrous men, quadrupeds, birds, marine monsters, fish, serpents, lowly creatures (*vermes*), trees, plants, stones, metals, the airy regions, the planets including the Sun, meteorology, the elements, and astronomy. Land and sea monsters are included as especially memorable examples of behavior. The work is a compilation based primarily on available texts (sometimes secondhand) by Aristotle, *Pliny, *Galen, Augustine, Ambrose, Basil, Isidore, Solinus, and Jacques de Vitry. While it is clear that Thomas took interest in the natural world, he makes little attempt to reconcile his book-learning with observable phenomena. Thomas interweaves with the natural lore (some accurate, some not) moralizations of use to preachers in indicating appropriate manners of social behavior, (thereby implicitly accepting humankind's animal nature). This work, just prior to *Bartholomaeus Anglicus's *De proprietatibus rerum* (pre-1260), is cited extensively by title in *Vincent of Beauvais' *Speculum naturale*, and used by Albertus Magnus (*De animalibus*); it formed the basis for two great translations, Jacob van Maerlant's *Der Naturen Bloeme* (c. 1270) in Flemish verse, and Jacob von Megenberg's *Buch der Natur* (c. 1349) in German prose, and was the direct source of the earliest natural history text (1460) of the modern age (rewritten in humanist Latin and shorn of moralizations), Pier Candido Decembrio's *De animantium naturis*.

Bonum universale de apibus (1246–1253) is an allegorical work on the life of the bees under their "king" bee (as the queen was considered until the seventeenth-century dissections of Jan Swammerdam proved the hive's central figure to be female). It consists of two main books, the second much longer than the first, and is extant complete in eighty-six manuscripts (fragmentarily in twenty-nine) and several early printed editions (c. 1472–1627). In it, the beehive is viewed as the perfect society, to be emulated by all monastic societies. The "king" bee is equated with the abbot, and the workers with the monks, obedient and silent. The structure of the work is based on the long chapter on bees in *De natura rerum*, greatly expanded and developed for moralistic purposes and as a preaching and teaching guide for the orders.

See also **Natural history; Zoology**

Bibliography
Primary Sources
Thomas Cantimpratensis. *Liber de Natura Rerum. Editio Princeps secundum Codices Manuscriptos. Teil I: Text*. Ed. H. Boese. New York: Walter De Gruyter, 1973.
Thomas Cantipratanus. *Bonum universale de apibus*. Ed. G. Colveneer. Douai: Baltazar Bellerus, 1627.
Thomas de Cantimpré. *Les exemples du "Livre des Abeilles" Une vision médiévale*. Intr., ed., tr., H. Platelle. Turnhout: Brepols, 1997.
Tomás de Cantimpré. *De natura rerum* (lib. IV-XII). Facsimile, 2 vols. Ed. Luís García Ballester. Granada: Universidad de Granada, 1974. (English Translation, Bks. IV–XII, by C. Talbot, Commentary Volume: 251–318.)

Secondary Sources
Aiken, P. The Animal History of Albertus Magnus and Thomas of Cantimpré. *Speculum* (1947) 22: 205–225.
Boese, H. Zur Textüberlieferung von Thomas Cantimpratensis' Liber de natura rerum. *Archivum Fratrum Praedicatorum* (1969) 39: 53–68.
Bormans, M. Thomas de Cantimpré indiqué comme une des sources où Albert-le-Grand et surtout Maerlant ont puisé les matériaux de leurs écrits sur l'histoire naturelle. *Bulletin de l'Académie Royale des Sciences, des Lettres, et des Beaux-Arts de Belgique* (1852) 19: 132–159.
Deboutte, A. Thomas van Cantimpré. Zijn Opleiding te Kamerijk. *Ons Geestelijk Erf* (1982) 56: 283–299.
———. Thomas van Cantimpré, als Auditor van Albertus Magnus. *Ons Geestelijk Erf* (1984) 58: 192–209.

Godding, R. Une oeuvre inédite de Thomas de Cantimpré La "Vita Ioannis Cantipratensis." *Revue d'histoire ecclésiastique* (1981) 76: 241–316.

———. Vie apostolique et société urbaine à l'aube du XIIIe siècle. Une oeuvre inédite de Thomas de Cantimpré. *Nouvelle revue théologique* (1982) 104: 692–721.

Newman, B. Possessed by the Spirit: Devout Women, Demoniacs, and the Apostolic Life in the Thirteenth Century. *Speculum* (1998) 73: 733–770.

Pollini, N. "Animals and Animal Lore in the 'Bonum universale de apibus' of Thomas of Cantimpré (c. 1200–1270)." Ph.D. Thesis, University of Oxford, 2003.

Pyle, C. M. Das Tierbuch des Petrus Candidus. Codex Urbinas Latinus 276. Eine Einführung. Tr. T. Honref, J. Schlechta. Zurich: Belser Verlag, 1984. (Codices e Vaticanis Selecti, LX.)

———. The Art and Science of Renaissance Natural History: Thomas of Cantimpré, Pier Candido Decembrio, Conrad Gessner and Teodoro Ghisi in Vatican Library MS Urb. lat. 276. *Viator* (1996) 27: 265–321.

Quétif, J. & J. Échard. "F. Thomas de Cantimprato." In *Scriptores ordinis praedicatorum*. 4 vols. Paris: J.B.C. Ballard and N. Simart, 1719 (rpt. New York: Burt Franklin, 1959). I, i: 250–254.

Roisin, S. "La méthode hagiographique de Thomas de Cantimpré." In *Miscellanea Historica in honorem Alberti de Meyer*. Louvain: Bibliothèque de l'Université, Bruxelles: "Le Pennon," 1946. pp. 546–557.

Van der Vet, W. A. *Het Biënboec van Thomas van Cantimpré en zijn Exempelen*. 'S-Gravenhage: Martinus Nijhoff, 1902.

CYNTHIA M. PYLE

TOLEDO

Toledo's image in the rest of medieval Europe as a capital of science was based on three related phenomena. First, Toledo was an astronomical center, symbolized by the *Toledan Tables*, *Ibn al-Zarqalluh's compilation of astronomical tables which made it possible to predict the movements of heavenly bodies with greater accuracy than those preceding them in the Latin world. Second, Toledo was widely viewed as the prime locus of astrological science, represented by the so-called "Letter of Toledo," a short prediction of gloom and doom associated with celestial conjunctions that appeared in the late-twelfth century and was disseminated throughout Europe over the following centuries, with the same format, though with changes in details to fit each situation. Third, Toledo was reputed a great center of black magic, a reputation very closely tied to popular conceptions of Arabic science.

Toledo came to be a center of science for much the same reason Baghdad had. The Taifa king al-Ma'mun—the same king who granted refuge to the young Alfonso VI of Castile—had gathered around him a group of scientists in emulation of his Abbasid namesake, who had patronized translation and presided over the *Bayt al-Hikma of Baghdad. The effort was organized by the qadi *Sa'id al-Andalusi and included mathematicians and physicians as well as astronomers such as Sa'id himself, al-Istiji, Ibn Khalaf, and the group's leading light, Ibn al-Zarqalluh, compiler of the *Toledan Tables* and author of its very influential canons, or instructions for use, who in turn was the intellectual heir of the great astronomer and mathematician *Maslama of Madrid—founder of a great dynasty of astronomers, created in Córdoba, at the beginning of the eleventh century and which included *Ibn al-Saffar and *Ibn al-Samh.

The *Toledan Tables* were the work of a group of Toledan astronomers during the reign of al-Ma'mun, working under the patronage of Sa'id al-Andalusi, twelve astronomers in number, according to the *Yesod ha-'Olam* of Isaac Israeli the younger (1310), among whom the leading figure was Azarquiel, that is, al-Zarqalluh himself. An early Latin translation of the tables in fact attributed them to Sa'id. Sa'id, however, in his account of Andalusi science (*Tabaqat al-'umam*, written in 1068), does not mention the *Tables*, and we know that Azarquiel carried out his first observations in 1061. Most of the tables, however, are not original, but represent a pastiche of those of *al-Khwarizmi, *al-Battani, and al-Zarqalluh himself. In terms of accuracy, the *Toledan Tables* were seriously flawed, with values for Mercury and Mars, for example, which erred by a figure of greater than ten degrees. The *Tables* were simply the result of the desire of Sa'id and his group to adjust preexisting table to the latitude of Toledo. Sa'id probably directed the effort to select and adapt existing tables and, after his death, al-Zarqalluh continued the project. The latter left Toledo for Córdoba in the early 1080s and it is not known who might have worked on the Tables afterwards. The Toledan Tables were not superseded in Spain until the 1270s when *Alfonso X the Wise oversaw the recension of new tables, known as Alfonsine. In England in the second half of the fourteenth century all tables were still associated with Toledo, partly because the meridian of Toledo had become standard. When the clerk in "The Franklin's Tale" brings out his "Tables Tolletanes," *Chaucer was most likely thinking of more recent tables (he says they are "full wel corrected") which retained Toledo as the meridian (North, 148–149).

From the late-eleventh century there ensued a feverish period in which recension after recension of tables were produced (tables need constantly to be brought up to date because the errors were cumulative; they also needed to be adapted to the latitude of the place of observation). The demand for astronomical tables was driven by the political elite's appetite for "political astrology," that is the casting of political predictions in the form of horoscopes. Taifa kings, in particular, wanted access to instant predictions: thus, al-Mu'tamid of Seville, before the battle of Sagrajas, asked his court astrologers how it was all going to work out! The typical Christian astrologer of the later Middle Ages was a courtier, casting horoscopes or making political predictions for monarchs and spiritual and temporal magnates. The sheer number of copies of tables (as opposed to recensions) is a mirror of the prestige accruing to someone from merely owning such a powerful scientific guide to human events.

A related phenomenon was the demand for simplified astrolabes which could be used by persons with relatively

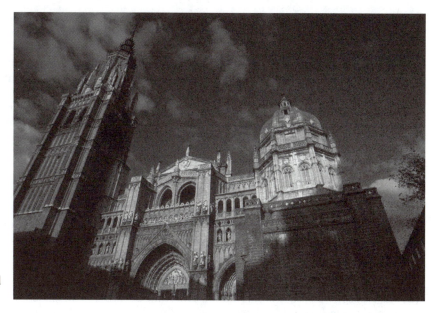

Toledo Cathedral. The foundation stone was laid in 1227 during the reign of King Ferdinand III. (Corbis/Macduff Everton)

little training. These were designed to obviate the chief limitation of the standard model which required a special plate for each latitude. Al-Zarqalluh was the first to design this kind of universal instrument which he called the Abbadiyya saphea (safiha), after the royal house of the Taifa kingdom of Seville. Later, he designed an even simpler model called al-Shakkaziyya. Both models lacked the "spider" or rete on which the rotation of the heavens around the Earth was represented on standard astrolabes. Thus Ibn Khalaf designed still another model in 1071, dedicated to Al-Ma'mun of Toledo, which had a simplified "spider." With the Christian conquest of the city, the fame of both Toledo's tables and her astrolabes began to diffuse northward.

Arabic into Latin in Toledo

Translation activity had begun in Spain in the Ebro Valley in the early-twelfth century. The early translation movement in Toledo has been associated with the French Archbishop Raymond (served 1126–1152) and with three dominant figures: *Gerard of Cremona, *Domingo Gundisalvo, and Abraham ibn Daud. But neither Gerard nor Gundisalvo can be documented in the chapter of the Toledo Cathedral until after Raymond's death, and Ibn Daud did not arrive in Toledo from al-Andalus until around 1160. Ibn Daud and Gundisalvo worked together on occasion, the former translating from Arabic into Castilian aloud, and the latter writing down a Latin translation. The attraction of Toledo was the ready supply of Arabic manuscripts there awaiting transplantation. Moreover sometime after the fall of Saragossa in 1118, the library of the Beni Hud, which was rich in scientific manuscripts, arrived in Toledo. Ibn Daud translated at least eleven astrological works of important authors like *al-Kindi, *Abu Ma'shar, and *Thabit ibn Qurra, and philosophical works by Aristotle, al-Kindi, Qusta ibn Luqa, al-Farabi, and Ibn Sina. Gundisalvo was a central

figure in the renewal of the *quadrivium in his book *De divisione Philosophiae* (*On the Divisions of Philosophy*), a free translation *al-Farabi's *Enumeration of the Sciences* (*Ihsa al-'ulum*). Gerard, who went to Toledo because he had heard that copies of Ptolemy's *Almagest* could be found there, worked in all fields, not only astronomy, astrology, and philosophy but in medicine as well.

In the course of the twelfth century, Toledo became associated with a style of science sensitive to the power of mathematics, particularly insofar as astronomy was concerned. This is why Gerard of Cremona went there specifically to study and translate Ptolemy's great astronomical treatise, the *Almagest*: he went there—"*Toletum perexit*"—for the love of the *Almagest*, which is minimally studied among the Latins—"*amore tamen almagesti; quem apud latinos minime reperti.*" Because of that translation specifically, "high-level mathematical astronomy there was introduced into a Europe." This too is why Daniel of Morley, among others, journeyed to Toledo some time in the 1160s: "When I heard that the doctrine of the Arabs, which is devoted almost entirely to quadrivium, was all the fashion in Toledo in those days, I hurried there as quickly as I could, so that I could hear the wisest philosophers in the world" (Burnett, 61–62). Daniel specifically went to hear Gerard lecture on the *Almagest* and the "fatal influence of the stars," and discussed philosophical issues with Gerard's Mozarab translation partner, Galippus, in the "tongue of Toledo," surely Castilian.

Natural philosophers steeped in the Toledan tradition of Arabic science produced propaganda endorsing the objectives and achievements of the new science. An example is the letter of *Pedro Alfonso known as the "Letter to the Peripatetics of France," in which he dismissed those scholars who studied mainly grammar and dialectic. Mathematics was the basis of learning, chiefly because without it, one cannot hope to master astronomy, just to learn which many people "traverse distant provinces and exile themselves in remote regions" (surely he meant Spain). Pedro spent a number of years in England, imparting the new science and preparing astronomical tables. According to Southern (167–168), Arabic science "made it possible for [English] astronomy to advance beyond the stage it had reached in the age of Bede." Walcher of Malvern's lunar observations provide "a visible witness to the union of the old Anglo-Saxon scientific curiosity and the new resources [imported from Islamic Spain] of scientific measurement and discovery."

The *Letter of Toledo*

The *Letter of Toledo* was an astrological prediction first issued in 1179 and valid until September in the eighth year following (1187), during which time there was to be a great conjunction of planets in Libra and the Dragon's tail, which indicated great perturbations in the places influenced by Saturn and Mars: there would be earthquakes, a great wind that would flatten cities like Mecca and Baghdad, and would be preceded by a total eclipse of the Sun and Moon. The Muslims would abandon their mosques and embrace Christianity. The *Letter*, which circulated in German, French, Italian, and Latin versions, was a landmark, "the first great chance [for astrology] to prove its value as a practical historical tool," according to Southern. That is, the new cosmology emanating from Toledo with its "precise doctrine of celestial causality" set in motion "the recovery of historical time proper to the astrology of late antiquity and of the Arab world: the great events which mark the history of humanity, migrations of peoples and succession of kingdoms, the birth of prophets and religions, are registered in the heavens: it was principally the great conjunctions of the upper planets—Saturn and Jupiter—which… act upon those historical events with universal significance, just as the lower planets preside over events of less importance and shorter duration."

A conjunction is the simultaneous appearance in the same house of the zodiac of two heavenly bodies. Great conjunctions involved three and were thought to produce religious upheaval, especially mass conversions. Hence they were the occasion for apocalyptic effusions in an epoch rent with religious confrontation and competition. In this sense did astrology, in Gregory's characterization, become "a hermeneutics of the Christian apocalypse."

In all likelihood, the Toledo letter had a Near Eastern prototype in a famous prediction based on the same conjunction made by the Persian poet and astrologer, Anwari, who, having earlier declared himself skilled "in every science, pure or applied, known to any of his contemporaries," was humiliated when the cataclysm he predicted failed to occur on the appointed day, which was August 13, 1186. Besides Anwari, Ibn al-Athir mentioned it, as did an anonymous fragment preserved in the Cairo Geniza.

The *Letter of Toledo* is not known in Spain as such and did not—apparently—circulate there until after 1200. Although one of the earliest manuscripts of the *Letter* was copied in the monastery of Ripoll around 1200, there may still be reason to doubt its connection with Toledo. In the early (and some later) recensions of the *Letter*, the word for "mosque" is rendered as *Machomeria*, *mahumeria*, *maumeria*, *synagoga maumertica*, etc. It is obvious that *mahumeria*, in the sense of "mosque," is a Gallicism, *mahumerie* or *mahomerie*, a term found in Latin as written by Frenchmen or Provençals and some Germans and Englishmen but not by Spaniards or Catalans. The mere presence of this word is not in itself enough to discredit Toledo as the place of origin of the *Letter*, but, at the very least, suggests the early intervention of a French-speaking Christian, either in the transmission of the *Letter* or the redaction of the original. The Spanish term *mezquita*, from Arabic *masjid*, mosque, was not known in Spain, either in Latin or Romance forms, before the First Crusade.

The authorship of the *Letter of Toledo* is ascribed in early recensions of it to Johannes David of Toledo. With the passage of time, authorship was ascribed to different persons, although the text remained substantially the same: thus MS Prague 1544, dated 1229, attributes the letter to a "magnus astrologus" from Toledo and MS Admont 318, from around 1200, to Gozwinus. Gozwinus is surely Qazwini, known for his writing on divination if not for astrology per se. In Roger of Hoveden's *Chronicle*, the expert is a mysterious "Corumphiza," perhaps a deformation of al-Khwarizmi.

The original 1186 prediction was adapted almost literally to the conjunction of 1229. Then in the mid-fourteenth century, around the time of the Plague and after, a spate of conjunction predictions involved various Toledo-based, including the association of the astrologers with the Toledan Tables and the simplified astrolabe, although the specific format of the Letter of Toledo was not generally used. The tables of planetary velocity of *Profatius (Profeit ibn Tibbon) and the *Toledan Tables* were the chief sources for the prediction of the conjunction of Saturn, Jupiter, and Mars that was to occur in March 1345. A notable participant in predictions around this conjunction was John of Lignères whose important tables of 1322 were highly dependent on the *Toledan Tables* in spite of John's acquaintance with the Alfonsine corpus. Lignères was also the designer of a saphea based on that of al-Zarqalluh. John of Eschenden, more in the tradition of the Letter, made a similar prediction of the conjunction of 1357, attributing its source to one "Milo of Toledo." This conjunction and that of 1368 were considered propitious for undertaking a crusade against the Muslims. Chaucer, who describes the conjunction of 1385, also in "The Franklin's Tale" was using his *Toledan Tables*, long after they had been replaced, in the rest of Europe, with the Alfonsine Tables, or versions derived from it:

"His Tables Tolletanes forth he brought,
Ful wel corected, ne ther lakked nought."

Alfonso X the Wise

The movement of translation and scientific creativity during the reign of Alfonso X the Wise of Castile

(1252–1277) is also associated with Toledo, even the court itself had no fixed place of residence. Associated with Toledo were the King's two most prominent Jewish scientists, Judah Mosca (fl 1231–1272) and Isaac ibn Sid ("Rabiçag," fl. 1263–1277). Judah Mosca worked with William the Englishman on a Latin translation of al-Zarqalluh's *Treatise on the Saphea* in 1231, and translated various astrological and astronomical works from Arabic into Castilian, including Ibn Abi Rijal's *Kitab al bari' fi akhkam al-nujum* (*Libro conplido en los iudizios de las estrellas*) and 'Abd al-Rahman al-Sufi's *Kitab al-kawakib al-thabita al-musawwar* (*Los IIII libros de las estrellas de la ochaua esfera*). Mosca and Rabiçag together composed the *Alfonsine Tables*, a work which included some direct observation, finished in 1277. Isaac ibn Sid was particularly adept at instrumentation, writing volumes on the astrolabe, the plane astrolabe, the quadrant, and four on different types of clocks.

Toledo: Capital of Black Magic

Toledo's reputation for black magic was owing to the association of Arabic alphabet and numerals with magical talismans. Because of the association of Arabic learning with astrology and alchemy, Toledo became linked in the popular imagination with magic and anyone studying there was de facto open to the accusation of necromancy. *Michael Scot, for one, who was in Toledo in the twelfth century, was never able to shake thereafter the suspicion that he had learned the Black Arts there. Scot's reputed wizardry, moreover, was of a specifically mathematical cast. There are many references: Caesar of Heisterbach tells two stories of students studying the "*arte nigromantia*" "*apud Toletum.*" In medieval French, "*jouer les arts de Tolède*" was a common term for running confidence games or card sharking:

> "Il fait d'un coq une poulette
> Il joue les arts de Tolète."

[He turned a rooster into a hen/he knows the arts of Toledo.]

How Toledo Got its Reputation

Toledo under al-Ma'mun did not have the outsized reputation in the Islamic world as a science center that it would later have throughout Christian Europe. Rather the process took around one hundred years and thus, in a sense, Toledo rode the crest of apocalyptic fervor attending the great conjunction of 1186 to world fame. The conjunction provided, in other words, an advertisement for Toledo's prowess in Arabic numbers, astronomical tables, astrolabes, astrological theory, and translations of manuals into Latin to master these new techniques. Toledo did not make the *Toledan Tables* famous: the *Tables* and the Letter of Toledo made the city famous, as both began their twin careers in the same decade. The *Tables* were compiled in the around 1080. Early in the twelfth century a small group of prescient European scholars reached Toledo. When they returned home they diffused a new kind of science, stressing mathematics, astronomy and astrology, whose key technical appurtenances were the tables—*zijat*—and the astrolabe. They in turn introduced the new program into a wider circle embracing all the courts of Europe.

Al-Zarqalluh's Latinized tables found a huge market very quickly owing to the pent-up demand for accuracy in prognostications. In subsequent recensions of the Letter of Toledo, therefore, the phrase "all the philosophers and astronomers of Toledo," or variants thereof, simply meant: "the Toledan Tables stand behind this prediction as a guarantee of its accuracy." Whatever the precise reasons for Toledo's reputation as capital of European science, by the 1190s that reputation was set. An anonymous manuscript containing the words of an enigmatic "Virgil, philosopher of Córdoba," asserted that "*apud civitatem toletanam essent studia instructa omnium artium per multum tempus*" (in the city of Toledo studies of all the arts have been imparted for a long time).

See also **Astrology; Astronomy, Islamic; Magic and the occult; Planetary tables**

Bibliography

Burnett, Charles. *The Introduction of Arabic Learning into England*. London: The British Library, 1997.

Gil, José S. *La escuela de traductores de Toledo y sus colaboradores judíos*. Toledo: Instituto Provincial de Investigaciones y Estudios Toledanos, 1985.

Grauert, H. von. "Meister Johann von Toledo." In *Sitzungsberichtes der (...) historische. Classe der Kgl. Bayer. Akademie der Wissenschaften*. Munich: G. Franz, 1901.

Gregory, Tullio. "Temps astrologique et temps chrétien." In *Mundana Sapientia: Forme di conoscenza nella cultura medievale*. Rome, 1992, pp. 329–346.

McGinn, Bernard. *Visions of the End: Apocalyptic Traditions in the Middle Ages*. New York: Columbia University Press, 1979, pp. 152–153.

Southern, R.W. Aspects of the European Tradition of Historical Writing: 3. History as Prophecy. *Transactions of the Royal Historical Society*, 5th series (1972) 22: 159–180.

Waxman, Samuel M. Chapters on Magic in Spanish Literature. *Bulletin Hispanique* (1916) 38.

Weber, Michael C. "The Translating and Adapting of al-Farabi's Kitab ihsa al-'ulum in Spain." Unpub. Doctoral diss. Boston University, 1996.

THOMAS F. GLICK

TORRIGIANO DE' TORRIGIANI

Pietro Torrigiani (Turisanus), Italian physician, was born in Florence between 1270 and 1280. He studied medicine at the University of Bologna where he was a pupil of the Florentine physician *Taddeo Alderotti. Between 1305 and 1319 he studied and taught in Paris.

Torrigiani's most famous work is an elaborate commentary on *Microtegni* by *Galen, *Plusquam commentum*, written before 1319. He also wrote a short treatise, *De hypostasi urine*. *Plusquam commentum* may be regarded as a statement of his teaching activity. It is not a simple account of the text by Galen, but presents a certain scientific originality, incorporating material concerning philosophy and natural science. At times it promotes new interpretations of classic topics of medieval medicine. Torrigiani depicts medicine as an active science that is divided into two parts: a theoretical part that is an intellectual speculation on the human body's foundations, and a practical part intended to produce physical change through therapeutic treatment. Torrigiani also deals with the scientific method. Following in the tradition of *Robert Grosseteste and *Albertus Magnus, Torrigiani examines the processes of resolution (demonstration termed *propter quid*) and composition (demonstration termed *quia*) applied to medical science methodology. Torrigiani frequently cites ancient authorities, in particular biological works by Aristotle and the medical doctrines by Galen concerning humors, elements, and complexion. He knew of these through the *Canon* and *De animalibus* of *Ibn Sina (Avicenna), classical sources of medieval medicine.

Like other members of the medical school of Bologna, Torrigiani engages in the medical-philosophical debate about *Aristotelianism and Galenism, discussing their differences and the possibility of their reconciliation. Unlike nearly all his contemporary physicians and philosophers, however, he sometimes takes doctrinal positions that favor the medical tradition, as represented by the anatomical and physiological knowledge contained in the work of Galen. These positions are more inclined toward safeguarding the methodological and theoretical autonomy of medicine than natural philosophy. An example of this occurs in Torrigiani's discussion of the Aristotelian doctrine of the supremacy of the heart over the other main organs. Torrigiani expresses great reservations about such cardiocentrism, stating that the brain, the liver, and the testicles have autonomous activity. Nevertheless, Torrigiani does not share Galen's view that such organs should all be placed on the same hierarchical level, since the function of the heart is clearly more important in its own right than that of the other organs. Torrigiani also takes issue with Aristotle about the role of the testicles in procreation. Aristotle thought that they had only the secondary role of delaying the emission of sperm, and that their role was similar to that of the counterweights on a loom. Torrigiani, however, took the view that the testicles, after receiving from the heart the *spiritus generativus*, are able to complete their operations on their own, particularly the conversion of blood into sperm.

In the Middle Ages embryology was one of the subjects that most deeply divided medicine and philosophy and brought some of the sharpest methodological and doctrinal confrontations between the two fields of study. One of the main reasons for the controversy was that all contemporary theories were derived either from Aristotle on one side or from *Hippocrates and Galen on the other. Regardless of which side they favored, medieval authors felt compelled to write *conciliationes* reconciling their own views with those of the other *auctoritas*. Like other pupils of Alderotti, Torrigiani's idea of conception and the formation of embryos is basically Aristotelian. Male and female are the two distinct principles of generation. The male is the active principle, the female the passive: The former has the generation principle, the latter simply supplies the substance to be molded, that is to say menstrual blood. Torregiani is important in the history of medieval scientific thought because he moved beyond the stylized *conciliatio* toward independent examination and judgment of the authorities in conflict.

See also **Elements and qualities; Generation; Medicine, practical; Medicine, theoretical; Nature: diverse medieval interpretations; Scholasticism**

Bibliography

Primary Source
Plusquam commentum in Parvam Galeni Artem Turisani Florentini medici..., apud Juntas, Venetiis 1557.

Secondary Sources
Martorelli Vico, Romana. *Medicina e filosofia. Per una storia dell'embriologia medievale nel XIII e XIV secolo.* Milano: Guerini e Associati, 2002.
Ottosson, Per-Gunnar. *Scholastic Medicine and Philosophy. A study of Commentaries on Galen's Tegni (ca. 1300–1450).* Napoli: Bibliopolis, 1984.
Sarton, George. *Introduction to the History of Science. III/1. Medicine.* Washington: Carnegie Institution, 1948, pp. 839–840.
Siraisi, Nancy. *Taddeo Alderotti and his Pupils.* Princeton: Princeton University Press, 1981.
Villani, Filippo. *Liber de civitatis Florentia famosis civibus.* Firenze: G.C. Galletti, 1848, pp. 26–29.

ROMANA MARTORELLI VICO

TRANSLATION MOVEMENTS

A comparative survey of medieval scientific translation movements (Greek into Arabic, Arabic into Latin, Hebrew, and European vernaculars) reveals some common patterns. The early phases of translation were marked by a preference for astrological treatises. But the immediate practical demand for astrological materials does not in itself satisfy the search for motive because the common pattern in these translation movements was for interest to quickly broaden out from *astrology and hermetic sciences generally to embrace the whole corpus of Greek or Greco-Arabic science.

Greek into Arabic

Gutas argues that the origins of Arab interest in Greek science are intimately bound up with the political ideology of the early Abbasid caliphs. When the Abbasids, who came to power in 750, removed the capital of the Islamic empire from Damascus to Baghdad in 764, they fell heir to the scholarly and historical traditions of the Sassanids who had formerly ruled in Persia and Mesopotamia. In order to co-opt the Persian elite, the Abbasids portrayed themselves as successors to the imperial ideology of ancient

Persia, one of whose cornerstones was the notion that Zoroaster had urged the preservation of all of the sciences of antiquity. Translation was thus deemed a worthy enterprise in itself and the Sassanids had already absorbed Aristotelian physics and logic well before the Islamic conquest. Moreover, political astrology—the notion that both history and politics could be interpreted by observation of celestial movements—was at the very core of Sassanid ideology. The Abbasids co-opted the Persian elites by translating the entire corpus into Arabic, including Zoroastrian texts which they used to argue against the same elites. In the bargain came an appreciation of secular knowledge.

The second ideological leg of the Abbasid translation movement was a deliberate policy of attraction directed at the large Greek-speaking Christian minorities of the Levant. In the reign of al-Ma'mun (809–833) the Byzantine Empire had entered a period of intellectual obscurantism and closure; classical texts were no longer copied. Al-Ma'mun, who had read Greek classics as a youth (and had, as a result internalized the values of the translation movement), justified the Abbasid war on Byzantium to his Greek-speaking subjects as a retrieval of the classical heritage. Byzantine decadence became a leitmotif among Muslim intellectuals, as Ibn Ridwan noted that al-Ma'mun had breathed new life into Greek medicine, while al-Jahiz decried the Byzantines as superstitious idolaters.

The Abbasid *Bayt al-Hikma is frequently referred to as a school of translators, but it was not a school. It is simply the Arabic name for a Sassanid palace library. In the Abbasid court, it was likewise a royal library where, in its early phase, books relating to Persian history and culture were translated. Under al-Ma'mun, mathematics and astronomy were added (Gutas, 83).

Early demand for astronomy (as in the transmission both of *Ptolemy's cosmological theories and of the Indian *zijat* or astronomical tables, particularly the *Siddhanta*, known in the Arabic world as the *Sindhind*), astrology, and mathematics (in particular Indian numerals, including the zero, and place unit system) produced the critical mass (both of texts and scholars) that generated demand for the translation of philosophy, leading to the rapid absorption of the entire Aristotelian corpus. The process fed on itself: the study of the first texts translated generated original treatises in Arabic commenting on them and refining technical vocabulary, which in turn required more accurate translations. These new scholars themselves became patrons of further translations (Gutas, 108, 110, 117).

The Arabic translation movement was associated with a technical innovation, *paper, introduced from China to Persia in the mid-eighth century, contemporaneous with the beginning of the translation movement. Paper made it possible to make copies on demand, at a reasonable price. Unlike the later Latin movement, which was executed on parchment, copied on a limited basis in monastic *scriptoria*, the Arabic movement was democratic and commercialized: the customer went to a book dealer and ordered a scribal copy of a manuscript which the dealer owned or had access to.

Arabic into Latin

The Latin translation movement of the twelfth and thirteenth centuries has not been successfully theorized. One hypothesis is that the interest in science was owing to a new social class—merchants—who were seeking a new kind of knowledge congruent with their world view (Gutas, 4). This solution cannot be sustained, first because the early translators were overwhelmingly churchmen; and second, because the undeniable merchant interest in precise measurement—of goods, time, and value—expressed in commercial arithmetic and the emergence of a theory of economic value, only found expression in the fourteenth century—much too late to explain the translation movement of the twelfth.

The inception of the movement can be dated to the Muslim loss of Zaragoza to the forces of Alfonso I of Aragon in 1110. That promoted a substantial inflow of foreign clerics in the Ebro Valley which became a focus of translation along with *Toledo, where much of the library, rich in scientific books, of the Beni Hud rulers of Zaragoza had been transferred. In the Ebro Valley, Robert of Ketton, an English archdeacon in Pamplona and his collaborator *Hermann of Carinthia produced a series of translations, particularly on astrological subjects (although Hermann also translated *Euclid's *Elements* and *al-Khwarizmi's important astronomical tables). Hermann's 1143 original work, the *De essentiis*, was the first application of Arabic astrology to Latin metaphysics. Hermann was a link between Robert, *Hugh of Santalla and Rudolph of Bruges—a distinctive northern group of translators, focused on astrology and astronomy (Burnett, 1977). The early seep of Arabic science into the Latin world was practical, linked to the astrolabe and simple (as opposed to abstract) mathematics. The first translator associated with Toledo was *John of Seville, who also began his career translating astronomy and astrology. He translated *Abu Ma'shar's astrology in 1133, influencing *Hermann of Carinthia's translation of the same work in 1140. Here we observe the same process as in the antecedent Greek-into-Arabic movement: multiple translations of key works, promoting constant refinement both of concepts and of terminology, as well as increasing mastery of Arabic. The mid-century activity in Toledo is variously said to have been centered around the Archbishop Raymond, ostensibly the patron of the group of translators; but Lemay regards John of Seville as the focal point; while Burnett promotes the candidacy of *Domingo Gundisalvo.

As in the Arab East, two approaches to translation existed side-by-side. *Boethius, based on his experience with translating from Greek into Latin, provided a long-lived rationale for literal, *de verbo ad verbum* translation which continued to be followed especially for Scriptural texts: one Latin word only was to be provided for each Greek word, and the word order could not be changed. It would have been presumptuous to do otherwise. The problem with Arabic is that its syntax and vocabulary, unlike those of Greek, were completely foreign to them. Thus, Hugh of Santalla observed:

"Often the translator gasps under the strain of the difficulties. He sees some strange word which resists being translated correctly because of either the variety of diacritical marks on the letters, or the lack of marks—often, too, because of the incompatible differences of languages in [each] of which the significance of the roots is different." (Burnett, 1997, 60)

Moreover, Arabic was prolix where Greek was terse, or so it seemed to the translators, some of whom viewed Arabic prolixity positively (because it made concepts easier to grasp), while at the same time it made de verbo ad verbum translations virtually impossible. The translators struggled with a Latin that could not adequately replicate the richness of Arabic expression. Thus in his translation of *Ibn Sina's Metaphysics, Gundisalvo was obliged to use esse ("to be") to represent thirty-four different Arabic expressions (Jolivet, 118).

Political astrology, which was the focus at least of the early translation movement, just as it had been in the East, was a fad. All rulers had court astrologers, some going so far as to take them into battle to check on the signs for each strategic move. It became part of the baggage of the nobleman not only to commission nativities and other auguries, but also to own an astrolabe and a set of tables (whether he used them or not). Translation itself might also be used as a political weapon. Translations commissioned by *Frederick II of Sicily, such as *Michael Scot's translations of *Ibn Rushd and also, interestingly enough, the Latin translation of *Maimonides' Guide of the Perplexed, were part of a deliberate policy to promote rationalist texts that were threatening to his papal enemies. In the wake of that translation, a short mathematical text of Maimonides on asymptotes (two lines that draw ever closer to one another without meeting) was rendered into Latin by Master John of Palermo as De duabus lineis. So here is an example of problem in theoretical mathematics that was translated from Arabic into Latin as an epiphenomenon of Frederick's war on the papacy (Freudenthal).

Arabic into Castilian

In general translations from Arabic into European vernaculars were not direct, but mediated by Latin or Hebrew versions. The Castilian movement was therefore something of an exception and was similar in dynamics to the Arab-into-Latin or Hebrew movements, with a similar focus on astrology and practical astronomy made more complex by the dynamic of vernacularization which embraces translation, as well as direct creation. In social terms, translation from Arabic directly or indirectly into vernacular languages, implies the diffusion of the new "Greco-Arabic" science beyond the circle of Latinate clerics or persons trained by them.

Although some scientific and medical texts had been written vernacular languages before the thirteenth century, notably in Anglo-Saxon England, the practice did not become widespread until the translation movement from Arabic in Latin had changed the content of science to the extent that demand for wider access was felt. Because Jews were more fluent in the vernacular languages than they were in Latin, they were as prominent in the thirteenth-century movement of translation from Arabic into Castilian, associated with the court of *Alfonso X the Wise (reigned 1252–1284), as they had been in the twelfth-century Latin movement. Indeed Américo Castro (1954, 490) went so far as to claim that "Castilian came into use as an instrument of high culture thanks to the Jews who surrounded [Alfonso X] and excited his extremely refined curiosity." Alfonso is also associated with a "school" of translators. It was not a school, more like a government translation bureau, where the king presided over the effort in science for which he recruited Jewish astronomers such as Isaac ibn Sid and Yehuda ben Moshe. Castilian was poor in abstract terms, so Alfonso's team created abstract nouns, creating a literary scientific language whose literalism, as had been true of Arabic translators from the Greek, was less a reflection of incompetence than the result of experimentation with new concepts.

Translations from the Arabic included Judah ibn Moshe's translation of 'Ali ibn Abi'l-Rijal's Kitab al-baric fi ahkam al-nujum (Libro conplido de los iudizios de las estrellas), on judicial astrology. Al-Sufi's Kitab suwar al-kawakib al-thamaniya wa'l-arbacin (Book of Forty-eight Constellations of the Stars) was one of the principal sources of Los IIII libros de las estrellas de la ochaua esfera, but the Alfonsine translators added other materials. Alfonso's method to have his translator/astronomers embellish on original texts and to use more than one source, as in the Ochaua esfera or the Lapidario, a collection of astrology treatises.

Arabic into Hebrew

Jews had virtually no participation in science in antiquity and were not drawn into the realm of classical science until the advent of Islam, when they participated in the Greek-into-Arabic translation movement and the early philosophical movement, in which all Arab speakers—ahl lisanina ("the people of our language"), as *al-Kindi put it—were welcomed. Arabic-speaking Jewish intellectuals were in awe of Arabic science. As Moses ibn Ezra (the great poet from Granada) observed:

"They have translated into Arabic all the sciences, ancient as well as modern, which they have appropriated and accomplished with explanations and clarifications. No nation has composed or translated such a quantity in the domain of science as has been translated and written by this nation. They were able to do this thanks to the richness of their language and the excellence of its rhetoric" (Barkai, 10).

Hebrew science—that is, science written in or translated into Hebrew—was an invention of two twelfth-century rabbi-savants, *Abraham bar Hiyya of Barcelona and *Abraham ibn Ezra of Tudela, whose scientific specialties of mathematics, astronomy, and astrology became Jewish specialties in Spain, but not elsewhere in the Arab world. In order to justify these activities, Bar Hiyya and Ibn Ezra both claimed that they were merely retrieving the "lost" science of the ancient Hebrews, a science which the gentiles had stolen from them—a myth of which they were perhaps the most influential perpetuators. Part of the myth was that the rabbis had kept their scientific method secret because it was the same method used in judicial astrology (Roth, Sela). When confronted with technical Arabic scientific terms, Ibn Ezra liked to represent them in Hebrew with words chosen from the lexicon of Biblical Hebrew. This strategy can be termed "Judaization," defined as an attempt to provide all aspects of social life and culture with a Jewish tradition stretching back to the Bible or, at least, the Talmud. Ibn Ezra was extreme in his willingness to stretch the meaning of Biblical expressions to fit concepts of Arabic science. He searched the Bible for "'original' Hebrew words endowed with scientific meaning, avoiding the creation of new Hebrew words based on cognate Arabic words or on loan translations of Arabic words" (Sela, 70).

As in the contemporaneous Latin translation movement, the early focus of Hebrew science and translation was astrology. Abraham ibn Ezra was the first Jewish author to interpret Biblical events astrologically "and to explain certain biblical commandments as defenses against the pernicious influence of the stars." He lived and worked in Tudela at the same time as Robert of Ketton, who had similar interests, was a canon in the Cathedral of Pamplona and when Hugh of Santalla was translating astrological treatises under the patronage of Michael, bishop of nearby Tarazona. In Spain during the twelfth century, "astrology had, among Jews, become the favored means of interpreting religious history and theology in a naturalistic manner" (Sela). The common focus of the Ebro translators and Ibn Ezra on astrology and the simultaneity of their activities, suggest a unified movement of transmission of Arabic science in two different languages, and with somewhat different justifications.

Ibn Ezra's role in the reception of Arabic astrology in Europe was singular. Judicial astrology, the *ahkam al-nujam* of the Arabs—judgments of the stars—was introduced by Ibn Ezra simultaneously in both Hebrew and Latin, using the terms *mishpatim* and *iudicia*, respectively. He introduced the term *mishpatim* in his Hebrew translation of Ibn al-Muthanna's commentaries on *al-Khwarizmi's astronomical tables. The Arabic original of this important treatise has been lost; it has been studied from one Latin and two Hebrew translations that survive. The Latin translation is Hugh of Santalla's. Abraham directed his Hebrew scientific writings to *professional* Jewish astrologers, people to whom he referred as *ba'alé ha-mishpatim* (masters of astrological judgments) or *hakhmé mishpete mazalot* (scholars of zodiacal judgments). He also wrote for Christian professionals, whom he called *doctores* or *magistri iudiciorum*, in particular his *Book of Astronomical Tables*, and another volume, *The Book of the Fundamentals of Tables*, which explained how to use them. He wrote four versions of the latter, two in Hebrew (lost) and two in Latin, which survive. This book's approach is observational, rather than mathematical. That is, he expected his readers to be able to use an astrolabe, about which he had also written a user's manual (Sela).

The switch from Arabic to Hebrew began with the Almohade dispersion of Arabic-speaking Jews from al-Andalus to the Spanish Christian kingdoms and to Provence, the destination of Judah ibn Tibbon (Hebrew translator of the Arabic works of Maimonides).

Arabic into Chinese

Of course, Arabic scientific ideas also moved eastwards contemporaneously with their westward movement. In this light, Ibn al-Nadim (*Fihrist*, 31) reports *al-Razi's anecdote about a Chinese man who had stayed with him in Baghdad for a year and, before leaving for home, asked al-Razi to dictate the sixteen books of *Galen to him. Al-Razi, along with students of his, complied after the man explained that he used a kind of shorthand for such projects. Al-Razi's anecdote appears to have been atypical. Chinese interest in Arabic science really did not gain momentum until the mid-thirteenth century and was mainly focused on calendrical applications of astronomy. The Il-khan ruler Hulagu was said to have "loved science and was infatuated with astronomy and geometry" (Allsen, 162). Astronomers from both China and the Islamic world frequented his court and around 1260 he ordered the construction of an observatory at Maraghah with Nasir al-Din *al-Tusi as its first director. Al-Tusi, together with Muslim and Chinese colleagues composed the "Il-khani Tables" (*Zij i Il-khani*), which had conversion tables for the Chinese, and other, calendars and seems to have been designed for administrators who had to convert dates from one system to another. The Chinese had been impressed by the accuracy of Muslim astronomical observations and Kublai Khan established an Office of Western Astronomy in 1263 with the Syrian *Isa kelemechi* as its head. This bureau was succeeded by an Observatory that Kublai founded for Muslim astronomers in 1271 with Jamal al-Din as director. The two astronomical traditions, Arabic and Chinese, were kept separate so that their results could be checked against each other. Although a few Arabic works were translated into Chinese there was no impact on Chinese astronomy or mathematics. In Medicine, notwithstanding Razi's anecdote, the theoretical basis of Chinese medicine in yin-yang and the Five Phases proved a solid barrier to the diffusion of Greco-Arabic humoral pathology. Only in Materia Medica can borrowing be detected. The use of rhubarb as a purgative spread from China through the Islamic World to Europe, while Arabic pharmacological recipes were translated into Chinese in the early Ming period.

Conclusion

Practical concerns provided the focus for at least the early phases of all the movements discussed—in particular issues related to the astronomical determination of the calendar (e.g., the advent of the new moon in Christianity and Judaism, or problems related to luni-solar issues, in China) or in the Islamic world, the determination of the *qibla* (the direction of Mecca) and canonical prayer times;

and astrology. What drove all this movements was the tremendous explanatory and predictive power in the new package of practical astronomy (Ptolemaic theory; Indian-inspired tables, and the refined astrolabe) which made the prediction of celestial movements not only more accurate but which was also accessible to persons of modest education.

China constitutes something of an exception, not only because of the cultural barriers to the diffusion of the Greco-Arabic corpus, but also because the phenomenon has not attracted as much scholarly interest as it merits

See also **Translation norms and practice; Vocabulary**

Bibliography

Barkai, Ron. *A History of Jewish Gynaecological Texts in the Middle Ages.* Leiden: E.J. Brill, 1998.

Burnett, Charles. A Group of Arab-Latin Translators Working in Northern Spain in the mid-12th Century. *Journal of the Royal Asiatic Society* (1977): 62–108.

———. "Translating from Arabic into Latin in the Middle Ages: Theory, Practice, and Criticism." In S. G. Lofts and P.W. Rosemann, eds. *Editer, traduire, interpéter: Essais de méthodologie philosophique.* Louvain: Peeters, 1997, pp. 55–78.

Castro, Américo. *The Structure of Spanish History.* Princeton: Princeton University Press, 1954.

Freudenthal, Gad. "Maimonides' Guide of the Perplexed and the Transmission of the Mathematical Tract, 'On Two Asymptotic Lines' in the Arabic, Latin and Hebrew Traditions." In R. S. Cohen and H. Levine, eds. *Maimonides and the Sciences.* Dordrecht: Kluwer, 2000, pp. 35–56.

Glick, Thomas F. "'My Master, The Jew': Observations on Interfaith Scholarly Interaction in the Middle Ages." In Harvey J. Hames, ed. *Jews, Muslims and Christians In and Around the Crown of Aragon.* Leiden: E.J. Brill, 2004, pp. 157–182.

Gutas, Dmitri. *Greek Thought, Arabic Culture.* New York: Routledge, 1998, pp. 29–59.

Jolivet, Jean. "The Arabic Inheritance." In P. Dronke, ed. *A History of Twelfth-Century Western Philosophy.* New York: Cambridge University Press, 1988, pp. 113–148.

Lemay, Richard. *Abu Ma'shar and Latin Aristotelianism in the Twelfth Century: The Recovery of Aristotle's Natural Philosophy through Arabic Astrology.* Beirut: American University, 1962.

Roth, Norman. The 'Theft of Philosophy' by the Greeks from the Jews. *Classical Folia* (1978) 32: 53–67.

Sela, Shlomo. El papel de Abraham ibn Ezrá en la divulgación de los 'juicios' de la astrología en las lenguas hebrea y latina. *Sefarad* (1999) 59: 159–183.

———. *Abraham Ibn Ezra and the Rise of Medieval Hebrew Science.* Leiden: E.J. Brill, 2003.

THOMAS F. GLICK

TRANSLATION NORMS AND PRACTICE

Essential for the advancement of medieval Western science and technology were translations that not only restored the full riches of ancient Greek scientific culture but also introduced the latest discoveries and theories of scientists writing in Arabic. Medieval scientists were well aware of the necessity for accessing works in other languages. *Roger Bacon emphasized several times that, for science and philosophy, one must know Greek, Hebrew and Arabic. He criticized extant translations for their failure to do justice to the original authors, but most scholars felt no need to learn foreign languages, and were happy to trust in the accuracy of translations. There were three main areas in which Latin culture was regarded as particularly lacking: mathematics, medicine, and philosophy. From the late-eleventh century a concerted effort was made to remedy this lack. First, *Constantine the African and his collaborators in *Salerno and *Monte Cassino established a comprehensive corpus of Latin texts in medicine by translating works on the theory and practice of medicine by doctors (Christian, Jewish, and Muslim) writing in Arabic. Then, in the second quarter of the twelfth century, the movement to translate from Arabic and Greek works on *arithmetic (calculation with Hindu-Arabic numerals, *algebra, and trigonometry), geometry (*Euclid's *Elements*), and the science of the stars (astronomical tables, *Ptolemy's *Almagest* and *Tetrabiblos*, and a host of astrological texts) got underway almost simultaneously in northeast Spain, Sicily, and the Crusader States. By the mid-twelfth century *Toledo had become the undisputed center for the translation of scientific works from Arabic, thanks to the combined efforts of *Gerard of Cremona and *Domingo Gundisalvo, who added philosophy to their interests. Gerard was responsible for the Latin texts which became the bases for the Western curriculum in medicine (*Ibn Sina's *Canon* and several works by *Galen), astronomy (al-Farghani and *Ptolemy), and natural philosophy (Aristotle and his Greek commentators), while Gundisalvo and his colleagues concentrated on psychology and metaphysics. Meanwhile, the full corpus of Aristotle's works was being pieced together, mainly directly from Greek, and this was complemented, from the early thirteenth century onwards, by Latin versions of the detailed commentaries by Averroes (*Ibn Rushd). By the mid-thirteenth century, just at the time when the *universities were getting started, the major translations had been completed. It was at this stage that Roger Bacon could criticize the translators, Gerard of Cremona and his successors *Alfred of Sareschel, *Michael Scot, and Hermann the German for their inadequacies. One of these was the dependence on Arabic versions of Greek texts, which was remedied by *William of Moerbeke in the late-thirteenth century (for Aristotle's works) and *Niccolò da Reggio in the early fourteenth century (for Galen). In the Renaissance, medieval translations were criticized for the barbarity of their Latin, and new attempts were made to render into humanistic Latin the authorities that were the staple of higher education.

There were two contrasting models of translation that medieval translators could follow, those of Cicero and *Boethius. Cicero described how he translated Greek "not as an interpreter (*interpres*), but as an orator (*orator*)," by which he meant not rendering "word for word, but [preserving] the general style and force of the language. For I do not think that I ought to count them out to the reader like coins, but to pay them by weight, as it were" (*De optimo genere oratorum*, V, 14–15). In deliberate reaction to this "rhetorical" translation, Boethius defended his decision to translate as a "faithful interpreter" (*fidus interpres*) when dealing with non-literary works, "since," he writes, "I have rendered each (Greek) word by a word extracted and obtained from it. The reason for this approach is that, in these writings, in which knowledge of things is sought, it is not the charm of limpid speech, but the unsullied truth that has to be expressed. Therefore I feel I have been most useful if, in the books of philosophy composed in the Latin language, through the integrity of a completely full translation, no Greek literature is found to be needed any longer" (*In Isagogen Porphyrii Commentorum Editio secunda*, ch. 1). Boethius's model tended to prevail among medieval translators. Among the most strenuous advocates of the *ad verbum* (or literal) style over the *ad sensum* (or rhetorical) style was *Burgundio of Pisa (d. 1193), who justified this method in prefaces to his translations of theological texts from Greek. He repeats the point that, for the translation of theological and scientific works, the *ad verbum* translation is to be aimed at, even at the expense of elegant Latin style, adding that any departure from this ideal must be regarded as presumptuous interference on the part of the translator, and he cites as models the translations of the *Septuagint*, of Justinian's Law Code, and the versions of Aristotle's logical texts made by Boethius. Burgundio put this method into practice in his translations of works by Aristotle and Galen, and the *ad verbum* style was followed by his colleague *James of Venice, by William of Moerbeke (who revised his own translations in the direction of literalness), and the majority of medieval Greek-Latin translators. *Robert Grosseteste, for example, has been described as producing "scholarly editions of the [Greek] texts. Besides the text itself, he provides manuscript variants, any Greek commentaries available and notes of his own.... For the use of a Western audience the texts had to be in some kind of Latin. But beyond that they are not designed to be read or referred to like translations" (Dionisotti, p. 28). In keeping with Burgundio's criticism of presumptuousness, most literal translators not only did not add anything of their own; they did not even include their own names on their translations.

To translate word for word from Arabic presented a greater challenge, since the structure of the Arabic language was so different from that of Latin. The incompatibility of its vocabulary with that of Latin and the ambiguities of its written form made it particularly difficult to translate, while the "prolixity" by which it was frequently characterized justified abbreviation in the eyes of some translators. Constantine the African tended to abbreviate by missing out passages of the Arabic medical texts he translated, while *Hermann of Carinthia and his colleagues in northeast Spain, under the influence of the French schools, aimed at writing succinct and elegant Latin versions. Nevertheless, the *ad verbum* method

became regarded as the norm. The translations of Gerard of Cremona are exceeding literal, to the extent of retaining Arabic syntax in the Latin, and transliterating Arabic terms where no direct Latin equivalent could be found. It is often evident, however, that the translator, while preserving his fidelity to the original in the body of the text, has added glosses rephrasing more obscure passages, and explaining the meanings of Arabic terms. Sometimes these glosses are prefaced by the words "*Sensus huius littere est...*,' i.e., they give the sense, while the text gives the letter. The literalness extends to the careful copying of diagrams and illustrations in the original texts, especially in geometry and medicine.

Another difference between Greek–Latin and Arabic–Latin translations is the more frequent recourse in the latter case to interpreters. Most Christian translators from Arabic are associated with an Arabic speaker (usually a Jew). Gerard of Cremona is said to have "Latinized" the *Almagest*, while the Mozarab Ghalib "interpreted" it for him. More telling is the testimony of the Jew Avendauth, who states that he "took the lead and translated the words one at a time into the vernacular language, and Archdeacon Dominicus [Gundisalvo] turned them one at a time into Latin" (Preface to Avicenna, *On the Soul*). The vernacular could have been the spoken Arabic of Toledo, or the local Romance, and the *ad verbum* method is clearly alluded to. In the third quarter of the thirteenth century, under the patronage of *Alfonso X, king of Castile and León, the vernacular versions (Arabic texts on astronomy, astrology, and magic, translated into Castilian largely by Jews) achieved literary status. The substantial body of (mainly) more popular scientific texts in European vernaculars outside the Iberian peninsula derive directly or indirectly from the Latin versions.

It is probable that native speakers provided the main resource for the translators' knowledge of their source languages (unless they were bilingual themselves). Dictionaries and grammars played a lesser part. The Arabic–Latin glossaries that survive (the "Leiden glossary" of the twelfth century and the *Vocabulista in Arabico* of the mid-thirteenth) are more likely to have been aids for missionaries, whilst the extensive lists of "synonyma," often in several languages, helped doctors to identify *materia medica*. There is, however, more evidence of language aids in Greek. Grosseteste arranged for a Greek grammar to be written for him by John of Basingstoke, and a comprehensive Greek–Latin dictionary (London, College of Arms, MS Arundel 9) may be a copy of glossary revised by Grosseteste from a south Italian exemplar.

Jews, as well as being interpreters, established a scientific literature in Hebrew from the early-twelfth century onward, based largely on Arabic writings. Here, too, the question of translation method arose, of which the most conspicuous example is *Maimonides' letter to Samuel Ibn Tibbon concerning the best way to translate his *Guide to the Perplexed*. Although Maimonides criticizes the literal method of translation, saying that "the translator should first try to grasp the sense of the subject thoroughly, and then state the theme with perfect clearness in the other language… changing the order of the words, putting many words for one word, or vice versa… so that the subject be perfectly intelligible in the language into which he translates," the *ad verbum* style became the norm in Hebrew too. It was adopted by the prolific translators of the Tibbonid family and Calonymus ben Calonymus, and, ironically, it was these literal Hebrew translations of the Arabic commentaries on Aristotle by Averroes and medical texts by Avicenna that were used when Renaissance scholars wished to revise and complete the medieval translations, whose style so much displeased them.

See also **Translation movements**

Bibliography

Primary Sources
Bacon, Roger. *De utilitate grammaticae*, edited by J.H. Bridges, Oxford: Clarendon Press, 1897 (see vol. I, pp. 66–69 and 81).
Boethius. *In Isagogen Porphyrii Commentorum Editio secunda*, ch. 1, edited by G. Schepss and S. Brandt. Vienna and Leipzig: F. Temsky, 1906.
Cicero. *De optimo genere oratorum* in Cicero, *De inventione*; *De optimo genere oratorum*; *Topica*, edited and translated by H.M. Hubbell. Cambridge: Harvard University Press, 1968.
Maimonides. *Letter to Samuel Ibn Tibbon*. http://www.sacred-texts.com/jud/mhl/mhl19.htm

Secondary Sources
Contamine, Geneviève, ed. *Traduction et traducteurs au moyen age*. Paris: Éditions du Centre national de la recherché scientifique, 1989.
Copeland, Rita. *Rhetoric, Hermeneutics, and Translation in the Middle Ages*. New York: Cambridge University Press, 1991.
Dionisotti, A. Carlotta. "On the Greek Studies of Robert Grosseteste." In *The Uses of Greek and Latin*, eds. A.C. Dionisotti, A. Grafton and J. Kraye. London: Warburg Institute, 1988, pp. 19–40.
Ellis, Roger, ed. *The Medieval Translator*. 8 vols (so far), various publishers; from volume 5 onwards Turnhout: Brepols, 1987–2003.
Hamesse, J., ed. *Les Traducteurs en travail: leurs manuscrits et leurs méthodes*. Turnhout: Brepols, 2002.
Lofts, Steve G., and Philipp W. Rosemann. *Editer, traduire, interpréter: Essais de méthodologie philosophique*. Leuven and Paris: Peeters, 1997.

CHARLES BURNETT

TRANSPORTATION

Transportation perhaps sits oddly in a volume dealing with medieval science, technology, and medicine, since it did not occupy a prominent position in the intellectual preoccupations of the time. Only in the consideration of lands and places far away did the issue of transport (how to get to these places, what lay there, etc.) enter into serious discourse. For issues closer to home, transport as an intellectual pursuit faded almost into oblivion. This is not to say that authorities and societies as a whole were not concerned about transport matters, but that these concerns operated almost solely on a practical level, responding to day-to-day challenges involved with the maintenance of transport systems rather than subjecting transport (and the policies regarding it) to anything like a broader, more abstract analysis.

A large part of this lay with the breakup of a strong coordinating regime in Europe from the collapse of the Roman Empire onwards. The smaller European states that eventually resulted, by and large, lacked the resources, the time, and the foresight to give transport anything but the most cursory attention. As a result, transport developments over the medieval period tended to be decided by a sort of natural selection, often steering a course between competing interests. Nowhere is this clearer than in the development of inland water transport systems. Water was one of the most contested resources in the Middle Ages (as it is today), being sought after by those who wanted river water for irrigation or hay production; by those who wished to use rivers as fisheries (particularly on the lower stretches of these rivers); by those who wished to use the power of rivers for mills; by those who wished to use rivers for essential waste disposal (particularly common for big cities such as London or Paris); and, finally, by those who wished to use rivers for boat transport. The balancing of these interests was reflected in myriad government and local pronouncements about—among other things—how far fishing nets could jut into streams; about the need of millers to maintain "flashes" (that is, removable sections of weirs) to allow a flow of water which boats could shoot when going downstream or be winched over when going upstream; about when water levels in rivers should be lowered to allow hay harvesting in riverside meadows; about the time when butchers in big cities like London could throw animal guts into the river so that the tide would flush them out to sea, and so on. Within this clamor of voices for water, only when commercial interests were at very high levels could rivers be kept sufficiently clear for the effective transporting of goods by boat. Although merchants often had the ear of government, royal pronouncements about keeping water systems open for commercial traffic almost always went unheeded unless local interests were sufficiently aligned with those of commercial traffickers to give this use of water a first priority. Sometimes this gave rise to complex compromises. One such was the Thames system in England, where not only were complicated agreements made with fishermen and mill-owners, but also in the development of specialized barges that could better negotiate the flashes at mill-weirs, such as the flat-bottomed boat which the English called a "shout", a design probably borrowed from the Dutch who called such a boat a *schuit*.

Within this Darwinian-like context some transport adjustments were nonetheless very far-reaching. One very important one was the large-scale introduction of the horse to vehicle hauling, both for goods and people. It is true that such use of horses was known for vehicle-hauling in the Roman period, particularly in Gaul, but, with the collapse of the Roman Empire and, more perti- nently, its vaunted system of paved roads, such haulage had to resort to the ox, whose slow, plodding but more relentless pulling power was more suited to the heavier hauling conditions on earthen roads. Only when a series of significant changes in the harnessing and care of equids coalesced around the time of the first millennium, featur- ing such things as the padded horse-collar and iron horse-shoes, did horses come in their own as haulage beasts. Their appearance in front of carts and wagons, particularly over the twelfth and thirteenth centuries, certainly transformed the look and effectiveness of road transport, probably allowing goods to be hauled from place to place at about double the speed previously possible. Alongside the age-old use of horses as pack- animals, a certain quickening of transport resulted, coinciding with the well-known "commercial revolution" of the twelfth and thirteenth centuries.

A similar sort of phenomenon was occurring with water transport. Some of this has already been indicated for inland river transport, in the development of more specialized barges, but the key developments were occur- ring on salt water. One was certainly the development of sturdier oceangoing vessels, such as the squat northern European cog, a reflection of the marked commercial reorientation towards the North Sea that characterized most of the middle ages. Such regional ship developments were not totally self-contained, however, and the period from the thirteenth century onwards saw the fruitful blending of Mediterranean and northern European ship designs to create, among other types, the rugged and maneuverable carrack. This featured such changes as supplementing the square sails seen predominantly on northern waters with triangular lateen sails from the Mediterranean, allowing a greater effective in sailing against the wind while retaining the ability to withstand the stresses of oceanic travel. Certainly, carracks, caravels and galleons would literally provide the platform for European world exploration. Probably even more important than this, though, was the rise of what has been called "quantitative navigation," centered mostly around the introduction of the compass to European waters in the twelfth or thirteenth centuries. This more methodical attitude to sea transport gradually saw the thirteenth-century introduction of portolan maps, with compass heading lines drawn from one port to another which mariners could follow; of astrolabes and quadrants to measure latitude by means of the sun or pole star in the fifteenth century; of sand-glasses, particularly useful in giving a sense of time passed in the crossing of the Mediterranean to provide warning if certain headlands were not spied at proper times, also developed in the fifteenth century; and the development of diaries or "rutters", as they were called by the Dutch and English (originally from the French routier), which provided a more permanent record of the experience gained by sailors, once again occurring in the fifteenth century. Although a certain amount of patronage accompanied these developments, particularly from such august personages as Prince Henry the Navigator of Portugal

(1394–1460), most developed rather naturally out of the needs of mariners and merchants.

One should not, however, overestimate the changes made to transport over the medieval period. The infra- structure for land transport in particular was very rudimentary. Paved roads, which had provided the communications skeleton for the Roman Empire, were in very short supply in the Middle Ages. Indeed, the paving of roads and streets occurred as little islands around towns and cities. Similarly, although bridges probably existed in numbers similar to those found several centuries later in the eighteenth century (such at least is the finding of one author examining medieval English bridges), they were almost all (with some notable exceptions: see below) made of timber and likely to have been much more flimsy and narrow that those later. The common categorization of bridges into those passable by cart (the widest), by pack- horse and by foot (the narrowest), suggests that, even if their numbers were about the same as centuries later, they were more of a bottleneck to certain types of traffic. On the other hand, the extensiveness of the road system was impressive. Except for the modern autobahns and motor- ways, virtually all routes shown on road-maps today existed in the Middle Ages along with the bridges to service these routes. Indeed, if we consider the modern road system in Europe to be like the circulatory system of a healthy young adult, the same system in the medieval period would have a much more aged look (that is, with a higher level of arterial constriction), but we could still recognize the "individual."

In short, transport in the Middle Ages often had an air of neglect about it. This neglect would be exacerbated by such things as tolls that landlords often charged at bridges or certain stretches of road. Tolls might have been benefi- cial in some instances—in the Alps, for example, it has been argued that the revenues from tolls were largely ploughed back into maintaining the material infrastructure of Alpine routes, and the same might have been said of the magnificent stone bridges sometimes built in the period (such as the great stone bridge crossing the Rhône at Avignon in France, begun in 1177), where tolls helped to defray maintenance costs of such structures. But in most cases the effect was parasitic as little of the revenues made its way back into the maintenance of the transport system. As mentioned above, this reflected the fact that transport was not in the forefront of intellectual concerns, perhaps partly because of the mainly spiritual concerns of the people at the time, certainly up to the turn of the first millennium. The travel or transport desiderata that existed for this period, such as in the "itineraries" common up to the twelfth century or the crude maps that were drawn during the period, pointed to a "literature" of curiosities rather than useful guides or tools for getting from place to place. The Crusades would signal a certain breaking out of this mold, and certainly the need for informed knowledge about the larger world would quicken afterwards, helped along by the Mongol expansion in the east. Even the cata- strophic effects of the Black Death would not dampen this and indeed may have accelerated it even further, as people grew more accustomed to travel and began to expect more

The remaining portion of the Pont St.-Bénézet on the Rhône River at Avignon, France. (Corbis/Franz-Marc Frei)

in the way of comfort. The development of inns as places of hospitality and conviviality was one reflection of this, as was the jolly traveling motif in such works as *The Canterbury Tales by* *Geoffrey Chaucer. Crucially, this popular embrace of travel and transport began to be accompanied by a more academic and systematic attitude to getting about. The period when navigation and other aspects of transport became truly "scientific" was still some ways off even by 1500, but the first steps in that direction had been taken.

See also Bridges; Canals; Navigation; Roads; Travel and exploration

Bibliography

Harrison, David. *The Bridges of Medieval England.* Clarendon Press: Oxford, 2004.

Langdon, John. *Horses, Oxen, and Technological Innovation.* New York: Cambridge University Press, 1986.

Leighton, Albert C. *Transport and Communication in Early Medieval Europe: A.D. 500–1100.* Newton Abbot: David and Charles, 1972.

McCormick, Michael. *Origins of the European Economy.* New York: Cambridge University Press, 2001.

McGrail, Seán. *Ancient Boats in North-West Europe.* London: Longman, 1987.

Spufford, Peter. *Power and Profit: The Merchant in Medieval Europe.* New York: Thames and Hudson, 2002.

Unger, Richard W. *The Ship in the Medieval Economy 600–1600.* London: Croom Helm, 1980.

JOHN LANGDON

TRAVEL AND EXPLORATION

The earliest expansion of Europe into worlds beyond its own borders was in the North Atlantic Ocean. Early Latin texts regarding the lives of Irish saints speak of the movement of brethren to some of the islands in the region, such as the Faeroes by 800 C.E., via the use of simple, wickerwork coracles. By the end of ninth century, however, Norse settlement had begun in earnest, and travel between Iceland and the Scandinavian mainland was in full force by 900 C.E. Norse movement, both in the Atlantic and, as raiders, in Atlantic and Mediterranean Europe, was made possible in part by their special skills in shipbuilding and, concomitantly, navigation. Usually slim, light, and propelled by rowed oars, the ships' hulls were built by the clinker method: first a shell, then overlapping planking with joints made watertight by the use of resin-soaked wool. The Viking *langskip* or longship, which was used mostly for the coastal movement of people, supplies, horses, and troops, had, as the so-called Gokstad ship demonstrates, up to sixteen pairs of oars and was crewed by thirty-five men. These ships were masted and hoisted sail and were not only quite mobile but could be easily used as mobile fighting platforms. Likewise, the Vikings employed the *knarr*, a medium to large merchant vessel used primarily for trading rather than raiding. More oceanworthy than the longship, the *knarr* was also more efficient in that it needed a much smaller crew. This is not to imply that the Norse were only fighting sailors. Norse military technology was developed for land combat as well, the most important piece being the double-edged blade sword, used primarily as a slashing weapon, often imported from the Rhine valley and finished in Scandinavia.

Western pilgrims and merchants had been a presence in the Levant long before Pope Urban II preached the First Crusade in 1095. Indeed, it was not until the 1090s that the pilgrimage routes were closed. The crusades saw a confluence of mercantile, religious, and military interests that allowed for the establishment of a Latin beachhead and brought news of the Muslim world, its culture and technology into much greater relief for the West than had previously been possible. As a military operation, the crusades to the East required the development of large ships capable of equine transport, as well as food and weapons. The terrain of the region also required new forms of siege warfare and, most particularly, the development of new castle-building techniques which allowed for the construction of castles on hillocks with deep defiles, sheer cliffs, and uncertain water sources.

Following the Mongolian invasions of Eastern Europe in 1240–1242, western travelers who ventured into Asia were repeatedly astonished, not only by Asian technological sophistication, but by the ability of the Mongols to move craftsmen and technological specialists from one part of their vast empire to another. Western reports, such as those by William of Rubruck, made note of Italian physicians and shipwrights, French and Flemish goldsmiths, Greek and Scandinavian soldiers, German miners and Alan armorers operating in the "east" while Chinese artillerymen, stonemasons, and engineers operated in Mongol-occupied Iran. One of the most notable technological exchanges of the Latin-Mongol encounter was the presence of Genoese sailors and shipbuilders in the Persian Gulf in the fourteenth century, working on the construction of ships for use by a possible Il-Khanid navy. If it were not for the internecine fighting that broke out among the Italians, it is possible that the Iranian Mongols would have become a naval power in their own right.

It was also in the late thirteenth century that we find the development of one of the most important tools of travel, the portolan chart. Likely used as an aid in navigation, it demonstrates how the knowledge of the extra-Mediterranean world developed. They also are the first maps with notions of scale, proportion, and distance, something which had been lost in cartography since the Roman Empire. The 1321 world map of Pietro Vesconte is so well developed as to include city plans at scale. Travels by *Marco Polo and others to eastern Asia, and by the Portuguese in the fourteenth and fifteenth centuries also came to be added to maps, extending Western geographical knowledge and conceptions even further. These were, of course, followed by the first Latin translation (c. 1406) of *Ptolemy's *Geography*.

It is an absolute certainty that Portuguese and Basque fishermen had been operating in the North Atlantic from the eleventh and twelfth centuries, if not before. Little is known of their techniques for navigation, other than oral knowledge and observational acuity of the patterns of tides and of migration patterns of cod. For the longer

The Gokstad ship, one of the best preserved Viking longships, (built c. 850–900) is now preserved in the Viking Ship Museum, Oslo, Norway. (Corbis/Richard T. Nowitz)

ocean voyages that the Spanish and Portuguese undertook officially in the fifteenth century, however, more ships, larger tonnages, and better ports were needed. The full-rigged ship, the carrack, was the most prominent of the larger vessels. Large, heavy, with a big spread of canvas, the carrack could support upwards of three watertight decks. The carrack was a workhorse, able to carry cargo of a thousand tons. The *Santa Maria*, one of *Columbus's first three ships for his transatlantic voyage of 1492, was a carrack, while his other two ships, the *Niña* and the *Pinta* were of the smaller, caravel, variety of ship. Designed for the Portuguese coastal voyages around Africa, the caravels were slim and able to sail. Needing small crews, they were ideal for ventures into unknown waters. The magnetic compass, astrolabe, and quadrant made sailing by the stars a more accurate venture. While the need for sailing by dead reckoning continued through the invention and common use of the chronometer in the eighteenth century, the cultural exchanges that took place during the fifteenth century resulted in the importation of new plants and animals, and, with them, new techniques for growing and raising crops and husbandry. Often, however, we find that the technologies needed for successful transplantation were not always readily understood in their new biotas and, as a consequence, crop failures were often commonplace. Orange groves, for example, that Muslims had planted in southern Spain were initially allowed to grow fallow by Christian reconqerors, unfamiliar with the special techniques required for growing citrus. Likewise, omnivorous European pigs proved so dominant in Mexico that they forced out indigenous domestic animals overnight.

Transportation, military and agricultural technology all were instrumental in the history of European expansion and exploration in the Middle Ages, and European techniques were exported globally as seaborne empires expanded in the early modern period.

See also **Geography, chorography; Shipbuilding**

Bibliography

Allsen, Thomas T. *Culture and Conquest in Mongol Eurasia.* Cambridge Studies in Islamic Civilization. New York: Cambridge University Press, 2004.

Falk, Hjalmar. *Altnordisches Seewesen.* Wörter und Sachen 4. Heidelberg: Winter, 1912.

Edwards, Clinton. Design and Construction of Fifteenth-Century Iberian Vessels. *The Mariner's Mirror* (1992) 78: 419–572.

Harley, J.B. and David Woodward, eds. *The History of Cartography.* Vol. 1: *Cartography in Prehistoric, Ancient, and Medieval Europe and the Mediterranean.* Chicago: University of Chicago Press, 1987.

Kennedy, Hugh. *Crusader Castles.* New York: Cambridge University Press, 1994.

Verdon, Jean. *Travel in the Middle Ages.* Transl. by George Holoch. Notre Dame: University of Notre Dame Press, 2003.

Watson, Andrew M. *Agricultural innovation in the early Islamic world: the diffusion of crops and farming techniques, 700–1100.* Cambridge Studies in Islamic Civilization. New York: Cambridge University Press, 1983.

ADAM KNOBLER

TROTULA

Trotula was originally the title of a compendium on women's medicine that was formed out of three independent treatises on gynecology and cosmetics sometime in the late twelfth or early thirteenth century. The title Trotula was soon misunderstood as the name of the compendium's supposed authoress. The figure of Trotula for many centuries hid from view a real historical female physician and writer from *Salerno, Trota (or Trocta, as her name would have been spelled in local Lombard sources). The complicated textual history of the Trotula accounts for the long-lived scholarly debate about whether an individual named Trotula really existed.

No detailed biographical information on Trota has thus far been found (claims, for example, that she belonged to the De Ruggiero family are unsupported), but it is likely that she lived in the early or middle decades of the twelfth century. She is credited with authorship of two works. First is the *Practica secundum Trotam* (*Practical Medicine According to Trota*), a miscellany of remedies for a variety of different ailments, from menstrual retention to snakebite, stomach disorders to eye problems. Trota's *Practica* was one of seven textbooks used to create a massive compendium of Salernitan medicine, *De egritudinum curatione* (*On the Treatment of Diseases*).

Trota was also the "authority" behind a collection known as *De curis mulierum* (*Treatments for Women*). This text served as the core around which two other Salernitan texts on women's medicine would become attached: the *Liber de sinthomatibus mulierum* (*Book on the Conditions of Women*) and the *De ornatu mulierum* (*Women's Cosmetics*), both by anonymous and almost certainly male authors. This ensemble became known as the *Trotula* (literally, the "little Trota"). Soon Trotula was misunderstood as the author's name and it was "she" who became the most widely recognized female authority on medicine in later medieval Europe.

Trota was not the only woman who practiced medicine in Salerno. Several male Salernitan writers note the practices of *mulieres Salernitane* (women of Salerno). But Trota is the only one who seems to have put pen to parchment; indeed, her works (which are poorly organized and display little engagement with formal medical theory) suggest that she herself was only marginally literate and was largely excluded from the theoretical discussions and textual exegesis that distinguished the work of her male colleagues.

Trota was known outside Salerno, apparently due to the influence of the Normans who controlled both southern Italy and England. The thirteenth-century French poet Rutebeuf crafted a devastating parody of her which, though vicious, is itself evidence of her fame. After the twelfth century, her *Practica* faded from view and only her *Treatments for Women*, once joined to the anonymous *Conditions of Women* and *Women's Cosmetics*, became influential. More than one hundred thirty copies of the Latin *Trotula* texts are now extant (compared to only two of Trota's *Practica*) and the works were translated into the vernacular languages numerous times prior to 1500. *Petrus Hispanus relied heavily on *Conditions of Women* in the gynecological sections of his *Treasury for Poor Men*, and *Gilbertus Anglicus similarly inserted major sections of Trota's *Treatments for Women* into his *Compendium of Medicine*. "Trotula" was also cited, independent of anything actually found in the *Trotula*, as an authority on "the secrets of women"—hence *Geoffrey Chaucer's inclusion of "Trotula" in the imaginary "book of wicked wives" in "The Wife of Bath's Prologue" in *The Canterbury Tales*.

The *Trotula* became less important after male practitioners began crafting their own gynecological texts in the late Middle Ages. It was "rediscovered" and printed as if it were an ancient text in 1544. In 1566, a philologist proposed that the name "Trotula" was really an error for "Eros," a freedman of the Roman empress Julia, thus leading to the modern debates about "Trotula"'s existence and the authenticity of the *Trotula*. In 1681 a local

Salernitan historian created the story that several women actually had held professorial chairs at Salerno, among whom "Trotula" was given pride of place. That element of the "Trotula" story has been one of the most persistent, leading to, among other things, a commemorative medal struck in "Trotula"'s honor in Salerno in the nineteenth century and a geological feature on the planet Venus named after her in the late-twentieth century. Findings about the work of Trota and the other women of Salerno suggest that there is still much to learn about women's medical practice in medieval Europe.

See also **Gynecology and midwifery; Hildegard of Bingen; Women in science**

Bibliography

Barratt, Alexandra, ed. *The Knowing of Woman's Kind in Childing: A Middle English Version of Material Derived from the 'Trotula' and Other Sources.* Turnhout: Brepols, 2001.

Green, Monica H. In Search of an 'Authentic' Women's Medicine: The Strange Fates of Trota of Salerno and Hildegard of Bingen. *Dynamis: Acta Hispanica ad Medicinae Scientiarumque Historiam Illustrandam* (1999) 19: 25–54.

————. *Women's Healthcare in the Medieval West: Texts and Contexts.* Aldershot: Ashgate, 2000.

————, ed. and trans. *The 'Trotula': A Medieval Compendium of Women's Medicine.* Philadelphia: University of Pennsylvania Press, 2001.

MONICA H. GREEN

TUSI, NASIR AL-DIN AL-

Abu Ja'far Muhammad ibn Muhammad ibn al-Hasan Nasir al-Din al-Tusi (1201–1274) wrote approximately one hundred sixty-five treatises, in both Arabic and Persian, on such diverse topics as astronomy and *cosmology, mathematics (geometry and trigonometry), medicine, as well as philosophy, ethics, jurisprudence, *logic, and history. Little is known of his early years aside from what he reveals in his autobiographical *Sayr wa-Suluk*. Apparently as a young man he traveled extensively to study with important scholars. He then entered the service of the Isma'ili ruler of Quhistan, and later worked in Alamut, the Isma'ili center of power in Iran, where he was active in political life, as well as in teaching and writing. When Alamut fell to Mongol forces in 1256, al-Tusi entered the service of Hulagu and his twelve-imam Shi'i Ilkhan successors as court astrologer as well as director of *awqaf* (foundations endowed for pious purposes). It was Hulagu who enlisted al-Tusi to oversee construction one of the largest observatories of the Islamic world outside the city of Maragha in what is now Azerbaijan.

Al-Tusi not only oversaw the planning and construction of the physical structure and its instruments, he also collected a large library and recruited scholars from a variety of backgrounds and geographical origins (a few even from China) to staff the observatory. It thus became an important center of research, teaching, and scholarship. The observatory survived the death of Hulagu (1265) and the death of al-Tusi himself, continuing to function under the direction of his sons, Sadr al-Din and Asil al-Din, for at least another thirty years. Such longevity in a medieval observatory is unusual; it may reflect an assignment of resources from the *awqaf* to its support.

Al-Tusi is best known to historians of science for his work in mathematical astronomy and cosmography. From an early period, astronomers in the Islamic world had been fascinated by the predictive accuracy and mathematical sophistication of *Ptolemy's *Almagest*, although they were deeply troubled by its physically problematic equant theory. It was here that al-Tusi made perhaps his most original contribution. His Tusi couple, as it has come to be called, combined two circular motions: a larger circle rotating uniformly on its axis and a smaller circle, with diameter equal to the radius of the larger circle and internally tangent to it, rotates in the opposite sense with twice the angular velocity of the larger. Al-Tusi showed that a point on the circumference of the smaller circle oscillates along a rectilinear path coinciding with a diameter of the larger circle. This result served as the key to allow al-Tusi to retain most of the mathematical features of the Ptolemaic system while preserving the uniform circular motions which the equant had seemed to violate. The success of al-Tusi stimulated others in his entourage to explore further non-Ptolemaic developments. This Maragha school of astronomy/cosmography has been extensively studied for several decades.

Neither the *Tadhkira*, al-Tusi's most complete description of his vision of the universe, nor the treatises of his colleagues and students who carried his studies further, were translated into European languages until the modern period. Even al-Tusi's *Zij al-Ilkhani* (*planetary tables), which did not incorporate either new observations or the non-traditional planetary theories, was known to the medieval world only as the *Persian Syntaxis* of Gregory Chioronides, whose connection to al-Tusi was not recognized. John Greaves, in his *Astronomica quaedam* (1650), believed that he was making his contemporaries aware for the first time of the value of precession recorded in al-Tusi's *Zij*.

Impact on Sixteenth-Century Science

Although al-Tusi's work was essentially unknown in European languages, Copernicus, in his *De revolutionibus*, used the geometry of the Tusi Couple when developing his lunar theory, prompting continuing speculation about possible lines of influence. The existence of Arabic manuscripts containing non-Ptolemaic discussions can be documented in Italy at the beginning of the sixteenth century, during the time that Copernicus was himself in Italy (1496–1503), ostensibly to study medicine. Attempts to argue from the fact of geographical contiguity to intellectual piracy have often foundered on lack of evidence that Copernicus had any familiarity with Arabic language. Recent documentary study shows that a Greek manuscript of the *Persian Syntaxis* (vat. Gr. 211), which contained notes on al-Tusi's lunar theory together with clear diagrams of a Tusi couple, was present in Rome by 1475. Further, even though Copernicus may have been ignorant of Arabic, some of his European contemporaries were already becoming interested in the Arabic astronomical tradition and were beginning to collect manuscripts. They studied their contents and sometimes annotated the manuscripts in Latin. Vat. arabo 312 is a copy of al-Tusi's *Tadhkira*, annotated in Latin, apparently about the time Copernicus was in Rome. Although the evidence is still largely circumstantial, claims of intellectual borrowing by Copernicus cannot be easily dismissed.

If this theory of planetary motion were his only contribution, al-Tusi would deserve an honored place in history. He did much more, penning a series of *tahrir* (redactions) of classic Greek mathematical works for students or novices. These works intended to present the author's essential ideas, simplifying and streamlining the language, while remaining close to the original presentation and avoiding unnecessary repetition. He often added notes to ease the student's entry into the study. The most popular was his *Tahrir* of *Euclid's *Elements*. Well over a hundred manuscript copies still exist, many heavily annotated by readers. The treatise was translated into Persian twice, as well as into Sanskrit during the late medieval period. Its long popularity is attested by the existence of several printings during the nineteenth century. Despite its long popularity in the East, it remains almost completely unknown among Western historians, eclipsed by an anonymous *Tahrir*, incorrectly attributed to al-Tusi, printed in 1594 by the Medicean press in Rome. The two share important technical *vocabulary and so may have a genetic connection.

Al-Tusi's *Tahrir* provides useful information on structural differences between Arabic transmissions attributed to al-Hajjaj and to Ishaq (in the revision of *Thabit ibn Qurra). Generally, al-Tusi follows the Ishaq–Thabit formulation (including vocabulary and terminology) of Group A manuscripts, while noting differences in numbering or ordering with the version of al-Hajjaj. His *Tahrir* contains some two hundred commentary notes, typically introduced by the phrase "I say." Nearly half of these notes present alternative demonstrations, most of which can be traced to the *Kitab Hall Shukuk Uqlidis* of *Ibn al-Haytham. These commentary notes also include added cases for a number of propositions in books I–IV. These cases are typical of the transmission associated with al-Hajjaj. The printed Pseudo-Tusi *Tahrir*, while it also contains some notes on structural differences, does not include many commentary notes. On the other hand, it makes constant reference to previous propositions and contains many more lemmas and corollaries.

Although scarcely known in the medieval Latin West, al-Tusi's work in mathematical astronomy was the foundation of an important research tradition and his student-oriented treatises or their derivatives came to have an important place in madrasa instruction in the eastern half of the Islamic world until supplanted during the colonial period by the introduction of European learning. The commentary on Book I of his *Tahrir* of the *Elements* composed by Mohammed Barkat (fl. 1750), for example, became part of the required curriculum in the Dars-i-Nizami curriculum reform in late-eighteenth-century Indian madrasas and was printed several times before the end of the nineteenth century.

See also **Astronomy, Islamic**

Bibliography

Cassinet, R. L'aventure de l'édition des Éléments d'Euclide en arabe par la Société Typographique Médicis vers 1594. *Revue française d'histoire du livre* (1993) 88–89: 5–51.

De Young, G. "The Astronomica quaedam of John Greaves: Oriental Interests and the Pursuit of Conservatism. In *Cosmology Through Time*. Edited by S. Colafrancesco and G. Giobbi. Milan: MIMESIS, 2003, pp. 167–173.

———. The Tahrir of Euclid's Elements by Nasir al-Din al-Tusi. *Farhang: Quarterly Journal of Humanities and Cultural Studies* (2003) 15–16: 117–143.

Mercier, R. The Greek "Persian Syntaxis" and the Zij-i Ilkhani. *Archives Internationales d'Histoire des Sciences* (1984) 34: 35–60.

[Pseudo-] Tusi. *Kitab Tahrir Usul li-Uqlidis*. Rome: Typographia Medicea, 1594. Republished under the title *Tahrir al-Usul li-Uqlidis: An Anonymous Commentary Upon Euclid's Elements, wrongly ascribed to Nasiraddin at-Tusi*. Frankfurt: IGAIW, 1997.

Ragep, J. *Nasir al-Din al-Tusi's Memoire on Astronomy (Al-tadhkira fi 'ilm al-hay'a)*. Two volumes. New York: Springer, 1993.

Rahman, A., et al. *Science and Technology in Medieval India—A Bibliography of Source Materials in Sanskrit, Arabic and Persian*. New Delhi: Indian National Science Academy, 1982.

Siddiqi, B. H. "Nasir al-Din al-Tusi." In *A History of Muslim Philosophy*. Edited by M. M. Sharif. Weisbaden: Otto Harrassowitz, 1963, I, 564–580.

Saliba, G. The Role of the *Almagest* Commentaries in Medieval Arabic Astronomy: A Preliminary Survey of Tusi's Redaction of Ptolemy's *Almagest*. *Archives Internationales d'Histoire des Sciences* (1987) 37: 3–20.

———. The Astronomical Tradition of Maragha: A Historical Survey and Prospects for Future Research. *Arabic Sciences and Philosophy* (1991) 1: 67–99.

———. "Arabic Planetary Theories and Their Impact on Copernican Astronomy." In *Cosmology Through Time*. Edited by S. Colafracesco and G. Giobbi. Milan: MIMESIS, 2003, pp.153–160.

Tusi, Nasir al-Din Muhammad. *Contemplation and Action*. New York: I.B. Tauris, 1995

GREGG DE YOUNG

U

UNIVERSITIES

Of the legacies of medieval Europe to world civilization, the university ranks as one of the most permanent. Its significance for the histories of science and medicine is difficult to overestimate; it even occupies a modest place in the history of the mechanical arts. The university gave the disciplines associated with the study of nature a new institutional home, which not only proliferated but also endured. Eight centuries later, the earliest universities (e.g., Bologna, Oxford, Paris, Montpellier, Salamanca) are still thriving, as are a host of later foundations. More importantly, this institutional model has spread throughout the world and continues to cultivate the sciences and medicine successfully (most Nobel Prizes go to university professors).

The universities gradually emerged in the late twelfth and early thirteenth centuries against a background of intense intellectual ferment. Trends toward naturalism (in philosophy, sculpture, and literature, for example) and rationalization (in administration, theology, and especially law) permeate the era. By the eleventh and twelfth centuries, the law regulated almost every aspect of life in European lands. For the first time, various bodies of law became systematic and principle-based: legal scholars appreciated existing logical tools, were eager for more, and gave much thought to the interaction of deduction and empirical consequences. Logic was not an esoteric discipline but an indispensable tool of thought, which leading *cathedral schools taught, along with the natural philosophy of *Plato's *Timaeus* and a new theology guided by rational principles.

An additional intellectual stimulus came from the translation of many Greek and Arabic scientific and philosophical texts into Latin (primarily from Arabic). Already well underway with medical works in eleventh-century Salerno, this trickle became a flood by the later twelfth century and extended to almost every field of learning. The influx included most of the Aristotelian corpus (with its logical, methodological, natural philosophical, ethical, political, and literary writings), a host of other works from the ancient mathematical and medical traditions (*Euclid's *Elements* and *Optics*, *Ptolemy's *Almagest* and *Tetrabiblos*, parts of the Archimedean corpus, *Galen, and *Hippocrates), and a vast library of Arabic scholarship that extended this work in new directions. Arabic scholars (mentioned here in their Latinized names) thus played a crucial role in the development of European science: Alhacen in optics and astronomy; in astronomy and astrology: Thebit, Alcabitius, Albumasar, Alfraganus, Alpetragius; in medicine: Rasis, and especially Avicenna's *Canon*; in natural philosophy: the numerous commentaries by Avicenna and Averroes on Aristotle's books. The emerging universities were poised to take advantage of this deluge of scientific material and to channel the intellectual excitement it generated.

The first universities were not founded, nor did they grow out of cathedral schools (Paris being the notable exception). They crystallized during the twelfth century in towns renowned for teaching in specific areas: law in Bologna and Oxford, the liberal arts and theology in Paris, medicine in Montpellier. Masters and students organized themselves into guilds or corporations—the original legal meaning of *universitas*, which quickly acquired academic connotations. The *universitas* of masters of arts at Paris and the universitates of the various nations of law students at Bologna were self-governing associations that used their bargaining power both to negotiate concessions from local authorities and to obtain "universal" privileges from the emperor or the pope.

The institutional variation among the first universities is consistent with their springing out of local circumstances rather than an archetype, whether indigenous or, more controversially, Islamic (as George Makdisi has argued). Paris was unusual in the early thirteenth century in that intense conflicts pitted the bishop and his chancellor against the masters of arts, who successfully appealed to the papacy over the bishop's head. These conflicts led to legal solutions that set precedents on which later universities would draw. In these struggles for self-determination, the masters often won with the aid of the papacy (against the bishop of Paris or the commune of Bologna, for example). This is an important point, for while the northern universities were officially clerical institutions under the jurisdiction of the church, in fact they were also largely autonomous and self-regulating bodies. They worked hard to ensure their control over their own affairs: at its foundation in 1425, the university of Louvain obtained privileges that put it largely beyond the reach of both the bishop of Liège and the duke of Brabant.

By the mid-thirteenth century, when they had secured full legal standing, the universities were doing something novel. They were certifying an individual's competence in various domains by awarding degrees for completing a sequence of prescribed courses to the satisfaction of the masters. Thanks to the pope's or the emperor's recognition of them as *studia generalia*, they had the legal power of conferring licenses "to teach everywhere." The universities had effectively created formal criteria for membership in a European-wide elite of Latin learning whose training included significant exposure to Aristotelian natural philosophy and, to a lesser extent, the mathematical sciences. Since these disciplines encompassed some thirty percent of the "arts" curriculum, they were prerequisites for study in the faculties of law, medicine, and theology, on which they had a notable impact.

In most early universities, this curricular emphasis evolved smoothly. Although exceptional, the conflicts at Paris illustrate the dramatic character of the transformation. Aristotle had long been admired for his logic, but in early-thirteenth-century Paris his newly translated natural philosophy proved controversial. His universe was eternal, not created; his doctrine of the soul stressed its physiological functions and left the immortality of the rational soul in doubt. Local ecclesiastical authorities therefore reacted defensively by prohibiting the teaching of Aristotle's natural philosophy in 1210 and 1215.

The Mob Quad at Merton College, Oxford. Construction was begun soon after the foundation of the college in 1264 and completed before the middle of the fourteenth century. (Topham)

Within a generation, however, the ban on Aristotle had been turned on its head. The 1255 statutes of the Parisian arts faculty placed Aristotelian natural philosophy at the core of the curriculum. At Oxford, another early university with a faculty of theology but with a more distant bishop, Aristotle entered the curriculum smoothly, a situation for which the theologian and Aristotelian commentator *Robert Grosseteste, deserves credit. Within this framework, no one could earn a bachelor's or a master's degree in arts without thorough immersion in the Aristotelian corpus and exposure to his Arabic commentators. When the universities multiplied in the fourteenth century and their enrollments expanded in the fifteenth, the study of natural philosophy, the mathematical sciences, and medicine diffused with them.

In a rough century-by-century schema, the thirteenth century was a transnational era of institutional consolidation and intellectual exploration and assimilation; the fourteenth was a century of institutional spread and of logical development and criticism, while the fifteenth century witnessed some unprecedented university enrollments and a more regional or national outlook, even as the intellectual life of the more than sixty universities in existence by 1500 remains a scholarly frontier.

Blurring Old Distinctions

The term "arts" in the eponymous faculty derives from the late-antique category of the liberal arts: the verbal trivium (grammar, rhetoric, and dialectic) and the mathematical *quadrivium (arithmetic, geometry, music, and astronomy). While these disciplines were taught in most medieval universities, the seven liberal arts no longer structured nor circumscribed their curriculum, which sometimes blurred the old categories. Logic, which dwarfed grammar and rhetoric in importance, was also the language of natural philosophy. It would develop spectacularly in the fourteenth century, blossoming into a host of technical subspecialties that impressed, if not the humanists, at least everyone who has tried to understand them, from Leibniz through Peirce to the present. Many of these logical developments were directly stimulated by the analysis of natural philosophical problems, actual as well as imaginary (issues of change/motion, such as the beginnings and ends of processes, rates of change, etc.), and some took on a strongly mathematical cast. Indeed, in the most sophisticated works of the genre (e.g., those of *Thomas Bradwardine, *William of Heytesbury, John Dumbleton, or *Richard Swineshead), logic, mathematics, and natural philosophy are so tightly intertwined as to be inseparable.

The four traditional mathematical disciplines of the old quadrivium also continued to be taught in most universities, sometimes from long-available textbooks, increasingly from new ones. In the thirteenth century, *John of Sacrobosco wrote introductions to arithmetic (*Algorismus*) and the reference frames of astronomy (*Tractatus de sphaera*), which the anonymous *Theorica planetarum* supplemented with a non-quantitative overview of Ptolemaic theory sufficient for understanding astronomical tables. Texts such as these have survived in hundreds of manuscripts. In contrast, the typical student read only excerpts of complex works such as Euclid's *Elements* or Ptolemy's *Almagest*, which only a small minority studied in detail, probably informally.

But the traditional liberal arts did not include natural philosophy, which had become the dominant category of scientific study in the arts faculty. Among these works were Aristotle's *Physics*, *On Generation and corruption*, *Meteorology*, *On the Generation of animals*, *On the Heavens*, *On the Soul* (the vegetable, animal, and rational souls), and *On Sense and sensation*. New mathematical sciences outside the quadrivium also made their way into the curriculum: in the thirteenth century, "perspectiva" (optics); and in the later fourteenth, courses on "the proportions of velocities in motions" and the *"latitude of forms," inspired by the mathematical natural philosophy of Merton College, Oxford.

Many more students were exposed to the arts curriculum than completed degrees. With attrition rates of eighty to ninety percent, only a minority went on to study in a higher faculty. Overall, law faculties produced by far the largest number of graduates, who staffed the growing bureaucracies of cities and courts, both secular and ecclesiastical. Medicine and theology were much smaller faculties. Universities organized on the Parisian model separated the arts faculty from those of law, medicine, and (after the mid-fourteenth century) theology. Universities organized on the Bolognese model retained a separate law faculty but joined arts and medicine into one faculty, recognizing the relationship, however contentious, between natural philosophy and medicine. Both theology and medicine show the strong imprint of this scientific curriculum. The place of medicine among the higher university faculties deserves emphasis. Whereas some earlier classifications of knowledge had treated medicine as a mechanical art, the university made it an academic subject, for which philosophical studies were a prerequisite, a striking inversion of some earlier priorities (but not of Galen, who believed that the good physician had to be a good philosopher).

The study of medicine usually presupposed a thorough familiarity with the core of the curriculum in arts, on which medicine built. At Bologna and Padua in particular, the masters' double degrees in arts and medicine are well documented, as is the crossover of their teaching. The theoretical connections between *astronomy and medicine were close, with *astrology providing the causal physical link between the stars and the body. Universities with leading medical faculties would continue to offer a strong stimulus to the teaching of astrology and its prerequisites (elementary planetary theory, the use of astronomical tables). In the fourteenth and fifteenth centuries, building on this legitimate foundation and on the availability of practitioners, judicial astrology, which was more controversial, seems to have been on the rise. The most lavish memorabilia of this growing interest, from noble horoscopes to decorative art and instruments, are associated with princely and ecclesiastical courts, but cities also used astrologers, which universities were in the business of supplying. Reflecting a growing demand, Bologna and Kraków each started with one chair in astrology, eventually adding a second in the fifteenth century.

Although university medicine included an important theoretical component, its purpose was the treatment of the sick. This focus on practice distinguished medicine from the other faculties and may have fostered more openness to hands-on instruction. Bologna inaugurated the dissection of human cadavers in the early fourteenth century, Montpellier at mid-century, and Vienna in the early fifteenth century.

The impact of medieval university medicine went beyond the classroom. Whereas other degree holders faced little external competition, university-trained physicians were a minority among healers. The universities thus thrust their graduates into the competitive world of healing, where they evidently did well, and sometimes good. With their criteria of medical adequacy and the legal power to grant licenses to practice, the medical faculties lay the groundwork for proto-professional standards and introduced a sharp division into health care, creating a class of learned physicians that used the law, sometimes heavy-handedly, to curtail the activities of competing healers.

Since all aspiring theologians who were not in religious orders had degrees in arts, they often retained their love of natural philosophy and its standards of knowledge when doing theology. *Thomas Aquinas's theological use of Aristotle is merely the best-known example of this trend, which blossomed in later centuries, from discussions of the created world, through the frequent question "Is theology is a *scientia?" to inquiry into the validity of Aristotelian logic in Trinitarian doctrine. Some of the best summaries of late medieval natural philosophy appear in Biblical commentaries (e.g., Henry of Langenstein's Lectures on Genesis, c. 1386–1392) while excellent natural philosophy and logic appear in the commentaries on *Peter Lombard's *Sentences* that marked the apex of study in theology.

The university formalized several characteristic approaches to the teaching of texts. Eventually surpassing the *lecturae* and commentaries, the *quaestio* (derived from the disputation required for the bachelor of arts degree) eventually came to dominate the format of natural philosophical and theological writing.

In addition to their task of transmitting received knowledge, the universities also played a role in both creating and diffusing new advances in various areas. The late-thirteenth-century astronomical tables originally produced for *Alfonso X of Castile have not survived. We know the Alfonsine Tables only in the version produced at the university of Paris with a new format and pedagogically appropriate instructions; it is the reworked university version that spread throughout Europe. The universities also created new knowledge. One of the most striking characteristics of the fourteenth century is the extent to which logical sophistication, often extensively tested in a scientific context, grew and influenced the way scholars pursued natural philosophy, medicine, and theology.

This development is noteworthy because logic was the chief tool of thought, including natural philosophy. In the fourteenth century, Merton was the institutional base for exciting developments at the interface between logic, mathematics, and natural philosophy. The "calculatores," as they were called, developed new analytical and logical tools to quantify and "measure" theoretically various qualities (speed, heat, whiteness, charity, etc.) These "languages of measurement" (Murdoch) characterize the intellectual outlook of the period. They spread into theology and medicine, without regard to differences in philosophical outlook (e.g., "nominalist" and "realist"). One approach, "the latitude of forms," probably derived from attempts to quantify both the "virtues" of medical compounds and the "just price" in economic theory at Montpellier. It assigned an extension (the latitude, literally "breadth") to a quality (the form), and analyzed various changes in the latter as a function of time (also treated as an extension or length). These and similar approaches to natural philosophical problems quickly spread from Oxford to mid-fourteenth-century Paris, to the new late-fourteenth-century universities in Germanic lands, and eventually to those of fifteenth-century Italy, where many texts from this tradition were copied and eventually printed. The fact that several universities eventually added these new approaches to the requirements for their degrees shows that the curricula were indeed responsive to new developments.

From the mid-fourteenth century onward, this diffusion took place on the heels of significant growth in the number of universities, in the territories of the Holy Roman Empire and beyond (Prague, Kraków, Vienna, Heidelberg, Erfurt, and Cologne, for example). Several of these foundations built on the diaspora of Germanic students and masters who were forced to leave Paris owing to the polarizations associated with of the Great Schism of the papacy, an incident that helps to explain the growing regionalism of the universities in the later Middle Ages.

The later fourteenth and fifteenth centuries proved difficult for Paris and Oxford but, as the preceding episode suggests, it is dangerous to generalize their institutional decline to include other universities. Remarkably, those of the Holy Roman Empire that have survived to our own day witnessed mid-fifteenth-century enrollment peaks unsurpassed until the late nineteenth and early twentieth centuries. Much of the intellectual life of these fifteenth-century universities, including their scientific activities, still remains to be explored.

Although the university excluded the mechanical arts from its curriculum, enough masters evinced manual skills to suggest that the academic environment was not inherently hostile to the enterprise. The inroads of surgery—a mechanical art—into Italian medical faculties in particular point to de facto accommodation, as does the appearance of human dissection. Instruction in the use of astronomical instruments was included in regular astronomical courses, while entire courses were sometimes devoted to instruments (e.g., at Vienna in the 1420s and 1430s). The invention of mechanical clockwork was perhaps the most striking example. It is a university text, Robertus Anglicus's 1271 commentary on Sacrobosco's *Tractatus de sphaera*, that first mentions intense research on the problem of the escapement, the eventual solution to which led two university-trained sons of artisans to construct the most sophisticated machines thus far devised—the astronomical clock of the St. Albans abbot Richard of Wallingford (d. 1336) and the astrarium of the Padua physician Giovanni Dondi (d. 1389). Not least, masters of arts were well represented among the first two generations of printers, including the astronomer *Johannes Regiomontanus (d. 1476), who specialized in printing mathematical and astronomical works.

From the thirteenth century onward, contemporaries noted that the universities had established themselves as a third power in their own right, alongside the church and the secular rulers. Although restricted to Christian men literate in Latin, the universities constituted a new socio-intellectual phenomenon of the first order, one that affected several hundred thousand individuals directly, and many more indirectly. Widely recognized as arbiters of competence, the medieval universities gave the scientific enterprise a semi-autonomous, permanent home and anchored it in European intellectual life.

See also **Aristotelianism; Ibn al-Haytham; Ibn Rushd; Ibn Sina; Optics and catoptrics**

Bibliography

Beaujouan, Guy. "Motives and Opportunities for Science in the Medieval University." In *Scientific Change*. Edited by Alistair C. Crombie. New York: Basic Books, 1963.

Berman, Harold. *Law and Revolution*. Cambridge: Harvard University Press, 1983.

Bullough, Vern. *The Development of Medicine as a Profession. The Contribution of the Medieval University to Modern Medicine*. New York: Karger, 1966.

Courtenay, William J. *Schools and Scholars in Fourteenth-Century England*. Princeton: Princeton University Press, 1987.

Courtenay, William J., Jürgen Miethke, David B Priest, eds. *Universities and schooling in medieval society*. Leiden: E.J. Brill, 2000.

Getz, Faye M. "The Faculty of Medicine before 1500." In *The History of the University of Oxford. Vol. 2: Late Medieval Oxford*. Edited by Jeremy Catto and Ralph Evans. Oxford: Oxford University Press, 1992, pp. 373–405.

Grant, Edward. "Science in the Medieval University." In *Rebirth, Reform and Resilience*. Edited by James M. Kittelson and Pamela J. Transue. Columbus: Ohio State University Press, 1984, pp. 68–102.

———. *God and Reason in the Middle Ages*. New York: Cambridge University Press, 2001.

Grendler, Paul F. *The Universities of the Italian Renaissance*. Baltimore: Johns Hopkins University Press, 2002.

Hoenen, M.J.F.M., J.H.J. Schneider, G. Wieland, eds. *Philosophy and Learning. Universities in the Middle Ages*. Leiden: E.J. Brill, 1995.

Kibre, Pearl and Nancy G. Siraisi. "The Institutional Setting: The Universities." In *Science of the Middle Ages*. Edited by David C. Lindberg. Chicago: University of Chicago Press, 1978, pp. 120–144.

Lawn, Brian. *The rise and decline of the scholastic* Quaestio disputata: *with special emphasis on its use in the teaching of medicine and science.* Leiden: E.J. Brill, 1993.

Leff, Gordon. *Paris and Oxford Universities in the Thirteenth and Fourteenth Centuries.* New York: Krieger, 1972.

Le Goff, Jacques. *Intellectuals in the Middle Ages.* Translated by Theresa L. Fagan. London: Blackwell, 1993.

Maieru, Alfonso. *University Training in Medieval Europe.* Leiden: E.J. Brill, 1994.

O'Boyle, Cornelius. *The Art of Medicine. Medical Teaching at the University of Paris, 1250–1400.* Leiden: E.J. Brill, 1998.

O'Boyle, Cornelius, Roger French and Fernando Salmón, eds. "El Aprendizaje de la Medicina en el mundo medieval: Las Fronteras de la Enseñanza universitaria." *Dynamis* (2000) 20: 17–393.

Ijsewijn, Jozef and Jacques Paquet, eds. *The Universities in the Late Middle Ages.* Leuven: Leuven University Press, 1978.

Rüegg, Walter, ed. *A History of the University in Europe. Vol. 1: Universities in the Middle Ages.* Edited by Hilde de Ridder-Symoens. New York: Cambridge University Press, 1992.

Shank, Michael H. *"Unless you believe, you shall not understand": logic, university, and society in late medieval Vienna.* Princeton: Princeton University Press, 1988.

Siraisi, Nancy. *Arts and Sciences at Padua: The Studium at Padua before 1350.* Toronto: Pontifical Institute of Medieval Studies, 1973.

———. *Medicine and the Italian universities, 1250–1600.* Leiden: E.J. Brill, 2001.

———. *Medieval and Early Renaissance Medicine. An Introduction to Knowledge and Practice.* Chicago: University of Chicago Press, 1990.

Sylla, Edith. "The Oxford Calculators." In *The Cambridge History of Later Medieval Philosophy.* Edited by Norman Kretzmann, Anthony Kenny, and Jan Pinborg. New York: Cambridge University Press, 1982. Pp. 540–563.

———. "Science for Undergraduates in Medieval Universities." In *Science and Technology in Medieval Society.* Edited by Pamela Long. Annals of the New York Academy of Sciences 441 (New York, 1985), pp. 171–186.

Thijssen, J.M.M.H. *Censure & Heresy at the University of Paris, 1200–1400.* Philadelphia: University of Pennsylvania Press, 1998.

Thorndike, Lynn. *University Records and Life in the Middle Ages.* New York: Columbia University Press, 1944.

Verger, Jacques. *Men of Learning in Europe at the End of the Middle Ages.* Translated by Lisa Neal and Steven Rendall. Notre Dame: University of Notre Dame Press, 2000.

MICHAEL SHANK

UQLIDISI, AL-

Abu' l-Hasan Ahmad ibn Al-Uqlidisi ("The Euclidean") lived probably in the first half of the tenth century in Abbasid Damascus. His *Kitab al-Fusul fi' l-hisab al-hindi* (*Book of the Sections on Indian Arithmetic*), written in 952, is the first extant Arabic work teaching the Indian decimal position system and its rules for calculation.

The book consists of an introduction and four parts. In the introduction, al-Uqlidisi undertakes to answer why the Indian methods—which he thinks are more powerful, easier to verify and better to control—did not manage to overtake the social and cultural spaces occupied by the more cumbersome methods of finger reckoning, which are open to cheating. As an answer he points to the instrumental side of Indian arithmetic, the so-called dust board, a board which is covered with sand and on which one writes the calculations, but cannot memorize them because of a lack of space. He proposes to replace the dust board by pen and paper. In the first three parts al-Uqlidisi teaches the methods of arithmetic as applied to the dust board. In the last part of the work he presents methods modified to the use of pen and paper.

In the first part, al-Uqlidisi introduces the basic concepts such as the nine letters or signs to be used for writing the nine Indian digits, a series of basic methods of calculation such as doubling and halving, multiplication, division, and extracting of roots and the methods applicable to sexagesimal numbers as used in *astronomy and *astrology. In the second part, al-Uqlidisi discusses various methods that are used for calculations including tricks and curiosities. This part differs from the first one by its higher level of complexity and comprehensiveness. The third part deals mainly with teaching how to check the result of calculating and discussing why the taught methods are justified. In the last part, after having discussed the modifications to what he had taught so far, al-Uqlidisi adds a few new points such as the description of a calculating tool for blind and weak-sighted people or the determination of the geometrical sum of 1 to 64, the so-called problem of the chess board.

The importance of al-Uqlidisi's work in the history of mathematics is usually seen in his representing in the third chapter of the second part some of the fractions he mentions in a decimal form. He does not claim, however, to be the inventor of this notation. Nor does he use it in a regular manner. His two standard forms of notating fractions are sexagesimal and ordinary fractions. Neither does he consider decimal fractions as a new type of fraction. As his text indicates, decimal fractions for al-Uqlidisi are the natural result of halving odd integers within the Indian decimal system.

The main importance of al-Uqlidisi's book lies rather in its author's substantial efforts to acculturate a foreign mode of calculating, to adapt its methods to local customs, and to improve its acceptance among local users by modernizing its technology.

See also **Arithmetic**

Bibliography

The Arithmetic of Al-Uqlidisi. Translated and annotated by A. S. Saidan. Dordrecht and Boston: D. Reidel, 1978.

SONJA BRENTJES

URSO OF CALABRIA

The medical writer and teacher Urso of Calabria is conventionally regarded as the last in the series of seminal figures associated with the "school" of *Salerno at its apogee (c. 1060–1220). The date of Urso's birth is unknown, but according to the confraternity necrology of San Matteo, Salerno, he died in 1225. It is doubtful whether he is identical with the Ursus Laudensis (Urso of Lodi) who composed the commentary on *Galen's Tegni preserved in MS Venice, Marciana lat. 2023, and who lectured in Cremona in 1198.

Urso's writings are closely aligned with those of *Bartholomaeus of Salerno and *Maurus of Salerno, particularly in their use of Aristotelian natural philosophy to construct a conceptual framework of medical theory, and in their approach to shaping medical knowledge into an academic discipline. He is the author of Aphorismi cum glossuli (a commented collection of axioms concerning the physical and physiological foundations of the processes, functions and changes characteristic of animated creatures), De commixtione elementorum, De effectibus qualitatum, De effectibus medicinarum, De gradibus de saporius et odoribus, and De coloribus. Two further treatises have been ascribed to him: De urinis and an Anatomia (the "Fourth Salernitan Anatomy"). In De commixtionibus elementorum, Urso mentions two other works: De pulsibus (possibly the De noticia pulsuum in Vatican City BAV Pal. lat. 1146) and De diebus creticis. This last treatise remains untraced.

Urso's writings extend the confines of medicine to embrace philosophy, physics, and even theological issues. Like Bartholomaeus and Maurus, he made creative use of newly available analytic tools, notably the Greco-Latin translations of Aristotle, particularly De generatione et corruptione and the fourth book of the Meteorologica. Urso may also have known the second book of the Meteorologica (translated from the Arabic by *Gerard of Cremona), and there are hints that he knew De caelo or at very least the pseudo-Avicennan De caelo et mundo. Following Maurus, Urso applied these to such topics as the nature of the *elements and qualities, the notion of mixture and complexion, and the biological phenomena that derive from these concepts. Interestingly, both men invoke the term elementatum (the "elemented," or the element as it exists in the real world, rather than in a pure state), which was a topic much discussed in the School of Chartres. Moreover they both furnished topics to the prose *Salernitan Questions—no fewer than ten in the case of Urso.

Urso was the most speculative, abstract, and logically sophisticated of the Salerno writers active in the later twelfth and early thirteenth century. Urso also departs from the pattern established by his Salernitan predecessors in another critical way: he composed no commentaries on the *Articella. Where Maurus discusses the elements in connection with the opening sections of *Hunayn ibn Ishaq's Isagoge, Urso devotes a separate treatise (De commixtione elementorum) to the subject. He glossed his own Aphorisms, rather than commenting on those of Hippocrates, and he composed his own treatise on pulses rather than expounding that of Philaretus. Nonetheless, it would not be entirely accurate to argue that Urso abandoned the textual and practical traditions of Salerno. In his seminal article on the School of Salerno, Kristeller comments that Urso's works, especially his commentary on his own Aphorisms, "contain a well developed system of natural philosophy intended to serve as a firm foundation for medical theory and practice. He establishes definite rules about substance, action, motion, and quality, discusses the effects of the four basic qualities, and attempts to derive from them the various diseases as well as their respective therapy." Despite his fascination with the study of matter and its transformation, Urso never loses sight of the physician's primary concern: the human body, its workings and its ills.

See also Aristotelianism; Medicine, theoretical

Bibliography

Primary Sources

[Aphorismi cum Glossulis]. Edited by R. Creutz, Die medizinisch-naturphilosophischen Aphorismen und Kommentare des Magister Urso Salernitanus. Quellen und Studien zur Geschichte der Naturwissenschaften und der Medizin (1936) 5: 1–192.

[De commixtionibus elementorum libellus]. Edited by Wolfgang Stürner in his Natur und Gesellschaft im Denken des Hoch- und Spätmittelalters. Stuttgarter Beiträge zur Geschichte und Politik 7. Stuttgart: Klett, 1976.

[De effectibus qualitatum and De effectibus medicinarum]. Matthaes, C. Der Salernitaner Arzt Urso aus der 2. Hälfte des 12. Jahrhunderts und seine beide Schriften "De effectibus qualitatum" und "De effectibus medicinarum." Ph.D. dissertation, Universität Leipzig, 1918.

[De effectibus qualitatum and De gradibus]. Edited by Karl Sudhoff, Die Salernitaner Handschrift in Breslau, ein Corpus medicinae Salerni. Archiv für Geschichte der Medizin (1920) 12: 139–143 and 135–138.

[De saporibus et odoribus] Hartmann, Friedrich. Die Literatur von Früh- und Hochsalerno und der Inhalt des Breslauer Codex Salernitanus mit erstmaliger Veröffentlichung zweier Traktate aus dieser Handschrift, Anonymous, De morbis quattuor regionum corporis, [Ursonis], De saporibus et numero eorundem, samt Wiederabdruck der Schrift, De observatione minutionis. M.D. dissertation, Universität Leipzig: Robert Noske, 1919.

[De coloribus]. Thorndike, Lynn. Some Medieval Texts on Colours. Ambix (1959) 7: 1–24 at 7–16.

[De urinis (ascribed to)]. Edited by P. Giacosa, Magistri Salernitani nondum editi. Turin: Fratelli Bocca, 1901, pp. 283–298.

[Anatomia]. Sudhoff, Karl. Die vierte Salernitaner Anatomie. Archiv für Geschichte der Medizin (1928) 20: 40–50.

Secondary Sources

Creutz, Rudolf. Urso, der letzte des Hochsalerno: Arzt, Philosoph, Theologe. Abhandlungen zur Geschichte der Medizin und der Naturwissenschaften 5. Berlin: E. Ebering, 1934.

Kristeller, Paul Oskar. The School of Salerno: its Development and its Contribution to the History of Learning. Bulletin of the History of Medicine (1945) 17: 138–194.

———. Studi sulla Scuola medica salernitana. Naples: Istituto italiano per gli studi filosofici, 1986.

Sudhoff, Karl. Constantin, der erste Vermittler muslimischer Wissenschaft ins Abendland und die beiden Salernitaner Frühscholastiker Maurus und Urso, als Exponenten dieser Vermittlung. Archeion (1932) 14 :359–369.

FAITH WALLIS

V

VINCENT OF BEAUVAIS

The Dominican friar Vincent of Beauvais (c. 1190–1264) was a prolific author who wrote many short pedagogical, theological, and devotional works. He is best known for a compendium or *summa* known as the *Speculum maius*. Divided into three parts, this colossal encyclopedia offered an overview of the classical and ecclesiastical knowledge available to late medieval scholars, as it mirrored the culture and thought of Scholastic society in the mid-thirteenth century. Until the eighteenth century it was considered to be the greatest European encyclopedia. Vincent's biography has been largely overshadowed by his voluminous writings. Modern scholars have only a brief outline of his personal life and activities, and some of those are more approximations than known facts. Apparently he was born and died in his native Beauvais. He joined the new Dominican Order around 1220 and studied at the University of Paris. Plausible conjecture has Vincent transferred to the new Dominican priory established in his home town ten years later. Vincent developed a very close relationship with the nearby Cistercian Abbey of Royaumont and with King Louis IX of France whose favorite residence was in the Royaumont-Beauvais area. Through their friendship Vincent enjoyed royal favor and was appointed lector at Royaumont.

Over the years Vincent developed a plan to organize all sacred and profane knowledge into a systematic compilation that would make the wisdom of earlier authors more readily available to his fellow preaching Dominicans. On hearing of Vincent's growing collection of quotations and excerpts, Louis IX requested a copy for himself and offered financial assistance to help finish the project. The *Speculum maius* originally was divided into two parts, the *Naturale* (description of the physical world), and the *Historiale* (a universal history from Creation to 1254). Vincent reorganized his encyclopedia several times; the first draft is usually dated 1244 and the last about 1260. He produced a third part, the *Doctrinale* (theoretical and practical arts and sciences). In the early fourteenth century, a fourth part, the *Morale* (drawn chiefly from the *Summa*

theologiae of *Thomas Aquinas) was anonymously added to the *Speculum*. All later printed editions contain these four parts even though Vincent compiled only the first three.

The *Speculum maius* covered all human history, summarized all known *natural history and scientific knowledge, and provided a thorough compendium on literature, law, politics, and economics. The *Naturale* consists of thirty-two books and 3,718 chapters, and is based on the scheme of the biblical six days of creation. It begins with an account of the Trinity, and then moves on to treat angels and demons, light and color, the four elements, cosmography, physiology, *psychology, physics, *botany, *zoology, *mineralogy, and *agriculture. Vincent's coverage of space, time, and motion; chemistry and alchemy; flora and fauna; air, rain, lightning, and clouds; mammals, birds, fishes, and reptiles; metals and precious stones; plants and herbs; medicine, organs, and the five senses; and geography, seas, and tides summarized all natural history known in thirteenth century Europe.

The *Doctrinale* consists of seventeen books and 2,374 chapters. Intended as a useful manual for students and officials alike, it deals primarily with the practical and mechanical arts. After defining philosophy, Vincent covers the liberal arts including grammar, rhetoric, and poetics; virtues and vices; economic topics such as building, herding, and vineyards; anatomy, medicine, and surgery; education; and politics and jurisprudence. Under mathematics he covers music, geometry, astronomy, *astrology, and *weights and measures. It is noteworthy that Vincent indicates exposure to Arabic numerals, even if he does not call them by that name. But he does talk about digits, place value, and the zero.

The popularity and influence of the *Speculum maius* are evident in the numerous extant manuscripts, excerpts, and summaries, as well as from medieval translations of all or parts of the work into French, Catalan, Spanish, Dutch, and German. It was printed four times in the fifteenth century, once in the sixteenth, and once in the seventeenth. The 1624 Douai edition, reprinted in facsimile in 1964–1965, is the most readily available and

Vincent of Beauvais reading in his study (miniature dated c. 1475–1500). (Topham/The British Library/HIP)

thus the most frequently cited version even though the 1473–1476 Strasbourg edition of Johann Mentelin is generally considered the most reliable text. The lack of a modern critical edition makes it difficult to study and evaluate confidently the organization, sources, and content of Vincent's encyclopedia.

While Vincent's masterful orchestration of divergent sources reveals a very logical and rational mind, he is somewhat gullible at times, intermingling superstition, myth, fable, and miracles with verifiable factual data and scientific knowledge. This master compiler is as good as his sources (more than four hundred), which are cited with amazing regularity and accuracy. Vincent's masterpiece is a composite of quotations and excerpts from earlier pagan and Christian authors. He made no claims to originality (his few interjections are designated with the word "actor"), and he took pride in being the great organizer who collected, classified, and arranged his summary of human knowledge into a single unified whole. Accordingly, Vincent's *Speculum maius* is the best and largest medieval encyclopedia. The three parts together consist of over three million words in 9,885 chapters in eighty books. According to current estimates, it would require over fifty modern octavo volumes to print the entire *Speculum* text.

See also **Astronomy, Latin; Encyclopedias; Music theory**

Bibliography

Aerts, W.J., E.R. Smits and J.B. Voorbij, eds. *Vincent of Beauvais and Alexander the Great: Studies on the Speculum maius and its translations into medieval vernaculars.* Groningen: E. Forsten, 1986.

Tobin, Rosemary Barton. *Vincent of Beauvais' "De eruditione filiorum nobilium": The Education of Women.* New York: P. Lang, 1984.

GREGORY G. GUZMAN

VOCABULARY

The language of science, technology, and medicine in the Western Middle Ages was almost exclusively Latin. This article will be limited to the vocabulary of that language, although the influence of Greek and Arabic in these fields was also very strong.

There were various names for the concept of science itself, the most important being *ars* (art) and *scientia* (science). The ancient distinction between *ars* on the one hand, for knowledge of a practical kind, and *scientia* or *disciplina* (discipline) on the other, for more theoretical knowledge, was often repeated, but in practice the terms became largely interchangeable. In the early Middle Ages, the sciences were classified according to the four disciplines of the *quadrivium: arithmetica* (arithmetic), *geometria* (geometry), *astronomia* (astronomy; *astrologia* was sometimes used for the same science), and *musica* (music; sometimes called *harmonia*). The quadrivium formed, with the three disciplines of the trivium (grammar, dialectic, and rhetoric), the seven *artes liberales* (liberal arts). In later classifications of the sciences, the four disciplines were often grouped with the theoretical sciences under the name *mathematica* (mathematics) or *scientia disciplinalis* or *doctrinalis*. Other sciences were added as *scientia subalternata* (subalternate science); these included *perspectiva* (optics), which was considered a part of geometry. The sciences of natural philosophy were called *physica* (physics) or *scientia (philosophia) naturalis*. From the discovery and translation of the Aristotelian works onwards, this natural philosophy was divided according to these texts. Thus, *meteora* (*meteorology) clearly indicated the science described by Aristotle in his book *Meteora*. The term *physiologia* was sometimes used for the particular science of physics, but after the entry of Aristotelian science into the university curriculum, and outside the classifications, *physica* was more usual in this sense. So, *physica* had at least three meanings: first, it could be the general name for the natural sciences; second, it might indicate the discipline of physics; and third, it could also be used for medicine. Some of the Aristotelian books were designated by the common name *parva naturalia* ("small books on natural science"). Among them were *De sensu et sensato* (*On sense and sense perception*), *De somno et vigilia* (*On sleep and being awake*), *De memoria and reminiscentia* (*On memory and reminiscence*), *De longitudine et brevitate vite* (*On the length and shortness of life*), which would all be within the modern notion of biology, along with Aristotle's books on the animals and, partly, his *De generatione et corruptione* (*On generation and corruption*). *Cosmology was not absent, of course. It was taught on the basis of Aristotle's *De caelo et mundo* (*On the heaven and the world*). In earlier times, the science of describing (parts of) the world was known as *cosmimetria* or *cosmigraphia*.

Magic was a very old art—in antiquity the *magicae artes* were mentioned by for instance Virgil—but it was for a long time excluded from the field of official science. In medieval classifications of the sciences it was often treated at the very end, after the scheme of the other sciences or given a place under the name of *scientia illicita* or *scientia inutilis* (illicit or useless science).

The technical terminology used by the various sciences is too large to be treated here. Some examples will be given from the fields of mathematics and astronomy. The science of mathematics itself was called (*ars*) *mathematica* (but this term can also designate all four disciplines of the quadrivium, as described above) or (*ars*) *arithmetica* (*arithmetic). The Latin tradition of the works of the Arab scholar *al-Khwarizimi led to the introduction of the word *algorismus* or *alchorismus* in the twelfth century. It was used for mathematics in general and implies the "Indian" art of calculation based on the nine ciphers and the zero, in contrast to earlier, traditional systems such as digital calculation. At the same time, the older terms *mathematica* and *arithmetica* remained in use, not only for arithmetic with Roman ciphers, but also for arithmetic or calculation with the decimal system. The abacus (calculatory table or reckoning board), used before the introduction of the Indian-Arabic tradition, was not abandoned as an aid to the practical technique of calculating. Masters called *abacisti* or *magistri abaci* taught their art in specialized calculus schools. The term *algebra, also introduced in the twelfth century, came from another work by the same Arab mathematician al-Khwarizimi, the "Compendious book on calculation by completion (*al-jabr*) and balancing." The word became common only in the sixteenth century. It was used for the technique of solution paradigms for different types of problems, using equations in which the actual numbers were replaced by symbols (for instance $ax^2 = bx$). In Latin treatises on arithmetic all kinds of traditional Latin words were used—examples include *adulterinus numerus* for the difference between a true root and an approximate root—but new words were also introduced, such as *cifra* (zero), *unitaliter* (in a manner equal to a unity). The word *computus* was used in the general meaning of reckoning or counting, but it had also the specific technical meaning of computation of time and it could name its products: a book containing its rules and methods, or a *calendar.

The terms *astronomia* and *astrologia* were both used for the science of the cosmos in general, including astronomy, the science of dimensions and quantities of the celestial orbs and bodies, and *astrology, the study of celestial powers and their effects on the terrestrial region. The modern distinction between the two concepts is also found in certain classical and medieval sources, but generally the two terms were interchangeable throughout the medieval period. One of the well-known instruments of astronomy, the astrolabe or flat disk reproducing the celestial sphere, was first called *walzachora*, but soon afterwards the terms *astrolapsus* and *astrolabium* were introduced. These last two terms were synonymous, but from the end of the eleventh century *astrolabium* imposed itself. The quadrant was first called *quadra astrolabii* before the word *quadrans* came into use. Other instruments for measuring time were the *horologium* and the *horoscopum*. The word *horologium* usually indicates the plate that enables the hour of the day to be read from the position of the Sun, although it sometimes means

"astrolabe." *Horoscopum*, another instrument that permits clockreading, can also be synonymous with astrolabe, but at the same time it kept its traditional astronomical meaning of "ascendant." Some Arabic words, through medieval Latin astrolabe treatises, have survived into modern times. These include "zenith," a term of spherical astronomy, indicating the highest point in the celestial sphere, and its antonym, "nadir."

Technology

The modern concept of technology is roughly equivalent to the medieval *artes mechanicae* (mechanical arts). In the early Middle Ages, the seven mechanical arts paralleled the seven liberal arts, and the expression is first found in the ninth century, but their rehabilitation as part of practical science occurred only in the twelfth century, when *Hugh of Saint-Victor included them in his classification of the sciences and defined them as follows: *lanificium* (fabric-making), *armatura* (armament and architecture), *navigatio* (commerce), *agricultura* (agriculture), *venatio* (hunting and food), *medicina* (medicine), and *theatrica* (theatrics). This scheme was taken over by other authors, with some variations. For instance, commerce was also known as *mercatura* or *negotiatoria*, the art of hunting and food was referred to as *ars cibativa* or *ars nutritiva*. Although the mechanical arts were sometimes given pejorative labels such as *serviles* (servile) or *adulterinae* (adulterous), this does not reflect the general estimation of manual labor or technological progress. Note that alchemy was sometimes, during the thirteenth century, considered a mechanical art and that the term *mechanicus* was used for alchemists.

Medicine

While *medicina* (medicine) was sometimes ranked as a mechanical art, generally it was considered a part of natural science and was as such called *physica terrestris* ("physical science concerning terrestrial or corporeal things"). In some contexts, the term *physicus* (natural philosopher) became the equivalent of *medicus* (medical doctor or physician). At university faculties of medicine the discipline was called *scientia* or *facultas medicine*, and also *physice facultas*.

At an early stage, medicine was divided into *theorica* and *practica* (theoretical and practical), the first being speculative, the second, sometimes called *cirurgia* (surgery), based on the application of the theory to physical reality. The two branches were intimately linked, and the distinction was not always easily maintained. For example, the vocabulary of theoretical medicine was used to describe the parts of the body, but that of practical medicine was used to describe the treatment of illnesses.

After the introduction of the Greco-Latin version of *Galen's treatise on the art of medicine, the term *doctrina* acquired a special meaning in medical vocabulary. It designated the teaching or organization of science in three steps: *dissolutio* or *resolutio*, dissolution by way of analysis; *compositio*, orderly composition or synthesis of the materials found through analysis; and *dissolutio termini* or *definitionis*, the dissolution or decomposition of the definition. This concept of *doctrina* was also applied to experimental science outside the field of medicine.

Another technical term is *ingenium*, which acquired a special meaning from the thirteenth century onward. It originated in the Arabo-Latin translation of Galen's treatise and appears mainly in phrases such as *ingenium sanitatis*, *ingenium sanativum*, and *ingenium curationis* ("methods and tools to reach health"). Two Greek concepts, that of method and that of artifice or device, are expressed by the single Latin word *ingenium*.

See also **Astrolabes and quadrants; Magic and the occult; Optics and catoptrics;** *Scientia*

Bibliography

Allard, A. "La formation du vocabulaire latin de l'arithmétique médiévale." In *Méthodes et instruments du travail intellectuel au moyen âge*. Edited by O. Weijers. Turnhout: Brepols, 1990, pp. 137–181.

Clagett, M. *The Science of Mechanics in the Middle Ages*. Madison: University of Wisconsin Press, 1961.

Craemer-Ruegenberg, I. and A. Speer, ed. *"Scientia" und "ars" im Hoch- und Spätmittelalter*. 2 vols. Berlin and New York: Walter de Gruyter, 1994.

Jacquart, D. "L'enseignement de la médecine. Quelques termes fondamentaux." In *Méthodes et instruments du travail intellectuel au moyen âge*. Edited by O. Weijers. Turnhout: Brepols, 1990, pp. 104–120.

Poulle, E. "Astrolabium," "astrolapsus," "horologium": enquête sur un vocabulaire. In *Science antique, science médiévale*. Edited by L. Callebat and O. Desbordes. Hildesheim, Zürich and New York: Olms-Weidmann, 2000: 437–448.

Teeuwen, Mariken. *The Vocabulary of Intellectual Life in the Middle Ages*. Turnhout: Brepols, 2003.

Weijers, O. L'appellation des disciplines dans les classifications des sciences aux XIIe et XIIIe siècles. *Archivum Latinitatis Medii Aevi* (1986–1987) 46–47: 39–64.

Weisheipl, J.A. Classification of the Sciences in Medieval Thought. *Mediaeval Studies* (1965) 27: 54–90.

Whitney, E. Paradise Restored. *The Mechanical Arts from Antiquity through the Thirteenth Century*. Philadelphia: Transactions 80: 1, 1990.

OLGA WEIJERS

W

WATER SUPPLIES AND SEWERAGE

The historiography of medieval water supplies has shifted away from blanket condemnations of medieval hydraulics and hygiene, and from linear narratives of technological progress. Recent scholarship presents a more variegated mosaic of local continuities and discontinuities, innovations and adaptations, successes and failures. Greater emphasis is being placed on the ways in which hydraulic technology was embedded in its social, economic, and cultural contexts. Although the majority of studies are still conducted within national or institutional frameworks, it is becoming clear that many of the technologies associated with water control were transnational in character, and that technical knowledge was diffused across social boundaries. The role of religion in technology transfer has been well established, but less is known about the diffusion process on the peripheries of Western Christendom, where crosscurrents from Byzantine or Islamic traditions may have come into play. Many researchers are adopting interdisciplinary approaches, bringing together evidence from documents (such as charters, administrative records, financial accounts, narratives, statutes, and court records), visual representations (art works, waterworks plans), standing structures, and archaeology.

Medieval water systems can often be dated with a high degree of precision, thanks to documents such as conduit licenses or land-acquisition charters. Since many of the components were subterranean structures, they have a good chance of surviving in datable archeological contexts. It is thus possible to chart the pace of technological change over a period of centuries, and trace the evolution of complex technological systems in a pre-modern society. There is also ample evidence for the technology's social context: the names and activities of patrons, donors, craftsmen, wardens, users, even accident victims and vandals are often preserved in medieval records. A complex pattern of technical discard and reversion as well as adoption and progress raises broader theoretical questions. Since advanced hydraulic technology was available for adoption, why did its diffusion remain so restricted? Which aspects of medieval society promoted—and which inhibited—technology transfer?

Although evidence for medieval hydraulic technology in general is relatively widespread, it is typically incomplete and fragmentary for any given water system. The parts are better understood than the whole. While it is possible to reconstruct the detailed hydraulic activities of some individual craftsmen, much less is known about broader mechanisms for the transmission of technical expertise. Overall, our knowledge of individual hydraulic components far outstrips our understanding of the configurations and flow efficiencies of complete systems.

Chronological Overview

The hydraulic technology of medieval Europe owed a substantial debt to Roman engineering. The gravity-flow systems of channels and pipes that conveyed water to towns and monasteries in the High Middle Ages were composed of hydraulic components that closely resembled their classical counterparts. Was this the result of an unbroken technological tradition in western Europe, or did it derive from a reintroduction of Roman-style engineering after a technological hiatus? The political collapse of the Western Roman Empire did not coincide with a parallel collapse of Roman traditions of engineering. The technology did not disappear—it was adapted to new ends in late antiquity and the early Middle Ages. Even before the "Fall of the Rome" hydraulic patronage was shifting away from the secular munificence of large-scale aqueducts and luxurious public baths to more modest ecclesiastical structures such as baptistry fonts, charitable baths, and atrium fountains. These new Christian waterworks helped to preserve the knowledge of subterranean pipes, hydraulic cement, and even inverted siphons. Some classical aqueducts were restored or remained in use during the early Middle Ages, often thanks to episcopal patronage. In Rome itself, the popes of the eighth and ninth centuries undertook the restoration of four aqueducts. Several early monasteries built entirely new aqueduct systems, or adapted Roman aqueducts to supply their cloisters. Secular patronage of water systems also persisted. The Ostrogothic king Theodoric restored aqueducts in Ravenna, Verona, and Parma, while Carolingian palaces at Ingelheim and Aachen had complex waterworks. The broader picture, however, was one of technological regression during late antiquity and the early Middle Ages. The majority of complex Roman water systems gradually decayed and were abandoned, probably due primarily to the breakdown of maintenance regimes in a period of urban decline and political instability. By the year 1000, most local communities were obtaining their water from rivers, wells, and cisterns, a simpler level of technology more appropriate to a less urbanized society.

In the eleventh and twelfth centuries, however, numerous new water systems were being constructed throughout western Europe. Most of the new conduits were initially built to supply religious houses or royal or episcopal palaces, but the technological revival soon spread from monasteries and palaces to the burgeoning towns, as well to as a few hospitals, castles, and gardens. The diffusion of technological awareness and know-how was stimulated by the rapid expansion of new religious orders, such as the Cistercians, Dominicans, and Franciscans, and by the widespread physical mobility of the High Middle Ages. Pilgrims, crusaders, university students, and merchants would have encountered conduits and fountains in the course of their travels. Expertise in hydraulic engineering was not confined to a single craft tradition: systems were built by monks and laymen, goldsmiths, masons, plumbers, and carpenters. By the close of the Middle Ages a number of cities were providing their citizens with piped water from public fountains, and a few were overcoming the topographical limitations of traditional gravity-flow systems by incorporating artificial lifting-devices and water towers. Nevertheless, advanced hydraulic engineering was still too complex and too expensive an undertaking for most local communities. The majority of Europeans would remain dependent on rivers and wells as sources of domestic and industrial water.

Hydraulic Technology

Complex hydraulic systems provided for the collection, conveyance, and distribution of water. At the source, water was collected into one or more receptacles (reservoirs, collection basins, or roofed conduit houses). Some conduit-heads included a series of settling tanks (some with perforated filters) which served to purify the water. Springs were the preferred source of water for systems catering to consumption and domestic uses. If springs were not available, fluvial water was used to supply conduit pipes. The capacity of most conduit reservoirs was modest, so even where piped systems were available, they might be complemented by open-channel systems fed by rivers. Such artificial watercourses could supply a greater quantity of water, even if the quality was compromised.

Conveyance subsystems were composed of pipes, channels, or some combination of both. Pipes were fabricated from lead, wood, or terra-cotta, and used both for intake systems and drains. Generally, pipe systems depended on gravity flow, although lead and wooden pipes were also used in low-pressure systems and inverted siphons. Most pipes were laid in subterranean trenches, although they might be carried across rivers on bridges. Pipe runs were often punctuated by small intermediate tanks, which could serve as junction boxes, inspection chambers, purification tanks, or manholes for maintenance and cleaning. These intermediate structures also helped reduce static pressure in the pipelines, and were sometimes used as dipping places for drawing water.

Channels were used for intake systems to convey fresh water, and as drains to carry off storm runoff, waste water, and sewage. Many channels were simply unlined ditches, but some had timber or wattle linings to reinforce the sides. Masonry channels are the best preserved. Most masonry channels had low gradients and rectangular cross-sections, but occasionally portions of a channel will exhibit a steeper gradient and trapezoidal or U-shaped profiles. These modifications generally occur in segments (such as those under latrine blocks) which were particularly vulnerable to blockage, and suggest that at least some medieval engineers had a good empirical knowledge of ways to optimize flow efficiencies. Open channels were often covered with planks or capstones, to protect the purity of fresh water or to contain noxious odors. Bridges and tunnels were used to maintain channel gradients across topographical irregularities. In a few places, subterranean galleries were themselves key components of hydraulic systems. In Iberia, a Persian-style qanat was used to supply water to Madrid, while more modest qanats were employed by peasant cultivators. Somewhat similar subterranean galleries occur in Siena, where a network of seepage tunnels fed civic fountains.

The end point of a water system was its distribution structure. This could be a simple standpipe or a sunken cistern, but often it took the form of a fountain. Spill fountains discharged water directly from a pipe or channel into a trough. Splash fountains used an inverted siphon to pipe water up a central shaft, from whence it cascaded from into one or more basins. In some systems several fountains were linked together in a chain of inverted siphons, so that the overflow water from one fountain fed the next fountain along the pipeline. Whereas most other components of a water system were hidden from view, fountains were highly visible structures, and fountain shafts and basins were often elaborately decorated.

The expansion of spring-fed, gravity-flow systems was limited by the amount of water available at the source, and the high cost of conveyance structures. By the close of the Middle Ages, artificial lifting-devices were being employed to raise water from rivers into water towers, which served as collection basins for piped systems. The technology of lifting-devices was not new: the Romans had been familiar with water-screws, pumps, and water-lifting wheels. In the Middle Ages shadufs, windlasses, and pulleys were used to raise water from wells, and, at least in the Iberian peninsula, norias (water-lifting wheels powered by the current or by animals) were widespread.

The German cities of the flat northern plains were among the earliest communities to apply the technology of water-lifting to urban water systems. Lübeck had a bucket-wheel by 1294 to supply the upper reaches of the town. By the fifteenth century lifting-wheels were civic status symbols in other Hanseatic cities, and the technology had spread to towns in southern Germany and Switzerland. More complex water engines were created by using pumps in addition to water wheels (an evolution stimulated, perhaps, by parallel developments in engines for draining mining shafts). The use of lifting-devices freed engineers from the topographical restrictions imposed by a reliance on springs, and enabled them to deliver larger quantities of water more economically to urban consumers. The hidden cost came at the expense of water quality: spring-fed conduits delivered water that was relatively pure, whereas untreated river water was far more likely to be polluted with sewage and industrial wastes.

Monastic and Urban Water Systems

Religious houses played a key role in the diffusion of advanced hydraulic technology. Although Cistercian water systems are the most famous, long-distance water systems were built to supply the houses of many orders of monks, nuns, friars, and canons. Both large and small religious houses built water systems, but cost could be a limiting factor. In England, few houses with incomes less than one hundred pounds per year were able to afford advanced waterworks, but for those above that threshold, rates of adoption seem to have approached twenty-five per cent.

Three surviving waterworks plans—those of the Benedictines at Christ Church Canterbury, the Augustinian canons at Waltham Abbey in Essex, and the Carthusians of London's Charterhouse—are among the most valuable sources of evidence for the configurations of hydraulic systems as a whole. Much of the best archeological evidence for medieval hydraulic technology also comes from monastic sites: recent excavations of the water system at Maubuisson, France, have been particularly thorough.

Medieval monastic waterworks were carefully planned and well-integrated systems that served small, cohesive communities. Monastic customaries called for regulated, synchronized patterns of water usage. At prescribed points in the day, all monks washed their hands and faces at the cloister laver. Shaving (also at the laver) or bathing in the bathhouse were activities performed by the entire community at set times. A complex water system was not a necessary feature in the life of a religious community, but a laver with multiple spouts or a reredorter with rows of latrine stalls could help that life run smoothly by accommodating the peak demands of simultaneous users. Besides feeding the main cloister lavatorium, water was piped to infirmaries, kitchens, brewhouses, bakeries, guesthouses, and bathhouses. Monastic houses also were furbished with sophisticated drainage networks. Smaller channels fed storm runoff and waste water into subterranean "great drains," large masonry tunnels which ran beneath the reredorters and were often flushed with running water.

Many medieval cities were situated on rivers or streams, and a number of communities created extensive networks of man-made channels and canals. Public or private dikes, embankments, and timber or stone revetments were used to control flooding. In some cities, such as London, the encroachment of numerous revetments into the streambed resulted in an extensive zone of land reclamation along the river frontage and significantly altered natural flow regimes. Watercourses (whether natural or artificial) could be used for defense, transport, mills, irrigation, fire-protection, and waste-disposal, and supplied water for domestic use, animals, and water-dependent urban industries (such as brewing, cloth dying, or leather tanning). Other common sources of urban water were groundwater (tapped by private and public wells) and rain-water (collected in cisterns or barrels). A minority of medieval cities supplemented these traditional water sources by building civic conduits, which supplied water to public fountains. The adoption of a public water system required a sustained commitment, as construction was expensive and could take many years. In order to mitigate the high costs, some cities collaborated with nearby religious houses. The public water systems in Paris, Dublin, and several British towns were linked to ecclesiastical water systems. Several Italian cities refurbished stretches of decaying Roman aqueducts or acquired private fountains and incorporated them into new municipal systems. Compared to other public works (defensive walls, bridges, public buildings), water systems remained uncommon, but once built they proved very popular. Municipal authorities who did adopt them found themselves fielding petitions for more fountains, additional water sources, and private branch pipes feeding off the public supply. They also had to find ways to ensure that pipes, channels, and fountains were properly cleaned and maintained.

City fountains provided numerous practical advantages. Conduits fed by springs which lay outside the zone of urban waste-disposal conveyed water of much better quality than that supplied by polluted urban rivers or groundwater. Aqueducts supplemented traditional supplies in hilltop cities which faced a dearth of accessible water in a period when urban populations and the industrial demand for water were rapidly increasing. A convenient neighborhood fountain reduced the arduous journey to fetch water from a distant source. The need for better fire-protection was another argument that was used to justify the construction of new fountains. In addition to these tangible benefits, a public fountain was an emblem of communal pride and a venue for displays of civic or national identity. Fountains such as Perugia's elaborately sculpted Fontana Maggiore and Nürnberg's soaring Schöne Brunnen were eye-catching focal points in core public spaces. London's civic conduits were decked out as stages for symbolic pageants during patriotic processions, and flowed with wine to celebrate events such as the victory at Agincourt or the birth of a prince.

Civic statutes, guild ordinances, royal decrees, fountain wardens, and informal social sanctions were all employed in an ongoing battle to protect public water supplies against pollution and vandalism. Conflicts between competing users forced civic authorities to arbitrate disputes, while citizens had to learn that not all activities appropriate to the riverbank were suitable in the basin of a public fountain. Brewers and fishmongers were accused of taking too much water from public conduits, while butchers, leather workers, and cloth dyers polluted streets, watercourses, and fountains with their occupational wastes. Some cities mitigated the problem by adapting their fountains to meet the needs of a wider range of users. In Siena, for example, the main public fountains were provided with specialized, subsidiary basins for rinsing water jars, watering animals, and laundering clothes.

Urban drainage systems were generally less sophisticated than their monastic counterparts. Sewage and other liquid wastes were deposited in cesspits, gutters, or watercourses. Street kennels were often simply open channels, but a few towns, such as Paris, provided covers for their municipal sewers. Several cities had public latrines, and many issued sanitation ordinances to regulate waste disposal and reduce the noxious odors in the interest of public decency and health. Nevertheless, the widespread reliance on pits and open watercourses for the disposal of wastes and sewage rendered urban groundwater supplies and streams vulnerable to contamination by waterborne pathogens.

Overall, the cities of medieval Europe lagged well behind religious houses in the adoption of complex hydraulic technology. The great majority of medieval towns did not even attempt to build public water systems. In part this technological "indifference" may be due to the fact that the scale of medieval hydraulic technology was a poor fit when it was set against the scale of an urban community. Local springs could provide a sufficient supply of clean water for a convent with a few dozen monks, but they could not supply a city of several thousand inhabitants. Even the most ambitious urban water systems (like the Roman aqueducts before them) did no more that supplement more traditional water sources. Spring-fed civic conduits did provide water that was clean, but they could never provide it in sufficient quantities to eliminate (or probably even seriously reduce) the citizens' reliance on rivers and wells. Systems with lifting-devices distributed greater quantities of water, but that water was no more potable than the local river itself. Civic water systems were viewed as prestigious and desirable urban amenities, but they were seldom seen as essential public services.

See also **Noria**

Bibliography

Glick, T. *Irrigation and Hydraulic Technology: Medieval Spain and its Legacy.* Aldershot: Variorum, 1996.
Guillerme, A. *The Age of Water: The Urban Environment in the North of France, A.D. 300–1800.* College Station: Texas A&M University Press, 1988.
Magnusson, R. *Water Technology in the Middle Ages: Cities, Monasteries, and Waterworks after the Roman Empire.* Baltimore: The John Hopkins University Press, 2001.
Skelton, R.A., and P.D.A. Harvey. *Local Maps and Plans from Medieval England.* Oxford: Clarendon Press, 1986.
Squatriti, P. *Water and Society in Early Medieval Italy, A.D. 400–1000.* New York: Cambridge University Press, 1998.
———, ed. *Working with Water in Medieval Europe: Technology and Resource-Use.* Leiden: E.J. Brill, 2000.

ROBERTA J. MAGNUSSON

WATERMILLS

In the Middle Ages water-driven mills were the most powerful land-based machines. Strictly speaking a machine for grinding cereals, legumes and other foodstuffs, the word "mill" (Latin *molendinum*, from *molere*, to grind) came to be applied to all subsequently-developed machines powered by water, so that contemporaries could speak also of mills for finishing cloth, or sawing wood, for example. (During the Industrial Revolution the word was further extended to apply even to textile and metal-working installations powered by steam). As might be expected with such an important technology, interpretations of its development and significance have differed, a situation accentuated by the uneven quality both of the surviving evidence and of twentieth-century research. In the wake of the still-impressive but perforce limited *History of Cornmilling* by Richard Bennett and John Elton, completed in 1904, a very few historians together constructed a perception of the mill that more recent—and more thorough—research has considerably modified.

The watermill was an invention of the ancient world, recorded from the first century B.C.E. It was for long usually accepted that mills were, nevertheless, little used in the Roman Empire, as a consequence of a mentality and an economy that preferred to use slaves rather than machines. In 1935 French historian Marc Bloch began to build a theory of medieval innovation on that perception: he believed, in effect, that the feudal lords of the Middle Ages discovered the hitherto little-used watermill to be an effective and attractive means of exploiting their social subordinates. Using their powers of local jurisdiction, the aristocratic class reserved to itself the right to build and own watermills (and later also *windmills) which they then forced their tenants to use—at an exorbitant price. The handmills the peasants would far rather have used were deemed illegal. The theory was further developed in a simplified form—that the watermill and other medieval innovations (whether genuine or supposed) showed that medieval people, inspired by western Christianity, were eager for labor-saving technological innovation. The theory was expounded by Lynn White, Jr., in a series of publications from 1940 and by his pupils and followers, and most extravagantly in a popular book by Jean Gimpel.

Little of that is tenable any longer. Modern archaeology is demonstrating that watermills were already frequently used during the late Empire, and continued to be used—probably without interruption—during the more troubled centuries that followed. Moreover it is clear now that mills were in early use outside the "civilized" world, and that historians must turn away from earlier prejudices that saw the watermill as an example of the sort of progress that only more "advanced" societies could achieve. Surviving remains show that watermills were well-known in non-Romanized Ireland in the early seventh century, with the oldest Irish literature and laws suggesting even earlier familiarity with the technology. The remains of more than thirty Irish mills have been dated to the early medieval centuries, a reflection both of the sophistication of modern dating techniques (in particular dendrochronology or tree-ring dating) and the impressive degree of preservation of ancient timbers in Irish peat bogs. If such evidence is lacking for other parts of Europe, this is more likely a reflection of the uneven survival of archeological remains rather than any cultural predispositions favouring or disfavoring watermill use.

Documentation for other parts of Europe during these centuries is poor, but nevertheless there are scattered references to early post-Roman mills in Italy, Gaul, and—from 762—in England. One must assume that had the quality of archeological evidence generally matched that both from late Roman settlements and from Ireland we should now see a pattern of very widespread watermill use perhaps by the third century, continuing without serious dislocation and probably indeed intensifying during the ensuing period of the establishment of the new barbarian kingdoms. The mills of Italy have been well studied, and the apparent appearance of so many mills there after 700 should be seen not as a new development in technology but a reflection of the survival of so much more documentation thereafter.

Bloch's theory of medieval innovation based on his case-study of the watermill is not supported by the facts, although his realization of how profitable the watermill would become to its owners was essentially correct. And unquestionably feudal lords in the regions studied by Bloch (northern France and England, essentially) were imposing a monopoly of milling on their tenants by at least the eleventh century. Whilst we do not know how far back in time that practice went, the watermill was surely well established and common in Europe long before the new feudal aristocracy learned how to exploit it for their own profit. The innovation we can observe, therefore, is not a development in technology but a new assertiveness on the part of the aristocracy, a significant extension of their authority over their social subordinates. What form did that new assertiveness take? As Bloch observed, territorial lords in many parts of western Europe claimed that only they had the right to own and operate mills, and that their tenants had a legal duty to use no other than their lord's mill—and certainly not a mill of their own, not even a handmill. Those claims were often only imperfectly translated into practice, but aristocratic ambition had legal backing. Whether lords rented out their mills or had them operated by an employee, we can begin to observe from the eleventh century onwards how great the incomes from milling could be, and how great the incentive was for any feudal lord with a suitable stream to own a mill. England was not the most

technologically advanced region of Europe, nor probably particularly backward. When its new Norman king, William I, ordered all the lands and properties of the kingdom he had conquered to be surveyed and valued in 1086, a total of 6082 mills were recorded—on average around two per settlement. Domesday Book was a unique survey in contemporary Europe, but as with the earlier Irish archeological evidence it would be perverse to interpret it as unrepresentative. The rest of eleventh-century western Europe, just like England, was full of watermills.

Although Domesday Book seldom provides details for each mill beyond its ownership, location and value, the exploitation of water resources was clearly advanced. The only parts of England with few or no mills were those lacking usable water resources (and indeed these were generally the areas which a century later would be the first to use the newly-invented windmill). Elsewhere, streams and rivers were intensively exploited and mills were found also in coastal districts where tidal waters must have been pressed into service. Tide mills have sometimes been represented as a new invention of about 1100, and even described in extravagant terms as a prime example both of the imagined inventiveness of medieval people and of their special drive to develop labour-saving machines; in fact, tidal waterpower had certainly been harnessed at least some five centuries before that, doubtless somewhere on the Atlantic coasts of Europe (where the tidal range is greatest), and most plausibly during the same period, the later Roman centuries, that saw the general adoption of waterpower across western Europe. The earliest known of the Irish mills were in fact tidal mills (at the monastery of Nendrum on the northern coast, and on Little Island, Cork Harbour, on the south coast, built in 619-21 and 630 respectively). In sheltered locations tidal mills could be and were viable, but the greater violence of the sea made many of them vulnerable: they were built because there was no alternative. The introduction of the windmill during the 1180s changed that, and indeed there is evidence for several cases from the thirteenth century of tidal mills on the English east coast being taken out of use to be replaced by cheaper windmills.

An apparent curiosity of medieval watermills is that over Europe and the Mediterranean world two quite different designs were to be found throughout the whole period (and indeed until the twentieth century), sometimes coexisting in the same regions. The design of the Roman mill, on current evidence, had been that usually termed the vertical (though more correctly vertical-wheeled) mill. An upright waterwheel had its lower part in a running stream or channel, and the flow of water turned the wheel and thus also the horizontal shaft on which it was mounted. The motion of the shaft was transferred by simple gearing through 90 degrees to an upright shaft which passed through the centre of the lower mill-stone, mounted above it, and rotated the upper millstone to which it was securely fixed. This was the mill that was described by Vitruvius around 25 B.C.E., and which is thus often called the Vitruvian mill. Medieval adaptation of the design was limited to nevertheless important developments of the waterwheel: the "undershot" wheel described by Vitruvius came to be replaced where appropriate by the more powerful 'overshot' wheel, driven by water falling on to its top surface, or by the "breast-wheel," essentially an undershot wheel but driven more efficiently by water falling high on to its backpart rather than running past its lower paddles. These two types of wheel, already familiar in the medieval centuries, thus exploited the power of falling water rather than simply running water, and could use smaller streams more efficiently. Their use normally entailed much greater investment in more elaborate hydraulic systems designed to bring water to the mill at as great a height as possible. In contrast to these highly sophisticated and expensive mills, most parts of Europe were also familiar with the horizontal-wheeled mill, a simple mechanism in which a horizontally-lying water-wheel was mounted on a vertical shaft directly connected to the millstones in the millhouse above. This mill required no gearing, therefore, and required only that the water should be directed in a concentrated form on to one side of the paddle wheel—preferably via a wooden nozzle such as a hollow tree-trunk. Many excavated examples were small and used no metals in their construction: this mill was thus easier and cheaper to build, in fact at its simplest requiring really no professional craftsmanship.

Speculation as to the reasons for the coexistence of these two very different mill designs is fruitless if it fails to take into consideration the varying relationship of milling to feudal lordship. It is clear that the horizontal-wheeled mill flourished whenever and wherever people without territorial lordship were able legally to operate their own mills: in those contexts where lords failed to establish a milling monopoly, or where they had no ambition to, or where lordship was different. Early medieval Ireland, England before the Norman Conquest, Scotland, Scandinavia—all preferred low-capacity, private horizontal mills, in the apparent absence of coercion from above. Technological backwardness can be ruled out as a factor, when more economically-advanced regions such as France south of the Loire, northern Italy and southern Germany, and the Mediterranean region generally, also continued to use the horizontal mill until the modern period—all regions where the feudal milling monopoly described by Bloch simply did not apply. The English evidence is perhaps decisive. With an increasing number of excavated horizontal mills from Anglo-Saxon England, their complete absence after 1200 (according to the copious evidence of mill repairs in manorial accounts, all to vertical-wheeled mills) points to a rapid changeover coinciding with the imposition of lordship on the northern French pattern. Domesday Book demonstrates many aspects of that transition, and perhaps shows us new, high-capacity vertical mills (built at great expense but returning good rents) in many places, with that significant group of mills returning low rents or none at all being the remaining horizontal mills, not yet taken into the lord's hand prior to replacement. The tendency for high-value mills to be found in well-populated areas may indicate that these were areas where lords gave priority to investing in a new mill.

The association of the vertical-wheeled mill with western-European feudal lordship is perhaps further borne out by the case of medieval Spain. Islamic society there developed its own complex hydraulic systems which inherited some physical remnants from Roman irrigation systems but otherwise were characterized by entirely new arrangements for the social distribution of water. The standard watermill in use was the horizontal-wheeled mill, most often of the type used in the Near East from the classical period onwards – that is, the mill powered by a vertical column of water delivered from a vertical penstock usually called an aruba. These penstocks could be as high as 46 feet (14 m), and thus their ability to deliver high-velocity water from an irrigation channel or a tank could compensate for deficiencies in supply. Where water was plentiful, Spanish mills used the penstock normally used in horizontal mills, an oblique wooden chute (sometimes a hollowed-out tree trunk). Vertical-wheeled mills were known in Islamic Spain, but the smaller horizontal mills were doubtless better-suited to the pattern of ownership and use—typically they were privately or communally-owned for domestic use. The vertical mill, with its far greater costs of construction and maintenance, was everywhere associated with large-scale milling. Whether milling was carried on in the modern period as a major capitalist enterprise competing for custom, or in the Middle Ages as a feudal one maximizing its profits through legal compulsion, the vertical mill with its greater overall efficiency and much greater potential power was likely to be preferred.

Without question the medieval period saw notable advances in milling technology, if the basic mechanism of the cornmill itself changed little. There is plentiful documentation and some excavated evidence for "multiple" mills, two or more water mills built in a complex under one roof and sharing one water-control system. It was doubtless a reflection of the limitations of the largely wooden mechanism of the watermill that one mechanism could drive only one set of stones: only with the extensive use of iron parts that began in the eighteenth century could more powerful and complex mill mechanisms be devised, capable of driving several sets of stones at once. Large rivers that were not easily incorporated into hydraulic systems presented problems of exploitation, particularly because their levels could vary considerably, and sophisticated wheels that could be raised and lowered were developed. These suspension mills were complicated to build, and were not widely used outside Italy and France. Medieval engineers experimented with building mills into the arches of bridges over larger rivers, where the flow of water was fast; the lack of success of at least some of them perhaps points to the difficulties of constructing mechanisms that were not easily damaged or even destroyed by rapid rises in the water level. A simpler and apparently effective form of mill on such rivers was the floating mill, an undershot watermill built into or on an anchored boat. Such mills were used—reportedly for the first time—by the Roman general Belisarius on the Tiber in 537 when the aqueducts of Rome (which drove the mills as well as bringing drinking water) had been cut by the besieging Goths. They were quite widely used on the major rivers of western Europe from quite soon after that time, so perhaps Belisarius' role as innovator should be doubted.

More important advances were made in adapting the watermill to a range of industrial functions. In many places fulling mills—using water-powered hammers to beat wet, new cloth to shrink it and felt it—replaced the men and women who had done this work with their feet. First recorded from the middle of the eleventh century, in France, the device spread over much of Europe during the next century, being first recorded in England in 1185. All but a very few of the industrial mills recorded in England were fulling mills; in France the figure was no more than 40 per cent, with many more mills for hammering iron during the smelting process and after, sawmills, mills for grinding bark for tanning, blade-sharpening mills and so on being recorded. If it is concluded from the English evidence—and the Italian, and the German—that industrial mills remained uncommon because in fact they brought in little revenue and were seldom worth building, the French evidence suggests that industrial mills could sometimes be more profitable there. It is as yet unclear why that should have been so. But however much industrial mills might have been used in some parts of medieval Europe, nowhere did they account for a significant proportion of production. There is no basis for the claims of an "Industrial Revolution of the Middle Ages" based on waterpower that some historians have written about, and which has gained a certain currency on the uninformed fringe of medieval studies. The water-powered cornmill was a legacy from the Ancient World, and it would be the nineteenth century before any substantial proportion of mills did other than that most important labour of grinding corn for the daily bread.

See also **Noria**

Bibliography

Barceló, M. "The Missing Water-Mill: A Question of Technological Diffusion in the High Middle Ages." In *The Making Feudal Agricultures?* Edited by M. Barceló and F. Sigaut. Leiden: E.J. Brill, 2004, pp. 255–314.

Bennett, R. and J. Elton. *History of Corn Milling.* 4 vols. London and Liverpool: Simpkin, Marshall, 1898–1904. Reprint ed. New York: B. Franklin, 1964.

Bloch, M. Avènement et conquêtes du moulin à eau. *Annales ESC* (1935) 7: 538–563; published in English as "The Advent and Triumph of the Watermill." In M. Bloch. *Land and Work in Medieval Europe.* London: Routledge, 1967, pp. 136–168.

Galetti, P and P. Racine, eds. *I Mulini Nell'Europa Medievale.* Bologna: CLUEB, 2003.

Glick, T. *Islamic and Christian Spain in the Early Middle Ages.* Princeton: Princeton University Press, 1979.

Glick, T. and H. Kirchner. "Hydraulic Systems and Technologies of Medieval Spain." In Squatriti, *Working with Water in Medieval Europe*, pp. 267–330.

Holt, R. *The Mills of Medieval England.* Oxford: Blackwell, 1988.

————. "Medieval England's Water-Related Technologies." In Squatriti, *Working with Water in Medieval Europe*, pp. 51–100.

Langdon, J. *Mills in the Medieval Economy: England 1300–1540.* Oxford: Oxford University Press, 2004.

Lucas, A. R. Industrial Milling in the Ancient and Medieval Worlds. *Technology and Culture* (2005) 46: 1–30.

Magnusson, R. and P. Squatriti. "The Technologies of Water in Medieval Italy." In Squatriti, *Working with Water in Medieval Europe*, pp. 217–266.

Squatriti, P. *Water and Society in Early Medieval Italy.* Cambridge: Cambridge University Press, 1998.

Squatriti, P., ed. *Working with Water in Medieval Europe.* Leiden: E.J. Brill, 2000.

Rynne, C. "Waterpower in Medieval Ireland." In Squatriti, *Working with Water in Medieval Europe*, pp. 1–50.

Reynolds, T. S. *Stronger than a Hundred Men: A History of the Vertical Water Wheel.* Baltimore: Johns Hopkins University Press, 1983.

White, L., Jr., *Medieval Technology and Social Change.* Oxford: Clarendon Press, 1962.

Wikander, Ö. *Exploitation of Water-Power or Technological Stagnation? A Reappraisal of the Productive Forces in the Roman Empire.* Lund: CWP Gleerup, 1984.

————, ed. *Handbook of Ancient Water Technology.* Leiden: E.J. Brill, 2000.

RICHARD HOLT

WEIGHTS AND MEASURES

The weights and measures of medieval Europe evolved from earlier Roman, Greek, Celtic, Germanic, and Near Eastern prototypes. Arising after the fifth-century collapse of the western Roman Empire and the ethnic and cultural transformations that ensued, medieval weights and measures mirrored a shift in civilizations. Unlike those used officially by the Roman imperial bureaucracy, which were relatively few in number, they were based on reliable standards, and were found everywhere in the Empire. Medieval metrologies differed by country, region, province, and a myriad of local urban and rural jurisdictions. Of the hundreds of thousands of individual units and their variants that emerged by the later Middle Ages, the vast majority arose from entrenched local customs, fierce ethnic and bureaucratic rivalries, profound economic and commercial developments, demographic and territorial expansion, urban proliferation, technological progress, and international exchanges. What follows is an account of the dominant characteristics of these medieval systems.

It should be noted from the outset that England had a slight advantage over other European states in attempting to secure a national system and curb proliferation because during the Anglo-Saxon period the weights and measures of Winchester were proclaimed as official standards. After the Norman conquest in 1066, London standards assumed this role. No national uniformity was ever achieved during the Middle Ages, but the English effort was the strongest in Europe. By contrast, France by the sixteenth century had more than one thousand units accepted as standards in Paris and the many provincial capitals, with approximately two hundred fifty thousand local variations. This condition arose despite several Parisian efforts to enforce uniformity based on its own standards. In Italy there were even more units, and attempts at simplifying the situation were thwarted by the existence of two competing zones with two different systems: a northern zone from Tuscany to central Italy and a southern zone which included all of southern Italy and the islands of Malta, Corsica, Sardinia, and Sicily. The situation in the Holy Roman Empire was even more vexed since there were approximately three hundred fifty territorial political jurisdictions by the middle of the fourteenth century, and most of them had their own metrological and coinage systems.

Unchecked Development

With no strong central governments enforcing metrological reform, medieval weights and measures developed unchecked and eventually fell into the following basic modes. First, various trades and professions got control of their own units to serve their own special purposes. In such cases the names of individual weights and measures were specific to those occupations. In Italy, the major groups were agriculture, architecture, science, medicine, pharmaceuticals, commerce, manufacturing, industry, logging, shipping, textiles, horticulture, viticulture, fishing, business, and metals and minerals. France had animal products, liquor, firewood, warehousing, merchants, ship cargoes, customs, maritime, mints, episcopal, mines, military, foundries, commerce, and cloth. Most other countries had similar categories.

In England thousands of such units were established for the sale of cloth, vegetables, fruits, glass, leather, jewelry, grain, coal, books, wire, skins, thread, yarn, dairy products, salt, metals, nuts, herbs, spices, soap, ale, and paper. Their counts, weights, or capacities depended on the physical characteristics of the products. Quantitative measure variants were just as prolific, and many of them were indefinite in count or based on an irregular assortment of variables. Most measures for wholesale shipments and for accounting purposes also displayed the same irregularities.

Central governments contributed to proliferation of measurement units by promulgating several national standards for each unit selected, and this practice was particularly evident in England and France. In the latter country there were multiple national standards for area, volume, and itinerary measures. In the British Isles there were different standards for the same units in England, Scotland, Ireland, and Wales. In some cases the differences were extreme. Regional and local multiple standards added to the problem.

With the rapid growth of towns after the eleventh century, weights and measures in certain areas became separated into different standards depending on whether they were used within the walled towns or outside them in the expanding suburbs. Similarly, some measuring units had different standards depending on whether they were used on land or at sea. Generally the maritime units were larger than their dry-land equivalents, especially among linear or distance measures.

Multiple uses and multiple names added to the general confusion. Some units, for example, were used for more than one measurement division, especially among capacity, volume, and area measures, and individual units could have many different names depending on local preferences. In addition, these and other units sometimes changed in size over time. When such changes occurred, most or all of a unit's submultiples were also altered.

Lastly, medieval weights and measures expanded in number because of certain traditional practices. For example, it was customary to base agricultural area measures of land either on coinage standards or on units of income derived through production. Naturally, the values of these coins fluctuated over time, as did the figures for those based on income. Land and product measures also were based on work functions, on the level of food production and tax assessments, on the physical attributes and time allotments of humans, and even on the production capability or strength potential of one or more animals. When these practices proved insufficient for national, regional, or local needs, the last resort was to create additional units by dividing existing weights and measures into halves, thirds, and fourths, or into an irregular assortment of diminutives. Such practices guaranteed the production of thousands of variations.

European weights and measures continued to proliferate after the Middle Ages. It took the metrological reform plans following the Age of Science in the seventeenth century and the Enlightenment in the eighteenth century to bring about radical change in, and eventual the abandonment of, these native systems. The final solution was the metric system first begun in France in the 1790s and eventually adopted by all the nations of mainland Europe at intervals during the nineteenth century.

See also **Agriculture; Coinage, minting of; Travel and exploration; Weights, science of**

Bibliography

Kula, Witold. *Measures and Men.* Richard Szreter, trans. Princeton: Princeton University Press, 1986.

Zupko, Ronald E. *British Weights and Measures: A History from Antiquity to the Seventeenth Century.* Madison: University of Wisconsin Press, 1977.

———. *French Weights and Measures Before the Revolution: A Dictionary of Provincial and Local Units.* Bloomington: Indiana University Press, 1978.

———. *Italian Weights and Measures: The Later Middle Ages to the Nineteenth Century.* Philadelphia. Philadelphia: American Philosophical Society, Memoirs 145, 1981.

———. *A Dictionary of Weights and Measures for the British Isles: The Middle Ages to the Twentieth Century.* Philadelphia: American Philosophical Society, Memoirs 168, 1985.

———. *Revolution in Measurement: Western European Weights and Measures Since the Age of Science.* Philadelphia: The American Philosophical Society, Memoirs 186, 1990.

RONALD EDWARD ZUPKO

WEIGHTS, SCIENCE OF

Two quite different approaches in the writings of antiquity influenced the science of weights in the Middle Ages: those of *Archimedes and of the author of the *Mechanical Problems* ascribed to Aristotle. Archimedes, perhaps best known for his geometrical books and for his solution to the problem of the composition of Hieron's crown, applied to the subject the principles of statics, treated geometrically. Thus he proved the law of the lever by appealing to the idea of center of gravity. In the *Mechanical Problems*, by contrast, we find dynamical concepts such as force, resistance, and velocity.

*Thabit ibn Qurra (d. 901 C.E.) is known as a corrector or improver of translations of scientific works from Greek into Arabic. His *Kitab al-Qarastun*—the last word is the transliteration of a Greek word meaning "balance"—which seems to have been based on Greek sources, uses dynamical ideas. This treatise is known in several versions and in the Latin translation by *Gerard of Cremona is different again—inter alia it has a prologue, an epilogue, and other material not in the extant Arabic versions. From this prologue we learn that the work is based on a certain *Causes of the Balance*, presumably Greek or of Greek origin. In the third of the eight propositions the law of the lever—that two weights hung from the ends of a balance arm are in equilibrium if they are inversely proportional to the lengths of the arms from which they are suspended—is proved by considerations of the power of the points on the beam, which is proportional to the distance from the point of suspension. Under conditions of horizontal balance it is stated that a displacement would be corrected and the horizontal alignment restored. The subsequent propositions are on the equivalence of several weights to a single weight at the appropriate point and on the heavy balance arm. Thabit's work seems to have had considerable influence on the science of weights among Arabic writers. For instance, al-Khazini (twelfth century C.E.) cites him, together with *Euclid, Archimedes, and Menelaus, in his *Mizan al-Hikma* (*Balance of Wisdom*) and presents a summary of his work.

The Latin West

In the Latin West a treatise on the balance, *De canonio*, was translated from Greek in the twelfth or thirteenth century. Its content has much in common with the *Liber karastonis*, as Thabit's work was known in Latin, but does not contain dynamical considerations. Two short pieces attributed to Euclid, a fragment on the Roman balance (i.e., one with unequal arms) and a *De ponderoso et levi* (*On the Heavy and the Light*) were translated from Arabic. The latter, in nine postulates and five propositions, is a general discussion of the force (*virtus, potentia*) of a body, the distance it traverses, and density. The *Liber Archimedis de insidentibus in humidum*, Archimedes' book on floating bodies, consists of fourteen definitions, six postulates, and eight propositions. It is probably not by Archimedes, although it treats the problem of determining the proportion of the substances in an alloy (the Hieron's crown problem) and the first proposition is the principle of Archimedes (the weight of a body in air exceeds its weight in water by the weight of the displaced water).

Jordanus de Nemore

There are several texts beginning "*Omnis ponderosi motum esse ad medium...*" (that the motion of every heavy [body] is towards the center...) associated with *Jordanus de Nemore (Paris, early thirteenth century). They have the same postulates and enunciations, but different proofs. One such text, *Liber de ponderibus*, was published by Petrus Apianus in Nuremberg in 1533, together with a fourteenth-century commentary referred to as "*aliud commentum*" (another commentary). The basic text is seven postulates and nine propositions. In the *Elementa* it is stated that when two equal weights are suspended at equal distances from the suspension, and if the equilibrium is disturbed, the balance will be restored. Such questions are discussed in terms of positional (*secundum situm*) weight, which is clearly distinguished from simple weight. Thus, when a weight is displaced to disturb the balance, it becomes positionally lighter. Virtual displacements are considered "as small as you please" (*quantulumque parvi*), and the consequent vertical motion of the weights is considered. Here we have not only the idea of virtual displacement, but also of components of forces. The proofs in the *De ponderibus* are in the main quite different from those in the *Elementa*. Added to the text are the four propositions from the *De canonio* (again with different proofs) and a prologue for the whole, in which the term *gravitas secundum situm* is explained. Motion downwards is considered "natural," and the curved motion that the weights must follow, according to the constraints of the system, "violent." This text has so little in common with the *Elementa* that it is possible that the postulates and enunciations were put together independently of either, but by whom and when are matters for speculation.

The most elaborate and most impressive of the "Jordanus" works is the *Liber Jordani de ratione ponderis* (*Jordanus's Book on the Theory of Weight*), a substantial treatise in four books. In the first book are two propositions that address the problem of the inclined plane. In Book IV there is a variety of dynamical ideas. Several of the propositions concern the effect of acquired velocity on force. The idea of impetus, later developed by *John Buridan, is adumbrated in this book. The *De ratione ponderis* was printed in Venice in 1565.

The Fourteenth Century

After 1269, when *William of Moerbeke translated the works of Archimedes directly from Greek, the genuine mechanical treatises of Archimedes became available among the Latins. They seem to have been little used in the Middle Ages. In the last quarter of the fourteenth century Blasius of Parma wrote a *De ponderibus*, a compilation largely of Jordanus's *Elementa* and the pseudo-Archimedean *De insidentibus in humidum*.

The medieval writers on mechanics preserved and developed the ideas inherited from antiquity and formulated, albeit sometimes obscurely, the ideas of work, of composition of forces, and of virtual displacements. They laid the basis for the mechanics of the seventeenth century.

See also **Jordanus de Nemore; Thabit ibn Qurra**

Bibliography

Knorr, W.R. *Ancient Sources for the Medieval Tradition of Mechanics. Greek, Arabic and Latin Studies of the Balance.* Florence: Istituto e Museo di Storia della Scienza, 1982.

Moody, E.A. and M. Clagett. *The Medieval Science of Weights (Scientia de ponderibus)*. Madison: University of Wisconsin Press, 1952.

RICHARD LORCH

WILLIAM OF CONCHES

The grammarian, natural philosopher, and Platonist William of Conches was born in Normandy by 1090 and was apparently still alive in 1154. He studied at the cathedral school of Chartres under its famous master Bernard, but by the 1120s had entered into his own teaching and publishing career. Among his students were John of Salisbury and Henry Plantagenet, the future King Henry II of England. In the schools he lectured and wrote commentaries on the great books of the age: *Boethius's Consolation of Philosophy*, *Plato's Timaeus*, *Macrobius's Commentary on the Dream of Scipio*, and Priscian's *Institutiones Grammaticae*. He styled himself not only as a grammarian, but also as a *Physicus* or physician, and had an abiding interest in both natural philosophy and medicine.

William's chief contributions to the advancement of science are two works of systematic natural philosophy, the early *Philosophy* and a late dialogue entitled the *Dragmaticon*. These two tomes serve as bookends to his career and treat the same material, albeit in different ways. The *Philosophy* was written around 1125, but the work was criticized, which led the author to revise, correct, and amplify its doctrines in the *Dragmaticon*, which was composed about twenty years later for Geoffrey Plantagenet.

The *Philosophy* is a relatively short work that summarizes the state of learning about the world as it was known in the early twelfth century. Book One treats what philosophy is, the Trinity, soul of the world, demons, and elements; Book Two considers the ether and the upper celestial bodies; Book Three studies air (including the operation of the winds and things meteorological) and water; and Book Four investigates the Earth both as an element and as a place (including its inhabitants, regions, and human beings, and medical matters such as reproduction, birth, growth, and the organs). The work ends with a consideration of youth and education, which brought William back to the classrooms in which he taught.

The elements served not only as an organizing principle for the presentation of material in the Philosophy, but also as the basic units of William's cosmology. Drawing on *Constantine the African, he said that "an element is the simple and minimal part of a body; simple in quality, minimal in quantity." The elements in turn are subject to the humors or temperaments of cold and dry (earth), cold and moist (water), hot and moist (air), and hot and dry (fire). He called visible and variable things that are subject to the humors "elemented things" (*elementata*), thus preserving the name of elements of the world for the pure particles. For William, then, as for the Platonists, pure fire was to be understood in the mind rather than detected by the senses. In his thoughts on the elements and human body, William was also influenced by the newly available *Isagoge* of Johannitius (*Hunayn ibn Ishaq).

The *Philosophy* may belong to an older encyclopedic form of scientific literature found in *Isidore of Seville's *On the Nature of Things* and in some of the works of *Bede, but William's tone and presentation of material were new and, indeed, pugnacious. He thought that after its creation the natural world operated by its own rational laws and was not subject to a capricious divine will. To the divines who claimed that God could do whatever He wished whenever He wished, William said: "As the peasant is wont to say, 'God can make a calf from a tree trunk.' But has he ever done so?" William thus stood at the forefront of a twelfth-century drive to recognize and engage the physical and rational nature of the created cosmos and in his *Glosses on Plato* he distinguished the various kinds of causes (efficient, formal, final, and material) that the natural philosopher should explore as operating features of the natural world.

The *Philosophy* captured the attention of a new generation of students, and *Hugh of Saint-Victor seems to have been influenced by it in the revision of his *Didiscalicon*. Over a hundred manuscripts of the *Philosophy* survive, and vernacular and learned adaptations appeared, thus making the book a fundamental and influential statement of twelfth-century scientific thought. A copy of the work was carried by one of William's students to William of St. Thierry who, following his successful attack on *Peter Abelard, opened up a new front against William. He characterized William as one who dangerously philosophized about the Trinity in physical terms and who rejected the literal story of the creation of Eve from Adam's rib. The charges must have stung, particularly in light of Abelard's condemnation, and William cleansed the *Dragmaticon* of those contentious teachings, but in that work he also reworked his natural philosophy and drew more extensively on Seneca's *Natural Questions*.

William missed the influx of new Aristotelian texts that surfaced in Europe in the second half of the twelfth century, but the schools themselves were changing late in his life. Students now sought an easier and quicker education than the laborious grammatical and textual training of which William had been a master. As a result of these developments, in the 1140s William of Conches abandoned the schools of northern France and retreated to the Plantagenet court, there to compose the *Dragmaticon*, his final great work.

See also **Aristotelianism; Elements and qualities**

Bibliography

Elford, Dorothy. "William of Conches." In *A History of Twelfth Century Western Philosophy*. Edited by Peter Dronke. New York: Cambridge University Press, 1988, pp. 308–327.

Gregory, Tullio. *Anima mundi. La filosofia di Guglielmo di Conches e la Scuola di Chartres*. Florence: Samson, 1955.

Lemay, Helen Rodnite. Science and Theology at Chartres: the Case of the Supracelestial Waters. *British Journal for the History of Science* (1977) 10: 226–236.

O'Neill, Ynez V. William of Conches and the Cerebral Membranes. *Clio Medica* (1967) 2: 13–21.

———. William of Conches' Description of the Brain. *Clio Medica* (1968) 3: 202–223.

Silverstein, Theodore. Elementatum: its Appearance among the Twelfth-Century Cosmogonists. *Mediaeval Studies* (1954) 16: 156–162.

———. Guillaume de Conches and the Elements: Homiomeira and Organica. *Mediaeval Studies* (1964) 26: 363–367.
PAUL EDWARD DUTTON

WILLIAM OF MOERBEKE

The Dominican translator William of Moerbeke was probably born between 1215 and 1235 in Moerbeke (East Flanders province, Belgium) or in Morbecque (departement Nord, France). Nothing is known with certainty about his entry into the Dominican order, or his study of the Greek language. In general, few documents about his life are available, although valuable information can be gained from colophons at the end of some of his works. They attest his translating activity from 1260 onwards in Greece, and later from 1267 to 1277 at the papal court in Viterbo, where he was appointed papal chaplain and penitentiary. William took part in the council of Lyons in 1274. On April 9, 1278, he was ordained archbishop of Corinth. He completed three translations in that Greek city in 1280, and afterward returned to Italy. In January 1284 he was on a mission in Perugia. He died some time before October 26, 1286, since a papal letter of that date confirms the nomination of his successor after a long vacancy of the see of Corinth. His place of death is unknown.

Works

William of Moerbeke translated virtually all the genuine works of Aristotle from Greek into Latin, either in the form of revisions of previous translations by *Boethius, *James of Venice, *Burgundio of Pisa, *Robert Grosseteste, and various anonymous authors, or new renditions of texts that had never before been translated directly from the Greek. Although some of these original works were already known through less accurate versions from the Arabic, several others were completely new to the Latin West, as in the case of *De progressu animalium*, the *Politica*, and Book XI of the *Metaphysica*. Moerbeke's philosophical works include translations of Aristotelian commentaries by Alexander of Aphrodisias, Ammonius, John Philoponus, Simplicius, and Themistius, and of Neo-Platonist treatises by Proclus. His translations of texts by *Archimedes, Hero of Alexandria, and *Ptolemy, and of two commentaries by Eutocius on works of Archimedes are preserved in an autograph copy, ms. Vatican Ottobonianus lat. 1850, which was almost certainly used by *Witelo for the composition of his *Perspectiva*. Moerbeke also translated *Galen's *De virtutibus alimentorum* and dedicated the work to the physician Rosello of Arezzo. His alleged authorship of a geomantic text is still open to debate.

Method

Studies have shown that Moerbeke had access to old and excellent Greek manuscripts. At least two of these have been identified, viz. ms. Vienna phil. gr. 100 (physical works of Aristotle) and ms. Venice Marcianus gr. 258 (Alexander of Aphrodisias, *De Fato ad Imperatores*). The latter contains his ex libris with the legend "*liber fratris guillelmi de morbeka ordinis predicatorum penitentiarii domini pape*" ("this book belongs to Brother William of Moerbeke, the book of brother William of Moerbeke, O.P., papal penitentiary"). His translations, in particular those of Aristotle, are marked by the careful rendering of the original's characteristics, such as the word order and the use of particles. Greek compounds are often translated by two Latin words to mirror the original, while technical terms are mostly transliterated, although sometimes with slight adaptations to conform to the Latin morphology or with marginal notes to explain the meaning of the Greek. Moerbeke obviously considered his translations as work in progress. He is known to have made second or even third revisions of the same texts, using different Greek manuscripts for comparison. For some translations two or three different versions are preserved in the manuscript tradition, reflecting successive stages of his work as it progressed, e.g. the Aristotelian treatises *Metaphysica*, *Physica*, *De Anima*, *De Caelo*, *Politica*, and *Rhetorica*. Earlier fragmentary versions of Aristotle's *Politica* ("*Politica imperfecta*") and Simplicius's commentary on *De Caelo* ("*Fragmentum Toletanum*") had limited circulation. The hypothetical relative chronology of his works, which was established on the basis of the dates from the colophons of some translations and on the study of systematic shifts in his vocabulary, is now commonly accepted.

Influence

Moerbeke was in contact with some of the finest scientists of his time. Witelo and Henri Bate of Mechlin dedicated works to him, and he is thought to have influenced *Campanus de Novara. *Thomas Aquinas and Henri Bate used his translations. Aquinas had access to the "*Fragmentum Toletanum*" of Simplicius's commentary on *De Caelo*, which survives in only two manuscripts, and

Bate quoted from Moerbeke's version of Ptolemy's *Tetrabiblos*, of which only one complete manuscript is extant. While Moerbeke's work is severely criticized by *Roger Bacon, many of his translations became the standard versions at medieval *universities. They laid the basis for the rich scholastic commentary tradition. Some texts are preserved in more than two hundred manuscripts and several early printed editions. The *peciae* system made it possible for numerous copies to be made at the same time, as separate quires of one corrected manuscript were loaned to various copyists. Still, not all of Moerbeke's works were transmitted through such a high number of manuscripts. Ptolemy's *Tetrabiblos* and the uncompleted version of Aristotle's *De Coloribus* are found in one manuscript each, while Ptolemy's *De Analemmate* and Aristotle's *Poetica* are extant in two. Since he mostly used Greek manuscripts of high quality as his model, Moerbeke's translations are still valued critical editions of the originals. In some cases where all Greek manuscripts are lost, his versions are the only complete witnesses to the text. In this manner, parts of the commentaries on Aristotle's *De Anima* (III, 4–8) by Philoponus and on *Plato's *Parmenides* (book VII, 141E7–142A9) by Proclus were preserved, as well as Proclus's *Tria Opuscula* (*De Providentia*, *De Libertate*, and *De Malo*) and two other treatises that have been partially recovered from Greek palimpsests, viz. Ptolemy's *De Analemmate* from ms. Milan, Ambrosianus gr. 491 and Archimedes's *De Insidentibus Aque* from a privately owned palimpsest which is now preserved at The Walters Art Gallery in Baltimore, Maryland. Fragments of Moerbeke's version of the latter text were retranslated into Greek in the sixteenth century, which caused some confusion about the origin of that version.

See also **Scholasticism; Translation movements; Translation, norms and practice**

Bibliography

Aristoteles Latinus Database. Release 1. Under the direction of Jozef Brams and Paul Tombeur. Turnhout: Brepols, 2003.

Beullens, Pieter and Fernand Bossier, ed. *De Historia Animalium. Translatio Guillelmi de Morbeka. Pars Prima: Lib. I–V. Aristoteles Latinus XVII.2.I.1*. Leiden: E.J. Brill, 2000.

Bossier, Fernand, ed. *Commentaire sur le traité du ciel d'Aristote. Traduction de Guillaume de Moerbeke*. Vol. I. Corpus Latinum Commentariorum in Aristotelem Graecorum VIII, 1. Leuven: University Press, 2004.

Brams, Jozef and Willy Vanhamel, ed. *Guillaume de Moerbeke. Recueil d'études à l'occasion du 700e anniversaire de sa mort (1286)*. Leuven: University Press, 1989.

Charlton, William and Fernand Bossier, tr. *Philoponus. On Aristotle on the Intellect (de Anima 3.4-8)*. London: Duckworth, 1991.

Clagett, Marshall. *Archimedes in the Middle Ages* (Vol. II: *The Translations from the Greek by William of Moerbeke*; Vol. III: *The Fate of the Medieval Archimedes 1300–1565*). Philadelphia: The American Philosophical Society, 1976–1978.

Cranz, F. Edward. "Alexander Aphrodisiensis." In *Catalogus Translationum et Commentariorum*. I: 77-135. Edited by Paul Oscar Kristeller. Washington, D.C: The Catholic University of America Press, 1960. (Addenda et Corrigenda by F. Edward Cranz. II: 411–422, and by Carlo Vecce. VII: 296–298).

Todd, Robert B. "Themistius." In *Catalogus Translationum et Commentariorum*. VIII: 57-102. Edited by Virginia Brown. Washington, D.C.: The Catholic University of America Press, 2003.

Vuillemin-Diem, Gudrun, ed. *Metaphysica. Lib. I–XIV. Recensio et Translatio Guillelmi de Moerbeka*. 2 vol. Aristoteles Latinus XXV.3.1-2. Leiden: E.J. Brill, 1995.

PIETER BEULLENS

WILLIAM OF OCKHAM

William of Ockham was born about 1285 in the village of Ockham, probably modern-day Woking in Surrey, near London, England. He died in 1347 and was buried in Munich in the cemetery of the Franciscan friary, now the site of the Bavarian National Theater. At the bottom of the stairs to the garage nearest the front entrance of the theater is a plaque commemorating Ockham, Orlando di Lasso, and others.

Ockham entered the Franciscan order as a boy of about twelve years of age, studied philosophy and theology, and completed his lectures on the *Sentences* of *Peter Lombard in 1319. At that time he was recognized as an *"inceptor,"* the Parisian equivalent of which was a bachelor of theology, and hence the reason for references to him as "Venerable Inceptor." Between 1319 and 1321 he revised the first book of his commentary, but did not complete his higher degree. Instead, he lectured on philosophy at a Franciscan friary, perhaps in London, and was not appointed to a lectureship in theology at Oxford. Around 1324 he was summoned to the papal court in Avignon to face charges that his theological views were heretical. He left Avignon in 1328 before the process was completed, joining a group of dissident Franciscans who opposed efforts to suppress what Pope John XXII regarded as radical views about poverty, the vow to which followers of St. Francis of Assisi were especially devoted. Ockham ended up in Munich, where, under the protection of Ludwig of Bavaria, he spent the remainder of his life, and died unrepentant while still fighting a papacy that he maintained was illegitimate.

Ockham is best known for his "razor," referring to the dedicated way in which he criticized and eliminated what he regarded as superfluous assumptions or entities in the views of his predecessors and contemporaries. Among social and political historians he is best known for his critique of papal authoritarianism. Although Ockham formed no school and had few, if any, followers, he influenced many of his contemporaries and successors by his incisive and sometimes devastating critiques and arguments. Even in cases where other authors rejected his bolder, reductionistic views, they modified their own opinions in response to Ockham's critiques.

Ockham was not strictly a scientist but a philosopher-theologian who wrote three commentaries and a collection of questions (1322–1324) on Aristotle's *Physics*, two of which were introductory summaries for beginners. Some of his most controversial views on natural philosophy, however, occur in his commentary on the *Sentences* (1317–1321). The interpretation of even his most fundamental views and opinions continues to generate controversy.

Scholars agree that Ockham was an Aristotelian, but his views provoked much reaction because of his interpretation and occasional rejection of Aristotle's views or the standard interpretations of Aristotle. It is precisely in that regard, namely as a critic of Aristotelian natural philosophy and as an anti-Aristotelian, that Ockham is sometimes viewed as having stimulated even more radical departures from Aristotelianism that, in turn, eventually led to the scientific revolution. The variety and eclecticism of later Aristotelians, however, led to interpretations of Aristotle that some tried to reconcile with anti-Aristotelian principles, even mechanistic ones. Under the influence of Renaissance humanists, some Aristotelians tried to purify interpretations of alien accretions, thus presenting Aristotelianism in a form that mechanists and other opponents of orthodox Aristotelianism could reject decisively. The story, in short, is complex.

Ockham's most important departures from the views of his contemporaries often constitute rejections, but his positive doctrine is difficult to reconstruct. Part of the reason is that the summons to Avignon in 1324 put an end to his plan to complete commentaries on Aristotle's *De anima* and *Metaphysics*. After 1328 he devoted his efforts to writing polemical treatises and never returned to the more academic philosophical works. Accordingly, his philosophy has rather the character of a program than a completed project, leaving later interpreters to complete it themselves.

Without further qualification we may summarize Ockham's views and suggest their significance for later developments. Ockham believed that Aristotle's texts approximated to the truth when they were interpreted correctly. He thought that incorrect interpretations generate numerous confusions that can be avoided by means of consistently applied logical distinctions. The upshot was that even common terms signify individual things, not universal things. There is no common reality existing in things, a doctrine usually referred to as "nominalism," although Ockham's version is more aptly called "realist conceptualism" because universal concepts or terms do signify real things, namely, individual things, not any common reality. Every science is of concepts, not things. A real science is one whose concepts stand for things, and a rational science is one whose concepts stand for other concepts. Accordingly, natural philosophy is a real science.

Ockham asserted the existence of only concrete individual things and qualities. Individual things are substances to which qualities are attached as extrinsic properties. He also adopted Aristotelian *hylomorphism, but he regarded matter and form also as actually existing internal parts, though not existentially separable from the compound of which they are a part. He also adopted from some predecessors the view that each substance contains a plurality of hierarchically arranged substantial forms. Because composite things are made up of several really distinct things, some later readers used his doctrine to construct mechanistic accounts of qualitative change.

Ockham's leaner ontology eliminated the existence of universals, common natures, quantity and relation as distinct from concrete individuals or qualities, the existence of motion as an absolute thing independent from bodies in motion, intellectual and sensible species interpreted as intermediaries between objects or objective qualities and the mind and the senses respectively, and the existence of place and time as independent of mental activity. In addition, he also restricted the Aristotelian prohibition of illicit *metabasis*.

Metabasis means "transition," and Aristotle objected to an illicit transition in a proof from one genus or species to another, based usually on ambiguity, which leads to fallacious arguments. Terms must be defined precisely and used consistently. A syllogism using a term in two senses is invalid because it commits the fallacy of four terms, thus yielding a false conclusion. Aristotle considered most, but not all, instances of sliding from one field to another in a proof or demonstration as an example of illicit *metabasis*. The arithmetical proof of a geometrical proposition is an example that he cited, but he did allow exceptions. In cases where a discipline is concerned with the collection of empirical facts while the other is concerned with discovering the reason for the fact, Aristotle judged the transition to be licit. There are cases where two disciplines are hierarchically ordered, for example, when physics provides the fact and mathematics the reason for the fact. In other cases, the two disciplines are equal: for example, a geometrical proposition provides the reason why circular wounds heal more slowly than other wounds. In other texts, however, Aristotle suggested that two disciplines remain separate, and that the apparent transition is actually a matter of considering a particular case as primarily physical or primarily mathematical. In the *Physics* he prohibited the comparison between circular and rectilinear motions as involving an illicit transition. He may have had the problem of squaring the circle in mind, but his view placed severe logical and ontological restrictions on mathematical analysis.

The consequences of Ockham's departures from standard approaches for numerous logical, physical, and theological discussions were startling. His rejection of species led him, for example, to affirm action at a distance. Likewise, he rejected the theory of *impetus on the grounds that the transfer of a force from one thing to another implied a magical event. Cause and effect, he argued, are simultaneous, requiring no intermediaries. The moving thing and the natural motions of elements, not an impressed force, are sufficient to explain the continued motion of a projectile. The rejection of motion as an absolute thing led to a focus on the body and the places it occupies at different times. The critique of quantity and the expansion of *metabasis* freed mathematics from Aristotelian logical and ontological restrictions.

Ockham's reinterpretation of Aristotle's view on *metabasis* followed from his theory of connotative terms and concepts, and from his consideration of *scientia* as a collection of intellectual habits that yield conclusions that can be ordered in a variety of ways. Ockham distinguished between absolute and connotative terms. Absolute terms can stand for real things (substances and qualities). Connotative terms can stand for one thing primarily (substances and qualities) and another thing secondarily (quantity, relation, and the remaining Aristotelian categories). Ockham denied the existence of distinct quantitative and mathematical entities for he interpreted quantitative and mathematical terms as connotative. This theory led Ockham to reject Aristotle's prohibition comparing circular and rectilinear motions, because in his view "circular" and "rectilinear" do not stand for specifically different entities but express nominal definitions that can be predicated of motions in a way that permits comparison. As for the conclusions of sciences, Ockham interpreted Aristotle as allowing for the subordination of a mathematical analysis to physical considerations, the subordination of a physical analysis to mathematical considerations, and even the partial subordination of one science to another. The consequence is that Ockham subdued the logical and ontological restrictions on mathematics, making it a suitable instrument for analyzing any problem that can be quantified or clarified logically by means of mathematics.

Ockham retained the principle of causality and the Aristotelian conception that things have the power to produce the effects that we regularly observe them to produce. "Nature" is a connotative term that refers primarily to sensible (non-artificial) substances composed of matter and form, and secondarily to some separate substances. "Nature" also refers to objects with an intrinsic principle of motion and rest. It is possible to construct a science of necessary and universal propositions, yet such assertions do not refer to natures but to individual things that God has created and endowed with the power to act for the most part in regular and predictable ways.

Ockham influenced some fourteenth-century Oxford philosophers (notably *William of Heytesbury and John Dumbleton) to use mathematics to clarify language about qualities, change, motion, and time. Heytesbury is famous for development of the mean-speed theorem. Ockham and Dumbleton made an important contribution to the notion of quantity of matter. They held that a given body had a finite and, in principle, denumerable number of parts. They explained condensation and rarefaction as the contraction and expansion, respectively, of the constant number of parts of the body. In other words, without loss or addition of parts, the same number of parts could occupy different volumes, thus reducing condensation and rarefaction to the local motion of the parts.

Ockham also influenced *Nicole Oresme to characterize terms like "motion" as connotative. Oresme's view was not as reductive as Ockham's but he too followed the Ockhamist-inspired critique in applying mathematics to problems of change and variation. He did not deny that motion is a real thing altogether, but affirmed it only as a mode of being. He denied the material or corporeal reality of species and their reality in the sensible world, allowing them only a spatio-temporal reference and thus rendering them intelligible in purely mathematical terms.

On the whole, one can see Ockham's critiques as provoking others to provide concrete, empirical support for theoretical, speculative, and hypothetical entities. The test to which Ockham consistently put such entities was to imagine whether anything was lost in explanatory power if the existence of the entity were denied. The challenge for his opponents was not just to argue for its existence but to provide concrete evidence. To several fourteenth-century thinkers Ockham provided logical support for a different understanding of the role of mathematics in natural philosophy. Proposals to make mathematical principles superior to the principles of natural philosophy, and the decision to represent mathematical explanations as causally explanatory were not shocking to those who had followed a more Ockhamist reading of Aristotelian natural philosophy.

See also **Albert of Saxony; Aristotelianism; Buridan, John; Grosseteste, Robert; James of Venice; Duns Scotus, Johannes; Kilwardby, Robert; Logic; Marsilius of Inghen; Petrus Hispanus;** *Scientia;* **Swineshead, Richard**

Bibliography

Adams, Marilyn McCord. *William Ockham.* 2 vols. Notre Dame: University of Notre Dame Press, 1987.

Beckmann, Jan, ed. *Ockham-Bibliographie 1900–1990.* Hamburg: Felix Meiner Verlag, 1992.

Brown, Stephen. "A Modern Prologue to Ockham's Natural Philosophy." In *Sprache und Erkenntnis im Mittelalter, Miscellanea mediaevalia,* Vol. 13, Part 1. Leiden: E. J. Brill, 1981, pp. 107–129.

Gál, Gedeon. William of Ockham Died "Impenitent" in April 1347. *Franciscan Studies* (1982) 42: 90–95.

Goddu, André. The Impact of Ockham's Reading of the Physics on the Mertonians and Parisian Terminists. *Early Science and Medicine* (2001) 6: 204-237.

———. "Ockham's Philosophy of Nature." In *The Cambridge Companion to Ockham.* Edited by Paul Vincent Spade. New York: Cambridge University Press, 1999, pp. 143–167.

———. The Physics of William of Ockham. *Studien und Texte zur Geistesgeschichte des Mittelalters,* 16. Leiden: E. J. Brill, 1984.

Livesey, Steven. William of Ockham, the Subalternate Sciences, and Aristotle's Prohibition of *metabasis. British Journal for the History of Science* (1985) 18: 127–145.

Ockham, William of. *Ockham's Theory of Terms (Summa logicae, Part I).* Translated by Michael Loux. Notre Dame: University of Notre Dame Press, 1974.

———. *Ockham's Theory of Propositions (Summa logicae, Part II).* Translated by Alfred Freddoso. Notre Dame: University of Notre Dame Press, 1980.

———. *Ockham on Aristotle's Physics (Brevis summa libri physicorum).* Translated by Julian Davies. St. Bonaventure: The Franciscan Institute, 1989.

———. *Opera philosophica et theologica.* 17 vols. St. Bonaventure: The Franciscan Institute, 1967–1989.

ANDRÉ GODDU

WINDMILLS

The evidence we have is that windmills appeared first in Persia. Towers built of stone, carrying a horizontal rotor on a vertical shaft, were at work during the Middle Ages and well into the modern period in areas of modern Iran and Afghanistan, being used both for grinding corn and raising water. It is less certain, however, when such mills first came into use. Their antiquity cannot be safely taken back before the ninth century C.E., although the possibility that they were in use long before that is not to be ruled out. The story that the assassination in 644 of Umar, the second caliph, was carried out by a Persian slave Abu Lulua whose profession it was to build windmills is known only from two centuries later and hardly constitutes evidence. On the other hand, traditions concerning memorable events are less easily dismissed than other orally-transmitted stories. It has not been demonstrated that knowledge of this type of mill spread outside the areas where it had long been in use. There is no reason to regard it as in any way the ancestor of European windmills, which were of an entirely different type and design, and most plausibly arose from a separate process of independent invention. It is conceivable that the idea alone of a mill powered by wind came from the east to the medieval west, although the lack of any evidence for intermediary examples seems to cast doubt on any such process of diffusion. Michael Lewis has argued that the western mill was derived from that of the east during the brief period in the late eleventh century when the Seljuks ruled western Asia Minor, and that the windmills of the eastern Mediterranean predated western European mills. The argument is ingenious, but lacks supporting evidence. All of the earliest known references to European windmills come from northwestern Europe, specifically from the lands on either side of the English Channel and the southern North Sea: from France and the Low Countries, but mostly from southern and eastern England. The two earliest firmly dated references to existing English windmills both come from 1185. Several writers claimed to have found English and European windmills recorded from earlier in the twelfth century, but none of these supposed discoveries bears close scrutiny. It is possible that new dating methods such as dendrochronology may one day modify the picture we have, but it seems unlikely. Telling evidence that the windmill was indeed new in the 1180s is the fact that it was only in the following decade that the Papal Curia was called on to address the question of whether this new source of revenue should yield tithes to the ecclesiastical authorities. It may be significant that the matter first arose in England. The judgment that windmills should indeed be so taxed, in a decretal issued under Pope Celestine III (1191–1198), came in response to a claim brought by two senior churchmen from the Fens, an extensive level area of eastern England where windmills were recorded in great numbers after 1200. The abbot of Ramsey and the archdeacon of Ely were pursuing a claim against a secular lord who was refusing to pay tithes on his windmill's income, and—clearly lacking any precedents which they could cite—these officials were forced to seek a ruling from Rome. Its very different mechanism alone marks this windmill as an invention made independently of the eastern mills. With its sails facing into the wind, and turning axially like a rotor rather than tangentially like the familiar vertically-mounted waterwheel, the windmill harnessed natural power in a new way. The rest of its mechanism—a simple gearing to turn its drive through ninety degrees to work horizontally-lying millstones—clearly drew on the mill-builders' experience of the watermill. The other original feature of the mill was that this was a building designed to be turned to face into the shifting wind. For the greater part of the Middle Ages most western mills were post-mills, their bodies balanced on, or suspended from, the top of massive wooden posts perhaps set into the ground and held rigid by pyramid structures of stout timbers. By means of a large beam attached to the mill, the whole body of the postmill could (with some effort it must be said) be levered round into position. The enormous stresses placed on this wholly timber structure, and the imperative that it should nevertheless be as light as possible so that it could be moved, meant that such mills could probably not have been built before the substantial improvements in northern-European carpentry techniques that archeologists have observed and dated to the late twelfth century. The post windmill was one of the most important inventions of the medieval West.

The extensive early manorial records available for England have allowed the first centuries of the English windmill to be studied in a systematic way, so that the known circumstances of its spread perhaps provide a model for what happened over western Europe generally. First appearing—and between 1200 and 1300 built in large numbers—in districts with poor water resources, it was slow to spread to regions that were well-supplied with water power where its impact would always be marginal. Vulnerable to the weather, the windmill was relatively costly to maintain; less profitable than all but the weakest watermills, the windmill thus came to supplement existing milling capacity. Only watermills of marginal effectiveness were replaced by windmills. Driving forward the adoption of the new technology was the power of manorial lords to force their tenants to use their mill: these English windmills all represented seigneurial investment in a new source of income. With a more static population by about 1300, the drive to build new windmills faltered; very few were built on new sites in the fourteenth century. With the substantial population decline that began later in that century, fewer mills were needed and perhaps more importantly the ability of lords to demand that their tenants should use their mill declined—certainly much lower incomes from mills are recorded everywhere, and many mills fell into disuse in the hundred years after 1350 or so. Significantly, windmills went out of use and became derelict in much greater numbers than watermills, emphasizing the inherently greater problems—and the greater maintenance costs—of harnessing this power source. By the middle of the fifteenth century perhaps a majority of the windmills built before 1300 had been dismantled. In the centuries following 1500 windmill numbers again began to increase, in line with the growing population.

The lack not only of early sources but also of extended studies means that we have a more fragmentary knowledge of medieval windmills elsewhere. In the northern parts of western Europe it was the thirteenth century, as in England, that saw the first windmills, as scattered references from France and the Low Countries make clear. It is often suggested that the new technology arrived in the Mediterranean rather later, in the thirteenth or fourteenth centuries, but problems of evidence need to be stressed. In the eastern Mediterranean, windmills are first recorded only in 1304, and in numbers only in the fifteenth century. But our sources are monastic, and the old-established Byzantine monasteries owned overwhelmingly watered, mainland lands where watermills had long been in use and where the windmill remained rare. The islands, the true home of the Greek windmill, are simply lacking in sources from before the fifteenth century, and it is thus not impossible that the Greek windmill (and by implication other Mediterranean windmills) could have been far older than it now seems. That can neither be proved nor disproved. An interesting feature of the Greek mills—and Mediterranean windmills generally—was that they represent an early form of the tower mill, as clearly illustrated in a picture of Rhodes from 1389. Tower mills, as far as we can judge from inadequate descriptions in building accounts and other sources, may have been appearing in tiny numbers in the west around 1300, although the design must in those centuries have presented problems. A period in which the design was being perfected would best account for the fact that it was only from the sixteenth century that the tower mill would begin to supersede the postmill—and indeed would never do so entirely, as the postmills still being built in the nineteenth century demonstrate. The successful form of the tower mill carried its sails in a cap that turned on runners, allowing its stone or brick body to be much larger and more robust than the postmill and thus contain a much more substantial mechanism. There is no evidence that medieval tower mills approached such sophistication, and indeed their lack of success indicates that their presumably rudimentary design as yet gave no advantage over the postmill.

Supporting that assumption is the fact that the wider potential of the tower mill was also not realized straight away. The design of the postmill allowed it to be used only for processes that could be contained within the turning body, and there is no evidence that it was ever used for anything other than grinding corn. In the late Middle Ages it was perhaps Dutch engineers who got round this limitation when they contrived the hollow postmill, which directed its drive along a shaft turning within the hollowed-out post. But that brought its own limitations and it was for the most part the tower mill that would be taken into use in the early modern period for industrial applications and most importantly for land drainage. These latter mills used turning scoopwheels rather than pumps to lift water from specially-constructed low-lying polders where it collected. The application of windpower to this process was regarded as new when it was first recorded in 1408 on the lands of the Count of Holland.

See also **Noria**

Bibliography

Bauters, P. "The Oldest References to Windmills in Europe." In *Transactions Of the Fifth Symposium of the International Molinological Society*. Saint-Maurice: 1984, 111–119.

Cheney, M. G. The Decretal of Pope Celestine III on Tithes of Windmills, JL 17620, *Bulletin of Medieval Canon Law*, new ser., (1971) 1: 63–66.

Hills, R.L. *Power from Wind: A History of Windmill Technology*. New York: Cambridge University Press, 1994.

Holt, Richard. *The Mills of Medieval England*. New York: Blackwell, 1988.

Langdon, J. *Mills in the Medieval Economy: England, 1300–1540*. Oxford: Oxford University Press, 2004.

Lewis, Michael J.T. The Greeks and the Early Windmill. *History of Technology* (1993) 15: 141–189.

Van Dam, P. "Harnessing the Wind: The History of Windmills in Holland." In P. Galetti and P. Racine (eds.), *I Mulini Nell'Europa Medievale* (Bologna, 2003), pp. 34–53.

White, Lynn Townsend. *Medieval Technology and Social Change*. Oxford: Clarendon Press, 1962.

RICHARD HOLT

WITELO

The little we know of Witelo's life comes from his two extant works, *Perspectiva* and *Tractatus de primaria causa penitentie et de natura demonum*, and from dispersed remarks in four thirteenth-century documents, stemming from Olesnica (1275), Vienna (1280), and Nuremberg (1281), and put to use for the first time in 1984 by Jerzy Burchardt in his biographical study of Witelo.

As Witelo himself says in proposition X. 74 of the *Perspectiva*, he resided in Poland, his *terra habitabilis*, specifically in Silesia, in the environs of Legnica, Borek, or the Silesian capital Vratislava (Wroclaw, Breslau). He must have been born there between 1230 and 1240, most probably about 1237.

The name Witelo is of Germanic origin, being etymologically the standard South-Germanic diminutive of Wito (North-Germanic Wido, Widelo), the Italian correspondent being Guido. Although the orthography of the name varies from source to source (in the printed editions, it is either Vitellio or Vitello), the manuscripts of the *Perspectiva* support overwhelmingly the correct form, Witelo. Witelo's parents were of mixed nationality, his father being Thuringian (identified by Burchardt as Henryk of Ciz or Zytyc), one of the German Thuringians who colonized Silesia in the twelfth and thirteenth centuries, and his mother Polish (belonging to a noble family of Borow), as his remark, "filius Thuringorum et Polonorum," is traditionally interpreted by historians.

Witelo's undergraduate education was acquired in Paris, where he was a student in the Faculty of Arts in

This engraving from a 1535 edition of Witelo's *Perspectiva* shows a range of optical effects. (Ancient Art & Architecture Collection)

1253, and where he became familiar with the works of *Plato, Aristotle, Averroes (*Ibn Rushd), Avicenna (*Ibn Sina), *Euclid, *Ptolemy, *Boethius, Chalcidius, Donatus, Priscianus, Porphyry, *Grosseteste, and others included in the standard curriculum of arts. Witelo obtained an M.A. degree, i.e., *magister artium liberalium*, most likely in 1258. After graduation he returned to Poland, where he may have been associated with the school of Legnica, whose program of study he unsuccessfully attempted to improve by raising the level of its curriculum from the trivium to include also that of the *quadrivium. He left the school in 1262 for Padua, where he studied canon law until 1268.

The cycle of jurisprudential studies at Padua then lasted six years. During those years, spent also with studies of psychology and cosmology, among others, Witelo wrote the treatise *On the Nature of Demons* and also, perhaps, other lost treatises, known only from being mentioned in the *Perspectiva*. It was also at Padua that his interest in optics was aroused by exposure to some remarkable optical phenomena and to the *Perspectiva* of Alhacen (*Ibn al-Haytham), translated anonymously in the twelfth century. From Padua Witelo went to Salzburg, intending to obtain financial support from the local archbishop (the Silesian Prince Wlodzislaw) to study theology in Paris; however, unexpected political developments caused the prince to send him instead to Viterbo, where he joined the papal court in late 1268 or early 1269 and befriended the translator and papal confessor *William of Moerbecke, to whom he dedicated the *Perspectiva*. After various further trips to Italy he finally returned to Poland (if we dismiss the unlikely hypothesis that he became a monk at the Premonstratensian Abbey of Vicogne), where he died at an unknown date around 1280.

The most important and influential of Witelo's works is the *Perspectiva*. Its last five books must have been written after 1270, since Witelo draws, in Book V, on Hero's *Catoptrica*, the translation of which was completed by Moerbecke on December 31, 1269. Books I–IV, on the other hand, could have been written, or at least begun, earlier. Other works, known to us only from being alluded to in the *Perspectiva* are: *De elementatis conclusionibus* (a supplement to Euclid), *Philosophia naturalis* (a general treatise on physics), *Scientia motuum caelestium* (an astronomical-astrological opus), *Naturales animae passiones* (a psychological treatise), and *De ordine entium*. The *Perspectiva* is Witelo's magnum opus. A mammoth work in ten books, it deals exhaustively with geometrical optics, and is patterned in all substantive matters after Alhacen's *Perspectiva* (*De aspectibus*), although Witelo never mentions the Arabic author by name. The only sources Witelo identifies explicitly in Book I are Euclid and Apollonius, although the other sources he used include *Campanus de Novara, Theon, Eutocius, Pappus, *Jordanus de Nemore, Theodosius, and Serenus. Throughout the *Perspectiva* he also displayed familiarity with *al-Kindi, *Galen, *Hunayn ibn Ishaq, Ibn Sina, and Ibn Rushd, as well as with *Robert Grosseteste, *Roger Bacon, and, probably, *John Pecham. Witelo's philosophical allegiance is the same as that of most scholastics in the thirteenth century. Not being able to distinguish between a pure *Aristotelianism and a syncretistic amalgamation of Peripateticism and Neoplatonism, they were prone to influences by Muslim philosophers whose works were translated into Latin about a quarter of a century before the massive movement of translation of the Stagirite's own works. To these ingredients must be added the influence of Platonism through Chalcidius. The Muslim philosopher who most influenced both Witelo's psychology and his metaphysics was Avicenna, who is the ultimate source of almost all Neoplatonic elements in Witelo.

The *Perspectiva* appeared in three printed editions (1535, 1551, 1572), and there are modern critical editions of Books I, II, and III (by S. Unguru), IV (by Carl J. Kelso, Jr., and V (by A. Mark Smith). Witelo's supreme model in his *Perspectiva* is Alhacen. Quite often Witelo appropriates verbatim Alhacen's proofs, occasionally adding, however, something original. The first, mathematical, book is absent from Alhacen's treatise. Its composition and place in the *Perspectiva* point to Witelo's systematic and didactic approach. It contains sixteen definitions, five postulates, and one hundred thirty-seven theorems. Euclid's *Elements* is assumed known, but Witelo adjoins to it other theorems needed in the remaining nine optical books and drawn from all the sources at his disposal. Book II treats the nature of radiation, the rectilinear propagation of light and color, and the problem of pinhole images. Book III deals with the psychology, physiology, and geometry of vision. Book IV, which is heavily psychological, discusses the perception of light and color visual stimuli and the errors arising in the process of their perception. Books V–IX are devoted to catoptrics, while Book X deals with refraction, the rainbow, and other meteorological phenomena.

The *Perspectivae* of Witelo and Alhacen, together with Pecham's more elementary *Perspectiva communis*, served as basic optical texts until the seventeenth century and exerted considerable influence in the field.

See also **Optics and catoptrics**

Bibliography

Primary Sources

Kelso, Carl J. "Witelonis perspectivae liber quartus Book IV of Witelo's Perspectiva: a critical edition and English translation with introduction, notes and commentary." Ph. D. Dissertation, University of Missouri-Columbia, 2003.

Paschetto, Eugenia, ed. *Demoni e Prodigi. Note su alcuni Scritti di Witelo d di Oresme*. Torino: G. Giappichelli,1978. pp. 89–132

Risner, Friedrich, ed. *Opticae Thesaurus*. Basel: Per Episcopios,1572. (The book contains the *Perspectivae* of Alhacen and Witelo. A facsimile reprint has appeared in New York: Johnson Reprint Corp., 1972 with an important Preface by D. C. Lindberg.)

Smith, A. Mark. *Witelonis perspectivae liber quintus = Book V of Witelo's Perspectiva: an English translation, with introduction and commentary and Latin edition of the first catoptrical book of Witelo's Perspectiva*. Studia Copernicana 23. Wroclaw: Zaklad Narodowy im. Ossolinskich, 1983.

Unguru, Sabetai, ed. *Witelonis Perspectivae Liber Primus*. Studia Copernicana 15. Wroclaw: Zaklad Narodowy im. Ossolinskich, 1977.

———, ed. *Witelonis Perspectivae Liber Secundus et Liber Tertius*. Studia Copernicana 28. Wroclaw: Zaklad Narodowy im. Ossolinskich, 1991.

Secondary Sources

Baeumker, Clemens. *Witelo, ein Philosoph und Naturforscher des XIII. Jahrhunderts*. Beiträge zur Geschichte der Philosophie des Mittelalters 3,2. Münster: Aschendorff, 1908.

Birkenmajer, Aleksander. *Etudes d'histoire des sciences en Pologne*. Wroclaw: Zaklad Narodowy im. Ossolinskich, 1972.

Burchardt, Jerzy. *Witelo Filosofo della Natura del XIII Sec. Una Biografia*. Wroclaw: Zaklad Narodowy im. Ossolinskich, Wydawn. Polskiej Akademii Nauk, 1984.

Lindberg, David C. The Cause of Refraction in Medieval Optics. *British Journal for the History of Science* (1968–1969) 4: 23–38.

———. The Theory of Pinhole Images from Antiquity to the Thirteenth Century. *Archive for History of Exact Sciences* (1968) 5: 154-176.

Unguru, Sabetai. Witelo and Thirteenth Century Mathematics: An Assessment of His Contributions. *Isis* (1972) 63: 496–508.

SABETAI UNGURU

WOMEN IN SCIENCE

The examination of medieval science entails, for the modern reader, a redefinition of the parameters and meaning of "science." According to the *Oxford English Dictionary* (*OED*), science is "a connected body of demonstrated truths... with observed facts systematically classified... under general laws, and which includes trustworthy methods for the discovery of new truth within its own domain." This definition reinforces the modern use of the word "science" as a term of approbation, as a source of proven truth. The *OED*, however, also provides a many-layered definition of the term, and defines science as "a state or fact of knowing," "knowledge acquired by study," "a branch of knowledge," or "a craft, trade, or occupation requiring trained skill." Through these less specialized definitions runs a common thread, the Latin root of the word "science" itself, *scire*, "to know." In order to understand medieval science, then, we must peel back these layers to the base, exposing an earlier meaning, a more inclusive meaning, of science. For the sake of this discussion, science is here defined as a set of skills and ways of knowing based in practice, in trial and error, and in observation of the results of these activities, without any theoretical overlay.

In order to examine the topic of medieval women as both subjects and practitioners of science it is necessary for us to narrow our definition of science even further, restricting our discussion only to the female body and to the healing arts. Male scientists wrote about women as subjects because their female bodies were different from what was believed to be the perfect male archetype; therefore, the evidence we have for women as subjects of scientific inquiry is primarily in the realm of human anatomy, physiology, and medicine. Women practitioners of science wrote few treatises; the female-authored documents that have survived are concerned with women's bodies and their care. The treatises of women such as *Hildegard of Bingen and *Trotula of *Salerno are invaluable as evidence of women as scientific practitioners; however, they are only the visible crests of much larger waves made up of the many illiterate medieval women who were pharmacologists, midwives, and healers, and who passed down their knowledge orally, invisible to the historical record.

The investigation of women as a category of scientific inquiry was limited primarily to the study of human anatomy and physiology, and later, the effects of women's unique physical qualities on the nature of women's minds and souls. One of the first scientists to deal with the subject of women's bodies was Hippocrates of Cos (460–370 B.C.E.). Of the sixty disparate documents included in the Hippocratic corpus, ten deal with the anatomy and physiology of women. The Hippocratic view of the female body was that it was very different from the male body, that it had processes and functions unique to itself (such as menstruation), and that these processes were natural, normal, and healthy. Although men and women had different humoral natures, with men being hot and dry and women cold and moist, these natures were not assigned qualities of good or bad. It was Aristotle (b. 384 B.C.E.), a philosopher rather than a physici!an, who would divide male and female into categories, with the qualities of the former being perfect and the qualities of the later being defective. Aristotle also posited that processes of menstruation, especially concerning the wandering womb, were dangerous and could harm men. From the ideas of Aristotle emerged the concept that women were unbalanced and therefore imperfect, since their bodies and souls were not in alignment. Prone to hysteria, woman was an irrational animal, which in medieval terms meant that she in no way could think clearly, and thus could not be truly educated in the manner of men.

Science in the Cloister: Hildegard of Bingen

Belief that women were inherently weak, both physically and spiritually, and therefore intellectually, disqualified women from participation in the *cathedral schools and *universities of medieval Europe. This does not, however, mean that women did not participate in scientific endeavors, nor does it suggest that they did not contribute to an ever-widening base of scientific knowledge in the eleventh through the thirteenth centuries. Because women rarely wrote treatises recording their activities, many of their experiments with materia medica, therapeutics, and healing procedures have escaped the scrutiny of the modern-day historian. Among the exceptions to this are the treatises of Hildegard of Bingen, a Benedictine nun of the twelfth century. The favored child of a noble family, Hildegard was given at the age of eight as an oblate at Disiboden, where she received both an education and mystical visions from God. Her most famous treatise, the *Scivias*, recounts these revelations in the allegory and symbolism of the Living Light. In writing her *Scivias* as well as her political letters and medical texts, Hildegard of Bingen was able to claim authority in a world that denied women intellectual power. Barbara Newman posits that Hildegard was able to claim this authority because of the belief in women's irrationality. Because her works were of such high intellectual quality, they must of

necessity have been divinely inspired; thus, Hildegard's authority was not gained on her own merit but instead given by the will of God. For this reason, Hildegard's works were taken seriously, and preserved for posterity.

In the years between 1150 and 1157, Hildegard focused her intellectual efforts on the human body, and produced her *Physica* and *Causa et Curae*. The former treated the structure and workings of the human body, while the latter described the causes and cures of disease and included descriptions of symptoms, therapeutic procedures, and recipes for medicaments. Importantly, her *Causa et Curae* also contained a list of *materia medica* written in German rather than Latin, and based on trial, error, and observation rather than the authority of *Dioscorides, whose vague descriptions and Mediterranean focus were of little practicality in northern Europe. Hildegard's medical works were not only read and studied in the male-dominated intellectual milieu of the cathedral schools and universities, but also circulated widely in convents, where the good sisters ran their own infirmaries and were charged with caring for their own.

Lay Practitioners of Science: Trotula

Not only women religious, but also lay women practiced the healing arts in various degrees. One, admittedly problematic, example of a laywoman practitioner who has left a written record is Trotula of Salerno. In her recent work, Monica H. Green has revealed that the Trotula Corpus, a collection of three treatises once attributed to a sole female author named Trotula, was the work of three separate authors, two of whom were men. However, the second treatise in the corpus, entitled *On the Treatments for Women*, was in fact the work of an eleventh- or twelfth-century woman at Salerno named Trotula. In her treatise, Trotula describes the nature and care of the female body in practical terms and details therapies, recipes, *materia medica*, and rituals of natural magic found helpful in the care of women during menstruation, conception, and pregnancy. Her discussion is free of theory and was probably meant to be used as a manual for midwives. This, of course, is problematic, since Trotula, like Hildegard, was exceptional in her literacy; the vast majority of women in the twelfth century could not read or write their own names, let alone a medical treatise. It is possible, however, that there existed a reciprocal relationship between the text and the midwife community, that the ideas in the text were already practiced among midwives who passed down their information orally, and therefore that the text evolved from oral tradition. The text, in turn, may have been read to healers of women, thus reinforcing their own practices and helping to codify procedures for future midwives.

Midwives and Healers

We must assume that from the earliest times women practiced some sort of healthcare within the family. Mothers would have treated the illness and injury of partners and children, experimenting with different herbs and remedies which were passed down orally from woman to woman, from generation to generation. Folkways such as these utilized natural remedies, therapeutics, and sympathetic magical practices, all combined in different proportions. What was most valued in a cure was what was effective. If a remedy worked once, it was remembered as a cure that might work again. These processes of trial and error remain hidden from our view because they were transmitted orally. Far from being unimportant, oral traditions that developed over the centuries were invaluable to the development of medieval manuals for midwives. Traditional practices emerge in the work of Trotula of Salerno, which by the fourteenth and fifteenth centuries had been translated, altered, and augmented to include elements from learned medical and theological treatises, local traditions, sympathetic magic, and tried and true recipes for success. One such manual for midwives was the fifteenth-century anonymous *Knowing of a Woman's Kind in Childing*, recently published in a critical edition by Alexandra Barratt. This treatise, composed in the vernacular, spoke directly to English women practitioners of healing, referring to local *materia medica*, localities, and personalities as proof of efficacy in certain remedies. The author's introduction to this text indicates that it was meant to be read by women who could read to those who could not to help educate the healers in the community. In this we can see the increase in the level of literacy among women, which would admittedly remain low for some centuries to come. However, as early as the fourteenth century, some midwives carried with them small handbooks detailing basic procedures and containing simple recipes. By the fifteenth and sixteenth centuries, many midwives no longer needed treatises read to them since they had attained a low level of literacy themselves.

Despite the sparsity of the written record, medieval women played a valuable role as practitioners of science, although their activities may not meet the modern criteria of the term. Women were involved in the daily experiments of survival, of childbirth, of healing wounds and easing pain. Not only their successes, but also their failures contributed to the base of medical knowledge, at first transmitted orally, next in writing for the few who could read, and then ultimately in vernacular handbooks to be read by a larger majority of women who had attained literacy. We might end with a vision of Martha Ballard, a woman who straddled two worlds and epochs, the Old and the New, keeping her diary in early eighteenth-century Maine, recording mundane details, weather, crops, as well as the daily-ness of her medical practice, the best herbs for fever, and the practical care of women's bodies.

See also **Aristotelianism; Medicine, practical; Medicine, theoretical**

Bibliography

Barratt, Alexandra. *The Knowing of a Woman's Kind in Childing: A Middle English Version of Material Derived from the Trotula and Other Sources*. Turnhout: Brepols, 2001.

Dean-Jones, Lesley Ann. *Women's Bodies in Classical Greek Science*. Oxford: Oxford University Press, 1996.

Gottfried and Theoderic. *The Life of the Holy Hildegard*. Translated by James McGrath, et. al. Collegeville: The Liturgical Press, 1995.

Green, Monica. *The Trotula*. Philadelphia: University of Pennsylvania Press, 2000.

Newman, Barbara. "Hildegard of Bingen: Visions and Validations." In *Church History* (1985) 54.2, pp.163–175.

Ulrich, Laurel Thatcher. *The Midwives' Tale*. New York: Random House, 1990.

BRENDA S. GARDENOUR

Z

ZACUTO, ABRAHAM

Abraham bar Samuel bar Abraham Zacuto was one of the most prominent astronomers of the late Middle Ages in the Iberian Peninsula. He was born around 1450 in the Castilian city of Salamanca, the university of which had a renowned chair of astrology. He studied medicine and astrology at that university. His scientific work began in the 1470s, and continued in exile in Portugal, North Africa, and ultimately Jerusalem.

Zacuto's most outstanding work is *Ha-Hibbur ha-Gadol* (*The Great Treatise*), completed in Hebrew in 1478. It is composed of sixty-five astronomical tables and the canons explaining their use. The tables have the year 1473 as radix and are arranged for the Christian calendar and the meridian of Salamanca. They give the positions of the Sun, the Moon, and the five planets, presented in the form of an almanac. Zacuto computed his entries according to the *Alfonsine Tables*. To do this work by hand required enormous effort, and the level of accuracy Zacuto attained required a high level of skill and careful attention to detail.

Together with the *Alfonsine Tables* we may find the influence of other astronomers, including Jacob ben David Bonjorn, the Catalan author of astronomical tables for Perpignan (1361) and a follower of Levi ben Gerson (1288–1344), *Ptolemy (second century C.E.), *Ibn Rushd (Averroes) (1126–1198), and *Alfonso X the Wise (1252–1284).

In 1481, three years after Zacuto finished the *Hibbur*, it was translated from Hebrew into Castilian, with the help of Zacuto himself, by Juan de Salaya, who held the chair of astrology at Salamanca.

Zacuto was one of the Jews expelled from Spain in 1492. He moved to Portugal, where he entered the service of King João II as an astronomer. After João's death in 1495, Zacuto performed the same service for King Manuel I.

In 1496 a Latin adaptation of Zacuto's *Hibbur* was published in Leiria (Portugal) under the title *Tabulae tabularum coelestium motuum sive Almanach Perpetuum* (*Book of Tables on the Celestial Motions, that is, the Perpetual Almanac*). Some copies have the canons in Latin, and others have them in Castilian. The author was Joseph Vizinus (Vizinho), a Portuguese disciple of Zacuto, who is mentioned in the colophon to the Castilian version as having translated the text from Hebrew into Latin, and then from Latin into Castilian.

The Latin version of the *Almanach* included a dedication, absent in the Castilian, to an unnamed dignitary of the Church of Salamanca. That could be Gonzalo de Vivero, Bishop of Salamanca, with whom Zacuto had some kind of relationship, although this dedication could also have been added by Vizinus as a tribute to *Johannes Regiomontanus, who had included a similar dedication to János Vítez (d. 1472), archbishop in Hungary, in his 1467 work *Tabulae Directionem* (*Tables of the Directions*).

The canons in the *Almanach* are different from those in the *Hibbur*, and it seems that Vizinus made a free adaptation rather than a translation. The tables, on the other hand, were largely taken from the *Hibbur*. From the contents it is clear that these works were addressed to two completely different audiences: the *Hibbur* to the Jewish community, the *Almanach* to the Christians. The *Almanach* is thus a distinct work, not merely a translation of the *Hibbur*.

An almanac consists of a set of positions for a given planet (including the Sun and the Moon), arranged at intervals of a day or a few days over the period of the planet's motion (ranging up to one hundred twenty-five years, in the case of Mercury). The advantage of an almanac is that it is "user-friendly," requiring only linear interpolation between adjacent entries. The first almanac in the Iberian peninsula was that compiled by *Ibn al-Zarqalluh (d. 1100), an astronomer from Toledo. The work influenced several later astronomers such as *Abraham Ibn Ezra (c. 1089–1167) and Ibn al-Banna (1256–1321). This tradition of almanacs in Iberia culminates with Zacuto. There were other almanacs compiled outside the Iberian Peninsula and its area of influence, for instance the tables drawn up in Paris in almanac form in the late thirteenth and early fourteenth centuries by John of Lignères and *John of Saxony among others. But it is unlikely that any of them was the basis for Zacuto's *Almanach*.

In 1496 the practice of Judaism was declared illegal in Portugal, and Zacuto was again forced into exile, this time in North Africa. He lived in Fez, Tlemcen, and Tunis where he wrote his *Sefer Yuhasin* (*Book of Genealogies*) and adapted the tables of the *Hibbur* for the year 1501. In 1505 he traveled to Damascus and Jerusalem where he compiled another set of astronomical tables, beginning with the year 1513, arranged for the Jewish calendar and the meridian of that city. Zacuto died around 1515, probably in Jerusalem.

As for the rest of his output, Zacuto wrote in 1486 a work on medical astrology entitled *Tratado de las influencias del cielo* (*Treatise on the Influence of the Heavens*), followed by a short text on eclipses: *Juicio de los eclipses* (*Judgment on Eclipses*), at the request of his protector at that time, Juan de Zúñiga y Pimentel, Master of the Order of Alcántara. Two other works on astronomy have been attributed to Zacuto: *'Osar hayyim* (*Treasure of Life*), and *Mishpetei ha-'istagnin* (*Judgments of the Astrologer*), a short astrological work concerning the years 1518–1524. Although Zacuto is mainly known for this astronomical activity, he also wrote on other subjects including lexicography and history.

Zacuto's work was highly influential, and made an immediate impact in Salamanca where we find texts in Latin and Castilian that are based on the *Hibbur* (independently of the *Almanach*). There were also several editions of the *Almanach* in Latin in the sixteenth century, attesting to its popularity, and there were at least two translations into Arabic. Zacuto's influence on Jewish scholars was most notable in the Eastern Islamic world, based in large measure on the work he did in Jerusalem shortly before his death.

Zacuto stands as an outstanding intellectual figure in the Spanish Jewish community of his time. He benefited from contact with Christian astronomers in Salamanca who, in turn, depended on a vast corpus produced by astronomers all over northern Europe. He also took advantage of the Jewish tradition in astronomy that developed mainly in southern France and Spain in the late Middle Ages.

See also **Almanacs; Calendar**

Bibliography

Primary Sources
Albuquerque, Luis de. Facsimile edition of Abraham Zacuto's *Almanach Perpetuum* (Leiria, 1496). Lisbon, 1986.

Secondary Sources
Cantera Burgos, Francisco. *Abraham Zacut*. Madrid: M. Aguilar, 1935.
Chabás, José and Bernard R. Goldstein. "Astronomy in the Iberian Peninsula: Abraham Zacuto and the Transition from Manuscript to Print." In *Transactions of the American Philosophical Society*. 90, Pt. 2, Philadelphia, 2000.
————. An Occultation of Venus Observed by Abraham Zacuto in 1476, *Journal for the History of Astronomy* (1999) 30: 187–200.
Goldstein, Bernard R. The Hebrew Astronomical Tradition: New Sources. *Isis* (1981) 72: 237–251.
Samsó, J. "La difusión del Almanach Perpetuum de Abraham Zacuto en el Magrib: Un ejemplo de cooperación intercultural e interreligiosa." In *La Civilización Islámica en al-Andalus y los aspectos de tolerancia* (Rabat, 2003), 57–70.
————. Abraham Zacuto and Jose Vizinho's Almanach Perpetuum in Arabic (16th–19th c.), *Centaurus* (2004) 46: 82–102.
————. In Pursuit of Zacuto's Almanach Perpetuum in the Eastern Islamic World. *Zeitschrift für Geschichte der Arabisch-Islamischen Wissenschaften* (2002/2003) 15: 67–93.
Vernet, J. "Una versión árabe resumida del Almanach Perpetuum de Zacuto." In *Estudios sobre Historia de la Ciencia Medieval* (Barcelona-Bellaterra, 1979), 333–351.

EMILIA CALVO

ZAHRAWI, AL-

Al-Zahrawi (Abu l-Qasim Khalaf ibn al-'Abbas) was known variously as Abulcasis, Albucasis, and Alzaharavius in the Latin medical tradition. In contrast to the subsequent impact of his medical work in Western Europe, medieval Islamic sources provide virtually no biographical information about him. Born in the first half of the tenth century, he is said to have died after the year 1009, and according to one source he died in 1013 at the improbable age of 101. His patronymic, al-Zahrawi, indicates that his native city was Madinat al-Zahra', the governmental center and cultural metropolis established in 936 near Córdoba, southern Spain, by the Umayyad caliph 'Abd al-Rahman III al-Nasir (r. 912–961). Al-Zahrawi's life spanned the government of three rulers—'Abd al-Rahman III, his son al-Hakam II (r. 961–976), and the dictatorial vizier al-Mansur (978–1002)—but whether he worked as court physician to any of them is a subject of speculation.

Physician, pharmacist, and surgeon, al-Zahrawi is credited with the first description of aural polyps, lithotomy with the aid of a special scoop and lancets, what is today known as the Walcher position in obstetrics, and the earliest recorded case of hemophilia, as well as with the pioneering use of animal gut for sutures. These and other medical procedures—some of which were already known in antiquity while the remainder still need to be fully evaluated historically—are described in his only preserved work, *Kitab al-Tasrif li-man 'ajiza 'an al-ta'lif* (the *Tasrif*). The title of this large medical treatise can be translated as "Arrangement of Medical Knowledge for One Who is Unable to Compile a Manual for Himself," although the final section has also been rendered in English as "For One Who Wants to Do Without Other Medical Works" or "For One Who Cannot Cope with Compilations." The compendium, written over a period of forty years, is divided into thirty sections or books of varying length, dealing with general principles of medicine (Book I), diseases, symptoms, and their treatments (Book II), and pharmacology (Books III–XXIX). The pharmacological section is presented in a variety of ways and includes simple and compound drugs, synonyms, substitutes, pharmaceutical manufacturing and techniques, weights and measures, and hygienic and dietary regulations. The thirtieth book, devoted to surgery, is thought to be the first to be illustrated with drawings of surgical instruments. Al-Zahrawi certainly devised a number of surgical instruments, such as a concealed knife for opening abscesses without alarming the patient, hooks of various shapes and sizes, cauteries, pincers, cannulas, probes, a scissor-like instrument for tonsillectomy, wooden instruments for bone-setting, a variety of obstetrical forceps, dilators, and vaginal specula. While the extent to which al-Zahrawi's writings were known to the medieval Islamic world has yet to be determined, claims regarding al-Zahrawi's surgical originality have been exaggerated, for he drew heavily on the Greco-Roman literary tradition, mainly Paul of Aegina. It is difficult to assess whether al-Zahrawi actually performed any of the major surgical operations he advocated. Given the author's comments accompanying some descriptions of surgical techniques and personal experiences, it seems unlikely that he did. None of the surgical instruments he designed has been preserved, although at the end of the twentieth century a number of them were reconstructed from manuscript illustrations.

The *Tasrif*, especially the surgical treatise, had an enormous influence in Western Europe, and helped to establish the high regard in which modern scholars hold medieval Islamic surgical methods. In the mid-thirteenth century, the first and second books of al-Zahrawi's treatise were translated twice into Hebrew, and then into a Latin version which was printed at Augsburg in 1519 under the title *Liber theoricae nec non practicae Alsaharavii*. The twenty-eighth book, devoted to the elaboration of simple drugs, was translated into Latin at the end of the thirteenth century by Abraham Judaeus of Tortosa and Simon of Genoa, and circulated separately as *Liber Servitoris*, which was printed for the first time at Venice in 1417. The thirtieth book on surgery was translated by *Gerard of Cremona, and also circulated by itself. Its influence is to be found in numerous medieval surgical writings, particularly *Guy de Chauliac's *Chirurgia Magna* written in 1363, printed editions of which (Venice, 1497, 1499, 1500) were bound with Gerard's translation. The reputation of al-Zahrawi's surgical treatise inspired a Turkish manuscript version, illustrated with human figures, in the mid-fifteenth century for the library of Mehmed II. In the eighteenth century, the surgical chapter of al-Zahrawi also became the subject of an edition with Latin translation by John Channing (*Albucasis de chirurgia Arabice et Latine*, Oxford, 1778). Some other parts of the *Tasrif* were transmitted to the West in vernacular languages.

See also **Medicine, practical; Medicine, theoretical; Surgery**

Bibliography

Abu'l-Qasim al-Zahrawi. Texts and Studies. Collected and reprinted by Fuat Sezgin, *et al.* 2 vols. Frankfurt am Main: Institute for the History of Arabic-Islamic Science, 1996 (Islamic Medicine v. 37–38).

Castells, M. "Medicine in al-Andalus until the Fall of the Caliphate." In *The Formation of al-Andalus*. Part 2: *Language, Religion Culture and the Sciences*. M. Fierro and J. Samsó, eds. Aldershot: Ashgate, 1998 (The Formation of the Classical Islamic World, 47).

Engeser, M. Der *"Liber servitoris" des Abulcasis (936–1013)*. *Übersetzung, Kommentar und Nachdruck der Textfassung von 1471*. Stuttgart: Kommision Deutscher Apotheker Verlag, 1986.

Hamarneh, Sami Kh. and Glenn Sonnedecker. *A Pharmaceutical View of Abulcasis al-Zahrawi in Moorish Spain: With Special Reference to the "Adhan."* Leiden: E.J. Brill, 1963.

Leclerc, Lucien. *La Chirurgie d'Abulcasis*. Paris: J.B. Bailliére, 1861 (repr. ed, Frankfurt am Main: Institute for the History of Arabic-Islamic Science, 1996 (Islamic Medicine v. 36).

Llavero Ruiz, Eloísa. "Estudio farmacológico de la Maqala XXI del Kitab al-Tasrif de al-Zahrawi." In *Ciencias de la Naturaleza en al-Andalus. Textos y Estudios*. IV. C. Álvarez de Morales, ed. Granada: CSIC, 1996: 235–255.

Savage-Smith, Emilie. Some Sources and Procedures for Editing a Medieval Arabic Surgical Tract. *History of Science* (1976) 14: 245–264.

——. John Channing, Eighteenth-Century Apothecary and Arabist. *Pharmacy in History* (1988) 30: 63–80.

——. "Europe and Islam." In *Western Medicine: An Illustrated History*. I. Loudon, ed. Oxford: Oxford University Press, 1997: 40–53.

——. "The Exchange of Medical and Surgical Ideas Between Europe and Islam." In *The Diffusion of Greco-Roman Medicine into the Middle East and the Caucasus*. J.A.C. Greppin, E. Savage-Smith and J.L. Gueriguian, eds. Delmar and New York: Caravan Books, 1999: 27–55.

This woodcut from the 1516 Valladolid edition of Al-Zahrawi's *Tasrif* (Book XXVIII) shows physicians holding a urine flask. (National Library of Medicine)

———. "The Practice of Surgery in Islamic Lands: Myth and Reality." In *The Year 1000: Medical Practice at the End of the First Millennium*. E. Savage-Smith and P. Horden, eds. Special volume of *Social History of Medicine* (2000) 13: 307–332.

Spink, M.S. and G. L. Lewis. *Albucasis on Surgery and Instruments*. Berkeley: University of California Press, 1973.

Ullmann, M. *Die Medizin im Islam*. Leiden: E.J. Brill, 1970: 149–151.

CRISTINA ÁLVAREZ MILLÁN

ZOOLOGY

Strictly speaking, there is little reason for including an article on "zoology" in an encyclopedia of medieval science. The term is unknown to medieval Latin and vernacular languages, and there are nearly no texts which might be considered as strictly zoological. Yet there is no doubt that most medieval people had a sound knowledge of the animal world, owing to their continuous contact with it in transportation, animal husbandry, medical use, hunting, and fishing. Many didactic texts devoted to animals were written during the Middle Ages, and they can be classified into four different groups, corresponding to different ways of looking at the animal world.

A first type of knowledge is biblical. The Bible mentions more than one hundred birds and quadrupeds, and the very fact of being quoted in the Vulgate confers on an animal the status of a commonplace for churchmen. As a consequence most biblical commentaries devote some attention to these animals, reflecting on their names and properties, and in some cases their symbolism. Particularly rich texts, such as the Book of Genesis, have been subject to special commentaries: the sermons on the *Hexaemeron* of St. Basil and St. Ambrose devote considerable attention to various animals, encouraged by the prominent place of the animal world in the story of the Creation. There are even texts especially devoted to biblical animals, but most of them are still unedited.

A second type of knowledge is reflected in *bestiaries. A selection of some forty animals, mainly of Biblical origin, was treated by the anonymous Alexandrian *Physiologus*. This Greek text, written in the second century C.E., was rapidly translated into Latin and circulated in many versions throughout the Latin West. From the eleventh century onward it developed into larger Latin bestiaries, finally including as many as one hundred twenty species of animals, often lavishly illustrated in de luxe manuscripts. In these texts, each animal is briefly described and some of its properties are evoked as a preliminary to a short allegorical explanation. The aim of these texts is in fact to give keys to animal symbolism, and they have provided a basic source of knowledge about animals to generations of churchmen and artists. A particular representative of this genre is the *Aviarium* (*Book of Birds*) of the Augustinian canon Hugo de Folieto (c. 1130–1140), describing the allegorical signification of some twenty-seven birds; his work combines text and illustration in many of the surviving manuscripts. But the expanded Latin bestiaries of the thirteenth century tend to reduce the allegorical comments, which causes them to be more informative and less symbolic. Vernacular translations or adaptations appear at first in Anglo-Norman during the twelfth century, then in continental French and other languages. In this way, the *Physiologus* and the bestiaries built one of the most successful literary traditions about animals in medieval Europe.

Encyclopedic Works

A third type to be considered is *encyclopedias. This genre, the medieval foundation of which was laid by the *Etymologiae* of *Isidore of Seville, developed mainly in the thirteenth century. The books on quadrupeds, birds, serpents, and fishes included in these works provide an extensive catalogue of animals: about two hundred twenty-five in Isidore, one hundred fourteen in *Alexander Nequam's *De naturis rerum* (c. 1200), one hundred forty-seven in *Bartholomaeus Anglicus's *Liber de proprietatibus rerum* (c. 1235–1245), four hundred sixty-three in *Thomas of Cantimpré's *Liber de natura rerum* (c. 1240), and more than five hundred in the monumental *Speculum Naturale* (c. 1250–1260) of *Vincent of Beauvais. The increase in the latter two works is due less to a discovery of new species than to an enlarged access to written sources. It was during the 1220s that Aristotle's books on animals, translated in Toledo from the Arabic by *Michael Scot, became known in the Latin world. Hence his extensive nomenclature of animals poured into encyclopedic compilations and the Aristotelian corpus produced a variety of secondary texts. The most eminent scholarly treatment of Aristotle's zoology is the *De animalibus* (c. 1260-1270) of *Albertus Magnus. This huge *summa zoologica*, as its modern English translators have termed it, offers a thorough commentary on the nineteen books on animals, interspersed with glosses, personal comments, local information, cross-references. and quotations from other sources. To this Albert added a revised catalogue of animals based on the encyclopedia of his former pupil Thomas of Cantimpré. The *De animalibus* is the largest medieval text devoted to animals, and it stands out as the most interesting zoological work of the period.

Another class of texts is the technical literature, which encompasses various genres. The largest and most rewarding of these, from the modern point of view, is the treatises on hunting. Medieval falconry has given rise to numerous technical texts, at first in Latin, the oldest one dating back to the tenth century. There are no fewer than eight treatises for the twelfth century, and their number increases over the next two hundred years. From the thirteenth century onwards there was a tendency to translate these Latin texts into the vernacular, followed soon by new treatises written directly in Spanish, Provençal, French, Italian, English, and German. They have a strong link with veterinary art: as a rule, the Latin treatises on falconry are mainly concerned with the manner of curing illnesses of falcons and hawks. Descriptions of the birds are brief, and technical data on how to train them are rare, but their various external and internal illnesses are treated in great detail, large numbers of recipes being written down in order to cure them. There are some longer and more descriptive texts, the most famous being *De arte venandi cum avibus* by the emperor *Frederick II of Hohenstaufen (c. 1240–1250). This text deserves a major place in the history of zoology. Its six books are concerned with ornithology (I), the method of manning and training falcons (II–III), and the special techniques for hunting cranes, herons, and ducks with gerfalcons, saker falcons, and peregrines (IV–VI). The first book is a totally new analysis of birdlife: the emperor elaborates a classification of birds according to their habitat, studies their nourishment, their migration during spring and fall, their reproduction, anatomy and plumage, their way of flying, their many forms of self-defense, and the annual mew. His method is very Aristotelian, although the information itself is not largely indebted to the antique zoologist. Occasionally, Frederick does not refrain from criticizing Aristotle on the basis of his own experience. Many new insights have been identified in his text about migration and about bird anatomy. Another eminent representative is again Albertus Magnus: in Book XXIII of his *De animalibus*, he includes a proper treatise *De falconibus* in twenty-four chapters, which is particularly rich for the description of falcons used in hunting. Other Latin treatises are less pertinent to zoology, but some vernacular texts provided important descriptive information. One of the earliest and richiest of these was the *Libro de la caza* of the Castilian prince Don Juan Manuel (c. 1320). The treatment of the species of game and of the various dogs used in hunting in the *Livre de chasse* of Gaston Fébus (written 1384–1391) is largely original, although other parts of the text draw on the *Livres du roi Modus et de la reine Ratio* of Henri de Ferrières, a major representative of the French cynegetical tradition. While mentioning Gaston Fébus, it is worth noting that there are far fewer treatises on venery, archery, and the cure of dogs than on falconry and the care of falcons and hawks. The anonymous *Practica canum*, which might be dated to the twelfth century, is the only Latin treatise dealing exclusively with the management and cure of dogs, and the situation does not differ much in the vernacular languages. Finally, one should note the absence of treatises on fishing until the very end of the Middle Ages, when they appear in southern Germany. On the whole, medieval hunting treatises deserve a place in the history of zoology, because their authors had a close knowledge of the animal world, both as game and as auxiliaries. Whereas the churchmen who wrote Biblical commentaries, bestiaries, and encyclopedias most often drew their information from preexistent written sources, the authors of hunting treatises could rely on their experience to expand earlier material.

Technical Literature

Technical literature on animals comprises other branches in medieval times, the most prominent being the hippiatric tradition. The antique Greek Hippiatrica were not

"How to go in search of high forests." Illumination from a medieval text of the *Livre de chasse*. (Topham/Collection Roger-Viollet)

known before the Arabic-Latin translations of the thirteenth century, but some Latin texts were available during the early Middle Ages, including those of Vegetius and the *Mulomedicina Chironis*. A new start was the *Marescalcia equorum* of Jordanus Ruffus (before 1260), who had been responsible for the stables of Frederick II in Sicily. His text was tremendously popular and was frequently translated into vernacular languages. Other major texts on horse medicine were those of Laurentius Ruzius and of Theodoricus Cerviensis (T. dei Borgognoni) in Latin, Juan Alvarez de Salamiella and Manuel Diaz de Calatayud in Spanish, and the *Rossarznei* of Meister Albrant, which was the source of many enlarged versions in Germany. These texts often include some descriptive information about horses, their anatomy, and their management. The amplitude and diffusion of this tradition are explained by the prominent place of horses in economic and military terms. Conversely, cattle were not subject to much technical literature; nor were oxen, sheep or swine. It is only through the bias of anatomical study that swine have a place in the history of medieval zoology. Due to the long-lasting lacuna in the dissection of the human body, a substitute was built by the dissection of swine, whose anatomy was considered—not without reason—as most comparable with that of the human. Hence there are several texts devoted to the anatomy of swine (*Anatomia porci*), which emerged during the twelfth century in the schools of medicine at *Salerno and Naples. Some information on animal husbandry can however be traced in larger works on domestic organization, such as the *Housebondrie* of Walter of Henley (c. 1250) and the *Liber ruralium commodorum* of Petrus de Crescentiis (beginning of the fourteenth century). Ultimately, one might also consult the pharmacological works in order to gather some zoological information: animals were part of the *materia medica*, many recipes in human medicine including some extracts from the body of animals (blood, fat, ground bones, excrement, etc.). Therefore, didactic works on the many available *simplicia*, or natural products with pharmaceutical effects, include sections on animals, often illustrated in miniatures. There were even specific texts on the *Medicinae ex animalibus*, going back to a model written in late antiquity by Sextus Placitus Papyriensis.

Representations of animals pervade all genres of medieval art. Iconographical documents can therefore also be included in this rapid panorama of medieval zoological sources. The best depictions appear in miniatures, but not necessarily in the illustrations of works as bestiaries or encyclopedias. Here the figures are very dependent on iconographic traditions, going back sometimes to antiquity. Rather, it is in marginal depictions of birds, quadrupeds, and insects that one will find the most adequate rendering of nature: birds in the margins of thirteenth- and fourteenth-century English manuscripts such as the Alphonso Psalter (London, British Library), the Peterborough Psalter (Brussels, Bibliothèque Royale), and the so-called Bird Psalter (Cambridge, Fitzwilliam Museum) have an astonishing level of naturalism. The same is true for manuscripts produced for Jean de Berry around 1400, or in some fifteenth-century Flemish books of hours. Very spectacular also are the forty-eight large images of birds painted at the very beginning of the fifteenth century in the margins of the Sherborne Missal (British Library). Some treatises on falconry also have accurate depictions: examples include the Vatican manuscript of Frederick II's *De arte venandi* or the *Moamin* of the Musée Condé at Chantilly, painted in Milan and dated 1459. The same is true of medical works, such as the four major illustrated copies of the *Tacuinum Sanitatis* (Vienna, Liège, Paris, Rome). Sketchbooks of the fifteenth century often include excellent drawings of animals, such as the famous *Taccuino* of Giovannino de' Grassi (Bergamo, Biblioteca Civica) or the albums of Pisanello (Paris, Musée du Louvre). Of course these examples have not been created with a scientific viewpoint, but they nevertheless have more than an artistic interest and deserve a scientific analysis.

See also **Aristotelianism**

Bibliography

Backhouse, Janet. *Medieval Birds in the Sherborne Missal*. London: The British Library, 2001.

Brunori-Cianti, Lia and Luca Cianti. *La pratica della veterinaria nei codici medievali di mascalcia*. Bologna: Edagricola, 1993.

Capponi, Filippo. Per uno studio sulle fonti naturalistiche dell'omiletica ambrosiana. *Rivista di cultura classica e medioevale* (1992) 34: 81–103.

Clark, Willene B. and Meradith McMunn, eds. *Beasts and Birds of the Middle Ages. The Bestiary and its Legacy*. Philadelphia: University of Pennsylvania Press, 1989.

De Clerq, Charles. "La nature et le sens du 'De avibus' d'Hugues de Fouilloy." In *Methoden in Wissenschaft und Kunst des Mittelalters*. Edited by Albert Zimmerlaltz. Berlin: De Gruyter, 1990, pp. 279–302.

Delort, Robert. *Les animaux ont une histoire*. Paris: Seuil, 1984.

Gaulin, Jean-Louis. "Tradition et pratiques de la littérature agronomique pendant le haut Moyen Age." In *L'ambiente vegetale nell'Alto Medioevo*. Spoleto: Centro Italiano di Studi sull'Alto Medioevo, 1990, pp. 103–136.

George, Wilma and Brunsdon Yapp. *The Naming of the Beast. Natural History in the Medieval Bestiary*. London: Duckworth, 1991.

Gerhardt, Mia. "Zoologie médiévale. Préoccupations et procédés." In *Methoden in Wissenschaft und Kunst des Mittelalters*. Edited by Albert Zimmermann. Berlin: De Gruyter, 1970, pp. 231–248.

Hicks, Carola. *Animals in Early Medieval Art*. Edinburgh: Edinburgh University Press, 1993.

Loncke, Jérémy and Baudouin Van den Abeele. "Les traités médiévaux sur le soin des chiens: une littérature technique méconnue." In *Inquirens subtilia et diversa. Dietrich Lohrmann zum 65. Geburtstag*. Edited by Horst Kranz and Ludwig Falkenstein. Aachen: Shaker Verlag, 2002, pp. 281–296.

McCulloch, Florence. *Mediaeval Latin and French Bestiaries*. Chapel Hill: University of North Carolina Press, 1960.

O'Neill, Ynez. Another Look at Anatomia Porci. *Viator* 1 (1970), pp. 115–124.

Pastoureau, Michel. "L'animal et l'historien du Moyen Age." In *L'animal exemplaire au Moyen Age (Ve–XVe siècles)*. Edited by Jacques Berlioz, Marie-Anne Polo de Beaulieu and Pascal Collomb. Rennes: Presses Universitaires de Rennes, 1999, pp. 13–26.

Poulle-Drieux, Yvonne. L'hippiatrie dans l'Occident latin du XIIIe au XVe siècle. In *Médecine humaine et vétérinaire à la fin du Moyen Age*. Edited by Guy Beajouan, Yvonne Poulle-Drieux and Jean-Marie Dureau-Lapeysonnie. Genève: Droz, pp. 10–167.

Schäffer, Jürgen and Klaus-Dietrich Fischer. "Tierheilkunde." In *Lexikon des Mittelalters*, vol. 8, 1996.

Simonetta, Alberto. "La conoscenza del mondo animale dalla Romanità al medioevo." In *L'uomo di fronte al mondo animale nell'alto medioevo*. Spoleto: Centro Italiano di Studi sull'Alto Medioevo, 1985, vol. 1, pp. 107–126.

Thorndike, Lynn. Early Christianity and Natural Science. Basil, Epiphanius and the Physiologus. *Biblical Review* (1922) 7: 332–356.

Van den Abeele, Baudouin. *La fauconnerie au Moyen Age: connaissance, affaitage et médecine des oiseaux de chasse d'après les traités latins*. Paris: Klincksieck, 1994 (Collection Sapience, 10).

———. Le "De animalibus" d'Aristote dans le monde latin: modalités de sa réception médiévale. *Frühmittelalterliche Studien* 33 (1999): 287–318.

———. "Quelques pas de grue dans l'histoire naturelle médiévale." In *Le réalisme. Contributions au séminaire d'histoire des sciences*. Edited by Jean-François Stoffel. Louvain-la-Neuve: Centre Interfacultaire d'Etude en Histoire des Sciences, 1996 (Collection Réminiscences, 2), pp. 71–98.

Voisenet, Jacques. *Bestiaire chrétien. L'imagerie animale des auteurs du Haut Moyen Age (Ve–XIe siècles)*. Toulouse: Presses Universitaires du Mirail, 1994.

Voisenet, Jacques. *Bêtes et hommes dans le monde médiéval. Le bestiaire des clercs du Ve au XIIe siècle*. Turnhout: Brepols, 2000.

Yapp, Brunsdon. *Birds in medieval manuscripts*. London: The British Library, 1981.

BAUDOUIN VAN DEN ABEELE

Index

Note: Page numbers in **boldface** indicate primary discussion of the topic; page numbers in *italics* indicate illustrations where no other discussion is present.